The author, Jeffrey Dudgeon, at the Ulster Reform Club, Belfast, 30 October 2018 (photograph by Nigel Macauley)

ROGER CASEMENT
THE BLACK DIARIES

with a study of his background, sexuality, and Irish political life

JEFFREY DUDGEON

3rd Edition

BELFAST PRESS

Published by Belfast Press
56 Mount Prospect Park
Belfast
BT9 7BG

Tel (028) 90664111 / 079 2125 1874

jeffreydudgeon@hotmail.com

1st hardback edition 2002

2nd paperback and Kindle edition 2016

3rd paperback and Kindle edition 2019

Typeset in Adobe Garamond 10.7
by *Books Ulster* https://www.booksulster.com

ISBN 978-1-9160194-0-9

This book has received support from the Northern Ireland Community Relations Council; promoting a pluralist society characterised by equity, respect for diversity and interdependence. The views expressed do not necessarily reflect those of the Community Relations Council.

About the author

The author, Jeffrey Dudgeon, was born in Belfast in 1946 and educated at local primary schools, Campbell College, Magee University College, and Trinity College, Dublin. He joined the Northern Ireland Labour Party while at school, and long campaigned for the right to join the Party proper. In the 1970s and 1980s, he was an active member of the Campaign for Labour Representation, and later the Campaign for Equal Citizenship. In 1975, he co-founded the Northern Ireland Gay Rights Association (NIGRA), and in 1981 was the winning plaintiff at the European Court of Human Rights in a seven-year suit against the British Government. This resulted in the decriminalisation of male homosexuality in Northern Ireland in 1982. It was the first successful gay case at Strasbourg and has been a precedent throughout the world, including the Supreme Court of the United States. He continues to work with NIGRA on legal and police issues.

After a long stint in shipping at Belfast docks, he was a civil servant for many years, working mostly in pensions. From 1995-8, he was parliamentary adviser and constituency office manager for the UK Unionist MP for North Down, Robert McCartney. For the following two years, he was engaged, full time, in researching this book, returning in 2000 to the Department of Health at Stormont to deal with health protection issues, including antimicrobial resistance, healthcare-associated infection, and screening. One-time honorary secretary of the Irish Association's northern branch, he stood as a liberal unionist for a Trinity College seat in the Irish Senate in 2011.

Jeffrey Dudgeon was awarded an MBE in the 2012 New Year's Honours List for services to the LGBT community, and, in 2013, was one of the two Ulster Unionist Party representatives at the Haass Talks on Flags, Parading and the Past. In 2014, he was elected to Belfast City Council as a UUP Councillor for the Balmoral area, and chaired the Council's Diversity Working Group. He is also a member of the City Growth and Development, and Licensing Committees.

In Council, he is majoring on achieving the erection of a Belfast Blitz memorial to commemorate the more than 1,000 victims of the two terrible German air raids of April and May 1941. He also works on a stand-alone municipal art gallery in the city centre and litter and graffiti issues in south Belfast.

The author continues to discuss, write and speak on issues relating to Roger Casement and his global significance, particularly so in this Decade of Centenaries, the high point of which was 2016 because of both the Easter

Rising and the Battle of the Somme. The authenticity controversy around the diaries reveals a still contested issue in modern-day Ireland, despite the immense strides made towards gay equality and emancipation, more so currently in the Republic than in Northern Ireland.

His more recent research in relation to Casement's time in Berlin involved transcription of much of the documentation of the key years, 1914-16, and culminated in the 2016 publication of *Roger Casement's German Diary 1914-1916 including 'A Last Page' and associated correspondence.* It detailed Casement's shadowy companions of that time and the role of British Intelligence.

A 2nd paperback edition of *Roger Casement: The Black Diaries – With a Study of his Background, Sexuality, and Irish Political Life* was published in early 2016. The 3rd extended and refreshed edition, with the 1910 and 1911 Black Diaries no longer abridged, came out in January 2019, with a further 10% of text and, again, a number of new photographs.

In February 2018, he published *H. Montgomery Hyde, Ulster Unionist MP, Gay Law Reform Campaigner and Prodigious Author.* Casement was one of Harford Hyde's major interests, alongside Oscar Wilde. Later that year he edited *Legacy: What to do about the Past in Northern Ireland?* being the proceedings of a conference at Malone House, Belfast in March 2018 on the government's proposed Legacy Bill. The conference speakers agreed that the proposed legislation with its myriad of new bodies was not human rights compliant, as well as being flawed, over-complex and unworkable.

All these books are available on Amazon and Kindle. The author's email address for contact or comment is: jeffreydudgeon@hotmail.com

Contents

Roger Casement, aged 25, looking somewhat roguish, in cravat and wing collar, jacket a little crumpled, signed "Yours affectionately", J. Thomson studio, Grosvenor Street, London

Illustrations

On the front cover, spine and back cover respectively:

Inside:

Identification of the locations and characters, both ethnographic and personal, photographed by Casement in Brazil and Peru (now in the NLI), and of the young men in the Bigger collections, has often to be speculative. Casement's camera in Peru was an Ensign de Luxe with a Cooke lens, bought, for £5.15.6 and £4.12.0, respectively, according to notes at the end of his 1910 Diary. The large number of young men who feature in the NLI photographs, many reproduced here, were donated by Gertrude Parry. They reveal more than she apparently ever recognised.

Those photographs and documents referenced NLI are reproduced by kind permission of the Council of Trustees of the National Library of Ireland. Photographs referenced BCL are reproduced by kind permission of Belfast Public Libraries to whom their publication rights are assigned. Photographs from the Ulster Museum are reproduced with the permission of the Trustees of the National Museums and Galleries of Northern Ireland. Prints of transparencies from the National Gallery of Ireland are reproduced by permission of Michael Purser. The National Museum of Ireland at Collins Barracks also gave permission for the use of photographs. Special thanks for permission to reproduce several photographs are due to Patrick Casement, while my gratitude for access to quotations from documents in their possession goes to The National Archives, the LSE Library and the New York Public Library. Those documents referenced PRONI are reproduced by kind permission of the Deputy Keeper of the Records of the Public Record Office of Northern Ireland.

Magherintemple, also known as Churchfield, Ballycastle, Co. Antrim

Reader's guide

- The single name, Casement, is used throughout and almost without exception for the subject of this study; Captain Casement is normally used for his father.

- The reader will have to consult the bibliographies early and often, as many previous Casement authors are quoted and their opinions assessed.

- The Casement genealogy is especially extensive, partly to clear up confusion as to precisely who Casement was within his family (compounded by the frequent occurrence of the name Roger), and also to assist the reader since so many members of the family appear in the Black Diaries and in later controversies. Millar Gordon's descent is included for local genealogical interest.

- Punctuation has been silently added, where appropriate for clarity, and abbreviations at times expanded. Certain spellings and accents have been corrected or rendered consistent.

- Pound and dollar signs are on occasions added for clarity. In duodecimal currency there were 12 pence to the shilling, 20 shillings and 240 pence to the pound. Therefore £3.14.11 is three pounds fourteen shillings and eleven pence.

- Casement put the names of animals and ships into double quotes. That style is not always copied within the diaries, especially where his oft-referred to bulldog, "John", is concerned.

- It is impossible to reproduce the placing of words, comments and calculations in the diaries. Entries are often out of time or order sequence; also, being hand written, they flow all over the page. Only a facsimile would serve to reveal the author's mode and precise intentions.

Abbreviations, nicknames and foreign words

ABIR — Anglo-Belgian India Rubber
BMH — Bureau of Military History
BCL — Belfast Central Library
BLPES — British Library of Political and Economic Science (at LSE)
Cholo — male with American Indian blood; a Mestizo (Spanish)
CMG — Commander of the Most Distinguished Order of St Michael and St George
Co. — County
DMP — Dublin Metropolitan Police
Doddie, Roddie, Rod, the O'Scodge, the O'Scodgin, Scodgie — Roger Casement
EDM — E.D. Morel ('Bulldog' to Casement's 'Tiger')
FJB — Francis Joseph Bigger
F.O. — Foreign Office
GAA — Gaelic Athletic Association
Gee — cousin Gertrude Parry (née Bannister)
GBS — George Bernard Shaw
HO — Home Office
IRA — Irish Republican Army
IRB — Irish Republican Brotherhood
Moço — lad, boy, young man (Portuguese)
NIGRA — Northern Ireland Gay Rights Association
Nina, Numkins — sister Agnes Jane Casement (Mrs G.H. Newman)
NLI — National Library of Ireland (in Dublin)
NYPL – New York Public Library
PAC — Peruvian Amazon Company
PRONI — Public Record Office of Northern Ireland (in Belfast)
QUB – Queen's University, Belfast
RDC — Roger David Casement (1864-1916)
RIC — Royal Irish Constabulary
RTE — *Raidió Teilifís Éireann*
Squiggy — cousin Edward Bannister
TCD — Trinity College Dublin
TNA — The National Archives (at Kew in London, formerly PRO)
UCC — University College Cork
UCD — University College Dublin
UVF — Ulster Volunteer Force
WO — War Office

Acknowledgments

My love and thanks go to the late Billy Adair for provoking me to write this book, keeping me well-fed and for being his amusing, sceptical and intransigent Ulster self; also to Cathy Gage (now Doig) for family histories in Ballycastle and Rathlin and grand explorations together in Co. Antrim;

Special thanks to Gilbert Hughes for the key Millar Gordon discovery, other genealogical searching, and for showing me the way around PRONI; and to Roger Sawyer for a vast amount of advice and documentary information, much encouragement and many answers;

Thanks to Hugh Casement for invaluable genealogical information and copy letters, and for answering my many questions about the Victorian personnel of his family, to his mother Mrs Lesley Casement for her kind invitation to visit Magherintemple (on the night of the great storm on 26 December 1998) to meet also her daughter Susie and her Brazilian husband, and to Patrick Casement for his later hospitality and permission to use several photographs. I hope the current family will forgive their relative being unearthed yet again;

To Mrs Elspeth Parry, heir to the Casement estate, for her kind permission to publish written and other material;

To the late Robert St. Cyr for research and arcane information in New York and Georgia and for guiding me around many of the United States; Brian Earls (who so sadly died in July 2013) for cuttings, advice and accommodation in Dublin; Andrew Finlay for help and accommodation, also in Dublin; Austen Morgan for accommodation in London and guidance on legal and Belfast historical matters; the late Norman Stevenson for support and guidance on literary questions; Erskine Holmes, Brendan O'Connell and Steven King for cuttings and much conversational diversion; Michael Lowry for encouragement and help, John Cobain and Gerry Lynch for vital computing advice and assistance, and my niece Jenny Shaw for scanning assistance after a floppy disk catastrophe;

To Bill Mc Cormack for holding the Goldsmiths College colloquium in 1998 (and two more) that started me on this journey into Casement; Hazel Armstrong for inviting me to address the John Hewitt Summer School in 1999; Maurice Leitch for writing such a great novel and for his Ulster certainties; Brian Garrett for legal advice and Ulick O'Connor for his book loan and some good natured disagreement;

To those sons and daughters of the Irish revolution who provided me with documents, information and advice: Declan Hobson, the late Ruairi and Máire Brugha (née MacSwiney), the late Joseph McCullough, and Máire MacEntee

O'Brien; and to their Unionist opposite numbers Mrs Macha Mackay, the Dowager Lady Brookeborough, and Lord Caledon for information on their Edwardian relatives in Ulster;

To Gerry Lyne and Noel Kissane of the NLI and their staff for friendly assistance on accessions and Casement research; Bruno Derrick and Michael Leydon of TNA in Kew for Casement catalogues and advice; Patricia Albright of Mount Holyoke College and Kevin Cahill, both in Massachusetts, for assistance on B.L. Reid matters; George Woodman, formerly of the Northern Ireland Assembly library, for details on the Catholic Apostolic Church, Martin Hayes of Worthing library for material on Casement's mother, and Linda Greenwood of Belfast Central Library for F.J. Bigger photographs;

To Paul Watters for his medical expertise; the late PA MagLochlainn for advice on matters Gaelic; Richard Kirkland, Shane Ross T.D., and Brian Gilmore for F.J. Bigger material and facts, and, in the last case, Armagh-related information; Dermot Gault for translation from Norwegian documents, Michael McAlinden (and latterly Robert Howes) for Portuguese translations, and the late Michael O'Sullivan for Belgian biographical detail; and to the late Dr Jules Marchal for invaluable Congo history and language guidance from his Belgian diplomatic experience in Africa;

To Timothy d'Arch Smith for Edwardian and Uranian detail; the late Peter Burton (*Gay Times* Literary Editor) for pointing me; Andrew Hodges for guidance on Room 40 and Bletchley Park; Ian Venables for assistance with the poetry of J.A. Symonds; AD Harvey for intriguing information on homosexuality in the army in the First World War; and Oliver Merrington of the Hall Carpenter Archives for cuttings;

To my fellow authors, researchers and perhaps rivals in the field of *Casementia* – Séamas Ó Síocháin, Reinhard Doerries, Lucy McDiarmid, Angus Mitchell, the late Lord Kilbracken, Paul Bew, David Rudkin and Roger Louis for assistance, many interesting and sometimes energetic discussions and the odd clue they perhaps did not intend to reveal; and to John O'Loughlin, a fellow *Casemental,* for so many documents on disk;

Finally, to the Royal Irish Academy for inviting me to speak at their key *Casement in World History* Symposium in Dublin in May 2000 and similarly to TNA and Goldsmiths College for the December 2000 colloquium at Kew;

This book is dedicated to Jit Ming Yap who would have prevented the Irish revolution had Casement met him first;

I am latterly indebted to Gordon Lucy for his encouragement and support in getting the 2nd edition[1] published for the centenary year of 2016.

The age of digitisation has brought a wealth of new information on the subject within official archives and family history while there have been numerous

Casement publications since 2002. The new, often fascinating facts discovered, tend to emphasise my earlier findings and none significant have been negated.

My thanks in recent years, especially in relation to the unravelling of outstanding mysteries go to Hugh Casement, now in Belfast having retired home from Germany, David Grant for his superb Irish Brigade website, Sheryl and Bill Christensen and Thomas Badamo, descendants of Adler Christensen's first and last wife respectively, Norwegian writers Bjørn Godøy and Gabriele Haefs, Jeffrey Panciera (US), and the many others who have provided me with articles, cuttings, leads and nuggets of information.

Thanks also go to those who have invited me to speak at many conferences and events since first publication: latterly, with talk titles in italics, in 2009, Jim Doan (Nova Southeastern University, Fort Lauderdale and Lynn University, Boca Raton); in 2012, Cillian O'Fahy at the TCD Sinn Féin Cumann ('Roger Casement: Separatism, Sectarianism and Protestant Nationalists'); in 2013, Brian Ó Conchubhair, University of Notre Dame for 'Casement: The Glocal Imperative', Tralee (*Casement and the Easter Rising: Berlin, Dublin and British Intelligence*); Edmund Lynch (Gay History Month, Dublin, *The Cult of the Sexless Casement*); Stefanie Lehner (Ulster Museum, Belfast, 'Location of Narratives: Storytelling and Archives', *Ethics of Archives*); and Mark Phelan (School of Creative Arts, Queen's University Belfast, *Roger Casement: Controversies in Script and Image*); in 2015, Professor Eunan O'Halpin (TCD Centre for Contemporary Irish History, 'The North Began? Ulster and the Irish Revolution 1900-25', *Casement and Ulster: Seeding Separatism and Misunderstanding*); in 2016, Fearghus Ó Conchúir (The Casement Project, *Hospitable Bodies*, symposium with David Rudkin, British Library, London); Dublin City Gallery Hugh Lane ('High Treason' exhibitions, Roger Casement 'Artist as Witness 1916-2016' *Researching Roger Casement's Role in Political and Cultural Controversies*) with Adler film by Alan Phelan; Brian Robinson (British Film Institute, London, 'Casement on Trial' with Peter Wyngarde); Kevin Hanratty (Northern Ireland Human Rights Festival, Black Box, Belfast); and Fionntán McCarry ('The Rogers Casement', Carey Historical Society, Culfeightrin Parish Hall, Ballyvoy, with Patrick Casement and Jordan Goodman); in 2017, Sinéad Nolan, 'Front Line Defenders', with Christopher McAteer ('Casement the Opera' The Mac, Belfast); and in 2018, Rev. Chris Hudson (All Souls Unitarian Church, Belfast, *Crime Against Europe* launch with Dave Alvey and Margaret O'Callaghan).

The diaries' controversy, of course, continues unabated, particularly through Tim O'Sullivan and Brendan Clifford's work in the *Irish Political Review* (which is also republishing Casement's writings) and by assertion in the Paul Hyde website www.decoding-casement.com/. That relating to Casement's role in the partition of Ireland has barely begun.

Preface

I attended the first Goldsmiths College Casement colloquium in February 1998 after fortuitously noticing a letter in the *Irish Times* from its organiser, Professor Bill Mc Cormack. I brought with me a small but significant piece of research done in the Public Record Office of Northern Ireland. It concerned the background of Casement's Belfast boyfriend, Millar Gordon, and had been enabled by the publication the year before of his full name in Roger Sawyer's book of the 1910 Black and White Diaries. I was also alert to the re-igniting of the dispute over authenticity involving a separate publication of the White Diary by Angus Mitchell, his former collaborator, who had come to believe the Black Diaries were forged.

The argument over the authenticity of the diaries which seemed to conclude after Brian Inglis and B.L. Reid published biographies in the 1970s was being rekindled, not by the older hagiographical defenders, but through an attitude apparently favourable to homosexual rights. In the new Ireland, being gay had taken on something of an iconographic status having become if not *de rigueur,* at least modish, in metropolitan circles. Prompted by Sawyer's 1984 book, nearly fifteen years previously I had written an article on Casement so I was well aware of his significance to Ireland. Similarly I was conscious of his importance in the history of homosexuality, almost as much for the denial of authorship of the Black Diaries as for their uniquely erotic contents. Both mundane and exhilarating, they are nonetheless a rare (and sparse) sexual memoir, while shining a shaft of intense light into one man's mind.

Resigning in June 1998 from my job with a Westminster MP, I was on the point of returning to the Northern Ireland civil service when I realised I was going to have to transcribe all the Black Diaries, especially Casement's never before seen, highly sexual diary of 1911. This consequent book consists therefore of transcriptions of the five Black Diaries in the Public Record Office in London (now unabridged in the case of the 1910 and 1911 diaries). For the first time they are all published together, beside comprehensive material about Casement's life, especially in Ireland, and his controversial homosexuality.

It became evident, researching Casement and the diary characters, that certain key areas of his life and work were little known, inaccessible, or myth-based. These were his family and early days, his sexual orientation, and his Irish political activity. The authenticity issue also needed a thorough assessment. So a biographical study came into being alongside the diaries. Much time was spent on constructing a necessary Casement family tree which, still lacking the precise origins of his mother Annie, tracks his unrecognised Australian connections. The project ultimately resulted in the creation of a Casement reader and source book.

The claims and counterclaims about the diaries reveal a story which takes on different aspects by virtue of changing values and events. In other words, there may never be a final settlement of the account. In the retelling, issues will be interpreted according to contemporary codes. While Ireland and homosexuality exist as discrete areas of dispute and conflict, so will studies of Casement. Despite the recent forensics tests, which only confirmed what any sensible reader of the literature already knew, the controversy shows little sign of abating. At the same time the BBC and RTE TV programmes in March 2002 failed to illuminate Casement's real life or his importance.

The actual mystery is how adults and whole nations could have continued to believe for a moment that the Black Diaries, after their emergence in 1959, were forged. Of course the diaries are authentic and genuine. Even the blottings are genuine. Some post-modernists may believe they are authentic and fictional. But believing in their authenticity does not mean you do not do the most rigorous checks on provenance and contents. The scholar who recently admitted that his computer analysis of the 578 lines of verse in *A Funeral Elegye* had erroneously attributed the poem to Shakespeare, rather than John Ford, accepted that "nothing can replace the value of close reading." Another writer added that close reading, "the idea of reading all of the texts and then reading all of the texts about the texts, although old-fashioned, was the winner." I would concur.

To those who would argue that there is little or no eyewitness evidence of Casement's homosexual activities I quote the remark made to me on the steps of the Royal Irish Academy: "When I came out, no one was more surprised than my wife."

No man can be a hero to his biographer. Consequently, the closer one gets to the mind of Casement, the less heroic will his decision-making process appear. All motives are mixed. Stripping a man down, as he famously did in his own diaries, renders an individual human, but it certainly makes it difficult to view them as saintly. That is all to the good. Too much popular history relies on a belief in humans based on perfection. A biographer knows both the humanity, and the ordinariness, at times the banality, of their subject. Perhaps I know Casement too well, sharing so many of his attributes and experiences, being someone of Ulster origin and gay, as well as Protestant; someone who, politically, resembled Casement for a time although not latterly.

Reduced to self-interest or the scarring of a disturbed upbringing, most subjects appear in a bad light. That is not to say that individuals do not do significant things, just that the causations may not in themselves be admirable. Most of those called to greatness stand out because of their family and their background. Casement, as I relate here, was no exception. His virtues were nonetheless many and varied: indifference to discomfort and pain, courage in the face of physical violence, persistence, love of humanity, kindness to animals, a refusal to see those of other races as subordinate by definition, and political effectiveness.

Casement can also seem unclear or contradictory. Was he, like so many notable figures in history, self-invented, governed by not being what he wanted to be, coming from the margins of his ethnicity? Although people have the right to be what they want, or what they believe themselves to be, historians must view them in the context of their choices and deeds. In the matter of Casement's homosexuality, I take the view adopted by Inglis and the under-read B.L. Reid; Casement enjoyed himself sexually, displaying little or no guilt and certainly no shame. He showed himself to be an early exemplar of what is now standard sexual behaviour for most gay men. I am using the word gay, even though it will jar with some who reckon it is historically inappropriate but then the word homosexual was a modern concoction from the 1860s, a word, to my knowledge, that Casement never wrote down. The word in use then, although gay has pre-Second World War provenance, was "musical", one spoken between the MPs Tim Healy and Joseph Biggar, but it no longer retains such a double meaning.

Casement had far greater influence on the politics of Ireland than is generally recognised. In particular his organising of arms shipments into Ireland in 1914 and 1916 put him into the category of that handful of individuals without whom there would be no separate Irish state. It was Yeats who presciently said after meeting Casement at William Rothenstein's studio, that his "mood of the mystic victim" personified "something new and terrible for Ireland"[2] It did, for within a decade the revolution he prepared had occurred.

To understand why the IRA's first arms were commissioned by someone also involved in the rebirth of northern nationalism is a necessary guide to how they might be decommissioned – alongside the mind-sets on both sides of the conflict. The thirty-year war in Northern Ireland also has to have its origins and longevity explained, for few have managed to address those issues effectively. This study of Casement provides a key to unlocking some of them.

The guilty or Anglophobic Protestant has been in many ways the cement for military Republicanism, its *sine qua non*, providing international respectability, by virtue of apparent non-sectarian credentials, for what might otherwise be seen simply as armed hibernianism. Casement was not a guilty but he was corrosively anti-English. Why was his hatred of England so pronounced and whence did such hostility come? What was the actual origin of his Irish patriotism? How was it that he failed to possess any Ulster Scots sympathies given that he was apparently a Co. Antrim Protestant? Why did he become a revolutionary separatist and not a Home Ruler? In what ways was his homosexuality the root of his radicalism? Was he governed by pro-German imperial sentiment? I hope I have been able to answer these questions. But of these, the last needs particular explanation here.

Casement openly expressed an appreciation for Germany; one ironically shared by some of his Ulster opponents – for the same and other reasons. They all viewed united Germany as a fresh power untainted by cynicism or a long history. The problem, unrecognised by Casement, was that a rapidly developing power is only able to expand its frontiers through a belief in its own virtues and superiority. Else why bother. And new world powers without a history, and worse, untouched by experience, once in an expansionist mode, are not going to operate a humanitarian regime. While living in Germany from 1914 to 1916, Casement saw the nature of the imperial German operation, even visiting the scene of massacres in Belgium, but his criticism was largely reserved for the thoughtless, sometimes deceitful way he was treated by the various parts of the Berlin military and government complex – not for its militarism or racism.

Contemptuous of every other imperial power, Casement was left with a single candidate to support. He had in turn come to dislike England, France (and its client Belgium), Portugal, Spain, the United States, Russia and Turkey. Each had been found wanting. His remedy for the ills of the underdeveloped world, by a process of elimination, was instead a relatively untried imperial power. He believed in the necessity of a period of different imperialism before self-determination or independence could flourish. That belief was most recently grounded in his South American experience where he had no time for the successor states of the Spanish and Portuguese empires, and repeatedly said as much, which is not to say he did not have ideas of a non-imperial or post-imperial nature. He did, and most of them in the form of decolonisation and the creation of a British Commonwealth of dozens of independent states came to pass in the half century after his death. They were for the most part inconceivable to those in the London of his time but would become commonplace during the life of many of his acquaintances.

The Taoiseach, Bertie Ahern, in an unexpected speech at the Fianna Fail, Arbour Hill commemoration in April 1999 called for, "A new and rigorous enquiry into the provenance and genuineness of the so-called black diaries." He added that "today under our legislation of 1993, sexual orientation is thankfully no longer even nominally a crime." In other words, Ireland could cope either way with an answer to the diaries controversy. This was a test of his government's own making. But could Ireland cope?

To take the study of Casement further, as the Taoiseach and his adviser Dr Martin Mansergh intended, it would have to risk becoming controversial, preparing to address Ulster realities as I have tried to do. Casement was no prissy operator when it came to revolution. But like all revolutionaries he must be judged carefully, and assessed sternly as he chose a course that would destabilise the lives of many people. Perhaps he did not grasp this fact, for from jail in 1916 he could still write "I feel like a boy and my hands so free from blood." In this volume he is assessed from the viewpoint of one of those people who have been affected by his activities, as I have affected others, for it is not just the Congolese or the Huitotos of the Amazon who have good reason to recall Casement and to judge his actions. Nor is judgment the preserve of Irish nationalists and humanitarians.

In May 2000, at the Royal Irish Academy Symposium on Casement, in the *Black Diaries: A Question of Authenticity* section, there was concern at the tone of several contributions and the direction latterly taken in the final framing speech of Martin Mansergh. He spoke fluently and with authority, and in the "battle for the truth", quite properly, made a case both for further scientific research and for the possibility, indeed as he seemed to indicate, the likelihood, of forgery. But he also said that the author of the diaries had "absolutely no conscience in regard to his own sexual life" and no "obvious concern about its impact on his life's work if ever revealed."

If not an Irish nationalist, it is easier to accept that the diaries are authentic, while it goes against the grain for someone who is. One cannot fail to be, to some degree, *parti pris* dependent on where you are coming from. Being gay makes acceptance of the diaries as genuine more likely although such an orientation does not always guarantee a belief in authenticity. However, it is one thing to argue forgery and quite another to regard the diarist as without conscience, indeed it is quite perilous if that person is proven to be one and the same man whom Dr Mansergh also stated it was "legitimate to co-opt…as a forerunner of Ireland's independent foreign policy." Some argue further, that Casement formulated and transmitted that policy of neutrality and independence in Europe. But what is that policy worth if its source is proven corrupt?

The Black Diaries do not depict a monster nor someone more hypocritical than most of us in the sex department. If thought crime was on the statute book, Casement could be convicted of offences at the graver end of the scale. But then Irish prisons would be jammed tighter than ever before. He certainly eyed and mused over many sexually mature males, regardless of age. But in an era, and in countries, in which there was no age of consent for homosexual acts, as all were illicit or illegal, his behaviour was unremarkable. Like Oscar

Wilde, his interest was frequently angled toward youths. Yet nobody today in Dublin would even dare say that Wilde should still have been jailed for his sexual acts. The diarist-as-paedophile accusation, with all the echoes that has in contemporary Ireland, is being raised by those who cry forgery. They must be held responsible if Casement's reputation is needlessly sullied as a result.

He did not exploit people and was no "sexual coloniser" or "sex tourist". The partners Casement described were largely urbanised and usually eager, consenting men and boys of many races. Despite Dr Mansergh's view that the diarist was "as predatory towards the natives as those he criticised", as someone who wrote of fondling testicles, he could never be put in the same category as Armando Normand whom Casement accused of smashing testicles of Indians.

Hopefully this volume will put the dispute over Casement's homosexuality and the authorship of the Black Diaries to rest, as it provides thoroughgoing, irrefutable evidence for authenticity. This permits the opening up of discussion of the effect Casement's sexual orientation had on the shape of his humanitarianism and his Irish political career (which it had) as well as his revolutionism. Dr Mansergh also stated that the question "over the authenticity of the Black Diaries is a significant obstacle to a definitive assessment of some of Casement's life and achievements." The question has been answered. The obstacle has been removed however I am not sanguine about the outcome.

It was a matter of some pleasure that when researching Casement one came across other figures such as the indefatigable Belfast antiquarian Francis Joseph Bigger; Ada McNeill, the first Glens *Feis* organiser; Denis McCullough, the key Belfast Republican who was briefly President of Ireland in 1916, being President of the IRB; the musician Herbert Hughes, who wrote *My Lagan Love* and *She Moved Through The Fair*; Harford Montgomery Hyde, the liberal Unionist MP with a passion for writing on sex and spying; the droll Tyrone Republican, Patrick McCartan; the early human rights lawyer George Gavan Duffy, who kept a very troubled ship afloat in 1916 as Casement's solicitor; Mrs Ellen Gordon, the mother of Casement's boyfriend Millar; and others like Rose Young, the Gaelic writer of Galgorm Castle where the orphan Roger holidayed; people fascinating and courageous in their own way who enable one to understand better what Casement lived through and what he represented.

Casement studies proved to be a crowded house but not a cold one; a field as well-populated as the material. He was a ceaseless correspondent and could no more stop writing than he could stop cruising – the 6 May 1911 Cash Ledger entry records him penning thirty letters. This correspondence was the chain with which he created his friendships and managed to achieve political momentum on the issues of the Congo, the Amazon Indians and Ireland, but it means that the amount of autograph material to read is mountainous. All who knew

Casement are now dead although there is undoubtedly unseen material in the hands of families (but no longer officialdom) with the potential for discovery.

There is a need, indeed it would be a great kindness, for the mammoth stock of Casement papers to be catalogued, indeed for a Casement library or documentation centre to be established: I would suggest Ballymena as its location, where Casement was educated and lived longest in Ireland although I recognise this would create a classic Ballymena spat.

Jeffrey Dudgeon
Belfast
September 2002

This 2nd edition of my book is expanded by some fifty pages, as well as updated and corrected. It includes improved and extended versions of the 1903 and 1910 Black Diaries. There are a dozen new photographs and a further bibliography of Casement-related publications, listing the nearly fifty issued since 2002.

New characters are outlined like the Bavarian schoolboy, Max Zehndler, and the Batavian Casement aficionado, Heinrich d'Oleire. The birth name and progressive origins of Casement's mother Anne, a Dublin Protestant, have been ascertained. The ultimate fates of Casement's comrades on the submarine and in Germany – Daniel Julien Bailey, John McGoey, and Adler Christensen are discovered and described. Newly revealed Gertrude Parry and Elizabeth Bannister papers, bought by the NLI in 1952, but never catalogued, have added considerably, since the first edition, to the documentation now accessible in digitised records.

Finally, I tracked down Casement's 1881 Scribbling Diary in the NLI within a batch of significant papers that had been catalogued and numbered, but not indexed. The diary was thought lost or stolen since B.L. Reid saw it in the 1970s. It tells more about 'The Sweet Boy of Dublin'. Later in 2016, I edited and published an unabridged version of Casement's German Diary. It is the last of the known journals.

Cllr. Jeffrey Dudgeon MBE
Belfast
February-June 2016

In this 3rd edition, the 1910 and 1911 diaries are now complete and unabridged while the 1903 diary is considerably extended. It is thus 10% longer than the 2nd edition in 2016 and has more than a dozen new photographs. There are many further bibliographic items due in large part to the 100th anniversary of the Easter Rising and of Casement's execution. Further discoveries, revealed by digitisation, shine a light on the Casement papers that George Gavan Duffy probably destroyed in 1915, explaining the absence of key correspondents from the archives.

This volume remains, as the title says, the unique and definitive version of the Black Diaries and their authenticity, alongside an account of Casement's family, sexual life and Irish politics. (If you wish to read more about the 1903 Congo and 1910 Putumayo investigations, or a comprehensive biography, the books by Séamas Ó Síocháin and Roger Sawyer are recommended).

New evidence has enabled me to exonerate the American lawyer Michael Francis Doyle of suggestions that he misappropriated the US Casement defence money provided by John Devoy. Through the descendants of Adler Christensen's wives and the Norwegian author, Bjørn Godøy, more on Adler's rackety life and early death has been revealed.

That the diaries are authentic has broad acceptance. None the less, a vocal, and growing, group of diary deniers is at work. The issue of Millar's motor bike obtained from Cyril Corbally, for example, has now been re-opened with assertions of MI5 forgery. The old faith has not gone away but is being reinvented within the same parameters of conspiracy and anglophobia. It operates alongside the anti-revisionist resistance to modern Irish historians, in particular Roy Foster and Paul Bew, who are seen as its high priests (then down the ranks to this author). Casement, for the anti-revisionists, is understandably the intellectual progenitor and hero of Irish separatism. Unwisely, a belief in the diaries being forged by the British has become integral to their resistance.

The Casement author and post-modernist, Angus Mitchell, continues to advise that "the Diaries are skilled forgeries", that their creation involved "re-written versions of existing journals" and also that the forgers "interpolated existing Diaries or manufactured a new set with the sex-centred narrative." Regardless of which, he is clear that if they were Casement's work, "he deliberately authored diaries that executed him, dramatically compromised his work as an investigator of atrocities and betrayed himself as 'a man of no mind'".[3] Mitchell also states they are "homophobic documents" portraying "a predatory sex tourist who debased and objectified the native."

Thus the authenticity debate continues, one which can never be resolved to the satisfaction of all, even if the evidence points only in one direction.

Cllr. Jeffrey Dudgeon MBE
Belfast
January 2019

Angus Mitchell and Jeffrey Dudgeon at Murlough Bay 2016

Casement family genealogy

Note: Those Casements named **Roger**, of whom there are ten, are highlighted in bold, as are characters featuring in the diaries or in later events related in this book, or who are connected to Magherintemple (Churchfield). Non-Casement surnames are in capitals while ancestors of Roger David Casement (RDC) are in bold and capitals. The term d.s.p means died without issue.

WILLIAM CASEMENT of Sulby, Isle of Man d. ca. 1733 at Lezayre, m. 1719 **MARY THOMASON** (1697-1729) their elder son being **HUGH CASEMENT (great-great-grandfather)** of Ballinderry, Co. Antrim b. 1720 d. 10 July 1797 m. 1740 **ELIZABETH HIGGINSON (great-great-grandmother)** d. 8 July 1801 aged 80, five sons and two daughters (inc. **Mary m. Hugh HARRISON** of Churchfield, Ballycastle, memorial in Ballinderry middle churchyard, also to their 4th son Thomas and his son Charles and 5th son Higginson):

2nd son George (Surgeon RN) of Invermore, Larne (in 1798 rebellion) d. 1834 m. 1st Elizabeth MONTGOMERY, two sons: John m. Mary McGILDOWNY, and **Sir William Casement KCB** b. 1778 d. 1844, Major-General, Military Secretary to Governor General of India. He m. 2nd ca 1783 Martha or Matilda MONTGOMERY, two sons Major Hugh and Lt. George Casement.

3rd son **ROGER CASEMENT (great-grandfather)** of Henryville, Ballymena solicitor and land agent to Lord Massereene, b. ca. 1756 d. 19 May 1832 m. 1st 1787 **CATHERINE COSNAHAN (great-grandmother)** of Peel, Isle of Man b. 1768 d. 10 October 1809: ten sons and four daughters; m. 2nd 1819 "his maid" Margaret McQUITTY b. ca. 1799 d. 20 November 1877 in Glenarm when RDC aged 13: four sons and three daughters. He had twenty-one children (fourteen sons and seven daughters) between 1789 and 1828, the last at age 74. Those marked (1) or (2) are the first or second having the same name:

The 14 children (10 sons, 4 daughters) of Roger's 1st marriage (to Catherine Cosnahan):

William	b. 1789 d. 12 March 1848, memorial stone in Culfeightrin but left nothing in father's will, m. Mary Anne KENNEDY Ballymena 1834 or 1839; dau. also Mary Anne bapt. Kirkinriola 2 May 1824 m. Belfast 1858.
John (1)	b. 1791 d. 1825 Australia on leave from India, Captain.

George (1)	b. 1792 d. 1822 attorney, Ballymena, m. Abigail McILWAINE d. 1868: son William b. 1819 d. 1904 Portstewart m. 1869 Mary HAYES d. 1899.
HUGH	b. 1793 d. 1863 m. twice (see below, RDC's grandfather).
Elizabeth (1)	b. 1796 d. in childhood.
Julius (1)	b. 1797 d. 1829 on way home from India, military surgeon.
Roger (1)	b. 1798 d. young by 1820.
Thomas	b. 1799 d. 11 June 1874 **(great-uncle)** of Ballee House; 1st wife Jane MAXWELL (sister of Rev. Ross Jebb's wife) d. 1839 m. 2nd 1848 Dorinda ABBOTT d. 1 October 1886: **Catherine** b. ca. 1849 m. 1869 (separated 1874) **Col. Eldred POTTINGER** (d. 1905 Portstewart): four daughters inc. **Kitsie** b. 1871 and Edith (**Edie**). Thomas and his second wife Dora adopted – or at least took under their wing – Tommy Jebb.
Catherine	b. 1800 d. 1873 m. 1825 William COULSON, Lisburn: four sons, five daughters inc. Catherine b. 1830 m. **Rev. Augustine FITZGERALD** d. 1900, and **Annie** b. 1834.
Robert	b. 1801 d. 1887, Curate at Culfeightrin m. 1834 Frances WARING, two sons, two daughters inc. **Fanny** of Ardnabreen, Ballymena d. unm. 10 July 1907.
Francis	b. 1802 d. 1 May 1868, of Brocklamount, Co. Antrim, m. 1834 Christina DICKEY d.s.p. 7 September 1881.
Cornelius	b. 1804 d. young.
Elinor	b. 1805 d. 1843 m. 1826 David TURNBULL of Glasgow, consul Havana 1842-44, wrote on Jamaican slave trade, d. 1851.
Rosetta	b. 1809 d. in infancy.

The 7 children (4 sons, 3 daughters) of Roger's 2nd marriage (to Margaret McQuitty):

Roger (2)	b. 1820 d. unm. 1843 Bristol, BA TCD 1842.
Margaret	b. 1821 d. between 1877 and 1883 m. 1851 Isaac HARDY, Loughgall, son Charles (Ceylon) and four daughters inc. Annie, Charlotte and Georgina (Guernsey).
George (2)	b. 1822 d. unm. 24 Nov. 1883 Fenagh, Co. Antrim, barrister.

Elizabeth (2)	b. 1824 d.s.p. 2 July 1905 m. 1853 Moore SMITH, Toome d. 1917.
John (2)	b. 1825 d. 1902, of Magherintemple (see below).
Annie	b. 1828 d.s.p. m. 1st Thos POPHAM, Dublin, m. 2nd Frederick ROSS, RIC, Croaghpark, Co. Meath.
Julius (2)	b. 1830 21st and last child, d. 6 June 1904, Cronroe, Co. Wicklow, m. Minie CLARKE (d. 1918) four sons inc. **Maj. Roger** b. 1864 d. 1917 consequent on war service, grandson **Roddie** (1907-1987); three daughters inc. Margaret (d. 1953) mother of *The Ot,* Irish History Professor Jocelyn OTWAY-RUTHVEN of TCD d. 1989.

4th son of Roger and Catherine: **HUGH CASEMENT (grandfather)** ship-owner and general merchant 15 Tomb Street, and Donegall Square South, Belfast (1820s & 1830s), Drumbo, and The Moat House, Sydenham, Holywood (until 1843), London, Australia and New Zealand, b. 11 December 1793 d. 29 January 1863 Melbourne m. 1st 8 March 1816 **AGNES** (or **ELIZABETH**) **TURNBULL (grandmother)** a "daughter of Adam Turnbull" d. May 1848 London, age 53, two sons and four daughters:

1. **ROGER CASEMENT (father)** b. 23 May 1819 d. Ballymena 26 May 1877 when RDC aged twelve, m. 24 April 1855 St Anne's Church Belfast, **ANNE (ANNIE) JEPHSON or JEPSON (mother)** b. 14 July 1832, baptised 16 September 1832 St George's (Anglican), Hardwicke Place, Dublin, d. 27 October 1873 in Sussex, when RDC aged nine, daughter of **JAMES JEPHSON** also **JEPSON** of Dublin **(maternal grandfather d. 1840)** said to be son (with brother John) of another James Jephson and his wife Mary Martin of Ballinahinch Co. Galway and "grandson of Norreys Jephson", and **JANE (or ANNE) BALL (maternal grandmother)** d. 1853 aged 46, said to be the daughter of Captain Ball and a granddaughter of an Adam Ball MP, two daughters and four sons:

    1. **Agnes Jane (sister Nina)** b. 25 May 1856 in Dublin, m. London 26 October 1887 George Henry NEWMAN b. 1852, soon separated, widowed 1911, went to USA 1915, d. Atlantic City 2 April 1927.

    2. **A son** b. at Rathmines 5 July 1858, d. in infancy.

3. **Annie Catherine** b. 14 September 1859 at Kingstown, d. 20 April 1864 d. of hydrocephaly at Long's Cottage, Islington Avenue, Sandycove, buried Carrickbrennan graveyard Monkstown.

4. **Charles Adam William Ball (brother Charlie)** b. 5 October 1861 in Park Row, Knightsbridge, d. 10 January 1932 m. 1st 1890 **Minnie BALHARRY** b. 1869 d. of typhoid 1898: two daughters **Blanche Constance (Nina)** b. 1891 d. 1972 m. 1919 Arthur AYERS (five daughters, one Nina; dau. Lesley McNaughton); **Kathleen Gertrude** b. 15 November 1894 m. 1928 Neville VAUGHAN d.s.p. 17 April 1969. Charlie m. 2nd 1901 (secretly) **Beatrice MacGREGOR**: one daughter **Joan** b. ca 1905 m. 1940 John STUART, d.s.p. 1963. Charlie was baptised in St Anne's Church, Belfast on 9 April 1862, his parents' address being given as 174 York Street. Blanche Ayers and Kathleen Vaughan attended the reburial in 1965.

5. **Thomas Hugh Jephson (brother Tom, his Jephson name was perhaps added later)** b. "at sea", birth reputedly registered 3 January 1863 Boulogne, d.s.p. 6 March 1939 Dublin m. 1st ca. 1892 **Blanche BALHARRY** Australia b. 1866 d. Melbourne 1946, sister of Charlie's first wife, divorced ca 1911; m. 2nd 1912 **Katje ACKERMANN** South Africa, artist b. 1878 d. 1970.

6. **ROGER DAVID CASEMENT K.B. (1911) C.M.G. (1905), erased from C.M.G. register 30 June; degraded from Knighthood 1 July 1916, b. Sandycove, Dublin 1 September 1864, d. unm. 3 August 1916, executed and buried in Pentonville Prison aged 51, reburied Glasnevin cemetery, Dublin 1 March 1965. Significant companions: Millar Gordon b. 1890, from 1907 to 1914, d. 14 August 1956 Greystones; and Adler Christensen b. 1890, from ca. 1909 to 1915, d. Fresnes Prison, Paris 1 December 1935.**

2. Agnes b. ca. 1820 m. 1845 in Holywood, Dr Thomas AICKIN of Dublin, migrated to Auckland, New Zealand 1859: two daughters; Agnes and Eleanor, and seven sons; John, William, Casement, Thomas, George, Reg and Arthur.

3. Catherine b. 26 August 1822 d. 1839 buried Drumbo, Lisburn.

4. Henrietta b. 6 November 1823 d 1837 buried Drumbo, Lisburn.

5. Hugh b. Belfast ca. 1825 d. 1861 Australia m. ca. 1856 Isabella HUSSEY of Dublin b. 1836 d. 1924: two sons Francis and Somerville b. 1861. She m. 2nd Charles J. PERRY b.1817 d. 1893.

6. **Eleanor** b. ca. 1828 m. 1857 **Rev. Somerville LANPHIER** (d.s.p. 1877) who had a niece **Eva** (father Rev. Joseph of Ulcombe Rectory) with whom RDC "fell in love" at age 17 (b. 1869 or 1870, so she was only then about 12) d. 29 June 1937 m. 1887 Rev Charles Symons b. 1864 ministering in China from that year, Dean of Shanghai 1920 until d. 19 January 1928 (*Times* obituary 27 January); children: Irene, 2nd Lt. Charles Handley Lanphier Symons, Royal Fusiliers, d. 20 November 1917 aged 29 (Cambrai memorial Louverval) and 2nd Lt Eric Clarence Symons, Machine Gun Corps, d. of wounds 1 September 1916 age 22 at Amiens.

HUGH (grandfather) m. 2nd London ca 1850 Rachel ATKINS (b. ca 1829 d. 1907) his first wife's "companion", three sons and one daughter:

7. **Roger** David Atkins b. 1852 London d. 1925 m. 1880 Melbourne. Anna Meyer, one son and six daughters.[4]

8. Christina Henrietta (1858-62).

9. William Wilson b. 1859, served Boer War.

10. Walter George Hugh (1863-4).

The Churchfield/Magherintemple Line

The 13th son of Roger Casement (great-grandfather) and his second wife Margaret: John (half great-uncle and RDC's guardian) of Churchfield/ Magherintemple b. 29 November 1825 d. 13 October 1902 m. 1st 6 August 1849 Charlotte NEWCOMEN (1827-1857) three sons; m. 2nd 15 September 1859 **Charlotte MILLER** of Ballycastle b. 1836 d.s.p. 1909:

1. **Roger (great-uncle's son i.e. RDC's second cousin) of Magherintemple**, founder of Ballycastle Golf Club DL JP b. 30 November 1850 d. 17 September 1928 m. 8 February 1877 **Susanna BEATTY** of Dublin b. 22 February 1852 d. 10 February 1915: five sons (see below).
2. **Brabazon (Australia)** b. 1852 d. 24 February 1910 m. 1st 15 September 1880 Henrietta BURKE (d. 15 November 1881): **Charlotte Mary (May)** b. 3 July 1881 d. unm. Holywell Hospital June 1952; m. 2nd 1884 Islet SCOTT (d. 1917): three sons, four daughters, including Kathleen b. 1898.
3. **John (Jack) of Glenville, Cushendun, Rear-Admiral**, b. 22 July 1854 d. 8 June 1910 m. 23 December 1892 **Maria (Mya) YOUNG** b. 1860 d. 3 April 1943 niece of Charlotte Miller (see above) father John Young of Galgorm Castle, Ballymena: one daughter **Charlotte (Judy)** b. 22 January 1894 d. unm. 15 February 1969.

Roger (above second cousin) and Susie's five sons:

1. **John (young Jack) of Magherintemple** Dartmouth Naval College, b. 19 March 1880 d.s.p. 2 December 1944 m. 28 December 1916 Anne HODGES d. 13 June 1975.
2. Francis of Craigtara, Ballycastle DSO, Major-General RAMC First World War, b. 19 October 1881 d. 14 August 1967 m. 19 December 1916 Mabel HARRISON b. 1886 d. 1972: one daughter Alison, m. Lord COOKE of Islandreagh, and one son **Francis Charles of Magherintemple** Major RA b. 1920 d. 1976 in tractor accident m. 7 November 1942 Lesley BROWN, three sons and three daughters: **Hugh** b. 20 November 1947 (family genealogist and historian, lived in Bavaria); **Patrick of Magherintemple** b. 28 February 1951, educ. Campbell College, Belfast m. 13 December 1975 Anne RUSH: Niall Francis b. 1980, Rebecca Anne b. 1985; Robert b. 1953; Sarah; Anne; and Susan b. 1964 m. 2 January 1996 Roberto MOREIRA, living in Brazil: daughter Mariana.
3. **(Roger) Hugh**, railway engineer b. 8 April 1883 d. India 2 March 1924 m. 29 April 1911 Mary COWIE b. 1882 d. 1973: one daughter Joan Mary b. 6 February 1917.

4. **Robert (Bertie)** James, Lt. Canadian Engineers First World War, b. 19 November 1884 d. 15 June 1946 m. 9 October 1917 Dorothy BUCHANAN: two sons and one daughter.

5. **Edgar Reginald (Reggie)** of Coolgreany, Ballycastle, Captain RE First World War b. 13 October 1886 d. 28 September 1962 m. 18 August 1920 Grace SAVAGE: one son and two daughters.

The Bannister Family

Grace Ann JEPHSON (aunt; sister of Casement's mother) b. 14 July 1841 15 Portland Street, Dublin, baptised 3 October 1841 St George's Church of Ireland, Hardwicke Place, dau. of James (Gent) and Jane Jephson of 15 Portland Street Dublin, d. Liverpool 29 April 1906 m. 30 October 1865 St Anne's Church of Ireland Belfast **Edward BANNISTER (uncle by marriage)** Congo vice-consul, d. 1907 Harrogate:

1. Edith b. 1868 d. 1882.

2. **Elizabeth Anne (Lizzie, Eilis or Eily, cousin)** b. ca 1868 d. unm. 16 December 1942 in Edmonton nursing home, living with Margaret Dobbs at *Portnagolan* at date of will, 11 August 1942. Left £635.

3. **Gertrude Agnes (also Una) known as Gee (cousin)** b. 2 September 1873 Liverpool d. Cushendall 23 September 1950 (will dated 12 February 1944), m. 5 October 1916 at Church of Holy Trinity Bermondsey **Sidney Methold PARRY** of Oxmead, son of Lieut.-Colonel Sidney Parry, d. Cushendall 17 August 1937 (will dated 26 June 1937). Sidney's second cousins Brigadier Richard (Rufus) Frederick Parry (1907-1994) m. Elspeth Bird d. 17 February 2010 (son, John and a daughter) and Major John Onslow Parry d.s.p. became residual heirs to Roger Casement's estate by Gertrude's will.

4. **Edward (Eddie) Jephson, aka Squiggy (cousin)** b. 14 March 1876 Liverpool d. New York October 1943. The 1881 census also records an African servant, Jane Grace b. ca. 1863 in "Colon (S W), Africa", as living with the Bannisters.

Casement's mother Anne and her Jephson background had been in dispute until it was recently discovered that she had been baptised in an Anglican church in Dublin under, however, the surname Jepson. This clarified that her birth religion was Protestant. A cousin may be Jane Jephson who was married on 6

December 1854 in St Peter's Church, Aungier Street Dublin to James Martin (clerk in holy orders) of 2 Richmond Hill (both were from that address); the respective fathers were Richard Martin (clergyman) and John Jephson esq.; witnesses were Charles. H. Jephson and Isabell J Gurnell.

Sources: Hugh Casement, formerly of Germany, the present family historian; *Burke's Irish Family Records* 1976; NLI 17595 which has a family chart "copied by G A Parry" from an original by Casement; also NLI 17602, and 36207/8 which includes what may be that original, an 1881 "Ironmongers' Diary." They have dubious details of Casement's mother's origins, indicating a line of descent through Norreys Jephson, son of Anthony Jephson and Hannah Rogerson, whom Burke records as dying without issue, and an Adam Ball, described as an MP and Irish Postmaster General who does not feature in standard listings.

Other sources include gravestones in Co. Antrim; original and copy wills in PRONI of Margaret Casement (d. 1877), George Casement (d. 1883), Robert Casement (d. 1887), Frances (Fanny) Casement (d. 1907), Sidney Parry (d. 1937) and Gertrude Parry (d. 1950); land purchase related copies of wills there of Roger Casement (great-grandfather d. 1832), his sons Roger Casement (d. 1843) and Julius (d. 1904); in the Probate Office London, copy will of Hugh Casement (grandfather d. 1863 in Australia), letters of administration for Grace Bannister's estate; in the General Register's Office, Southport, the birth certificate of Charlie Casement and death certificate of Annie Casement.

Prologue: the execution

Casement signed off the last letter he would ever write, the last of very many thousands, with the salutation, "Ever defeated – Yet undefeated". Writing of the cause of Ireland "Surely it is the most glorious cause in history", he called on his compatriots to "think of the long succession of the dead",[5] a succession he would be joining in a few hours. This was the letter still warm in Casement's coat that Father James McCarroll copied surreptitiously. Had he not done so, it would have joined all the prisoner's recent notes and correspondence in the furnace, including his jail journal, a document headed *My Prison Diary*.

This mean-minded destruction was ordered by Sir Ernley Blackwell, chief legal adviser to the Cabinet and Home Office official, as dedicated as Casement to detail, although in Blackwell's case to imperial not Irish or humanitarian interests. The "properly detained" documents "sent up now from the prison should be destroyed forthwith" ordered Sir Ernley, a deed he neatly marked "Done EB 16/8/16."[6] There would be many more such little tasks undertaken by Blackwell before his retirement fifteen years later. No Casement matter was too trivial for him to deal with. Thus did the last of Casement's diaries go unread into the flames along with a letter to Agnes O'Farrelly, reckoned treasonable and martyr-fixated, which called on his friends to "roll away the stone from my grave."[7]

Even for a man long conditioned to the fate intended by his enemies, Casement admitted to feeling the strain: "The long waiting has been a cruel thing, three months and eleven days now." And though he always gave the impression of certainty about execution there had been flashes of hope. "They dare not hang me",[8] he told his solicitor on 14 June. When the Cabinet decision against a reprieve came through, it was just a matter of waiting for a few more hours. "And if I die, as I think is fated, tomorrow morning I shall die with my sins forgiven and God's pardon on my soul." Casement was concerned about how he would face the last moments, and consoled himself by writing "I hope I shall not weep, but if I do it shall be nature's tribute wrung for me – one who never hurt a human being – and whose heart was always compassionate and pitiful for the grief of others."[9]

During his last evening walk Casement was observed in the prison yard by an English prisoner, a conscientious objector, Fenner, later Lord Brockway, who recounted how "Casement's gaze was fixed steadfastly in the direction of the setting sun which he watched disappear below the horizon of the prison wall for the last time. His face was wonderfully calm and he seemed already to be living in another world; there was not a trace of fear or anxiety in his features."[10]

On the night of 2 August, after his first confession, Casement slept peacefully. At 7.30 a.m. at Mass in the prison chapel in Pentonville he took his first and last Roman Catholic Holy Communion. Refusing breakfast, he instead expressed a desire to go fasting to the scaffold, so that his God might be the last food he had on earth: "He took off his shoes (as a sign of humility) and as he raised his head to receive the host, his face was transfixed and he remained a long time at prayer at the altar rail"[11] one priest reported. From then until nine o'clock was passed in further quiet prayer in the condemned cell.

The Governor and the executioners duly arrived to take him to the scaffold. As the party walked toward the execution shed, Father Carey recited the litany for the dying and Casement made the responses, marching "with the dignity of a prince."[12] There awaiting him was the hangman John Ellis, a hairdresser from Rochdale, and his assistant Robert Baxter. Casement had already been weighed and measured for the drop. His height was just short of 6' 2"; his neck was assessed as "muscular" and his weight given as 168 pounds – exactly 12 stone. With these details, and according to a mathematical formula, the drop was calculated to ensure the prisoner was not decapitated nor left with his neck unbroken to experience the long and intense torture of asphyxiation. Maurice Joy, later that year, wrote of his friend "He is dead this Knight of the Flaming Heart, hanged by the neck with a rope manipulated by a Rochdale barber."[13]

Father McCarroll remembered how Casement quietly "submitted to the attentions of the executioner. With his hands bound, he walked calmly to the scaffold, repeating the words 'Into thy hands I commend my spirit'. His last words were 'Lord Jesus, receive my soul.'"[14] While Canon Ring, in a 1935 memoir of the horrible event, wrote that after Casement's hands were pinioned behind his back "like an uplifted lance, he raised himself to full height, saying 'For God and Kathleen ni Houlihane'…a white wrapper was drawn over his head, his feet were gently strapped together, I watched the noose drawn round his neck with the knot under his jaw. The bolt was drawn and the tall, silent frame of a great man dangled in the pit from a rope-end, and his soul had winged its way to the Great Tribunal where so many sentences and judgments are reversed."[15]

Ellis, the chief executioner (later a suicide), having placed a rope round Casement's throat, a few moments later pulled the lever. He dropped through the trap and the noose instantly tightened over his Adam's apple, hopefully to break his neck. If not it would start to strangle him to death. Casement was now apparently unconscious but since it could take up to twenty-five minutes to die from suffocation his body was left dangling as a precaution. It was, however, a highly satisfactory job as the prison's governor and medical officer attested in the paperwork.

Cause of death was given as a "fracture dislocation of the cervical vertebrae."[16] Casement was buried in quick lime in the prison yard, but not immediately. Dr Percy Mander, the medical officer at Pentonville, had still to perform a special service for Sir Ernley Blackwell. He duly reported to him: "I made the examination which was the subject of our conversation at the Home Office on Tuesday, after the conclusion of the inquest today, and found unmistakable evidence of the practices to which it was alleged the prisoner in question had been addicted. The anus was at a glance seen to be dilated and on making a digital examination (rubber gloves) I found that the lower part of the bowel was dilated as far as the fingers could reach. The execution went off without a hitch and prisoner was dead in forty seconds from leaving the cell. The vertebrae were completely severed and spinal cord also, so that death was absolutely instantaneous."[17] Thus was Blackwell provided with more evidence of what he described to the Home Secretary as "the most engrossing pursuit" of Casement's life.[18]

Father Edward Murnane of Holy Trinity, Dockhead told Casement's friend Sidney Parry on 30 September 1916 about the behaviour of the crowd: "This is the most Irish church in London and the majority of devout souls who were present outside Pentonville and fell on their knees and prayed for dear Roger and thereby stopped the barbarians' booing and cheers were from here."[19] The foundation deed of Holy Trinity indeed stipulated that one of its priests should be an Irish speaker.

In stark contrast to the intense spirituality building around an Irish martyr, Ernley Blackwell had been continuing to excavate Casement's other life. After the trial two Harley Street doctors, R. Percy Smith and Maurice Craig (who was also Rupert Brooke's physician), were given the 1911 Black Diary and Cash Ledger to inspect. On 10 July 1916 they provided the Home Office with its first professional opinion on Casement's sexuality and state of mind. The two doctors deduced his writings "contain definite evidence of sexual perversion of a very advanced type...long standing and chronic." The detail, and the intermingling with everyday material, were particularly unusual, they thought. There was, however, "no evidence of delusion or general intellectual defect, but that he should permit himself to write such compromising and obscene matter in his diary and ledger they thought indicated that the writer was a man whose disordered instinct and feelings influenced and outweighed his judgment."

The frequency of the obscene incidents proved "how absorbed his mind was on this subject." He therefore "must be regarded as a mentally abnormal individual" although he was not certifiably insane, the facts being too meagre.

However, Casement's "absorption in the subject and at times his conduct suggest much more mental disorder than is usually met with in a person who is suffering only from a perverted instinct."[20] The doctors seemed more disturbed by the writer's effrontery in describing his (enjoyable) sexual experiences than about his supposedly diseased state of mind, one they were quite familiar with.

Others were surprised and disturbed by what Ernley Blackwell triumphantly showed them. The Archbishop of Canterbury, Dr Randall Davidson, was asked by John Harris, a former Baptist missionary in the Congo and a friend and ally of Casement in the Anti-Slavery Society to sign a petition "in favour of a mitigation of the capital sentence passed on Roger Casement." He refused, writing instead to Herbert Samuel, the Home Secretary with what was in effect a character reference: "I think perhaps I ought to write a few lines to you on account of the relation I formerly had to Casement when I was promoting the protests or agitation about the Congo, and subsequently when the Putumayo atrocities were being investigated. At each of these times I saw something of Casement and was always impressed by his capacity, his enthusiasm and his apparent straightforwardness…I am aware of course that there is another element in the question, namely, the accusations which are current against him respecting unnatural vice."

The Archbishop (whom Casement had previously categorised as an "old shifter") then reported that John Harris had assured him "from intimate knowledge of Casement's life in the close intercourse which Casement and Harris had during the Congo days he is able to say without hesitation that at that time he was one of the purest of men at a time when opportunity of vice was not only easy but was commonly yielded to."

These opportunities for vice were attested to by another of Casement's colleagues from Congo days, Dr Fred Puleston, who wrote in his book *African Drums* of how the most moral of young men would eventually succumb to the lure of African women. He made no mention of boys being as easily procured. Puleston did note that Casement had been given two native names *Swami* or Woman's God, and *Monafuma*, Son of a King, which suggest he was attractive to women but reckoned too lofty or perhaps too distant, to misuse them.

The Archbishop, like many other sympathisers, then tried to promote the insanity argument in order to encourage a reprieve: "If Casement is now guilty in the vicious way alleged it may be taken as further evidence of his having become mentally unhinged. I have to do pretty frequently with problems of vice of that sort, and I suppose it is indisputable that sometimes a mental upset takes the shape of vicious behaviour, especially of an unnatural kind."[21]

The mood of the time was plainly unfavourable to a straightforward reprieve and the insanity angle seemed at first the only runner. It is likely the Archbishop felt that attaching his name to a public petition was inappropriate given his station, while the sexual rumours made it even more so. He chose instead to apply pressure from within the establishment.

The Home Secretary declined a request from John Harris for an interview, offering him only an audience with his legal adviser, Ernley Blackwell. Harris was quite confident that the stories were false. In his letter of 17 July to Herbert Samuel "with reference to the other charge which is being circulated" he said "in spite of appearances there is some dreadful mistake…I am absolutely convinced, and with solid reason, that Casement is innocent of moral depravity and think I could give you good ground for saying this."

Certain that he was going to turn the tables on the authorities, and unlike the Archbishop who had declined an invitation to view the evidence, Harris turned up to be shown "the diary and other 'exhibits' bearing on it." Ernley Blackwell did the honours personally.[22] Harris brought with him a copy of his memorandum to Archbishop Davidson on Casement's "alleged depravity". It outlined a number of reasons for disputing the government's "serious mistake", all six of which the writer Angus Mitchell quotes.[23] The first was that "Casement's whole life and conduct was a perpetual and vigorous protest against the prevailing immorality." On his copy, Blackwell later noted tartly "1–5 may be regarded as withdrawn."

After an hour alone with the material, the man who had been "firmly convinced that the diary was not Roger Casement's handiwork" believed otherwise: "Alas when it was put before me and I had examined certain parts, my confidence was shaken. Then I came upon two or three facts only known in Europe to Casement and myself and then my hopes were shattered, for I realised that the wretched thing was genuine."[24]

The naming of one particular boy (a native servant) particularly turned Harris.[25] He was so upset he went pale and needed water, describing the diary as "the unfolding of a life which for years had been poisoned by disease." The likeliest candidate for the boy was Richard Koffee who appeared in the 1903 Black Diary in May, involved in sexual chatter with Casement. Harris felt somewhat consoled, as he described to the Archbishop on 19 July, to find that there "appears to be no certain evidence that these abominable things were practised in the Congo – it may be that our presence checked them." Harris did offer to visit Casement in Brixton but he declined, indicating that they could only have a few minutes together in the presence of a warder, which would be "painful."[26] Casement plainly did not relish a conversation about the diaries or his sins.

His name was subsequently to be omitted from Harris's 1933 book *A Century of Emancipation*, instead he was referred to, where relevant, as "the British consul". However, he does appear by name in an unpublished autobiography of Harris, presently in the papers of the Anti-Slavery Society. Harris, later a Labour MP was also a Home Ruler, but despite his progressive politics seems to have been less liberal and certainly less worldly than the Archbishop. Admittedly Dr Davidson being an Anglican would have, as he said, more experience of the subject. Lady Harris, forty years on, remembered Casement more fondly than her husband, describing him as a man with "a good figure and a great attraction for the ladies."

Dr Davidson exhibited due Christian charity when he replied the same day to Harris: "One feels that an incident such as this sends us all to our knees and that is really all we can say, but it is the best." The Home Office was by now satisfied thinking it had finally seen off church-related reprieve agitation. The Archbishop, however, was to make a final plea instead to the Lord Chancellor, Lord Buckmaster, on 1 August, two days before the execution. By this point he was, in a last artful throw, trying to turn the circulation of the diaries to Casement's advantage. He adduced the fear that people in America and Ireland would make mischievous capital of the execution "far more so if they could (as they would) spin a tale to the effect...that the authorities had been privy to the trumping up of an infamous story about the man's immorality, an accusation with which he had never been confronted."[27] This somewhat disingenuous try, given the verification of the diaries provided by Harris, was not to succeed, but it proves the Archbishop's persistence in seeking to save Casement's life.

In a final defence of his mission, one at odds with the moral and medical conclusions above, Casement declared, "My dominating thought was to keep Ireland out of the war. England has no claim on us, in law or morality or right. Ireland should not sell her soul for any mess of Empire. If I die tomorrow bury me in Ireland, and I shall die in the Catholic Faith, for I accept it fully now. It tells me what my heart sought long – but I saw it in the faces of the Irish. Now I know what it was I loved in them. The chivalry of Christ speaking through human eyes – it is from that source all lovable things come, for Christ was the first Knight.

"What was attempted so valiantly this year by a handful of young men is the only episode of this war that should survive in history. The rest is either mistaken slaughter of brave men or plotting to destroy an enemy by hate for motives of greed and dominion. I cast no stone at the millions of brave dead throughout Europe – God rest their souls in peace... [but] Ireland alone went forth to assail evil,"[28] he argued.

In the summer of that year of 1916 thousands of Ulstermen (and Irishmen) died at the Somme. Five hundred Irish people and British soldiers had died at Easter in Dublin. The hanging of this one man was, however, unique in that so many were aware both of who he was, and of it happening. He was known by hundreds of people and had influenced a generation of Irish nationalists, more perhaps than they knew. Many were devoted to him. All were aware of the indescribable pain he was experiencing and of the mental torture suffered that comes from the knowledge of knowing weeks in advance of the precise moment of one's death.

Casement's life had enormous width, ranging over four continents and many countries. Unlike most of his contemporaries he had had a career of so many segments that he knew individuals from every class, race and nationality. His charisma and the sheer force of his personality had entranced the famous and the powerful, and those survivors of the rising in Ireland who were soon to become famous and powerful.

On that Thursday morning his friends, family, acquaintances, and casual intimates were contemplating what was about to happen to the man they knew. Some loved him, many admired him, some had had sex with him. The small number of his private enemies, and the vast number of people who wanted him to die because of his treason, were also considering his imminent hanging, in their case, with some satisfaction. Some, especially those sharing his name, were in a quandary. In Ireland a few were frightened, while hundreds of thousands were beginning to sense martyrdom and were part-fascinated and part-sickened.

In Ulster in Ballycastle, Ballymena and Belfast – Antrim towns all – there was a complex mix of expressions and feelings from those who knew him. Most of the Protestants of Ulster were pleased to see a friend of Germany die to pay for the loss of so many of their sons at the Somme. In Dublin, Cork and Donegal they would mourn him. In regaelicised Ulster he was already a saint. In London and in Liverpool they knew him well. Many of those in England's establishment were acquainted with him and had fought with him, or like F.E. Smith prosecuted him, but by no means all were his enemy.

Wee aunty Bannister and her three children, his cousins, Gee, Eddy and Eily knew him. He changed the girls' lives forever, as much as any husband ever could.

They knew him in Paris, in Brussels, in Lisbon and in Naples. In Germany he had been amongst them for his last eighteen months of relative freedom – in Berlin, in Hamburg and Munich. For twenty years he had been among them on the Congo river and in Nigeria, Liberia, Angola, Mozambique, and South Africa and they knew him, whether they were native, trader, explorer or settler; in the case of the Congo Africans they also had cause to be grateful to him.

They knew him in the ports and towns of the Atlantic, in Madeira and the Canaries, and in Barbados, where he took his leisure. In Australia and New Zealand, where successive Casements, including his grandfather had migrated, he was family, while his execution was about to take its toll on his brother Charlie in Melbourne. In Brazil, in Pará, Manaos, Santos, Rio de Janeiro and Petropolis they knew him; in Peru, in Iquitos they also knew him biblically and diplomatically, and on the Putumayo river and its tributaries, many Indians were alive because of him, while certain local Spanish were now gleeful, having lost their living and in some cases freedom because of him.

In America, in New York, Philadelphia and Washington, Joe McGarrity, John Devoy and John Quinn knew him and loved him, and with them now was the woman who loved him longest, his sister Nina.

They knew him in the consular service, in the Foreign Office, in the Anti-Slavery Society, in the Liberal Party, even in the Conservative Party, amongst the Irish Volunteers, in the Gaelic League, in Sinn Féin circles, at Irish language schools. The old boys of Ballymena Academy knew him, as did the new boys of every town and city he visited or frequented.

Millar Gordon and Adler Christensen knew him, loved him and in the latter case betrayed him. John McGonegal, Francis Naughton, José Gonzalez, Ramón Tapia, Bernardino, Welsh Will, Casaldo, Fortunato *et al.* had been enjoyed by him although they did not object.

Francis Joseph Bigger from Ardrigh on the Antrim Road in Belfast, Cathal O'Byrne, Denis McCullough, Bulmer Hobson knew him. Miss Cox and Miss Vigrass and Mrs Thomas, his landladies in London and Belfast knew him. Ricudo and Omarino, the Putumayo boys knew him. Dick Morten, Herbert Ward, E.D. Morel (EDM), William Cadbury, and Sidney Parry, had known him for years, loved him, funded him (or were funded by him) and only in Ward's case felt betrayed by him.

At the same time he had betrayed those many from the Casement family who were serving in the wartime forces (some his precise namesakes) and their wives and children. They knew him, had given him a home, a county and an identity and would pay an unwelcome cost for three generations. Yet in Antrim and all around Ireland other members of that same class did not feel betrayed by him – rather the opposite; Rose Young, Margaret Dobbs, Ada McNeill, Jack White, Alice Stopford Green, Eva Gore-Booth; they shared his new nationality and understood his treason was their patriotism, as they threw in their lot with the revolution.

Had he not been captured immediately he landed off the German submarine at Banna Strand or had his trial and appeal been spun out for a few months more, the reprieve already granted to de Valera and Markievicz and the early release of those imprisoned, like Eoin MacNeill and W.T. Cosgrave, would have propelled him into the War of Independence, partition, the Civil War and the new ascendancy in the Free State with the Fianna Fail and Fine Gael parties, and finally into a Republic. It is a speculation too intriguing to ignore, to place Casement in a post-independence twenty-six county Ireland.

His career path had perhaps half a dozen directions to go. Judging from his class, caste and cohorts his fate might have been that of Bulmer Hobson (1883-1969), Denis McCullough (1883-1968), Erskine Childers (1870-1922), Constance Markievicz (1868-1927), Patrick McCartan (1878-1963), Ernest Blythe (1889-1975), Alice Stopford Green (1847-1929) or Douglas Hyde (1860-1949). An unintended destination might have been that reached by another Irish Protestant whose life patterns and national sympathies were remarkably similar, Oscar Wilde (1854-1900). To go into reverse, to go back to Unionism (whence he had never actually come) like the Abbey playwright St John Ervine or the peculiar Herbert Pim (who stayed a Catholic, becoming a confrère of Lord Alfred Douglas) was never a possible eighth option for Casement.

Bulmer Hobson suffered the ignominy of being excluded from the inner IRB conspiracy in the Volunteers and being arrested "all in a tremble" by his own side on Good Friday 1916, and held as a precautionary measure until Easter Monday at the Phibsboro house of Martin Conlon whence he had been lured. His conclusion in 1953 on the whole enterprise was "The Phoenix of our youth has fluttered to earth such a miserable old hen."[29] Hobson was never forgiven, indeed he was almost ostracised. A rare few like Cathal Brugha and later his son Ruairi (formerly *Ruadhrai*) maintained social contact. He played no further part in mainstream Irish politics despite his earlier critical role and ended his days a forgotten remnant. Hobson was fond of quoting the remark "not having been in jail, as MacNeill had said, I had no political future." He was to be written out of the new ruling class despite his unlikely position as an Ulster Protestant, indeed a non-ascendancy Quaker dissenter, and an early and seminal Republican organiser.

Denis McCullough, Hobson's colleague in early Republican Belfast, prospered and did the state some service in peacetime business development. Erskine Childers took the Republican side in the civil war and was shot, almost out of hand, for possession of a revolver – by his erstwhile Free State colleagues. Alice Stopford Green became an ornament of the Irish upper house, the Free State Senate, while Constance Markievicz, the first ever woman MP, fought in the Civil War and was elected a Fianna Fail TD in 1927 only to die soon afterwards. Ernest Blythe, another Ulster Protestant, became Minister of Finance in 1923 and a steely managing director of the Abbey Theatre for twenty-six years until 1967. Patrick McCartan although latterly a Senator, like his fellow Ulster revolutionary Bulmer Hobson never fulfilled his early promise.

Douglas Hyde became the first President of Ireland in 1938, a job that would have been Casement's for the asking had he survived (and whose funeral would at least have been attended by the Irish Cabinet, unlike Hyde's); that is if he had not taken some appointment on the international stage. Casement would probably have given his reluctant support to the Treaty, like his solicitor in 1916 George Gavan Duffy, while his stand in the Civil War might have tended to the neutral as happened with the other older Ulster revolutionaries he knew so well. Then again partition might have driven him to the extreme edge of Republicanism where nearly all the female Irish revolutionaries ended up.

Or might he have been disgraced? In an unhelpful view, one English writer, John Sparrow, asked "What would life have had to offer to the ageing Casement on his ultimate release? He might have grown hard – 'withered old and skeleton-gaunt, an image of his politics'; or (worse fate) he might have grown soft, the fine figure of his early manhood, declining entirely into the epicene Casement known of old to Agostinho. Either way, it was better to die in mid-career, 'changed, changed utterly' by martyrdom."[30] Not so the latter, anyway; Casement would never have stood still long enough, although he might have gone a little dotty like Nina, and as his brother Tom increasingly became.

The historian and IRB Supreme Council member, P.S. O'Hegarty (1879-1955), asked a key question for revolutionaries in his 1924 book *The Victory of Sinn Féin*, and for those legitimate governments who enter wars swiftly and casually: "We adopted political assassination as a principle; we turned the whole thoughts and passions of a generation upon blood and revenge and death; we placed gunmen, mostly half-educated and totally inexperienced, as dictators with powers of life and death over large areas. We decided the moral law, and said there was no law but the law of force, and the moral law answered us: Every devilish thing we did against the British went its full circle, and then boomeranged and smote us tenfold; and the cumulating effect of the whole of it was a general moral weakening and a general degradation, a general cynicism and disbelief in either virtue or decency, in goodness or uprightness or honesty."[31]

Casement, had he survived, might have started to ask important questions such as that posed by his former comrade but it is doubtful if he was psychologically or politically equipped to do so. He was a radical and a romantic.

1

Introduction

For its percentage of the British population, Victorian Ireland was particularly well endowed with grand families whose sons were increasingly available, and called upon, to service the ever-expanding empire. Africa was being opened up. Australia required colonists, while India needed soldiers, officials and modernisers. Throughout the nineteenth century, transformation of Ireland's political, economic and power structures was also gathering pace. Catholic rivalry over Protestant predominance in jobs, places and land necessitated a response from the dominant classes, and from southern Protestants in particular.

One response was to resist the coming changes or at least try to postpone them with delaying tactics. Another response, favoured more by women – Oscar Wilde's mother Speranza being an early example – was to link into the coming power, at first only into the Gaelic cultural and language revival, but slowly from there into nationalism, separatism and inexorably into Catholicism, by conversion or marriage.

The third, the option of Casement's family, one especially for younger sons, was emigration or the armed forces (which had always drawn a high proportion of Casement males). No longer did Irish Protestants head only for America. That was now predominantly a Catholic escape route. They were directed instead to the newer British Empire. With ever fewer traditional openings in Dublin's administrative or commercial life, boys who did not have the background, drive or finance to participate in the building of an industrial society (the new frontier within Ireland) moved out. Only in Ulster, and then from a different class and to an extent another ethnic group, the Scots Presbyterians, did such an industrial aristocracy emerge. The Casement family was Anglican (Church of Ireland), it was gentry (if only recently) and it was land-owning. Having no industrial connections, it had little spare wealth. So the colonies were the outlet for surplus Casements, those who did not welcome the military life.

In the century before Ireland's partition, southern and northern Anglicans of the gentry class were one breed having more in common with each other than with any Presbyterian neighbours. They intermarried within and without the island, and provided the political and legal class in Dublin. Opportunities in that capital city, however, were diminishing with the rise of the new, driving Catholic classes keen to intrude upon Protestant monopolies, and overthrow what was looking more and more like a caste system. The law and politics were increasingly Catholic but administrative power was reserved to London and, alongside finance, lingered under the control of Unionists – of both religions. Ironically, with the collapse of Irish Gaelic, there was now a common language spoken by both the Catholic majority and the ruling Protestant minority.

The disestablishment of the Church of Ireland in 1869 was a harbinger of an imminent and sharp decline for southern Protestants. The confidence of that ruling class (though not a governing class), with its sense of certainty and right to predominate, was ebbing away. The Church had now gone. In a sense the State had gone with the Act of Union in 1801. Catholic emancipation in 1829 put politics literally into the hands of Catholic parliamentarians for the first time, and increasingly so with an ever-extending franchise and the advent in 1872 of the secret ballot.

It took the best part of a century for the Catholic population to escape from under their Protestant masters and put themselves into power in the 1920s, alone, and without them. As late as 1890 a Protestant landlord, Charles Stewart Parnell, was leading Catholic Ireland. Perhaps because of that he exacerbated the dispute with Ulster by use of uncompromising Ireland-a-Nation rhetoric. Not being Catholic, he could not afford to display any weakness to northern Protestants. He became a messiah, a Bonaparte figure to his followers, including the teenage Roger Casement. Having fused within himself the characteristics of two cultures, Parnell was able to call himself the leader of the Irish Nation, not the Anglo-Irish or the Gaelic Irish, but the *Irish* Nation.

Ulster, however, was continuing to operate on the lines of a frontier society where nothing was inevitable and anything could happen. The class structure was fluid. Men made themselves economically and then became politically powerful: Edward Harland and Gustav Wolff, the Belfast shipyard pioneers, became Westminster MPs. The new frontier in Ulster was industry and its pioneers were most often Presbyterians. They rose out of Scottish backgrounds, often aided by Jewish expertise and finance. Many such new men were actually born in Scotland which should be no surprise as, at its closest, Scotland is ten times nearer Co. Antrim than Dublin. Indeed, from large parts of the Antrim and Down coasts, Scotland is visible and accessible. However, the last thing frontiers people are able to do is blend into the ethnicity of those on the far side of the frontier. They exist not to. The exception is through marriage. However, the 1907 *Ne Temere* decree of Pope Pius X, on the faith of the children of such mixed marriages, ensured that that traffic would be one way and largely the reverse of earlier times.

Frontiersmen are often rough. Life is perilous and frequently short. Identity is largely negative, being defined by what one is not. Refinement and culture must await the third generation. And there is an enemy across the frontier, be it mental or physical, which does not go away. It is not for nothing that in America the Scotch-Irish, as they later became known, were the best at clearing a frontier. They had 17th century experience of doing it before in North Ireland, and did so again in 18th and 19th century North America. The downside was an inability to settle, especially a failure to tend the land, and a propensity to crude religiosity and drink. These failings were often allied to democratic instincts, which can make a heady brew.

The contemporary United States frequently reveals the influences of that first Irish migration out of Ulster. If the Protestant community was ever to be obliterated in Northern Ireland it could assuredly rest happy genetically, knowing it had successfully replicated itself, under another name, across the Atlantic. But that culture was never going to attract Irish Anglicans of a certain sensibility like the Casements.

Each new generation has a preordained role, hinged to its family's then status and history. Individuals may break free but often only in reaction to their background. Many start off as rebels and return to the fold. The question is, did Casement carve out a radical and novel path or was it one well trodden? Did he betray his family, class, religion, his gender and his nation, or did he act out the suppressed or residual dreams of his people? Did he, as a political front-runner, offer them instead a long-term future on the island of Ireland?

Exactly who Casement's people were perhaps needs answering first. He was so many, often contradictory things; an Irishman and an Ulsterman, British Imperialist and Irish Republican – although never Scottish or Presbyterian. Confirmed an Anglican, he was both a Protestant and a Catholic; apparently heterosexual yet unquestionably homosexual. From the very beginning he was different, more varied in every sense than others in his family or class. He came from a disturbed family unit which was to get more disturbed. Every indicator was therefore present to predict an unsettled or original future, one which could bring little satisfaction to him but a great deal of good or damage to others.

He was born near Dublin on 1 September 1864 and named Roger David. Although David was not a regular Casement family name, Roger certainly was, being the name of his father and great-grandfather. It was a name that was to be used ten times over four generations before it died out for obvious reasons. The last boy so called was to be listed permanently as Roddie, his full forename remaining unused for the rest of his life. Being only nine in the key year of 1916, this Roddie's parents were able to stick with the diminutive and not advance him to the unwelcome Roger.

With such a confusion of Rogers, Casement was, as he explained in about 1882, even being called "occasionally, but rarely now, Doddie."[32] Later when writing home from Africa to Ballycastle he signed himself Roddie, sometimes

David, but ultimately become Roger to his eponymous cousin in a last letter from the death cell. He was fond also of humorous variants like Scodgie, and an Irish version, The O'Scodge, especially in letters to his favourite cousin, Gertrude Bannister.

The name Roger, however, did live on, but in Irish Republican families. Eamon de Valera named one of his sons for Casement, that born three months after the execution on 3 November 1916. Dev, however, used Ruaidhri, a Gaelic version of the name. The West Belfast Gaelic Athletic Association sports ground was named Casement Park (*Parc Mac Aismaint*) at its opening on 21 June 1953 which ensures the surname has a daily resonance in Belfast Catholic circles, and will have for decades to come. Casement would be hugely pleased to know that splendid boys abound in Belfast wearing sweatshirts with his name emblazoned on their backs.

In contrast, the sculptor Herbert Ward, a great friend of Casement's from Congo days, had his own son, at Eton, unnamed 'Roger Casement' Ward. The first petition for a change was made as early as January 1915 "in consequence of unfavourable views to which the utterances of the said Sir Roger Casement have lately given rise in the public mind." The Wards' fear was that the name was detrimental to their son's career, destined as he was for the Grenadier Guards. Ironically, another mutual friend, J.H. Morgan, who had just defended Casement at his treason trial, took up the pleading in September 1916, declaring that bearing the name "of a convicted felon" was ignominious, would bring undesirable notoriety and carried a real stigma for the boy. Ward, he told the Home Secretary, would be satisfied with "nothing less than a Royal Licence or an Act of Parliament."[33] In the event, he had to make do with a deed poll name change which was gazetted in November 1916.

Both Herbert Ward and Casement had worked for General Henry Sanford in the Congo in the late 1880s; Ward was also on Stanley's Emin Pasha Relief Expedition in 1887 so Africa still coloured Ward's life when the replacement names of 'Rodney Sanford' were selected for his son. Coincidentally, his wife's maiden name was Sanford, which provided a safe alternative source for the boy's new second prenom should the American diplomat also be revealed as having a murky past. The Wards lost one son killed, and had another captured during the First World War which added to their desire to distance themselves from a traitor and his name. Their prisoner-of-war son was actually the first to escape from a German camp and get back to England.

Herbert Ward, an author as well as a sculptor, majored in African and primitive art. Some of his magnificent African pieces are in the Smithsonian Museum. He had published, in 1910, a vivid picture of the man he came to hate, one that mirrors many others, for Casement had something spectacular about his presence that captivated those he met, especially women. He also magnetised Ward, who in his book *A Voice from the Congo*, described him as "a tall, handsome man, of fine bearing; thin, mere muscle and bone, a sun-tanned face, blue eyes and black curly hair. A pure Irishman he is, with a captivating voice and a singular charm of manner. A man of distinction and great refinement, high-minded and courteous, impulsive, poetical. Quixotic perhaps some would say, and with a certain truth, for few men have shown themselves so regardless of personal advancement."

Critical, if at times adulatory, assessments of Casement come in contrast from other friends who knew him too well, especially when they had to listen to his rants against England and the incessant talk of Ireland. Joseph Conrad and John Devoy who met and saw him for shorter periods were better able to penetrate the carapace of his charisma, having their own reasons for scepticism. Yet another key Irish-American, Joe McGarrity, politically a hard dynamiter, was plainly distressed when seeing him off to Germany in 1914. "I felt blue" he wrote as Casement took his leave, calling him thereafter "the Blackbird because of his dark hair and beard."[34]

2

The Casement family

Roger's great-great-grandfather, Hugh, immigrated from the Isle of Man, and by marrying locally introduced the surname of Casement to Ulster. He leased farmland in Ballinderry, an old Co. Antrim area of settlement near Lisburn which still has a distinctly English, if not Norman feel. The Manx Casements were Anglicans and remained so in Ulster. At this time Man by virtue of the easy sea access was linked with east Ulster more than were most other parts of Ireland.

The surname Casement derives from the Norwegian Asmundr, a combination word meaning the tutelage of the Norse God As. It became Mac Asmundr – son of Asmundr, and wound its way through Mac Casmonde, Mac Casmund, Casmond, and Caisment before settling on Casement. His Viking ancestry intrigued the young Casement. Indeed he put some effort into seeking out those Manx origins in his revealing search for a past in order to decide on a future. This hunt also took him on several vain searches to discover his maternal background.

It was great-grandfather Roger (1756-1832) who founded the Casement dynasty. He was a prosperous solicitor with offices in Ballymena and Dublin and became a more prosperous landowner. Significantly he was attorney to a bankruptcy commission in 1784 and to the Court of Exchequer in Ireland in 1788. It was, however, as land agent to the Earl of Massereene in the town of Antrim that he achieved his greatest advance. The second Earl, Clotworthy Skeffington (1745-1805), a notorious gambler and womaniser had run up enormous debts in France because of speculative investments. He was also unhinged. One of his lesser eccentricities was to insist on walking with his arms crossed, his hands on his shoulders.

Lord Massereene stubbornly refused to attempt a settlement and in 1770 was consigned to a Parisian debtor's prison. As his mother had control of his estates she chose not to pay the full debt off, knowing only more would be run up. The Earl was to be imprisoned for over eighteen years. Yet life was not entirely without comforts as he married a woman he met in gaol, much against his family's wishes. His wife was to organise two attempted escapes from La Force prison. Finally in early 1789, taking advantage of the revolutionary times, the new Countess paid a mob to break down La Force's gates, allowing the Earl to escape. Together they headed for England.

Baby Roger and his parents ca. 1865

Life in London was a repetition of Paris, including a further debtor's prison. He eventually separated from his French wife, who died soon after. She was replaced by Mrs Elizabeth Blackburn, "a menial servant in a house immediately opposite his lodgings." It was said "she possessed a peculiar dexterity of twirling her mop", one "his Lordship admired."[35] They married in 1803, at which point Massereene's long established land agent was dismissed and replaced by Roger Casement, regarded as a man wholly subservient to the interests of the new Countess and her lover George Doran, son of "Priest O'Doran." George was later to marry her.

Roger Casement drafted Lord Massereene's last will a year before his death. It left everything to his new wife bar a guinea to each of his brothers. One of the Earl's final eccentric exploits, followed the death of a favourite dog which was first waked then placed in a lead coffin for burial at Antrim Castle. Fifty local dogs were then ordered to attend in scarves. The will was inevitably contested in a series of messy court cases with Casement's reputation becoming an issue in that of March 1809. Arthur Macartney, counsel in the Massereene family's interest, did not spare Casement despite his apparent embarrassment when he first showed the offending will to the late Earl's brother, Chichester.

Calling him "a celebrated conspirator", Macartney declared, "I have heard of this Roger Casement upon a former occasion, and you will be able to appreciate his character when I tell you that, upon prosecuting a gentleman for gross scandal, the jury gave him a verdict with damages of one penny."[36] No hint survives of what the gross scandal was but it could well have been an accusation of financial impropriety. To unravel the whole disastrous episode, despite the will being overturned, Elizabeth Massereene was eventually bought off, with an £800 annuity.

Roger Casement's career as a land agent was over. But his fortune was now such that he soon advanced to becoming a big landowner himself. His springboard to this new status may have occurred during the attempted unencumbering of the Massereene estates. One way or another a large number of his land acquisitions are reckoned (even within his family) to have come about through insider trading on land leases, as both agent and solicitor. His earlier work dealing with the estates of bankrupts may already have laid the foundation for his growing land wealth.

In 1787 he had married his first wife, a Manxwoman, Catherine Cosnahan. She died in childbirth in 1809. Through her, and a second marriage in 1819 to a Ballycastle girl Margaret (Peggy) McQuitty, his children's nanny or maid (stories differ), he fathered twenty-one children over nearly forty years. This and the repetition of names explain the generational confusion that has afflicted Casement researchers and the family itself. Only a couple of those twenty-one

Captain Roger Casement, father, Isle of Man studio

children died young or as infants which was remarkable for the time. One who did was a Roger, born of the first marriage. He was to be replaced by another of the same name from the second marriage. Unfortunately, despite surviving to graduate from Trinity College Dublin in 1842, he too was to die prematurely in Bristol, at the age of twenty-three, probably from tuberculosis, that great scourge of Victorian times and of this family. It was known then as the White Death, or, as Casement put it later, "the national complaint".

The patriarch and his family lived at Henryville, Ballymena in a large house beside the Braid river. In time Henryville was to go down market – in more ways than one, turning into Harryville and a council housing estate. It became notorious when the Catholic Church was picketed, besieged even, in the 1990s as a response to Orange Order marching restrictions. Roger had bought the lease for Churchfield House near Ballycastle in 1790 which was later to become the family seat. The lease cost £4,600 and was purchased from his father who had acquired it from his own daughter Mary, the widow of Hugh Harrison.

Neither the patriarch nor his father, who resided in a substantial seventeenth-century thatched farmhouse at Bessvale, Ballinderry (which is also still extant), appears ever to have moved to Churchfield. Hugh Harrison had died in 1786 leaving Mary with ten children – another classic bourgeois brood of the time – but without the means to keep up the rent. The house was therefore saved for the Casement family, by purchase and retention of the lease, while Mary was left in place to bring up her family.

Great-grandfather Roger made his own will in 1831 at the age of seventy-five, a year before his death, and at a moment when seven of his children had already predeceased him. The last so to do was Julius who died in 1830 aged thirty-three, although he was to be replaced in the same calendar year by another Julius, the twenty-first and final child. Of the seven children who died before their father, five were to be reborn in name at least, through the second marriage. In his will, Roger humbly asked that God "will mercifully forgive me my manifold sins and transgressions." He was known to be "a hard man" and like most rapidly successful men may well have had many sins to forgive.

Division of his extensive estate was complicated by the number of his children and the fact that the eldest child of the seven born of his second marriage was only eleven, and the baby, Julius, only a year old. His eldest son William should have been his heir-in-chief but all eight other surviving sons, with one exception, received a due share of money and land. His five surviving daughters were only willed money.[37]

A trust was set up for his widow Peggy and she was left £25 to buy mourning clothes. She was permitted "for the term of her widowhood and no longer" to stay in the family house at Henryville, although at "a very reasonable rent of £46.3.1" which her husband fixed in his will. It also ordered that no land in the Barony of Carey which included the townland of Churchfield was to be sold by the trustees. The Churchfield house was in the parish of Culfeightrin and a short distance from the church itself. The adjoining farmland had been owned by the Stewarts of Ballintoy and originally leased to Mary's father-in-law the Rev. Michael Harrison, vicar of the parish from 1741, who died in 1765. The house, described in 1835 as "2-storey, plain and pretty" had, according to local lore, brought grief to the family because of Hugh Harrison's plundering of a large portion of the walls of the old Culfeightrin church for its building material. Harrison was said (recorded in 1838) "to have subsequently experienced much distress and calamity in family and effects."[38] No mention of the consequent fate of the ten Harrison children is to be found. It may have been gloomy.

Ultimately the house was to become the home of three of the patriarch's fourteen sons: Rev. Robert Casement, a curate at Culfeightrin; Thomas Casement, before he moved to Ballee House in Ballymena; and, finally, John Casement (1825-1902), who lived there until his death. It was he who over the years opened up Churchfield to a number of young relatives who had need of a home or a base because of parental service abroad or death.

The Church of Ireland parish of Culfeightrin (and Ramoan) is largely to the east of Ballycastle heading along the coast toward the Glens of Antrim and the villages of Cushendun and Cushendall which featured so prominently in the lives of Sir Roger Casement, his friends and relations. The house's mundane but historically accurate name of Churchfield was, however, regaelicised, presumably by John Casement, into the evocative Magherintemple. Churchfield was the name of the townland in which the house was situated, being a translation of the earlier Gaelic name of Magherintemple, "plain of the church", a name that bears a hint of a pagan structure. An adjacent townland is called Magherindonnel, Donnel being derived from the name of the dominant local chiefs and landowners, the McDonnells, Earls of Antrim.

Ownership of the house and its 3,300 acres of predominantly sheep-grazing land passed to John Casement who, despite a medical degree from Trinity College Dublin, seems not to have practised. He made two marriages to women from wealthy families, the Newcomens, bankers in Dublin, and the Millers, merchants in Ballycastle. He had a shareholding in the local railway on top of his farming interests but no other commercial involvement. Having inherited land from his father, he was to be left more in 1843 by his oldest full brother Roger (as were all the other surviving siblings from the second marriage). John had therefore the time and the means to develop and extend the family seat, which was in time to provide Casement with his adopted home and county in Ireland and his Irish pedigree.

As the name of the Casement dwelling changed, so did the house itself. Churchfield, as it was, has been described as a modest Ulster farmhouse but is closer to a gentleman's residence. It is in a grand location with a sweeping frontage of tree-lined land looking down to the Culfeightrin church and the coastline – with Rathlin Island beyond. It is also only a mile or so from the steep winding path that leads to Murlough Bay, Drumnakill Old Cemetery and the ruined oratory of St. Mologe, in other words to old Ireland.

Murlough Bay has been the scene of frequent Casement commemorations by Republicans, including a famous visit in 1953 by de Valera when he was Taoiseach that involved a parade of the old IRA which particularly aroused Unionist ire – and Republican dissension over his Fianna Fail intrusion.[39] Later commemorators included Conor Cruise O'Brien in 1966. The bay has a breathtakingly beautiful setting with verdant wooded cliffs, a bright sandy beach, rocky pools and views across to Donegal, Rathlin Island and over to Scotland. In 1905, Casement wrote of Murlough "glorious as ever – a veritable bay of paradise."[40]

In the 1930s Murlough also became a popular holiday spot for Belfast's artistic and progressive set. The dramatist John Boyd described how "The Murlough holidays began before war started, and some of our number, including Bob

Davidson's younger sister Georgie and her husband, an Englishman,[41] kept returning to Murlough year after year long after war was over…It was a romantic place, having associations with Roger Casement who, according to the old people, had slept in the cottage and loved to scramble over the scree and along the shore…Sometimes we saw convoys of ships in the North Channel on their way to America…War was tacitly a *verboten* subject, Eva Gorstein and Linde Ewalt were émigrés from Germany…the German girls surprised us by swimming naked and the rest of us immediately followed their lead."[42]

Casement would have approved of the swimming. At this time, however, radical Protestants were allied to the Soviet Union, no longer to France and certainly not to Germany as he had been. Those who were or became members of the Communist Party of Northern Ireland were by the 1950s to be linked yet again to Irish Republicans in a common anti-imperialist cause. This replaced the brief wartime pact of Communists and Ulster Unionists which started after Russia was invaded.

Before his execution Casement expressed the desire to be buried at Murlough. His wish was not to be realised and remains an outstanding demand of Irish separatists. It is probable that he will never leave Glasnevin cemetery in Dublin – short of a united Ireland – since this (temporary) resting place for his remains has become the measure of an unrealised dream. To go back while Northern Ireland continued to exist would not be appreciated by his ghost nor would it seem appropriate, given his view on the exclusion of any part of Ulster from an autonomous Ireland.

John Casement attached a Scottish baronial residence to the original Churchfield, making it, as has been written, "something of a mongrel." The new house merited a new name although it is noticeable that some locals like Rose Young persisted in using the old into the next century, despite her love of Gaelic. In truth the two houses were (and are) like Siamese twins joined at the thigh, rather than a hybrid. It could have been worse in that the original house with its elegant and simple lines might have been demolished, although a new porch was to be slapped over a quarter of the frontage of the old dwelling. This has left the imposing entrance hall lacking in light and, when filled with antlers and an enormous tiger skin, as it is today, somewhat eerie.

The formal and severe add-on with matching gatehouse was built in and around 1874, which might be the year the boy Casement first came to live in Co. Antrim, his mother having died the year before. John Casement's family consisted of three sons from his first wife Charlotte. Ultimately, but not initially, he became adviser and a substitute father to the orphaned boy, his half great-nephew Roger. John's first wife died of consumption aged thirty. His second wife whom he married in 1859 was also named Charlotte. Under the influence, it is said, of the second of the name, John took the pledge and had inscribed over the new front door the injunction; *In all thy ways acknowledge Him and He shall direct thy paths.*

These then were the words Casement would see every time he came and went to Magherintemple over the next forty years and which he would unceasingly ignore even if he remained a Christian. Little wonder that at times he found the house hard to take, although the critical remarks noted in his 1903 diary may have had as much to do with the European winter, a cold he was starting, and his initial reception, or lack of same, when he arrived on Christmas Eve for a four day stay at Magherintemple: "…on to B'castle, train late, 20 minutes stoppage at Armoy. No one to meet me. Cold and black I will not go up there again. Aunt C. [Charlotte, by then uncle John's widow] up, all well. House changed, but not improved at all, on the contrary…Miserable place to stay in, this, beautiful day down to golf club…Spent day in house, cold worse – much worse, very miserable place during day. Others to Church, I to bed early…".[43]

Ada McNeill of Cushendun, in a 1929 memoir, saw Magherintemple differently. Her father was a first cousin to Charlotte Casement who "was hospitality itself. They kept open house. Her relations were always welcome." In 1885 Ada was twenty-four, Casement only twenty-one but he taught the older woman: "I criticised the Irish, but he always made excuses for them. At Magherintemple were delightful books which would never have been found in our house. I remember rainy, grey days in the dark old library there – which were anything but grey for me – with the open doors of the big bookcases, and Roger refuting my arguments with quotations upon which he could always lay his finger. I learnt a lot like this and I learnt to read for myself. Then there were more walks at home, over the moors, and along the Tor Road, and life seemed to hold only Ireland."[44]

Magherintemple's new extension is believed to have been designed by John Lanyon, a relative of Charlotte, and there is a date stone with John Casement's initials to be found above the drawing-room window. The design has found few favours, being described as "a very Scots, very plain, very porridgy composition, executed in Ballyvoy stone, somewhat grim except for the lavish crowsteps, finials and chimney stacks; not a turret or bartizan in sight."[45] Whether or not this harsh assessment is entirely fair, it must be said, given the exposed location, the high ceilings and the excessive roof area, that the house was bound to be draughty and cold – especially at an Edwardian Christmas. Magherintemple is still in the family's ownership, being lived in and the land farmed organically by a fourth generation descendant of John Casement.

The Casements were now gentlemen farmers – no longer just rising middle class. However, class lines in Ireland were by necessity less rigid than in England, so becoming gentry was a matter more of what you felt you were, allied to living in a country house or having a title. House or title normally incorporated grand words like Mount, Mont or Temple to mask the brevity of much of the Irish upper class's existence and compensate for its comparatively tenuous hold on the land. Adherence to Anglicanism and church office were other points of entry to the gentry and the Casements scored on both.

There were any number of nearby big-house families to mix with. But none were that big nor the occupants that grand or aristocratic. The Boyd family was predominant in Ballycastle's arrested coal-based industrialisation while nearby houses and estates, belonging to the McGildowny, Woodside, Miller, Traill, Macnaghten (of Bushmills), Gage (of Rathlin Island), McNeill, Montgomery and Alexander families, and especially the Youngs (of Galgorm Castle, Kintullagh and Fenaghy), provided an adequate stock of social and, in at least four cases, marriage partners for Casements. Many of these names, in time, crop up in Casement's diaries or correspondence.

The one old aristocratic family in the North Antrim area with a peerage, in this case only carrying the right to sit in the Irish House of Lords (up to its demise in 1800) were the McDonnells, the Earls of Antrim. They had an immensely long history and dominant landowner association with the area, and beyond in Scotland, as the Antrim earldom and the subsidiary title of Viscount Dunluce (and the doubly extinct marquessate) indicate. Ironically the McDonnells were largely old Catholic and had moved down the coast from Dunluce Castle to Glenarm Castle. They looked now to London and sometimes to Rome but not Ballycastle or Belfast. Indeed in a letter from Ecclefechan, Dumfriesshire, responding in 1889 to a request from John Young of Galgorm Castle, the 11th Earl declined to assist the cause of the 'Loyal Irish Union'. Writing later that year from a different Scottish address, this time Elgin in Morayshire, he declared, "You are regarded more or less as criminals by the radicals, who will eventually govern the country...You will never see me back in Ireland. I object to living on my estate as a rent charger and not as a proprietor."[46]

Anyone who was ever a reader of the novels of Mazo de la Roche whose family saga dealt with the multi-generational colonial dynasty of the Whiteoaks of Jalna, which covered in part the same era and the same colonial and imperial aspect and grew exponentially as the series gathered pace, will appreciate the complexity of such a family as the Casements. But no Canadian novelist could match the reality of the life and romance of Casement, whose career, politics, and sexuality were to involve so many of these recurring issues and themes in world affairs.

It was to be a significant part of Casement's political and cultural development that the Catholics he first associated with in Ireland were from the Glens of Antrim. Like the east Down Catholics, they were then a breed apart from those of Tyrone, south Armagh (or later Belfast). The Glens people still seemed Scottish and were plainly so in speech, as well as other ways. In east Down the fact of Norman ancestry would, for its Catholics, act as a drag on separatist tendencies. Old English stock was not virulent in its nationalism. And not to be a nationalist in these parts, if a Catholic, would not be unusual until a further century was to elapse.

One must return now from the Magherintemple story to Casement's eponymous great-grandfather in order to track forward his grandfather Hugh and father, also Roger. With so many children, it was inevitable that most from the patriarch's first marriage would move off to provide space for the second brood. His widow Margaret was considerably younger than her husband, surviving him by forty-five years. She died in 1877 over one hundred and twenty years after her late husband's birth. She did not remarry but by the time of the early death in 1843 of her own first-born child (another Roger) she appears to have moved to Belfast. From Casement's own birth in 1864 up until his arrival in Co. Antrim, Margaret Casement, who was not even his great-grandmother but a step-version, was the grande dame of the family.

It was her own son John Casement, born in 1825, the eighteenth child of his father, and now the master of Magherintemple, who would take over the role of parent or guardian to the teenage Roger. By that time John had married a second time and his new wife Charlotte Miller, herself from Ballycastle, whom he wed in 1859 had already become a stepmother to three boys, the twins Roger and Brabazon born in 1852, and the youngest, Jack, born in 1854. Jack was later to become an Arctic explorer and a Rear Admiral, marrying into the Young family of Galgorm Castle to which his stepmother Charlotte was also connected. Jack's grave in the New Layde churchyard in Cushendall is beside that of another Glens Protestant turned separatist, John Turnly of Drumnasole, who also paid for his Republicanism with his life when assassinated in 1980.

The first wife of Roger Casement, the solicitor, had died in 1809, the year of the final Massereene court case. Ten or eleven of her fourteen children were still living – born during the period when their father was making his fortune and becoming a man of substance in the county. Two boys died abroad, having served in the army in India. The two oldest surviving boys, William (who may have married a Roman Catholic) and George, marry and disappear into obscurity. It was the fourth oldest child, Hugh, the grandfather of RDC, who featured prominently and exceptionally in his father's will. Hugh seems a chip off the old block. A general merchant and ship-owner in Belfast, he was probably enabled to expand by virtue of his father's generous financial assistance.

From the 1820s to the early 1840s he operated as Casement & McClean out of Academy Street and Tomb Street in the docks area of the city, living lastly at a town centre address in Queen Street.

In his father's will, it was explained at some length that Hugh had been loaned an initial £2,000 of "late Irish currency" and then "considerable sums of money and bills of exchange and securities to enable him to enter into business." In return, Hugh had in 1829 "executed to me a mortgage of his properties in the town of Belfast for the sum of three thousand pounds sterling." Ominously, the will stated that "the said Hugh will be found at the time of my death considerably indebted to me."[47] After allowing him clearance of the £2,000 loan as a form of inheritance, he required and directed his executors to call in the mortgages to clear Hugh's other debts to him. The money so realised was to be paid into the residue of the estate.

It is obvious reading the will's provisions that, by the time his father died in 1832, his faith in Hugh was at a low ebb, although he still named him as an executor trustee along with Thomas and Robert, two other brothers. The effect of calling in the remaining debts may have been to leave Hugh especially vulnerable to any recession. Either way he was soon borrowing again from other family members. His student half-brother Roger nearly a decade later in 1843 refers in his will to an enormous outstanding debt of £1,670.[48]

Grandfather Hugh's business was inevitably of a speculative nature given the nature of the rapidly expanding city of Belfast where he operated. Devastating losses in shipping were experienced and he was forced to declare himself bankrupt in 1842, although not entirely without assets, as he paid his creditors eleven shillings in the pound. In a letter dated 21 December 1842 to a significant creditor, Colonel John Garnier, who had only that year loaned him £3,000, Hugh promised "that Divine Providence would strengthen his desire and determination on his part and enable him to fulfil it, namely not only to pay the above notes but also to pay him and all his creditors in full."[49] Despite these somewhat guilty words only another shilling in the pound was ever forthcoming. This further £113 for Col. Garnier, it must be said in Hugh's favour, was an entirely voluntary payment.

Plainly Hugh Casement's finances were complex and would remain so, but in the entrepreneurial spirit then prevailing in Ulster, he was not put off. Instead he moved to London with his second son, also Hugh, and started up as a provisions merchant. In London, he lost a wife and luckily gained a second, a young woman named Rachel Atkins, said to have been his late wife's companion. They married in about 1850 when she was twenty and he fifty-seven. After a decade in the English capital he migrated to the Antipodes. His commercial operations certainly prospered there and were such that by his death he had considerable interests in both Dunedin, New Zealand and Melbourne, Australia.

When it came to writing his own will, Hugh's previous financial difficulties in Belfast plainly still haunted him: "I was at a past period unfortunate in trade and obliged to effect a compromise with my then creditors", he stated. If any who had "acted liberally with me" should "now be in difficulties" he ordered that £1,000 be put aside for any such part-paid creditor who so applied. Failing any claims being made, the money was to be given to the Belfast Fever Hospital. This act of charity may be connected to the deaths, said to be from diphtheria, in the late 1830s of his two teenage daughters Catherine and Henrietta, buried in Drumbo near Lisburn.[50]

Col. Garnier's son who was by then in Auckland, New Zealand, was informed by Hugh Casement, as late as 1862, that "it was still his wish and intention to pay off the debt although legally under no obligation to do so and that he hoped to contribute a little more in the ensuing February if spared in life." His life, however, ended on 29 January 1863 in Melbourne public baths, two days before that February ensued. Garnier was advised by Hugh's London solicitors that a later codicil to his will, made in London, had revoked the section ordering that old creditors be paid in part. That interpretation remains open to question but was accepted then as accurate. Hugh's assets in New Zealand were of the order of £3,500, while in Melbourne he was reckoned by Garnier to have "prospered in his worldly affairs and to have amassed a considerable sum of money."[51]

In London, Hugh had also become an Adherent of the Reformed Apostolate, a newly burgeoning religious sect. The Catholic Apostolic Church, as it was later to be known, was developing from a peculiar mix of High Anglicanism and Presbyterianism, combining initially fundamentalist doctrine with later ritualist practices. Its liturgy was said to be the most elaborate ever devised while its buildings (like the Gordon Square church in London) were appropriately splendid in design, if rarely finished. Founded by Edward Irving in the early 1830s with the financial assistance of a rich banker and former Tory MP Henry Drummond, the church gathered members from the upper and middle classes.

Irving, a powerful preacher and mystic who died in 1834, had been expelled from his Church of Scotland ministry at Regent Square chapel in London for heresy. An episode of miracle cures combined with speaking in tongues at Port Glasgow in 1830 had been the key to his conversion to this millenarian cult.

The Catholic Apostolic Church had one great flaw in that the original twelve Apostles selected by Drummond to await the imminent second coming of Christ were not given the power of replacement, although the lesser rank of Angel could ordain. Only Apostles, by crossing someone's forehead with

Mrs Grace Bannister, maternal aunt, Liverpool photographer

Casement, aged 25, signed "Yours affectionately, Rod Casement. April 25th 1890", J. Thomson, Grosvenor Street, London studio

consecrated chrism, could "seal" the recipient into eternal life. The Church therefore petered out after the last Apostle died in 1901, although the fact that the imminent second Advent had not occurred was already eroding Adherents' faith. That an Ulster Anglican like Hugh Casement, along with his family, could be drawn into this church is significant. Plainly he was dissatisfied with the old conformities, susceptible to prophetic voices and appreciative of the Roman and Orthodox rituals. Although there is no evidence that his eldest son became an Adherent (or that he was not), he must have been well aware of its peculiarities. Something of its wayward radicalism certainly drifted down to his grandson.

The Casements were to be linked in Australia for several generations with another Adherent, Charles James Perry (1817-93), a member of the Victoria State Assembly and ultimately an executor of grandfather Hugh's will. Another executor, in London, John Saffery an accountant, was also an Adherent. Hugh's eponymous second son, with the status of Angel, died before his father and his widow Isabella then married Perry. In time, two of Perry's grandchildren, sisters Minnie and Blanche Balharry (through his first marriage), would marry Charlie and Tom Casement, two of Hugh's grandsons and the brothers of Sir Roger Casement.

The impression given later by Hugh's eldest son Captain Roger Casement is that Perry and Saffery had intruded themselves into his family and were determined to do him down. The will, however, was rigorous in providing for all Hugh's living descendants, including his two daughters Agnes Aickin and her many children (she was by then living in Auckland) and Eleanor Lanphier (who was to end her days there). The problem of the will was its trusteeship complexities, an apparent lack of ready cash to meet all the immediate legacies, and the executors' decisions as to arranging the investments and dealing with the property. It was 1902, forty years after Hugh's death, before the estate was finally wound up. In 1905, Casement was still talking of going "to New Zealand where I have a share in some property left by my grandfather."[52]

In all there were three sets of Casement migrants to Australia in the second half of the nineteenth century: Casement's grandfather Hugh, his cousin Brabazon, and his brothers Charlie and Tom. Indeed he could well have ended up there himself had his own father managed to go with his young family and, as was notioned, settle after the death of Hugh.

Hugh Casement's eldest son Roger (father of RDC) was born in 1819 and brought up at agreeable addresses just outside Belfast – The Moat, Holywood and Pine Hill, Drumbo. Before his Belfast business crashed, Hugh arranged an army career for his son in a regiment then in India. A cornetcy in the 3rd (The King's Own) Regiment of Light Dragoons was purchased for the standard price of £840, then a great deal of money. An impression of desperation to get an undisciplined first-born son off his hands and into the army, rather than into the family business, is further evidenced by an 1840 letter to the War Office seeking expedition of the posting.[53] The fact that he was apparently shipped to India in one of his father's own vessels (which was said to bear the patriotic name of SS John Bull) also tells of a certain eagerness to speed the start of his army career. Roger had already been on the Grand Tour, it was said,[54] which could well have unsettled as much as educated him.

That 1840 letter to Lt.-Gen. Fitzroy Somerset made great play of the fact that Hugh Casement's first cousin was General Sir William Casement KCB (1778-1844). Sir William was the son of the unfortunate Dr George Casement who was targeted by the United Irish rebels in Larne in 1798. Knighted in 1837, William had risen to become Military Secretary to the Governor General of India and since 1839 was a member of the Supreme Council. Casement was aware of a monument to his kinsman in Kensal Green cemetery, London,[55] and was able to quote his father reminiscing, "They were like all Iro-Indians, full of India and the things of that country."[56]

The cornetcy was gazetted on 16 April 1841. Almost immediately the young soldier was involved in a disastrous British expansion into the North West frontier to counter the somewhat imaginary Russian threat. After his participation in the 1842 Afghan campaign when the regiment under General Sir George Pollock obtained battle honours for its part in recapturing 'Cabool', Cornet Casement was, in November 1843, promoted lieutenant. Another Irish officer in that campaign, although in the 4th (The Queen's Own) Regiment of Light Dragoons, was Lieutenant Martin Kirwan, who was to figure in the Dublin Castle scandals of 1884.

The First Sikh War of 1845-46, that ended with the incorporation of the Punjab, was one which saw the 3rd Light Dragoons being reduced to half strength after the December 1845 battles along the River Sutlej of Mudki and Ferozeshah. There were further terrible casualties at Sobraon in February 1846. As the Second Sikh War gathered pace in 1848, Lieutenant Casement was growing disillusioned and in August asked to retire from the army by selling his commission. He even promised to pay the purchaser's travel costs out to India. Perhaps the horror of incessant and bloody frontier wars was making him question earlier values and turning him off imperial expansion. After being in the army for nearly eight years he was replaced by a Cornet Chaplin, who bought out his commission in November 1848 for only £350.[57] Casement's father was not yet thirty.

In 1872, he was to write about this decision to his half-brother John, suggesting he was later doubtful about its wisdom: "My father condoned my questionable act of retirement from the Army, because he thought my health not strong enough for India, and he was reduced to inability to purchase me up, or to give me an allowance in a regiment elsewhere, besides he said if my conscience had an active part in my act, I was right to follow its dictates even if in error."[58]

In 1849, returning home from India, he indulged his romantic if not radical outlook when he assisted the Hungarian rebel leader Kossuth by delivering a plea from Widdin, his sanctuary in Turkish controlled territory, to Lord Palmerston in London. It asked, successfully, for intervention on the defeated army's behalf to prevent it being handed over to the Austrians or Russians. This was later described as a passion for the rights of small nations. In *The United Irishman* of 25 February 1905 under the title *Kossuth's Irish Courier* Casement told the story, heard as a child from his father, of his dealings with Kossuth and the ride through Transylvania. The creaking dialogue (taken from Kossuth's memoirs) opened: "Good Day Sir. What can I do for you?"; Lt. Casement: "I am come from India to fight for Hungarian Freedom." Kossuth unfortunately described his saviour as English.

A matter-of-fact description of the episode by the father comes in a letter dated 20 December 1872 about unlikely journalistic jobs applied for. One was as war correspondent in Abyssinia with the *Daily News*. He wrote that he urged "some claims I had as having aided the Chief Editor in 1849, when I brought Despatches to Lord Palmerston from Turkey at my own expense as an Amateur Queen's Messenger, with an Official Bag from Belgrade, and also letters to the *Daily News* from its correspondent there."[59]

Another description was published in the Belfast *Northern Whig* just ten days before his wedding. Under *Latest Intelligence* in a primitive gossip column, the writer told of a recently noticed article in the *Westminster Review*. "Our readers will recollect the danger to which Kossuth and his companions were exposed when they were offered the alternative of embracing Mahometanism or of being surrendered to Russia." It continued with the lifted story of how one Roger Casement had followed Kossuth through Hungary to Widdin before carrying Kossuth's letter from there to Palmerston in ten days. While on a visit to the United States in 1851, Casement, "the person who carried your letter from Widdin", gave Kossuth a book, *Brace's Hungary*. The story ended, "If we are not mistaken the Mr Casement here referred to holds a Captain's Commission in the Antrim Rifles." It seems that the Captain was doing a little self-publicity in Belfast or spending too much time in the company of journalists.

The following somewhat fanciful view of his father, who had died when the boy Casement was only twelve, was also outlined in the 1905 article: "Although an officer in the British army, [he] was, throughout his life an ardent and sincere lover of Ireland – one who had sacrificed something to his country, and never wavered in his loyalty to her National claims… [having] an overmastering love of freedom born of a close perception of the evils of Irish misrule." Commenting elsewhere, his son was to write, "This friend of Hungarian freedom was one in heart and soul with the cause of Ireland."[60]

This impression was carefully drawn with the inclusion of the undeniable fact of British Army service, yet omitting entirely the detail that he had later taken a commission, this time as a Captain, in the North Antrim Militia (The Queen's Royal Antrim Rifles) – not a force with a kindly reputation when dealing with the United Irish rebellion of 1798. At his marriage in April 1855, the Captain gave his place of residence as Belfast. After only three years' service from 1855 to 1858, and six years before his famous son's birth, he resigned from the Rifles on health grounds. That was his last known remunerated employment. Indeed between leaving the Indian Army in 1849 and his marriage in 1855 nothing is remembered of his career or activities except the visit to the United States where he squared Kossuth on the matter of his nationality – Irish not English.

Aside from his military service, and until his relatively early death, Captain Casement's life appears unrewarding despite a marriage and the birth of four children over the decade to 1864. Perhaps his whole life was one of regret, missed opportunity and resentment. His photographs certainly suggest that, depicting a heavily-bearded man with seriously grim, set features. Yet the Captain's niece, Elizabeth Bannister, recollecting her impressions many years later was positive. When about seven years old she said she had seen a man who looked "tall and striking…in his long military cloak."[61]

The Captain and the family's addresses were to be legion, even if some of the locations are vague or unverified. They are known or said to have lived in the Isle of Man and the Channel Isles. His only daughter Nina wrote of being "in Jersey near St Heliers for the benefit of my father's health." Her brother Roger, she said, was taught to swim there. Their father used to "heave off the wretched quaking boy" into the sea, an old-fashioned teaching method that worked well in this instance, as Casement became addicted to swimming.[62] Gertrude Bannister wrote of her cousin Roger living "on the continent" with his parents, France and Italy being mentioned,[63] while his brother Tom was supposedly born at sea and had his birth consequently registered in Boulogne in January 1863. Imprecise mention is made elsewhere of the family "travelling in Europe"[64] in the period 1856 to 1862. However, more mundane, suburban, then outer London addresses predominated on letters addressed to Magherintemple from Dalston, Surbiton and Dorking. Poverty took its grip, grinding the father ever further down.

In a letter to John Casement from London, dated 24 January 1871, Roger's father revealed the parlous financial state he had got his family into. They were reliant on handouts from relatives, since he was unremunerated and because his own father's legacy was still subject to fits and starts in payment – eight years after the death. This Dickensian situation of unsettled estates and lawyers' disputes, in both England and Australia, continued long past the father's own death in 1877. A first indication of near paranoia about lawyers, and other villains, in or near his family, is displayed in this letter although it may have been long-seated.

Addressing the letter to "My Dear John", the Captain wrote, "Your kind note & very generous inclosure reached me last evening, and in thanking you very sincerely for the latter, let me explain that for nearly four years, I have not received so much as a single penny from my father's legacies. Indeed it was owing to the stoppage of all income that my kind Uncle Thomas [of Ballee House Ballymena; JP and High Sheriff 1874] made me the allowance of which I told you.

"I shall not worry you with any sad details, but I shall add that I am quite able to prove that my troubles since my father's death, have been brought on by incapacity & devilry, chiefly the latter, on the part of those who had charge of his affairs, including the lawyers."[65]

This sad letter exemplifies the unsettled state of the boy Roger's childhood. It was nomadic and involved living in a series of rented rooms. It was one he recalled later in life when writing to E.D. Morel in about 1905, "If my father had not been so extravagant I should have been well off – as it is I am without a penny."[66]

A further missive on 18 October 1872, from Norton Cottage, Ewell Road, Surbiton tells the same tale in greater detail, although it seems to have failed in its primary purpose of eliciting another fiver since the Captain was obliged to write again two months later: "I am afraid the sight of my name or handwriting will hardly have a cheering effect upon you nowadays, and I am heartily sorry you may be sure for the cause of this, as well as the result. That 'long lane' of trouble I have been so many years now in passing through, has brought me to no <u>turning</u> yet, though for some months during the past summer, I took to advertising again for some sort of employment.

"My good and kind Uncle Thomas continues his voluntary allowance every month, and now gives me an extra £5 at Xmas, but you know practically what the expenses of a family like mine must be, with every possible economy I may be able to practice.

"It is always excessively difficult to find lodgings where people are content with rent alone, as the class who rent furnished lodgings generally expect to make something out of their lodgers besides, and when they find, as in our case, that the expenditure of the lodgers does not admit of this, 'notice to quit', is the usual consequence. I think we were in Dalston in the London suburbs when I last had the pleasure of hearing from you and receiving an Xmas box that allowed some most urgent necessities about last New Year's Day.

"Soon after that we had to 'turn out' of our lodgings and were able here in a more countrified suburb, to find lodgings at our terms, no easy matter any where. But we have had to change more than once here, and now have had 'notice to quit' at the beginning of next month again. On such occasions, paying up of any little arrears, if any has to take place, and it is a great pressure of this kind that forces me terribly against my mind, to ask you to compliment me with another Xmas box this year and to antedate the gift, for the purpose of meeting this great pressure now, as we are being dunned for a month's rent and fires etc. due, which I have been totally unable yet to pay.

"A similar presentation to your last, viz £5, would do us more good than you can well imagine, and less, would not actually meet the case. How am I to make any return to you or other kind relations who have sometimes aided me, I cannot tell, but unless I am able to do so before I die, I will not die happy. I beg you will not think I make light of troubling you in this way for it grieves excessively to do so. Yours affectionately, Roger Casement."[67]

As that letter does not seem to have produced any useful response, another dated 8 December 1872, was written from St. Leonard's Road (a different Surbiton address). It reveals further interesting facts, fills in gaps and tells the story of an unlucky man riven with self-pity. He writes to his uncle, a man six years his junior: "Without wishing to press you too much, as to what you may be very averse to I can hardly avoid again writing this Xmas month, to say how very black it appears to me at present. After my usual severe illness of weeks ushering in each winter, I have now, such prospects from ill health and penury together with little or no sympathy anywhere, that I would feel death itself to be a happy release. Nor have I now, as I once had, any hope of my rich Uncle Thos. putting me beyond a disgraceful state of poverty at his death. [Thomas was not to die for two more years having one child, Catherine, who had married in 1867.] I say disgraceful only in reference to that sense of humiliation which society imposes on the poverty stricken without the slightest consideration as to the cause of misfortunes. Mine I know have not been brought on by wastefulness or follies, as so often is the case…

"If he [the Captain's own father Hugh] had always been as clear sighted and reasonable with me, things would not have come to this pass. He left me without any status to act regarding his Will and Uncle T. particularly advised me, against my own views, to go out to Australia to counteract the costs there. To have done that right, I ought to have had the means of taking my family with me, to remain there, and so see that fresh costs would not occur as soon as my back was turned. But no, I was hounded out there to my doom, to ask thieves to disgorge their ill gotten half, or the Court of Equity to judge between us. The thieves got other thieves to help them for other pay, and carried all before them, and when the Executor here [J.J. Saffery] afterwards pressed my Uncle Thos. to purchase up my otherwise lost life Interest for me and save me from complete ruin, he refused because he thought surely I must have mismanaged. Then four years ago when I told Julius [his Co. Wicklow uncle] some of this, and asked him to help me get back to Australia, he would have done it, if on speaking to Uncle Thos. about it, the latter had not turned him round. Yet neither would tell me then or since, what it really is they have against me, except misfortune, though I have often pressed to know.

"Under these circumstances, not knowing that I can ever return you any little sum you might feel inclined to send me, as you once did before for our benefit under difficulties, I will not press, but only say we are in such a shocking position, that even a £5 Xmas box, would be a great temporary boon.

"I have been trying hard for all sorts of employment, but without success as usual. The War Office though still retaining my name on list of Official candidates for a regimental Paymastership, never shows any sign of seriously considering my many good recommendations for that appointment: Just return a stereotyped communication meaning little or nothing, and give the posts I understand to those only who know the backdoor entrance with a few hundreds at their back, or to some strong friend of the Minister for War.

"Pardon my troubling you, for I don't intend it again, and believe me. Yours affectionately, Roger Casement."[68]

Only this letter tells of the Captain making it out to Australia where his father was buried. It was a place he had apparently never been before. There he must have met for the first time his two young stepbrothers Roger David Casement and William Casement. He would also have been introduced to the Perrys, the Catholic Apostolic family that was now linked to his by marriage, and would eventually be so, twice more, through his older sons Charlie and Tom. Ironically the thieves mentioned can only be the same Perrys and their cronies. Their grip on his inheritance may have further jaundiced him about clergy as his major enemies all appear to be men of the cloth. Had he been enabled to take his young family to Australia as he had wished and start afresh, the boy Casement would never have been or become an Irishman and Ireland's history would be significantly different.

In response to the speedy delivery of the desired gift from John Casement, a second letter, this time of thanks, was written back to Ballycastle on 20 December 1872 some twelve days after the first:

"Your most kind and welcome Xmas box of £5 reached me safe this morning, and will stop the mouths well of the two tradesmen who threatened us. I am very much indeed obliged for it, and will now reply to your kind suggestion and compliment as to me trying for employment as a writer, because you consider me very competent. First I must say, that I have been trying in other quarters for a Xmas box, antedated, like yours, for present wants in the house until 1st proximo, but without success, and that as Uncle Thos. evidently allows himself to be influenced by jealous enemies of mine, connected with the Casement family by marriage, [seemingly his sister's husband, the Rev. Somerville Lanphier] and I believe now is not disposed towards me as formerly in consequence, I see no good in being (or continuing) an encumbrance to my family, as I did feel myself to be in various ways. For I cannot get any sort of employment. As to writing for newspapers or even acting as a copyist, I have repeatedly tried for both. I have written often for years as an amateur, not only for the sake of good generally, but hoping thereby to gain a footing somewhere. Public writers as a rule are an unscrupulous unconscionable lot, though clever – corrupt; writing for pay.

"When the 'Daily News' became a penny paper and made staff changes, I applied either for employment at home with that Staff, or as Correspondent to the paper in Abyssinia when the war there broke out…I also replied to a Hastings little newspaper advertisement lately for a Sub Editor, offering my services cheaper than others. Got no answer in either case.

"All last summer I got from a friend payment for weekly advertisements in London papers for various sorts of employment, but any replies that came shewed dodges, usually wanting a deposit of money, or aid in money somewhere. Generally advertisements are not what they appear to be, and people replying have their peculiar reasons for it too I found. [This sounds as if those replying to the Captain's ads were making fraudulent suggestions or even sexual offers.]

"As soon as I die, some arrangements will have to be made for education of my family by law, as although owing to Legacy having invested contrary to my expressed wish in Consols, and not in real estate, or not in the Colonies under jurisdiction there at higher interest, there would only be some £40, a year, if that much coming to them through London Court of Chancery, but the Vice Chancellor I suppose would interfere perhaps, and Uncle Thos. and perhaps Uncle Robt. would <u>then</u> help, to save scandal. For this last reason, I have been suffering torture for years, the rather prolonged useless sufferings, I have been enduring mentally and physically. I look to heaven for both pardon and recompense…

"21st PS. I used to consider Revd. Mr Lanphier (my Sister's husband) my greatest enemy in undermining me with my Uncle T. for his own ends and had proof of much, but latterly, I believe he is "out Heroded" by Revd. A. Fitzgerald (my cousin's husband) in that particular line. [This particular animus against clergymen does suggest they were of an interfering and moralising nature, even within families.] If I thought it would be any good, I would ask you to try and remedy these things for me, as I don't think you would likely entertain bad impressions towards any one, or be influenced by what interested parties might say of another, without giving that other a fair chance of clearing himself. But I fear the matter has gone too far in my Uncle T's mind, and in addition that my wife's name has been made very hateful to him by many, who thought that blasting her (unjustly or ignorantly) would serve the same purpose as attacking my character more directly. Both of us would like nothing better than meeting enemies or charges, face to face."[69]

This mention of "blasting" his wife Annie is mysterious. Given the likeliest complaint against him is that he is idle and useless, or a spendthrift, that against his wife, if not about her mothering abilities, which seems unlikely, might be more about her reputation or past. Possibly she was thought to have exercised some malign, perhaps papist, influence over her hopeless husband and children. But in life she was inscrutable. The only photograph of her gives the impression of a big-faced, slightly mannish Victorian lady, certainly quite tall and by no means badly dressed. In it she is holding a large, maniacal-looking baby, said to be Roger, dressed as was then usual in girl's clothes.

The Captain does display a certain hauteur about traders, who callously insist on payment, which must have been passed down to the children as they were all to exhibit a significant degree of *noblesse oblige*, and a form of expectation that others will and indeed should provide. The corollary that the favour ought to be returned was also part of their make-up. Privilege did carry responsibilities. His talk of imminent mortality indicates his annual winter illnesses were worsening but he was not to die first. Things had taken a sad and perhaps unexpected turn when exactly a year later on 8 December 1873, he approached John Casement for a further Christmas box:

"Since I had the great pleasure of hearing from you this time last year, when you so kindly sent us a most welcome 'Xmas Box', even before the day itself arrived, I have experienced a variety of troubles, but none equalling, or approaching to that which I and my poor children have had to bear, in the loss of my wife and their mother, on the 27th of October last.

"The great extra expenses I have been involved in by this, have been partially defrayed by Uncle Thos., and Julius also added a very opportune present of £5, but I have had more annoyances of a pecuniary kind than I can quite explain to anyone, having had claims for arrears of rent & other things pressing upon me even before my wife's death or illnesses lately. Indeed had it not been for them,

I would have had a more experienced and expensive Medical adviser with her than I was able to afford, and then the result would likely have been different.

"However I do trust now that you will not think me troublesome under these sad circumstances in prompting your good nature again as to a Xmas Box this December just similar to your last one. I am sure you won't, and as I have not yet got a permanent lodging, landladies having so much aversion to boys generally, and have some rent to pay on leaving the place I am now in, a week hence, I hope you will ante-date like last year, a present of £5, to help to stem the tide of my difficulties.

"I am trying very hard to get something to occupy me, even slightly remunerative, just to supplement Uncle T's allowance, finding it almost impossible to gain the very smallest competence, or promise of it for my proffered labours or services, and the War Office still shows no sign."[70]

The Captain was obliged to write this letter from the address of his father's executor, J.J. Saffery, at 14 Old Jewry Chambers, London E.C., his then home address being especially temporary. Annie, his wife, was dead. The version handed down through the family was that she had apparently died shortly after giving birth to another child.[71] Yet no child survived or was detailed in any way. Mention was made in correspondence to Ireland of her dying in East Preston, Littlehampton, a Sussex seaside town. It is also suggested that she may have been sent there in an attempt to restore her health. She was not yet forty years old. Her youngest son Roger was nine, her oldest child, Nina, being seventeen.

The childbirth story has been published so often that it has now become given fact. But the location of her death is peculiar in that it was in Sussex and not with her family who then lived in Surrey just outside London. Her death certificate, however, tells another story and provides a melancholy explanation both for the silence surrounding her life and the mysteries developed after her death.

She died on 27 October 1873 at 11 Warwick Buildings in the town of Worthing, not at East Preston. The death was registered the next day by a Jane Taylor who gave that address as her own residence. It was a lodging house and she a lodging-house keeper. Jane and her husband Richard, a carpenter, are recorded in the 1871 census as living there with at least three children. The village of East Preston near the town of Littlehampton was then best known as the site of a huge workhouse that covered the greater Worthing area of West Sussex. Captain Casement had no money and from his remarks was obviously distressed that he could not afford better medical assistance for his wife. Whether she had been forced to rely on the workhouse system is unclear, as is the reason why she was living in Warwick Buildings with the Taylors, who were not medically qualified.

The secret shame is revealed on Anne's death certificate where the primary cause of death was certified to be cirrhosis. A secondary illness was given as asthma. In other words, Annie was most probably an alcoholic. The asthma contributed to her dying so early but her liver ailment must have been acute. Her age was given as thirty-seven on the death certificate, one or two years fewer than previously mentioned. It is indeed possible that she was thought to be pregnant since she may have suffered the classic cirrhosis symptom of abdominal enlargement, caused by accumulation of fluid. Or that condition may have been passed off as a pregnancy to disguise the truth.

The fact of her drinking clears up the baffling remarks made by her husband about his clerical kinsmen "blasting" the name of his wife. If her drinking was sufficiently noticeable and known about to be of concern to relatives in Ireland it must have brought a further dissonance into the boy Roger's upbringing. A biographical line in an 1895 poem talks of "a weak child dandled on a weak woman's knees"[72], while to confuse the issue there is an isolated remark which the young Casement jotted down in a teenage notebook amongst his poetry, without further comment, "Annie the Drunken man's child."[73] If his knowledge of her disease and ultimately mortal illness was limited, Casement knew precisely where his mother was buried, as in July 1916, from prison, he instructed Gertrude: "Take my body to Ireland. I would like to have my mother's remains there too from Worthing but – *mavrone* – they must be lost sight of now. It is so long ago."[74]

Such a letter and Annie's death were plainly the precursors of imminent family and domestic breakdown, which was going to necessitate and require intervention by those back home in Ireland to protect and secure the youngsters. Captain Casement's track record was not encouraging, while the state his five-strong family unit was in would have been no surprise to any of his uncles. His career to date had involved very little in the way of stability or reliability, while his health was poor. Therefore things were only going to get worse. Although he lived over three years more, he was to leave London and return in the end to Antrim, where he died.

His character so far as is known was formed by a number of circumstances: prosperous early days in Belfast; military service in India; his marriage to Anne Jephson; and his failure to make anything much of himself, except as a father, over nearly thirty years thereafter. He plainly had a masculine love of fighting, quite standard at the time, perhaps also an excess degree of militarism which was manifested in a tough disciplinary regime within the family. Gertrude Bannister, who was too young to have her own memories of her uncle, instead quoted details given to her by his youngest son Roger who "told stories of his father who was stern and harsh with his children but who nevertheless inspired

Roddie with affection. Uncle Roger visited any breach of discipline with sound thrashings. This awed Charlie and Tom into meekness." But not apparently Roddie. He defied him.[75] Nina made the excuse for her father that "ill-health made his temper despotic."[76]

Yet, within this image of a man who was in contemporary eyes cruel, there is evidence of a different kind. He apparently loved animals and was involved with the society for their protection from cruelty, the RSPCA. The Captain's political views were not conservative as he indicated in various of his Letters to the Editor. One such to *The Daily Telegraph* on 21 November 1870 opened "I feel constrained as a Liberal…".[77] It would be a miracle if it had been published as his handwriting was almost illegible. Writing to newspapers was a habit he passed to his son. An essay on spiritual matters derived from his Indian experiences survives, suggesting a man with a yearning for alternative explanations of life.[78] Indeed he is said to have conducted séances in Ballymena in the hotel where he died.[79]

As is often pointed out, when Ulster Protestants go to England they too are regarded, pejoratively or carelessly, as indistinguishably Irish. Being an unhistoric people, the English, not unreasonably, regard all those from Ireland as Irish. As they all speak English, they cannot see why these Irish people do not get on with each other since the Irish are an apparent subspecies of the English anyway. The use by F.J. Bigger of the title and refrain *We're Paddies Evermore*, in a sentimental story about a United Irishman, reveals that 'Paddy' was being thrown back by some Irish Protestants at the English even in the nineteenth century. The corollary of this is that once out of Ulster such migrants often develop an artificial Irishness, a love for 'a nation' which they never were of, nor perhaps felt part of, when living on the island.

A significant number of Irish separatists of this era and the revolutionary period of 1916-23 had slender or tenuous connections with Ireland and frequently lived large parts of their lives elsewhere. Father and son Casement were exemplars of this and of the fact that the shallower the connection the more rabid can be the nationalism. As another son Tom developed the same patriotic sentiments despite living much of his life abroad, it is probable that their father did imbue his children with some sort of romantic Irish and anti-English sentiments of his own. Those sentiments were also likely to have been accentuated because of his failure as a provider in England. His diffused resentment may well have led to blame being attached to those English who failed to employ a military man who had risked his life in India for the Empire, to the clergy who cemented the system in, and thus to England itself – especially in Ireland.

Casement's sister described in an Irish-American newspaper series how Annie Casement had dreadful difficulty on one critical occasion containing her husband's political enthusiasms, writing of "the terrible struggle she had to prevent father from joining the Fenian bands and 'going out' as it was then called." The Captain was "polishing up his cavalry sword and a pair of pistols." But Annie must have succeeded in dissuading him with her cry, "O Roger remember your wife and young children."[80] If this story was even remotely true it proves that there was in Roger's upbringing a strong atmosphere of sympathy, not just with Irish nationalism, but with actual rebellion. The father's notebook in the NLI[81] reveals that he was no monarchist; indeed, he was a committed republican in relation to America. Significantly, he detailed making an effort to become a US citizen during his 1851 visit.

The Irish Republic was proclaimed on 4 March 1867 by the Fenians and there were a number of skirmishes, most notably at Tallaght then outside Dublin. The Fenian leadership was arrested early and the rising petered out. It did, however, leave a long and well-populated legacy. The Manchester Martyrs were a trio (Allen, Larkin and O'Brien) of hanged Irishmen of whom Casement was particularly fond, describing them on 23 September 1906 to Gertrude as the "loving, sacrificing young Fenians of 1867."[82] He also recalled them in his last written words as he prepared to follow his heroes to the gallows. The conspiratorial Irish Republican Brotherhood was another part of the legacy. It formed most of the inner junta within the Irish Volunteers that finally took the decision to rise in Easter 1916.

That Casement had an early family association or rebellious sympathy with nationalism explains the fact of his teenage identification with Gaelic Ireland and his continuous and total absorption in it. There was to be no other analysis or outlook where Ireland was concerned. Given the uniformity of the views of the four children who all had anti-English opinions – in the case of Nina and Roger almost pathologically so – it has to be accepted they were received early and directly. It is, however, probable, as Nina was five years older than any of the boys and effectively in charge of them in their teens, that she also transmitted her own received version of Ireland's history. "I have been a Nationalist all my life and even as a boy I was furiously so", Casement confirmed in 1916.[83]

Another possibility, if tenuously evidenced, is the influence of a "nurse" by the name of Mary Monaghan whom Nina mentions as accompanying the children to stay with some cousins of her mother at "Bally-brough a delightful old place not far from the Powerscourt Demesne" in Co. Wicklow.[84] This was in 1864 at the time of Roger's birth. He was, inevitably, as she wrote, golden curled, while their mother was kind and gentle. The fact that Nina remembered her maid's name is significant, as the influence of Catholic servants and nannies is one of the great unresearched areas of Irish Protestant history.

A servant girl from Newry was reputedly the source of Ernest Blythe's enthusiasm for the Irish language and thence Republicanism, and possibly also Herbert Hughes' love of Irish music – years later he was able to recall the name of his family nurse, Ellen Boylan. Ada McNeill learned her good Gaelic from talking in Irish with a native-speaking servant from the Aran Islands in Galway Bay.[85] This author has also met Protestants who recognise that their later nationalist outlook was shaped by Catholic domestic help, their own parents being distant and uninterested.

The dysfunctional nature of the children's upbringing is highlighted by the appearance in court in January 1876 of Thomas aged 13 and Roger aged 11 on a charge of book stealing from a newsvendor in York Road, Lambeth. The boys had admitted "they took the books to make money of, as they had none."[86] "The prisoners' father, a respectable-looking man, here came forward, and said he could not account for the lads taking the books unless it was to pay for the loan of them some other day. They were inveterate readers of juvenile literature…He allowed his boys money to buy books and would have paid for them. He believed that the showy covers and sensational titles attracted their attention and desire to read them. He assured his worship that they were not thieves." Their father, described as a captain in the militia residing in South Lambeth, was ordered to enter into recognisances for their future conduct.

The family's perpetual moving resembles in many ways the upbringing of an Irish contemporary, James Joyce, for whom such instability was to work its way through, and out, in his writing. Without such a problematic family background, complicated by the early deaths of his parents, Casement may not have become homosexual or a rebel searching for a better and different background, and a new family.

It is striking that all three of Captain Casement's sons were to follow in his footsteps, getting out of the British Isles and into the colonial or imperial world, across three continents. All four children were to live abroad and two to marry there. In the Captain's case, army service had been in Asia like at least five other Casements of that and the previous generation. In the next generation, Charlie was to go to Australia and Tom, quitting Australia, headed for South Africa. He was to end up in Dublin in the 1920s. Described as "a fervent nationalist" and "a convivial rolling stone", Alice Stopford Green apparently on one occasion in the 1920s had the task of calming him down and decommissioning his gun. Nina eventually departed for the United States, while Roger of course worked in both Africa and Latin America.

At some distance in time from the hurts of childhood, as happens, Roger was to forgive his father and romanticise his faults. He turned in that direction to seek solace, and in due course found strength, from re-invention of his father as a patriotic Irishman. The boy seems on the surface to have coped with the death of two parents in such rapid succession, although one would have thought the second only compounded the first. Perhaps it was the other way round and his father's departure was a blessed relief, life with him in the final years having become intolerable. Thus was Casement consolidated in new Co. Antrim surroundings and enabled to pursue his life in relative calm. However, his adolescent rebellion did not come then; it was inverted, instead gathering pace in middle age. It was as if the early loss of his parents at age nine and twelve forced him to become serious and secretive. His hobby then became Ireland, one to which he returned in early middle age.

Becoming an orphan by the age of twelve with a peripatetic childhood was sure to make Casement an outsider, able to look after himself whilst also forcing internalisation of his anger and frustrations. The series of London lodging rooms may have made the youngster streetwise, giving him the later adult confidence to cruise effortlessly around the cities of three continents and operate two separate lives – one as a sexual being, and the other as a gentleman and British diplomat.

Boys of nine or ten may not grasp the nature of a father's desperate financial plight, but the older brothers, and their sister Nina in particular, now seventeen, must have been obliged to grow up quickly. She had to substitute as a mother for the boys then aged twelve, ten and nine, and three years later on to take up the responsibilities of a father. The quick temper and oddness attributed to Roger's father, especially in his last years, will have had the inevitable effect of further destabilising the four siblings. Consistency in treatment was probably not a feature of either parent while living on one's wits was a trait passed on from father to son, as well as the ability to keep on the move without being overtaken by a desire to settle down. Constant changes in surroundings gave the boy the external appearance of confidence – an ability to cope with new people and places, and an extra skin to deal with the scorn of others.

With two brothers, one only a year older, Casement might have been able to be enclosed in a world of boys where he was protected as the youngest, and thus socialised into male ways. But there is unintended evidence, from his cousin and champion Gertrude, of significant sibling rivalries, and of the ganging up by the two older brothers against sister Nina and young Roger. These fights, involving Roger's use of head-butting and fists to protect a girl seven years his senior, seem a little unlikely but reveal a history of childhood dissension and of two hostile camps; indeed Tom and Charlie were known as "The Terrors."

Roger may also have been pushed into earlier adulthood both by these internal feuds and the rootless life the family led, giving him the necessary brass neck to do, so early in life, those sexually exceptional things he did; things the vast majority of his homosexual peers either never did or only commenced when they were well on into adulthood. If a homosexual in this era, it was rare to be free of an all-consuming guilt, but Casement seems to have managed it.

Money, the getting of it and the accounting for it, was to be a dominant feature of the boys' lives; Tom in particular was to exist like his father in a state of perpetual financial crisis, with madcap business schemes going awry; Charlie's second marriage necessitated further loans from his consul brother. Roger was to be without a home of his own his whole life, which probably cost more than it ultimately saved, although it enabled him to be fed and entertained at others' expense. While he was reliant on rented rooms, he was, however, a much sought-after and obliging guest, brightening the lives of many hosts. This gave him an invaluable opportunity of networking through the relevant power structures; an opportunity that was just not available to other men who could not afford such frequent absences from wives and family.

The registration of Roger's birth in 1864 as from *Doyles Cottage* reveals the home of his parents to have been an artisan's dwelling. Despite its location in Kingstown, a respectable south Dublin suburb on the road to elegant Dalkey, it was plainly not a gentleman's address. In 1932, when a Casement museum was being contemplated there, it was described as "a decayed terrace of houses on the tramline beyond Dun Laoghaire."[87] It has since been demolished. Kingstown was to become Dun Laoghaire after independence and is best known as the passenger port of exit and entry for Dublin. His father, by this time forty-five years of age, is recorded as "Late Captain in the Antrim Militia", while his mother's name is given as "Annie Casement formerly Jephson."

Ostensibly the influence of the boy's mother on Roger appears remarkably slight. This may be simply a matter of being almost imperceptible herself, while her antecedents remain obscure or obscured. Little is recorded of her life, in fact next to nothing before she married Captain Casement. Her family name was Jephson according to both Roger's birth and her marriage certificate, and her mother was named Anne Ball according to family notes. Perhaps the diminutive Annie, used on the boy's birth certificate, had come about to distinguish her from her own mother Anne but it is striking and indicative to a degree of an informal upbringing. However, the newspaper report of her marriage in Belfast's *Northern Whig* of 26 April 1855 describes her as Anna and adds the detail that she was the "eldest daughter of the late Jas. Jephson esq. Dublin." This reveals her father was by then dead and also indicates she had at least two sisters, one more than is spoken of.

She seems to have been a Dubliner, yet her residence is given on the marriage certificate as Belfast. The wedding was in St Anne's Church the precursor to the present Church of Ireland Cathedral in Donegall Street. The legend of a Paris wedding and indeed of a first meeting there appears fanciful, yet the fact of a newspaper write-up and the prestigious church chosen prove this was no hole-in-the-corner event. The groom was thirty-five and the bride twenty-one. Uncle John Casement supposedly received the couple at Magherintemple after their nuptials which would confirm there was no frostiness in that quarter.

The fact of Annie being born a Roman Catholic had been a moot point. If she had been, she apparently adopted the Anglican faith on marriage. But the notion of her cradle Catholicism – accepted and emphasised by Casement – was disputed by Gertrude who wrote that Roger's mother "though brought up a Protestant became a Catholic when her children were still young", and revealingly explained the reasons: "Her father was a Catholic and her mother a Protestant and as was usual in those days the daughter of a mixed marriage followed the religion of their mother. Anne was brought up a Protestant but the warmth of her nature and a certain emotional strain revolted from the coldness of the Protestant faith and shortly after her marriage she found the Catholic faith...The Casements had in all eleven children but only four survived infancy...Anne Casement's nature was too expansive, too beauty loving, too vivacious to find consolation in a religion that cramped, that denied, that suppressed and so she joined the Catholic Church and had her children baptised as Catholics."[88] She added that Casement's "mother absolutely adored" Roger.

On 16 September 1832, Anne was baptised an Anglican in St George's, Hardwicke Place but under the spelling Jepson which prevented earlier discovery of this detail. Her address was given as 48 North Strand, Dublin. This was where her mother, from 1835, ran a Ladies Seminary under the name Miss Jane Ball, and Mrs Jephson from 1842 until 1853, the year of her death. School education for girls was then a rarity, indicating a very progressive family background to Casement's mother and aunt. Such an outlook plainly travelled forward two generations to Jane's grandson Roger and his three siblings (not to mention his Bannister cousins). Their parents, Anne and Captain Casement, seemed to share a world view not dissimilar to that of Oscar Wilde's parents Speranza and Sir William.

Interestingly, Anne's sister Grace married the Liverpool shipping agent Edward Bannister in the same church, St Anne's Belfast, as she had married Captain Casement ten years earlier. That Grace married an English Protestant and brought up her family as Protestants again confirms the sisters were not raised as Catholics, although in the case of one at least of Grace's daughters, Gertrude, a religious conversion took place in 1916, the same year as her cousin Roger's.

What is evidenced by document is that Anne had her three boys conditionally baptised as Roman Catholics by Father Felix Poole SJ in Rhyl, North Wales on 5 August 1868. They were detailed as "*Carolus Gulielmus, Thomas Hugo et Rogerius David, filii Rogerii et Annae Casement (olim Jephson).*"[89]

Theologically this second baptism was somewhat pointless as their first Anglican baptism would normally be regarded as sufficient and valid. In emergency, baptisms by lay people are permitted in the Catholic Church. Indeed folklore exists about Catholic servants in Ireland secretly baptising their baby Protestant charges. The Rhyl baptism would have been conditional upon their never having been previously baptised – an unlikely event in those days. Anne's discreet visit to the Welsh resort may well have been occasioned by a desire to extend and complete the process of her own change of faith.

The baby Roger, born in September 1864, had not been (first) baptised until 20 October 1865 on the Isle of Man,[90] over a year after his birth, suggesting at least a disorganised family where religious duties were concerned. Casement was aware of the location of this earlier baptism. Writing from Ballycastle in September 1905 to Gertrude who was visiting the island with her sister Lizzie, he remarked, "I've not been in the Isle of Man since I was baptised. I often think of going there to hunt up Casements – Macasmund is the rightful name of them you know and they came from and still come from Gaelic Mann."[91] The choice of the ancestral home island for the baptism is interesting but indicated just another example of the family's frequent moves. Casement's own description about religion and his early days is that he "was brought up really nothing." Given his family circumstances this rings very true but more so by virtue of his father's probable indifference to formal religion.

The Jephson family of Mallow in Co. Cork is upper class and southern Protestant with a past dating back to the Tudor era, Ascendancy in a way that the Casements were not, and with many more centuries of Irish residence. Despite valiant efforts, including those of Casement himself, only the most tenuous and inconclusive connection has ever been made between Anne and the Mallow Jephsons. As she died when Roger was only nine, it is not surprising that he would be unable to recall much of her talk about her family or upbringing. But he certainly heard something. In an enquiry of 1 June 1895 to Louisa Jephson-Norreys at Mallow Castle, he explained that his mother "spoke of being related to Jephsons of Mallow, in my hearing, and since her death I never met with anyone whom I might make enquiry."[92] He had first come across this lady in Las Palmas in 1892 and another of the family, Arthur Mounteney Jephson, in 1887 in the Congo. Casement was there with the well-equipped Sanford team while Jephson was on the Stanley expedition to relieve Emin Pasha. In fact Casement had assisted a very ill Jephson with ten grains of quinine and the loan of four of his bearers when he was too weak to walk.

That Anne (according to Lizzy Bannister) was "a tall, graceful woman" while Roger at the age of seven was "even then tall for his years"[93] and good-looking, and her sister Grace Bannister ("wee aunty") dumpy, are the only facts passed down the generations. But Nina disputes even that, describing her mother as graceful though "slight", noting wrongly that she was twenty-five years younger than her husband.[94] Gertrude reckoned twenty years younger.[95] Facts were, however, not Gertrude's strongest point, and less so Nina, although whether Gertrude was sometimes inaccurate or easily deceived is not always clear. Another notion was that Annie had been a music teacher. If so, her musicality was passed on to the youngest Casement son and his sister Nina. He played the piano and had apparently a beautiful baritone voice, often singing Moore's Melodies, in particular *Silent O Moyle be the Roar of thy Waters*, and other Irish airs. He would at times be accompanied by Nina, who herself played and sang in public. She remembered him, earlier in England, at the age of seven as a chorister in his surplice. There is no musical tradition in the Ballycastle family, according to the present Hugh Casement, so Anne must indeed have been the source.

On a single sheet torn from an 1881 *Ironmongers Diary & Text Book* Casement had, as a boy, written out his Jephson descent. The source is unspecified. Elsewhere in the NLI papers, however, there is a long, handwritten, mainstream Jephson genealogical account in which Casement wrote near the end that "the family of Jephson is a Roman Catholic one although originally Protestant." This is inaccurate and cannot apply to the main family as they were undoubtedly Protestant. The February 1881 page veers off the main genealogy at one Norreys Jephson and ends with Annie, Capt. Casement and their "four children, Agnes Casement the eldest, Charles, Thomas Jephson and Roger Casement."[96] The cadet Norreys Jephson could have married a Catholic but Casement records no wife's name. At that time such a marriage would have ended his links with the family. But the Jephson family genealogist details the appropriate individual, one "Norris Jephson" (1727-1767), as marrying a Deborah Lombard and dying without issue.[97]

In the 1 June 1895 letter to Mallow Castle, Casement "groping in the mists of early recollections" tentatively proposed that his Tipperary grandfather was the descendent of an entirely different member of the family, one Lorenzo Jephson, who sounds Italianate if not Catholic. "Of course I know the account Burke gives of the Jephsons", he wrote, but he hoped nonetheless he might be able "to ascertain the descent of my grandfather 'a typical Irishman' from the Jephsons who came to Ireland in Queen Elizabeth's reign. I have no doubt of his descent from them – but the occasional remarks of a long dead mother are not sufficient warrant for my considering it sufficiently well-established for our 'family tree' up here."[98] He was to be disappointed. The name Lorenzo Jephson occurs in three generations of this Carrick-on-Suir branch of the family but there is no record of any of them having a son called James. Neither were any

Roman Catholics. The suppositions in Roger Sawyer's 1984 book concerning an unrecorded son of the first Lorenzo (1773-1820) called James are entirely dependent on the reliability of Casement's facts. If the original story was invented then there was no such son.

These detailed notes of 1881 might evoke wonder at why a boy of sixteen could be so taken up with questions of ancestry at a time when most of that age are rebelling against their families and origins. That the details seem to be false or falsified, both then and in 1895, is another strange aspect. Accepting that Casement was hoping to find an aristocratic Jephson origin for his mother we are left with another unexpected motive and need. From these notes and the inferences drawn, it appears that Casement was also desperately seeking to find an Irish Catholic element to his family background, and that he was willing to delude himself in the process, although more so when a teenager than later.

Gertrude discovered more of the boy's research notes from 1881 which unfortunately are now missing. She did, however, transcribe from them that Anne's maternal grandfather was a Captain Ball, his father being Adam Ball MP who was Postmaster General of Dublin and that that family was connected to the Martins and the Herveys.[99] There is, however, no Adam Ball visible in the Dublin directories of the era and certainly not one who was an MP. There is one so-named, Adam Gustavus Ball, born in 1821 who died in 1882 in Australia leaving two daughters, and whose brother John was an MP and became Irish Lord Chancellor. It is possible he was the template for the Ball story if it was entirely a fiction. There is verification available of some Martin connection and that is a regular £5 quarterly allowance which Grace Bannister received from a long-established timber merchant, Richard Martin & Co., situated on Sir John Rogerson's Quay in Dublin. Martin had at one time been the Prussian consul and the firm was also engaged in shipping. Casement for no obvious reason possessed and kept the accompanying letters to his aunt, dated 1898 to 1907, including one brusque rejection of a request for further advance payments.[100]

There is also a problem with Casement's note that his grandfather James Jephson was the son of "Mary Martin of Ballinahinch Co. Galway."[101] There was such a Mary Martin born in 1815, a novelist, and daughter of 'Humanity Dick' Martin from whom she inherited Ballinahinch Castle and a vast, although encumbered, estate. Known as The Princess of Connaught she, by then Mrs Arthur Bell, died in childbirth in New York in 1850, the same year as her famous novel *Julia Howard* was published. It is too much of a co-incidence that Casement should have been advised of an ancestor who was in her day quite famous. Although he himself may not have recognised the identical name, it does seem to be another example of exaggerated ancestry sourced from his mother.

Given that Casement lived with the Bannisters in Liverpool for three years from 1880 and kept in close touch for many more, he must have had ample opportunity to reminisce with his aunt about her family. It is therefore odd that he chose instead to make his adult round of genealogical researches directly to the Jephsons in Mallow. Perhaps Grace Bannister was reluctant to open up on the subject and he felt embarrassed questioning her, yet he was happy, indeed eager, to tell relatives of new knowledge about the Manx (and in this instance the Viking – not the Gaelic) origins of the Casement family. Writing in 1902 to his cousin Roger he insistently recommended the purchase of "Moore's *Names of the Isle of Man*."[102] It may well be that Grace was reluctant to disclose any of her sister's history to avoid going into detail about her character.

Casement appears to have been searching for the mother he hardly knew and the desired outcome was someone at least as well connected as the Casements, if not better bred. It seems he felt his own identity to be marred by dubious ancestry, while his Casement father, who had been inadequate in both career and domestic matters, was still someone for whom he had little respect. Sensitive children will be dissatisfied and feel inferior to their apparent peers, no matter how grand their own origins.

These periodic outbursts of genealogical fervour are a classic symptom of someone with identity problems or uncertainties. It is therefore no surprise that gay people are noted for being overly well represented in genealogical, historical and archaeological circles as well as in librarianship. Casement wanted to recreate the past in an idealised form, with his mother's origins being long established and aristocratic, rather than that of an ordinary Dublin family, albeit with their own lore of Mallow Castle origins. In tune with his own anti-Scottish, Irish Gaelic sympathies he also wanted a Catholic background although the Tudor Jephsons were precisely the class he abhorred historically for extirpating the Gaelic kingdoms.

He admitted deceiving his Jephson correspondent about his grandfather James ("or John" as he also wrote). Casement first stated that he had died in a hunting fall and then switched to the wildly improbable tale of him having been killed jumping Dublin's Grand Canal for a wager. Either way, his apparent death on a horse gave him a touch of class. The wager story with its romantic daredevil air is more likely to be a remembered version of a family fable, where accuracy about ancestors is rarely a requirement. It also usefully explained the loss of the family fortune, "as to his property, that I knew went in some such way."[103] But it could not have brought any ease to Casement that he failed to find the needed link that would elevate and catholicise his mother's origins. The sad truth is that the only member of his family to die in the Grand Canal was to be his brother Tom.

3

Ballymena schooldays

When Captain Casement returned to Ireland it did not involve the wholesale transfer of a family of five. With a penniless father and four children, the oldest Nina being seventeen in 1873, a number of relatives in England, Ireland and Australia were asked to assist. Information is sparse on the precise share-out of responsibility and the exact sequence of events but it seems a split-up was inevitable, with the two older boys being prepared for a seafaring career. There were presumably some residual connections left from grandfather Hugh's days as a ship-owner in Belfast and in London, and the brothers were first sent to sea on a sailing vessel *The Euromene*.[104] The merchant navy had the advantage of not only providing a job for young teenage boys but also a home for long periods while at sea. It was eventually to get them to Australia.

Obviously there was no certainty over the timing of the death of their father but he appears to be now a spent force. The evidence is of a man increasingly divorced from reality, conducting, after his return, séances at the Adair Arms Hotel in Ballymena. At first glance such a location would not seem to be fertile ground, it being the most Presbyterian town in Ireland. But even in Ballymena and its environs, there were spinsters, widows, and retired colonial servants with enough time on their hands and a sense of spiritual or semi-religious curiosity to keep him busy. It was also a garrison town.

Despite Ballymena's hard-line reputation, it is no distance from Ballymoney, where the famous Home Rule Presbyterian Rev. J.B. Armour ministered and where Casement made his first notable speech in October 1913. Ballymena was also where he gave what may have been his first public address in Ireland: Rose Young of the Galgorm Castle family, recorded with pride in her diary on 10 November 1891 "Father, Rosie, Willie and I went to a lecture on the Congo by Mr Roger Casement in the Protestant Hall."[105] This was a hall that was to be wrecked by an IRA bomb in 1990, losing for ever its elegant Italianate frontage.

His father's physical health was not good as was so often the case with those who had served in tropical climates. In 1858 illness had caused his second retirement after only a couple of years in the North Antrim Militia, although there is a suggestion in family letters of an objection to the eviction of crofters. He had rejoined the army in the year of his marriage in an obvious attempt to regularise his life and of course his income, especially as Annie would soon start a family. His mental health in the few years between his own and his wife's death may also have deteriorated further as the few written items to survive from around that era indicate a bizarre whimsicality. They were on diverse topics such as horses and the Paris Commune, and bird keeping. His son was to be similarly afflicted by a series of debilitating ailments that sapped his mental strength as much as his physical, and frequently kept him away from his consular duties. Indeed as a chain smoker with innumerable sexual partners and tropical diseases, it is a wonder he survived so long.

When death came for the father (described as a gentleman on the death certificate) it was sad and lonely. He died suddenly on a Saturday morning in the Adair Arms Hotel where he had been living for the previous six months. Within twelve hours a jury had been sworn and an inquest held that evening in the same hotel. The verdict returned was that Captain Casement's death was due to a "haemorrhage arising from a long continuing pulmonary disease", presumably tuberculosis. It was reported that he had been "for a lengthy period in ailing health" and that despite medical aid being procured a second severe haemorrhage quickly proved fatal. He died relatively young, in his late fifties, although the registrar recorded his age as fifty – whether through error or guesswork remains unknown. Yet another Casement had succumbed to the White Death.

The boy Casement was thus aged twelve when in May 1877 he became an orphan. He was (or was to become) a boarder in the nearby Diocesan School, now Ballymena Academy. His career there can only definitely be confirmed, or more accurately inferred, for the three academic years from September 1877 to the summer of 1880. It is probable that he had only started at the Diocesan School the year before, consequent upon his father's move.

The fact that Catherine Pottinger makes the remark "he has been at school before, he told me", in April 1878 to her uncle John Casement, suggests that the Ulster Casements were not well-informed about the boy and were only now becoming aware of such simple facts about him. They certainly seemed to accept as unsurprising the fact that the children of Roger and Annie might be strangers to schooling.

A letter from John Young[106] jnr. of Wellington St. Ballymena to John Casement, probably also written in 1878, reveals what happened to the boy from the time he arrived in Ireland in 1876 until his schooling began. He was "kept" by Mrs. Pottinger for the first two years, "not having been at school for three years before" and commenced Latin in September 1877 when just thirteen, probably his first month at the Diocesan School, or possibly a year earlier.

There obviously had been behavioural difficulties and his future was uncertain, "Mr King gives a very good report of him & says he is getting on very well indeed & he thinks it is very unfortunate he has displeased Mrs Pottinger & that he really thinks it was not the boy's intention or fault…I think he is much to [sic] gentle & nice to rough it at sea, he is much more suited for an office or land life of some kind I think & would learn more this year at school then too again he is only fourteen years of age which is almost too young for any profession except sea." He concluded by saying, "I think Rodger [sic] would like to go into the constabulary but I daresay that would be impossible as they are not taken until they are eighteen now I think. I think he is willing to do anything that would support him as a gentleman. He is very unwilling to be a burden on his sister." The *Belfast News Letter* carries a report on 29 September 1879 of those pupils successful in the 'Intermediate Education Examinations,' one name being 'Roger D. Casement' of 5 Wellington Street, Ballymena.

A note made by the Casement author W.J. Maloney confirms that father and children remained in England for some time after Annie Casement's death in 1873: "Numkins (Nina) led me to believe that they drifted from lodgings to lodgings for these three years, her father being so crotchety and restless he would not stay put…This may be merely malice on Numkins part."[107] It seems not, as Gertrude wrote "after his mother's death Roger spent two rather lonely years with his father and brothers in London and elsewhere."[108] Nina also told Maloney that Roger had been educated for the previous three years in London, remarking "the boys went from one board school to another." Elizabeth Bannister added "Roddie was sent to school in Ballymena to the Revd. J King who prepared boys for the Army and various professions…He made many friends and was a favourite with both masters and boys."[109]

There were just half a dozen other boarders at the school which was essentially one for day pupils. No school chums apart from Travers King (the seventh of the headmaster's sons) were ever mentioned, so it is probable Casement made no lasting friendships in Ballymena nor found anyone greatly to love or admire. The atmosphere there, despite its location in the capital of Antrim Presbyterianism, seems to have been scholarly and unoppressive. The boy Casement was as well connected locally as any boy could be, so he was unlikely to have been put upon or bullied.

The fifteen-year-old was also something of a cricketer, being recorded as playing for three separate local teams in the months of June and July 1880 including one from a school in the nearby Moravian village of Gracehill. His scoring was not impressive although in his second game he made five runs out of the team's total of twenty-two. Failing to register a run in the other two games, he did catch a batsman out in the first. Match scores were then tiny due to the poor state of the pitches.[110] There is a hint here of an enthusiastic teenager helping to make up the numbers, especially as he switched sides from

Cullybackey to Ballymena for his third game on 20 July 1880. Not particular about which team he played for, it is probable that Casement was lending a hand to the men of the Young family who were associated with Ballymena Cricket Club, and with whom he was staying at Galgorm Castle.

The evidence is that one way or another Casement became very well educated. His surviving exercise books in the NLI tell of classical studies, in which he excelled, apparently winning prizes. His French was good and stood him in good stead in the diplomatic world. He was reasonably fluent in Portuguese which he learnt through conversation, not in class, although he does not appear to have had the facility for composing in it. Latterly he was able to translate from Spanish. He developed a taste for poetry especially Keats, Shelley and Tennyson and was to spend many a quiet moment in Africa and elsewhere honing his own poetic efforts. They were normally torn from him through emotion. The evidence in his notebooks reveals that writing poetry was a habit he started in Ballymena.

The Diocesan School was of course an Anglican establishment; an island of educational Anglicanism in a sea of Presbyterianism. Rev. Robert King, the headmaster, and his predecessor, Dr William Reeves were both Cork-born. They also shared the distinction of being Gaelic language scholars and heritage enthusiasts. Reeves (1815-92) became Bishop of Down, Connor and Dromore in 1886. His translations included *Adamnan's Life of St Columba* while he is also remembered for his learned researches in the antiquarian field with works such as *The Ancient Churches of Armagh*.

Rev. King, described as "the father of modern Irish church history" published in 1860 *The Book of Common Prayer* in an Irish translation. Nina was to describe him as "the greatest Gaelic scholar then living" and with "a large family of sons, seven in all."[111] She was two out as he had nine. Despite this proximate scholarship, Casement was to state categorically that he was not given any Irish language or history teaching, although he told Alice Stopford Green in 1906 that "Dr King spoke Irish as well as he spoke English."[112] It seems impossible to believe that the atmosphere at the school was in any way antagonistic to matters Gaelic. Indeed Gertrude took it further, writing of King as "a great Irish scholar well versed in the ancient literature of Ireland and from him Roger learnt to appreciate the literature of his own land...Roger's years under Mr King's care were fruitful in cultivating his fine intelligence and literary turn of mind."[113] Casement certainly managed to steep himself in Irish history and legend from his early teenage years, and become an early devotee of Parnell.

John Casement could hardly have been expected to accommodate a slightly dotty father as well as four children at Churchfield. Indeed he was that keen to have even the one boy, Roger, around him. This contrasts with the fact of other children, Robertsons for example, being boarded with him in later times while their parents were abroad. In contrast to the accepted view of Casement as an adopted son of Ballycastle and Magherintemple, things were not so clear-cut, certainly not in the first instance.

Two fascinating letters to John Casement from the daughter of his stepbrother Thomas have survived and reveal things to be quite different from that previously assumed view. The thirteen-year-old Roger was a problem in more ways than one: he was already showing signs of turning out a rebel, and had ideas way above his station – that of an impoverished relative who would have to get an everyday job after an early departure from school.

That niece was born Catherine Cosnahan Casement. She had four daughters, but by 1875 was separated from her husband Col. Eldred Pottinger whose family reputation was that of "an awful tartar." The Colonel and his daughter Catherine, known as Kitsie, both ultimately merited mention in the Black Diaries. Why Catherine Pottinger was taking such an interest in young Roger's future remains unclear, although in the second letter she displays what appears to be a degree of rivalry with the Young family. She wrote from *Lis-an-Iskea* in Castleroe, Coleraine, firstly on 29 April 1878 nearly a year after Roger's father's death:

"My dear Uncle John, I am much puzzled about little Roger Casement and want your help in advising me if you will kindly give it. He seems not very strong and is growing rapidly, but at the same time appears to have such a foolish and undue estimate of himself as to his future position and present style of dress that it is needful not to encourage it by over carefulness or attention. Mr King tells me he is getting on well with Latin which he commenced with him in September last (he was just over thirteen, rather late in commencing). In History and Geography he all [sic] does well but his arithmetic is not good and he appears to make little progress, and gives little or no attention to it, so that if he does two exercises in an hour and a quarter which is given to it three times a week, he thinks it wonderful. He has been at school before, he told me, so I do not think him ignorant of school studies or quite a stranger to application.

"Now as to his future I was thinking of the Constabulary, or a Bank Clerkship or in a mercantile house. I do not know the way to proceed for the Constabulary but suppose examinations are necessary. The qualifications I don't know – or the necessary expenses. I was also thinking of his going to Canada like Tommy Jebb, who is doing well. Neither health or finances are suitable for a learned profession. He holds no text but for the army and being a 'dashing young fellow like Grant's Heroes'. I don't admire them, and it is absurd enough poor boy – if he seems turning out well I would not object to giving a helping hand but his ideas are magnificent. Could you give me any advice on the subject for which I would be grateful. If it would not be too much to ask to let him go to you for a week or two in the summer vacation you could tell his character better, if not inconvenient to you and Aunt Charlotte – With much affecte. love to you Aunt Charlotte, Roger, Susie, Brab and Jack, believe me ever dear Uncle John your affecte. niece."[114]

Plainly Roger had neither seen uncle John nor yet been to Magherintemple. His term-time home was the schoolhouse in Ballymena while some free time was spent in the town with the Young family. He also holidayed there, while every weekend he joined the headmaster and Mrs King for Sunday lunch. Early days with his parents had been unstable and disorganised. Things had not changed much where his home life in Co. Antrim was concerned.

In August 1879, a year and two summers later, Catherine wrote to her uncle John again. Roger was now fourteen. The idea of his emigrating had firmed up, with Canadian relatives of the Pottingers (the Evans) living in Quebec province being sounded out. By this time Roger had obviously been entertained at Magherintemple but Nina was now an issue. Her famous contrary streak must already have been on display just as her carelessness in money matters was well recognised although she was still only twenty-three:

"I cannot say about Roger David that I think it satisfactory that Nina should be his only guardian if he went to the Evans – as she might direct his doings there, and his leaving anytime which if he went, whether withdrawn or not, they would expect the £30 annually until his coming of age. Besides he and she could make themselves most disagreeable to the Evans when there was no power to interfere with them, thus I would not be inclined to do anything if you do not see your way to be guardian. I know how reckless they are in money matters and not until they have 'eaten their cake' do they think of the consequences.

"Uncle Robert will not assent he told me as much, early last month – and he thinks as the Johnny Youngs interfered and took him they ought to provide for him! Annie Coulson has much at present to do with her money and I know is very much "put to" to do all that is expected of her. She is paying many expenses she need not but still if she did not, no one else would do so – and I know she feels like Uncle Robert for I sounded her ideas on the subject. I do not think the boy would go, unless he is compelled. And if so will he do any good?"

With the Rev. Robert Casement refusing to assist, and with the generosity of Annie Coulson (a daughter of great-aunt Catherine, living in Portadown) already stretched, not to mention the fact that the boy who wanted to be one of "Grant's Heroes" was not enthused about Canada, the family was preparing to wash its hands of providing the young Casement with a future, or any position locally. Nina was another fly in the ointment.

The complaint about the Johnny Youngs revealed a critical fact. It was they who had taken him in; not the Johnny Casements. Gertrude largely confirms this outline when she stated that Roger lived with "an old friend of the family" near Ballymena, while Nina never short of a harsh word for anyone, described Mrs Johnny Young (John's second wife Rose Miller) as "a bit of a martinet" who with no children of her own had provided an Easter holiday home. Outwardly the Youngs were a conventional family. Loyal in 1798, during the American Civil war they favoured the Confederacy, in particular Generals Robert E. Lee and Stonewall Jackson, where the young Casement admired the Ulster-origined General Ulysses S. Grant.

Crucially it was the first Mrs Young, née Grace Savage, an Anglican married into a staunch Presbyterian household, who was the key to her daughter Rose's nationalist outlook and who may well also have indirectly influenced the young Casement's early political development. Her son William recorded Grace Young's outspoken remarks about the Manchester Martyrs with astonishment. While staying in Forfar in 1873 with the former Lord Chancellor, Earl Cairns, and in the presence of another of Disraeli's 1867 Cabinet, Viscount Cranbrook, Mrs Young launched into a defence of the Manchester Martyrs. Grace argued that "they only intended to burst the lock when firing into the door of the prison van."[115] Espousing the cause of the Martyrs was of a piece with her general romantic view of history and her particular hatred of informers.

The various Young families lived in or near Ballymena and were innovative linen manufacturers and merchants. The John Youngs had bought several thousand acres of cheap encumbered land from Lord Mountcashell of Co. Cork in 1851, and now possessed the town's most prestigious address of Galgorm Castle. John's brother William had a large house there, Kintullagh, now the St Louis Convent grammar school. Another Young branch lived at Fenaghy near Cullybackey. The connection to Roger, distant, yet locally sufficient, was with John Casement's second wife Charlotte Miller whose sister Rose had married the Rt Hon John Young as *his* second wife.

John Young, from his first marriage, had had a large number of children. One daughter Maria (Mya) Young was to marry John Casement's son, Captain Jack (later Admiral Casement), in 1892, but another, Rose Young (1865-1947), was to provide important influences and contacts in the Irish cultural movement, critical to Casement's developing Irish Irishness.

Despite the heavy Unionist (and later UVF) involvement of the Young, McNeill and Dobbs families there was a gender split over culture and nation which was remarkably common in Co. Antrim. The more muscular tended to Unionism while the more gentle gravitated to the Gaelic League, and in time Catholic nationalism. Rose and to a lesser extent her sister, another Charlotte, learned Gaelic and steeped themselves in the language and literature. One of her closest collaborators and mentors was Bishop Reeves, the former headmaster at Ballymena. In time as *Róis Ní Ogáin* she published an anthology of Irish verse in three volumes, *Duanaire Gaedhilge,* some of it transcribed from old Glenswomen she heard singing. In the last days, Casement would send out of prison through Gertrude, "Love to R.Y. and to Charlotte."[116]

The Young girls were far from alone in this pursuit. The names of the Protestants in the Gaelic League or the various associated cultural and educational bodies can in most cases be individually identified. In Ulster they are a roll call of the entire literary, progressive and humanising establishment, ranging over archaeology, folklore, nature, geology and literature. The Belfast Naturalist Field Club was a key meeting ground where Protestants collided with modern attitudes and ancient Gaelic ideas. The various individuals became increasingly interlinked although in many cases they already knew one another. The commercial class, however, was almost entirely absent, certainly in the first generation, from this intellectual resurgence.

Partition and the formation of Catholic and Protestant states in 1921 snuffed out that crossover culture. Though these Irish Ireland Protestants are occasionally rediscovered or reappear, they were not able to resolve the intra-Unionist dispute of whether to throw in their lot with nationalism or stay British. Casement did not give much thought to this dilemma, probably because he never felt himself representative of Ulster Protestants, although at times he announced he was. In truth he never was, having so early given his allegiance elsewhere. He therefore contributed to that tradition's failure to modernise and to the other community's inability to understand the nature (and necessary intransigence) of Unionists.

That these Protestant women were dilettantes, toffs with time on their hands, is an argument that fails by virtue of the intensity and longevity of their attachment to the language and "the native Irish tradition." That tradition, "was in reality a set of values, a vision or view of the human condition, an outlook, a storehouse of human experience." One writer in his learned article *Womenfolk of the Glens of Antrim,* puts it thus: "In the early years – before politics took over – the language movement was a force for drawing people together; it broke down the barriers between the well-off, the middle class and the poor mere Irish; it gave the opportunity to people, regardless of sex or background or religious persuasion or political affiliation to come together for a common purpose – the cultivation and sharing of a rich and varied human tradition."[117]

The movement, particularly for Protestants, was an engaging alternative to the conventional. For wealthy women who were broadminded and adventurous, it provided a purpose and a function which before the advent of careers were otherwise denied. Marriage was obviously the path laid out for such women but there was a dearth of eligible young men by virtue of the high proportion who left for the army and the empire, and of course Dublin and London and the universities. Many girls were thus left high and dry. The huge numbers of male casualties in the First World War only worsened matters. Today in metropolitan Ireland there are innumerable outlets for such energies, including a life independent of men. Cultural nationalism, however, is no longer the intellectual draw it undoubtedly once was for Irish women.

The 1898 centennial celebration of the United Irish rebellion was a key moment for a revival in Protestant folk memory regarding the Presbyterian role in the birth of separatist Republicanism. But at about this time it also became increasingly difficult for Unionists to maintain involvement with matters Gaelic, for the very reason that as the movement grew in popularity it came into conflict with that for the maintenance of the Union. As Unionists existed not to be nationalist – being defined by what they are not – only the radically minded would join organisations like Sinn Féin. The perhaps 10% of Irish Protestants who remained Home Rulers or non-unionists until 1916 and partition, however, continued to influence, and to provide significant leadership in the separatist movement, even in Ulster.

The future of the Casement boys meanwhile was being determined by a serious lack of funds. In August 1877 after their father's death, Nina, who was then twenty-one, and her uncle Rev. Somerville Lanphier were appointed guardians of the three lads. On Lanphier's swiftly following death she was to become, in November 1878, their sole guardian in charge of the continued distribution of the English monies from grandfather Hugh's legacy. Money expended on "providing the two elder boys with suitable outfits for sending them to sea and paying any premium that might be necessary for apprenticing them" had to be repaid to the Lanphiers. Later a sale of investments was made "for their outfit on their return home and for the next voyage."[118] Thus were Charlie and Tom launched into their life at sea.

Nina and young Roger also went on holiday to various cousins in England or in the south of Ireland. Gertrude Bannister recalled one of the few, if not the unique occasion, that Casement was to express any interest in the opposite sex, when she wrote of his love at age sixteen or seventeen for Eva Lanphier, his aunt Eleanor Casement's niece she having married the Rev. Somerville Lanphier (or Lamphier). Born in Co. Cork around 1830, he had a Ballymena connection, having been a curate in the town for a decade from about 1865. His last posting, however, was chaplain to the county asylum in Nottingham. The brief summer attachment to Eva possibly flowered there, or at Magherintemple which she visited. It was not to be pursued.

As a boy Casement loved animals, having a rabbit at one time, while his favourite childhood poem was *The Careless Chicken*. In 2006, the NLI bought in America the original "Illustrated fable by Roger Casement for his godson signed 'To Reginald Dorsey Mohun from an admiring Godfather R.C. September 24th 1896.'"[119] Richard Mohun was U.S. Commercial Agent at Boma in the Congo Free State from 1891 and was probably the former US Consul in Zanzibar that Casement quoted approvingly on Arab slavers.

Nina says there was nothing girlish about her brother although she and her girlfriends were happy to see him dressed up in girls' clothes, and he was more than willing to oblige. She described a particular incident with some relish in one of a series of articles in 1918 in the *Philadelphia Irish Press*.[120] If nothing else it reveals Casement's ease in the company of girls – a setting other boys would normally avoid. A contemporary view would be that he liked girls as friends and they reciprocated. Most boys do not, or more probably cannot, make such friends and so it can be seen as an early indicator of a pattern of non-heterosexual behaviour, that would become homosexuality.

Gertrude also recalled his fondness for dressing up. In a deception on her girlfriends, Nina dressed Roger up in a small toque of her own, while she pulled his hair into "a fringe or 'bang'." Then, as she wrote, "a spotted complexion veil, a loose sealskin coat, muff and skirt of dark green completed the attire of this lady-like and pretty, but astoundingly tall young friend of mine." To strengthen the ruse she "drilled him carefully how to walk, with small steps and not to fall over the train." Much shrieking ensued when such a thin, lean boy was unmasked as hoaxing them with a girl's dress. Other more serious pursuits were also reported such as "long walks and visits to historic remains of antiquity." On such walks Gertrude noted evocatively a boy not settling into English life, one who "picked clover and made it into bunches and fixed it to the dog's collar and told it that it was now an Irishman."[121]

Of Casement's opinion of his education we know little beyond the much-quoted 1912 letter which he wrote to his old school after a request from the headmaster for a donation. It is a bitter denunciation of what he was not taught, and is suspect for two reasons, over and above the fact that it was written so long after his attendance there.

The letter may have been largely designed to prompt the school to rethink its teaching of matters Irish. Secondly, Casement maintained very friendly relations with the widow of his old headmaster. She had been school matron while her husband was godfather to one of John Casement's boys. That Casement called on Travers King in Ballymena as late as May 1910, and earlier in 1903 (according to the Black Diaries of those years), indicates a warmth that belies the hard and propagandist nature of his 1912 letter.

It was probably the case that the teaching was British-based and only thus minimised or excluded Irish history. This was the major fault in Northern Ireland's Protestant schools until the recent era of education for mutual understanding. Nothing was anti-Irish, or pro-Unionist, but the schools operated on, and were linked to, an English-hinged curriculum. Although many guilty Protestants harp on about being denied the Irish side of their history, this author can attest to a diet of 1798 Presbyterian Republicanism from an A level history teacher at his Belfast public school, while his long-time companion recalls being instructed in the evils of the Black and Tans at the nearby secondary modern school, also in the 1960s. Teachers are not known for being averse to the radical or alternative view.

Casement replied to the headmaster, "I fear it is not in my power to give you any substantial help, for I am already committed by promise to aid several educational movements in Ireland of a distinctively national character which must have the first claim on my sympathy and support. These are a training college in Donegal, [Cloghaneely] an Irish school in Galway [Tawin] and a school in Dublin, St. Enda's where the course of teaching is Irish throughout – that is a course devised primarily to interest boys in their own country and make them good useful citizens of it. Now from my own recollections of the old Diocesan School and from what I know of similar establishments in Ireland, their aim is not so much to fit a boy to live and thrive in his own country as to equip him for export from it.

"I was taught nothing about Ireland at Ballymena School. I don't think the word was ever mentioned in a single class of the school and all I know of my country I learnt outside the school. I do not think that is a good and healthy state of mind in which to bring up the youth of any country – and while it endures, as it unhappily does in so many of the schools in Ireland – we shall see our country possessing inhabitants fit to succeed and prosper in every country but their own – citizens of the world, maybe, but not of Ireland.

"As an Irishman, I wish to see this state of things changed and Irish education to be primarily what that of every healthy people is – designed to build up a country from within, by training its youth to know, love and respect their own land before all other lands...Patriotism has been stigmatised and often treated as 'treason', as a 'crime' – or dismissed with superior scorn as 'local'.

"I shall be happy to give a little help to your school for the sake of old associations and boyish memories, if you care to accept it after this letter, and feel that your course of instruction justifies you in receiving support from a very pronounced Irish Nationalist."[122]

The mention of "boyish memories" and the absence of any complaints about his schooldays reveal that his time at Ballymena must have quite gratifying.

He may well have been a scholastic favourite of the Rev. King, being seen as a pupil willing to learn and with great potential. Casement was certainly to hold his own and impress in literary and linguistic matters with many who attended more distinguished institutions and, unlike him, had a university education. At the Diocesan School he won prizes in classical studies and developed his love of poetry and history. It was the absence of money not academic talent that saw him depart Ballymena, and formal education at the age of fifteen and a half, in order to seek a career in England.

Casement received an unexpected reply to his letter, one which was quite shocking and disarming. It was not to be replied to, simply being noted as "R. 18 June" [Received on 18 June 1912.] This response letter is rarely if ever quoted yet it merits close attention. It was from the headmaster, Mr J.A. Fullerton, and he knew precisely what to say to his haughty respondent, outpointing him in the democratic ring and upstaging him from the left: "I have to thank you for your extremely interesting letter which came as I admit as a great surprise. I naturally imagined you to be the usual product of the 'ascendancy' type of school. You naturally took me to be the direct successor of the Diocesan type of pedagogue. Well we were both badly wrong. So instead of being annoyed by your letter as you seem to fear I have quietly enjoyed the heaviest of your hits.

"You see I was myself at the Diocesan School as dayboy and being the son of a national teacher I came early to appreciate the vital distinction of class and of creed too, for I happen to be a Presbyterian. Things, however, have changed in Ballymena. The landed gentry, the county families, the army men, the rectors, the enriched business people all now give the school a wide berth; and they are perfectly justified in their action. What they want they get elsewhere. Instead we have the confidence of the middle and lower-middle classes and our 170 pupils are children of farmers, shopkeepers, dispensary doctors and National Teachers.

"We do our best to prepare them for their life work. We train them to be obedient, to be straightforward, to work methodically at whatever course they are taking up, to hear the other side, to recognise the rights of others, to shun bigotry and class prejudice. So far I dare say you agree with us but I am sure we fall short of your ideals. We do not teach the Celtic myths and legends. We do not dwell on the wrongs of Ireland, nor talk of patriots and traitors.

"We probably do not teach Irish History and Geography as you would like them taught though you will see from enclosed History sheet – last week's work for one of the grades and the only specimen at hand as I write – that the pupils have to know at least something of their native land. Personally I am untouched by the charge of turning the children of Ireland against their parent and I would feel no qualms about accepting help for the academy building fund from the most pronounced nationalist that ever lived.

"As for the Governors it would be presumptuous of me to speak. If you sent them a cheque accompanied by some home truths for the Ulster ascendancy they would probably have enough humour to pocket the subscription and chuckle over their epoliation of the Egyptian. That however is a matter entirely for your own consideration…".[123]

Casement had met his match and certainly knew it. He had engaged with a liberal but still indomitable, view of Ulster, very different from his own view of Ireland, one where the native Irish and the upper-class or intellectual Protestants came together and the Scots/British had no place, although they would be welcome. He may have retained this unanswered letter but it left no mark on his political outlook.

Rathlin, off Ballycastle, Antrim's only inhabited island, where Robert the Bruce met his spider, was to entrance the boy and be the stuff of later poetry, as was the nearby dramatic ruin of Dunluce Castle. But it was Irish Gaels, not Scots Gaels, who peopled his list of heroes. Casement's adolescence on the north coast was also to see the development of a life-long pursuit of bathing and swimming which was to bring him much pleasure, and many sexual opportunities. This form of exercise, which was almost to become an obsession, was described in an 1898 letter from Ballycastle to his friend Dick Morten, "I bathe too in the deep blue sea, off rocks, two or three times daily – glorious dives of over twenty feet into the deepest blue imaginable – blue and sparkling, and painted red, green and white by sea-weed (rack we call it here) and sands of varying depths."[124] This poetic, almost sexual enthusiasm for swimming in what are pretty chilly waters confirms that his love of bathing was genuine and not just a ploy to eye up locals. Yet he obviously observed any companions, as is evidenced in a question to Morten the next year, "Do you ever see Lady Young now? What became of her son [Winthrop] the one bathing with us?"[125] Nude swimming was quite usual until the end of the nineteenth century; indeed the Amateur Swimming Association did not introduce a bathing costume rule for schoolboy racing until 1890.[126]

If Magherintemple had been more generous, Casement's future might have been Trinity College, Dublin, a professional career there and the extensive homosexual social life that the great Dublin Castle scandals of 1884, and the theft in 1907 by Francis Shackleton of the so-called Irish Crown Jewels, brought to light. Instead he left Ireland for over twenty years, headed to his aunt and uncle Bannister's house in Liverpool and a job that was to lead to Africa. But not before he had developed a love for his family's county, once the land of the O'Neills. In time, that love extended to the whole island, the nation and the country.

A certain mid-teens conformity is evidenced by Casement's confirmation aged sixteen into the Church of England at St Anne's Church, Stanley on 20 May 1881, near where he lived in Liverpool. Gertrude recalled that rite of passage romantically: "I can remember him in dark clothes, very tall, very slim and very handsome...I think he went off by himself for a long walk afterward."[127] Another sign was said to be the poem he wrote celebrating a shoot and a stay in Portglenone House near Ballymena. It was the home of a big landowner, Robert Alexander, who had connections to the Earls of Caledon and the Young families, one member, Annie Young, controversially inheriting his estate. Rose Young's brother William was also a keen shooter and field sports enthusiast, staying there often. That poem is comic and where it talks of Bob Alexander seeing off Home Rulers like the notorious Joseph Biggar MP (second cousin to F.J. Bigger), it is descriptive and not, as some writers have suggested, sympathetic to Unionists. Entitled *Portglenone*, it was written by Casement "when a boy" in February 1883 [aged 18] a few months before his first voyage to Africa.

And if a Home Ruler should be such a fool or
Ass as to come with his preaching up here –
He'd get a backhander from Bob Alexander
Would lave him a black eye for many a year...

And though Biggar or Healy, may mouth it so mealy
Far down in the South
Yet they'll alter their tone
Here in swate Portglenone
or not open their mouth.

Casement also recorded the bag of that day's shooting, by seven guns, "20 pheasants, 2 woodcock, 87 hares, 13 rabbits; and 3 owls by the keeper."[128]

His other political poetry was far from unionist and it was heartfelt. Gertrude recalled that in his attic room in Liverpool, "The walls were papered with cartoons cut out of the *Weekly Freeman* showing the various Irish nationalists who had suffered imprisonment at English hands for the sake of their belief in Ireland a Nation."[129] The titles of his long romantic poems gathered together as *Dream of the Celt* in 1901 tell of his unflinching loyalty to the heroes of the Irish past, those who had seen off the Saxons and the Scots, especially in Ulster. *The Triumph of Hugh O'Neill* recounts the 1598 victory of the Ulster woodkern over the army of the Earl of Essex under Henry Bagenal at the Battle of the Yellow Ford. The 1642 victory, two generations later, of Owen Roe O'Neill over General Robert Monro's Scottish army, also along the Blackwater river, is memorialised in *Benburb*. The contents of this poem are equally unforgiving and unforgetting and oddly blind to the fact of his own and his family's comfortable existence in Antrim, courtesy of those Scots and English:

Since treason triumphed when O'Neill was forced to foreign flight,
The ancient people felt the heel of Scotch usurper's might;
The barren hills of Ulster held a race proscribed and banned
Who from their lofty refuge viewed their own so fertile land.
Their churches in the sunny vales; the homes that once were theirs,
Torn from them and their Faith to feed some canting minion's prayers.[130]

Absence abroad did not mean Casement lost his interest in Ireland or changed his basic views. In May 1884, aged nineteen, he can be found writing to *United Ireland* asking for back numbers and enquiring if "the subscription to present a testimonial to Mr Parnell is still open."[131] Much later, in 1898, as he remarked from Ballymena, "It is still *Erin go Bragh*."[132] In contrast to his love for the Gaelic element of Ireland, he averred in 1907, "The Scotch are the Jews of the western world."[133]

Casement's career and consular postings 1880-1913

Born 1 September 1864.

Summer 1880: left school in Ballymena, aged fifteen, and went to live with the Bannisters in Liverpool.

1881-83: clerical job with Elder Dempster & Co. in Liverpool.

1883-84: purser on Elder Dempster's SS Bonny sailing to and from west Africa.

1884-autumn 1886: in Congo working for King Leopold's International Association under Sir Francis de Winton (successor to Henry Stanley), and Camille Janssen; met Herbert Ward. Casement later stated, "I left its service of my own volition as soon after it became a recognised government as I conveniently could – not without some little pecuniary sacrifice."[134]

September 1886-February 1888: with the Sanford Exploring Expedition, a company formed in mid-1886, working on river transports, as was Herbert Ward; then briefly in charge of a trading station in the upper Congo.

1888-November 1888: "elephant shooting", then engaged on the Matadi-Stanley Pool railway project as transport manager and director of native black personnel for the advance expedition of the *Etudes du Chemin de Fer*.

December 1888-July 1889: "lay-helper" with the Baptist Missionary Society under Holman Bentley at Wathen near Stanley Pool, and then home (with Major W.G. Parminter of the Sanford Exploring Expedition).

1890-92: organising labour and transport to Stanley Pool from Matadi and operating a trading station for the Belgian-based *Societé Anonyme Belge pour l'Industrie et le Commerce du Haut Congo,* founded by Captain Albert Thys. This association had absorbed the Sanford Exploring Expedition in 1888. (Casement first met Joseph Conrad at Matadi on 13 June 1890.)

Late 1892-95: on staff of the Survey Department, assistant Director of Customs at Old Calabar in the Niger Coast (Oil Rivers) Protectorate, and acting vice-consul.

1895-97: consul at Lourenco Marques in Portuguese East Africa (Mozambique).

1898-99: consul at St Paul de Loanda in Portuguese West Africa (Angola); also covering the Congo.

1899-1900: in South Africa on Boer War service that included a spying mission to Delagoa Bay in Portuguese East Africa.

1900-1903: consul at Boma in the Congo Independent State (from 1901 also accredited to French Congo); Congo investigation from July to September 1903.

1904: *Correspondence and Report from His Majesty's Consul at Boma respecting the Administration of the Independent State of the Congo* (Cd. 1933) published in February; briefly consul-general in Lisbon.

July 1905: honoured with CMG, a Foreign Office decoration.

August 1906: appointed consul at Santos (São Paulo state) in Brazil.

December 1907: transferred to Pará (Belém) also Brazil.

March 1909-March 1910: promoted consul-general in Rio de Janeiro, residing at Petropolis; technically in post until 1913.

August 1910 and 1911: investigatory missions to the Putumayo, knighted July 1911.

1912: *Correspondence respecting the treatment of British Colonial Subjects and Native Indians employed in the collection of Rubber in the Putumayo District* (Cd. 6266) published in July as a Government Blue Book.

1913: House of Commons select committee's report on Putumayo published in June (H of C paper 148); Casement formally retired from consular service on ill-health grounds in July with a pension of £412 p.a.

4

Africa 1880-1903

Despite Catherine Pottinger's suggestions, there was not to be a police job or emigration to Quebec. Nor was Casement enabled to follow in the footsteps of his father and pursue his interest in an army commission. John and Charlotte Casement had obviously provided holiday hospitality and love, sufficient for the boy to adopt that family as his, make Magherintemple his home and to deem Ballycastle (and not Ballymena) his town. Nina too adopted the area and came to inhabit the north coast of Antrim and various boarding houses in its seaside resorts although she does not appear to have been invited to stay at the family home. Yet all this was to be in the future, as it was his mother's sister in Liverpool who was now offering the boy houseroom and a career.

It is significant that, in 1904, he later explained, "Without asking a penny of help from a single relative, without one of them lifting a finger to help I went off into the world straight from my old schoolmaster's house here in this county, a boy of fifteen and a half to face the world, and that entirely off my own bat I got every step in life."[135] His resentment and pride jump off the page in a statement that is largely true but based on a certain falsehood. He did have assistance and financial help but he was underprivileged compared to his Irish second cousins. It was, however, his own sturdy, even courageous, and persistent efforts in Africa that got him noticed and as he survived, he advanced.

So when almost sixteen he went to England, to a city not unlike Belfast. He seems to have met relatively few people, mostly neighbours of his aunt and made no lasting friends. There is a suggestion in Denis Gwynn's 1930 biography of the boy first seeking to enter the civil service, an option necessitating tutoring, but that, if accurate, came to nothing. He was therefore inevitably pointed toward his uncle Edward Bannister's world of shipping and foreign trade. Grandfather Hugh Casement had been a ship owner so there was involvement in that industry on both sides of his family. This could have been the point of contact between the two sisters Anne and Grace Jephson and their future husbands. Whatever their own origins, both were to marry men with shipping and mercantile backgrounds.

Grace's husband, Edward Bannister, was a man of substance in Liverpool in the Africa trade, and it was to be Bannister's career path which directed and channelled that of his nephew. Ireland was now to recede into the background during a period which co-incided with the debacle over the relationship between

Parnell and Kitty O'Shea. This debilitated Irish nationalism for a generation, turning the Irish, as some argue, toward a preoccupation with re-imagining themselves. Instead, for Casement, Africa and a series of different jobs and chance encounters leading in time to the consular service, were to make the man, and most importantly his reputation.

Casement's first post in Liverpool was with Elder Dempster & Co., a big shipping concern which majored in the West African trade. At this time with much of Africa unmapped and its boundaries unclear, trading and shipping enterprises had a semi-governmental role to play, similar to that of the East India and Hudson Bay Companies in earlier times. They were in place before the flag and it was their needs and ambitions which fed into decision making in the European capitals. The companies therefore had a critical part in political life and the national rivalries that made Africa, for thirty years, the key component in the territorial disputes that were to culminate in the 1914-18 war. Casement could not have started his career in a more crucial continent. He was well placed to become somebody if he did not succumb to disease, crocodiles, or rebellion.

The boss of Elder Dempster was Alfred Jones who was later to figure in the Congo controversy as an opponent of both Casement and another former Elder Dempster employee, E.D. Morel, in time an influential Labour MP. These two great radicals were not to meet until 1903 but immediately became firm friends. Interestingly, the Elder Dempster company was to develop an increasingly interlocking ownership relationship with Belfast's premier shipbuilders Harland & Wolff. In the early 1900s Alfred Jones had a monopoly on the Congo-Antwerp mail traffic as well as consular duties representing Leopold's Congo State in Liverpool. Described by W.T. Stead as the "Uncrowned King of West Africa", Jones, who was knighted in 1901, had a myriad of interests. He developed the tourist trade in the Canary Islands and the banana industry there and in the West Indies. He helped found the Liverpool School of Tropical Medicine and was chairman of the Bank of British West Africa. Born in 1845, the indefatigable Welshman died unmarried in 1909, the same year as King Leopold, a co-incidence that would be noted with some pleasure by Casement.

Edward Bannister worked for another big Liverpool firm, Hatton and Cookson, at one point the only British company in Congoland. He was initially a trading agent in Loanda in Portuguese West Africa. It was through Bannister's connections with Alfred Jones that Casement obtained his clerical job with Elder Dempster. That job lasted some three years but was plainly unsatisfying for a boy who did not take kindly to office discipline, liked the open air, and had a sexual life perhaps only in his head in his late teens, but one which required the freedom of living outside of a family. He is said to have been insubordinate to Jones and was only saved from dismissal by a proposal to send him to sea as a purser on one of the company's ships.[136] So in 1883 he left for the first of three round trips on the S.S. *Bonny* to west Africa and to Boma in the Congo where his uncle then was. These voyages also introduced Casement to the pleasure islands of Madeira and the Canaries which were to be happy hunting grounds for thirty years on his journeys to Africa or South America.

The dispute with Alfred Jones may, however, be a fable as in 1884 he certainly seemed on reasonable terms with his boss. Writing to his uncle, John Casement, for further advice on an offer of employment from the Congo International Association, he explained that he had to see "Messrs Elder Dempster & Co and obtain a testimonial from them". This he had done "and Mr Jones one of the firm in giving it to me told me I was certain of getting the appointment. He is acquainted with Col. Strauch the President or head of the Association in Brussels."[137] This Association was to transmute after the 1885 Berlin Conference into the administration for the Congo Free State, under its sovereign, King Leopold of Belgium.

In the event, another trip intervened before Casement started for a job in Africa. On July 2 1884, at sea, he wrote again to his uncle John in Ballycastle relating that Colonel Strauch's (underpaid) offer had come too late since Elder Dempster "had nobody ready to take my place as Purser of the 'Bonny', so that I, not wishing to cause them any inconvenience promised to make this voyage in their service, and leave the Congo question over until my return – a decision in accordance with your advice too."[138]

As a consul he was later to correspond with Sir Alfred Jones, pointing-up opportunities for the company, and quite properly, offering his services as a British representative. So good relations after Liverpool and before the breach over the Congo did exist despite Casement's harsh words to Morel in 1905. In a tirade against employers generally, including his then Foreign Office masters, he raged "If I went round begging for a job the very fact would turn them against me and induce them to exploit me, just as that cad Jones did when I was a boy of sixteen, or Strauch three years later. All men are snobs and they worship assurance and position."[139] An accurate assessment but one by his definition applying also to himself.

The Englishman Edward Bannister now became the dominant male role model in young Casement's life, whether he noticed or not, and one of two relatives to substitute as a father figure for the orphan. In an under-remarked way, Casement followed in almost every one of Bannister's working footsteps. They appear to have had the same outlook on African life even though one was a modest person where Casement was wilful and somewhat vain. There being no genetic connection, it is quite plausible to argue that Casement was moulded by his uncle, or perhaps he simply adopted the views and concerns of the older man. His personality which was gradually maturing into a certain rigidity was thus being shaped by Bannister through his uncle's experiences in the Congo and Angola. Both were to display a similar pattern of consular responses to Congo State excesses, driven by a humanitarian sensibility which was to transform itself into anti-Belgian feeling.

The main issue facing Atlantic consuls, aside from reporting to London on trade impediments and opportunities, was representation of British blacks who had gained employment in every port and country around that ocean. The Congo State recruited labour extensively in British West Africa and the Caribbean, and an ever-rising tide of complaints ensued. In 1893, from May to December, 1,851 such black British were enumerated (by Bannister) as arriving in the Congo while thousands more were scattered throughout the State, said mostly to be soldiers.[140] These men, somewhat inaccurately termed Kruboys – Hausa from the Niger as opposed to the Kru coast were especially sought for heavy work and still so-called – were mistreated, in fact treated as the native Congolese were treated; flogged to death, imprisoned on a whim, pressed into military service then gaoled or executed for desertion, and if alive (and even after death) forbidden to leave the state with their earnings.

In consequence, London eventually decided to appoint a second, and this time dedicated, consular official in the Congo; the first appointed in 1888 had been diverted north to Old Calabar more often than not. In 1893, Edward Bannister who had had honorary consul experience in Angola on and off since 1885, and had operated as a trader in the Congo itself, was appointed vice-consul in Boma, the then Congo capital. This was soon after his nephew had moved out of the Congo to work in Old Calabar. There he took up the government employment that led him into the consular service. Five years later, in 1898, Casement was posted to the very same town of Loanda in Angola which his uncle had left to go to the Congo. By that time, however, Bannister was three years out of his Boma job.

Casement's consular appointment at Loanda was interrupted by his South African War missions. In 1900 he again followed in his uncle's footsteps, this time to the Boma posting, one now uncoupled from Loanda. Kinchasa, the present day capital, further up river and on the opposite shore from Brazzaville, was London's preferred location for a consulate but one rejected by Casement. Despite being of different generations, uncle and nephew were to be only some five years behind one another in their Angolan and Congo appointments.

Unsurprisingly, Bannister was obliged to deal with many more of the abuses for which he was appointed. His despatches were moving and lengthy. Although well constructed and convincing, by being delayed many weeks in order to

Roger Casement (at back, marked 9) with other Congo Free State officials including Sir Francis de Winton (marked 1) and Camille Janssen (marked 2) in Boma ca. 1886

accumulate evidence, and thus dealing with series of incidents, they tended to lose immediacy and force. That of 17 June 1894 ran to thirty-three pages with seventeen enclosures. In it, he spoke of the acting Governor General Félix Fuchs (a man Casement would communicate with in his 1903 investigation) causing the death of seven recalcitrant Barbadians "by having them fired into, when huddled in a mass on board ship." In a similar incident on the *Gretchen Bohlen*, Bannister had interposed himself, declaring, "You may send for your soldiers and fire but you will have to fire on me as I shall stand in front of these men." He also told of the beginnings of State reprisals for his brave stand: "Fourteen Accra men were brought right in front of the consulate and I found them all chained. I cannot but think that this was done purposely to try and impress on me that my interference would not save them."[141]

Bannister excused himself at one point for his use of very plain language with the public prosecutor, and honestly admitted getting "very indignant." An indication of an increasingly emotional involvement is his sarcastic definition of "Congo Free State dress", as seen on a "living skeleton" of a prisoner. In classic Casement-style phrasing, he dubbed Free State dress – "an iron collar with a chain attached."

Governor General Théophile Wahis whose "ungovernable temper and arrogance would not allow him to be even commonly polite", when he did receive the British consul, kept him standing throughout the audience "with an expression of rage on his face." Plainly the local officials could no longer tolerate Bannister. (Casement was later to concur regarding the Belgian official, although in more measured tones, advising London that Colonel Wahis, now en route to Brussels, was no "friend to, or admirer of those principles of free dealing and equal opportunity identified with our treatment of Colonial affairs.") The Colonel's earlier military experience had been with the Empress of Mexico, King Leopold's sister, in the ill-fated Mexican Legion under her executed husband Maximillian. Wahis was to stay Governor General for twenty years from 1892 to 1912.

On the evidence of Baptist missionaries, a massacre ordered by a State officer of seven native carriers in the upper Congo, who had gone on strike until they were paid and allowed first to return home, to "enjoy a little rest with their relatives", was also reported to the Foreign Office.[142] In October 1894, Bannister repeated his serious concerns in a letter to the Governor of the Gold Coast (forwarded to London) about the Congo State hiring Accra men as labourers, only for them to discover they were now soldiers under military discipline; "fraudulent enlistment" as he stigmatised it. The consul asked at least that copies of employment agreements be sent to him. "I had hundreds of complaints, and am still occupied with grave charges of cruelty practised on thesc men by officers of the State who stop short of nothing in brutality under the guise of *discipline*" he added. His efforts, he said, were "met by remarks from the Governor-General...that it was not my business to interfere, I must confine myself to commercial questions, pure and simple." That he added "did not deter me in the least, it simply had the opposite effect."[143]

If one did not know that this was the uncle writing it could easily be taken to be the work of his nephew. The length of his letters and his manifest dedication to core human rights bear an uncanny resemblance to Casement's *modus operandi,* and official style, down to the use of a favourite archaism of his – anent (about). That the cruelty in the lower Congo was insignificant compared to what Bannister said was "perpetrated in the regions of the Upper Congo"[144] was a fact also passed to London, laying the base for the wider investigation, ironically to be undertaken by his own nephew nearly a decade on.

London did put in place various restrictions on recruitment (agreed with the Free State), including a requirement that contracts should be executed in front of the British consul. Ultimately, despite Congo State protest, a ban was applied in late 1894 by the Gold Coast administration whose Governor reckoned Bannister was entirely accurate and reliable. In 1896 it was extended throughout all the West African colonies by Joseph Chamberlain, the Colonial Secretary. Promises of better treatment by Leopold's officials were, however, joined by commercial pressures arguing that the prohibition tended to throw the Congo more into French hands. As a result the ban was amended later that year to allow for engagement of such labour by the Congo Railway company in which there was substantial British investment.

This reform was Bannister's great achievement in Africa but by the time of its promulgation he was no longer in post. He had returned to England on leave, having been convicted by a Congo court of assaulting an official. Back home he was to suffer the ignominy of reprimand and peremptory replacement. The vice-consul was judged guilty of taking his set tasks too seriously – this despite the Foreign Secretary, Lord Kimberley's order of April 1894, on reading an earlier Bannister report: "These abuses must be put a stop to."[145]

The incident that finally provoked Bannister's downfall occurred on 2 June 1894 when he boarded the *Akassa* and demanded to see a list of its West African immigrant passengers and their terms of engagement. When the official declined his request he snatched the papers that revealed "unlawfully enlisted recruits from Sierra Leone." For shoving the official "along the deck" he was provocatively charged with assault, fined and ordered to pay costs. This peccadillo occurred in a state where massacre and mutilation, if not official policy, were certainly widely tolerated.

Bannister apologised on 28 December 1894, offering his sincere regrets to the Foreign Secretary through his consular superior W. Clayton Pickersgill for the annoyance he had caused. He then proceeded to relate an earlier series of outrages that had culminated in a flogging for a headman who had complained to the consul about his Kruboys being denied repatriation. The State Captain on seeing Bannister's card said to the old African "I'll teach you to go to the Consul!" Fifty lashes were then administered. "He did certainly teach him – Congo Independent State fashion!" was Bannister's ironic comment. The Governor's further complaint to Bannister was that he was being seen to act "in favour of the blacks." Having justified his actions with extra contextual detail, Bannister concluded by promising "I will endeavour to suppress my personal feelings in future for the sake of my position and my obvious duty as an officer of the government and not a private irresponsible personage."[146]

This letter was urged on him by Pickersgill, who did add in his enclosure to the Earl of Kimberley, "The incidents he describes are such as not to escape your Lordship's attention although they cannot be regarded as offering him any excuse."[147] Such a inculpatory yet self-justifying letter ensured Bannister would not be returning to Boma, but the process was opaque. Kimberley, after reading the Gold Coast Governor's trenchant views, noted on 13 February 1895 that he did not entirely trust Bannister's reports. He then contradicted himself by writing that there was "abundant reason" to proceed with the policy of stopping recruitment because of ill treatment. Brussels was duly informed and told that unless guarantees of proper contractual arrangements could be entered into, the ban would stay in place.

The notion of a British diplomat being arraigned in a foreign court for attempting to protect the lives and liberties of British subjects, and then being sacked, is still hard to credit, especially as the Congo was subject ultimately to British (and other) control through the Berlin Act. The matter, however, seems to have gone unremarked at home which gave the Foreign Office a certain freedom to dispose of Bannister. By July 1895 officials were discussing who would replace him. H.P. Anderson who in March had minuted "Until the regime in the Congo is completely altered, it may be impossible for any Vice-Consul to hold his own"[148] was three months later singing a quite different tune. Recommending to Lord Salisbury the name of an "intelligent soldier" as a replacement for Bannister, one who might go up river to discover "what the Belgians and the French are doing in the direction of the Nile", he declared that "Mr Bannister the Vice-Consul in the Congo cannot return there. He was intemperate in his actions and injudicious in the tone of his correspondence with the authorities (though his intention was good) and the State Governor asked for his recall which was agreed to."[149] Salisbury concurred.

In one key respect this was untrue and it is surprising that Anderson's minuted assessment, and the detail about agreeing to the Congo State's wishes – let alone acquiescing with its actions on the consul went unchallenged. The geopolitical problems of the upper Nile may well have required reassessment of Foreign Office priorities and an opportunity having presented itself was duly taken to swap a humanitarian-minded consul for someone who would concentrate on Britain's wider interests. But the notion that London should and did agree to Bannister's recall on the say-so of the Congo State Governor is inherently unlikely, especially as the archives in Brussels give no indication of any such request, rather the contrary.

Dr Jules Marchal, a Congo historian and a former Belgian ambassador in Africa, suggests "Bannister as an older man could not adapt to the ways of the consular-diplomatic caste, could not refrain from calling a cat a cat. Having no esteem for the Congo authorities, he told them bluntly what he had to... This lack of 'good manners' was a cardinal sin in the eyes of the Foreign Office."[150] Whether he was simply "quick-tempered and possessed more zeal than tact" as has been suggested[151] and was thus the victim of a ruthless Congo administration is one argument. Somebody, however, within the Foreign Office conspired, or at least deceived, to ensure the consul's demission or transfer, by neglecting to tell the Foreign Secretary that King Leopold had actually disagreed with his Congo officials about Bannister. However, it remains unclear who precisely, and why.

On 16 May 1894 the Governor-General had urged Leopold to ask for Bannister's recall because he had written that the public prosecutor was a liar. The King replied that such a request was not appropriate especially as the prosecutor was himself unfit for the job. Later when Leopold learned of Bannister's conviction, he ordered, on 30 July 1894, the remission of the fine, observing that the Congo justice system had been so maladroit, its proceedings could well lead to the establishment of the mooted system of British consular courts. In both instances Leopold faulted the Congo authorities and not Bannister whose defence of the interest of the black British he seems to have respected.

The Foreign Office, regardless of Leopold's view in Brussels, laid the blame for the incidents solely on their own man and a note was sent from the Brussels embassy to the King on 28 September 1894 stating that his assault on the government clerk was clearly improper and indefensible. It did, however, ask for the fine to be abated as the conviction was contrary to normal diplomatic immunity, and ended by stating "the Vice-Consul will be censured, and will be warned to be more careful in the future." The bemused Belgians responded by advising that Leopold had sent instructions to the Congo over a month earlier that the fine be remitted. What cannot have gone unnoticed was that the British were not backing up their man on the ground, ensuring the Congo authorities knew they need not worry about further pressure from London concerning treatment of their own, let alone British, Africans.

Oddly, in Casement's extensive surviving correspondence there are no letters from his uncle or any mention of this remarkable affair or of his effective dismissal, and almost no references to him otherwise. When Casement came to be given the Foreign Office's documentation on the Congo question prior to his 1903 investigation there was nothing about his uncle. The saga cannot have gone unremarked although Casement chose to ignore it in his writings. Nina, after 1916, recalled a family version of uncle Edward's court appearance. In her somewhat embroidered account he had rescued an African put in a barrel by a Belgian official which was then thrown into the river. Bannister, in the process, hit the Belgian for which he was fined 500 francs.[152]

Anderson further minuted to Lord Salisbury "Mr Bannister, who has only held one post as Vice-Consul, has little claim on us and need not, I think, for the present at least receive any other appointment."[153] This was inaccurate as he had had previous honorary consular appointments. In anyone's book Edward Bannister was an unsung hero of the Congo story, a trail blazer who paid an apparently high and unheralded price for his courage and persistence. According to his daughter Gertrude, her father "retired"[154] after his dismissal, as has been accepted. In fact this was not the end of his career.

From a cursory reference, by Casement, to his uncle having worked in Brazil, a sequel was to be uncovered. Writing from Rio de Janeiro in 1909 he had remarked to Gertrude how he often thought "of your poor father when he came here from Africa. No wonder he resigned and fled in despair."[155] Such a posting is to be found in the diplomatic list of the time which has Bannister appointed as vice-consul in the Brazilian capital in August 1895 – but only up to March 1896. The Foreign Office, perhaps because of the discreditable treatment it meted out (or for fear of Bannister making an issue of the matter), had had second thoughts about simply discarding him. He was sent to Rio de Janeiro, a more agreeable Portuguese-speaking territory than Angola, spookily prefiguring his nephew's movements once again. Like Casement, he was reluctant to take up his new post, and was in September 1895 certified by his Liverpool doctor as unfit due to "catarrhal influenza." The doctor added that he still needed a couple of months in Europe to complete his recovery.[156] The Foreign Office granted the request but declined to commence paying Bannister's salary.

Arriving in January "he showed unmistakable signs of illness that he was unfit for this post" and on 3 February he was so certified by Dr Raymundo Bandeira who added "Through his long residence in hot climates and having had a chronic and severe malarial infection in Africa he is in such a state of debility and weakness of his nervous system (neurasthenia) that it is impossible for him."[157] This medical description is eerily similar to one his nephew would obtain, some twenty years later, when he too, having also displayed an inability to settle in, or warm to, Brazil and unwilling to face further time in Rio de Janeiro, was to seek a medical retirement. Bannister resigned to seek "some other post in a cooler climate" and sailed out of Rio on 17 February 1896.[158] There were to be no further appointments. He died in 1907.

Consciously or unconsciously Casement learned from his uncle's fate that if one was going to survive in the Foreign Office (and be controversial) one needed to become political and have journalistic allies as well as political friends. Indeed Edward Bannister's dedication and subsequent destiny taught him how to be a political consul and how to prosper as one. In part, this was how Casement's future career path was decided upon.

British concerns over the administration of the Congo were to make Consul Casement, whereas they broke Consul Bannister. Under a Conservative administration, the Foreign Office chose to make Casement their trouble-shooter on slavery issues both in the Congo, and later when the Liberals were in government, along the Amazon. Even with an official licence to interfere he was, like his uncle, incapable of just carrying out orders. He expanded his role and acted in a partisan and political fashion in the controversies pertaining to both regions. It is a measure of the greatness of individuals that they can make systems bend to their personalities and needs. This Casement did. Operating wildly beyond his consular, and even his special reporting remit, there were to be remarkably few reprimands over the decade, despite his political activities coming to the attention of his superiors. He got clean away with it. Probably he was discreetly encouraged to cross the line by one wing of the diplomatic service. Bannister certainly was not.

The Congo State was a peculiar institution. Britain as a signatory to the Berlin Act had certain powers and responsibilities without the means of enforcement. The State had been set up as a compromise entity with a private sovereign, King Leopold II of Belgium, to stymie German and French expansion threatening British commercial and colonial ambitions in Africa. The preferred British option had been an extended Portuguese buffer state but that idea was abandoned. London's interest remained free trade but the absolutist Leopoldian system needed revenues, especially seeding money for infrastructural development and cash for security and administration. It came to rely on taxation through forced labour, monopoly control in areas such as Leopold's *Domaine Privé*, and the offer of trading concessions to obtain a guaranteed income flow. Fine, if like Sir Alfred Jones, you were offered concessions or exclusive company territory but for other traders a point of resentment.

Britain was in advance of most other powers in its abolition of slavery

– Portugal and Brazil only abandoning the system during Casement's time on the Atlantic coast. There was therefore a British desynchronisation by virtue of its enlightened imperialism, humanitarianism, and enthusiasm for free trade. Such an outlook easily brought it into conflict with a weak and badly financed Congo entity. But Britain was slow to act. It took campaigning and campaigners to bring Leopold down just as he had campaigned so effectively to be granted a huge slice of Africa to be his private estate.

The story of Casement in Africa is one of a man moving through and gaining experience in various commercial, imperial and even missionary operations, initially Belgian not British. He was drawn from pioneering into public service and, given his nature, towards a predominantly humanitarian outlook. This was done while maintaining a free trade imperialist outlook. Few of the other pioneers who survived had such a breadth of experience in Africa. Most wanting some sort of family life, did not remain in the area for as long. After a decade, Casement was well vaccinated against most African diseases, retaining as a consequence a permanent low-level series of ailments, especially malarial and gastric complaints. Or as he wrote, I was "deeply inoculated with malarial poison."[159]

In the Sanford Collection,[160] in the Florida city bearing that General's name since 1877, there is a series of revealing letters that give conflicting views of Casement in the Congo.[161] It would be fair to say that, wherever he went some people loved him and, as with his father and sister, others could not abide him.

An American naval officer, Emory Taunt, wrote to Sanford on 22 August 1886 saying he had taken "over from the State two white Agents, Messrs Ward and Casement (English). They are by far the best men I could get…Mr Ward at 170 per year Mr Casement at 150. This is an increase of 40 for Ward and 20 for Casement…I know Casement to be an upright honourable gentleman and he will carefully look after our interests." He was certain he had a competent man in Matadi to attend to "the assorting and forwarding of our loads, and also building our store there." In time, he felt, if business prospered up country, Casement could be given more responsible work. And Charles Ingham, a month on, was to write to General Sanford saying that Mr Casement was "a very good hardworking man, a gentleman and with some principle about him, he was in the stores at Vive, a hard and thankless task."[162] Later Taunt wrote of a punitive expedition involving Casement: "I took with me 14 Langibons, Mr Casement, and gave the "State" 11 Kabindas for porters, all for nothing… The fight was a complete "fizzle"…The chief was killed and about ten others but I fancy the State will keep it quiet."[163]

But another colleague, Baron Fritz von Rothkirch, disagreed.[164] Writing on 10 March 1887 from Matadi, he remarked "I think it will be inevitable to employ here a white man, and I dare say anyone but M. Casement." The views of Anthony (Antone) Bannister Swinburne from 1886-88 are also of interest: "Mr Casement I am sorry to say is little or no good far too much of a boy however, I have no one else and must use him for Kassai" adding, "Mr Casement is utterly useless as a trader and I shall have to try and get rid of him."[165]

However, in December that year, E.J. Glave, a man Casement loved, told Sanford he always found him willing and obliging, although, "I have heard him spoken badly of but I think myself he is a scape-goat for everyone's faults. But all agree that he displayed great energy whilst on the road." Casement composed an *In Memoriam* poem for Edward Glave, after his early death in Matadi in 1893 which opened:

He sleeps himself, whose hand has often made
The simple grave wherein lost comrades lie.[166]

In 1897, some of Glave's papers condemning the Congo Free State's developing forced labour system for rubber gathering were first published, providing an early warning to King Leopold.

Major Edmund Barttelot of the Stanley expedition (which included Herbert Ward) and Casement, then working for Sanford's Exploring Expedition, were co-incidentally together for five days from 16 to 21 April 1887. The Major's comments from his diary give a rare, and very favourable, impression of Casement. He was obviously taken with the 23 year-old, met at the Inkisi River: [16th] We "encamped on the other side, just the far side of a camp of Casement, an uncommon nice fellow belonging to the Sandford expedition... [17th] came across Casement and had lunch with him; also Jephson, who was bringing up the boat... [18th] Stanley and Casement came up in the afternoon and camped with me. We dined together... [19th] Casement helped my Soudanese on tremendously; he is a real good chap... [20th] Tried to send my Soudanese soldiers on earlier, but Stanley stopped them – perfectly unnecessarily, only he hates them so. However, I got to camp at Makoko village at 11.35 a.m. Jephson had a slight fever here. The king of this village, also Makoko by name, has a wonderful beard, which he keeps plaited up in two rolls under his chin, but when let down it reaches the ground, so that he can stand on it. Casement came up late at night, and camped near me. Our sugar was finished to-day... [21st] Breakfasted with Casement; left camp at 5.45 a.m."[167] Barttelot became commander of the famous rear column of the Emin Pasha relief expedition. He was to die the next year on 19 July when shot by a Manyuema porter called Sanga, employed by the Zanzibari slave trader Tippu-Tib, after complaining one morning about Sanga's wife's incessant drumming.

In a typically long letter to General Sanford, of August 1888, after his

February resignation, and written from Kasai province, Casement described his view of the Congo and its economic prospects. Given "the general disinclination of all the Congo natives to anything like disciplined labour" there were serious obstacles. Ironically the Leopoldian system which Casement in due course brought down, was designed in part to meet this problem. In explaining his departure which he regretted, he told Sanford it was involuntary "although at the end I quitted the Expedition willingly. However I do not wish to re-open that question now – for, unfortunately, it involves personalities." So many incoming letters with comments on Casement suggest that Sanford was making something of an investigation into the man.[168]

Later, writing from Matadi, in a letter dated 1 July 1890 to John Young of Galgorm Castle, who was interested in starting a trading company on the Congo, Casement outlined his career in Africa since 1884. He confirmed his time with Sanford's "exploring expedition" whose object he said was the "opening up of the tributaries of the Congo to intercourse and trade with the Europeans." After arranging the transport of a steamer for Mr H.M. Stanley he travelled further up river "so far as it was possible for a steamer to go, effecting friendly relations with Balolo tribes living on the banks of those rivers." In what was a copy of a job application, he explained unconvincingly that he had quit the Sanford expedition "with the intention of returning home, somewhat weakened after three and a half years service in an exceptionally unhealthy country." But he did not leave until July 1889, eighteen months and two jobs later.[169]

There are a number of other assessments of Casement made by associates in the Congo, most notably and perceptively (and most often quoted) by Joseph Conrad. Writing in 1916 to John Quinn – with the assistance of hindsight – he memorably stated "But already in Africa I judged that he was a man, properly speaking, of no mind at all. I don't mean stupid. I mean that he was all emotion. By emotional force (Congo report, Putumayo etc) he made his way, and sheer emotionalism has undone him. A creature of sheer temperament – a truly tragic personality; all but the greatness of which he had not a trace. Only vanity. But in the Congo it was not visible yet." The words Conrad used in his 1890 diary when he first met Casement at Matadi on 13 June are, "Made the acquaintance of Mr Roger Casement, which I should consider as a great pleasure under any circumstances and now it becomes a positive piece of luck. Thinks, speaks well, most intelligent and very sympathetic."[170] In his next note he contradicted himself, revealing doubts about his fellow whites, "Intend avoid acquaintances as much as possible." Nonetheless the two were to share a room for several weeks, barring a period when Casement went down river to Boma escorting "a large lot of ivory."[171]

Congo comrades, from left:
Edward Glave, William Parminter, Herbert Ward, Roger Casement

Perhaps the most famous description by Conrad about Casement comes from a letter to Robert Cunninghame Graham dated 26 December 1903: "I send you two letters I had from a man called Casement, premising that I knew him first in the Congo just 12 years ago. Perhaps you've heard or seen in print his name. He's a protestant Irish man, pious too. But so was Pizzaro. For the rest I can assure you that he is a limpid personality. There is a touch of the conquistador in him too; for I have seen him start off into an unspeakable wilderness swinging a crookhandled stick for all weapon, with two bulldogs, Paddy (white) and Biddy (Brindle) at his heels and a Loanda boy carrying a bundle for all company. A few months afterwards it so happened that I saw him come out again, a little leaner, a little browner, with his sticks, dogs, and Loanda boy, and quietly serene as though he had been for a stroll in a park...I have always thought some particle of La Casas' soul had found refuge in his indefatigable body...He could tell you things! Things I have tried to forget, things I never did know. he has had as many years of Africa as I had months – almost."

The most detailed contemporary appraisal, however, is that of the Baptist missionary W. Holman Bentley. Although he only had a few months to observe

Casement in his 30s. Regent Street photographer, wing collar, check jacket

him, Bentley's letters in 1888 and 1889 tell a rounded story: "Casement is very highly esteemed by everyone out here, a perfect gentleman, and very good and patient with the natives." He had, when about twenty-four years old "been led to Christ" as his fellow missionary, T.H. Hoste, had mentioned. Bentley added, "I managed also very delicately to get an assurance that there had been nothing in his manner of life out here which would not cast reflection on us did he become identified with us. I do not think we have any grounds of apprehension on those lines. Then as to his religious convictions and experience: He speaks very definitely of his conversion and faith in Christ which he dates from the early part of this year & attributing much to the influence and conversation of Mr Hoste." A certain volatility was indicated, with mention of an earlier job on a station in the Kasai area lasting only a single day. It ended as Casement "had a difference of opinion with the manager and left." Bentley noted that Casement was Irish and well connected, as his aunt was married to "Mr Bannister the Vice-Consul at Loanda."[172]

Bentley did fault Casement for his failure to drive a hard bargain when buying food from the locals. This was not appreciated, there being "far too much of this throwing away money out here, on the part of state men, and we in the missions have great difficulty in keeping prices down...I only mention this to show how fair, generous and good hearted he is. His work was well done and the books well kept."[173] Unlike most Europeans in the Congo, despite their pre-existing religious scruples, Casement had not given way to temptation where native women were concerned which was probably the question Bentley posed first. He would be unlikely to have asked about boys and in these regions, as the 1903 diary illustrates, Casement had few if any sexual opportunities. His people were from the islands or the coast, urbanised and European, or Europeanised. Up-country, and chaste for long periods, with death all around, especially the deaths of his colleagues, he was susceptible to becoming 'saved' in a Protestant religious experience. Casement never lost a belief in God but from this moment in Africa, until his prison conversion, religion rarely intruded.

Proving that the feelings of respect were mutual, Casement went out of his way to pay a return visit less than two years after he had left. In a letter home, dated 2 March 1901, Casement reported "Coming down from Pool I walked 140 miles to Ngombi Mission Station to Mr Bentley an old friend of mine." In the same letter he expressed a classic Casement combination; rage at high prices and rage over the standard (and growing) British racism of the era. Going from Matadi to Stanley Pool by train, as he wrote, cost £20 first class or £2 second class "the so-called second class is only for blacks, and would in any ordinary European community be held cruel even for the transport of hardy animals." He went second class on a two day journey which "created excitement: the idea of H.M. Consul going 2nd with 40 dirty 'niggers'. I did it on purpose as a protest against the gross robbery of the 1st class fare – and also as an example to all my Countrymen out here – who think it infra dig to go 2nd with blacks." However, he returned first class as there were over fifty "chiefly naked savages from Upper Congo" in a carriage for forty. He admitted, despite the £10 cost, "Even my free and easy way of travelling could not stand making the 51st in such a crowd."[174]

While Casement was in the Congo, from 1884 to 1892, what evidence there is suggests he did not see any particularly harsh treatment by the new State or its officials. Most of his work was on the lower Congo littoral, and within Europeanised areas which is not to say he did not see death and cruelty. He left for Nigeria in 1892 some seven years after Leopold had been made sovereign. What he was more aware of was "the terrible misery of Arab robbery and oppression" which was only recently suppressed, not to mention the barbarities inflicted by one Congo tribe upon another. His views were of the traditional variety, favouring the civilising of the Congolese through regular labour rather than "idling in villages", along with revenue-raising measures like the Hut Tax imposed in Sierra Leone. It, he felt in 1899, was "calculated to bring home a sense of individual responsibility...there we see the African savage being brought to individual participation in the public affairs of his country – and despite all the turmoil and uproar that has been made over the Hut Tax I am sure – from my knowledge of Africa – that Col. Cardew and Mr Chamberlain are right."[175]

Interestingly, such a view was expressed personally to King Leopold at breakfast on 10 October 1900. Casement noted its "appeal to His Majesty who said that that he had wished not to levy direct taxes upon the natives, but to induce them to develop their country by working its india rubber to their own benefit and to the profit of the companies interested." This, the King ominously added "was not forced labour, although it was necessary to insist that that the natives should work."[176] Such a position put Casement entirely at odds with two significant African activists and commentators, E.D. Morel and Mary Kingsley, who, together with Alfred Jones, vainly attempted to have the Hut Tax abolished. It had led to rebellion in Sierra Leone in 1898 and of course serious disruption of trade.

Although Casement, the public servant, was taking an opposite view on such a matter, it is interesting to note here the critical link that was to bring Casement from Africa to Ireland; Alice Stopford Green had been a great supporter of Mary Kingsley and her native cultural approach to Africa. Kingsley died in 1900 whilst a war time volunteer nurse in South Africa. Green founded *The African Society* in her memory, working closely with Morel who with Richard Dennett[177] were, in time, to draw her and Casement together – with all the repercussions that their meeting would have for Ireland.

Like many adventurers, as opposed to settlers, Casement grew in affection for the various native peoples he was put amongst, but it was the three years in Nigeria that were his closest to conventional colonialism. Britain was extending its protection up-country from the coastal ports like Old Calabar in an attempt to prevent the hinterland becoming attached to France or Germany. In the latter instance, delimiting the frontier between German *Kamerun* and the Niger Coast Protectorate was an early responsibility of Casement's. For the first time he had become a civil servant with only an indirect commercial role.

Casement once remarked (in 1903) that "Africa needs special types of character as well as men, and unless a man is the peculiar type required he might as well go to the churchyard at once."[178] He was obviously referring to himself as an eccentric survivor, and perhaps also his cronies. Yet as can be gleaned from official reports, it is in his Niger service that Casement's most remarkable and admirable characteristics were displayed. He undertook three, increasingly effective, surveying expeditions, often unarmed. On one such he was the only white man on the journey into the interior, with admittedly forty-three native

Casement in consular dress

companions. On this occasion he was captured by hostile villagers only to be released by the local monarch. Plainly he was intrepid and brave, perhaps even foolhardy, but he was opening up Africa without the use of the gun.

A.C. Douglas, in his 1927 book *Niger Memories*, provides a classic quotation, with Casement saying, "I am seldom sick, and not often sorry. I don't wear a helmet as, personally, I don't feel the sun" while recording a rare drunken episode, conspicuous by Casement becoming unusually polite.[179] At the party to celebrate Casement's departure, the question was apparently asked, "What's come over the ruddy vice consul that he's blanket-blank polite to us all tonight." Was it Casement or his successor Digan? Both were acting vice-consuls and present, but it was more likely Casement.

As these Niger territories nominally constituted a protectorate, Britain was not yet in a position to outlaw slavery. The hope was that it could be whittled away so as not to leave thousands of slaves suddenly high and dry. But Casement was enraged at the needless cruelty associated with the absolute power the institution allowed over enslaved individuals. The worst aspect, he wrote, being exemplified in the ritual burial of slaves alongside a deceased king, or even their being eaten during the funeral ceremonies.[180] That, and the prolonged crucifixion of virgin girls, appalled him most.

As acting vice-consul in Opobo, Casement told his boss, Sir Claude MacDonald, on 24 November 1894, that despite a personal warning, three of four persons, one female and two male, recently condemned to be sacrificed in connection with the funeral rites of the late Chief Wankwanto, had been put to death. The fourth intended victim who was younger had been purchased and become another headman's property. Casement had pointed out that human sacrifice was cruel and wicked and a practice the government was resolved to suppress. In response, he had been advised that the "practice of sacrificing of slaves at the death of a chief was one these Nigerians had no intention of giving up." He proposed therefore a punitive expedition to arrest the two main culprits and impose a fine on the town.[181] Only in 1900 when Britain finally become the colonial power in Nigeria – annexing that which she was supposedly protecting – was slavery formally abolished. And not until Casement reached the Putumayo in 1910 would he come across a more terrible form of slavery, worse because it was genocide, in the truest sense of the word.

Casement also found a bit of Antrim in Nigeria. He is recorded as making regular visits to assist the Qua Iboe Mission which had its headquarters in Belfast. Mr S.A. Bill who kept a diary for many years, mentioned him frequently in 1892 amongst reports of rescuing twins, a phenomenon feared by the locals. The Belfast missionaries obviously communicated their concerns over this issue to him since he wrote in an article, *Negroland*, how "in one district a woman bears twins and superstition demands they should all three be put to death."[182] Casement's "very kind" letters were welcomed as was the ten shillings he gave a missionary's baby for a birthday present. "He seems a nice kind of man" wrote the missionary, adding "Mr Casement went to Old Calabar this afternoon. I killed a snake in the river as we were leaving him down in the boat. It is the poisonous kind."[183] A museum room presently exists in Old Calabar dedicated to Casement, indicative of continuing respect in Nigeria for his efforts.

The last strong sense of religiosity expressed by Casement before 1916, comes at this time in a 1894 official report. Suggestive of missionary influences, he digressed "Our ways are not their ways. They have made evil their good; they cling to their cruelties and superstitions, their idion crowns, and symbols of fetish power, to their right to buy and sell men...To all such, the coming of 'the Consul' means 'red ruin and the breaking up of laws'..."[184]

Reporting later, from the borders of Ibo territory in March 1894, to his best friend Dick Morten (whom he had known since 1891), Casement also reckoned life in Nigeria was not like "the old days" in the Congo. He noted "the Ibibios are a dirty misshapen very very ugly race." In a flash of good humour, he continued archly that whereas the Inokims, and their women in particular, were clean "their coiffures are masterpieces...the general *chignon* is an arrangement of hair with grease and camwood powder into a huge crown of seven or eight inches, resembling the fan-shaped tail of a pigeon spread out – all stiff." In comparison with southern Africans, he observed "the Nigger is totally different from the Bantu; the former is stubborn and obstinate and by no means so ready to sing small to the Whiteman."[185]

In the Oil Rivers Protectorate, Casement's surveying activities were supervised within the consular service while he increasingly stood in for consular colleagues. His worth came to be recognised and a posting to Uganda loomed. Instead events in South Africa came to dominate the next five years of his life, just as they would interrupt Britain's imperial progress. Although entry to the consular service was usually by examination, in his case this was dispensed with and he was sent in 1895 to Lourenco Marques, his first posting as a consul. An experienced Africa hand was obviously reckoned of greater value than a raw recruit in such a critical location so close to Pretoria.

Writing home on 2 March 1896 from Lourenco Marques, to his uncle John and thanking him for a £100 loan, Casement revealed what he reckoned was his critical involvement in the Transvaal affair: "I may as well tell you in confidence, that I was the direct cause of the German 'scare' early in January: as I have every reason to believe it was in consequence of information I wired from this and Durban, that the Government took such prompt steps to mobilise the Flying Squadron – and to send ships here to counteract the German designs. I think we have effectually checkmated them – and my German colleague Count Pfeil has been rendered ill I fear by the failure of the Emperor's little game to be Suzerain of the Transvaal."[186] Germany was contemplating annexing Delagoa Bay where Casement was posted. He was not yet a Germanophile.

Although he later regretted some of his views and perhaps his actions of this time he was not embarrassed to approve of the war once it started. He could hardly have done other given that he and his brother Tom were engaged in the fight against the Boers. Writing to Dick Morten, as early as July 1899, Casement's opinions were blunt: "To me the South Africa question is in a nutshell. It is either Boer or British. It can't be both. There isn't room for a divided rule." It was the time to be absolutely unflinching, he continued, taking the opportunity to slag off Kruger's adviser, Dr Farelly, as "a big, fat, gross, Irish idiot."[187] He was not the only Irishman working, or indeed fighting, for the Boers. Other notables included Major John MacBride, a Mayo man although like Casement one with Antrim forebears and also Arthur Griffith. Before the end of the South African War there were to be Irish POWs recruited into the Boer ranks and Boer renegades enrolled by the British to fight against their former comrades, a concept Casement never forgot. He was to talk it over with MacBride fifteen years later, the prelude to an Irish Brigade being formed in Germany.

Casement's strategic opinions remained consistent during the conflict. This is confirmed nearly two years into the war in a letter of 2 March 1901. Writing from Matadi in the Congo to his cousin Susan he told of his brother Tom being tasked by the commander-in-chief Lord Roberts, and outlined his own rigorous views: "Tom says Lord R sent for him, spoke awfully nicely to him, wished him luck, and promised him a good billet in the Administration if he got back all right from the mission he was then giving him. I've not heard a line since from him – or of him – and as there has been so much sniping by brother Boer, and so many night attacks and captures, it's quite possible I never may again. I wish the war were over – although it can only end on our terms – never the Boers' terms. It would be a huge crime now, after all this bloodshed to give in and build up only a bigger day of reckoning in the future. We must end the war at all costs of men and money according to our views of settlement not the views of anyone else."[188] Casement in his notes to Counsel in 1916 tells of doubts when home on leave in July 1900. "I was then becoming a pro-Boer… [having] come to look upon myself as an African."[189] It is probable such a view was not then as far advanced as he wished to believe in 1916.

An even more rigorous view, apparently at odds with the policy of concentrating Boer women and children, was, "We should have cleared the country of every male inhabitant as we moved on from Paardeberg. You can't make war and peace at the same time – and while war lasts it should be thorough and severe – so that it may sooner be over."[190]

This is *realpolitik* talking, the views of a committed individual. Of course Casement was not anti-imperialist. He accepted that powerful states were going to have colonies in Africa and also spheres of influence. If anything, a certain consistency in his political views can be traced in relation to the Transvaal, the Orange Free State and Ulster, with echoes even around America. The Boers and the Orangemen were settler peoples who had not melded with the natives, by virtue, in particular, of a distinct religion, and a differing ethnicity. The Boers no longer had an imperial homeland in Holland to rely upon directly, although they had much sympathy in northern Europe. They were thus on their own. But having become economically powerful through their gold fields they were more than just an impediment to British predominance in south and east Africa, and would have to be crushed. Being also faulted by Casement because of their harsh treatment of the native Africans, their national rights were not regarded.

The high point of his direct involvement in the war once posted back to Mozambique on a roving, espionage mission was his proposal adopted by Sir Alfred Milner, the High Commissioner in Cape Town, and sanctioned by Lord Roberts, to blow up the railway line between Lourenco Marques and Pretoria so as to cut off possible munitions supplies from Germany. This proposal was accepted despite Casement's own intelligence reports that the Portuguese were maintaining their neutrality by an embargo on arms imports. Although Casement set off from Natal in April with over five hundred men, moving in two contingents, the mission was to his great chagrin aborted as Roberts felt other needs were more pressing, while the Foreign Office was dubious about any long term gain or advantage. The war did get Casement a medal if only after some later prompting.

By this time Casement was beginning to exhibit two key characteristics that would predominate in the remaining fifteen years of his life. He was now in his mid-thirties and just starting in the consular service but already communicating directly with ministers in London and interacting with top officials in South Africa. Firstly he had a confidently high opinion of himself and great certitude of view, often expressed in sweeping form. Secondly he was suffering frequent bouts of illness.

Together these two attributes made him believe he had a degree of immunity from the everyday discipline imposed on other consular officials. Permission was constantly being sought for ever more extended home leaves due to his various medical conditions. Yet on one occasion, in 1912, he sought cancellation of leave of absence despite it have been granted on medical grounds.[191] The illnesses were unquestionably exaggerated as his malarial fevers rarely laid him up for more than a few days.

London was sympathetic, and fearing the high death rate in Africa built extra years for such "unhealthy service" into consular pensions, Casement in 1913 receiving eight. Even so it was the threat of necessary and imminent surgery that most often ensured his leave was granted. Casuals were then hired to cover his mundane consular duties. Casement could see his talents were recognised yet he felt he was not at first given concomitant absorbing postings at sufficiently elevated level. Indeed his dissatisfaction was ceaselessly expressed to colleagues in the service. He hoped to be out of Africa soon.

The South African War was in the end a watershed for Casement as it was for so many others. He had seen imperial power in action and although supportive at the time, he reckoned he was not the same man after it. In 1907 he explained to Alice Stopford Green what had happened: "I was on the high road to being a regular imperialist jingo – although at heart underneath all and unsuspected almost by myself I had remained an Irishman. Well the war gave me qualms at the end – the concentration camps bigger ones and finally when up in those lonely Congo forests where I found Leopold, I found also myself, the incorrigible Irishman…I was looking at the tragedy with the eyes of another race."[192]

After the South African War concluded, the Congo became the issue, which as Sir Edward Grey the Liberal Foreign Secretary said, aroused British public opinion more than any other in thirty years. Casement was therefore fortuitously well placed to shape policy. His accumulated life parts – genetic, environmental and experiential – were poised to be an instrument of fate in both African and world affairs. Belgium, and its role in the Congo in 1903 can be traced forward over a decade to that country's pivotal position regarding the outbreak of world war in 1914, and the death of millions. But Casement did not foresee that chain of events nor even the Congo's imminent arrival at the centre of European affairs.

His posting at Loanda in Angola was one that covered the Congo, and in 1899 Casement was back there making representations in person to the State authorities on the issue of the treatment of British West Africans. He reported to London that the Vice Governor General "Major Wangermée, impressed me as being a man most desirous of impartial dealing." Another Gold Coast Governor, writing in October to London, noted "the energetic action of Mr Roger Casement in behalf of these natives", a commendation that prompted a Foreign Office order to "write to Mr Casement that Lord Salisbury has much pleasure in sending him a copy of this letter."[193] Casement was being praised by the Prime Minister for his restrained interventions but he was no less radical than his uncle in the nature of his views about the Congo State.

Meantime in a letter of 30 April 1900, he was explaining from South Africa

Casement in 1903 with urbanised Africans when consul at Boma

to Sir Martin Gosselin at the Foreign Office's Africa desk – to a man who liked and looked after him – that he was still unable to recommence his Loanda job. He explained, referring to his South African military operation, that "Sir Alfred Milner has asked me to stay on until a final decision has been come to, and it is possible I may take a more active part than by mere assisting in discussions. I hope so, and I conclude there would be no objection on the part of the Foreign Office to my giving the matter any personal help I could – even if by doing so I must remain still longer absent from Loanda and the Congo. I feel it somewhat on my conscience being so long away from my post."[194]

In a world changing over to rapid communication it was plainly still permissible for officials on the ground to make their own decisions as regards their movements and location. Casement was a free agent so far as the Foreign Office was going to be concerned. And they were learning to respect that, despite grumbling notations on his minutes. But he was also suggesting to Sir Martin that after the war Britain might "join Germany or any other interested power in putting an end to the veritable reign of terror that exists in the Congo." The State was nothing but an oppressive trading monopoly where "everything else is subordinated to the lust of gain. As long as it remains so clearly 'on the make' it were hopeless to expect improvements in either the conditions of the natives or the Government influences directed to that end."

Casement then quoted at length the views of an unnamed American naval officer, once US consul at Zanzibar, and now a high military official in the Congo. He, Richard Dorsey Mohun, had had experience of the Arab slave wars which "we were all called upon to admire as an achievement of civilisation over barbarism." However, he felt that "slavery still exists...For the native I believe the change has been for the worst as they certainly haven't the same respect for a dirty native chief as they had for the powerful Arab always clean, and even the worst of them with the manners of gentlemen." The American, in a turnaround of which Casement obviously approved (and one shared by Casement's friend-to-be Major Berry) asserted "I believe the Arabs when they permanently occupied a country did a very great deal of good, much more than they will ever be given credit for."[195]

Casement's exclusively Congo appointment, at the handsome annual salary of £1,000, was gazetted in August 1900. But he stayed on in London until late October telling the Foreign Office not to expect him in post until December, and even then, as there was no house in Kinchasa, he was going to stop in Boma. On 11 December, he announced both his arrival and that he was renting a house there. His first (lengthy) despatch concerned the matter of 10/- levied by his predecessor, a sum of money he had just discovered.[196]

In a letter home to his namesake's wife, Susan Casement, dated 2 March

1901, he told a moving story of loyalty and tragedy over the response to Queen Victoria's death on 22 January: "We held (at my request) a Memorial Service in the Mission Church on 3 February – it was one of the biggest European gatherings I should think there has ever been in Central Africa – all the Congo State officers came in full uniform (about 50 of them) and I went (knowing they were to be in uniform) also in my uniform.

"The clergyman who officiated, died five days ago! He had just arrived there on 25 January – both got ill together ten days ago & he died after 5 days – she, poor soul, is going home to her children. I got a lot of black cloth and had the church draped – also a very big Union Jack...I also sent a telegram to F.O. expressing our heartfelt sorrow (we all indeed felt it) and loyal devotion to the King. It was sad news – but after all the Queen had lived her life – lived it splendidly and beautifully every day of it – and she has left a memory I suppose no other Monarch in the World ever left before."[197] Although partly phrased to please the loyal denizens of Magherintemple, they were Casement's true sentiments.

A week later he sent much the same letter to Francis Cowper in Lisbon whose job he was sizing up. Casement was now at Stanley Pool, and he wrote "the sad news of the Queen's death reached me. We were all (Belgians too) greatly grieved at that, to us, well nigh irreparable loss. Now that the Great Old Lady is gone one realises how vast was her place not only in the history of our country but even in the daily lives of each of us. I cannot think of an England without 'the Queen'."[198] Casement certainly seems to have had a special place in his heart for old Queen-Empresses as in a letter to Gertrude of 28 August 1901 he had written "I have just heard of the Empress Frederick's death – I am very sorry and we are half masting all flags here."[199] She, Victoria's eldest child, also named Victoria, was German Empress for a few brief months in 1888. Her husband died of an untreated throat cancer and was succeeded by their son Kaiser Wilhelm, another monarch whom Casement found especially admirable.

For reasons of health, and normal or extended leave, Casement was to be out of area, in Europe or travelling for large parts of the next two years – from September 1901 to May 1902 and from late October 1902 to April 1903. These periods of absence co-incided with several visits to Italy. The frequency of his absences may well have been prompted by pleasurable Italian experiences. Yet he was also fuelling the fire where Leopold's sovereign rule was concerned, with more letters to the Foreign Secretary which told of a belief that the whole basis of the sovereign's position was untenable. This was Casement effortlessly entering into diplomatic territory although the concerns expressed were still hinged to consular interests such as trade and the mistreatment of British subjects, matters he dutifully continued to attempt to rectify.

In 1901 he was being reprinted in a Foreign Office Congo Confidential, *Further Papers Respecting Ill-treatment by Officials in the Congo Free State.* Casement detailed on 28 June 1901 the case of a Lagos man Cyrus Smith who was convicted in relation to the deaths of numerous prisoners taken by his company under the orders of its Belgian director, Hubert Lothaire. (Smith's name and trial details appear in Casement's 1901-02 Army Notebook below.) The prisoners, mostly women and children, had starved to death, although in mitigation Smith evidenced his sending out of armed men to forage for victuals. His men then proceeded to kill a chief and a number of villagers who were under the impression, wrote Casement sarcastically, that "these innocent food-seekers were a band of government marauders." Lothaire had a reputation for brutality having hanged a former British missionary in 1895 on the spot for selling arms to Arab slave traders.

Casement continued "Nothing that has been alleged against the methods of the Congo State authorities in their dealings with the natives of Central Africa need, I fear be greatly doubted after the exposure effected by this case." It was, he declared "a case of 'King's Evil' not cured, but promoted by the Royal touch." Casement complained further of the ABIR company recently importing thirty cases of rifles while the same steamer took home a record cargo of 600 tons of indiarubber and 60 tons of ivory – "red" rubber for rifles, he called it. Summing-up, he stated "The only hope for the Congo should it continue to be governed by Belgians is that its Governors should be subject to a European authority responsible to public opinion, and not to the unquestioned rule of an aristocrat, whose chief pre-occupation is that this autocracy should be profitable."[200] Mentally, his 1904 report was already being written, with the Congo Reform Association also taking shape.

E.D. Morel, working separately with both his trading and humanitarian allies, had managed to get a Congo resolution, proposed by Herbert Samuel MP (Home Secretary in 1916), through the House of Commons on 20 May 1903. It called for action by the Berlin Act signatories "to abate the evils prevalent in the State." Sir Charles Dilke, in the debate, memorably described the Congo State's military technique as one of employing tribesmen whose rations consisted of the dried bodies of those they had recently killed. The allegation, which Dilke first made as early as 1897, had been countered by Stanley but it was still being repeated. The explorer explained it was a misplacing of the earlier fact that auxiliaries of a cannibalistic disposition had been used successfully in the war against Arab slave traders. London would obviously need dependable materials for an indictment, reliant as it was on occasional cases involving British subjects, and newspaper stories, many originating from the Morel camp alongside elderly tales of the Dilke variety.

Even when he managed to be in Boma, Casement was in no position to provide definitive or first-hand evidence of atrocities. From his preferred base at Loanda, he had, in May 1902, already proposed a mission of enquiry into the rubber region of the Congo river basin. But his mind was as much on his next posting. En route back to the Congo, he told Cockerell of the Foreign Office, on 28 April 1902, that of the posts being hinted at "my inclination is more for Manila than Haiti" although "I hope to accomplish one journey at least in to the interior."[201] More leave and illness were to intervene. Although the Foreign Office concurred, they were to find, in September 1902, the mission unaccomplished and Casement telegraphing "I have abandoned journey to Upper Congo, propose return Europe, leave Loanda by mail packet of 10th September for Lisbon. Existing consular accommodation Boma most uncomfortable, rendering difficult work there. I think it better to hasten plan for house than go journey interior. Consulate at Boma closed. No local representative. Nightingale will attend to correspondence forwarded here. Please sanction."[202]

This was another *fait accompli*, and taken as such in London. One official noted on the message his belief that "the poor man must have gone off his head. There is nothing to do but sanction his return." Another more charitably wrote "He is a good man, has had fever, and he would not telegraph like this unless it was really necessary." As always in the Foreign Office there were two views and given the distances involved, and Casement's increasingly exceptional position, his will prevailed, free of strong discipline. Strangely, however, he hung on in Loanda for a further month before departing, despite the urgency and precision of his demands.

The Foreign Office briefed Casement in London early in 1903 and before his departure provided him with a vast amount of documentation on the diplomatic history of the Congo. Ironically it was to be lost for months on the voyage out, as was referred to so often in the Black Diary of that year. In April 1903, finally back in the Congo from leave, Casement once again set about an expedition up-country. Initially he advised London he was starting out at the end of May. As there were parliamentary developments, he was told to hold off until further notice. Two days after the House of Commons debate, Lansdowne cabled with an order to proceed.

From this journey came the Casement Report. Although lengthy in duration and distance, his journey covered but a small proportion of the Congo State. It involved those territories coming within the direct economic control of Leopold and in particular those where rubber was the primary commodity. Some parts of the country Casement travelled to he had seen previously – over the years 1884 to 1892. He was therefore well able to make comparisons with earlier circumstances. While London sanctioned the start of his mission on

22 May it was not until 2 June that Casement, in Matadi, got a wire from the Boma consulate to say he had messages from London there – two in code and one in cypher. They included the order to proceed. On 4 June he received and deciphered the critical wire and set out the next day.

While on his investigations, on 8 August 1903, a note was finally sent by London to King Leopold. It complained of forced labour, ill treatment of natives, and trading monopolies but was as yet not particularly hard hitting. Leopold replied to the note on 17 September and unwisely chose a cheeky and hectoring tone. He accused the British of similar, if not worse, crimes in Sierra Leone. Although he accepted that the Congolese were obliged to pay their taxes by means of labour – a form of serfdom – he reminded London that this was a practice approved by Joseph Chamberlain. He was in no mood to accept criticism, particularly not from a rival imperial state. He had failed, however, to recognise that if he lost any one of the big powers' support, or at least their acquiescence, he was doomed. A state created by the great powers, but one which was not free of them although behaving as if it was, would be reconstituted.

In his 1901 minute to Lord Lansdowne, Casement had foreseen the Congo's switch into standard European state control and out of Leopold's rule. But it was still to be half a dozen years before Belgium annexed Leopold's colony to stave off its total loss. In the meantime he had lost it so far as the Foreign Office was concerned. The death in 1901 of Queen Victoria, his close Saxe-Coburg relative, also removed a certain immunity he had enjoyed. And Leopold had made one more implacable enemy when he suggested Casement was a hypocrite, being on record as having praised the Free State in a 1901 letter.[203]

Casement set out on his investigation without a sense of destiny. He was just another Atlantic consul. By the time he came back he was ever more self-regarding and he had a mission, a task in life, one that reflected his newly politicised view of the world. By becoming a man who believed in himself, as well as someone with a reputation and the right connections, he had passed over into that select group who can make history. He was to seize the time by being instrumental in setting up the Congo Reform Association although abandoning his consular career for a number of years. Remaking Ireland was a new departure and a mission looming up at speed.

5

1901-02 Army Notebook

The 1901-1902 item[204] is notorious for being ordinary. It is not a Black Diary at all, and it suggests that rather than other diaries being destroyed by Casement, they may never have existed or were little more than jotters. It is in fact a field service notebook manufactured by Waterlow & Sons. Secured with a leather strap and backed in red leather it came with an elastic closer. In a little pleated slot, Casement placed a news cutting of advertisements, the most striking depicting an "Evans Vacuum Cap for Hair Regrowth" plus one for *Homodont* tooth powder. The paper is very flimsy and perforated at the top for the removal of carbon copies, as if intended for use as a tiny despatch book. The National Archives at Kew refers to it as "Army Note Book 153, containing notes and sketches relating to Casement's service in the Congo." Nobody has bothered suggesting this item was forged. Within, Casement drew a map marked "*Terrain choisi pour l'establissement de la Consulate Britannique*" presumably for that house (and office) in Boma whose construction only begins in 1903. Other writings are also in French. He sketched out the case of Cyrus Smith "arrested 29th June 1900; tried in Oct 1900" while mention is made of Accramen in chains and one James Kudjoe. Cyrus R.E. Smith "a native of Lagos colony [who] did not bear a good character"[205] was sentenced to ten years imprisonment, commuted on appeal to twelve months, for atrocious, murderous crimes in Leopold's Domaine Privé. A rare and nearly complete sentence in the notebook reads "20 April 1899 Wangermée [then the Congo Vice-Governor General] 1000 francs fine etc for not giving notice of anchors lost." Some 80% of the pages lack any inscription at all while it contained nothing of a personal nature beyond the address of a Mrs George Cornwallis (of *The Anglo-Saxon Review*). It would have been pointlessly manufactured, if the whole set of five was.

Casement's movements during 1903 Black Diary

14 February 1903 in London

22 February left Liverpool by ship

28 February arrived Funchal in Madeira

20 March arrived Las Palmas on Grand Canary

26 March left for Africa

6 April arrived Banana in Congo thence to Portuguese Loanda and Cabinda

1 May arrived Boma

22 May left Boma for Matadi and other towns, making preparations for expedition

20 July commenced investigatory voyage

27 September returned to Boma via Brazzaville, thence to Banana and Cabinda

3 October arrived Loanda

6 November set off for Europe, calling at São Thomé

24 - 26 November at Lisbon

30 November arrived in England

22 December left for Ireland

24 December arrived Ballycastle via Dublin and Belfast

1 January 1904 arrived London, thence to Liverpool

6 - 8 January 1904 back in London.

6

1903 Diary

This, the first Black Diary, is a "Letts Pocket Diary and Almanack for 1903."[206] What follows is an abridged version, this author's annotations being within square brackets, and in bold. The diary measures approximately six inches by four inches and is bound in blue-green leather (and rebound in 1972 by the PRO). Priced on the spine at 4/-, and inside in pencil at 3/-, it is the smallest of the five volumes obtained by Scotland Yard in 1916, yet remarkable for so much information being packed into such a small space. The Home Office typists, presumably, have numbered the pages to 130, starting with "1 done".

A page of French words with Casement's own translations appears first including terms for braces, pumps and "to suffer for his faults". He offered "sometimes pretty" for "*parfois mignard.*" Pasted-in are a couple of cuttings about ship movements from, as Casement noted, "Glasgow Herald, Monday 19 Jan. 03." and "Morning Leader Feb 13. 1903." Oddly, neither details African voyages although some are trans-Atlantic.

The diary is ruled in blue horizontal lines with cash columns. There are some fifty pages of preliminary printed material including lists of contemporary MPs and peers which go entirely unmarked. On its calendar, Casement has numbered the first eleven weeks of the year, up to 21 March, marked several days in January and also written "Mrs Windsor paid to 28 Feb". Saturday gets a page to itself where other pages cover two days.

Casement has also inscribed a Munich address for one Helene Hofmeister. The same address on a scrap of paper in the lady's own Germanic handwriting and style is pasted onto the earliest blank page.

Helene Hofmeister, München, Jahnstrasse, 15/1st floor, Bavaria

Books to get. Tennyson – By Sir Alfred Lyall, K.C.B., Macmillan.

Today & Tomorrow in Ireland by Stephen Gwynn 7½ by 5, 233 pp., Hodges & Figgis, 5/- net.

E.D.M. wrote H.W. on 13th Mch/03 "Did you see Stephen Gwynne's article in the Fortnightly Review?" This à propos of Congo affairs.

There is some act, design – some holy strife
That leads us **[soon?]** to a larger life

Name for Novel "The Far from Maddening Crowd" by R. Mc. Asmunde. **[This**

is a gaelicised version of Casement's name, derived from its Viking Manx origin.] Serene enclosings of a mightier self… **[There are a number of notes here about sailing durations and distances in the summer Congo investigation.]** Morgan wrote 1.7.03 about hire of "Pioneer" if C.B.M. at Lulanga agree – "Accepted – number of months time of possible arrival." – He lent me 2 pillows & 4 pillow slips for my bed…

[The diary proper opens on 14 February 1903 and continues until entries end on 8 January 1904. The earliest daily entries, up to and including 13 February, were crudely torn out and shown to journalists in London in 1916. This was a preliminary and unsophisticated effort at exposing Casement's homosexual life, designed to weaken any campaign for clemency on his behalf, especially in America. As Casement wrote a seriously sexual poem on 11 February 1903 which opened with the line "A big mouth choked with love", it may well be that those torn out pages included details of especially torrid encounters.[207]

Later, photographs of diary pages were made and circulated. Later still, through July 1916, a transcript of this, the 1910 Black Diary and the 1911 Cash Ledger was typed up in Scotland Yard from which the text for the 1959 Singleton-Gates publication was taken – still without the pages for 1 January to 13 February 1903. They are forever lost. Singleton-Gates was not given the transcript of the 1911 Black Diary by his source (Sir Basil Thomson, the former Metropolitan Police Assistant Commissioner) so that diary's existence remained unknown for forty years. There is no record of what the police typists, who were probably male, thought of their task. Their instructions must have been to type what they saw, not what would make sense or be consistent. Concern was certainly expressed in Naval Intelligence that women working there should not get to see the diaries.[208]

The missing forty-four days of diary entries cover part of a period of special leave. Casement arrived back in London in December 1902 after his unilateral decision to return from Africa. Between initial jottings, some above, and the address below, and until the first (surviving) dated entry of 14 February there is an extended extract, with comments, from an 1891 taxation decree *et seq* on King Leopold's *Domaine Privé*, outlining the powers granted for exploitation of the wealth of the Congo and rules on the treatment of natives plus other notes by Casement relating to voyages. These rules required payments in kind by villages, including provision of workmen or soldiers – an interchangeable concept in Leopold's Congo. They imposed certain responsibilities on recognised chiefs to establish plantations of cocoa and coffee and obliged locals to clear and work them. Since an 1896 decree the King had absolute control of the *Domaine de la*

***Couronne* and *Domaine Privé* – 100,000 square miles of the richest rubber between the Kasai and Ruki rivers. There was also a decree specifically dealing with indiarubber exploitation.]**

The Lady ffrench, St. Josephs, 29 Ailesbury Road, Merrion, Dublin. [**This Lady ffrench was the mother of Casement's old friend and fellow Africa hand Irish peer, Lord ffrench. Charles's wife Mary née Corbally, like so many others, was to describe Casement memorably but also critically: "I had been told that he was extraordinarily good-looking, and on first sight I recognized that it was true. He had, without doubt, great charm. One's critical faculties are all awake when one meets someone who has been highly praised. Something contrary in me, anyhow, makes me look out for the faults, but though Roger Casement was far from dull perfection, there was nothing ugly or ordinary about him. He had a most romantic personality and an ideality of mind which was expressed in his type of looks at once Spanish and Irish. He was the strangest person imaginable to come out of Ulster. This was all very intriguing, but although I liked him and we made friends, he did not fire me to any great extent with enthusiasm for his causes and ideals in the way he did most people who admired him. I felt that mentally he lived on a different plane. I am quite sure that Roger Casement, even in his most condemned actions, had the highest motives for what he did. He saw things like that and he could not see them otherwise. Moreover, unlike most idealists he was prepared to sacrifice himself. He was the only man of my acquaintance who could wear a beard and get off with it".[209]**

Lord ffrench was not without his critics, being vilified in correspondence from German East Africa in 1912 and 1913 by Hans Coudenhove, another crony from Casement's days in south and east Africa: "I knew of course that he was a crook but I did not want to tell you as I saw you were such pals. In '99 or 1900 a high British official warned me against him." Coudenhove then detailed one charge – of defrauding his servant Matteo, "I put his accumulated six years wages in one of Lord ffrench's undertakings and he lost every penny."[210]]

FEBRUARY

14 SATURDAY Writing in morning – Labelling G.Bs' heads for Club. [**George Brown's 'Darkie' heads**] Then to 53 Chester Square to lunch – Mortens there – with them to Paddington 3.35. Then to Nina to tea [**Casement's sister, christened Agnes but always known as Nina was now aged 46 and separated after a brief marriage to George Newman.**] then to studio (H.W. gone) Then to Club – H.W. [**Herbert Ward**] Cui, Collis & I. Then to Collis' to dinner.

Did not wire Dick Morten as agreed. Home early on bus 10.15 to Nina. She still seedy. To bed at 11.10. Slept very long. No letters. Very interesting articles in "West Africa" about Burrows' book. **[Guy Burrows, whom Casement met in 1901 in Matadi and distrusted because of his intemperate habits, as he warned Lord Lansdowne, had changed sides and was now damning Leopold in a second book. His first, published in 1898, *The Land of the Pygmies*, had praised the anti-slavery efforts of the Congo's sovereign.**[211] **Casement asked the Foreign Office to forward him a copy of the second, which arrived during his stay in the Canaries, as he diaried on 21 March.]**

15 SUNDAY **[At top of page:]** Bought at Stores £4.1.6
Up 9.40. Dressed quick. Wrote long Congo Concessions Memo. for Farnall – Sent it in at 4 p.m. with private wire. Went Princes for an instant – & then on to 53. **[Chester Square]** Not in. Up to 30 Hemstall Road **[This was the West Hampstead home of George Robertson whose mother was a sister of uncle John Casement's first wife]** – saw all. Brought Bertie back to Nina **[John's grandson Robert Casement, born 1884]** still seedy. Went supper with Cui (and Mrs Cui **[the Cui Bonos were Congo-connected friends]** – at Carlton home at 11) Walked home via Oxford Street. Goodbye to Cui & Collis y'day.

16 MONDAY Wired Dick. Went 53. Bade Mrs W**[ard]** goodbye at 10 clock. Then to Stores – bought things for Congo. Then to Hoste and back at 4. Out to Dick's at 6.5 with Darkie' Head. Very tired after dinner fell asleep. Miss Lathbury there. Turned in at Dick's. No letter from States – Mail possibly delayed. **[Casement is anxious to hear from George Brown and has only to wait one more day.]**

17 TUESDAY Left Denham 9. **[Dick and May Morten lived at *The Savoy*, in Denham, Buckinghamshire.]** Uxbridge 9.32. Saw in paper "Saxonia" arrived Queenstown 16th & proceeded immediately. Back to pack up at Aubrey. **[Aubrey Walk was Casement's address in London, a flat borrowed from a friend, Count Blücher.]** Lovely weather. Sharp frost – but at 11 bright glorious sunshine. Lunch with Nina. Then both of us to Park & saw Troops from Parliament & then to H.W. studio & then home. Letter from G. Blücher to Mrs Tyrrell with it at 8. **[Wife of William Tyrrell, private secretary to Sir Edward Grey 1907-15. Casement had hosted Tyrrell in Mozambique. He, unusually, was trusted by Casement who pleaded to see him during his interrogation in London. Tyrrell, by then Lord Tyrrell, was later as British film censor involved in a dispute around a possible Casement film.]** Then club dinner with H.W. Then walk. Papers. Saw (Enormous – youthful). Home – letter from G.B. of 6 Feb. at New York, **["6 Feb." not "6 File" as the biographer**

B.L. Reid reckoned, drawing the erroneous conclusion that Casement kept files on boyfriends.[212]] & from Parkinson about "Rags".

18 WEDNESDAY Beautiful frosty morning. Busy writing all day. Intended leaving "Bonny" today too late for her. Nina went Kings [**One of these letters was to F.H. Cowper, consul-general in Lisbon. Dated 18 February 1903, from his Aubrey Walk address, and enclosing a letter for Parkinson about his abandoned bob-tailed sheepdog, Casement announced "I think there is little doubt I shall get Lisbon when you go...Don't tell 'Rags' this." Where sailors had girls in every port, Casement had dogs, and trunks.**[213]] Drew £50 & cheque book for 50. Sent clothes (2 packages, Hat Box & Trunk) to 55 Ebury Street, E. Peacock. [**Mr Edward Peacock, Casement's tailor and occasional landlord; an Ebury Street address was where this diary was to be found in 1916.**] Went to "Aladdin" with Nina. Awfully stupid piece. Wrote G.B. to New York, Hartford Hotel, 309 Pearl Street, N.Y.

19 THURSDAY Went city got ticket £49 from E.D. & Co, [**Elder Dempster, the shipping company Casement had worked for in Liverpool as a teenager**] self & Charlie to C. Palmas. [**this Charlie is not Casement's brother.**] Lunch Oxford Street. Wired H.W., Bertie & Miss H to come dinner. Found card from Nisco at G. Central. [**Baron Nisco, an Italian judge in the Congo, was to serve on the enquiry team appointed by Leopold after Casement's report. An unwise choice from the King's point of view as Nisco was on good terms with Casement. He, however, reckoned it a poor choice since Nisco's knowledge of the Congo was restricted to the capital. Nisco's view according to Sir Constantine Phipps in Brussels was that the Congo Belgians were often "'ne'er-do-wells', drunkards, failures or cast-offs, but the class was now improving." "Not true", responded Casement. In May 1904, explaining his acquaintanceship with Nisco he told Lord Lansdowne**[214] **that he had dined with the Boma judge on 18 February 1903. He was a day out but a forger working from Foreign Office material would not have made the same mistake.**] All dined there – & met others before dinner. La Bohème after. Home – saw Miss H. home. Back tired after walk. Last day in London.

20 FRIDAY Went ~~city~~ Euston with Nina & Charlie, Bertie, Nisco, H.W. & Miss Heath there to see me off by 12.15 train. Lime Street [**Liverpool railway station**] 4.50. Went E.D. & Co. & got tickets & good berth. Sent Charlie to theatre with porter. [**Casement was staying at the North Western Hotel in Liverpool from where he wrote his cousin Gertrude Bannister five minutes after his arrival**[215]] Went Auntie's. [**Casement's mother's sister, Mrs Grace Bannister**] She, Lizzie, Ed [**his cousin Edward**] well. Back by Frederick St.

at Sailor's Home. Henry Abrahams from Demerara 6" Arthur ". **[second measurement was never inscribed]** 11/6. Drove to Park. Home, supper & to bed. Paid all bills at 22 Aubrey Walk. Medium – but mu nua ami monene monene beh! beh! **[These and subsequent African language phrases are in Kikongo, the language spoken in the funnel of the Congo and around Boma. Translated and decoded, it reveals that Henry Abrahams had a penis of medium size (6 inches) but Arthur (whose length was left uninscribed – with just an inches symbol following an empty space) had one significantly larger, "monene monene" being Kikongo for "very big." Arthur was taken "mu nua ami" – in my mouth.]**

21 SATURDAY Auntie & Lizzie to breakfast. Went stage at 10 a.m. Luggage by hotel porters to "Jebba". Got off about 11 A.M. Good cabin. Beastly ship. Egerton again Purser. **[Casement's first job at sea on the S.S. Bonny in 1884 was as a purser, a ship he missed.]** Bad weather outside. Lay down in afternoon trying to sleep, weather getting worse. Turned in at 12.

22 SUNDAY Beastly weather, "Jebba" a tub & rolling fearfully. Past South of Tuskar at noon – Going worse in evening. Food very bad. Charlie sick in bed – poor little beggar. ~~Ran 184 miles~~.

23 MONDAY Sea bad. Wind S.S.W. Ran 184 miles at noon. Ship rolling fearfully. In evening sea somewhat better & as night went on it got quieter.

24 TUESDAY Sea got worse at 9 A.M. Wind became gale. Ran 187 miles are 840 from Madeira. Ship doing about 5 Knots now. Gale freshened in afternoon sea very bad. Awful tub. Very uncomfortable indeed.

25 WEDNESDAY Ran 157 miles only! Alleged Gale in our teeth – She is a Tub & Horror.

26 THURSDAY Wind abated. Ran 239 miles. Madeira 448 distant. Weather warmer – To get in Saturday morning.

27 FRIDAY Weather better. Ship going well. Wrote 9 letters home. Wrote F.O. in evening also for Burrows' book on Congo – to Farnall & Spicer, Nina, H.W., Kings, Roger Dennett to go by Jebba. Beautiful day.

28 SATURDAY **[Casement was now arriving in Madeira, a Portuguese island territory, where he holidayed for nearly three weeks before departing to the Canary Islands for a further week. During his visit to the island's capital of Funchal, he went to the Casino every one of the nineteen nights he was there, except for that of 6 March. He managed inevitably to lose**

more than he ever won which irked him. The Casino doubled up as a social club for upper-class English visitors escaping to the sun. It was, however, to be a vacation marred by rain and cold.] At 6 a.m. past Fora Island. In to Funchal at 7.30. Perestrello – as in Sept 1897, on "Scott" with photos – grown tall – eyes beautiful. down on lip. curls. **[Perestrellos Photographos Lda, a well-known photographic shop, is still in existence at 30 Barreiros, Funchal with a branch at Galerias Casino.]** On shore with Reid to Carmo. At café in square & coffee & *Carro* offered. Lunched with Hon. A. Bailey. **[Hon. Arthur Bailey, born 1868, son of the first Lord Glanusk and a Nigerian resident]** They off at 3. "Jebba" 3.30. Walked Alameda, types – dark distressful. Then gardens at 4. Band of "Majestic" – Prowse R.N., of "Jupiter" came up & spoke. Squadron goes on Monday. Dinner very stupid. Hotel Carmo bad. Out at 8 to Old Town – same place as in Feb. 1885!!! 18 years ago. **[Casement was twenty in 1885, revealing his cruising skills were long established.]** Then to Square. Two offers. One doubtful. The other got cigarettes – same I think as in Alameda in afternoon. Whiskey drunk by waiters 8/- bottle – 16/- a day at Carmo far too dear. Went Casino at 5. 1 milreis on Roulette lost.

MARCH

1 SUNDAY Lovely morning. Slept very badly. Bed too short & carros **[car or carriage]** up to 3 A.M returning from Ball at Palace. Manoel. to Paseo do Pico – Went up hill past Santa Clara Hotel. Met Dr Connolly – $1.250 Saw Sir Ernily **[??]** on Square. Went Casino. Called on Spence, not in. **[John Bowring Spence (1861-1918), Consul in Madeira since 1897]**

2 MONDAY Went up to Monte with the jones. Laura Lady Wilton there. Delightful. Beautiful creature by stream coming down – at tramlines. Called on Spence. not in – on "Hogue". – 19 – Cigarettes. Clubfoot **[nickname for a partner]** Went Casino. Lost about 3 dollars. Connolly to dinner. Then Café – Eveng. in Square. Turned in early.

3 TUESDAY Went to Perestrellos. Bought 2/6 photos. Lunched with ~~Connolly~~ Spence & Mrs. Spence. On to Mr Fletcher till 5. At Casino. Won four times. about £4. To dinner and then again to Casino at 10. till midnight. Did not play at night. American won about £600. Cape Liner arr. Home mail steamer will take our letters. Que Ser Senhor **['What would the gentleman want?']** $3.800. Went Quay to steamer

4 WEDNESDAY Smoked too much y'day. Walked up hill to Mount Church – Beautiful there. John Hughes an Irishman at Hotel. Beautiful types – on

Carro – and Belmonte. Stayed all day there – Lunching at Reids – nice waiters. “Kildonan” arr from England – very bad weather reported. Back on carro $1. Dinner & then to Casino. Lost £2.10/-. Home early – Turned in 11.

5 THURSDAY Stayed in garden & reading papers. No news of interest. After lunch to Mount by train. Beautiful not there. Hughes. down by train at 6. Lovely evening – to Casino at 10. Played – won on 33 $7.500 on 200. Back at 10.30 – In Bullock Carro. Tired. Turned in at 11. Slept better.

6 FRIDAY Lovely morning as usual. Walked up to first Station – then train. Young P [**Perestrello**] in, at Belmonte Hotel. Looked camera – took photo asked. White said Homão [**Armão??**] de Administrado. Vierya de Machico. Walked about all day. Beautiful there. Josiah 115, Carreiro do Monte. Lunch at Belmonts & Dinner at Reids. Down by 8 train. Lost cigarette case – Walked a bit. Home at 10.

7 SATURDAY Went Perestrellos with roll of films for developing to try & get V. de Machicos done asked his address. Told out by Jones’ Hotel so walked there – Quinta Nunes [**a country estate**] – Lovely spot – but Jones told me it belonged to Blandy. Ordered dinner at Casino invited Connolly. Back to lunch & to Perestrellos again. Developed, asked prints & Machicos address in Funchal. [**The pursuit of the young photographic assistant at Perestrellos became something of a holiday obsession, having had its origins in a visit six years earlier and plainly losing none of its drive in between times. What the boy made of the increasingly obvious attention which he was being paid and the ever-tamer excuses used by Casement to justify seeing him, remains unknown.**] Saw very beautiful near Casino at shop door & again at Bridge. When going back to lunch. To Casino in afternoon with friends – Band very good. Spence there. Played & lost about 27/-. Back to dress for dinner & then with Connolly there. To Casino at 9. Many people there, dancing & playing, including Spences. I lost about £2. They went & Connolly at 10 or so. Lieut. of “Dom Carlos” there – splendid. Then servant in gardens with Senhora Cosham [??] Quinta? [**Thursday**] Bastante [**Quite a lot**] there. Muinto frio [**Very cold**] – many times $4.000. Tomorrow & Agostinho **X**. About 17½. Segunda feira [**He was, however, not seen on Monday. Casement was stood up as he knew to expect since such lads were seldom reliable.**]

8 SUNDAY “Cameroon” came and left. Up Mount with photo for Viera – then to Spence’s to lunch – then on board “Dom Carlos” to Dance. To English rooms & back to Casino. Music good – Not played. To dinner thro’ Gardens. All Madeira there listening to band. To Casino at 9. Lost $2.500. Smoked too much at Bar. Back walking lovely night. No sign of Agostinho. Waited long.

Slept fairly well. Played won $6 & then lost it & £2.

9 MONDAY Beautiful morning. Waited all morning for Viera de Machico – but no visit. Went Casino in afternoon to music – played & lost. After dinner walked there, played & lost again. Many types – two Rua do Carreira up to Sao Pedro & then in Praça. **[Square]** Sailor to sea. Walked home stranded and stony – Lovely night. No Agostinho. Lost about £3.

10 TUESDAY "Norman" arrived at 10. Joe MP **[Joseph Chamberlain was visiting Madeira]** on shore at noon. Went with Miss Rolland to snapshot him, & to club. Many beauties there – exquisite eyes. Joe & others after lunch to Mount. In Square most of day with Miss Rolland. Bought dog for 600 reis. Went Casino at 8.30. Won £3 nearly & lost but came away with 30/- clear & all expenses paid. Home. Met Alvaro gave $2.000. Poor boy. 19. Is a clerk in an office. Mother a seamstress.

11 WEDNESDAY Cold night. "Saxon" in at upgetting. Went up Mount with Miss Rolland. At Reids with Hughes. At Belmonte waiter said had given letter to Veira who would come Carmo to thank me. Down in Carro with Miss R. Lunch noisy as usual. At 4 to Mrs Spence – then to Casino together with black pup – After dinner to Casino and lost 30/ - At one point had lost £2.10/ -, & then got it back with about 3 Dollars over – but played too late. Home at 12 on foot.

12 THURSDAY Better day at 7 a.m. Sun out again. But cold. Went up Mount to Belmonte. Left 4 photos for Vieira **[The spelling of this name, probably that of the Perestrello boy, as with Agostinho's, varies on most inscriptions.]** with waiter at noon & card. Walked down. Slept after lunch very tired. To Casino at 4.45. Many people there. Band good. Played & lost £2 about. Introduced to Mr Stanford & Lady Edgcume. Invited to lunch tomorrow. Spence to dinner in carro. Dined in private room. To Casino after. Spence went early. I played hard. Won pleno on 19 & side = 20½. Then lost a lot & then won again pleno on 19 & on 9. Total gain after all losses about £3. Home in rain – very heavy.

13 FRIDAY **X** Friday 13 **X** Stayed in bed till 12. Then to lunch at Quinta Stanford. Duke of Montrose there too. **[That Duke (1852-1925) was not "a young man of 25 years" as Singleton-Gates emphasised. However, his son then was. As the 6th Duke, he was the chairman of the Scottish National Party for ten years until 1934, while his son, using his courtesy title of Lord Graham, came to fame in Rhodesia as Defence and Foreign Minister in the illegal regime of Ian Smith in the 1960s. He was notorious for an**

after-dinner routine involving a penny clenched between the buttocks, a party piece that seriously upset Harold Wilson in 1965.] Then to Mrs. Fletcher. All day rain. Then to Spence. Long yarn. He to Casino. ~~Then Spence to~~ I won about £8 on 27 pleno and on 9 pleno = 55 dollars. Dinner – to Theatre – only a minute. Then to Casino & back to Theatre. Augustinho – Kissed many times. 4 dollars. To Casino lost £3.

14 SATURDAY Stayed in bed till 12. After lunch to Convent at Rua dos Cruzes – then to Cemetery & then to Casino. Lost £3.10. Home to dinner. Dressed & to Casino again. Lost £3. Total losses today nearly £7. Plenty of dancing – but nearly all English. Portuguese beauties not there. August not there. Walked about – talked to Lady Edgecume **[wife of Sir Robert Edgcumbe]** & then home at 11 walked in rain. No good today. Have finished all my money but 20 dollars. Heavy rain since Thursday 7 p.m. almost without intermission night & day. One is never sure of not getting wet.

15 SUNDAY **[At top of page:]** Still raining. Agostinho & <u>whiskers</u> **[The boy may have complained about Casement's beard when kissing him.]** Have left exactly $17.000 – @ 5610. <u>£3.0.6</u> out of £29 a fortnight ago – Have spent £26 in 15 days. Today: Boots ~~$8 000~~ Carro to Reids 17 00 & down 2000 3700. Perestrello for 3 dozen photos 2500. Lost at Casino 2500. To Club foot. <u>1.000</u> 8700. To Agostinho. no tua dinheiro **[not your money]** **X** 5000. Have left <u>2500</u> 16 200. Went Reids with Connolly – Then to Bucessia. Then after dinner Agostinho splendid. Casino lost. Home. 10.30. Boas nata **[great cream]** up sidewalk with <u>cape</u>.

16 MONDAY Stayed in all day – not feeling well. Lay down in afternoon with 3 overcoats on. So cold. After dinner to Casino with Somersets. Took £3. Won plenos on 31, 27 and 19 and came away after much play with £4.6/- to good. Mrs Raglan Somerset gave me a Hymn book – Came back with Somersets at 10.30 walking & turned in at once. Slept nearly all day feeling seedy.

17 TUESDAY **[St Patrick's Day]** Since y'day £5.9/- won. Got Shamrock. Stayed in all morning. Went Stanford's call at 4. Mrs S. ill. To Casino met Duke of Montrose played with Lady Edgecume & lost about 25 dollars then won it back & 10 dollars to good. In evening again with $26.800 to Casino. Lost it all. Borrowed £3. & lost it – altho' once I got 18 dollars on 31 pleno on small Table. Home with Nelson-Ward at 11.45. Stony broke, having lost $43.600. Club-foot a Traitor. **[Disaster all round what with huge gambling losses and being stood up, yet again.]**

18 WEDNESDAY Beautiful morning. Went Club. Read papers & after to lunch with Spence's. Duke of Montrose there. Charming again. After lunch to Casino. Lost ~~£8.10/-~~ £3.10 43.000 dollars. Then won 2 times on 3rd dozen close on $60.000 – but blew it again in four or five coups. "Tenerife" arrived. After dinner to Casino again – & lost £3 – bid Lady Edgecumbe goodbye & on board at 10.20. Tenerife vile. Left at 11.30. **[Casement then sailed to the Canary Islands.]**

19 THURSDAY Going to Grand Canary on the worst ship I've been on yet. Vile Germans on board. Reading "Daily Mails" lent me by Mrs Sexton.

20 FRIDAY Arr. at Las Palmas 9.30. To S. Catalina. Charming. Old waiters' faces just same all welcome one. Swanston at door. To Town by tram Many beautifuls out with Swanston & to lunch with him & Mrs S. Loafed in garden. In to town at 6.5 by tram Dinner (vile) at Union restaurant in old square! To Cathedral Square. Beautiful & then on bridge followed – No offers – save one that ran. Home on foot at 10.15.

21 SATURDAY Juan 20. Left in "Viera y Clavijo" at 10.30. Tenerife at 4 p.m. Letters at Consulate. Two from George Brown with photo & two from Nina – three from Tom with wretched story of deception & misery again unfolding **[Casement's older brother Tom had settled in South Africa from Australia but without his first wife Blanche.]** – To Pino de Oro. Poor show. Stayed with Olsen on way up. Some types at pier head on landing. Did not see M. Violetta. After bad dinner at Pino & learning that my big basket of official papers is lost by Charlie **[The saga of the missing basket went on for weeks. Charlie who was looking after their baggage thought it had gone on board the *Teneriffe*. In correspondence, Casement suggested its absence was so devastating as to stop him continuing his journey. The contents of this large, wicker, padlocked basket included official Blue Books, stationery, half a dozen private books, Foreign Office canvas letterbags, eighteen volumes of Congo *Bulletins Officiels*, and a large Union Jack. It weighed 60-70 pounds.[216]]** went down town. Filled with Spaniards on Square. Home by Plaza de Constitucion at 10.30. Sat down and then to waste ground. Came **X**. Not shaved – about 21 or 22. Gave pesetas 13. about. To meet tomorrow. Slept many mosquitoes in bed and badly. Got Burrows' book by post.

22 SUNDAY Went to Laguna by 11.30 train. Broke down. Innocencio there. Lunched at Aguerre. Then to Crokers & saw them all there. John in great form. **[This is the first mention of John, the male who would dominate this diary and Casement's life for most of 1903. In April 1902 Casement was explaining to Cowper in Lisbon that Croker "gave me a beautiful bulldog**

who is going to the Congo with me. His name is "John." "Rags" would be fearfully jealous if he knew what was happening."[217]] Down by 6 tram. Many most beautiful in the day. In evening to Square to Band. Beautiful in white exquisite. Home at 12 after music & stroll. Wired to Reid for basket & to Catalina again.

23 MONDAY **[Inserted at top:]** Young, fair hair, blue eyes, brown clothes, about 16. Reading Burrows book & wrote to Spence about basket **[This letter survives in the PRO. Another of 26 May illustrates Casement's increasing desperation, when he wrote of being caused such serious trouble over the basket's loss that he would "pay a lot of money to get it back." Perhaps there were also some private letters or pictures amongst the official papers, most of which otherwise appear replaceable.[218]**] & to Davis at W.O. Wired again to Las Palmas about basket. **[sentence inserted between lines:]** Enormous at 1 o'clock in Square. Lunched with Cambrelyn at Paris Rest. Then to Camachos where met Errol McDonel with Croker. **[Casement duly reported to Cowper that both "young McDonnell from Liberia" and Croker looked very seedy, the latter seriously so. He added that Errol MacDonnell (1874-1928) was also after Cowper's Lisbon job, although Casement was sure he himself would get it – as he did.[219] MacDonnell ended up with a posting in Greece, but not until 1906. Cowper's wife was co-incidentally a cousin of Janet (Sinead) Flanagan – the girl who would marry Eamon de Valera in 1910.]** Home to lie down. Dined with Olsens nice waiters. After to Plaza – Weyler and Whip in hand to Avenida. by new road. **X** *Mu nua ami malumi maudi matuved ikembela gidikili.* **[The first three words mean in my mouth, while the next are a comment in plain Kikongo about ending with oral as opposed to anal sex. *Gidikili* means to tidy oneself up once sex is over.]** 25[note] & 13 pesetas.

24 TUESDAY Slept badly. Lovely weather. Not well. Went Paco's house to 11 Breakfast. Back lay down – then to Laguna feeling very seedy. Got "John". Dined with Croker and Mrs C. at Tenerife. Drove back in carriage at 9 p.m. arriving about 10. To bed. To WC 11 times awfully bad attack half dysentery – "John" barked all night – Charlie's fault leaving him out. Feeling very ill – lots of blood passing. **[This complaint may well also be connected to recent intercourse.]** **X** "Mucho amigo." **[Very friendly]** **X** **[In a letter dated 24 March 1903, Casement complained bitterly about Madeira to his colleague in Lisbon, Francis Cowper, "The British colony there is a most objectionable one to my mind – a narrow minded greengrocer community."[220]**]

25 WEDNESDAY Not at all well. Very bad night between John and

dysentery. Lying down nearly all day. Dr Otto advised going to bed and not leaving for Congo. In afternoon slightly better so decided to go. Phillippeville in all day – sailed for home at 5 p.m. After dinner went Olsen's to pay for dinner of Monday. 3/5. To waiter. In street & to Avenida. Juan 20. *mu nu ami diaka Nsono.* 18p. 20 years. Back to Olsens – Pepe 17 bought cigarettes – *mucho bueno – diati diaka moko meoslela mu mami mucho bueno – fiba, fiba* **X**. p.16 **[The first phrases translates as Juan 20 in my mouth again with a hint of shame, while the second encounter, decoded, suggests oral sex with Pepe, one party embracing hard; *fiba* is Kikongo for suck. Some of these words are not easily deciphered and cannot be translated.]**

26 THURSDAY Lauro his name. "Anversville" in when got up. August says Captain is giving me the best room on board No. 14. Went aboard at 10.30 after leaving card on Don Paco. Photograph boys there Bought £1. Same as last year but grown most exquisite. M. Violetta at Las Palmas – but this one on "Anversville" too last year. Smiled often. Gave 2.00 p. in copper. Left Santa Cruz at 11.15 about. Steamed splendidly. Blom **[Gustave]** & Vourland on board also Weber & Madame Weber. Thought of Pepe **X** & his pellos **[hair]** of y'day. Saw Croker's son at E.D. & Co's. office – got letter from Georg.

27 FRIDAY "Anversville" steaming splendidly. 312 miles at moon. Got up at noon. Read "Le Temps" lent by Blom & lay down most of day. Georg wrote from New York – will send him £20 from S. Leone – cannot spare more. **[The George Brown crisis was deepening and Casement earmarked a large sum to bail him out.]** Trade winds – but not too strong. "John" behaving very well, but poor "Jack" catching it.

28 SATURDAY Manoel Violetta at Jordao Perestrello. **[For a number of days the names of boys are written at the top of the page. These notes are like written conversations with himself that occur while Casement has time on board ship to ponder the lads of the Atlantic islands by jotting down their names. There is no-one else he can confide in except his diary which serves now, and again in 1910 and 1911, more as a friend than an aide-memoire. Writing-up a diary may in fact have become part of a release technique to make up for not sharing the great secret with anyone from his daytime world.]** No breakfast. Stayed in bed till 9.30 – Dressed slowly – Read papers. Rye has followed Woolwich giving Liberal huge majority. Now Chertsey has to poll. North Fermanagh too may give Russellite & then Camborne where Caine has died – his majority was only 108 – so the Tories have a chance there. a/c Seat. N. Fermanagh polled Sat. 21st Craig (U) Mitchell (I) I.C. seat by Big Majority. **[The election was actually on the Friday – the result being announced on**

Saturday. These last five words and the inaccurate polling day may be a later insertion; Casement seems to have laid the page out for the results of the by-elections while those words slightly overwrite the line below. The issue is confused by the fact that Mitchell, who is described as running under the title of Independent Conservative (I.C.) had not won by a big majority. In a poll of 2,255 to 2,407, on a classic Fermanagh turnout of 90%, he had won by 152 votes. His predecessor, Edward Archdale, had been returned unopposed in 1900 so a comparison of majorities cannot explain Casement's description.] Chertsey – polled 26 Thursday Fyler (C) Longman L. **[The Conservative candidate John Fyler won the Chertsey by-election only to resign the following year by taking the Chiltern Hundreds due to bankruptcy.]** Ship ran 321 miles today –only 197 from Cape Verde. Should be in S/Leone by 5 p.m. on Monday. The voyage like all on this Coast is very wearisome.

[This Fermanagh election entry has been used on several occasions, most recently in 1998, in a somewhat desperate attempt to prove forgery, by revealing inaccuracies or inconsistencies in the Black Diaries. The problem, as always, is that if you are wrong and shown to be grasping at straws your case is terribly weakened. The old-timers of the forgery school rarely entered the text proper to make their case, and one can see why. Relying instead on slagging off the British establishment in time-honoured tradition, and presuming infinite resources to accomplish such a grand deception, they avoided evidential investigation. Given Casement's habit of non-specificity where subject and object, and the order of events is concerned, and his lack of self-analysis or explanation, it is surprising that more has not been made of the opaque nature and the sequencing confusion of so many diary entries.

In the *Irish Democrat*, the newspaper of the once influential Connolly Association in London, a dispute arose between former editors which was to be settled in the columns of its February 1998 edition. Gerry Curran triumphantly drew attention to the above entry of 28 March 1903, stating "It was discovered that the entry in the 1903 diary referring to the Unionist Captain Craig winning the North Fermanagh seat was premature as the election did not take place until 1906!"

But this misinterpretation and a consequent inaccuracy, as notioned by Curran (and others), was not that of a forger. Casement wrote initially in ignorance of the result of the by-election and seems only to predict, hopefully, a Russellite win – as did occur. It is true the defeated candidate Captain James Craig did become an MP but only when returned for East Down three years later, in the 1906 general election. To further confuse the

issue, his brother, Captain Charles Craig (1869-1960) was coincidentally elected a month earlier in 1903, at a by-election for a seat in South Antrim, which the Russellites had expected to win. But Casement did not record a victory for James Craig who was to become Ulster's first Prime Minister dying in office in 1940.

The victorious Russellite, Edward Mitchell, a Fermanagh farmer "reared on 15 acres of land" favoured compulsory land purchase, unlike his predecessor. He had the support of many Methodist and Presbyterian voters and of the entire Catholic electorate. Nominated by the Ulster Farmers and Labourers Union, he joined the Liberal Party in 1904 and was then defeated in 1906. The man who gave his name to this brief liberal Unionist movement was the Scots-born Sir Thomas Russell (1840-1920). He was South Tyrone MP from 1898-1910 and eventually became a Liberal government minister while representing North Tyrone from 1911-18. The anti-Anglican Russellites won seats with Catholic support in those quieter years, dominated not by Home Rule, but by the land issue. Russell gradually drifted into a Home Rule position which is the fate or destination of most liberal Unionists once they slip the tribe.

In rebuttal, Martin Moriarty, another former Irish Democrat editor, relied on the texture of the descriptions in the uncontested 1910 White Diary (or Amazon Journal, so named by Angus Mitchell) which suggested "erotic engagement" with the male bodies Casement frequently wrote about. And they were almost always male. "A handsome face and shapely body" are not, he says "sexually neutral words" but have a "romantic or erotic charge (which) is difficult to deny." Moriarty, in a riposte over nitpicking about apparent inconsistencies in the diaries, reminded the forgery school of Joyce's *Ulysses*, "a text which amply demonstrated the paradoxical authenticity of internal contradiction."

For Edwardians brought up on a diet of Baden-Powell, Cecil Rhodes, Kitchener and General Gordon talk of "bronzed beautiful limbs" and Indians like Inca princes with "soft gentle eyes" was unremarkable. Moriarty, however, writing nearly ninety years later believes that this is convincing evidence of same-sex desire. These apparently masculine, if not macho, British heroes were not revealed until much later to be of mixed motive in their interest in boys and their love of young male companions. Indeed at this time interest in women was seen, to an extent, as a non-masculine trait.]

29 SUNDAY 17 Lauro of Santa Cruz. Manuel Violetta 19 gone to Las Palmas. Pepe & Juan again – Stayed in cabin. Feeling very seedy. Bleeding badly aft as in Santa Cruz **[Another anal operation ultimately became necessary,**

taking place in Belfast in January 1905.] – Ran 372 miles from S/Leone 393. Will not get in until about 7 p.m. tomorrow – so will probably be kept all night there. I rather hope so as it will give more time make enquiry for basket. Hope to find it or hear of it. Feeling very seedy indeed. Turned in 10.30 after talk with Blom.

30 MONDAY Much hotter today. Busy writing in cabin in morning. Wrote many letters. Borrowed £20 from ship for G.B. Ran 327 miles – S. Leone 66 off. Arr. there about 5.15. "Teneriffe" in – no sign of basket. **[In a letter, again to Consul Spence in Madeira, from Sierra Leone on this date, Casement wrote "There is no trace here of the missing basket. I have boarded the 'Teneriffe' here – they have it not."[221]]** Wrote G.B. with £15 to go by "Jebba" tomorrow & other letters about basket. **[The intended £20 of three days earlier is, on reflection, cut back to £15. In the event it was not enough to get Brown out of his predicament]** On shore to agents with Captain. Left at 8.35 a.m.

31 TUESDAY Pepe of Guimar at Tenerife 17. Ran 201 miles to noon. Splendid. 288 left to Cape Palmas & total from S/Leone 66 to Axim 840. Read Loti's "Mon frère Yves". Bboy – on board. Read "Smart Set." Very hot indeed. "Mon frère Yves" is peculiar. **[Given the fact that Casement copied a lengthy and torrid description of Yves and his beauty out of this book (see end of diary) it is reasonable to assume by "peculiar" he meant homoerotic.]** "John" not very well poor old soul with the heat.

APRIL

1 WEDNESDAY Very hot, only did 286 – two miles short of Cape Palmas. Passed along near it – a steamer there. 344 to Axim. Passed Cavally **[Charlie's home]** & then to sea. Read "Les Carnets du Roi" stupid exposition of a Beast-King.

[2-5 April: Travelling further along the West African coast for four more days, reading books in French including one by Henri de Régnier, *The Double Mistress,* and Marie Corelli's *Soul of Lilith.* She was later to be a proposed speaker at a Congo Reform Association meeting.]

6 MONDAY **X X X** "Accra" Enormous. Beautiful morning – in Congo water. At noon 296 miles – at 12.30 saw the tree tops by Red Point or Kabinda only 44 miles to Banana. Captain says will try to go in. Monrovian. **[two lines stroked out and unreadable]** Down. X oh! oh! quick, about 18. ~~wants~~ much ~~in mouth~~ **[This shipboard encounter was perhaps with James W. Hyde, of**

Jamestown, Accra who appears in Casement's address book of the time, there described as an "Accra Steward."[222] The "Monrovian" reference (to Liberia's capital) confuses the issue.] Arrived Banana 4.30. On shore to Wright. Back to dinner at 7. Plenty people and noise all night.

7 TUESDAY Did not sleep last night. Left Banana at 8.30 for Boma. Struck twice on sand – last time badly. Did not see "Accra" again. Invited for tonight Underwood & Barrow at 2.30 on board. Went to Chiquenge – dinner awful as of old. Slept better. Walked a bit – Boatboy talked of "Doctor". Kruboys of Cape Palmas only a few there. John & Charlie together. Lots of letters.

8 WEDNESDAY Up at 8. Letters from "Anversville" were interesting. Blom called. "Tarquati" down at 8.30. Went on board at 10.30. Left for Malella at 11.30. called here & Banana & off for Loanda at 5 p.m. Walked with John on board Whitman played with him. Captain Harry good sort.

9 THURSDAY Arrived Loanda at 11 p.m. On shore to N's. Dined at Julius Caesar's with him and Dr Ansorge. Waiters clean nice Angolan lads. John ate good dinner. Nothing interesting. Home to bed with N. at 11.

10 FRIDAY – Good Friday Wrote F.O. & sent duplicate Life Certificate by "Ambaca". Took passage by her to leave tonight for Ambriz & Cabinda. Went on board after dinner –Lots of people there as usual. Left about 11. No sleep all night – Had to sit up with "John".

11 SATURDAY At Ambriz at 6.30. Left 12 noon. At Ambrizette 4 p.m. Left 8.30 p.m.. No food all day – beastly dirty boat "Ambaca" and a rotten lot on board. A. Nightingale & I squared up – he paid me £5.15/- for Saidu Kabu & charged me £3.15/- for another S. Leone man he repatriated named Movella or some such name. Gave him cheque for £21.13/8 to send £20 to G Brown from Lisbon by Notes or postal order. **[Arthur Nightingale, a fellow consular official was thus tasked on 11 April to send more money to George Brown in New York despite £15 having been forwarded on 30 March]**

12 SUNDAY – Easter Day Arr Cabinda at 7.45. On shore at 8.20 with A.N. Bought things for Davis & A.N. He off after breakfast. "Ambaca" sailed at 3. Young Martens, John & I to sea side. "John" got sick with salt water poor old soul. Jones sick. Royle all right – Standing. Turned in at 9.30 in old room on top. Cabinda quite dead like Loanda & Boma too. Jones not lively. Mosquitoes are lively.

13 MONDAY Beautiful morning. Getting rooms ready. In Hand. Gold

Fcs. 130 Silver 22.50 **[ditto]** 2/- = 2.40 Fcs = 154.90. Spent quiet day. "John" got better after y'day's debauch of salt water. This day last year I arrived at Lisbon and curls & green in Avenida. **[The previous April, Casement was on convalescent leave from the Congo after a recurrence of malaria. Either he confused Lisbon with Las Palmas or his dating memory was faulty by a few days as he wrote to his cousin Roger from Grand Canary on 12 April 1902 describing a pleasant three days just spent in Lisbon. He had then gone "by train via Seville to Cadiz" catching "a Spanish South American steamer for Tenerife."[223]]**

14 TUESDAY This day last year **[More likely 10 not 14 April, but Casement is plainly unclear about the precise day he met the curly haired boy since he had just recalled the anniversary as a day earlier.]** Another beautiful morning. Sun & clear. Weather cool & agreeable. Got very hot. Royle sick. Walked with John to Obras Publicas **[Public Works]** & back. Heavy rain & lightning.

15 WEDNESDAY Last night's rain tremendous. It rained from 12.15 to 8 A.M and most of it very heavy. "Wall" arr. from Congo at 1 p.m. with letters for me – one from Ry. Coy & one from home & from Underwood. Bouriez & another to dinner. Talked until 10 p.m. Then to bed. Read Conan Doyle's "Mystery of Cloomber". Rather good. Walked to Mission with Gibson and "John". Latter pigged.

16 THURSDAY "Wall" left. Wrote one F.O. by her. Africa 3. Also to Cowan & to Wilkes C.B.M & Under. "Tarquati" in at 7.30. Got 6 Irish whiskey – She left for Landana at 12 p.m. No news. Wrote official letters and fixed up Registers. to find out missing corr. in Basket lost at Canary. Rain in evening. Two fights between "John" & "Snap" & later with Jack. Both fled – "John" with both eyes bunged up Master of Ceremonies. Turned in tired "Nigeria" at Tenerife. **[The black bulldog John, his behaviour, adventures, health and eating habits are an ever-present feature of diary entries from now on.]**

17 FRIDAY Cool morning after the rain. "John's" eyes very bad swollen. Got Hot later. H.M.S. "Odin" arr. Brought news of Sir Hector Macdonald's suicide in Paris! The reasons given are pitiably sad! The most distressing case this surely, of its kind and one that may awake the national mind to saner methods of curing a terrible disease than by criminal legislation. **[This entry, and the two later of 19 and 30 April, are almost unique in their discursive comments by Casement on homosexuality as a condition. Sir Hector Macdonald had shot himself in the Hotel Regina in Paris on 25 March, having read that day, in an American paper, the first news story of his disgrace. He was returning to Ceylon, where he had been appointed Officer Commanding in 1902, to face**

a court martial on indecency charges which were, according to the Governor "not punishable under Ceylon law."[224] The complaints, it was suggested, involved a party of Sinhalese boys and two Anglican clergymen on a train in Kandy which indicates indecent exposure on a heroic scale. Nonetheless an "habitual crime of misbehaviour with several schoolboys" was formally recorded which more likely was to do with rumours surrounding the two sons of a Sinhalese-Portuguese, Burger (English speaking) family named de Saram that Macdonald had befriended.

Born in 1853 on a croft near Inverness, and an enlisted man, Macdonald was an especially popular general having come up from the ranks, commanding the Highland Brigade in the South African War and being wounded at Paardeberg – a rare victory. He had been appointed an honorary ADC to both Queen Victoria and King Edward VII. His marriage was informal in a Scottish custom and he rarely saw his wife or son. There was some gossip about his sexuality, including a story that he had had a relationship with a Boer prisoner but he had largely sublimated his sexual desires in military discipline and campaigning. Before leaving London for Paris, Macdonald had had a difficult interview with King Edward VII. Like his son George V, he was of the belief that the revolver was the proper course of action for someone in Sir Hector's position.

Macdonald's popularity in Scotland was such that his funeral nearly became an occasion for mass demonstration and public resentment. Despite intense pressure his wife insisted on a private burial, at dawn, in Edinburgh. Thousands came later to pay respects to their hero 'Fighting Mac'. The nearest equivalent to Macdonald's passing would be the intense displays of loyalty and adulation in Ireland that marked Parnell's career (and funeral). After his death despite the accusations, and indeed because of them (as with Casement), he was much commemorated. In 1907 a giant tower was erected in Dingwall as a monument in his honour.

Obviously Macdonald's suicide troubled Casement and he pondered his own fate should he be exposed in similar circumstances. This almost inevitably happens with famous men who do alfresco sex or get involved with boys. Casement was potentially liable on both counts, although his luck held until Norway in 1914. It has to be said that since same-sex sex was entirely prohibited there was no age of consent. But the penalties were going to be more severe if the boy concerned was in his early teens. Ironically it was (and is still potentially) the case that teenage boys often got charged alongside any older man accused of corrupting them.

Suicide is, and does, remain a horrifyingly frequent response by otherwise respectable and ordinary men to a public indecency arrest. Indeed it has almost become an imperative. Casement must have pondered what he might do if it came to him. Being thought to be homosexual, even then, was a world away from five fatal lines in a local newspaper. People were, to a degree, allowed a private life. But after exposure, if a personality collapse had been avoided, disappearance by flight and emigration were essential. Oscar Wilde (unlike the East Belfast MP, Edward de Cobain, the first prominent victim of the new 1885 law) declined to leave the country, losing his freedom, reputation and health. Casement knew all this but ploughed on regardless, adding further sexual and political outrages to his enlarging collection of rebellious activities.

His diary comments on Macdonald are, however, somewhat mechanical and distant – perhaps a test run for arguments that he was beginning to adopt for private use in discussion, or for his own psychological purposes. In the wake of the 1895 Wilde trials which were based on the 1885 Labouchère amendment that introduced the 'gross' indecency charge for every homosexual act other than buggery, Casement must have known law reform was almost inconceivable. His second shot of treating homosexuality as a disease was to be the special pleading of many well-meaning reformers for the next half century, and something Casement must have already heard discussed in liberal circles.

Such sentiments, including the compulsory words of condemnation Casement includes in these diary entries, were still being uttered by certain MPs and peers in the law reform debates of the 1960s – people now known to have been homosexual themselves. Self-regard, in early 20th century England, was the attitude of only a tiny number of homosexual radicals, like the campaigning writer Edward Carpenter. Casement may have already come across such ideas from some of his sex partners, or later from his Advanced Liberal allies in the Congo Reform Association, but they did not colour his written opinions, on this or the other two occasions that the matter surfaces in his writing. When undertaking the act, or dreaming about sex, it was, however, a different matter. He was neither guilty or ashamed.

Casement was probably only testing out an argument of whose validity he was not convinced. Nearly a century would pass before gays in the military ceased to be subject to courts martial and dismissal. Anyway, if the under-age element had been proved, Macdonald, then as now, would have been liable to imprisonment for the criminal act and dismissed from the army. Casement was never going to abandon his pursuit of sex contacts, rather it would intensify but he would not break-out from his habit of secrecy. There is never a hint of any discussion with his partners after

sex. He was therefore to remain a sexual loner devoting himself to other radical causes.

This is not to say he was an unemotional man without a capacity to love, as the Oxbridge don, John Sparrow (a discreet homosexual), argued in 1960. He reckoned Casement's "emotions were as shallow as the intellect revealed." And that he could be summed up "in four short syllables: no thought, no love."[225] But he did love, and was intellectually sturdy and well read. He just did not settle down. The older Casement became, the less likely the younger objects of his affections – and they were invariably a lot younger – even if socially equal, would be willing or able to make a long-time commitment. Anyway he loved his other causes too much.

Dr Letitia Fairfield (a sister of Rebecca West) in a letter published in *The New Statesman* on 25 May 1957, responding to Robert Kee, argued in favour of the diaries' authenticity against the then, newer, interpolation theory. Her case rested on an enumeration of the number of "objectionable passages" that just could not have been added later by virtue of their position or length. She recorded that in 1903 there were only 39 such entries compared to the 70 in 1910, some 25 of these latter being almost entirely given up to actual sexual encounters. But, in passing, she made the interesting point that after the first Macdonald reference of 17 April 1903 "there are no improper entries except for two mild comments, until October 6, when he had a relapse on his return from a very trying voyage up the Congo." The suicide might have dampened Casement's appetite for a while but lack of opportunity during his investigation up-country surely played the greater part.] The commander of "Odin" on shore with his 1st Lieut. Turned in fairly early. Wrote S/Leone about estates.

18 SATURDAY ~~Sent S/leone letter by "Odin" to Banana~~. The foregoing is Saturday's entry. My letter to S/Leone Gov. is Confidential & the Commander of the "Odin" takes it for postage at Banana. Another dog fight between "John" & "Snap" Bad night. Stuffy & Headache.

19 SUNDAY Wrote Underwood & Wright to go by "Odin" today to Banana. Rain again this morning. "Odin" left for gun firing practice at about 3 p.m. Walked to Dutch Ho with "John" Royle and the Trust. Very sorry at Hector MacDonald's terrible end. Poor old Mrs Young with her love for him. **[There is a plethora of Youngs in Casement's life. One candidate is Mrs John Young jnr., née Elizabeth Dickey, but not Mrs John Young of Galgorm Castle, who had died in 1894. Another mentioned in letters is Mrs (Margaret) Young, married to John's brother William, and whose family resided at Kintullagh in Ballymena, and holidayed at Lisnavarna House in Portrush.**

She or Elizabeth turns up in Cushendall in 1906, as Casement wrote: "Mrs Young is down there with Jennie's sister and James and the pony. She - Mrs Y is quite without the use of her memory now and is very frail on her legs... but she seems quite happy and takes a great interest in all going on round her."[226] That "Poor old" Mrs Young – "aunt Min" to Rose Young, died on 25 August 1911 at Kintullagh.]

20 MONDAY I had a very bad night with Mosquitoes & heat & sand flies. Reading Gertrude's present of the *Reminiscences of an Irish RM.* They are delicious. [**and written by Edith Somerville and Martin Ross (Violet Martin), two West Cork Protestant ladies. Edith outlived Violet and experienced the anti-Unionist terror there during and after the so-called War of Independence, including the assassination in 1936 of her brother, retired Admiral Boyle Somerville. He was shot in Castletownshend by the IRA on the tenuous grounds that he was recruiting for the Royal Navy. She later developed a friendship with Dame Ethel Smyth, the composer who was relentless in her pursuit of females. This diary entry is confirmed by a letter to Gertrude Bannister of the same date in which he said he read her gift from 2 a.m. until dawn "under my mosquito curtain with a healthy crop of large mosquitoes also under it, and 'John' my bulldog giggling to himself under all as I laughed at each page." Casement wished he had more books by the same author, "I fancy one of them is a woman – don't you? It is the best Irish book I've read for a long time – and I think I like it better than any Irish book (of the lighter kind) I know."[227]**] Wrote to Lagos Govt about several matters. Arengo & Alewode. Coolish evening. Bought four suits from H & C. [**Hatton & Cookson**] at $6000, 2000 & 8000, 16000 = $28000 reis – not bad. Mosquitoes, very tired at night.

[**21-28 April**] Beautiful morning – very tired after another bad night – mosquitoes & all other horrors...Centipede in bed – no sleep all night...No sleep on account of centipede last night. A huge thing all over mosquito curtain & then it disappeared and I lay in dread...

29 WEDNESDAY Fever on me – all thro' night. First attack since I came out! Took 16 grains quinine & lay down til 3 p.m. "Hirondelle" arr. with local letters & Karl Sanders on board. "Vilhena" arr. & then "Benguela" about 2 p.m. Her mails not interesting. Young Martins of Beira baixa (Castello Branco) left for Loanda. I decided to go Congo in "Hirondelle". Governor of Cabinda called on me at 5 p.m.

30 THURSDAY Packed up everything – Left Cabinda [**the Portuguese enclave north of the Congo river**] at 9 A.M. Royle taking me off in his

warm-hearted way. Arr. Banana at 4. Got a letter from Reid of Madeira about basket – not there. Mrs. Wright in rather weak state I fancy. Capt. Wright all right. Called on Etienne. "John" seedy– a dreadful room at Hotel. Sandflies. Did not close my eyes. Hector MacDonald's death very sad. 5 francs for room.

MAY

1 FRIDAY Left Banana at 7.30 – 50.$^{\underline{00}}$ francs passage from Cabinda to Boma. Very hot. Arr. Boma 3. Underwood came. Lots of letters for me. From F.O. several interesting ones – S.S. "Nigeria" in Capt Flemyng. He says he has my basket from Tenerife. He cannot find it. It is on ship's manifest. Shipped by H.B.M. Consul to me on H.B.M**'s** Service & yet Flemyng says he remembers it did not come. **[The basket saga continues and must have been enough to exasperate a saint.]**

2 SATURDAY More letters by P'guese mail – from Charlie, Tom & Blanche. All three affairs more & more complicated. B. had got my letter of 15 Jan. with £20 in. She sends two of Tom's letters to her – but in them he tells her little of what he tells me. Went on board "Nigeria" – saw the manifest – but alas! no basket – Got letter (undated) from Evisbury at Grand Canary saying they had found basket upstairs & were sending it across to me at Pino. "Nigeria" went on to Matadi. Weeks & large party on board going up River. Called on Fuchs – he was <u>very</u> amiable – too much so. Called in evening on Gohr **[Director of Justice]** & met his wife also – on Van Damme **[Secretary General in Boma]** not in. Went tennis & said How do to Sweerts & Mdme S – to Horstmans & Dupont. Weather very hot indeed. Turned in at 9.30. Lots of mosquitoes – Heavy rain in night.

4 SUNDAY Lots of rain last night. Rain again today in deluge. Very cool after it. Wrote letters all day to Coast Govts & fixed up things. "John" fever. Gave enema of 6" quinine. Shanu called **[H.A. Shanu, a successful Nigerian businessman who had worked in the service of the Free State]**. Turned in early. Read M. Posts. Poor paper on the whole.

[4-8 May: The dog dominates.] ...& the Thrust. "John" caught child pig & then a fever..."John" very sick – stayed up with him most of night till 3 A.M. Poor old Soul! Nice morning & cool. "John" worse. Vomited and an enema 6" quinine he refused. Castor Oil also vomited. "John" got better at 8 a.m. Came to breakfast & at midday eat a lot so too at dinner...Turned in early at 10.30 with "John" sleeping tranquilly & happily..."John" up and out. Learned of Ingmohl's death this morning very suddenly – Went funeral at 5 p.m. V der

Most greatly cut up…"John" seedy again. **[With the dog's temperature over 106 degrees, a distraught Casement wrote on 7 May to Gertrude Bannister "I fear John is going to die here."[228] But the bulldog who is treated better than any servant and given all the paternal love a male human could muster, is nursed back to health and all of his many excesses again excused. During this week Casement managed only to start preparations for building the new consulate, and take a walk on 5 May "in evening with K.B. [Kru Boy] of Bow. Splendid." The day before there is a largely indecipherable passage that refers in part to "the same K.B. as first night."]**

9 SATURDAY Close morning. Wrote Whittendale before breakfast. "John" better –poor old soul. A lot of men came with complaints – but I sent all away refusing to give ear to their grievances – only pointing out the Notices in their own Colonies warning them against seeking work here upon Local Contracts. **[Casement's uncle, Edward would not have been quite so indifferent, his strenuous efforts costing him his job at Boma.]** Mon. & Mdme Sweerts to tennis. Also Van Damme – I played – first time since August last year – played very badly. In evening at billiards with Trust & McKay – They beat us by 20 out of 126. But we should have won! I played U. after for 20 for who should pay the losses & beat him easy. A lovely night. "John" ever so much better. "Craw Craw" troubling me dreadfully.

10 SUNDAY A beautiful cool morning. Engaged two Masons for tomorrow to begin on ground. Heavy rain from 7.30 to 10 a.m. Beeckman called in afternoon – also Captain Whitton of "Lagoon". Went up ground with Beeckman to see site for Consulat. Too much grass. Beautiful evening. Moon glorious.

11 MONDAY Wrote Charlie sent £15. Wrote Tom and Blanche – Hopeless affair that is. I see no possible outlook. Wrote to Nina all about the Balharry question. Called on Waleffe and Madame Waleffe – also Horstmans. Went with the Sweerts down the hill. Madame S. very pleasant. Rain threatening. Played billiards – the "Trust" in form – Fat "John" played till 12 midnight. Bow. Jupiter. Began grass clearing. 2 Masons engaged.

12 TUESDAY Military music all morning. Up hill to ground. Sick S/Leone Sandiki turned up – gave him food &c. 7 francs worth & sent him up to Gohr. Went up to tennis played badly – still nervous at the service. After dinner played billiards very badly. Bright lightening & thunder & rain. Turned in at 11.30 in rain. Tall – "How much money?" Watch going. "John".

13 WEDNESDAY Heavy morning. Very dark. Rain in quantities lying in clouds. Rain fell most of morning. At midday saw "Bow" enormous at

River – also garden beautiful. Wrote final letters & to F.O. on land & house. Wrote Timi [**Congolese name for Alfred Parminter**] & Cust. In afternoon Horstmans called. "Ville de Maceio" arr. Letter from Dennett & from Pino about basket. Played U & I 121 & Trust only won 126 by potting us. Then I challenged T. for 25 & won by 4!!!

14 THURSDAY Last day of Trust! Beaten. Poor old Trust. Saw him off on Champagne breakfast. "Nigeria" left at noon. "Heron" also for Banana & Cabinda. Two wires from F.O. important. At last they are taking action! Very busy all day. Very hot. Letter from Dennett. Shanu called. Will do ~~levelling~~ stone work. Costa wants fcs 2.500 for the levelling. Too much. Will not accept. No billiards. Turned in early. Did not sleep well.

15 FRIDAY The F.O. wires I got y'day will cause me a lot of trouble I fear. Put the Accras on House clearing ground for Shanu's men on Monday. On ground most of morning. Made arrangements with Underwood for helping the carpenter and getting House on shore when it comes. Gohr called in evening. Entreprise Africain will sell Bricks at 50 francs the 1000. Played billiards with McKay he beating me badly.

16 SATURDAY Cloudy morning & close. Air very heavy last night and lots of flying bats "Vilhena" arr. last night, goes on today. She left at noon for Matadi. U got 30000 bricks for me at 50 francs the thousand. Cleared ground. Dupont, Swerts (2), Van D. came. He Mdme & I beat U – S & Dup 2 sets each game 6 us none them. Got wire from Fuchs to déjeuner tomorrow. Played good tennis. Dupont said Bentill's case settled y'day verdict in B's favour for 1800 fcs. I won one game billiards against McKay.

17 SUNDAY Fuchs père, Gohr, U, Brandel S.C.S. Went Déjeuner. S. & Mdm. S. Gohr. Brandel. U. Pere Superior – 8 in all. Pleasant morning. Brandel played in afternoon tennis on top till 6.30. Excellent but missed winning – Horstmans Swerts & I against Van D.U. & Dupont. Plenty Beer. Dark night – after dinner turned in after slight stroll. "John" slight fever. I drank much beer.

18 MONDAY Went out to ground. Two masons at work. Shanu came with planks for his men's hut. Got a letter ex French mail at 10 a.m. She came down & went on to sea. The flies are absolutely hateful – buzzing all day. Hope "Albertsville" brings my basket. Played tennis. U. beat Jennings & I. 6 to 4. Then I beat U & Jennings 6 to 3. In evg. Billiards. I beat U. 50 to 33. Then he beat McK. & I 63 up. We played awfully. Walked till 1 A.M. Still evening. "John" going strong. "How much." cigarettes.

19 TUESDAY Out on land all morning. Kboys clearing grass away. Did a lot. Wrote very little. Shanu's House finished. Missa Ansah engaged from y'day at 15 francs the month with the Accras. Ordered 20 metres cubic of stone from Magalhoes. Played tennis in evening on top. Mdm. S. U & I winning. Beer at Sweerts'. No news of mail. Billiards after dinner until 11 p.m. Very good. I beat U badly. Saw pelicans at 5.30 p.m.

20 WEDNESDAY Dry season morning. Cool & excellent. Certainly dry season from y'day. The pelicans never fail! The "Albertville" arrived at 2.30 p.m. or 3. Got mails. Nothing interesting. Long letter from Nina. Also H.W. & his Statues excellent. Congo going strong in papers. Wired F.O. (2 wires) about House and the Illtreatment of Br subjects out here. Cockshut arr. by "Albertville", also the Basket from Croker. **[It has finally turned up.]**

21 THURSDAY Very busy getting Basket dispatches arranged and all the things put straight. Sparrow called in afternoon & played tennis – the Swerts coming down. Went up with Underwood after dinner to them. Decided to go Matadi tomorrow by "Albertville". Walked "John" a little on return. He goes home by "Albertville" too. "Wall" left for Loanda with my wires for F.O.

22 FRIDAY **X.** Left Boma. Packed up and got on board "Albertv" with Masamba – leaving "John" with Charlie to go by "Albertville". Got Hair & beard cut – first barbering since "Anversville" in early April or end March. Arr. Matadi went to see Barrow who is sick – Then to Sims who came to meet me. Richard Koffee still there. Turned in early after light meal.

23 SATURDAY Very busy getting Mrs. Meyer palaver and Akinwuumi written out for F.O. Called on the Substitut **[Deputy Prosecutor]** & Mrs. Weber. Wrote all day until 5.30 p.m. Turned in at 9 – but wrote Mrs M. palaver until 10 p.m. or later. Got a bottle of whiskey. Left Vanadium with Sims to experiment with on cases in his hands. Hope to get up country now in a few days. Beautiful weather for travelling – and with poor old "John" in safety all will be well.

24 SUNDAY Glorious morning this. Old Queen's birthday **[typical example of Casement's affection for Queen-Empress Victoria, the Queen Mum of her time]** Went to Forfeitts – then on to Nkala & stayed. Chop at Noon. Sleep & up to "Albertville" – the "Prince Baudouin" arrived with passengers for Leo. Wrote by her to U at Boma for "John" & Charlie to come by "Heron" on 28th or earlier. Stayed at Albertville coming back. After dinner talked to Koffee a bit & to bed at 9 p.m.

25 MONDAY A beautiful morning – cool and dry. Bad night the Dr.'s Dog's crying. Poor dog – Old S castrated it he tells me. The boys not castrated. Say they are "Kiadi beni" [**'very sad' in Kikongo**] for poor "Tinker". Very busy Forfeitt & Mayo called. Went there to tea. Back at 8.30. 4 francs "Dash" to Boatboys.

26 TUESDAY Called on Commissaire De Raash [**Gabriel de Rache**] and on Juge Territorial Cuchinello [**Michel Cuchiniello**]. Former not in – latter in. Kyffin came down from Tumba. Wrote Underwood to send John & Charlie up. Former to go home by Anversville. Got S African War Medal from F.O. via Kinchasa. 23 April.

27 WEDNESDAY Busy writing hard all day to get my Mail to F.O. off in time by "Albertsville". Beautiful cool weather. Delightful season now.

28 THURSDAY Finishing F.O. Africa 8 on the hardships inflicted on Br. Subjects. "John" arr. with Charlie. Very badly burnt on Nose. Brutally burnt by Underwood [**Casement's vice-consul in Boma**] over some dirty pig of his. Took "John" on board in the evening to go to Antwerp. Left him with Sparrow. Heard awful barks as I came back. Ominous. [**The diary is verified here by a letter Casement sent home to his cousin Roger at Magherintemple, dated 28 May 1903.[229] He wrote of family news told him by his sister, which would be the "long letter from Nina" of 20 May above; of his dog's imminent departure which was to be thwarted, but not until the following day: "I am out now some time and getting on fairly well – with my lunatic bulldog 'John'. He goes home by tomorrow's mail steamer – very much the worse for the Congo climate – poor old soul."**

In a postscript Casement also confirmed his 26 May entry of two days earlier, saying "I got the South African War Medal (of 1900) day before y'day – sent me by the Sec. of State! Three years old, but better late than never." The medal had first gone "to Foreign Office 21.4.03" according to the War Office file.[230] On the FO note accompanying the medal when sent out from London, Casement very precisely inscribed "Received at Matadi Tuesday evening 26 May 1903 from Kinchasa."[231] In 1916, justifying the fact that he had sought this award and knowing how his British honours made him appear hypocritical, if not more treasonable, he explained to his solicitor "After my war work, not because I wanted it but as I had felt I had really earned it and it was being given to many who had not seen active service as I actually had, I demanded it."[232] This was to be the first of his three deserved honours (plus the 1911 Coronation medal) of which he was to be divested in 1916.]

29 FRIDAY Chief Officer came at 5 a.m. asking to go on board, John in possession of Captain's cabin & refused to give way. Took him back. **[This incident is confirmed in a letter to Cowper, dated 3 August, with Casement explaining "I had to take 'John' back from the steamer (in May last) by which I was shipping him home. He took charge of the Captain's cabin who sent up a piteous appeal at 5 a.m. before he got under way for me to come down and quiet 'John' so that he, the skipper, might get into his cabin to change his clothes."[233] John, whom no other human or animal appreciated, was to prove ever more troublesome during the voyage into the interior, in which he was not intended to participate.]** All day on shore. Decided to go Pool on Monday if possible. John very well and flourishing.

30 SATURDAY Beautiful weather. Spent quiet day. Wrote more F.O. despatch – on Mrs Meyer Africa 9 & sent it before 11 a.m. by reg'd. post in copies of corr with Gov. about the £35. Went to Nkalankala in afternoon & to Forfeitt, also called on Kyffin & Carl. "John" with me. Barrow very well. Read old Blue Books on the Congo Treaty of 1882 & 83 with Portugal which never came off. Beautiful night. Also on the Ry. Employés here, the old corr. between the English Govt. & the Belgian recruiting for workmen on the West Coast.

31 SUNDAY **[In margin:]** Alleged rain fell last night.
Went out for walk to Prison. Just the same as last year no change except whitewash. No beds. Looked in one of the three cells. Bare cement – blankets rolled upon it – saw no jailer. Three police in yard at back. On to Domenjoy's grave & round by Ravine Léopold – new Ry bridge fine. Church Parade before, Dr. after. Walked to town. Kyffin called on me. Long talk.

JUNE

1 MONDAY Very busy all day writing for F.O. and hearing complaints. Four in morning – and one in afternoon. None of them got any satisfaction out of me. All S/Leone men! Of course. They are often a rotten bad lot. Went into Matadi to Weber first about contracts – and then to Bampton. Back at 7 & yarned with Doctor until 9.30! Interesting.

2 TUESDAY Read Irish magazines. In Night Dreamed splendid plot of Novel. Got up at 3 A.M. & sketched it out. Wd would make splendid story. Got wire from U. at Boma asking me go telephone at 11. Went 3 Govt wires for me & local letters. Also a Mr. Giles **[Childs]** American Consul at Zanzibar who is visiting Congo. Sent Forfeitt's boat down for the wires & to bring up many of my things I want. Went to Kyffin. Had a lot of S/L men in the

morning with complaints. Got letter from Gohr about S.C. Bentill [**British West African**]. Very cold grey morning.

3 WEDNESDAY A really glorious day. Wrote another F.O. despatch on faulty judicial system out here – with Ali K's, S.C. Bentill's[234], Bongura's S. Tucker's & John Jumbo's cases as illustrations. It will be a terrible bulky thing for poor F.O. Went to Forfeitt's and on to NkalanKala in evening – and back by latter boat at 9.20. 5 francs dash to Boys. Slept very badly.

4 THURSDAY Busy all day – writing & packing for tomorrow's journey. In evg Kyffin called – and at 5 or so Tubs & the Boat from Boma came with 3 F.O. Wires. Two in Govt. Code unintelligible – the other in cypher Africa 4, about Congo misgovt. – to go to interior as soon as possible & to send reports soon. The Debate in Commons has been terrible attack on Congo State. Morrison to lecture too! Kyffin to tea & at Midnight I to bed. Wired F.O. to go by German S/S if she comes in.

1.08	£1.40
30	35
	1.75

[From 7 June, Casement continued to maintain daily entries in his diary, but extracts of significance in relation to his family, his private and sexual life or to his personal and political views predominate here over the Congo investigation. It and the controversy over the official report and its considerable consequences, which included the making of Casement as a public figure and his development into a British radical, have been covered elsewhere, notably by Peter Singleton-Gates and Roger Louis, and in the Brian Inglis biography. The 2003 book of Séamas Ó Síocháin and Michael O'Sullivan, *The Eyes of Another Race: Roger Casement's Congo Report and 1903 Diary* is unabridged and with detailed information on the Congo at that time.]

5 FRIDAY Left at 7 A.M. Fare 200. Boys 50. Luggage 60. Sims 70 for Chop – also Potatoes 10 – Onions 14. Rice 14 = 38. Left £5 for Bannister child [**Could this mysterious gift refer to an adopted child of Casement's uncle, Edward Bannister?**] & £5 for Distressed people. Two passengers only & a priest at Kimpese. The country a desert – no natives left. At Tumba 3.30. To Baluti's & then to Abreos & to Commissaire. He said 5 women to one man in the country now – Sleeping Sickness! I said also Transports!! Beautiful cool at Tumba. Dined Abreo. Lovely Ngombe Mawuku. [**This Ngombe man, Mawuku, was later employed by Casement.**] "John" caught NKewa. Horatio Will brought contract. No term fixed.

6 SATURDAY Delhaie (Commissaire) de District. Gave Mawuku 2 frcs. Left Tumba at 6.30. Cold & nice. NSona NGunga splendid. High wind & cool. Congo people now on line instead of Coast men. Latter very few I'm glad to say. No signs of improvement – save a few broader paths to the water where we swam of old. Morgan met me & Mr Meyer & with former to Dr.'s old brick house – Very comfy. At Kinchasa "John" caused great interest. Mrs Morgan looked well. Very comfortable in Sims' old brick house. "John" sleeping splendidly. Mawuku of Wathen **[Baptist Mission station]**. Beautiful 6th June & 5th June.

14 SUNDAY Wrote to Vass & Howell about S/S. Busy writing all morning. To Kinchasa afterwards with Childs & higher – 8 kilometres. "John" went well. Made up bag (F.O.) to go by Childs tomorrow. Dinner with Malets. Back from Kin. 10.30.p.m. Mails up River left.

15 MONDAY Saw Childs off at 6.45 a.m. Gave him F.O. Bag. Mrs. Sjoblom also left. Got letters from Boma – inclu F.O. 8. 9. 10 & 11 Africa. At last they are moving! My despatches have sown the good seed. Very busy correcting Lord L's proposed draft to Brussels on my last years Africa 10 of 18 July.

16 TUESDAY Sent F.O. further reports includ Police at Boma & John Marshall's case at Léo. Sent these all by Sr. Amaro to go by Dr. Sims on "Anversville" on Thursday afternoon. (got letter from Captain L. all received &c.) Wrote till after midnight. Wired F.O. to await reports due 10 July – This goes down by post in morning.

17 WEDNESDAY Sent letters to post at 5.15 a.m., one for F.O. (Farnall with J. Marshall's case) & wire for F.O. via Loanda. Rested most of day. Mr. Morgan went to Br'zville to send his wire. Very tired after my recent long exertions. I have really got thro' a lot of writing for F.O. of late. It would make a big book if published Malet called in afternoon. to go to Kinchasa tomorrow.

18 THURSDAY Went to Kinchasa on foot with John & Charlie. Pleasant day with the Malets who go up in "Flandre" on Monday. Called on Dr Villa in afternoon & back on foot. 11.5 p.m. Very dark night. "Punch" from Gee there. "In the Congo 'Free' State." Malet's Coffee Works are interesting. Read till after 12. & slept well. Maps & Stationery from U. arr.

19 FRIDAY Up at 8 A.M. Very tired. Very cool morning. Delightful. Did little, very little all day. Too tired. Walked to cataract in afternoon. In evening came back by the Native Hospital – it is far worse than the thing at Boma – Deplorable – I never saw anything like it. Police in evg. Caught one of Morgan's

boys. Palaver with Jevons. Fire at camp in evening. Turned in at 11 p.m.. Mr. McGhie of H. & C.s with me.

20 SATURDAY Beautiful cool morning. Spent morning writing many letters to local people. Including 2 to Gov-General &c Director of Justice. Walked to Spring with McGhie in evening. Got some letters & "West Africas" &c. **[magazine edited by E.D. Morel]** in evening. Terrible attacks on Congo Govt in them. Portuguese mail arrived. Got letter from Blanche with many from Tom – It is a sad sad business for her poor thing. **[Tom's deserted wife, despite all pleadings, will still not yield, although at the end of the 1903 diary a note by Casement indicates Blanche is about to book a passage on the *Persic*. However, the impression is that Casement was noting the prospect of her arrival in England, where he was, not South Africa where Tom was.]**

21 SUNDAY **[In margin:]** Anversville sailed for Europe.
Spent morning at Church & in palavers with some of the Local D.B.S (Lagos & Accra men). Afternoon with Mr. & Mrs. Morgan, McGhie &c. to hill to view Cataracts & then round by Hospital – Again the same terrible spectacle. Mrs M. shocked. The poor woman lying on the ground by the fire. Upset her cooking pot. Saw about 50 cases guns for Abir in State Store. Dead body lay there.

22 MONDAY Left Léo at 9 a.m. for Kin. The 3 Lagos men followed me there. Tommy came told him to follow to Kin. At Kin. ~~"Hainault"~~ "Flandre" still lying there – thro' some mistake. Saw Malets at 5. Stayed with Gordons at Mission – Very comfy. Wrote to Cooper at B'zville to say I was going over there tomorrow. Sail by B.M.S. canoe.

23 TUESDAY Very cool. Went with 3. Lagos men to S.A.B. Saw Thierry who promised to see into the matter at Molundu. Will write down in a month & say the result. He then offered me a passage up to Chumbiri in his S/S – own ship. I accepted. Very kind of him. He goes up to Molundu day after tomorrow. In afternoon called on Cuthbert Malet & went to Villa's at Belgika. Malet calls all his workmen "slaves" & says they have to pay 50 fcs. for their wives' passage when they go home. Is this true?

24 WEDNESDAY Dr. Villa sent his boat for me & I crossed to B'ville – Cooper received me very civilly. Wrote Governor – Vice Governor Des Bordes. I should call tomorrow at 10 a.m. Went for a walk afterwards. I like B'zville. It is the beginning of a town – not as at Léo., only a Great Govt factory. **[While relaxing in Brazzaville, the capital of the French Congo, Casement wrote on 24 June to Gertrude telling her a tale of animal mischief: "There is a**

chimpanzee here very tame that runs about and gets drunk daily. It stole just now a glass of gin from one of the whitemen here and goes around the town getting Absinthe and then has to be brought home by the police."[235]] The road from Dutch House to Govt Station is about 2½ miles long. After dinner played billiards with Cooper and Clark.

25 THURSDAY Went to B'zville & called on M. Des Bordes, the Vice Governor of the Congo français. I like him. B'zville I think is better in most ways than Léo – there is freedom here. Gov. calls on me this afternoon. Plenty mosquitoes here – far more than at Kin. Greshoff's place is very fine indeed. M. Des Bordes returned my visit at 5 p.m. Charming man. Played billiards in evening. James Daniel came to see me. Fine lad. **[In 1908, Casement received a strange letter from James Adeshand Daniel (or Daniels – both spellings were used) who was still living in Brazzaville. He wrote in proper yet nearly incomprehensible English which suggests he was a coastal Kruboy. James wanted his address in order to send him an "ivory walking stick and some napkins." In return, he asked "that you will kindly forward me your photo…for I beg to says I need to see your face daily of my life any pity your poor boy to says so sir and in what possesion will you wanted your poor boy to be?" The letter ended with him praying that he "accept the little compliment of your poor boy…in hope his lord is quite well daily."[236] Casement had plainly captivated yet another individual.]**

26 FRIDAY Up & to M. fluviales about several cases. Lots of men complaining. Baptiste an Accra Mason – a bad case – 1048 fcs due on 30 Nov. last & not paid yet. Came back with Dr Villa at 10. & breakfasted with him. He gave me a good breakfast & we discussed the State. To Malet's in afternoon & then on to supper at B.M.S. & to bed at 10.30 p.m. Gave B –2 francs.

27 SATURDAY Wrote Shanu. Saw Accras from B'zville. Went S.A.B. The Steamer will only go on Thursday morning. M. Rozez showed me wire from Deuster saying "Consul Casement peut prend passage à bord P. Brugmann pour Chumbiri". It seems the State forbids the S.A.B. by Special Convention to carry passengers! Rozez will not allow me to pay my passage. I went on to C.T's about the Accra pay. Captain of "Valerie" not there. Will be back at 5 p.m. Gave the men 2 francs to get food & wait till 5. Then to Malet's & looked through State papers for the passage Order of 50 fcs. per wife. Could not find it. Went again to "Citas". Captain not there – passed homewards by Dr. Villa's – and to B.M.S. for tea. They are very kind there. Dr. Villa told me of a recent visit to a village near Madimba & the people seeing a white man all ran away. His Senegalese dresser got some back.

JULY

… 1 WEDNESDAY Morgan says get "Bongudi" at Bolobo for engineer of steamer. Billington knows of Dupriz at back Chumbiri killing people & going home first class. He went with Morgan. Mr. and Mrs. M. came over – letter for F.O. Gave M. Wrote several more to go tomorrow. Morgan's boys ran away. Called on Malet.

2 THURSDAY Went S.A.B. "P. Brugmann" not ready. Went lunch with Villa & at 2.30 p.m. got off by "B" around French bank. Beautiful Dover Cliffs – lovely view. Camped on Island in Pool at 6.30 about. Hippo down stream. Saw three pelicans feeding close to us. Also saw a beautiful Egyptian Ibis. Black body & white wings – a lovely fellow in full flight over us for his home in the woods below Dover cliffs – white-winged too.

3 FRIDAY **[In margin:]** A very few canoes of Batiki fisherman.
Left camp at 6.45. Saw "Harricamb" going down State side of Pool. Passed Rabinek's Grave at 11. Wood post just at entrance to Pool. On past a State wood post – two French ones & a telegraph post. To the bank at 10.30 about – where we anchored for the day to get wood. Elephant hippo & buffalo tracks. Disturbing ibis. An antelope came down to drink in eveg. Passed State barge full of Rubber towed by small steamer – down.

… 7 TUESDAY **[In margin:]** At Chumbiri.
Wrote Howell at Bolobo – & to Vass by "Brugmann". Money left Fcs. 298.50. Canoe left for Bolobo. "Brugmann" left 8.30 for Kasai– Good chap, Captain Loppers. Much hotter at Chumbiri than at Pool. Glad to change clothes twice daily. Wrote a little. Hairy B is a good sort. "Reed" will go up with me to Bolobo & there we may make other arrangements for chartering her &c.

8 WEDNESDAY Not well today. Walked a little bit and wrote out a/c Current & other things – Headache all day getting worse in eveg. A German Sud-Kameroon came up on her way to Sangha – She slept at Kwamouth with "Brugmann" who was wooding there. I do not like Chumbiri at all – neither place nor climate. Poor old Hairy Bill! A queer life!

9 THURSDAY **[At top of page:]** Soup boiled Sugar for change. & Custard – Hot in morning – same one cold in eveg.
Packed up all day & wrote one or two letters – Two to F.O. routine only. Henry Reed ready for tomorrow – got chop from Billington. They both go up – sent most things on board "H. Reed" ready for early start. Close – Hot day – but little sun. Most things on Reed by teatime. Very glad to be leaving Chumbiri

– chicken, chicken, custard custard every day – come Sunday. God then.

10 FRIDAY Leaving about 8 A.M. this morning. Delayed in starting by the Infallible Cause of all Delay & Every Miscarriage since Eve first ~~slew~~ upset Adam's apple cart – Woman! 9.5 when we left Chumbiri. Deliverance I arr. 8.30 – No letters. 15 bottles Claret. ~~40 francs freight !!!~~ Passed two State wood posts at which "Deliverance I" stopped. She caught us up & passed us after one of them but we got to Bolobo before the second could be made good. 6.55 p.m. We had boiled sugar gain for change also custard on board. Howells met us.

11 SATURDAY **[At top of page:]** Met Hansen & Fornascieri.
B.M.S. Bolobo is a regular town – Lots of people there. Got "Reed" on slip by 8.30 A.M. Good work. Hairy B is an excellent chap & good worker. "Roi des Belges" went down – we missed her for mails as she left at once. Called on Miss de Hailes in her hospital in afternoon. She complains of State Exactions bitterly upon the people. Went to the Clarkes in the Evening – a blessed gathering – all silent & all diligently damned like Wordsworth's or Justin McCarthy's tea party. Back at 10. I turned in, but no sleep till 1.30 a.m. owing to infernal noise made by the Bolobo boys of Howell. A regular Hello. This place – built by **[??]**

12 SUNDAY **[At top of page:]** "Phillippeville" sails for Europe July 26th July 31st.
Goats at 5.40. began bleating, awfully loud. Delicious breezes at Bolobo mornings. At Church about 400 there – mostly males. To 12 lunch with Miss de Hailes. The "Valerie" arr at 2.30 & went on at 3.30 up Sangha way. Close in evening. Turned in 10 p.m. High wind at 11.30 arose blew throughout night a queer time for the wind to begin.

13 MONDAY Not feeling very well. Went down to Reed at 10. All hard at work scraping & painting her. Basakos splendid types – Two magnificent. Hairy B. **[Billington]** says he may go with me. I hope he doesn't mean to bring the Apple of Discord – That would be too much – stewed NSusu & Custard again twice daily for a month wd. beat me hollow! Besides sleeping & bathing &c. Nothing important. At State Beach photo'd pier & Loango – about 9" – Young probably Hansen's. **[i.e. Captain Hansen's servant]**

14 TUESDAY French National Fête. Thunder in night! Very cool breeze in morning. This must be Auntie's birthday. Poor wee soul. I will send her a present **[Mrs Bannister, "wee auntie", was sent a fiver on 20 July.]** A small French S/S went up. In turning ships &c. excellent work. Hairy B. says we will get off on Monday next he hopes & to Lulanga about 30th – when I shall really begin work. "John" caught Fataki's goat by forearm – choked him off. Prayers

in evening. **[Casement was taking hospitality from Baptist missionaries]** Decided not to take Bongudi Hairy B goes himself.

15 WEDNESDAY Lovely morning. Wrote a little & began draft of F.O. despatch on state of country up to S. Pool. Called on Miss Hailes who gave two quango – one a State –one from Litimba the other an ordinary one – ea. 1 Rod. Capt. Hansen called to bid goodbye and made some strange remarks on Belgian officers. Three or four peals of thunder in night.

16 THURSDAY Whale boat with Hansen returned to Yubi. Howell got telegram from Morgan saying "Livingstone" was coming down & ought to be here today. He can give her some tons of cargo at Pool – I can get something too. I wired Barrow for 1c/s W. & 2 c/s Claret. A small French steamer came down & then the "Dolisie" – a fine ship. Morgan said "Hainaut" had left with letters for me – & Telegraph clerk said she left Kwa this morning – so we should get our mails tomorrow. Very heavy afternoon – one peal thunder. Wind arose to a gale from 8 p.m. to 10. Strong. "Livingstone" did not arrive – She may have turned back or gone into Mantumba.

17 FRIDAY Beautiful morning. Slept well. Breeze not too strong. "Hainaut" up at 11 or so. Mails arr. Lots of them also papers with news of Debate. "Livingstone" arr. down at 5 or so. Got Danielson for Engineer of "Reed". Went tea with Clarkes. Heard from G.B. poor old chap. **[George Brown would seem now to be in deep trouble despite the money funnelled to him by Casement. The notion that Brown was a boyfriend is not an entirely unreasonable assumption if based on the amount of money Casement has been sending off as he travelled down Africa. But Brown was actually the supplier of the "Darkie" heads that Casement was labelling for his Club on 14 February, one of which he also took to Dick Morten on 16 February. Boyfriends aren't usually dealers in shrunken heads.**

The mystery can be unravelled since Casement recorded a location for George Brown, other than the New York hotel diaried on 18 February. He is in gaol. Brown's illicit trade in heads must have been rumbled. In Casement's address book of the period,[237] Brown's address is given as care of Sheriff T.B. Blunte in Darien a town in McIntosh County, a majority African-American coastal region in the state of Georgia. This suggests he may have been a Liberian or Kruboy met in the Congo. Darien was then a bustling little port exporting lumber to Europe on Norwegian and Russian ships, and an early wintering spot for New Yorkers. The Blount family (as spelt) were prominent citizens. A large curly 'L.' enigmatically prefixes the entry for Brown's name.]

18 SATURDAY Very busy all day at F.O. corr: going strong. Everything ready on "Reed" Wrote Farnall. Got papers &c. from H.B. dealing with Dupriz outrages. Howell & Clarke read over to me the draft of the letter of protest they sent to Baynes on the Deputation – It was a very emphatic protest indeed & does them credit – I wish they wd publish it. They ought to. Everything ready on "Reed" – Small Belgian steamer went up river. H.B. read over the contract of Reed. I am responsible for compensation if she is wrecked! How much I don't know. **[For the next two months Casement was to traverse the upper Congo investigating abuses of the Africans in Leopold's personal fiefdom. His previous experience in the region and his ability to compare the current state of depopulation with earlier prosperity, alongside the detailed stories of mutilations by collection enforcers and Congo State troops were to make his report especially credible and powerful.]**

AUGUST

… 1 SATURDAY Rained in night – but later a beautiful day. "John" caught three goats today. One into Lake. Wrote out a rough account of yesterday's visit. Rationed the men. Nothing in particular. Rain again – but afterwards delightful. Roman soldier. Coliseum. August 1900. Carte de Visite. Fortunato. **[Casement permits himself a nostalgic look at previous August highpoints, in this instance three years earlier with one Fortunato whom he had met in Rome's Coliseum. This remained a favoured cruising area as Dr Alfred Kinsey observed in 1955 when researching his never-published book on homosexuality. His American biographer, however, did write "Its many dark passages teemed with sexual activity. In his trip notes, Kinsey stated that he observed two soldiers masturbating each other, a male on one side of an iron fence showing his erect penis to another male on the other side of the fence, and a priest 'who was certainly cruising the Coliseum for sexual contact'."[238]]**

2 SUNDAY **[At top of page:]** Albertville sails. Home Augt 20th.
F.O. Africa 29. A beautiful morning – cool fresh breeze. At service some 220 people. Wrote a little. Gave 10 Francs to Church. Wrote to F.O. on Cranbourne's speech on 20 May. Ibrahim Jacob **X** Wrote Howell about Bolobo boys returning. **[The next day Casement wrote to Francis Cowper in Lisbon "from a small steam launch", replying to a letter received on 17 July: "The people round here are all cannibals. You never saw such a weird looking lot in your life. There are also dwarfs (called Batwas) in the forest who are even worse cannibals than the taller human environment. They eat man flesh raw! It's a fact." These dwarfs or pygmies, now known as Twa, were largely eradicated during the Rwandan genocide of the 1990s. Casement**

then described, somewhat enthusiastically, how the taller peoples would, by arrow, "bring down a dwarf on the way home, for the marital cooking pot...The Dwarfs, as I say, dispense with cooking pots and eat and drink their human prey fresh cut on the battlefield while the blood is still warm and running. These are not fairy tales my dear Cowper but actual gruesome reality in the heart of this poor, benighted savage land."[239]]

3 MONDAY Left Ikoko in "Reed" for Ituta. She going on to Irebu with the Bolobo men. I stayed at Ituta – on S. bank of Mantumba entrance. "Peace" arr there coming into lake at about 4.p.m. "Reed" back from Irebu at 5.30. All slept at Ituta. Interviewed Frank Eteva and drew out a long story from him of recent "indecents" of State. Mr. & Mrs. Stapleton on "Peace" going down to Bolobo.

4 TUESDAY Left Ituta at 6.30 a.m. "Peace" following about 8 minutes after. She caught us up and passed us and got in some 4 minutes ahead – a gain of possibly 12 minutes in some 18 miles. Wrote most of day – not feeling well at all. Difficulty in getting a crew here. Wrote F.O. 29 & 30 Africa on state of country & Italian officers here & movement towards Lado enclave of troops & c'tges. **[By an 1894 treaty the Lado enclave was only to remain in the Congo until Leopold's death. In 1910, it thus reverted to Britain.]**

5 WEDNESDAY Wrote Farnall to go by "Peace" today with other F.O. letters. "Peace" left with letters 10 a.m. Mr. & Mrs. Stapleton are convinced the rule of the State has swept off the population wholesale. He thinks the Missions have been too quiet & laughs at the "Commission". He does not approve of Grenfell's acquiescence in State rule & methods & says his own Yakusu district is the severest condemnation of State rule here.

6 THURSDAY Left in our boat for Nkaka Creek with 12 paddlers. Clark & Frank. Up to Ikakima first – then on to Bokoti & then down to Nkaka & home. About 12 to 15 miles up Creek. I should say to Bokoto. Left at 8 A.M. Back at 7.30. Very tired – took copious notes from Natives – all they say points to great maladministration. They are cruelly flogged for being late with their Baskets to Bikoro. Very tired after recent sailing. Turned in before 9.

7 FRIDAY Thunder & heavy rain in night. Cool morning. Busy writing out afresh my notes of y'day.

8 SATURDAY 8.5 left Ikoko. 10.15 at Mwebi. On to Ngandi passed Nko – & to Ngire Bombwa & then to Montaka. People every where fled from us until we cried out – & some at long last timidly came – finding us Mission folk & not the Govt. they returned.

9 SUNDAY At Montaka. Sir R. Moor's address is Limehurst, Kingston Road, Roehampton.

… 16 SUNDAY Spent quiet day at Bolengi – Walked to Bolengi native town. Wangata Island in mid stream – poor old Glave with all his memories round me – His people these.

17 MONDAY (Anversville State mails leave Léo.) Sent men for wood to island opposite. Poor old Ted Glave. His land. Went to Nganda with Faris – saw his Evangelists go out – Prayed with them. In evening to Wangata Village to Botolo's town. S.A.B. abandoned – a State sentry lives there to look after some State plantations. Excessive taxing. Saw Ifodji, Botolo's nephew who is pawned to Iso of Bolengi for 1000 rods to pay the tax & fine. Back in canoe. Botolo & others paddling. Past down Old Ted's! beach ah! in Sept 1887. What a change.

18 TUESDAY Whitman left in boat for Ikoko. I sacked two of the men. Botolo came & told me all the story of the taxing of his town. Disgraceful. Went into Wangata in afternoon & right thro' it. Visited Ifodji and his family and saw whole extent of town. It is 20 times at least as big as Botolo's. Back in canoe with Faris.

19 WEDNESDAY Rained all morning. Left Bolengi about 9.45 a.m. 11.35 arr. Coquilhatville. Commis there. 3.10 left Do. Passed across mouth of Ruki. Fine Station. Met Stevens & Substitut at Déjeuner with De Bauw. Talked of Habibi's affair – Left again – & steamed slowly up past Ikelemba to a (good) wood place on South bank. Boys worked well. Will have plenty wood for tomorrow. "La Lulanga" passed down towards Equator.

20 THURDAY 6.20 Left camp for Lulanga. Excellent wood last night. 11.5 Tube burst in boiler. N blown up Water ran out & steam too. Towed to island close to shore – fortunately made fast to tree-swampy island. 4.15 Tube repaired & got off again. 8.20 Arr Lulanga C.B.M. Letters from Coast & down country. Underwood congratulates me on my appointment to Lisbon! Messrs Gilchrist, Whiteside & Bond here.

21 FRIDAY Lovely morning. Bright sun. Went in afternoon to Walla to see people there & hear about the fine. Waded knee deep over a part of the way – Heard the story of the fines from their own lips poor souls. Fine Balolo or Mongo people – good straight limbs and nice faces.

22 SATURDAY Fearful rain in night and all morning. Made further enquiries from Mission men & others as to recent fines. Bought good leopard skin from

Bokungu for 350 rods. 1.10 left Lolanga at 1.10 for Bolongo. Beautiful on beach – 3 Tribal slits on cheek. John plunging & Major excited horribly. 4.45 off Bolongo. Quite dead. I remember it well in 1887. Nov. Full of people then. now 14 adults all told. I should say. People wretched – complained bitterly of Rubber tax. 5.30 Left Bolongo for Bonginda. 6.30 passed deserted site of Bokutia. 10 months ago Monzede says the people were all taken away by force to Mampoko. Poor unhappy souls. 8.0 Passed Mampoko without stopping. 9.18 arr. Bonginda. = 7½ Hours. – Met by Armstrong and Walbaum & 2 ladies. 7.30 N. Steaming.

23 SUNDAY **[At top of page:]** "Anversville sails". Home Sept. 10
Lying at Bonginda. Cool after rain. Finished Bentley's "Pioneering on Congo". "Ville de Paris" went down river with India rubber to Coquilhatville – She does nothing else. Remember A.B.I.R cap guns at Léo. Walked into Bonginda to Bokonzi and further down. Slept in good room on shore. Canoe from Lulanga – 2 Boy. A's mails leave.

24 MONDAY Lovely morning. Three Stripi came standing looking at John & Major pulling incessantly *locus standi ludusi* **[(Latin) the rightful position for play]** Busy writing all morning to Coast & elsewhere – Wrote Blom to B'zville. Bought a lot of lady's dresses for ½ franc each – 10 B. Rods. Major pulled out up river. two others after verbal offer. Gone to Ifumi for canoes. **[At margin:]** Bought 16. Black dyed Bangala women's dresses @ 10. Ea = 16 rods. 5 white undyed 10 " = 50 3 do 5 " 15 " 225

25 TUESDAY **[At top of page:]** Decided to go Ifumi when 15 sentries were there a short time ago.
7.30 Cool morning. Heavy Rain at 11. Decided leave for Ifumi. 12.15 Left at 12.15 p.m. 3.26 Boyeka – deserted line of bank – once (1887) very populous stretch of towns. ~~Had~~ A Station of La Lulanga Cie. This was the island town of 1887! 5.25 Stopped for wooding. Up in night watching wood cutters. Got up 1.40. Turned in again 3.10 A.M. Read Burrows' book. Horribly true.

SEPTEMBER

… 6 SUNDAY Quiet day – Wrote a lot letters to Local auths: enough of this to keep me some days at work. In eveg. Bompoli came with wounded boy **[Ikabo]** – hand off. Awful story. [**This detail is confirmed in Casement's (copy) letter dated 12 September to the Acting Governor General, Félix Fuchs: "On Sunday last, the 6th instant, about 9 o'clock some natives… brought with them a young lad aged about 16 years whose right hand was cut off at the wrist."[240]**] Decided to go to Ekanza.

7 MONDAY **[At top of page:]** Anversville's mails at Lulanga D.V. P's mails leave Pool.
More Ngombu came with a man, a Chief Mbuoko of Lobolo shot there, arm – showing both sides, by a sentry ~~Ekanza~~ Itelo of La Lulanga in about February last. "It was in the time of the clay"! – i.e. the beginning of the C.B.M slip here. Then they poured in. See depositions! Went to Ekanza with Armstrong & D. in two canoes. Fearful state of affairs. **[Also in his 12 September letter to Fuchs, Casement wrote "On Monday, the 7th September, accompanied by the Revs. W.D. Armstrong and D.J. Danielson[241] of the Congo Balolo Mission…"[242]]** Canoe with Spielier from Bokakata passed down.

8 TUESDAY Writing all morning – Bokotila men came to say Spielier going to lodge a complaint against Bonginda because the boys jeered when he passed y'day! Absurd. "Ville de Paris" went down stream stopped for letters. Big canoe with two Boiyeka agents of La L. went down stream. Decided take Epondo to Substitut at Wangata. Charge Kelengo **[the offending sentry]**.

9 WEDNESDAY 9.0 Left at 9 A.M. for Lulango. 11.10 Passed Bolongo again. The poor people put off in canoe to implore my help. 1.10 Lulanga. 2.37 Left Lulanga for Wangata. 5.25 Camped at good wooding place all night.

10 THURSDAY 7.00 left camp at wood. Passed Ikelmba – where right bank is grassy plain with smoke of frivolous grasses ~~blowing~~ hanging in trails. 8.30 Arr. Wangata. Stevens. Charged Kelengo with his abominable crimes. Told Steevens I denounced the System which permitted armed savages to go about the country. Lunched with Malets – they told me of Mpailo's tour round Lake Ikoko after me. On to Bolengi & stayed all night. Overland to Bongandanga.

… 14 MONDAY Philippeville mails (13 Augt) leave Pool. 6.30 Left Chumbiri. Steamed well until Kwamouth when breeze sprung up – wrenched boat away twice – had to put in to French side two hours & then on again till about 5 p.m. when camped on State bank just above Lysa Pt. Had we continued running all day till 6 we should have been in Pool. Drafted letter to Gov. General on atrocious system.

15 TUESDAY 5.50 Left Camp. Good wood last night. Beautiful morning. Very high wind, going badly on account of it. 9.15 Stopped meeting "Peace" On to Pool. Stopped at B'zville and then on to Léo. 3.45 Landed poor old Danielson at Morgans. Big palaver on, M. says. Danielson seedy went to bed. Wrote F.O. all night. **[Describing himself "as a self-appointed Criminal Investigation Department", Casement informed Lord Lansdowne, in a note of this date, that with his evidence of "wholesale oppression and shocking misgovernment" he had now**

"broken into the thieves kitchen."[243]] Return Ikau.

16 WEDNESDAY I returned to B'zville with "Reed" at 8 a.m. Captain Shaw navigator. Stayed at Dutch House with Cooper. Shocking stories of the mutilation & illtreatment of natives in French Congo **[a country to which Casement was also accredited as British consul although his investigation was restricted to Leopold's Congo. Oddly, given E.D. Morel's virulent Francophobia, these stories were either not told to him by Casement, or Morel felt restrained in the matter. He had already published a denunciation of the French Congo for its use of the concessionary system, forced labour and atrocities against Africans. Much later, in a 1909 letter, Morel complained to Casement that the French "introduced the detestable theories and practices prevailing in the Congo State into French Congo", and that conditions in certain areas there were still "as bad as the conditions of the Belgian Congo."[244]**

In 1905 the French had sent their explorer hero (and Casement look-alike) Pierre de Brazza out on an earlier and similar mission of enquiry to investigate the scandal of cruel murder by French officials. He died en route home and his report was buried with him. In 1925, André Gide's report for the French Colonial Ministry was actually published, despite accusing the regime there of a system of shameless exploitation] Very tired and used up. Over excitement of last few days. "Reed" leaking. Return Bonginda.

17 THURSDAY Lots of papers not many letters I am sorry to say. I am wondering what to do. At B'zvill all day writing away.

18 FRIDAY at Lulanga. Dr Villa **[Italian Consul]** called on me. Told him much of what I had seen up river. He was furious and begged me to continue my "work of honour". Going to the President of Tribunal. Went there. Got paid grants against La Lefini for over fcs 8000. Walked there & back.

19 SATURDAY Spent a busy day – writing many letters to Gov. &c. Walked to Mpila Upper River with toothache but wanted certainly. "John" enjoyed his walk poor old soul.

20 SUNDAY **[At top of page:]** Phillippeville sails for home with Danielson and F.O. letters.
Quiet day. Walked in morning and evening – but not far. To Mpila Stream first. "John" fool. Wrote still today also chiefly to D. & S. & other local letters. Decided to go Kin. tomorrow & (D.V.) if Billington comes down to Matadi on Wednesday – or Friday. Phillipeville sails for Home with Danielson & F.O. letters.

21 MONDAY A fine morning. Not very well. Deaf & eyes troubling. "Les Cloches de Corned Beef" Opera en 365 Actes [***Les Cloches de Corneville* by Planquette was Casement's favourite opera.**] – The daily Chop Bell on the Congo [**chop is slang for food**] 1.25 Left Brazzaville for Kin. 1.50 arr. Kin. B.M.S. Went to Malets to dinner. Gave "John" a fearful hiding, broke my stick over him. Malet walked back. [**This is unusual behaviour for Casement who often wept for animals if they were cruelly mistreated, although John was a remarkably aggressive dog.**]

22 TUESDAY [**At top of page:**] (Left Sept 3) "Albertville " arrives. Monsembe. Cool morning very – Writing & waiting for "Goodwill". Went to Station in afternoon & on to Dr Villa where again a long talk over Congo affairs. He told me of S.A.B. guns. 200 Mausers coming away Oké of Lagos with Oko MKubwa to line – To arrange his palaver tomorrow with Obroko & Colibole.

23 WEDNESDAY Oké came & the others & I went S.A.B. and got 50 francs for each of them. Oké goes Kasai he says if I will give him a "book". Will give paper of Nationality. Sent 8 packages down line to Matadi. Hope Hairy B will come today & I can get off on Friday. Sent Loppers 18 bottles of Beer. Dined with Villa. Talked too much in denunciation of B.M. I can see.

24 THURSDAY At Kin – Waiting for "Goodwill". Busy writing F.O. about the Accras at B'zville. "Goodwill down about 10. Went on Léo & returned with Morgan at 4 p.m. All well. Paid off the crew all good lads – They go back on Monday – Billington going to take the Steamer up again to Chum. I go Matadi in morning. [**Casement's two month up-river investigation is now over, and the chartered steamer is relinquished.**]

25 FRIDAY 7 A.M. Left Kinchasa at 7 A.M. Billington, Gordon, Williams & Villa came to see me off. Beastly journey down in foul smelling smoke. 4 p.m. Got Tumba & went Baluti. Found Mawuku out of job so took him on. Revd. Sutton Smith there on his way up country – Brought me my latest papers & letters from Underwood.

26 SATURDAY Left Tumba at 8 A.M. Brought Mawuku with me. Arr at Matadi at 3 or so – met by Simms, Kyffin, Tubbs & Sparrow. Asked latter for his launch to go down to Banana en route to Loanda. Agreed at 3£ per day. Wrote a letter late at night. Sat up late writing out fresh plain copy of my letter to Gov. General of 12 September on condition of the country in interior. Will leave it at Boma to go up.
X Coffee at last [**a later, inserted comment**].
Richard Coffee took letter 9 p.m. & returned with answer & then we talked

and he said Yes – true Massa, a big one and I swear god Sir – and so to bed at last! **[Koffee having featured briefly in the entries for 22 and 24 May above was obviously someone Casement had marked down for sexual conversation and probing. His relief at finally getting this servant to talk dirty is palpable, but it ultimately did him damage, probably for a minimum of pleasure. It seems on this occasion he may have obtained little more than a brief look, something which came at a price, paid for in 1916, when the Archbishop of Canterbury's public support came to be sought for a reprieve. This particular diary entry was the cause of some of his reticence.]**

27 SUNDAY Finished the letter to Gov. Tired after writing most of night. Arranged "Albertville" steam launch to go down today. Bid Ruskins good bye & left Matadi at 1 in boat & Nkala at 2 in Launch. Got to Boma – Tubbs with me – in Launch at 5.15. Went over Consulate & then to AJ. U's who was up at tennis. Slept very badly.

28 MONDAY P's mail at Lulanga. Sent the letter to Gov. General under cover to Van Damme – privately saying I was staying too short a time in Boma to call. **[This extremely courteous letter majored on the case of a second mutilated boy Epondo. His right hand had been chopped off by a native sentry called Kelengo or Mbilu for failure to obey orders "to insure their working india-rubber for his employers." Unfortunately Epondo was later to recant, declaring instead that a wild animal had bitten his hand off at the wrist. Casement, however, disputed this change of story, aware that the lad, who had an adjacent gunshot wound, had been suborned. He also wrote that he accused not an individual but the system – a phrase that should have been a warning to Leopold. Otherwise, in his letter, Casement had nothing but praise for his time in the Congo Independent State.[245]**

Epondo's story prompted a discussion with Joseph Conrad on whether this was an indigenous custom. He advised Casement on 17 December 1903, "During my sojourn in the interior and keeping my eyes and ears well open too I've never heard of the alleged custom of cutting off hands amongst the natives. I am convinced no such custom ever existed along the whole course of the Ludin river to which my experience is limited. Neither in the casual talk of white men nor in the course of definite inquiries as to the tribal customs was ever such a practice hinted at."

Casement after responding received an assurance from the novelist dated 21 December saying, "You cannot doubt that I form the warmest wishes for your success."[246] There was ample, photographic evidence of dismemberment being a regular local practice, and a crude regime punishment. One Belgian newspaper quoted by Morel lamely argued that those like Epondo

were "unfortunate individuals, suffering from cancer in the hands, whose hands thus had to be cut off as a simple surgical operation."[247] Phipps from Brussels on 12 February 1904 gave Lansdowne a more sophisticated explanation for the boy's mutilation, "An independent declaration made by a certain missionary proved that Epondo's hand had been mutilated by a wild boar and that on gangrene setting in, pieces of the hand had fallen off and it has finally been amputated at the wrist."[248]] Went on in Steam Launch at 9. Broke down several times. Got Banana 7.45 only under paddle – steam finished. Spent evening with Wright & talked a little. Eat some dinner at 9 – & to bed in next bed to Wrights.

29 TUESDAY Left Banana at 7.30 in "Hirondelle" for Cabinda. Nisot Captain – comme toujours. Arr Cabinda before 12. On shore to old quarters. No news – Sleep Town as of old. "John" very frisky. Went out past Mission. Reading "Times" & thinking of effect of my letter to Gov. General.

30 WEDNESDAY <u>Upoto.</u>!!! Raining drizzle all morning <u>N'ot</u> at Upoto. Writing F.O. to send them copy of my letter to Gov. General. Wrote Lucas for passports &c. to Loanda to go by today's mail. Wrote F.O. enclosing copy of my letter of 12th September to Gov. General [**Although Casement writes earlier in the diary of drafting this harsh letter to Fuchs on 14 September, and having it delivered on 28 September, it is actually dated by him 12 September – perhaps the day he started it, and thus use of that date would be accurate. What is also interesting, although Casement seems unaware of it, was that his uncle Edward, only seven years earlier, had expressed concerns to London about the murderous cruelty of Fuchs.**

That Casement in 1903 does not record any mention of his uncle makes one suspect he felt talk of his family history in the Congo might not be well-received, or that he was nervous of a charge of nepotism. Either way, his uncle who lived until 1907 must have been proud to know that his nephew ultimately succeeded where he failed, and, remarkably, by identical evidential rigour. Of course London was by now better disposed to findings critical of Leopold than it had been] & sent by Nisot to Banana to go by "Albertville" under cover to H.S. King & Co. Moron to lunch & dinner – Royle to Mission.

OCTOBER

1 THURSDAY No sign of "Benguela" – She got to San Thomé on 24th they say! Wrote to Gohr two letters & to Sims about Abir & C.B.M. matters. Sent Nisot a case of Port wine. To call on Gov. of Cabinda. Walked up hill – Cabo Verde sentry – 5.$^{\underline{00}}$ Royle on board "Hirondelle" at night.

2 FRIDAY "Benguella" arr at 11 from Landana. Took ticket for Self & 3 Boys $28.500. John 2.000 30.500. "Benguella" left at 5. Very comfy ship indeed. John, Charlie, Masamba & Mawuku all forward together. [**Casement's dog and his three servants, or boys**] all forward together [**From 3 October, Casement is back in Portuguese territory, "installed" in the Loanda consulate, awaiting the call to go to London, which came on 4 November. He dines unusually frequently with Paul Dorbritz, the German consul who was a native French speaker from Lorraine.**]

3 SATURDAY Got Ambriz about 10 A.M. or so. Left it again about 5 p.m. Arr. Loanda at 11.20 p.m. Some boats off but did not go onshore. Very comfortable ship "Benguella".

4 SUNDAY [**At top of page:**] Albertville sails, arr. home Oct 23.
Came ashore at 9 A.M. up to Consulate. Got in all right over wall and so installed. Boat $1.700 Luggage 1.000 Charlie 200 Sending wire to F.O. to say "arrived staying several days" Sent it at 4 p.m. No news. Brock to lunch at Café Paris & the Jewboy. Dined Dorbritz – the German Consul – Talked Congo after

5 MONDAY Wire from F.O. to say to stay at Pool but only got here. Alas! Wired long wire. 3.15. "Wall arr. from Congo probably also to wire about me. A day before her time! Got letter from Wright by her saying governor very vexed at my going from Matadi. Hardwick changed £5 gold of mine @ $5645 = 28225.

6 TUESDAY [**At top of page:**] Wire from F.O. to say they have noted corr. Beautiful day & night. Full moon. Band in evening – walked & talked there with Dorbritz, Brock &c. – They to Bungo to play – I home with John – Saw en route enormous with matches. Band not bad at all. Many at it. Dinner at Café Paris which is good as good can be. Bourriez to dinner. He on board tired. [**In margin:**] I lay down all day.

7 WEDNESDAY Spent quiet day tried to write but could not do anything at all. Hopelessly lazy. Dorbritz to dinner – went up with him alone to his house to whiskey & smoke – Talked Congo & home at midnight. Brock & Hardwick there hard at it.

8 THURSDAY [**At top of page:**] Band in eveg. Invited Nuno &c. to dinner on Sunday.
Tried to write again but failed – Went to Island at 7.30 & played tennis – Then bathed and then to lunch on "Bartolomeo Diaz" with Nuno & Sosa – &c. Afternoon slept – & then "Lagoon" arr. & "Melange" Rapido arrived from

Lisbon. To dinner – certainly huge & after a walk sans incident to bed with John snoring fearfully. Lagoon left about 4.

9 FRIDAY Slight rain at 7-8 A.M. Very nice but not enough. Saw ~~Davis~~ Hardwick off to "Melange" at 9.30. Then walked & turned in for good. Wrote one despatch to F.O. about Dorbritz's views on Humanity in Africa. Sent it by ~~Davis~~ Hardwick to Lisbon. He Drunk and Smiling. **[Overwritten scrawl in margin:]** Very big Abruba Restaurant

10 SATURDAY **[At top of page and in margin:]** Melange sailed about 11 A.M. Phillippeville's mails probably at F.O. today
Went for a walk with John to beyond the old fort house & stone work – where he bathed. Then back to breakfast with Askell – Hardwick who is only a boy – but rather a decent boy – who told me all about himself & his plans. He & Brock go shooting today. Dined at home also after 7 on Bread & Cheese for dinner on John & self. Turned in 10 p.m.

11 SUNDAY Went to Island with Dorbritz & played tennis – B'fast on Bartolomeu Diaz & then home sailing. Slept – at 4 for a walk – out Musekes & home by Ingombota. Cabinda Enormous "Adios ser" & then to dinner with Nuno, Souza, Captain & Dorbritz – Enormous – Stiff. Music & to D's house after with Nuno & Co

12 MONDAY Stayed in all day. **X X** Twice enormous of dinner to me came. Called on Goma de Souza & then on Davis – Gomez not in. To dinner at Frazao's – big on right – waiting at door with John & Charlie. Afterwards with Dorbritz to talk politics of Congo. **[Dinners with the German consul at a local Italian restaurant are enlivened by an Angolan waiter who provides Casement with an unofficial floor show, distracting him from the business at hand. This was discovering Germany's intentions locally, and privately encouraging Herr Dorbritz to take up the cause of humane treatment of the Congolese.]** He gave me the gov general's letter exempting him from Customs duties to copy.

13 TUESDAY **[At top of page:]** Left Sept 24. Anversville arrives.
Wrote to F.O. Sent on A/C Current with Bill in my favour for £108.12.6. Dined with Dorbritz & Purser of "Benguella" at "Areas" in Upper City. Then to music till 10.30 & home to "Johnson" dear old snorting soul. "Benguella" sailed for home at 11 p.m. Due Lisbon 6 or 7 Nov. Got Guinea fowl & franklin from Hardwick.

14 WEDNESDAY A lovely morning. Eat franklin & gave guinea fowl to Davis. Wrote out Etat 31. Total £312.1.1 less Consular £7.16.0 fees. H.M.S.

"Thistle" arrived from South for Setta Cama, Gaboon, Bonny & S/Leone. Sent all Etats 31 by her. Lt. Commdr. Houseman. She goes in morning. Walked with Dorbritz & then to Frazao's Found "Joe" of Accra. (Sept 1901 here at Loanda! Ah! me!) there as waiter. Big one transferred to both sides holding. "John" – whiskey.

15 THURSDAY **[At top of page:]** Phillippeville sails for Congo
Damp misty morning – Wrote a little to clear up back work – got rid of several outstanding things & then to F.O. corr. Got off Africa 40, 41, & 42 & 43. Latter very long. "Thistle" left for North. Got wire to say "San Thomé" had left Ambriz at 6 p.m. "San Thomé" arr. at 8 pm. Went for walk to Coshats.

16 FRIDAY No news by "San Thomé". Wrote more F.O. things but not very much. Got wire from F.O to say they wish to publish Grenfell's statement about the Commission of Protection being useless. German S/S "Aline Woermannn" arr. **[The *Deutsche Afrika-Linien's* second ship of that name.]**

17 SATURDAY Went aboard "Aline Woerman" with Dorbritz. Sent long wire to F.O. advising them to wait till I could ask Grenfell if he would object to publicity. Not well. Kept waiting for nearly an hour by Dorbritz on Quay & no food till close on 2 p.m. On shore – at Dinner not well. Gave poor old "John" a hiding for not following me & up after a few minutes at Bungo reading papers – Turned in in fearful sweat feeling very seedy.

18 SUNDAY In bed all day & night – not well. "Aline W" sailed for North.

19 MONDAY Up again feeling seedy – in house all day writing some F.O. despatches about guns & Mola. Went down to dinner at Frazao's – Big was bigger – about 9" & awfully active. Ernesto at it again! **[The show continued, providing ever better entertainment]** Came home at 9 & turned in after short stroll.

20 TUESDAY Got letters from Congo by "Sokoto" which was in at 7.30. Also some clothes from Boma. Also a letter from E.D.M. who says letters from Congo people for him should be put under cover a/d to J.W. Richardson Esq. Stoke House, Revelstoke, S. Devon (Revelstoke). "Sokoto" left for Benguela at 4 p.m. Got two wires from F.O. today about Congo – one to go home and prepare report.

21 WEDNESDAY Wrote to Morel about Congo also writing Poulteney Bigelow on the same subject & to Joseph Conrad – & telling E.D.M. to send

his pamphlet to them. **[In this letter from Loanda, dated 23 October 1903, Casement told "Mr Morel" to address the pamphlet to Fisher Unwin, Conrad's publisher's. He added "Conrad is a charming man – subtle, kind and sympathetic and he will, I hope move his pen when I see him at home."[249]**] Shall (D.V.) **[God willing]** go by Rapido on 8/9 Nov. due at Lisbon on 26th – but am not decided. Shall wait till F.O. wire me what they think of my private letter to Gov-General. **[Casement might not have been too happy to read the (ultimately minority) views of F.A. Campbell an "unsentimental Foreign Office official" who noted on 18 October 1903 "He has the system on the brain…we ought to have as British representative someone not harder hearted but harder headed."[250]**] Dined with Dorbritz alone My Congo clothes came – nothing I want!

22 THURSDAY **[At top of page:]** "Sokoto" seen about 6 miles out steaming North.
Busy writing all day – F.O. & other matters – for Hmwd. bound P'guese steamer – will send the Congo boys home by "Heron" or "Wall" (Heron 26th here – Wall 5th). Dined with Dorbritz again. Turtle Soup – excellent dinner. Brock & Davis there also. I left at 11. Straight home. **[that going straight home was worthy of comment indicates a cruise around Loanda before turning in was Casement's norm]** Mawuku with me to 7.

23 FRIDAY "Sokoto" must be Ambriz. Another busy day – writing Congo letters chiefly to go by "Heron" or P'guese mail. Another dinner with Dorbritz – who was not well poor chap. He is busy getting wall-papers for his house – some pretty but mostly fearsome things. Back at 9.30 & walked to Bungo.

24 SATURDAY A lovely morning – Wrote Nuno to say tennis tomorrow and to come dinner in evg. with me. Invited Brock to dinner tonight at Areias. We went there & passed a pleasant evening – Dorbritz, poor soul in bed with fever & stomach. Too much Turtle. Brock home about 9.45 or 10.15. I forget. I to bed. Very heavy, splendid rain in night – Began 3 A.M. & went on in copious downpour.

25 SUNDAY **[At top of page and in margin:]** ~~Anversville sails home Nov 12.~~ Heron arrd.
Went Islha – Had to wait 2 Solid hours for Boat – only got there 10 A.M. Enormous Ambundu stroke oar – Bow also young – Nuno & Souza but no tennis possible. Returned after Dejeuner on "B. Diaz" at 1. Lay down – Got wire No: 8 from F.O. about arms imported to Congo State. Nuno & Brock to dinner at Areias & then the Band till 9.45. Then to my House to whiskey until 11.40 p.m.

26 MONDAY **[At margin:]** ~~Phillippville's~~ Albertville's mails probably at F.O. today or tomorrow.
"Heron" in dry dock. Got big mail from Congo by her with papers up to 24th Sept – The British Note to the European Powers published – I am referred to as a "Consul of Extensive African Experience". Well – we'll see. Two letters from H.W. & several from Morel. One from Charlie. Dined with Brock at Frazao's. Albertville's mails probably at F.O. today or tomorrow.

27 TUESDAY **[At top of page:]** "Anversville" due to sail for home.
In writing all day – but did not do much. Y'day wasted by the mail which came so late by "Heron". Dined with Dorbritz who was full of Congo owing to my papers y'day. A bad dinner. Home at 10.20 to bed. With "John" & Charlie. Still reading papers of "Anversville".

28 WEDNESDAY "Portugal" Rapido in from Lisbon. Nightingale is not on board the "Phillippeville" S/Leone tells us. I suppose he is being kept by F.O. over the Congo palaver to advise them. They need an adviser but A.N. knows but little on the subject. Still is good to have him even – but he will give them wrong advice I fear. He is not very pro-native, & is after all, a trader at heart. Dined with Dorbritz. Mawuku & John with me. M. – big at last.

29 THURSDAY Not very well. Brock **[acting British consul]** up to Breakfast put me off my work all day. Dined with him in the evening at Frazao's. Music after with Nuno and Arez at Biker's Café **[a German beer hall]** 'till 11.30 p.m. Up after too many cigarettes.

30 FRIDAY A very bad day – Spent it nearly all in bed – and not feeling at all up to mark. Joe Hammond of Accra called with charge of shooting against Davis. **[Joe is unfortunately calling in debts rather than offering diversion, as previously.]** Dined with Dorbritz, Brock there. Mawuku & "John" also with me. Gaw **[??]** big flying but "John" caught all.

31 SATURDAY S.S. "Cazengo" in from San Thomé &c. "San Thomé" sailed last night for home The "Zaire" from L.M. will get to Lisbon as quickly they say – so keeping all mails for her. Spent stupid day – mostly in bed all the time – No breakfast at all. Went to dinner with Dorbritz in evening at 7.15 and came back without Mawuku and "John" to Home. "John" did not go out today much the old snooker.

NOVEMBER

1 SUNDAY Ikona. Went over to Island with Charlie, John, Mawuku & Masumbu. Played tennis & then with Nuno & Brock to Shore & Dr. of

Casement under tree in Lourenco Marques with 'bald headed' Fritz Pincus ca. 1900 (NLI 36208/4)

"Cacongo". To Bicycle & Meeting. After dinner with Nuno, Brock & a Mr. Wolf, who wants to go to Benguela but is not going Very tired after tennis, bath, Sports (2½ hours standing) and so home at 10 with Nuno & Fortaleza. X

2 MONDAY Bells ringing in all Churches. Spent rather a busy day. Wrote 14 official letters – chiefly local & coast. Dined with Dorbritz who goes to Benguela in "Cazango" tomorrow – Our farewell dinner. Gave him my last Neapolitan pin as a Keepsake [**The German should have been honoured, as memories of Naples preoccupied Casement. To him it represented a city of love. This month of constant contact with Dorbritz is suggestive of a new theme in Casement's life – the adoption of younger men, with or without sexual promise, but with potential for carrying forward his dreams and missions. Series of such seemingly paternal relationships now begin to develop. Although he was to describe the Congo Reform Association as his "son and heir"[251] there is clearly an attempt to reproduce himself through other men. As someone approaching forty, Casement is determined to**

leave an ersatz genetic imprint, entwining himself and his outlook, like ivy, around a hopefully willing host.] Back with Charlie Boy and "John" at 12 midnight.

3 TUESDAY **[Top of page:]** Left Oct 15. Philippeville arr.
A beautiful morning. Slept well last night. Sent "John" out with Mawuku. Dorbritz's last day in Loanda. "Zaire" will arrive 6th Wrote various letters for Congo and Colonies. "Cazengo" left 4.15 for Benguela. **[with Dorbritz]** Went to dinner at Frazao's with Brock. Home at 9. Lovely night – walked – long way round by Calcada & Station.

4 WEDNESDAY Two wires from F.O. one about Consulate building at Matadi. Next a long F.O. wire to come home & prepare my report there. A.N. goes to Boma to act for me. Wired back leaving on Friday in "Zaire". Dined at Frazao's with Brock. Charlie & ~~Mawuku~~ "John" with me. Beautiful night. Full moon and delightful weather.

5 THURSDAY Another wire from F.O. Busy writing – Not very well. "Zaire" expected at daylight & to go tomorrow night. "Wall" in sight before 2 p.m. Bourriez called. Told him I was going home on "Zaire". Turned in seedy.

6 FRIDAY Last day. Paid off Masamba & Mawuku at Loanda & Charlie Boy **[although he was also soon to go north.]** Dined with Bourriez & Brock at Loanda & then on board "Zaire". Nuno & Sousa there. Got "John" fixed up in Browne's room for night. Turned in at 2 A.M. We never stopped till then.

[Casement was travelling by steamer for more than three weeks from 7 November until his arrival in England on 30 November, with stops at the island of São Thomé and Lisbon. Apart from one encounter on 25 November, he was not sexually active. Indeed the general lack of such opportunities while he was in Africa confirms the adage – the less you get, the less you want. In Casement's case the inverse was certainly also true. 7-21 November:] Steaming splendidly. Did 191 miles to noon. "Zaire" very pleasant. Distance Loanda to San Thomé is 670 miles...At S Thomé at 5.30. Crouch off at 9. On shore with him to Ceffala and Wright...Mrs. Sheldon **[See photograph of Mrs May French Sheldon and Casement on the island]**.[252] called with Capt. Harrison of Sekondi & Egerton Purser & Dr. Camden. Walked a bit. Mozambique, Guinea & then Sena...3402 miles from S Thomé to Lisbon...Concert in evg – P'guese Naval officer sang charmingly. Sat up all night reading *Woman in White* till 4 A.M...Blowing strong all day – many sick – but ship going well. Slept in smoke room. Very badly up to 4 pm...Nous verrons. Lovely morning – with sun & sea & fresh wind...Passed

German Ship also going north – left her far behind. Saw Grand Canary at 3 p.m. Peak of Tenerife well in view at 5 on port side. Got W.A. Mail Nos. 26 & following of 25 Sept 1903...Passed Las Palmas about 9 p.m. "John's" son there. "Bill" unknown to "John"...

22 SUNDAY Beastly night and morning. Ship kicking like a colt. High half starboard – beam – Sea & high wind. Will not do more than 270 today. Many sick. Ran 264 miles. (264) 289. Lat. 30° 39′. Long 14′ 00′. Heavy sea still wind dropped – but screw racing continually. Sea still bad. Slept in smoke room very miserable. **[At top & margin:]** 264 528 803 264 539

23 MONDAY Lost The **[gap]** my diary. Found again at 12 noon! Will go probably 276 miles to noon. Ran 275 miles 350. Lat: Long: **[in margin:]** 539 275 264

24 TUESDAY **[At top of page and in margin:]** Left Nov. 5 Anversville arrs. Drew £30.
Bad night. Up at 2 & again. Cape Espichel & Cintra at 7. In River at 9 & at Lisbon 10 A.M. Excellent run. Cowper sent down to meet me & then to Central & Cowper – Letter from A.N. & to Sir M. Gosselin. Not in. Saw Dom Carlos in carriage to Cowpers. "John" with me. Dined Central & than walked. Note from Gosselin. **[This phrase is repeated the next day. Sir Martin Gosselin (1847-1905), the British minister in Lisbon since 1902 had helped get Casement earlier consular jobs, and probably the aborted 1904 promotion to Lisbon. In the second note, Gosselin insisted on Casement dining with him despite his excuse of a lack of clothes. On the back of the first invitation Casement has cryptically written "Jaime (?) Tame Dogs".[253] Even though he tried to avoid him on this occasion, Gosselin's sudden death in 1905 deeply upset Casement, not least because he had just posted him a very personal letter which he declared "contained some private reflections intended only for Sir Martin's own eye and heart – and I wonder who will open and read it."[254] The letter has not survived although there a couple of earlier letters in the Hertfordshire County archives. In one, dated 14 August 1902, Casement wrote, "The Congo State is a horrid sordid sham". He enclosed a photograph "of some of the maimed beings of the Domaine privé...they are I think some of Fievéz's [Leon Rom] victims." Casement spoke of showing it to "Our King." Gosselin noted that he had so done at Balmoral on 5 October.]**

25 November Note from Gosselin. Went out with "John" to Vet. Left him with Parkinson **[John was now to join the sheepdog Rags at Parkinson's]** A. Brown to luncheon. Dined with Self at Central. Walked – Spanish type.

Mrs May French Sheldon with Casement on São Tomé and Principe Island 1903 (Wellcome Library)

26 November Lunched at Legation with the Gosselins and then on board "Ambrose" & off from Belem at 5.30. **[Writing to Francis Cowper on 3 December 1903, from the Wellington Club, Casement said he was sorry to have seen so little of him "especially that last day at luncheon…with my anxious expecting to be called back in street to the 'Ambrose'…Tender love to dear old 'John'."[255] Despite many expressions of concern about John to Cowper, there was soon bad news from Lisbon where these animals were stacking up. On 7 June 1904 Casement was to reply "I am very sorry about dear old 'John'. I have no luck with the dogs I take to Africa."[256] Few others mourned his passing.]**

27 FRIDAY On "Ambrose" of Booth Line. At Noon about off Finisterre. Weather got bad.

28 SATURDAY Weather beastly, gale and sea.

29 SUNDAY Weather beastly, gale and sea. Passed Tuskar some time & then later saw Small's Light.

30 MONDAY Got L'pool at 8. & on shore at 10.30. To Hotel at H. & C.'s & off to London by night train.

DECEMBER

1 TUESDAY Arrived London. To Stores & then to F.O. where saw many men including Villiers – They are a gang of Stupidities in many ways. Dined with Sanford at 102. Eaton Square Ordered to make my report at once. Cold coming on. **[On arrival he wrote excitedly to Gertrude (from Herbert Ward's house at 53 Chester Square) "I have just this instant arrived and find your letter of 13 Nov. awaiting me. In <u>what</u> paper and on what date did you see my movements chronicled?...Write me at once with dates and names and outline of offensive paragraph in public press."**[257]**]**

2 WEDNESDAY Up early – cold getting worse – shall be seedy I fear. Note from Farnall Lord Percy wished to see me. Went & saw him & had a long talk. Think I gave him some eye openers. Then with Roupell & Strachey to Wyndham to lunch. Then home. Note from Barrington telling me Lord Lansdowne wished to see me at Lansdowne Ho at 11.30 tomorrow **[This entry is precisely verified by a note in Casement's papers from a Foreign Office official, Eric Barrington, dated 2 December. It reads "Lord Lansdowne would like to see you and would be glad if you would call tomorrow Thursday at Lansdowne House, Berkeley Square at about 11.30 a.m."**[258]**]** Expecting type writers & then to report. Dined with Cui Bono.

3 THURSDAY Went Lansdowne House – Saw Barrington & then H.L. He was very nice & after hearing my dire tale said "Proof of the most painfully convincing kind Mr Casement." **[Henry Petty-Fitzmaurice, 5th Marquess of Lansdowne (1845-1927), was an Irish peer, his seat being at Kenmare in Co. Kerry. A former Viceroy of India, he was married to an Ulster Duke's daughter. The Lansdowne subsidiary titles include the earldoms of Kerry and Shelburne. He was Foreign Secretary from 1900-05. In the Cabinet again, during the war, he was to be found arguing for a negotiated peace with Germany in 1916, and was one of a number of ministers and ex-ministers to advocate a reprieve for Casement. Lansdowne's politeness was legendary although he was also famously described (by his tutor) as "talented without imagination." His son was to become a Free State Senator.]** Dined at Club & went for walk in rain after & so home at 11. across Park.

4 FRIDAY Type man called. All going well – to begin tomorrow. Bertibus called **[This was Robert James Casement, born in 1884, the fourth son of**

cousin Roger who had become in 1902 the Master of Magherintemple. Use of this pet name in the diary is confirmed and explained by the author himself: In a letter of 15 August 1909 from Rio to his eponymous cousin, Casement asks "what news have you of Bertie – 'the Bertibus' as I always called him?"[259] Robert migrated in 1904 to Vancouver, enlisting in the Canadian Engineers during the First World War. He was awarded the DCM for bravery in 1915, obtaining a Commission the following year.] & we dined together at Club & then to King Richard II at H.M's Not good – scenes grand. Walked home, delightful walk after and so home to by & by & sleep and doodle do.

5 SATURDAY **[At top of page:]** Phillippville due S'thampton
Typer came & hard at work all day – Began dictating my Report. Got 4500 words of it typed & wrote more. Many letters & various people seeking to interview me – including Reuter's Agency. Dined at Club – with newspapers to 9. & then home about 10.30. After a good hard day's work with typer who seems a good boy named Jordan. He left at 5.30 p.m.

6 SUNDAY **[At top of page:]** "Albertville" sails. Home Dec. 24
Very busy on Report with typer. Did 6000 words today & revised a lot. Dined at Comedy Restaurant alone. First time there in life – porter gone. Excellent dinner. French chef. Then walked. Dusky – depredator – Huge. Saw 7 in all. Two beauties.

7 MONDAY Very busy again – got some 15000 words typed of Report since Saturday. At it all day. Papers full of my Congo journey. D.M. got leader & Pall Mall too at night! Awful mistake. Dined with Cui B. & Mrs C. jolly dinner. Strolled. Dick West End – biggest & cleanest mu nua ami **[in my mouth: that Casement has to remark on the cleanliness of this particular man's penis indicates that he was frequently obliged to deal with and be repelled by unhygienic members, and that many of those he met were probably poor and ill-housed.]**

8 TUESDAY Busy all day & then to Robertsons at 30 Hemstall Road **[The home of these distant relatives was a regular port of call for Casements when in London – "George was looking very old and broken down – a complete wreck" according to a 1902 letter home. George Robertson, secretary of the Institute of Chemistry and a fellow of the Chemical Society was to die in 1903, not long after this letter, at the early age of forty-five.[260]]** – Home by Marble Arch. D.W. 14 C.R. £1 – Drizzle – Home tired & to bed, Bertie walking part of way.

9 WEDNESDAY Up early & hard at work on Report – Hope finish it this week. Working till late. Dined Royal Academy Club with Goscomb John. In train & home from Underground.

10 THURSDAY Very busy but tired. Getting near end of report thank goodness. Grattan Guinness called on me in afternoon **[who worked at the Congo Balolo Mission. The Balolo, or Iron People, were noted for their cicatrization. The sculptor Herbert Ward, for one, was fascinated with the three separate lumps as large as, and similar in shape to, pigeon eggs, scarred into the bridge of Balolo noses.*]** & then E.D.M. (Morel) first time I met him. The man is honest as day. Dined at Comedy together late & then to chat till 2 a.m. M. sleeping in study. **[Morel described it thus: "I slept in my clothes upon the sofa; while its author (the report's) sought his bedroom above." The meeting was at 53 Chester Square.[261] This was a fateful event, described by Sir Arthur Conan Doyle, somewhat enthusiastically, as "the most dramatic scene in modern history."[262] Plainly EDM made an immediate and deep impression. Morel, now thirty, was to become Casement's most important, and long-lasting political ally and correspondent. He fulfilled, however, a greater role as one in a line of males who were assigned the mixed parts of the wife and son Casement never had. In a sense he was collected, quite willingly. A rare note of concern expressed by Casement about his associate, does, however, come in a letter of 1913 when he complained "I too never hear from Mr Morel...I sometimes think he is far less altruistic than I once thought him – and that he, too, would compromise on things when there can be none."[263]**

Morel's own words about their first meeting are worth quoting for their eloquence and passion: "It was one of those rare incidents in life which leave behind them an imperishable impression. I saw before me a man, my own height, very lithe and sinewy, chest thrown out, head held high – suggestive of one who had lived in the vast open spaces. Black hair and beard covering cheeks hollowed by the tropical sun. Strongly marked features. A dark blue penetrating eye sunken in the socket. A long, lean, swarthy

---

* "Slave-trading canoes are to be seen coming out of the river daily with their cargoes of wretched humanity. The slaves are the Balolo branch of the Bankundu, and a very inoffensive tribe. They are distinguished by their tribal mark, which is a large tattoo cut on the forehead, just between the two eyes, and again on the side of the temple, between the ear and the eye. It stands out like the half-shell of a walnut. Often they supplement these standard marks by smaller ones, like hazel-nuts, along the bridge of the nose right up to the end, and sometimes on the chin and dotted about the face. It seems to be a type of beauty to have as many hideous protuberances as the face will admit of." Herbert Ward *Life Among the Congo Savages*.

Vandyck type of face, graven with power and withal of great gentleness. An extraordinarily handsome and arresting face. From the moment our hands gripped and our eyes met, mutual trust and confidence were bred and the feeling of isolation slipped from me like a mantle. Here was a man indeed. One who would convince those in high places of the foulness of a crime committed upon a helpless race, who would move the bowels of compassion as no one else could do."[264]

A couple of years later Morel was less certain of Casement's sanity, when on 3 May 1906 he wrote wearily to John Harris, concerned about unwelcome letters, "I am very sorry for him, and his troubles have made him unreliable."[265]]

11 FRIDAY Morel off after breakfast – & then to hard work all day worked like Trojan – practically finished Report – read & revised till 8 p.m. Then to Comedy to dinner & then for long walk to Holborn Viaduct &c. & home at 11. or so. To bed.

12 SATURDAY Revised report again – at it all morning – and then took it to Farnall. Later got F.O. despatches from Brussels by bag – Congo have begun their anti-Casement campaign. Cuvelier launched his first dart against me over the Spillier incident. Tired & did little. Called on Mrs Sanford afterwards & her niece. Did not see old S. at all. Dined at Gatti's Adelphi & then home on foot in rain.

13 SUNDAY Busy all morning dictating Inclosure 1 (Basingili refugees) & then wrote reply to De Cuvelier's mendacious note to Grattan Guinness. Jack Jr. R.N. **[This was Captain John Casement (1880-1944), a submariner and ironically a naval intelligence operative attached to Room 40 in the First World War, and later Master of Magherintemple. He was another son of cousin Roger and Susie Casement.]** & Bertie called on me & latter stayed to dinner at Gattis Adelphi restaurant. Home on foot at 10.30. Slept well.

14 MONDAY Letter from Morel. "African World" got "curious particulars of Mr R. Casement's tour "which it proposes publishing "after his report is issued." This is poor boy child Askell Hardwick – at my breakfast at Loanda. **[Presumably Hardwick was trying his hand at journalism, and capitalising on his acquaintance with Casement in Africa. Worryingly, the particular publication that Morel mentioned was said to be an apologist for Leopold's regime.]** Dined with Mrs. Sanford & pretty Miss Miller and then to Earls' Court called on Miss Heath and Miss Redmayne there – nice girl.

15 TUESDAY Very busy finishing notes all day. Got mostly all thro'. At Victoria

Street – beautiful fat type. Walked to City & to Docks. & home to Strand where Lewisham & Dulwich elections out. Supper at Press Café. & home tired.

16 WEDNESDAY Finished many things & took notes for Report to F.O. Saw Villiers who again gave me impression of being abject piffler. Went to Club. Got letters & then to dine with Cui & then to Ennismore (as ever was) & Wolf at Hans Crescent Hotel – & so home. [**Viscount Ennismore, when writing in 1904 to "My dear Roddie", was plainly not convinced by Casement's reawakened enthusiasm for the Irish language and replied in the same manner as did others: "Your eloquence on the subject of the Irish language is lost on me. If you want to improve this people, preach temperance, not two tongues. Drink is the curse of the country and the publicans wax fat."**[266]] Many F.O. letters &c. One a wire from Nightingale to say Mr Kempton eye witness on way home.

17 THURSDAY Phillipeville leaves Antwerp Due Congo Jan 5. Foggy morning. Villiers says he wants report out before end of month. All complete so far as I am – [**Despite Casement earlier describing him as 'an abject piffler', Francis Villiers, in contrast to his unsentimental colleague F.A. Campbell, noted that the report was "terse, full of matter and written in a quite dispassionate style…free from all trace of exaggeration." Unknown as yet to Casement, the publishing delays were in part due to pressure from Sir Alfred Jones, his old employer in Liverpool. Somewhat typically Casement exploded at Foreign Office indecision, being unable to recognise the web of conflicting interests on this and other issues that the officials had to resolve.**[267]] Ennismore wants me to go to Convamore [**the family seat in Co. Cork**] Drove Office of Works – Walked back. Missed Collis. To Club. Found him & then home. Miss Heath, Bertie, Ivy & Mrs. G. with me at Great Central. Drove Miss Heath home & back in same cab to bed.

18 FRIDAY Busy again at additions to report. & then with them to F.O. to Farnall who seemed very desponding. Villiers again at his "indecisions". My report not likely to come out until February now when Parliament meets. Lunched with Cust at United Services. Beautiful there! [**at side**] **X.** Uniform Hoste to dinner at my Club & then to his house & home after stroll.

19 SATURDAY [**At top of page:**] Phillipeville leaves Congo Jan. 17 1904. Home Feb. 4.

Got statement of position of W.A. Mail from Morel. About £1800. needed to bring capital up to authorised amount. This is my last day with Typewriter Jordan. His a/d is "Writers London" Went to Sanford in evening & tried to interest him on the situation of W.A. Mail. [***The West African Mail* had been**

started by Morel in 1903 as a rival newspaper to *West Africa* on which he had previously worked. It had come into existence by virtue of investments from the Liverpool traders Sir Alfred Jones of Elder Dempster and John Holt. Jones withdrew his firm's advertising in 1904 over the paper's attacks on the Congo Free State, with which he had a shipping contract due for imminent renewal. Morel came then to rely, like Casement, on the financial assistance of William Cadbury. On Sir Alfred's death in 1909, Casement wrote to Morel from Brazil (on 15 December) to tell him how his heart jumped when he read of it, alongside the illness of King Leopold. "So he has just preceded his Royal Master", he thrilled. "What did he die of?" was the enquiry, followed by the insertion of an obvious guilty afterthought – "I am sorry for his friends and relatives."[268]]

Then left for Uxbridge at 7. & got there 8.20. Found Dick, Mrs. M. Tommy & his Mother there. Talked Congo, myself and "Love's Horizon" in "Daily Mirror". **[Confirmation of his appreciation of this poem occurs in 1916 when William Allan Hay mentioned it in a letter to Casement's solicitor. Hay, who had met Casement in Africa, took the opportunity to say there was no truth in the aspersion cast upon his service in Lourenco Marques although he did not explain that particular allegation. Hay had earlier written that "after perusal of Mr (as he then was) Casement's poetry", he gathered that he had lost his (female) lover by death.[269]]**

20 SUNDAY Out at Morten's – Seedy with cold. No breakfast. Drove after lunch to Swakeleys – the Gilbeys – a beautiful house Charles I or II's time? Dark & cold coming back.

21 MONDAY Left Morten's & into town at 12. Lunched at Club & drew £20. Home. Letter from Sanford – no go. Wrote various letters mostly private & off to Dublin at 10.30. Called on Sanfords & saw Charlie Boy before going away. Good wee soul. **[This reference to "Charlie Boy" being at the Sanford home helps unravel the mystery of his identity and origins. Charlie had accompanied Casement to Africa from England without any background detail or explanation in his diary. He was instrumental in the loss of the basket of official papers, although little admonished. The 'boy' appellation indicates he was both African and a servant. He must have been attached to this Eaton Square household from whence he left in February. The Sanford in this case, however, was not General Henry Sanford (1823-91). He, formerly American minister in Brussels had employed Casement for a surveying exploration in 1886 with the Congo International Association. This Sanford was instead Charles Henry Sanford, Herbert Ward's father-in-law and another very wealthy American.**

Casement had written to Gertrude on 20 April 1903 saying "Charlie my Kruboy servant is with me but he will go home to his own people soon for a rest."[270] The Kra (Accra) or Kru people form a language group in Liberia and elsewhere along the West African coast. They, or the generalised group so known, speak Creole and have their origins in liberated slaves and other anglicised Africans. Charlie lingered on in Casement's address book as "My boy Charlie at Grand Cavally, native name Wa, care of. To write Ba – Grand Cavally via Cape Palmas." The river Cavally forms the frontier between Liberia and the Ivory Coast. Whether Charlie was a Wa or a Ba, Cape Palmas is definitely on the Liberian coast in Kru territory and was sufficiently magnificent for Casement to write a poem so entitled: ..."On the dark Liberian shore where the stately palm trees soar/.../Where the tides of God must set them, tho' the ways of love deplore."

Indeed Cape Palmas crops up frequently in Casement's notes. In an 1898 letter to Gertrude he wrote of a particular, white bulldog: "Patsie lies long sunk beneath the Atlantic off Cape Palmas."[271] A photograph exists in the NLI of Casement and an enormous white bulldog who is surely Patsie. During Casement's shipboard illness, the dog's fate was decided by a ship's cook who claimed to have forgotten that he had closed him up in a locker, wherein he proceeded to suffocate. If Patsie had John's temperament then his fate was hardly surprising.

Rider Haggard's name is also to be found in this address book which suggests that Casement may have been providing him with African colour and stories for his best selling books.[272]]

22 TUESDAY Bad crossing to Dublin. At North Wall. Went Bray. Francis Naughton not there – back to Westland Row. At Harcourt Street J.B. grown greatly in <u>all</u> ways. £1. 6/- Xmas Dinner at Dolphin – Home to Hotel – nice fire. In bed & off to sleep. [**There is an entry in Casement's address book for a "W 'O' Byrne, Dolphin Hotel, Essex Street, Dublin". One can only deduce that Casement put the 'O' in inverted commas to indicate that this was an unusual, Gaelicised form of the name. He sounds as if he was an employee of the hotel (one frequented by Irish nationalists) and had attracted Casement's attention because of his looks or views or both. The firm of Dollards who supplied Casement with his 1910 Office Diary and fulfilled other orders for Irish stationery, which Bulmer Hobson was often deputed to arrange was also situated in Essex Street. In an out of sequence comment, Casement added:**] J.B. 1/8/- Enormous. came, handled & also came.

[In the absence of Francis Naughton, Casement came across another

acquaintance who was favoured with a considerable amount of money for mutual efforts. The character Naughton was documented in Casement's papers outside the Black Diaries, according to B.L. Reid, in a way he regarded as implicit confirmatory evidence of the homosexual nature of Casement's link to him. He discovered in the NLI a loose undated note-book page reading "Francis Naughton, Station Hotel, Bray, Co. Wicklow. Home address Cavan House, Bundoran. He gets £20 a year and his keep at the Station Hotel in Bray: Is a Catholic and has both parents living at Bundoran. Has been living only 9 months in Dublin."[273] Naughton (see later chapter) was therefore one of a hundred or more males who were to live with the key to a mystery that they could not reveal for fear of literally incriminating themselves.]

23 WEDNESDAY Left Amiens St. at 10.30 but held up at Donabate owing to accident. Got Drogheda 2.30. & Belfast at 6 p.m. Wired from Drogheda to B'castle. Dined at Northern Counties **[Not the hotel of that name in Portrush but the Northern Counties Railway station hotel in Belfast's York Street. In Casement's absence, in July 1903, the Midland Railway had absorbed the Northern Counties Railway and renamed its flagship hotel the Midland.]** & then to Uncle Tom's Cabin. Fearful. **[This performance, according to Belfast press advertisements, was at the Theatre Royal in Arthur Square where "John Tully's well-known company of American Actors, Dancers &c. and Full Chorus of Real Negroes" were all week putting on *Uncle Tom's Cabin – a Grand Plantation Festival.* The Empire Theatre around the corner in Victoria Square (site of a famous urinal now preserved in the Ulster Folk Museum) was trying to compete with a "Grand Xmas Attraction" of "Black Troubadors."]** Fred Mcarthy after amusing Accra. **[This cryptic comment may have been evoked by a nocturnal meeting with someone from the chorus of Uncle Tom's Cabin or one of the Black Troubadors.]** Foggy night.

24 THURSDAY Left at 12 for B'castle. Saw Mrs. Johnnie at B'mena train in passing. **[Mrs John (Mya) Casement, formerly Maria Young, of Galgorm Castle (1860-1943), was one of several Young sisters who entertained the boy Roger during his school holidays. Two younger sisters, Rose and Charlotte, become Gaelic Leaguers, at political odds with their Carsonite father and brother. Mya was the exception to the rule about the distaff side of Ulster's Protestant elite becoming nationalist: she and her car had a part to play running guns for the UVF on the night of 24-25 April 1914. According to Mary Young (née Macnaghten), Mya's sister-in-law, "Every car and every lorry was on the road that night. All the police were kept shut up and the organisation was wonderful. Of course it was a very**

anxious night. Mya made tea and read the most bloodthirsty Psalms of David. Our cars got home about 3.30 a.m. Was it right or wrong? Politics reached fever pitch and we had to man our guns having secured them." The 216 tons of arms were landed at Larne Harbour having been shipped out of Germany on the SS *Fanny* and reaching dumps throughout Ulster that night in a naval and military operation of great precision.] Tea at Ballymoney and then on to B'castle – Train late. 20 minutes stoppage at Armoy! No one to meet me. Cold & bleak. I will not go there again. Aunt C. up & all well. **[born Charlotte Miller in 1836 and from a substantial Ballycastle family, Aunt C. had been uncle John Casement's second wife since 1859. Nina described her as "the out-of-date type of Ulster Presbyterian…one of the best but with a gruff brusque manner."[274]]** House changed but not improved at all – on the contrary.

25 FRIDAY Miserable day – Did not go out till afternoon with Roger. Busy on my Report revising it which I found here from Farnall. Went to Club & then home with Roger in cold. Glorious light on Cantyre in sunshine. **[old spelling for Kintyre in Scotland, visible across the North Channel.]**

26 SATURDAY Again in bed till lunch at Report – but not finished. The additions came from Farnall **[Harry Farnall of the Foreign Office's African Department, and its Congo expert.]** – with excellent opinion of my report – "Could not be better – admirable both in style and substance." Good – A.L. Jones will not succeed in getting it wilked out I see. Sir Lamp's?? influence will fail too I am sure. **[Casement's comments on his old boss, Sir Alfred Jones may well have been prompted by reading an irritating news item in a Belfast paper, the *Northern Whig*, on 22 December. Over the headline "Congo Atrocities" it quoted Sir Alfred in an interview saying that a "conversation regarding the Congo with the King of the Belgians (had been) very satisfactory…in a great territory like the Congo where the natives had so long been cannibals, the Belgians had done a good work." Leopold's fight back was under way.]** Miserable place to stay in this. Beautiful day. Down to Golf Club. **[Thereafter Casement spent his time in Ballycastle in hotels and guesthouses such as the Antrim Arms Hotel, Atlantic House, and The Quay. During the Ulster crisis he would not have been welcome in Churchfield anyway, but he had already chosen to keep his distance, not least because of the cold in such a draughty house.]**

27 SUNDAY "Anversville" sails. Home Jan 19. Spent day in House. Cold worse – much worse. Very miserable place – Dreary day. Others to Church **[Culfeightrin parish church where many of the Casement family are buried**

is about a mile from Churchfield and has two prominent standing stones in the graveyard.] – I to bed early. Kitsie arr. y'day. **[Cousin Kitsie (Dorinda Catherine) Casement, born in 1871 and a grand-daughter of Thomas Casement had left home after disagreements with her father Col. Eldred (Eddie) Pottinger. She lived in London and was a "Lady in Waiting to several Royal Ladies" but unfortunately was in trouble in 1917 with a court appearance on a shoplifting charge. The war and her cousin's execution may have disturbed her, not to mention her own mother's committal to a lunatic asylum. It was that mother, Catherine, who was most exercised about the boy Roger's future when she corresponded on the matter in the late 1870s.[275]]**

28 MONDAY Finished Report & sent it to F.O. by 3.20 train by regd post. Left with aunt C. She to Nanaveere – & I to Ballymoney & then on to Portrush. Wired Nina. Beautiful got in with sister at B'money. Nina met me at station & dined together at Portrush.

29 TUESDAY Pleasant day at Portrush – Writing in morning & in afternoon called at Pottingers, Youngs & Cunninghams. Dined together and then to the Boy's Club at Huntingtown Hall. "Wee Dougal" sang a song & McAllister recited a lot of things Paddy in the Butter the best. **[One of the letters written from the Northern Counties Hotel in Portrush, during this stay, was to Dr R.F. Scharff, keeper of the Natural History Section at the Science and Art (now the National) Museum in Dublin. Dated 30 December 1903, he asked "I wonder if you would care for some Central African (Congo) curiosities for the Museum. I am just back from that part of the world…I got no Monkey or live thing for Dublin Zoo I'm sorry to say – altho' I had you always in my mind – but the difficulty of travelling with Monkeys is great!"[276]**

Casement finally handed over the promised extensive material, which included specimens of native bread, India rubber, a basket of Gum Copal, wicker shields, spears, a pair of handcuffs and a native guitar, in person, on 10 and 25 June 1904. He also deposited, perhaps unintentionally, as he did not list it, a Swazi war cap in ostrich feathers. It had a label, endorsed in his handwriting "Roger Casement H.M. Consul Loanda etc. Cap to be kept at Churchfield till claimed – October 1898."[277]]

30 WEDNESDAY A lovely day. Walked about all day and to Miss R.'s Cottage Hospital with Numkins. Then lunch & then to Nina's for tea and songs **[Casement's sister (Numkins) was sufficiently talented to be found performing in public in Portrush on 6 April of the following year, as Rose Young wrote in her diary "Mr R.D. Casement called at Lisnavarna. Mrs**

Newman's concert in the Town Hall."[278] In an article in *Irish Life* of 7 July 1916, Nina's repertoire was described as "Irish folklore ballads."] – No news – Japan & Russia still threatening peace – but war likely to end their instigations. **[The war actually started six weeks later on 10 February 1904. Britain had just intervened to "maintain the balance of naval power" by snapping up two warships that Chile had put on the market, ones the Russians had been attempting to buy. The newspapers of that day also reported that Englishmen were already enlisting to aid their Japanese allies. The Russians who were in league with France lost what was to be largely a naval war.]**

31 THURSDAY Again lovely morning. Paid Hotel bill & off with Nina for B'mena – At Mr Y's to luncheon & then to Galgorm & Mrs Kings **[Mrs King was the widow of Casement's old headmaster, Robert King who had died in 1900. Mr Y was Rose's father, the Rt. Hon. John Young. In 1912, Casement was raging about his boyhood host, being on the "precious Standing Committee of the Ulster Unionist Council." He was, Casement declared "a man I've known all my life – John Young of Galgorm – my cousin married his daughter. He ought to know better."[279] Like many liberal Ulster Protestants, Casement was seriously illiberal about people who held to Unionist views, although the strength if not the source of his antagonism might well have been his own rebellious sexual orientation. Another revealing poem written on 19 May 1895, on Rathlin Island, defending the "beauty in the devious path" reserves its strongest anger, like Christ, "for that rigid school who measure virtue, like a gown, by rule, who wear their righteousness as Sunday clothes, that would be soiled by meaner people's woes"[280] – Ulster Scots Presbyterians.**

Rose Young diaried Casement's previous visit to Galgorm Castle on 25 May 1898 thus: "Mr R.D. Casement dined at 9." Three years before, she recorded time spent on Rathlin with Casement, his cousin the Rear Admiral and his wife – her sister, writing on 18 May 1895 "R.D.C. and R.Y. to Rathlin on Coyle's boat to stay with Jack and Mya."[281] The next day, an Ulster Sunday, Casement was working on two of his most religiously justifying, homoerotic poems "looking over to Jura & Islay over the blue and white sea."[282]] & then to Larne by 5 train. Over in "Princess May" – 3rd class all the way 27/6$^{d.}$ to Euston. Cold bitterly in train. Did not sleep much at all – nice quiet fellow passenger all the way. Scotch brute got in at NStewart. **[Newton Stewart in Scotland]**

JANUARY 1904

1 Jan FRIDAY 1904 Arr. Euston 8 A.M. Home lots of letters & papers of 31 Dec. M. Post has Poulteney Bigelow's article on me. It is a rummy one. **[Bigelow later refused to take Casement's Gaelic language revival arguments seriously, telling him "you may let your Irishman talk Dutch or English it can't make him into a Dutchman or a Cockney."[283]]** Busy writing all morning. Called at F.O. saw Farnall & Villiers & had long yarn over my Report. Both offer many compliments on it. I am to decide its fate practically. To Cunninghame Graham M.P. at Devonshire [??] **[Robert Cunninghame Graham was a Liberal/Labour MP, representing North Lanarkshire from 1886-92. He had been a cattle farmer in South America and became a famous travel writer, and in 1928 the first chairman of the Scottish National Party, also described as a "socialist favouring legislative independence for Ireland." In 1916 he turned against Casement.]** & then to Harley House. Bow.

2 SATURDAY Writing Morel again. Prepared Memorandum showing that to press the Congo Govt we must resume our extra-territorial jurisdiction. The other Memos are L. Percy's, Villiers and Farnall's – the former for an International Commission the two others urging objections to it – I did the same & suggested the alternative of the Consular Jurisdiction. **[Critical discussions on Congo policy ensue over these eight diary days in 1904 with various Foreign Office personnel, suggesting different diplomatic options.]** Lunched with Gerald Spicer at Carlton Grill Room. Met Nascimento there & we talked of Parminter's nephew and L.M. the Notorious. Back to F.O to Farnall. Sent Minute on Consular Jurisdiction to Villiers. Saw Roupell at C.O. Went E – early. Dined at Press Café.

[There are no specific days for 1904 printed in the diary after 2 January. Casement's later daily entries are placed where he can but before them are two pages of old notes about postage costs and Foreign Office repayments for Kru repatriations.]

for 2nd Quarter of 1903

Postages at Aubrey Walk		12 6
[dittos]	Madeira $2.000	
	Tenerife pesetas	6
	S/Leone	1 0
	Loanda $<u>440</u>	
	Cabinda	
	Boma	

From F.O. £100.00 for repayment & fund.

Repaid by Arthur. from Gold Co.	10.	6.	0	
[ditto] [ditto] Congo govt. Saidu.	5.	15.	0	**[see 10-12 April]**
[ditto] [ditto] Lagos govt. Akin.	2.	5.	0	
Expended by A.N. on repatriated S/L				
	£3.	15.	0	
by Dr. Sims on Lagos	2.	5.	0	
Repaid by Lagos	7.	5.	4	

Sunday 3 Janry Went to Conrad at Pent Farm Stanford, Near Hythe **[Casement writing to Morel on 23 October 1903 told of "Joseph Conrad the author of some excellent English – a Pole, a seaman and an ex-Congo traveller. I knew him well – and he knows something of the Congo – indeed one or two of his shorter stories such as 'The Heart of Darkness' deal with his own view of Upper Congo life."[284]]** & spent a delightful day with him. Back by last 8.20 train & home to bed. Revised report in train.

Monday 4. Jan. At F.O. Saw Farnall but no Villiers. F. read my Memo all right. Wired Forfeitt Took Revised Report to Farnall today. Dined at Café Regina & to Olympia. **[the Exhibition Hall]**

Tuesday 5 Jan <u>1904</u> Forfeitt could not come – Wrote many things all morning & then off to L'pool by 2.15 train – 2nd Class. Wired Morel about Scrivener to publish this week & in train wrote a heading to Scrivener's article. M at Lime St. – Dined there & then to Hawarden. Talked all night nearly. Wife a good woman. **[Mrs Mary Morel was the mother of three boys including a son called Roger, so named before any physical meeting, and a daughter. E.D. Morel, known as Georges to a very few, had joined the Liverpool firm of Elder Dempster in 1891 as a shipping clerk, some seven years after Casement had departed to work for Leopold's Congo International Association. The pair of former shipping clerks had remarkably similar careers and an uncanny resemblance in personality, manner, and charisma.**

EDM has been described as a tall, thin, handsome man with a commanding presence but a solemn sense of purpose which deprived him of any humour or wit. Catherine Cline in writing also of Morel in this way is aware that it could just as easily have been Casement: "Certain of his own righteousness, Morel was equally convinced of the wickedness of his opponents; the possibility that his adversaries might, on occasion, have been as well-meaning as himself seems never to have occurred to him. His enmities were as passionate as his friendships, and his sense of grievance was highly developed."[285]

He also had identity problems having been born in Paris in 1873 and

been brought up there for eight years with the name Georges Edmond Pierre Achille Dene Morel de Ville. His father died when he was four, and back in England with his mother, he gradually abbreviated himself to E.D. Morel. As the degallicised name reveals he had no time for the French, while Casement developed similar views on the English. Neither had the slightest sympathy for Belgium although Morel was never other than patriotically British. Both in effect adopted new countries. Their prejudices led eventually to flirtation, and in Casement's case alliance, with Germany. And both were in Pentonville prison during the First World War although Morel emerged alive to defeat Winston Churchill and become a Labour MP for Dundee in 1922. His six-month gaol term in 1917 on a trumped-up charge for transgressing wartime rules regarding correspondence with Switzerland broke his already weakened health.

Two weeks after his re-election in 1924 Morel died of angina before he had a chance to fulfil the promise that saw him tipped as a future Labour Foreign Secretary. Ramsay MacDonald had failed to so appoint him in his brief administration earlier that year to avoid offending France. EDM's largely successful struggles in the Congo Reform Association, and later in the Union of Democratic Control, against the secret diplomacy blamed for starting the First World War were both popular and ideological. However, they brought, like Casement's Irish and German efforts, their own bitter legacies. Each man was to die at the age of fifty-one.

In both cases a commendable humanitarianism when mixed with too much of that inevitable national prejudice to which everyone is prone – in their respective views England and France were intrinsically evil – created an explosive mix. Morel attacked the reparations which Germany was obliged to pay after the Versailles Treaty and linked them to the territory forcibly ceded to Poland, an act he described as "rape" and "an astounding act of robbery." In his haste to ascribe every conceivable crime to French militarism he only helped to advance German revanchism and British appeasement.

In 1920 his dangerously popular pamphlet *Horror on the Rhine* railed against the use of French colonial troops in the occupation of the Rhineland. The lack of evidence of ill-discipline was brushed aside with a certainty about the consequences of using "African troops who in their natural condition are polygamous." If "quartered without their womankind upon a European countryside" their stronger sex drives, designed (as Morel thought) to ensure reproduction in tropical conditions, would have inevitable results, be it ten or ten thousand such cases. Both he and Casement ascribed serious virility to African males although Morel's experience would have been less personal than Casement's.

This last campaign was Morel at his worst, appealing to racial fears, while in alliance with a German women's league financed by Krupps. His lurid prose described how "big stalwart men…living unnatural lives of restraint, their fierce passions hot within them, roam the countryside. Woe to the girl…home alone hoeing in the fields. Dark forms come leaping out from the shadows…" This he said was "the hell created west of the Rhine by French militarism."

If these two men were such clones in their humanitarianism and their hating, one wonders did the similarity extend into their sexual lives? The two men within a year of meeting, started using the chum names of Bulldog and Tiger for each other in their voluminous correspondence but there is no hint of shared sexuality. Morel was apparently an uxorious man with time only for his family, though not that much time. There were "various charges and innuendoes" in circulation about him, which he referred to in a plea in January 1924 to Ramsay MacDonald for a government post, but he did not outline them to the prime minister.

The only person (Sidney Parry aside) now known to have been homosexual that Casement, and in this case also Morel, associated with was Earl Beauchamp, President of the Congo Reform Association from 1904. The Earl was to become a Liberal Cabinet minister before his ultimate disgrace and hurried departure for the United States in 1931. It was of him that King George V famously said "I thought men like that shot themselves." However, his Beauchamp's increasingly open lifestyle would probably have repelled or frightened Casement. As Lord Warden of the Cinque Ports, he lived at Walmer Castle. One young man was recorded there playing tennis "nude to the waist and covered with pearls." His excuse (to Lady Aberconway) was "that he had the right type of skin to heal pearls." The same individual is credited with the famous description of action at the Battle of the Somme "Oh the noise and the people"; not an appetising milieu for The O'Scodge.

Morel initially chose not to visit Casement in prison. However, in a letter to Alice Stopford Green, of 25 May 1916, he made it plain that this failure was governed by political considerations and fear of the damage his opponents could do to him in relation to Germany, as opposed to any possible taint regarding Casement's sexual life.]

Wednesday 6th Jan. Back via Chester. Lloyd George in train – We talked much of it [**Congo presumably**] – & other things. Arr. 3.30 Home. Many letters. To F.O. at once by taxi. Saw Farnall & Villiers. Consular jurisdiction &c. * [**at side**] Dined Cafe Regina. Bad Headache. Home to bed.

Thursday 7. Janry. Forfeitt came up from Worcester & called. Long talk with him & then on with my writing till dark. Got another Congo Memo. done on the Administration of Justice in Abir Concession. Took it to F.O. & left it on F's desk – he not in. Then to Cui B.'s to dinner. Long Fiscal yarn. Met his brother in law Dick Hodgson of Yorks & so home as Mr Pepys hath it to sleep.

Friday 8th Jan. At Final Revise, I hope, of my Report, taking out the names of Wauters & Lejeune &c. Decided to go to Ireland again tomorrow. Left final Revise with Farnall at 5 p.m. & yarned about Ireland. Then to Sanfords & yarned Congo & home. Went to see Miss Heath at 44 Longridge Rd. not in. Dined at Café Regina The old clergyman of 15 Lowndes Square there. Home to bed.

[Daily entries terminate on 8 January 1904. There follows sixteen pages of notes comprising addresses, Congo information and various reminders. Book and Foreign Office details plus a sexualised extract from a French novel also appear. Another sequence of notes refers back to Casement's birthday, the cost of telegraphing cypher messages from Loanda and a memory of his ghastly bulldog John. They range from the practical to the sentimental, from the self-regarding to the self-pitying:]

Lokola of Mpelenge, 3 miles from Bonginda. Taken by Revd. W.D. Armstrong of C.B.M. at Bonginda 27 Augt 1903. Sir D. Plunkett, Science & Art Museum, Leinster House, Dublin. No. 57/173/03 to send List of Curios. Blanche Balharry, 436 Collins St., Melbourne, 25 Nov. 1903, recd 1 Jany. said. Hopes to sail by "Persic" on 22 Janry or if not then on 19th Feby. **[This is the Australian address for Blanche in Casement's address book in use from about 1899 to 1909. It also contains a series of temporary London addresses dated 1905 for Emily Balharry – a third Balharry sister who became a musician. Emily reappears mysteriously in this story in 1916. She died in England where in her old age she was sent money by her Australian relatives.[286]]**

Mrs G.H. St. Hill, 6 Princes Gardens, S.W.

Francois Léopold, Receveur des Postes & Telegraphes a Carimama, At Dahomey, Nov. 1903.

Revd. H. Nelson Ward, Newdigate Rectory, Surrey.

H.W. Dec. 29. from Paris. Palace Hotel, Caux, Suisse, above Montreux up by Rochers de Naye.

Lawson Forfeitt, Cowsden Hall, Upton-Snodsbury, Worcester. Jan. 1st '04,

F. Dormer Jordan, Writers London, York Typewriter Co. Ltd., 32 Holborn

Emily Balharry, 2 Jan. 04, 18 Norfolk Square, Lancaster Gate, W.

Eva Symons, 78 Range Road, Shanghai, Feb. 07 1903.

J.G. Whittindale head, Lime House, Bishop's Waltham, Hants. **[Dr J.G.**

Whittindale was a member of the Royal Colonial Institute.]
Mr. Hewitt-Helctum, **[Perhaps Brewitt Hilliard]** 5 Palace Mansions, Addison Bridge, Kensington, W. Dec 8/1903.
Captain H.E. Purey-Cust R.N., 15 King Edward Road, Rochester.
H.W. Balharry, c/o Ambler Farrell & Co., 46, 48. 50. 52 King St., Melbourne. Charlie owes him £33 which he writes about to me on 19 May/03. Sent his letter to Charlie on 16 Jan/04. **[More sibling debts – the Balharry creditor may be a brother of Charlie's first wife Minnie Balharry.]**

Sept 15 1903. "John" on "Henry Reed". "A thing of beauty is a joy for ever" Innocence personified. Sitting down evening among Love songs & water lilies & weaving with enormous paws the mystic darkness in to speech like Helen at Naples in "Sir Richard Calmady". To "repeat" a cypher group of five figures by W.A. Telegraph Coy at Loanda costs $5.120 – & to be refunded if the error is found to be due to a mistake of the cable staff.

My motto in Ellery's Birthday book at Ikau – when I wrote my name on 4 Sept – for 1st Sept Sept 1. 1903. **[Casement's 39th birthday]** *'I have fought a good fight, I have finished my course.'* 2. Tim. IV. 7. **[The next line from the book of Timothy, which he omitted, reads: "Henceforth there is laid up for me a crown of righteousness." That the biblical quotation stuck in Casement's mind may well be connected with Ramoan parish in Ballycastle. Its energetic 1840s Rector, Rev. John Monsell, is world famous for his hymn *Fight the Good Fight.*]**

His work was done, and like a warrior olden,
The hard fight o'er, he laid his armour down,
And passed all silent thro' the portal golden,
Where glows the Victor's (victim's) crown.
R.H. Baynes.

[Rev. Robert Baynes was a writer and editor of sacred poetry "designed to suggest thoughts of solace and of peace amid the trials and sorrows of our earthly life." His style matches that of Casement.]

"Mon frère Yves"

[Casement, next, laboriously inscribed a two page extract in French from the novel by Loti, *My Brother Yves,* which he recorded reading on board ship on 31 March, noting it then as "peculiar". The whole section is a detailed and romantic description of Yves, a tanned 24 year-old boy from Finisterre, with an athlete's body and carriage, whose smile had the sweetness of a

child, illuminating him like a ray of sunshine passing along the Breton cliffs. There is much more in similar vein, giving the impression of an author enticing readers with overwrought and sexually suggestive male imagery.]

State passage Upper Congo	Fcs
1st Class Pool to Lulanga	135
2nd Class (2 boys) 25 =	50
Compulsory ~~Cabin~~ Food	
12 fcs per day & Cabin 5 fcs	
for say 10 days	170
Excess baggage say	100
	Fcs: 455

The immutable rights and wrongs of life
La Verité sur la Civilization au Congo. 1903 Brussels. J Lebeque & Cie 46 Rue de la Madeleine.
Fox-Bourne's Civilization in Congoland.
E.D. Morel's "Affairs of West Africa"
also La Verité sur le Congo No. 2 Aout 1903. J Lebeque & Cie Bruxelles 46 Rue de la Madeleine Prix 25 cts.
Potier – was at Bolobo fully 3 years ago. He was followed by a young Belgian officer – name forgotten. It was either Potier or Catasani who sold Fataki the Gun. Many were sold for ivory. Léoni was the Officer here last year in Oct who arrested Fataki. He showed Howell his orders from the Govr General – which were that he was to get the cap-guns in by hook or by crook. If other means failed he was on every occasion to impose fines on the native Chiefs & make these fines payable only in guns. Mr H saw this order with his own eyes. Léoni showed it. He was a Lt. in the F. Publique.
Earl of Roseberry (Sir T.H. Sanderson) Confidential No. 13 of 5 Sept 1892.
Mr P's appointment to Congo £200 per annum Travelling Expenses.
Final paragraph points out as a temporary measure waiving of Consular Jurisdiction over Br. Subjects but to report on working of judicial system in Congo State.
Alfred Emmott M.P., Spring Bank, Oldham & 30 Ennismore Gardens, S.W.
Moor! 23 Carlisle Mansions, Victoria St. S.W. **[street mentioned in 15 December entry]**
Monsieur James Daniel Adeshend, Macon, Travaux publics, Brazzaville His father and Mother are both alive in Lagos & he writes to them. **[In Casement's address book, James is noted as an "old boy of mine at Loanda."[287] See also diary entry for 25 June 1903.]**
... Blom. Ban ~~ylmb~~ ilimby, Ubanghi; Rue Pasteur, Bois Colombes (Seine).

Raw Rubber at Pool. Product of Landolphia Tholloni Olitandra Gracilis **[plant]** – or raciness de Gaukele.
Bokakata, Boiyeka, Mampoko **[towns]** – Directors: La Lulanga 3 Stations many sentries & outposts.
J Hames **[??]**, 98 Westbourne Terrace, Hyde Park
John Hughes, Maryville, Blundell sands
Robert W. Jones, Holly Bank, Garston, L'pool
Mrs Clifford England, Rock Ferry, Cavendish Park, Cheshire.

7

Ulster 1904-14 and F.J. Bigger

Casement's report was published on 12 February 1904. Despite the disputes about identifying places and people, and disagreements over the policy London should now pursue, this was double-quick time. For the next months "Congo Casement" was the centre of public attention, and of Foreign Office machinations to effect a change in Leopold's method of exploitation and administration. The level of his Congo reign of terror and the subsequent loss of population, let alone his profiteering, has been a matter of historical and academic dispute ever since. For Casement there was no question but that he was a man of epic malevolence who must be done away with. "Leopold = Hades = Hell" he told E.D. Morel in 1906. When the King counter-attacked and started to impugn Casement's motives and evidence, the conflict took on a personal aspect and Leopold's overthrow became an even greater necessity.

All sorts of cross currents, however, swirled around the issue, such as the growing entente between England and France, and the perceived Protestant edge to the Liberal and radical campaigning on Congo reform. One writer, Henry Wack in 1905, suggested that the Protestant missionaries in predicting the end of the State were inciting insolence and subversion amongst the Congolese by offering an alternative power structure. Ireland intervened, sadly on the wrong side where Casement was concerned, when on 9 June 1904 in a House of Commons debate, the MP for South Armagh, John Campbell, "deprecated the Protestant attacks on Catholic Belgium."[288] In contrast, Alfred Emmott, a Liberal MP and a Casement friend, was critical of the Foreign Office for its failure to back him in public, especially with the further evidence against Leopold it possessed.

All the time, Casement's *bête noire,* Sir Constantine Phipps, at the British legation in Brussels, was doing what diplomats do. Just short of going native, he was explaining and justifying the King to whom he was accredited. Phipps incurred Casement's wrath to such an extent that he exploded to Morel, in 1906, writing "I shall not spare the cur. He is beneath contempt – but I'd like to lay that same contempt on with a good thick Irish blackthorn." Calling him "a thorough going blackleg", he added that Phipps might be willing to take a bribe instancing the "service of plate" he once got from the French government.[289]

That Casement was instrumental in setting up and funding the Congo Reform Association must have been reasonably well known and had it not been for his reawakening Irish interests, a career in Liberal politics could have been his. It, and Ireland, made a return to humble consular service uninspiring although the Foreign Office was faultless and patient in its provision of the long-heralded Lisbon posting. In July 1904, as Casement was preparing to depart for Portugal, Leopold appointed his own Commission of Inquiry without any British representative, despite, or perhaps because Casement's name had been suggested. And the issue went off the boil for several years so far as London was concerned while Leopold attempted to stave off his encircling enemies.

Lisbon was the jewel of the Atlantic consulates. The incumbent, Francis Cowper, was known to be in ill health and contemplating retirement. Casement's opening shot to Cowper as early as 1900 was that his "successor was quite to be envied, I think – whoever he may be."[290] In the myriad of letters Casement subsequently wrote to Cowper, he was, at first, haughty about the common mob of his fellow consuls who were feverishly positioning themselves in expectation of the imminent vacancy. Critical of those who were canvassing for the post and disdainful of any trying to exploit contacts in London, he was also careful to describe the awfulness of his job in the Congo where nothing thrived except disease, death and mosquitoes. "I positively loathe the sound of its name…I shall be glad not to go there again", he wrote. While from Tenerife, en route to the "curse of Central Africa" for his last and most important stay in March 1903, it had been "I go on to my local hell."[291]

By late 1902, he had, however, shifted his ground and was rather obviously cultivating Cowper: "I think I shall try for Lisbon and I shall quote you as a well-wisher for my chances. Am I really at liberty to say you contemplate soon going and asking for the reversion of your post?"[292] In the same letter Casement even offered to stand in for his friend to give him a break. Soon he was quite shamelessly canvassing inside the Foreign Office. With his intelligence work in the South African War and the high-level diplomatic activity that the Congo posting had come to involve, Casement had moved up several notches in the consular pecking order. By February 1903, before leaving London, he was telling Cowper he was sure he would get Lisbon. In August 1903, he heard that he had been definitely selected. However, by this time the key event that was to change his life, the official Congo investigation, had commenced and his heart's desire for Lisbon would begin to abate.

It was to be the juxtaposition of Casement's developing radical politics on the Congo issue and the linked re-opening of his interest in Ireland that brought about his squandering of this cosy billet granted to him by a grateful Foreign Office; that, and a concurrence of his two endemic health problems. Reading the torrent of notes, penned almost hourly to Cowper as Casement inched his way to Lisbon to replace him (changing his travel plans frequently and managing to approach Portugal from the south of Spain), one is left with the strong impression that he was willing incapacity along.

In perhaps the longest missive, writing on 27 July 1904, from what he described as a remarkably agreeable hotel in Algeciras in Spain, he graphically detailed his problems: "I got a bad attack of diarrhoea which has been followed by a very severe attack of my old African complaint – piles." He was living on milk and beaten eggs and had lost over a stone in weight. It was "dysentery with piles" prefaced by "two days of enforced constipation – no WCs on these filthy Spanish trains."[293]

On 26 August 1904 he was telling F.J. Bigger "I have been very ill for six weeks – and fear I must return home to get cured. I hope (D.V.) to sail for Liverpool on 30th to put myself in my own doctor's hands. My visit to Lisbon has been disastrous to my health."[294] To Gertrude, signing himself, Thine Scodgingly Scodge, it was, "I don't like Lisbon at all, and am not sorry to be leaving it."[295] Back in September, having hardly set foot in the city, he told Cowper what his doctors had decided, "I must undergo two operations. One for fistula which is not very grave and another for the appendix which has to be cut out! The attack I got abroad was appendicitis."[296] After a final desultory trip to Lisbon, Casement put in his resignation to London.

Francis Cowper's last words to Casement came in July 1913, from Sydenham, in London. Like his former colleague he was contemplating a retirement in South Africa and accurately he surmised, "I suppose we shall never meet again on this side of the unknown!" To Cowper, Lisbon had become "an impossible place since the Republic...I dislike it more and more every day." Somewhat wearily, alluding to the Putumayo, he added "What a lot of wrongs there are in this world which have to be righted!"[297]

Casement was obliged to go to Belfast in early 1905 where a second operation on a fistula *in ano* was to be performed. He preferred to keep it hidden, Maurice Joy, writing in 1916, remembering "how anxious he was that his illness should not be made known."[298] The operation, performed by Surgeon Kirk, cost £21.0.0.[299] However, it was in fact "two operations done together" as Casement "from bed and bandages"[300] told Morel in a letter dated 10 January 1904, a turn of the year mistake he often made. (It should have been dated 1905.) By 14 February the wound of the operation had not healed as "the surgeon had to perform two operations but they came off together so the one lying up, alone, was needed."[301] His appendix was not removed.

Ireland was in the ascendant during the next two years until 1906, yet Casement still managed to give about half his time to the Congo. With a prodigious effort that involved an industrial output of letters, he got the Congo Reform Association up and running, cutting through a thicket of conflicting interests and egos. Typically, he remained off platform even at the notable Holborn Town Hall meeting of 7 June 1905, which he had organised. This was largely due to the need to keep a fig leaf of cover as between consul and campaigner, a modicum of distinction his civil service employers had to be able to perceive. But he also had a morbid dislike of publicity, derived from a certain modesty and a desire not to be conspicuous. From 1913, once retired and speaking at nationalist meetings and march-pasts, he was obliged to overcome this fear. Indeed by May 1915 he was thrilled to be filmed or "kinematographed" as he put it, in Germany, writing enthusiastically to Joe McGarrity in Philadelphia, "I was 'kined' lately at the request of one of the U.S.A. war correspondents – a good fellow who wrote me up in an interview for Washington Herald and McClure's Syndicate, etc. etc. I expect the film is across now."[302]

Channel 4's 2003 series *The First World War* shows those unique moving pictures of Casement in episode 8. He is pictured writing a letter while seated at a desk, finding and trying to fill an envelope which irritates him. The scene is the same as in a photograph on the RTE website, signed and dated 17 April. It lasts some 35 seconds. John E Allen Inc. of New Jersey has the original with the extra 13 seconds of footage which also includes Casement smoking, badly, and with even the ghost of a smile. All 48 seconds can be found on YouTube.

There were thus three strings to the Casement bow until Irish separatism predominated: the Congo (and then the Putumayo) campaigns carried out largely in England, the cause of Ireland which flowered from 1904-06 and then again from 1912, and his ordinary consular work in Brazil during the politically lean years from 1906 until 1910. In those years, other than during periods of home leave, Ireland and the Congo had to be addressed from abroad through correspondence and exhortation, especially with Bulmer Hobson and Alice Stopford Green. He also kept in constant and detailed contact with E.D. Morel, the Congo Reform Association secretary. Casement's final return from Brazil in 1911 was to coincide with the five key years that dynamised and remoulded life on the island of Ireland for almost a century, changes for which he and the Belfast revolutionaries were in many ways most responsible.

In his German diary (written for publication, as did happen) he recalled the 1904-06 period, "I was purposely idle at the time, having practically retired from the Service over the Congo controversy. I had been so anxious to support Morel in his Congo fight – more with the Foreign Office almost than against Leopold – that I had asked to be seconded (without any pay) from Lisbon whither the Foreign Office had sent me after the publication of my Congo report in the beginning of 1904. Lisbon had not agreed with me – still less the Foreign Office method of conducting the controversy with Leopold, which consisted largely of running away from their own charges and offering apologies for my report. So in December 1904 I seconded myself and remained a freelance, devoting myself to Irish affairs, until in August 1906 Sir Edward Grey wrote to suggest my return to the consular service, when I went out first to Santos, then to Pará, and finally to Rio de Janeiro en route to Putumayo."[303]

The 1906 offer had developed out of a meeting with Lord (Edmond) Fitzmaurice, a brother of Lord Lansdowne, but a Liberal, Foreign Office minister. It had been set up as a response to Casement's concerns about not being offered a new post, and the remarks in a recent letter of Sir Eric Barrington when he admonished him by writing "It was most unfortunate that you should have so hastily resigned Lisbon, which is one of the nicest posts in the service."[304] Barrington had previously been Lansdowne's Private Secretary and had dissuaded Casement from a somewhat self-pitying threat to resign in March 1904. He was probably instrumental in the decision to honour Casement with a CMG, a decoration many officials would, and probably did, kill for. The arcane rules of the Most Distinguished Order of St Michael and St George – about the precise cloaks to be worn by a Companion, and when – made up a small pamphlet issued to Casement although he never opened the package containing the actual medal.[305] By mid-1906 he was without any income or reserves and obliged to borrow money from a missionary friend, T.H. Hoste. A job was therefore vital although he reckoned that with his unwelcome honour he was almost unemployable, being overqualified in class terms for anything otherwise suitable.

In a foreign affairs debate in the House of Lords, Fitzmaurice was fulsome in his praise of the consul, deplored the unjust attacks upon him and emphasised that he had been out of post since 1904 only for health reasons. He pointed out that the fruits of Casement's efforts were to be found in Leopold's new reforming decrees, proposed by the King's own Commission of Inquiry, one involving Casement's friend, Judge Nisco. An obligation to reappoint was thus created, and duly exploited with a parliamentary question about Casement's lack of a new posting, given his recovery in health. Fitzmaurice who had told his boss, the Foreign Secretary, that Casement (like himself) was "an Irishman – of a very good type – but a bit hot headed and impulsive"[306] was now instructing Barrington to hunt out a vacancy. Bilbao was first proposed, to be swiftly followed by a better paid offer of Santos in Brazil.

Thus Casement entered the second phase of his consular career, one that would bring him a further opportunity to use his meticulous talents of investigation on behalf of a benighted jungle people, one in greater peril than the Congolese.

Casement's active participation in Irish affairs and public life covered little

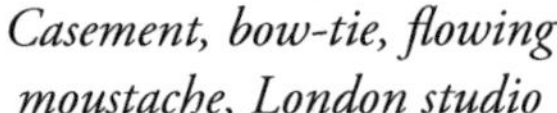

Casement, bow-tie, flowing moustache, London studio

"Yours affectionately Davie Casement". Falk Studio, 949 Broadway, New York

more than the dozen years between 1904 and 1916. Indeed for nearly two thirds of that period he was out of Ireland, but the effect he had on his country was to be profound. His two seminal years were 1904 and 1905 when he visited large parts of the island for the first time especially the Irish speaking areas of the west. As early as March 1904 he was involved in preparations for the first Glens *Feis* although he was, in many senses, a latecomer, following a path well-trodden by others.

By the end of the nineteenth century a retrogressive or anti-modernist cultural movement had been in existence for several decades and was gathering pace. It was born out of a rewriting of the legendary histories and fictions of Ireland. Part-antiquarian but part-popularising, this awakening of enthusiasm for Gaelic culture was led by Standish (James) O'Grady (1846-1928). The Cork-born son of a clergyman, he published a series of books graphically portraying the nobility and vigour of the Ulster, Fianna or Ossianic cycles, tales of Ireland in the first millennium. Starting with his 1878 *History of Ireland: The Heroic Period*, O'Grady prophetically wrote back into the popular imagination Finn MacCool, the Dé Danann, Medb and Cuchulain. No separatist, he saw the task of his Anglo-Irish class as providing leadership for the mass of Irish, although he foresaw that the cultural renewal was developing a dynamic which could well result in a separatist, military movement. That sense of a historic task survived amongst other Protestants like Casement, a patronising outlook yet in so far as the Anglo-Irish could hardly become Irish Irish through will, their only possible stance. That would continue until social change and events permitted a melding of the two ethnic groups as had happened with the Old English.

The next wave of writers brought about the inception of the Gaelic League (*Connradh na Gaeilge*) in 1893 to revive Irish as a living language. Its first President was Douglas Hyde. Eoin MacNeill was amongst the other founders of the League whose branches spread amongst the towns and cities of the island. By 1908 there were over six hundred groups, almost entirely in English-speaking Ireland. Prefigured in 1884 by the Gaelic Athletic Association, the two organisations provided unusual opportunities for the young of both sexes, mostly from the new lower-middle class, to meet and to become politicised. The GAA can also be credited with turning the Irish county into a unit of local patriotism.

In Belfast, the key event for bringing politics into the Gaelic revival was the centenary of the United Irish rebellion and the consequent 1898 celebrations. Alice Milligan, born in 1866, was the organising secretary in Ulster. She and Ethna Carbery (a cousin of Joseph Campbell) founded first *The Northern Patriot* and then, in 1896, the influential, separatist magazine *Shan Van Vocht* (The Poor Old Woman, after Ireland's 1798 Marseillaise – *Yes, Ireland shall be free/ From the centre to the sea.*) They also published the earliest writings of James Connolly. Milligan, from a well-to-do Methodist family, was the daughter of an Omagh antiquarian. Her initial mission was rallying the few who had not lost faith after Parnell's death. Later she turned to radicalising with a *Life of Wolfe Tone* and her play *The Last Feast of the Fianna*, staged in 1900 by the forerunner of the Abbey Theatre. It was credited with being the first play to dramatise Celtic legend for an Irish audience while the Tone biography created Tyrone's primary, indeed only revolutionary of the period Dr Patrick McCartan. He called her book "The first real foundation I got for my national faith."[307]

The inscription on Alice Milligan's gravestone in Drumagh churchyard in Tyrone reads poignantly "She loved no other land but Ireland." By the time of her death in 1953 she was a forlorn remnant trapped unhappily amongst Unionists. Her most famous poem, evoking a childhood memory, symbolises the conversion to nationalism of many from Unionist backgrounds, and could as easily apply to Captain Casement's children:

Then the wind-shaken pane
Sounded like drumming;
'Oh!' they cried, 'tuck us in,
The Fenians are coming!'

But one little rebel there,
Watching all with laughter,
Thought, 'When the Fenians come
I'll rise and go after!'

Meanwhile the re-genesis of the language, aided by Church of Ireland clergymen, was quietly under way in Catholic Belfast and amongst the women of Antrim's big houses. Yet there were competing historical and cultural outlets, embodied in organisations like the Belfast Naturalists' Field Club, in which could be found Casement's great friend Major Robert Berry (1870-1947). It emerged from and appealed to the Protestant community while its equivalents could be found in many other British cities of this era. A number of key individuals like the antiquarian Francis Joseph Bigger, for seventeen years editor of the *Ulster Journal of Archaeology*, Herbert Hughes the musician, and Mrs Mary Hutton straddled both wings. The Field Club's Irish language classes actually predated the Gaelic League.

Casement's interest in Ireland had been rekindled by a series of chance encounters and connected individuals although it was a path he was plainly going to take one way or another. He was never susceptible to joining one of the Home Rule parties, hinged as they were to Westminster. It was his experience that every Irish MP "I meet there gives me qualms. They have lost their souls and are merely club members in one of the great illusions of the modern world."[308] In 1904 he fell in with an established network both in Antrim and in Belfast, the city, as he later pointed out, of his father and grandfather, although not of himself.

He came in 1904 to Irish Ireland obliquely. Having met Alice Stopford Green through the Africa movement germinated by her friend Mary Kingsley (whom Casement had actually been introduced to in Nigeria in 1902) it was but a single step to his destiny. Green was the wife of an English historian and the daughter of a Co. Meath Archdeacon. An early widow, she herself became a distinguished mediaeval historian, concentrating later on Ireland. In 1908 she published her controversial book dealing with the "English extirpation of Irish Society" (from 1200 to 1600), *The Making of Ireland and its Undoing*, and then in 1911, *Irish Nationality* which had an even greater impact. That was the book which had Casement take on the role of a one-man publicity department and distributor, according to the 1911 Cash Ledger.

Green's Irish interests had, in turn, been reawakened by an unrequited relationship with John Francis Taylor QC, a "brilliant failure" of an Irish barrister. Described by Yeats as the "greatest orator he had ever heard", Taylor's views can be heard tumbling down through the decades. His nationalism "compounded of a real love of Ireland and a vehement distaste for what remained of the

Mary Kingsley, Casement's bulldog Patsie, Lady MacDonald, Sir Claude MacDonald and towering Casement, Nigeria 1895 (NYPL)

Protestant ascendancy and Unionist Ulster" was not of the inclusive variety: "There is nowhere in Ulster", he declared, where "a gleam of national kindness is to be seen [instead there is] gloom, hate and bigotry... Wherever the English have come they blended with the people...but these unthinkable Scotch, why indeed were they kept upon the planet?"[309] On the ethnic question, Casement was honest enough to write to Mrs Green "We two implacable Celts (or whatever we are)", knowing full well they weren't.[310]

Casement credits a Scots Gallic enthusiast, Miss Louise Farquharson, from a big estate in Ballater, Aberdeenshire with providing his entrée to the Gaelic League itself. Although they met in London she was a regular visitor to Ireland, in particular to Armagh, and a frequent correspondent until an abrupt cessation. This suggests a parting of the ways or a failure of reciprocation as her letters were quite intimate. She also was a great hater of Irish Unionists, calling them "garrison people", despite having been a lady-in-waiting to Lady Cadogan in Dublin Castle. She had apparently not been a year in Ireland before perceiving the need for Home Rule.[311]

In Casement's correspondence and up to the very end of his 1903 diary, there is no mention of any of the Belfast or Irish characters who in a few short months were to take over and populate the rest of his life. 1904 in Ireland was to be a dramatic year which he had had to fit in and around the beginning and end of his Lisbon appointment. Recalling that year he later wrote, "I got back to Ireland early in 1904 – got to find the Gaelic League at once and all the old hopes and longings of my boyhood sprang to life again."[312]

Once he had met Bigger, he had not only a home in Belfast but access to a stream of young, energetic, politically involved individuals who, like himself came and went to Bigger's house. In 1916, Maurice Joy recalled Casement "back in 1905" as looking like "a buccaneer of the Spanish Main…standing on the steps of Ardrigh that quiet sunny morning when I saw him first. He had a cigarette in his hand and the tall dark figure was relaxed…a subtle quality not always certainly distinguishable from dilettantism."[313] Before 1916 was out, Joy, who was in New York, had collected together a memorial volume to the Fenian dead of the Easter Rising and was able to offer an unusually discerning (pre-cultic) view of Casement. He described him as one who "spoke in low musical, kindly tones without a trace of arrogance, though with a great deal of self consciousness." He added "I felt sure that Casement hated the compromise of ordinary politics too much ever to get the best out of them and therein would be his weakness as a national leader…I greatly doubt if any man's opinions but his own ever influenced his major actions." Casement, he concluded was "not easily amenable to discipline he had to work in his own way…impatient of mediocrity, he therefore could not nor did not conceal his contempt for his superiors."[314]

The gathering strands of the Irish movement in Ulster can be seen at their best in the first Glens *Feis*, of June 1904, in Glenariff at Waterfoot. For an opening event it was magnificently well organised and visually memorable, down to the pipers' costumes based on Armenian folk dress designed by F.J. Bigger. Sectarian differences were presently invisible as the upper and intellectual classes of the north combined with the coastal Catholics of Antrim in a celebration of Irish life, locality and culture.

The names in the *Feis* programme, illustrated by John Campbell, are a roll call of Casement's people.[315] Ada McNeill of Cushendun House was the secretary, F.J. Bigger, one of the treasurers. "Consul Casement" represented Glenshesk on the Committee of the Nine Glens, Rose Young (Glencorp), John Clarke (Glenarm) and Frances Riddell (Glentaise). Prizes were presented by Sir Horace Plunkett. Those donating included Mary Hutton (for the best written copy in Gaelic of the Lord's Prayer), 'Moira O'Neill' (Nesta Skrine, née Higginson, of Cushendall, author of *Ballytearim*, and mother of the novelist Molly Keane), Monsignor O'Laverty (for best oral knowledge of history of the Glens), Lord McNaghten (best telling of a story in Irish), Major Berry, and Alec Wilson (best hank of Irish yarn).

Some who gave prizes were not known for being nationally minded: Ronald

McNeill (for best spinner of lint at the wheel), John Andrews (best baker of a griddle of soda bread), R.P. Woodside, and Francis Turnly (best set of toys or models). Stephen Gwynn and John (Eoin) MacNeill adjudicated on the literary and Gaelic competitions.

The consul and his sister, "Mrs Newman", also presented prizes, two of his being for the best dressed boy and girl in Irish materials made up in the Glens, and another for decorative work in Irish wood. Tom Casement, back from South Africa to get his knees operated on in Belfast, was also present. Ada McNeill summed it up, writing of that romantic time "A spirit was awakening in Ireland. Even in the sleepy old Glens, people turned out to meetings and worked on committees. We tried to revive Irish dancing, and Roger took his place in the fourhanded reels. He strode about the roads, hatless, encouraging and working up interest in the movement."[316]

John Clarke whose pen name was *Benmore*, in a memoir of Casement at the 1904 *Feis* wrote of "a man of splendid physique, well-built, towering conspicuously above many of average height, keen grey eyes, a beard raven-black and pointed, with curls of loosely arranged black hair covering the brains of a man of genius." Aside from the standard devotional language which tells of Casement's potential for messianic rank, it is the sense of his height being so noteworthy that stands out. He was 6' 2" which was remarkably tall for the period, a fact that can be attested from the photographs of Casement's guards in 1916 and the soldiers of the Irish Brigade (and the British Army), so many of whom were diminutive – bantams to a peacock.

By October 1904, Casement was telling Cowper in Lisbon, "You see I use Irish postcards...the Language movement is steadily progressing and I am in the thick of it – God bless It!" Another postcard from Lisbon, this time to Gertrude, depicted the old Irish Parliament, on which Casement inscribed, "It will meet again, please God."[317]

The two most political of these young Irelanders were Denis McCullough and Bulmer Hobson who, between them, can be credited with the revival of the Irish Republican Brotherhood, an oath-bound conspiratorial organisation; the rebirth of the *Fianna*; the creation in 1913 of the Irish Volunteers; and the commissioning of arms for the Volunteers – out of which came the IRA. McCullough (*Donnchadha Mac Con Uladh*) became involved before 1900 with the Gaelic League and was one of the founders of the first hurling club in Belfast which led to the foundation of the Co. Antrim Board of the GAA. He was inducted into the largely moribund IRB by his Fenian father, a Belfast publican, after 1903. At Donnelly's pub on Belfast's Falls Road, McCullough swore allegiance for life to the Irish Republic "now virtually established." Recruiting like-minded young men, he quickly brought the IRB back into

RIC men and unhappy looking Belfast Republican

Bulmer Hobson, Herbert Hughes and another friend on Donegal folkloric hunt

business. Indeed this was done partly by excluding veterans like his father and other older men who were not always sober or disciplined. John Devoy himself an actual Fenian, was a much earlier organiser in the IRB, his *Clan na Gael* being its American sister operation.

Co-opted to the IRB's Supreme Council in 1908, McCullough was by the next year the senior Ulster representative. After a similar process of elimination in Dublin, he became, in 1915, IRB President chairing the meeting which decided on the rising. His political activity went alongside maintaining and developing an instrument making and retail music business in Belfast's Howard Street, generated from his original trade as a piano tuner. Frank Bigger encouraged its growth with orders for bagpipes for his boy bands. In time, after the move to Dublin, this became McCullough Pigott of Suffolk Street and marked the beginning of a highly successful and influential Free State business career. The most notable of the innovative native industries in which McCullough distinguished himself (inspired by Michael Collins) was to be his formation of the New Ireland Assurance Company. A director of Clondalkin Paper Mills, he also had a role in the Army School of Music, and the Gate Theatre. While in America as Special Commissioner for the Free State (leaving his wife in charge of the music business) his new premises in Dawson Street were entirely destroyed by an IRA land mine as a reprisal.

Bulmer Hobson, born in 1883 the same year as McCullough, was a pre-teens subscriber to *Shan Van Vocht*, a teenage member of the GAA, establishing the first hurling team in Ulster, and of the Gaelic League's *Tir na nOg* branch. A schoolboy debater and proselytiser, he founded the young person's Protestant National Society which developed into the Ulster Literary Theatre. His first go at creating the *Fianna Eireann* came in 1902 when, hoping to interest working-class youths in Irish-Ireland culture and politics, he drew interested GAA lads into meetings in the Catholic Boys' hall on the Falls Road.

As northern Protestant males were few and far between in the national movement, it is enlightening to try and look for the origins of Hobson's outlook, and for the reasons why so few of his contemporaries took the same path. The Hobsons were Quakers although Bulmer later resigned on principle soon after the Howth gunrunning. His son Declan Hobson,[318] has told of the difficulties his Catholic mother faced in getting a dispensation from Rome for her marriage. Bulmer's father was from Monasterevin in Co. Kildare and said to be a Gladstonian Home Ruler in politics while his mother was radical and English. In 1911 she is to be found on a suffragist procession in London but, as noted, was long involved in Belfast cultural activities. She gave a lecture (entitled *Some Ulster Souterrains*) as the Field Club's representative in 1901 at the British Association's annual meeting in Leicester. With Alice Milligan, she organised the Irishwomen's Association whose home reading circle met in the boy Bulmer's house, presumably within earshot. In many ways he had a background typical of middle class members of the Communist Party in Britain around the 1930s.

Casement must have known Bulmer's father, as in a 1907 letter from Lucan in Co. Dublin, he wrote "I dreamed of your father" adding a familiar refrain "There's mighty little nationality in these parts."[319] Effectively a journalist, although an apprentice printer from 1901-03, Hobson was not noticeably religious, not married until he was over thirty and definitely not involved in the great commercial enterprises of Ulster.

According to Alice Stopford Green, Hobson was not particularly effective, as she told Casement in 1914, perhaps unfairly: "His lack of training shows itself. His Volunteer office is wholly unorganised."[320] However, until Redmond's intervention in the Irish Volunteers, he was always at the cutting edge – one of the implacable. Compromising then, and thereafter marginalised, he remained a radical to the end of his life. He, Patrick McCartan, Dinny McCullough, and to a lesser degree (in America), Joseph Campbell, and Padraic Colum maintained after 1923 a political position between the two civil war factions. To early Ulster revolutionaries, a settled and increasingly Romanised Free State was not quite so appealing, most especially alongside a partitioned Ireland. George Gavan Duffy too despaired of the illegalities to which the factions descended after independence, and stayed aloof from politics thereafter.

The atmosphere in which most Ulster Protestants were cultured was not one to which Hobson or Casement could warm. The vast majority of those people had a portmanteau culture, largely British, a little Irish, and where it was local, it might be Scottish, Orange, Presbyterian or just parochial; also anti-Catholic, for they were mostly defined by what they were not. Their memorable successes were not in art or writing but in enterprise, invention, manufacturing and commerce, with people like Lord Pirrie, Lord Kelvin, John Boyd Dunlop and Harry Ferguson. Nonetheless the culturally minded sons and daughters of Ulster's Protestants in every generation have with monotonous regularity either departed or followed the path set by Hobson and Milligan into radical nationalism.

In 1904, McCullough was responsible for swearing his friend Bulmer Hobson into the IRB: both 21 year-olds were "handsome, gay, eloquent and with a frightening simplicity, impatient to get on with the work of overthrowing English rule in Ireland."[321] Between them they organised a revolution. The pair started the Dungannon Clubs, an open political organisation of young men and boys whose name, suggested by Padraic Colum, evoked the Volunteers of Grattan's Parliament, a movement first convened in that Co. Tyrone town.

The spirit of those 1782 Volunteers had been a significant precursor to the development of the United Irishmen. The separatist Dungannon Clubs, with membership in both communities, involving "young men at a white heat of enthusiasm" had as a constitutional objective the building up of Ireland intellectually, materially and "by the popularisation of physical culture and training and the spread of our national games." Clubs were formed as far away as Dublin and even London,[322] their first serious propaganda campaign being opposition to recruiting for the British armed forces, one in which Casement eagerly participated as a (resting) British consul and thus at a certain risk to his future employment.

Hobson had some of the markings of a Lenin although never susceptible to class politics. In Belfast he did experience the disputation between nationalists and socialists, and like James Connolly, debated with the municipal Labour leader William Walker, being denounced as a "rent collector" for his trouble. The Dungannon Clubs intervened in the 1907 Belfast labour troubles adding sectarian fuel to a combustible conflict. Later, Connolly's whole political outlook was to come under the influence of Casement. His daughters who were more openly nationalist than he was, often visited Ardrigh and met Casement, but it was the consul's foreign policy writings rather than personal contact that went to create the final Connolly outlook so visible from the outbreak of war.

Some illustration of what Bulmer Hobson was about can be gauged from reports going from the Police Crime Department (Special Branch) to the HQ RIC Office in Dublin Castle: on 18 April 1905, he was recorded addressing a meeting organised by R.C. (Dick) Bonner at Tirlane Mountain, Magherafelt in Co. Derry. The observer calling it "a violent speech" noted him declaring "What was desired was the severance of all connection with England." A few days earlier on 13 April, "Denis McCullagh" (as spelt) was noted presiding over a similar event.[323]

On 11 July 1905 an informant to the Dublin Metropolitan Police is to be found telling of anti-recruiting literature being "printed and published by F. Bigger of Ard Righ, Antrim Road, Belfast and being issued to Gaelic Clubs etc. at ½d per copy." The Belfast police, however, found it "difficult to probe the matter to the bottom owing to Mr Bigger's position."[324] The text of this Dungannon Club pamphlet was written by Alice Stopford Green and Hobson but the involvement of Casement is also detectable. Entitled *Irishmen and the English Army*, its widespread distribution and contents caused serious concern to the authorities. On 5 June, the Glenarm police reported finding seditious anti-recruiting material stating "any Irishman joining English Army, Navy or Police force takes his stand in the camp of the Garrison. He is a traitor to his country and an enemy to his people." Two prosecutions at least were launched by the RIC, one in Belfast and another earlier in Ballycastle where Stephen Clarke was charged with causing "to be published a scandalous and seditious libel." In August 1905, John Butler of 112 Divis Street, who ran a stationers shop appeared before the Belfast Assizes also on sedition charges.[325]

The pamphlet dealt at length with the events of the South African War, the part played by Irish troops, and the legality of militia regiments being sent to serve overseas. It read in part "Some men were known to say that they could not see why the Boers should lose their land or that they should be used in inflicting such hardships on the farmers." Declaring that the Royal Dublin Fusiliers had had 600 out of its 800 men killed (Hobson's statistic), it charged that by its recruiting of Irishmen ("second to none in the world" as soldiers) England "leaves this land weak and defenceless."

Stephen Clarke, who had a cottage at Murlough Bay, was ultimately acquitted of the charge but not before Casement had taken the remarkable (and fruitless) risk of intervening with Sir Charles Mathews, the Director of Public Prosecutions. A decade later, in prison, he recalled telling Mathews that although he had not written the item in question he "had got the leaflet printed."[326] Mathews was still the Director in 1916, on which occasion, perhaps armed with the 1905 memory, he undoubtedly got his man. Bigger had briefed an "Orange" barrister for Clarke who ensured a mixed jury and thus a split verdict.

Another police report, indicating how close a watch was being kept on Bulmer Hobson, although to no immediate purpose, told of rifle practice being observed at a house rented by him and James McKittrick on Ballygomartin Road at the top of Belfast's Shankill Road. In February 1906 in Glasgow, Hobson was at his most martial (according to Dublin Castle's intelligence sources)[327] when he "advised every Irishman to have a rifle in his house and to be proficient in its use."

In 1907 the Dungannon Clubs merged with Arthur Griffith's *Cumann na nGaedheal* to create the Sinn Féin League. The next year Bulmer and Seán MacDermott, who along with Patrick McCartan were the most prominent of the new recruits and organisers in the Clubs, moved to Dublin to crank up the propaganda machine from the capital. Within a few years Denis McCullough would, in the RIC's eyes, be "one of the most dangerous suspects in Ireland."[328] McCartan's assessment of MacDermott was cutting: "bright and energetic but mentally superficial. He had not an idea in his head when Hobson took him up and directed his 'education'." Yet, tellingly, of his own mentor it was, "I loved Casement almost to the point of adoration."[329]

Writing to Gertrude on 5 September 1898, six years before meeting any of his future Irish Ireland comrades, Casement announced "Belfast no doubt thinks the North Down election or the Revd. McQuinzy Drivelbag's last Orange harangue of far greater interest and importance than the breaking up of empires or the repartition of continents. Belfast is really I think a very stupid ill-bred town and although I have not (fortunately) been in it for seven years until this visit I hope it may be fourteen before I come to it again. I've been cheering all through breakfast over the London news."[330] That news was the capture of Omdurman and the Khalifa's defeat.

With views like these, Casement still lacked the necessary animus against the British Empire to be an Irish separatist. However, his anti-Unionist position was set in stone. Later he explained how his radicalism had developed with one issue interacting on the other, "It was only because I was an Irishman that I could understand fully I think their whole scheme of wrongdoing at work in the Congo."[331]

His attitude to Belfast was mirrored by Paul Henry, perhaps its greatest artist. Repeating the lament of the Ulster Protestant middle classes he wrote "I had been brought up in the most narrow and arid religious atmosphere, and the longing to get away from home, and its atmosphere was stifling me. I had to smoke in secret, drink in secret, and think in secret. These were the three most unpardonable sins. There was a fourth more deadly still, though it was never mentioned."[332] On 22 September 1912, writing to Gertrude from his rooms at 105 Antrim Road, Casement was echoing Paul Henry's remarks, "The church parade has begun past my windows. Heavens! How appalling they look with their grim Ulster Hall faces."[333]

This cry against their own people has seized Protestant intellectuals from that day to this. It has detached them from their own community driving them to the other. Unsoftened by their absent intellectuals, the Orange element thus retains the necessary intransigence to survive the verbal and other assaults of Irish nationalism, duly joined each generation by a further batch of guilty or aggrieved Protestants. Thus is created the Catch 22 of Irish and Ulster politics.

Casement experienced a number of reinforcing episodes with fellow North Antrim Protestants. Kathleen Boyd, the last remnant of Ballycastle's premier industrial family, responded unfavourably to his request for a donation to an Irish language cause. From the Manor House, she wrote "In the first place I am not an Irishwoman and secondly I do not sympathise with the study of Irish literature and the Celtic language. I fail to see of what possible use either of these can be, either to the country or individuals...whereas Irish is not of any use commercially. I am very sorry to be obliged to refuse to subscribe but I have already so many calls upon me that I am afraid I cannot add to their number."[334] Of course she was an Irishwoman, by birth, but she declined to accept that that was her nationality.

Further disillusion occurred when Ulster hardhearts failed to subscribe sufficiently large amounts to a charity appeal Casement chose to make in 1906 on behalf of a local acquaintance, Mrs Mary Dunlop Williams. She was in unspecified difficulties. The fund only reached £8.10.0. (Mya Casement gave the ten shillings.) Ascribing its relative failure to an ethnic defect, Casement raged "Some of the north of Ireland hearts are not Irish at all and do not please to compound those basaltic compositions, imported from Scotland or God knows where, with anything native to the Irish temperament. It makes me angry to hear those people presuming to call themselves Irish – when they have no drop of Irish blood in their hearts."[335] In this vein, ironically, he was sharing and encouraging Mrs Boyd's self-exclusion from Ireland.

The subject of the collection, after emigrating to California, did not forget his altruism. Hers was almost the first letter to reach Casement in gaol in 1916. Yet she was plainly something of a sponger, money troubles plaguing her to the point that she even denied receiving a cheque from Casement in 1912. He then asked the consul in San Francisco to investigate, only to be told it had been endorsed and cashed by her. The consul advised that "Mrs Williams from time to time received a great deal of aid from the Benevolent Society and also from other societies in San Diego. She also receives monthly help from the county. Her son seems quite able to support her if he would."[336] Perhaps some of the Ulster hardhearts had good reason to keep their purses closed.

Again, in 1906, when the Glens landlord Francis Turnly, who had provided a £1 prize for the 1904 *Feis*, tried two years on to stop one of his tenants lending a field for the event, Casement went into rage mode "God's wrath upon all 'Loyalists', the brand is always the same", adding, "'Loyalists' are the devil and it is enough to make anyone who is decent and kind-hearted declare himself a Fenian just to differentiate himself from them."[337]

Yet the year before in Dublin, awaiting the opening of the Oireachtas, Casement had been in more constructive mood. Having been to see "Lord Edward's coffin yesterday in the vault of St Werburgh's Church" he mused to Bulmer Hobson about a strategy: "We should found the nucleus of a national government...have a Cabinet, a Prime Minister, a Secretary of Foreign Affairs... They could in five years, or more, build up an Irish State and create a confident, reliant national mind in the country."[338] In 1907 he was suggesting an Irish Olympic team, after the formation of an organising committee of "Unionists and Nationalists, Sinn Féin and Loyalists."[339]

In June of that year, writing to Alice Stopford Green's brother Edward, Casement tried to explain his feelings about Ireland, evoking the heightened sense of place that animated him. It was, he said "Something more than race; more than nationality; more than any reason I have yet seen put forward. There is something in the soil, in the air, in the inherited mind of a country that is as real, nay more real than the rocks, the hills and the streams. No historian defines this thing, yet it exists in all lands."[340]

Sir Shane Leslie's considered view was that "English or Ulster Protestants who become Irish nationalists either remain half-baked constitutionalists who shed their teeth as well as their tears; or they become more fanatically Irish than the Irish. In fact, the gentle Gael through the centuries has learnt from English and Protestants how to hate, resist and extirpate the English."[341] Casement was meant to feature in Leslie's second category along with Tone and Mitchel, although Leslie too, had come under the influence of Bigger and the University of Ardrigh, standing as a Home Rule candidate for Derry City in 1910. In the *Irish Times,* on 23 April 1956, he was to advise, revealingly, "Above all let us distinguish between a born and a practising homosexual – Christian charity and law here intervene." Leslie later likened Casement to General Gordon, deciding that both acquired "ascendancy over the native by detachment from wealth and women."

Despite all this, there were moments when Casement could not stop returning to his roots. In 1909 for example, he was telling Bulmer after a brush with the Catholic Bishops, "Freedom to Ireland can come only through Irish Protestants." Condemning many Irish nationalists as "Cawtholic and shoneen", he also declared, "It would be a very excellent thing if Ireland could relapse into brilliant Heathenism for a year or two. When she got converted again the Bishops would all be gone...It is a hopeless thing to think you can free Ireland when she licks her chains."[342]

There was even a momentary sympathy for a certain minority outlook in Republicanism which saw the Roman Catholic Church as damaging to the cause of Irish freedom – more so than the Church of Ireland for which a few actually left. Writing in 1907, Casement lamented "If only they had taught the people to fight for Ireland as for their faith, both would have been saved." The Church of St Patrick "has done more to injure Ireland than the foreign Church could ever accomplish."[343] This was not a heartfelt view as his antagonism to Anglicanism was deep, although Ireland, for him, would always be a greater religion than Rome – until the last day.

A couple of examples tell of Casement's impatience with the Irish Parliamentary Party under Redmond and of his lack of faith in Sinn Féin's Arthur Griffith, and of his coherent ideas for a future Ireland: On 10 August 1905[344] he wrote to Bulmer Hobson saying, "If the "Party" were not so hopelessly in the quagmire of Parliamentary waiting – waiting but not doing – expecting something to "turn up", now from the Liberals, now from the Conservatives, – it might be possible to form a national executive within and from them. They should have a Cabinet – a Prime Minister, a Secretary of Foreign Affairs, of Agriculture, of Home (& Police) of Education, and so through the list. Those men should make a special study of the departments of Irish life they were to overlook. If, instead of wasting their time and energies at Westminster they met in session and had their office in Ireland, they could do more in five years to build up an Irish State, and to create a confident reliant national mind in the country than by all the Parliamentary "successes" they will achieve in 50 years."

And on 7 September 1909,[345] again to Hobson, it was, "I presume the Daily "Sinn Fein" is out. Is it any use? I cannot believe it can be. Griffith has not been able for over 2 years now to make that tiny weekly Sinn Fein of any weight or real feeling – I often wondered which was the poorest production "Sinn Fein" or "The Peasant" – and it certainly does seem as if our claim to possess any national character was indeed a poor one with such solitary exponents of it. I sent Griffith £50 for shares in the Daily Sinn Fein but I fear it is money thrown away – only I had promised it long ago – and wished for <u>his</u> sake I could have made it more. I have never felt confidence in him as a leader I may tell you, but I did not like to say a word to anyone that would weaken their faith. The meeting I attended in Dublin in December last convinced me of his narrowness – and that we cannot stand in our far too narrow Ireland."

Casement's attitude to Ulster veered from the apprehensive to the severe. One year it was, "I go to Armagh for 12th July to an Orange gathering! I shall wear a green tie and probably be stoned to death."[346] Another, this time 1912, he was declaring to Gertrude, "Sometimes the only thing to bring a boy to his senses is to hide him, and I think Ulster wants a sound hiding at the hands of her that owns her – Ireland's hands. Failing that I pray for the Germans and their coming. A Protestant to teach these Protestants their place in Irish life is what is needed."[347]

In a draft written in Cushendall on 7 November 1913, Casement was blaming the Unionists for being misled by Englishmen and Tories, "The 'Ulster' resistance to Home Rule is a combination of the sincerity of deep ignorance, – that of the rank and file; of deeper bigotry – that of the 'Churches'; and of political immorality – that of the politicians and agitator elements such as the Carson's, Smiths etc etc."[348] Four days later, on 11 November 1913, it was, "If only that infernal British Providence would withdraw from Ireland and leave us each face to face we'd soon settle the gang of terrorists who rule 'Ulster'."[349] This was simple bravado as the Catholics of Ulster were neither mobilised, nor of his opinion. Belfast, in particular, did not even vote Sinn Féin in serious numbers until the 1980s, seventy years on. De Valera failed to win the West Belfast seat by 8,488 to 3,245 votes when standing in 1918 against the city's Home Rule leader, Joe Devlin, another charismatic bachelor who could charm women off trees, and who, after F.J. Bigger's death, bought his house, Ardrigh. Ulster Protestants were, and remained, overwhelmingly Unionist even if a few thousand individuals were Home Rulers, or in a handful of cases, separatists.

It was a common view that Ulster was both bluffing and misled by others. Casement normally believed both and relied on those views as a sufficient justification for ignoring the Unionists. On a few occasions, however, another more realistic outlook could be heard. Also in 1913, he offered Alice Stopford Green a more sophisticated, if premature, opinion, "Two factors are against Ulster – time and the tendency of the British people to regard Home Rule as inevitable and as a good thing imperially."[350] By 22 June 1914, reality about the Home Rule Bill and Ulster's self-exclusion was beginning to stare Casement in the face. He told Gertrude "I think Carson will win. That has been my view all along."[351] The effect of this, actually quite recent belief, was to strengthen his separatist enthusiasm and rage against England, rather than the opposite.

If nationalism is a positive force it is also, and by definition, negative in that it defines itself against another nation. In Casement's view Ireland had two antagonists: England and Scotland. One was an imperial power and the other was represented by a colonising people. Britain and the British were not then phrasings in significant usage; it was always England and the English. An early private expression of Casement's view comes from an unguarded jotting of around 1900 in his address book, "England just struck me with enmity the minute I saw the face of them."[352] This suggests an early juvenile antipathy, perhaps born of childhood experiences in the south of England.

Casement's Anglophobia – for it does reach near pathological proportions – was the major and recurring theme of his last twelve years. This is not to say that, like paranoia, it cannot be justified, and certainly explained by a history, over many centuries, of conquest and domination. But it did not allow for the nuances of a millennium of shared experiences on the island not to mention the waves of settlement which included the old English of the Norman era who assimilated, and the newer English of the Cromwellian and Plantation period who did not. There is no large European country that did not either absorb neighbouring territories or insist on a key role in the affairs of contiguous countries. Economic imperatives alone will make this happen.

But Casement who accepted and understood the value of trade in Africa was not one to give credence to such market forces in the north of Ireland. He had therefore much the same brand of certainty that enabled Britain (England) to gain an empire in the nineteenth century; except that his certainty was now in opposition to Britain's empire – in particular to the colonising and control of Ireland. "Irishmen are to her, cattle either to feed her workers in one shape or when they are not castrated to fight her battles", he would declare.[353]

Writing to the Home Rule MP, Hugh Law, about the Congo, Casement ingratiatingly sought his support "in the light of our past history and of all that the native Irish suffered at the hands of exploiters and exterminators."[354] Invoking these memories was entirely genuine on his part but the words exemplify his central historical fault in that his separatist activity was directed to the unwriting of history, the return to a golden age before the English came, at least before the Tudors ruled, possibly before the Normans, and perhaps even before the Vikings landed.

Given his affection for the Kaiser ("Wilhelm will yet do great things in Europe") it cannot be argued that Casement was intrinsically anti-imperialist, rather he was anti-England and pro-Irish. In a letter of 17 January 1914 to the *Freeman's Journal* he insisted, "As a matter of fact the people of Alsace-Lorraine today enjoy infinitely greater public liberties within the German Empire than we are ever more likely to possess within the British Empire", adding praise for "the extraordinary liberty German imperialism accords a lately conquered territory."[355] He was a progressive, only marginally different from those of the same outlook in England, except that in Ireland such strength of politics made one a revolutionary.

What is difficult to accept or understand is why Casement felt the Ulster Scots so unworthy of consideration or affection. In his German diary he gratuitously wrote of Scots accents: "I know no language that fills me with the sense of nausea that Glasgow or Butter Scotch does."[356] Despite this, Gertrude believed "the Ulsterman never excited his enmity – only the English politicians."[357] What she said might at times be true but his view remained that the Ulster Protestants were either misled or just unpleasant. He never once considered their predicament in terms of their having any national or group rights. Such neglect of empathy by a man of Casement's stature and background enabled later generations of Irish Republicans to operate entirely without consideration of the true nature of the ethnic nature of the conflict.

In February 1914, England was "the fat man, the Stranger in the House"[358] another time the Emerald Isle's giant parasite.[359] In the accent department she did not get off lightly either, "England 'curse of Europe': The horrid English speech, the twang, the dropped h's and the rasping voice."[360] He was also withering about her soldiers, "an English Tommy is a liar and a cad."[361] Of the English race it was, "Individually I like many – collectively I loathe them."[362]

Casement's Irish nationalism could at times be couched in positive terms as he expressed to his favourite Englishman, Dick Morten, as late as 29 June 1914, "A free Ireland means a close friend Ireland…Leave Ireland's hands free and they will never do a dirty deed."[363] By the outbreak of war in August his regular and arguably only theme was, "England made the war inevitable. She leagued herself deliberately against Teutonic commerce and industry."[364] Six months into the war and after London had prohibited cable traffic from the continent, Casement excelled himself, reaching perhaps the zenith of his abuse of England, "My God! How much more will the world have to stand from that Bitch and Harlot of the North Sea"?[365] No crime was forgiven. Soon the United States began to come under the same lash. Writing to Countess Hahn on 22 February 1915, and before its May sinking, Casement retailed the latest Berlin gossip, "I hear that the *Lusitania* brought two American submarines for the English on her last voyage, under the American flag too. That is a queer manner of being 'neutral'."[366]

To know about Francis Joseph Bigger, and his personal and political life, is to understand the spirit of the times in the two decades before the Irish revolution. More than any other, he was the father of twentieth century Republicanism, especially of that Belfast variety, which saw that century out. Many now would see him and Casement as virtually indistinguishable in Belfast terms. Although categorised as romantic, both were also practical revolutionaries. But it was Bigger's ability to educate the young of Ulster, to cultivate them, and by providing the critical venues, tasks, romances and organisations, to bind them into what became a movement that mattered, indeed what mattered most to them. Bigger was the chief promoter of all aspects of Irish culture in the north and as such moulded a generation. No other intellectual force in Belfast as that around him has ever been as strong or as dominant.

Casement and Bigger shared a remarkably similar early life. Born a year apart, both spent their pre-teen years in England and found the place unwelcoming. Frank lived in Liverpool where his father Joseph's shipping business had taken him. He was miserable there until the age of eleven when the family returned to Belfast. Where he was of Presbyterian background with lowland Scottish antecedents, Casement was not. Bigger was therefore initially taken with the largely Presbyterian heroes of 1798 in Down and Antrim. However, the closest his family got to the United Irishmen was a grandfather in the 1782 Volunteer movement. Shane Leslie reckoned Bigger, in his dreams, was The O'Neill returning from the past (while in his memoirs called Casement "an Irish Quixote mixing some brave qualities with a bubbling vanity").

FJB's father's cousin was Joseph Biggar (as spelt), the famous (and famously ugly) obstructionist MP for Cavan from 1874 to 1890 and one-time IRB member. Any influence he brought to bear has not been recorded but this hard-line nationalist differed from his second cousin in two areas; he was a notorious womaniser, if never married, and he did convert to Rome. Lacking any such Presbyterian heritage, Casement was obliged to kindle his historic enthusiasm in the O'Neills and the pre-1600 Gaelic chieftains, despite the absence of any Celtic genetic inheritance or Gaelic family tradition, rather the opposite.

Remarkably, Bigger was the seventh son of a seventh son of a seventh son although never credited with healing powers. From the time of an early illness he was thought a delicate boy and sent to roam the nearby Carnmoney Hill for his health. He was his mother Mary Jane née Ardery's dearest child. In return, it was said "his ardent affection grew stronger and stronger with her years." In return, it was said "his ardent affection grew stronger and stronger with her years." They were never parted as he lived with Mrs Bigger (née Ardery) until her death. This was at Ardrigh, the big family house and garden, almost an estate, on the slopes of Cave Hill overlooking Belfast Lough.

Bigger attended the liberal Belfast school, Inst (RBAI), in Belfast where his father Joseph was a governor and, later, the then Queen's College. After graduation he pursued law studies in Dublin where he commenced his antiquarian pursuits and book collecting along with a fellow school-friend George Strahan with whom he was to set up a solicitor's partnership in Belfast. This partnership was to last thirty-seven years and was only dissolved by death.

The greatest influence, in relation to Ireland, on both Bigger and Casement probably came from John Mitchel (1815-75). Directly or indirectly, this 1848 Young Irelander's views moulded three generations of separatists, especially those of his fellow Ulster Protestants who came to share his hatred of England. Mitchel's ideas can be traced through a line whose cultural apogee was Douglas Hyde. A contemporary and friend of Bigger and Casement, Hyde was resolutely non-political within the Gaelic League. However, with his 1892 address *On the Necessity for De-Anglicising Ireland*, he lit a fire that was not to be quenched.

Mitchel was born in Limavady the son of a liberal Presbyterian minister. Educated in Newry, Co. Down he became a solicitor and was to be married in the famous Drumcree Parish Church. His inherited separatist instincts were sharpened by the famine. Mitchel had "a holy hatred" for English rule in Ireland. Some said he hated England more than he loved Ireland. True or not, he was so pathological on the matter that at times he could not even bring himself to name his foe, instead referring to it as The Thing.

Mitchel's writings, which Casement loved to read and encourage others to read, indicate not a man who was selling out his own people but one who perhaps naively believed he could risk them not following where he led: "The Anglo-Irish and Scottish Ulstermen have now far too old a title to be questioned: they are a hardy race and fought stoutly for the pleasant valleys they dwell in." In 1846, in a famous Dublin speech, he told his audience, "I am one of the Saxon Irishmen of the North, and you want that race of Irishmen in your ranks more than any other...Drive the Ulster Protestants away from your movement by needless tests and you perpetuate the degradation of both yourselves and them."[367]

He risked and they did not follow. His successor Protestant nationalists played out the consequences. The price his people paid was for Irish nationalism to be enabled to don and keep the non-sectarian Republican mantle. Transported to Tasmania for treason-felony in 1848, Mitchel escaped several years later and reached America. In one sense his Ulster Protestant frontiersman instincts survived, and resurfaced there, through his attitude to those he saw as less advanced peoples. He was notoriously prejudiced on race and skin colour. An open and unabashed advocate of the institution of slavery, Mitchel paid a high price with two of his sons dying for the Confederacy in the American Civil War.

In answer to a question about his precise religious persuasion, F.J. Bigger stated on 8 May 1910 that his mother had been an Anglican "and I (with the rest of the family) was so baptised, and so far as conviction can go with me, am so inclined. Locally I am 'deemed' a Presbyterian but not a 'staunch' one."[368] The question was posed regarding an appointment to the National Board of Education that Alice Stopford Green was trying to arrange - unsuccessfully as a paid-up Presbyterian was needed.

Despite the impression left in some of his writings, Bigger was never an actual Presbyterian, a distinction that mattered then, where today it hardly does. Inter-church marriages, for example, no longer rate even a murmur of a problem as to whether the Anglican or Presbyterian partner's faith will predominate. In truth, Frank was a high Anglican, perhaps of such height that a conversion to Rome would have been superfluous. In 1907, Casement remarked truthfully, if with some disdain, "Mr Bigger is of course deeply in with the Cardinal and Bishops."[369] He attended St George's, the highest Anglican church in Belfast, where his funeral was to be held in 1926. His parish church, St Peter's, on the Antrim Road, was also tolerably high. Bigger would certainly have counted himself amongst those Anglicans who then (and now) define themselves also as Catholics.

St Peter's was to be the setting for a youth group named *The Neophytes* which Bigger founded and organised in the first years of the 20th century. Where Casement was given to collecting flotsam and jetsam, Bigger concentrated his efforts on acculturating young enthusiasts and idealists. His Neophytes were not deliberately nationalist, although it seems from some of their writings that Bigger would, if anything, have had to restrain their flowering in that direction – one he had admittedly evoked. What he started, before the Baden-Powell scouts were even contemplated, was an intellectual Boy Scout troop.

Photographs of the lads, who ranged in age from early teens to early twenties, survive, depicting various summer camps. In one, the row of remarkably substantial tents was erected in mediaeval style with flowing banners. In another, a boy is pictured in full doublet and hose. Bigger had a noted passion for dressing

Neophytes stretching near tents

Older neophytes lounging at camp

up and in a sign of the unselfconsciousness of the times found no difficulty in persuading others to join him. His most fanciful headdress design for an Irish piper was an extended goose wing, otherwise pheasant feathers predominated.[370]

The Journal of the Neophytes, "A Guild of Boys in the Parish of St Peter" founded in 1900, details the many outings and cultural events in which the lads were eagerly involved, and which were assiduously written up on return. The Guild's motto was *Per Severentia*. Bigger was President and the Hon. Secretary was Herbert Hughes (1882-1937) of Thornleigh, the musician and song arranger, who revealingly said of Standish O'Grady, "I loved him with all the fervour of adolescence."[371] (Herbert's father signed the Ulster Covenant. His influence was plainly secondary.) The boys assumed various pseudonyms such as *Portcullis* (Hughes), *Rouge Croix* and *Phiocene Wanderer*. Philip Reynolds was the photographer. Heraldry and gravestone rubbings were popular pursuits, while lectures on the Gaelic revival and the writings of Sir Samuel Ferguson are also recorded in the Journal. Herbert reported to the other Neophytes on his travels with Bigger around the cathedrals of England.

Described as having an "ardent and self-confident manner", Hughes is first heard of in an Irish musical capacity (beyond being honorary organist at St Peter's at the age of fourteen) collecting traditional airs and transcribing folk songs in North Donegal in August 1903 with his brother Fred, Bigger, and John Campbell.[372] Dedicated to seeking out and recording such ancient melodies as were yet to be found in the remoter glens and valleys of Ulster, he produced in 1904 *Songs of Uladh* with Joe Campbell, illustrated by his brother John and paid for by Bigger.[373] Continually encouraged by Bigger, and in collaborations with the poets Joseph Campbell and Padraic Colum (met at Ardrigh), and Yeats himself, Hughes arranged and produced three celebrated Irish songs that have and will long outlast his memory: *My Lagan Love, She Moved Through The Fair,* and *Down By The Sally Gardens*. A dispute with Hamilton Harty over related copyright was on Bigger's advice never pursued. Married to Suzanne McKernan, Herbert had three children one of whom was the jazz musician and music writer Spike (Patrick) Hughes. Unfortunately the brilliance of Herbert Hughes' talent was to consume him and he died at the relatively early age of fifty-five.

The closest one gets to a first-hand, private and critical opinion of Bigger comes from an obscure young man who slips into this story only in 1904 and 1905. This only extant letter was signed "Mac" although his full name was Henry McNally. It was written to Casement from 34 Leoville Street off Belfast's Falls Road, near Clonard Monastery. The 1905 street directory lists one H. McNally as a Gaelic League organiser at that address but in no subsequent year. A Mr MacNally or Macanally is variously mentioned in news reports as being present at the 1904 Glens *Feis*. On 26 August 1904, Casement, writing to Bigger, stated "I got your letter about McNally. I am sorry to hear of his illness poor lad. My contribution for one year is certain – after that I cannot say. We will see." A month later on 24 September 1904 from the Shelbourne Hotel in Dublin he asked, "How is McNally doing? I hope he is better poor boy."[374]

That one letter by McNally was dated 15 September 1905. In it, Mac cheerfully replied to Casement despite his apparently refusing a loan. McNally recounted enthusiastically a moneymaking hosiery sales venture he had in mind. Continuing, and after advising Casement about England: "You would be far better away from the Saxon", and mentioning Ada McNeill, he told of Frank's failing. "Bigger's all right. I suppose he thought he was right and I think I was too but I may be excused for taking a fiendish delight in hearing that his bike suffered. I had no money to bring it home. It needed repairs and he refused to give me my pay so I came home on my own. It was unfortunate of course that the bike was so done up but it was his own fault. I can't agree with you and Miss McN. that he was a good friend of mine. I would be ungrateful if he had been but lowly as he is I gave him far more than ever he gave me. Still I forgive him and moreover I think he's genuine in his love for [the Irish language.]"[375] Despite his earlier serious illness, Henry died in 1946.

With archaeology as Bigger's guiding passion, this resolute protector of ancient monuments spared no effort to save heritage sites all over Ireland, at a time when government took no part in the matter. Typically, in 1910, Bigger re-activated at Cranfield old church on Lough Neagh the *Bealtaine* (May) festival with its Stations and Processions to the Holy Well.[376] The origins of his key sentiments can be traced in his speech that May. "*Ochone*" he lamented, talking to an audience he called of "the old race and the old faith, [living] on Lough Neagh's banks 'ere the despoiler set cruel and wicked hands on everything that appertained to Irish civilisation, prosperity and nationalism." Casement (as diaried) and Bigger visited Cranfield the next April.

Earlier in 1908, unveiling the re-erected statue of the Madonna and Child at the church of Our Lady at Dunsford, which he himself had discovered at Ardglass golf club, Bigger made the heartfelt declaration, "It is Erin we are restoring and healing and placing on a new pedestal, and it is fit and right that a Protestant should make some substitution for his creed of the past." He added, with pride, "Cardinal Logue has blessed it and me."[377] Shane Leslie comes nearest to Bigger with a character in one of his novels, described as "a Protestant with Franciscan leanings."* Another classic endeavour was the placing

---

* Sir Shane Leslie dedicated (inaccurately) his book The Irish Tangle "To the memory of Francis Joseph Biggar of Ardrigh, near Belfast: An Ulsterman devoted to all Ireland: A Presbyterian in theory and a Franciscan in practice: lover of bees, flowers and relics: who gave counsel and courage to all Irishmen desirous to help a cause or

of a giant granite slab over St Patrick's supposed tomb outside Downpatrick Cathedral, as was the restoration of the Monastery of Nendrum on Mahee Island in Strangford Lough.

But better than preservation, Bigger tried to restore life to those buildings that could be revived. Just as with the *Bealtaine* festival, so with Castle Seán in Ardglass where he dressed up as if The O'Neill himself, wandering amongst the many guests said to be from every walk of life. The castle was in effect an inhabited museum. Snatching ruins, as was said, from the decay of time, he then furnished them, literally or metaphorically. Known locally as the Chieftain of Lecale, a guide to the interior of his castle read "...off the dining hall we visit the Oratory with its stone canopy and beautiful altar, suitably equipped with crucifix, candlesticks and embroidered linens." What had been little better than a roofless ruin, untenanted save by rooks and ravens, now rang to the noise of laughter, and music conducted by the kilted host. The visitor's book from 1916 significantly contains many names written in Gaelic, with some others boldly marked "Irish Republican Army".[378]

Monsignor O'Laverty, the Down and Connor diocesan historian, admiringly described Bigger as "Everybody's friend" an epithet that apparently fitted him like a glove.[379] Nothing pleased Frank more than getting into his kilt although he needed training, as is revealed by his ownership of a book *The Kilt and How to Wear It.* And he was photographed in it, the print being captioned "An Irish Chieftain of Today."[380] Others photographed in the new Irish dress, sent their pictures to him for his collection. The singer and journalist Cathal O'Byrne was especially fond of so kitting himself out, as was Joseph Campbell who apparently turned girls' heads in London. Credited with a staggering 387 periodical articles in *Hayes Sources for the History of Irish Civilisation,* Bigger also had many books of poetry and prose dedicated to him, before, and after his death.

Yet his interests were by no means all in the past. He set up the Ulster Public House Association to transform the province's bleak spirit grocers into English-style taverns. *The Crown and Shamrock* pub not far from where he was to be buried was restored and given a classic Biggeresque name. It and the purpose-built *Dunleath Arms* in Ballywalter, a handsome building in the Arts and Crafts manner, are still extant. He also designed and built a series of labourers' cottages with one large downstairs room and no hall. In a 1907 pamphlet he declared that previous designs (with two rooms and a hall) "savour of a smug respectability." He wanted no such impositions in a country like Ireland "where the pleasant face or the cheery wave of the hand from an open

a craft honourable to their country: who committed the high crosses of the north to the care of Orangemen: who, while he lived, gave Belfast the distinction of the most cultured home in Ireland. His Friend Shane Leslie of Glaslough in Monaghan."

Boy in Tudor costume on mound

Kilted piper (F.J. Bigger collection).

door comes like second nature." One row of houses was named Sally Gardens after the Yeats poem. Bigger's house and money were thus used generously not just for patriotic and cultural causes but also for uplifting charitable purposes.

Casement complained about Bigger's increasing corpulence on a number of occasions and did not always appreciate the entertainment at Ardrigh, solemnly advising Mrs Green on 8 September 1906, "I shall see the 'boys' in Belfast soon – but I am not going to be present at one of Mr B's ceilidhs – those gatherings are amusing but one does not want too many of them."[381] Nonetheless on 23 September 1913, writing from Ardrigh to Gertrude, he positively glowed in his affection, "An Biggerac was in great form; not a chief merely but an Emperor! Kilted."[382] Bigger stated: "Sons of the Empire! Children of the blood! Will the sun never set on this Great Empire of ours? Which was greeted with a howl of "Never! never!" immediately followed by the chauffeur, decked out in Orange robes, declaring he would "Never, never surrender". The fun is the chauffeur, an Orange boy, is a Scotch Protestant, and so everyone took part, the three constables of Ardglass, poor souls, belts off, caps gone, marching round the room up to 2.30 a.m. with the rest and the pipes skirling like the devil, all singing "God save Ireland"!"

There are hints of Bigger permitting himself to be exploited. Casement, when warning Alice Stopford Green in 1906, spoke volumes to a contemporary mind, "Yes the 'boys' are a good lot – a dear lot of youngsters altho' I think Mr B. is a bit foolish over some of them but he is a boy himself and that's all to the good."[383]

Bigger had a remarkable gift for inspiring ordinary people who would otherwise never have become interested in history or heritage. There can also have been few Belfast intellectuals or nationalists who did not attend his Ardrigh salon, described as a centre and "rallying ground for a host of young Gaelic enthusiasts."

...A dispenser of gifts and hospitalities;
A diviner of thoughts, a patron and friend of boys;
An urger of native effort – ah the loveliest soul,
The lordliest type of mortal Irish man
It has been, or will be, my lot to know.

These were the lines written of Bigger by Joseph Campbell in his 1904 poem *A Character – after Walt Whitman.* That Frank Bigger was homosexual[384] has led some into disparaging his efforts as only antiquarianism and boys. Others have made the unlikely suggestion, given the frequency of his stays at Ardrigh, of a physical relationship with Casement. There is no evidence of that, nor indeed of any improper behaviour directed toward the many boys and young men he knew well. It is possible, although again unlikely, that he led an entirely non-sexual life. The police and others did not think so.

Several peers, in end of 20th century House of Lords debates, regretting any lowering of the gay age of consent, spoke of how some of the best teachers and youth workers that they had known, loved boys. They felt the existent law was a psychological barrier to any misbehaviour. Without it, such men could no longer work in that field. The argument did not convince but the perception is accurate. It has to be said that today with the relentless hunt for paedophile rings (instead of corrupt individuals), such apparently blameless mentors like F.J. Bigger could not now provide the same service to youth that used to illuminate so many of their lives.

He was also an early aficionado of motoring, whizzing around the countryside like Mr Toad in *Wind in the Willows*. In correspondence with Alice Stopford Green there are many mentions made by him of one, Tommie, who appears to be a chauffeur or at least someone who drives his car. There is a photograph of a handsome man in his mid-twenties with a peaked cap in Bigger's car, although in the back seat.[385] In 1908, he recounted how, "The rascals (Tommie and Denny)…sang all the way in the big brake, nothing but '98 songs" indicating Tommie was politically a separatist and probably a member of one of Denis McCullough's Dungannon Clubs.

Later, in 1910, there was discussion about Alice Stopford Green coming to live at Ardrigh. Frank seemed keen on the idea. Explaining the domestic arrangements he described someone he called "Jones" (presumably Tommie, the chauffeur) as living in. There was, however, a problem about his housekeeper Brigid whom he said would resent another woman living there. The scheme, perhaps for that reason, was never taken forward.[386]

Bigger's activities did not go unobserved. Despite the cheery nature of much of what he organised, Ardrigh was also the centre of an incipient revolutionary movement. In 1907 he was complaining to Alice Stopford Green that Dublin Castle's "spies in Belfast are ghosting people in a very Russian way." Over fifteen years, most of the prominent personnel of the 1916 Rising passed through Ardrigh, although Padraic Pearse preferred to stay at Deramore Park on Belfast's Malone Road with Mrs Hutton, a fellow language enthusiast and translator of the *Tain*.

Unrelenting where England "our most bitter enemy"[387] was concerned, his rhetoric was boundless, and thoughtless as to its consequences. Even Belfast's Linen Hall Library, a haven of liberalism, was obliged to discipline him for a lecture he gave there, innocently entitled *The Holy Hills Of Ireland,* which turned out to have been a pretext for "ventilating political prejudices" on English government in Ireland "calculated to rouse party and political bitterness." In

F.J. Bigger and Herbert Hughes making gravestone rubbings

South Armagh, where he frequently spoke, while praising the Middletown Pipers in 1912 and presenting them with a new flag – "such splendid types of young men", Bigger was calling up the spirit of Owen Roe and Shane O'Neill, leaders who predated "the Anglicising influences…when the 'National' schools were unheard of." He added, encouraging the wearing of Irish-made material, that he would "rather see them clothed in orange made in Ireland than in the most nationalist colours made in Manchester. (Laughter and cheers)."[388]

RIC intelligence, of a fairly low grade, went to Dublin Castle telling of the goings on at Ardrigh. In November 1914 a résumé described "a Francis J. Bigger, solicitor, Belfast" whose associates were "all extremists…He is a Protestant and lives at Ardrigh, Antrim Road." Inaccurately linking his origins to those of Casement, the collator continued, "He is well-to-do and comes from the same locality as Sir Roger Casement with whom he is intimate. Mrs Stopford-Green who is suspected of pro-German activity has stayed at his house. Mr Bigger is constantly visited by leading Sinn Féiners such as Bulmer Hobson, John MacDermott, Denis McCullough, Ernest Blythe and others. He has also been seen with James Connolly of the TWU. He does not bear a good moral character and is said to hate British rule."[389]

F.J. Bigger at Ardrigh reclining on grass, with Tommie Jones, his chauffeur

The tone of this intelligence report typifies much of the RIC's outlook and output. Slightly under-educated, it manages to be respectful and where Bigger's "moral character" was concerned, unwilling to call a spade a spade, perhaps even frightened to delve into the matter. No sense of enthusiasm, no missionary zeal permeated this seemingly demoralised police force. They also recorded Casement as being at Ardrigh for a week from 6 June 1914 and detected him visiting Castle Seán on 14 July – ten days after he had left for America!

In contrast, MI5's assessment tended toward that of the amateur psychologist. It was provided to London on foot of Adler Christensen's mention at the legation in Christiania of Bigger. "Originally a 'Protestant Home Ruler' of the ordinary type", whatever that meant, it described him derisively as "personally enthusiastic and unbalanced, although not lacking in a certain type of intelligence. All this makes it quite possible that the extreme party are using him as an unconscious tool...or at any rate as an 'accommodation address'. He would be a very suitable agent to select for any gunrunning scheme." This report was noted as passing through the Foreign Office on 2 November 1914.[390]

After 1914, Frank Bigger pulled in his horns and there is little evidence of vocal enthusiasm for revolution. Noticeably, he kept well clear of London during Casement's imprisonment although he did assist in several discreet ways. In 1916, in Holy Week, when Joseph Connolly, later a Fianna Fail minister, asked Bigger to draw up his will in anticipation of his likely death in the rising, he recalled that "Frank shied away from the whole business" telling him to have sense, "and not to be worrying about a will or anything else." Connolly after his release from gaol made the appraisal that for Bigger "the whole period must have been a nightmare of shock and apprehension."[391]

On Easter Saturday 1916, Denis McCullough and Herbert Pim took the Belfast Volunteers to Coalisland on a fruitless, if non-sectarian, diversion but Bigger did not participate. He was, however, mentioned in April's police report to Dublin Castle, doing what he loved best: "Suspect F.J. Bigger, Solicitor gave a lecture in St Mary's Hall on 8th ult. on 'The Penal Days'. About 200 members of the Gaelic League were present."[392] An example of Bigger's continued willingness to assist Republicans, indicating he never fell away from his attraction to the heroic, came with the attempted arrest of Denis McCullough at Ardrigh after the rising. Tipped off about a raid, Bigger rang his housekeeper who hauled McCullough out of bed and pushed him through a hole in the hedge on to Fortwilliam golf course. Later he erected a little archway in the hole and placed a wooden cross there in memory of McCullough's deliverance.[393]

Partition utterly disheartened Bigger and on principle he apparently never crossed the new frontier. Not without some belated recognition in his own city, he was awarded an honorary degree by Queen's University Belfast in July 1926. The following month, after a visit to Lindisfarne, Whitby and the Low Countries, his appetite fell away. Friends noticed he was losing flesh, and he declined rapidly, to die on 9 December aged sixty-three. He was interred in a family plot at the old burying ground in Mallusk behind the grave of Jemmy Hope, the 1798 veteran, under a high cross he himself had erected. Its base is carved with a Gaelic inscription of a Psalm verse: "Then they are glad, because they are at rest; and so He bringeth them into the Haven where they would be." Not entirely forgotten by his loyalist enemies, his tombstone was beheaded by a bomb in 1971, and remains so.

After his death, Alice Stopford Green, who had a knowledge of such matters possibly gleaned from her late husband who had spent a lot of time in Italy, wrote to Bigger's housekeeper. Regretting that the Master was dead, she told Brigid, "R.C.'s table you should have", adding in a minatory tone, "Perhaps it is well to say nothing as to some things that were collected for fear of raising gossip in Belfast. There is much you should keep carefully in your remembrance where it should be safe."[394] Later, on 1 July 1927, reminding her "You can certainly trust me as a good friend" she told Brigid about a difficult visit from FJB's brother, Sir Coey Bigger (an eminent physician and later an Irish Senator). Calling on her recently, he had been "very silent and reserved." She further observed, "I don't think he will come again." Alice dilated, it being Palm Sunday, "I went to Westminster Cathedral this morning to be among good Irish friends but I would not take a paten from Cardinal Bourne, the enemy of all Irish things."[395]

Controversy about Bigger was to rage, immediately after his death, in the pages of *The Irish Statesman* from late December 1926 to the end of January 1927. This started after its columnist *Spectator* belittled him in the 18 December issue: "I am sure no other solicitor could have kept Unionist clients had he appeared in public in a saffron kilt or outraged convention by substituting bottle green for the formal black of evening clothes. Bigger carried off these things as he did the pipers band with which on state occasions he manned the battlements of the tumble-down castle at Ardglass, which he had crammed from cellar to parapet."

Switching from scoffing to a harsher vein, *Spectator* continued, "Needless to say his archaeology was sentimental rather than scientific. The trappings of history, not its realities appealed to him, and for this reason most of his writings suggest the litter of a curio-shop...All his life he had been glorifying the romance of Irish revolution which as he saw it, seemed to be a matter of waving green flags above an array of nicely polished pike-heads. He lived to pass through a revolution where nobody showed a flag from first to last and the most thrilling battlefields were empty streets sprayed by the bullets of hidden snipers."

The affection in which Bigger was held is revealed by the long series of responding letters. The first published was from Evelyn Gleeson of the Dun Emer Press who wrote on 25 December 1926, "I have often heard strong loquacious pillars of the Empire mingling their scorn for 'Bigger's Doings' with an unconscious pride...and a humorous twinkle of enjoyment." Replying to the comment on Castle Seán, she declared, "The tottering tower of Ardglass to my knowledge is a solid structure with walls six foot thick; it is a model of a local museum full of interest and beauty." Recalling memories of speeding "through Down and Antrim" in Bigger's motor and stopping "with reverence by the crumbling ruins where the saints lived in earlier centuries" she added it was only then that "the treasure-house was opened and chronicle and legend poured out from the storied richness of his mind."

Touring: F.J. Bigger and chauffeur in back seat

Bigger's car broken down at Errigal, Co. Donegal

Alice Stopford Green 1849-1929

Bulmer Hobson at United Irishman Jemmy Hope's grave, near the Bigger plot in Mallusk cemetery

Colm Ó Lochlainn, a regular visitor to Ardrigh, and one remembered by Casement from Pentonville prison, entered the correspondence on 1 January 1927: "A kindlier word might well have been spared to one who – whatever his faults and foibles – and God knows I would as soon deny his as my own – was a notable figure in that far-off time, ten or twelve years ago, when great men were not so scarce as they have become…Anyone who was really intimate with Bigger in the decade before 1916, can tell of the many students he helped with notes, books and encouragement to attain that perfection of scholarship which was never his." Ó Lochlainn had been on the 1913 committee of the Irish Volunteers and taught at St Enda's although he later fell away from the political movement, disillusioned by the degree of 'deceit and duplicity' involved in the engineering of the rising, deceit in which he was reputedly involved himself.

In a restrained letter, Alice Stopford Green pointed out on 8 January 1927, that Bigger "had a jealous care for the preservation of old monuments, and carried on a ruthless and necessary war against their desecration…In this generation which lives practically without any historical background, we miss an

Irishman whose range, if not scientific, was large and true." Later in a tribute in *The Gaelic Churchman's* January 1927 edition she wrote, somewhat cryptically, "If he himself faltered once or twice he led the right forces with the right spirit."

Finally a Protestant "Ulsterwoman" (L. Rentoul) on 29 January outlined his other great achievement, "We simply did not know that there was any history beyond a record of internecine strife between semi-civilised or, indeed, quite barbarous people, bearing uncouth and unpronounceable names, and who were deservedly swept out of existence by our 'planter' forefathers." For that he deserves much credit. Castle Seán was later granted to the government of Northern Ireland by Frank's nephew, Professor Joseph Bigger, on condition that no flag decorate it save one bearing the "Red Right Hand of Ulster on a white ground" to be flown on 17 July – FJB's birthday. One wonders if that condition was ever met, given that it was then, accurately if unromantically, renamed by officials Jordan's Castle.

8

Brazil 1906-13

In the four years between re-entering the consular service and his commission to undertake the Putumayo investigation, Casement was trapped in several Brazilian cities. (See Roger Sawyer's *The Flawed Hero* for an informed account of the consular service and Brazil in Casement's time there.) At first it was Santos, where Francis Cowper had been posted in the 1880s. If the homosexual world in which Casement moved was small, the world of consuls was tiny. Santos was in the booming coffee-producing area of southeast Brazil. Casement's tasks there were undiplomatic and mundane, being linked to trade, the port and, as always, representation of British subjects in difficulties, whom he interviewed behind a wire-netting screen. He threw himself into his bureaucratic duties with so much enthusiasm that Louis Mallet at the Foreign Office, dealing with yet another complaint about stationery, noted, "He will always be a source of trouble."[396] Despite this view, Mallet was later to be helpful on the Putumayo issues.

The Santos posting was an especial torture for Casement as he was away from Ireland and had to live his obsession, vicariously, through correspondence with Bulmer Hobson and Mrs Green. Santos was not attractive, another predecessor, Sir Richard Burton, describing it as the Wapping of the West. It was a futile and absurd post, Casement declared, while Africa was the only place for him "if it can't be Ireland."[397] Brazil with its appreciating currency was also exceedingly expensive. Leave "on urgent private affairs" was applied for and granted from 1 July 1907.[398] On 1 October, Casement recorded from Ballycastle that he had been absent "with sanction during the whole of the quarter ended yesterday" on full pay.[399] He was not to return to Santos. Instead, having complained further, he was offered Pará to the north at the mouth of the Amazon. In February 1908 he therefore arrived at another Brazilian port city not happy that a better posting had been withdrawn.

Consulting W.A. Churchill, a Pará predecessor, Casement was given the low-down in a letter dated 15 December 1907. "Now about Grand-Para" whose population was reckoned to be 120,000, Churchill first advised "It will not be necessary to take out an earth closet as I did on my first visit." However, "drunken sailors and beach-combers are unfortunately to be found" there as in most such places. "The best hotel" in the city he advised, "a sort of cow-shed called the Grand Hotel da Paz [has] a good reputation from a hygienic point of view." After Casement took up the post and was duly horrified, Churchill wrote again in June 1908 from his Amsterdam consulate, "Your idea in securing permanent offices over the London & Brazilian Bank is an excellent one but it is very near bars and beach-combers and tipsy shell-backs." He was shocked by Casement's addition of the word Ireland to his consular notepaper: "I like the heading of your paper. Has not the FO asked you to explain why you include in it John Bull's other island?" In his usual droll style he concluded, "I shall understamp this letter because taxed correspondence usually reaches its destination quicker and safer than that which is registered."[400]

But Pará was actually a more elegant city than Santos having some pretensions to European cultural norms. This produced a frisson of distaste in Casement who, in despatches to Lord Dufferin at the Foreign Office, was quite free with his opinions: "They are nearly all hideous cross-breeds – of Negro-Portuguese, with up here in the Amazon, a very large admixture of native Indian blood… The 'Brazilian' is the most arrogant, insolent and pig-headed brute in the world I should think" he pontificated in a letter of unprecedented distaste for racial mixing.[401] A couple of months on, he appeared more settled, writing of a "good-natured and cheerful" people "amiable, gentle and…caressing in their manner with much passive goodness of disposition."[402] Someone, or something, had obviously been soothing the Consul.

His most memorable attack came later, in 1910, in a letter to Dick Morten marked, SEE THAT YOUR PURCHASES ARE BRANDED WITH THE IRISH TRADEMARK. Therein Casement opined, "I don't want any more Latin Americans for you; Heavens! what loathsome people they are! A mixture of Jew and Nigger, and God knows what; altogether the nastiest human black pudding the world has yet cooked in her tropical stew pot."[403] Such language should not be taken to mean Casement was, for his time, particularly anti-Semitic or racist. In 1901, when only a junior consul, he vigorously defended the reputation of a German Jewish merchant named Pincus with whom he had lived in Lourenco Marques the previous year.

In a series of forceful letters to Lord Lansdowne, Sir Alfred Milner and William Tyrrell, he described the unstated allegations made against his "poor, fiddle playing, bald headed" friend in Durban as "spiteful absurdities." He even threatened to resign, and "direst" of all, to "turn Irish Home Rule Member of Parliament."[404] (There is a large cache of Casement's letters to Pincus in TCD which reveal they met again in Germany in 1915.)

His views on the virtue German imperialism were also taking shape. Perhaps developed from antipathy to the "abominable Monroe doctrine" which England now backed, he opined to Gertrude, "Someday Europe will challenge this pretence of the USA and put it to the great arbitrament of battle, and I sincerely hope Germany will win and erect a Great German State with honest clean laws and institutions here under the Southern Cross."[405]

Two overdressed spivvy lads on quayside. Note the shadow of Casement as photographer in foreground who complained of how Brazilians dressed themselves up like Parisians. He also wrote "Pleasure, amusement, social life, companionship all are wanting in Brazil — altho' in a city of close on one million people I am far more alone in this sham, pretentious copy of civilization (without any of the reality) than I was away up the Congo. The Congo naked natives were far nicer people, sincere and real, than these overdressed vain, empty minded humbugs with their extraordinary vanity and arrogance."

Another shadow of the future was momentarily visible in June 1908 when Casement reported from Pará to his superior in Rio on alleged atrocities in the Putumayo: "I send you a fresh cutting of the horrors in the interior – this time between Peruvians and Colombians."[406] These involved one Julio Arana, and his company, reducing Indians to slavery, and worse. Yet Casement was not pressing on the matter: the press stories "are greatly exaggerated I fancy…much of it may not be true" he wrote, attributing a certain amount of their strength to Brazilian fault-finding in order to carve fresh territory "out of Peruvian soil." Casement's anti-Brazilian prejudices seem to have been running in front of his humanitarian instincts at this point although he did add, with satisfaction "A party of Colombians described quaintly enough as 'missionaries desirous of converting the Indians' were recently reported in the Pará papers to have been all massacred (save one wounded man) by a surprise party of the very Indians they set out to 'convert'. As the telegram states, they were armed with guns as well as Bibles. I fancy the repugnance of the Indians to such attempt at conversion was not illegitimate."

The whole Putumayo area abounded with territorial disputes although the biggest losers were the Colombians whom Arana had seen off, by both purchase and armed evictions until he had "squatters rights" to a territory larger than France. Casement only had the most peripheral responsibility for this area, which was in another country disputed by a third.

In November 1908 he went home on leave, which after an apparently less than successful Barbados cure was extended, on application, to allow for further convalescence. During this vacation he was pleased to be selected for promotion to consul-general at Rio de Janeiro, Brazil's federal capital. Thus was Pará vacated, not to be seen again until he passed that way in 1910, en route to the Putumayo. Reaching Rio in March 1909, he had a year in post before his next leave and that first Amazon mission. By August 1909 Casement had chosen to move out to the diplomatic town of Petropolis, high above sea level, and commute down to Rio to his office, a worthwhile but "somewhat fatiguing journey."

One of his few recorded endeavours was arranging the appointment of Brian Barry as a vice-consul on a visit to the coastal city of Victoria, north of Rio. He was one of two Irishman there, the other "I know from schooldays in 1879" as he told Dick Morten in 1909. Barry was chief agent of an American coffee firm, Hard Rand & Co. as Casement advised the Foreign Office on 2 August 1909 when he had appointed him acting vice-consul. He felt the Irishman was eminently suitable and that the appointment should be made "with the least possible delay."

On 26 August, London telegraphed approval, but four days on, Casement wrote to say Barry had asked to be relieved of his duties. This was on account of strained relations with the President of Espirito Santo state – he had refused to transact "a financial job" for him, while the trouble caused by a British seaman off the *Aboukir* completed Barry's disillusionment with the honorary post. Unfortunately Casement had earlier quoted the President as greeting his protégé's appointment with great pleasure. Effortlessly he switched to a new tack and asked for London to sanction abolition of the post. The next day, to Lord Dufferin, he further emphasised the case for abolition, saying, "I see no earthly reason for maintaining or trying to maintain a useless post where the people it is designed to assist have no use for it."[407] Regardless of this embarrassing fiasco, Casement kept in touch, for on 1 July 1910 Barry was telling him, more in hope than expectation, that he would "start for the Cradle of Christianity in May next, after eleven years absence. I fear my best girls will be looking old and I have no fancy for marrying an older woman."[408]

The evidence from Casement's diaries suggests a fairly robust sex life in the Brazilian capital with a number of names recurring – Bernardino, Mario, Antonio and Gabriel, not to mention Ramón and Francisco in Buenos Aires. He frequently travelled around Brazil, partly to see his junior consuls, while also spending a month in the Argentine on his way home in March 1910.

The Putumayo problem was brewing in London but Casement was still marginal to the dispute. The controversy had started in September 1909 with the first of a number of articles by an American traveller, Walter Hardenburg, in *Truth*, entitled *The Devil's Paradise,* and ominously subtitled *A British Congo*. Parliamentary questions followed, as not only was the Peruvian Amazon Company, British registered, but it employed several hundred black Barbados British as overseers. They were in effect indentured labourers unable to leave through indebtedness to the company. In many cases, as Casement discovered, they were complicit in the murders of Indians, and were trapped in a spiral of viciousness from which he managed to rescue them. Arana's justification to his shareholders in December 1909 was the defence that "some of our employees were sacrificed at the cannibal feasts of certain tribes." Casement was not impressed, writing in blue crayon over his copy of Arana's pleading "How naughty."[409]

The company Casement would be asked to investigate had become the Peruvian Amazon Company, having earlier dropped Rubber from its name. Since 1907 it had been registered in London acquiring four British directors and raising £135,000 through a speculative share issue. It remained under the control of the Arana family in Iquitos, especially of Julio Arana. Being a British company, however, made it susceptible to concerned Liberals and humanitarians in London.

These two British aspects enabled the Foreign Office to encourage the company to send out a high-powered team. This became the Peruvian Amazon Company's commission of enquiry, headed by Col. Reginald Bertie with Louis H. Barnes, a tropical agriculturalist, Walter Fox, a botanist and expert on rubber, Seymour Bell, a commercial expert, and Henry Lex Gielgud, the company secretary in London. Casement was then attached to it, ostensibly to investigate the position of the Barbadians. Advised in June by his Congo ally, John Harris, that his name had been suggested, he received his orders to proceed from the Foreign Secretary, Sir Edward Grey, in July and was in Pará on 10 August. The 1910 Black Diary (and its White counterpart) track Casement's year in a gradual build-up of entries from 13 January. Initially sparse, they become denser as the investigation proceeded upriver in August.

Casement's movements during 1910 Black Diary

13 January 1910 in Rio de Janeiro/Petropolis (Brazil)

1 March left for São Paulo and Santos

8 March left Brazil for Buenos Aires and Mar del Plata (Argentina)

5 April left Montevideo (Uruguay) for England

1 May disembarked at Liverpool

18 May left London for Dublin

26 May in Belfast

21 June left for England

16 July left London for Dublin, returning 20 July

23 July left England for South America

8 August arrived Pará (Brazil), left 12 August

16 August arrived Manaos (Brazil), leaving next day

31 August arrived Iquitos (Peru)

14 September set out upriver on Putumayo investigation

25 November returned Iquitos, leaving 6 December

10 December arrived Manaos, leaving same day

13 December arrived Pará, leaving for Europe 17 December

28 December arrived Lisbon

31 December 1910 in France

9

1910 Diary

[The 1910 Black Diary[410] printed by Dollards in Dublin has a dark blue satinised cover and a red spine, with space for three daily entries per page (none for Sunday). It is strikingly large, measuring thirteen by ten inches. Best described as a desktop diary, most entries look as if written by someone seated at a desk or table. Priced at three shillings when "Interleaved with Blotting" it indeed has thin, pink blotting paper like the 1911 Black Diary. What follows is an abridged version, this author's annotations being within square brackets, and in bold.

Some of the actual blots come from external documents, such as an envelope address for Wyndham Robilliard "c/o Booth & Co. Manaos", detectable opposite 3 February. Entries run only from 13 January 1910 and are initially intermittent. They start when Casement is in Brazil. Inside the front and back covers, which Casement twice endorsed "Private Diary", there are pages of expenditure details and additions, both official and personal.

A typed timetable of "Approximate Sailing Arrangements" for the Iquitos Line out of Liverpool and New York to Iquitos and back, is glued into the front. It appears to be amplified and annotated in two hands. Inserted in the diary is a set of comic verses entitled *A Knotty Problem,* spoken by "Miss Marguerite Tariff-Reform", mocking women's suffrage and, according to Casement's note, clipped from the October 1909 edition of *Truth.* Its concluding verse begins "When Christabel a vote has got/And horses fly and fishes trot." The postal regulations printed in the diary indicate that in 1910 an inland letter cost 1d. and that there were five deliveries in Dublin every day except Sunday which had only one.

Two specific mentions of Casement's mysterious friend Millar are to be discovered in the flyleaf; a 7/6 lunch at Belfast's Grand Central Hotel and a two shilling tie pin. Both these items are mentioned later. There are also "Photo Frames" bought, one to enclose Ramón's image and another for Kate Parnell's, marked later with a cross. B.L. Reid in his 1976 book suggested Millar had an artistic bent as "Japanese Books" at a cost of 1/2 were bought for him.[411] However, closer inspection provides an accurate reading for the word he took to be Millar. It is actually Mullans, Belfast's then major bookshop at 4 Donegall Place. The Japanese books were for Casement himself. A present of a hat rack for Mrs G. also merits a cross. One stray local note amongst a host of South American items in the seven inscribed pages of endnotes reads "Egg Julep for Hair, 2/- big bottle, prepared by B. Ranagan, Donegall Place, Belfast." Ranagans was

a "Ladies and Gentleman's Hairdresser and Wigmaker" at 15 Castle Lane, off Donegall Place.

There are several pages at the front and back of the 1911 Cash Ledger devoted to "Expenditure at Rio" from March 1909 to April 1910, with fragmentary notes about events and characters like Ramón. This suggests Casement's diarying was spasmodic but building up to a climax in 1910 and 1911.

January, 1910.

13, Thursday Gabriel Ramos – **X** Deep to hilt. Last time – "palpito" at Barca **[throbbing or fluttering at Ferry]** at 11.30. To Icarahy "*precisa muito*" **[needed a lot]** – 15$ or 20$. Also on Barca the young caboclo **[mixed Indian and white]** (thin) dark gentleman of Icarahy. Eyed constantly & wanted – would have gone but Gabriel *querido* **[dear Gabriel]** waiting at Barca gate! Palpito – in very deep thrusts. **[Until 24 February, there are only entries for 20, 21, 22 and 24 January]**

20, Thursday Valdemiro – $20

21, Friday To Petropolis **[Brazil's diplomatic capital]**. Sick.

22, Saturday Sick in Petropolis.

24, Monday Down to Rio to O'Sullivan Beare. **[Daniel O'Sullivan Beare M.D. (1865-1921) ultimately Casement's successor as consul-general in Rio was a man like him of Irish background with anti-slavery credentials and African experience.]**

February, 1910.

24, Thursday Valdemiro – Rua 20$.

28, Monday Deep screw to hilt. **X** "*poquino*". **[like a poker]** Mario in Rio – 8½" + 6" **[Presumably length and circumference although Casement's assessments of size may be inflated if Kinsey's supposedly scientific statistics are anything to go by.]** – 40$.000. Hospedaria. **[guest house]** Rua do Hospicio, 3$ only fine room. Shut window. Lovely, young – 18 & glorious. Biggest since Lisbon July 1904 & as big. Perfectly huge. "Nunca veio maior! Nunca" **[You've never seen a bigger one! Never]**.

March, 1910.

1, Tuesday Left for São Paulo.

2, Wednesday Arr. São Paulo. Antonio 10$000. Rua Direita. Dark followed & Hard. Teatro Municipal **[famous cruising area in the gardens below]**.

Breathed & quick enormous push. Loved mightily. To Hilt Deep **X.**

3, Thursday Saw Antonio at Cafe – watering plants.

4, Friday To Santos **[São Paulo's port and the location of Casement's posting in 1906-7]** ~~& Kee~~ **[Keevil presumably]** Parminter. **[This is Alfred (Timi) Parminter, nephew of Major William Parminter of the Sanford Exploring Expedition and Casement's favoured successor as vice-consul in Lourenco Marques. Casement several times generously assisted him when he was out of favour in London including finding him a job with a coffee firm in Santos. Alfred's son Reggie was the fourth of Casement's godsons.]**

5, Saturday At Santos & to Guaruja. **[A resort seven miles outside Santos where Casement had boarded with John Keevil and his family. See Sawyer (1910) p. 44 where he writes "For most commentators the presence of '& Kee..', above, rules out any involvement of a forger, at least with this part of the diary." Robert Berry visited Casement in Guaruja. Keevil, writing to Berry in 1907, reported that Casement seemed terribly careworn and absent minded. Two years later Casement was to be chirping "I expect Major Berry here very soon from B. Aires and we shall talk nothing but Ireland."[412]]**

7, Monday At Guaruja.

8, Tuesday Left in "Asturias" for B. Aires.

[9-10 March blank]

11, Friday Arr. B. Aires & on shore to the Hotel of before. Algerian.

12, Saturday Morning in Avenida de Mayo. Splendid erections. Ramón 7$000. 10" at least. **X** In.

Sunday 13 To Hurlingham to Warden – Lunch. **[This lunch at the Hurlingham Club was with William Warden who may have been an Ulsterman. He was certainly interested in Ireland and corresponded with Casement as early as 1907, being instrumental in an Argentine collection for the relief of distress in Co. Galway prompted by Casement's 1913 appeal. However, he was of an imperialist outlook. Writing to Casement about the results of the appeal he affirmed "by helping to solve the Home Rule question you will be putting the heart of the Empire right."[413]]** Saw Ramón get off tram at Zoo & sit down on seat & read – pencil under ear – watched long & then on to station. Back at 10 p.m. Met Ramón after sailor with request of fleet. Ramon 10$000 to meet tomorrow.

14, Monday Ramon. At Zoo entrance & Ramon to breakfast at Restaurant there – no it was in Chocolate House & name written on paper & "his pencil

Casement reading Somerville and Ross in Guarujá near Santos ca. 1910 (Consuela Keevil)

mine". Gave 20$000. Again at night.

15, Tuesday Ramón. Breakfast at Restaurant, arrived at Plaza Hotel at 11 p.m. **[In his 1911 Cash Ledger, notes by Casement about the dates 12-15 March 1910, to enumerate sessions with Ramón, are marked 1 to 4. Session number 8 is reached on 3 April:**

1	**Sat 12**	**X**	**Ramon. Three days in B. Ayres.**
2	**Sun 13**		**do. Ramon & sailor & Francisco. Cabs lunches & Hurlingham tips to steward 1.0.0 & 7/-**
3	**Mon 14**		**Ramon Do. X To Mar del Plata & hotel**
4	**Tues 15**		**Nothing spent at Mar de P.]**

16, Wednesday Left for Mar del Plata.

17, Thursday At Mar del Plata

18, Friday At Mar del Plata

19, Saturday At Mar del Plata. Ramon 20$

Sunday 20th Mar del Plata [**In a letter to Gertrude Bannister of 21 March 1910, Casement described Mar del Plata as "the Brighton of the Argentine…a very fashionable place indeed" adding, "I go back up to Buenos Ayres tomorrow probably."**[414]]

21, Monday Returned to Buenos Aires.

22, Tuesday Ramon at Zoo again & in the *Bosquet* [**forest**] afterwards – By train to Belgrano & back. [**Cash Ledger: Ramón 11.0 B'fast 5.75… 5**]

23, Wednesday Ramon **X** In. 4 this year. To La Plata & lunch at Hotel there. Lay down after for an hour & then to Gardens & tea & back at 5.30 train. At Club & arranged go San Marco tomorrow. [**Cash Ledger: Ramón 25 000 La Plata 6**]

24, Thursday To San Marco by 6. Trains with Eddy Duggan. Brothers there & played Bridge. [**The Duggans were Irish-Argentines, like John Nelson and his family, who all contributed to Casement's appeal for the impoverished people on the islands off Connemara.**[415] **The magnificent sum of £2,500 was raised in this, Casement's last, humanitarian venture.**] to San Marco interesting but very wet.

25, Friday At San Marco

26, Saturday At San Marco

Sun 27 Returned to Buenos Aires. At Station & sailors again.

28, Monday Ramon. At Zoo & lunch & walk to Gardens of Palermo.

29, Tuesday Ramon. Left for Mar del Plata but sick of night train – so stayed behind. Many types. Especially Martinez of Entre Rios. [**Cash Ledger: Tues 29 Ramón Zoo 20.000 & to M de P 7**]

30, Wednesday Left for Mar del Plata by Day train – seeing hares & birds – & enjoying the journey.

31, Thursday Mar del Plata

April, 1910.

1, Friday Mar del Plata. Left Mar del Plata at 3 train & arrived B Aires at 11 p.m. To Hotel & bed.

2, Saturday Wrote Ramon – Drew money £80 & got ticket for L'pool by Lamport & Holt "Veronese". **[A cheque stub, dated 2 April 1910, for "passage per Veronese" exists. William Warden's name is also on the stub indicating the cheque may have been made out to him and that he was a shipping agent.[416]]** Met Sailors of fleet & others. At Club with "Amethyst" officer. **[Cash Ledger: At B.A. Wrote Ramón.]**

Sunday 3rd Last time Ramon at Tigré. At Hurlingham **[Club]** & then to Tigre with Ramon from Belgrano. Saw last time at Belgrano. Never again. **[Cash Ledger: Ramón (45.000) to Tigré 8. Last saw at Belgrano Estacion.]**

4, Monday Left B. Aires in "Veronese." Wrote Ramón from Montevideo.

5, Tuesday At Montevideo. Posted Letter to Ramon. Sailed 4 p.m.

11, Monday at Bahia. Type at night on board. Stevedore.

23, Saturday At Las Palmas. Three types – one beautiful – Bathed with C.S.P. daughter B.M. Moule. **[Mrs Bill (Katherine) Moule (1884-1947), daughter of Kitty O'Shea and Charles Stewart Parnell]** Mason.

24 April At Tenerife all day – gardens & types. Left 2 a.m.

25, Monday Left Tenerife at 2 a.m. On board about 11.30 after a pleasant day.

28, Thursday At Vigo. Left early morning. Lovely – but cold. Left Finisterre at 12.50.

29, Friday In Bay of Viscaya

30, Saturday Approaching Lands End & in Irish Sea. Saw Ireland – & Lugnaquilla & pointed it out to Katherine Parnell.

May, 1910.

Sunday 1st May Arr L'pool & to London to Euston Hotel.

2, Monday At London. To Mrs Green & Col. Stopford **[her brother Edward]** & to Earls Court to 110 Philbeach Gardens. Miss Cox. Euston Hotel £1.18.6.

3, Tuesday At London. At Miss Cox 110 Philbeach Gardens Earl's Court. Greek £1.0.0.

4, Wednesday at London

5, Thursday At London

6, Friday At London. King Edward died. At F.O. & saw Tyrrell who told me King was very ill in evg & prophesied it! At E.D.M.'s

7, Saturday Death of King announced in press. To Savoy & Dick – poor old chap.

8th Sunday at Selous with Dick & Mrs M. Selous.

9, Monday Left Savoy for London again. Nina

10, Tuesday In London.

11, Wednesday In London. To "Tales of Hoffman".

12, Thursday At Caversham with Gee. **[Gertrude Bannister was employed for nearly seventeen years at Queen Anne's, Caversham, a Greycoat Hospital school, latterly as assistant headmistress, until her contract was peremptorily terminated in 1916 with a £40 pay-off.[417]]** Milano Francesco. 1.0.0.

13, Friday In London

14, Saturday At Theatre with N, Gee & Miss Colles. At Robert Lynd's till 8 p.m. At Exhibition & saw Formosans & Japs afternoon.

15th At Kew with N & girls. Gardens. Fine day.

16, Monday In London at Exhibition with Nina. 519,000 people! Miserable.

17, Tuesday At Exhibition by self. Formosans & many others.

18, Wednesday At Exhibition. Japs Exhibition good. Left Euston for Dublin. John Redmond on board.

19, Thursday In Dublin at Miss Ffrench's & at Irish Opera 'Eithne'. Rotten. **[In this he concurred with Forrest Reid, the Belfast novelist and lover of boys, who briefly attended F.J. Bigger's salon at Ardrigh. Reid declined W.B. Reynolds's request to write about Irish Opera in his short-lived but influential magazine *Uladh* (Ulster) describing Stanford's opera *Semus O'Brien* as dreadful. He provided instead "a short story about a little boy" entitled *Pan's Pupil* which he remarked was received "in silence".[418]]** Stayed at Gresham. Very comfortable.

20, Friday Sent Ramon a post card of Zoo here. In Dublin at Zoo. **[Ramón's**

favourite haunt in Buenos Aires was the zoo.] King's Funeral Service but did not go.

21, Saturday In Dublin. In Phoenix Park,[419] & lovely – at **X** where F. Cavendish killed.

22 [**Sunday**] At Tara – with Harrie & family. [**Harriette Wilkinson's family house, not that of John Harris of the Anti-Slavery Society, as has been proposed. It had been a port of call for Casements as far back as the 1880s. He was in her company again on 7 August 1911.[420] A young man, Pat Wilkinson, presumably a son of the family was an irreverent correspondent from Quebec in 1913: Casement had introduced him to Count Markievicz whom he had frequently met thereafter, remarking of him in his letter "my admiration has always been divided between his rival capacities for childlike enthusiasm and for the wine of the country."[421]**]

23, Monday In Dublin. At "Memory of the Dead". Big party. Douglas Hyde & Mrs Hyde, Miss O'Farrelly & Arbuthnot [**of Dublin Zoo**] & the Wilkinsons. [**This was probably a reception given by the Association for the Preservation of the Memorials of the Dead in Ireland. F.J. Bigger frequently contributed to its valuable antiquarian magazine which recorded and reproduced gravestone inscriptions. A different explanation could be derived from the fact that *Memory of the Dead* is a famous United Irish song written by John Kells Ingram. It opens with the words: *Who fears to speak of '98.***]

24, Tuesday In Dublin.

25, Wednesday In Dublin.

26, Thursday 'See it coming'! In Dublin. To Belfast, John McGonegal **X** 4/6. Huge & curved. Up by Cregagh Road met by chance near clock tower & off on tram – it was huge & curved & he awfully keen. [**The Albert Clock, Belfast's leaning tower of Pisa, is near the river Lagan. This was then an established cruising area due to an extensive public toilet at the nearby Customs House. At night it was a red-light district, the adjacent pubs servicing the needs of sailors for generations, while before the Second World War, one such, DuBarry's, doubled-up as a gay bar. The actual location for the sex itself seems to have been the woods in the glen at the top of the Cregagh Road, just beyond the tram terminus. John, who was either very camp or whose trousers did not disguise his rampancy, features again in May 1911. He is credited with five shilling in the tots in this diary's flyleaf.**]

27, Friday Gresham Hotel bill £7.7.5 [**The following words were properly the previous day's entry and Casement crossed them out, re-entering them in differing form, above:**] Left 3 train for Belfast at Royal Hotel. Ormeau

Park & Gardens. Met J. McG. 4/6 Huge & curved. **[Not crossed out:]** To Richhill Castle To Mrs Berry. Gordon & Art. Last time 4/6. **["Richhill is charming. All it lacks is Berry himself", he wrote to F.J. Bigger that day.[422] However the mention of "Gordon & Art" has led to confusion as to the identity of this particular Gordon. By virtue of Casement's consistent use of his Christian name when referring to his boyfriend, Millar Gordon, he can be ruled out. Roger Sawyer, with the help of Bulmer Hobson's sister Mrs Florence Patterson, pinpointed W.R. Gordon, an art and crafts teacher at RBAI (Inst) in Belfast as the Gordon in the diary. She was the first Irishwoman to become a licentiate of the Royal Institute of British Architects – indicating the progressive nature of the Hobson family, but was wandering somewhat by the time of this interview.**

Major Berry had connections with Inst and its finances (as had F.J. Bigger who became a Governor) which gave a proximate correlation to the option but still provided no explanation. W.R. Gordon, by 1910 aged thirty-six, had been a folk singer and "a man of wide culture and accomplishments" who experienced "the perfect contentment of a happy domestic life" according to a history of the school; Not quite a Casement person. In fact he did have a theatrical connection to Bulmer Hobson and others in the Bigger set. In 1904, with the closing of the old Belfast School of Art, its drama group or 'Sketching Club', which included W.R. Gordon as a member, had merged with the Ulster Literary Theatre. By 1905, Gordon's "fine interpretation" in the role of the old farmer McKinstry in Lewis Purcell's *The Enthusiast* was being noted by Forrest Reid.[423] The Art School actors brought practical skills of painting scenery and costume design to the dramatic originality of the Gaelic revivalists. But Casement does not mention attending any such plays in Belfast in this period.

Sawyer was right to think there was a Berry tie-in, but it was far simpler. The Colonel, as he became, had a number of sons, one named Gordon and another Arthur i.e. Art. Mrs Berry was concerned about the boys' schooling, and in her husband's absence, talked the matter over with Casement during this visit. Berry was away in Sierra Leone where he "assisted in the suppression of the cannibal rising" – leaving for this dangerous climate very much against Casement's advice. Berry later wrote a detailed history of the origins of West African peoples and of the gory doings of the Sierra Leone cannibals. His comment that "on the Congo, herds of human cattle are preserved and fatted for the table" may well have been suggested by a conversation with Casement.[424]

Casement wrote to Berry from Ballycastle on 6 June 1910 saying "I spent a happy day and night at Richhill and saw Arthur, Gordon and Desmond. I've also seen Mrs Berry – needless to say. You must come home in July and help her with Gordon's school future and Art's."[425] (Bigger was to describe the family's (rented) castle at Richhill as one smelling of rent and aggression.)

Roger Sawyer relates how the Colonel, who had even been to see Casement in Brazil on a botanical expedition finally fell out with him[426] after a friendship of many years. That was in 1913 when Casement tried to draw Berry from the British Army to the Irish Volunteers. His nationalist proselytising was now of such a level that he was willing to jeopardise long-established friendships. Indeed he was in the process of breaking free of his past so drastically that he could disregard the feelings and loyalties of those, like his Ballycastle relatives, who could not share his extreme politics.

There can be little doubt that relations were already distinctly frosty after Casement had got onto his high horse in a different matter, a year earlier. Mrs Berry had given birth to another boy in 1912 and invited Casement to be a godfather. A response came on 27 August, alternatively lecturing and hectoring, and at the same time revealing of Casement's politico-religious views: "With regard to the christening of the boy and your kind thought of me as godfather I fear it is not possible. I am not a member of that church to begin with – and I think that is essential. The only Christian Church in this country, in my opinion, is the Roman Catholic church." After much more in the same vein, he continued "It is a horrid and silly sham…I mean the Godfathering and Godmothering of the English Protestant Churches in their various aliases [i.e. the (Anglican) Church of Ireland.] I never set foot inside those Churches – and never will, please God, while they preach intolerance."[427]

Col. Berry's father, a surgeon practising in Belfast and Larne, was oddly a Count of the Brazilian Empire. Like his friend Casement, Robert Berry served in the South African War – on the same side, although not in the First World War when Berry was a Lieutenant Colonel in the R.A.S.C. Of his boys, Gordon died within his lifetime while Art, an Army lieutenant, died young in 1930, on service in Egypt. His first wife, Georgina Hannay, also died young, in October 1914, only a couple of years after this correspondence. The Colonel, a polymath, wrote extensively in learned journals on topics such as *The Scandinavians in Ulster* and *The Royal Residence of Rathmore of Moylinne.*[428]

Further confusion over this day's entry has reigned with what was taken to be a second person called Gordon featuring in the phrase "Ormeau Park & Gordon"[429] but close inspection of the diary, allied to Belfast knowledge, reveals the word to be Gardens not Gordon. Walking to Ormeau Park from the Royal Hotel which was situated in Belfast's Wellington Place, Casement would have gone through Botanic Gardens, a cruising area well into the 1980s and still known locally as 'the Gardens'. He would then need to cross the river to go into Ormeau Park. If all this confuses modern writers it would have been a near impossible task, not to say largely pointless, for any forger to research, let alone write.]

28, Saturday Left for Warrenpoint with Millar. Boated & Huge Enjoyment. Both Enjoyed. He came to lunch at G Central Hotel. **[In the flyleaf Casement inscribed its cost: "Lunch Grand Central, Millar & I 7/6". As the Grand Central Hotel was in Belfast's Royal Avenue this lunch was before their departure to south county Down and Carlingford Lough.]** Turned in together at 10.30 to 11 – after watching billiards. **[This is a rare example of Casement sharing a room and presumably a bed. Sleeping together was not his usual sexual expression.]** Not a word said till – "Wait – I'll untie it" & then "grand" **X** Told many tales & pulled it off on top grandly. First time – after so many years **[Perhaps not since 1907, the year they first met]** & so deep mutual longing. Rode gloriously – splendid steed. Huge – told of many – "Grand".

29 **[Sunday]** At Warrenpoint & Rostrevor. **[Casement's accounts at the front of this volume reveal that the Warrenpoint hotel bill was £2.9.9 while costs in Rostrevor only amounted to 7s. 3d.]** Enormous over 7½" I think. Asked after friend – repeatedly. **[The friend could have been John McGonegal. If so, Millar was keen to learn more about other like-minded acquaintances of Casement in Belfast.]** Millar again! Back – Back voluntarily. First time he turned his back. "Grand" **[Casement revisited this entry on an unusual number of occasions judging by the four or five types of pencil and colour of pen ink used in his comments.]**

30, Monday Left Warrenpoint to Belfast together. "Aye! if she's running to time like" **[Casement here records a little piece of Millar's Co. Antrim idiom.]** Saw F.J.B. Ned Dickey. Bulmer. "It's Grand". Green jersey at 11 – at Hotel. Did not **[pursue?]**

31, Tuesday To Giant's Ring with Millar. **[The Giants' Ring, a two-acre site, consists of a Neolithic passage tomb at the centre of an impressive high-sided circular theatre. It is to the south of Belfast near the river Lagan and a cruising area today. This 1910 visit by the pair of lovers was of an archaeological nature.]** Wrote "Northern Whig" "Irish in Ulster". **[A controversy on whether Ulster Protestants had ever been Irish Gaelic speakers was raging in the *Northern Whig*, a Belfast Unionist newspaper. Indeed this is a dispute which continues to this day having political significance for those Republicans who see Unionists as part of a single Irish nation and thus a people to be wooed, not bombed and driven out. In the paper a writer signing himself 'Ulster' had rubbished both Douglas Hyde, and John (Eoin) MacNeill for relating what he described as a myth about Irish-speaking Scots in Co. Down – evidenced by a Presbyterian minister, Rev. William Neilson, reportedly preaching a sermon in Irish at Rademon near Crossgar. Neilson actually ministered in Dundalk, Co. Louth and was a guest preacher. The event was explained away as insignificant by the hostile writer.**

Casement's letter, dated 31 May 1910, as from Belfast, was published the very next day under the name 'Another Ulster'. He accepted that "Dr Hyde may have slipped into some inaccuracy when he alleges that the lowland Scots settlers habitually spoke (Gaelic)." Describing himself archly as "one of those wandering propagandists whose little candle flickers for a moment in the morning papers" he added that he had "but yesterday reached Belfast from a very distant country" where his library was still situated. The evidence he managed to adduce included a reference to bilingual girls at Ulster hiring fairs wearing ribbons in their hair – "a gay tribute to superior learning." Concluding his letter, which he acknowledged was "far too long", he said "I found a hamlet of Scots Presbyterians in Donegal in 1889 who certainly spoke Irish for I heard them conversing in that language."

The editor allowed 'Ulster' one more throw the next day (2 June) while announcing "This correspondence has already far exceeded reasonable lengths" and bar a possible Gaelic League response was closed. 'Ulster' quoted Rev. James Bryce of Killaig near Coleraine, grandfather of Lord Bryce, as reporting in 1803 that the people there spoke the "broad Scotch of Ayrshire and Galloway." Accepting many of Casement's points, he admitted the census probably under-recorded Irish speakers but warned "the danger is now slightly in the other direction, and that perfervid Gaelic enthusiasm may induce some to return themselves as 'Irish speaking' who would fare badly" if tested by a particular, named, Irish language professor. MacNeill did manage a final response two days later arguing that the Ulster Scots were formerly Dalriada Gaels and thus one way or another were Irish whether they knew it or not.

In a note to MacNeill dated 31 May, Casement told him he had written to the *Whig* under the name 'Another Ulster' "as I personally don't want to get drawn in to a controversy." He was now hunting down "books of reference which will give a different complexion to Mr Ulster's diatribes" although he admitted "I don't think all the Scottish lowlanders, or anything like all, knew or used Gaelic but far more of them did than is generally supposed."[430]]

June, 1910.

1, Wednesday Wrote many letters. Sent £100 Rio for Brian B. [**Ernest Hambloch described a reported incident during a visit to Brian Barry (who came originally from Castleblaney in Co. Monaghan) when Casement flung several vases of harmless yellow flowers out of a window thinking they were orange lilies. The story was told to prove the author's theory that Casement was that "saddest of God's creatures: an Irishman without a sense of humour."[431] Eoin MacNeill "as someone who knew him intimately in his latter years" disputed Hambloch's assessment, declaring in 1938 "He had a keen sense of humour and was always bright and cheerful. Far from taking**

himself too seriously, he had no vanity and seemed almost unconscious of himself."[432] Wrote Rio & others.

2, Thursday At Belfast.

3, Friday At Belfast. Left for Ballymena – Lunched Travie & Bertie Orr & Mrs King [**Casement's fellow diners were Travers W. King, his mother Mrs King, Casement's old headmaster's widow, and Travie's solicitor colleague R.H. Orr. The closeness of the King family to Casement's is revealed by the fact that his great-uncle Francis Casement was godfather to one of Rev. King's brood of sons, some one of whom attended the funeral of his father, Captain Casement, in Ballymena in 1877. Travers King died unmarried in 1933.**] – On to Ballycastle by 4.29 train. At Brannigans.

4, Saturday At Ballycastle. Dined Roger & Susie. [**His second cousin Roger who was nearly fifteen years older than him, farmed at Magherintemple.**]

[**Sunday**] At Ballycastle & Hurling Match & to Woodsides. [**This family of gentlemen farmers lived until recently at Carnsampson on the other side of Ballycastle in a remarkably similar house to Churchfield, and with a 'Jungle Room' full of colonial trophies and artefacts.[433]**]

6, Monday At Ballycastle. Aodh Ua Dubbthaigh [**Hugh Duffy**] called on way to Feis na nGleann.

7, Tuesday At Ballycastle.

8, Wednesday At Ballycastle – & to C'dall to 'shesk, but heard of Jack's sudden death at C'dall & up to Glenville – & Home at 8.30. [**In a letter to Bulmer Hobson, written later that night of 8 June, Casement described the sudden end at Glenville of Mya Young's husband, the Rear Admiral: "My cousin died of heart failure – without any warning – in his sleep really. He was not 56 yet and was as well as I am yesterday and last night – about and all over the place and he died without waking this morning. I am very sorry for his wife." Belfast newspaper obituaries however spoke of the Admiral being "in failing health for a couple of years past."[434]**]

9, Thursday At Ballycastle – Lunched with Roger & Susie & walked down with Mrs Robertson. [**See 1903 diary for details of this Casement-related family.**]

10, Friday At Ballycastle all day. Wrote M[**illar**] & others. Drew £10 from Bank. (First since £20 on 20 May)

11, Saturday Over to C'dall with Roger & Reggie to Jack's funeral. Then to Cushendun & up with Miss MacNeill to Shane O'Neill's Cairn. [**O'Neill was**

hacked to death here at Glendun on 2 June 1567, by the MacDonnells, with whom he was attempting a reconciliation. Their behaviour was not entirely unreasonable as two years earlier Shane had destroyed their Scottish settlements in Antrim and murdered Sorley Boy MacDonnell's brother James.] Ethel Johnston came.

Sunday 12, June. At Cushendun all day.

13, Monday Left Cushendun with young C'dall car boy driving. He is 19 on 29 August next **[Casement was given to recording the birth date (and age) of young men he met along the way because it was both a good conversation piece and an item of knowledge which he could return to on a future occasion to illustrate his interest in the individual.]** Tiny wee Jack MacCormack talked Irish on road – To Dobbs to Lunch & then up by Parc mór's car to Ballymena & to tea with Kings. **[Born in 1871, Margaret Dobbs lived at *Portnagolan* near Parkmore railway halt above Cushendall. She was from a cadet branch of the Dobbs family and died in 1962, unmarried although much loved locally because of her Gaelic revival activities and her Republican past.**

She had been secretary of the Glens *Feis* for half a century almost from its inception in 1904. She was a playwright and a prolific writer on old Irish and Celtic studies who described herself as a "dead nut on history." In 1909 she was to be found giving a lecture to the Belfast Naturalists' Field Club entitled *The Dawn of History in Ireland.* Miss Dobbs's funeral was intended to be private but the Glens people turned out in their hundreds to make it a public event. A retired, local journalist who witnessed the funeral somewhat disparagingly explained to this author that these spinster Protestant ladies took up the Irish language for want of anything else to do.[435]

Dobbs was a member in 1914 of the provisional executive of *Cumann na mBan*, precursor of the women's IRA, as were Agnes O'Farrelly and Caroline Bloxham. In 1916 she donated £10 to the Casement defence fund. At a presentation in 1945 for her contribution to *Feis na nGleann* she gave her life-view: "Ireland is a closed book to those who do not know her language. No one can know Ireland properly until one knows the language. Her treasures are as hidden as a book unopened. Open the book and learn to love your language."[436]] & on to Coleraine by 6.51 train & to Clothworkers Arms. Lovely room. Millar & Argentine sailors X. X **[The sailors were present only in the mind on this occasion. That particular fleet had not been in since Casement's visit to Buenos Aires in April. Millar was also absent, suggesting the double Xs record sexual fantasising.]**

14, Tuesday To Portrush during day – Nina came over & called on Edie Pottinger & to Miss Reynolds where Mrs Dobbs of Castle Dobbs was with others. Back by 4.25 train & at home at 6.10 & found letter from Millar. **[None of Millar's 1910 letters are to be found in the Casement archives – this one may have set up the arrangements for 20 June.]**

15, Wednesday No letters of any interest. At Ballycastle all day.

16, Thursday At Ballycastle – Up Glenshesk to Glenbank & then Dunlops with Hoppy **[Gertrude was so nicknamed because of a bad leg]** & Nina.

17, Friday At Ballycastle – up to Magheranteampul **[his spelling]** by myself. Got letter from Anti-Slavery people about Putumayo River & the Amazon Rubber Coy. Answered by wire at once & wrote also. **[This letter from Rev. John Harris was the initial sounding out of Casement for the job that would crown his consular career. Harris was suggesting his name to the Foreign Secretary in a move indicative of the influence of advanced Liberals over Asquith's government. Rubber was certainly a boom market although plantations were starting to replace wild collection. Co-incidentally three days earlier the Belfast *Northern Whig* was advertising the share prospectus of the "New Peruvian Rubber Co."]** Called on Father Eardley & gave £1.

18, Saturday Lovely weather. Gave £10 to Rathlin School Fund to Miss Gough of Coleraine & at meeting with her & Miss MacNeill. **[Miss Emily Gough, said by Casement to be a niece of Lord Gough, was an Irish language teacher on Rathlin and an early Gaelic Leaguer like Ada McNeill. Relationships with Mrs Norah Gage, the island's chatelaine were to become frosty. Writing to Alice Stopford Green on 29 October 1913 Casement reported: "An awful visitation has emerged out of Rathlin. That Woman of the Hair and the Voice has risen and scattered you and me as 'those people', 'people like that' in a letter of reproach she wrote Alec Wilson anent our visit to 'her' island!" Describing the Belfast-born widow as a petty despot, one that Alice had "smelt a mile from the shore", Casement's room for manoeuvre was, however, limited by the knowledge that the islanders showed great respect to, and affection for the Gage family. His letter of complaint to Mrs Gage in the event went "no further than Miss Gough" as he decided on reflection "to let the matter drop in the interests, I hope, of family peace."[437]**

Alice Stopford Green may have been a comrade of Casement but she could be quite acid in her attitudes. In 1913, she is to be found, after listening to "a particularly vehement Irish tirade" from him, once the hall door had closed, exclaiming "Sometimes when I listen to that man I feel I never want to hear the subject of Ireland mentioned again."[438]] Further letter from Putumayo people – also from E.D.M. Very seedy all day – lay down. Drew £10 at Bank. Going to London on Wednesday morning.

Sunday 19th June – Rathlin Island. Lovely day.

20, Monday Gave £2 for Irish prize on Rathlin to Father MacKinley. Left Ballycastle at 4 train. Millar to dinner at N. Counties Hotel. Splendid. [**The location for this particularly memorable sex with Millar Gordon is something of a mystery. On first reading one assumes it was in Portrush where the Northern Counties Hotel was situated. But Casement in his 1903 diary was still calling Belfast's Midland Hotel by its previous Northern Counties appellation. The mention of a tram also suggests Belfast, but a recently reinstated tramway to the Giant's Causeway from Portrush existed in 1910. The Midland Hotel location is supported by sight of a letter written to Eoin MacNeill on 31 May 1910. Here Casement stroked out the words "Midland Station Hotel" on the letterhead and replaced them with "Northern Counties Hotel", while leaving the word "Belfast" untouched. Plainly he was irked by the English rail company's takeover of the local Northern Counties Railway.**[439]]
Gave Millar pin for tie [**The cost of Millar's tiepin is recorded in the diary's flyleaf as two shillings which was paid to Mrs Frances Riddell. She had set up the Irish Home Industries Workshop in Ballycastle whose manager/ instructor was Stephen Clarke, a Glens *Feis* organiser. It was also the basis for a local Irish toy industry. He was charged in 1905 in connection with distributing anti-recruiting leaflets, in whose publishing Frank Bigger and Casement were involved. Bonfires were lit in Ballycastle on Clarke's acquittal. During the war he stayed constant to the cause, unlike most others according to Nina: "The Ballycastle Irish Volunteers have gone rotten – the few good ones being unable to save them...The S.C. is all right."**[440]] & stayed till 9.30 & in Room. **X X** Then to his Mother's on foot & by tram. In deep & warm. [**Mrs Gordon's address after she was widowed in 1907 is unconfirmed for five years although she is possibly the Mrs Gordon, of 4 Myrtle Terrace, Lisburn Road, Belfast who first appears there in the 1907 street directory. She would have been expected to vacate her bank manager house in Larne rapidly after her husband's death. She is definitely in the 1912 edition living with her son and a maid in Belfast. Her new house, named Carnstroan, was on Myrtlefield Park off the Lisburn Road, and a tram ride across the city from the Midland Hotel. This diary reference is the last to Millar in 1910.**]

21, Tuesday At Belfast. To Castle Dobbs in afternoon & lunch there. Coming back with medical student in train – Charming view – & nice face. Medical student – smiling face. Left for L'pool – Bulmer to see me off. Charming day. With A. Dobbs at Castle Dobbs. Eden S.O. Carrickfergus. [**Castle Dobbs, near Kilroot, is a grand 18th century country house, secluded within a wooded and walled demesne. The biggest house in Co. Antrim, described as "without equal in Ulster", it was built in the 1750s by Arthur Dobbs,**

an early Governor of North Carolina. In 1910, Archibald and Edith Dobbs were the master and mistress of the castle.]

22, Wednesday In England. Arrived L'pool & to London at noon. To Exhibition – Takayaki Morohoshi Morohoshi.

23, Thursday In London. To Anti-Slavery & House of Commons. Dilke, Wedgwood & other M.P.s – Splendid talk – Noel Buxton.

24, Friday To dine with Conan Doyle. Morel there & to "Speckled Band" after **[This was a play by Conan Doyle, a man reckoned to have lost out on a peerage because of his efforts in 1916 to gain a reprieve for his friend Casement.]** 1 a.m. H.B. 10/- & 1.45 a.m. Jamaica! 6/6. 16/6 **[a tot of the two sex payments]**.

25, Saturday To Carlton Park **[Lord Norbury's country seat near Market Harborough – not to be confused with the Earl of Caledon's London home at Carlton Park Terrace]** at 4.55 train. Lady S. Lady Caledon. Lady Morgan.

[Sunday:] At Carlton.

27, Monday Left Carlton & to London. To Exhibition. Greek Fled **[This sounds as if a rampant Athenian was getting out of hand in a toilet cubicle in the Exhibition hall, discretion calling for Casement's hasty departure before the authorities were alerted by the noise.]**

28, Tuesday In London. Lunched at Prince's with Lady Caledon & sisters – Lady Caledon, Lady Margaret, Lady Charlotte. **[Elizabeth, the Dowager Countess of Caledon, was a daughter of the 3rd Earl of Norbury and sister of Lady Margaret Jenkins, and Lady Charlotte Graham Toler.]** Last time of seeing Sheelagh. **[Miss Shelagh Alexander, born in 1886, was a granddaughter of the 3rd Earl of Caledon and another of those progressive Edwardian ladies with something of a soft spot for Casement. The "last time" remark is one often used by Casement and does not necessarily mean final ever sight. She was an assiduous attender at the House of Commons select committee enquiry on the Putumayo atrocities, three years later in 1913. In one letter to him she remarked "The Ranee of Sarawak (Lady Brooke) was there one day. She told me she had such an admiration for you. I felt inclined to say 'no use my friend, his eyes are on the hill tops!'" The Brooke family were hereditary Rajahs of the Borneo state of Sarawak, and so remained, for a century, until 1946.**

There is an overtly flirtatious edge to Shelagh's correspondence although she seemed to sense the cause was hopeless. This may only have encouraged her. The reason for Casement's indifference must have eluded her, despite her writing in one letter "How well I read your character the first time I

saw you!" Reading that sentence may have given him a momentary weak turn but he knew a captivated female when he saw one especially when she started sending him her poetry for critical assessment. Addressing him in one instance as "Dear Don Roderigo", she admitted her suggestive remarks were ones he would "hate being told." An example was her requesting him to "lurk in the moonlight near some balcony" without knowing he frequently did. She instructed him to "send me the poem that came out in *The Nation*" asking despondently "I suppose there's no feminine or romantic element in it?"

Shelagh also tried to give him political advice on Ireland. Trying to moderate his hardening posture she wrote "It's so funny my writing and preaching to you this way, because I'm constantly told how over enthusiastic and one-sided and so on I am myself." She and her sister Cethlyn had lived for a while in their ancestral seat in Caledon, Co. Tyrone, a village that was the scene of the opening political shots of the 1960s Civil Rights campaign in Northern Ireland. Ultimately Shelagh went to live in Nova Scotia from where her grandmother hailed. She drove an ambulance in the First World War and though never marrying, unusually for the time, adopted a daughter. Shelagh died in 1970.[441] Lady Charlotte Graham Toler, another Norbury daughter, seemed also to have taken a shine to Casement, remarking in one letter to him "I think you are very plucky."]

29, Wednesday In London

30, Thursday In London.

July, 1910.

1, Friday In London. Welsh Will. Splendid 6' 3½" 10.0 & Japan.

2, Saturday To Savoy to Dick. Very pleasant.

[Sunday:] At Savoy.

4, Monday At Savoy

5, Tuesday At Savoy

6, Wednesday Left Savoy for London. To Gloucester Road and lovely type **X** to Bolton Gardens & home. Marylebone at 1 p.m. Lizzie.

7, Thursday At London. With Lizzie to Hampstead. Lunched at Metropole with Doyles. Called Lord Listowel. **[This was the 3rd Earl of Listowel (1833-1924). His son and heir, Viscount Ennismore, was a South Africa War veteran and a friend of Casement's from his time in Mozambique where he first made the acquaintance of two other of his greatest chums, Lord ffrench**

and Count Blücher (and also Lord Tyrrell). The Listowel family seat was burnt in 1921. The 5th Earl, an internationalist, was in Attlee's Cabinet as Secretary of State for India and, keeping up the Africa connection, became Governor-General of Ghana in 1957 with Kwame Nkrumah as his prime minister. President Nkrumah sent Dublin a message of African gratitude for Casement's life on the occasion of the 1965 reburial.]

8, Friday Dined with Mrs Hicks & Mr Hicks at Les Lauriers. Home & out Carlo Zioni 12/6. **[F.R Hicks, writing on 22 February 1911, the next year, was joshing Casement about his endless travelling. He said "I hope your godson won't want to follow." The godson was little Roger Hicks whose photograph is to be found in the 1911 Cash Ledger. In the very letter which may have enclosed that photo, his father added "Ever since I married, Providence has made everything smile for me. I hope you'll do the same one day." Casement was then aged forty-six.[442] From prison on 14 July 1916, he asked that a copy of the poem *Easter Week* be sent to "a little godson of mine", and "another in France named fully after me", happily unaware of Herbert Ward's desperate efforts to have his son, that particular godson, renamed.[443]]**

9, Saturday Lunched with Mrs Green at 1 o'clock. To Louie & together to Savoy.

[Sunday] At Savoy

11, Monday At Savoy. Left at 3 p.m. to London. Lay down awfully tired. Dined Blüchers. Morel Testimonial Lord Cromer's letter appears in "Times", "Morning Post" & other papers. Wrote to Tyrrell, saying had heard I was to go to Putumayo & was ready if Sir E. Grey wished it.

12, Tuesday At London To Lunacy Commission for Mrs Beere – & to EDM. To Louie **[Heath]** at 4 p.m. Morel Test'ial. Splendid leader in "M. Post". Packed up to go to Ireland but got a wire from Tyrrell asking me to call noon tomorrow F.O. To Welsh Will – but too late 9 p.m. **[Will must have received callers at home]** on & many types. Wire from Tyrrell.

13, Wednesday To F.O. & Mrs Green. Carlo but did not go. **[This is Carlo Zioni who was paid 12/6 on 8 June but who was now being stood up on a second date.]** to F.O. at 12. & then at lunch Mrs G. & then at 3. Sir E. Grey & others at F.O. Putumayo. To F.O. & saw Tyrrell who told me Sir E. Grey was decided to send me to Putumayo & wished to see me at 3 today. Lunched Mrs G. & then back to F.O. Saw Sir E. Grey & long talk with him. **[This repetitious entry involves much heavy scribbling, indicating notes written and expanded as the day went along – some for immediate guidance.]**

14, Thursday At F.O. from 12.30 looking at Putumayo papers. Lunched Spicer & to Booth Line for passage to Pará. Lizzie to dinner.

15, Friday At F.O. from 11.30 looking over papers till 5. Home to Lizzie & Louie & after dinner to Brompton Rd. & Albert (10/-) **X.** in Park. Then M. Arch & fine type in Park but fled & home at 12.50. 15½ years Albert. **[Notes in margin:]** Morel Testimonial Letter of Committee Splendid. Albert 10.0

16, Saturday At Alisons' to get things. **[Casement's shipping and storage agents Allisons who also acted as a *poste restante*.]** Lunch Holborn & then home & Lizzie & Louie Dinner at Holborn restaurant & at 8.45 to Dublin by Euston. Lizzie to see me off. Very tired of London.

Sunday 17 July. Arr Dublin 6 a.m. In Phoenix Park after dinner at Zoo. Fine type. Stiff. **[No other purpose for the visit was recorded but to Casement an overnight journey was as insubstantial as a ten mile bus trip is today.]**

18, Monday In Ireland.

19, Tuesday In Ireland.

20, Wednesday Return to Sasana **[Gaelic for England]** – beastly Hole. At F.O.

21, Thursday Morel Testimonial Lunched with Doyles. He reports £350 only in. **[To which Casement adds £217 that he has collected, including £50 from himself. As the Congo issue came to a close in Casement's life, he was thrown into a brand new slavery controversy and investigation for which the establishment considered him the obvious, if not the only suitable, candidate from within their ranks.]**

Add to this:	A. Emott	£ 50	217
	R.C.	50	567
	Dick	10	
	F. Ware	5	
	Mrs Green	30	
	Collected by her	70	
	Lizzie	2	
	Will Reid?		
Stationery for my Journey		1.0.0.	

At H. of C. & Emmott.

22, Friday Busy all day. At "M. Post" 3 times, at H of C. Lunch with Emmott. Met Hugh Law & Boland & others **[Law was a Home Rule MP for Donegal West. Casement had earlier tried to get support from such MPs for Congo reform, the difficulty being that Leopold was a Catholic monarch and there was a Protestant edge to the campaign against him. In 1905 he had written to Law, a convert to Catholicism, accepting that there were "attempts to import religious differences into the discussion" but pointing out he himself was impeccably nationalist.[444]]** To Lizzie & to Gilmours at Fagan of British Museum. Wrote E.D.M. letters until 2 a.m. – Wrote to "L'pool Courier" & "L'pool Daily Post". Wrote many letters.

23, Saturday Expect to sail by "Edinburgh Castle" ??? Cabs 5/- Luggage 7/- Ticket to S'hamp/ 11/- Typed copy of Anti-Slavery matter **[1.3.0 and 5 are inscribed in the far right £ cash column]** To Southampton. Mrs G., E.D.M., Harris, W. Reid. **[the farewell party]**

Sunday 24 July 3/6. At sea on "Edinburgh Castle" Ran 261 miles. No meals because "Commission" at my table. **[Total of previous two days' expenses:]** 7. 3.0.

25, Monday 3/6 At sea Rather rough. Writing many letters about E.D.M. testimonial. Ran miles. No meals all day!

26, Tuesday 3/6. ~~Madeira?~~ No meal till dinner time. Wine 10.6

27, Wednesday Madeira? Tips to Stewards. Luggage on shore – 1.5.0.
Hotel 1. 0.

17 **[the boy's age]** Carlos Augusto Costa 12.6.
189 Rua dos Ferreiros,
Funchal
Madeira

28, Thursday
10.12.6 **[in total column]** Hotel 1.0.0.
Splendid *testemunhos* – soft as silk & big & full of life – no bush to speak of. Good wine needs no bush. Carlos Augusto Costa – 189 Rua dos Ferreiros, Funchal 7/6 Very fine one – big, long, thick. Wants awfully & likes very much. João – Big £1.12.6. Internacional Hotel. Bella Vista.

29, Friday Hotel 1.0.0. Carlos Augusto Costa 1.10.0. Total **[of the three payments to Carlos:]** £2.10/-. Last time Carlos. 9 to 11. **[the two hours together]** Huge Extension.

30, Saturday Hotel 1.0.0. 13.12.6 **[This is the total of the journey's non-sex expenditure since 21 July, as detailed in the far right column. The following set of totals reveals João as the recipient of a massive second payment:]** João £10.0.0 Total 11.12.6 C.A. Costa 2.10.0. **[Total sex expenditure:]** £14.2.6 in Madeira **[Carlos plainly left such a big impression (although he was not so hard on his pocket as João) that Casement, in just a few lines, records his name five times and his address twice, not to mention his attributes. He is also so cheered that he makes a literary pun about his "bush". Some of the Carlos commentary is his later insertion.]**

Sunday 31 July. Sailed from Madeira in "Hilary". Hotel 13.12.6. 1.0.0. **[In a letter dated 19 July 1912 another, presumably female, admirer Carnegy Johnson wrote to Casement from Abruzzo in Italy with "a mite enclosed for your Putumayo mission from one to whom (you will have forgotten) you were kind during another lonely week at the Villa Victoria, Funchal two years ago."[445] Getting no diary mention, Carnegy was correct to assume she had not been remembered. Casement's eyes were not on the hills for those four nights, but on Carlos and João.]**

August, 1910.

[1-7 August: On board the *Hilary*, en route from Madeira to Pará in Brazil where Casement had been consul in 1907-8, doing little but losing money at bridge.]

1, Monday At sea – not well at all. Feel very low. Lay down all day – & Read a bit. Ran 333 miles in 23½ H.

Sweep	2/0
Bridge	2/6
	4/6

[Doodling on blotter:] Errin, Eren Dublin London Era Erie Eire Eire.

2 Tuesday	Ran 343 miles.	Bridge 3/0	Sweep 2/-	5/-
3, Wednesday	Ran 348 miles.	Bridge 12/6	Sweep 2/6	14/6
				1.4.0

4, Thursday Losings on board 1.4.0. Ran 351 miles, only 1376 miles from Pará – 19/- Lost at Bridge 4/6. Sweep 2/- 6/6.

5, Friday Hot morning. 344 miles.

6 Saturday 337 miles. Current against us.

Sunday 7 August **[blank thereafter]**

8, Monday Should arrive in Pará and get on shore by 6 p.m. Will go Valda Peso – & Cafés first – then to Theatre & then on to Cafe in Independencia – & back to Theatre about 10.30 & Valda Peso at 11. *Camerinos'* first. **[*Camarim* means a theatrical dressing room revealing that cruising went on within the theatre.]** Arrived Pará at 3. Alongside 3.30. Tea & at 5 with Pogson to Vaz Cafe. Lovely moço **[lad]** – then after dinner to Vero Pesa. Two types – Also to gardens of Praca Republica. 2 types – Baptista Campos one type – then Senate square & Caboclo (boy 16-17). Seized hard. Young, stiff, thin. Others offered later. On board at 12 midnight.

9, Tuesday Called Pickerell. Shall I see João – dear old soul? I'll get up early & go to Ruy Barbosa by 6.51 & wait till 7.30 – & on all morning till 9. No sleep hardly – Up at 5 on shore at 6 a.m. Lovely moço in tram – to Cemetery & lo! João coming along. Blushed to roots of hair with joy – handfast & talked. Gave 10$ – Said he thought it was me. To Consul USA & then to Marco. Lunch Pogson. Dined Barry. Left 11.10 Barry. One type 11.30. Too late. Rain & on board midnight. João Anselmo de Lima – 251, Baptista Campos. **[In conjunction with the United States consul, George Pickerell, Casement had been making efforts to keep the local cemetery in good condition and thus had justification for his frequent visits.[446]]**

10, Wednesday On shore at 6.35. Met João again at Cemetery. He gave roses. Promised to call on him later & he said roses. To stream in forest. Two caboclo boys there at hut. Bathed & back in "Hilary" at 10.30. Very tired. Letters from home – Kate Parnell & others. Afternoon on shore a minute – too hot. Then after dinner to big square & all over place – including Baptista Campos – but none – altho' several possible types.

11, Thursday Out to Ornstein's **[a friend from his consular days in Pará]** & on to Forest Stream & bathed – Huge caboclo – thin, 40 years. Antonio & Francisco out at Charcoal. Policeman at Station. At Zoo & Museum & breakfasted with Jimmy Hall & Mrs Hall at 143 Ruy Barbosa. Very good breakfast indeed. Back on board. Barry, H, Pogson & Davis dined on board with me. Left at 10 with them to Square & all over. No type – but at 12.30 Darkie policeman "em paisana" **[out of uniform]** – enormous = 5$.

12, Friday Very hot day. To call on Governor, but owing to Pogson's folly failed to find him high or low. Pogson is an ass! Back after luncheon with Barry & H. (Bertie there) and on board. Left wharf at 4 sharp. Pogson arrived 5 minutes too late! He is an ass! Out to bay & anchored till 12 midnight & then up anchor & off up River! Nice pilots on board – one Paraense boy of 18 or so.

13, Saturday Steaming up to entrance to creek. Due to arrive at Manaos on early morning of 16th. Pilot boy is Augusto de Maranhaos – 18 of Pará. Steaming all day. The *praticante* Augusto is the son of Rubim of Port Works and very like him.

Sunday 14th August Lovely weather – Lovely All day steam. Talked Pilot Augusto 7.50-8. Passed Obidos 8.30 p.m. Lights.

15, Monday Passed Beautiful cliffs at 7. Augusto said were named – forget name. Lovely Banks. Col. Bertie advised by Dr. to go home at Manaos. I agree. **[Bertie was the leader of the Peruvian Amazon Company commission of enquiry. His brother was the Ambassador in Paris, whom Casement recorded dining with in early January of the next year, on his way home from Brazil. Louis Barnes, now assumed command of the Commission, Casement not being a member as such, merely an accompanying consular observer.]** Stayed at Itacoatiara at 5. But Brazilian Customs refused to allow the cargo to be landed for the M-M Railway. What utter Rotters. They had telegraphed from Para to Manaos on 11th for this permission! As "no cargo, no mails", said Skipper Collins & on to Manaos! A beautiful instance of Brazilian competency.

16, Tuesday At Manaos Arrd. Manaos at 6 a.m. Lovely view over broad bay of Rio Negro. On shore at 10 to Booth's & Chambers to Breakfast – after b'fast out by Flores tram. João Pensadors shut up but to further stream. Filthy Portuguese vendors – Back to J. Flores & on board at 4. Wrote F.O. of Col Bertie's return & on shore at 6. To Gardens by Lyceo & Barracks. Several policemen wanting, I think. One lovely schoolboy. Back & forward several times & at 8.15 to Chambers & stayed all night there in good bed & room. **[Casement left Manaos for Iquitos in Peru on 17 August on a voyage that lasted a fortnight. No significant diary entries were made. The investigation was to get under way once Iquitos was reached. Those interested in Casement's detailed examination of what he saw, and sought out, as soon as he reached Iquitos, might read Roger Sawyer and Angus Mitchell (both 1997) for their versions of the 1910 White Diary. Casement's thoroughness – there was something of the auditor in him, created a formidable inquisitor. His dedication to the written word, almost a vice in both his private and public life, was the weapon with which he attempted to save the Indians from their genocidal masters.]**

17, Wednesday Left Manaos for Iquitos. Up at 6.30. Down to Theatre and town. Wire from F.O. John Brown **[interpreter]** can't come he is sick in Montserrat. Called Aranas & got card of Colombian Consul in Manaos – Dr Rozo. Refused to meet him. Lunched at Derings out by Igarapé Grande – Beautiful water. Manaos a horrid town! Very hot. No Barbadians came. At 4 on board, cleared out luggage & to "Huayna". Beastly ship. Left anchorage at

5. Israel & other passengers on board – including Javari family with boy Luiz, 17 on 15 July last, returning from Lisbon after 6 years. Entered Solimoes before 6 p.m. Dark Brown water again. Steamed all night.
[In margin:] Luiz de Veiga son of Pio d'Azeredo Veiga.

18, Thursday Steaming along South Bank. Passed Purús main entrance about 10 a.m. Very hot morning. Only one bath & W.C. for all Men passengers – 27 of us. Food bad. Ship old & smelling. Great tornado in afternoon, cooled air greatly. Talked Luiz & others especially after dinner. Steaming slower, Solimoes current is stronger than that of Amazonas. Turned in at 10.15 after chat with Luiz. Cool night. Anchored from about midnight as pilot was sick. Lost clear 6 Hours.

19, Friday Not well. Headache. Air in cabin very confined. Food abominable & ship dirty. No bath today! Passed beautiful banks – often high red clay today. River often 3-4 miles broad. 7 fathoms & no bottom at a point 4 miles broad at 4 p.m.! Passed Camara in morning – Coary in ~~evening~~ afternoon. Cool day & night. Slept on deck till 10 and then turned in at 10.15 in cabin. Cool night. Passed 'Athualpa' at 3. She reports only 18 feet of water – we draw 21.
[in margin:] Passed Ega or Teffe of Bates at 5.30 a.m. 20th.

20, Saturday Warm & brighter morning. Near mouth of Japura. –
[In margin:] 380 miles from Manaos at 5.30 a.m. Doing about 150 miles per day
No bath again! Feel seedy & bored. We shall be stuck very soon now – after Jurua. Did not see Japura at all. Steaming well. Banks often high 50 or 60 feet. Splendid trees. Birds often – eagles & gulls. Saw turtle at 5.30 swimming. An Indian boy on board 3rd class. River still splendid stream. Expect reach Jurua in night about 3 a.m. Slept till 1.30 on Deck. Passed Fonte Boa at 5.40 Sunday morning.

Sunday 21 Steaming well. At Jutahy R. will be half way to Iquitos. Anchored at 11.40 a.m. to take soundings about 25 miles below Jutahy. Launch returned at 3 – with a hatfull of turtle's eggs in Antonio's hat. Anchor up – plenty water – and at 3.10 off = 3½ hours. Steamed past Favorima – high red banks & anchored at 6.30 p.m. close to Jutahy River.

22, Monday Up anchor 5.45 & off at 6 a.m. in lovely cool morning. River like silver. Don't suppose will do 80 miles today – probably 60. Passed Jutahy R 6.35 a.m. 5-7 fathoms. 2 p.m. anchored in 60 feet – sending out steam launch at 2.26 only for soundings – below Timbatemba Island. We have steamed about 46 miles I reckon since this morning's start. A loss of ½ hour from anchoring & nearly 40 mts. from time we slowed (1.53) down. Stayed at anchor all night – Launch returned at 6 from sounding, reporting plenty of water all the time.

Wasted 16 hours! Slept on deck, fearful flies & mosquitoes. Heavy rain – but my bed good & I got none. Off Timbataba Island.
[In margin:] ½ way to Iquitos

23, Tuesday Up anchor at 5.45 & on. Off Putumayo River mouth at 1 p.m. High land on left bank since this morning – with many very pretty places & clearings like Missions perched on the hills. Read over all papers of the Enquiry. 3.45 Passed on right bank, south one mile & half, high red cliff & fine houses – Colonia Rio Jajo. On across River to Maturas Island & then steep banks both sides – river (whole of it) some ¾ mile wide or less. Very deep, swift current. Maturas town – very pretty. South bank with <u>Church</u> – the first seen from Manaos – & after about 6 miles more we anchored at 6.10. about 12 miles below Larangol. Miserable!
[In margin:] Colonia Riojano

24, Wednesday Plenty mosquitoes. Up anchor & off at 5.50 in misty morning. At 7.10 ran on a bank but getting off quickly – 'deep six' – cool and rainy. Expect "Urimaguas" tonight possibly – but more likely not before Tabatinga on Friday. Passed Recreio at 10.45. Passed São Paulo de Olivença at 1.10. Steaming badly – about 44-46 miles since we started at 5.50. At 2.5 passed N. bank. Plantation with English flag called Tupenduba (9 miles above Sao P). Half speed at 2.20. On again. Passed "Bom Future" at 3.50. Many Siphonia Elastica trees – some tapped. Steamed on splendidly till 6.30 in sight almost of Boa Vista. Have done about 82 miles today. The chief Pilot, Noronha, has bet C/S Champagne will be in Tabatinga tomorrow night. It is about 92 miles away. Actual run about 85 miles.

[On blotter facing 22-24 August:] 3½ Hours anchored from 11.40 to 3.10. 6 Hours – on night of 18th. At anchor 11½ Hours. Total to date <u>21 Hours</u> 33 minutes lost from time we slowed ship to departure of Steam Launch. Should be 770 miles instead of only <u>620 about!</u>
22-23rd At anchor 15¾ 36¾ Hours

124

<u>84</u>

213 miles from Putumayo to Tabatinga

<u>289</u>

502 miles from Iquitos to Putumayo

Another all night sitting <u>12</u>

48¾ Hours

At 10 o'clock we are 129 miles from Tabatinga. 418 807
With good luck we should reach it on Friday afternoon some time. Then left 289 miles to Iquitos.

25, Thursday Up anchor at 1.27 a.m. Full speed 1.33. Passed Boa Vista at 2.10. steaming well. At 6.10 Belem and on full speed. Noronha has done the trick! Should be in Tabatinga at 4 p.m. Bath in Dr's bath. Very seedy feeling. Slept from 8.30 to 3 when out on deck. Orique – 9.40 a.m. (45 miles from our starting point 4 miles below B. Vista). Only 44 miles to do now at 9.40 to Tabatinga = 4 p.m. At 2 at Guanabara, close to S.E. mouth of Javari – a Brazilian flag at a good house & party on verandah. They fired three shots, we stopped – I presume a half caste pic-nic wants a passage! Brazilian Customs come off for newspapers and ice! Detained 40 minutes. On at 2.40, Esperanza at 3.35. Mouth of Javary. Landed Luiz & father. ~~On at~~ On again at 4.53. Lost 1.17 Suddenly struck ground just past Javari 2nd mouth & anchored all night in 23 feet.
"Liberal" launch reported at Guanabara as having cleared there at 7. a.m. for Iquitos from Ica, with 45 tons Rubber & a lot of "sick people" on board.

10.5 fathoms =	63
add rise	27
	90 ft.

[On blotter facing 25-27 August:]

Carried Forward	48¾ hours
24-25th Anchored	7
	55¾ hours

24) 161 (hours 144 **[divided by]** 17 8_17.0
Lost at Gate & Esperanza (Javari)

	2
	57¾
25th-26th At anchor	
off Javari all night till 9 a.m.	15½
	72¼
26th at Tabatinga – noon	1¼
	73½
26th 27th Leticia (say 18)	17¾
	88¼

If "Urimaguas" left night of Friday 19th she will be 8 days out tonight – Say she makes average 100-110 miles per day, she will be tonight from 800-880 miles from Manaos. By distance chart Tabatinga is 861 miles. So she cannot well be there before tonight or tomorrow morning.
After Juana Island & Parana the water of the river is much clearer. Why – because Current very slow.

27th At anchor Loreto Channel	6¼
	94½
Night of 27th-28th anchor	11¾
	106¼

26, Friday Steam launch out at 5.45, sounding. Return reporting only 24 feet. At anchor till 9 a.m. – & on to Tabatinga in less than 6 ft. At 10 a.m. getting near Tabatinga & arrived 11.15. Brazilian military post – 2 small field ~~guns~~ pieces on earth platform & a house of Commandant. Anchored within 15 yards of shore in 12½ fathoms. River dead low, breadth 1000 yards, depth say 100 feet. Current very slow, less than 1½ miles per hour. Below at Javari current about 5 miles per hour, but depth only 21-24 feet. Group ½ doz. soldiers by guns. The Commandant came on board, but we had to send a boat for him. What is the use of this post? They do nothing. It will cost us some £30 to pay this absurd visit, as well as the delay! The soldiers all visibly niggers, the 1st Liberian Army Corps over again! Left Tabatinga 12 noon for Leticia just up stream. Arr. Leticia at 12.15 and anchored near "Esperanza". She high and dry on the bank in midstream. 5 Peruvian soldiers off – Cholos – fine chaps. One splendid fellow, gave cigarettes. Also Brazilians from "Esperanza" & at 5 all bathing on sand bank & summersaulting.
[In margin:] See from Tabatinga the "Esperanza" aground at Leticia.

27, Saturday All night at Leticia. Expect "Urimaguas" hourly! Wasted 6-7 hours at Leticia. Proceeded at 5.45 a.m. after 18 hours wasted deliberately at Leticia – pretext steering needed attention. Pilots all went for a spree to "Esperanza". Bright sun this morning. Soundings across river from Xinari to Ronda gave least water 6¼ fths = 37½ feet. River about ½ mile wide or less, current slow. Islands few & small. Similar to Lulanga at junction of Lopori, but rise here very marked on bank – fully 35 to 40 ft I should think. Steaming very well. Near Loreto (39 miles) at 9.50. Captain timid however, & stopped on N. bank "in no bottom at 10" (60 feet). Launch for soundings ready. We could easily go on to S. P de Loreto, another 40 miles. Anchored 9.53 in "no bottom at 10". Launch did not leave till 11.10 = 1 h. 17 deliberately wasted. She takes 6 hours coal. Launch returned 3.45, reports 22 feet. Captain I can see will stay all night! He is talking of whirlpools in this calm, lake like river. He fears everything – not the man for the job. 4, under way again till 6. (2 hours lost over & above the time needed!). 6.10, slowed for anchor. Very shallow in Loreto channel. Only 22 ft and we heeled over twice. Launch "Inca" came up from Javari & anchored.

Sunday 28. Up & off 5.45. "Inca" left at 5. At Caballo Cocha at 7 stopped. Launch left 7.32. River dirty again & evidently rising. Huge logs, trees & grass

& scum floating past. Launch returned 10.45 a.m. We started 11.10. SS "Javari" passed down 12.15. Reports "plenty water" in channel right up to Iquitos. She was ashore at Tigre – 3 days anchored. 4.17 – Launch not off till 4.55. (38 minutes lost.) Launch returned 7.30 – 22 feet. "Inca" passed up. Turned in at 10 "Urimaguas" reported. Came alongside 11.30. Anchored.

[On blotter:] ½ hour lost in sending launch

Carried forward	102		15
Launch about 3.15			
28th Hard off Caballo Cosha	4.		10
10½ Hrs anchored 4.10 = 6.20			
steaming = 38 miles at outside			
At 6 a.m. 29th "Huayna" at anchor			
all previous night from 7 p.m.	13.		43
	120	Hours.	8

29, Monday No sleep. Getting ready to tranship to "Urimaguas" at 5 a.m. Did so, along with four others – Israel & Kouriat & two more. Left "Huayna" about 6.30. Passed steam launch sounding up above. Waved farewells. All party on board. Steaming well, but not so fast as "Huayna". Passed San Juan and later on San Pablo de Loreto (187 miles from Iquitos). "Urimaguas" is a Launch of 110 tons built at Glasgow to order of E. de Costa & Co of Liverpool. She burns coal or wood. Our supply of former running short they say – we must stop to buy wood. Will not reach Iquitos till Wednesday morning. Day delightfully cool. Many Indian houses on the right, or South bank, which we are skirting most of the time. Better built houses than those one sees in the Brazilian woods, & some small plantations around each. Cassava, mealies & so forth. Many more people too & they look happy – are certainly Indians – not mulattos – altho' clothed. Even the children are clothed. Played Bridge with Barnes, Gielgud & Fox till 11 or later.

30, Tuesday Going well. Stopped for an hour owing to fog from 4 to 5.15 a.m. Passed Pebas in the night – 114 miles from Iquitos. "Urimaguas" does not do more than 5 knots over the ground I think. We should be at Iquitos early morning. There are many more Indians & inhabitants along the Peruvian than the Brazilian Amazon. Stopped at La Colonia Braziliana for firewood. Saw two Boras Indians. Caught young – Dark, fierce, brutal faces. Other Indians. Wood is sold at 30 Soles the 1000 billets = £3. On again & passed mouth of Napo about 5 p.m. Will anchor in night so as to reach Iquitos early morning.

31, Wednesday Arrd. Iquitos at 8. All on shore. To Booth's office & then Consul Cazes. Lunched his wife & he. Took room "Le Cosmopolite". Hotel dreadful. **[Perhaps because of this, as Casement wrote on 3 September "I became the guest of Mr David Cazes, the British consul here."[447]]** Called on Prefect Dr Paz Soldan at 4 to 5.45. Talked fully. He declared the stories 'fables' – but much that he said confirmed to my mind their truth. Very hot at Iquitos, & lots of mosquitoes. The town is very well situated, but horribly neglected & dirty. The 'streets' atrocious, the houses poor. **[Responding to the Foreign Office, Casement described how "Iquitos remains in a condition of filth and neglect well nigh indescribable."[448]]** Hundreds of soldiers in blue dungaree – splendid looking Indians & Cholos. Nearly all are Indians – a conquered race held by "blancos". They are finer men than the "blancos" & with gentle faces, soft black eyes with a far off look of the Incas. **[The blotted name and Chepstow address of "Col. Hon. R.H. Bertie" on the pink blotting paper opposite this date's entry can be deciphered at Kew with a mirror.]**

September, 1910.

1, Thursday On board "Urimaguas" for bag. Met Lizardo Arana & to his house for Barnes. He spoke of the great prospects of the Putumayo. Its many Indian tribes, its fertility, etc & hoped the result of the visit of myself & the others wd be the introduction of "fresh capital". The late acting French Consular Agent Vatan called on me & told me that the condition of things on the Putumayo had been disgraceful – that the existing method was slavery pure & simple – but that it was the "only way" in Peru as she exists. The evil inheritance of an evil past – a conquered race outside the constitution & the law with "no rights" – the Indians had to be "civilized" & this is the way it is done. Interviewed two Barbadians just from Putumayo. One confirms well nigh everything. Engaged him to return with me – the other two saw only good & gave a clean bill.

[On blotter:] Interview with Vatan. Interviewed Bishop & Nellis Walker

2, Friday The Iquitos "El Oriente" of last night has long account of the "Commission" declaring it is solely to get fresh capital for the Putumayo – in fact the article is clearly dictated by Lizardo Arana – acting on the lines of Julio's letter to Cazes. Interviewed Dr. Pizarro – Federico M. Pizarro – who "knew nothing". Also A. Guichard who equally knew nothing about any of the "Truth" deponents. Spoke again to the Barbadian, – Frederick Bishop, who seems a little bit afraid now & hopes there is "nothing political" to get him into trouble. Cazes says the Prefect thinks me prejudiced and taking a partisan view – another Arana insinuation I presume. In evening "El Oriente" a telegram from Lima saying the Govt are going to enquire into the Putumayo charges, – a letter from Barcelona to the "Comercio" having excited great sensation from Deschamps a French geographer.

[On blotter:] Pizarro and Guichard. X

3, Saturday Called on Barnes & others suggesting to take the statement of Bishop when I can get him – all of them to come. In house all day getting things unpacked & writing to F.O. Bishop came at 5 – & told me further horrible things recently done on Putumayo by Moung or Montt. Macedo is supreme he says & the Peruvian soldiers at La Chorrera a farce – & the Indians all slaves. He flogged them for not bringing rubber. Cazes wrote also to say an important witness from Putumayo had come down & in evening told me it is a Spaniard who declares that all in "La Felpa" and "La Sanccion" was true! & he will prove it. After dinner Cazes & I talked till 11.30 on this Putumayo Horror. He explaining his reasons for not having taken action.

Sunday 4 Sep. Interviewed F. Bishop & Juan Guerrido on Putumayo. Dreadful story – all Commission present. Went tram ride with Mr. & Mrs. Cazes – & then Gielgud & Barnes to dinner, played Bridge.

[On blotter:] Interviewed Juan Guerrido Ditto Bishop – By all Commission.

5, Monday Heavy tornado last night & rain & another this morning at 6.30 a.m. Very heavy rain often all day – & apparently throughout the night. Cazes told me of Burga, the Comisario of Govt. in the Putumayo – also of the Peruvian Captain & the two Indians in guns at Nazareth on Javari – for "running away" – also of young Borda, son in law of Morey, the leading merchant of Iquitos, who is now trying to filibuster & seize by force an 'Estate' down at Caballo Cocha which he Cazes, is agent for. Threats of force are being used, on both sides. Young Borda says he is a "brave", a "valiente" & no one shall stop him – the owner threatens his rifle. Played Bridge with Commission at their House.

6, Tuesday Heavy rain still, River risen 18″ last two days. Another statement by Bishop, dreadful! – perfectly awful. Told Commission of it – ~~who are now as convinced as I am of the horror of it all~~ Have invited them & Zumaeta & Arana to dinner tomorrow with Com. & Consul. River risen over 1 foot last night = 2'6" in three days. Wrote F.O. & wrote out Bishop's Statements telling Commission all the added facts. Bishop's statement today incriminates Macedo & Ocano of Savana and worst of all Martinegui who went to Lima by last "Liberal" with the plunder of <u>Atenas</u> – leaving the Indians starving.

[On blotter:] Bishop again

7, Wednesday River risen a lot in night. A Govt. Launch left early down river. I wonder where for? I am terribly suspicious of the Local Authorities! – more so of them than of the Coy. Warm day again. Three Peruvian gunboats came, led by "America" bringing back 123 soldiers "Volunteers"! from the Napo. Splendid men – all Indians nearly – sturdy & fine, gentle-faced, handsome chaps. Poor Indian people. In house all day nearly, save for once to Booths' to get Time Table. Reading 'Forest Lovers', after many years. Today 88th anniversary of the Independence of Brazil. Dinner at 7.30 – Lizardo Arana & Pablo Zumaeta, Cazes & the four men of the commission. Drank health & prosperity to Peru.

8, Thursday Lovely day at 7 a.m. River risen again fully one foot or more. Sandbank getting covered. Huayna's passengers all came up yesterday. Met some of them. Out by train to forest pool – Morona Cocha. Fine types, one with shotgun lovely & strong. Indian Cholo in Brick Works. Stayed at Britos' house (£1500) & saw nice children & then back at 11 & a fearfully hot day. Did little or nothing – it was too hot. At 5 out to Shooting range but did not find it with Fox & Bell & then stupid dinner & out again to Commission & played Bridge till 11.30 winning two Rubbers. Home at 12 & young Cholo policeman on Malecon – splendid young Indian. Turned in 1 a.m very hot still. Shall be glad to get off from Iquitos – hope on Monday. Hear that the Interpreter at Copal Urcu is not to be found. Nous verrons when Argentina comes.

9, Friday River risen steadily since Monday. The big sandbank nearly covered this morning & various channels through it. "Argentina" returned 11 a.m. No Interpreter! Alack. I walked Punchana 9 to 10.30 a.m. Wretched. No plantation or life at all. Women bathing in stream. 2-4 Cholo **[Indian]** soldiers discharging "America" in blazing sun. Almost all Indians & a few half-castes, all fine, splendid youths. One half-white muchacho **[boy in Spanish]** magnificent display & a young Cholo with erection as he carried heavy box. Down left leg about 6-8". They are far too good for their fate. It was not the "Argentina" after all, so there may still be a chance. Called at Vatan's store and asked him to call. At 4.45 began taking statements of 4 Barbadians & one of them amply confirmed Bishop's story. The others had seen nothing, but had been on the Launches all the time. Turned in early not feeling well at all. Took 16 grs. Quinine in night – no sleep at all. Terrible storm. Rain, thunder & Thunder bolt! 2 a.m.

[On blotter:] Walcott Jones Ford Labadie

10, Saturday River still rising. Heavy rain last night – torrents. "Liberal" returned, reports "Huayna" may arrive today. My wine a/c £4.3/9 on Huaynas – & 6 bots of whisky for voyage £1.10/-. Also £5 given to Stewards on board, poor souls. Informed that Stanley J. Lewis, a Barbadian referred to in Declarations is on board "Liberal". Sent for him twice. He came to Cazes' first in forenoon, but as soon as Cazes told him that I wished to see him he bolted C. says. Said he had to go to Prefectura with a paper & that he wd. come back. At 3 I sent Bishop for him & he returned saying Lewis would not come! He did not know why. I said nothing only "I'd see him later on" and it did not matter. The Brazilian

Consul General called – "A. Aranjo Silva, Consul Général des E.U. du Brésil, Iquitos (Peru)". Why the French? I was out. My washing back today 16.80 + 7.80 + 7.50 = 32.10 = £3.4.2. Cheaper than I expected. The dinner to Arana & Zumaeta was 120.00 = £12. Turned in early on my own bed and slept all night – God be praised. Cool & nice. Heavy rain and tornado of wind at 8 p.m.

Sunday 11. Sept. Lovely morning after rain. River rising. Sandbank shows big heads only. River risen still more all day. Called on Mrs. Prefect, Ernestina G. de Alayza, a nice woman. The Alcalde, Dr. Lucas Rodriguez called to return my visit, but I was out. Barnes & Co. examined the Peruvian interpreter I sent them who speaks Huitoto & Boras & was in Arana's service. His evidence incriminates Miguel Flores & he will prove it.

12, Monday "Urimaguas" leaves for Manaos at 2 p.m. with mails. I am not writing officially by her as Arana goes on her & all letters might easily be opened. The two Barbadians, Gibbs & Lewis asked to come to see me refused to come. "Argentina" returned from Copal Urco without the Interpreter, who was in the bush. A great pity in every way, but will get the Peruvian now. Very seedy all day altogether quite unable to do anything. Running blood last night and left me weak & faint & my head aching dreadfully…I spent a truly awful night. Mosquitoes like drops of fiery poison all over me – pale yellow beasts & horrors. Bishop says Gibbs tells him of Norman[**d**]'s doings – burning people alive often & killing them. Gibbs is on the "Liberal". "Argentina" returned from Copal Urco. No interpreter!

13, Thursday A fine morning indeed, but going to be stifling. Adolphus Gibbs came at 9.30 & told his story of service at Abisinia & Morelia. At latter saw Jimenez chop off the head of a Boras cacique who had been in chains for 2 weeks & tried to escape. Saw heaps of floggings but had not flogged himself. Looks a rascal. Busy writing out depositions of the Barbadians, with Mr. Osborn as copyist. He is willing but slow. Dr. of "Huayna" to breakfast with me at Bella Vista - it cost 17 soles = £1.14/- for 2 of us! Carlton Morris did not come. Went to Booths at 5 & sent letter to F.O. to Spicer with depositions of Barbadians to go down by "Huayna". Met Jensen who told me much about the Indians and about Arana getting hold of the Putumayo & killing Serrano etc. & starving the others out.

[On blotter:] Adolphus Gibbs
Carlton Morris – The 'Barbadian Consul' did not come – will await my return – he said to say He is a carpenter in Iquitos.

14, Wednesday Packed up & down to "Huayna" for breakfast and then at about 1.30 p.m. Left in "Liberal" for Putumayo. Gibbs & another Barbadian deserted! After getting advance too. The swine. Captain Carmino Regado furious

& no wonder. Cook drunk. A Peruvian Engineering Officer on board going a trip from the Putumayo to Lima. Our interpreter looks a decent muchacho. About 23, wild hair, dark eyes, splendid teeth & a bright smile. He is half caste & looks good sort. Indian pilot young man – fine chap & Cholo steersman too. Ship is comfortable & quiet & better than "Urimaguas." Played Bridge after dinner until 8.30 & then turned in in a hammock on deck. Cold & not nice.

[On blotter:] Left Iquitos

15, Thursday "Slept" or rather lay in hammock on deck last night – Beastly – will not do it again. Got sore throat badly from it – no blanket. Anchored in night from Storm 10.30-12 midnight. Carmino told me of Burga & his Cia Cohero de Alto Maranon at Morona & Santiago. Wiped out by the Huambisas who killed 2 sons, 2 priests & all party. Burga about. These Indians big strong fellows – got guns & use them & shoot well. They are now going to be conquered. "Cosmopolita" passed Ponga de Manseriche 4 months ago with Lores as Captain & the American prospecting party. At 2.30 near "Santa Sophia" tremendous hurricane – fearful storm, nearly swamped. Captain said the worst he had ever experienced in his 14 years of Amazon life. Lasted ½ hour & rain another ½ hour. Near Leticia saw "Perseveranza" steaming splendidly up stream full speed for Iquitos. Alack, our mails on board & so near & yet we shall not get them until end of October. At Leticia. "Esperanza" has 3 feet of water. River risen some 5½ or 6 feet since I passed up on 26 Augt. Practicantes on board. Gave cigarettes nice Paraense moco. On to Tabatinga & Javari. Many mosquitoes. Left Javari at 9.30 & on to Putumayo.

16, Friday Out on the bosomy Solimoes ("only Lemons". River's Eng Portuguese navigation!) Hot enough, but night was cool. I have a very bad sore throat from sleeping in Hammock. Passed S São Paulo de Olivença at about noon. Beautiful situation. It has clearly deserted the high steep cliff Herndon & Bates speak of for this cliff lies about 1½ miles up stream & the town with its Church is on high sloping green pasture. At 2.30 coming to Maturas which passed on 23 coming up at about 5 p.m. then. Heavy tornado from down stream. Turned nose up River to avoid it and lost fully ½ hour. Coming to Colonia Rio Jano at 3.30 p.m. for mules. Cooler after rain. On shore Colonia Rio Jano. Got 12 mules with great trouble, but a tremendous storm first below Maturas. Left Colonia at 10.30 after long delay & mosquitoes & got to Putumayo Mouth at 11.30 but I in bed. A few miserable Indians at Colonia Rio Jano. We started up Putumayo – white mist at 4 a.m.

17, Saturday Delayed in Putumayo early morning 2.30 a.m. to 4 a.m. by white mist. Up only at 9 a.m. ill with fever & saw little of River at all. The Banks seem of clay – hard caked clay. Stone sand shown & a few sandflies. Steaming all day – at 5 p.m. passed mouth of a biggish tributary on S.W. bank

– sandflies not so bad as I expected. Mosquitoes none at all. At dinner heard of the attack on La Union in Jan. 1908. The Engineer now on board was here then & our Indian pilot was shot in ear & head. River is deep & connects with Amazon by side channel but the phenomenon of this depth is that of the Amazon itself – not the great quantity of fresh water delivered by this region, but the great quantity held up & restrained by the influence of the Ocean. "Liberal" steams 7½ knots, cannot say 2-2½. It is 42 Hours steaming from mouth of Igaraparana to Caraparana, says Captain.

[On blotter:] Ocean level The young Quichua pilot on Liberal is named Simon Pisango – a pure Indian name – but calls himself Simon ~~de la~~ Pizarro, because he wants to be civilised! Just like the Irish Os & Macs dropping first their names or prefixes to shew their respectability & then their ancient tongue itself, to be completely Anglicised. Simon Pisango still talks Quichua – but another generation of Pizarros will speak only Spanish! Men are conquered not by invasion but by themselves & their own turpitude. The man who gives up his family, his nation, his language is worse than the woman who abandons her virtue. What chastity is to her, these essentials to self-respect & self-knowledge are to his manhood.

Sunday 18 Sept. Mist in night & anchored. Cold – pleasant. No mosquitoes at all. Many sandflies this morning, but not so many as I expected. Lots of small green parrots in bushes – tiny chattering things. No araras. Many assai palms & bactois. Herons too. Stopped twice today at Brazilian stations. Military post and Customs station. Latter had 3 white Brazilians – dreadful hole. Then at 5 at Cotuhi River. 2°53′. 12. S. – 69°. 41.10″ West Greenwich.

19, Monday Lovely morning – Passing a new palm, the Punchana pilot calls "Pona" – a lovely thing indeed. Fox raving about it & well he may. Beside the assai it shoots up its graceful stem with from 6-12 magnificent fronds like those of a hart's-tongue fern on top – & then a green bulging head to its long stem. Five lovely and quite differing palms growing here close together & in enormous numbers. The young pilot calls the ground – an "island" probably – "achawa". 8.30 a.m. a deer swimming down midstream at tremendous rate. Lowered canoe & after long chase, deer often turning up stream & beating canoe, one man jumping over, but being beaten hollow by the deer, the poor little chap was caught by the hind leg, after many failures & dragged into canoe, tied by legs & hoisted on board. I should like to save him & take him home to Ireland. He richly deserves his life. I do not want to eat him! Captain Carmino, decent man, won't kill him, but has put him in a fine cage to keep & tame him. The Quichua name is "Juíchu". On thro' desolation of desolations – at 9.30 passed "Pupima" river) – misnamed so as they are not puprima palms at all, but pona.

[On blotter:] Immense numbers of "Pona" (Quichua) Ariartea orbigniana.

Also of Javari (Astryocaryum) the spring palm and of Assai (Enterpe precatora). Bates lovingly calls the Assai palm the Enterpe oleracea. Urucuri attalea excelsa were Splendid leaves & fronds, at 3-4 p.m. only a few of them. of D'Orbigny Ariartea. Orbigniana

20, Tuesday Hot morning. Interviewed Stanley S. Lewis at 8.30 to 9.30 & got revolting particulars from him which I could check by Marcial G's & from Juan Castono's statements – all true! Stopped at Pescaria a fishing station of Coy's, 10 hours below Arica & mouth of Igaraparana. Several women of Huitotos there in sexual servitude. A "whiteman" from Lima with certainly two Huitota concubines, mothers of two, separate, boy children. Two dead monkeys smoking on fire on verandah. Bought a piraracu lance of hard wood. On at 11 a.m, the river broader than ever. Magnificent palms, & innumerable too, a real forest of them. Splendid sunset over broad reach of river, often ¾ to 1 mile broad. Clear beautiful night. Arrd Mouth Igaraparana at 9.30 p.m. About 150 yards broad or less. Putumayo sweeping from a South reach some 500 yds broad. We are about 400 miles from mouth of Putumayo.

21 Wednesday Steaming very fast up Igaraparana – it is less than 100 yards broad, but looks deep & current not nearly so strong as Putumayo. Rise of 6 feet–8 feet apparent in mud of overhanging bush. Water clearer than it looks – In general more like pea soup or lentil broth. In night steaming round a sharp curve vessel listed & my Winchester fell on filter, smashed basin & I cut my finger. We must be doing 5½–6 miles an hour now in this weak current, so that at 9.30 we shall be some 70 miles up this Canal in the Woods. At 8 a.m. a good sized muddy & lazy tributary from South bank. Name not given. 9 a.m. arriving at Indostan, some 65-70 miles up from mouth. Found prisoner heavy chain ("Bolivar", a Boras boy) crime trying to escape. The "hands" absolutely miserable – starving. 2 girls in dreadful state & high fever. Gave Quinine. 2 lads also ill. Woman sleek & fat – the concubine. Others loading wood – 2 girls & 6 lads (one a half-caste) all starving. Gave Biscuits & bread to them. Indostan has about 50 acres cleared with casava, rice, sugarcane, coca, lentils, pine, etc., etc. Passed (ruin) Santa Julia at 12 noon – Fine clearing.

[On blotter:] Told that there are about 15 "hands" all told. The Chief "poor white" (with revolver on hip) named Sumaran. Says he needs 50 hands – he explained the chained Bolivar by saying he had tried to escape to Brazil (Escape to Brazil!) by stealing his only canoe with "four others" & had taken a "cup of wine". He explained with great emphasis on it that "he had not flogged" Bolivar. Bolivar said that he had been "castigated". We released Bolivar and took him on board (in new pants & cap) for La Chorrera. Left at 11.40 or 12 say.

22, Thursday At 7 a.m. in sight of high forest land in West. About 450-500 feet the beginning of La Chorrera cutting. First high land since Santarem. River swifter – Banks steep, clay, rock & soundings 38 feet, breadth 60 yds-80-100. Steamed all night without stopping. Dreamed & planned a great Irish romance of the future. Interviewed James Clark of Barbados. Interviewed Stanley S. Lewis again this morning & got the most disgraceful statements about Ultimo Retiro & J.I. Fonseca from him – murders of girls beheadings of Indians and shooting of them after they had rotted from flogging. Asked he wd come with me he said yes only Fonseca had threatened to shoot him if he ever saw him again! Arrd. At La Chorrera at 12.30 & Macedo, Tizon, Dr Rodrigues and Ponce and others came on board to welcome us. Also 7 Boras Indians, nude save for their bark covering, to carry our Baggage. 5 Barbadians there also to drive them. Three of the Boras show broad scars on their bare buttocks – some of them 1½" or 2" broad. Weals for life. This is their wealfare, their daily weal-fare. All slaves. Walked to cataract with Cipriani. Played Bridge with Tizon. Macedo looks a scoundrel. The whole place is a Penitentiary.

[On blotter:]

2. Matanzas	
1. U. Retiro	9
4. Santa Catalina	
3. ~~Abisinia~~ Savana	
1. Oriente	S. Lewis &
3. Abisinia	Ultimo Retiro
2. Steam Launches	
16)	
3 ~~Another man~~ Cho	19)
Headman	Donal Francis
The Baker	Greenwich
Cook	Lawrence
Commission	= James Chase)
Do	Stanley Sealy (Sily))

23, Friday Heavy rain in night. A young Englishman Parr in Store here. Talked to him. Got in the five Barbadians in the Station this afternoon before Sr. Tizon & Mr. Barnes & interrogated them. Three had "seen nothing", two, Stanley Sealy and James Chase, spoke out like men and told of dreadful things. They had flogged men and seen them flogged & killed too – often, & said so & maintained it. Tizon did not like it at all but bore it and in evening began flattering me after dinner & saying nice things about me and how glad he was my Govt. had sent a man like me. Is it sincere or is it a part of the game?

24, Saturday Interviewed Dyall who accused himself of <u>five murders</u> – in presence <u>Barnes</u> – atrocious crimes. Bell seemed to think that everything was right, so I asked him to come with all Commission this afternoon to my room & Tizon, where we had his Statement read over and confirmed, & I then called Bishop and S. Lewis to confirm and they did and we thrashed the matter out. Tizon practically chucked up the sponge and admitted that things were very bad & must be changed. In evening he complimented me – said he was very glad I had come, that the F.O. had chosen the right man. We decided to take Sealy, Chase, Dyall up with us & to confirm on the spot their charges – but late at night Tizon asked me to try & stop this & promised to carry out <u>sweeping reforms</u> & to dismiss all the incriminated men. This up to midnight & later.

Sunday 25th Another general meeting of Commission & Tizon & myself. I insisted on acceptance of Barbadian testimony if the men did not accompany us to press their statements & he made his promise in face of Commission.

Pilot in peaked cap

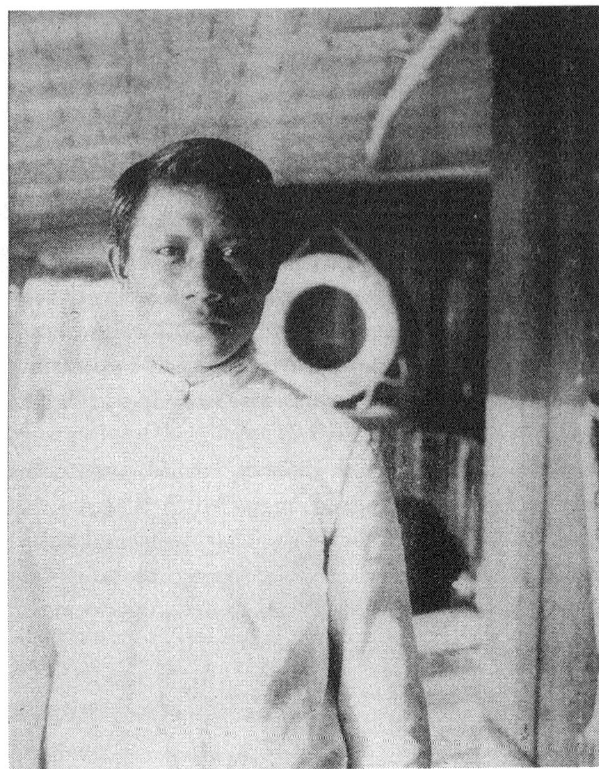

Boy steward with lifebelt behind him

26, Monday After yesterday's dreadful "field day" I feel tired out – but I have practically done all I can do now. There are only 9 more* Barbadians in the Company's service – 4 at Savana – 2 Matanzas, – 1 at Ultimo Retiro and 1 at Abisinia, & then King at El Encanto, the Arch-Murderer. "Liberal" left for El Encanto at 9 a.m. & I bid Cipriani goodbye. His name is César A. Cipriani, Ingeniero Civil Lima (Peru). Goodbye. Sick Boras Indian (no medicines) the eighth man. Also the "Muchacho de Confianza" – I gave him a magnificent pyjama suit, for his three photos. Flores & his woman & the 8 Boras & other 'muchachos' (Machetes) went on board, with a stack of Winchesters. 7 of the Boras in Singlets & trousers – the sick man in none & no medicine either. Decided to take Sealy, at his request, up country with us. Rain & packing up. Very tired – very tired, very sick of everything. God help all.

[***On blotter:**] + 2 slaves actually 11

27, Tuesday Left La Chorrera in "Veloz" launch – Commission, Tizon & myself. Also the Mayor Domo and Bruce & Garrido = 9 whites. 3 Barb – Bishop, Sealey & Chase – arrd Victoria & discharged some of our grub – the lighter we are towing is too heavy. Current very strong, river deep, a deep forest river between silent walls of trees. Generally 80-100 yards broad, sometimes broader. Arr Naimenes Sucursulo at about 4 p.m. the Chief Rodriguez (Colombian) & a second man Acosta in charge. Found here the very girl Bishop had flogged at orders of Elias Martinengui & on whom that wretch had inflicted the nameless crime. She had a Baby by a whiteman, José Maria Tuesta, who died of fever in the Caqueta last year, so Acosta said. I told Tizon & Barnes. Former refused to investigate, threw up sponge again & said "he accepted, he accepted". I gave the woman tins & things thro' Bishop & we steamed on again at 6 p.m. All night in great discomfort on launch. Stopped for hours. On at 3 a.m.

[After arrow from 27 September entry:] Tizon assured me at dinner that since his promise before he had issued a Circular to all Sections & Chiefs saying that if any more cases of flogging came to his knowledge he would at once dismiss the employé & hand him over to the Peruvian authorities. He had issued the Circular with Gielgud he said. I said good, but that the Coy must go further & prosecute – not sit by with closed hands but give the evidence and press the charge.

28, Wednesday Arrd. at Occidente at about 9 a.m. Very tired, no sleep. Found Velarde. Torrico in charge, & Rodriguez also, came overland to greet us, arriving long before we did. A fine station – big house & clearing & a huge Indian Maloca behind. Cheery boys, "muchachos" to clear our luggage. All of us tired & slept most of day until nearly 5 p.m. Commission deciding on rest of route. Andokes for cigarettes at 4 & asked me to give them, looking so gently & fingering anxiously his pierced ears. He said several things to me in a soft low voice, asking questions, I thought & looked longingly. I gave him a packet of cigarettes but he did not want to go. Played Bridge this evg until 11.25 with Tizon as partner. He & I won 2 out of 3 Rubbers. The Commission talked over their plans with Tizon & Velarde asking latter many questions as to rubber production & natives of his District. He expects 500 "men" to a Dance tomorrow.

[On blotter:] Saw James Chase again about flogging & killing at Abisinia. John Brown's credit 301 – 85 + £ 30. Captain Whiffen to F.O. claims that he had taken over this & paid John Brown the £30 – & that the money is his. To write to Chief of ~~Station~~ Putumayo Sr. Macedo & suggest that this money be remitted to the Governor of Barbados. R.C. 26 Sept 1910
"Andokes" huge erection at 3 p.m. – in stern asleep. Small boy on Launch.

29, Thursday Up till 3 a.m. hunting out the record of Velarde in my documents – it is a bad one. He is one of the chief criminals. I slept from 2.30–3 a.m. only after finding out about Velarde. Then wrote it out & put a few questions to Bishop about Ultimo Retiro & Aquileo Torres. Velarde was his jailor for a long time at Port Tarma. Poor Tizon. I am sorry for him! but I am far, far sorrier for those wretched Indians. God help them. Tonight's dance promises to be a big thing. Lots of Indians arriving from 11 a.m. onwards – the women mostly stark naked, the men (all undersized), some in dirty pants and shirts, but mostly in "fonos". Many of them whose limbs are bare show clear marks of flogging – one small boy, a child, quite recent red weals unhealed & many other small boys show marks of flogging. There will be near 1000 people here tonight, all the population of this District. I see many faces I saw Naimenes. The dance a Success – those poor gentle creatures have few occasions like this. I photo'd a lot of them. I never saw anything more pathetic than those people. They move one to profound pity.

[On blotter:] Fidel Velarde. Dance.

30, Friday Another long talk with Tizon. He admits practically everything? The Dance stopped only at 5 a.m. I was up in night from 2.30 till a glorious sunrise. Bishop told me that "Francisco" the capitan of one of the "Nations" & another had come to him in the night complaining of recent grave illtreatment here – one of them even having been drowned by Acosta in the river – the new method of torture being to hold them under water while they wash the rubber – to terrify them! Also floggings & "putting in guns" – & flogging with machetes across the back. Told Barnes & Bell & they interrogated Francisco & then I told Tizon at 1.30 when he came to talk to me. He went – I sent him – to B. & B. & they sent for Francisco & will interrogate later tonight. I bathed in river, delightful – & Andokes came down & caught butterflies for Barnes & I. Then a Capitan embraced us, laying his head against our breasts, I never saw so touching a thing! Poor soul – he felt we were their friends. Gielgud must be told to drop calling me "Casement". It is infernal cheek. Not well. No dinner.

[On blotter:] At Ocidente. The Capitan Francisco tells his story to Bishop who comes to me. I sent Barnes & Bell after him, Bishop having stopped him. They took his Statements and then I told Tizon who spoke nicely to me after lunch & sent him in to them. He said he would question. Tizon told me of his intention at Matanzas.

October, 1910.

1, Saturday October 1st The Commission & Tizon off to see the actual method of tapping Rubber trees by the "Labourers" of the Coy. They took Rodriguez, Torrico, Acosta to guide them as they "know the labourers". They found two Indians, rubber tappers, the only "labourers", & seemed surprised! I asked Barnes if he had not yet grasped the system – that I was surprised he was surprised. We were simply in a Pirate Camp, nothing more. The Indians the absolute slaves of the pirates, who then is **[undeciph.]** Velarde, then Fonseca, & so on. I stayed at home and interviewed Stanley Sealy, both on his own acts

& then on the Commission. On one of the latter with Jiménez and Caneta to Caqu in May or June of 1908 he was eyewitness of three awful & hellish acts committed by that monster. I took down his statement almost word for word, and I shall never forget the effect it produced on me. It was told with a simple truthfulness, and even grace of simplicity that would have convinced anyone in the English-speaking world of the man's absolute good faith and scrupulous exactitude & control with appropriate gesture and restraint of gesture too. Wrote out Memorandum on the stations and their personnel. Very hot day. The others returned at 1. p.m. & all did nothing till dinner, & then Bridge. Another talk with Tizon & Bell this time.

[On blotter:] At Ocidente. At dinner time Bell assuring Tizon all must go & complete change of system.

Sunday 2 All off some 4 miles through forest to Indian House of rubber workers. 6 there, but 2 away, saw 4 of them loading rubber – all bore evidence of flogging, one man dreadfully scarred & further round in Hut, – there were 11 Indians. All had been flogged they said. Back on foot, beating launch with Gielgud. In bed early, very tired. In night Bishop brought letter from Herman Gusman.

3, Monday Asked Tizon & Commission to come together. Could not discuss anything in the House, as all is open & the pirates can overhear. Suggested Indian House. We went out, all pretending to catch butterflies & when there I asked Sealy & Chase to stand & deliver the appalling story of Jiménez. They did so & again a veritable tussle – this time chiefly with Gielgud who opposed much. Tizon bewildered – after another battle Royal carrying Barnes & Bell absolutely with me (& Fox of course) we agreed to accept Sealy & Chase & that Tizon should of course dismiss Jiménez. He is in despair – so am I. Garrido called, went back on everything he said at Iquitos. A cur! I gave Tizon Gusman's note implicating Alfredo Montt, explaining its coming by Bishop last night. I told Tizon coming back from Indian House of the murder of the 4 muchachos in January last at Ultimo Retiro, by Rodriguez & Lopez & the others. Played Bridge and to bed.

[On blotter:] Dreadful nightmare. I yelled for help in night. Waking all House! Sent Bishop down to Chorrera by launch. I protested against feeding with Jiménez – the thrice accused murderer. My clothes brought by Sealy at 3. When I went to pay find they have been washed by one of Velarde's "four or five wives"! Measured stocks in "Cellar" – 21 Holes. In 5th, holes 33″ apart.

4, Tuesday Heavy rain last night, & afternoon. River rising again. At 9 to bath & found "Andokes", the light boy & a little boy in their hammock outside bathroom, all doing what **[Hans]** Coudenhove once said of the boys of Rome & Johnston of the Nyasaland Boys – without concealment! The boat servants looked on practically while these three boys played with each other with laughter & jokes! A fine beastly morality for a Christian Coy at 9 a.m. with three of the domestic servants [**The White Diary has an entry describing the same sight: "No one works. Even the table boys go to their hammocks at 9 a.m. and lie down three deep playing with each other."[449] The private diary, surprisingly, seems to condemn such activity more than the diary which would eventually be provided to the Parliamentary select committee. These two entries of the same date have been used by both sides in the forgery argument. One saying that no forger would invent for Casement what appears to be a censorious view of activity he normally recorded as stimulating, while the other points out that no man of Casement's alleged tastes would write so disapprovingly of such a public display.**

There is something of a contradiction in these two entries and neither interpretation is entirely convincing. Indeed Angus Mitchell argues that the forger had "twisted"[450] the sense of the White Diary's "general unspecific observation by Casement about the table boys lazing around in their hammocks." This is an odd view given that the supposed forger ruins his own effort by adding "fine beastly morality for a Christian Coy." Some forger.

It can be argued, on close reading, that Casement in both diaries is actually denouncing idleness and a lax approach on the company's part. His views on the innocent display itself are actually confined to well-remembered conversations about boyish homosexual activity, with two old friends from his Africa days. It is possible too that Casement just did not like activity, which he rather appreciated, being laughed at and becoming subject to ribald comments from onlookers who were trying to erase such cultural distinctions.] Wrote till late last night. Aquileo Torres from U. Retiro. Talked to Barnes & Bell. Wrote out a lot of my Diary [**presumably his White Diary**] since Friday. Several Capitans came in to be instructed by Fox in better methods of preparing latex. Called Sealy to explain to Bell & Barnes the method of collecting the Indians every 10 days or 15 days, as he had done it at Sabana, Abisinia & Ultimo Retiro. Bell thinks it is quite differently done. He got explanations from Torrico of the mode per at Occidente & Torrico says it is the "Same at all the stations". Bell is a queer character. He is frequently taking the explanation of these people as final. I don't!

[**On blotter:**] Aquileo Torres arrd on foot from Ultimo Retiro on way to Chorrera.

5, Wednesday Charlie's <u>49th Birthday</u> – I will write to him. Did not write to dear old Charlie – will do so by this mail (28 Oct). Spent a lazy day, writing my notes of things, discussing with Fox & G., who are still of opinion it is a trading Coy. G.'s naivete delicious. It is commercial if you please "because it buys things" (His very words to my objection that I could see no element of Commerce in the whole structure). I retorted "So do I buy things" – "But it sells them." When I said – not here – "Yes it sells bottles of Scott's Emulsion at La Chorrera to its own staff – the Baker – at £1 per bottle." He shut up. Aquileo Torres contd his journey to La Chorrera I am told today, early morn. One less to encounter at U. Retiro, thank God. Gusman arr on foot from Naimenes & reported "Veloz" left there at noon. He arrd about 4 p.m. She came only at 8 p.m. Bishop reports Mings from Sabana was there with sore feet but working. No incidents at La Chorrera. I turned in without bridge tonight, tired. We are to leave in morning. Did not write much tonight. Too tired altogether. Slept till 1 a.m. or 2 & then very badly later.

[On blotter:] Aquileo Torres on to Chorrera.

6, Thursday Always cold coffee at these abominable stations. Cold & late rarely before 7 & often nearer 8. Left Occidente at 9.20 a.m. The Staff standing to see us. The Cholo man-servant Pena shook hands with me gracefully – this for a bottle of Jameson I gave him. Shook hands all round but no farewells. Many Blue Emperor butterflies – splendid things, lots of others. Measured the "stocks" before leaving by myself. See page 13 small green book & up to p. 19 **[White Diary]**. Same for notes on this day written in the Launch. We had one fine passage of what Tizon said was a Chorrera at low water – took us all our time to get past. Passed Emeraes Rion about 4 p.m. Nothing of interest all day beyond the butterflies and my reflections, if these could be called interesting which I doubt. I am wondering how to convert Fox & G. to a healthier frame of mind. Arr. Puerto Peruano at close on 7 & up to the Shelter house with Tizon. Dined on board & then on shore to sleep at 8.30 in this House. F. & G. one room, Tizon & I the other. I like Tizon.

7, Friday Heavy rain in night & on to this morning. Up at 6 a.m. but did not leave till 8.10. How these Peruvians mismanage things. This tiny launch could have been easily off by 6.30. On the Congo we should have left at 5.30, firewood & all. Nobody of the crew gets regular meals, or rations. Scraps are hoarded. I had to give my private stores both today & yday to the 3 Barbados men, altho' one of them is the Coy's servant (Chase) & Sealy is supposed also to be chiefly theirs – only Bishop wholly mine. So with the Steersman, table boys, wood boys, etc. all are hungry, & always hungry, & get no regular meals but "bits" over that Garrisi the Steward chooses to spare them. Again today magnificent display of Butterflies – beats anything I've seen yet. For most of today see Note Book (green) 20-27 **[White Diary]** & my following notes. Arr Ultimo Retiro at 4 p.m. Jiménez & his Staff the greatest set of villains yet. Concubines everywhere. The stocks in place of honour amidships – the house built like a ship – a Pirate Ship. Each room named after the Captain "1st officer" etc. I am in **[blank]**. The bows front river – the thick stockade of basement walls (16') rises 2' above verandah & makes the bulwarks. A sentry at night. Warned Bishop and B's to sleep together & no girls!

8, Saturday A sentry, I think, pacing all night – someone certainly shaking the ship. Please God I'll shake this ship of state to its bilge. We are going to have a demonstration of the "cepo" **[stocks]** today. The black hole, too, with its trapdoor. The vile, squalid place is filled with women & concubines of all ages & is a den of vice & degradation. Eighteen women making steps to privy under direction of a "whiteman". 3 Naked as born, rest dressed – but all women. How paid? Nothing in Store. Examined Edward Crichlow – another tale of shame. Also of brutal ill-treatment of himself by Aurelio Rodrigues and F. Velarde. Had Barnes & Fox to it. It took all afternoon – also raid to Japurá & invasion of Colombia, a truly fine proceeding for an English Company, in May 1910. I wrote all day nearly – very tired indeed. Macedo ordered the raid to Colombia. This alone warrants his dismissal from the Coy's service.

[On blotter:] On 8th Oct at Ultimo Retiro. Measurements of one man & a woman. The man's name "Waiteka", the fearless skeleton of my Diary, **[see White Diary entry of 8 October]** who denounced the "cepo". Age about 35-40. Weight say 120 lbs. Height 5'6". Chest 35". Thigh 17". Calf 11¼" (his ankle in "cepo" just fitted in). Biceps 9½". Forearm 8". Stomach 32".
Woman Theorana by name. Age say 22 yrs. Weight 104. Height 4'7". Chest below breasts 31". Stomach 33". Thigh 19¾". Calf 12¼". Biceps 9½". Forearm 8".
Edward Crichlow very damaging statement. Capture of 21 Indians in Colombia and three Colombians.

Sunday 9 Oct All of us off to Meritos Indians. One family makes this Nation. I photo'd all of them at once. Road made by slave labour, no pay, food supplies. Monkeys etc. Butterflies & all. (Gave food to Indians). Swam river & returned to Ultimo Retiro.

10, Monday Took name of one Indian boy Riaquéro – flogged by Velarde whom I think of taking home if possible. The Commission, all except Bell, out to forest. I stayed with him. Gusman arrived from Occidente with 3 more loads of ours – 18 hours behind the Indians he came with. They had already started for home this morning. No pay at all. Commission returned. Fox & Barnes thoroughly disgusted at the floggings they had seen traces of – one on a tiny boy of 10 or 11 – "Cut to ribbons", Barnes says. They photo'd him. My eye is very bad indeed – left eye, and I have it bandaged with ~~Carbolic~~ Boracic lotion and the Dr. of Hilary's stuff. Turned in early with wet bandage over eyes. Took details of Crichlow's raid across Caquetá to Colombia. Twesta died there he says – the husband of the unfortunate girl at Naimenes, I think. Heavy rain in night.

[On blotter:] Riaquéio X Riaqueyo – Naimenes below Occidente.
the boy in red jersey, is a boy of Francisco.

Told Tizon and Gielgud that Barbadians intended to claim compensation and that I should support their claim. I called Crichlow & Bishop.

11, Tuesday Heavy rain delayed our leaving Ultimo Retiro for Entre Rios. We are to start now after lunch – & stop at Puerto Peruano tonight instead of going on today to the Indians' house in the forest. Rain stopped at 10 a.m. I am far from well, my left eye very bad. Pig Killed "Bridget". Stern morality of the place that she was at once taken out & shot! – Playing with Fox! Jiménez saw us off toward his camp & waved his cap. Pity we cannot wave his head, the scoundrelly murderer. Steamed down river to Puerto Peruano. Left Ultimo Retiro 1.21 Arr. P. Peruano 4.34 = 3H 13M @ at say 6 miles p.h. = 20 miles – it may be more. Found about 40 Indians from Entre Rios waiting for us. Camped the night there. Fires etc below house. Indians sleeping there, sent down to Chorrera for more food. All these Indians flogged too, but not so badly as the Occidente or Retiro ones. Heavy rain in night. An Indian recently flogged, within 30 days, by Borborini **[sometimes spelt Barborini or Barbolini]** – the white executioner at O'Donnell's. Shows himself to Bishop who showed him to Fox.

12, Wednesday Left P. Peruano at 7 a.m. Bruce on launch to Chorrera. Indians the most dreadfully willing carriers in the world. The "road" atrocious & such as it is all due to the Indians' slavery. Trees down, bridges made, saplings made, steps often 100 feet high up & down inclines, all by these poor patient beings. I will pay my carriers anyhow. Got to Monones – deserted Indian house – on road & lunched. A "blanco" there named Borborini with mule & horse. Fox & Bell on them. On to Entre Rios arr about 3.15 – total distance from Puerto I should say 12-14 miles. Soon after Peruano steep hills & streams all to Igaraparaná – then space & then the river to Cahuniari – so the steep hills & heights about 100 feet above Igaraparaná are the divortium aquarium between Japurá & Putumayo. Entre Rios in midst of fine plantations, a circular clearing about 1¼ mile diameter, largely cleared & planted. O'Donnell far the best looking agent of the Coy we've met yet, honest even & certainly healthy. Has been shot at often – even here on river bank bathing. Turned in early without dinner. Martin Arana here, said to be a brother of Julio Arana.

[On blotter:] Borborini

13, Thursday Bell already again gone astray. Thinks Jiménez "all right" in spite of the evidence of his crimes. This not to be regarded now, because the Indians at R. "seem to like him". I am disgusted with the lack of character & humanity of these shifting, vacillating men. It is not a Commission at all. Bad night. Liver deranged badly. Took medicine. Bishop spent one year here – flogged and flogging he says – once ordered by Borborini to shoot an Indian & refused & even the muchacho refused to do so. Bishop says the Colombians did treat the

Indians much better than the Peruvians. He saw it. Armando King murdered Justino Hernandez at Loayza's direction, so he says. Visited Rubber Store – a great deal of Rubber & very big lumps & loads. The cepo here has 24 foot holes & one head hole in centre. Must weigh their loads. All furniture in my room made by Bishop including the door to "sitting room" – he got nothing for it, but had to go on Commissions too. Then got Chase up & took his Statement of all his term of service at Abisinia, the most awful things happening right up to three or four months ago. Perfectly atrocious. Took all morning at this. Heard O'Donnell lying to Commission. Afternoon Bishop & to Cahuinari with him to write down further Statements. Evening Bridge & bed.

14, Friday Busy writing all day. There is to be an Indian "ball" tonight – but it is raining & I don't think they will come. The Manguari is beating its summons. Got Sealy in to confirm Whiffen & Celestine Lopez & others in H documents. He does so in some cases but not in all & he & Chase show that some of Broga's statements are lies. The Dance afterwards – about 500 Indians – O'D. says, I should say 350 at outside in to it. Bathed in Cahuinari.

15, Saturday 'You buy these with the rubber we produce.' Indian Chief looked thro' glasses – like the entrancement by Una. Weighed rubber in store and photo'd a lot of carriers of rubber. Interviewed Pinedo (with Bell) to confirm his statements to Sealy of the recent brutal murders by Aquileo Torres on march & at Ultimo Retiro. Told Pinedo to tell Tizon. Busy writing and talking to Indians all day. Took measurements of one & gave away small things. Bathed twice in Cahuinari – only 3 feet deep now, or less – it rises another 3-4 feet in flood. A narrow ditch about 8-10 ft. deep (at highest bank) and about 20 feet broad. Played Bridge with Fox & won Rubber. Turned in early.

[On blotter:] Borborini then cut the Indian's head off himself. Chase second Statement. Sealy in to confirm Whiffen. Pinedo.

Sunday 16 Left Entre Rios for Andokes. Many streams, some bigger than Cahuinari, & lovely water. Slept at Muinanes house, deserted & a nightmare in night. Rain too. We have about 40 Indians. Picked up crumbs.

17, Monday On from Muinanes House by atrocious 'road' thro' forest at 8 a.m. A lovely river named **[blank]** the clearest water yet, and then a big, deep river. Bathed in both. Indians got a little beans at starting & at 11.30 a pot of rice. Enough to give each man about 3-4 ounces of it. They scoffed it in a brace of shakes. They picked up the crumbs from our table again – tiny scraps of biscuit – like birds. All beg & beg for food. On & passed a Muinanes house that Normand burnt & killed its people – so Andokes says. Heavy rain in afternoon, a deluge came on: Indians made umbrellas of palm fronds. Trees much bigger, at last, about Andokes. Arr. there in deluge 3.30 or 4. Normand absent on a 'correria'. Did not expect us. Had sent for. Bustamante recd. us. Cannot go down stream, save with four guns guarding. Normand arr. 5 or 5.30. A rifle shot & he came! A loathsome monster – absolutely filthy. Played Bridge & turned in at 9 p.m.

18, Tuesday 7 Harems arrived. Normand's Harem arrived 2.30 a.m. & tried to get into his room where Barnes & Bell were! I up & saw all. They had his tula **[rubber collecting back pack]** & other things. He had "run" on the road. Up at 6.30. Levine is still out at Normand's House – only James Lane here now. Will see him today & sent for Levine. Told Tizon I would leave tomorrow for Entre Rios. James Lane again at 9.30-11. Again disgraceful things revealed & brutal murders. An Andokes man flogged to death last month at La China. Later on Westerman Levine who arrived – He is a blackguard, but I made him speak. He lied first & then admitted all. I told Tizon & brought him in to the confrontation of the two when Lane forced Levine to admit his lying. A disgusting day. Found "cepo" covered with palm thatch. Two prisoners sent off previous day by Bustamante. Down to stream. A dance in evg of the Boras Indians who brought in enormous loads of Rubber – some of them 140lbs weight I fancy. Women & children. Several women & tiny children flogged.

19, Wednesday The Boras Indians despatched with rubber at 6.30. I followed at 7 with Bishop, Sealy & James Lane (Lane & Levine both discharged at my request). On road found a "boy" of Matanzas with rifle lying on road in dying condition. Has been 12 days out without food to look for the "wife" of Negretti who had "run away". I tried to help him on & fed him, but he could not walk over fifty yards without falling. So I left him at last under shelter with my umbrella to keep off the rain & sent Sealy on to get 3 carriers to go back & help him on to Muinanes where I decided to sleep. Then an Andoke woman with heavy load of rubber absolutely incapable of walking, so I laid her load down & helped her on to Muinanes **[These are typical examples of Casement's immediate response to finding individuals in perilous condition – people whose lives would have been casually discarded had he not happened upon them.]** My 3 Indians came in at 5.30, turned back by Negretti, who refused to allow the "sick "boy" this way. Had sent him to Matanzas. But he cannot walk half a mile! Negretti is expected & B. says will insult me! – purposely.

[On blotter:]
5 Hours march – took us 6¾) Total distance
5 Hours march = about 6 Hours) 28-30 miles
Very heavy rain storm at 2.30-3 p.m. Poured a deluge on us in the forest.
James Lane & Westerman Levine at Matanzas 18 October 1910.
From Matanzas to Entre Rios 19 Oct but slept at Muinanes owing to the sick boy & Andokes woman ill on road.

20, Thursday Normand came to Entre Rios (without Levine) who passed on road to Puerto, & stayed the night. Tried to talk to me to convince me of his gentle treatment of the Indians & to make me change my "assertions". I said, "I make no assertions." Left Muinanes House at 8 a.m. or 7.45 a.m. The beast Negretti arrived at 7, bringing up the rear of the fabrico caravan – 42 people, all except 12 women, & tiny boys with small girls too. All carrying heavy loads. Four women left sick, including my poor old woman unable to proceed. The Boras left at 5.15. I followed at 8, leaving Lane to guard the sick woman & inform Barnes (by letter) of the state of things. Passed Negretti and the Boras rubber carriers, & on to nice stream near the Savana where bathed & breakfasted. On at 11 – fearful road. Inca sent out by O'Donnell just past Indian house & in at 1 a.m. at Entre Rios. Met by Fox & O'Donnell. Very glad to see both. Latter quite an angel after Normand. The poor Rubber caravan arrived at 5.15 – exactly 12 hours – the beast Negretti bringing up the rear. He drove them on. Hiti, hiti! without pause – & Fox got only two photos of them. He stayed to sleep & eat. They to be all night in open.

21, Friday Negretti did not turn till 8 a.m. on road to Peurto. God help these poor people. I am writing up my Diary since Monday. He slept & got food here. They lay in the open. Then some stragglers came at 10.30 or 11. One tiny kid of a boy & others. I photo'd several but they were in fear. One boy had 37 kilogs on his head. I photo'd him & weighed it. Then just before breakfast a poor being staggered in & fell – in a faint almost. He lay groaning & saying he was dying. I sent whiskey & food & got him into the store on a rug & weighed his rubber – 50 kilogs! Not a scrap of food with it. The man lay like a log. Then another while we are at breakfast, bent double & feet dragging, but he passed on. No one to help him! Then Normand himself. Wonderful flight across "Chacara" & then he came. 2 shots and then the Commission with news of the boy & the 'old lady'. Both better. Thank God. Normand tried to talk to me. I left him to Fox. Stayed in room, writing till nightfall. Played Bridge till 9.30 & turned in.

22, Saturday No water hardly in Cahuinari. Up at 5.20 decided to stop Levine going down with Normand to Chorrera. Asked G. tell Tizon to give the order. (N. green with rage.) He had decided, I am sure to bribe Levine to retract & then he, Macedo & Levine would be free to corrupt all the 8 Barbados men who are waiting my arrival. 8 of them to be there by end of month. I further determined send Bishop to Chorrera to spike their guns. Got B. off ostensibly to send me up things I need & with letter for Macedo. Normand off at 9 a.m. & Bishop too. Will Levine return? I fancy not, altho' G. says T. gave positive orders. Tizon must find me an abominable nuisance, but I cannot help it. I will take no risks, & playing with the Devil I'll not go Spades & leave him to double. Heavy rain at 1 o'clock & got heavier & heavier. Down to stream at 4.30 – risen only about 10". Rain cont'd in night. Huascar & Lincoln playing by kitchen. Played 3 Rubbers of bridge. Lost 2. Turned in 11 p.m.

[On blotter]: Heavy rain.
He was a thin fellow with ~~legs~~ arms like a child's.
Heavier rain. Break-up of recent dry weather, Fox thinks. Glad of it. Sandflies dreadful – the rain will clear them out.

Sunday 23. Rain all night. Levine should return today. Nous verrons. Some of the men came up. No Levine. At 2.30 a letter from Bishop saying he refused to come as I fully expected & that Normand & he were plotting. Tizon sent imperative order for his return at once.

24, Monday Heavy rain all afternoon of y'day & night & some of today. Cahuinari nearly full again. Some of the Boras & Andokes – some 60, passed back today. Two very sick old men. No scrap of food! I gave tins of meat to several. I want to get Doi a Boras boy home with me. A large wood ibis at lunch sailed round & alit close to House. Fox & I saved it from being shot. It was like a stork, a big white bill, white body & broad black ends to the wings. Extraordinarily tame – it was within 20 yards of the house & wheeled off twice & returned. I tried to photo, but failed. It then soared off higher & higher. The Indians said a bad sign! Tizon got letter from Normand refusing send back Levine, alleged a bad leg! A lie. Tizon knows now the trouble begins. We had long talk till 7. I told him all my fears. He sees their force & agreed to go to Iquitos with me if necessary. Played 33 hands & 2 Rubbers Bridge.

25, Tuesday The Commission & Tizon left for Atenas. Atenas, the city of Montt. I stayed with O'Donnell. Wrote Gordon, John Gordon, of the 33 bridge hands last night. **[The White Diary of the same date records the event as "I wrote a note to John Gordon with the Bridge record of last night." In the Black Diary entry for the previous day (24 October) Casement wrote "Played 33 hands & 2 Rubbers Bridge" while the White Diary has "Played bridge – 33 hands in two rubbers. I should think a record. First rubber was 17 hands and second 16. I kept the score of the first to send to John Gordon."**

Angus Mitchell makes much of the differing phrases "33 hands & 2 Rubbers" and "33 hands in two rubbers" suggesting the use of the word 'and' (actually an ampersand, or possibly even 'in' since it is a microscopic squiggle) is "another revealing slip of the forger's pen." Although rubbers in bridge are composed of a number of hands it seems a very insubstantial point to claim that the use here of and is suspicious. One can just as properly write of "33 hands and 2 Rubbers", especially when emphasising the small number of rubbers as opposed to the large number of hands.

Mitchell also insinuates that the greater emphasis on playing bridge in the Black Diary betrays the forger's métier since "Bridge has long appealed

to tacticians and plotters."[451] That view has the unintended effect of ruining his case as one would assume that any forger addicted to bridge could at least get his bridge terms right.] Think I'll go over to Atenas tomorrow to lunch & return in evg. Hot today after the recent rains. Read thro' last night & today E.P. Oppenheim's "The Yellow Crayon". 4 Boras (a young man, splendid type, a boy of 12, & 2 women) came down, guarded by 1 armed footpad from Matanzas, with 2 loads of rubber. I photo'd them & gave a tin of meat. The boy terribly flogged, all over his backside & thighs. Enormous weals. A beautiful boy. The young man fine fellow – very light skin. Heavy rain in afternoon, a deluge. Rode with O'D. all round his chacara – it is some 300 acres of felled forest, about 50-60 acres planted with yuca, maize, sugar cane. Old Indian house in midst. Sick (skeleton) brother of ~~Muinane~~ Muitudifos chief in maize. Splendid deer brought in. Weight (cleaned) 36½ kilogs. Also squirrel. Fine Muchacho carried deer, beautiful limbs, thighs & chest – light coffee colour. Rain much in night.

On 25 October 1910 in the Black Diary, Casement wrote "Four Boras... a boy of 12... I photo'd them and gave a tin of meat. The boy terribly flogged, all over his backside and thighs. Enormous weals." In the White Diary of the same date he wrote "The boy bore brands of flogging all over his nether parts" (TNA FO 371/1455)

26, Wednesday Left E.R. 8.5) 2.45. Left Atenas 3.) 2.54.
arr. Atenas 10.50) arr. E.R. 5.54)

I off to Atenas with O'D. It is reckoned 3 Hours. We went very quick & got there 2 H. 45 M. I reckon it 12 miles. Past 2 fair-sized tributaries of Cahuinari. Bathed Atenas in Cahuinari – splendid stream there 8 feet deep. Strong current. Old Bridge 10-12 ft above river which rises to great volume very quickly O'Donnell says. Montt is insignificant looking little wretch. The one-legged man here. Rubber is very thin – Putumayo sausages – M. says 24 tons. Had 790 men. Now about 250. Says Indians "very bad" – cannot coerce them. Not enough *empleados*, only 4 all told. About 12 muchachos. Station in ruins. Enormous clearing, but no planting to speak of. Very badly flogged specimen – old thin man – called by Sealy. Left Atenas 3. Terrible rain, all way nearly. Tried Banana leaf – caught blue & brown butterfly, magnificent specimen. Walked very fast back & arr. just before 6. Dinner & turned in. Reckon it 24 miles today – O'D says fully or even more. Many sandflies in night – awful biting. could not sleep. Commission leave for P.P. tomorrow direct. I go down with O'D on horseback.

[On blotter:] Puma shot by muchacho. O'Donnell said my letter to Bishop had been delivered & then Tizon showed me Normand's. Bathed at 2-3 in Cahuinari with a boy dreadfully flogged. Was a carrier to Andokes. I noticed then, but now worse. Awful scars. A nice lad of 17 about & six tiny boys – gave all soap. They revelled in it.
2 p.m. On their way to P. Peruano, the footpad carried only his gun, one woman a basket & tula, the others food I presume of sorts. The footpad gave them a small bowl of cassava & bean broth – cold water!

27, Thursday Leaving E.R today to return to P.P. & get Veloz tomorrow mg for Chorrera where the big row begins. Normand, Macedo & Co. there with their beautiful Levine. Tizon I to fight. I go down today with O'D, I on horse he on mule. I made him run y'day sometimes but he could beat me on the hill. I am going down Hill! 47th year & he is only 27. Rather weary, but more from bad night. Read "Yellow Crayon" again in night. Left Entre Rios about 8.30, I on horse, O'D on mule & to Monanes house where we lunched, Borborini cooking it. Luggage by "muchachos" – one very fine lad, fair skin & nice face, about 19. Met "Muchacho" of Occidente at ¾ hour from E. Rios with letter for O'D. On & met Commission at Lunch & then on together to P.P. over Nimue, a fine stream. Heavy rain. Atenas carriers of Commission absolutely skeletons – Photo'd four ~~boys~~ skins of bones. Gave meat to them, all the tins I had left, after Sealy kept for himself & Chase. Played one Rubber of bridge & turned in at 9 p.m. in same room of house. Arevalo in charge of Launch. Hear that Normand etc. went by land. A batalon with rubber is lying in port. Caught three splendid butterflies on road. O'D & Sealy in fingers. Beauties.

28, Friday Left P. P. at 7.18. Before going, the beautiful muchacho showed it, a big stiff one & another muchacho grasped it like a truncheon. Black & thick & stiff as poker. On boat Lincoln & Occidente muchacho doing same.

		H	M	Miles
Left P.P. 7.18 Arr. Occidente 11.10 ½ =		3	52	25
Passed Naimenes	3.11 – slower current	4.	00	20
"Victoria Beach	5.28 ½	2	17	11
Arr. Chorrera"	5.37		8½	1
From P. Peruana to La Ch: Roughly				57 miles

River about 7 feet lower at Port Victoria, but below rapid at Chorrera it is fully 16 feet down. Bishop brought a written statement of all that has transpired since he left me. Amusing in its way. Told Tizon & talked with him till near midnight, after one rubber of Bridge.

29, Saturday Boy of Launch also stiff, y'day & again this morning, pretending to do it with small boy with huge thrust. Swam in river which is fully 16-17 feet lower – big sand islands showing in mid-pool, & the fall sunk to very narrow confines. It has gone down 16 'feet' I found. Bought things from store and wrote up my diary since Entre Rios and got various papers in order. Normand is here but goes back to Andokes & will not sail in this "Liberal", so Tizon says. All goes well. N. wanted to go to Iquitos by her – but Tizon stopped it. Very hot today. I bathed in river in morning. The Indian boys are swimming all afternoon. Lovely bodies out in the stream, & the girls too, paddling logs across to the islands & lying awash by the hour. After dinner talked two Risigaros – muchachos – one a fine chap. He pulled stiff & fingered it laughing. Would have gone on & other too (keys on chain in left pocket) looking for cigarettes. Awfully exciting & stiff stiff work too. Thought of João & Flores.

[On blotter:] This day last year "Vaseline" at dear old Icarahy – To think of it!

[Sunday 30th] Lovely day. River dropped over a foot today. "Liberal" will not be able to get in here. N. returned to Andokes early at 2 p.m. by launch. Doi to come down. Sabana Barbados men arrived. Got Greenidge's contract & papers from Fox & wrote a good deal.

31, Monday Saw "Andokes" bathing. Big thick one as I thought. Called Batson & took his Statement, a dreadful one. Then Sur Rubber arrived. Huge loads – lots of Indians, fine, handsome types of Naimenes Indians of Sur. Chose one small boy, a dear wee thing named Omarino. His weight 24 Kos in fono & his load of rubber 29 Kos. Weighed a load 63½ Kgs & another 50. A fine muchacho named Arédomi wants to come. Very fine lad – would like to take him. He followed like a dog all afternoon. Gave breeches to him.

His beautiful coffee limbs were lovely. Promised to take him home if I could manage it. Spoke Tizon. Bought Omarino. More Rubber in evg from Sur, 9 or 10 tons of it. Miranda at head. All slept under House – his Indians. I looked & saw several & one boy caressed hand & shoulder. River falling enormously, down a foot today. Equal Bridge. Won 2, lost 2. Stiff asleep ones. [**By the end of this month of October, Casement is beginning to resexualise his thoughts, first by describing the attractive looks of individual boys and men and then by being able to observe more explicit sexual activity amongst the local Indians, porters and sailors. This sexual activity was of a casual type quite normal in the region amongst young Amazon males – a sort of cheerful, mutual, self-pleasuring that carried no shame or guilt. Various anthropologists have recorded such inter-male genital stimulation as being both commonplace and insignificant amongst Amazonian groups, and Casement's observations confirm this. Apparently joking sex-play among unmarried men was normal, anthropologists noting that it often involved a boy lying in a hammock with a friend nuzzling him and feeling his penis while talking about sexual exploits with women.**

Indian boy, with necklace, in ill-fitting European clothes, thatched longhouse behind

Ricudo (Arédomi) in a feather headdress as worn for the Rothenstein portrait: Casement wrote in his White Diary on 7 November 1910 "I took Arédomi up to the hill to the cataract — and photo'd him in necklace of 'tiger' teeth, armlets of feather plumes and a fono."

It was certainly true that the combination in younger Indians (and indeed those of mixed race) of minimal clothing and unashamed erections left little to the imagination. Buggery itself is said not to be a characteristic of such overt male sexuality in the Amazon, whereas in Mediterranean and Arab cultures it is, being utilised as an alternative to unavailable heterosexuality – often performed on willing Europeans. In the Amazon, women were not so unavailable to men, indeed sex was given something of a higher value above simply marriage and procreation. What is frequently described as the adolescent homosexual phase – a diversion rapidly going out of fashion – is probably more precisely an undifferentiated sexual phase, and in this uncondemning and more innocent culture it found full flower amongst younger men and boys.

It was now six weeks since 14 September when Casement had left Iquitos, and in that time, no sexual opportunity had presented itself or been taken advantage of. Indeed his last recorded cruising was detailed on 8 September in Iquitos, and previously on 16 August in Manaos, while the last mention of any action was nearly three months earlier on 11 August with a

Omarino (with distended stomach), older Indian and third person in European dress

policeman in Pará. This was an unconscionably long gap for a regular cruiser, one who was in a climate and society where success seemed almost guaranteed. It reveals that opportunities during Casement's Putumayo voyages were few while he also recognised it was not the time or the place to be activating potential partners. However, once sexual sights hove into view, Casement's imagination is provoked and his mind turned to the matter more and more.]

November, 1910.

1, Tuesday River still falling in morning. Arédomi I saw for a moment & then no more. Fear he has been sent off. Very heavy rain in afternoon, pouring & River began to rise almost within 1½ hours of it. Took Statements of Sidney Morris, Preston Johnson & Augustus Walcott. All from Sabana. All wish to go away with me. Dreadful deeds by Normand. "Huitota" arr up River from S. Julia with Aguero & his Rubber & Alcosta of Oriente & his Rubber & Ocainos Indians. I was too busy right up to 6 p.m. with the Barbados men to see any of it. Met Aguero & Alcosta at dinner. Velarde also down from Occidente – going home with me! Told Tizon of Batson's Statements and of Morris on Normand & of Aurelio Rodriguez. Saw big ones on Indians at dinner & before.

Casement with Juan Tizon, newly appointed head of the Peruvian Amazon Company in the Putumayo

Man with moustache and sleek hair; river background

2, Wednesday Up early. Ocainas & others about, & some of the Sur Indians & Miranda's. One boy with erection, fingering it long & pulling it stiff. Could see all from verandah. <u>No fono</u> – only grey twills. The River has risen fully 3 feet in night, & is a good deal bigger now than when we came on Friday. Sent Bishop at 6.30 to look for Arédomi. Fear the poor boy was sent off with the Naimenes men yesterday with one Bowl for his Rubber! Bishop reports he is over on the Chacara cutting firewood for the launch – & soon I saw him turn up smiling. I interviewed Five Barbados men today. It took me all the day. Their Statements cover a lot of ground and in some cases show grave illtreatment of themselves, particularly by Normand. Further infamous acts of cruelty against Normand and Aguero & the rest of these monsters & infamous treatment of Clifford Quintin by Normand. Wrote till 5 p.m. or later. Mapp & others back to S. Catalina to get their things down. Acosta, Rodriguez & others from Occidente. A holy gathering. Very little rain today, but still it passed St Swithun's without rain. Walked after dinner & turned in early.

[On blotter:] Evelyn Batson's statement 4
<u>Hallow Eve</u>
Walked till 12 with <u>Arédomi</u> **X** <u>& Others</u>
Sidney Morris X Preston Johnson X Augustus Wallcott X
James Mapp 3 Alfred Hoyte 2 Reuben Phillips Clifford Quintin X Allan Davis 1

3, Thursday Lovely morning. River risen some 7 or 9 feet since 1st instant. Cataract Huge now. <u>Davis too</u>. <u>Chase told</u> Bishop he saw it. <u>Rajina</u> – her <u>name</u>.

Huitota woman. Arranged with Macedo to take Arédomi. He has no objection. Gave Garece £5 for the recent journey & all his trouble. Arranged Sealy to stay with Barnes & go on with Commission at £7 per month & be repatriated by them. Bishop says the Atenas carriers of rubber not allowed over this side. They came in during evg & even long after nightfall. These were the lights we saw on the opposite hillsides last night. They did not want us to see their starved condition. So after a march of 13 days (two days with rubber) these poor boys are hunted back without food. We saw the skeletons at ~~E.R.~~ P. Peruano. Last night Aguero took away the sweeping woman from this to add to his Harem. A shame & disgrace. Told Fox & Commission at breakfast. Busy all day over A/cs of the Barbados men & with Tizon on the subject. He offers to take away 25% as their back a/cs on ground of overcharge. they accept gladly. Also the 50cts. per £ for the men with sterling contracts & the <u>medicines</u> altogether wiped out. Then to pay compensation to the men grossly injured by the Servts. of the Coy – Crichlow, Quintin, Dyall & Augustus Walcott. Very busy all day at this & wondering what is the best course to take. I think the interests of the men should be the first & that seems to demand acceptance.

4, Friday A poor sick man at Sur called me "<u>Mare Capitan</u>" & patted me. Commission went to Sur at 7.30. I followed at 8 with Sealy carrying coat etc. & Arédomi small tula. Took names of the buried at Cemetery. Found an orchid on road. Arrived Sur 9.30 & bathed. Arédomi carrying clothes showed huge. Told him bathe too, and he stripped. <u>No fono</u> on – Carbolic soap – glorious limbs, a big one. Back & pineapples. A Decayed Station. Big cepo in the stockade is under post. Miranda alone. The road ½ trees, some 20,000 at least. Counted 9 to the yard & 2 miles of this = 30000 saplings. Returned with Sealy & Arédomi at 4. Heavy rain on way & thunder. Arédomi's wife & brother came. Gave salmon to the family. She wants much to go with him. I can't take her & fancy it is scarcely fair to take him, altho' he is most anxious to go & says she will be well cared for by her mother. River still rising – the ledge of rocks across the fall nearly covered now. Velarde & Juanito Rodriguez at dinner & talked of walking. Bishop says Juanito threatened to flog an Occidente Capitan I dared to give a knife to! Told him he was to say nothing to us that "The Englishman" had nothing to do with the Indians & they were not to speak to us. <u>The brute</u>.

5, Saturday Bishop says some of the Indians have broken into the Store & stolen – dug a hole & took some rice & food & fled in Greenidge's boat. They think it is the decent Boras Indian with the child's face who wanted to return to his wee son at Abisinia. Commission to return from Sur today. Expect "Liberal" today. Barnes, Bell & Fox arr. before lunch, G & Tizon stopping for an Indian dance at Sur till tomorrow. River rising fast now. Again rain today – but not so much. Many of O'Donnell's Indians are down from Entre Rios – sent beforehand to help carry the rubber over from P. Victoria. Such a waste of their lives after all they have suffered. Read over several of the B'bados men's statements to them & got them signed by them today. Find Allan Davis was sent to Encanto y'day just to guard an Indian boy sent there for a case of Soap. A nice use to put civilised beings to at £7 per month. They are hunting for the runaway Boras Indian & those who are supposed to have stolen the things. They may be some of Velarde's Occidente Indians of whom many are down waiting for that fabrico. River rising all day & night. Bathed with Arédomi in hill stream. Second time. [**"A married man of 19 probably or 20...This youth's name is Arédomi, but he has been called 'Pedro' by these civilising gentlemen! He has the fine, long strong hair of the Indians, the cartilage of the nose and the nostrils bored for twigs and a handsome face and shapely body. I gave him a pair of pantaloons and he stripped the old ones off and stood in his fono. A splendid shape of bronze."**[452]]

Sunday 6 Did more of the Barbados men's statements this morning & got their signatures. Rain came today again, fairly heavy. No sign of Liberal. Arédomi & his wife together all the time now. Bishop wants me to take them. River rising – well – cataract a line of snow. Barbados men from S. Catalina with Fonseca himself came down by the road & crossed over. Bathed.

[**On blotter facing 6-9 November:**] Sunday 6th Nov. New moon on 2nd Nov. 4 days old.
Lunar Rainbow at Chorrera. 7.30-7.45 p.m. seen first by me who called Fox, Bell, Barnes, 8. Tizon, Macedo & F. Velarde all saw.
9th October [**sic**] "Liberal" arrived. Mail from home, but really no news of any interest and nothing in papers about Putumayo.

7, Monday [**Over written:**] This is Sunday. One day out
Took further Barbados signatures this morning – S Morris, Preston Johnson & Augustus Walcott. Then looked more & more into their accounts and compared the prices charged them with those charged to me at Iquitos by The Iquitos Trading Coy & I find in some cases nearly 400% on top! Rice is 200% on top and Butter some 350% Nothing less than 150% to 200% and a great many over, & then the Iquitos price represents itself fully 150% on European price. It is monstrous & I fear I cannot agree to the men accepting 25% reduction, for their sake as well as for other reasons. It is a pity but I think I have no right to compromise or accept anything without permission of F.O. At night a lunar Rainbow, 7.30 to 7.50 in the East & then rain. River rose since last night 5-6 feet & is now almost to the steps where it was on our arrival on Liberal. It had fallen 20 feet below that. Rain came 7.45 & dissipated the lunar rainbow. Played Bridge at 9.30. Won 1st rubber with Tizon. Lost 2nd thro' Fox's bad play. I went once No trumps. Barnes doubled (24) I redoubled (48) & he redoubled (96). I got 4 tricks = 384 below. Aces easy! Wild ducks on diminishing edge of the sandbank at 5 p.m. B'bados went to shoot them & killed one with a Winchester but did not get it.

8, Tuesday **[First version crossed out:]** Lovely morning at 8 a.m. Reading Lt Maw again about the Indians & Putumayo in 1827. Hope "Liberal" comes today. They are trying to put the "Alvaringa" on barge "Putumayo" into the river today – the high waves are awash of her.

8 Tuesday Made a mistake of a day since Saturday!
River dropped since y'day evening, best part of a foot up to noon today. O'Donnell arrived from E. Rios by Veloz, bringing letter from Crichlow asking me to recall him. 'Huascar' arrd with O'D – & smiled on me with big left erection. **[O'D is Andrés O'Donnell, who was to show up in Barbados in 1911; Huascar his boy servant.]** Butterfly. Very hot afternoon. Fonseca going away for Saban. Saw his head muchacho & tulas paddle across at 12 noon & then Huascar with butterfly. Expect "Huitota" surely today, and hope Liberal also today. O spent a lazy day. Walked to hills in evg. by stream & at 6 Arédomi came with a plume head-dress quite well arranged, for me as a present. Poor boy. He had been home for it – far off all day to show his gratitude. A little rain, but not enough to influence river – it is still falling steadily. It rose 16 ft from Tuesday to Sunday – 5 days.

9, Wednesday Did nothing all morning. No sign of "Huitota" or "Liberal". What has become of both. Such a waste of time as they manage to get thro' here! I am heartily sick of this place. Rain at 1.15. River fallen a lot – fully 2 feet in night – and still falling. The Entre Rios rubber coming over all y'day & today from P. Victoria – about 10 of these poor Indians are down here at the miserable job. Velarde has disappeared! Gone back to Occidente I presume. "Veloz" left early today for Ultimo Retiro & to bring Crichlow down. He wrote me he was not safe there & wished to return. Looked at mules – they made 10 journeys today to the port. Misused dreadfully. Called Tizon, Barnes to see. "Liberal" arr. at 5.45. John Brown arrd. – useless brute. A big mail from home, nothing interesting in these surroundings. Mrs G. as usual good beyond measure. All well. Davis, King & Dyall from **[continued on blotter:]** Encanto. John Brown from Barbados.

10, Thursday "Liberal" brought some Peruvian soldiers under a Captain Delgado, to go to Encanto. Their passages not paid! As I fully expected all along. Very busy day. Went over remaining Barbados Statements & got them signed. Took King & J. Minggs two Statements. Both liars! Told Tizon feared could not accept his offer without first reference to F.O. & begged him to refer to Coy. He has read full P/A from Iquitos house. What right have they to grant it? He says Columbia **[sic]** is going to invade the Putumayo & is making a road from Pasto. Peru getting ready, Prefect writes him. Also Lima "Commercio" has article about forthcoming enquiry into the crimes here. Attorney General has moved for it in consequence of Deschamps letter to Barcelona. Why not have done this when all the facts were stated in Iquitos. Went on board Liberal

& saw C. Reigado & two new men from Coy – 'agricultural experts'!!! Burke there. The three Barbados men, J. Mapp, R. Phillips & A. Hoyte returned by the "Huitota" without going to S. Catalina, owing to conspiracy to murder them on way by Blondel & Aguero, so they say. I told Tizon & he heard Mapp's Statement. The men say there was a plot to kill them, Batson says to frighten the Commission from going to Abisinia. I was busy all day with the Barbados men's accounts until 5, when on "Liberal". The men very anxious for my accepting the offer of 25% reduction. I can see. Gielgud agrees with me, before the Coy, that matter ought to be referred home to his Board. Learn of the Revolution in Portugal & flight of King Manoel & his mother to Gibraltar by Brazilian Dreadnought, S. Paulo. The Peruvian soldiers under Delgado left for Iquitos. They do not pay their passages. Gielgud admitted it & Bell said they appeared as debtors.

[On blotter facing 10 November:] Liberal's mail Joseph Minggs, A. King recalled Dyall and Allan Davis who returned from Encanto y'day & got all remaining Statements signed except Greenidge & P. Lawrence.

11, Friday Another long day – The rectified a/cs of the Barbados men brought to me by Tizon. They show, when gone thro' a gain of some £650 to the men., who accept gratefully, again going thro' them, checking & finding errors, and the men putting forward further claims that will bring the amount up to over £800. Incidentally I find that while much of their indebtedness arises from gambling debts with Chiefs of Sections & other employés, the notes they gave for their debts are sometimes forgeries by the Peruvian who presents them. Specific charge of this made by Levine against F. Borber **[probably the same person as Borborini]** now at Andokes, also against Bustamante. Tizon present asked him to take Levine to Macedo to repeat the charge. This he did. Tizon brought two signatures of Levine's – the 'forged' one & an admitted one. They resemble each other, an expert could decide. I think personally it is not Levine's signature – so did Batson who was present when Tizon brought it. Davis thought it was Levine's. The whole thing is disgraceful, another illustration of Macedo's principles of management – the booking of gambling debts & carrying them to debit and credit through the Coy's books. The cheating of the men has been colossal and the deliberate neglect of any attempt at decent control or protection of their interests. All the men now say they will go home, save Francis, Greenidge & Lawrence the Cook – also King, of course, who returns to El Encanto. He is a cut-throat scoundrel. I shall leave the men complete liberty of choice. There will be another & I hope the final row. It cannot be helped, for I cannot act as arbitrator, or bind the hands of my government. I have no authority to do it.

12, Saturday Again a lazy day. I am waiting developments. The a/cs of the men will, when completed, be brought to me to hand out to them. I shall refuse & tell Tizon it must be done by the Coy, that I am not paying the men but he. Had a long talk with him after lunch. He was very frank and said he was going to do his duty & polish off Zumaeta, Arana & all, that he was now "a member of the Commission". He begged me to go see the Prefect and talk to him "frankly" and urge him to come round to this. I said I should do so. Velarde is not going by this steamer, but by next. Torrico is in charge since 1st. Got all the a/cs back from Tizon of the 19 Barbados men. They show a gain to them of some £850. Not bad. Told Bishop I should advise none – that they were to choose for themselves. Up the hill and bathed with Arédomi in upper river.

Sunday, 13 Nov. Sealy came to report that Borborini (O'Donnell's man) had cut a Sur Indian's head open last night with a fillet of firewood. Found the man & sent him to Tizon all Bleeding. Via G. Tizon dismissed Borborini on the spot to go home by this steamer! Good. **[Señor Juan Tizon when appointed manager ended the reign of terror on the Putumayo but the relief was short-lived as his health gave way and he was replaced around 1913. Casement, in a note quoting Tizon, declared in late 1910 "His views are practically my own. He says they are starved – starved to death; That the carrying of the rubber must be stopped – it has killed hundreds and hundreds; That they have no time to attend to their own wants or to make plantations and prepare food. They are literally done to death. The thing must be stopped and at once."[453]**

According to Dr Dickey[454] Tizon's successor was one Jorge Meave, the book-keeper at La Chorrera, and a former painter. He reinstated the stocks or *cepo* and shackling for rubber carriers. The return to cruelty co-incided with a rise in Indian acts of violence – effectively slave rebellions by the Boras and Andokes. The post-Casement reforms were largely abandoned. Dickey also remarked that the Franciscan mission priests Casement arranged to install in the region were ineffectual.] Very hot day. Looked at papers & decided <u>not</u> to take Mrs <u>Arédomi</u> home & told Miranda about her who pledged to see her safe.

14, Monday A busy day. Gielgud & Tizon with the a/cs of the Barbados men all morning. The men accepted the gift of 25% back and the matter is settled thus. There were incidents I did not like but they must pass. Crichlow came down from U.R. with Jiménez who came to me after lunch to protest against the "Truth" charges with Bruce interpreting. A queer scene indeed! recorded more fully elsewhere **[as it is extensively in the 'White Diary' of the same date.]** A very hot day – river falling fast. Some Entre Rios Indians also down here now – altogether then there must be 70 of these beings here. I am thinking all evening of possible trouble in Iquitos on arrival there with all these Barbados men. Their evidence constitutes the case against Peru, more really than against the P.A. Coy, & I fear Tizon & the Prefect acting on T's advice will try to nobble these witnesses. I told Barnes of my fears at night, talking to him till near midnight. Told him I should put matters to a test tomorrow by saying I wanted the passage tickets made out to Javari in Brazil & if they object I shall know the plot that is in view.

15, Tuesday A very anxious day. My last in Chorrera. I told Gielgud after lunch that I should like the passenger tickets for the men all to be optional either for Iquitos or "intermediate" ports. He went to see & came back from Macedo to say this wd. be done provided the Brazilian authts. allowed it. I visited the Brazilian Customs officer on "Liberal" (Mathias) & he said there was no objection at all. I then again saw G. & made sure the tickets were as required. I had told Bishop in the morning of my fears & that I thought it might be very well to land him & all the men at the Javari to await my coming down river on "Athualpa". I could go on to Iquitos & collect their money & pick them up on my return in a few days. I spent a very anxious day, meditating all sorts of ways of getting away, but there seems no way except by "Liberal". I finally decided to go by her with all the men, & with this option of landing at Javari all may be well, & I can leave all or most of the men there if necessary. Heavy rain all afternoon, & got cooler. River began to rise again, the sandbank showing. Talked to Burke after dinner & he like Bruce gave the show away completely. Played Bridge for E.D.M. testimonial & got £1. 18/ - (G. £1. Fox 10/ - & Bruce 8/ -). Called on Mrs Macedo & bade her goodbye.

16, Wednesday River has Risen 6" inches in night. My last hour in Chorrera. Poor Donald Francis came & cried & cried & cried in my room, wanting to go home with me to his old mother in Barbados. Poor boy. I was sorry for him. A scene with Dyall & his 9th or 10th wife, she refusing to be parted from him & even trying to get on board the "Liberal" but turned back on gangway. All settled & all on board at 9.30 a.m. & off at 9.45. Last I saw of Chorrera was the group of Tizon, G, Barnes, Bell & Fox with Sealy, Chase, Francis & Greenidge waving adieux. Sealy & Chase came to bid me goodbye after drinking. Four of the Boras 'wives' with them. The skipper C Reigado gave me assurances in front of Tizon, Gielgud, Barnes that the men could land where they pleased. So off on my last fight! Passed Port Tarma at 11.30 – naked Indian women, the last I shall ever see probably. Came to the great highland forested ridge at 12.15. – it is over 500 feet high, fully 600-700 I think, a curving sweep, three or four parallel ranges of forested upland. Jeremias Gusman on board, and Garrido the traitor, sent back by the Commission. Eclipse of the moon, just as it rose at 6 – half covered. Became total eclipse at 8. **[In the White Diary of the same date, Casement wrote "A total eclipse by Regada's almanac. The whole visage was obscured by 8, and then clouds came and covered the subsequent stages." The forgery school disputes the former timings but the issue is confused by the fact that the region's time zone apparently changed when it became Colombian territory.]** Lovely night.

17, Thursday Very handsome Cholo sailors on board. One is a young Indian moço of 18 or 19 – beautiful face & figure – a perfect dusky Antinous, would make a fine type for Herbert Ward's statues of the Upper Amazon. Steaming down Igaraparana & at 10.45 saw Putumayo & entered it about 10.50 **[Casement had left La Chorrera the day before on the *Liberal* with many of the British Barbadians, after a three-week sojourn there.]** It is very low & a huge sandbank blocks mouth of it. Called Arédomi to see it & explain thro' Bishop – he calls it Haumia – & Igaraparana is Cottué. He came to my room & I showed him many pictures of Bates' book & others to his great delight. It got up I think – was thick anyhow. **[This 1883 book by Henry W. Bates is *Naturalist on the River Amazona.* The session with Arédomi bears a strong resemblance to the prolonged teacher/pupil tutorials that Casement contrived with José Gonzalez the following year in Iquitos.]** Passed Puerto Parana at 12.12 on left bank. High ground, cleared but house gone as at Arica at mouth of Igaraparana. On to Puerto Parana, another abandoned site on left bank & then at 4.30 to Pescaria, where the beast Cerra came on board. Sandflies & other horrors. At 5.30 off again down the Putumayo of the Palms. Wondrous palms on left and right. The river ½ to ¾ mile or more broad, nearer 1 mile I think. Captain says about 20-25 feet deep. Current slow, not over 1 mile I should say. Splendid moonrise. Turned in at 9 p.m. & slept well.

18, Friday In Yaguas River 9'27 = 3'45° to Recreio. Steaming fast down Putumayo to get to Yaguas River today. 10.8 entered Yaguas – a fine river about 250 yards broad at mouth. Called up all Barbados men to see what they wish to do. 1.53. arrd at small palm house on right bank. This is Recreio. River evidently rises 12 ft. No current to speak of at all, just a deep ditch where level depends for miles on that of the Putumayo. On to Trunifo an hour later & left it at 4.15 & got to Putumayo 7.35. Many palms along Yaguas banks, especially this beautiful Assai & the queer looking popunha – but not popunha. No moon to speak of. Arédomi at 7.30 nude torso beautiful bronze for medicine against sand flies. Gave it to him & rubbed it on his beautiful body, poor boy. Young pilot prentice again on deck. Arranged (I think) to leave the men at Javari.

19, Saturday We arrived at the 1st Brazilian post at 2 a.m. & anchored alongside & got papers & then on to the second. 1st the Custom House at 2. & then the military post till 5. 3 hours lost – We bought wood at the post. £3 per 1000 billets – 1½ tons. Coal in Iquitos is 38/ – per ton of 1500 cwt, only. It is called a ton of measurement but works out at 15 cwt. 10.50 a fine tributary on right bank, 150-200 yards broad – "Urute" river – & then at 11.20 a Brazilian trading house, served by two launches from Manaos at the mouth of this fine deep river – its own river, no one else allowed up. This house has Ticuna Indians as its slaves Reigado says. Then a Columbian main hut & clearing on a parana and we went down it six miles. An old negro, his wife & baby in a canoe going down stream waved to us. More huts & we bought firewood at one & saw several other houses on left bank of Putumayo – also a biggish canoe going up with a sail, and then another with four Indian or cafuzo paddlers, a woman & a boy steering. A dark night & we got to Amazon about 1 or 2 a.m. = 76 hours down from Chorrera – or about 620 miles I should say.

Sunday 20 Nov. A bad night with skin eruption like heat bumps. In Amazon & stopped off Colonia Rio Jano till daylight. Then on to Amatura (Matural) where we bought firewood. I on shore & visited church – no padre for three years, many children to baptise. Left Matural 8.15 a.m. Hear "Javari" & "Athualpa" have both gone up, one of them on 14th. Captain's steward an Indian boy of 19, broad face, thin. Huge soft long one. Also Engineer's steward, big too. Steaming up Amazon all day. Very slow & tired. 4.30., 6 Ronsocos on bank, quite close. They stood watching us 40 yds off.

21, Monday A big sea-going steamer with green & red lights passed down last night at 9 p.m. Fear it is the Javari gone down. We stayed a long time at Boa Vista getting firewood from about 3 a.m. to near 6 a.m. this morning. On in drizzle. Deck hands washing decks – then lovely Cholo types, three big ones. Cholo Steward too, (young 18) enormous in new bags. To decide now if the men for Javari or Iquitos. 10 a.m. Stopped Palmeras. Beautiful soil, forest etc. 1 Hour stop. On at 11 – & at 11.45. passed Belem with church & many buildings. River Calderon – & Launch. On to Cacaus river, 80 yds, & alvarenga & canoe two Indians 12.15. Same owner. River for 6 Hours in big Steamer. Mafra (Peruvian of Italian descent) the owner. Our pilot Manoel Lomas has been up Cacaus 6 hours in big launch. Says Ticuna Indians work the rubber. On slowly, the firewood very bad, the Captain says. Steaming very slowly indeed. The river deeper than I thought – it has risen a great deal since end of August. Shall not get to Javari till 10 p.m. the Captain says, but at 11 we are not there. Turned in. Made all arrangements for landing 14 men, 4 women & 4 children at Javari **[Casement was leaving the Barbadians at a river junction so they could head down to Manaos in Brazil. He, Bishop, the two Indian boys and four others instead cut back up the river to Iquitos and into Peru once again.]** Bought a lot of food for the men from Reigada.

22, Tuesday We got to Javari at 1 a.m. Reigado told me the "Javari" S/S had gone down four days ago, and the "Athualpa" had passed up on 13th! Landed all men & women &c. Young Brazilian Customs officer very kind & pleasant face too. He embraced me! It is very good of him to take the men so willingly. Got off at 3 a.m. Dyal **[sic]** tried to sell his son, or rather the Chief Engineer tried to bag him! I stopped it. One of these Peruvian beasts, the 2nd Cook Bishop thinks, threw his puppy dog over in the night. Bishop is very sick about it. Took 3 hours from Javari to Tabatinga!!! Only 6 miles. River rushing down. Brazilian troops & young striped sergeant on board, off at once. At Leticia delayed for 2 hours by the lazy Peruvian brutes there. River risen about 8 feet since Augt. Captain says he must get to Iquitos on Thursday. I doubt it. The Peruvian Comisario & Lt here wanted seize Liberal to go back to Brazil to catch 4 soldiers who ran away last night. Good soldiers. On at 11.15 after 4 hours delay over this folly. Got wood & popuncha peaches at a clearing at ancient Loretto. All on shore & then on at dinner time steaming badly. Turned in early, seedy

23, Wednesday A hot day. Steaming past Peruvian chacaras all day. Some good ones like San Tomas. Saw mills. River rising. Read Johnston's 'Negro in the New World'. Very good. After dinner spoke to Steward Indian Cholo about *frejol* [**food – black beans**], & he got <u>some</u> for me & then another thing. It was huge & he wanted awfully. He stood for hours until bedtime & turned in under table – also small party Engineer's youth & pilot's apprentice too – all up – till midnight & then at Yaguas & saw two Yaguss Indians in their strange garb of Chambira fibre died [**sic**] red. On at 1 a.m. after wood & palm at Yaguas. Three Yaguas Indians on board, I think. Steward's Cholo very nice. Smiled & fingered & hitched up to show. [**There is evidence that Casement's interest in the crews of the Amazon steamers did not go unobserved although it is unlikely that the Cholo sailors complained. They were plainly happy to display their charms yet his enthusiasm may have become conspicuous. In a letter to Alfred Noyes, dated 17 May 1956, a voice from the past resurfaced. "Sir", wrote Jasper Moon, from an address in Montgomeryshire, "The late Captain Good who was Master of the Steamer in which Casement travelled to Iquitos told me that he nearly decided to put Casement ashore in the matter."[455] This letter certainly did not appear in Noyes's book. Jasper Moon can be found in 1908, during Casement's recuperatory stay in Barbados, billing Casement with an account from his firm, Fletcher & Moon.[456]**]

24, Thursday Due at Iquitos today. Will it be peace or war? Gave small boy Victor Tizon 2S/P. Very rainy morning. Cleaning brass work. Cholo steward did mine & Captain's & showed it again <u>huge</u> & stiff & <u>laughed</u>. Smiled lovingly. Got cheques ready for Iquitos. All hands cleaning up. Engineer says we will be in Iquitos by nightfall. I doubt it greatly. At earliest 9 p.m. & probably midnight. Slept better last night but fear attack of <u>gastritis</u> is coming on as in Pará. Stopped for wood at Murupa, opposite the mouth of the Napo & at 3 on again – very hot. Nice Indians at Murupa. Many small chacras. Passed mouth of Napo at 3.30 & slowed down as cannot get to Iquitos tonight in time for landing. It is 8 hours steaming from Napo. Will be there this morning. Steward showed enormous exposure after dinner stiff down left thigh. Then he went below & came up at St Thereza where "Elisa" Launch was & leant on gunwhale with huge erection about 8" – *"Que,* [**word unclear**] *Señor*?" Garrido watching. I wanted awfully.

25, Friday Gave Engineer's small boy 2s/1 & Steward [**??**] £1.0. Asked <u>my</u>

Steward his name. Ignacio Torres he said [**a name that will rattle around the diaries and Casement's correspondence for a year or more**] & I asked him come to Cazes' house. Arrived Iquitos at 7 a.m. On shore to Cazes & then to barber with Arédomi & Omarino. Met Sub-Prefect there who gave me warm welcome & then told me an 'Auto' had been opened & all was to be investigated! Cazes said the Judge from Lima is a fraud that all is a sham! Visited Booth & down to "Athualpa". Doctor of her, an Italian, gave me a medicine. Saw Reigada & his Cholo sailors – all had been drunk & he put them in the hold, the brute, "to sweat it out." Saw Ignacio Torres on the deck looking at me. Visit from Prefect A.D.C. & also from Pablo Zumaeta but I was out. Spent pleasant day & was very tired at nightfall. Lots of mosquitoes again & I could not sleep well. Talked to Cazes till fairly late. I am very tired of the C's & Iquitos. "Athualpa" does not sail until 2nd or 3rd I hope I will catch Clement at Manaus.

26, Saturday Called on Prefect with Cazes. Long interview from 10.15 to 11.40 a.m. Told him much & promised to send Bishop to him on Monday at 10. He says the Commission of Justice will sail next week. A Doctor goes too and officers & soldiers. In Govt. Launch. Doubtless "America" which is being fitted up already I see. He says they will punish as well as reform. Asked me for help to see that the Commission went straight when there. Heavy rain at 6.30. Went to dinner at Booth's house & played bridge. Rain all time. On board "Athualpa" again & saw young Customs officer from Manaos – great. I will indeed, only a boy almost – pure Indian too. Also fair-haired pilot boy, tall & nice, from Pará. Took my room No 1. "Athualpa" leaves only on 4 Nov., Sunday next. Will miss "Clement" at Manaos. She sails on 7th.

Sunday 27. Off in "Manati" pic-nic to Tamshiako 25-30 miles up river. Prefect brother & Lt. Bravo & all, etc., etc. Pleasant day. Again told Prefect many things of Putumayo. Pleasant day. Saw Indian cook boy on "Inca" – enormous, lying down & pulled it often. Huge, thick, big lad 17. Also Ignacio Torres & told him come 8 a.m. tomorrow. Saw him twice. Told Pinheiro come too. Told Bishop get Lewis.

28, Monday Heavy rain all night & this morning pouring. 9.30 No Bishop, no Ignacio, no Pinheiro & no Lewis. What is up? Ignacio Torres came at 10 a.m. Clean & nice. Gave him £1 & a portfolio for Captain Reigada – asked him to return with the cover. He has not been to Brazil. Running from Iquitos – in bare feet. Gets £3 per month. Bishop late. Sent to Prefect at 10.30 only. He returned 11.15. had told him everything (in 30 minutes!) & I saw John Brown & S. Lewis & will send them tomorrow. Saw Ignacio Torres below at 2.30 looking for me with my portfolio. J. Clark with him. Door shut, so he went on to the office, poor boy. I should like to take him too. Saw him later when with Cazes & he said he was coming at 8 a.m. tomorrow & then saw

1st of 2: young man in hat with heavy belt, three-quarter length

2nd of 2: young man in hat with heavy belt, full length

him at band. Also saw Viacarra who shouted at me again & again & looked very nice. He was talking to Bishop. Manuel Lomas the Pilot stood me a drink of ginger ale & begged me to visit Punchana & see him. Regretted church not here in Iquitos. Played bridge with Cazes & Harrison & walked with latter until11.30. Fireworks. Cazes says the Judge Belcarce is very well spoken of locally as honest.

29, Tuesday Expect Ignacio this morning – am on look out for him. He came at 8.10 with my portfolio & I sent him for cigarettes. He brought wrong kind & I gave him 2/- & patted him on back & said 'até logo' [**'See you later' in Portuguese**] & he said 'Hasta luego' [**the same in Spanish**] & he left at 8.20. Last time of meeting probably. Will go to Manoel Lomas [**pilot**] today. Expect Jeremias Gusman this morning to send to Prefect. He came at 10 & I sent him along with Brown & Lewis. Prefect not in. Told by orderlies to come in 3 Hours. They went, all three at 1-3 & waited but Prefect could not see them & told them to come tomorrow at 10. I walked to Booths & on to Punchana & to

Manoel Lomas house & then talked to Vatan about things. He said my coming was a blessing to all (not only to Putumayo, but to the whole Department. That the Prefect had acted in a very bad way over the Dutch Expedition & that were it not for my official position I'd have been shot in the bush & now they were afraid of me & my evidence & wd. do something. Walked after dinner to Booth's House & then with Harrison to Square. Walked round it. Many beautiful types Indian & Cholo. Saw Ignacio at Merry go Round & pulled. He rushed & approached. Another Cholo with him. Waited longer hoping, till 10 p.m. & home to bed.

[On blotter:] Ignacio at Merry go Round 10 p.m. Last seen.
John Brown & S. Lewis to Prefect. He took their Statements in writing.

30, Wednesday Saw "Liberal" Cholo sailors going home at 5.30. All smiled. Wrote to Vice Consul at Manaos to send by "Clement" the 7 Barbados men who wish to be repatriated. Sent for John Brown to go to Prefect & Lewis & Guzman. They all went as far as I know at 10 a.m. but have not seen one of them since. They are lazy swine. Lent J. Clark £3. Saw Vatan again & asked him for Memo: on the Dutch Expedition. Went on "Athualpa" to lunch. Afterwards back to the house in atrocious heat. Called on Mrs Prefect and told her a great deal of Putumayo. Heavy rain at 6.30 all night. Spoiled all attempt at going to the Cinematograph at Alhambra. Walked round Square with Mr & Mrs Cazes. Atrocious dinner! Played Dummy bridge - a very stupid party. I am as sick of the Cazes as a man can be! & of Iquitos. No sign of Bishop since this morning. I will pay him off tomorrow & finish with him. The "Rio Mar" left for Manaos with Philip & J. Clark. I wrote down twice to Manaos about the men there.

December, 1910.

[On blotter:] "Rio Mar" left. Guzman to Prefect but told come today.

1, Thursday I fear the "Athualpa" will not sail until Monday 5th, certainly not till Sunday 4th Huge erection Indian boy at C. Hernandez corner at 3-4 a whole Hour. Up at 5.30 & out for coffee. All closed at 7. Fingered & pulled. Back to tea & out to Booths at 7.35. a.m. again. River risen 7' since Athualpa arrd. on 13th. It is now 62' – was 48' when we were here – a rise of 14 feet since Sept 6th or 10th. Its highest is about 80, but no one seems to keep any record! A lazy shiftless lot. Went to Booths to meet all the Barbados men. Only two came and I sent them to Booths' office to get work. Walked to Morona Cocha with 'Wags'. Very muddy indeed. Letter from Simon Pisango against Captain in "Loreto Comercial" of 30th. With Brown in afternoon & he dined with me at Bella Vista & then to Alhambra to Cinematograph & Pablo Moronez came in – & lots of Indians & peons. Splendid chaps & Cholo soldiers. Back at 11.30 in rain. Brown told me of Lt. Bravo's estimate of the Judge Valcarce as a man <u>who could be bribed</u>. Brown says the Indians are <u>all</u> treated badly & tells me of the killing of Valdemiro Rodriguez on Madre de Dios by 8 Indians only a month ago. The news came first by the Indians themselves who talked of it on the Plaza. No sign of Ignacio Torres since Tuesday night. Not a glimpse. Fear he has gone in Launch. Saw "Julio" in white pants & shirt at Alhambra. <u>Splendid stern</u>. **[In the White Diary entry for 2 December, Casement wrote, "There was not a very big crowd at the Cinematograph. I counted 62 men in uniform – including the band – the so-called military band of Andean Cholos – fine chaps to look at, but the devil to play. The row was infernal... The things shown were of the usual Latin-American type – of the amorous seduction and outraged husband setting – although immoral and nasty and the very worst thing to put before an audience mainly composed of young Indians, soldiers and work boys whose natural simplicity can soon be corrupted by what is offered to them thus in the name of civilisation. Higher civilisation! God save the mark."[457] Casement reveals himself here as something of a hypocrite, preferring that his lads were kept in a state of adolescent innocence rather than beginning Europeanised adulthood too soon. He masks his contradiction with a politically correct tirade against commercial exploitation by film industry moguls.**

This commentary on filmic values was preceded by a further discussion of the difficulties facing the Portuguese who had in October, and in Casement's view, foolishly, overthrown their monarchy. "Portugal is less fit to be a republic than Ireland – an Egyptian republic would beat a Portuguese one...the poor people are simple, kind and brave – and as ignorant as the Egyptian fellaheen. An Irish Republic, but better still an Irish state not a republic – if the Protestant and upper classes could be induced to join – would be a fine thing but with the tenant farmer, the County Councillor and the Dublin Corporation in charge – Ahem!"[458] Casement, in 1899, had encouraged his eponymous cousin in Ballycastle to run for Antrim County Council, calling the new local government system "a very interesting experiment in Irish history." He was plainly not yet a Republican.[459]]

2, Friday Heavy rain in night & all y'day afternoon & it will quite spoil the discharge of "<u>Athualpa</u>". Saw "Julio" at Pinto Hess **[Casement has begun to transfer his loyalties, or more accurately, his interest to Julio, "A strong-limbed, very sturdy chap about 22 or 23 years of age" according to the 18 November White Diary entry. Julio was also said by the skipper to be naive and trusting regarding money and little more than a slave.]** Gave cigarettes. He said "*Muchas gracias*". Enormous limbs & it stiff on right side, he feeling it & holding it down in right pocket. Saw <u>Huge</u> on Malecon. Looked everywhere for Ignacio. No sign anywhere. Very sad. Guzman <u>not get</u> see Prefect. Saw Guzman at 10 a.m. Waiting for Prefect with elderly Indian woman. Prefect "too busy" again! – Bishop tells me. At 5 p.m. Guzman was told to come at 3 p.m. This is Friday & he was first sent on Tuesday! To Booths & with Brown – saw "Julio" again at Store & asked him come to Punchana. He said "*Vamos*" but did not follow far. **["I walked part of the way to Punchana in the afternoon trying to get Julio the Huitoto off the *Liberal* to come with me" Casement wrote in the White Diary of this date.]** He asked when I was going to Manaos. Saw some really stiff ones today on Cholos. Two Huge erections & then four boys at 5 on seat in front – & then lovely type in pink shirt & blue trousers & green hat & later in Square with "Wags" the same who looked & longed & got Huge on left. To Alhambra with Cazes at 9.30 seeing many types & "Julio" in white again in a box. Met outside & asked him come Punchana tomorrow. He said "*Vamos*" & asked when to meet. I said at 10 a.m. but he probably did not understand.

3, Saturday Went out at 9.30-10 to look for Julio but saw no sign of him. Took John Brown's Statement up to 9.30. Bishop says Guzman saw the Governor only a short time y'day and that he told him to go back at 8.30 today & wd. probably send him back to Putumayo as Interpreter Viacarra is going down to Manaos on a Launch. Good riddance! altho' I like the Rascal's bright face & Indian skin & splendid teeth. Went on "Athualpa" at 10 & talked skipper & Brown & then lo! Ignacio on the Mole shovelling potatoes into a sack! So I asked him to come & see me today at 6 p.m. He said "Where" & I told him at C's house. Reygada called on me at 3 & told me he leaves for Putumayo on 7 Decr. Waited till 6.40. No Ignacio, or sign of him! Alack! To Booth's to dinner after turn round Square. Saw Beauty last night first in work clothes & then again in pink shirt at 5.30 in front of Cazes. After dinner round Square very many times till near midnight & saw types especially Cazes' office or shop. 'Passeando" **[strolling]** & feeling left pocket. Took photo of young Booth Customs' Clerk, Antonio Cruz Perez.

Sunday 4 Decr. Very hot morning. Looking out window saw Ignacio waiting. Joy. Off with him to Tirotero and Camera. Bathed & photo'd & talked & back at 11. To meet tomorrow. Gave 4s/. At 5.30 Cajamarca policeman till 7 at Bella Vista & again at 10.30 passeando & at 8. long talk. Shook hands and offered. Tall, Inca type & brown. Cards & Bridge & stupid party till near midnight **[This was at the Cazes's house where Casement was staying. Not having private rooms in Iquitos cramped his style on this visit.]** Saw Cajamarca **[the person not the town]** several times from window.

5, Monday Ignacio at 6.30 & off together to Tirotero & bathed. On to Indian chacra & mule boys (brown legs etc.) with lina passed into town. Gave £1 "tanto ufano" (so much contented) but no more! On to Hospital & to Itaia River by Telegraph - pretty & sat down by "Azul". He comes from Tarapoto, is 19½ & left the soldiers in August. When with 72 Tarapotanos he had volunteered for eight months. Poor lad! "Some day will go to Brazil for caucho". **[rubber collecting]**

What a fate! **[In the White Diary of the same date, Casement expanded on Ignacio's biography, adding "He says he is of the "*raca Española*" whereas he is almost a pure Indian and speaks Quechua as his native language I find. What a pity that all these people desire to shake off their Indian birthright and pretend to be part of the race of their oppressors."[460] Casement will not accept the reality of such imperial domination and the need of people to at least adapt to, if not join (if allowed) such a ruling culture, in order to survive, let alone prosper.]** To store & ginger ale & gin & on slowly, painfully dragging back towards House. At length the parting – & at Factoria Calle said Adios, for ever! He nearly cried I think. I gave him 2s/ more – & I think he was wretched. He said *"Hasta luego"*. I turned back & found him still standing at corner, looking straight in front. I to Fotografia & he crossed street. Last time I saw him was there standing and looking. Poor Ignacio! Never to see again. Wrote a little & out to Booths to get tickets (£37.10/-) an awful fraud. After dinner out to Square & saw several types, one young & lovely & a soldier from Lima – also the huge Cholo policeman with his sweetheart. Drank beer. Looked for Ignacio but no sign anywhere. Turned in at 11.45. Very hot. Pablo Zumaeta called on me at 2.30 for a list of the criminals!

6, Tuesday Packed up early & called on Prefect. He had properly been fooled. Told me Dublé was going round to Putumayo! Dublé. I wrote Barnes & all. At stage Zumaeta & Raygada **[sic]** & others to bid me goodbye – including the Prefect's ass of an A.D.C. – a young ruffian that. Zumaeta going also to Putumayo! A nice beginning to the Judge's "mission"! "Athualpa" off at 11 – a crowd on pier – but no sign of Ignacio. I thought he wd. have come, but he has not. Poor boy. Said farewell to Iquitos with every joy but regrets for Ignacio & the Indians all. God bless them. Steamed down river. Lots of people on board & had to shift cabin. The Franco-Dutch people (2) on board. Some fine Cholos going to Manaos to go up to Acre for *caucho*. One tall six foot lad told me for 3 years. Poor boy. Gave many cigarettes & sat up till 10 on lower deck. Some of them willing & soft.

[On blotter:] Left Iquitos. Goodbye Ignacio! Never to see again! **[Appropriately, the White Diary, the template for his official Foreign Office report, concludes on this date.]**

7, Wednesday Rain in night & I out at 3 a.m. & moved chair. At Leticia at 6.30 a.m. & on to Tabatinga & Esperanza at about 10.30 a.m. The Customs officer of "Liberal" came off & I learned from that the Barbados men had gone down to Manaos in the "Andresson" two days after I left them at Javari. 15 days ago I left there, so they have about 13 days start & must be in Manaos about 5 days already…I talked to tall *seringueiro* lad from Iquitos, José Gonzalez born there 1885 & going up Acre for 3 years – a fine young chap. Turned in at 9.30 or 10 p.m. after talk with Engineer.

8, Thursday Passed Jutahy at 8 a.m. Great firing of guns to us as "Athualpa" was once 4 months aground there, & all full speed. Made out accounts of Bishop & of the B. men at Manaos to be ready for arrival there on Saturday morning. The day passed quietly, and rain in night. We passed many seringals and pretty places on the river bank. Heavy rain in night.

9, Friday Heavy rain all morning & most of day. Passed a lot of places – lakes & rivers without end. We are steaming very well and shall be in Manaos soon after midnight. Passed Purus river at 5 p.m. a fine broad opening. A lot of the poor Iquitos folk who came down by "Rio Mar" are camped there on both banks, waiting the launch that will take them up – Their 'patrons' on to Manaos. At midnight saw the glare of the electric lights of Manaos (12 miles N.E. of the intervening peninsula) & we got there at 3 p.m.

10, Saturday On shore at Manaos at 9 a.m. & arranged with Dering for paying off the Barbados men. Most of them are going to Madeira Mamoré Railway, only 5 to Barbados. At Booths' office & then to Chambers to lunch & meet Laughlin & at 1 back to Booths & paid off the men losing some £40, at least, by the transaction. On board at 5 p.m. & off in "Athualpa" to Pará. Poor wee Ricudo is sick – temperature 104° in hospital. In Manaos saw the results of the bombardment of two months ago. Quite disgraceful the whole thing. All our Iquitos Cholos left at Manaos – poor boys – they go to that hell the Acré. We hope to reach Pará on Tuesday afternoon in time to land. I hope so. I shall go to the Hotel & have a good time of it – at last! **[After a frustrating time in Iquitos, the recharging of Casement's sexual batteries in his old consular stamping ground of Pará was to be a concentrated three-day affair.]**

<u>Sunday 11 Dec.</u> Steaming well down river. Splendid breeze. Ricudo sick & in Hospital – poor wee chap. New pilot from Manaos, a fine chap indeed & huge Pará caboclo. Passed Parintins. Villa Bella first and on all day till Obidos at 7.30 steaming fast. Santarem at 12.20 midnight. Long talk with Dr. (an Italian).

12, Monday Very cool strong breeze. Passed Monte Alegre at 6.30 or 7 a.m. in haze. To reach the Narrows this evening, and it is very doubtful if we shall get to Pará tomorrow in time for the visit. I hope so, as I want much to go on shore & find João. Have a lot to do in Pará – & will certainly see him this time – poor old José is dead & gone. I think of Ignacio all the time. Steamed down past mouth of Xingu at 5 & to Gurupa island & town at 6. Saw the great flood of the Amazon going N.E. as we turned into Gurupa entrance. Adios. Talked to the pilot who told me lots of stories of Xingu Indians & others & at 9 entered the Narrows – a fine night. Turned in at 9 & read till 11 & slept all night.

13, Tuesday Out of Narrows about 4.30 & steaming across the beauty expanses of clear water by Marajo, a wondrous inland sea, but fresh water &

delicious water. Passed between Murumuru Island & Javaeita, & many houses & canoes & they put off to avoid swamping. Mouth of Tocantins at 12.30 & on full speed on falling tide to round the lower island & sighted Mosqueiro at 3 p.m. a steamer going up. Turned up stream at 4 p.m. opposite Mosqueiro & arr. off Pará – 5.15. "Trader" behind us. Customs & Dr. visited & on shore with Atahualpa Purcell at 7.30 to Hotel do Commercio where got room & out to Marco by tram for a cool ride. O 14$000 A 10$000 & Beer etc. 5000 = O. 29$000 A 10000. "Olympio" first at big Square, then Polvora & followed & pulled it out & to Marco when in deep. **[In the pages of accounts at the back of this diary there are further references to these sex costs, replicating the above details of 29$000 paid to "O & A Olympio & Alves" plus 1.000 for the former's tram fare, and a further 10.000 for Alves three days later. Expenditure of 10$000 on "Guavo jelly" is also recorded there.]**

14, Wednesday

Lib	191
La	35
Irish	63
	289

Nice day – out for a walk & at Cemetery after going round Baptista Campos etc. met João at 8 a.m. & he gave me a big bunch of flowers – very nice indeed. To meet at B. Campos. Pogson called. To lunch with Southgate in S. Jeronymo 111 – & then got things out of Customs & all bags on shore & at Hotel. Letters from home & by telegr. see that General Election is nearly over = 518 seats filled with a Liberal-Labour-Irish majority so far of only 60. Conservatives 229 & the others all told 289. After light dinner out to B. Campos till 8.10 & then to Valparaiso & back home at 10.30. Theatre & grounds lit up finely. Sorry I did not meet João this evening, as I wanted to give him something. **[On blotter:]** Last time of meeting João Anselmo de Lima at Cemetery corner at 8 a.m.

15, Thursday Not feeling well. In Hotel all day nearly writing & getting ready to go home by "Ambrose". She arrived at 6 p.m. or so. Saw Kup at lunch & arranged for Lewis to work here at Port Works. Bishop & the Indian boys to go to Barbados & wrote to Father Smythe at St Patrick's about them. Also had Kup out to dinner in evening & talked to him & a Frenchman till 8.30. Then out for a stroll. To Big Square by Palace & then to B. Campos – none & on to Nazareth & Valparaiso, where soldiers wanted to enter the Show. Back to B. Campos & down to Palace Square. Two – one same as Nov. 1908. Grown bigger & well-dressed. This is at 10.35 or so p.m. Back to Nazareth at 11.20 & down to Paz for Beer & thro' gardens. Home on foot to Hotel at 12. "Sereno" in hammock at door. Enormous, only 18. Huge.

16, Friday In House all day. Got £60 from Bank. Bill No. 4. They gave me only 882$800 = I have lost about £6, I think between them & Booth's over the tickets in this exchange business. Boyd of the Amazon S.S. Coy to lunch & complained bitterly of the Minister & F.O. not backing them up more. They got £50,000 from Port of Pará. Boyd says that all the Brazilian Rivers for Rubber are worked by slavery pure & simple. The men don't get down. It is the "Cuenta" business & the "rule of the rifle" begins right here at Pará, so he says. Sent most of my baggage on the lighter to go off to "Ambrose". A very little rain at 3 p.m. the first since I landed on Tuesday night at 8 p.m. & yet this is the "rainy" season! It is hot daily, & I am ill & glad to be going. Gave Bishop letter for Governor of Barbados & £2 for the boys & a cheque for £20 also some milreis: Lewis 15$000. **[This money, including some Brazilian currency for the voyage, was not to be used by Bishop for its intended purpose leaving the boys in serious difficulties. Casement was easily conned having declared "I found Frederick Bishop a thoroughly trustworthy man."[461]]** Dined & Pickerell called & at 9 to Anderson till 10.30 & then to Theatre & met Alves & another type & to Independencia. "Soldado", **[soldier]** he said. 10$000 & back at midnight. Into Alves back door. **[This indicates, contrary to horrified statements in 1916, much repeated since, that Casement was simply passive, rather he was both bottom and top.]**

[Commentary on voyage home: The next day Casement left Brazil on the *Ambrose*, another "old tub", skippered by a Captain Jones. The voyage to Europe lasted ten days with the first landfall at Lisbon. Casement feared quarantine difficulties there, as happened, but only for one night, because two 1st class passengers had died on board: "young Boyd", a Casement informant, succumbed to yellow fever (known locally as *vomito negro*) and an "elderly Portuguese" to beri-beri.

Casement was able to pick up some useful information from a fellow passenger Julien Fabre about Arana's offer (through Pablo Zumaeta) to sell his share of the Peruvian Amazon Company to Fabre's Dutch-French Colonizing Company, partly because of fears about the Colombian boundary conflict. Julio Arana, Casement now believed, wanted to clear out and had been rushing rubber through to heighten his final share. "What a murderous ruffian! By God's help I'll unmask him" he wrote. And he was as good as his word.

It was a rough but otherwise dull voyage; no passengers or crew were recorded as providing any sexual comforts – visual or physical. Casement was reduced to pleasuring himself with thoughts of seeing "Agostinho and Antonio too!", if the quarantine authorities allowed disembarkation at Lisbon.]

17, Saturday Left Pará in "Bullrush". Bishop & Ricudo on board "Ambrose" with Kup & others & off at 10.30 or so. Few passengers. Fine breeze blowing up the splendid estuary of Pará. Pinheiro & Mosgueiro passed & blue sail flying before the wind. Far distant line of Marajo island. Off Bragança & Dalinas & out to sea with splendid trade wind blowing right in our teeth. Ship has about 400 tons rubber. Captain Jones in command. A Heavy head sea & very strong Trade wind as soon as we got to the open. Ship pitching a lot.

Sunday 18 Very rough. Everyone nearly seasick. At noon 337 miles from Pará.

19, Monday Heavy head seas & Trade wind very strong against us. At noon 330 miles. A poor elderly Portuguese died of Beri-beri – our second 1st Class passenger dead since "Ambrose" arrived in Pará.

20, Tuesday Sea slightly better. M. Julien Fabre gave me the Quito paper "El Ecuador" of Wednesday 1 March 1910 with a long translation of a "Truth" article on the Putumayo & 3 Declarations I have never seen as to the infamies of that hellish Peruvian region. How can it be ended for good? How? Ran 329 miles. Very heavy head sea & wind. Played Bridge – Captain Jones, Nurse Thomson, Norwegian Laurens & I.

21, Wednesday Ran 309 miles only. Sea worse & much stronger. Such trades. Played Bridge again – impossible to write or do anything. Ship like a girl on a skipping rope, jumping & kicking. Half passengers still seasick.

22, Thursday Ran 281 miles. Very head sea & wind. Quite a gale. Never saw Trades like these. Mon. Fabre told me today that Pablo Zumaeta came to him 3 or 4 days before he left Iquitos at the Hotel (introduced by the Hotel proprietor) & told him Julio Arana was trying to sell his shares in P.A. Coy & wd. give them for a very good bargain. He pointed out that J.A. held the bulk of shares & if Fabre's Franco-Dutch Syndic. bought them they wd. possess the Putumayo. He gave Fabre J.A. address in London. The affair had not been going well lately owing to 'various causes, partly the boundary conflict with Colombia. He said it would be a 'coup de fusil' (!) – for whom? What d-d scoundrels. Fabre evidently wanted my opinion. I said only 'Prenez garde'. This confirms Cazes' opinion that J.A. wishes to clear out & had been rushing the rubber in order to raise his share. What a murderous ruffian! By God's help I'll unmask him.

23, Friday Sea a little quieter & wind too gone down – & we seem at 8 a.m. to be making better way. Skipper said yesterday that to reach Lisbon by noon on Tuesday we had from noon y'day to make 13 knots = 312 per day. This we can easily do if the weather doesn't get infernal, but it may be touch & go. I do want to get to Lisbon by daylight on Tuesday in time to land if one can land – after our two deaths on board – one of yellow fever, poor young Boyd at Pará & the poor old Portuguese at sea three days ago. I fear we shall be quarantined at Lisbon, but if not I hope to go on shore & see Agostinho & Antonio too! Ran only 291 miles. Sea fell slightly, but got up again in night. Wind shifted to N.N.W.

24, Saturday Wind N.N.W. or more N. Ran 319 miles. Are now 1070 miles from Lisbon. To get in by say 5 p.m. we must do 330 miles or 13.7½ miles per hour. This tub cannot do that except in quite smooth water – as soon as there is any swell she skips & loses way. We are now well out of tropics & getting colder too. Very tired of this voyage I must say. This is Christmas Eve, Play Bridge every night with Captain Jones, Nurse Thomas & Mr Laurenson, a young Norwegian from Carnolin & Christiania.

Sunday 25th Decr. Ran 342 miles. Lisbon 728 miles.
Stupid day. Played Bridge & lost 4 Rubbers after dinner.

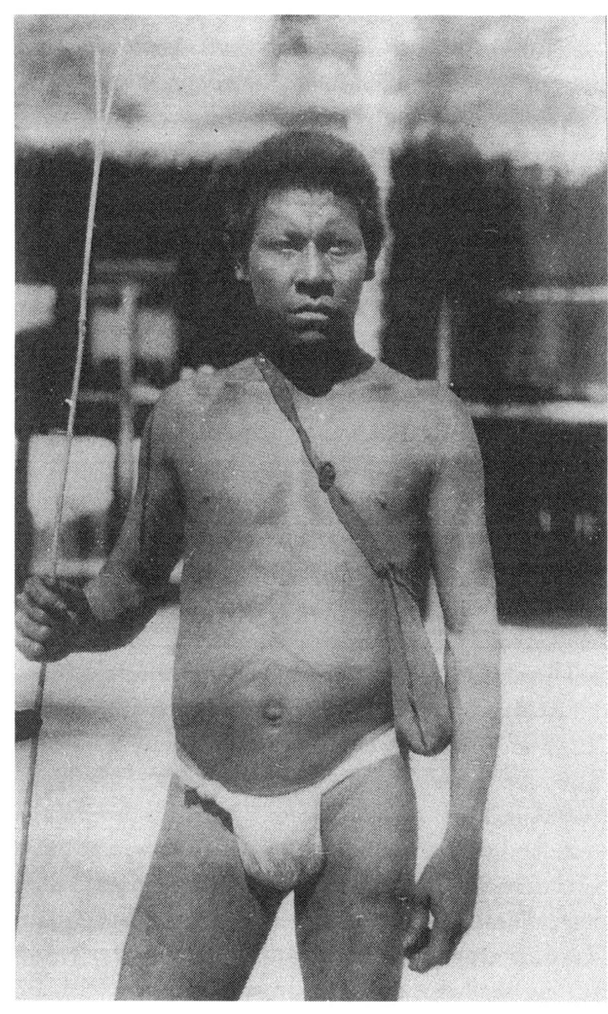

Sturdy, tattooed, Indian male: thatched longhouse behind

26, Monday We pass Madeira about 1.30 a.m. Lost 15/- at Sweep y'day & today 5/- to Dr. on bet that we should do nearer 350 than 346 miles. The "Ambrose" an old tub. Ran 339 miles – Lisbon distant 389 miles. A wretched performance. Everything favourable, wind, sea & all & yet this is all the so-called 15 knot "Ambrose" can do. We may arrive about 4 p.m. at Lisbon, in good time for the visit. Lost my 5/- bet with the Doctor, or rather this miserable tub lost it! Stone of Serpa told Laurens of the killing of the Cearenses up the Acre when they have a credit. Boy was to 'come tomorrow' & get his Saldo. Warned in night to scoot. Had 3½ centos due & fled rather than be shot 'by others'. So got down river & Stone engaged him. Is there now on Stone's farm. Many similar cases occur & this is further Brazilian testimony supporting Boyd of Amazon Coy who is also a Brazilian.
[In margin:] 10/- to Band – an awful fraud.

27, Tuesday Read y'day splendid speech of Thys on Congo govt. & future of the natives. A very fine statesmanlike pronouncement. I will write & congratulate him. This morning we have head sea & wind again & ship pitching & rolling heavily once more.
Ran **[blank]**
Arrived in Lisbon 4.30. but the idiots wd. not give us *pratique* & quarantined us all night. I never knew such rubbish.
[Inscribed earlier:] 5 P.M. Should be in Lisbon roads off Carcavalhos. (Sat. 24 Dec)

28, Wednesday On shore at Lisbon at 10 a.m. & to Avenida where long-legged boy types & sailor. Then to Largo Camões & to Taurus to lunch & then Largo again & young soldier lad (18 or so) in grey twill – Splendid – followed. To O'Neills house [***The* O'Neill lived in some splendour at 59 Rua das Flores in Lisbon; at Estoril; and on the Boulevard Haussmann in Paris. In 1904, when Casement was consul-general in the city they had met twice – just prior to his two departures for home. On the second occasion Casement dined with the family "in old Irish intimacy" as O'Neill described it. Sadly, he reported to F.J. Bigger on 11 December 1904, "I had only one moment to introduce him to my wife and family – and I can only add that we all like him very much." Related to Hugh O'Neill, the Earl of Tyrone, who reluctantly departed for the continent in the 1607 Flight of the Earls, Jorge O'Neill was recognised as titular head of the clan, hence his various titles – Prince of Tyrone and Comte de Tyrone.**

Casement described Jorge as "the undoubted lineal descendant of Brian Ballagh (Brian the freckled) and of *Aodh buide* (Yellow Hugh) "who crossed the Bann" in that memorable expulsion of Norman settlers from Antrim, far back in the making of Ireland."[462] The modern Prince of Tyrone was seriously taken with Casement, whose interest in his other predecessors, extending to the more famous Shane and Owen Roe O'Neill, provided

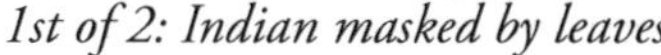
1st of 2: Indian masked by leaves

2nd of 2: Indian masked by leaves, hair shading only appreciable difference

a welcome link to Jorge's ancient homeland.* It also boosted Casement's long-held view that the O'Neills and their successors were the rightful rulers of Ireland as opposed to the Norman, English and Scots intruders. Yet things were always more complicated. Casement did not recall Yellow Hugh's marriage alliance and treaty of 1269 with the Norman Earl of Ulster, Walter de Burgo.

For a quarter of a century, the Count corresponded with Bigger in Belfast about antiquarian and religious matters and especially over an introduction he had commissioned him to write for *The History of the O'Neills*. He donated £10 toward the 1907 Glens *Feis*. Constant enquiries were also made about Casement, especially about his state of health because of the illness that led to him abandoning the Lisbon consulate. "Have you heard from that charming fellow Casement?" he asked on 31 January 1907, "I heard he was now Consul at Santos." O'Neill was also a provider of port for

* Hugo O'Neill of Clandeboy presented President Mary McAleese with a batch of letters from Casement to his ancestor in 2002 during her state visit to Portugal. Dated 1904 and 1905, they are now in NLI 36,650 (1-7).

Ardrigh, frequently sending F.J.Bigger a case "of our country's nectar."[463]] & down to Largo near Consulate where arranged things & on to Arsenal & Necessidades Palace [**Ministry of Foreign Affairs**] & several types & back to Avenida & then by Banco de Portugal an enormous offer about 9", lying on one side like Agostinho, but too late & so to Consul Somers Cocks & off at 4 on board & "Ambrose" sailed for Oporto.

29, Thursday Oporto & Vigo
Lovely day, sea like pond & bright sun, altho' very cold. At Leixoes at 7 a.m. Glorious sunrise & everything beautiful. Left at 10 a.m. for Vigo by Spanish coastline. Exquisite winter's day. Very cold but delicious sunshine. Arr. Vigo at 3 p.m. Wrote to Ramón. Poor Snra. Villalaz, her daughter, & other passengers from Iquitos were quarantined for 5 days at Vigo – had to go in a barge to Lazaretto with 27 Deck passengers – poor souls. The wee girl cried. "Avon" off at 4 & we at 5, following her. Glorious day & sunset. Cool & clear & delicious air.

30, Friday ~~Cherbourg in evg.~~ Overhauled "Avon" at 3 a.m. but then we slowed down, Captain says, and she went away. Lovely day over bay of Biscay, we should do 360 miles easily. Wrote to Tyrrell at F.O. saying I was going to Paris from Cherbourg & sent Life Certificate to Chief Clerk. Cannot get to Cherbourg till 8 or 9 a.m. tomorrow morning & hope to get to Paris by 6 or 7 p.m. Sending most baggage to Liverpool.

31, Saturday Fishguard tonight & probably London. Arr. Cherbourg – early on shore & to Station & at 12.56 after rotten lunch to Paris. We were Lorentzsen, Van der Est, Fabre & the train very slow. Due 6.58 but arrived only at 8.25 Gare St. Lazare. To Hotel Terminus & got vile room. Out to Place de L'Etoile after dinner & 32 Artillery. Denis Hilaire there & to Grand Armée. Later in Champs Elysée soldiers & then in B. des Capucines green hat & small. Two last no copper – but Denis 10/-. Mild evening, great crowds. Boulevards & Capucines & everywhere silly songs being sung & pretended gaiety without heart in it. Wrote F.O. Life Certificate & so to bed at end of year – already in 1911.

Casement's movements during 1911

1 January 1911 in Paris

4 January arrived London, leaving for Dublin 21 February

6 March left Ireland for London

14 April in Belfast, arriving back in London 30 April

4 May left for Belfast, returning to London 17 May

26 June meeting Indian boys in Southampton

5 August arrived Dublin, finally returning to London 14 August

16 August left England for South America

28 August arrived Barbados, leaving 4 September

10 September arrived Pará (Brazil), leaving 23 September

28 September landed Manaos (Brazil), leaving 3 October

16 October arrived Iquitos (Peru)

13 November left Iquitos to go upriver on investigation

23 November back in Iquitos, finally leaving 7 December

11 December arrived Manaos, leaving 17 December

20 December arrived Pará, leaving 24 December

28 December 1911 arrived Barbados, leaving 31 December for USA

10

1911 Cash Ledger

The 1911 Cash Ledger[464] is a blank, hardback notebook measuring eight by five inches and follows on seamlessly from the 1910 Black Diary. It is the first of two journals Casement maintained in 1911. Bound in black half-leather the pages are lined blue horizontally, and red vertically. There is an entirely unused set of alphabetically indexed pages at the front. The word Ledger is stamped in gilt lettering on its spine while a price of 1/6 is marked inside in pencil.

1911 opens with Casement, aged forty-six, returning to London via Paris from the first Peruvian investigation. His task now was to write a report for the Foreign Secretary. During the first half of the year he visited Belfast and Dublin before returning to South America in August on a follow-up mission.

This Cash Ledger acted as a small accounts system, one kept by a man who had no permanent base to store his papers or bills and who was ceaselessly travelling. It should be read as such. About two thirds of the money notations are omitted as mundane, repetitive or uninteresting, although some of the most banal are of historic relevance in assisting understanding of the detail of his and others' lives, and of the relative cost of living in Edwardian England and Ireland.

Despite having a separate, proper diary for 1911, Casement did not persist with it. Although well intentioned, his resolution only lasted until 18 January. Consequently he permitted his necessary expenditure records here to be enlivened by some of the more dramatic happenings he experienced from January to October. On 13 August, when back in South America, on mission, he recommenced use of the 1911 Black Diary having made a few sporadic jottings and drawn a map in between times. Entries from then to 31 October are written up in both volumes. The Ledger ran out of space at the end of October and he therefore continued with the Black Diary alone from 1 November to 31 December 1911.

Cash totals on the right hand edge of the page, added-up by line across, and by day down, are omitted unless they are themselves significant or instructive. Monthly accumulations and other occasional calculations are also omitted. The 'cash for sex' calculations (and totals) usually appeared in the left margin, at times out of date order. Here they are normally placed below the related daily entry. Expenditure on Foreign Office matters was also accumulated in the margins but is not reproduced.

Casement was not a mean man, as many have suggested by virtue of his recording of tiny payments – literally even the spending of a penny in a lavatory. Far from it, he was constantly giving his money away. But he did want to keep track of his spending. Such accounting is best done comprehensively or not at all. Casement in 1911 chose the former, although he did not always manage accurate monthly totals. He also needed a record of his expenditure in order to reclaim from the Foreign Office money spent on official business.

The notion propounded by some, and oft repeated, that his precision regarding expenditure had some sort of psychological connection to his homosexuality – evidencing an anal personality, is thinly based given the lack of other cash ledgers. Jeffrey Meyers in a 1973 article stated, "For Casement's compulsive and repressed personality, the spending of money was closely related to the spending of sperm and the former often financed the latter in remote places where bed and boy were easily available."[465] Such a view is momentarily convincing but the unquestionable fact that Casement wrote so ceaselessly meant it was a small extra effort to keep daily accounts. There is also a near universal truth, evidenced by joke, that gay men make lists and are notoriously tidy which undoes a compulsive personality theory being uniquely attributed to Casement.

For those unfamiliar with pre-decimalisation currency, one pound sterling (i.e. £1.0.0) consisted of twenty shillings (e.g. 3/- or 3.0) while each shilling had twelve pence or 'd' (e.g. 4d.) making two hundred and forty pence to the pound. £2.16.11 is therefore two pounds, sixteen shillings and eleven pence. Casement often left blanks when there were no pence (or shillings) involved in a purchase (e.g. £4.5) and at times just inscribed a dash (£4.5 -). Neither was he consistent in his use of stops between cash figures (either £4.2.10 or £4 2 10 can appear). For clarity, such details are here regularised <u>with</u> stops, <u>omitting</u> dashes and blanks. Nor did he always use pound signs. To bring amounts up to present day values a rough multiplier would be between thirty and fifty.

On the cover there is a typed note reading "This Ledger, formerly the property of ROGER CASEMENT, was forwarded to the Home Office by the Commissioner of Police on 23rd January, 1925 – see correspondence in file 311,643/206a." Ominously, it is signed by Casement's most dedicated adversary in 1916, "Ernley Blackwell."

In the flyleaf, Casement stuck a photograph of a standing toddler on which he inscribed "My godson "<u>Roger" Hicks</u>." Baby Roger had been

christened on 15 February 1910, in Casement's absence. The baby's father Lt. Col. F.R. Hicks was an officer at Fermoy, Co. Cork and Dick Morten's brother-in-law. It is this sort of private, human detail, as Roger Sawyer notes, that precludes the likelihood of forgery.[466]

This version is abridged with, as before, annotations being within square brackets, and in bold.

On the first two pages or flyleaf there are a few notes, mostly addresses of foreign males picked up in London during 1911:
1/6 **[this ledger's price]**

Amron Kali. Ahmed Khaled. 7 March **[Casement overwrote a figure 8 with a 7 and the episode is duly diaried on 7 March below.]** 12.35 a.m. New Oxford St. **[An arrow from this note then points to]**
Mr Gatty.
9 Jensen Street Jansen John's (? Johnson Street) Jones St.
Farringdon Road. E.C. **[The precise address of this individual annoyingly eludes Casement.]**

25 July. 12.15 p.m. T Court Road corner
Jean of Algiers. Clerkenwell Rd.
Enormous. twice as big as Amron's.

Master E.K. Biddy.
Bishop's Court Hill. **[See 29 August and 1 September entries for more on Teddy Biddy.]**
Bridgetown.
Barbados.

[Before and after the Ledger's dated entries there are four pages of notes to do with expenditure in 1909 and 1910 (some which tally precisely with entries in the 1910 Black Diary) indicating that the book had been around for a year and was previously, if briefly, in use. Those at the front are labyrinthine in complexity and in tiny writing. A few that are more comprehensible or relevant now follow:]

Expenditure at Rio.
February 1910.

Previous to Janry 1st 1910
1909 in Rio from 22 Mch 1909...Decr...9 Months 9 Days = R 9:825.400... to Tuesday 18 Jan- ...20 To Petropolis Ticket 9.600...24 Lunch O'S.B **[O'Sullivan Beare]** ...Pedro 60.000 **[Pedro, although unrecorded elsewhere,**

is presumably a sexual partner and one who was considerably rewarded.] ...Icarahy 221.000...Less Petropolis journeys 4. 4. 4. £80. 1.0
18th won at Bridge 16.000 Bridge 37.500...Pedro 5000...Tue 22 **[22 February 1910]** *Lunch 50.000 **[at top]** *Nordenflychts lunch...Thurs 24...Pedro 10.000 **X** ...Val 20.000 **[Black Diary on Thursday 24 February 1910 – "Valdemiro – Rua 20$"]** ...Sat 26 Pedro* 10.000...Monday 28 ...Mario Rua Hospicio **[See graphic 28 February 1910 Black Diary entry for Mario, $40]** ...743 000 less won at Bridge 10 800 R. 732 200 Add – Total 732 200 Icarahy 100$000 Petropolis Pension Central 578$000 Pedro 60$000 Do. Boots &c. 40$000 **[Mario]** 40$000 English hotel 24-28 103$000 **[grand total]** R. 1:613 200

Sat. 19. Saw "Beauty" at Raiz da Serra in down train. Smiled & looked: but turned away – alas!

"Beauty" on *Barca* – Would not like – cut me dead – alas! – followed in Avenida to General Camara – last saw going along it in black.

March 1910

... Wed 2 Antonio 10.000...Frid 4 S Paulo Hotel...Lottery...Fri 11 arr B.A. on shore...Sun 27 Left San Marcos for B.A. **[Notes inscribed here of assignations with Ramón can be found in the 1910 Black Diary at dates in March and April.**

As there are no pre-printed dates in the Cash Ledger, Casement had to inscribe them daily. His style of dating varied considerably, as did the month abbreviations he chose to use. The 1911 dated entries now start:]

JANUARY

Janry 1st. 1911. Sunday. In Paris with Denis **[Hilaire]** first 30 fcs.
To Prefecture and Quai d'Orleans and Montparnasse and back to Place de l'Opera and Pierre – "*bien servi*" 40 fcs.
Say 80 fcs.

Janury 2nd Monday. To dinner with Dick **[Morten]** and Barrons and then service 90 fcs. **[The service charged was not actually provided. Casement was robbed of 90 francs, nearly £4 – see 1911 Black Diary for same date.]** Lunch with Bertie at Embassy **[an invitation from the Ambassador for the next day.]**

Jan 3. Tuesday. In Paris. Bought clothes. M Clothes. Lunch with Bertie. About 100 fcs. **['About' written twice]**

Friends in Janry in Paris 7. 5. 0
in London 7. 0. 0 **[actually £6.19.0; this calculation is a**
£14. 5. - **later insertion]**

Ernest Lift of Philadelphia.

Jan 4th. Wednesday. Date of arrival in London. Hotel bill Terminus fcs. 50... Lunch in train to Calais...Railway fare etc. 75 fcs = £3.0.0...Dinner 4/6. Cgttes 7d.

Ernest 6/- Cab 2/-. Ernest 10/-	**X**	18.0
...Whiskies 1/- and Cigttes 1/-... Fred 15/-		15.0

18.0 **[paid to Ernest]** Enormous
15.0 **[paid to Fred**
1.13.0 **1st accumulating total of sex expenditure in 1911]**

Jan 5th. Thursday Arrd. in London from Paris at 8 p.m. Wed 4th Janry. Sweeper 6d. Train 9d...Lunch 1/10. Dinner 1/1. Cigarettes 1/6. Matches 1d. Whisky 4/6.

Ernest	**X**	2. 4.6
S/Leone **[probably Fred – see entry for day before]**	**X**	10.0
...Cabs 5/6	**X**	5.6

Supper at Gatti's 10.15

1. 13. 0 **[previous (1st) sex costs accumulated total**
2. 4. 6 **paid to Ernest**
10. 0 **paid to "Sierra Leone"**
5. 6 **price of cabs**
4. 13. 0 **2nd 1911 sex costs accumulation]**

None of your "Swank". **[A comment from the American, Ernest, who did not come cheap. Singleton-Gates in *The Black Diaries* left out that part of 5 January's entry after "Ernest X 2.4.6" plus the entries for all four days from 6 to 9 January 1911.]**

Jan 6th Friday ...Parliament Guide and Diary 2/6. [for significance of "Diary 2/6" see 31 January entry] Novels 2/2...Tea with Robert Lynd.

Saturday Jany 7th 1911 Bread – stone milled…Bottled fruit and cake…Jacob's Short Bread. Above bought on 5th Jany at Irish Stores…Nina and self dinner…

Sunday Jan 8. Dinner 5.6. Train 4d. Bus 5d. Cgttes 3d.
Matches 1d. B **[a line is drawn from B to Bush]** 8/- 8.1
Bush Soldier Grenadier Cardiff in Park.

4. 13. 0

8. 0 X **[Welsh Grenadier**

£5. 1. 0 **3rd sex costs accumulation]**

4 **[This is Casement's first personal, as opposed to cash, sexual accumulation in 1911. It seems that he is counting individuals rather than sexual events although those in Paris appear not to be included.]**

Monday 9 Jan. …Tea with Nina…Taxi to Hampstead 2/2 and tip 8d…

P. Order to Dublin for gift for Captain Jones "Ambrose". 1.0.0
[*Ambrose* was the ship which had just brought Casement from Brazil]

Tuesday 10 January F.O. **X.** Typed copy Hardenberg M/S from Anti-Slavery. 6. 6.0

….Dress coat from Paris which I did not want and had to get for H.W.'s **[Herbert Ward's]** dance – worse luck to it. 6.18.0
…To Mrs Jerome, Robuchon's book 10.0. **[Eugenio Robuchon's book *En el Putumayo y sus afluentes* was published in 1907 – after his disappearance and death. He was a French explorer commissioned by the Peruvian government which used his findings to enhance Lima's territorial claim to the Putumayo region. It was his ill fortune to be eaten by hostile Indians. Lucien Jerome, a British consul in Peru, was acting chargé d'affaires in Lima at this time, and as he said, a "paddy". He advised Casement that other London rubber companies were enslaving Indians although Arana's enterprise was the worst, especially as he had "bought up the government" in Lima. He added that the Peru's was "one of the worst presidents South America has ever had."[467] Casement's annotated copy of the Robuchon book survives in the NLI.[468]]**

[11-19 January: These ten days were unremarkable, involving as they did much work on writing a report of his findings. Expenditure on associated typing and stationery was recorded. Nina gets three mentions. On 16 January, Casement finally saw Colonel Bertie who had been writing about arranging a get-together for some time. They dined at their mutual club, the Wellington.]

Friday 20 Janry 1911 Telegram Mr Morel…Train 5d…M. Lane E. India Dock 2d. Trams 1d. Cgttes 6d. Tram 2d. (Many Chinese 28 of them) (& Lascars) Bloomsbury Italians and then Fanti 15. **X**

To Him 10/-. Taxis 4/-. 14 0

…Beggars [**payments to beggars are almost a daily occurrence**] 1.0

5. 1. 0
14. 0 [**Fanti**
5. 15. 0 **4th sex costs accumulation**] (5) Fanti [**5th sexual encounter**]

Saturday 21 Janry 1911 …Rooms and grub Miss Cox from 2nd Week to 18th Jan. 5.10.5. [**Miss Cox was Casement's landlady at 110 Philbeach Gardens, Earls Court**] …Luggage to Denham… **X** Fanti (Did not come, up to 6.20) [**Typically an arrangement had been made for a second round of sex with the young Italian although there appears to have been a no show.**]

[**22-23 January: At Dick Morten's in Denham, and back to London**]

Tuesday 24th Jan. 1911 2 Photo books 1 @ 6/-. 1 @ 5/9. 11.9. 1 India Rubber roller 2.9…

Wednesday 25 Janry …Handkerchiefs (to B'mena) 1.0.9. Bag &c. for Olga von Nordenflycht (Duncan) 2.0.0 [**"A very handsome present"[469] trilled Baron von Nordenflycht, who was the German consul-general in Rio during Casement's time there, and a close friend. This gift is confirmed in a letter from Casement to Evelyn Gleeson of 28 January 1911[470]. Casement was to avail of the Baron's hospitality in Germany in May 1912. He also stayed with the Nordenflycht family in Berlin during the war. In February 1915, the Baron was flattering him over the Findlay affair, "If diplomacy consists in obtaining from other people by their doing what you want and what is contrary to their interest I don't hesitate to declare you a consummate master in this art."[471]**] …

Thursday 26 Janry …Night bus 6d. Turkish Bath 2/6. Tips 10/-… [**Unfortunately uneventful, but tips of 10/- indicate Casement was displaying conspicuous generosity perhaps in the hope of sexual credits.**]

Friday 27 January 1911 …Telegram Miss Gleeson…To Blucher dinner… To W.I. Docks 4-6 p.m. [**10 transport journeys including another visit to dockland are listed for this Friday – by bus, train (tube) and taxi.**]

Saturday 28 Jan. 1911 Miss Cox room etc. to 25 Janry 4.3.0

2 Photo frames for Mrs Cazes. F.O. Iquitos a/c 4.7.6

F.O. (Iquitos a/c)...Books for B.M.S. Postage on parcel to Iquitos say 1/3... Doll for R. Lynd's girl...Taxi to Hampstead (R. Lynd's)...Beautiful at 12 30 midn. at T. Court Road.

Sunday 29 Janry 1911 Cigarettes (on Saturday) 6...Trains to Victoria...Seats Queen's Hall, Nina & Liz...Abdulla Cigarettes 1/7 **[Casement was fond of foreign cigarettes asking his cousin Gertrude from prison in 1916 to get him fifty "de Resky's."**[472]] ...Dinner Austrian Café Oxford St.

X Poor Jew 7/6 Piccadilly **[met in the notorious toilets]** 7.6
Sundries and train home. 1.0

£5. 15. 0
7. 6 **["Poor Jew"**
£6. 2. 6 **5th sex costs accumulation]**

Monday 30th Janry 1911 Nina to lunch at Harrods...On to Anti Slavery Society and F.O...

My tickets 3/-. J's. 4/-. Him 12/6 **X** 19.6
...Wash up 2½d... 6 **[6th partner]** To Harrow Jew – **X** Enormous and liked greatly.

6. 2. 6
16. 6 **[Harrow Jew; Casement's own train fare of 3/- is excluded.**
6. 19. 0 **6th sex costs accumulation in 1911]**

[Significantly, Casement notes here that he, the Jew, "liked greatly" what was happening to him – rather than the other way round. This is recorded on other occasions. It is obvious that Casement found particular pleasure in the fact of another male's erection welcoming him, feeling it a psychological turn-on. To be appreciated sexually by a much younger, and well-equipped, person was a great boost to his self-confidence.

This may partly explain why and how Casement was able to take on his work-superiors about all sorts of issues, given that so many of them were of the highest social and political status alongside making himself attractive both to radical politicians and those same establishment figures. It was not, as has been suggested, that Casement "loved a Lord" but that he frequently felt himself one, and believed no-one his better, especially when

boosted by attractive males wanting to have sex with him. Being Irish, and becoming Irish Irish, also gave him an effortless sense of superiority over mere Englishmen.]

Tuesday 31 January 1911 Train Parry's…Total a/c kept of Janry (I spent more because my first days in Paris are not included or remembered.) I spent some £18 in Paris). Total say £90.0.0.

Summary of January Expenditure

Coming from Paris to London, etc. 7.2.6
Friends 6.2.6 **[The 16/6 spent the previous night on J, the Harrow Jew, is omitted from the January cumulative sex account which should total £6.19.0, a figure returned to later.]** …F.O. a/c. Stationery: Book 6.6.0. **[the Hardenburg manuscript]** 2/6. 1/6 **[see below for significance of this item]** 2/2. 10.0. 2/4…Gifts – 1.0.0 "Ambrose" **[Captain Jones's postal order of 9 January]** 4.7.0 Mrs Cazes **[Louie, wife of David Cazes the outgoing consul at Iquitos]** 2.0.0 Nina…

[Responding to a 1960 article in *Threshold* by the forgery proponent Professor Roger McHugh, Letitia Fairfield wrote "The 1911 diary cost 1/6, and, as I had expected from knowledge of his habits, I found an item of 1/6 under "Stationery" in the summary of expenses incurred in London at the end of January's cash account." This explained that the diary was not bought until Casement reached England and seemed to clear up the mystery, developed by some into proof of conspiracy, as to how Casement had obtained and entered up a 1911 (English-printed) diary from 1 January when he did not arrive in the country until late on 4 January 1911.

Fairfield put it this way "Obviously when Casement found himself in Paris on January 1 without one, he did what any confirmed diary-keeper would do. He used an old notebook for a few days as both cash book and diary. Arriving in London he bought a diary into which he copied the entries in a slightly expanded form."

Working from Peter Singleton-Gates' book, she was unaware that there was an entry on 6 January specifically recording the purchase of a diary. The reason for her ignorance is that 6 January is one of the four days missing from that book *The Black Diaries*. The missing reference would have confirmed her hypothesis precisely. However, the 6 January entry does not perfectly distinguish a cost of 1/6 for the diary as it is incorporated with another item, a "Parliament Guide". This made up a total cost of 2/6.

Dr Fairfield had, according to a letter in the *New Statesman*, access to

copies of the diaries in 1957 – two years earlier than their first publication in 1959. A suggestion has been made that her diary source was from within the Irish embassy in London. But this may be a story derived from the fact that Dr Richard Hayes of the NLI had, before 1959, purchased a copy of the typescript from Singleton-Gates in London while promising to keep it under wraps for a decade. Whatever her actual source, the text she worked on, if not directly from Singleton-Gates, was cloned from his typescript as neither of them had the key entry of 6 January.

So she was wrong. The 1/6 she homed in on appeared in the January summary of expenditure, in a sub-list headed "F.O. a/c. Stationery". It would not have included a personal diary. All the other stationery amounts in the list tally with items in the diary margins between 6 and 14 January which Casement had marked "F.O." Dr Fairfield's explanation of the sequence of events and the diary purchase was perfectly credible, but in this one respect inaccurate and dangerous, as the list of Foreign Office stationery items was staring her, and others, in the face. The truth of this matter – the missing 6 January entry – was only available in the Public Record Office from 1959. Like all such Casement confusions or inconsistencies there is rarely a cast-iron answer. The nature of the diaries is that, being for personal use, so much of the information is implied, and thus unclear and open to question.]

FEBRUARY

[1-2 February: In London, to the pantomime with Nina, Louie Heath, and Lizzie Bannister, supper at Gatti's.]

Friday 3 February 1911 Out in Parry's motor with Mrs Green. Telegram to Charlie. Tip to Parry's motor man 4.6. Mrs Green gave 5/6...To Mark Lane and W.I. Docks Young Japanese sailor and then back. Nil. **[Nine bus journeys are made plus four by tube or train – Casement rarely distinguishes between the two – in an ultimately fruitless day's search. By this time, already a month back in London, he must have been well known to, and recognised by, the other denizens of the cruising areas, as well as being appreciated by London's transport companies for his custom.**

4-6 February: Telegram to Sir Edward Grey, the Foreign Secretary, to Denham for Saturday night, four dress circle tickets bought for Coronet Theatre on Wednesday; Louis Mallet at Foreign Office presented with a preliminary Putumayo report and photographs.]

Tuesday 7th February Lunch with typist. Beggar 2d. Bus 3d. (To Dr Long). Evg Busses many. Dinner Grand Hotel Grill Room…
"Welsh" 4/6. Splendid **X** 4.6 in Park 3 times **[most likely St. James's Park]** and also outside several and to Buckingham Palace at 11.45.

6. 19. 0

4. 6 **X [Grenadier**

7. 3. 6 **7th sex costs accumulation]** 7 **[7th sex partner]** Grenadier Huge

Wednesday 8 Febry. …Train Richmond 1/-…Beecham's Pills 2/6… Programmes at Coronet 1/-…

Thursday 9 February 1911 Porridge milk 6d…Postcards 6d…
Welsh Rarebit at Sloane Sq. 6.0
Supper Gatti's 3/1…

7. 3. 6

6. 0 **X [“Welsh Rarebit”**

7. 9. 6 **8th sex costs accumulation]** 7 **[7th person, “Welsh” a second time]**

Friday 10 Febry 1911. …Ticket Windsor 3/- Lavatory 6d. 2d…. Heavy rain at Windsor and Cold stream chilliness at Hyde Park Corner. **[presumably a wry comment on a Coldstream Guardsman failing to accede to a suggestion or proposal]** Dark eyes and beautiful…To Windsor 5.5 p.m. Return 9.52 p.m. in Rain and wretched night.

10/6

3/- **[3 shillings for the Windsor train**

13/6. **February sex costs total to date]**

Saturday 11 Febry 1911 …Miss Cox. Lodging &c. to 8 Feb. 2.11.1
H. Compton. **[Ballymena]** Tailor's Bill, overcoat and two suits. 11.15.0
Took Nina, Lizzie and Gee to lunch & theatre…4 Upper Circles Apollo 4/-.
…Taking Nina & Girls out 1.12.0
… **X** Laurens at W.I. Docks 4/6. Bus 4d… 4.10

7 .9. 6

4. 6 **[Laurens**

£7.14. 0 **9th sex costs accumulation]** 8 **[8th partner]** 18/- **[February's costs to date]**

Sunday 12 Febry 1911 Book for Cricket, Oscar Wilde's "Happy Prince"... **[Cricket was a daughter of Herbert Ward]** Went to Poplar. Laurens not **[Striking while the iron is hot, within 24 hours of a sexual transaction, perhaps hoping to develop a more substantial or regular relationship, was a common occurrence with Casement. Addresses must have been exchanged but Laurens was not in.]** ...Lovely Italian – Clerkenwell Rd. on tram – off at bridge – Huge. No Laurens "Alack" **[Casement is still grieved at his failure to pin down the Nordic sounding Laurens.]**

Monday 13 Febry Return ticket to Groombridge... 6.6

Train to Victoria & paper 1d. 5d...

X Clarence Gate 3/6 Soldier **X** 3.6

Lavatory 1d...Down to Old Lodge Ashdown Forest to Lord & Lady Norbury. **[The 4th Earl of Norbury, a big Irish landowner]** Scots at Victoria 6.30 & Irish after dark.

7.14. 0

3. 6 **["Soldier"**

7.17. 6 **10th sex costs accumulation]** 9. **[9th new associate: These rising numbers come in different forms. Usually in pencil, some are ringed, and some are in brackets. They are not as prominent as might be the case if inserted by a Home Office enumerator.]**

Tuesday 14 Febry. Telegram "Cui" 1/-...Welsh Rarebit 10/-. Lost at Gate **X** 10. 0

Victoria Station 11 p.m. 2/6 **X** 2. 6

Walked Paddington to Park. Wales lost at gate.

1. 1. 6

12. 6

1. 14. 0 **[February's sex costs total]**

7.17. 6
10. 0 **["Welsh Rarebit" again**
2. 6 **Victoria Station person**
8.10. 0 **11th sex costs accumulation]** 10. **[10th partner, Welsh already counted]**

Wednesday 15 Febry 1911 Telegram Lady M. Jenkins [**Lord Norbury's daughter who later informed MI5 about Casement's favoured coastal resorts in the west of Ireland**] ...Postage on Irish history to Katie Parnell 4d. "Ireland" [**Casement is obviously concerned about Parnell's daughter, and her lack of historical knowledge so she is issued with another copy of Mrs Green's book. Katie never used the surname Parnell although she was his child, not Captain O'Shea's.**] "Oscar Wilde"! Train to St. James Park. Parry not in – so to Mrs Green till 7. (Lovely type at Westminster tailor) [**Casement continues his relentless wandering through the city, having in the strictest sense no home to go to, rarely spending an evening in.**] ...

Thursday 16 Febry ...Taxi to Bluchers 1/-... [**Count Blücher was another old Africa connection, a descendant of the Prussian general Marshall Blücher who with Wellington was victorious at Waterloo. In 1904, the Count, trying to lift his friend out of a depression, unprofitably recommended marriage "the haven of helpful and intelligent simplicity which only a union can give in this world."[473] He took his own advice in 1907. Later the Count and Countess would be met in wartime Berlin, Casement then noting sourly "Blücher's interest is solely in himself, and his chances of besting his unscrupulous old father."[474]**]

Friday 17th Feb ...Train 5d. to Parry...Miss Cox – my bill to 15 Feby. 2.8.1. Also Miss Cox. Rooms to 1st Feb. 2.7.5. Cheque sent to Father Smythe at Barbados for Boys 10.0.0. [**This money for Father Frederick Smith was to pay for the upkeep and education of the two Indians who were being prepared for a London propaganda debut after selection in the Amazon. In truth, the older boy selected himself. The younger boy whose parents had been killed "by this rubber curse" was bought for a shirt and a pair of trousers. Nina's affectionate name for them was "forest devils."**] ...

Saturday 18th Feby ...To Albert Hall Nina & I. 2/- each...Dinner at Gatti's.
Busses after all over 1/-. "Scotsman" 2/6 3.6
...To Aldgate and on to W.I. Docks only Chinese and none. Thin long type about 16. Small sturdy and firm. Later Scot in Sl. Sq. till 8.

8.10. 0

2. 6 **X** **[Scotsman**

8.12. 6 **12th sex costs accumulation]** 11 **[11th partner]** £1.16.6 **[February total]**

Sunday 19 February To Denham asking Nina to go too. **[to Dick Morten's residence at Denham, a house later owned by Sir Oswald Mosley]** ...Evg. train to Victoria...

X Scot 12/6. Trains and Bus 7d. 13.1

[As normal, Casement returns at speed to the previous night's encounter with the Scot and isn't disappointed, as he had been by Laurens]...Putney Bridge. **[location of the meeting with Scot?]**

8.12. 6

12. 6

9. 5. 0 **[13th sex costs accumulation]** 11 **["Scot" for 2nd time]** £2.9/-. **[February tot]**

Monday 20 February 1911 Nina to Lunch...To Anti-Slavery and saw Buxton and Harris. Telegram to Hebblethwaite. Book to Cricket in Paris. **[Frances Ward (Cricket) had married a diplomat in 1911 ironically the son of Casement's arch-enemy Sir Constantine Phipps, British minister in Brussels in 1904 and defender of Leopold. Replying to Casement from the British legation in Sofia in August 1912, after another gift, she was to write "Thank you – Oh thank you many times for the beautiful poems of Yeats. I love the book."[475] In a letter to *The Tablet* (18 May 1957) she recalled how Casement who had "quarrelled finally and irretrievably over Ireland" with her father "had an infinitely humble suffering soul...when he came to stay, if possible, we never left his side."]** ...Bus to Col. Stopford **[Alice Stopford Green's brother Edward]** and back 2d...

Tuesday 21st Febry 1911 Leaving today for Dublin...Porridge 4d. Bus to Brompton Road and back. Lunch with Hebblethwaites 9/-...Flowers 5/-.

Ticket to Dublin and back L.& N.W. 2 .16.10

Miss Cox's Bill. 2. 9. 6

...Tea at 2.30 a.m. ss "Ulster" 1. 0

Wednesday 22 February 1911 In Dublin...Books and Sinn Fein etc...Dinner

(Eddie Wilkinson) 9.2. Lunch 2/3 (Dolphin)…Supper (Dolphin)…Hair cutting 1.0. Ramon. Heard from **[He was last seen by Casement in Buenos Aires in March 1910, but his letter has not survived which confirms there was a cull of boyfriend correspondence.]**

Thursday 23 Feb. 1911 In Dublin "Larzoy the House" Xmas NO **[meaning unclear]** 1.0. Sinn Fein 1d …

Friday 24 Febry …Dr Fitzgerald – Eyes 1.1.0. Dr Coffey's book (Miss O'Shea) 2.0…To dinner Marcus Matthews…Ill with cold coming on.

[25-28 February: ill in Dublin:] Sick in bed all day…Turned in at 3.30 p.m. Ill with fever not out at all. Sick…To Mrs Green for 10 copies her "Ireland" 2.0.0. To dinner Dr Sigerson (John Daly there). **[George Sigerson (1836-1925), was, like Casement, a man proud of his Scandinavian ancestry, being a descendant of the Norse invaders of Ireland as he put it. Father to the poet Dora Sigerson Shorter, he was Professor of Zoology at UCD and an influential author and translator of Irish poetry, most notably the anthology *Bards of the Gael and Gall.* He provided Casement with a medical certificate for the F.O. in 1913 when he needed evidence of illness for sick leave.[476] Eventually Sigerson became a Free State Senator. The GAA's prestigious universities' cup is named after him.]**…Only got up at 1.30 p.m…In bed all day still ill…Books at Gills 4/3…

Total in February £69.19.9…

MARCH

March 1911 Wednesday 1st March Ada Yeats typing Barnes letter for F.O. entirely F.O. 2.6…Turkish Bath 2/-…To Oculists. First out since Sunday.

1911 Thursday 2nd March …Week's bill at Gresham including washing, Bulmer, and many paid out items £5.19.3. Message to Miss O'Farrelly 1.0…

Friday 3 March 1911 Spectacles from Prescott's Dr Fitzgerald's for Eyes	17.8
To Bulmer for journey up to Dublin. From Tuesday to Friday.	1.0.0
…Tawin School subscription	5.0
…Tip to Night Waiter	1.0

[The Belfast-born Bulmer Hobson, like Eoin (John) MacNeill (a Glens of Antrim Catholic) and Casement, all opposed the starting of the 1916 Easter

Rising, largely on logistical grounds. Casement, because of his execution, achieved iconic status despite his stance on the rebellion. MacNeill who countermanded the order to commence the rising was rehabilitated and selected to serve on the ill-fated Boundary Commission where he failed again to enhance or protect the Republic. He then lost his seat in the Dail. Hobson was effectively exiled to obscure civil service departments and Co. Galway, dying at his daughter's house in Limerick over fifty years later, a largely forgotten man.]

Saturday 4th March …"Graphic" & Ill. "London News" "Erin"…
Irish books at Gills… 5.6

Sunday 5th. March …Trams 1/-. "How"? 2/6 **X** 3.6
Enormous 19. about 7" and 4 thick. **X** 2.6
…Supper at Jury's…Enormous Dublin under 19 Very fair – thin leg knickers & coat. White scarf. Blue eyes & huge huge. Stiff long & thick – a limb.

9. 5. 0
2. 6 X **["Enormous Dublin"**
9. 7. 6 **14th sex costs accumulation]** 12 **[12th person]** 2/6 **[March sex tot]**

Monday 6th March Bill at Gresham 7.5.8…Cab to W. Row **[Westland Row station]** …Train to Kingstown 1/8…Hibernian Academy 4 tickets 12.0 & programme 1.0…Brushes at Varians 10.0…Lozenges 2d…Left Ireland for England.

Thursday 7 March 1911 Cab at Euston…Postage Ramón and BA **[Buenos Aires]** Bernardino and Rio…
"Park" 5/-. Amron 10/-. Ahmron Kali. Taxi 2/-. Cab 1/6. 18.6
[An opaque note inside the front cover reads "Amron Kali. Ahmed Khaled 7 March 12.35 a.m. New Oxford St." The names suggest not two people but a question in Casement's mind as to his precise moniker.]

9. 7. 6
18. 6 **["Park" and Amron Kali plus transport**
10. 6. 0 **15th sex costs accumulation]** (13) **[13th person]** £1/1- **[March tot]**

To Norfolk Hotel for night and then to F.O. saw Tyrrell and Sir Ed. Grey. Wrote to Ramón – posted. **[This is a classic inverted entry, with earlier Foreign**

Office meetings and the posting of Ramón's letter positioned after the evening sex in the park. Because the later events were fresher in his mind, they were inscribed first.]

[8-31 March:] To Denham Bill at Norfolk Hotel 7.7…Ticket to Denham 3.0…**[Casement was now setting off to Dick Morten's house where he stayed for a month, allowing himself only half a dozen day trips to London. The task in hand was the writing of the final version of his report. March was therefore a cheap month with next to no lodging charges and sexual costs of only a guinea. The expenditure total of £41 compared favourably to January's £90 and February's £70.]** Got letters from F.O. and very nice ones too…Telegram Lady Charlotte **[another Norbury daughter]** … Began my report on Putumayo…Very weary work – in pencil all. Eyes giving out…Heard from Millar. Private letters posted by Parry at his expense… Ended it practically to-day **[15 March]** about 28,000-30,000 words in six days, not bad work…Patrick's Day **[17 March]** Mrs Green refunded the £2 on her books. It is good of her. I sent it to the Irish boys in Dublin. **[i.e. to Patrick Pearse's school, St. Enda's]** …Miss E.M. Stear, Typist…Very cheap good typist. 10d. per 1000 words…Washing clothes at Savoy…Motored with Dick to Cricklewood through Willesden Green etc to Metallurgique Car Coy. **[Dick Morten indeed had such a Metallurgique car which is pictured on page 104 of the privately printed memoir of Herbert Ward written by his eponymous son.[477]]** Letters from Iquitos and Rio. Cazes of 22 Feb… Chestertons to lunch…To Pinesfield with Sandy. Kate out…Heard from Parry to go to South of France…Wrote to Lord H. de Walden, Mrs Green, John Holt about E.D.M. Testimonial…Snow storms all day…Snowy winds of E. Anglia!…Wrote Miss McNeill about Raghery. **[Ada McNeill was a cousin of the Unionist propagandist and Conservative MP, Ronald McNeill. Despite writing in a private notebook, Casement did not refer to her as Ada nor even by the Irish name of Ide that she adopted. The letter was about Rathlin Island. Unfortunately most of Ada's incoming correspondence has disappeared.]** … **X** Tip to Reggie Parminter my Godson – by letter to Dover 1.0.0…To London to Misses Armstrong, Mrs Green and Nina and Lizzie… To London to F.O. to revise Report and give album to Sir E. Grey with photos of Putumayo. Then to Countess Blucher and Richard Coudenhove and home by 7.20 train…**[Three days into these weeks of hard work, Casement noted on Saturday 11 March "Heard from Millar." Arrangements for an Easter visit to Belfast were obviously being made to meet him for the first time since 20 June 1910.]**

APRIL

Saturday 1 April 1911 Train to London to Nina…Lavatory 3d. Train to E. Court etc. 1/8 (Nina). Zoo Nina and Self…To Zoo with Nina, at Gloucester Road Station waiting for E. Court train saw lovely fair hair 20 or 19 big, Fingering and stiff – wanted – nice respectable. Looked often and often. [**After a month of celibacy, largely in the Buckinghamshire countryside, Casement was unable to capitalise on the eager fingering youth observed in the station toilet, as he was with his sister. This meant a torture of frustration over a lost opportunity, tempered a little by the above, fondly described memoir.**]

Sunday 2nd April 1911 At Savoy. Letters from John Holt. [**The Liverpool trader, John Holt, was offering to add £1,000 to the Morel testimonial fund if £9,000 was raised. Casement marked Holt's letter "R. 1 April 1911 at Denham" verifying this entry.**[478]] Decided not to go with Parry and Dick. Richard Coudenhove down. [**another old Africa hand**] Spent pleasant day.

Monday 3rd April. To London to E.D.M., Forfeitt and then Parry. [**Sidney Parry was a rich Malayan rubber planter. It is unclear how he first met Casement. He was involved with the Congo Reform Association and had a pecuniary interest in civilised rubber production. He seems also to have been in Dick Morten's circle – "Mr. M. Sidney Parry J.P." chaired the South Perak Rubber Syndicate Ltd's general meeting in London on 4 November 1935 while he was noted in a 1919 newspaper report as chairman of the Beaufort Borneo Rubber Company Ltd.**] Latter gave £40 to E.D.M. testimonial…Beautiful fair hair type at Oxford Circus and Regent St. Young country. **X** Cheque sent to R. O'Dogherry 5.0.0. Rathlin School 10.0.0…

Tuesday 4 April 1911 At Savoy all day writing. Snow fell. Cheques to Nina £35.0.0 **X** [**Casement's Xs signify emphasis and are used, on occasion, for amounts of money requiring special note such as refundable Foreign Office expenditure or gifts and payments to his siblings. They were also used to mark memorable sexual encounters.**] Bulmer for *An Fianna* 10.0.0 [**This £10, according to Casement's cheque stub dated 4 April, was to pay for "Irish kilts for Dublin boys" – the *Fianna Eireann* being the separatist movement's youth wing. organised by Bulmer Hobson.**[479]] …Arthur Griffith marriage present 2.2.0…

Wednesday 5 April <u>Heavy Snow</u>! <u>Bitter cold.</u> To London to take Nina out to luncheon…Books at Mudies. "*Through Mexico*" Lumholtz 18.0. Cross River [**Nigeria**] Inbis 5.0: 1.3.0 [**These purchases are verifiable through a cheque stub dated 6 April 1911 and duly noted "Mudies Library £1.3 Mexico".**[480]]

Barbarous Mexico 7/6 **[This 1911 book by John Kenneth Turner on the near extermination of the Mayan and Yaqui Indians left a great impression on Casement. He now railed against the Mexican leader Porfirio Díaz "another Leopold" enslaving his people. For Mexicans there were only "cornstalks and the whip, the chain gang and the murderous lash." At the same time he was saying the Yankee Oil Kings in Mexico were fast exposing the Monroe Doctrine as "a crime against the human race."[481] Four days hence from Liverpool, Casement was telling Alice Stopford Green "Do get *Barbarous Mexico* and read some of it yourself – it is atrocious."[482] He bought a second copy on 13 April, and later recommended it to William Bell jnr.]** …

Thursday 6 April Snowing Cold!…Wrote 30 letters packed and up to London to leave tomorrow for L'pool. Sent Father Smith £20 for Indians.

Taxi 2/6. Karl 12/- (Baden) "Fat" 2/6 **X** 17.0

Busses 1/6 (Saw many types Ritz's Karl)…Hotel Ritz…Saw Welsh Rarebit **[not so rare since last seen on 14 February]** M. Arch 11.25.

	10. 6. 0	**X**
Karl	14. 6	
Fat	2. 6	
	17. 0	
	£11. 3. 0	**X** **[16th sex costs accumulation]** 14 **[14th partner]** 17/- **[April tot]**

7 April 1911 To Liverpool today. To servants Savoy Nellie 10/-. Annie 10/-. Cook 5/-…

Saturday 8th April 1911 At Liverpool…

X Pasto 5/- (South American 21) 5.0

11. 3. 0	**X**	
5. 0		**["Pasto (South American 21)"**
11. 8. 0	**X**	**17th sex costs accumulation]** 15 **[15th liaison]**

Sunday 9th April 1911 In L'pool…Taxi 1/3. £1.2.6. "Pasto" 1.3.9.

11. 8. 0

1. 2. 6 **[nearly five times yesterday's payment to Pasto!**

12.10. 6 **18th sex costs accumulation]** 15 **[second time the number 15 is inscribed**

1. 2. 0

1. 3. 9 **Taxi fare (1/3) included in this April sex costs tot, but not in**
2. 5. 9 **the 18th above]**

[10-12 April: To and from Manchester arranging a public meeting:] Message to Bishop of Liverpool...Beard trimmed y'day...At Manchester with Dean... Tip to Bishop's Butler 5.0...Hire of Room at Town Hall Manchester for 20 April 10.0...Telegram Reggie...

Thursday 13 April "Barbarous Mexico" 2nd copy...My bill at Exchange Hotel 4.14.6...Ticket to Belfast 12/6.

Friday 14 April Good Friday Arr. Belfast...Motor to Donegore Mrs Green and F.J.B. **[Francis Joseph Bigger, a Belfast solicitor and seriously romantic, cultural nationalist was also a practical heritage protector and an early environmentalist. He had an elegant motor, a shooting brake, with the registration number IJ 82. The choice of Donegore was hinged to the celebration of the centenary of the birth of Sir Samuel Ferguson, organised the year before by Bigger. Ferguson, a fellow Belfast antiquarian who translated and popularised the verse epics of ancient Ireland like *The Tain* and *Deirdre,* was raised on the slopes of Donegore Hill and buried in the Church of Ireland graveyard there.**

Bigger had laid a wreath of bays from his own garden during that 1910 ceremony. The hill was also the site of the main assembly point for the Antrim rebels of 1798 prior to their defeat at the battle of Antrim town where Viscount O'Neill was killed. Led by Henry Joy McCracken, the Presbyterian United Irishmen had had several successes earlier in Ballymena and in Larne, where ironically Casement's kinsman, Dr George Casement RN and his family, came under prolonged attack. He had been a juror at the 1797 trial of the hanged patriot William Orr.] Then down to "News Letter" Office for Circular printing **[Belfast's morning Unionist newspaper, publishing since 1737 and the oldest surviving in Europe; it failed to bill him until 30 May.]** Then round town and one splendid strong type. **X** Clean and offered again and again **[the sex was only visual as no payment (or lack of same) is recorded.]** Letter from Putumayo all were – all good. **[This will have been the letter from PAC Commissioner Louis Barnes, still in Iquitos, which Casement records as receiving at Belfast on 14 April 1911. It mentions the accidental drowning of a suspect, Aquilo Torres, and also Hal**

Gielgud's of 5 March on board the S.S. Liberal "nearing Iquitos". In it, he advises of Paredes appointment as Putumayo investigator and Zumaeta's bond for the production of Aurelio Rodriguez, while adding "No trace of Agassiz. I'm afraid" (the book).[483]] Glorious weather. Divine day. Beautiful Irish young man in Belfast. **[Casement's mood is now as sunny as the day.]**

Saturday 15 April Telegrams Manchester cancelling meeting on 20th over Putumayo…Cheque to Bishop Welldon for E.D.M. cause £15.0.0.

Sunday 16 April 1911 **[Easter Sunday]** At Ardrie **[Life-long home of F.J. Bigger, high on the Antrim Road and overlooking Belfast Lough, now replaced with a block of flats named Ardrigh Court, although a walled garden survives. The English language version of the house name eventually mutated from Ardrie to Ardrigh although the Belfast Street Directory typesetter for a while favoured Airdrie. Bigger and his housekeeper Brigid may have been hospitable but Casement, wanting some peace and freedom, left on Tuesday to his regular rented rooms lower down the Antrim Road.]** To lunch with Alec Herdman and family, and then up Madigan with Mrs Green and A.H. and his daughter. Lovely day.

Monday 17 April 1911 <u>Easter Monday</u> To Cranfield **[This very English-sounding location comes from the Gaelic, *Creamchoill* or wild garlic wood. The remarkable, round walled site at Staffordstown is on the shores of Lough Neagh and includes St. Olcan's old church and its circular graveyard, and a holy well. Bigger was that year resurrecting the annual May feast of *Bealtaine*.]** via Shane's Castle demesne **[Lord O'Neill's walled estate in Randalstown – the castle was burnt by the IRA in 1922]** in car with Mrs G, Father McKenny and F.J.B. and Tommy **[the live-in chauffeur.]** On to Toome and a tent gathering. Bought sweets there 2/6 to give the children. **[Bigger was concerned about these events getting out of hand and announced that the boys and girls assembling at Cranfield would be under the control of "a local committee supervised by the clergy who will see that no irregularity will be allowed or tolerated." The festival there had previously been terminated by the Church due to excesses of drinking and sexual licence.]** Very cold wind. Back and turned in early very tired.

Tuesday 18 April In Belfast. Leave Ardrie for 105 L. Terrace and so away. **[His rooms at 105 Antrim Road, prop: Mrs Elizabeth Thomas, were on Laburnum Terrace. The house, near the junction with the New Lodge Road has since been demolished and replaced with another in pastiche-Georgian style.]** Car from Station 1/8. Luggage…Trams 5d. Dinner 2/- (8d. really!). <u>Friend</u> 3/- (small knickers) 3.0 **[a scant type of knicker trousers remained**

in style for younger men until after the 1st World War.]

12.10. 6
3. 0 **X** **["Friend (small knickers)"**
12.13. 6 **19th sex costs accumulation]** 16 **[16th partner]** £2.8.9 **[April tot]**

Wednesday 19 April In Belfast...Mrs Green's book 1/-...Trams to French football (Lovely boy in Ormeau Park legs)...Mrs Green's history 1.0 Cigttes... Heard from Millar. **[Casement wrote to Bulmer on this date, saying, "I came here after Ballymena. I shall make these old rooms my headquarters for some time."[484]]**

Thursday 20 April To Ballymena **[town where Casement went to school]** Return ticket Mrs Green's history 1.0. Hair and beard dressing in Briens 5.0... Fire in Evg in Donegall St. Gloriously beautiful type. Loveliest ever saw in life. Soft and auburn and rose. None all evg.

Friday 21 April ...Very busy all morning writing E.D.M. testimonial business. Sent out 750 Circulars. Heard direct M **[Millar]** can't come this evg...

Saturday 22 April In Belfast all day...P.O. to Tom Clarke "Irish Freedom". **[Clarke, an Ulsterman, led the 1916 Easter Rising]** Trams 1/5...Car 1/3. Small friend Ormeau Rd. 4/6. Dunggan Boy (Dungannon) 8/- "Like it rightly". 12.6

[Neither boy merited an X despite the Dungannon lad expressing his satisfaction in Ulster idiom. The "small friend" on the Ormeau Road was probably met in the public convenience that used to be set into the Gasworks wall near that road's junction with Ormeau Avenue. The frustration of Millar cancelling is plainly beginning to tell with Casement trolling all over Belfast, a single encounter being insufficiently satisfying.]

12.13. 6
12. 6 **["Small friend" and Dungannon boy**
13. 6. 0 **20th sex costs accumulation]** 17 **[17th sex partner**

2. 8. 9
12. 6
3. 1. 3 **April sex costs tot]**

Sunday 23 April To Ballycastle and Chdun…At Cushendun with Ive, Gee and Lizzie [**Ive is Ada (Ide) McNeill but pronounced Ive. She frequently wrote to Casement in Irish Gaelic, indeed her first ever such effort went to him. Casement tried to keep a due distance, avoiding being alone in her company as she had overly strong feelings for him. With his Bannister cousins, Gertrude and Elizabeth also at her Cushendun residence he probably felt there was safety in numbers.**]

Monday 24 April At Cushendun. To Muirbolg Bay [**Murlough Bay where the much vandalised Casement memorial cross was – with F.J. Bigger's name also inscribed on its trunk. It is now levelled after several Loyalist attacks. Casement requested that he be buried at Murlough, but his wish remains to be granted.**] via Cushleake Culrany etc, with Gee and Lizzie. Car 10/-…Lovely type by Ballytearim [**townland near Cushendun.**]

Tuesday 25 April At Cushendun walked to Mya [**A big Easter re-union in Ulster with five of Casement's most favoured women in Antrim; Gee, Lizzie, Ada, Mya and Alice.**] and then on to Parkmor [**station near home of Margaret Dobbs.**] Fine types…Train Ballymena to Belfast…Porter Belfast 6d. Dennis 4/…Beggar 1/-…Letter from darling Bernardino at Rio, also card from Millar [**neither item survives.**]

Wednesday 26 April Lovely morning in Belfast, to sleep with Millar to-night. Washing 3/5…Telegram to Miss O'Rorke…Trams 3d. At Carnstroan with Millar and Mrs G. [**Millar and his mother Mrs Ellen Gordon lived at Carnstroan**] **X** Entry at 12.50 a.m. [**the Home Office also noted this entry with an X**] 18 [**Millar gets enumerated as 18th partner**]

Thursday 27 April At Carnstroan. Trams in with Millar 5d…Telegram O'Rorke 6. Trains Emma and Self to Greenisland 1/6…Wrote long dispatch to F.O. on Putumayo [**a response to Mallet's enquiring letter of 25 April "R at Belfast 27 April 1911."**[485]] To Miss O'R's to dinner [**Miss Emma O'Rorke was from a Co. Antrim legal family. Writing to her at *Tinnemara*, Greenisland, on 10 September 1913, Casement enclosed some new Irish "labels resembling postage stamps" prohibited, as he put it, by an "Edict, Bull, Ukase or Firman of the Postmaster General." The envelope bearing two George V stamps was delivered despite the Irish label.**[486] **Casement, in time, appeared on two Éire stamps, a 5d black and 1/- brown, issued in 1966 to mark the 50th anniversary of his execution, and again in 2016 on the centenary.**] and late to Millar. Both tired so turned in alone.

Friday 28 April Left Carnstroan with Millar on Trams together. Cigttes and Matches 9d…Tram 1d. 5d…Pasting in photos nearly all day…Heavy rain all day nearly – at night colossal rain. **[He advised Bigger that day, "Can't go tomorrow to Ceilidh in Templepatrick or in evening. Busy".]**[487]

Saturday 29th April …Irish and Dimples. F.O. Telegram ¼.

P.O. order for Miss Gleeson's rugs.	10. 0
Bulmer for "Irish Freedom" one year's subscription.	2. 0
Fleetwood to London ticket.	1. 8. 6
Mrs Thomas' bill – rooms to 25th.	1. 5. 0
Carriage for baggage – 3 Trunks.	11. 7

[These trunks, which Casement is obliged to cart around like the shell on a snail's back, will figure later when some are left in 1914 at Bigger's house and others at Ebury Street in London.] …(Cashed a Cheque at Biggers for £10 Cash)…Boy 2/6 Trams 4d. Sundries 1/-. "Dungannon" **[last seen on 22 April.]**

13. 6. 0
2. 6 **[Dungannon boy**
13. 8. 6 **21st sex costs accumulation]** 19 **[19th partner]**

3. 1. 3
2. 6
3. 3. 9 **[April's monthly sex tot]**

Sunday 30th April Arr. London via Fleetwood to Mrs Green's…Dunraven, Macdonald and Sir J. Solomon to lunch **[MacDonald may be the future Labour prime minister but Sir Anthony McDonnell is a likelier candidate according to biographer Séamas Ó Síocháin. The Earl of Dunraven and Mount Earl (1841-1926) was a liberal Unionist and later an Irish Senator. The usual monthly tot follows. There is a list of "Cheques out" (totalling £117.2.0) including £10 for Sinn Féin, and the £15 for "Rex O'Doherty & Rathlin." Late mention is made of £10 "Lent to Mrs McCullagh of Belfast." She is described as "Caroline Bloxham (Mrs McCullagh)" on the cheque stub[488] and under her Bloxham name became a member of the Provisional *Cumann na mBan* executive in 1914. The April total comes to the startling figure of £163.9.3 despite many nights of free hospitality.]** …

MAY

[1-3 May: Casement is in London at Mrs Green's working on the Morel Testimonial going also to the Foreign Office for a meeting and to the House of Commons. He recorded seeing "Sir Richard Staples" on 1 May. This may be Robert Ponsonby Staples (1853-1943) an artist and Protestant Home Ruler, from Lissan House in Co. Tyrone, who turned up mysteriously in Germany during the war. However, Robert did not inherit the baronetcy until the death of his brother John in 1933. The Irish Volunteers were to drill at Lissan House on his Cookstown estate in 1914.

Casement in his second last letter to Count von Wedel in Berlin, on 31 March 1916, is baffled by the information Wedel has provided about the "intended visit to Germany of one Ponsonby Stalleys, believed to be a British spy who represents himself as of Irish descent." Imminent departure made this visit irrelevant as in a few days Casement would no longer be in Germany "although probably near to other British spies" as he put it. The mystery was cleared up in 1919 by Major Frank Hall of MI5: "Ponsonby Stalleys...is no doubt a misspelling of Ponsonby Staples. This man is an eccentric Irishman who was anxious at one time to go over to Holland to secure the release from a private lunatic asylum of a relative who was confined there. Staples' movements excited our suspicion at one time but to my knowledge he was certainly never employed by us."[489]]

Thursday 4th May Return to Ireland today...Mrs Green's book 1/-...Harrods Sweets (Nina) 3/-...Ticket to Belfast via Heysham 1.8.6...

Friday 5th May ...Porter 1/-. Tea and Steward 1/-...Lunch 3/3. Trams 2d. Tram 3d. 3d. Biddy. Bigger's servant 4.6 [**As normal, Casement commenced his Belfast visit at Bigger's house, Ardrigh (High King in English). Biddy Mathews "a pure Gael" was left an annuity by Bigger at his death in 1926 while all his other worldly goods were left to a nephew Joseph. The exception was his library and certain correspondence which were given to Belfast's Central Library. Biddy was to be the recipient of a famous letter from Casement's death cell.**] ...

Saturday 6th May Lovely day in Belfast...telegram Mrs G...In house nearly all day cold and wretched. Thinking of Ignacio, Bernardino and Mario [**Last mention of Mario was in Rio on 28 February 1910 "Biggest since Lisbon July 1904 and as big."**] ...

Sunday 7th May In house all day till 5 p.m. then up A.[**ntrim**] Road to dine with W. O'Rorke, [**lawyer from Ballymena**] met Miss Dickey [**Emma Dickey**

also from a legal family; Cunningham & Dickey] ...To Miss Gleeson Dun Emer (Dimples wedding present). 4.7.6 **[Evelyn Gleeson, with the Yeats sisters, ran Dun Emer Industries in Dublin, an Arts & Crafts workshop]** H. Compton, tailor **[of Church Street in Ballymena]** 6.14.6.

Monday 8th May. ...Train to Marino 1/3...**[Bulmer Hobson's family lived at Marino around this time]** Heard from Millar suggesting he should call tomorrow evening at 7. Replied yes. Saw glorious type at Co. Down Ry Stn, **[station for the seaside town of Bangor (and Marino) across Belfast's river Lagan]** huge one and stern too, young and knickers.

Tuesday 9th May. 33 copies of Mrs Green's Book for sale at Ulster Hall. Lunch with Bulmer 4/4...Lunch at Castle Restaurant with Bulmer and then to E. Mayne's who accepting 200 to 300 of Mrs Green's book. Only 52 all told in Belfast! **[In a letter to Bulmer two days later Casement fumed over sales and distribution problems, and in his frustration proposed a trick on Erskine Mayne's, a bookshop on Donegall Square Belfast beside the City Hall: "E Mayne has ordered 400 copies of her book and proposes to sell it at U Hall on Friday." The number of copies ordered had risen since first mention yet Casement declared he was now going down to the shop "'on my own' to demand 100 copies of her book. I know I'll not get it! I shall not say what for and they'll be on tenterhooks of inquisitiveness and may write for more."[490] On 16 June he was artfully telling Mrs Green "400 copies nearly gone – in one Belfast shop."[491]]** Home at three...for Millar Trams 3d. Saw fair hair grown and all July 1906 and do. 1907. Last time, at Carlisle Circus **[now reduced to a windswept roundabout at the bottom of the Antrim Road, its statue of 'Roaring' Hugh Hanna blown up by the IRA in the 1970s.]** Met him at corner of Donegall St. waiting for Crumlin Road tram. He saw me and got on it and up. **[the tram]** I longed. Long limbs as of old. Joe McCullagh! Splendid. **[in margin]** Touched. **[The events of five years before were not to be repeated on this occasion. A frustrated Casement instead returned to his rooms that afternoon to await someone else.]** Millar came to tea but altho' standing clean and strong nothing – did not go room **[Serious disappointment, since Millar declined to retire to the bedroom, despite Casement being ready, washed and obviously eager.]**

Wednesday 10 May 1911 Glorious day. May day. Season surpassing! ...To Ballymena and back 4/-...Millar **[in margin]** Postages 6d. Telegrams 8d...To B'mena demesne 3d. Beggar 3d. To Ballymena to Comptons. **[his tailors]** Very hot indeed. To old Turnpool by Braid and Devenagh Burn of Nov. 1877 !!! Rippling in brown and swift, and there too when I plunged across in Mch

1879! Glorious boys of Erin, big and fair. **[This note is very revealing as Casement is reminded of events and boys, out swimming in 1877, when he was thirteen, and later in 1879, when fourteen. It seems he was observing other males sexually as a young teenager and that his desires and sexual orientation were already fixed. It also appears he was not, even at that early stage, riven by guilt. This (deep) turnpool in the Braid river is on the Galgorm Castle estate, the home of the Young family where the boy Casement often stayed.]** Back at 5 train very tired. **[but still able to cruise around the woods at Fortwilliam Park off the Antrim Road, and tip a boy twice for services rendered:]**

"Harry" at Fort William. 10/-. 2/- 12.0

Trams 3d. Sundries 1/-. The most surpassing day and night glorious sunshine. Night of heaven. Venus like an orb of gold over Cave Hill. All heavenly. **[The Cash Ledger, despite its intended function, is developing into a journal, and reflecting Casement's moods, which veer from the lyrical to the depressed while providing a home for ever lengthier descriptions of past events and present longings. Warm weather brings the diarist's feelings as well as his sexuality to life.**

Cave Hill is the mountain that looms over the Antrim Road and above Ardrigh. Mac Art's fort is at its summit. This was where Wolfe Tone, Henry Joy McCracken and Thomas Russell, leaders of the United Irishmen, swore a solemn obligation in May 1795 "never to desist in our efforts until we had subverted the authority of England over our country and asserted our independence." All three were to pay for rebellion with their lives three years later or, in Russell's case, after the Emmet insurrection in 1803. Casement followed in many of Tone's footsteps but allied with Germany not France. Like McCracken he too was hanged. Both had loving and loyal sisters. Rather than submit to hanging, Tone committed suicide in a Dublin gaol.

In 1924, Bigger was in receipt of the comparative views of another of Belfast's antiquarian solicitors, C.H. Brett, on Thomas Russell, the Linen Hall librarian (and *The Man from God-Knows-Where*), whose rising in Loughinisland in Co. Down was a hopeless failure: "As to Russell his story is a very sad one but his actions were so foolish that he could not expect any other fate than what overtook him. He was nearly as senseless as Casement in our day. But Russell was a much better class of man than Casement." Bigger would not have appreciated this critical opinion of Casement from another of the city's (liberal) establishment, seeing it as an unwitting attack on him as well. By this time, however, his hopes of a Tone Republic were at a very low ebb.[492]]

13. 8. 6
12. 0 **[Harry**
14. 0. 6 **22nd sex costs accumulation]** 20 **[20th person]**

12. 0 **[Harry on 10 May**
10. 0 **Harry on 11 May]**
1. 2. 0

Thursday 11 May 1911 Glorious day...Bath Swmg 3d...Saw the man, a glorious type get in Belfast. Fair hair and blue eyes and tall strong well dressed at "Junction". He looked and smiled and felt again and again. To Swimming Bath and four Beauties...
Harry 10/- **X** ...at Northern Ry Coys 10 .0
[The young man, a classic Ulster Protestant, sighted at Castle Junction in the city centre has sparked Casement off on a round of activity, inducing a visit to a Belfast swimming pool for visual pleasure. This only whets his appetite further so Harry, yesterday's catch in Fortwilliam Park, is discovered again in the railway station toilet at York Street station.]

14. 0. 6
10. 0 **[Harry**
14.10. 6 **23rd sex costs accumulation]** 20 **[20th person repeated – Harry again]**

Friday 12 May 1911 Another heavenly day Letter from Millar agreeing to Newcastle **[a response to his of 10 May; Newcastle is a Co. Down seaside resort.]** Mrs Green's book 6/-. (I bought 7 copies I think.) Trams 3d. (Met Millar in Street).

Saturday 13th May Lovely day. To go Newcastle with Millar. "Grand" 5 times I hope! Draw £10 at Bank...Hair cut 1/4...Cgttes 4/6. Grattan & Co Hair and Vaseline. 2.6 **[Grattans, a large chemist's shop in Belfast's Corn Market]** ...
Train with Millar to Newcastle 13/-. 13.0
Papers for Millar 9d. Whiskey 6d. 1.3
Arr. Newcastle. Huge! In Bath Splendid. Millar into me **[these three words underlined on the police typed copy]**

Sunday 14 May **[in heading:]** At Newcastle with M.
In to Millar! and then he came too. At Newcastle. Mist and rain. No go for Sl.

Donard, **[Slieve Donard, highest of the Mourne Mountains which also gives its name to the magnificent golfing hotel in Newcastle where Casement and Morel met in 1904 to plan the Congo Reform Association]** so took car to Annalong along the "whin-litway". Car 7/6 Drinks 2/6. Imagine! Both. Hard luck **[The Home Office reader queried the word 'luck' on the Special Branch typed copy, suggesting instead 'work'. He was obviously getting into the swing of things wielding his blue pencil and mimicking Casement's markings with an outbreak of crosses of his own over both Millar days.]**

Monday 15 May Bill at Hotel 2.13/2 Tips 1/10 **[then back to Belfast and business]** ...Telegram Barnes...Telegram from L'pool. No meeting there.

Tuesday 16 May 1911 To leave Ireland again today!...Washing 3/2 at 105 Antrim Rd...Beggar girl 6d...To Sharman 2/6. Mrs Green's book to Lady Sheelagh 1/- **[actually Miss Shelagh Alexander]** ...Lovely one at Post Office and then John McG **[McGonegal]** in Ormeau Park. **X [Former estate of the Marquesses of Donegall, Belfast's ruling family the Chichesters, and location of another wrought iron Victorian public toilet.]** Telegram Miss Cox. My bill at Mrs Thomas' 105 Antrim Rd. since 29 April Rooms 1.11.0. Food &c. 3.15.0. Sundries 12.2. £5.18.2 **[previous visit included as well]** ...Fare via Heysham to London 1.8.6...

[17-19 May:] Arr. *Sasana* (Heysham) At Crystal Palace 1/-...Maoris 6d... Taxis to Blucher's...Burns evg. Piccadilly &c. Cgttes 6d...To Harbour. To Harboro'...At Carlton Park.

Saturday 20th May Left Carlton and returned to London. Servants 10/-. Fly 5/-...Crystal Palace 1/6 (No Maoris)...Earls Court Exhibition (twice) 2/-... Somalis 1/-...Left Carlton. No Cadburys. To E. Court Niggers. Then to Crystal Palace. French type splendid and soldier G.G. **[Grenadier Guards]** big. To E. Court. Egyptian and then White City all through Exhibition, but see nothing. **[Crowded exhibition halls are a favourite venue for Casement's cruising, giving him the chance to wander aimlessly in circles spotting foreigners and then make repeated visits to the toilets.]**

Sunday 21st May To Savoy to Dick's to lunch...Stayed all night. Mrs Pat and John there.

Monday 22 May In with Dick on Car to Cricklewood. Taxi from his Club to Victoria...White City 1/-...Mrs Green's book. Cheque to Bulmer to buy 50 copies Irish Nationalist 2.10.0. E. Court Exhibition 1/-...Beer 6d. Cgts 4d. Beggar 6d. Dinner 3/9...

Friend 4/- Do. **[abbreviation for ditto]** 10/-. Taxi 3/-. 17.0
Bus 6d. Algerian 1/-. Train 4d. **[A taxi ride under sexual expenditure (as here) indicates a visit to a partner's lodgings, confirmed by the bus and tube costs detailed immediately afterwards for the return journey. The occasion must have been unmemorable as names and descriptions go recorded and only the word "Friend" appears.]**

14. 0. 6 **[Incorrect running total; it was £14.10.6 after Harry on 11 May**
17. 0 **"Friend"**
14.17. 6 **24th sex costs accumulation]** 21 22 **[21st partner, 22nd perhaps the Algerian]**

1. 2. 0
17. 0
1.19. 0 **[This May monthly sex sub-tot was actually slotted in at the 20 May entry, adding Harry's three payments of £1.2.0, in all, to the 17 shillings for "Friend".]**

[23-28 May: A week of meetings and visits] ...Lunch with Putumayo Commission...Arr. Cadbury's and talked Putumayo...Left Birmingham for London...Taxi 1/- (to Parrys)...(Nina's Birthday) **[25 May]** ...Taxi 1/- to Station. Good Mistake (?) Lunch Nina 6/8. Nina present £1...To Malling and Putumayo...Sweets Mrs Barnes children 3.6...Entry to Exhibition S. Bush 1/- Maoris 1/- **[They're back!]** ...To Hampstead to Mrs Dryhurst **[Nannie Dryhurst, mother of Robert Lynd's wife Sylvia, was a journalist and hostess who in Dublin had made protégées of the many Gifford sisters, two of whom married executed signatories of the Easter Rising proclamation. She was pleading in vain for a visit to her old friend on 28 July 1916 "before his barbarous sentence is carried into effect" and valiantly proclaimed to Basil Thomson that the diaries were "transcripts of evidence he was collecting against the Peruvians of the atrocities committed in the Putumayo [and that Casement] had copied them himself because he could not trust them to a woman typist"[493]]** ...

Morel Presentation Monday 29 May 1911 ...At F.O. (Dufferin and Mallet) **[2nd Marquess of Dufferin and Ava, of Clandeboye in Bangor, Co. Down (1866-1918), Under-Secretary at the Foreign Office since 1896.]** Morel Luncheon **[This was the testimonial luncheon at which EDM was presented with the proceeds from a national subscription for his work with the**

Congo Reform Association. Casement had devoted significant energies to help raise the money. The public luncheon presided over by Lord Cromer was at the Whitehall Rooms. As well as a cheque for 4,000 guineas (John Holt, the Liverpool trader, kindly added a late one thousand) Morel was presented with his portrait by William Rothenstein.] and then dinner Gee and Lizzie…Taxi etc. home after Dinner to Morel 11/-. 6/-. Small chap Euston Square "Fanny" **[a ubiquitous camp name.]**

1.19. 0

11. 0 **["Small chap" and Fanny**

2.10. 0 **May's monthly tot]**

14.17. 6

11. 0

15. 8. 6 **[25th sex costs accumulation]** 23 **[23rd partner]**

30 May 1911 To Miss Cox to 24 May 2.1.8
To E.D.M. Printer 1.7.9 **[This invoice from the *Belfast News Letter* inscribed "Apl 19. 1500 circulars Morel Testimonial" was receipted on 31 May, Casement writing on the back "This account should have been rendered long ago. It is a very slow way of doing business"[494]]** …Taxi 3/6. Lunch Putumayo Commission. Taxi home 3/6. Do. Nina and cousin…Exhibition 4/- 8/- 3/- 3/6 3/- 1/6 2/- 2/- **[items of expenditure unspecified]** 1.7.0

31 May 1911 Nina to Eastbourne. I to Dicks. Miss Cox's bill to date 2.7.6 …Putumayo 2/…Taxi to F.O. 1/-. Not going to Dick until tomorrow… Exhibition 1/-. Somali 6d…Presents at Exhibition to Nina, Louie and Lizzie 4.6.

Total for May £64.0.6

Add cheques from Mrs Green. Cancelled cheque returned Bulmer.

…First six months of 1911 £515.11.7

…Recd W.A.C. for Indians 50.0.0 **[This gift of £50 was from William Cadbury of the Quaker chocolate family who had commercial interests in African cocoa production. He was a supporter of the Congo Reform Association and a frequent correspondent and host. Casement later sought further financial assistance from Cadbury for the Indian boys and for his feckless brother Tom in South Africa.]** …

JUNE

Thursday 1st June 1911. To Peruvian Amazon Coy's meeting! No go! [**"All commissioners there. No go!" – the identical phrase is to be found elsewhere on a Casement note.**[495]] To Savoy to stay there.

Friday 2nd June At Savoy writing letters. Cheque to Booth & Co for Indians 40.0.0

Saturday 3 June 1911 To Miss Cox Balance due	13.0
Lizzie Donnelly. Putumayo Photos	1.15.3
Patterson Boots [**"Samuel Patterson, Bootmaker" of 23 College St.**[496]]	1. 1.0
Cyril Corbally and his motor bike for Millar.	25. 0.0

[**4-7 June:**] ...At Savoy nil. At Savoy Nil. [**nil expenditure**] To London to Duchess of Hamilton [**to talk of Christian missions going into the Putumayo**] and Robert Lynd. Saw Gardiner! [***Daily News* editor**] Hair and Beard cut 1/3...To Mr Doyne, Oculist 2.2.0. Ticket to Savoy Return 1/6. Lavatory 1d...J Keetes 1/-...

Thursday 8th June 1911 To London to lunch with Collis and Wolf and then E.D.M. Dinner etc Mrs Green at E.D.M. 7. Gift of rug. Rug £1.0 0. Cab with it 4/-...Lavatory 2d... [**in margin**] Rug to Mrs G. Carriage of Motor Bike to dear Millar 18/3. 18.3

[The Scotland Yard typed copy is marked here with an X for this was the Triumph motor bike bought second-hand by Cyril Corbally in 1910 whose purchase for Millar Gordon and subsequent re-registration to him by Essex County Council on 10 July 1911 enabled War Office Intelligence to discover his identity. The substantial transport costs of 18/3d were paid five days after the purchase money of £25.

Casement's Africa friend, Lord ffrench was married to a Mary Corbally from an aristocratic Catholic family in Co. Meath. She had a brother called Cyril. A champion croquet player, he lived at that time in Bishop's Stortford in Essex where he managed a golf club. It is reasonable to assume Casement became aware from Lady ffrench of the motor bike being for sale. Indeed in July 1911, he twice diaried meeting the couple while in London. Again the assumption is that in 1916 Cyril Corbally's name struck a bell with Major Frank Hall of MI5 who contacted him in pursuit of Millar's address.[497]

At the end of the month, Casement wrote "Epitome of June A/C. Present

etc. to others Cyril Corbally… 25.0.0." A separate note elsewhere listing and totalling extensive expenditure includes "Millar 25.0.0".[498]]

[9-10 June:] Lovely day at Savoy. Writing all day…6 Seats at E.D.M. Lunch *1.10.0 *Cancelled. Mrs Green refused cheque…At Savoy, going to R. Lynd's to dinner. **[Robert Lynd (1879-1949) essayist and Sinn Féin member was from a Belfast Presbyterian background, and literary editor for the *Daily News*. Described as a man with "lustrous eyes, waving hair and an arresting face", he once shared a studio and flat with the artist Paul Henry. Lynd, although a loyal friend, apparently convinced Michael Collins of the diaries' authenticity.]** Dined with R.L. and then to Norfolk Hotel for night.

Sunday 11th June To Dine to Parminter's…Busses in London on return (some types – one stout Japanese in Oxford Street. Wanted!) Tip to Reggie Parminter **[a Casement godson]** 10.0…At Dover – lovely day and back at 9 and out for 2 hours walk in London. Very crowded. Seamen at P. Circus.

Monday 12th June …Books of Mudies 17/11 (5/5 to Reggie Parminter) My lunch at Inns of Court 2.0…Kate and Don – bill lunch 8.8…Hotel at Norfolk Hotel &c. Tip 15.6. To dine with Phoebe Williams and others. Chaplin at Beaconsfield.

[13-14 June:] Eyes: To Mr Doyne. Oculist…	1.2.0
X Presents to Charlie in Melbourne	10.0.0
X and to Nina my niece	5.0.0

[In a letter dated 13 June 1911, Casement wrote to this niece in Australia telling her that the enclosed money was "a present for you and Auntie Blanche to spend together on anything you would like to get." Blanche was Tom Casement's recently divorced wife who seems to have been involved in the care of the two children of her deceased sister Minnie, first wife of Casement's other brother Charlie.[499]] Medicine for Eyes by Doyne…To 5 Carlton House Terrace to Lady Cs **[Elizabeth, Countess of Caledon]** …

Thursday 15th Letter from Sir E. Grey telling me of Knighthood! Alack. **[This letter is marked by Casement "Rec'd 15 June 1911 at Denham." The Foreign Secretary, later Viscount Grey of Falloden, explained that the knighthood, given on his recommendation, was "in recognition of your valuable services in connection with your recent mission to the Putumayo District".[500]]** To Uxbridge. Lovely Boy Scout and Chaney's baker lad. Cgttes 10d. **[After being underwhelmed by the proposed Coronation honour of a Knight Bachelor**

award, although less unhappy than when he received the CMG in 1905, Casement returns immediately to his more immediate concern of eyeing delivery lads and boy scouts. Gertrude believed that when congratulated about the award by someone who had seen it in the newspaper, Casement said, "It's the first I've heard of it." He plainly put something like this version about to excuse his acceptance, coming in time almost to believe it. The list did not appear in the press until 20 June so he would just have had time to turn it down. *The Northern Whig* in Belfast thrilled about local men so honoured. Oddly short of fresh biographical material on Casement (and lacking a picture), the newspaper noted that he was "greatly interested in the Celtic Revival Movement." Home Office markings around this diary entry reach blizzard proportions, indicative as it was of *lèse majesté*. The actual knighting ceremony by the always-bearded King George V took place on 6 July.] ...

Friday 16th June 1911 Cancel £2-10/- for Mrs Green's books of 15 May, refunded by Bulmer. Train to London 3/-...Japanese youth 25. G. Miyagawa. Kingsway W.C. 63, Craven House.

Saturday 17 June At Savoy all day, played Croquet. Was to have met Miyagawa at 4 at Gr. W. at Paddington but did not go. **[If Miyagawa was the Japanese of 11 June who "wanted" so much, Casement plainly lost interest and stood him up. Getting his address rather than having sex then and there, indicated a lower level of enthusiasm. The enterprise was plainly doomed.]**

[18-23 June:] ...At Savoy all day. Many came to Lunch and play Croquet. To London to F.O and other places...Lunch Fox at W.P. Hotel...At Denham... Telegram for Barbados about Boys...Coronation Day! **[22 June]** ...Stayed at Savoy all day. Writing Putumayo...2 Irish Pamphlets of Gill's...

Saturday 24 June To London for Rooms...Exhibition (Splendid Japan Wrestlers). Got room for Monday at 71 Warwick Rd. **[to board the Indian boys.]**

Sunday 25 June To go Southampton for Ricudo and Hammurummy... Dinner Southptn 2/8...Ticket Spton 13/-...Porter (Denham) 1/-. Lovely French lad or Italian. 20. Dark cap, fair, very tall. Strong sailor in Ship St. and then thick young German or Italian sailor round Gardens.

Presents to Dimples	Rug Dun Emer	4. 5. 0	
	Sarita	2. 5. 0	6.10. 0

[Sarita is Mrs Herbert Ward; the payment to Miss Gleeson of Dun Emer Industries is confirmed on a cheque stub.[501]]

Monday **[no 26 June date inscribed]** at Spton to meet Ricudo & H. Boys Stewards 15/-…Lovely Italian Ice Boy 18. Tall splendid loved. Also young dark boy huge wanted awfully. To West Station and there darkie by Watts Grove Orotaru 2/-. Lovely boy wanted too. **[Watts Park, also known as West Park, is in the centre of Southampton near West Station and is named after the hymn writer Isaac Watts whose statue it contains.]**

Tuesday 27 June. At Southampton To leave today with Ricudo…Hotel Bill Self 1.0.9. 2 Boys 10.0. Tips 5.3 **[they stayed at the South Western Hotel[502]]** Luggage 1/- (Porter E. Court). Exhibition 6/6…

Wine 6d. Taxi 2/6. Donald Ross 1.0.0 of Egypt **X X X** 1.3.0 (3 tickets from Spton 19/6.) **[A mixed-up day with entries time-jumbled, but Casement had returned to London with the two boys. He was still able to find time to meet up with, and go off to, Donald Ross's house. Unless he figured previously, which is unlikely given the "of Egypt" description, Donald was probably encountered at the Exhibition.]** …

15. 8. 6 **[last such total was a month back on 29 May**

1. 3. 0 **Donald Ross**

16.11. 6 **26th sex costs accumulation]** 24 **[24th person]**

Monday 28th June Meeting of P.A. Company in Club Room **[at the Naval & Military Club "nothing good or serious."[503]]** Suit for Ricudo Irish Stores 2.5.0 **[confirmed by a bill for this amount, dated 28 June 1911, paid to New Irish Direct Supply Ltd & Irish Art Companions of 94 Victoria St.[504]]** …Gaelic Button 1d…Evening with Louie Heath **['Uncle Roger' has roped in Louie, a girlfriend of his cousin Lizzie Bannister to help out with the boys, taking them to a fun fair.]** Boys and Louie Exhibition 3/6…Wrestlers 2/-. Joy Wheel 2/-. Chute 2/-. 6/-…Self 11 to 12.30. Donald 10/- (11.30) **[see also 2 July]** Bus 6d.

16.11. 6

10. 0 **X [Donald Ross**

17. 1. 6 **27th sex costs accumulation]**

1. 3/-

10/-

1.13. 0 **[May sub-tot of two sex payments, both relate to Donald Ross]**

Thursday 29 June 1911 At E. Malling **[where Louis Barnes who had been the acting leader of the Amazon investigation team lived]** with Ricudo. Ricudo at Stores. Lunch Strachey **[Probably St. John Loe Strachey the editor of *The Spectator* although the Foreign Office, when checking, thought he might have been an official with that surname.]** ...

Friday 30 June At East Malling. Lunch Ricudo 3/11...Evg. Dinner with Gardiner. "Daily News". **[A.G. Gardiner was the editor in 1912 when his newspaper (owned by Cadbury) nominated Casement as a Man of the Week. He also signed Conan Doyle's reprieve petition in 1916. *The Daily News* later transmuted into *The News Chronicle*.]** ...Boys to Exhibition with Nina. Entrance 2/6. Shows etc. 6/-...

Total in June £124.7.5

Epitome of June A/C

...Present etc. to others Cyril Corbally...25.0.0 **[This £25.0.0 was for Millar's motor bike, bought from Corbally who was Lady ffrench's brother.]**

JULY

Saturday 1st July 1911 In London – Took Ricudo and H. to Booth & Co and on to Fisher Unwin. **[The firm that charged Casement £48.11.0 for publishing his book of poems *Dream of the Celt* in 1901.[505]]** ...Two knives boys 3/-. Ball for H. 5d. Clothes for Hammurummy 1.9.4. In evening out with Nina and Lizzie to theatre. Three stalls Court Theatre 15/-...Refund from F.O. in June £104.5/-...

Sunday 2nd July 1911. 10/- **[for Donald Ross and the miner, below]** Boys to Richmond Park with Nina and Louie. Boys to Mrs Green. Paper 1d. Bus 6d. Taxi 1/8. Taxi 3/-. Beggar 2d. Dinner 1/8. Paper 1d. Trams 6d, Train 4d, do 2d. 2d...Bus 2d. 2d. 1/-...bus 4d. **[This frenetic travelling around London involved getting the boys taken to the park by Casement's sister and later being left with Mrs Green. It then culminated, more than satisfactorily, with two partners, one having featured before:]**
Italian miner 4/- Donald Ross 6/- at Regent Park. 10.0

17. 1. 6
10. 0 **[Donald Ross and the Italian miner**
17.11. 6 **28th sex costs accumulation]**

Monday 3rd July One week of Ricudo & H. 1.10/-. My own room 1-10/-... Paid to Mrs Selby. Paid to Maggie 4/-...Fruit 1/-. Toys 2/8. Exhibition 12/6... Tuesday 4th July 1911 **X** to Nina Her quarter **[a regular payment]** 35.0.0. For Ricudo Watch and Chain 11/-. Tooth paste 1/-...Eye Medicine 2/-. Purse for Ricudo 1/-. Evg Exhibition 1/-...

Wednesday 5th July 1911 Putumayo and Board meeting...Ricudo – Goods at Irish Stores 16.7...self 3.9. Message F.O. for C.M.G! **[Casement had had to arrange with the Foreign Office to borrow a CMG badge to wear at his knighting, a point he made to his trial lawyers to prove his indifference to the award. Indeed he was even uncertain as to where it was. When in 1916 the Order's registrar plaintively asked for the badge back, Casement was very helpful, suggesting to the prison governor on 24 July that it might be in Ireland, and that he would ask his sister to hunt for it, as he did.[506] However, an engagement with the hangman a week later overtook a resolution of the matter, and when the badge was eventually found, his cousin Gertrude gave it to the Heraldic Museum in Dublin's Kildare Street.]** To tailor at Nathan's...Shamrock 2/6. **[For Casement to buy shamrock in July can only suggest it was to be worn as an Irish gesture on his dress uniform before the King.]**

Thursday 6 July 1911 Meeting of P.A. Company. To St. James Palace to be knighted by George V. **[the actual event, notably, warranted no detail]** Taxi there 3.0. Taxi back 3/-...Dinner Nina and L. 6/-. Bus 3d.

Friday 7th July Under drawers 3 Ricudo 7.6. Self Do. 7.6...Under drawers Ricudo and Self 14.9 **W.J. Goult, hatters of Earls Court, was paid this amount for six pairs of "pants" according to the receipt dated 7 July. Whether Casement bought a dozen pairs of such pants that day or just duplicated his recording of it here is unclear.[507]]** ...

Saturday 8th July 1911 ...2 tickets R and self to Poole return 1.9.0
[While Ricudo was going to stay with the Duke and Duchess of Hamilton in Dorset, Omarino was with Mrs Louis Barnes at East Malling. She wrote to tell Casement "The little boy is quite good and happy now, I think he missed Ricudo at first. He enjoys doing his lessons. After seeing him I don't wonder at you feeling so strongly that the poor Indians must be protected somehow."[508]] ...
To Nathan & Co Uniform for Levee 5. 5. 0...
[This bill, to be found in Casement's papers, was from L & H Nathan, "Court Costumiers." Dated 6 July, the day of his knighting, it was receipted on 10 July 1911.[509]]

Sunday 9 July 1911 At Duke of Hamilton's Knoll House. Nil. [**The 13th Duke of Hamilton (1862-1940) was President of the Animal Defence and Anti-Vivisection Society. He and his wife Nina donated money toward the Putumayo mission. They had a summer house, Knoll, at Swanage near Poole. Casement had first met them through T.H. Hoste, a Congo missionary who seems to have been a part-resident, spiritual adviser to the family. In 1905 Casement had been borrowing large sums of money from him. Lending him over £150, Hoste explained "Your friendship for me has been one of the brightest things in my life." The feeling was mutual, Casement describing in his 1916 "Notes to Counsel" how the missionary "had a great influence over me at that time."[510] In 1913, Hoste reported that the Duchess "longs for an influence like yours over the boys." Unsurprisingly, in 1916, things were not so trouble free. Calling on Alice Stopford Green, Hoste came to say he felt obliged to withdraw the application he had made to visit Casement in gaol.[511]**]

10th July Monday Loan. Makes £15 she has promised to repay. To Caroline McCullagh 5.0.0 [**Evidence of this loan is found in a letter written from 70 Cliftonpark Avenue in Belfast on 6 July. It seriously irritated Casement as he had already lent the lady £10 in April; She wrote "My dear Roddie, I got your letter but was very disappointed you did not send me the cheque for £5 that I asked for. Will you think over it again and try and do this for me? It is a matter of very serious importance to me that I should get this money at once. As I said in my other letter it will be as easy for me to repay you the £15 as the £10. Please do this for me. I am in great trouble. I am ever your sincere friend. Caroline A. McCullagh. PS If you just send me the cheque you need not write."**

Casement did send the money but noted sourly at the top of her letter "Sent £5 on 10 July. Makes £15 due from her." She replied on 12 July saying "Many thanks for cheque for £5. I shall return it as soon as I possibly can." The initial letter does not survive while the "trouble" remains unknown, as does the matter of repayment.[512]] To Ricudo "Buster" 1/6 [**a comic**] ...At Duke of H.'s...

Tuesday 11th July Left Knoll House. To William the footman 10.0. Cab (Poole)...Called Mrs Green and then home to letters and unpacking. To Exhibition at 8.40 p.m. 1/-...
Miss Cox one week and things for Boys. 3.2.2

Wednesday 12th July To Mrs Selby 1 week of the Boys £3.0.0. Their washing 5.0. My own washing 5.5. Boisragon called. [**This individual had been**

recommended as a travelling director for the Peruvian Amazon Company. Casement reckoned he was, in fact "Alan Boisragon, a former Major, who was a colleague of my own in the old Niger Coast Protectorate many years ago. He got into trouble over the Benin massacre – being one of the two survivors who escaped." On 22 June, he had been telling Spicer, "Boisragon, I find, behaved with great weakness at Shanghai when in command of the police and was compelled to resign...It is 16 years since I saw him on the Niger. He was told off to accompany me at the head of troops on a journey I made against refractory natives in Oboto which I settled without bloodshed or firing a hut – in Feb – March 1895 – and without calling into action a single rifle – to Boisragon's disgust at the time. I liked him then – as a man – and I am sure he is quite incapable of any dirty act or connivance in wrongdoing – but he is a weakling I fear – and the Coy. wants a strong man on the Putumayo to think for himself and insist on his views being put into execution. You should choose a good man for Consul at Iquitos – a young man (not too young of course, but one who can stand the climate and the heat) – a man like Hambloch with brains, intelligence and a good honest nature who can put two and two together is what you want. I'll invade you all next week with my Indian slaves – you will like them I know, poisoned arrows and all!"[513]]

Thursday 13th July To Rothenstein Studio with Denet **[for the painting of the boys' portrait]** ...Gubbins called. **X** £80 To Charlie in Melbourne. **[These regular and occasionally large payments, as this, to his siblings indicate that Casement recognised he had a duty to help keep them afloat. His brothers relied on him to get them out of financial problems or assist in enterprises and property purchase, while Nina appears to have lived entirely on such handouts. He had initially been distributing dividends from their grandfather Hugh Casement's estate, forty years after his death, but later used money from his own salary. The last of their grandfather's capital had been handed over by Casement's London solicitors, Hammond and Richards, in 1902. They also stored his will of the time in their "Strong Room" and had informed his sister Nina accordingly.[514]]** To Exhibition 1/-...

Friday 14th July Putumayo Board Meeting...To City, Horner and Putumayo Coy...Telegram 10d. Boisragon. Clothes for Ricudo collars expended by Nina on them 4/9. Dinner Nina and Self...Busses 8d. Exhibition 1/-. **[As soon as Nina is fed and returns home, Casement sets off to an Exhibition.]** ...

Saturday 15th July St. Swithins Day Sweets Boys 2/-. Their fare and messengers to Hampstead to Rothensteins 3/-. **[Later that day Rothenstein wrote**

to Casement from his Frognal address saying the boys "put on their ornaments with care – almost with pedantry, with the help of comb, water and a looking glass and then stood like rocks."[515] Casement was particular that Rothenstein did not give any money directly to the boys although the painter was keen to pick up any expenses involved. The ensuing portrait depicts the boys in loin-cloths and necklaces; Arédomi (Ricudo), adorned with headdress and armbands, looks quite plump and grave, having his arm around a somewhat apprehensive Omarino.] ...Busses night 1/-...

Sunday 16 July To Zoo with Nina, Dennett and Boys...Buns for animals 2/4...To dinner at Lady Caledon. Lost 466 1d. points to Col. Sydney 2.0.0... Aldershot 6/6. Cab 1/6 8. 0

6. 6 **[For "Aldershot" whose descriptor suggests a soldier based there**
1. 6 **Cab**
8. 0 **items missed out from annual accumulation]** 25 **[25th partner]**
18/- **[July's tot to date; the previous 10/- payment was on 2 July]**

Monday 17 July 1911 To F.O. and Lord & Lady Ffrench. To Exhibition 9.45 p.m...

Tuesday 18 July ...Taxi to Lord Ffrench and then with him and Lady Ff. to Exhibition and her car there 5/-...Saw Ev. Fielding **[Everard Feilding]** at lunch, Mnsr. Bidwell at Cathedral. **[This was Monsignor Manuel Bidwell of Westminster Cathedral, secretary to the Cardinal Archbishop, who was helping to arrange a mission to go to the Putumayo region. Problems included a sectarian row. Bidwell, writing to Casement, was troubled by a letter from Rev. John Harris: "I do not see how we can avoid stating the fact that Peru does not allow and therefore will not recognise Protestant missions."[516] A Protestant mission connected to the Evangelical Union of South America was in fact to be proposed for "a part of the Putumayo distant from the Catholics." This indicated "a friendly spirit", Travers Buxton told Casement in 1912.[517]]** ...Bell in morning to breakfast with me. Turned in 11.20 after Exhibition. Boys with Nina to Rothenstein.

Wednesday 19 July To G.M. Booth today. Boys to Thompson the photo **[This entry is confirmed in a letter that Casement wrote to W.A. Cadbury on 19 July: "A big photographer is today taking anthropological photos of them."[518] These photographs were recently discovered in the University of Cambridge's Museum of Archaeology and Anthropology. The boys were there identified as "Two slaves from Putomayo (sic) river, Up. Amazon,**

Colombia".] ...To Ricudo etc for Exhibition 4.0...To Miss Cox for rooms 2.2.0...Busses 1/-. Dinner 1/8. Cgttes 9d. Train 4d.
X Mexicano 12/6 Cab 1/6 14. 0
20. (Freid) T.**[ottenham]** Court Road...G.M. Booth no use! I knew it before – still more now. **[Booths, the shipping company were showing no interest in funding the proposed Putumayo Franciscan mission.]**

17.11. 6

14. 0 **["Mexicano"**

18. 5. 6 **29th sex costs accumulation]** 26 **[26th partner]** 1.12/- **[July tot]**

Thursday 20 July Ricudo C.**[rystal]** Palace 10/-. Goods Hopes 9/8 **X** 19. 8
Do. breakfast 1/10. tele 7d. Tea 3d... **X** 2. 8
[Something unclear, possibly purchases, prompts this outbreak of Xs by Casement.]

Friday 21st July Refund by Allison on Charlie's telegram...Lunch 8/-. (Bell & Self)...Busses 6d from City mostly as home at 5 p.m...Train (to Brixton)... Huge one all day!

Saturday 22 July Glorious day and morning. Ricudo suit 1/7/6...(To Lever's on Soap!) (Notting Hill – Huge!) Busses on to M. Arch &c. &c. 1/3. Dinner Marguerite. (Lovely Italian.) Cab(s) 3/2. Cigarettes 2d. Many types. One showed big red head. Hard stiff wagging H. Park Corner. **[Casement's randiness of the day before is partially quenched by a tour of the usual haunts, including the toilets at Marble Arch, on a hot July day, with good visual success. The evening is also enhanced by the first sighting at Marguerite's restaurant of an especially attractive Italian waiter.]**

Sunday 23 July To Denham and Dick...Returned 7.37 to Paddington. Dinner Café Marguerite (Dear free again!) **[perhaps a reference to Freid, see 19 July]**
Dinner 3/- Waiter 6d. Dear Free 1/- Looked in eyes 1/- 4. 6
Busses 1/-. Cgttes 9d. Walked about till 12 p.m. and then home.

Monday 24 July ...Afternoon train to Lady Caledon...To Caxton Hall in evening. Rotten performance...Dinner Marguerite 9.30. (Fear Free gone!)

Tuesday 25 July ...Blue Life Guard at Knightsbridge wanted 1.30 a.m. To Duke of Norfolk 11.15 a.m. **[15th Duke (1847-1917) England's leading Roman Catholic layman]** Ricudo's Rooms etc at Miss Cox 2.10.0. My own rooms 2.2.0...Boots Bartley & Son 3.10.0. **[Casement's bootmakers were**

paid for these "patent wellingtons" on 25 July.[519]**]** Putumayo typing at City meeting 6 July 1.18.4. **[A Queen Anne's Typewriting Office invoice for this amount is dated 24 July.**[520]**]** ...Boys – Nina with R. & O to Hampstead... Lay down till 7.10 and then in Mrs G.'s motor to Archbishop's. Papers 2d. Bus 2d. 2d. 7d. Cgttes 1/4. "Jean" of Algiers. 20 enormous. Oui M'sieu. il est tres grand, mais est joli aussi. Que j'amais ça **["Yes sir it is very big but it's pretty also. How I used to love that"; the sentiment in the second sentence is surely Casement's own. The encounter also merited a note at the beginning of the Ledger.]** 7.0. Promised £2 tomorrow 9.

18. 8. 6 **[At the last tot this was £18.5.6; the missing 3/- may have been spent on "red head" and "Free/Freid"]**

7. 0 Jean

18.15. 6 **[30th sex costs accumulation]** £1.19.0 **[July's tot to date]**

Wednesday 26 July Telegram Cadbury and Horner **[J. Stuart Horner of Birch & Co, 2 London Wall Bldgs.]** ...Saw beautiful type Oxford Circus and some huge ones. In City with Horner, Laidlaw and there Van Oppel. No go! **[The proposal that Horner and Hobson were putting together involved Mrs Julio Arana. The Peruvian Amazon Company had few tangible assets and no title deeds to land just the "squatters claim of J.C. Arana."**[521] **Mrs Arana was Zumaeta's sister and according to Casement "by mortgage now represents all the properties in Iquitos recently owned by the English company."**[522] **The proposal was to be declined unceremoniously by Casement who wrote to J.J. Hobson about the meeting "with you and your friend yesterday afternoon in the City" saying "you might let Mr Horner know this too" while declaring "I am not prepared to discuss further steps of the kind suggested."**[523] **Horner, trying to draw in a mutual acquaintanceship with Lord Milner, reported to Casement, of course "he knew you in the old days" during the South African War.**[524]**]** Jean. To meet my Algerian at 9 p.m. to Harrow. Friends 2.12.0.
Went and there already beautiful. To H. 9.15 and 10 mins after in Huge spit and clasp. **[Jean appears to be the same character as that recorded on 30 January 1911. The clues are the identical description of his male member "enormous", a significant step-up from the standard "huge", the initial J, and the fact that he is visited at his house in Harrow, on both occasions after an initial street meeting the previous night. Although defined as Jewish in January and French Algerian here, there is no necessary contradiction between the two details. So many such second meetings got taken no further forward. One wonders why and who it was that lost interest? In July**

it took another chance encounter out cruising, for a further arrangement to be made.] Back 10.41 – 11.8 Supper and at Piccadilly. Young. Trains 3d. To Harrow 1/4…

18.15. 6

2. 6. 0 **[Jean of Algiers in Harrow] X**

21. 1. 6

6. 0 **[young Piccadilly friend**

21. 7. 6 **31st sex costs accumulation]**

27 28 **[Confusion here as Jean, the French Algerian Jew, got no numbering for the previous day's action (but does today) while the young man at Piccadilly is allocated the 28th partner number]**

1. 19. 0

2. 6. 0 **[for Jean only**

1. 6 **unclear – possibly the ticket to Harrow**

4. 6. 6 **latest July sub-total]**

Thursday 27th July, 1911. To Southampton today… **X** Friend German Jew 16/- **X** …Spton.

21. 7. 6

16. 0 **[German Jew**

22. 3. 6 **32nd 1911 sex costs accumulation]** 29 [**29th sexual partner]**

4. 6. 6

16. 0 **[German Jew**

5. 2. 6

6. 0 **late inclusion of "Young" at Piccadilly**

5. 8. 6 **final July sex costs accumulation]**

Friday 28th July. Bath at Spton. Fearful heat. Hotel 10/-…Returned 2.59 train…Mr Harris 6/- Whiskey 1/8…French from Paris.

22. 3. 6

6. 0 **[Payment for Mr Harris who does not sound French**

22. 9. 6 **33rd sex costs accumulation]** 30 [**30th partner, last so recorded]**

Saturday 29th July 1911. Ricudo and O. Hair 2/-. Nina for them £1.10…To Spicer at F.O. and offered to go out to Iquitos. To St. Pancras for Warlies and Buxton. Train 6d. Boys 6d. **[Warlies, the Buxton family house, was at Waltham Cross near Waltham Abbey]** To Sir T. Fowel Buxton. **[The 1st Baronet, also Sir Thomas Fowell Buxton (1786-1845), was so created as a reward for his "philanthropic exertions to abolish slavery." He replaced Wilberforce as leader of the anti-slavery cause in the House of Commons.]** …

Sunday 30th July. At Warlies. Lovely youth there 18, coal black, **[the boy's hair presumably]** Alexander Scot. Son of Master of Polwarth. Magnificent one. Huge. Bathed together in pond. **[The Master, Walter Hepburne-Scott, later the 8th Baron Polwarth, was married to Edith Buxton. She was the sister of Sir Thomas and of Noel Buxton (1869-1948), President of the Anti-Slavery Society. In 1930 he was created Baron Noel-Buxton being Minister of Agriculture in both of Ramsay MacDonald's Labour Cabinets. A Liberal MP from 1905-6 and 1910-18, and a Labour MP from 1922-30, Noel's wife Lucy was also to be elected (in his stead) as a Labour MP.**

Casement recorded that "in July 1911 Mr Noel Buxton MP invited me to accompany him to the Balkans on a private mission to investigate alleged Turkish atrocities,"[525] an invitation probably made during this visit. This would not have been a task with which he would have empathised, but Casement was able to decline gracefully having just been ordered back to Iquitos. Noel Buxton, for his pains, was wounded by Turkish political assassins in the Balkans in October 1914 whilst on a mission to rally local support for the war. His was the classic career path of so many of Casement's Advanced Liberal milieu; those who managed to avoid Ireland and or disgrace.]

Monday July 31st 1911. Back from Buxton's after early bath with Alex – perfectly huge head and circumcised. Splendid. He is lovely **[Sadly, Alexander was not granted much time to enjoy his manhood if he ever did, being killed in action in May 1915 at the age of twenty-two, less than four years later. He was by then a Second Lieutenant in the Scots Guards, and died unmarried. The entry in the police typed copy for this day is marked with two giant Xs indicating it was to be photographed, presumably with the added intention of showing copies to any Buxtons clamouring for a reprieve.]** …Ricudo & O. to Exhibition 4/-. Hobson to lunch 14/8…A Mr Reynolds called to interview Boys for "D. News" Hobson **[not to be confused with Bulmer Hobson]** called about Putumayo. Told him it was off…

Nett outlay. **[for July]** 199. 6. 2

AUGUST

1 August 1911 …To City and P.A. Co. and Horner…Miss Cox's bill. 6.0.2. **[The notepaper for this bill is headed "Misses Cox & Vigrass" revealing she had a partner.[526]]**

Wednesday 2 Aug. F.O. sends orders to go out to Iquitos 3 Aug. **[The actual departure was a fortnight later on 16 August, after two trips to Ireland, one lasting barely twenty-four hours.]** At West Hill with W.A.C. **[Cadbury]** Nil.

Thursday 3 August. **[In margin:]** Me to Iquitos. Train from Birmingham… Train to F.O. 3d…Boys To Exhibition Ev'g. Self. To Notting Hill and dinner with Ethel Young **[of Galgorm Castle in Ballymena]** and husband and then to Exhibition…Bus back N.H. **[Notting Hill]** 1d.

X 5/- **X** Soldier 5/-. 3rd Bat. G.**[renadier]** Guards 5. 0
[The predilection for soldiers amongst London's homosexual community at the time was known as 'Scarlet Fever'. Obviously availability had a lot to do with their popularity since many young guardsmen were happy to enhance their earnings by such trade, and did so well into the 1960s.] Busses in to M. Arch 10d. Many types Park and H.P. Corner. **[Hyde Park]** Beauties…Marching orders to Putumayo again today from F.O.

August 4th Friday. …Busses Hampstead with boys to Rothenstein. I to lunch Cheapside…Out at 10.30 p.m. to supper. Train Sloane Square…Supper Sl. Square…

August 5th Saturday. To Ireland today 8.30 a.m. Taxi to Euston 3/10…Arrived Gresham, **[hotel in Dublin's Sackville Street, later O'Connell Street]** Letter from Millar. Good on for Tuesday. Hurrah! Expecting! Out after dinner with J. Nelson and Family in Gresham. **[The Nelsons were living at one point in South America and were obviously patriotic as Casement bought John Nelson a present of "a '98 pike" for £2 in 1907.[527]]** Lovely ev'g. To Harcourt St. **[railway station]** and one Huge exposure, red head and all and then Wicklow lad, knickers "His alright" stiff. **[The large X here on the police-typed copy indicates a photograph was made of the entry]** To Burlington Road 3/-…

Sunday 6th August 1911 In Dublin. To Zoo and Arbuthnot **[Captain L.C. Arbuthnot of Dublin Zoo to which Casement presented an ocelot, making a welcome breeding pair.[528]]** …Entry 2d. Cgttes 3d. To Sandycove 5d. **[Although Sandycove was Casement's birthplace, it is also the location of the Forty Foot, Dublin's only gentleman's bathing area where swimming costumes were traditionally not worn. This particular trip certainly owed**

Sarah Purser's portrait of Casement painted over ten sessions in June 1913 and presented to the National Gallery of Ireland in 1930 by William Cadbury. The other 'sketch' is on this book's cover.

more to the chance of an ogle and possibly an encounter than nostalgia as he hardly lived more than his first few months there.] Back 6d. 2d. Called at ffrench's **[Lord and Lady ffrench lived at Ailesbury Road.]** and on to O F. Tram 2d. 1d. To dinner at Gresham with J. Nelson. Out at 9.30 Lovely evening to Harcourt Street and Hatch Street and several, and then all at once the lad of 5th of March. "How?" **[This lad was previously diaried as under nineteen, and with a penis seven inches long and four inches thick. Three months earlier he had also said "How?" and was to be similarly gifted a half crown.]** To Burlington Road and pulled it out.

Huge 2/6. 8d. Car home 1/6 4.8
[In margin:] Huge Irish

22. 9. 6 **[The 5/- spent on Thursday's Grenadier Guard is omitted**
3. 2 **2/6 and 8d for "Huge"**
22.12. 8
Car 1/6
22.14. 2 **34th sex costs accumulation]** Huge thick as wrist.

Monday 7th August 1911 In Dublin…Beggar 4d. Harrie & Annie Trams to Zoo 1/-. Entrance 1/-. To lion keeper Flood 2/-. To Rotunda Irish Pageant 3/-. Whiskey 6d. Harrie and Annie back at 6 to Baronstown. **[Harriette Wilkinson and her daughter Annie lived at a house named Tara in Barronstown, Skreen, Co. Louth, which Casement visited in 1898, for the first time in over eight years, as he wrote. The Wilkinsons including a sister Emma Dickey/Dickie were old family friends about whom Nina was naively concerned when, after the events of 1916, they failed to answer her letters from America.[529]]** I to meet enormous at 9. Will suck and take too. He was not there! **[There are huge Xs on the Home Office typescript here. It is also a very rare use by Casement of an indelicate word, but an example of entries being written-up during the day because of his enthusiasm. It further indicates the likelihood that Casement kept this Ledger on his person.]** I waited till 9.30. No sign. To H. Bwait **[?Herbert ?Place]** & Park. None…

Tuesday 8th August 1911 Leaving for Belfast. To sleep with Millar. **[in margin:]** About 11 p.m. I trust and shall thrust too! My last night with Millar was 12th May at Newcastle. Slept with Millar. In at once. Turned and pushed on to it **[actually the last night together had been 14 May 1911.]** Hotel Bill at Gresham. 2.0.5. Ticket to Belfast 9/5…Extras on 3 3rd Tickets. Mine and Miss O'F's 14/5 **[On 24 August 1916, Major Frank Hall of MI5 described**

Professor Agnes O'Farrelly (of Gortahork) to Ernley Blackwell as "a member of the Provisional Committee of *Cumann na mBan*. She is an extreme Gaelic Leaguer and was always mixed up in Sinn Fein."[530] O'Farrelly became a Senator in 1932 having kept clear of the military struggles of the previous decades.] Lunch Belfast 2/1…Hair etc. 5/5…

Wednesday 9th August 1911 …Fare to Ballycastle 1/-. 9/-…Lunch in Belfast 8/6…Bulmer 2/6…

Thursday 10th August **[At top of page:]** Death of Johnnie Bell. Told by letter. On 10th October 1909. **[Casement was in Brazil on this date]** Poor darling wee boy. At Ballycastle. With Roger and Susie, Irish button for Joan, Charlie's daughter 4.0 **[This Australian niece, later Mrs Joan Stuart, was the only offspring of his brother's second marriage.]** Telegrams Nina and Gill…Letter from William Bell telling of Johnnie Bell's death.

Friday 11th August Telegram Royal Mail and Elder Dempster passage. Replies paid 1/- Nina Plymouth…Archie 2/-…

Saturday 12th August To leave Ireland today. Return London from Belfast. Mrs Thomas' Bill washing 5/9. Eye lotion 3/7…"Agassiz" Journey to Brazil 14.0 **[Pickering & Chatto invoiced Casement for "Agassizs Journey in Brazil" at a price of 14 shillings on 4 August 1911.[531] Casement, in a letter, had been told on 27 December 1910 "Your Agassiz – Tizon said he gave it back to you", so it remained missing and a further copy had to be purchased.[532]]** … Out to Breda House Cregagh Road to Johnnie "Jock" Bells. Oh! Dear God To think of it. Dead and Gone! Old father and mother and sisters. **[The precise details of Casement's relationship with Johnnie Bell may never be known but his death affected him more deeply than any other he recorded in his diaries apart from Sir Hector Macdonald's in 1903. Indeed his comments and actions, including this visit and the later purchase of a photo frame so that Johnnie's picture could be preserved and enshrined, suggest that he was much admired and probably loved. His father was first recorded in the 1904 Belfast street directory as living at Breda House on the Cregagh Road.**

The mystery of the initial connection is only deepened by Casement's inscriptions on an undated sheet of Grosvenor Hotel (Belfast) notepaper which indicate he is both trying to find the Bell family's address and doing some family research. Copying, as he wrote, from that same 1904 street directory, he had transcribed "Wm Bell traveller Breda Hse" and "W Bell & Co wine and spirit merchants 18-21 Gordon Street."[533]

This suggests he was trying to track Johnnie Bell down, while his detailing of three unrelated Casements living in working class areas of Belfast

– George, Joseph and William, a joiner, a tailor and a paper cutter respectively – also reveals a continuing genealogical interest in searching for missing or unknown relatives. It may be that a speculative letter to Breda House produced the terrible news just received. Plainly Casement did not know the lad's address (the wine merchant was unconnected) which indicates a fleeting relationship with the boy, not involving correspondence, and one unlikely therefore to have been of a political nature.

The young man's death certificate revealed the sad fact that, actually on 14 October 1909 (not as advised on 10 October), he had suffered a fatal accident at Belfast's Harland & Wolff shipyard on Queen's Island, where he was employed as an apprentice plater. The news report in the *Northern Whig* on 15 October told of "terrible injuries" sustained after a fall of forty feet: "The ambulance was at once telephoned for and he was removed to the Royal Victoria Hospital but there his condition was seen at once to be hopeless and he succumbed to his injuries shortly after admission." His age was given very precisely on the death certificate as seventeen and nine-twelfths (and that he was a bachelor) although he was said to be nineteen years old in the press reports of the fatality, and the inquest, which his father attended to give identification evidence.

According to the death notice in the *Belfast Telegraph,* "John (Jack)" was the "youngest and dearly beloved son of William and Sarah Jane Bell, Breda House, Cregagh Rd. His remains will be removed from above address this day (Sat) at two o'clock for interment in the City Cemetery. Friends will please accept this intimation." In the tradition of the time an inquest was held the day after his death, before the city coroner, Dr James Graham, with HM Inspector of Factories in attendance.

A fellow plater, David Morton, also engaged on "ship 400", *The Olympic*, sister ship to the *Titanic* which was 401, on the main deck who was working with John, gave evidence of the boy "lowering a pattern a few pounds weight to the tank top [when] standing on a plank about nine inches wide." The height from the tank to the main deck was about 32 feet. Although he was "only a few paces away [he] did not see deceased fall" nor did he know of anyone who did. No one else was with them. He "could not at all account for the deceased falling", the plank was steady although not fastened. A juror asked if he could have tilted it up or if it could "have shifted in any way out of its place." The answer was no to both questions. John Bell, whom he last saw stooping, fell through a gap in the staging purposely left open "to lower patterns through." "The high wind had nothing to do with it?" Morton again replied no. At this point the Coroner emphasised "So far as I can see it was a pure accident."

Another witness, James W. Britty "said as he was passing along the tank top the deceased almost fell on top of him." He did not know what caused the fall or what deceased had been doing. Dr Joy stated death occurred five minutes after arrival at the Royal Victoria Hospital and was due to a "cerebral haemorrhage following upon fracture of the skull."

In conclusion, the Coroner stated it was evidently a pure accident of which there had fortunately been very few in recent years in either Harland & Wolff or Workman Clarks. "To him that was a particularly sad inquest as he had known deceased from infancy and he also had known his parents for very many years. The Cregagh district would miss this young man very much as he was a pioneer amongst his companions in every manly and athletic sport." The *Irish News* reported that John Bell was "very popular in the Cregagh district." The jury returned a verdict of accidental death.

Such inexplicable, unnatural deaths involving young men would today leave a suspicion of suicide and there is a hint of this in the Coroner's efforts to direct the jury toward the verdict of accidental death. Perhaps he wished to spare the feelings of John's father by even speculating about or investigating such a possibility. There was no evidence either way. If as seems likely, John was homosexual, he was a respectable boy in a working man's job yet one who had thoughts and did things that would not be tolerated if discovered, or so he might increasingly think. People were not as harsh as he feared although he would never find that out. Even in these vastly more liberal times the rate of suicide amongst young gay males is inordinately high.

John did have a brother, William, who corresponded with Casement about Irish political matters in 1912 and 1913. In his letter of 9 May 1912, William Bell opens with the salutation "Dear Sir" which is either indicative of an acquaintance that has not previously involved a meeting or a respectful attempt at the written style for addressing a knight. His address was then 4 Stranmillis Gardens, Belfast where he lived, as he noted, with his wife. In another letter he enclosed "a small sub" of five shillings in response to Casement's recent newspaper appeal "to provide a daily meal for the poor little school children of 'the Connemara Islands'."[534]

No mention was made of his late brother in these letters but William thanked Casement for various books that had influenced him greatly, especially "Mrs Green's 'Irish Nationality'." He added that he had again read this book and was "now a convinced supporter of the cause of self-government for Ireland."

There is a tone of naive and humble enthusiasm in the letters of the young William Bell which resembles the sentiments expressed in some of Millar

Gordon's correspondence with Casement. These two male Ulster Protestants with a somewhat similar background, are perhaps the only two of that tribe who were converted to Casement's Irish political views by his influence. William Bell senior died in 1922 aged 73; a retired commercial traveller. His address was by then *Laurelbank* on Belfast's Knockbreda Road. The executors of his will were named as William, described as an auditor, and a further son Hugh, a cashier.]

Mrs Thomas food and rooms 12/-...Telegrams 6d (Gill)...Decided to go to Dublin see Gill...Ticket £2.5.6 **[This was T.P. Gill, a onetime nationalist MP and pamphleteer, later a civil servant whom the Chief Secretary Augustine Birrell was to deny an honour. Striking his name off an awards list he described Gill as "a scribbler and a humbug who already had too much pudding."[535] From Santos in 1906 Casement was hoping he and Mrs Gill were well and the boys flourishing[536] but by 1914 it was "He is a real snake the one Patrick omitted to evict."[537]]**

Sunday 13th August **[This is the first entry since 18 January duplicating one in the other 1911 journal. Casement continued such double entering until 31 October when this Ledger was abandoned. The diary then took over for the remainder of the year.]** Arrived Dublin 5.20 a.m. To Gresham... Out to *Syral Sanna* **[in Gaelic script]** with Gill and Mespil House. Miss Purser **[This is the artist Sarah Purser RHA (1848-1943) whose beautiful painting of Casement is in the *Seanad* at Leinster House (with the study in Dublin's National Gallery). It was commissioned by W.A. Cadbury at a cost of 50 guineas. Casement called his portrait a great success, saying that Miss Purser had named it "Colmcille in Iona", adding in a letter to Gertrude "So I am an Irish Saint you see after all, even in Exile."[538] The artist ran a renowned literary salon in Mespil House on the banks of the Grand Canal in her "huge damp drawing room." One (unionist) Dublin exile of the time described Miss Purser to this author in 1999 as "tinged with green." Ever a friend, she wrote in 1916 to Gavan Duffy saying "I think of him constantly and with the greatest sorrow." Casement's solicitor replied gloomily: "Had there been a little more charity in Dublin I should be less anxious about a reprieve."[539]]** ...Supper on board 2/6. 3d. Extra fare to Euston 18.0...

Monday 14 Augt. Arr London. Cab 4/9. Porter 6d. Paper 1d. Grantham Hotel writing 2/3 (Porter)...To F.O. (Saw all final words. Royal Mail)...Lunch (Gatti's) 3/-. Busses 6d. Dinner 3/-...

Friend "8 inches" Brass worker 5/-. 5.0

[Possibly, and unusually, this was an Englishman as his nationality is not mentioned.] ...

22.14. 2

5. 0 **["Brass worker"**

22.19. 2

8. 0 **Recipient of this amount is not specified**

23. 7. 2 **35th sex costs accumulation]**

[In margin:] 1 Jan-14 Augt **X** To date Friends £23.7.2 **X** 31 **[the partners since 28 July went uncounted when making up this figure of thirty-one, the final so inscribed.]**

Tuesday 15th August In London. Packing up. My passage to Barbados 21.12.0. Ricudo and Omarino 36.0.0. Miss Cox My rooms 2.2/-...moth paper 2/-... photo frames 2/1. Mudies 2 Copies of C. Markham's "Incas of Peru". **[The author of this title, geographer Sir Clements Markham, is accused by Angus Mitchell in the May 2001 edition of *History Today,* of being "one historian capable of masterminding (but not executing) the forgery." Unfortunately Markham died in January 1916, in his eighties, before the Black Diaries were discovered. Mitchell adduces no evidence of his involvement except to say that as Markham "enjoyed the company of naval officers he would have known some of those recruited in to Room 40." His was the third proposed name for the supposed master forger emerging in a twelve month period in 2000-2001 after Frank Ezra Adcock and Donald im Thurn.]** One of them for William Bell of Breda House. **[An interest in matters Latin American by William Bell junior is confirmed in the correspondence, mentioned above, when Bell wrote of a book on Porfirio Diaz's Mexico, recommended by Casement, and of a seamen's strike on the Olympic Line which he found encouraging.]** ...Hope Brothers: Shirts for Boys and Self 4.19.7 **[On both Tuesday and Wednesday hectic shopping and allied arrangements were made and many payments recorded prior to the departure for Iquitos.]**
...Donald Ross (or Kimfull) **[word unclear, police have Kingsfield]** 23 Gower Street. 10.0.
To Louie in afternoon at 4-6. Dinner with Barnes.

22.19. 2

10. 0 **[Donald Ross**

23. 9. 2 **36th sex costs accumulation, the unexplained 8/- added above now expunged]**

Wednesday 16th August Leaving England to-day by Magdalena for Barbados. To Servants at P. Gardens 10/-...Ticket to Southampton 1st class 13/6...Left S'ptn 12 noon. Cherbourg 7.20. Left 8.20. Fabre and son **[of the Dutch-French Colonizing Company]** on board bound to Quito.

Photo Frame at Harrods Johnnie Bell 2.6

...Tip to steward for boys 4/-. **[The boys "look quite happy and smile at all around them" wrote Casement to Cadbury on board ship that day outlining his change of heart on the decision to take both back to Iquitos.[540]]** ...

[17-27 August: en route to Barbados] At sea on Magdalena...Ship not comfortable as I am double bunked and no need for it at all. Heaps 2 vacant cabins...Sweepstake 1/- **[entered each day except both Sundays; eight draws but never a winner]** To arrive at St. Michaels (Azores) **[Sunday 20 August]** ...Arrive Ponta Delgada 3.40 p.m. and on shore...Boat 2/-. Wine 4/-. Marino Cabral 3/-...Left Ponta Delgada 6 p.m. and on to Barbados...

Sent to Nina Extra Strike Pay 5.0.0.

Monday 28th August Arr. Barbados and landed. Wine a/c Barman for Boys 1.0.9. Steward 2nd Class for boys 5.0 **[Casement went 1st class while the two Indian boys who were being returned home after what must have been the experience of a lifetime, travelled 2nd class. Nina described them as "light-mahogany coloured, their skins smooth as satin; extremely clean they would bathe if permitted half a dozen times in a day."[541] Happy and well-looked after, as they were in England (particularly by Casement's women) re-entry to a dangerous and primitive existence after such cultural novelty and material wealth might have been very unsettling.]** Evening in Barbados To Club and Pier.

Tuesday 29th August At Barbados. At Sea View Hotel...Boy to bathe 6d. **[In margin] X** 6d. ...2 boys to swim today. Expect Teddy at 4. At 4 he has not come so I fear he is away in St. Vincent.

Boys R. and O. for spending 3.0.

Teddy came, met on bicycle and back to room and dinner. After dinner to room and he looked and looked. I saw his big huge and felt mine and he looked all the time and back on bicycle...Teddy to come tomorrow at 5 to bath. Then will see and feel. **[This day's entry is marked on the government's typed copy with a forest of crosses. Teddy Biddy, a previous acquaintance, must have been summoned immediately on arrival. The youth has a never-before noticed, or revealed history, dating three years back to the two month convalescence Casement spent, in 1908, in Barbados, when suffering terrible gastritis. In another cash ledger, a *Cyclopean Exercise Book*,**

Teddy Biddy, Barbados boy

inscribed "Notes at Barbadoes" he merited his own entry headed "Teddy a/c." Casement carefully recorded eight different items in it amounting to "1.3.0". They included "4.2" for a "Ticket" which from the price of four shillings for his own "Bath Ticket" suggests it too was a season entry to a swimming pool.[542] This item is compelling, corroborative evidence of the authenticity of the Black Diaries.]

Wednesday 30 August To Hastings Bath 7.50 and several and then nice fair haired boy, blue pants and thick and stiff. To bath together 11.30. Bath 3[**d.**] Cgttes 1/-. Bath (11.30) 5d. He then glorious form and limbs and it...Teddy and "Budds" at 5.30. Latter lovely and huge one too. Only 11 years old on 17th July. [**Details underlined in the police-typed copy. Indeed Home Office markings here become febrile with Casement heading into under-age territory.**] Bath Budds present 5/-...

Seen to-day 1 oldish man huge one
2 clergyman small
3 lovely youth thick fine one
4 big youth nice clean one
5 lover, only top stiff and lovely [**presumably Teddy**]
6 Budds beauty

[The ten days on board ship crossing the Atlantic were followed, as on other occasions, by an explosion of sexual activity with frequent visits to a local seaside park, Hastings Rocks, to scrutinise boys – some of them disturbingly young, if apparently sexually mature. For another brief period, Casement's erotic musings obliged him to write-up his accounts in the extended form of diary entries – which duly caught the attention of his enemies.]

Thursday 31 August To Hastings Bath 5d, clergyman there told me was father of beauty. Returned 11 and beauty came glorious limbs but did not show it alas I love him…Walked to Father Smith and the Convent and then to Club. **[Father Frederick Smith S.J. of St. Patrick's Church, near the Ursuline Convent, had been made guardian of Ricudo and Omarino in Barbados. Casement forwarded regular cheques from England during their stay. On the island, Frederick Bishop, a Barbadian whom Casement came to trust, despite his cruelty, when working for the Peruvian Amazon Company, had on 16 December 1910 – the day before Casement's departure for Europe – been given £22 to look after the boys. Within a fortnight, according to Father Smith, Bishop had squandered half of what was then a considerable amount of money.**

Writing from the "Catholic Church" on 6 February 1911, Fr. Smith commenced a repeated refrain "Mr Bishop brought the boys and asked me to take them but as I am not Superior of the house and as the Superior would not let me take them I am not at liberty in the matter." Another Barbadian from the Amazon, Stanley Sealy, then looked after them. On 21 March 1911 Father Smith wrote again "Fr. McCormick refused to let me have anything to do with the boys at the beginning. When your cheque for £10 came Fr. McCormick received it without saying anything so I suppose he will make no difficulties." If, however, he, Father Smith, had been the Superior, "I would have found a place where the boys could sling their hammocks." Father John McCormick was parish priest from 1908 to 1914 at St Patrick's church in Bridgetown, now the Roman Catholic cathedral of Barbados.

On 2 May Fr. Smith reported "The older boy Ricudo seems to wish to return to Putumayo. There is a fellow countryman of his here and I suppose this has put it in Ricudo's head." As an old Amazon hand, himself he reminded Casement that Indians as a rule do not like to stay in any one place for long. After a time they like to "take a walk." He had other concerns about Ricudo: "He takes a little liquor now and again…(and) has a little looseness of the bowels for a day or two, perhaps from the Rum… They are both slow in picking up English. The little one Umurummy seems to get a little better."

On 13 June, the day before the boys left for England, he wrote to say "They are in excellent health and well stocked with clothes." He also had bad news: "I did my best to get your parrot but I could not find Mrs Bishop and I have not been able to get it yet." And a fortnight later he reminded Casement yet again "not being the Superior I could do nothing."[543] Heavy rain all night. Got wet twice…

Total spent in August £168.10.10…

Epitome for August

…Net expenditure outside special £60.4.9

SEPTEMBER

September 1911.

Begins at Barbados in Seaview Hotel.
Friday September 1st My 47th Birthday!

To Bath at Hastings to meet Beauty for last time. Bath 5d. His name is Hughes. Born March 16. (Did not come) Stamps 1/- Cg'ttes 1/10 Sweets 2/9. 5 7 Trams 8d. - Lunch with Crawford. Then a lovely Meztise boy **[a Mestizo is a person of mixed race, born of Indian and Iberian parents]** of 16 or 17 in blue at Church Sq. Longed for & talked to & asked to come to bath Sunday & was most willing. The Biddys at 6. Teddy looking often – They went 6.40. **[The reference to "The Biddys" is only explained by inspection of the inside cover of this journal. Alongside addresses for other sexual partners such as "Jean of Algiers" and "Amron Kali" is one for "Master E.K. Biddy". These notes were not published in *The Black Diaries* and can only be detected in the original journal. (See also the 1911 Diary on this date: "The Biddys came at 6. Very sick at sight of them. They are beggars like all here.") These Biddys were not Irish or some form of Barbadian street youths but a local family he had befriended, possibly to gain access to Teddy, who when met three years earlier in 1908 must hardly have been pubescent. From Casement's scornful remark, the Biddys appear to be poor whites although his address was the former Bishop's Palace. The same boy, Edward Kay Biddy, a clerk, born in 1895 in St. Vincent is recorded as travelling from Barbados to Hartford Connecticut in 1912, with his mother and five siblings. By 1917, he was an officer in the US Army only to die in the 1918 flu epidemic. He was an engineer with at least one patent to his name.]** To Hastings Rocks & then to town. Club 1/-. Darkie guide 1-. Trams 2d. 2 2 £0 8 2 **[This day's entry in Scotland Yard's typed copy is marked with two large crosses by the Home Office reader.[544]]**

Saturday 2 Sept. 1911

Trams 6d. Paper 1d. Cgttes 3/8 Club waiter 4/-	8.3
Cotton wool 1/. Beads for Nina 3/-.	4
Passage to Pará by Boniface **X**	16.13. 4
X St. John's poor white boys **X**	6.10
Clothes for Ricudo and Omarino	1.17. 6
To waiter 3/- Tel 1/- Trams 1/-	5 0

Coleridge King. **[a line with an X connects his name to the above "poor white boys"]**

£23. 9. 2

6.10

23.16. 0 **X** Coleridge King **[37th sex costs accumulation]**

Sunday 3 Sept 1911 Spent in Barbados…Still at Barbados. £20.3.1 "Boniface" not in during night. Hair cut 1/6 Cocktail 6d. Bathed at Light House. Fine big Darkie 1/-. Trams 6d. Club 1/6. Saw several beauties. Sundry 1 …

Monday 4 Sept Out to Light House & saw a nice boy. Asked him to bath & he came on bone. Stanley Weeks 20. Stripped. Huge one – circumcised – swelled & hung 9" quite & wanted it awfully – asked come at 11.30. Boniface arr. & out at 12 & Stanley again & wanted it fearfully. His stiff & mine stiff. Then had to leave. Farewell to Stanley! **["Stanley Weeks" is also written in both margins and once underlined while Xs appear in a snowstorm around the description. Connected expenditure of two and then three shillings is set within it. The whole entry is a classic stream of consciousness of which James Joyce would be proud. The late and badly-timed arrival of Casement's ship, the *Boniface*, intruded in fact, and in mid-memoir, on the frustrated opportunity for significant sexual contact with the apparently eager Stanley Weeks.**

There then follows the usual rush of items of expenditure to do with departure – the hotel bill, customs charges, tips, the luggage car and porters (with nine shillings going on chairs for the two Indian boys). Finally there is a record of an assignation made the day before:] Coleridge King 5/- who left his address with Mrs Seon **[note, as in this case of leaving an address with the hotel proprietor, the cool demeanour of Casement and so many of his casual partners, who assume correctly that others are oblivious to anything untoward going on.]** – I want Stanley Weeks **[phrase underlined by the Home Office on their typescript.]** Left Barbados at 4 p.m £28 15 4…

23.16. 0
5. 0 Stanley Weeks 5/- **X X**
24 1. 0 **38th sex costs accumulation**]

Tuesday 5 Sept 1330 miles to Pará…On Boniface. A filthy tub. She has legal accommodation at N. York for 5 passengers, and has 16! A barefaced swindle – These Booths are blackguards [**a regular complaint about other ships and shipping companies but Casement was now especially antagonistic to Booths.**] …~~Tuesday~~ 6 Sept At sea in Boniface. Dr Dickey of Dunmór of Moylinney on board. Nil. [**Dr Dickey was Presbyterian, and there is a Moylinny near Lord Massereene's demesne in the town of Antrim. These two facts suggest the doctor's family may have originated in Ulster. Casement and Nina were great friends with a Miss Emma Dickey of Portrush while Roger, their great-grandfather, managed the notorious Lord Massereene's affairs. The Dickey name and Moylinny would therefore have registered with Casement, explaining the above phrase.**

Dickey, an employee of the Peruvian Amazon Company, writing many years later, said he had first come across Casement at the Marine Hotel in Barbados. He recalled a "great multicoloured macaw…a pet most obnoxious to everyone but Casement." This must be the lost parrot for which Father Smith had been searching apparently now reunited with its owner. When Commander Mendez on the Pará-Manaos run requested that Casement should wear shoes at dinner, the response was uncompromising "Go to hell."[545] Apparently no other concession was made to the heat, with Casement wearing a tweed suit throughout. Anyway "formality is the refuge of the ignorant - of the mannerless", as Casement jotted down on the back of a 1910 Booth invoice.[546] Dickey also records the fact that "Casement seemingly had forgotten how to smile", a facet of his demeanour others reported, and some denied.]

[**7-9 September: sailing for Pará and the mouth of the Amazon:**] Still on "Boniface" Talking to Dr Dickey about Putumayo…Full moon. [**Dr Dickey was to feature significantly on the side of the forgery school, when he swore an affidavit in 1938 stating he was a medical doctor with thirty years' experience. He had responded to Casement's request for details of sexual perversions among the Amazon Indians for Sir Arthur Conan Doyle, which were then recorded copiously in a notebook. Also a medical doctor, Conan Doyle was stated by Casement to have used his stories as source material for previous books, having also asked for and been told "of numerous examples of sex depravity among the Congo natives." Dr Dickey enlarged**

on the matter for up to three-quarters of an hour while Casement recorded the steamy testimony. This little charade was supposedly concluded by Casement remarking gravely: "What terrible stuff to entrust to the mails!"

Dickey swore that he had encountered many homosexuals "but if Casement was one of those unfortunates, I am a rotten diagnostician - and I shouldn't be." But the Casement defenders of this era, like Dickey, had never seen the detail in the diaries and assumed it to be on a par with foreign or tropical pornography, rather than numerous daily recollections of sexual rendezvous and comments. Dickey, with his recollections of the time spent together, remains a key character for forgery theorists who were previously reliant on the Normand diary explanation as to how sexual material got into Casement's writing. Indeed, Angus Mitchell has described Dickey as someone who could deny that the 1911 voyage took the form of "a sexual odyssey – an officially sanctioned cruise along the harbour fronts of Amazonia."[547]]

<u>Sunday</u> 10 Septr. <u>Arrive Pará</u>. To arrive in Pará to-day off S.S. "Boniface". Home [**sic**] meet João tomorrow. [**João was last seen on 14 December 1910 "at Cemetery corner at 8 a.m" when he gave Casement "a big bunch of flowers – very nice indeed"**] Wine Bill 1.0.6. ...Sub Life Boat fund 5/-. Going ashore baggage. Beer 1/-. Lent Cashier 1 3 Stewards 13/6. Carpenter 2/6... Arrived Pará 1.30. Alongside 4 p.m. & on shore at 5. To Hotel do Commerc. [**Dr Dickey recalled[548] his amazement that Casement chose to stay at a "very second rate house", as the Hotel do Commercio ("a Baptista & Alves") was, but attributed it to Casement's charitable instincts which had eroded his financial resources. Plainly Casement knew exactly where to stay in order to be near, if not in, the action.**] Sereno gone! – Out after dinner & Baptista Campos & Nazareth – None. Huge exposure B. Campos with girl & in Nazareth nice Paraense – young 16, big soft...

Monday 11 Sept. 1911 [**At top of page:**] Saw João Anselmo de Lima <u>7.30 a.m.</u> *Serzedello Correa*...In Pará – Out at 7 saw João Anselmo at corner by Cemetery, but did not speak. He busy but I am sure saw me. Poor small cart. Trams 300...

Tuesday 12 Sept. <u>At Souza.</u> Vermouth 1000. Biscuit 500. To lunch with Pogsons. Awful muck! [**George Ambrose Pogson was British consul at Pará. The "muck" comment is explained in the 1911 Diary as being the vile grub served up by Mrs Pogson.**] ...

Wednesday 13 Septr. 1911 Lovely day. Out to Una & Val du Caens & back & then dinner with & Andrews & McH. & Huge Tram Inspector's after 9.10 p.m. at Palace Square. <u>Stiff as sword & thick & long</u> **X** Big Tram <u>Inspector</u>. [**5 tram journeys are paid for that day**] ...Ricudo 200...

Thursday 14 Sept 1911 To Zoo. Met João Anselmo – & talked it big…João 10.000. Breakfasted Andrews & Mac H…Afternoon lay down. Then to Pogson 7 p.m. Cgttes 400. Trams 600. 200.
Friend **X.** Augusto Gomes dos Santos. [**name inscribed later**] Entered strong at Cemetery 10.000. Whiskey 500 500…

£24. 1. 0

13. 4 [**Augusto's 10,000 or 13/4, not João's gift**

24.14. 4 **39th sex costs accumulation**]

Friday 15 Sept 1911 …Postage stamps for Father Smith at Barbados. [**On 3 October, Smith wrote back saying "Your kind letter of September 15 came safely and I thank you for your great kindness…in sending such stamps." Father Smith was a keen philatelist and had asked for some low denomination Brazilian issues.**] …Val du Caens to lunch with Harveys. Back 6 p.m. & after dinner out…Tip 200 boy. Tram 200. Huge exposure 8" in Kiosque at Palace Square 8 p.m.

Saturday 16 Sept. War between France & Germany! [**Not quite, the Agadir crisis about conflicting spheres of influence in Morocco did not yet result in armed conflict between these two imperial powers but it was an indication of how close war was.**] Tram to Marco & back 880. To Andrews & MacHaffie…
X Augusto Tavares dos Santos 10.000…
X Met him at 8 Cemetery & in at once. "Gosto" [**A pleasure**] – Police. [**In a cryptic note in his address book, Casement inscribed "Stern Reprisals. The surest nocturnal pick me up is the policeman,"[549] words which may relate to his experience of police at night pursuing more than criminals.**] Then Spaniard theatre & a small thing at corner offered.

24.14. 4

13. 4 [**Augusto's second 13/4 is converted from 10$000**

25. 7. 8 **40th sex costs accumulation**]

Sunday 17 Sept 1911 **X** – Friend 17$ = £1.2.0. To Sacramento & bathed… To Zoo twice & huge ones. In at 5 p.m. & beer & lay down till 7 & out to Palace & Co. at once. Huge & furious. To Him 17$000. "Rio!" 17.000
[**13 tram tickets recorded as bought on this one day**] …

25. 7. 8 **X**

1. 2. 0 [**for "Rio"**

26. 9. 8 **41st sex costs accumulation – total later ignored**]

Young man, in light suit and hat, stone wall background

Waiter with black bow tie, elegant house or hotel setting

Monday 18 Sept. ...£24.14.4 **X X X [the sex total inscribed three days earlier on 14 September and used again on 30 September. The change is related to Augusto declining gifts.]**
To Augusto of Tavares for his tram from Marco 1000
Refused to accept.
Did not meet "Rio."

[19-21 September:] ...Drew £40 Bank at 16¼d. per dollar...Sandwich & Chop ...About 14.762 to £...Stamps for Father Smith at Barbados 5.400... Hotel Bill to date 18th. Myself 80$000 Ricudo 80$000 – Extras 74$500. **[No mention of Omarino who presumably shared Ricudo's room.]** ...Ricudo 500...Hammock 8.000...

Friday 22nd Sept. Leave Pará in "Hilda". Passage to Iquitos 302$000...Hotel Bill at "Commercio" 130.000. **[The bill paid on that date actually totals 140,000 but marks indicate 10,000 have been deducted.[550]]** Tips to servants Manoel 5.000 Joaguim 15.000 José 15.000 Jorge 15.000 other with 5.000 Cook 8.000...Left Pará about 2.30 a.m. on Saturday after being 14 hours on this detestable craft there. God! how hopeless this people is!

[23-28 September: On board *Hilda*:] To Cloghaneely College from Pará 11. **[Cloghaneely is the Irish school in Donegal which Casement both funded and attended to learn Gaelic.] ...**On "Hilda" Steaming across Tocantins. Nil on board...– Up Narrows...At Santarem – Bought – 4 parroquets 8.000 100 oranges 2000...near Solimões mouth...At Manaos. Landing boat 2.000...

Friday – 29 Sept. ...Boys 7000. Boat 2000. Bird seed 1.000. Wine Bill on Hilda 33.000. Trams 1.000. Grenadine 1.000...

Saturday 30 Sept. 1911

...Papers 200. Haircutting 3.000. Bath 600	3.800
Boots **[cleaned]** (Italian boy. Big one)	400
Stout 2000. Schopes Dr. 2.600	4.600
Cg'ttes 1000. Caboclo followed.	1.000
Vermouth 2000. Trams 600.	2.600
Indian of Madeira - Mamoré **[railway]** "*Não me falta*".	4.000
[See 1911 Black Diary for same date for explanation of this phrase.]	
Cafuzo in Square.	18.000

X. X. Evg.

24.14. 4 **[Previous two totals ignored, reverting to 14 September's**
X 1. 9. 9 **for the Indian and the Cafuzo, converted from above 22.000.**
£26. 4. 1 **42nd sex costs accumulation]**

...Total in September £100.2.11...

OCTOBER

Sunday 1st Oct. **[last month of this Cash Ledger]** ...Gave Booth & Co Cheque for £29 7/- for Milreis 441$700...In Manaos.

1	Raymundo. Aprendiz Marinheiro	12.000	
2	Sailor Negro of "Commandante Freitas".	15.000	
3	Agostinho de Souza.	40.000	
		67.000	4.9.4... **X X X**

26. 4. 1
4. 9. 4 **X [the three lovers @ 67.000 or £4.9.4**
30.13. 5 **43rd sex costs accumulation]**

...3 Lovers had & two others wanted... **[The use of the word 'Lovers' where normally 'friend', or the unemotional 'type', would be written, indicates a relaxed happier Casement.]**

Monday 2nd Oct. ...Whisky 4000 Ginger Ale & Cgttes 2000...Boots 400. Schopes 1200. Cgttes (50 pkts) 26000. Bramlio 15000...

X
30.13. 5
1. 0. 0 **[Bramlio; the exchange rate used is 15 to the pound**
31.13. 5 **44th sex costs accumulation]**

3 Oct. Tuesday ...Goods Booth 13.700...Liquors 26.000 Lewis 10.000...
Hotel Bill 125.500...Postage 200...
Cheque to Pogson for £18-10-0 for Brazilian money and stamps.
Tuesday 3 Oct 1911 **[Casement dated this day twice as the entry crossed to another page]**
To Agostinho de Souza, 24 Rua Mons Coutinho. Night of 2nd 12-1 a.m. 25.000

Total Agostinho = 2.13. 4
1.13. 4
£4. 6. 8

£31.13. 5
1.13. 4 **[Agostinho**
£33. 6. 9 **45th sex costs accumulation]**

…To Nina 3rd Oct £35. 0. 0…On board "Hilda" Tuesday from 5 p.m. on 3rd Oct.

[From Wednesday 4 October, during a fortnight's voyage up the Amazon from Manaos to Iquitos, Casement noted only four purchases or items of expenditure; "matches 1.000"; "Wine bill 3.8.0"; "Leticia etc. 51.000" (Leticia is a river port on the Brazil-Peru frontier); "postage 1.000" and made no other remarks except to state "on Hilda" each day and inscribing the name "Remate" on 12th October. This town, Remate de Males, 'Culmination of Evils', on the Brazilian side of the Javari river, is now known as Benjamin Constant.]

25 REMATE DE MALES, OR "CULMINATION OF EVILS"

Remate de Males or 'Culmination of Evils', Amazon port in 1912 on the Brazilian side of the Javary River, since renamed Benjamin Constant

Monday 16 Octr. 1911. Arr. Iquitos, in "Hilda" 9 a.m. and on shore 11.30 a.m. Passages by "Hilda" of Ricudo. R. 135$000 Omarino 135$000 **X** 18.0.0… (270$ @ 15$ to £ = £18)…Drinks etc. self and others and R. & O. (Ginger Ale at Muelle).

Tuesday 17 Oct 1911 At Iquitos [**in Peru**] in Brown's House. Very hot. Out for drinks.

Wednesday 18 Oct. "El Oriente". [**Earlier a "disgraceful little paper,"[551] written-off as an organ of the "Arana gang" edited by Dr Paredes whom Casement described as "a former paid defender of Arana." Yet a "great eulogy of me in today's Oriente!!!" according to the 1911 Black Diary entry for this date.**] Met José.

Thursday 19 Oct **X.** José Gonsalez. Young Pratico [**pilot**] (Present) 10.0 [**shillings**] Wine bill on "Hilda" 21.000 paid on 16th on reaching Iquitos.

33. 6. 9
10. 0 **X** [**José's present**
33.16. 9 **46th sex costs accumulation**]

[**20-21 October**] …Beer 1. Pen 50.

Sunday 22 Oct. At Iquitos. Out with José Gonzalez to Ignacio's stream 8 a.m. To Morona Cocha [**a forest lake and pool**] with José. (9/6 Food 2/0 Canoe 2/0 Tram)…Present to José 4$ 8.0. Evening drinks cocktail with Hdg. and ginger beer [**Casement's favourite fizzy tipple – not Cockney rhyming slang for queer**] Brown. 6.0.

33.16. 9
8. 0 [**the above 4$ present to José**
34. 4. 9 **47th sex costs accumulation**]

Monday 23 Oct. 1911 Out with José Gonzalez to Swim. Ginger ale 2/-. Him 4/-. Ginger ale 1/-. 1/-. 2/-. Soldier "Manuel" 3$. No. 7 Regt.

34. 4. 9
4. 0 [**José**
6. 0 **Manuel's 3$**
34.14. 9 **48th sex costs accumulation**]

[24-29 October] …"El Oriente" 2.0. Ginger Ale 1.0. "El Oriente"…Ginger ale and cakes 1.20. Cazes drink Pisco 40…Ice at Café 40…At Iquitos – Friday 27th. Advance to John Brown **[interpreter]** 3.0.0. Ginger ale 50…Ices. Mrs Cazes and self 80. Cazes and self drinks 1.60. Matches 10. Heavy rain…4 Ices (Omo and Browns) 1.60…17, 18, 19, October: 3 days meals R. O. **[Ricudo and Omarino]** and Brown @ S6 ea. = S18.00.

Monday 30 Oct. Cart for baggage 8S. José Gonzalez came but nothing. Arranged péon. Amer picon 40. Ice etc Brown 60. Ginger 80. 1.80 Ginger ale 50. Matches 10. Dr of "Napo" attending me 2.2.0.

Tuesday 31st Octr. **X** To José 2.60. Present after swim 2.60. Amer picon 80. Ginger ale 50. Whiskey 50. Cgttes 50. Matches 8.

34.14. 9

5. 3 **[José's present goes down in sterling under sex costs**

35. 0. 0 **49th and final sex costs accumulation recorded in this Cash Ledger]**

In Octr.	£113. 0. 9
less Pogson refund	18.10. 0
Actual Expenditure	£ 94.10. 9

[And so the 1911 Cash Ledger ends – on the purchase of a box of matches. The alternate 1911 Black Diary had been gathering pace in the meantime. It makes up in colourful detail for the dull October entries here. At the end of the Ledger there are the following items relating, however, to 1910, with a line under them to enable Casement to carry on with 1911 calculations. The same blue crayon is used here as in the 1910 details at the front. The style of handwriting is similar to one Casement utilised many years earlier.]

…Ramón H. Tapia, 1860 Alvarez, 1860 B. Aires. (11 March 1910, 12 March 1910, 13 March 1910). **[Ramón features prominently in the 1910 Black Diary from 12 March to 3 April. Met at the Zoo in Buenos Aires, he became the subject of a Casement obsession. As soon as his ship left Montevideo for Europe, letters started to be written to him while yearnings lingered on for eighteen months. The other financial and personal weight details for 1910 are precise but obscure.]**

Mch 1910 B. Ayres (Mch 12 13 14) Ramon 22 pesos = 2.0.0 gold 2.0.0. 13 Mch. Francisco 7$ **[Francisco has to be the "sailor with request of fleet"**

John Brown, Casement's Montserrat-born interpreter in Iquitos, in a collar of jaguar teeth 1909, from the book of photographs of the 1912 Viaje de la Comisión Consular al Río Putumayo y Afluentes (p. 101)

noted on 13 March 1910] Pampa 7$, Plaza 1$, Cabs 4$, Trains 2$, Sundries 3$ = 2.6.0.
Mch 15 Weight on getting to Mar del Plata **[in 1910]** K 74.100... **[end of 1910 items.]**

[There is next a mix of financial calculations and currency conversions for the first ten months of 1911, laced with memories of old 'friends', and a list of Iquitos anticipations and expectations, checked off against meetings and sightings so far:] Expenditure 1911: 1 Jan to 30 June 552.18.10, July 206.16.2, August 168.10.10, September 110.2.11, October 113.0.9, November, December **[amounts for these final two months never filled in]** My cheque to Pogson at Pará for £18.10.0 made up as follows...Stamps Father Smith 5$400; His cheque for Dickey £8...Should be only £18.3.5 but I made the extra to cover possible loss of exchange. I suggested he should return it in settlement of the furniture.

To see (D.V.) in Iquitos – Oct 1911 **[Casement had been in Iquitos, in 1910, from 31 August to 14 September and from 25 November to 6 December. His time then had been high on visuals but low on sexual product, largely because he was staying at the home of David Cazes. He obviously intended to rectify this.]**

Ignacio. **[Ignacio Torres, then a nineteen-year-old steward on the *Liberal*, the flagship of the Peruvian Amazon Company, featured in a number of**

ways in both the White and Black Diaries of 1910. He had a "huge erection" on 24 November 1910 but was not to be found in 1911. Ignacio, a former soldier from Taropoto, claimed to be Spanish yet Casement described him on 5 December 1910 as "almost a pure Indian" who spoke Quechua as his native language. Unsuccessful attempts were made to contact him earlier in 1911 from the UK.[552]]

Simon Pisango – seen **[Indian pilot "with a nice face" also on the S.S *Liberal* in 1910 who again saddened Casement by abandoning his ethnic roots and Iberianising his name. The new moniker, however, eluded Casement who variously called him Pisgara, Pizarro, Perez and Pisango, as well as both Simon and Samuel.]**

"Cajamarca" – seen

Beautiful legs

Young big eyes

Huge one. – Police **[word bracketed over all three descriptors]**

Office boy Cazes – (gone) – saw night.

Shop boy Do. – gone **[On 3 December 1910 he was "feeling left pocket."]**

Antonio Cruz Perez. – seen **[Obsession of 1910, photo taken on 3 December.]**

Huge one plain clothes – Yes. **["The huge Cholo policeman" of 8 September and 5 December 1910; featuring in 1911 from 9 November.]**

Julio. – no sign of. **[Julio, a well-dressed Huitoto Indian boy and tease, got a number of mentions in November and December 1910 in both the White and Black Diaries, once "feeling it and holding it down in pocket." Whether he was servant or slave was an unresolved issue in Casement's mind, although the evidence points to the former.]**

Brown legs, woodcutter. – no sign

Soldier Boy. – no sign of **["Young and lovely and a soldier from Lima", he had been spotted in 1910 on 5 December.]**

Do. of Photo. – Gone, I fear.

Pink Stout Beauty – no sign of **[On 3 December 1910 Casement had noted "Saw Beauty…in pink shirt."]**

Pilot's boy José Gonzalez – came 18th & 19th Oct. et seq. **[These October dates relate to 1911 as do the other follow-up remarks, above. Boys simply marked "seen" or "gone" and José Gonzalez have their names stroked out. One José Gonzalez had been mentioned by name on 7 December 1910, a tall rubber tapper born in 1885, but he was on board ship heading "up Acre for 3 years – a fine young chap" and is not this apprentice pilot who took up so much of Casement's time in Iquitos in 1911.]**

Spent first 6 months 1911 £515.11.7…

11

1911 Diary

Due to its heavy sexual content, this is the one Black Diary which has never been published before. A "Letts Popular Desk Diary for 1911",[553] it measures ten by eight inches and is interleaved with thin pink blotting paper. It is remarkably heavy, and was extensively restored by Kew in 1972. The green leather jacket is covered in advertisements on the back of which are a few doodles; "W.C." in large stylised lettering is one, and "Coleman Coffee Coup" another. These words must be prompted by one advertiser's Coleman Street address. There are alternatively three and four days on each page of the diary which has horizontal and vertical blue lines. Initial entries appear from 1 to 18 January. The duplicate 1911 Cash Ledger was maintained from 1 January to 31 October 1911. Double entries therefore exist in January, and again from 13 August until the end of October 1911 with this diary concluding on 31 December 1911. On the front, faintly written, is the diarist's note: "Begun in Paris. Ended in Barbados at sea in S.S. France." At the end there is a page of ads for The Yorkshire Insurance Company and Dr J. Collis Browne's *Chlorodyne* for coughs.

This is now an unabridged version of the 1911 diary. As before, the author's annotations are in bold within square brackets.

As with the 1903 and 1910 Diaries there are a number of opening and end pages of notes and memoranda. In this instance there are four at the beginning and two at the end related mostly to Casement's second Putumayo journey in 1911. They deal with Amazon history, populations of Indians, a figure of 15,000 being "asserted" for Iquitos (although many Indians would not have been counted), flora and fauna and the fate of the men of the Peruvian Amazon Company guilty of atrocities. The second page after a detail of the numbers and nationalities of electors in Iquitos ends with several quotes from a local newspaper, the *Loreto Comercial*. The third page consists largely of quotations from the 1883 book by Henry W. Bates *Naturalist on the River Amazona*. On the fourth page there are two paragraphs in Spanish on Putumayo history copied from an Iquitos newspaper of November 1911.

According to the 1912 edition of the *Statesman's Year Book* the main currency unit in Peru was the sol or half sovereign, that in Brazil the milreis (indicated by a dollar sign) which traded at just over two shillings. The

Casement in the black morning coat bought for Herbert Ward's Paris party on 3 January 1911, with top hat, cane, gloves, Regent Street studio

Well dressed Iberian with bright, protruding tie

1876 Peruvian census counted a population of 2.6 million: 2% negro, 14% white, 25% Mestizo ("Cholos & Zambos") and 58% Indian although it was also stated "many uncivilised Indian numbers are absolutely unknown." By 1908 the population of Peru was estimated to be 4.5 million. Brazil had 22 million, Pará state having nearly half a million, and the Amazon city of Manaos 50,000 inhabitants. It was noted that the Peruvian constitution prohibited the public exercise of any religion but Roman Catholicism. This later creates problems for Casement. In 2015, the population of Iquitos (both Europeans and Indians) was 437,000. It remains inaccessible by road.

Cesar S. Goyzueta was asst. of Normand in Matanzas when he saw Normand bake a small Indian boy on the ovens. He shot the child. Peruvian soldier now was "sacked" for this! Probably in the Putumayo.
New York Spanish & Peruvian rendezvous
Hotel America (14th Street) Union Square kept by a Peruvian – all go there. Spanish spoken. Macedo may be there.
Elias Martinengui at Callao
45 000 Indians
15 000 in Dr Dickey's time 1908 by the Jefe's…
Fonseca & Montt have ten (10) Boras Indians at Santa Theresa on Javary.
Aurelio Rodriguez broke bail £2000 6 Augt. Harding of J. Lilly reported to Dr Dickey & got off. But Macedo caught by wireless [??]
Commandante at Tabatinga is Manfredo de Miello.
Peruvian Lt. who went down to Nazareth is Lt. Riocco.
José P. de Campos Junior (at Manaos) Brazilian Police Officer who was sent to Remate de Males.

[2nd page:]
No. of Municipal Electors in Iquitos in Oct. 1911 was 7500 – out of asserted population of 15.000 ("Loreto Comercial 13 Nov 1911)
The Register of Electors was published for the first time in 1903 & 1905 when there were only 463 electors subscribed, composed of
304 Peruvians &
159 foreigners
463
The Foreigners consisted of Spaniards 63 Italians 37 Portuguese 16 French 10 Brazilians 8 British 2 Moroccans 2 Russian 1 Dutch 1 Mexicans 1 Ecuadorian 1 142
leaving 17 not denominated – probably Germans.

[At edge] 14. Nov. 1909

The U.S.A. Consul Charles Eberhardt left Iquitos in the "Elisa" to explore the Javari both commercially and industrially. — *Loreto Comercial* of 14 Nov. 1911

1898 – 14 Novr. – with No. 260 & after nearly 5 years of life expired the Iquitos weekly "El Independiente" of which was editor since its founding Benjamin C. Dublé.

[3rd and 4th pages:] Bates on the Hyacinthine Macaw.
p. 67 *Naturalist on Amazon.*
First saw this bird at Patos up the Tocantins. Name – *Macrocereus hyacinthinus* of Lath. Guarani name Araruna.
"One of the finest & rarest of the Parrot species. Occurs only in interior of Brazil from 16°.5 latitude to southern border of the Amazon valley. 3 feet long from beak to tip of tail. Entirely of blue save around the eyes where the skin is marked & white. It flies in pairs. Feeds on the hard nuts of several palms, but chiefly on the Mucujá palm (*Acrocomia lasiospatha*)
p. 247 He killed 6 Hyacinthine Macaws at Tapajoz at Cupari River waterfall – Their craws were full of the pulp into which they had crushed the nuts etc. Tucumá palm (*Astrocaryum Tucumal*)
They were found feeding in flocks on this palm.

Grand Para owes its name to the Tupi original being only a corruption of Parana guassie – "Great River" 13 Nov. 1499 – from Puerto Palas sailed Vicente Yánez Pinzon to discover the Amazon which he called "Santa Maria de la Mar Dulce".

From "Loreto Comercial" of Iquitos of 16 Nov. 1911…Harding says this protest was mostly "political" – and dealt with the then proposal of Peru in favour of Colombia.

JANUARY

1 SUNDAY In Paris all day. Went Av. du Bois & met Denis & then to Prefecture & Quai d'Orleans to lunch. Back to Hotel & out to Boulevards. Met Pierre & to Gare du Nord. Enormous. & fine – Back & turned in – "Oui! Msieur. Je suis bien servi." Took in mouth – with much groaning & struggle & moans of love. **[Pierre is quoted as saying just bien servi – 'well served' in the 1911 Cash Ledger where he is costed at forty francs.]**

2 MONDAY In Paris. Went to H.W.'s & saw them all. Lunched there & then to Br. Embassy & saw Bertie **[Sir Francis Bertie, Ambassador in Paris from 1905 to 1918]** who asked me to lunch tomorrow at 1. Went to Prefecture of

Police – no one there [**These frequent calls with the police are most likely to do with Casement obtaining a *billet de sour* or sojourn ticket, a necessity for foreign travellers when in France, until the 1950s.**] – & on to Montparnasse. No models – Cold. Up to dinner with Dick & Noisy Nick at Hotel Mercedes. [**Dick and Nick were in fact Dick Morten and an entirely peripheral individual, Harry Nicholson "a retired but energetic R.N. Captain" hence the 'Noisy' epithet. This is according to the privately printed biography of Herbert Ward, *An Erratic Odyssey* compiled by his eponymous (clergyman) son whose wife was Noisy Nick's niece. No forger could surely have contemplated introducing such obscure individuals and then hiding them under a nickname. All Herbert Ward's (and Casement's) old Africa cronies seem to be gathering for the party. Ward entertained royally courtesy of his wife's money.**] Could not leave at 10 so missed poor Pierre in Place de la Bourse – & met Beast at Place de l'Etoile who got £2 gold & 30 fcs gold & 12 fcs silver = 92 francs! [**Casement was rolled, that is robbed of ninety-two francs, by someone pretending to offer gay services who turns on his client usually when he is at his most vulnerable. There are a number of mentions in the Casement documentation of robberies (including one, surprisingly, by a Maltese ruffian) and other unexplained losses suggesting he was prone to such occurrences. In 1890 he reported his watch was lifted by a pickpocket at a public meeting in London addressed by the explorer Henry Stanley for whom he once worked. The event was attended by the Prince and Princess of Wales. It is possible he had been rolled on that occasion too, a pickpocket substituting for the robber. Casement complained bitterly to Gertrude "I had my watch stolen in the hall – so that was all the profit I had from my visit there." That watch, Nina recalled had been presented to him "by a dear dead friend...when a boy at the Ballymena high school."**[554]]

3 TUESDAY In Paris – Went to H.W.'s Studio & with Dick down town. Bought hat, gloves, collar & Hkfs at Paquins & to Embassy at 1 to lunch. Sir F. Bertie & Lady Féo – & Lady Hardwicke & Sir H. Austin Lee & young Phipps & Bertie's son & son's wife there. Told something of Putumayo to them. Like Lady Féo. [**Sir Francis Bertie's wife was born Lady Feodorowna Wellesley**] To H.W's studio with Mitchell [**correctly spelt Michell, he was to be appointed later in the year to Iquitos**] the Vice Consul who was on Congo as a tame Vice Consul & got sick. Big dance in Washington Palace in honour of Cricket & Dimples, about 180 there. [**Ward's daughters were nicknamed Cricket & Dimples, Casement sometimes calling the latter Mac Dimpler**] Did not leave till 3.30 & to bed at 4.15 a.m. Coat from Tailor Hill. [**The dress coat cost him the then enormous sum of £16.8.0, as Casement recorded in the Cash Ledger on 10 January, and "worse luck to it." The**

full-length photograph of the tall Casement in his tails with hat, cane and gloves makes him look like a spindly giraffe.[555]]

4 WEDNESDAY Left Paris (Very glad to do so indeed) with Dick & Noisy Nick – Cold journey & bad crossing of the channel – swell & cold. Late at Dover & Victoria only 8 p.m. Luggage out & took Dick to Marylebone Station & then on to 110 Philbeach Gardens & got rooms. Out for dinner at 9.10 p.m. & to Gatti's via Leicester Square where Ernest.
Cab to Euston 2/- & "Fred" after 15/-.

17 0	**[Fred and cab**
16 0	**Ernest**
1 13/-	**Total]**

Letter from Nina saying she wd. be at Ly. Rd. on Friday.
[In margin:] Ernest "Enormous" **[He was gifted 10/- and 6/- according to the Cash Ledger on this date.]**

5 THURSDAY Ernest. To Allison's – & got trunks thence & sent off the plates & things of Barnes & Gielgud. Then home changed clothes & to F.O. Saw Malet **[Louis Mallet]** & long talk with him about Putumayo & the horrible illtreatment of the Indians there. Saw Sperling too (whom I don't like) and missed Tyrrell who had gone to a wedding. I like Malet – he was full of sympathy for the Indians. Spicer away till Monday. Back & cheap dinner at Earls Court & then to Ernest in Chandos St. & Compton St. – 8.40. 9.50. Things in town. After saw several Darkies – 9 Japanese (fine types) & 4 Chinese all on look out & one young Italian model **[possibly contemporary slang for rentboy]**. Cold night. Also 11" in cab to Westminster Bridge.

	2. 4. 6	**[Ernest]**
Cab	10/-	
	5/6	**[Second cab]**
	3. 0. 0.	

6 FRIDAY Wet day – Wrote letters all morning – To Tom & others & then lunch at Stewarts at 1.30 & on to A. Slavery Soci[**et**]y where saw Harris & Travers Buxton for a minute & Gooch & got papers I wanted from Harris. They will cost £6.6/-. Awful. **[This huge cost merited an X when accounted in the Ledger entry for 10 January.]** Home after seeing R. Lynd at "Daily News" office & to dinner at 8.30 p.m. at Stewarts. Reading & writing most of the day & all evening & feel very tired. Saw Gooch **[G.P. Gooch, a former**

Liberal MP, and historian who signed the London reprieve petition.] who said Mrs. Green in Rome – coming home soon.

7 SATURDAY Expect meet old Nina today. Called on her in evg & out to dinner with her at Stewarts & then home & turned in tired early. At F.O. at 3. & got note from Louis Mallet asking me to write a short preliminary report to try & get some of the criminals hanged. Alas! no chance of that – Home & started it and did most of it before 7 p.m. when out for Nina –

8 SUNDAY Finished report – preliminary one on Putumayo – wrote also F.O. two letters for Departmental control – Chief Clerks – & in house all day. Out to dinner late at 9. in Knightsbridge & then to Park & Gate There splendid types & to Oxford Circus & home by Bus & foot – pleasant walk. 8/- **[Welsh Grenadier in Park as per Ledger]** **X** 8/-

9 MONDAY Busy first draft of Report & long letter to Mallet which sent by special messenger to F.O. at 11 a.m. Wrote Fraser too on Life Certificate & lunch in house & out to tea with Nina at 4. Called Louie Heath, but she in Droitwich & then at 6.40 to Paddington & there till 7.10 **[station toilets presumably as no train met or caught.]** – No sign & on by taxi to Robert Lynd & very pleasant evening there with Sylvia & R. & a friend named Riddell from Belfast – talked till 11.15 & home by Tube – got "American Egypt" & letters from Harris, Bertie & also got photos from photoman. Many Amazon prints I fear spoiled.

10 TUESDAY Very cold morning. To Allison's with photos & keys & to get a typist to come. Got things needed. Lunch at Holborn – some <u>beautiful</u> types in streets. Back at 3 after visit to Anti-Slavery & C.R.A. but no one in at either. Wrote letters & to Nina for a moment and then to Sloane St to dinner & Nina & out busing to Oxford Circus, Marble Arch &c. Very cold night. Another letter from Julio C. Arana tonight to see me. The swine! From Mallet also a letter about Iquitos Indians.

11 WEDNESDAY Cold miserable morning, drizzle. Letter from Moule. Katie gone on stage as a chorus girl at Sheffield! Alack! – Alack! **[Katie O'Shea had married a West Africa acquaintance, Bill Moule, whom Casement thought "an ass". She was not living up to her Parnell inheritance in his eyes.[556]]** EDM's article in Manchester Guardian. In to F.O. I saw Spicer – awful ass. He put on the usual official asinine attitude. To lunch with Strachey at Carlton Grill Room (£1.3/-) and then to Mallet. Saw Turkish ambassador. **[There is an unconfirmed story that Casement was being sounded out for a job as some sort of observer or administrator in Macedonia.]** Mallet had not

yet got the Report – the special one – I sent by hand on Monday morning for him! Spicer had intercepted it & "sent it to printer". The pig-dog – to prevent speedy action if he could. To Fulham Theatre with Nina to "Tales of Hoffman" – not good or well done either. [**According to Nina, Casement thought of theatres as "frivolous amusements." It is certainly true that he rarely had a good word to say about a performance. In contrast "movies he told me he liked because you could go in when you liked and leave the same way."**[557]]

12 THURSDAY In house all day writing & getting ready for the typist tomorrow – wrote letters and got my a/c in shape. My expenditure all told in Putumayo £508 odd of which only £239 is personal for 164 days. It is less than 30/- a day – wonderfully cheap for a journey to heart of S. America of such a kind – yet the F.O. kicks! In after dinner & turned in at 10 p.m.

13 FRIDAY In house all day till 7. Typist came at 10 – a stupid fellow from Yost's – not like the Congo man – This one no good. He muddled the a/cs & did very little all day. I did most by hand – & got a lot of the things done. To dinner at Stewarts & turned in at 10.30 after.

14 SATURDAY In house all day till 6.30 with typist to 1 p.m. & then alone – when I finished the FO a/cs of my journey. They have been vexatious because so many trifles to be remembered & vouchers hunted up. To dine at 7 with Gee, Lizzie & Nina at Stewarts [**according to the Cash Ledger, Sidney Parry was also with them**] & then all to my rooms & talked till 10.20 & gave them Indian collars of animal teeth. They are to come to lunch tomorrow.

15 SUNDAY In house all day writing out my statement of a/c for F.O. Dinner at 8 in Victoria I think 2/3 & a walk and home.

16 MONDAY In house with typist dictating to him the first part of my report on Putumayo concerning the ~~Indian~~ Barbados men & their treatment. He is an ass & cannot type or take down dictation either. Gee & Liz to tea & Eddie also at 4. – 5 [**the three Bannister siblings together.**] Dined with Colonel Bertie at Wellington Club. Saw "Cui" who is being divorced by Mrs Cui. Home at 1.30 a.m.

17 TUESDAY In house all day. With Gee & Lizzie to lunch at 1.30. Gee to Paddington & Reading. I to dinner at Stewarts & then walked all round to Oxford St. &c. &c. none. A little dictation today – less than 1 hour, but the man is so slow.

18 WEDNESDAY About 1½ hours dictation – but he is no good & I wrote

to say he must go on Friday. Dictated down to Stores & peculation by the Company. Invited Nina to dinner. **[The 1911 Diary ends abruptly here and is not taken up again until Casement resumes entries on Sunday 13 August, just prior to the commencement of his return journey to the Amazon and Peru. In the intervening months there is a scattering of notes and jottings: A street plan runs over the three days 20 to 22 February, while on the blotter opposite 3 to 5 April the words "A. Pogson, Esq., H.B.M. Consulate Pará" can be read. Opposite 27 to 30 April on the blotter is the diarist's full new title (from July that year) of "Sir Roger Casement C.M.G". These half dozen legible items are actually blottings of separate letters or envelopes. Some can only be read with the use of a mirror as the ink has not penetrated through to the other side. Opposite 8 May the blotted phrase "keep them in your house" can be distinguished. Those opposite 15 to 17 May include the words "Reported lost or stolen. Please look", while another is an address for "D. Brown esq. Booth & Co, Iquitos" and is dated 6 November 1911. It is hardly credible that these blots have been forged.**

On 24 May Casement deleted "Empire Day" and substituted the words "Queen Victoria born." This reflects Casement's sentiments about the long-serving monarch about whom he wrote a dreadful poem in 1897: "…May we from out the scattered race/Which looks to Britain and to thee/ As one, to draw our heart to thee/Altho' we have not seen thy face…".[558]

On 13 August, the 1911 Black Diary recommenced following a somewhat pointless one day trip to Dublin. Only sparse notes and reminders are inscribed until Casement reaches Barbados on 28 August 1911.]

AUGUST

13 SUNDAY Left Dublin for Sasana. **[Gaelic for England or Saxony]**

14 MONDAY Arr. London at 7.30 & to Philbeach Gdns.
Took tickets by Royal Mail to Barbados.

15 TUESDAY To Barnes at Club.

16 WEDNESDAY Sailed from Sp'ton on "Magdalena" for Barbados at 10 a.m.

My passage	21. 12/-	
My two Indians	36. 0. 0	
	£57. 12/-	**[identical amounts are in the Cash Ledger]**

Arr. Cherbourg 6 p.m. – sailed –
M. Fabre & his son embarked there.
[Cash Ledger: Left S'ptn 12 noon. Cherbourg 7.20. Left 8.20. Fabre and son on board bound to Quito.]

17 THURSDAY Crossing Bay of Viscaya **[Biscay]**

18 FRIDAY Out towards Azores – Getting wireless messages. **[No entry for Saturday]**

20 SUNDAY Arr. Ponta Delgada at 2 p.m. in St. Michael's **[island]** of the Azores. All shut up. Stupid old town – clear sea in harbour. On shore & young Portuguese (22) took me to gardens. Told me all were monarchists on the island. Bought 3 bottles very good white wine for 10d. each. Soldier in grey (26) at pier head – big erection – looked & love long after my boat – would have given much to stay & see later.

21 MONDAY On for Barbados. **[These words are repeated, sometimes only by the ditto abbreviation, "Do." for the six days from 22-27 August.]**

28 MONDAY Arrived Barbados on Magdalena S/S & on shore at 10 a.m. & to Seaview Hotel after seeing O'Donnell at Ice House. **[Andrés O'Donnell was, in Casement's eyes, something of a lesser Putumayo criminal, being part Irish. He had migrated to the island, taken a grand house there and was now preparing for his marriage to a Barbadian lady, Miss Turney, "daughter of the man who had charge of the public gardens" at Queen's Park. He was also intent on starting a hotel business. Next day Casement passed on the intelligence to the Foreign Office which resulted in an extradition warrant issuing from Peru for O'Donnell on a murder charge. The marriage nonetheless went ahead at Christmas and was "a feature of the day"[559] according to Lt. Col. R.I. Kennedy who kept Casement posted on the saga.**

The couple were married "by Father McCormack SJ", the priest who had refused to board Casement's Indian boys Ricudo and Omarino. Writing a year later on 20 December 1912, the Colonel explained that O'Donnell had beaten the rap and was now "liberated". He had "had a very clever coloured barrister named Reece" and the magistrate accepted Reece's view that the Peruvian warrant was defective. Lt. Col. Kennedy felt the Peruvians had not tried too hard but O'Donnell did take the island's general advice and, in fear of another warrant arriving "cleared out leaving his wife about to be confined."] Fabre & son & rest went on in "Magdalena" to Trinidad & Colon.

29 TUESDAY In Barbados. **[Casement knew Barbados well having recuperated there for two months in 1908 after one of the most serious of his myriad illnesses, acute gastritis. One author aptly described Casement as "a connoisseur of fevers."[560] On 20 August 1908 he had complained of Barbados to Bulmer Hobson, calling it "This ghastly little Britannic island of prigs and paupers."[561]]** Wrote Spicer about O'Donnell. **[The entry for 30 August is simply "Do.".]**

31 THURSDAY Called at Ursuline Convent on nuns & Father Smith.

SEPTEMBER

1 FRIDAY My Birthday 47 today. Nina is over 55! At Barbados. The Biddys came at 6. Very sick at sight of them. They are beggars like all here.

2 SATURDAY In Barbados. Tried to get Dudley Stanson by telephone from Bathsheba. Poor boy could hear nothing of him. Saw Coleridge King & the other poor white boys.

3 SUNDAY Bathed & read novels.

[At top of page:] 4 Sept. Met Stanley Weeks at Barbados. Came back from Trinidad by "Voltavia" on 28 August & is looking for work at the electric. 20 years old. **[See below and Cash Ledger entry for 4 September 1911 for more on Stanley Weeks.]**
4 MONDAY Out at 8.30. Met Coleridge King & took his a/c at Mrs Seon's. **[She ran the Sea View Hotel in Hastings. Her letterhead read "Proprietress Mrs I. Seon. Cuisine properly attended to. A well stocked Bar."[562]]** Gave him 5/-. **[In margin: X** 5] Then to Bath & met Stanley Weeks 20 years. Has certificate from Trinidad Electrical concern – trying to get work here at the Electrical. Bathed together first 9 a.m. Huge one & then 12.45 – Huger still. Hung down curved & swollen & wanted awfully. **[In margin: X** 5] Poor boy. Wished I had taken him. Will try & get him to Iquitos **[Casement's fantasy collecting syndrome again.]** Was waiter once in a B'bados Hotel. Two scars on face from fall. One on thigh too – & it – off in Boniface for Pará with Ricudo & Omarino.

5 TUESDAY "Boniface" is a filthy tub. Has 16 passengers with accommodation for 5. A Dr Dickey on board – was the doctor at El Encanto once. Speaks Huitoto. Told me that Fonseca & Montt are at Sta Theresa, about 7 hours up Javari on Brazilian side. Working under contract for a firm called Edwards

& Serra – Fonseca is a ~~West Indian~~ Mauritino darkie – latter a Brazilian. Normand said to be in Argentina at Mendoza. ~~Gesuito~~ Goyzueta (a former man with Normand) told Dickey a letter had been received from Normand from Argentina. Dickey says that Aurelio Rodriguez escaped – broke away. Wireless sent to Lima for Macedo's arrest. O'Donnell had a bill for £680 protested by the Coy. in London. He leaves for Manaos by "Clement".

6 WEDNESDAY Dr Dickey was 14 months on Putumayo. He came overland from Colombia – down Caquetá to Putumayo. Thinks the Colombians are much better than the Peruvians. Gesuito is a soldier now of Peruvian army. He told Dickey that Normand once at Matanzas when he was there put two little Indian boys on a kitchen fire across the bars & roasted them alive. The skin peeled off & they were baked – but still living – so he, Gesuito, for pity shot them both to end their agony. He was dismissed for this & is now in the army. Dr Dickey says the Colombians are much better than the Peruvians. He likes the Tarapoto and Moyobamba & Urimefury Indians, like Ignacio Torres – but not the Quechua or Corteño – Dublé, he tells me is a blackmailer – his own words. He got money from the Masonic Lodge at Manaos for his wife & children & spent it on a motor car & two harlots. Then got more from Iquitos Masonic Lodge.

[At top of page the address of an old friend from 1908:] Dr Carlos Ornstein – Medico – 173b Benjamin Constant. Pará
7 THURSDAY Still at sea entered Amazon water this morning when over 700 miles from Pará & about 520 from central mouth of Amazon itself. The greenish -black hue has replaced the blue clear strain of sea. Ran 221 miles yesterday – 240 – & Monday-Tuesday 186 & 647 miles leaves 683 miles to go to Para. & 573 to Salinas. **[At side and in middle:]** 186 240 221 683 1330 Should be in Pará & alongside wharf at 4 p.m. So they say. Shall go on shore to Baptista Campos & look for João Anselmo at 251.

[At side:]
256 miles run
903
1330
427
110
317

8 FRIDAY We have come 903 miles from Barbados and are about 430 from Pará. Should get to Salinas at midnight tomorrow, Saturday, where we must anchor for the night, and so will not get to Pará till Sunday afternoon – Mate

says we shall go alongside wharf at 4 p.m. If so I'll go to Hotel do Commercio & after room & dinner will be out to Praca do Palacio where I hope almost at once to run across a good big one. Will grasp & off to Marco. It is delightful to think of Olympio & the others.

9 SATURDAY Steaming in Amazon water some time now. Since 7th really – but did not see the line of division. Thinking much of poor young Stanley Weeks at Bridgetown and his beautiful specimen and his gladness in showing it and youth and joy. His glorious limb of Antinous! **[The Emperor Hadrian's much sculpted boyfriend Antinous drowned while swimming in the Nile at Alexandria in 120 A.D.]**

10 SUNDAY Should arrive Pará – Will go shore & to Hotel do Commercio for night. **[It is situated at "Boulevard Da Republica e Rua da Industria."[563] Casement noted in his Cash Ledger "arrived at 5 p.m."]** Expect find Olympio & I hope the Grand Mulatto **[mixed race, African and European]** – & others. Arr. Pará alongside 4 p.m. On shore to Hotel do Commercio. After dinner out to Palace Square. None. To B. Campos – some & one Huge standing on young Portuguese & girl. To Nazareth & Paz & Palace again till 12.40. Not one.

[At top of page:] João 251 Baptista Campos. Will (D.V.) go Baptista Campos at 6.30 a.m. & find I hope before 7.30. João Anselmo de Lima – If I do I will instantly give 15$000 & invite for tonight without any misunderstanding. **[This resolve about unambiguous generosity, after a typical private conversation with himself, did not come to pass. João, a flower seller at the cemetery got only 10 milreis.]**

11 MONDAY Saw João at 7.30 a.m. but did not speak – too many about – He looked poor. To Pickerell & Cox – & then to Pogson **[Picky and Poggy, the American and British consuls, respectively.]** & Niece & Customs & got baggage after. Rain at 5 p.m. Saw a magnificent caboclo boy at 1 p.m. – white pants & huge *testemunhos* **[The word in Portuguese actually means witnesses but Casement enjoys the literary allusion based on the ancient Greeks' custom, when swearing an oath, of holding their testicles as visual proof of their sincerity.]** & stiff, also; 7½" lying – thick across thigh. Wired F.O. about Fonseca & Montt. 4 p.m. out after dinner to Palace Square. None. To B. Campos, Beer. Not a soul & to Paz Square. None anywhere – all in theatre. To Palace Square again. Saw Barber of 1908. Huge exposure long snake & *testemunhos*, grey pants & then a Portuguese about 27. well dressed, huge one. Stiff all across square to Palace & sat down. Very shy wanted! hugely – about 9" – I think. Left & home after long stay at Theatre at midnight. Wished I take Portuguese. He sat beside me on seat & wanted awfully.

12 TUESDAY Tuesday 12. Sept. Out to Souza. Seeing glorious Ceará caboclo type in Nazareth Square on seat. At Souza, Vermouth – then back to breakfast with Pogsons at 12 but it was 1 a.m. **[sic]** before we sat down to a vile grub. Fine Cockatoo – Back at 3 & lay down with headache. Out after early dinner 6. to Big Square. None – & then B. Campos – beer – & round several times – none. To Nazareth none & to Paz Gardens. One possible offer – but small & dirty – so back to Palace Square & there on seat "Passear" of long ago – Bared but I none & home 9.15 & turned in in new room.

13 WEDNESDAY Lovely morning – intend going Val de Caens on foot today. **X.** Left 7.30. Tram to Marco. Saw lovely boy yellow pants on way at Tram corner. Huge one. Soft face. To Una. Bathed. Big caboclo – small one. On to Val de Caens. Mrs H. in bed. so turned back. Bathed Una & old Indian – long one – & to Public House drinks & back to Marco at 1 p.m. & home 1.30. tired & hungry. No food since 6 p.m. last night! Dr Dillon Jones to lunch. Cards Ornstein & Chaplain. Then Harvey called & found me with Dr Dickey in room. At 6.30 out to dine Andrews & MacHaffie. Lovely caboclo moço well dressed in corner – Huge exposure – Dined & talked till 9 p.m. & then back to town. Off at cg'tte shop corner where big exposure of morning – but now down. To Palace Square & saw a fat Portuguese middle aged & then suddenly "Whist" under trees on pavement & Tram inspector called & said "Venha ca." **[Come here]** He entered Kiosque I followed & he put hand at once softly fingering & milking – I put hand & found, in dark, a huge stiff one – long & thick and firm as poker. He had near to the dark caboclo.

[At top of page:] Met João Anselmo de Lima at 9 a.m. & gave 10$000. To meet tomorrow at 7 a.m. at Cemetery – but I did not.
14 THURSDAY Saw Enormous one on poor dungaree boy (17 or so) from Hotel window watering spare ground in front. Bare feet & it a huge soft one wobbling under pants. Out to Zoo – seeing many – and on way met João Anselmo de Lima & shook hands long & softly – gave 10$000 He wanted to give me roses but I said tomorrow morning. To breakfast with Andrews & MacH. and back at 2 & lay down & then to Pogson & after light dinner out to Baptista Campos & Cemetery after Paz Theatre where Friend appeared & said "Gosto" **[a pleasure]** – & tried awfully hard – saying "much milk" – worked like Oscar round & round & deep. Back at 10.30 & dressed again & out on a walk but all deserted till after midnight. **X** Friend "pequeno" **[small]** to meet Saturday at 8 p.m.

[On blotter:] **X** Augusto Santos entered

15 FRIDAY Bad headache – did not go out to João at 7 a.m. as was too

seedy. Poor boy – will try & see him later. To Val de Caes at 10.30 to lunch with Harveys and then they brought me back in Lotus. Jig Saw at 7 to 8 p.m. with Ricudo & Dickey. Then out to Palace Square & at once entered Kiosque **[Dispute rages over what exactly a kiosque was with the suggestion that Casement is writing of some sort of shelter. Angus Mitchell displayed a picture of what looked like a small bandstand to the Casement Symposium in Dublin in 2000.]** & huge long one (about 7½" lying), tried to get me. Man of 27 or 28, like Barber wanted awfully. Saw "Passear" too, after at 8.30. so left to B. Campos – Whisky – None & then Paz none & Nazareth (twice) none & Theatre Square & round & round several times. None at all. Saw caboclo Indian at Paz who looked lovely but still at 12 none after another wait at Palace Square. It is the best. Jig Saw till 1.30 a.m.

[On blotter:] Augusto mtg. Saturday **[??]** hard

16 SATURDAY Up tired after Jig Saw & finished it at midday only. After lunch to Andrews & MacH. Expect meet friend tonight at Cemetery & will to Independencia & enter. Returned at 2.30 from Andrews & at 5. to Pogsons till 6.30. Then dinner & at 8 p.m. out to cemetery & met Friend who entered at once – Huge *testemunhos*. Police passing behind paling – but he laughed & went in deeper 10$000. Then to Nazareth & B. Campos & at 9.10 to Paz & there Spaniard young shirt sleeves offered – & also a poor thing & then other fine young, dark haired work Spaniard of Thursday evg at Theatre – on seat in Avenida – & he to theatre & spoke. I came & so home – He wanted & suggested good for Sunday to passear **[walk out]**. Turned in at 9.40 & slept. Sereno called at 4. Huge one – Brown face. Works at Reducto! Shook hands! **[Cash Ledger: X Augusto Tavares dos Santos 10.000... X Met him at 8 Cemetery & in at once.]**

17 SUNDAY To Sacramento with Andrews at 9. after many types & there after 6 for it then to Zoo – & Huge ones on several & so home at 4.45. to beer & then my diary. In evg after rest, out at 7. to Palace Square & almost at once a beautiful moço in white looked & entered Kiosque. Met outside & invited to *passear* and away we went. Felt in darkness big head – & then to B. Campos & on by Souza tram to Marco where in dark travessa **[lane]** he stripped almost & went in furiously – awfully hard thrusts & turns & kisses too & biting on ears & neck. Never more force shown. From Rio. Returned 10 changed & out till 11.30. Huge one in café on moço.

[On blotter:] **X** "Rio" entered huge thrust.

[At top of page:] Felt tired all day. "Augusto" in Tavares Cardozo & Co.

Livraria. **[a book shop]** João Alfredo. **[a street name]** Would not take any present! First since Dublin. **[The last such unremunerated person, "Fine type. Stiff", was found on 17 July 1910 in Phoenix Park. This remarkable note confirms Casement's total acceptance of his status as an older (and richer) man who would not only be expected to pay by gift, but indeed is cheerfully aware that it would be bad form not to offer a present. In João Anselmo's case Casement was annoyed that he had not made this clear earlier. This reveals that he had long recognised the nature of the transactions. The boys are not prostitutes, indeed those on the street are usually eager, but they have self-respect which entails a certain recognition for pleasing a well-off gentleman.]**

[On blotter:] X Augusto Entered hard.
Saw my crested screamer in Zoo. Local name is Seriema. Cariama Cristata (L). **[a red-legged bird]**

18 MONDAY Stayed in house most of day till 7.30 p.m. writing letters & reading a little and then after dinner with Dr Dickey at 7.30 out with "Agassiz" **[a book which later was lost]** for Pickerell & then at corner waiting for tram saw a fine type who looked across street at me too. I waited for 2 trams to pass & then walked along & was looking back at a lovely Ceará caboclo sailor when a moço hurried over & held out his hand & it was this boy. He had followed – At once took my arm & squeezed & led away side – & arranged meet at Nazareth Square at 8. To Dickey ill & then to Nazareth & at 8.15 he came & at once led me off – Felt. Huge – thick as wrist. Only 17 or 18. From Lisbon. 4 years in Pará. Walked to Sao Braz. he squeezing hand & wrist all time & there "assenta!" **[sit down!]** on grass in dark *travessa* he admitted his wish at once & so I took it. First spittle but so big could not get in – then glycerine & honey **[Casement obviously went equipped on these occasions.]** & in it went with huge thrust & he suck on me & worked hard. "Calor"! **[hot!]** Refused any present. **[The Home Office reader left an instruction to "Photo" this and the next two days of entries.]**

[Cash Ledger: To Augusto of Tavares for his tram from Marco 1000 Refused to accept. Did not meet "Rio."]

19 TUESDAY I went to Pogson & Andrews at Pará Electric, where saw a most lovely moco I've ever seen I think. Big soft gazelle eyes, tiny moustache & sweet chin & oval face. Well dressed sitting down. We looked often at each other & smiled. Back & Andrews & Mac to lunch. Then Customs to try & get Baggage by Andrews Despachante **[Customs agent]** – but failed. Inspector refuses allow it to go! Said I'd leave it altogether. Read "The Heart of Rome".

Out to Ornstein at 6.45–7. Left card. After dinner to cemetery & saw waiting there Augusto dos Santos – but passed saying "Boa Noite" **[Good Evening]** & as he did not follow returned to Palace Square – none at all – & to bed at 9 p.m.

20 WEDNESDAY "Hilda" sails today for Iquitos & I can't go in her on account of this baggage delay. Will probably go by "Rio Negro" & try & ship the baggage as cargo by "Javary". Out to Duff & Cole & Zoo. Fine caboclo keeper big one – & then some huge ones and finally "Passear" emerged from office of trams in white & went passed **[sic]**. Will do it with him tonight! **[No. Casement's interest was directed to a better offer which was thwarted by a rival cruiser.]** In evg out to Andrews, but he out. Found MacHaffie in & stayed till 9.30. Then down by Circular to Palace & a caboclo in striped jersey on seat. Looked & wanted & got up to mooch off thro' to shade of trees of Square. I knew he meant it – but while waiting at Kiosque corner a fine caboclo – about 24 – innocent smiling face – broad thick set – in white & bare feet came up softly & timidly & said "Passeando"? I said "Yes" "Si" & then "segue" **[follow]** & he followed. But striped jersey followed too. Caboclo on after me up to jail – but then lost sight – as I hurried on to avoid striped jersey. It was a pity, as his rose stiff as iron pushing out his loose pants straight in front.

[At top of page:] Quinta feira. **[Thursday]** Hope tonight 8.30 meet "Augusto".
21 THURSDAY Spent day in Hotel mostly. To Pogsons sent telegram for Rio about Customs inspector & got reply at 5. Good. Then at 6.20 out to Nazareth & got sandwich & down to Baptista Campos at 7.10. There a glorious young moço, smart set of Pará, came & sat down & talked & asked if "Orenta" – and then got his up stiff as poker & hand in pocket. Wanted it awfully. Literally begged for it. Put arm round neck on seat but had to go for "Augusto". He wanted to come with me. Shook hands & off at Nazareth 8.10 to 8.50. No Augusto – as I feared. So missed both. To Palace Square 9.15 – & there till near 11 but save "Passear", **[i.e. the tram inspector]** none. Last night in Pará & this bitter disappointment. "Passear" got into Ascural tram with me – but I left it soon & back on foot.

22 FRIDAY Leaving today by "Hilda" for Iquitos with Dr Dickey. Pogson down at 9.30 to report his utter failure to get my things out of Customs! The Inspector declined all recognition of telegram or Governor's. So I have to go up river with all my equipment & gear in the hands of the Pará customs! On board "Hilda" at 12.30. A filthy pigsty – I am very sorry I came! What a fool I've been! Even the "Napo" were better than this. We lay to all afternoon – so on shore for a bit & saw glorious type with huge erection on young 16 Portuguese shop boy in Camisaria Moderna, lovely face too in João Alfredo. Left wharf

at 4.30 Andrews & MacH. just in time to cheer & after vile dinner & evg. turned in at 8 p.m. & groaned in travail all night.

[On blotter:] Left Pará in "Hilda"

302$000 **[costs of passage to Iquitos calculation]**

	1.	4¼
		10
	13.	6½
		10
6.	15.	5
		3
20.	6.	3
	1.	8½
£20.	7.	11½

23 SATURDAY Under way at 2 a.m. & soon after got fearful rocking that capsized deck cargo all over place – thought it was a rebellion of the Deck hands. Lovely day. Arr. Tocantins Bay, splendid mouth & tide & sea & breeze and got to mouth of narrows at 5 p.m. "Hilda" is doing 8-9 knots certainly – Pilot says will be in Manaos in 4 days. Thank God! Poor Ricudo & Omarino seem very miserable – altho' I feel less sympathy for the latter who is a wee fox. **[The reality of a uncertain future looming ever closer, seems to have dampened the boys' enthusiasm; Omarino's crime remains a mystery.]** Am awfully hungry all the time. Did Jig Saw puzzle till 3 p.m. Heard from Avellino at Pará – will write him tomorrow. **[This young man first features in a letter to Casement from George Pickerell, the American consul in Pará dated 2 February 1909: "Avellino – I have paid him his salary as you desired and have his receipt for same. He is working away on his lessons about all the time and to date I have no complaint to make."[564] Pickerell does not sound enthusiastic, Avellino bearing all the hallmarks of a classic Casement lame duck. They were usually more trouble than they were worth, as Adler Christensen later evidenced.**

Ernest Hambloch who was Casement's vice-consul in Rio from January 1910 was one of the few of his acquaintances to publish (in 1938) an antagonistic view of him. He describes incidents indicating that his homosexual status was recognised at the time. Avelino, as he is spelt, also features in the book: "One of the clerks at the Consulate was a Portuguese youngster, Avelino. He knew no English and could not write Portuguese correctly.

I could not understand how he came to be there. Pullen told me he had been with Casement at Pará and that Casement had sent for him to come to Rio. He was bitterly distressed when Casement went on leave and left me in charge. I dismissed him when Casement ceased to be titular Consul General, for he was an obstinate youth. He and Casement corresponded frequently, and he regarded himself as Casement's special *protégé*."[565]

A dispute was then to arise over £20 spent by Hambloch in late 1912 for Avellino's passage to Lisbon. Casement reluctantly forwarded half the money, complaining about the decision to use private funds and saying he would write to the consul in Lisbon "to make enquiries for him."[566] The lad's sad fate is further alluded to by Hambloch in a 1913 letter to Casement where the tone is now mixed and suggestive: "How sad about Avelino...I am afraid it is a case of the sins of the fathers...he seems very bad and apparently knows it."

Later in 1913 the gloves come off and in a letter unequalled in rage (except to some that Casement and Nina wrote to supposed friends) Hambloch laid into Casement. "I consider your action in opening a letter plainly addressed to my sister in a clear and legible hand most unwarranted while your excuse for such action given in your letter to my sister is ludicrously inadequate." There are three such furious pages by Hambloch in all. Casement had not been able to contain himself when he was mistakenly sent the sister's letter, but being Casement he had admitted his fault to the lady on resealing it and sending it on.[567]] My passage to Iquitos on "Hilda" is 302$000 = £20.7.11½ @ 1/4¼d. per milreis.

24 SUNDAY At Marajó 6 a.m. where Captain's brother has seringal [**rubber estate**]. On shore & stayed there & next place for some four or five hours. On again at 11. towards Gurupá – "Hilda" steams 9 knots. A young mulatto boy of 16 or 17. on board going to Coary [**Coari**] on Venezuelan frontier to join his father's detachment – the 46th Regiment. Will take him 2 months from Manaos. He has soft, smooth face, tall & thin & huge pisa. Sleeps in hammock outside my door – Huge exposure stiff across left thigh at 5 p.m. Got to Amazon main stream at 3 p.m. – 28 hours from Pará of which some 5 have been stopping = 33 hours steaming as against 24 hours in "Atahualpa" down. "Hilary" overtook us 10.45 & Ambrose past down 11.15 p.m.

25 MONDAY Lovely morning. Due in Santarem at 6 p.m. today. Passing the high hill of Mt. Alegre at 9 a.m. about 6 hours down stream in "Atahualpa" – it will take us 10 hours at least I should think up. Arrvd Santarem at about 4. – A pretty little place – with fine beach and the dark green black water of the Tapajoz scarcely flowing. Many whites & half whites off. Bought 4 parroquets

for 8$ & 100 oranges for 2$. Offered a dear wee monkey for 5$000 – but too young. Many painted cuyias [**type of fruit**] – one fine boy of 18 – dark eyes – born there, but pure white. I thought of Bates & the arrest of Lt. Smith – left Santarem at 7.30. “Hilary” passed up at 11 a.m.

26 TUESDAY Steaming well. Finished “Pilot” jigsaw at 4 p.m. – only 12 hours over it. It is a beast. One parroquet dead – escaped from cage when Ricudo cleaning it. Passed some pretty spots by devious channels. Off Villa Bella at 4 p.m. Very hot day – but not quite so bad as yesterday. A lovely pilot boy on board – young (15) & face like girl – with long lashes & peach cheeks. Expect get Manaos at noon on 28th. “Hilary” will arrive tomorrow. Passed Parintins the boundary between Pará & Amazonas. Stopped to cut grass once & once for fish & so on up sideways.

27 WEDNESDAY Lovely morning – We should pass Itacoatiara tonight & be in Manaos tomorrow. “Hilary” must have got there last night. Passed Itacoatiara at 11 a.m. In sight of it at 10 a.m. Saw big steamer of Madeira Mamoré Ry. Coy. & their lighters. After Itacoatiara steamed past mouth of Madeira & then on left bank past the cattle ranches of Silverio & Constanino Neri – two rogues of the first Amazon water! On in cooling breeze. Passed “Crispin” steaming down river – she must have left about 11 a.m. we have passed miles of cleared ground for cattle on left bank since Itacoatiara – most of it looking parched & burnt. Should be in Manaos at 12 midnight – “Hilary” arr at daylight today. Cool evg. – steaming well – Turned in 10.30 p.m.

28 THURSDAY Stopped in dark and wasted many hours at mouth of Solimões coming into main stream – trying to make fast to right bank of Solimões mouth to cut “capim” for the cattle. Hours wasted. Arr. Manaos 9 & on shore to Hotel Cassina & out after. Met at once lovely caboclo (22) strong & thick one. Smiled & looked many times. Wanted. Then Miguel Gomez of Pará in Tabacaria Cubana & milk & gave cigarette. Took to Alhambra & promised to meet there at 8 tonight. At 7 saw in Avenida with a friend & as awful headache I turned in at 9.30. Saw several beauties, and one distinct offer from a workman in bare feet & whites in Cathedral gardens – but altho’ I said “Boa Noite” I went on after an instant’s pause. Out to Flores at 3 & bathed there – two caboclos, one from Pará, young & graceful & pulled it stiff & wanted – saw mine too. Lovely type of soldier in Barrack Square. Cearense [**from Ceará province**] in tram – perfectly glorious (the loveliest I’ve ever seen almost.)

29 FRIDAY Rather tired today. Sorry I did not see my Paraense friend at Alhambra – Again out to Flores today & bathed. Feel awfully the heat here in

Manaos. Sent to ask if Governor would see me – he said tomorrow only. Spent day mostly in bed lying down & after early & very bad dinner at the Hotel out again – all round Cathedral Square & on up to Bijou where took Grenadine. None that I could see – so I again turned in very early.

30 SATURDAY Young Portuguese in hotel gardens. Asked to *passear*. Hair & beard cut = 4/- ¾d. Life certificate should go home today from Manaos. Saw Dr Dickey & with him to Schopes in afternoon. Indian caboclo boy (19) or so, well dressed followed & smiled. In evg. as I was walking up to Alhambra he overtook me & smiled so I said "passear" & he at once agreed & told me he had been thinking of me all day since first saw me & came out only to "procure" me. Walked to old Palace – squeezed soft, cool hand – saw his honey & then he to Alhambra (4.000) till 8 p.m. tomorrow night. His last words were "Nao me falta." [**'Don't stand me up' – the same words in Portuguese are written in the Cash Ledger alongside mention of a gift of four dollars. Despite Casement's two entries for this day the order of events and people is difficult to follow. Perhaps since expectations were dashed on both occasions, he did not bother dwelling on the precise details. It is also the case that when the sex gets more frenetic and the partners more numerous the clarity of Casement's handwriting diminishes, as well as the sense. This deficiency may reveal a degree of cautious embarrassment, whereby the words are not as readable and therefore less shameful. If so, an ostrich could have done better.**] Later a caboclo work-servant boy – sturdy limbs in Gardens mine huge & he pulled it out. Others came so I fled – leaving him on seat without word.

OCTOBER

1 SUNDAY Dr Dickey to b'kfast & Schully. Then at 2 out & saw young sailor *apprendiz*. Pure Indian boy – only 16 I should say – to Kiosque & agreed meet at 7. Met at 7 at old Palace where I put it in mouth. It got huge & curved down & thick & stiff as iron – Said he wanted to enter & so did – he took off boots & trousers & gave a tremendous one – Then darkie sailor at corner. Lovely neck & asked – Said yes & followed to Palace & in twice – kissing on neck & hugging – awfully strong, huge arms & stiff one. Then a huge darkey 9 inches long & thick & stiff but no chance beyond feeling & then Agostinho of Madeira & home with him all night. [**This must be the same Agostinho whom Casement met in Madeira in March 1903, when the boy was seventeen. Then he complained about Casement's whiskers. He would now be twenty-six. If it was Agostinho again, and he appears to be on closer terms than most partners, with a surname – de Souza – detailed in the**

1911 Cash Ledger and an overnight stay mentioned, it confirms the small, closed homosexual world in which Casement travelled.]

[**At top of page:**] Huge one on caboclo clerk. Stiff & said laughing he wanted to spend night "com rapaz" [**with a boy**]. Up at 5. Stars cooling the sky. Took shower bath & Agostinho in again awfully kind – Three times he did it & three times from the two sailors – in all Six times tonight. [**The 1911 Cash Ledger records the sixteen-year-old Indian sailor's name as "Raymundo (12$)"; number two as "Sailor, Negro" off the "Commandante Freitas (15$)"; the third, Agostinho, merited 40$ or forty Brazilian milreis. Casement then added a comment about the day, "3 lovers had and two others wanted." Angus Mitchell, however, regards so many partners and so many sex acts as proof of forgery, observing "that the climate there is such that to have one partner is heroic – five would be downright impossible." See also the list of gifts and partners' names at end of this diary.**]

2 MONDAY Out to coffee & then by tram to Brewery & to Flores – lovely morning. Bathed at João Pensador's stream & back to hotel at 9 when met Dr D. & Stanley Lewis [**Barbadian steward on the *Liberal* who was assisting the investigation**] & the boys. Then to lunch with Robilliard [**Wyndham Robilliard, British vice-consul in Manaos**] out at Virtue Villa & Macaw Hall. Back at 2 to Hotel where Dr D. called to say "Hilda" not going until tomorrow morning! So out & in Book shop young Barbados man very smart & huge one. Looked at once at me & smiled & came over & asked "if American" & agreed to meet at Bar Vaughan at 8. There but did not see him. Then met young Paraense of Oct 1908 & again last year. [**Possibly Olympio who was "in deep" on 13 December 1910 in Pará.**] Very sweet – smiled & followed – stiff & long about 7" & said loved it. Got it in fearfully long time – clasping & kissing & pushing hard. Bathed in sweat – said he liked it awfully but was afraid & "Vergonha" [**ashamed**]. Then lovely ~~Rio Grande~~ Pará boy too Sul [**south**] (22) caboclo – & got it huge. Said he wd. come but was shy & refused 20$000 but it got stiff & I knew he was warming – he asked where I lived. Then to Agostinho at 11.20 till 12. Bathed & then he entered & did it hard & kissed & loved & so to bed at home at 12.30. [**Agostinho's address of 24 Rua Mons, Coutinho, appears in the Ledger entry of 3 October 1911 followed by the cash detail – "night of 2nd 12 – 1 a.m. 25.000."**]

3 TUESDAY On board "Hilda" at 8 a.m. after paying bill. [**This bill from the Grande Hotel Cassina of Praça da Republica in Manaos dated 3 October 1911 has survived.**[568]] Pilot's apprentice came up smiling & feeling it clearly under trousers – Looks lovingly. Gave cigttes & to João too. "Hilary" sails at

10 a.m. for Europe. Sent Nina £35 & then wrote to Loughlin for Stanley S. Lewis & gave him 10$000. "Hilda" by wharf all day – so out to lunch with Robilliard & Dening **[perhaps Derring, a vice-consul in Manos]** & got splendid Blue Macaw as present from R. Back at 2 p.m. & on "Hilda" & waited till 5 – seeing "Madeira-Mamoré" S/S along side & several fine types – including one young giant Brazilian sailor of 20 "about", speaking English – asked him to come to Iquitos with me & he went for things but we left before return. **[One wonders if this was a cruel hoax or just a notional remark.]** Awfully hot night – & ship crammed.

4 WEDNESDAY We stopped at two spots during night to land "passengers". A fearful crowd on board. The police officer called on me with card from governor of the state at 8 a.m. – so that's all right. Fearfully hot day. One young Brazzy on board about 22 – strong face, long Indianish hair, bronzed & a <u>huge</u> exposure under loose white pants. It is a big curved giant fully 7½" long lying down & thick as a plantain. Lay down most of day – having tried to sleep last night on deck in a long chair – but utterly miserable. At 2.30 passed Purus – about 4. To Anuri, on left bank, long street – by a creek landed passengers & on – At 10 or so got to a night port – Codajas & landed passengers – Very cool delightful night. Breeze across up river delicious but had to sit in chair as Dr Dickey took cabin with fever.

[At top of page:] Charlie's Birthday– He is 50 today! **[brother]**
5 THURSDAY Arrived at Camará, on right bank at 6.30 a.m. & landed some passengers – very happily getting rid of some of the <u>Cows</u>. My Blue Arara is a glorious bird & sleeps in my cabin. On after capim **[grass for fodder]** & landing goods & passengers – and about 130 or so entered Coari inlet – Clear outflow of olive water – very deep – white clay banks – river rises fully 25 feet there – seems tremendously deep & <u>full</u> of fish. A wretched little town – with an Intendencia! Awfully hot! Tried get bath but failed. On shore with Omarino & left again at 4.45. Very glad to get away & out in river again to try & get breeze. Dr Dickey bad with fever – poor beggar. Ricudo & Omo all right. Washed my clothes today & look after parrot. Feel seedy – fear it is the old complaint of Lisbon <u>1904</u> & <u>1909</u>. **[Casement's doctor in 1904 thought he needed an appendectomy. Since the King had recently survived such an operation it was now a fashionable procedure. Suspecting there was nothing operable, as such, Casement declined to proceed. Now his old rectal problems of that time and before were also back. Variously described as a fistula or piles, this region had haunted him for nearly twenty years.**

Energetic anal sex when there is "bleeding aft", as Casement described in his 1903 diary, was hardly likely to encourage healing. In 1893, he had

been obliged to borrow £30 from his uncle John to pay for an operation in St Thomas's Hospital in London. He explained how the operation was "consequent upon my journeys down the West Coast of Africa last year – when the exposure to damp and bad food etc. – brought on an attack of piles which now call for this immediate remedy."[569] In August 1900, his surgeon was advising the Foreign Office "Casement operated on for *fistula in ano* five years ago, needs further surgery; run down, return to tropics highly undesirable."[570] This was not to have the desired effect as he did return to Africa.

There is every indication that Casement's body had been overloaded with malaria and other tropical ailments and that the gastric complaint was prompted by his immune system having been long compromised. His perpetual illnesses reveal a man deteriorating – yet one whose body had hidden strengths. Casement's liberal use of quinine which has something of a narcotic effect could also have had unusual consequences. He justified his quinine habit in a letter of 24 November 1902 to Francis Cowper, remarking archly, "I attribute my good looks to quinine and think of recommending that drug to all ladies in search of new complexions."[571]]

6 FRIDAY Feel better today. Called at many places during night & day. Stopped early at Caiambé on right bank where I went ashore with Ernani, the pilot's boy to try & swim in the lake but it was dirty & no sand. Saw 4 Mutums & 4 Trumpeters here. On again after some hours here & at 2. entered Teffé stream & steamed up it until Teffé Mission where anchored until 8 p.m. Mission steam launch came alongside & took cargo & passengers up to Teffé & we could not go until she returned. A lot of the cargo is bricks! & the clay soil at these spots wd. make glorious bricks. The strong-faced youth with Huge one came & talked to me at 6.30. Is a Cearense & splendid type.

7 SATURDAY Stopped at several places again in night. There are 55 mail ports on our list from Manaos to Tabatinga! & 38 other passenger & cargo ports!! It is perfectly insane the way time is wasted. We are now 15 days out from Pará – with certainly a good fortnight yet before us to Iquitos. Damn Dr Dickey say I! [**These five words are crossed out. Was Casement's ire due to Dickey's fever depriving him of his cabin or had he failed in some other respect?**] On, stopping many times for letters & small loads & cargo. Heavy rain at 5 –6. & earlier. Cool evening & night. Passed Porto Zeco on left bank at 4.30 – & will be at Fonte Boa at 2 a.m. and land cargo there tomorrow morning. Should reach Jutahy tomorrow also – 569 miles from Manaos. I am due now 8.30 p.m. to meet Bramilu at Julieta in Manaos. Poor wee boy!

8 SUNDAY Stopped once or more in night & on again about 5.30 I think– at Fonte Boa at 4 a.m & on again about 5 .30 I think. Landed some passengers there – thank goodness. Rain in afternoon. Bought two turtles for 2$ each. Making very poor going indeed. We stop constantly – to give one letter or pick up one. Towing two huge canoes shaped like Noah's arks – with Indian crews. All here seem Indians probably Ticunos but Lingua Geral dead & gone.

[At top of page:] Took Candy – enema broken I find – only ear syringe left. One week after event. **[Casement is suffering from constipation now and with no enema has to improvise.]** Jutahy to Putumayo 79 miles 15 Hrs.
9 MONDAY Passed Jutahy River at 12 midnight = 569 miles from Manaos in 5d. 7H. Learn that "Napo" was aground there for 3 days. Stopped nearly all today buying turtles – at two places. They have got some hundreds on board I fancy – 60 at one place & then a tremendous lot at a bank covered with them – tame Ticunos Indians did the selling – a profit of 200% at least on Javary = 100 Turtles will give a clear profit of a *conto*. Owing to waste of time will not reach St. Antonio (Putumayo) today. Alack! Altogether near 200 turtles on board. Oluru to Bank. Met "Rio Curaça" at Timbotap & communicated. She is fine boat & lovely young officer (Huge one, long & big) also Indian table boy & others. On at 5.30.

10 TUESDAY Passed S. Antonio do Ica at 3 a.m. Learn of wreck of "Asturiano" a launch chartered by P.A. Coy with 30-40 tons Rubber & that crew & passengers to 40 are waiting for us at Colonia Rio Jano! Pretty good that! Gave medicine to young Practico "Antonio" – Found early at Colonia Rio Jano that the shipwrecked crew &c. had been taken on in "Elisa", Levy's launch of Iquitos – so we are saved that – No! We found them there above Matura, on sandbank about 30 of them. Officers & soldiers have gone on in "Elisa". This is crew & Woodroffe of El Encanto. 32 tons Rubber gone **[Years later, Dr Dickey described how Mr Woodroffe, a very short man, was kitted out in other people's clothes and ended up looking a "sartorial monstrosity."[572]]** & launch of Barcia Hs? ! Tizon in Encanto. Miranda lying by Caquetá. On to S.P. de Olivença midnight. Landed many Turtles. Left there 1 a.m. & on stopping often.

[On blotter:]
213
84
129

Putumayo R. to S.P. de Olivença 84
S.P. de Olivença to Tabatinga 129

Tabatinga to Leticia	2
Leticia to Bocca do Java	10
Bocco do Java to Nazareth sq.	<u>25</u>
	250

"Rio Curaça" leaves Remate de Males every month

11 WEDNESDAY We seem to stop about every 5 to 10 miles on this miserable craft. Heavy misty morning. 131 miles from S.P. de O. to Tabatinga, or say 123 to Esperanza & then 25 from that to Remate de Males = 148 miles to do to get in today. Expect will be tomorrow. Simon Pisango is pilot of wreck. On board. Gave him photos and Whiskey. One fine Cholo **[mixed race male with Indian blood]** boy with big thick one. Gave cigarettes. Also a handsome Cholo 1st class boy of 22 or so. My young Cearense is 22 also. Today must arrange with the Police officer about F & M. Did so. **[Casement was organising the extradition of the two criminals, Fonseca and Montt, by the simple device of landing them on the Peruvian bank of the river.]** He is to go up to S. Theresa at once & try & get F. & M. & put them over on Nazareth where the Comisario will arrest them. I hope it will succeed. Woodroffe of La Chorrera on board. Awful liar. Tells me that Guzman was Paredes' interpreter – Good – I did hear that I think. A fine Cholo, Manuel Bazan, on board. Beautiful Hair & Eyes. Big tall young fellow – got only £5 per month. Passed many places during day including St. Cruz & Belém & at 8 at Capacete near mouth of Javary.

[At top of page:] Gave Cortes shirt. Son of Papayan man. Came to Las Delicias on Orteguason?? of Caquetá & arrested by Peruvians there & mistreated. Fed by Cholo soldiers. Lost all in wreck of A.

12 THURSDAY Anchored at mouth of Javary till early morning from about 11 p.m. On at 6 a.m for ~~Remate de Males~~ Capacete **[inserted]** Customs House. Again there ½ hour & then up Javari by middle entrance of Whirlpools. Anchored ½ way up to fish (!) in a lake – & twice to land food &c. & letters, & arr. at Remate de Males about 2 p.m. The Police officer from Manaos told y'day exactly what to do. At Capacete we took on board Hahn, the police officer of R. de Males – a big degenerate German Brazilian – Both up together to R. de Males & when there on shore to drink with Serra. Dr Dickey reported 5 p.m. that both were drunk &d that Hahn had been bribed by Serra. Da Cunha (my man) informed Dr Dickey that F. & M. had "gone away day before yesterday." He could not say <u>where</u> or anything more being then half drunk & an evident ass. Walked on shore & talked to Colombian boy Cortes, wrecked in Asturiano.

13 FRIDAY (Should arrive at Remate des Males today!)

We are now 17½ hours in Remate de Males & have not yet landed one box of cargo! No attempt made all y'day afternoon. We could easily have arrived here yesterday morning at daylight & have got to Tabatinga & Leticia last night. I never saw such people to waste time. All they can do is spit and eat &c. Paid wine bill 51$000 for a few bottles of Caxambu – each bottle is 2/9d! The Police officer da Cunha shows no sign – Dr Dickey gone down to Pombo to a sick person. After long, hot day left & down past R. de Males at 6 p.m. for up stream to land planters & left that at 9.30 & down past R. de M. & Nazareth to Esperanza where stayed long time & then at 2 a.m. landed the girl from Pará at the Fazenda **[plantation]** & on to Tabatinga where we stayed till 7 a.m. No sign of ~~Da Cunha~~ De Campos, the Police officer.

14 SATURDAY At Tabatinga. Brazilian lady & 2 children came on board, probably wife of the officer. I counted 9 soldiers besides the officer – on to Leticia at 8 a.m. We have wasted time fearfully since Capacete on Wednesday evg. having made less than 25 miles in 2½ days. The "Immediato" **[First Mate]** says we shall get to Iquitos in 2½ days from R. de Males! Nous verrons! **[We shall see! – This tell-tale Casement phrase (in the 1910 Black Diary on 23 October) also crops up in a letter written from Santos to his friend Robert Berry way back in 1907 – "mais nous verrons" and elsewhere.[573]]** The bank at Leticia where "Esperanza" was covered with rich grass about one foot out of water. River is some 8' feet higher than in Augt. 1910 when I went up in "Huayna". Caballa Cocha at 4. & landed & took passengers & on at 6. Lovely evening – Sunset over Maranon splendid & then stars & planets. Talked Manuel Bazan of Caxamarca. Fine cholo.

15 SUNDAY Passed Pebas at 4 p.m. Stopped at 7.15 to come to with "Hamburgo" & take a Peruvian officer on board. Then on. Learned "Huayna" downward bound, aground. Came to [??] at 8 p.m. stayed two hours. Then on & anchored again for fog 2 – 4 a.m.

[At top of page:] Arrived in Iquitos.
16 MONDAY Arr. Iquitos 9 a.m. Delayed landing by funeral of John Lilly's son Lionel – died y'day of Yellow fever. Yellow fever outbreak in Iquitos very bad. Prolonged dry weather. Fearful heat. **[Casement told London of this death, advising that the illness of the English merchant's son's lasted "only four days." Yellow fever, he wrote, was known locally as "Black Vomit."[574]]** On shore. B'fast Cazes. No sign of Ignacio Torres or Antonio Cruz Perez. Went Brown's house. Cazes took 2 rooms for me (£9 a month) but they are useless – & so am let in for that! A nice waste of money! Met Vatan & Brown. Called Guy's to condole with John Lilly. No news from Cazes. Letters from

Nina & others (Gee & Lizzie). Fearful heat – atrocious. Nearly fainted. Sent boys dine Bella Vista. Dinner 2 soles = 4/- Stayed in & talked with Brown & captain of "Napo".

17 TUESDAY Slept well. John Brown came. Sent boys to breakfast with him. He lives Punchana **[an Indian village down river from Iquitos]**. The restaurant wants 12/- a day! for two meals for these two boys. Outrageous! I shall be ruined here. On board "Hilda" & "Napo". Got telegram F.O. saying Mitchell **[sic]** sailed 12 Oct. (to come on by "Manco", she left Lisbon 11th Oct.). Letter from Mitchell **[whom Casement was standing in for until his arrival]** – a very stupid one it seems. Very bad cold & sore throat. Out after dinner to Malecon & met Cajamarca for one – & then a lovely boy on seat – talked to for an hour. He had been in Putumayo. Then in Square a beautiful young Policeman of Chosta. Splendid type & big one too. Asked where I came from. Gave him cigarettes.

18 WEDNESDAY Saw the young Peruvian negro soldier leaving barracks with erection under white knickers – it was half way to knee! fully 1 foot long. Cold is worse – Went to John Brown's house at Punchana & his Cafuzo wee boy **[someone of mixed African and Indian race]** kissed & hugged me. Called on Prefect who said the Putumayo mystery had been solved by me – the honour was mine. It had been a "mystery" even here in Iquitos! Don Pablo was hidden here in Iquitos the Prefect says, waiting the result of his appeal against the Judge Dr Valcarel's order of imprisonment. Dr Paredes' report covers 80 pages & goes to Lima "next mail"! Just the same as mine. Got the order for Montt **[who had murdered Omarino's brother]** & Fonseca to go down by "Anastasia" with J. Lilly tomorrow. Called on Mrs Prefect & at Mrs Cazes's – & then talked with Harding & home to dinner & turned in at once after with fearful cold. Sneezing & blowing my nose terribly – & in real pain. Visited two empty houses today. A great eulogy of me in today's "Oriente"!!! Met young pilot Practicante **[Cash Ledger: Met José."; and later "Pilot's boy José Gonzalez – came 18th & 19th Oct. et seq.]** at 4 of "Liberal" – the boy with the big exposure. Lovely face & huge. Shook hands & begged him to come at 9 a.m.

[At top of page:] ~~Probably will reach Iquitos today. 4 weeks less one day from Pará.~~
19 THURSDAY Cold awfully bad. Took lots of quinine & stayed in bed. Sending Ricudo to Putumayo today by "Beatrice". Young Pilot came at 9 a.m. Very well dressed. Sat down & I stroked knee & gave 10/- & cgttes & photos. **[Cash Ledger: X. José Gonsalez. Young Pratico (Present) 10.0]** Would like it I am sure. Caressed hand too. His is a big one I know. To come on Saturday

1st of 4: José Gonzalez, fully dressed, smoking, hat on cactus

2nd of 4: José Gonzalez, side view, shirtless, hat on wall

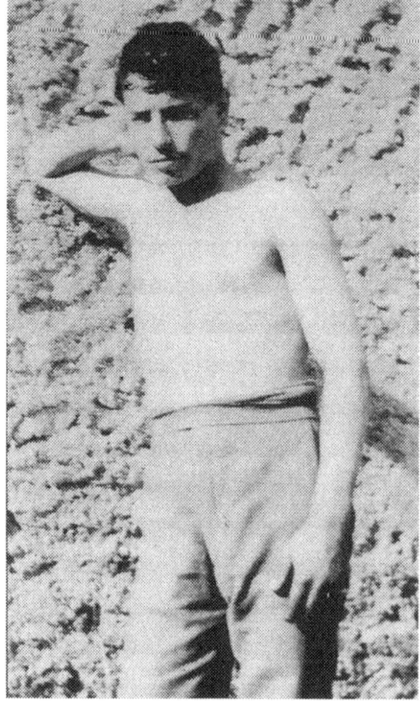

3rd of 4: José Gonzalez, front view, shirtless against wall

4th of 4: José Gonzalez, shirtless against wall, displaying armpit

to "passear" with me & get his photo taken. He is beautiful. Tells me Ignacio Torres is on S.S. "Ucayali" as steward. She is now "on voyage". Will tell Ignacio to come to me on return. Cold got much worse so to bed and Doctor of "Napo" came to me. Great pain & trouble. Got quinine & to bed. Saw some splendid ones too again today and such lovely faces. Very heavy rain – began at 8.30 p.m. & till 11 in deluge – then stopped & then began again till 5 or 6 a.m. **[Although some progress is being made in rounding up Putumayo criminals everything else is grinding Casement down – the weather, the Yellow fever and his own ailments. The appearance of José is a precursor of better times.]**

20 FRIDAY Ricudo left for Putumayo in "Beatriz". Prefect's A.D.C. called for him to take him to Captain Zubiarr. In bed all day. Saw from my window splendid type – one young lovely Indian. Thick limbs & sturdy with big one – found him to be steward on "Rimac". Then to quay as "Javari" arr. at 4 p.m. & saw a glorious type – young, tall (about 18½) with big limbs & a huge one. Pensive Inca face & long Indian soft hair. Also green-eyed boy who looked at me. Back & turned in after Doctor called at 8. Jansen dined with me. Others to Cazes. Captain Barnett's story of the Manaos caboclo 15 years ago who showed large & had one below knees he could kiss! Did it for fun for a plug of tobacco.

21 SATURDAY Expect José González at 9 a.m. but am too seedy to go out with him today. Will give him a present and ask him to return on Monday early to go out to stream with me. He came at 9. New pants, showing much & bowed from street & then up to my room. I shut door & took his hat & almost at once I saw his getting stiff & bulging out sideways his pants. We sat down side by side & looked at Enock's book [***The Andes and the Amazon – Life and Travel in Peru***] & I caressed & held hand & thigh & sometimes back. He blushed & hand hot & wanted awfully – leaning close to me & hand against my thigh. Bad cold. Told come 3 p.m. 3 o'clock. Waiting for José my fly open. **[This entry is further and conclusive evidence that Casement wrote up his personal diary, on occasion, as the day went along especially when he was using the process as an anticipatory erotic aid. In other words, writing down what he was doing, thinking about doing, and hoping he would do, was itself a turn on.]** Have just seen young Cholo boy 17 thick set, splendid legs & huge erection down left thigh opposite window. Will José's be up too? He fully expects it I am convinced & is coming express. Had hair cut too! José came 3 & stayed till near 5. Got stiff & fingered it. I photo'd him often & tried get it. Mine up & I pulled it & he looked often & got redder & his very big. After dinner to band & saw lovely boy of Tuesday 17. Going home.

[On blotter opposite:] Gave José necktie poplin & new Hkf also medicine.

22 SUNDAY José Gonzalez to come at 8 a.m. & take me out to stream. Will show him mine. Went 8.30. No stream. Dried up. On to Morona Cocha, embracing hand, shoulder & waist often – in Laureto Tram. **[Cash Ledger: Out with José Gonzalez to Ignacio's stream 8 a.m. To Morona Cocha with José...Present to José 4$ 8.0.]** Lunch & in together to Plaza. To go tomorrow Itaya. Afternoon to Cazes & then evening Malecon & Square. Some fine types & met again Beautiful of 17[**th**]. Asked to "passeando" on Malecon with me – but he shy & went. I believe wants it as always alone. Back 10.20 & turned in. Saw on seat on Malecon 9.30 p.m. Cazes' former shop boy "Passeando" splendid limbs & grown. It huge. Was with a gentleman!

[At top of page:] Young municipal chap, blue uniform with huge one – splendid and on several Indian boys – very big exposures.
23 MONDAY Up at 6 & out to meet José Gonzalez at Hospital 8.20 a.m. He there first, ill poor boy with fever. To Itaya River together where we swam – but he kept his calzonzillas on **[Spanish word for underpants – correct spelling is calzoncillos.]** However, it got up after & was stiff & if not for his illness would have come off. Gave milk & money. **[Cash Ledger: Out with José Gonzalez to Swim. Ginger ale 2/-. Him 4/-. Ginger ale 1/-. 1/-. 2/-. Soldier "Manuel" 3$. No. 7 Regt.]** To "Napo" at 5 & then to see house on Malecon of Moreys which will take probably – After dinner out to Bella Vista & round Plaza. Some splendid Indian lads with huge ones & beautiful sterns – & tried with several & then a lovely Lima boy of 19 with glorious face, a gentleman. Finally coming home a young soldier, thick-set Inca Indian – & gave cigttes & 3S/P – & he accompanied me. Mine up & he looked & wd. have done it. "Manuel" is going to Caquetá –Very sturdy. He was quite ready I could see.

24 TUESDAY Very tired. Waiting for "Napo" mail – due to leave tomorrow. Lovely young Indian boy about 16 gone past window, bandy legs like Cazes' shop boy & huge long one on right side of dungaree knickers. Saw Manuel (the Corporal) twice this morning outside barracks. He is splendid type of sturdy young Indian, grand calves & thighs & thick set – upright body. It must be a good one! Last night he was quite ready for it! Played snooker pool after dinner – then out stroll to Plaza & Malecon – latter quite deserted. Saw fine big one, as tall & small boy at Café listening to piano on right side & also in afternoon outside Mrs Cazes on a sturdy fine moço of 18, bare feet. In evg. several soldiers but not Manuel – followed one white one – young & tall and sat beside one in blue a minute.

25 WEDNESDAY Saw the nice boy of 17th & Sunday last at 6.25 a.m. returning from market with bag to House of *Despachante* opposite. Probably cook there. Wrote many letters (F.O. & others to go by "Napo" today). She catches "Lanfranc" & will reach England 23 Nov. probably. Saw one Inca soldier from Brown's window at 2 p.m. with huge one all down left knicker – also young guard of y'day constantly feeling – slim limbs & lovely face. Then one came from Malecon feeling it & making signs to others as if entering! Then young white soldier (same as I walked partly with last night from Square) talking to others in shirt (open bosom) & knickers & one put hand on his & he showed enormous extension – as long as palm" & big *testemunhos.* They all gathered round & looked & it was lying down all time, thick & about 7" or 8" long lying! Saw three bathing lovely colour & limbs & one big one. In afternoon lovely green eyed boy of 20th to Reuss Store underneath. He has a huge soft long one. I saw it plainly on left side loose pants. Smiled at him. To Hardings – whose store boy has a beauty too & smiles shyly. Sat in Square with young boy & splendid limbs, 6.30 – 7 till darkness came & home to dinner & turned in after.

[On blotter:] Manuel the young "Loreto" battalion Corporal – Gave 6/- (3 dollars) & shook hands & stroked. He is very cheery & nice & wants it.
Met Paredes at Harding's at 4 p.m. Long talk. He complimented me mightily.
Met Lincoln of Benito Lores on "Liberal".
Saw José on Malecon with long legged boy with fine stern & huge *testemunhos* & later two or three young boys in Plaza with very big ones from 5–7. Cold worse.

[At top of page:] Up at 6.30. Heavy rain all night. Took Quinine. Soldiers out & "palm" of yesterday in his knickers & other one embracing young thick set soldier of 18 – a beauty.
26 THURSDAY The lovely boy of 20th came to Reuss' store at 7 this morning & two carters to shift whiskey etc. He smiled & bowed. I love him – also one of the carters, a big Inca (white) péon with blue shirt & pants & a perfect monster. It swings & shows a head about 3" in diameter! He has enormous shoulders & curved strong back about 27 – & is as strong as stallion. Saw it at 9 a.m. swinging & I'll swear it is 3" across. Lovely boy looked up & smiled – his is a big long soft one, or his pants are loose & yet it & his bags hang down a lot. He has a lovely gentle face (about 19½). Expect José some time today. River 63' 8". Out to **[??]** ground & then by Javary at dusk. 5.45 – & the young guard of y'day (& today) went past. Manuel splendid – both. I saw from window. Then Cazes' old shop boy well dressed & splendid legs went past & hugged a bigger boy. Out after & met & shook hands. Said he was sick – brought him in & gave him quinine. He said "I have grown much, haven't I?" His name Alcibiades

Ruiz – works John Lilly – & him on "Napo". After dinner to Malecon & Lima soldier. 2 Cigarettes. Met Antonio Cruz Perez, much grown too.

27 FRIDAY Lovely morning & very bright sun all day. In house all day nearly. Saw "Manuel" in morning, on guard, with bayonet at side in blue & in afternoon at 3.30 several times on guard. Running & straight splendid legs & twirled round once & clasped a man around waist, holding him lovingly thus. It looked pretty big even at distance. Thinking of Manuel often & hope to meet soon now. Saw him often, in afternoon from window. Saw Antonio Cruz twice – very stout strong young man now. Promised y'day to photo him again. Stayed in house all day till near 6.30 p.m. when out to Plaza for a bit – & after dinner and a game of billiards with Brown out at 9 –10 to Plaza & Malecon seeing none – and no sign of Manuel, altho' some soldiers to be seen. "Vaseline" at Nictheroy two years ago. "<u>In sua bode</u>"! **['In his money pouch!' – an amusing memory of a past encounter in Nictheroy, a Rio resort now spelled Niterói, returns to Casement's mind. It is referred to in the 1910 diary on 29 October as happening that day the previous year in Icarahy which is a cove and beach in Nictheroy.]**

28 SATURDAY Lovely morning – but my cold is worse & has turned into a steady, dry "'acking cough". Will not move today to new house now. No news of Michell I fear now for over a month. Saw Manuel several times during day & at 9 p.m. with two well dressed boys under umbrella going up town. Also saw Beautiful green eyes Reuss Store often & at 5 p.m. when going home he smiled twice very warmly & kindly at me. Also saw Antonio Cruz Perez twice. Round Square at 6 p.m. (none at all) & then out at 9 in rain to Malecon & Square. Some soldiers & one brown one of 9th gave cigarette to – a big strapping Indian of hills. "A mañana". Moved in at 10 with port wine.

29 SUNDAY River 65'00 at 10 a.m. "Javary" sailed. Began breakfast &c. at Continental good & cheap. Walked Plaza with Brown after dinner. Met Reuss' beautiful boy in Sunday best. I love him – also Alcibiades looking splendid. Also a dark eyed lad who said "Buenos noches" as he passed. Some fine soldiers too, of 9th Battalion – but no sign of "Manuel". Turned in at 8.10. Rain & visit from a Major of 17 Bat. till 9. Then bed & slept well.

[At top of page:] <u>In New House</u> at <u>Belen</u>. **[a rough district of Iquitos]**
30 MONDAY
Heavy rain all night. Packed up & got ready for flitting to new house. Awaiting José. Saw Reuss beauty arrive & new shirt & pants. It fine hanging & swinging loose. Also <u>huge</u> Carter of 25 years – a beautiful splendid péon. Saw fine big Indian with huge on right side & then outside my new house small lovely boy

with huge one too on right side. Moved into house – horrid. José came with me & said wd. arrange a péon & water for tomorrow. **[Cash Ledger: José Gonzalez came but nothing.]** Péon to clear out the filth at back. Out at 6 to Cazes & Malecon & round square till 7 – seeing a lovely boy with legs stretched in front & huge long one under white pants & beautiful thighs. After dinner with Brown till 8.30 & then round square & Malecon & turned in at 10. Very sick. River was 66ft at 4 p.m. on Monday.

31 TUESDAY New house is a pig stye – literally – It will never do for the Michells. Infested with mosquitoes & every noise & syllable next door heard. José Gonzalaz came & we went to Itaya where bathed. He stripped all today & I saw it, small, but it got big after & has large head. It was quite stiff after in his *calzoncillos* & stuck out straight. **[Cash Ledger: X To José 2.60. Present after swim.]** Back & breakfasted with Cazes. The Itaya had risen fully 8' since 23rd when last bathed. Gave milk José & told come on Viernes **[Friday]** 3rd to go to Guayobamba. Slept afternoon & then to Bella Vista cocktails at 6 p.m. (having lunched with Cazes) & asked Cazes to dinner at "Continental". After that at 8.30 round Plaza & on Malecon till 10 p.m. None – but in Plaza a splendid young moço who looked & looked & I thought wanted & followed but he stopped & talked. Also small boy to cigarette but he would not. River 66' 6".

NOVEMBER

1 WEDNESDAY Lovely morning. Very bad night. Awake a great deal in night – & bad cold still. Wrote to Jerome of Lima about local things a long letter. Breakfasted alone. Public holiday. After breakfast to Mole & saw "Anastacia" & walked a bit. Called on Dr Vigil – but ill. Called on Cazes & out with him & Mrs C. to German house in bush but did not reach it. Dined with Harding, Paredes, Lanetta & Captain of "Anastacia". Learned of Zumaeta's release by the "Judges" & dismissal of Dr Valcarel – Harding says it is a conspiracy against right. Paredes is coming to see me tomorrow to talk "largely" about it. Harding says he is furious. **[Dr Valcarcel was being replaced as the Peruvian judge investigating Casement's Putumayo allegations. Casement's initial opinion of Dr Romulo Paredes, on 3 December 1910, in his White Diary, was not flattering: "The Judge Paredes, editor and leader writer of 'El Oriente', is another of the scoundrels here."[575] Paredes, however, had the political strength of being a friend of the Peruvian President Leguia, and it was to show. The John Lilly company's A. King Harding was later to congratulate Casement. Home ill from Iquitos in 1912, he wrote, "You really deserve to see your efforts for the humane treatment of those unfortunate Indians**

crowned with perfect success. Such at any rate are my prayers and hopes. There is a lot to be done on the same lines for the Indians up river."[576]] Walked a bit looking for "Manuel" – but lots of other soldiers &c. – but never him. "Anastacia" back from Javary – but no news. River at 1 p.m. 66' 10" & evidently rising. Sandbank completely gone & submerged trees also all swept away. The river has risen almost if not quite 10 feet since I came on 16 Augt. D. Brown **[of Booth & Co.]** says it is unprecedentedly high for this date. "Marco" expected up on 12th. Harding says 8th now – & that she left Manaos yesterday.

[On blotter:] Letter to Jerome went by "Adolfo" today. Should be in Lima by 28th or 30th.

[At top of page:] River at 5 p.m. Dined with Paredes, Lanetta &c. &c. at Bella Vista. No sign of Manuel. Looked all night to midnight.

2 THURSDAY Lovely morning – but I should much prefer heavy. Another 5 fresh cases Yellow Fever on 31st – none reported in paper. Hair cut by Spaniard & beard only 1Sp = 2/- in Manaos $3 = 4/3¾d or more than double! Barber told me that "Don Pablo" **[Zumaeta]** was out! Great news he said – he talked as if he didn't like it. He is a Coruna man. After noon with Hagenau & saw a fine Indian moço on seat in Plaza & when he stood up it was sticking out hugely & he arranged with hand. Walked about after dinner & sat beside a big Indian lad in Plaza & then Alcibiades & mine as stiff as a poker – but he wd. not come & finally just outside my house at 11.35 met young soldier who asked & mine up & gave 1$ & he shook hands. Saw many soldiers all after women. Asked Alcibiades to come house. River fell slightly.

3 FRIDAY Out with José to Guayobamba via San Juan where we bathed both going & coming in a pretty little stream of cool water. Weather good except on way back when it got very hot. Arrived at 2.40 & turned in tired till 5. & then at 6.30 out to Cocktail at Bella Vista & on to Cazes where I stayed to dinner – Mrs C. going to bed ultimately at 9.30 or so with an impudent glare. She is an awful vixen & leads that poor man a dreary life. My house is atrocious – a cesspool of the backyard & a d. neighbours dumping heap. Turned in 11.30 waiting for rain – It came on slightly at midnight.

4 SATURDAY Wakened about 3. with long steady rain & slept little after. It poured on till near 5 I think. I did not get up till 8.50 a.m. Streets soaking. Sleep very badly in new house. To breakfast at "Continental" seeing splendid type on way. Out to Muelle **[dock]** & Punchana way & back at 2.35 & lay down till 6. Then to Bella Vista to dinner & after on Malecon where at 8 met the young soldier of Thursday night. He stopped & offered himself at once "muchacho" & felt it & asked me "why not – Comes from "hills, 2 months

away." When "en paisana" **[in civilian clothes]** never went with mujeres **[women]** – now often. Was in Javarri & Purus. Is quite lovely & begged to get me a "muchachita". After with Harding & then by self till 12. looking for young soldier – in vain or Manuel.

5 SUNDAY Lovely morning – dry & glorious sun. Breakfast at Bella Vista 2.90. Last night's dinner cost 6S = 12/6d. After ~~dinner~~ lay down & the young soldier came & stood by house but did not see me as I leaned out of window. No dinner – only some fruit & Ginger Ale at Continental & then at 8.40 turned in. Rain in afternoon – and again in evening – In bed at 9. very tired of Iquitos & sick with indigestion & sciatic pains.

[At top of page:] Called on Brazilian Consulate. At 1.30 returning from lunch met Beautiful of Reuss' Store.
6 MONDAY Rainy, gloomy morning. Told José to come today – but will not go with him – as don't feel well enough. He came at 8.30 & showed him books & told come at 3. He came then. I alone on bed, & his got up & he pulled back coat & stretched out legs to show it – & looked at mine. Gave him £1 for boots. Then to Celandine with him & to house of German once in Cameroon with José & back 6.30. After dinner at Bella Vista – outside which I saw my "Muchacho" soldier boy pass at 7 to Plaza when Harding came – several beautiful types listening to Paredes etc. on elections & Alcibiades then & I think wanted me, as he came past several times – with his splendid legs & white pants. His up too I think. Harding with me all time.

7 TUESDAY Heavy rainy morning – awfully heavy now and rainy sky. Still ill with cold and indigestion. Have not met "Manuel" for 15 days & nights & seen only at distance! Alack. He may be off in "Liberal" which leaves tomorrow for Putumayo – with Alcibiades on board. He said he was to go to Caquetá next month. Breakfast at Continental – then a walk to Mole – seeing one fine one on way. Coming back met the small boy, with nice stern in Prospero & his was up. River 65' 3" only a drop of 1' 8" since Wednesday, a very big one sticking out pants on left side as he walked & big balls underneath. Met Beautiful Reuss at 12.50. Heavy rain from 11.40 a.m. Saw small mestizo boy of about 9 (tall & slim, perhaps 10) tossing himself off in street, from window – close to me. It was fully 7" long & sticking out about half a foot – a huge one & a very nice looking boy indeed, but quite a child.

[Continuation of 7 November but on blotter facing 9 and 10 November entries:]
Señor José Gonzales
Calle de Arica No. 281

Iquitos.
To send photo to him.

7th Novr. 1911 Out to Morona Cocha 4-5.30 meeting José & a girl. 3.30 p.m. a minute after preceding exhibition two Cholo boys came along, & one about 14 (with fine square shoulders) pulled his out to pump ship [**urinate**] & I saw a big yellow beauty – thick and fine with good long foreskin. Quite a young boy & when he put it in it bulged out his blue dungaree knickers. After dinner at Continental to Malecon in moonlight & there saw Alcibiades with the man & after in Square with him. At 10.10 he returned alone and saluted me at table & I followed him & found him lingering for me & looking back. Clasped hands & spoke lovingly – asked if alone & then said Adios for ever. Told me wd. be back in a month – & I said I should be gone. He looked lovely. Has grown into a magnificent youth – broad chest, shoulders, hips & matchless thighs & I could see under his whites the curved line of the splendid tonga. Turned in at 11.15.

8 WEDNESDAY Nice morning. "Liberal" sails at 1 or 2 today with Alcibiades Ruiz on board – Adios! Adios! I love him and his beautiful face & body &d mind. Just at 10.15 when longing for him I saw from window José coming along & he stopped & shook hands & I asked him to come at 3 today – mine being stiff as a poker under sill. He felt his & looked glad & said "Yes – *Está bien señor*" – So I feel I may really have him today. To breakfast at 11. saw Manuel Bazan as Sergeant of Police & shook hands. Talked Harding & then back at 1 to wait for José. On bed & at 3 he came beautiful – new pants, clean and lovely & it bulging. He wanted at once – but Brown & Omo came & heavy rain. So for a time at window – he looking at mine up – & then I sent Brown & O. home & took José to room & his got up too & he wanted awfully. His lovely face suffused with glorious Indian blood & eyes glistening. I refrained with enormous difficulty & at 5.30 he went with pineapple – after talk about Mexico. Heavy rain from 2.30 to 6 p.m. After dinner B. Vista to Cazes & talked to him till near 11. Gave notice to Morey wd. not keep on the house.

[**At top of page:**] In today's paper "Ucayali" is timed to arrive 11th. Then Ignacio!
River today at [**sentence ends abruptly**].
9 THURSDAY Fine morning after rain – cold night Therm 75 degrees. Harding expected "Manco" last night. Liberal expects 40 tons of rubber, Cazes says. No breakfast. Staid [**sic**] in house all morning. At 1 p.m. magnificent young Cholo policeman passed with fine big one – and splendid calves. Strong as a tapir. [**Calves were a Casement speciality as he remarked in similar**

vein in his German diary about those of a French POW "fair, strong – in blue puttees showing splendid calves and with the figure of a young Hercules."[577]**]** Immediately followed by another with a Huge one on right side. Could see it plainly stiff & long & thick (about 7") wobbling down right thigh – peaked Inca nose & pure cholo (about 30). 1.16 p.m. "Muchachita" just gone past. My window wide open but he was looking across street or wd have seen me. I flew to window & looked after – lovely stern, thighs calves in blue & blue putties. He stood a minute upright & strong & then down side street. Will watch for return. He did return now at 1.26 & I saw him coming but hid. He glanced in window as passed but did not know I was there! And so I have again sacrificed love to fear. To dinner B.V. after Malecon & Plaza & soldier 9 Bat. – cigarettes, but wd. not & then José to House at 11 p.m. **[The Home Office photographer was ordered to take pictures of the entries in their typed version from 9-12 November 1911 for distribution. Plainly Casement was writing up this diary almost minute by minute as the feast of visual stimulation in Iquitos so energised him. Apart from the time taken up by this viewing most of the myriad of sightings and contacts were of the briefest duration and he would have been able to complete his usual work quite satisfactorily.]**

10 FRIDAY José to come at 8 after last night's visit at 11 p.m.! To go to S. Miguel, but it is raining. He came at 8.10 & we went away at 8.25 first to S. Miguel & then on by new path to S. Juan where we bathed & after coming out mine under H'Kf **[handkerchief]** got stiff & he did same with his H'Kf & fingered it too & it got huge. I saw it swelling & at last under h'kf got glimpse of it & it was a tremendous one with red head. Nearly did it. Back at 11 & told him come 3: to breakfast Cazes', seeing huge one on Wesche's shop boy in store & then to Morey's & now at 2.45 I am waiting for José naked with mine ready! He came at 2.48 and on till 5 stayed with me – mine huge & his up too stiff. He wants it! He is quite ready – but if I do it I must take him with me to Rio! **[Casement's collector mentality again]** After dinner met Manuel. Gave good evg. To Malecon to wait him and there Indian "muchacho" from "Tapiche" wanted awfully. Splendid thighs. Tried feel it but got match box instead. Agreed to come with me but afraid of soldiers. Then a Colombian on Vatan launch & showed him mine & felt his.

[On blotter facing 12 November but continuation of 10 November:] Indian Muchacho at 2.35 opposite (about 17) called to two girls & waited, leaning on wall to show limbs – girls came & one patted his cheek & he followed close, almost covering his prick showing enormous propulsion of his old pants right down left thigh, rising bigger & longer – about as much again – so marked a

Chinaman (young) looked back twice at him. Boy followed girls close & they turned down river side together! A nice boy too, he had given me a good day previously when passing my window. At 2.20 this young Cholo moço passed down with a huge one on right side. We greeted each other & I had a good look at it. It was thick & big & long & good *testemunhos* behind it, to help bulge out his pants. A thin tall lad with Inca face.

11 SATURDAY I hope "Manco" today – also "Ucayali" and to see dear Ignacio tonight! After last night's two on Malecon I am tired and a bit afraid. The "Tapiche" boy said that the soldiers "agarrar" them **[grab them roughly]**. His thighs as firm as rocks & felt it & wanted awfully. Rain came on I asked him to follow. José now at 9 here reading "Carlo Magno" & "Don Quihote". Expect Ignacio today. At 6 p.m. no "Manco" & I have not heard that Ucayali arrived. José came at 1 p.m. staying till 3.20 or so writing English exercises & Spanish. Poor boy. I am sorry for him. To dinner at Bella Vista & then after to Brown's where fell asleep with a headache after y'day. Very tired – Back at 10 p.m. & turned in straight to bed & slept. Heavy rain all last night – but river I fancy still dropping slightly.

12 SUNDAY Rain in night but fine morning. Writing letters for "Manco's" mail. **[That to Gertrude, dated 12 November 1911, describes the Peruvians as "all bandits and pirates when not worse – 20th century Pizarros without the courage but all the crime." It also mentions that "the small Indian boy is with me and the big one who went to the Putumayo to look for his wife I expect back very soon now."[578]]** She is due on 14th and I shall miss my mail by her. Out after lunch at B. Vista to pier & then to Celandine stream with splendid young Chachapoyas Cholo (carter) to show the way. He had a monster & fine limbs – but wd. not bathe (too shy) but showed about 8" lying down & a thick one. Coming back met his young friend – wood cutter – with only blue drawers on – naked torso below navel & calves & a huge one too – a lovely type. After dinner to pier to "Ucayali" which arrived at 2 p.m.

[Top of page:] Left in "Anastacia" at 10.40 a.m. River 66' 5" at 10 a.m.
13 MONDAY To "Ucayali" but could see nothing of Ignacio – so sent Brown on board with photos to ask for him. Steward says he left ship last voyage Oh! sick – & he has been in Iquitos all the time! Told Brown to find out where he is at all costs. Saw Antonio Cruz at wharf looking awfully nice – shook hands & asked him to come to M. Cocha with me when I returned from this trip. **[Casement was now starting his only (and somewhat pointless) journey beyond Iquitos in 1911. It lasted barely ten days. The official Peruvian government response was beginning to peter out, or be sabotaged, while**

the company itself was going into liquidation. With Arana as liquidator, London's leverage would disappear. The feeling now was that Casement's report, about which the Foreign Office had been vacillating, might as well be published. There was less to lose and it might evoke international pressure, especially in America where an effort to open a second front against Peru's Indian policy (or lack of one) was under way. Sir Edward Grey, however, decided to await Casement's return before going into print. The company was not finally dissolved until 1927.] Some huge ones on wharf. Two on board – one Inca type – lovely face & small boy with huge one – Juan Garcia Buenaño* on board going overland to Putumayo. We dropped him at a Colombian place on bank when he comes to Napo in 2 hours to Elias who send him on – spoke strongly to him thro' Harding & he seems straight.

[There have been many commentators who cannot believe that Casement could be so brazen in his cruising in his hunting, gathering and collecting individual males. Some suggest he was fantasising, others that the diary entries just could not be authentic. It must first be remembered that much of what appears in this diary is what he saw not what he did. Although some might reckon he must have been conspicuous just in his looking at young males on the street and especially at their groins but one must recognise that most people are quite self-contained and observe only what interests them or what is necessary for them just to get from one place to another. And if they notice they are being observed, rather than becoming hostile can get nervous and look away, as the other's intentions are not necessarily clear or indeed friendly.

For centuries and until very recently, gay men have relied on those facts to indulge in the most outrageous behaviour within earshot and at times even within sight of others, and get away with it; one reason being that it never crossed the mind of many people, indeed it could not even have been conceptualised that something homosexual was going on. Internal mechanisms would find ways of ignoring or re-labelling untoward actions such as men endlessly lingering in toilets. If given a sideways glance, these men might be seen manipulating and at times displaying erect members, but then straight (and many gay) men are embarrassed enough urinating in public and so rarely risk looking around. Indeed if one was to look in that direction a self-accusation of undue interest might form in the mind.

---

* In a dispatch to the US Secretary of State, the American Consul in Iquitos, Stuart J Fuller, wrote on 15 July 1912, "The comisario is a man named Juan Garcia Buenaño. He is fairly well spoken of as a man, but stated by many to be in a position where he can do little or nothing to better things, even though he might wish to."

As an evidential example, in the 1940s hardly thirty years later, Dr Alfred Kinsey was showing a researcher the toilets in New York's Grand Central Station, pointing out that "eight or nine men were migrating from one urinal to another, washing their hands, drying them, milling around and then coming back to the urinals." He told the researcher "Those are homosexuals. They are looking for partners. So now what do you think about the incidence of homosexuality?" The anthropologist confessed he had been to that rest room a dozen times without seeing a thing. "You never looked" was Kinsey's reply.[579] Thus he had seen nothing.

By 1911, Casement was a veteran of thirty years world-wide experience in outside cruising and of the limits to which he could go. On any one of the thousands of previous occasions he could have been exposed and destroyed. Indeed it is a wonder that any prominent men in his position survived. However, he and the other survivors were wily. Only if reckless would he be really vulnerable. It is the inexperienced, the married man for example, who falls victim most often to the police. The critical fact for understanding why Casement's sexual contacts, even if they were lukewarm like José, who participated minimally and reluctantly, maintained, silence is that they could never reveal the facts else they would be incriminated as well.

Rent boys have a trade to protect, and enhance, and are therefore not interested in making life difficult for clients. Camp, streetwise youngsters could embarrass or present difficulties but Casement seems normally to have given effeminate youths a wide berth. His interest, in Latin America, was largely directed at sexualised Indian males aware of their own pleasuring needs or respectable European working boys not always certain of whether they wanted adolescent sexual activity with this older man but happy to be taken notice of, and perhaps rewarded.

A reason why so many find it difficult to accept this 1911 Black Diary in particular as credible, is of course the notion that Casement was now well known and conspicuous, not to mention the fact that he had enemies in these river ports. But he was happy to rely, in part, on his position as an investigator whose job it was to find out from all sorts of sources, many of them disreputable, what was going on in the Peruvian rubberlands up river. This explains how he was able to pursue Ignacio, and later instruct Brown of Booths so forcefully to track him down, without any embarrassment. He was the boss and had a degree of diplomatic immunity, because of his status and mission. Harassing him could just as easily backfire. He was a man to please not pick off.

When he first visited the region he did it attached to a team appointed by the Peruvian Amazon Company itself. This was partly to evade the Monroe

Doctrine as no British diplomat was normally allowed to involve himself in South American affairs. But the fact remained that he was acting on behalf of a London-based, City financed company and the Arana brothers were officials of that company. They would be unlikely to try to destroy a Foreign Office official who was in effect part of their company. To have Casement followed or to harass him would be counterproductive. That is not to say the Aranas were incapable of blackmail and bribery and worse. They were. Julio Arana even tried to blacken his earlier American accuser, Hardenburg, by means of a suggestively homosexual bed arrangement he had engineered.[580] But in 1916, and afterwards, despite Julio Arana's triumphalist attitude, there is no record of him adding sexual charges. It seems he just did not know what Casement was up to in his free time.]

14 TUESDAY On "Anastasia" – very cold & nice – Writing letters & expecting to see "Manco". We passed "Manco" I learn at anchor at 3 a.m. in night. Stopped at several places and at 5 p.m. got to Leticia & got "Manco's" passenger list. 75 Cabin passengers & 69 Deck. No Michells & No J.C. Arana or Macedo. Both may now come by "Ucayali". The small steward boy has a splendid big one – & the Indian Inca boy too I fancy but I can't see it as his breeks **[trousers]** are loose. The others tight showing a monster. To Javari at 8 p.m. & on up.

15 WEDNESDAY Very cold last night in Javari. Arr. Nazareth about 3 a.m. & alongside. Heavy rain at daylight – Javari high & sweeping huge logs down. Stayed at Nazareth till 3 p.m. & just as we left saw the Brazilian mail steamer coming up with flags flying. Long talks with young Escurre, J. Lilly's agent. He left Chorrera 2½ years ago & knows all about it. He denounced it at once to Dr Cavero the Fiscal of the Iquitos Court on arrival – who told him he "would speak to Sr. Arana on his arrival"! Escurre tried to see the Prefect (Leon) who "was sick". He denounces his own Gov't firmly – both for their crimes against the Indians as against the Colombians. On up Javari, the river growing quite interesting with steep clear banks, real trunks & splendid tree. A new kind of tree tall & rugged bark, I've not seen on Amazon – steaming up river often stopping – sand flies very bad.

[At top of page:] A lot of fine trees on Javary – two notable ones over 100 feet high.
One Carpa and the other Cupadon in Peruana.
16 THURSDAY Stopped often in night. Did not turn in till near midnight owing to sandflies. The two Indian Steward boys both asleep – one on trunk on back. River retains a breadth of 300–400 yards, steep banks, high trees &

very deep about 50-60ft. At 8 passed Campina on right bank, high ground & steep banks – very pretty. Many logs floating down –many miserable "barracas" **[huts]** of Cearense gatherers. All is Brazilian on Javari – the Peruvian side only so in name. The Brazilian is a better worker than the Peruvian. Mostly Cearenses and Cafuzos. Stopped a batalón **[canoe]** & took her rubber from her to help pay debt much against the owner's will. We chased her & made her fast. A very handsome young Cearense on board about 22 or 23 – lovely cafuzo hair, great big eyes & a huge thick one, skinned head under pyjamas. I gave him cigarette & looked in his eyes. & longed. At 8 to a beach and lovely young Cearense boy – talked to him & felt. He looked & felt too. From Sobral in interior of Ceará. **[Casement, when he writes 'felt' does not mean he felt this particular young man's skinned organ, or that the Cearense youth touched him. What has occurred is a ritualistic self-touching of the crotch, by both parties. Amongst macho, heterosexual males this is indicative of self-confidence, but if mutually repeated, almost imitatively, is interpreted as a come-on signal. The trick is to judge correctly when what the world sees as seriously masculine behaviour has actually crossed over into homosexual mating display. It is vital to be sufficiently restrained to avoid getting it horribly wrong. Ironically the man who feels himself more often may be seen as more male so long as he does not reveal he is indulging in a homosexual display.]**

17 FRIDAY At mouth of Rio Curaça at 6.30 a.m – fine broad stream from S.E. a Brazilian Customs post at mouth on an island. On up the narrower Javari about 200-250 yards broad & deep. A few parrots & first Hornbills seen today & at 10.45 to "Venezia" – a solitary hut – the first since Rio Curaça I've seen. At 5.30 arrd. at mouth Javary Mission & up it S.W. about 3 miles & then down again & up Javary. Heard many Trumpeter birds this evg. & have seen today 5 splendid ducks – as big as geese – quite black with a broad white band on each wing. Some parrots and araras too. Took a fine photo of the <u>only</u> decent house on all Javari on Brazilian side – all the rest is misery, dirt & squalor – No food, no plantation only rubber piracy! A Quack doctor on board with a *batalón*.

18 SATURDAY Foggy at 6. But soon cleared & are now some 250 miles or so up the Javary still very deep & about 150 yards broad. Passed some miserable palm huts during the day with Cearense workers – always Cearenses. The Quack left in night to cure a seringueiro **[rubber tapper]** who fell from ladder put up rubber tree to tap high up. This destroys the tree! A few Macaws – more palms than below – and sometimes wild <u>ducks</u> & once the geese of yesterday. No Indian or single <u>native</u> inhabitant all along the river – all imported – all

1st of 2: self assured, shirtless boy, full-length

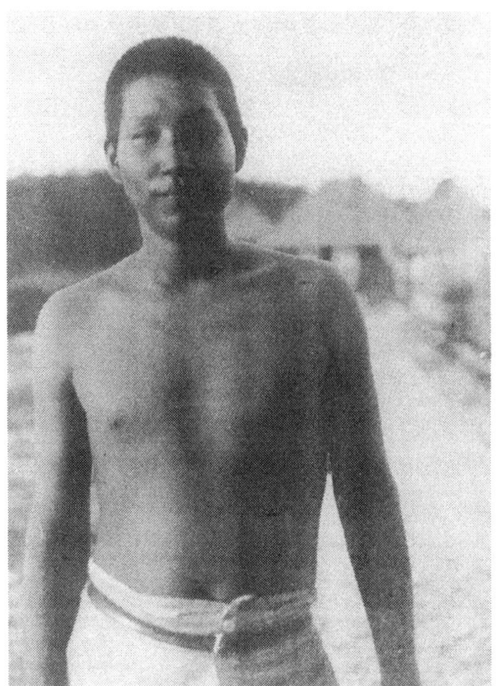

2nd of 2: self assured, shirtless boy, half length

Guy with moustache, in longs, thatched dwelling behind

wretched & all squalid & yet £2,000,000 worth of rubber in Javari annually. One house with a clearing at 11.30 & five cattle & a mule! The only instance of domestic economy in 400 miles. Arrived Palmeira at 11.20 p.m.

19 SUNDAY We reached Palmeira before midnight & left again – no rubber. Down stream – the Acurana is 5-6 hours higher up. At daylight were far down river again and so on all day. Rain in afternoon, first since entering Javari. Got turtles once or twice & passed Javary Mission at 5 p.m. Huge snake in a pool at one point we passed. Harding says they declare it a monster. He saw its red eyes at night once – coming down stream.

[At top of page:] Amazon snakes are the originals of all snake stories.
Dr Dickey & now Harding – a 2nd fool – with me **[?? ??]**
20 MONDAY At 6 a.m. saw mouth of Rio Curaça again. The river on upper Javari had dropped while all bellow is rising. Story of the Cearense on "Brazil" whose wife went always with him with rifle. We shall get very little rubber. Down stream fast stopping rarely. Many wild ducks – beauties. Stopped at Mucuà at 4 p.m. & saw two rubber trees in tapping. Young Cearense of Sobral still there – splendid stern, thighs & *testemunhos* – a lovely boy. On to Antequera where we landed the worker?? – & then the sick man – and so thro' night till at 4 a.m. on Tuesday arrd. at Boa Vista where Edwards came on board – a pretty tough rascal – Fonseca at Santa Theresa higher up – it is Peruvian territory. **["Fonseca and Montt reported to me by Dr Dickey on being (in July) at Santa Teresa" was how he advised London on 6 September at that time diarying correctly that they were on the Brazilian side of the river.[581]]**

[On blotter:] 20th Monday Got some mails by "Manco" today at 10.30 a.m. meeting "Hamburgo" on her way up. She reports "Manco" at 11 a.m. on 15th at Iquitos. She left at 4 p.m. – mails only at 2 p.m. on shore. Saw fine Indian boy in Janissius canoe that brought him over. A big strong fellow – nice face & great thick stiff one which he felt often under grey pants.

21 TUESDAY At daylight steaming down fast to Nazareth – stopping only briefly. Arr. Nazareth at 10 & after some hours there up to Marius Levy's where shipped 65 cases rubber (10½ tons weight) & saw Jacami bird & fine monkey. Back to Nazareth – young Italian stout but very nice face, huge stern, thighs & immense big one, long, thick, soft, he fingered often & one could see it hanging down 6" or 7" inches – through very thick trousers too. Left Nazareth at 5. with "Le Journal" from Belem up to 5 Oct. giving Italy – Turkey war & strike in Ireland. At union & mouth of Javari at 9.30 & on to Leticia.

22 WEDNESDAY At Leticia since 11.30 p.m. Left only at 7.30 a.m. taking up Peruvian officer & family & enormous mass of rubbish of furniture including 5 jerrys! Cold is again very bad. Left letters to Tom, Gallwey, O'Reilly & Bernardino with Peruvians. Amazon is up – risen a lot & huge lines of trees & logs going down stream right across river diagonally sometimes **[??]** of them without ceasing. Hope "Ucayali" will be up by 28th. At Caballo Cocha at 4.30 – river risen I should think fully 6 feet since 13th – Stayed there only a few minutes & out again. Clock on church is painted strip of canvas always at 11.45 a.m.! Rain but not heavy. Met "Elisa" & got papers – including a "Truth" with part of Paredes' summing up. José came & asked me for photo in Iquitos – looking lovely & then at 8.30 for cigarette papers & later I called & pulled mine & asked for water. Also with Pilot's boy.

[At top of page:] Return to Iquitos.
23 THURSDAY Lovely day. We are steaming very well & expect to be in Iquitos before 10 a.m. tomorrow. Read letters and drafted a long despatch to F.O. giving as my opinion the unlikelihood of Peruvian Government acting seriously – hope to send it by "Manco" if we get up in time. Passed Pevas **[Pebas]** at 2 p.m. (102 miles from Iquitos 186 from Leticia which we have done in 30 hours including several stoppages. "Manco" passed down at 5 p.m. Saw Brown on board. River is not so high up here although lots of logs still – often striking them hard. At 8 p.m. a huge one nearly swept away a man & case of rubber. River dropped I think 5".

[On other side of blotter:]
River was 69' 11"
I was only 7" out in my guess!

24 FRIDAY River at 10 a.m. 69'- 11"-
Steaming along left bank close to shore – fine land trees & flowers. The river here is certainly not so flooded as down below. No logs to speak of & high water mark visibly fully 10ft. I expect at Mole the height may be 70.' 6" – a rise of 4'1" since 13 Novr. arr. 9.55. Antonio Cruz came on wharf & will come Sunday 8 a.m. Saw some big ones on Indian boys & then up ladder at top a young Spaniard with huge soft big one under blue pants. At my corner the lovely 6 foot young Inca policeman & his up at full half cock! Simply enormous, all down left thigh & thick too – fully 7½" & huge *testemunhos* too. I now am sure of the Indians! Many letters from Mrs Green & others. Saw the Cholo policeman again going to lunch & it was huge, half down his thigh & he 6 foot & lovely. Then the small policeman passed & his too enormous. Then Paredes young Editor also very big. José came at 3.15 looking very nice & it was half

up & showed big. Gave 5/8 for Spanish book. Saw the young policeman while talking to José & it was simply huge. Both pure Cholos.

25 SATURDAY Lovely morning. Busy with mails of "Manco". Wrote F.O. & at 8.30 José came with primer & sat beside me. His was swollen & fine all time & I felt his thighs close to it. He proposed to come in evg. & I said at 8. Out to Booths' & hair cut – "Adolfo" arr. Also at 4 "Beatriz", with I presume Ricudo & Humme [**Omarino**] & letter from Tizon. Saw Antonio Cruz & he said "Manana" with bright smile. Ignacio Torres, José says is at a rubber place on Tapiche River named Nueva York. After dinner at Bella Vista back at 7.50 for José. He came at 8.10 – sat down beside me with coat off & we started Spanish exercises – my hand on "muscles" & felt it often. Then got him to stand against wall & to measure & it was up & I put my hand on it often & felt it swelling & stiff. He wanted awfully – blushing & loving & gleaming eyes. [**José may have "wanted awfully" but it is plain that he is somewhat reluctant and that Casement is trying to wear down his resistance and stimulate an interest, incrementally, by calling up the youth's high sexual feelings.**] Sitting again – it up huge & I played with it. Ricudo & wife returned by "Beatriz" at 4 p.m.

26 SUNDAY Heavy rain in night. Up for Antonio Cruz at 7.30. He came 8.15. Lovely & huge legs. Is only 20. I photo'd him. He is an Iquitos boy & half Indian. Heavy rain last night & again this afternoon. Dined with Cazes & turned in at 9.30. Saw the splendid young Cholo policeman at 11.30 & gave him good day. Saw it was huge under loose knickers – He is splendid.

[**At top of page:**] Cazes states "Beatriz" brought 41 tons of Putumayo river [**sic**] no freight! All free [**??**] all the time. Indians with them. Zubiarr reports that many of the criminals have bolted taking 500 Indians with them. Saw "Muchachita" go past at 9 a.m. Slowed & showed big stern. I hid behind window.

27 MONDAY Expect José tonight at 8.30 when I fear it will come off surely – as he is now so anxious for it & it will be well nigh impossible to be close together our thighs touching for 2 hours & not to go further when both will be up & stiff. His was very stiff on Saturday night as he held the head & I fingered the back of it. It is about 7". I measured him all over & pressed mine against him as I did it & his responded at once. I felt it rising & pressing against me & then I clasped his stiff & swollen & then it got quite erect as he sat down. [**This is being written during the day to heighten anticipation, which for Casement was almost as important and as much of a turn-on, as the sexual act itself.**] Out to stream & bathed with two Indian boys from

Ucayali – both had nice ones, long & clean & lovely skins (only 15 or less). Back at 3 very hot & lay down till 6 & to dinner at Bella Vista & at 7.50 back for José. He came – quite lovely – but he did not want it tonight. Mine stiff & I pulled it out, but he would not look & his was not up for I laid hand across it more than once.

[On blotter:] 28 Nov.
River at 8 a.m. = 70' 4" –
a rise of 5" since Friday.
"Liberal" returned from Putumayo. 25 tons
Escurre called with Lima telegrams

28 TUESDAY Gun signal at 7. I thought "Ucayali" & went out but it turned out to be "Liberal" with 25 tons rubber. Greenidge on board & many agents. Greenidge reports Donald Francis stayed in Brazil (by her) helped by the Captain. Took Escurre & he to breakfast. Paredes got letters confirming the telegrams from Callao & Lima. Lay down afternoon & wrote F.O. too & then at 5 out & bought an owl for £1 – a lovely young thing at El Pollito. Talked Israel, Harding & Osborne till 7. Lovely evg. Dined again Bella Vista – very bad indeed & back at 7.30 for José. Lay on bed. He came at 8.15 & sat beside me & after a minute to table. Till 10.20 – but he persistently refused all my efforts – I tried hard – at end about 10 his got half up & I touched it once & felt its hard curve & he showed it too. He left at 10.30. Rain at 8 a.m. Expect "Ucayali" maybe up today.

29 WEDNESDAY Heavy rain – awful downpour at 2.10 a.m. & kept on all night. At 8.30 it is still falling soft & slow. No sign of Ucayali – or of the boys & bird. José came again tonight. I asked him to go on Sunday to Guayobamba & bath. Escurre **[who worked for the Amazon Freight trading company of John Lilly]** came to show me the actual telegrams & letters of the Lima men to Paredes – says many more were received by the Court & by the Prefect too – that not one of them is sincere or honest in the matter. He is to go to Dr. **[Alfredo]** Borda at 2 p.m. today to be interrogated in – Dr. Borda's House if you please privately, but not in the Court House! He will come & tell me tomorrow – Gave him an owl I bought for £1. A lovely young thing. José came at 7.50 (before the time!) & wanted it from the first & I felt it often – Stiff & fine – He let my hand rest on it often & looked at mine. He went at 10.30 & I turned in. River today 70.' 5".

[At top of page:] River 70' 10½" at 1p.m.
[ditto] 71' – at 6 p.m. Rising fast.
8" in two days

30 THURSDAY Fine night – many stars & cool & this is a nice morning. See no sign of "Ucayali" which was due at Manaos 17 Novr. Out to breakfast at 11.30 after visit from Dr Paredes & Escurre who gave me full particulars of latest fiasco on Putumayo & P. showed me his report confidentially – listing those allowed to escape. **[Judge Paredes had written a 1,300 page report vindicating Casement's allegations over the Putumayo atrocities, despite his previous harsh doubts about the judge's objectivity. Paredes then issued 237 "apprehension" warrants.]** Escurre to breakfast & at 12.30 gun of "Ucayali" – so off to meet her. At wharf most glorious type of Indian purser moço on "Victoria". I fell deep in love with him – perfectly divine face and limbs. Also white moço gentleman with huge one. Friend of many & then my darling "Beauty" of Reuss store talked & beamed on me. The Michells came & took them all round & to Escurre's house & Cazes. Dined on "Ucayali" & then to Cazes to billiards. A few letters – two from Nina & Tom & Gee & Lima. No news. Turned in reading Manaos papers but equally no news in them. Hope to leave by "Ucayali" about 10.

[On blotter at top:]
Dr Paredes & Escurre called
Former's report & telegrams.
Lovely Cholo moço – on launch Victoria – thought of him all day & night & Reuss boy too –wished for both very much.
[at end] Gave back Report to Paredes.

DECEMBER

1 FRIDAY Fine morning. Writing till 10.30. Then to Muelle to Michells. Me and them – River slightly over 71' 1". To Michells in afternoon getting their house in order – poor souls. Gave several things & £10 to G.B.M. **[George Babington Michell (1864-1936) was coming to replace David Cazes as the new consul in Iquitos. This was to be a full-time appointment where Cazes, a Jewish Gibraltarian, had been doubling up as a trading agent. Casement was instructed to introduce Michell to the Peruvian Amazon area as he was tasked by the Foreign Office to follow up the Putumayo issue. Michell had been posted as vice-consul to Stanleyville in Katanga in 1905, and immediately previously to Paris partly on Congo business. He found time to publish on native Congo languages. On 24 July 1911, Michell, who was part of the wider Casement Africa web, wrote thanking him: "I appreciate very highly your recommending me for the post at Iquitos." He was apparently eager for another consulate away from civilisation. Despite the health dangers in**

Iquitos, Michell was accompanied by his wife Marion and two daughters. His two younger children stayed in England at school. Casement's opinion of him, expressed in the diary in January 1911 when they met in Paris, was typically unflattering.[582]] Invited them all to dinner at 7. Cost 20 soles = £2.0.0. Met Alejandro Alaysa who complimented me on my Spanish – with Paredes. Reading latter's report all day. José waiting at 8.20 in doors. I left room open – & I left him till 9.20 as I stayed with Michells till then. He stayed till 10.30 & I helped him on with his English. Have (D.V.) decided to go by "Ucayali" on Thursday next (D.V.). Felt José's once or twice & clasped him often.

2 SATURDAY Lovely morning. Wrote Hambloch, Barry (Pedro) & Avellino. Finishing with Paredes Report – it is very well done. To Harding at 5. Got letter from Lugard in Hong Kong – & Eva [**Frederick Lugard, a Nigerian administrator from 1894, was Governor of Hong Kong from 1907 to 1912. Later Lord Lugard, he was between 1912 and 1919 Governor General of Nigeria. Here he congratulated Casement on his knighthood and belatedly on the Congo report. The tone of the letter, which Casement marked as received on 2 December in Iquitos, and as answered from Manaos on 12 December, suggests they knew each other in Africa.[583]**

The letter from Eva is also marked by Casement in his usual style – "R. 2 Dec 1911", and is signed "Eve Symons". Her address was then 89 Range Road in Shanghai although Casement has earlier addresses of 9 Rifle Range, Shanghai and c/o the Church Missionary Society, Salisbury Square London, for her in his address book and yet another at the back of the 1903 Black Diary. She is the missing Casement cousin with whom he was said to have been "in love" as a lad of seventeen.

Mrs Eve Symons was born Lanphier. Gertrude was unclear as to whether Eve was the niece or daughter of Rev. Somerville Lanphier who had married Eleanor Casement, Roger's aunt. The evidence suggests she was a niece, the daughter of Dr Richard Lanphier of Lincoln. Their mutual uncle Somerville Lanphier was born in Cork and had been a clergyman in Ballymena in the 1860s, before an appointment as chaplain to Nottingham's County Asylum around 1874. He died in 1877 having been briefly the boy Roger's guardian and the family's financial controller since the death of their father. And this despite being considered by the father as "my greatest enemy in undermining me with my Uncle Thomas for his own ends and had proofs of much."[584] Aunt Eleanor Lanphier was last heard of in New Zealand where her sister Agnes Aickin lived. In July 1904, Casement sent a cheque for £10 to her son Casement Aickin, a timber merchant in Auckland. No reason for such a large gift was recorded but it reveals a continued connection with the families of his father's sisters.[585] He also recorded in his address

book[586] the name of Josiah Martin in Auckland who had provided "photos of New Zealand types", presumably Maoris.

In the letter dated 4 August 1911, Eve offered "warmest congratulations on the Coronation Honour" and wished him "happy return of the 1st.. The birthday wishes for 1 September took four months to find and reach him from China. After complaining as to why the British were allies with the Japanese, a "clever but conceited little race", and detailing her husband and children's activities (cricket, carpentry and Jardine Mattheson), she asks him to "give my love to your sister when you write. I often think of my happy days at Ballycastle."

This was an intimate letter but very much a family one, not that of an old flame. There is an echo of time at Magherintemple spent together. Although Gertrude believed Casement had a teenage crush on Eve – born five years before him, there is nothing here to suggest anything so romantic. The teenage Casement's strong feelings for Eve, if such they were, are still being quoted as evidence of a heterosexual orientation.[587]]
– Bought bed for Ricudo. "Truth" (18 Oct) a further attack on the Putumayo. Michells to dinner with me again. It cost 21 soles £2 2/- – They have Brown & Ricudo in house with them. [**No mention of "the wee fox" Omarino, but both boys were now installed as servants in the Michell household. Casement had so written to Gertrude a fortnight earlier saying "I shall leave both here with the new Consul." He had thus solved his, and their problem, but at the risk of being called a hypocrite since he had railed against "gentle docile" Indians being effectively "purchased" for domestic service in Iquitos.[588]**] Met Paredes in evg. with Harding after seeing M's house. He says he wd. be in jail too if it were not for his paper. Macedo is at Manaos. Today's "Heraldo" has an attack on me he says by Rey de Castro! [**Peruvian consul-general in Brazil**] & a letter from Macedo. [**Victor Macedo was the Arana agent at La Chorrera the company's main trading post, a man Casement described as "swarthy, thick set with bloodshot eyes and looks like a mixture of hyaena and panther."[589]**] Zumaeta elected President of new Club!

3 SUNDAY <u>River 71' 7".</u> at 6 p.m. Paredes called to say he considered the whole thing a farce. Lanetta [**lawyer, and then Mayor of Iquitos**] is retained as Macedo's advocate! All are against Paredes. He fears assassination & again warns me not to go to Putumayo. Says I will be attacked too – just like Hardenberg & if I go to Putumayo, in danger. He goes Lima this month. José for an hour 10.30 to 11.30. Gave 15/- for M. Cocha & then at 3.30 to Michells & with them until 7. Dined with Harding at B. Vista & walked after on Malecon till 11 p.m. seeing Arequipa soldier – huge one who wanted it & sat beside me.

[At top of page:] River today
4 MONDAY Rain y'day & cold morning. Busy getting papers for Michell to read & writing too. Hope sincerely now to get away by "Ucayali" on Thursday morning. I am tired of Iquitos! God help the Michells. Gave Michell long account of the Putumayo beginning of things – & some of my despatches to F.O. recounting latest features of the whole dirty business here. Then to call on Mrs Cazes & wish her many happy returns as it is her birthday. Back to house & wrote more till 7 & then dinner with J. Lilly & G.B. Michell at Bella Vista. José at house at 8 waiting. Left him writing till 9.15 when joined him till 10.15. Mine up huge again as usual & once more nearly did it in garden with him pumping & after told him I was leaving by "Ucayali".

5 TUESDAY Hope to catch "Rio Curaca" today at Remate de Males (12 Nov.) – (Alas! I did not – I am still in Iquitos!) Lovely morning (awakened with vivid dream of 1887-1888 going up Mazamba Hill* – Oh! God – to think of it – "The fields of Heaven" from Congo dia Lemba – 24 years ago in the hey day & glowing flush of my youth – just 23 years old – more than half my life gone since then). Expect Dr Paredes now with telegrams. Ignacio Torres is at Nueva York Estate on Ucayali River with Daniel Fachin. José knows & will send photos. Out to Michells & Cazes. Got cloth for Ricudo's mosquito curtain. Dined with Michells. Left door open for José. Back at 10.15 & found him there & talked & felt – stiff as poker till 10.45. Lovely night with full moon & glorious sky & air as light & fresh as possible. Read El Oriente of today & Pableto. Paredes called on me earlier today with news of wire from Lima to Corte **[court]**.

[On blotter:] 5th Felt José's stiff & really this time. It was very big & he allowed me to do it just as I liked – never moving all the time.
Got long Cipher wire of 29 Novr. from F.O. most of it unintelligible but clear they are making strong representations to Lima. 4 p.m.

---

* Mazamba is mentioned in Casement's memorable final letter to Dick Morten of 28 July 1916 (NLI 17044) where he wrote of Ward, "I am very sorry for Herbert and Sarita losing their Charlie – tell them so – someday – not now. I am sorry Herbert has not a more understanding mind – I should not have treated him so – but I do not think of it and when I think of him it is of earlier days when the good things of life were all contained for him and me in a Huntley & Palmer Biscuit tin – and we were lugging the Crank Shaft of the "Florida" over Mazamba Hill down to the Bumbizi & up again, to the night camp when the red ants came. Oh! So long, long ago – (February-March 1887 it was)." He concluded with, "I made awful mistakes – did heaps of things wrong – confused much and failed at much but I very near came to doing some big things...Goodbye dear old Dick and don't forget me & forgive everything wrong."

6 WEDNESDAY Fine morning. In house all day nearly. Dr Paredes called in the morning and I gave him letter to Anti-Slavery Socty. to Travers Buxton & told him call on **[Pedro]** Zulen & Jerome in Lima (to latter also a letter of introduction). He promises to get me the telegram the Court is sending to Lima. Asked him for his Report again & got it back at 9 p.m. & will copy much of it tonight. José came at 6 & I gave (lent) him £6 for a suit to be repaid later on. Gave him the photos for Ignacio Torres to post & write. He says Daniel Fachin is a Loretano **[from Loreto, the Peruvian region along the Ucayali river, whose capital is Iquitos]** and not very honest. "He robs the a/cs of his péons" – is half an Indian & Loretano. Harding & Paredes came at 9 p.m. & I gave latter final advice as to his action in Lima & promised to get the whole of the "processo" sent to the Minister of Justice, so that he can judge of the enormity of the crimes & remove the matter from the hands of these d-d rascals here. José at 9.20 to 10.30 & felt his & laid his hand on mine – stiff. Gave him 1$ for Punchana on 8th – Now to copy out Paredes report at 10.45 p.m. Bid José goodbye. Up till 4 a.m. at it.

[At top of page:] Up till 4 a.m. & only 2 hours sleep. Up again at 6 a.m. Gave José the photos for poor Ignacio & £6 loan.
7 THURSDAY I hope to be leaving today at 11 a.m. in "Ucayali". Up early packed & off to Michells & to Hardings. Paid bills & bid goodbye all round & then to "Ucayali". Nice young corporal on board of Loreto Regt. with a fine one. He saluted me & smiled. All down to bid goodbye. Off at 11 a.m. with hat waving & so to the downward path. I don't suppose I'll ever see Iquitos again – altho' it is quite possible I may – but I do not want to. **[Casement reported to his cousin Gertrude that Ricudo could not make the actual parting – "the big boy got an attack of something the day before I sailed, and the morning I came away he seemed very ill indeed, and could hardly walk. He had been to the Putumayo, found his wife and brought her back to Iquitos, and she was going to live with the Consul's family too, and do the cooking."[590]]** – "Ucayali" steaming well and at 5.30 we passed Pevas & so into the night – Sleeping on deck on my campbed. No cabin available at all. Work in Stewards' room. River on leaving Iquitos had dropped 2" or 3" – it stood 71' 9" or 8".

8 FRIDAY At Leticia at 6 a.m. & soon off again & at Tabatinga & on to Esperanza where we finished before 10 a.m. & away downstream. Passed São Paulo de Olivença at 6.10 p.m. – 2 hours ahead of "Atahualpa" last year. Rain in night several times, but it did not touch my camp bed. Writing to F.O. all the recent developments at Iquitos & Paredes complaints to me.

9 SATURDAY At daylight steaming past Jutahy, prettily perched on steep red clay banks on downward bank of the mouth of the Javari – the black clear water of which refuses to mingle with the red flow of the Amazon for some distance. Many birds at Jutahy – the town small & pretty. We are steaming 15 knots – 350 – miles per day & should reach Manaos about 12 midnight or possibly earlier on Sunday – a thousand pities not in time to land on that festive strand on its gayest night of the week. Wrote to F.O. a long despatch I had drafted y'day.

10 SUNDAY Copied my F.O. despatch for Lima to go on by "Ucayali" to Barbados whence to Colon. Passed Cámara in its lake at 6 a.m. looking very pretty – on well & cool. Writing all day to F.O. & Lima till evg. & then Bridge with Captain, Engineer, Mrs Gye. Slept only to 12. when we got to Rio Negro & anchored at Manaos at 12.30 a.m.

[At top of page:] at Manaos again
11 MONDAY (Hope to arrive today in Manaos – 11 Dec) Robilliard & Dening off & I on shore & to Hotel Cassina & out to lunch with them at Parrot House. Then to Hotel & wrote till 5 (after getting things from Customs) & after a light & vile dinner out to walk around till 11.20 p.m. No good at all. Saw no one I knew & very few I liked – one lovely lad in Bar at 9 with paper. He quite beautiful & Huge one. Only ~~16~~ 17. & sturdy splendid limbs. Some police wanting & one grand mulatto at 7.30 in Gardens. Tall & huge one – 8" long at least. Pumped & then on seat showed it huge. I spoke. It about 8" lying down under duck pants **[work pants]** & thick too.

12 TUESDAY Rain in night but very little. Writing private letters most of day & talking Savage London – Beard cut 1$ at 6 p.m. Awful heat. Early dinner & out at 6.30 & heavy tornado during which I sat in Café & then to Kiosque & then a few minutes up & down when saw nice white work boy eye me. Asked time & he fingered it & said "Cedo" **[early]** – so I "passeando" & he at once – just 7.30 & then Agostinho "whished" & followed & promised to go at 11. Up with work boy to old Palace & there he entered, hard & loving much, feeling stomach & "mamilos" **[nipples]** – "Antonio" of Cabedello. Back to Avenida & up & down often & one big Black in whites wanted badly. Saw two police ones. Then at 10.40 to Agost. & he in hard & loving. To meet on F. at 11. At 11.30 two guarda mor moços **[young policemen]** & one young one (boy) lovely & huge long stiff one – 8" tight pants. Café terrible. **[If, as Casement often noted, a considerable number of those out cruising or expressing interest were themselves policemen, the chances of being exposed or arrested were significantly lessened. Because of internal and external**

threat these Amazon towns were cluttered with young soldiers and various types of local guards and police.]

13 WEDNESDAY Tired after y'day & wrote very little indeed. Changed bedroom at 4. Sent all mails home, including £10 for Nina by "Hilary", due 31 Decr. Saw Shandon again & lunched together and after then lay down in bed. Changed bedroom at 4. Very hot day again & bathed in perspiration. Called at M-M R'y only to find that May gone by "Hilary" to Pará. Strange not to tell me. Early dinner at 6.30 & out with raincoat to meet Antonio of Cabedello at 8. Left Hotel 7 & almost at once met the tall mulatto boy of Monday walking round by Cathedral. Said "Boa Noite" & he greeted too & instantly I turned & he shook & I asked to walk & he said yes. So away first to Cemetery where I asked if big & he smiled & he said yes & then I put hand on it & found it huge & stiff as policeman's truncheon. Asked if he liked to enter & he said "Yes" at once so on at last to alugar **[rented room]** & he entered with a will. To meet tomorrow & go Flores. He did not ask for or want any money. Is "Aprigio" of Alagoas. Back too late for Antonio but waited there till 8.15 & no sign of him there. To Café & lovely moço again with it stiff. The young Bombeiro **[fireman]** & Aprigio passed at 9 p.m. & then a Darkie with Huge one wanted me & followed & asked after pumping. He certainly wanted much it is stiff & very big. He about 24 or 25. Aprigio is 22. Caboclo of Maceio. Then a white moço tall – 6ft 1" – thin & Inca nose – huge. Wanted longingly.

[On blotter:] Lost 50$000 note out of pocket at 7.50 p.m. with Aprigio **[Ironically he had not sought money.]**

[At top of page:] Slept well – after Aprigio – Thinking often.
14 THURSDAY In room all morning – tired & very hot. Lunched alone & a talk with **[name left blank by Casement]** of Booths. Then to Tram centre at 1.15 & shoes by young Italian Imp who offered "Alguma coisa" **[something]** – I agreed to do it later. Out to João Pensador by tram, bathed there & walked back to cricket & to the bathing pool there. Seven school boys (one a cafuzo of 17-18) & 5 of them white & 4 had huge ones & all pulled & skinned & half cock all time. One a lad of 17 had a beauty all "gentlemen". After dinner out at 7.10 met Aprigio on seat. Stiff as poker & huge. So together to terracos baldia **[uncultivated terraces]** where sucked & then he in. Left & met Antonio my sweet Caboclo of last time & he followed & showed place & in too – hard. Huge *testemunhos* & loved & kissed. Nice boy. Then young *Alfandega, Guarda mór* darkie, big & nice – bayonet & felt it huge & stiff as his bayonet. Awfully warm. Nice lovely Italian boy passed at 11 & smiled & so to bed.

[On blotter:] Aprigio **X**
Antonio **X**
Grande moço **X**

15 FRIDAY Warm day. Out to Café & met "Grego" **[Greek]** of last Sept. who came & shook & told me he lived in 20 Sarmento ("Leilões".) Then to M-M & asked Woodroffe to lunch. He came & told me of Julio Arana waiting here till the process is "dead" & then getting the Putumayo "straight" after our demoralization. Trams round town & then out to Flores & back at 5. Missed Arana Bros visit – Thank goodness. Out at 7. & almost at once met Antonio of Cabedello & fled. Then Aprigio in gloom of trees, then Antonio Caboclo at Café – also met Agostinho – & at 9.30 a lovely Pará Moço boy gentleman who wanted & said yes & tried hard come, but I "away in breeks" & promised for tomorrow at 8.30 at Terríveis. To Agostinho at 10 & home at 11 very tired & disgusted. **[Casement is suffering from a sexual surfeit and subsequent ennui, and is not prepared to repeat last night's performance, although the intent is there.]**

16 SATURDAY Saw Woodroffe in morning & talked about Putumayo devils. Out after lunch (& before it too) & went all round on Cachoeirinha **[little waterfall]** Circular tram & back at 2 to Booths. Saw none on journey – but some after. The route round Manaos quite interesting. To Café dos Terríveis At 7.50 till 8.40 – but the young Paraense did not come & so up & down all night till at 10 met one I had seen often before, a young lad in white trousers & blue coat & he offered and so after a little away together to same place as Antonio Caboclo where I to him – he refusing – soft & nice. Saw the *Guarda mór* darkie **[Casement has the name of a "guarda mór", Jose Lobo Viarma, in his address book[591]]** once or twice – & at Alhambra & fine young Darkie sailor boy – from Bahia.

17 SUNDAY Left Manaos at 10 a.m. in "Hubert" for Pará – very comfortable ship. I don't feel well & lay down all day.

18 MONDAY We had to anchor 8½ hours in the night, at Serpa Island, on account of smoke. Steaming down river all day. A Mr Sanceau on board who has been right across Brazil & Bolivia & then through Peru too. He declares the Bolivian & Peruvian Indians are all slaves & agrees in his statements with Nordensjkold. "Hubert" is very comfortable and clean & good stewards.

19 TUESDAY Steaming down river – past the hill of Premha & Sierra Jutahy and at 5. near Gurupá entrance of channel. We should arrive Pará before 6 p.m. tomorrow evening I hope – but I am not sure of it, as we behind where Athualpa was last year. I am a bit better but not very well – & wonder what

news I may get from Tyrrell – if any. 1/20 **[long line drawn to next day's entry]** Arr. Pará 5.40 anchored & found guns but no 'San' & no agents!

20 WEDNESDAY Health visit 7.10 & Customs 7.20 & Booths & got ashore just 15 hours after we arrived. To Hotel do Commercio & after bath down to Camisaria Moderna & lo! there he was at door in new pants & It down left thigh – huge & enormous – & he lovely beyond words. Went in & tried to buy necktie asking him – saw him often after & met in street. He is quite splendid. To Tavares Cardoso too – several times – but no Augusto! To Pogson & letter from Tyrrell saying B.A. is given to Mackie of Congo! Alack – alack. So I am clear done out of that. What a shame. **[The Foreign Office had appointed Horatio Mackie, another old Africa hand, to the desirable Buenos Aires consulate. In 1905, Mackie had followed Casement from Dakar into his Boma and Loanda postings.]** After b'fast to B. Campos at 11.30 till 12.30 & also to Palace Square & saw many on seats & in trams & lots of huge ones – perfect monsters. A lovely young policeman at Hotel. Caboclo with big limbs, hands, soft face & huge curved one. He shook hands & we clung long. I loved him & followed to street. Out at 6 after early dinner to Palace & then very soon white work boy – nice – followed long but I to B. Campos when practicante of "Hilda" wanted & a small boy (lovely) with huge one. Tried but practicante spoiled by intercepting. To Nazareth where Huge one on seat (biggest ever seen) & after long rounds to Paz Theatre &c. &c. At last a Darkie there with very big one. Wanted & I pulled it & gave 5.000 & home at 1 a.m. New police in Pará – many caboclos.

21 THURSDAY See yesterday's entry – in error under Wednesday. I only landed today at 8.30 a.m. **[Casement's entries on this return leg of his journey are sparse and he must have failed to fill in one day, entirely, leading to this mistake.]** Got a few letters by "Anselm" today, but none from Nina – poor old soul. Charlie & Miss **[Margaret]** Causton & Mrs G**[reen]** & Agnes O'Farrelly.

X 5.000 **X** to Darkie at Paz Gardens

22 FRIDAY In house & out at 8.30 to ~~Pogson &~~ Pickerell & got my luggage from Customs only at 5 p.m. near 48 hours after landing & with immense difficulty after 5 visits to the Customs warehouse. To dinner on "Anselmo" after a visit to B. Campos 6-6.30 seeing one fine type on seat. After dinner with May &c. on "Anselm". Left at 8.40 & to B. Campos – none & Nazareth none & then Paz where a young moço tried – & then the Darkie who entered fiercely & hugely, pulling down pants & stripping. Again later on met him again & still more furiously – never anything like it. He asked "E bom?" **[What about that then?]** when putting in with awful thrusts. Saw several others.

23 SATURDAY Spent day mostly in Hotel. Kup & Coulson to lunch & then on "Anselm" to see Mays off at 1. Then to B. Campos for an hour but none & back to Hotel & to Pogson but Darkie came just near door, so I crossed Paz Gardens & on to Mrs Kup & Ornsteins [**Not the time or place for more of yesterday's vigorous action, so a diversionary tactic is adopted. Anyway Casement was off to bid farewell to chums from his old days in Pará. E.A. Kup who lived at Barbosa in Pará had stood in for him as acting consul in 1908 when he was recuperating in Barbados having cleared out of the "yellow fever hotel of Para".[592] Casement was under instruction to bring two bathrobes back from Barbados for Dr Ornstein which were wanted for his wife during the rest of her pregnancy.[593] Kup and Ornstein may well be the friends Dr Dickey was to describe as the people he normally saw Casement with in 1911 – a Eurasian and a nondescript English-speaking Swede.**] & then after dinner out to Palace Square & B. Campos & Nazareth. At Palace S. several & one splendid young mulatto like "Aprigio" beautiful limbs & clothing & huge one on seat at corner – but shy & finally home with none all night.

24 SUNDAY Embarked on "Denis" for Barbados at 9 a.m. Fine boat & only 5 passengers for Galveston – so heaps of room. [**This was to be Casement's last ever day in Brazil although he remained technically in post as consul-general at Rio de Janeiro for some time.**]

25 MONDAY Christmas day on "Denis". Spent day reading mostly – old books & loafing. Weather cool & fine – Ran 258 miles from 10.56 a.m. on Sunday. Bbados 941 miles. Poor old Hyacinthus is not well & won't eat. [**She is the parrot eventually given to W.A. Cadbury. He later wrote, "Polly is quite at home, has chewed up one perch – I am now doing her a new trapeze business."[594] Her behaviour was to worsen and she was subjected to discipline for pecking Emmeline Cadbury despite an otherwise poor appetite. Casement wrote in 1913 that he was "sorry to hear poor Polly is becoming all ravening in beak and claw." He was sufficiently concerned about the bird's future treatment to say the peck had gone to his heart.[595]**]

26 TUESDAY Cold morning – & sea – Ran only ~~287~~ 301 miles leaving 640 miles to Barbados.

27 WEDNESDAY Ran 287 miles only leaving 358 to Barbados so I fear now we shall arrive too late to land tomorrow. I wonder if I shall see Stanley Weeks – I hope so – very much.

28 THURSDAY Cold morning. & showers of rain at times. We may arrive at Bridgetown before 6 p.m. but I doubt it.

Run today = 254 miles only
Leaving to Bridgetown 100 – We got into Bridgetown at about 9 p.m. & Dr Bridges came off & the three tourists went on shore. I stayed on board. I just missed the Royal Mail at 1 p.m. for Cherbourg & the "Verdi" at 8 p.m. for New York. Bad luck.

29 FRIDAY On shore at Barbados with "Polly" to Sea View Hotel. **[The stay cost six shillings per day from 29-31 December, according to Mrs Seon's bill.[596]]** & on board in afternoon for baggage – as find there is a Lamport & Holt vessel on 31 for New York – the "Terence". To Point to bath – but none at all – to Club with Dr Bridges at 2 p.m. After dinner in to Bridgetown & out to Hastings Rocks **[scene of much eyeing in August]** & Marine Hotel to a dance.

30 SATURDAY To "Denis" with Polly & leaving some baggage on board. Took ticket for New York & drew £40 from Bank. Ticket $50 = <u>£10.8.4</u> deposit 4$. In to town & meal & nice sodawater & milk & to Fontabelle & then to Dr Deane's at 8.15. **[Frederick Deane had been Casement's physician in 1908 charging him £5.15.0 for medical services.[597]]** Back on foot at 10 p.m. & turned in. To St. Lawrence Hotel to see young Dickey Indian. **[This was presumably a Putumayo lead provided by Herbert Dickey.]**

31 SUNDAY S.S. "Terence" arr. in night. To Health Office 8 a.m. & to Bank & then to RC Church to Fr. Smith & Fr McCormick. On board "Terence" at 2.30 p.m. and reached her 3 p.m. She left about 3.30 or so for New York & so ends 1911. **[And also this last of the Black Diaries.]** I am the <u>only</u> passenger! **[a fact confirmed by the passenger manifest on the Ellis Island website]** Turned in early & slept very badly.

[Casement was to make his way to the United States where the British ambassador, James Bryce (1832-1922), himself a South American expert and also an Ulster man was to arrange for him to see President Taft in Washington. The State Department was always concerned about breaches of the Monroe Doctrine while London wanted to enlist U.S. support in putting pressure on Peru to clean up the Putumayo. Taft is said to have succumbed to the force of Casement's arguments, a meeting that was likened by one British diplomat to that between a black snake and a wombat.[598] The first and last Viscount Bryce, so created in 1914, had been Chief Secretary for Ireland from 1905-06. Born in Belfast, he was educated at Belfast Royal Academy and later in Scotland. Although he declined to sign a petition, he made an attempt, in conjunction with Eva Gore-Booth, to gain a reprieve for Casement by getting across the fact that his intention after landing in April had been to stop the Easter Rising (for lack of sufficient German assistance).

There are then a final two pages of entries in the diary, both carefully filled with accounts, calculations and currency conversions. The first is private with Casement calculating the cost in local currency of gifts to partners in Pará and Manaos in September and October 1911 which came to 273$500. It is instructive to read his view of these costs in that they are not payments for sex but described as gifts to individuals who were largely enthusiastic parties.

Gifts [**to sex partners**] in Pará & Manaos Sept & Oct 1911.

Pará		
2 Augusto Gomez dos Santos	20$000	[**14 & 16 September**
1 Rio	17$000	**17 September**
João Anselmo de Lima	10$000	**14 September**]
1 Augusto	47$000	
	1 500 tram	
	48$500 Pará	

[**Numbers of sexual occasions, name and gift amount list. (These cash figures appear in the related Ledger entry):**]

4 Agostinho	65 000	[**1 & 2 October**
1 Bramlio	15 000	**2 October**
Cafuzo (surprise)	18 000	**30 September**
2 Commandante Freitas	15 000	**1 October ("Sailor Negro")**
1 Raymundo	12.000	**1 October ("Aprendiz Marinheiro")**]
	125$000	– Manaos
	48$500	
[**Divided by**] 15	173$500	£ (11.11.4
	15	
	23	
	15	
	8	

173.500

add Sundries	100
	273.50

The last inscribed page, numbered 106, relates to the official costs of his journeying to Iquitos which reveals that a total of £131.19.0 had been spent. This amount covered Casement from leaving London in August 1911 until his arrival in Iquitos via Barbados, Pará and Manaos and details fares, hotels, landing fees, porters, stewards' tips, wine bills etc. It would be reclaimed from the Foreign Office although the costs for the two boys were removed from Casement's letter to Sir Edward Grey giving the actual amount of his disbursements. Sent from Iquitos, it was dated 23 October 1911 (NLI 13081/2). The total amount claimed came to £90.4.6. Casement also explained why he had travelled via Barbados. The final page of the diary, numbered 107, consists of advertisements.]

[Pre-printed:] **NOTES FOR 1912.**

...

...My passage to Iquitos. begins 16 Augt. 1911.

16 Augt. – "Magdalena" to Barbados	£21.12.0
4 Sept "Boniface". Bbados to Pará	8. 6.8
23 .. "Hilda". Pará to Iquitos	20. 8.0
	£50. 6.8
Train to Sp'ton	13.6
Cab & porters London	9. 0
Landing & going off Barbados	10. 0
Luggage transfer Barbados on shore...	
Hotel at Pará 12 days	12. 0.0
	£73. 5.8
Hotel at Manaos 5 days	5. 0.0
Actual expenditure was as follows.	
My passage to Barbados.	21.12.0.
2 Boys	36. 0.0.
Tickets to Spton self 13/6. 2 Boys 19/-	1.12.6
Cab (London) 9/8. Porters 7/- 4/-	1. 0.8.

Tips Stewards "Magdalena" 4/- 5/- 2.11/-	3. 0.0
Landing &c. Boat 3/3. 5/9. 1/-	10.0
Hotel 6.8/-. Tips. Going off boat 6/- 6/7 =	7. 0.7
"Boniface" Passages –	
Self 6.6.8. 2 Boys 6.6.8 Tips 1/2.2	14.15.0
Landing Pará 10$000 – going off $20.000.	2. 0.7
Hotel Pará –	
Self 80$000. 40$000. Extras 104$500 = 224$500	
Boys 80$000. 40$000 = 120$000	23. 5.11
Tips at hotel 63$000 =	4. 1. 9
	£113.19.0
Boys Passage to Iquitos 270$000 =	18. 0.0
	£131.19.0.

[By comparison with the other journals, the 1911 Black Diary stands out for its near-narrative mode and the remarkable frequency of the sexual accounts. For the most part it also lacks Casement's trademark Xs. Sex references were so commonplace Xs were hardly necessary. The diary does give the impression of not being revisited by Casement to the same extent. Perhaps its density or even its explicit nature repelled him. More likely the lack of financial detail made it less relevant especially as he had the 1911 Cash Ledger for that purpose.

To explain this heavy sexualisation, one must first note that Casement was nearly fifty. He was now in middle age and would have reckoned his opportunities were going to dry up. Ironically, at the same time, the sex was getting better as he became more experienced and calculating. The many José episodes, of course, add to the high frequency, but as the pursuit progressed, writing the diary itself became part of the turn-on. Casement also had much more time on his hands in 1911 with no particular task, no team accompanying him, and no visit to the Putumayo itself. In Iquitos he had a dwelling of his own and on the return journey through Manaos and Pará he was no longer encumbered with Ricudo and Omarino.

The sheer repetition of his sexual sightings, let alone the uniformly enormous size of members noted, has raised suspicion. Of course his visual sample would have been much greater than those he recorded, the less well-endowed or invisible simply not getting a mention. The lack of underpants then, as can be seen from photographs of the era, alongside the

crude tailoring, were (with the Amazon sexualisation) probably key factors in the frequency of such spectacles. Underpants were hardly invented at this point only starting to appear in the early twentieth century. They were undoubtedly rare in South America compared to their near universality today (alongside the ubiquitous uniform of blue jeans).]

Sir William Rothenstein's 1911 portrait of Ricudo (Arédomi) and Omarino

12

1911 Amazon coda: Ricudo and Omarino

There is a sad, if predictable, coda to Casement's journeys and journals of 1910 and 1911 concerning the ultimate fate of the two Indian boys. They had been taken out of the Putumayo and after six months in Barbados sent to England. Casement's intentions toward the two boys were entirely humanitarian and he behaved impeccably, keeping them well clothed, well fed and watered, and royally entertained. On several occasions in 1910 he did record his impressions of the older boy's body: 4 November "Arr Sur 9.30 and bathed Arédomi carrying clothes showed huge. Told him bathe too, and he stripped. No *fono* on – Carbolic soap – glorious limbs, a big one." A *fono* is a small bark penis sheath or strap. Both boys were to be memorialised in paint by Sir William Rothenstein (although he felt he needed more time to finish the portrait) before returning with Casement to Peru in August 1911.

Casement had initially made arrangements for one of the boys to go instead to Ireland to be educated. He chose St Enda's, the bilingual school founded by Patrick Pearse in Rathfarnham, where Mary Colum also taught. Pearse, in a letter dated 15 June 1911, replied to Casement, accepting Omarino as a pupil, and writing "I shall be very glad to receive your young Indian at St Enda's. Indeed I think it will be a very interesting experiment for myself personally. I am sure he will be at home among our boys…We break up for the summer vacation on Wednesday next, but I could easily arrange to keep the boy during July and August. I shall be in the west during July and could take him with me to my cottage there where I generally take one or two of the boys in the summer…Let me know when you expect to arrive here with him…I sincerely hope that between us we shall make a great success of this barbarian. It is work that appeals to me very much."[599] The annual fees were £45 which included a uniform and a kilt for drill.

Pearse's own sexuality has been the stuff of controversy and dispute. One camp suggests he was terminally naive about sexual matters thus rendering his innocent writings prey to mocking innuendo. The other believes that no-one could have written the poem *Little Lad of the Tricks*, first published in Irish in 1909 – before his significant (and brief) political phase – without having some sexual yearning for boys, no matter how unrequited, and without knowing that he had. It has to be said that there is a similar intensity and sense of illegality to Casement's feelings as expressed in *The Nameless One*, that version written in 1900.

Ricudo, the older Amazindian boy brought to England, wearing necklace and armband in 1910 (NLI CAS 21C)

There is a fragrance in your kiss
that I have not found yet
in the kisses of women
or in the honey of their bodies.

Lad of the grey eyes,
that flush in thy cheek
would be white with dread of me
could you read my secrets.

He who has my secrets
is not fit to touch you:
is that not a pitiful thing,
little lad of the tricks.

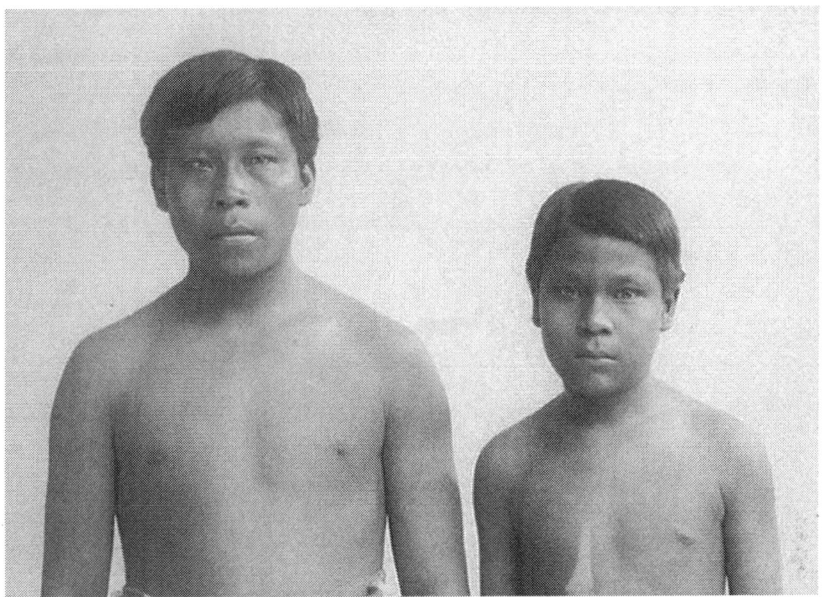

Ricudo and Omarino, shirtless, London 1911, Museum of Archaeology and Anthropology Cambridge

Whether the secrets are Pearse's improper obsession with his own death or a shameful passion for the boy himself, they seem, given his longing for death, to be sourced from one and the same thing. In another poem, *Why Do Ye Torture Me*, he complains of his heart's desires driving him inexorably, night and day, to a doom which would complete his earthly task. Again there is an echo of Casement's frequent assertions of the virtue, even the necessity for him, of death at a young age. In the latter case this is the classic theme of those men whose preference is for boys or younger men and who know their sexual days will inevitably run out early, leaving them, they fear, riven with frustration.

For no recorded reason, the St Enda's proposal and Pearse's offer were not taken forward, so there was to be no Amazonian involvement in the Easter Rising or the War of Independence. Instead the boys returned to Peru. Cadbury, their Bourneville benefactor, writing on 9 August 1911 must have been consulted as he was responding "I can understand your anxiety about the Indian boys but fancy you are right in taking them with you – they would feel dreadfully lonely by themselves in this country."[600] Casement promised on the day he left England that he would "not leave them in the desolate forest – but in Iquitos with a friend there."[601]

Ricudo went home from Iquitos to collect his wife after his year long absence but difficulties had arisen, as Juan Tizon wrote to Casement: "Your

Ricudo and Omarino in European clothes, J. Thomson studio London 1911, from the book of photographs of the 1912 Viaje de la Comisión Consular al Río Putumayo y Afluentes (p. 235)

boy Ricudo came, but unfortunately his wife is now the wife of another Indian, the boy Nicholas, who you perhaps remember. A boy in this house who used to clean our rooms. The woman will not follow Ricudo, she says that he left her alone and that he has no right to claim her now, & as I don't think I can oblige her to go, he is returning alone. The boy Ricudo said that he should like to remain here with me, as my boy. I am sending him back now, but if there is no objection on your part, he might come back, and I would be glad to keep him as he is a good boy…PS In the last moment I arranged the matter of the boy satisfactorily and Ricudo is leaving with his woman and Nicholas is perfectly satisfied."[602] Tizon's letter is dated 15 November and confirmed in Casement's diary entry for 25 November when their return on the "Beatriz" after a month is mentioned. He also noted, "Ricudo says things are much better – little floggings now, and that Tizon does his best for the Indians – but then Ricudo never left La Chorrera! He never went near Naimenes or to see any of his people. What a race!".

In the event, Casement arranged for them to be taken on as servants by the new, dedicated, British consul, George Michell and his wife Marion. This was not to go unnoticed or unremarked. Louis Barnes of the enquiry team passed on a conversation with another member, Hal Lex Gielgud, saying that "the consul in Iquitos had the two boys…working as servants and that everyone in Iquitos called them slaves and it was creating a very bad impression." Barnes asked "Have you heard anything of this? I think HLG is a bit inclined to run with the hare and hunt with the hounds."[603]

Despite Gielgud's later chirpy and sincere letters to Casement, he was of course a company man and the sentiment about his two-sidedness was one which Casement had already noted in his diaries, describing him also (on 19 November 1910) as "a nonentity, a paid servant of the Company with really no mind of his own, – an absent-minded beggar."* But he was open to accusations of hypocrisy since he had complained about Indians in Iquitos being effectively enslaved as domestic servants.

David Cazes kept Casement informed about his successor as consul, telling him in April 1912, "I persuaded Michell to take our place. I thought it would be more comfortable and healthier for them." Later he advised, "You have no doubt heard that Mrs Michell and daughters have left Iquitos and are on the way home."[604] Both Michells also corresponded in 1912, relating how the boys had fared in Iquitos. They had not adapted to urban or European ways.

George Michell wrote first, on 7 March 1912, hardly three months after Casement's departure. The letter is marked as received in London on 9 April: "All the Indians have left us. 'Omo' is I hear working on board and has gone down river. Ricudo and his wife took themselves off early on Tuesday morning with all their traps and went on board the 'Liberal' wanting to go back to Chorrera. I had told them they would not be allowed to return there and I thought they had given up the idea. But they did not get away after all as the Captain turned them off and said that he had orders to take no Indians either as crew or passengers. They have not come back to us yet and I don't know what they intend to do. I had been paying them two soles a week each for the month or six weeks. But they said "they were tired of work." I am sorry as we tried to be as kind to them as possible. I did as much housework as they did and my wife and the girls more! …We have moved into Cazes flat and find it much healthier. But the girls have fever today. The first any of us have had so far, happily."[605]

* As Lt.-Col. Henryk Gielgud M.C. of the Norfolk Regiment, Hal was to be killed aged 36, in 1917, at Cambrai in France.

The girls' malaria obviously distressed Mrs Michell, especially as her husband was away much of the time checking up on conditions in the Upper Amazon.[606] Dickey recalled meeting Michell (and the new American consul), on the Liberal, near the mouth of the Putumayo, accompanied by Julio Arana. The Doctor was heading into the region to start another well-paid and ill-judged medical job offered by Arana. On 20 July 1912, Mrs Michell advised Casement of her imminent departure, as her husband "has to be absent from Iquitos so constantly it is better for us to get back to England – at any rate for the present."

Then on 3 September, by this time living in Weston-Super-Mare, she wrote confirming her husband's earlier story: "About Ricudo and Omo, I was very sorry to leave Iquitos without knowing their whereabouts. I tried again and again to find out where they had gone but unsuccessfully, except for a report from a Spanish woman in the Arica who said Omo had gone away on a launch as he was bent upon getting to the Putumayo. When we moved to the Cazes' flat, Ricudo and his wife seemed very pleased with the change and quite happy and we thought would perhaps stay especially as the Captain of Arana's Company's steamer refused to take them – but Ricudo hated work and said he was "tired of it" and must get away to the woods! We could not think where they had gone and never saw them after they left us. I knew you would be disappointed but it was inevitable."[607]

Father Smith (who had experience of nomadic Indians) when explaining their situation to Casement earlier in 1911, from Barbados, reckoned the boys, especially Ricudo would not settle. The draw of the woods despite all the dangers and the hardship remained too strong. Nothing further is ever heard of them. Fêted in London, they chose to return to their own state – the forests and rivers of the Putumayo region. Not necessarily an unwise decision on their part.

13

Millar Gordon

Until the 1997 publication of Roger Sawyer's second book on the subject, *Roger Casement's Diaries – 1910: The Black and the White,* the mystery of the identity of Millar, Casement's only significant Irish boyfriend had not advanced beyond assumption and dramatic invention. He was frequently recorded by name, initial and anatomical description in both the 1910 Black Diary and the 1911 Cash Ledger. Having been a point of controversy in the 1960s when Herbert Mackey insisted that Millar was a misreading for Bulmer, he remained a tantalising area for further and future excavation. Apart from Adler Christensen, whom Casement granted recognition in Germany as his official companion (as opposed to *diener* or servant), no sexual partner other than Millar gets as many mentions in his diaries and letters, or in Casement literature. There was even some unlikely discussion between the Casement writers Peter Singleton-Gates and Roger McHugh that Millar was "the boy of Oscar Wilde."[608] They were presumably referring to Christopher Millard, Wilde's bibliographer, who was only ever a friend of his executor Robbie Ross, not Wilde himself. Millard died in 1927 aged fifty-five.

By the 1990s, there was now no prospect of any of Casement's friends or acquaintances being available to advance the search, had they even been willing to help. Millar would surely have had to have been born by 1885 and would therefore, if of average male life expectancy or even with better luck lasting until the age of eighty, be dead by 1965 at the latest. He would also have had to be fortunate enough to have survived the First World War which cut such a swathe through Ulster's young men, particularly at the Somme in July 1916.

The lack of conscription in Ireland did make it more likely that Millar might not have been in the army, thus avoiding death in the trenches. That being the case, it might have been Casement's influence that discouraged Millar from opting for military service. He was certainly old enough to have joined the UVF in 1912 and might have been, like many a young Ulsterman, especially those from Co. Antrim to this day, keen on motorbikes. His peers were already using their motor cycling skills in 1914 as despatch riders in the army of Craig and Carson, the UVF, during the Larne gunrunning in particular. Indeed Casement received a mysterious letter addressed from the Ulster Signalling and Despatch Riding Corps (O.C. A Sayers), Old Town Hall, Belfast as at the Despatch Riders Camp Magilligan in June 1914: "Will be very pleased indeed to meet you and talk over the matter referred to."[609] Departure to America intervened before he was able to pursue this Carsonite liaison.

Millar certainly wasn't to be spotted amongst the oldest denizens in or around Belfast's tiny gay scene – which this author discovered and entered in 1965. At that time the only gay venue in the north was the public bar, in Rosemary Street, of the Royal Avenue Hotel, which was just across the road from its superior rival, the Grand Central Hotel. The Royal Avenue Bar was to be memorialised in Maurice Leitch's 1965 novel *The Liberty Lad,* a remarkably sympathetic account of gay life, indeed probably the earliest set in an Irish city. The Grand Central was to figure in an entry in the Black Diary of 28 May 1910 when Millar "came to lunch." This memorable meal was also recorded as "Lunch Grand Central, Millar & I 7/6" in its flyleaf. Casement occasionally stayed there but used many other hotels when not on the Antrim Road.

In the preface to his 1997 book, Sawyer makes the point (needless in the event) that as the "black portions are personal and private" the publication in 1959 of *The Black Diaries* by Singleton-Gates only "forced" the issue. Although he became convinced they are genuine, a case could be made, he felt, for withholding access under the terms of the hundred year rule until "well into the 21st century" to spare the Casement and Parry families further hurt.

However, like the atom bomb, once published there was no going back and uninventing the matter. As the Singleton-Gates version of the 1910 Black Diary was "garbled" – which it was to a degree – Sawyer stated "a principal justification for republication today is to resolve the forgery issue once and for all." Well, resolved it wasn't as the mission ended in splitting the publishing team of Sawyer and Angus Mitchell and inaugurating the first post-modern case for forgery, by Mitchell, who proceeded to bring out his own book on the 1910 Amazon investigation, putting the opposite view as to whether Casement wrote the Black Diaries.

In rectifying errors and clarifying the confusions, Roger Sawyer's assiduous researches picked up perhaps the only other reference to Millar in official papers, ominously originating from the War Office Intelligence Department. The document, released in 1995, provided the vital clue for tracing the person who had until then had been masquerading under what was thought to be a surname. If a surname, it had been reckoned that Millar was a somewhat subservient individual who not only signed himself so but despite the hot intimacy recorded on a number of occasions was so referred to by Casement. It was, however, not a surname. That turned out to be Gordon, a seriously Scots name. The War Office document was quite informative but was only a cover note describing a letter that was still being withheld for security reasons. That was until the advent of a new British government prompted a policy change in May 1998 after pressure from the Irish peer, Lord Kilbracken.

Northern European young man with very short tie, possibly Millar Gordon

Casement in his thirties, in pin striped jacket, thick beard, looks somewhat haunted

The unsigned minute prefacing the, as yet unseen, item read: "See also letter within dated 31.7.16 from Major Frank Hall of the War Office Intelligence Department reporting that the person referred to by Casement as 'dear Millar', and to whom he says he gave a motor bicycle, has been identified as Joseph Millar Gordon: and that the transfer of a motor bicycle from Cyril Corbally to J.M. Gordon in 1911 has been traced."[610] This minute appears to have been written in the early 1930s by a Public Records Office archivist and also carries a paragraph stating that other Foreign Office correspondence in the file lists "incidents which would not be known to anyone contemplating the production of a forgery." Although the aforementioned letter remained withheld for a further three years, there was enough information provided to track Millar down. The reference to the gift of a motor bike bought from a Cyril Corbally is from the Cash Ledger entry for 3 June 1911 and the confirming price of £25 mentioned on that date crops up a couple of other times in Casement's papers.

If the diaries were forged, military intelligence was now on a wild goose chase which could collide with the truth. For if Millar was interrogated and convincingly denied any sexual aspect to his relationship with Casement then the whole conspiracy could come to grief. This of course underlines the fact that no one would be so foolish as to invent a homosexual character who was alive, Protestant and respectable. And one also living in Belfast from where Major Hall at times operated. His letter was to Sir Ernley Blackwell of the Home Office who was co-ordinating the diary verification in a cross-departmental investigation. Categorised "Private and Confidential" Hall's letter was significantly dated 31 July 1916.

Addressed from Adelphi Court, York Buildings, in London, it read: "Dear Sir Ernley, re Casement's diary: I have ascertained that the individual referred to as "dear Millar" in the entries under date May 28th/29th 1910, May 13th/14th & June 3rd 1911 is a young man named JOSEPH MILLAR GORDON aged 26, a clerk in the Donegall Sq. Branch of the Belfast Bank who resides with his mother at CARNSTROAN – Myrtlefield Park Belfast. We traced him through the Motor Cycle which Casement gave him. (One Cyril Corbally registered a TRIUMPH Motor Cycle F3044 in 1910 and in 1911 the number was transferred to J.M. Gordon.) Gordon has not been interviewed but if it was considered advisable to approach him on the subject we could easily arrange to have it done discreetly. Yours very truly, Frank Hall."[611]

The letter was written three days before the hanging at a time when Ernley Blackwell's mind was on other aspects of the matter, specifically the Cabinet's capacity for doubt over an execution. The reprieve bandwagon had gathered considerable pace, obliging him to circulate his famous memorandum "The Question of Expediency"[612] for the final Cabinet meeting of 2 August. Therein he argued that the rebellion itself, not the executions had brought about the change of attitude in Ireland. (He wrote separately on the reprieve itself, noting at the end, "I have dealt in a separate memorandum with the question of his diaries and the bearing they may have upon the decision".) Argument on Ireland took up the opening part of his text being unusually sensible and prescient, perhaps due to Blackwell's Scottish origins:

"I understand that several members of the Government are inclined to the opinion that it may be inexpedient to execute Casement. I suppose it is feared that in addition to the American question the hanging of Casement may interfere with the Irish settlement.

If Casement had been taken to Dublin a few days later he would of course have been court martialled and shot and would have been a 15th martyr.

The shooting of the 14 leaders is said to have given a great impetus to the Sinn Fein movement. I am inclined to think that the rebellion itself and its results have given the impetus and that the situation today would have been much the same whether Pearse, Connolly and the rest had been shot or merely sent to Portland with a confident expectation of amnesty and early release.

Casement's value as a martyr is already a good deal discounted. His private character is by this time pretty generally known in London. The 'Daily Express' on three occasions has openly stated that he is a moral degenerate addicted to unmentionable offences and has cited his 'diaries' in proof.

But assuming that the view is right that on national grounds it is inexpedient that Casement should be hanged I am quite at a loss to understand what it is hoped to gain by a Statutory Inquiry as to his sanity before a reprieve is announced. From the report of Drs. Percy Smith and Maurice Craig it is practically certain that Casement cannot be certified insane and sent to Broadmoor.

If the intention is that the report of a Statutory Tribunal of Alienists; which would probably be in similar terms, is to be made an excuse for respiting Casement on account of his mental condition he will have to be sent to penal servitude with a 'stigma' upon him which he and his sympathisers will say is far worse than death. There will be a demand for the evidence upon which the Alienists have based their opinion. Is the diary then to be published and in what form? It will of course be called a forgery and the original will somehow or other have to be proved. Mr. Doyle is now doing his utmost to inform the American President and public that attempts are being made to spread false reports of Casement's vices!

It appears to me that British public opinion has been entirely left out of account. Are the Government prepared to face the storm of indignation with which the reprieve will be greeted in this country? The public know that Casement is not insane, as they understand insanity, and they will simply regard the Inquiry as a subterfuge. It will be said that Casement has been reprieved not upon national but upon party grounds to further what is and always has been the policy of a section of the Cabinet in Irish matters."

In defence of Blackwell, his choice of the word expediency was to address the fears of those who saw an execution as inexpedient. He was convinced the national interest required execution, not least because of the storm of indignation that would otherwise have to be faced. Pretending that Casement was insane was, he felt, a transparent subterfuge that would just open up the demand for the diaries to be published. That the Foreign Office had already been judiciously using the contents of the diaries seems something Blackwell was not aware of. Asquith finally authorised Cecil Spring Rice, ambassador in Washington, to use them, "confidentially", around 29 July, although copies had been sent earlier on 21 July.

"Had Casement not been a man of atrocious moral character, the situation would have been even more difficult" wrote Blackwell's political master, the Liberal MP, Herbert Samuel. This remark of the Home Secretary confirms that Casement being reckoned "a moral degenerate addicted to unmentionable offences" and, of course, the diaries themselves, had done the trick. Blackwell's general and specific pleading certainly sealed his fate. Ironically, in 1905, the same Herbert Samuel was being fancied by Casement as something of a kindred spirit[613] although by 1914 he had changed his mind, reporting instead "Most Irishmen refer to Mr Samuel as an 'asiatic half caste or half-bred Jew."[614]

Millar was not needed. Indeed there was insufficient time to introduce Millar into the issue, nor was this the right moment. And Sir Ernley was the last man to complicate matters with a potential wild card. If an interview ever took place, no evidence to that effect has been found. To the modern eye it is remarkable that the police and security machine did not exploit or simply crush lesser characters like Millar. But it has to be pointed out that in many ways the London system was not thorough. It was understaffed and often quite gentlemanly in its treatment of suspects. The example of the kid-glove approach to another gay traitor Sir Anthony Blunt, also springs to mind. He was not even stripped of his knighthood until many years after he had confessed when his treason was publicised.

Up until the 1995 release of Millar's surname only two documented references to him, outside of the diaries had been discovered, both published by B.L. Reid. The earliest and most noteworthy occurs as early as 1907 when we now know Millar to have been just seventeen years of age. This mention was on a Foreign Office letter to Casement. In a rough scrawl he had pencilled "from Alston" below the date 23 August 1907 on the three page crested and embossed quarto item. Above the date, this time in ink, he also wrote "Rec'd. Saturday 24 Augt/07 Just before Millar came!"[615] This was a typical example of Casement's method of recording a letter's date of receipt. Rarely was there a comment, and only a handful of a sexual nature.

The contents of the letter from Sir Beilby Alston, who in a second missive on 5 September announced that Lord Dufferin was replacing him, were not entirely welcome: "It really seems unnecessary that you should return to Santos at the end of your leave, so you had better apply for a two months' extension from Sept 20. Haiti will not be vacant…". The job in Port-au-Prince which had been promised and about which Casement had already been researching was no longer forthcoming. In recompense, he was offhandedly told he could have his leave extended. Casement had already initiated a correspondence with the outgoing consul, A.G. Vansittart, who had thoughtfully advised him that in Haiti "you cannot possibly trust any Black man." He had therefore employed "a negro Danish subject" to deal with the "Black Britishers who infest the consulate."[616]

An attractive diversion from this Haitian disappointment was the arrival of Millar and sex to orgasm, later that Saturday. B.L. Reid commented "I do not scruple to argue that this is a homosexual explanation point"[617] And there is really no room for argument on the point. But there has been, this author in 1999 hearing Reid described as "the inventor of the homosexual exclamation mark."[618]

The second uncovered item was a letter from Millar to Casement in London, dated 19 November 1913, describing his successful completion of a mission to purchase two pictures, being exhibited in a Belfast gallery by Ada McNeill. She had been pursuing Casement off and on since they first met in 1885 despite his repeated failure to respond. In 1905, writing for advice on her future, she had confided "You have been most kind to me, more so than anyone I ever met before or since."[619] In 1913, Casement obviously felt the gesture of a friend, as opposed to anything else, would be to pay homage to Ada's artistic talents by buying one of her paintings.

It is worth quoting Millar's letter in full for it says so much, and yet so little. Reid describes it as written "in a neat clerkly hand and the general effect is somehow shabby-genteel."[620] Another opinion is that while pointing out that it is in the most legible hand in the NLI's huge Casement correspondence collection, it is rather the letter of a somewhat pedantic young man of a certain class, innocently trying to please. The £2 spent on "a writing desk for Millar" diaried earlier, suggests Casement was encouraging a prolonged correspondence. The letter, in black ink, is without an address and covers the four sides of the, then very popular, folded card.[621] At the top, on the left, in two different inks, Casement noted "R. 22 Nov 1913" and "an'd 26 Nov" (i.e. received and answered on those dates):

"My dear Sir Roger, I went to the exhibition about the pictures and have secured a pair by Miss MacNeill which I think will please you. There were none of hers above £2 = 2 = 0 in price, most of them being small ones from 10/6 up to £1.1.0, but there was this pair and another pair each picture being £2.2.0 so by taking two I was able to approximate to the amount you mentioned. The titles of the two pictures are "Evening on the Moor" and "A Grey Day in the Glen" both extremely nice & the tone very well done probably the dull effect in each case suggested by the titles. They are both Irish scenes and I shall find out the exact places and let you know. The man in the place was not sure of that but can find out.

"The other two pictures were "White Lines on a Sullen Sea" – an impression of a rough bit of sea with a rocky shore & the waves coming in with white crests – and some coast scene in India. They told me Miss Mac Neill had been in India some little time ago and painted this while there. I chose the other pair for two reasons first the scenes are Irish & I know you would like that best & second the frames and mount are much nicer being gilt & well finished whereas the others are stained wood of some kind & rather coarse.

"The pictures must remain in the Exhibition till 15 Dec. as if everyone took away his picture as he bought it towards the end there wouldn't be any exhibition! But I suppose you are not in any particular hurry for them & you can just let me know where you want them sent to & I'll look after them you may be sure. It's a jolly nice show, quite small you know, but some very nice little pieces of work. There are one or two little Egyptian scenes, I forget by whom at the moment, one of a bridge of boats, which is very nice. There are also some bas reliefs or mouldings apparently of some kind of clay. There are an astonishing number of works sold already, a red star on each one sold & you may be surprised at the number of red stars.

"Mother was unfortunately not able to go with me as some friends arrived unexpectedly and prevented her but I told her all about it & she concurs with what I have done. Excuse the writing as I am doing this down town. With every kind thought & hoping this will please you. Of course I did not give your name, but my own. Ever yrs, affectionately Millar."

The letter reads like a written conversation. Millar is plainly wearing out near the end, but determined to fill all four sides of the card. He knows that giving Casement's name is inadvisable, one assumes because Casement is by now a prominent and outspoken separatist, not overly welcome in Belfast. What is also of some significance is the fact that Millar's mother was involved in the whole enterprise, before and after the gallery visit. Plainly she was on proper, indeed close social terms with the knight and was pleased to assist him in ways other than providing him with occasional accommodation. The pictures were probably showing at Rodman's Gallery which was advertising its annual exhibition in the *Belfast Telegraph* on 31 October 1913.

Angus Mitchell has pointed out that Millar's letter was written "nine days before the Irish Volunteers were founded and uses the language of respect and affection found in much straightforward communication among men of that period" and that "there is neither blatant nor indirect sexual innuendo in the letter."[622] All of which may be true, except that it is written in an unusually intimate manner, in full recognition that the addressee will appreciate such apparently trivial detail. The remark about Casement preferring his choice of Irish over Indian scenes reveals Millar is well tuned to his politics.

Before the May 1998 release of Millar's home address and employer, this author had, with the assistance of a local genealogist, Gilbert Hughes, become aware of precisely who Millar was. Tracking Millar backwards, turned out in the end, after much other effort, to be a matter of searching through the wills of people named Gordon probated in Belfast since the turn of the century. This was actually a stroke of luck since, as it happened, Millar had not died in Northern Ireland. Because he still made use of his former employer, the Belfast Bank and its Executor and Trustee Company, of Donegall Square, his will had also been proved in Belfast.

And so through census details, electoral rolls, birth, death and marriage certificates as well as wills, the picture gradually clarified. It was to be a miniature image of the development of Ulster over a century from rural to urban, rustic to urbane. Millar was born on 23 June 1890 in Larne, the seriously Protestant port town just south of the Catholic Glens of Antrim. His father, James Andrew Gordon, was then a bank accountant aged thirty-six. He had been married for almost two years when his only child was born. By the time of the 1901 census he had been promoted manager of the Belfast Bank in Larne and was living in the extensive bank house at 11 Main Street. It ran to sixteen rooms with ten outbuildings including a stable, coach house, cow shed and piggery.

Both parents were recorded as Presbyterian and they had a Roman Catholic servant called Margaret McCallion. All four, including Millar, could read and write which was a change from 1890 when their illiterate maid, Matilda Martin ("X own mark"), managed to allow the registrar to record her own Christian name, instead of Ellen's, as the baby's mother, creating a parent named "Matilda Gordon". While his father came from a long established Ballymoney family of watchmakers and jewellers, his paternal grandmother, Mary Sharpe, was from Moyarget in Ballycastle. His mother, Ellen Millar Hunter, was also from the north coast from a farming family. The couple, when both in their early thirties had been married in 1888 at her father Isaac's house in Corstown, Portrush.

The politics of Ireland only appear to have intruded once previously as the Gordon family meandered up the social scale from their Ulster (Scottish) origins in the Antrim countryside. That was when a great-uncle of Millar's father "became implicated in the troublesome period of 1798" and as a member of the United Irish Society had to fly the country for America, continuing in the family trade as a watchmaker in Rynder Street, New York. It was this George Gordon whom Francis Joseph Bigger wrote up as the source character of a romantic story, titled after the song, *We're Paddies Evermore*. George after his capture had, so Bigger crafted, been personally tortured in Dublin by Luttrell (Lord Carhampton) the army commander for his wearing of the green. Bigger sketched George Gordon (much as George Birmingham's hero Neal appears in *The Northern Iron*, a novel dedicated to FJB): "He had scarce finished his boyhood days, the dawn of manhood had not yet dulled the clear bright blush of youth upon his cheek, although his manly form was well developed, strong, straight and tall. His shapely head was poised upon broad shoulders; his curly hair hung about his neck. He was a comely youth and fair to look upon. Every grace of mind was his."[623] This was probably how the seventeen-year-old Millar appeared to Casement in 1907.

What may have been a happy childhood in Larne was marred by his father's illness. For two years Mr Gordon was in failing health with kidney disease. He then suddenly deteriorated, dying "at the Belfast Bank House" aged only fifty-two on 27 April 1907. Millar was only sixteen. The obituaries, in both the Belfast and Ballymena newspapers recorded the shock felt at his early death, his rise to manager in the Larne office and the esteem in which he was held. He was buried in Ballymoney, his home town. Great sympathy was felt for his "widow and one son, who is also in the service of the bank."[624] So Millar, like Casement, had already left education in his midteens, and started on what was to be a successful career in banking and finance.

No university education for him, indeed his schooling remains a mystery although he definitely did not attend 'Inst', the liberal Presbyterian establishment in central Belfast, of which F.J. Bigger was a governor (and old boy), W.R. Gordon later a teacher, and Forrest Reid, Robert Lynd and Paul Henry, pupils. It is probable Millar was, in 1907, already working in Belfast which would explain why his widowed mother had left Larne and followed her son to the city – to provide him with a comfortable home. Millar's personnel file in the Belfast Bank was lost when its Waring Street head office (where this author's father was then working and where Henry Joy McCracken was tried in 1798) was badly damaged by a German incendiary bomb in one of the two huge air raids on the city in 1941.

The earlier failure to identify Millar resulted from Casement never transcribing his surname. It was therefore erroneously assumed that Millar was not his Christian name. The nearest Casement got to writing Gordon in his diary was on 26 April 1911: "At Carnstroan with Millar and Mrs G". The Mrs G. was read as Mrs Green by early researchers.

The obvious answer to the riddle was of course from within Casement's Ulster. It was and is a Presbyterian tradition having something of a feminist tinge for parents to name sons with the surname of the mother or an earlier surname in the female line. This was to be the case with Millar, and perhaps doubly so as not only was Millar's mother, Ellen Hunter, herself blessed with the middle name Millar but a paternal ancestor was Mary Miller from Buckna. He would hardly have welcomed being christened 'Hunter Gordon'. A paternal uncle was named Joseph Miller Gordon – one a Millar, the other a Miller – separated by a vowel. This Joseph had died aged only 22 in 1881 and was to live on in name with the birth of another, nine years later in 1890. It was, however, to be by his second Christian name of Millar that the later Joseph Gordon was to be known by family and friends. These were people from Casement's county; Antrim Presbyterians. They were not, however, of Casement's faith nor of his class. He was an Anglican although he was also on paper a Roman Catholic, and a gentleman although with no local land or standing. As a place, Carnstroan, meant nothing to most researchers especially as it was misspelt in *The Black Diaries.* It was in fact the name given by Mrs Gordon to her prestigious Myrtlefield Park residence, built in 1902. A large long house just off the Lisburn Road in Belfast, it is situated on an attractive tree-lined avenue which was developed in the late 1890s, its Edwardian houses being built in the then fashionable Arts and Crafts idiom. The choice of the name Carnstroan for this new house, first inhabited by Mrs Gordon from about 1911, was no chance thing. It was an indication of a sense of history and family continuity, Carnstroan being the name of the Co. Antrim townland in which the Gordons had farmed since the early eighteenth century. Carnstroan, the place, is in the parish of Racavan near Broughshane, on the lower western slopes of Slemish Mountain where St. Patrick tended his sheep.

Carnstroan, the house, still in good order at the turn of the twentieth century, is situated opposite the local library and in the next street from the Public Record Office in Balmoral Avenue, two valuable resource and research locations for this author. According to the 1911 census, it was of the premier class and had fourteen rooms. It has a central staircase featuring a stained glass window, with a corridor along the upper floor. Millar was recorded in the census as a bank official while the general domestic servant, a 27 year-old member of the Church of Ireland was Sarah Anne Walker. Only Mrs Gordon was on the electoral register in 1912 and 1915. As the inhabitant householder she alone had a local government vote. Nobody at Carnstroan was yet eligible or enfranchised to be a parliamentary elector.

The connection between Carnstroan and the Black Diaries was first resolved by the author on finding in the 1912 Belfast & Ulster street directory's name index that a Mrs Gordon was living at a house of that name and remembering that the Carnstroan name featured in the 1910 Black Diary. But the connection had actually been spotted before. Roger McHugh had also discovered and noted down in his papers[625] the fact that Mrs Gordon lived at Carnstroan but despite finding Millar's surname and Belfast address he apparently chose, perhaps now aware of coming too close to something untoward, not to follow up the lead. When researching for Alfred Noyes in 1957, he had asked Bulmer Hobson about certain of his memories of the period. McHugh noted Bulmer's reply: "Motor bikes were very unusual then. He never owned one himself."[626] The impression given is that McHugh was trying to make a political link between Bulmer and Millar (and Casement's gift of a motorcycle).

More recently, the same notion has fed into Angus Mitchell's imagination when he asserted that "rather than performing sexual favours, it is equally probable that Millar was part of Casement's own inner circle of rebels and worked as a courier for the nationalist sympathisers."[627] That theory suffers from the fact that the motorbike was gifted in 1911 while Casement was still under Foreign Office orders, and two years before the Irish Volunteers were set up. The newly turned-up fact from PRONI's website that Millar Gordon signed the Ulster Covenant in 1912, as did his mother, finally undoes the theory.

Finding an explanation of how Millar and Casement first became acquainted is quite another matter. And if they first met in 1907, as Casement's jotting revealed, or at least first engaged sexually with one another that year, how did their relationship develop to the point of Casement overnighting with Millar at Carnstroan when his mother was also there. Assuming that Mrs Gordon was completely unaware, at this point, of any sexual activity at Carnstroan, or elsewhere, it stands to reason that there was some prior connection between the two families. That is unless the pair had met in some venue frequented by homosexuals in Belfast, or Millar had been cruised on the street, which again is a little unlikely, given that he was only seventeen and surely inexperienced, if not unworldly.

Even if they had met in such a fashion it would still not explain the apparent intimacy of Mrs Gordon who seemed quite happy to accommodate Casement. Unless she was bohemian or easily fooled there surely had to have been a formal introduction. Nonetheless and despite this, Casement was undoubtedly bold enough to engage in sex with Millar while Mrs Gordon slept down the corridor. One advantage of a new house like Carnstroan was that the corridor floorboards would not have aged sufficiently to start creaking. Similar perilous ventures have been undertaken many times by gay people, before and since. Casement's diaries reveal how he often took such risks of exposure, risks necessary to achieve coition, not indulged in for their own sake. They also told of how he would engage and develop the sexual instincts of teenage boys.

Millar was from Larne but his father was from Ballymoney, both Co. Antrim towns. This was not quite Casement country but no distance away. In October 1913, Ballymoney was to be the scene of the famous meeting of Protestants opposed to the 'Lawlessness of Carson'. There is, however, one connection with this town detailed in both the White and Black Diaries of 1910 which provides a plausible tie between the two families. That is the mention of the existence of an otherwise undocumented friend of Casement, one John Gordon, a bridge enthusiast like the diarist.

On 24 October, in his White Diary, Casement noted "Played bridge – 33 hands in two rubbers. I should think a record. First rubber was seventeen hands and second 16. I kept the score of the first to send to John Gordon." While the next day in the Black Diary, Casement recorded "Wrote Gordon, John Gordon, of the 33 bridge hands last night", and in the White, "I wrote a note to John Gordon with the Bridge record of last night." So we have three mentions of a bridge partner called John Gordon who merits a letter from the Amazon on the matter of an unusual number of bridge hands. It is unlikely that Casement knew the Lord Lieutenant, the Marquess of Aberdeen and Temair whose name that was. Significantly, the name is clarified, on this third and last occasion, as not just Gordon, but specifically also John Gordon. This reveals the existence of an important other person called Gordon – Millar Gordon one assumes.

There was a John Gordon in Millar's family – his uncle, who took over the family jeweller's business in Ballymoney. Born in 1863, a year before Casement, he died a bachelor in 1927. It is not unreasonable to hypothesise that the two men met at a bridge club in Co. Antrim or possibly had been at school together in Ballymena. Thus acquainted, further introductions may have led to the recently bereaved, fatherless Millar, now in 1907 in Belfast, being committed informally to the care of Mr Roger Casement C.M.G., the distinguished diplomatist when he was in Ireland.

Millar disappears from the written record in 1908 and 1909 while Casement is in Brazil on consular duty. He then re-appears in the 1910 and 1911 journals when Casement is at home, before and between his two Amazon investigations. The boy's sexual enthusiasm was still present but less strong than Casement's and not constant, which is the mark in some ways of a man who experiences homosexual feelings of differing intensities; someone who might be significantly heterosexual. Casement twice records disappointing sexual non-events, while there is a tendency for engagements to be broken by Millar for minor reasons. Another clue to a mixed sexuality is the ease of his sexual enjoyment with a much older man which is something more often associated with males who occasionally have sex with other men, but who are not predominantly homosexual.

The first documented appearance of Millar in 1912 comes in a letter of 20 April to Gertrude Bannister, addressed from "Carnstroan, Myrtlefield Park, Belfast". In it, Casement remarked "I got over all right after a very good (voyage) in the new Belfast boat 'Patriotic'." He was also being wise after the event, complaining at length of British disregard for marine safety: "She has accommodation for 1052 passengers and only life saving room for 304." It was indeed not a good time to be in Belfast even if he was staying with Millar once again. The city was in mourning for the *Titanic*, which five days earlier had sunk after striking an iceberg, 1,513 lives being lost.

Apart from the drowning of a large number of Belfast shipyard employees including its chief designer Thomas Andrews, the nephew of Lord Pirrie, the loss of the *Titanic* like all major disasters came to be seen as emblematic of the end of an era and the harbinger of dreadful times to come. It was a shock to the confidence of a city that had grown enormously in wealth and industry in fifty years, even overtaking Dublin in population, only to have such a famous ship, built on Queen's Island by Harland & Wolff sink on its maiden voyage.

Casement continued on his own disappointments, "Belfast is looking very well and nobody talks of Home Rule, it is not thought of even at the moment, as everybody is thinking of the Titanic...It will be hard to get people to feel for the far off Indians when they have had this calamity so near." Three days later Gertrude was sent a further letter from Carnstroan in which Casement only related that his "cold is a bit better but not much."[628]

So the relationship with Millar was flourishing. Knowing Casement it was bound to have other facets. Proselytising was one of his accomplishments: writing on Christmas Eve 1912 to Alice Stopford Green, from 45 Ebury Street in London, Casement was triumphant, "Here is a letter from Belfast may please you – from a young 'Unionist' now converted to Ireland."[629] Three months later on 21 March 1913 he was writing to Gertrude, this time from Rydal Mount in South Africa where he was visiting brother Tom and his second wife Katje. It is in almost identical language: "Here is a letter from a Belfast youth (a Presbyterian) I've turned into a truculent Home Ruler. Read it and burn. He is a decent soul."[630] It is a pity these two letters have probably been lost for ever as it would be intriguing to know what had made the young man, an apparently conventional individual, so truculent.

There is only one credible candidate for this new recruit. The fact that Casement, normally a correspondence hoarder, was happy to pass on (and order the destruction of) Millar's letters, reveals both the extent of his pride and a degree of security consciousness. Millar was, as ever, the soul of discretion in his missives and nothing untoward, aside from his newfound political views, can have been included. That he was now a Home Ruler, perhaps even a separatist was not totally unheard of for young Protestant men of his class but surprising nonetheless, given the growing intensity of the events then raging around him. On 28 September 1912 the Ulster Covenant had been signed, with Carson steaming up Belfast Lough on the *Patriotic* to watch bonfires blazing on the hills and headlands, including a spectacular (and symbolic) fire on Cave Hill. In January 1913 the UVF was formally instituted.

There are two further chirpy bits of Millar correspondence surviving, unnoticed until now, in the Maloney Papers in New York. Casement presumably had left them with Joe McGarrity when he departed for Germany in October 1914 although Maloney did mysteriously get hold of other original material of earlier date. The two items are both postcards although only one carries a photograph. It is of perhaps the ugliest looking scene ever depicted; a blocky "Larne Harbour and Curran, Larne." Both are meticulously addressed to "Sir R Casement CMG." so Millar, despite his new politics, was no believer in disregarding British titles. Although Casement was using the same rooms where Millar first came six years earlier, the young man remained uncharacteristically uncertain of its precise Antrim Road number, having to define the house as "c/o Mrs Thomas (opposite Messrs McKenzie Painters)." J. McKenzie & Sons, Painters and Decorators were indeed located opposite, at 114/116 Antrim Road, according to the Belfast street directory.

Both cards are annotated by Casement as received "at Ardrigh 3 Sept 13" with the second also bearing his comment "Wired to say coming tomorrow." So the cards were sent up by Mrs Thomas to Bigger's house. Casement was therefore obliged to head down the Antrim Road later that evening to meet Millar, who was certainly not economising on communications in this attempt to ensure the assignation finally took place.

The first card, postmarked Larne, reads "Delighted to have got your card with the good news [**unexplained**]. This is where I am for the week-end. See you next week. Hav'nt we had some grand weather, hope September will be the same. Yrs M."[631] Note Millar's little Ulsterism "grand" which Casement enjoyed replicating in his diary entries on both 29 and 30 May 1910.

The second dated "2/9/13" and postmarked 3 September reads "Sorry I was not able to go up to-night to see you as I am feeling a bit seedy, but hope to go up to-morrow night about 7.45. Hope you are very fit and enjoying the glorious weather. I was down in old Larne over Sunday and sent a PC which I hope you have got. I always enjoy going back there – most people like to revisit the scene of their childhood Ever yrs. M."[632]

And so the documented side of the pair's relationship ends. Although they may have continued meeting up to the first half of 1914, Casement was getting busier and more prominent politically. It is unlikely he communicated from

Germany as it would have put Millar in serious jeopardy. Up to this point no harm had probably been done by Casement's early form of attention. If there was any corruption it could be argued it was more of the mind than the body.

Millar's change of politics may well have precipitated, or at least encouraged, his next career move although the arrest and execution of Casement, as well as the newspaper publicity about the diaries must have had a devastating effect. If, as Gertrude wrote on 19 August 1916, Bigger was "in an awful fright…for fear he should be connected with him."[633] Millar's predicament was a thousand times worse. He had not been party to the treason but he was open to prosecution by a vengeful state who had evidence of his criminal sodomy with Casement. Major Hall may or may not have knocked on his door, as he was proposing in his memo of 31 July, but even if he had not, Millar must have been expecting the worst, awaiting his own crucifixion.

As early as 17 May 1916, one acquaintance of Casement, William Allan Hay, a mercantile clerk who described himself to Gavan Duffy as once a "lone, young Scot in St Paul de Loanda" to whom Casement had been very kind, apparently without a hint of impropriety, was horrified by the press campaign. He enclosed a cutting from a Glasgow newspaper which talked of the diaries and the fact that "nothing so filthy, so pornographic, so infinitely disgusting as what Casement set down in black and white can be imagined. The things which he narrated as personal experiences over which he gloated were so horrible as to be revelations to experienced men of the world – things that had not been heard of by those that thought they knew what sin was like."[634]

With stuff like this in print, not just Millar but Mrs Gordon, who had in all innocence so graciously hosted the eminent man, must have felt imperilled. What conversations ensued at Carnstroan may have been quite painful unless the pair had already broached the subject. Mothers tend to know more than they say or more than they even know they know about these things. Whatever was said, Millar was shortly to leave Belfast for Dublin where he would spend the rest of his life.

Mrs Gordon was not slow in joining her son. She had been on the Belfast Bank's Widows and Orphans' Fund since 1907, and as the wife of a manager would have received a generous pension. Its records note her date of death as 26 September 1933 so she outlived her husband by twenty-six years. Her Widows Fund file with the Belfast Bank carries an opening note "one boy in bank aged 17" to which was added in 1922 "now a Stockbroker."[635] On her estate duty form it was indicated that she had come to reside in Dublin in 1920.

The fact of Millar's arrival in Dublin is first confirmed in the 1920 edition of *Thom's Directory* which details him being in business as a government stockbroker in a partnership, Kennedy and Gordon, of 12/14 College Green ("Telegrams KENGOR"). Given that Millar worked in a city centre branch of the Belfast

Bank (which merged with the Northern Bank fifty years later) it may well have been in its stockbroking arm, probably the same Trustee and Executor section which dealt in time with his own will. The fact of a partnership and the chosen field of dealing in government stocks, suggest both a high degree of planning for his departure from the north, allied to the necessary experience and contacts. It was plainly no sudden flight. Of course without other evidence being found, Millar may have quit Belfast anytime between 1916 and 1920. A year later in 1921, Kennedy & Gordon had moved around the corner to 102/103 Grafton Street, an address shared by the Brazilian consulate.

Millar next enters official records with his unexpected marriage to Mary Helen Martin at Rathgar Presbyterian Church in Dublin on 22 April 1925. He is now thirty-four while his bride is a young nineteen. Her father is a contractor named Henry Herbert Martin of Temple Road, Rathgar. Millar's address was given as Selma, 4 Neville Road also in Rathgar. The first witness at the wedding was Geoffrey L. Kennedy, his stockbroker partner, although hardly five years later Millar is in business on his own. In 1943 Geoffrey Kennedy is to be found at another Grafton Street address while Millar's office is at 8 Anglesea Street.

To all intents and purposes Millar has thrown off the legacy of Belfast and Casement, and progressed, unfazed and successfully, in the path that his own father would probably have set out for him. The marriage must have been a great satisfaction for the now dowager Mrs Gordon who before her death seven years later, at the age of seventy-eight, was also to become a proud grandmother. Millar was named administrator of her estate which included shares in Shamrock Shipping.

The nagging fear of exposure if the diaries were ever to be made public can never have gone away. The uncertainty must have been especially stressful, for Millar could not have been aware of how little or how much Casement had written about him, but the lurid stories must have made him assume the worst. Each new surge of publicity can only have left him in a cold sweat. The 1936 Maloney book which produced an enormous trail of articles and further controversy had at least one upside – the diaries, if produced, might be able to be discredited as fakes as Maloney argued. But mud sticks, perception being more important than reality in sexual scandals. Once outed as a homosexual you are not able to go in again if that is your wish.

In the event Millar's luck held on that score. He was to die aged sixty-six on 14 August 1956 of "malignant hypertension – 6 months certified", three years before the 1959 publication of *The Black Diaries*. By this time retired, and a resident of Greystones Co. Wicklow, he was buried ("funeral private") from St Patrick's Church in the town. In his will, dated just six months prior to death he left almost all his substantial estate to his wife, in trust for his two student sons.

Family descent of Joseph Millar Gordon (1890-1956)

John GORDON of Creevamoy, Racavan b. ca. 1661 d. 6 May 1738, the father of **Thomas E. GORDON** of **Carnstroan** b. ca. 1706, d. 27 October 1787 m. **Susan WILSON** d. 2 April 1767 aged 47, parents of:

Millar's paternal great-great-grandparents: Joseph GORDON b. 1747 d. 20 October 1815 m. **Mary MILLER** of Buckna b. ca. 1759 d. Ballymoney 20 April 1823, aged 64, watchmaker, journeyman to William Harpur of Antrim; Ballymoney business established 1777. Joseph's brother was George Gordon, about whom F.J. Bigger wrote a romantic tale *We're Paddies Evermore*. He was supposedly a member of the United Irishmen who had to fly the country, going to the United States where he kept a watchmakers at 66 Rynder Street, near Grand Street, New York.

Millar's paternal great-grandparents: The only child of **Joseph and Mary GORDON** was **James GORDON** also a watchmaker in Ballymoney b. 1786 d. 15 January 1852 in Ballymoney aged 66 (or 64), m. 1st 16 November 1819 **Elizabeth DICK** b. Garry 1792 or 1793 d. Ballymoney 22 April 1822, mother of James' only child, **Joseph**, m. 2nd Mary MOORE b. Dunluce 1787 or 1791, d. Ballymoney 22 February 1854, no issue:

Millar's paternal grandparents: Joseph GORDON b. 17 December 1821 d. 22 May 1891, third generation watchmaker, of Ballymoney where he was born and died; m. 10 November 1853 **Mary SHARPE** of Moyarget, Ballycastle b. ca. 1832 d. 1 March 1911, parents of seven sons and six daughters (six dying young):

1. **James Andrew b. 25 July 1854 d. 27 April 1907 (father).**
2. William Thomas (twin) b. 3 February 1856 d. 16 February 1856.
3. William Sharpe, agent Belfast Bank, Portrush, from December 1901 in-Coleraine, b. 20 February 1857 m. September 1890 Annie MASTERSON: one son John Moore Sharpe b. Portrush 21 November 1892 and one daughter, Eileen Mary b. Portrush 12 May 1896.
4. Joseph Miller b. 15 November 1858 d. 20 September 1881 aged 22.
5. John Sharpe (uncle, see below) b. 9 February 1863, fourth and last generation watchmaker/jeweller, Ballymoney, d. 3 January 1927, unmarried.
6. George Wilson b. 18 September 1865 d. 11 February 1869.
7. Robert Alexander b. 19 June 1874 d. 2 February 1921, Ulster Bank, Strabane m. Kathleen McCUTCHEON, d. 26 October 1971 at 90, issue.
8. Jane Moore (twin) b. 3 February 1856 d. 19 May 1863.
9. Elizabeth Dick b. 21 October 1860 d. 2 November 1863.

10. Mary Matilda b. 6 February 1862 m. 14 December 1887 William MASTERSON: daughter Mary Gordon b. and d. 1869.
11. Janetta Elizabeth b. and d. 1867.
12. Annie Wilson b. and d. 1869.
13. Florence Wilhelmina WOODS, provider of information to genealogy compiler Philip Crossle, and residuary legatee of her brother John.

Millar Gordon's maternal great-grandfather was Andrew HUNTER (1770-1842); **maternal grandparents, Isaac HUNTER** (1819-1896) and **Jane McCORMICK** (1822-1912); their children **Ellen Millar (mother)**, John McCormick (1857-1918) and Elizabeth Ann (1860-1916).

Millar's parents: The oldest of thirteen children, **James Andrew GORDON**, agent at Larne for the Belfast Bank, later titled manager, b. 25 July 1854 d. Larne 27 April 1907 (when son, **Millar** aged 16) m. 27 September 1888 **Ellen Millar HUNTER** of Corstown, Portrush, b. 1855 d. in Dublin, 26 September 1933, resided at Carnstroan, 7 Myrtlefield Park, Belfast from about 1911 to 1919, and in Dublin from 1920.

James and Ellen's only child was **Joseph Millar GORDON** b. Larne 23 June 1890 d. Greystones 14 August 1956 aged 66, m. 22 April 1925 aged 34, **Mary Helen MARTIN** then aged 19. Millar and Mary Gordon had two sons; **James Herbert GORDON** b. 1928 and **David Millar GORDON.**

Will of **John Sharpe GORDON (uncle)** jeweller of Main Street Ballymoney, dated 12 January 1925; handwritten. Executor Wallace McClure, merchant. Probated in Belfast 11 April 1927. Estate £1846.15.7. He died with neither widow nor children on 3 January 1927 aged 63. Bequests were made to: Mary Matilda Masterson (sister) – £1000; Florence Woods (sister) – £1000, and the residue; William S. Gordon (brother) – £500 and his daughter Eileen, £100; the children of Robert Gordon (brother) – £1000: These children may have been Frances Mary, wife of Capt. Charles B. Baillie d. 29 January 1952 aged 39, and William John Gordon d. 17 December 1977 aged 63, m. Margaret Elizabeth d. 7 February 1974 aged 60. Millar Gordon was left nothing.

Details are derived from newspaper cuttings in the Gordon scrapbook in the F.J. Bigger catalogued collection at Belfast Central Library, and from gravestones in Racavan Old Cemetery and in both Ballymoney Old and New Cemeteries. Some dates of birth and death, of Millar's paternal great-grandparents differ as between the cuttings and the gravestones.

14

Ireland and USA 1912-14

On his return to England in January 1912 Casement had another eighteen months left in the consular service. He had first to write a further report on his second Amazon mission which told of how the first rush of enthusiasm by the Peruvian authorities, and Judge Paredes in particular, was beginning to come up against the reality of legal systems and their inability to change the world quickly. Having to be in London on call as required by the Foreign Office, he still managed a round of visits to friends in England as well as trips to Belfast, Falmouth (with Nina) and to Germany for three weeks with Dick Morten. From August to October, back in Ireland, he divided his time between Donegal (Falcarragh), Dublin and Belfast.

In Angus Mitchell's extensive 2012 *Field Day Review* articles there is an interesting misinterpretation, derived from an overheated desire to see connections where they don't exist, about Casement's 1912 tour of Germany and to what became the Belgian war zone. He wrote – with a typical touch of conspiracy – that he travelled, "in a car provided for by the German government [in what seems] was much more than a motoring holiday but a carefully planned route through the region, interspersed with meetings, discreet intelligence gathering operations and moments of historical and cultural contemplation."

The story of the car is quite properly sourced to a section in a published memoir by Casement's fellow consul Ernest Hambloch who quoted[636] him saying, in 1912, of his recent German visit, "I have been spending some time there motoring through the principal towns and studying their municipal organization. They put a car at my disposal. They are magnificent organisers." But that simply wasn't the case. Hambloch either got it wrong or Casement was spoofing. He had travelled to Germany with his friend Dick Morten, whose car it was, and a 21 year-old German admirer, Heinrich d'Oleire. Together they toured Luxembourg, Belgium, Germany and France.

Casement earlier explained to his cousin Gertrude Bannister, without a hint of a state-sponsored journey, "I am off with Dick Morten tomorrow to Germany for 3 weeks on a motor…We pick Heinrich up at Strasburg & go to Lake Constance probably first and then to Nuremburg and Coblenz &c."[637]

In his later correspondence with Gertrude and her sister Elizabeth, there is absolutely no mention of anything by way of official dealings, only impressions, for example, "We ran through Heidelberg without stopping – it looked so studenty & they are so ugly with their pork chops of cheeks criss-crossed as if for cooking. The people are not pretty – but very admirable & their form of work & application and organisation wonderful. I would much like to see them in Ireland for fifty years!"[638]

Heinrich d'Oleire, who was born in Strasbourg in 1890, was to surface several more times. His rubber plantation work in Asia seemed to have connections which brought him into Casement's circle of friends in London, although he is listed in the 1911 census as living in Hampstead.

Interned in Ceylon at the beginning of the war, he wrote some years later from Batavia in Java to Gertrude's husband Sidney Parry in a newly discovered letter. He congratulated him on his marriage (in 1916) which one George Perry had told him of.

Dated 4 November 1921, it read, "I do not know how to thank you for the dear kind words you have for dear Roddie. You cannot imagine how dearly I loved him & how willingly I should have given all for him. To me he was absolutely an ideal & the noblest man that ever lived. The hours I was allowed to spend in his company are for me the most beautiful recollections of England. Just to sit near him & to listen to the dear voice & to look into his soulful kind eyes so he still lives in me. This picture & his last letter to me is a most precious treasure to me."[639] He added that he had not married Miss Brandon "perhaps for the better" while indicating his mother was living in Frankfurt (at Sachsen Lage 4).

In 1913, Casement was sent a postcard picturing the Kerkhoof by his admirer in Medan, Sumatra, which ended with "Kindest regards to your sister and cousins."[640] Casement then advised Dick Morten from Ardrigh on 29 June 1914, "I will write from abroad and tell you more; meantime all good luck and love to you and May. I heard from H. on Saturday – getting on very well indeed. He has changed his work to some other Estate and likes it better and gets much better pay. He asked after you and S. [Sidney Parry] How is the latter?"[641]

Heinrich d'Oleire later wrote a shocked note to Casement from Colombo on 16 August 1914, "My dear Roddie, On my way to Strassburg I have been restrained here with 24 other germans. Tomorrow we will be escorted up the mountains to some camp where we are to await peace. A shameful thing indeed but not to be helped! If I only knew this safe in Strassburg! If war is over I shall hasten home. I only hope my ticket will then still be of value as I only got £4 beside it."[642]

On 15 October 1914, Casement in Philadelphia told the story to Dick Morten, "The war has upset & changed everything – including my heart. It is a crime. Grey & Asquith are greatly to blame. England cd. have prevented this war altogether had she wanted to – but she wanted to get Germany down &

could not resist the chance that came – as the direct result of her own planning & contriving with France & Russia. Now England will pay dearly & bitterly in the end – but God knows all will pay – It is a monstrous crime & calamity & will ruin half the world.

Here is a letter from poor Henri – but no I'll keep it – It came too last night – He was seized & is in a Concentration Camp in Ceylon – Just a few lines to say they got him on his way to fight for his country…I am with good friends here. I am sorry for Heinrich – I'll keep his letters. Tell Sidney Heinrich's letter is from Colombo, Ceylon, 16 Augt. He says he is there with 24 other Germans & that they will be taken up the mountains next day to some camp to be "Kept till peace." Tell Sidney to try and help him – He had only £4 on him."[643]

The summer of 1912 had commenced with the July publication of his Putumayo report (or Blue Book) which brought his name back to the attention of the public. Instead of a Peruvian equivalent to the Congo Reform Association, he devoted further and considerable energy, entirely beyond his necessary official duties, to the formation of a Franciscan mission on the Putumayo to provide some church protection for the benighted Indians. To his rage, his picture appeared in a favourable article in the *Illustrated London News*. Casement had always resisted his photograph being used in the press, presumably fearing some rent boy or other casual acquaintance might spot it, connect the consul and the cruiser, and try to blackmail or expose him. He was unforgiving of the culprit who had provided it.

Indicative of the fact that he was prolonging his home stay on his own say-so rather than returning to his consular duties in Rio, was the Foreign Office decision to put him on half pay from July 1912. This was not well-received by Casement who was generally restless and undecided, and beginning to feel his health worsening. Although the Ulster crisis was coming to a climax, Casement was torn between a quiet life, indeed an early retirement, perhaps in South Africa, return to Brazil or a political strike. In the autumn of 1912 the last stage of the Putumayo affair, so far as he was concerned, began to be played out through a rigorous House of Commons select committee enquiry on the atrocities.

Casement gave evidence over three days in November and December. He was subject to close scrutiny as to the state of his own early knowledge, when Pará consul, of the Peruvian Amazon Company's misdemeanours. Indeed he was obliged to reveal that he had dined with Julio Arana on board a steamer whose captain, in 1908, had then called to see him with shocking stories about murder and oppression in the Arana territories. The select committee continued its hearings into April 1913 due to an added task of assessing the efficacy of the consular service as an agency for the protection of aboriginal peoples. Its report published in June 1913 found the English directors of the Peruvian Amazon Company guilty of culpable negligence, having unearthed documentary evidence indicating that their state of awareness about the suppression of Indians was more extensive than Casement's lesser charges of sloth and complacency revealed. But no charges were laid against the directors, nor were the Aranas disgraced locally even if the company was now in ruins. Undoubtedly the Indians were given a breathing space, or more, by the various consequences of Casement's activities, official and unofficial.

The Consul's worsening state of health had been revealed, after an extensive medical check, to be due to a recurrence of his old appendix problem, X-rays having uncovered nothing more sinister. He was constipated, his appetite was poor, yet examination *per rectum* only showed up evidence of the old fistula problem. A "full and very tender" liver and "an ovoid swelling" in the appendix area, also tender, suggested the need for an appendectomy. This was familiar territory and as happened almost a decade earlier Casement fiercely resisted the surgeon's knife in that region. So fiercely, one suspects he knew the doctors listening to his complaints were determined to prove their worth by putting a name and a curable diagnosis to something imprecise, better described as growing old (with arthritis), or just a desire for extended medical leave and early retirement. Casement was certainly not so ill that it prevented him arranging a revolution over the next three years.

He was adamant however, telling a concerned Mrs Green, that he was going to Canary in particular, regardless of his doctor's opinion: "I do not share his alarm as to the appendicitis trouble" was his response to her fear of him being out of reach of a good surgeon.[644] His three months leave started with a leisurely voyage to South Africa lasting many weeks, punctuated by long stops in the old stomping grounds of both Las Palmas and Teneriffe. He then sought to extend it by a further two months to include a rest cure, as he told Sir Edward Grey, at a "sanatorium in the hills of the Orange Free State" – actually his brother Tom's new hotel venture.[645] Recognising he had exhausted the goodwill of his employers, he finally chose early retirement rather than a return to Rio de Janeiro, and after an extended correspondence was granted his ill-health pension of £421 p.a. After a stay in France with Herbert and Sarita Ward, Casement commenced his key year of public and energetic involvement in Irish politics. He first took rooms in Baggot Street, in Dublin. Of his fellow tenants, he remarked in June 1913 "all the rest is Old Maids. And Unionist Old Maids too! They pass me on the stairs with arrested eyes – a thing of horror."[646]

Casement made one noted effort to take on Carson and those Unionists within the heart of the beast, Carsonites who were not old maids, rather decidedly butch. He chose the town of Ballymoney where there had been a tenant right movement in its surrounding area, The Route, and a surprise Liberal victory in the 1906 election, with the return of R.G. Glendinning for North Antrim, and even memories of the United Irishmen. However, he was not one to notice that the vast majority of Ulster's 1798 survivors came to terms with the 1800 Act of Union, appreciating, particularly, the dissolution of the Anglican and Ascendancy parliament in Dublin. They and their children had thence devoted themselves to the new Gods of manufacturing and technological progress, while the Unionists had regained the North Antrim seat in 1910. Casement's road to Germany and the gallows was to commence in Ballymoney but he failed to check by rational assessment whether what was to meet him there was in any way typical of Ulster. The large audience of about four hundred, representing competing strands of non-conformity, clapped him on his way regardless.

Writing to Alice Stopford Green from Ardrigh, on 2 September 1913, Casement was trying to put a platform together, "I want you to come and speak at a North Antrim Home Rule meeting. I see a big chance of a huge breach in the enemy's wall there, and with the help of every drop of my fenian blood in my soul I hope will light a fire there may set the Antrim hills ablaze." He added in forlorn hope, and "unite (for I think it possible) Presbyterian and Catholic farmers and townsmen at Ballymoney in a clear message to Ireland."[647]

Another speaker, Captain Jack White, an early socialist from the Whitehall estate in nearby Broughshane, complained "when Casement heard that the meeting was incubating, he descended on the town and the Committee." Failing to notify White of either his intentions or of what he had done, "made subtle changes in the spirit which I had intended the meeting to express."[648] White's intended title 'The Lovelessness of Carson' was not adopted – Casement winning out with 'Lawlessness' instead. A fight was developing between the two which, in different forms, would see out the century: Should Labour Wait (on nationalism)? Casement and White duly set about each other: "We'll get on all right if you're honest" said the Captain, his "rival Messiah" replying "I think you are most insulting."[649]

By 13 September, again from Ardrigh, Casement was musing over the problem of speakers; "possibly FJB although Capt. White fears he is too much of a Papish. His kissing Cardinal Logue's ring has upset the midriff of the Antrimers."[650] A fortnight on, the platform and theme were firming up. An Irish Ireland meeting was out of the question. Casement was still defending Bigger but knew he was not going to be chosen as a speaker, "Mr B is seen as a crank, a banner and piper maniac or thing of that kind. Well they are wrong." Lord Ashbourne was also out, being perceived "a papist". Casement then gently put the knife into his adversary, "Captain White is not a 'lunatic' but I am not very sure of his ability."[651]

Rev. J.B. Armour ('of Ballymoney') the most prominent of Ulster Presbyterian Home Rulers and an opponent of landlordism, explained the arrangements to his son: "Sir Roger Casement the consul who exposed the atrocities of the slavery sanctioned by the late King of Belgium who was a crowned villain worse than Pharaoh, and the worse state of slavery in the rubber fields of Putumayo, had written to suggest a meeting here to attack the policy of Carson." He continued "I had written Sir Roger suggesting the lines on which the resolution should be drawn. He had suggested that Lord Ashbourne, the head of the Gaelic Leaguers and a Protestant who had turned Catholic, should be asked to take part as a speaker – a proposal that I vetoed quietly by saying that no Catholic should be asked to take part as a speaker."

It was further reported that Capt. White had called on Armour in his two-seater Ford, along with his wife "a handsome woman a Spaniard it is said." She was Mercedes (Dollie) Mosley "a half-Spanish Roman Catholic" met in Gibraltar where White's father "the Hero of Ladysmith", noted locally in song as "Our Irish General", had been Governor. After discussing arrangements for the 24 October meeting "before he had gone a mile his motor punctured, and he had to return...his wife seemed to think the puncture was not of good omen."[652]

Casement later told of his recent difficulties with the Captain. There had, he said, been a big quarrel over speakers and who should chair the meeting. Armour's account of precisely what was stated suffers from what always seems to happen on Casement documents – just when they are at their most intriguing, words are indecipherable or pages are torn. But from the remnants of his letter what can be detected is that White had "opened on Sir Roger, accusing him of every type of crime winding up with the charge that he was not an honest man: There was a casting of the creels there and then", Armour concluding with relish "Sir Roger's explanation of the matter is that there is a slate off."[653] Patrick McCartan described (in 1924) how Casement made his judgments of people, explaining he had a mind "like a rat-trap and when suspicious it snapped before the rat reached the pan."[654] Jack White with his seriously advanced views on marriage, morality and secularism was plainly the object of such suspicion.

Dealing with the local police on security, Armour drew on his regular and influential contacts in Dublin Castle. (Birrell, the Irish Secretary dined with him later in the month.) He told the RIC to permit no-one to enter the Orange Hall opposite "and begin a drumming to drown the speakers: 'Oh that cannot be, we have not the right'. 'That can and must be', was the reply." Armour then played his trump card: "Suppose they begin drumming in the Orange Hall and fifty from the other meeting go across and lather them, splitting their drums – there will be a riot and you will be responsible for a breach of the peace."[655] The event was thus heavily policed, with no disturbance permitted.

In the hall, a banner was hung above the platform reading "No Provisional or Provincial Government for us." It was the finest gathering ever, earnest and high toned, noted Armour who arranged that as White and Casement had had "a tiff" the former should lead off. He added that the latter's speech was "very fine".[656] *The Times* reporter described Casement as one "who combines citizenship of the world with an enthusiastic attachment to romantic nationalism", to which Casement responded by emphasising his local roots: "I have lived amongst Ulster people many years of my life and in quiet and daily contact with them I have learned to know them well."[657] In his speech Casement was on one point absolute, the exclusion of Ulster from Home Rule was unacceptable.

The next day he was writing to Armour from the Marine Hotel in Ballycastle where he, Alec Wilson and Mrs Green had gone, saying the speeches should be printed as a pamphlet, especially Wilson's. When done, it appeared under the title *A Protestant Protest.*[658] Enclosing a future article, he apologised for his phrase about "the Rectory capturing the Manse" in case it offended the Presbyterian Armour. He was, however, "sorry that there were so many references to the Catholic Church" at the meeting.[659] This criticism was probably directed at Captain White who had chosen to assert that Rome had always supported England in Ireland, while he had also argued for non-sectarian state education – not an attractive option to many Catholics.

Jack White was critical of what he saw as his rival's hypocrisy: "In his appeal against lawlessness Casement was not even sincere. At Ballymoney he protested against the 'Lawlessness of Carsonism'. At Cork a little later he called for three cheers for Sir Edward Carson, from a fervidly Nationalist audience, and explained just in time to prevent the platform being stormed – that it was because Carson was the first in this generation to teach Irishmen to fight."[660] Writing in his autobiography, *Misfit*, he gave as his belief a slightly sophisticated version of Connolly's famous remark that partition would lead to a carnival of reaction in Ireland: "Ulster's exclusion and isolation, her lack of faith in the dynamic quality of her Protestantism have allowed those influences to envisage the conversion of twenty-six counties of Ireland into a Papal State, and to make some headway to date towards its achievement."[661] The unwelcome results of partition were still blamed by White on the Ulster Protestants for not leavening the dough of Irish nationalism.

A variant of that view, expressed in David Rudkin's famous radio play on Casement, is that Protestant Dissent was needed for "the pluralising of a future Ireland...All societies need dissent or they rot and die – the way de Valera's Ireland very nearly did."[662] But the Home Rule that the Presbyterians of Ballymoney sought was far along the Redmond scale towards Unionism, while that which Casement was arguing for, was at the opposite end. He complained of the slimness of the devolved powers on offer, believing in separation, while Ballymoney's view was not even in the middle ground of nationalism.

Jack White was gaoled in Swansea during the 1916 events for trying to encourage a revolt amongst Welsh miners in order to prevent Connolly's execution who because of his wounds, was the last of the rising leaders to be shot. Transferred to Pentonville the day before Casement's death, Jack White was within earshot of the next morning's hanging. In a 1936 speech he recalled "I felt no horror at Casement's passing. I felt his death was as purposeful as his life, and perhaps more powerful than his life for the achievement of his purpose."[663] In the final set of his life's rebellions, White went out to organise the Connolly Column in Spain to fight Franco, fell out with the Communist Party for its deceits, and teamed up with the anarchist movement where he was obviously much more at home. Many years earlier his Unionist (and Tory) friend Ronald McNeill had joshed him "Jack you're a very decent fellow but there are three ways in which you make things very difficult for yourself and your friends. You want to change the whole world; you want to do it at once; and you want to do it all by yourself." White agreed, saying "I admitted the justice of the criticism."[664]

The Unionist fightback started in a *Times* editorial on 25 October 1913. It categorised the Ballymoney assembly as "a small and isolated 'pocket' of dissident Protestants, the last few survivors of the Ulster Liberals of the old types. Ulster Liberalism is very like the Cheshire cat in *Alice in Wonderland.* It has vanished till only its grin lingers furtively in a corner of Co. Antrim. The one small effort of Protestant Home Rulers in Ulster serves, however, a useful purpose, because it reveals the scantiness of their numbers." Ronald McNeill also tried to underplay the event calling the organisers "a little handful of cranks."

In his book on Armour, *Against The Tide,* J.R.B. McMinn is perhaps unfair in that part of his commentary where he wrote "Since White, Casement and Mrs Green were all romantics, essentially out of touch with the realities of Ireland past or present their emphasis [on 'the spirit of 1798'] was hardly surprising."[665] Despite not being resident in Ulster or experienced in public speaking it did not stop Casement and Alice Stopford Green from commissioning arms for the Irish Volunteers and ultimately setting a lot of fires over the hills of Antrim. Romantic Ireland was to become a reality.

Ballymoney boosted Casement's morale sky high. On 25 October 1913 he was already spreading the news "The Meeting was a grand success: Hall packed, smiling good-faced farmers of the Route in hundreds." A couple of days later he was expatiating on a series of further meetings being planned in his head, "The local devils are choking with rage; they'll choke deeper yet when Crossgar, Saintfield, Garvagh, Portglenone, Ballycarry and Islandmagee follow the lead of

Ballymoney." Signing off this letter, "*Mise*, O'Scodgin", indicated an unusual cheeriness.[666] But these meetings were never to take place. A second, this time in the less propitious town of Coleraine, was stymied by local councillors. Casement, now a public and political figure was increasingly drawn to more fertile ground to advance Irish Ireland.

The territory of Ballymoney Town Hall was symbolically regained less than a month later, on 21 November, with a bigger Unionist meeting addressed by James Craig. According to a partisan Armour, it was an "omnimixum" gathering with nearly two hundred trained in "on the Ballycastle Railway and a similar number brought from Portrush, with the Orange contingents from far and near…Craig fell on Mr Alec Wilson for his statement, which is as true as the gospel that thousands of Protestants were dragooned into signing for Carsonism…Dunville[667] in this case was clearly the inspiring spirit."[668]

According to the Ballymoney solicitor and Liberal Party organiser, Thomas Taggart, when writing to Casement on 14 November, there had been a mysterious shooting in the meeting's aftermath, that of young John Dinsmore. However, he was inclined to think it was not intentional, more of a prank. He understood nonetheless that Dinsmore had been warned not to attend, coming as he did from Ballymena "a very impossible place."[669] Dinsmore had also made the hardest-hitting speech of the night, attacking "the great linen magnates of Belfast" for manipulating sectarianism in order to distract their workers from poverty wages: "When they asked for bread they were given *The Boyne Water*" he had bravely declared. What exact price he paid for his temerity was not detailed.

Events and Casement moved rapidly after the Ballymoney meeting. He was now a public figure on the Irish stage although still trading on his Ulster Protestant origins and his fame as *Congo Casement*, advanced by his knighthood in 1911, and yet further fame on the strength of his Putumayo report

When the third Home Rule Bill was passed by the House of Commons, and duly rejected for a second time by the House of Lords in early 1913, the following year was destined to be the moment of truth for Ireland and Ulster. The third Home Rule Bill's third time round the parliamentary course was timetabled to reach its climax in the middle of 1914. That Bill still carried no compromise so far as Ulster was concerned. Despite that, Casement remained a rare opponent on the grounds that it provided, he said little more than local government for the island.

Were the Unionists bluffers as many in the Liberal government, like Winston Churchill, and Irish nationalists (including Casement) insisted on believing? Or, emboldened by their allies in the Conservative Party, now led by a man of Ulster origin, Andrew Bonar Law. Was Ulster going to resist? For if Ulster opposition to Home Rule would dissipate like snow off a ditch, all was fine, but if because of either local or Tory agitation the province would do battle, nationalism needed to compromise, or arm and fight; and fight to win. In the event, arming and fighting occurred but the issue was not to be Ulster exclusion, rather "English" rule or separatism.

With the passing of the Parliament Act in 1911 the blocking power of the Lords now only ran for three years. There was thus a date-specific crisis with the three years now being up in 1914. But the Unionists had a three year start in the mobilisation department. Major Fred Crawford (who was to sign the Covenant in his own blood) had been tasked as early as November 1910 by the Ulster Unionist Council to obtain funds and prepare for the importation of weapons, and to undertake the creation of an Ulster army. There was no bluff to be called.

The UVF had, by the end of 1913, reputedly enrolled 90,000 members and was organised into regiments with signaller, despatch rider, medical and nursing corps. Its key figures were General Sir George Richardson commanding, Captain Wilfrid Spender the youngest staff officer in the British Army, and Captain Hall its Military Secretary. Almost as ominously the Ulster Unionist Council approved the setting up of a Provisional government, with Carson at its head, for the moment Home Rule was enacted.

The tempo was heightening and Casement was unable to resist the denouement. He was, he said, now obsessed by Ireland although he had been all along, putting his consular career in jeopardy as early as 1905 with his anti-enlistment activity. The frequent prophecies of his life ending on the gallows for treason were now to be tested and could be fulfilled. They were, however, not so much a death wish as a perceptive assessment of the consequences of the direction his opinions were taking him. The disparity or contradiction between the extremity of his views on Ireland (and the hard certainty with which he spoke and wrote), and his personal status within the British Empire, indicated an inevitable and climactic struggle.

Casement was totally embedded within the nationalist and separatist camp, indeed more than most who were, in 1916, to crash into armed politics. With a history dating back a decade, he was on intimate terms both with the personnel in Belfast and, increasingly, with the revolutionary wing of the movement in Dublin. Indeed he was outranked in seniority by few, if any who were not also members of the IRB, a group he never joined or appears to have been asked to join. If he had doubts they rarely surfaced.

He had, however, no ability to judge the Craig and Carson Unionists. Being so out of sympathy with them he could only sneer or make the self-deceptive error, common to most nationalists to this day, that Unionists were misguided

Irishmen and, given their suspicion of England, people who would easily turn into Irish patriots – even into Irish Irelanders like him. An example of this view is a draft letter to Col. Maurice Moore, dated 6 December 1913, in which he wrote of "the northern Protestants who, I am confident are only for a moment and under a misapprehension in an opposite camp."[670]

Bulmer Hobson was not so sanguine. As perhaps the earliest military-minded separatist and since 1911 on the IRB's Supreme Council, he proposed in July 1913 to the Dublin Board of which he was chairman, a plan of action in response to the UVF. As he wrote "it was decided, that the members of the IRB in Dublin should commence drilling immediately."[671] Largely under the instruction of his *Fianna,* this began in a National Foresters Hall on Dublin's Parnell Square. But what Hobson was noising abroad, in particular, was a unified national force inaugurated by someone of prominence who could become the focal point of a movement. He was also concerned "that the IRB must not show its hand."[672]

Then in the autumn, Eoin MacNeill published an article entitled *The North Began*, in a Gaelic League journal edited by Pearse, calling for an historical repeat of the organising of the Irish Volunteers. In 1782 they had effected legislative independence for Ireland, an early form of devolution or home rule, although only for the Irish Anglican caste, the Protestant Ascendancy. Indeed the UVF already displayed many of the same attributes of its eighteenth century predecessor except that it was integrationist not devolutionist.

MacNeill was Professor of Early and Mediaeval Irish History at UCD and not a revolutionary or separatist. Significantly he was averse to any adventures in the north, indicating that Ulster Catholics were too prone to violent responses. He was also susceptible to the remarkably common fantasy that Carson was a secret home-ruler.[673] His article duly ended with another fantasy, originally uttered some years earlier at the Toome *Feis*: "I said that the day would come when men of every creed and party would join in celebrating the Defence of Derry and the Battle of Benburb. That day is nearer than I then expected."[674]

Bulmer Hobson brought flame to the fire by seizing the opportunity MacNeill's article presented. After discussions with MacNeill, facilitated by The O'Rahilly, a giant public meeting was arranged to establish a modern version of those earlier Volunteers. The thirty-man Provisional Committee of the Irish Volunteers selected included Hobson, MacNeill, Joseph Campbell, Casement, MacDermott, Pearse, The O'Rahilly, and Larry and Tom Kettle of the United Ireland League. Col. Maurice Moore (brother of the writer George Moore), also a member of the League, was to become the Volunteers' Inspector General. Hobson ensured his own people, such as Campbell, were involved and that Casement became Treasurer. Although Arthur Griffith chose not to join, the new organisation did represent a wide range of opinion and bodies. Some committee members were Redmondites others spoke for the Hibernians or represented the National Foresters but the core was separatist.

The 25 November meeting in the Rotunda rink, a large concert hall, was stewarded by IRB men like Liam Mellowes and addressed by MacNeill and Pearse, while Seán MacDermott spoke in one of the overflow halls. Father Eugene Sheehy and the first Free State prime minister W.T. Cosgrave were on the platform. Common sense prevailed with a prohibition on street demonstrations in Ulster being adopted as policy. Indeed later in August 1914, Pearse, for whom England was the enemy, would come into conflict with Redmondites on the Volunteer Committee because a Hibernian MP linked to Joe Devlin sent sixty of the Howth rifles into South Armagh.[675]

Being a makeweight for the UVF, the Irish Volunteers gathered enormous support very rapidly. Perhaps five thousand people including a large body of UCD students were at the inaugural meeting, so many that the application forms ran out. Amongst them was a former British soldier and Boer War veteran, Robert Monteith, who was later to join Casement in Germany. On 1 December, he paraded the first squad of the Irish Volunteers while still a civilian employee of the Army's Ordnance Department at Island Bridge, a job he was to keep for nearly another year. The response from Dublin Castle within a week of the Rotunda meeting, one he characterised as "imperialism's tomb", was a proclamation prohibiting the importation of arms into Ireland.

The enrolment form for *Oglaigh na hÉireann* read "I, the undersigned, desire to be enrolled in the Irish Volunteers formed to secure and maintain the rights and liberties common to all the people of Ireland without distinction of creed, class or politics." It is noteworthy that although the English version of the organisation's name was later to evolve into the Irish Republican Army, it has remained throughout its existence under the same title in Irish. The present IRA can thus be regarded as a true and unbroken successor of both Hobson and McCullough's IRB and MacNeill's Irish Volunteers. Yet the Volunteers were not specifically separatist. MacNeill was unaware of the IRB grip on the new organisation, while Pearse was only sworn into the IRB by Hobson, in December, after the Rotunda meeting.

Monteith recorded that after the meeting "there was no great rush homewards. Little knots of men stood around until after midnight discussing the issues."[676] He suggested the seismic nature of the night's events by pointing out how many "by virtue of their attendance and subsequent activities...took an Empire by the throat and shook out its teeth."[677] The huge crowd was indicative of a growing national mood displaying a very real sense of a people's government preparing to take over power.

Separately, a first Irish Citizen Army had already come into being, prompted by the strike led by Jim Larkin, and the consequent Dublin employers' lockout. It was being trained by Captain Jack White to become a workers militia, and members started to disrupt the Rotunda meeting with cheers for Larkin during the reading of the manifesto. This was until White joined the platform party and order was restored. Casement astringently commented on 26 November "The Larkin men tried to break it up. That speaks badly for their need of discipline. Jack White has his work cut out for him in bringing order to that disorderly mob."[678] The IRB under Bulmer Hobson, however, managed to contain the socialists' early efforts at infiltration. A second version of the Citizen Army, later to come under James Connolly's command, was put together in March 1914. Based at Liberty Hall, the headquarters of the Irish Transport Workers Union, it sought to complement the Volunteers not compete with them. Countess Markievicz who was to be a significant combatant in 1916 joined Connolly bringing in her valuable *Fianna* experience. He and the Irish Citizen Army were no longer revolutionary socialist, but now left-nationalists.

Casement co-wrote the Volunteer manifesto with MacNeill. In contrast to the sparse and telling prose of the Ulster Covenant it was long and dull. The promise was made that the Volunteers "under a national government" would become in effect the army of the nation. The resistance of Ulster was ignored and the northern difficulty laid entirely at the door of an unnamed English political party. Enthusing in a letter to Alice Stopford Green, Casement contrasted the fine spirit of the Irish with the "sordid, cowardly gang of curs" represented by the English aristocracy. Warming to his theme once again, he added "I sometimes in my heart long for the thud of the German boots keeping guard outside the Mother of Parliaments", hoping also for *The Times* office to become the Headquarters of German Intelligence.[679]

Indeed eighteen months earlier, writing to his cousin Gertrude from Falmouth, where the people looked "tame, dull and dreary" compared to the Irish, he had said of the Germans that he "would like very much like to see them in Ireland for fifty years."[680] Dispatched to England before the meeting to explain recent developments, he gave a number of press interviews, one appearing under the headline "Why He Is Organising the National Volunteers." In it, he announced support for the Ulster Volunteers if their liberties were attacked, and promised that the Irish Volunteers would not be used to coerce Ulster.

Meanwhile, up in Belfast at his home under Cave Hill, Bigger was organising a New Year's Eve party which was a cross between a pageant and a Volunteer drill. He described it to Alice Stopford Green in a letter of 7 January 1914: "New Years Eve at Cave Hill – all the boys present – some in kilts, others in old Volunteer uniforms – all armed fully with rifles & pikes – pipers go lear

& drums with standard. I received them at the door (a lovely clean cold frosty star-lit night) at midnight – then we had heavy firing of shot from the balcony and 'a Nation once again' from the pipes – then a quick march in fully drilled ranks down the road and then up the road ½ mile in tense excitement. The local police on night duty are very interested but come in for refreshments – after saluting the standard. And so we heralded in 1914."[681] Plainly the RIC were not too sure whether such play-acting was for real and, as often was the case, held back from intervention. It was, however, the start of something that would, in Belfast, see out the century.

After the Volunteers were founded, Casement took speaking engagements and made public appearances, especially in the west and south of Ireland. At a famous meeting in Cork which was partially disrupted by Hibernians when both Casement and Eoin MacNeill enthused overmuch about Carson and Ulster's resistance to England, seven hundred recruits were enrolled. Writing to Gertrude he trilled, it "was a grand success; the press reports lies…The reporters bolted when the row began, and we held our place, and then when the tumult died The O'Scodge called the sea back from its bed."[682] In another letter of encouragement, this time to Alec Wilson in Belfast, he eagerly reported "The loudest cheers I've heard have been when I said I was a Protestant" – not a description he adopted privately.

Nonetheless he appeared convinced of the need to blend the two opposing forces, also writing of "The Antrim Papist and the Antrim Protestant, the two leading Irish Volunteers who have made the Gospel of goodwill for 'Ulster' the outstanding feature of the Irish Volunteers." To a different audience, he drafted a letter at Ardrigh on 14 June, with the same initial words but with a sinister change, "Eoin MacNeill and I, 'the Antrim Papist and the Antrim Protestant' have brought the Gospel of the Gun to Ireland…An armed Ireland will be a friendly Ireland – if we could keep the politicians out and send all editors to jail for six months…we'd have a united Ireland. There is no ill will at heart between the people – it is the old game of the conqueror and plunderer."[683]

By February 1914, in an article under his name in *Irish Freedom*, Casement was openly calling for a new anti-British alliance of peace-loving peoples "a friendly Union of Germany, America and Ireland." By 17 March he was reviewing the Limerick Volunteers and marching at their head. On 19 April he was in Tullamore where it was the turn of Kings County to have a Volunteer corps established. There the message was protecting Home Rule, however, if force was threatened two could play that game thus he reckoned the Volunteers' first duty might be to protect the new Parliament. The knight and former diplomat was about as prestigious an ornament as the Volunteers could get so he was much in demand yet he was much more critical than that as his strategic speeches at these events were beginning to reveal.

A campaign to get the *Hamburg-Amerika Line* to replace the White Star and Cunard lines in use of the Cork port of Queenstown (Cobh) for transatlantic traffic took several months of his time in the early part of 1914. The British lines had chosen to abandon calls there on speed, economic and supposedly safety grounds, which was a great blow to the local economy. Working with a somewhat underwhelmed John J. Horgan in Cork (later to feature as an important source in René MacColl's book) he nearly pulled it off, until he so politicised the reception for the first German ship that *Hamburg-Amerika* got cold feet and backed out. Frank Bigger had been commissioned to divert from a gig in Clonmel and bring along his saffron-kilted equivalent of an Irish boy band, while Casement ordered that every ship in the harbour be decked out in German flags.

Horgan was the recipient of a large number of letters in which Casement expatiated on his motives and feelings. Writing from Malahide on 16 February 1914, he told him "I feel for you my Catholic countrymen perhaps more even than you feel for yourselves – I feel for Ireland – as John Mitchel felt for Ireland – the shame and ignoring of our race – the white slave race of European peoples. But I don't despair – because I believe with John Mitchel that the manhood of Ireland will outlast the British Empire." Later he advised "Be prepared to die for your country and John Bull will pass from our shores like a bad dream...I'll get you arms yet – don't fear 50,000 of them if you'll get the men ready." Nearly twenty years later, writing to Denis Gwynn, Casement's first biographer, Horgan gave his considered opinion of the man: "I do not think he was altogether normal...He took an exaggerated view both of the wrongs and the remedies...He gave an impression of instability and restlessness bordering on hysteria where Ireland was concerned."[684]

Although there were many other Protestants around the national movement including peers, politicians and literary figures, none had a reputation beyond Ireland or the international experience that Casement could bring to the Volunteer movement. That is not to say certain old Fenians and IRB personnel like Tom Clarke and John Devoy were not constantly dubious about someone of Casement's background, especially because of his career in the British diplomatic service. But conspiracy was their forte while Protestant nationalists were people to cherish. That they were also suspicious of them (as well as of socialists and radicals) could only be expected.

As Ulster prepared politically and militarily, the government began to face up to what it had somewhat naively brought about, and of the new realities now appearing. Various options based on the increasingly popular two nations theory began to be suggested for the province. The exclusion argument, anathema to one-island/one-nation believers, did reflect the reality of two peoples with differing ethnic origins. They had no economic, religious interests and beliefs in common and most importantly fairly distinct territories, albeit on the one island. The proposal mooted for Ulster which was to be put into the final piece of Home Rule legislation, an Amending Bill – that was ultimately shelved – was initially a six year opt-out for those Ulster counties so electing by vote. The Unionists were not impressed: "Sentence of death with a stay of execution for six years" Carson described it. Redmond on 2 March, however, acceded to a three year compromise on condition that if rejected by the Unionists and Conservatives, the unamended Bill would stand. A week later Asquith announced it was to be for six years despite his initial agreement otherwise. In July he yielded to indefinite exclusion.

At the same time elements of the government, acting unilaterally, chose to display an uncompromising face with the First Lord of the Admiralty, Winston Churchill, ordering a naval cordon around Ulster. The War Office in a letter dated 14 March instructed Sir Arthur Paget, officer commanding in Ireland, to reinforce his vulnerable military barracks in Ulster. He foolishly chose to test his officers with a loyalty question. They were required to resign instantly if they were not able to promise obedience – or be dismissed. The result was the so-called Curragh mutiny. Had they been simply ordered to do a particular task in Ulster, most would have obeyed but a test almost by definition produces a united and antagonistic response. This initially firm, indeed provocative attitude was at the end of March aborted by a climb-down on the part of the War minister, Sir John Seely. He gave a written assurance to the sixty cavalry officers under General Gough at the Curragh Camp in Co. Kildare, who had indicated resignation, promising instead that political opposition in Ulster would not be crushed by the army. Seely's subsequent enforced resignation was followed by Lord Milner's announcement of a British Covenant to support Ulster. Britain was seriously divided while the army, because of Churchill's failed *coup de main*, was needlessly demonstrated to be unreliable.

By virtue of his dominant Anglophobia, and the conflicting messages coming out of Carson, who although Ulster's titular leader was still an Irish Unionist in many of his sentiments, Casement maintained a naive hope of a coming together of the two sets of rebels. He frequently notioned the idea of talks with Carson to bring this union about. When in the House of Commons on 14 February 1914, Carson challenged Redmond, presumably rhetorically, to either take Ulster "or go and win her", Casement was impressed.

Two days later, in a letter to Horgan, he contemplated writing to Carson asking him to join him in Cork. "He could save Ireland and make Ireland... Shall I ask him? I don't know him at all, and I've blackguarded him openly in the Holy of Holies (Co. Antrim) but he knows I am honest and sincere and fearless – qualities he himself I think possesses…I like him far better than those craven, scheming, plotting Englishmen whose one aim is to see how little freedom they can give Ireland."[685] Yet again Casement would give no thought or credence to the dominant Ulster, and particularly Scots Presbyterian, element in resistance to Home Rule. He even "tried to speak to Carson to get him to parade at Clontarf on 23 April"[686] but could not get near him. This was in Belfast but "Carson [was] hedged around with bayonets."[687] He could not see or speak to him and anyway thought better of it.

Despite Churchill's naval cordon, on the night of 24 April 1914, the UVF's complex gunrunning plan, put together by Fred Crawford, came to fruition. The arms bought in Germany were taken through Danish waters (and nearly seized there), and after transhipment off the Tuskar Rock brought into Belfast Lough on the *Clydevalley*. It was a vast 200-ton armoury consisting of 25,000 German, Austrian and Italian rifles and three million rounds of ammunition that arrived in Larne. Under the guise of a full test mobilisation, and organised by Captain Frank Hall, the arms were, by dawn, successfully distributed in motorcars around the province. The die was cast so far as Ulster was concerned. But in Casement's words to Alec Wilson "It has been the manhood of the Ulsterman that has brought the guns back to Ireland."[688] He was better pleased that England's beard had been tweaked than disturbed that Ulster was more implacable than ever.

By March 1914, however, Casement's views as to the purpose of the Irish Volunteers had hardened up. Carson's remarks at a Dungannon meeting attended by both him and Erskine Childers, although a truism, were sobering: "All government rests on force; all law rests on force."[689] The Curragh events and the Ulster exclusion proposals told him enough of what was in store, not to mention the apprehension induced by his own psychological profiling of Carson; "I think the man is very unhappy – he looked wretched, gloomy, dark and foreboding."[690] On 28 March, in a joint letter with MacNeill in the *Irish Independent*, he said that Ireland was a conquered country under military occupation as the Curragh events proved. The only policy to flow from such a statement was evident.

Plainly the Unionists were the first to mobilise and arm in this crisis but to blame that minority in Ireland – who could only lose once – for having re-introduced the gun to Irish politics misses the point about democracy being invalid, indeed useless, if it governs without sufficient consent. This was a lesson the Unionists would in turn fail to learn. But there is a simple lesson here: if in ethnically disputed areas, people are mobilised either on to the streets or into organised formations, the consequences will be conflict, no matter

Kilted band at Ardrigh with, from left: Casement, Father Kelly, Lord Ashbourne, F.J. Bigger, and Alice Stopford Green (seated) ca. 1913

Casement with other members of the Gaelic League at an Irish language school on Tory Island

any well-meaning intentions, while the conflict will take totally unexpected directions. Casement was duly reminded in 1914, by an old Fenian, of earlier nationalist moves in this area, of how "several boatloads of arms mostly Martinis were landed in Ireland by my party in 1881 to 1884 and are supposed to be still taken care of."[691] And these Martini rifles did indeed resurface over the years of rebellion.

In early April, Casement told Maurice Moore, the Volunteer's training director that they must have arms. "Had we only rifles and officers" he told him "we could have 150,000 splendid men in six months."[692] On the occasion of his Tullamore speech, he was if anything upstaged by Tom Kettle, a former Irish Party MP for East Tyrone, who declared the Volunteer movement's object was an adequate force of trained men armed with modern rifles; not an orator's movement but a drill-sergeant's movement. The arming of the Irish Volunteers was therefore conceptualised before the UVF landing at Larne while there was already a small number of privately owned or previously imported weapons at their disposal.

On 9 May, Redmond, McNeill and Casement met at the House of Commons without coming to any agreement. The next day at a critical meeting at Alice Stopford Green's London house with MacNeill and Darrell Figgis, Casement observed that by arming the Volunteers one could keep them out of Redmond's control. It was Figgis, an Englishman living in Ireland and whose love life was to end in a messy court case and his own suicide, who provided another of those many evocative portraits of Casement: "His face was in profile to me, his handsome head and noble outline cut out against the lattice-work of the curtain and the grey sky. His height seemed more than usually commanding, his black hair and beard longer than usual…as I spoke he left his place by the window and came forward towards me, his face alight with battle. 'That's talking', he said…Language had wandered far from its meanings when one man could say to another that he was talking, when his appreciation and brevity betokened an end of talking."[693] By the conclusion of the meeting Figgis, for ever captivated, had offered, once sufficient money was gathered in Ireland, to go to Germany (as Crawford had done) and negotiate an arms shipment.

"When you are challenged in the field of force" said the Volunteers' Treasurer "it is upon that field you must reply" so Casement brought Figgis and Childers to meet the London agent of an arms dealer. But there was no cash forthcoming in Dublin so he had to arrange a whip-round in London as he had done for so many other causes, notably the Congo Reform Association and the Morel testimonial. In the upshot, it was Alice Stopford Green who put up most of the purchase money, a loan of £750. The £1,500 raised from Alice Stopford Green, Mrs Childers and the Hon. Mary Spring Rice was small beer compared to the UVF's bankroll but it was enough to buy about a twentieth of its number of weapons – 1,500 somewhat antiquated rifles and some 75,000 rounds of ammunition. Instead of chartering steamers, for which there were no funds, Mary Spring Rice imaginatively proposed the use of private yachts. Childers and Conor O'Brien (Mary's cousin) provided the *Asgard* and the *Kelpie* respectively. That of Childers, skippered by him, was womanned by his American wife Molly, and Spring Rice – as the famous photograph depicts despite both being trammelled by long skirts. After transhipment off the Scheldt the yachts evaded the Royal Navy cordon and landed separately to the north of Dublin in Howth on 26 July and Kilcoole in Co. Wicklow on 1 August.

In Patrick McCartan's view "Casement originated and was responsible for the scheme"[694] for arming the Irish Volunteers but its execution was a group effort. The reasons this collection of upper-class Irish Protestant women, and Anglo-Irish and English men organised such a key importation of rifles bear a certain similarity to a later period and are perhaps thereby more explicable. Many non-communists, particularly notable nuclear scientists, either conscientiously or because of the manipulation of agents and fellow-travellers, betrayed the West's nuclear secrets to the Soviet Union. They argued that it was vitally necessary to maintain a balance of power in the arms race. Without a reasonable balance, deterrence would be eroded and war inevitable. Casement would have concurred, although in the case of Ireland he needed no secondary excuse.

Given his role in the founding of the Volunteers, their arming, and his increasing journalism, more of it now under his own name, it is little wonder that the authorities were to come to the opinion that he was the political leader – the brains behind the 1916 Rising. Progenitor or midwife, Danton or Lenin, without him the Irish revolution would have taken a different course, or perhaps no course at all: No Rifles no Rising. For all that, on 21 June, he was declaring to Gertrude Bannister from Buswell's Hotel in Dublin "I think Carson will win. That has been my view all along."[695]

Before the landing of the arms, indeed starting as far back as March, there was a fightback by Redmond who saw an alternate power base coming into being. Having thrown in his lot with the Liberal government, and with Ulster starting to gain legislative concessions, he needed no private army run by separatists, one largely manned by his supporters yet outside his control. In June 1914 he was at the height of his popularity with the Home Rule Bill in the bag. Yet, as he said, the effect of Carson's threats, the Curragh incident and the Larne gunrunning vitally altered the balance and made it desirable to encourage and if possible arm the Volunteers. To do this and leave them in the hands of the separatists was unthinkable, so Redmond required that it become 'representative' through the admission of twenty-five of his nominees to the Provisional Committee.

Casement's alternate proposal of a system of county delegates found favour except with Redmond. Hobson and Casement, to avoid Redmond gaining unilateral, unchallenged control of a movement which now had tens of thousands of members throughout the island, changed their mind about resigning. To abandon the Volunteers now just when an arms shipment was about to arrive would have put paid to the developing momentum for action. Either way with the IRB secretly in the centre of the organisation, Redmond was never going to succeed in dictating military policy. As events were to prove it was a small military sub-committee that made the critical decisions in 1916, decisions which would be kept even from Eoin MacNeill.

For Bulmer Hobson his concession was the beginning of the end. Fellow IRB men were not approving of compromise. Indeed when Tom Clarke and Seán MacDermott in a last minute attempt to get a change of heart spoke to Hobson (and Casement), he was asked "How much did the British pay you?"[696] He was

Bulmer Hobson and Joseph McGarrity ca. 1910, Philadelphia (Villanova University)

showing himself to be a trimmer in a group of absolutists, or perhaps more accurately a revolutionary and not a rebel. The arms importation may have permitted his reprieve within the IRB until his resignation but a strategic difference had opened up. Clarke apparently never spoke to Hobson again. In the event, the extra names for the committee, except for Joe Devlin, were not particularly worrying. They included four priests and Redmond's brother William. Many rarely attended meetings. Administrative control stayed where it was.

The final passage of the Home Rule Bill coincided precisely with the outbreak of war and the two issues became irretrievably connected and dependent upon one another. Casement left Belfast discreetly for North America in early July 1914 in an effort to rustle up more cash and arms for the Volunteers. America was the key element in Irish nationalist operations, better organised and with a clearer head than was to be found at home. By virtue of the enormous numbers of Irish there, their increasing power and wealth and the fact of the United States becoming an imperial player on the world stage, a small number of Irish-American would facilitate and indeed arrange a revolution back in Ireland.

The trip had been arranged by Bulmer Hobson who had recently returned from another visit there. But by the time Casement reached New York he was no longer welcome. John Devoy of *Clan na Gael* was aware of Redmond's intervention and the divisions in the Volunteers, and blamed Hobson for his decision to accept the Redmond ultimatum. Devoy wrote to Hobson telling him that Casement's visit would be useless while sacking him as Irish correspondent of the *Gaelic American*. But the letter crossed in the Atlantic with Casement himself.

On 18 September the Home Rule Bill became law (after a Conservative walkout in Parliament) but with the war starting on 4 August for both Britain and Ireland – the day after the Germans invaded Belgium – its commencement was postponed for at least a year by means of a Suspensory Act. The prime minister, Asquith, having already gone along with certain Unionist demands by allowing at least a four county Ulster exclusion now had to address the length of that exclusion. This was to be dealt with by an Amending Bill but inevitably it was itself amended in the Lords, to full nine county, permanent exclusion. A similar attempt in the Commons by a dissident Cornish Liberal, T.C. Agar-Robartes, was voted down. Ultimately Asquith acceded to no time limit on exclusion although he sought to limit the area to four counties, but the imminence of war saw the Amending Bill abandoned on 30 July to everyone's relief. The matter remained to be resolved.

The Germans were to a degree emboldened in their aggression by a belief that Britain would be diverted by an imminent civil war in Ireland. In time they were to be persuaded by Casement to do more than just hope for a rebellion.

But they had not reckoned with Redmond's complete endorsement of the war or indeed the total capitulation of the Liberal Cabinet. On the night of 3 August in the House of Commons, Redmond proudly promised that "the armed Catholics in the South will only be too glad to join arms with the armed Protestant Ulsterman…In comradeship with our brethren in the north we will ourselves defend the coasts of our country."

And thus thousands more Irishmen than ever were to die in the seven years of conflict from 1916 to 1923, started toward their fate. They went to the thanks of Sir Edward Grey, for whom Ireland "was the one bright spot in the very dreadful situation."[697] This was, however, initially only a commitment to relieve the government by enabling its soldiery to switch from garrisoning Ireland to active service in Europe. A second statement by Redmond in Co. Wicklow came two days after Royal Assent to the Home Rule Bill. In a euphoric atmosphere, on 20 September, he announced "It would be a disgrace if Irishmen refrained from fighting, wherever the firing extends, in defence of right, freedom and religion in this war." Extending the commitment to fighting outside Ireland was a step too far for MacNeill and the separatist Volunteers, who had coped with Redmond's first pronouncement on the war.

This is not to say that his line was not popular in nationalist Ireland. It was, as the recruiting figures were to show – immensely so, not least because of the fact of Belgium being a Catholic country. At the moment of war, Tom Kettle was in Belgium buying arms for the Redmondite wing of the Volunteers, which were handed to the Belgians because of their perceived greater need, so split was plainly inevitable. Hardly five per cent, some 11,000 of the Volunteers (albeit most of the activists), stayed put after Redmond's nominees were excluded from the committee. The majority then took the name Irish National Volunteers. Asquith pledged to arm and equip them; a pledge he did not keep. Indeed they were not even allowed to form a distinctive division within Kitchener's army, like the UVF was, and initially were dispersed. Redmond had got everything, and nothing.

Bulmer Hobson put together a plan to bring sufficient Volunteers and their womenfolk, discreetly to Howth on Sunday 26 July 1914. They were to abandon their ladies on the arrival of the *Asgard* and, on landing the cargo, use the waiting taxis, to get the ammunition away and dispersed into the city. Once on shore, the rifles were distributed to upwards of seven hundred men under Cathal Brugha who marched back into Dublin. At Clontarf they were confronted by hastily mobilised soldiers and police. By dint of confusion and argument most Volunteers got through, retaining their rifles. Significantly some Volunteers did open fire, wounding soldiers, while the police showed an understandable unwillingness to effect the intended disarmament. It was only later at Bachelor's

Walk in the city centre that the army inflicted fatal casualties on the jeering populace who were stoning the unprepared Scottish soldiers. These first three dead in a generation (a fourth died later of wounds) were given a memorable funeral. The day after the killings Austria declared war on Serbia.

When Casement got to see John Devoy on 20 July, he received a frosty reception. Devoy was not going to put himself out as regards fund raising although he was impressed with Casement and the potential of the gunrunning project. In many Irish-American eyes the successful arms importation was to turn Casement from an unwelcome guest to an overnight hero. He was invited to address a myriad of meetings and the compromise with Redmond was forgotten. He also had an enabling cablegram from Eoin MacNeill: "Reaffirm my former letter asking for arms. Ireland's urgent need today is rifles. The whole nation is aroused and determined. The crisis demands exceptional sacrifices and prompt aid is essential."[698] Howth and Bachelor's Walk had provoked a mood of militancy in Ireland.

Casement was in Philadelphia at the moment the news came through and spoke on 2 August at a protest meeting on the killings, as news of the event spread across the Atlantic. All his favourite lines were delivered down to the

Casement and John Devoy, USA 1914

fact that "if every Irishman has a gun there would still be no civil war."[699] He was also getting to know all the key players and, in particular, became very friendly with Joe McGarrity (1874-1940), an Ulsterman from Carrickmore, and an implacable Republican, for whom Casement became a "reincarnated Tone".[700] Even Devoy, a hard-bitten old Fenian, was inspired as Casement wrote to Alice: "Old J.D. says with a glow of joy 'the greatest deed done in Ireland for 100 years' – and keeps on repeating it."[701] In time, Devoy would lose his enthusiasm for Casement but McGarrity stayed loyal to his memory.

With the outbreak of war and the passing of the Home Rule Bill after a quarter of a century of effort, Redmond's popularity, even in America, stymied much of Casement's fundraising efforts and he collected only some $7,000 not the $50,000 anticipated. And this despite some excellent press coverage. One interviewer, telling of his "striped gray suit and straw hat" added, "He is tall… possibly the most distinguishing thing about him is his utter kindliness. It shines from his blue-gray eyes and radiates from him like an aura."[702] Regardless of his success, limited or otherwise, the strategic push towards Germany which had been developing for some time in Casement's mind, perhaps for a decade, now came increasingly to the fore.

When Bulmer Hobson was in America earlier in 1914 (with Pearse) he had brought with him a memorandum by Casement on Irish-German relations in the event of European war. Devoy had passed this to Count von Bernstorff, the German ambassador in Washington. After the outbreak of war Devoy and other Clan members met von Bernstorff and Franz von Papen, the military attaché, with a view to interesting them in supplying arms and officers for an Irish rebellion. A meeting then occurred between von Papen and Casement on 18 September when the possibility of raising an Irish Brigade from captured Irish soldiers was discussed and, in effect, agreed.

Casement noted on Captain von Papen's confirmatory note "R at 2 a.m. on return from meeting…I pointed out on no account to exchange Irish prisoners…He told me…Paris again in panic and that the German position was 'overwhelmingly strong'…Good – the meeting was good." The Captain wrote again, cryptically, on 30 September, "Cable was sent over concerning the news of Dublin and will interest the people over there. Papers for the Holyman are ready and I shall keep them there until I see you Friday. Nobody on the other side will mention your projects. Baron v. Horst can be released only by exchange of prisoners; we see no other way."[703]

"God save Ireland now is another form of God save Germany"[704] summed up Casement's unstinting view of Germany. Another time it was: "I prefer the Germans – the brutality of men not afraid to die for their country or to pour out their blood in rivers for their faith in their fatherland." But a slightly cooler head, like Devoy, although described by the Germans as one of their "Confidential Agents", simply sought to exploit the first multilateral European war for a century. An address to the Kaiser was drawn up by the Clan and a representative sent to Berlin to lay the ground for political and military support to bring about Irish independence. That agent travelled on from Berlin to Dublin to advise the senior IRB man Tom Clarke of the grand design, and thus the seeds of the Easter Rising were sown.

Despite opposition from the devoted Francophile, John Quinn, whom he was staying with in New York, Casement recognised that in the new circumstances extreme measures were appropriate, measures happily in tune with the extremity of his own pro-Germanism. Every aspect of the conflict of the Great Powers was such as to point him toward Berlin. He was opposed to French colonialism, Russian oppression, and English supremacy of the seas, and of course England in Ireland. He also believed that the British policy of encircling Germany with alliances and naval power and depriving her of colonial possessions had forced Berlin to go to war.

Casement had a coherent, if rarely heard, attitude towards German expansionism. On 14 September 1909, from Rio, he was complaining to E.D. Morel "From the intense fear of and jealousy of Germany our Cabinet have tried to prevent German expansion on all sides and the Moroccan tomfoolery was one of the most fatal steps taken in that direction. The right policy would have been give and take with Germany – not bitter opposition – and seeking means to aid her to some safe outlet for her growing powers and population."[705] The next day, he added "I would have invited Germany into Morocco or anywhere she wanted to go – to Brazil for one. We have tried to bottle up very new wine indeed in very old diplomatic bottles...Now things have reached so evil a pass that peace between the two great Powers of Europe can hardly be kept. Both are preparing for war and faster than the world suspects – but the fault lies far more with England than with Germany."[706] His Brazilian hosts would not have been too pleased to hear how Casement would casually transfer them to Berlin to assuage the German appetite, but it had been done elsewhere within the decade, not least in the Congo, while Portuguese territories were always vulnerable.

But Casement was also positively pro-German, taken with their Teutonic freshness and relatively unblemished, if brief, imperial record. He had a naive belief in Germany, a place he had recently visited and a number of whose citizens he knew and liked, although he did not know it well, and the language not at all. In a 1913 book review, for example, he picked out a photograph of a young German soldier whose face he wrote was "typical of the courageous and good-humoured goodwill of the German race."[707] Of course it was a country of hardly fifty years standing, newer in many ways than the United States.

In August 1914, in a letter to a New York newspaper, signed "a lawyer", he was writing from the heart, in jingoistic mode: "England relies on money, Germany on men. And just as Roman men beat Carthaginian mercenaries, so must German manhood, in the end triumph over British finance…Germany fights today as the champion of Europe, nay more, as the champion of Christendom [against] the hordes of Russian barbarism, the sword of French hatred and the long purse of British greed…as an Irishman I say from my heart – God Save Germany." Where England had an "avarice of freedom" which she was unwilling to impart to others, Germany was "fighting for light, for air, for freedom" and hoping to build "a loftier and larger dwelling…for a numerous and growing offspring."[708] In other words, *lebensraum*.

Quinn, however, was advising caution in every way, and warned Casement not to "fall a victim to Devoy's obsession that England has paid spies all over America. That is an especial bug of the old man…Devoy is very fond of using the word gold in connection with the English."[709] But Casement did not care to temper his certainties and Quinn soon lost any confidence he had in his new friend, calling his German mission absurd and saying he was "always fighting for lost causes or slaying dragons."[710]

Casement finally translated his sentiments into a public statement thus pinning his colours firmly to the mast. Published in the American press on 17 September (before Redmond's fuller commitment to the war effort), he penned "An Open Letter to Irishmen." He opposed enlistment in the British Army, it being designed only to "aid the allied Asiatic and European powers in a war against a people who have never wronged Ireland." He stated that the Liberals had pledged to give self-government to Ireland for twenty-eight years, a pledge unfulfilled except to enact a Home Rule Bill "and defer its operation until after the war, and until an 'amended bill' profoundly to modify its provisions has been introduced and passed." What was on offer now, he wrote, was only "a wholly hypothetical and indefinite form of partial internal control of certain specified Irish services, if in return for this promissory note (payable after death), the Irish people will contribute their blood, their honour, and their manhood, in a war that in no wise concerns them." Irishmen instead should "save their strength and manhood for the trying tasks before them, to build up from a depleted population the fabric of a ruined national life."[711]

The nature of these sentiments was on a par with those published in pamphlet and poster form during the 1905 campaign against enlistment, his first and serious anti-British intervention. Indeed similar sentiments can be found in many of his letters from Brazil to Morel. In one, dated 15 May 1908 from Santos, he asked "Who shall restore the destroyed Irish race – the dead Irish tongue – the murdered Irish music – the wealth of gentle nature, lovable mind, high temper and brave generous heart which made of the Irish people a race we shall not see the like of again."[712] The answer was of course himself and he was no slouch in the matter.

Although his open letter was not honestly pro-German, it was sufficient to prompt a response from Arthur Nicolson at the Foreign Office. Casement was asked, somewhat needlessly, if he was the author of the signed letter which urged "that Irish sympathies should be with Germany rather than with Great Britain and that Irishmen should not join the British Army."[713] It was many months before Nicolson's letter found him, by then in Germany. (Note the English inability to utilise correct nomenclature – Ireland not being part of Great Britain although part of the United Kingdom.) Sir Arthur also pointed out, humbly, that Casement who never drew his pension again, was "liable in certain circumstances to be called upon to serve under the crown." This was icy understatement. Plainly he would be put under some threat if he returned. After fussing as to whether he had the power to stop Casement's pension, the Foreign Secretary, Sir Edward Grey finally suspended it when faced with a parliamentary question on the subject.

Casement was now treating with the German enemy in a way which nobody in Ireland was yet doing, although for Irish nationalists in America this was almost second nature. It was his peculiar position that permitted such a unique stance: he loathed England with a venom that only certain Protestants like Douglas Hyde and Frank Bigger could summon up. He knew the personnel of London's governing class and had no respect for them. He was entirely dismissive of their reasoning and motives yet was able to think in their terms. Exceptionally, he could be strategic, by virtue of his diplomatic training and experience. And being without ties in the form of a wife or children, or the need to consider consequences for others, he was perfectly positioned to become an active traitor. He was, he knew, committing treason, a concept he certainly recognised, even if it was one he denied in this instance by virtue of his changed nationality.

One author's critical interpretation reckoned Casement's "admiration for Germany was a compensating mental mechanism for his hatred of England. But in the end it too became an obsession." He cited as evidence that, in early September 1914, on the German defeat at the Marne, John Yeats, father of the poet heard him intoning "Poor Kaiser Poor Kaiser [with] tears in his voice."[714] Casement was certainly not simply anti-imperialist. If the peoples were Irish, or not of European origin like the Turks or Zulus, then they had right on their side, if not, his Anglophobia took precedence. A hint of future political development, had he survived, are his remarks in 1907 about Britain that "until a real Socialist upheaval comes to sweep the whole building away, nothing will really be changed."[715] However, rather than Casement going so far as adopting a Marxian world view, it is possible more to see him coming into his own at the end of the 20th century as a conscience-based, third world liberationist, or in mid-century as a left wing anti-colonialist socialist knowing the cruel facts of empire and finding it easy to attribute fault to his own people.

From September 1914 until April 1916, Casement was not alone when communicating across the Atlantic or with Ireland. Telegraphic messages to and from the German embassy in Washington were being intercepted and his discreet letter arrangements through Holland were also compromised although many American letters did get through unnoticed. London was listening to his messages and reading his mail. Though to what useful purpose is another matter. Knowledge may be power but what you do with the knowledge is still critical.

In the 1921 government Bluebook, *Documents Relative to the Sinn Fein Movement*, many of these intercepts were published. In its introduction there is also a description of a collection of Casement articles that was translated and published in Germany and which were widely disseminated in English language versions in Ireland and America. The collection's title was *Ireland, Germany and the Freedom of the Seas* with, as one subtitle, *A Possible Outcome of the War of 1914.* One of the items was his 1911 article, *Ireland, Germany and the Next War.* Casement explained his purpose as the author then, and his present position: "The vital needs of European peace, of European freedom of the seas and of Irish national life and prosperity were indissolubly linked with the cause of Germany in the struggle so clearly impending between that country and Great Britain. The war has come sooner than expected. The rest of the writer's task must be essayed not with the author's pen, but with the rifle of the Irish Volunteer." The world and his former employers were well warned.

An intercepted despatch of 27 September 1914 from von Bernstorff's embassy to Berlin told London of plans afoot and of certain diplomatic options proposed by Casement. The writer felt American public opinion would favour Germany giving freedom to "oppressed people such as the Poles, the Finns and the Irish" although in the event of German victory the fear in the U.S. would be of any "excessive extension of our frontiers over areas where foreign languages are spoken." If there was to be no understanding with England, and instead a life and death struggle, he reckoned "the formation of an Irish Legion from Irish prisoners of war would be a grand idea if only it could be carried out." Bernstorff was something of an Anglophile, unlike von Papen who was to become Hitler's deputy in 1933, and twenty years later still, write an introduction to Monteith's book on Casement. One senses the ambassador's regret could the war not be settled by compromise. On 1 October, Casement was first mentioned with his imminent departure being signalled to Berlin. On 3 November, Zimmermann was telegraphing back to the Washington embassy saying "his proposals are being carefully gone into."[716]

It is unclear from the Bluebook exactly when these messages were decrypted or made available to the British authorities, and to whom, precisely. Indeed the hugely significant details provided by the "Irish Revolutionary Directory" in America both about the arms importation and the timing of the rising seems to have been given little value or circulation. One explanation is that London was so concerned not to give Berlin any clue about such messages being intercepted it, underplayed both the facts and their import.

Casement recognised his proposed mission to Germany was both military and diplomatic. Indeed he was as well suited as anyone to effect an advance in that latter department. In effect he became the first Irish ambassador sent into Europe since Wolfe Tone arrived in Paris in 1796. Diplomatic recognition of a country's right to independence is a critical first step, and ultimately a *sine qua non* for a state coming into being. Of the three tasks he set himself – German recognition, an Irish Brigade and arms deliveries it was only that first which Casement was to bring about satisfactorily.

Whether in the long run it was all that significant is another matter. As America was to enter the war in 1917, despite much Irish-American opposition, and Germany was to lose it, the results of Casement's alliance were doubly diluted. If any country was able to put effective pressure on London it was America. And Casement, by his alliance with Berlin, not to mention his willingness to assist in sabotage within the U.S. (and indirectly to encourage Mexican revanchism over their lost territories), all before America's entry to the war, ensured pressure from that quarter would be muted. The ceaseless comings and goings to the U.S. after 1916 by de Valera, Patrick McCartan, Denis McCullough and Joseph Connolly (the latter three, oddly, all Ulstermen) were vital for the course of the Irish revolution, but largely in terms of Irish-American assistance and money. The U.S. government was never to become actively supportive of separation; just not actively pro-British.

On 6 January 1915, Richard Meyer, Casement's long-suffering Foreign Ministry interpreter recorded: "The Admiralty Staff requests to instigate Irish in America, through intercession of Sir Roger Casement, to far-reaching sabotage in the United States and Canada."[717] Meyer was a Jew personally turned down for citizenship by Hitler in 1936; interestingly German-American Jews were another group targeted by Berlin in 1914. Taking the matter further, the Wilhelmstrasse Foreign Ministry advised von Papen on 26 January of people "indicated by Sir Roger Casement" from whom the names of "persons suitable for carrying on sabotage in the United States and Canada" could be obtained.[718]

The first of the three names was that of Joseph McGarrity. The deciphered message concluded by advising "In the United States sabotage can be carried out on every kind of factory for supplying munitions of war. Railway embankments and bridges must not be touched. Embassy must in no circumstances be compromised."[719] This message may have also become Casement's death warrant, perhaps being of greater significance than the Black Diaries in President Wilson's failure to respond to pleas from Capitol Hill concerning a reprieve.

"It would be inexcusable to touch this", Woodrow Wilson told his Irish secretary in July, adding "It would involve serious international embarrassment."[720] His coolness on the matter was put down by many to his Ulster Presbyterian origins. But he would also have been well aware of intelligence that put Casement and the German embassy at the centre of a web of intrigue opposed to his country's best interest. For the next twenty years, the process of trying to obtain reparations from Berlin through the Mixed Claims Commission for the damage caused by sabotage, not least in the July 1916 Black Tom railway freight yard explosion in New York, would keep lawyers busy and the issue militating against rapprochement between the two nations. In that sense, Casement's overblown, indeed careless, pro-Germanism was to have unforeseen effects on German-American relations for a generation – through to another war.

His reception in the U.S. was tending toward adulation, with Casement being "appealed to again and again to come out and be a new leader – a sort of aged Parnell" as he told Dick Morten.[721] He was to tell much the same story to Mrs Green: "They are setting their hearts on a Protestant leader and they think poor souls, I may be the man" and a few days later "They are mad for a Protestant leader."[722] Casement also came under sustained attack from Redmondite advocates, one Michael Wade of the United Irish League declaring in the *Philadelphia Inquirer* of 30 July 1914: "As for the titled gentleman who is visiting the city he has all his life been in the pay of the British government, was one of the individuals who denounced the King of Belgium in order that England might get control of the rubber fields, and denounced the Boers so that England would have an excuse in seizing Transvaal."[723]

But Casement was not happy in America. He never was anywhere, except Ireland. He had already started complaining about the country's failings while there, indeed the more he saw of the country the less he liked, he told his cousin. Redmond's apparent success with Home Rule, the differences of opinion over the war, not to mention the disputes within Irish America which were to erupt later into a state of hostility particularly between Devoy and McGarrity, distressed him. As Devoy was willing to fund Casement into Germany, indeed was keen to see him out of the States, as he was showing signs of taking on a leadership role above and beyond *Clan na Gael*, the solution was clear. He was now to be shipped to meet his destiny.

On 28 November 1914, Casement wrote a letter (which London was to read) to Eoin MacNeill distilling that destiny for Ireland: "Tell all to trust the Germans – and to trust me. We shall win everything if you are brave and faithful to the old cause…Tell me all your needs at home, viz rifles, officers, men. Send priest or priests at all costs – one not afraid to fight and die for Ireland…We may win everything by this war if we are true to Germany: and if we do not win today we insure international recognition of Irish nationality."[724]

15

Germany 1914-16 and Adler Christensen

Casement was not to travel alone to Germany. On the July day he had arrived in New York he met a young man who was to come perilously close to destroying him several times over. This was Adler Christensen, a 24 year-old Norwegian. Described by some as an adventurer, he was the classic projector once found working with Tudor intelligence. His schemes took over a large part of Casement's life in Germany and fuelled the paranoiac and conspiratorial side of his character. Indeed without Adler the homosexual aspect of Casement's life and the Black Diaries might never have surfaced, for it was the Norwegian who first opened that closet door to London officials.

Casement had spent the best part of a year in the public gaze in Ireland with many normal outlets denied by virtue of political commitments. Knowing his propensity for looking forward to cruising big cities on arrival, it is plain that having booked into his hotel, Casement set out on such an errand the night he arrived in New York. He was staying at the Belmont on 42nd Street, opposite Grand Central Station. The hotel was staffed by Irish men and boys, "Some" as Casement diaried "had even the brogue still lingering round the shores of that broad estuary of smiles, that takes the place of a mouth in the true Milesian face."[725]

Later, he wrote: "Strolling down Broadway [probably at Times Square] in the thought of perhaps locating old points of view, like Ponds"* and the hotel he lived in in 1890, a young Norwegian sailor spoke to me – and him I befriended and told him to see me next morning…He had run away from his father's house after getting a severe beating for playing truant at school and had stowed away on an English collier. This when he was 12 years old. He was landed at Glasgow and left there, and some Norwegian sailors took him and so he became a fireman on a succession of Norwegian steamers. When he met me he was out of work, starving almost and homeless. He was grateful for my help and I saw him once or twice in New York where with the help I gave him he got work."[726]

His description of the meeting was probably accurate so far as it went. It is taken from the journals he wrote explicitly for future publication, as he said on 9 April 1916, when handing them over to his American friend, Dr Charles

* Pond's Celebrity World Tours had a Union Square office. James Pond specialised in explorers and in 1891 had hired Casement and Herbert Ward for a US tour.

Studio photograph of Adler Christensen in 1915 in Berlin aged 25 (NLI)

Curry: "The Diaries are very poor stuff, very poorly written and hastily put together and would need much editing by a friend for I often say things in them I should not like to stand for ever."[727]

If Adler had worked as a fireman on board ship he was certainly neither slight nor delicate as it was an arduous, backbreaking job and one that could be bettered on shore. Having gone to sea as early as the age of twelve he undoubtedly came up against sexual proposals if not actual abuse. The question is whether that night in New York he was selling sexual services and whether Casement partook, for in certain ways Adler was neither a classic rent boy nor just a cruiser collecting cash gifts. He seems to have lived on his wits but not to have been entirely self-interested since he could get into his projections, indeed be taken over by them.

Casement expanded on his motives for befriending Adler in a letter of 12 November 1914 to the Gaelic scholar Kuno Meyer, a German patriot who had left Dublin at the outbreak of war. He spun a tale to convince a possibly sceptical Meyer of how Adler "was starving, looking for work, to whom a stranger (myself) had been kind – that was all – then my taking him across to Norway with no real knowledge of his nature beyond my instincts for an honest heart – and the fact that on the voyage he became aware of my identity" adding the pathetic detail that he "has not seen his parents for twelve years."[728]

Christensen was the only one of Casement's companions or partners to take flesh, outside of his diaries and correspondence. A fair number of his friends met and got to know him and some like Captain Robert Monteith, of the Irish Brigade, were in Adler's company for lengthy periods. His time with Casement is normally thought of as the years from 1914 to 1916, however, although not generally known or at times accepted, Adler had a life with Casement before those years.

He was born Adler Eivind Christensen on 3 May 1890 and baptised a Lutheran on 20 July in Moss, a coastal town south of Christiania (modern Oslo). At that point Norway (once a Danish possession) was part of Sweden and remained so until its bloodless separation in 1905. Adler's surname was initially spelt Kristensen. His father, a steamship engineer, Aksel (Emil) Kristensen, was born in 1861, and his mother Henriette née Brynildsen, a housewife, was born five years later in 1866.[729]

In the 1900 census his father was stated to be away in Russia – presumably working. Adler was recorded as one of eight people living together, of whom three girls, Ingrid, Aslaug and Ellen appear to be his younger sisters. A Hans Brynildsen, probably his uncle, born in 1869, and a woman born in 1879, Malla Gjersze, a servant "employed with housework" along with his parents completed the household. The family lived in a four-roomed upstairs apartment with a kitchen at 12 Fleischers Gade (Butcher Street). Later his mother had another son, Rolf, eleven years younger than Adler. Contrary to a statement by the Casement writer and campaigner Herbert Mackey, Adler is not registered as having died in Moss in 1926. The time and place of his demise remained unknown for many more decades.

His only published photograph, in Curry's 1922 book, depicts a different looking individual to the pen portrait drawn by René MacColl in his 1956 biography. This studio photograph was taken in Berlin on 24 June 1915, according to an inscription, in what looks like Adler's own handwriting on the face of the NYPL print. He was then twenty-five years of age. It shows a beefy,

Adler Christensen suited and outdoors (NLI Ephemera, A 430 Prints and Drawings)

Adler Christensen (2nd right, back) with his parents, three sisters and younger brother Rolf ca. 1920

almost florid, well-dressed man with a lined forehead; not boyish at all, nor a classic Casement sex partner. The print in the NLI" is inscribed on the back, by an unknown hand, "Sir R.C.'s Norwegian servant." He led a rough life although there is only one mention of him being a drinker which is somewhat indicated by the sitter's looks. He certainly does not look camp or flighty but a lot nattier than a stoker, indeed as a confidence trickster or con man might appear. Courtesy of Princess Blücher's memories he has been condemned in most histories as essentially a screaming queen, thereby proving Casement's homosexuality.

Although he ran away from home, he ended up following his father's profession but as a seaman not an officer. He was obviously a difficult and perhaps unhappy boy not willing to subject himself to family discipline yet his early circumstances were by no means impoverished. A decade later he was a man of the world, a survivor and, by necessity, an accomplished operator. He may well have been charming in an enthusiastic Scandinavian way but was certainly not domesticated. The German ambassador to Norway reported in late 1914 from enquiries made locally that Christensen "had caused his parents a good deal of trouble as a boy, but was said to be 'talented'…and to have once been a secretary to a millionaire."[730] Berlin seem to have naively accepted such a fanciful tale at least until different evidence surfaced. In 1916, British investigators were to prove more thorough, unearthing a considerable amount of damning evidence, even if some was plainly extravagant.

Casement must have seen something in Adler beyond his value as an accomplice or agent on the German mission. It may be that he was just another in a long line of Casement lame ducks but he did have useful qualities of guile and criminality. As well as that he spoke some German, although at the time of this July meeting in New York, Casement was not necessarily expecting to go there or need such assistance. Normally he travelled alone even if the thought of being accompanied by attractive young men was often on his mind – a notion he frequently proposed to himself.

Adler may indeed have been sexually memorable although no longer in the first flower of his youth. So they kept in contact through that summer and when in October a voyage to Germany via Norway was decided upon, he came back into the frame. The problem was Adler was no servant, but an official companion, one with a mind of his own. What was not made known to Casement's Irish-American colleagues was that the two had met before, in similar circumstances in that Adler was again broke and Casement cruising. There are three confirming references to this previous meeting, one from Casement himself. In a statement by Adler "upon oath at the Consulate-General of the United States of America at Berlin", after setting out his place and date of birth and parentage, he stated he was "engaged by Sir Roger Casement, whom I had previously known, in a confidential capacity."[731] Although this could refer to their July meeting it is more likely in this context to mean a longer-standing connection.

The fact of revealing a meeting earlier than 1914 was obviously in Casement's mind when he started drafting an unfinished history for Adler. It is in Casement's handwriting and has neither introduction nor any explanation as to its intended purpose. Plainly he thought better of utilising it, as it was full of holes and could only have led to more questions than answers. Written in the first person, it was either a script for Adler to memorise, or an affidavit to swear to. Given his misbehaviour in Germany, it was probably also designed to be available as a defence for Casement, outlining the charitable nature, of not just their second, but their first meeting, should his choice of companion ever become an issue.

Adler was supposed to relate their opening moments thus: "When I first met Sir Roger Casement I am sure he never thought he would ever again meet the Norwegian sailor he had helped as he has surely helped many others who were in similar trouble. I had run away from my ship at a South American port as many sailors do; and after wandering around for a bit I got so hungry and tired that I did not know where to turn. I did not go to the Norwegian Consul for I was a deserter and liable as such to punishment, and I had no claim on any other consulate. But I wanted to get to work again and so I thought I would try the British Consulate where there are always many sailors engaged and wanted. I had no discharge papers from my last ship and so they would not take me."[732] The story which was written by Casement on the same paper as a ten-page self-justification on the question of his treason, the British newspapers and Sir Edward Grey ends abruptly here.

Plainly, Casement began to despair of this tale being persuasive and abandoned the project. It had several flaws if it was ever to be convincingly used. According to a later statement by Adler himself, they had actually first met in Montevideo, a city where Casement was not a consul. Notice he had left the port's name unspecified while the reasons adduced for Adler calling at the British consulate in the first place were plainly specious. Whether Casement was to appear in the story and reverse a junior official's decision or simply meet Adler by chance and assist him, will never be known. But by Casement's admission they had met before their New York encounter.

The saga of Adler becomes ever more convoluted and critical to the whole German enterprise, calling into question the balance of Casement's own mind and his judgment. Up to this point he was able to divorce his private life from his official and public life. The extremity of his views *vis à vis* the Foreign Office had been pursued vigorously but just within the rules. With friends he let his pen and tongue rage. However, where Ireland was concerned he had now crossed irrevocably over into radical opposition, both to moderate nationalism, and to England. The circumstances of the war had turned him from a militant separatist into a one-man military opposition to the enemy: Casement v. England.

But the stress of war, treason and his inevitable fate were to accentuate the sillier not the heroic side of his character. A noble enterprise dependent almost entirely on him, one for which he was uniquely qualified, and for many other reasons seriously unsuitable, was to be jeopardised over and over again, largely because of Adler. Casement's associated lack of security, his ever-flowing mouth and writings, alongside his kindly and humanitarian nature were to finish him and the enterprise off. Although, unexpectedly, it came to ultimate fruition in twenty-six counties of Ireland because of its initial failure and his death.

What was Adler to Casement? How could Casement have allowed someone, who was increasingly obviously trouble, to be privy to so much of his mission, and who with his projections would almost take it over? The answer to date has been to write Adler off as an outrageous homosexual as if that can explain his involvement in the matter, or to portray him as an unfairly maligned, faithful servant. The truth does not lie between the two. The evidence suggests that Adler had a pathological personality. Indeed he was a sociopath, entirely self-interested but not averse to becoming emotionally involved in whatever scheme he had in progress. He had the mind and outlook of a double or triple agent but at times had difficulty deciding which way to jump. Just such a moment presented itself in 1916 in Philadelphia but more prominently earlier, in October 1914, in Norway.

Why did Casement need Adler? The third reference to a previous meeting explains in part. He had been a sexual partner and one sufficiently memorable to justify a reconnection after the chance meeting in New York. But Adler was no teenage lad. Rather he was of a different disposition, being butch, bisexual and closer to the rough trade Casement also appreciated.

Within weeks of Casement's capture Adler had resurfaced, unexpectedly, at yet another British diplomatic mission. This time it was the consulate in Philadelphia. On 10 May 1916 London was told of "an offer from a man named Adler Christensen to give evidence against Casement and if necessary to proceed to England." When questioned by detectives sent out from London, Adler told of meeting Casement some ten years previously in a hotel in Montevideo in Uruguay. Casement "who was on a visit to the German Minister Baron Nordenflecht [sic] followed him into the lavatory and they afterwards had drinks together at the bar and became very friendly." Adler also mentioned he had just jumped ship, adding "I frequently saw Casement and he visited me at my rooms… [He] gave me a present of jewellery and money to the value of $900."[733]

Casement was briefly in Montevideo in April 1910 but did not diary a mention of Adler. Baron von Nordenflycht was a German diplomat in South America whom Casement had known in Petropolis in Brazil and was later Minister in Montevideo. If this event occurred even eight years previously, Adler was then eighteen years old, and already using his survival skills. Not a rent boy by profession he was willing, and importantly able, to service men for necessary reward. With his propensity for the easy life he was obliged to live off his wits and any other assets. As the record later proves that Adler was a bigamous heterosexual it would seem the homosexual side to his nature was secondary and largely mercenary.

Being a sexualised individual with a preference for women, it seems likely that he was happy to perform vigorous anal sex on Casement but otherwise was not overly interested, and content to be excused such duties. That is not to say that there was not also the semblance of a mutual father/son relationship between them, one which Adler appreciated. Perhaps as he had found himself at odds with his own apparently harsh father, Casement's affection, kindness and attention were a welcome substitute. "I am always thinking of you. I remain as ever your loving faithful servant Adler" was his method of signing off letters to "My Dear Sir Roger!"[734] But as he was not faithful to Sir Roger and was ever willing to betray him (for money) his love may also have been of the cupboard variety.

It is that ersatz paternal relationship with Adler that explains Casement's foolishly trusting behaviour in relation to him. Adler was a lame duck, sex partner and son all rolled into one. And where youth was concerned, be it imperial powers or lads, Casement's judgment went out the window.

Together they sailed for Europe on a Norwegian liner the *Oscar II*, which left New York on 15 October 1914. Casement travelled, beardless, on an American passport using the assumed name of James Landy. He and Adler had taken elaborate precautions to ensure they were not tailed before their departure. On board, Casement went first class and Adler second. The vessel, as they feared, was intercepted by a British warship, HMS *Hibernia*. Casement, writing to his sister, nonetheless enthused "when I saw that on the caps of the men I nearly kissed them."[735] The ship was obliged to put into Stornoway in the Outer Hebrides and detained for several days. Casement's disguise held despite the seizure of half a dozen German suspects of military age. Adler later stated that "there were eight German officers on board the *Oscar II* who escaped being taken off…owing to their having false passports; some harmless bandsmen were removed."[736]

It was plain that London had no idea Casement was on board which was to mystify John Devoy when the British legation in Christiania, a few days later, was apparently so well informed about the pair's arrival in Norway. First continental landfall was on 29 October, Casement noting: "The Norwegian girl was very useful and got me a cab and got my things through the Customs… drove up to the Grand Hotel at nearly 2 a.m. with the Norwegian girl. I made her sleep next door to me and we both went to bed very tired."[737] He added in this letter to Nina that "she was penniless when I helped her first [and] had gone from job to job in America."[738]

The "Norwegian girl" was quite busy after they arose that first morning in Christiania. Once Casement went to the German legation, Adler now on home territory, chose to go to the British. On his first visit he was fairly circumspect, neither giving Casement's name nor asking for money. His was a mission of projection and he could never have guessed to just what extent it would be successful. Asking to see the minister, Mansfeldt Finlay, who was out, he made do with a lesser official, Francis Lindley. Adler explained he had accompanied an English "nobleman" from New York who was in league with the Germans in order to stir up trouble in Ireland. He had pencil copies of a German cypher and a letter which he had steamed open while entrusted with them during the *Hibernia* arrest. These he allowed Lindley to transcribe, informing him also "that his relations with this Englishman were of an improper nature."[739]

Lindley was plainly too much of a gentleman to inquire further about these unsettling remarks but their import was also passed to London by Findlay who stated that Adler "implied that their relations were of an unnatural nature and that consequently he had great power over this man who trusted him absolutely."[740] The earliest mention on official records of Casement's sexual preference being for his own sex is therefore the message of 29 October 1914. Lindley also noted that Adler spoke with a strong American accent and was very nervous. The British diplomats were plainly unprepared for Adler's arrival and did not even know what Casement looked like. Findlay, when writing by hand to Sir Edward Grey on 31 October, asked for a photograph of Casement so that Captain Consett, the naval attaché, who had observed someone "very tall, dark heavy-jaw, [and of] rather distinguished appearance" on the Copenhagen train, could identify him. He added, however, he had little doubt it was Casement and that Adler's story was true. "What blackguards!"[741] Findlay exploded, in his childish rage. Captain Consett had also been flabbergasted to observe Adler and Casement get into the same sleeping carriage as the King's Messenger, Mr Park Goff, and hastened to warn him that the two men "were dangerous rascals."[742]

At this point Adler either chose to play both sides or on second thoughts abandon entirely his first treachery, a pattern of behaviour he repeated in 1916.

Casement in Germany ca. 1915

Returning to the Grand Hotel, he told Casement an unlikely story that a man had brushed up against him in the hotel lobby and given him a telephone number to ring. Which done, he was asked to take a car to an address which transpired to be the British legation. There he was astonished to be told they knew of two telegrams, one sent the day before by Adler to his father in Moss, and another to New York. These details are as recorded by Casement in his diary.[743] For the British to have such accurate knowledge, of course required either fortuitously good connections to the Norwegian telegraphic service or an intimate relationship with Norwegian Intelligence and an amazingly speedy and efficient operation at that.

Or, self-evidently, if Casement had bothered to stop and think – that the legation only knew of the telegrams because Adler had so advised them. But Casement was impressed and suckered in, and like his erstwhile colleagues happy to believe almost anything Adler said. After a further visit, this time sanctioned by Casement, Adler was able to reveal that the British minister was willing to pay the enormous sum of £5,000 for his capture. The minister was also happy for Adler, albeit discreetly, to do away with Casement saying (as Adler reported) that operating under the name of a man still in New York, he did not properly exist at all in Europe. Ironically the 'fact' of the legation knowing of Casement's arrival also led John Devoy to conclude, after a systematic assessment of all the information by Judge Cohalan in New York (whose professional judgment Devoy was proud to trust) that someone in New York had betrayed Casement's movements, but that the information was too late getting to London for the *Hibernia's* crew to unmask him!

More spies, but for all Devoy's certainties he did not initially suspect Adler, despite later, in 1916, implying he knew he was a crook from the start: "One of the worst crooks I ever met and...in the pay of the English all along."[744] Devoy then added the unconfirmed comment "He, Casement was warned of that from Ireland and the first thing he did was to tell the fellow himself."

Casement advised Berlin of the Christiania affair, and realising London now had precise information about his arrival, his concern intensified about the possibility of the papers at Bigger's house being found. On 6 November 1914 therefore, an intercepted message for New York was wired (in English) by Arthur Zimmermann at the Wilhelmstrasse through the Washington embassy. It read "Casement begs that the following intelligence be transmitted: For Judge Cohalan, 51 Chambers Street, New York. Landy's identity discovered by enemy who are greatly alarmed and taking steps to defend Ireland and possibly arrest friends. They are ignorant here [word missing, actually "true"] purpose my coming Germany but seek evidence at all cost. Here everything favourable, authority helping warmly. Send messenger immediately to Ireland fully informed verbally. No letter upon him. He should be native-born American citizen, otherwise arrest likely. Let him despatch priest here via Christiania quickly. German legation there will arrange passage. Also let him tell Bigger solicitor Belfast to conceal everything belonging to me. Roger."[745]

There is no hint that Bigger's houses were searched as a consequence of this message although there is an indication from certain action taken that Casement's warning was received. That London deciphered Casement's assumed name of Landy as Lody, a German spy who had been arrested in Killarney on 2 October and executed in the Tower of London on 6 November, the very day the Berlin message was dated, might go some way toward explaining their inactivity.

Casement presciently expressed his worry in a letter to McGarrity on 11 November 1914, "My chief concern is for my sister in Ireland & for my papers with Bigger and at the Agent's in London. How foolish of me not to have got them over to the USA. Now the enemy will get them I fear. They are in a state of mind that sticks at nothing."[746] In the event, it took London nearly two years to get hold of what he feared they would.

Findlay later provided the Foreign Office with a memorable description of Adler: "Age 24, about six feet, strongly made, clean-shaven, fair hair, blue or grey eyes very small and close together, gap in front teeth...speaks English fluently but with Norwegian-American accent...has a fleshy dissipated appearance, has been wanted by the New York police as a dangerous type of a Norwegian-American criminal."[747] The thought of dealing with Adler turned Findlay's stomach but he persevered despite calling him on 14 January 1915 a "most loathsome beast [with] a mind unregulated by any rules of morality or intelligence...(one) guided by low cunning."[748] He added naively "all these people are more or less mad." Significantly the outcome was an Adler win on all counts which resulted in Findlay having to grovel to his bosses, both about the much publicised note in his handwriting, offering £5,000 for Casement's capture, and for believing so many of Adler's projections. However, he was not initially generous, as he told London: "I gave him 25 kroner, about 30/-, the traditional price in such transactions."[749]

This farrago of nonsense should have been put to one side by Casement but instead it became his personal crusade to turn Adler into a double agent (which he already was) and to revenge himself on Findlay and the Royal Navy. Casement was in many ways still an English gentleman and was horrified by the thought of Findlay's dirty tricks, many of them inventions or exaggerations passed on by Adler, but which were now his meat and drink. And so Adler's scheming took root to the point where he became as addicted as Casement – "Please be quick about this, and this bastard I will get"[750] instructed Casement's "treasure" from Norway on 26 November.

The initial scheme may have been an insurance policy against imminent unemployment for it was unclear what future Adler now had with Casement in Germany. Adler's plan was to see if British warships could be lured into the Baltic or, if submarines, could be persuaded to surface, in a deception about Casement's movements at sea which also involved providing charts detailing non-existent minefields. The Germans were sceptical and on one occasion in November detained Adler for two days when en route to Norway with manufactured documents. These were seized and read. Worse, they replaced his gold coin with paper money and forced him to pay for his meals.

London was less sceptical of Adler. On receipt of various fraudulent papers concocted by Casement and Adler, suggesting they would soon leave for Ireland, London prepared to intercept. Prime Minister Asquith, Kitchener, Churchill and Birrell were given sight of the papers from the beginning while Captain Reginald Hall of Naval Intelligence and Basil Thomson of Scotland Yard set in train various absurd marine wheezes. Sailors' lives were put at risk. When Casement disclosed the fabricated scheme in an open letter to Sir Edward Grey on 1 February 1915, they must all have been acutely embarrassed to read that "The stories told Mr Findlay at these interviews should not have deceived a schoolboy. All the pretended evidence of my plans and intentions that Adler Christensen produced, the bogus letters, fictitious maps and charts and other incitements to Findlay's appetite were part of my necessary self defence."[751]

With the Germans not getting involved, instructing their man in Christiania that direct relations with "Christensen shall be limited to the indispensable" and worse, Adler switched to blaming them. This new attitude worried Casement and made him, perhaps for the first time, concerned about the lad's reliability: "Also I am <u>not</u> sure of Adler! His air and manner have changed greatly since he came back or rather since he went away. He confesses that he now "admires" Findlay! Findlay "is a man" "he sticks at nothing. He would roll these God d–d Germans up." For the Germans now, since they held him up at Sassnitz, Adler has scorn and a sense of outraged pride. They treated him badly there stripped him, split his gloves open, took his gold coin and gave him paper money, extorted 7 Marks per meal, while he was detained 48 hours their prisoner pending the order from Berlin to release him, and read aloud to the crowd my letters to my American friends. This last extraordinary piece of stupidity it was that chiefly affects Adler. He says they "are fools" and trying to fool me and get advantage of me and Ireland and give nothing in return but empty words.[752] Casement just could not conceptualise a man whose first, and perhaps only, loyalty was to himself and not some high-flown historic dream or a modern ideology.

Instead he began to fear, as he might, how a developing Norwegian anti-Germanism could turn Adler, given ominous remarks about Findlay being a man who could take the Germans on. This was the same Findlay about whom Adler wrote, on 23 January 1915, from the Continental Hotel in Berlin "I told him to go and fuck himself…I bet you nobody ever talked to him as I did. He was right pale in the face." Such profane language horrified Casement who was something of a prude in this department, certainly in his letter writing. The Black Diaries are remarkably restrained in the naming of parts, very rarely does such street or sex talk intrude except when the remarks of others are quoted, while Casement did not diary his own mono-sexual activity nor gave a description of his own particular sexual needs. The 'f' word never appears. Indeed when recounting this story of Adler's he left a row of dots for the word fuck, calling it instead "the most filthy expression."[753] In the same account, he also told of Adler suggesting to Findlay's footman, who "had a smile on his face", that he should go and tell the diplomat to fuck himself. Casement stroked out the 'f' word.

"Knowing now all I do of his character, of its extraordinary complexity, I should feel gravely disposed to mistrust his fidelity in a matter where German ships were the issue as against British ships. I should even now, be indisposed to trust myself to his schemes" became the view in Casement's diary.[754] Adler's sociopathology was such that like any perpetual liar he took up the viewpoint of those he was apparently favouring. He had no ultimate loyalty and rather than switching his favours as appropriate, his loyalty was to some extent to all, but not all at the same time. His sexual *modus operandi* was similar in that he tried to keep at least one man and several women on the go at once.

In a remarkably frank yet self deceptive analysis of Adler and one, despite which, Casement cannot bring himself to believe the worst part he diaried: "He is clearly beginning to feel that Findlay is a bolder, more uncompromising and reckless rascal than myself and Adler's deepest affection is won by extreme rascaldom. Utter unscrupulousness of action, so long as it succeeds, is his ideal he confesses. He was won to my side, he admits, only by my extreme trust in himself. Seeing how fully I trusted him on the voyage over, his honour (or what corresponds to it) came to the top and he determined to be true as steel to me.

Now that he sees me going off on my Irish "journey" and he not to take part any more in my efforts, and this due to the evil (and indeed quite untruthful) reports of the Berlin police as to his conduct here, his rage against the Germans is almost swallowing up his affection for me. His face is changed. The old, boyish eyes and smile are gone and he does not look me openly in the face.

I think he is in his heart really regretting that – but no! I will not think that even. But I must see that he is ill disposed to the German cause and losing interest in mine, since he can no longer be associated with me in it and since he is aware that the Germans have "scandalised" him so much."

The Norwegian in him did mean Adler had a certain hostility to Germans who had anyway started advising of some (unclear) misdemeanours. Casement diaried first, on 3 December, that Professor Schiemann ('a political agent of the Wilhelmstrasse') "called late at night with disquieting statements about Adler that were unwarranted and malicious. Poor Adler! God knows he is bad enough without these professional inquests on him. I was annoyed beyond words – and disgusted."[755] A fortnight later he wrote of "the resentment he feels, the very deep resentment at the allegations against himself and his conduct in Berlin to which Schiemann referred and which Blücher told me had been conveyed in a police report to the F.O." adding, "I told Adler of this report last night – giving it as the reason why I found it impossible to take him on with me to Limburg and the Irish Brigade."[756] The Casement biographer, René MacColl, commenting on this diary entry cruelly wrote "One feels that the appearance of Adler at Limburg would have been all that was needed to touch off a full-scale riot among the POWs."[757]

One might jump to the conclusion that the allegations concerned homosexual activity, as a number of commentators have surmised. But that would have set alarm bells ringing all over the show. There is no suggestion in official German records of concern about the pair's sexual relationship nor of any homosexual activity locally, by either. It is unlikely that a homosexual aspect to either Casement's or Adler's life, particularly if in a public setting in Germany, would have gone entirely unnoticed or unrecorded. As Casement could not speak German, he aroused suspicion wherever he went and therefore had difficulty travelling about. Although he took to wearing a small American flag badge in his lapel, it seems likely that he did not indulge in nocturnal cruising for fear of becoming so conspicuous that the police might be called. One of the few mentions, of even a sexual thought in Germany, comes in a classic Casement annotation on a letter from Count Blücher "R. at Limburg 14 Jan/15 11.30 am by smiler – soft extension."[758] Smiler presumably refers to a cheerful orderly, delivering the Count's letter from Berlin, and his trouser contents. Casement's unusual use of the word extension for penis occurs several times in the Black Diaries, yet this letter, it is worth noting, was never in London's hands.

What emerges outside the remarkably discreet and unspecific correspondence concerning Adler, on both sides of the Atlantic, is a pattern of dishonesty regarding money, allied to deceitful relationships with women. It is probable that financial matters first brought Adler to the attention of the German police. In the event, Casement diaried, typically non-specifically as early as 18 December 1914, "I feel it would be far safer for all concerned to send Adler back to Norway and let him return to U.S.A. to work there. I told him much

The Irish Brigade in Germany prior to a boxing match in camp ca. 1915

of this last night – and said I would try to get him good work there, if he would promise to go straight and quite give up doing the things he confessed to me the last night before he returned to Moss he had done. And so there I left him this night."[759] Casement reveals here about as much understanding of how to deal with the youthful and amoral Adler as one who advises an alcoholic to take up sport in an effort to stop drinking.

The major antagonistic witness to Adler's demeanour, outside of Casement's German diary, has been Princess Blücher. She was an English Catholic, born Evelyn Stapleton-Bretherton, who for many years lived in a world, not unlike Casement's, of mixed loyalties. In 1939, and by then a widow, she featured in British Intelligence files as a member of the Nordic League, which described itself as one of "those patriotic bodies…engaged in exposing and frustrating the Jewish stranglehold on our Nordic realm." Effectively she was in the British branch of international Nazism, preparing to collaborate with a future occupying German regime.

Yet in 1919, she and her husband were passing to British Intelligence typescript copies of letters Casement had left in their care for eventual delivery to Eoin MacNeill and E.D. Morel. The three copy letters had been written to Count von Wedel in March and April 1916, and of course told any reader everything one would have needed to know about the details of the Easter Rising and the gunrunning. The Blüchers handed them to the General in charge of the British military mission in Berlin. After passing through many hands, including those of Major Frank Hall, who reckoned that "passages in the letters, however, show clearly his treasonable intentions towards this country"[760] they ended up with Sir Ernley Blackwell at the Home Office in March 1919. If anything, Evelyn Blücher was more pro-German than her husband who was educated at the famous Catholic public school Stonyhurst. By 1919 however, she was keen to distance herself from others seen as traitors. Her stories are inconsistent and at times untrue as regards her own responses at critical times.

The Princess's later statements contrast with Casement's account to Count Blücher (as he was until the Prince, his father, died in 1916 after falling from a horse) "of Schiemann's remarks about Adler – and then of the truth – of Adler's confession to me the night before he left for Christiania. Blücher agrees with me about him, that there is an innate sense of honour and courage that make amends. I went to von Wedel [head of the English desk at the Foreign Ministry] at seven to tell him too – I felt it necessary to be frank."[761] They also contrast with her flattering attempts to engage Casement in rewriting her memoirs. "If I sent you some of my notes now and again you would embellish them and put a little more force and life into them"[762] she asked in January 1916. He agreed to do what he could but earned her eternal enmity when his response was critical of her literary efforts and he curtly declined to assist further.

René MacColl wrote "The Princess tells me (London March 10th, 1954) that Casement's perverted tastes quickly became evident in Berlin and caused scandal. Christensen's appearance and mannerisms were very feminine and he habitually made up. The last point we have confirmation of from Casement himself. A year later he wrote a letter to 'dear, good, faithful old Adler' chiding him on his extravagance 'Don't go & be foolish with the money – you will soon have not a cent…You are fearfully wasteful of money…much more so than I am even, because you buy things you don't need at all, like that raincoat and the gloves etc. I have no gloves and you have about six pairs! And face and complexion blooms'!"[763]

It is the remark about his complexion that is taken as evidence of Adler putting on slap or women's make-up. Oft repeated, it has become the standard, prejudicial view despite the notion of anyone's complexion blooming once covered in cosmetics being an unsatisfactory reading. But as Alfred Noyes wrote in defence of Casement, the omission of the immediately following words "And God knows what. All you need is some healthy good work to keep your mind occupied" casts a different light on the matter. His assessment, as opposed to René MacColl's, is probably accurate since everything about that letter, and many others in similar vein, suggests paternal advice, "Remember when young, work plenty is a good proverb for the heart as well as the head"[764] was another Casement admonition. Noyes accurately remarked that such counsel "might have been written by an army chaplain."[765]

By 1956, when interviewed by Roger McHugh, the Princess was only up to "hinting a good deal about allegations of Casement's immorality" describing Adler as "a horrible type."[766] She also said she had ultimately shown Casement the door because of his scandalous reputation and treasonable talk, although given her life in Germany one would have thought accusations of treason unwise.

It was Adler's extravagance and his enjoyment of the high life that continued to worry Casement, especially as it was at his expense. As he told McGarrity on 22 March, he wanted him back in America "to land work. This loafing intriguing life...is bad for him." Worse, "Christensen is spending his head off and is a heavy charge."[767] There is a stream of letters to Adler on money, all of them totally ineffective, one assumes. In February 1915, Casement was advising from Hamburg "Don't spend all that 250 marks on the suit. Remember once you begin spending on things you like...soon the money is gone...Don't put things off – but sit down now like a good private secretary and write both [notes on the Findlay affair] out plain and clear."[768] Telling an obvious shopaholic this was about as pointless as his advice about working. Casement was never to learn how to cope with streetwise youths although he did treat Adler as a political equal, for in the same letter, commenting on Italy entering the war and trying to raise a laugh over his erstwhile beloved country, he wrote "Everyone expects Austria and Germany to give the Maccaroni's the greatest hiding they ever got."[769]

After Adler first surfaced in Christiania, the lines to London purred with telegrams about Casement and his relationship with the Norwegian, yet nothing was leaked to the London press. Indeed once Casement issued his open letter on the Findlay affair, revealing once and for all that Adler had been (so far as Casement was concerned) operating simply on Casement's behalf, London's greatest fear was of being embarrassed by the reward letter and their apparent gullibility. Further publicity would only cast Findlay, in particular, in a worse light, the legation having observed of Adler and his scheme that "he was not clever enough to invent it." Only in Norway was much prominence given to the matter, with newspapers criticising the British for exploiting a young Norwegian. Despite Adler's name being all over the papers in February 1915 there is no suggestion of the legation exploiting their knowledge of the homosexual aspect.

Elsewhere, and within Germany, the Findlay/Christensen affair was thought small beer – nothing that could not be expected in wartime. Shading his loyalty back to his master, Adler lived to betray Casement another day. But London was pondering over whether to capitalise on the matter, Lindley indicating that Casement was evidently unaware that Adler ("the informer") had divulged the unnatural character of their relations. When Findlay asked Arthur Nicolson on 27 February 1915 for information as to why Casement left the consular service and if the reason was sodomy, he also wondered if Casement was "generally known to be addicted to sodomy?"[770] As a result Casement's enemies in the Foreign Office opened a file on this aspect of his activities, not knowing when it might come in useful.

This was hardly reprehensible activity in an era when homosexuality was criminalised. Allegations of buggery in high places had been successfully used as political ammunition by Irish nationalists, like Tim Healy, at the time of the Dublin Castle homosexual scandal of 1884, Dublin badinage of the time suggesting that Earl Spencer, the Lord Lieutenant, be elevated in the peerage to become the Duke of Sodom and Begorrah. While in Germany itself, after the von Eulenburg affair was used against him politically, Kaiser Wilhelm supposedly had to be rescued from a homosexual milieu – one overly familiar with Naples. This left him, in consequence, more susceptible to the militaristic elements at court and in his government.

While devoting so much of his time to revenging himself on Findlay, and generally trying to ensure that his motives in coming to Germany were seen as honourable and untainted by any suggestion of being bought, Casement still managed to take two of his primary tasks forward. After discussions with Zimmermann and von Wedel at the Foreign Ministry, a policy was agreed that Irish Catholic prisoners of war were to be removed from the various camps and concentrated together, pending Casement's attention, and the arrival of the required priests. The Protestants were first "weeded out" as Bryan Kelly, an Irish student whom Casement had managed to get repatriated, told London[771] although English-born Irish were not. Many such were to be described by Casement as "undesirables" when he wrote to von Wedel in April 1915 calling for those he listed to be removed at once from Limburg concentration camp. Father Nicholson had told him of how such "British flunkeys in the Camp" were terrorising those sympathetic to the Brigade. Casement named sixty-six prisoners who were "either not Irish at all, or are so strongly Pro-British" as to hinder progress. "They should be carefully collected together and disposed of in other camps."[772] The General Staff apparently obliged.

Germany also decided to announce on 20 November 1914 that "the well known Irish Nationalist Sir Roger Casement" had been received at the Berlin Foreign Office. This was to be seen in the context of scare stories being circulated by John Redmond, in particular, that a "German victory would inflict great loss on the Irish people whose homes, churches, priests and lands would be at the mercy of an invading army, actuated only by motives of pillage and conquest." Consequently the statement continued "Sir Roger sought a convincing reassurance of German intentions towards Ireland that might reassure his countrymen all over the world, and particularly in Ireland and America."[773]

This was duly provided in terms that did not commit Berlin to the rights of small nations or to the principle of national self-determination. That would not have been the German view, except where Ireland was concerned, and even then the pledge remained somewhat imprecise.

By virtue of the German Chancellor's announcement, Casement had within three weeks of his arrival achieved his greatest diplomatic advance: "The Imperial Government formally declares that under no circumstances would Germany invade Ireland with a view to its conquest or the overthrow of any native institutions in that country. Should the fortune of this great war, that was not of Germany's seeking ever bring in its course German troops to the shores of Ireland, they would land there not as an army of invaders to pillage and destroy but as the forces of a Government that is inspired by goodwill towards a country and people for whom Germany desires only *national prosperity and national freedom.*"[774] Casement, feeling "my country can only gain from my treason", diaried in justification that "the blow struck today for Ireland must change the course of British policy towards that country. Things will never be quite the same."[775] The cause of Ireland was now on an international plane.

The Declaration was not all that felicitously framed even if Casement had a large hand in its drafting. Its intention of undermining Redmond's scare mongering might instead have sent a few shivers up those Irish spines not previously contemplating German pillage. But it was much appreciated in New York. Devoy congratulated Casement on his splendid work saying it was everything "that could be expected in the present military and naval situation."[776] And the German embassy in Washington on 5 December reported that the Declaration had "made a splendid impression", even if it was also relaying Judge Cohalan's recommendation, undoubtedly agreed by Devoy, that Casement should stay silent about the Findlay affair "until actual proofs are secured."[777]

The consequences in Britain and Ireland of course were quite different and mixed. If Casement had been a minor player up to this moment, well known only to Liberals and Irish nationalists, he now burst centre stage. The press attacks in London were matched in Belfast. But feelings of revulsion amongst Casement's acquaintances at home were by no means universal. Alice Stopford Green dropped him – leading to the Chief Secretary Augustine Birrell telling his Under-Secretary Sir Matthew Nathan, about their mutual friend: "I don't know where she stands in the hierarchy of treason but I should put her low down."[778]

Rev. J.B. Armour of Ballymoney was not especially fazed. Writing to his son on 3 December, he remarked "Carson and Captain Craig coquetted with the Kaiser and brought on the war sooner than it would have come…Sir Roger is doing what they did from all accounts…Many of the Orangemen through the north are credited with the wish that the Kaiser should win as they regard him as the only real Protestant king in the world." Referring to one of Casement's friends who had gone into print, he added "Conan Doyle's explanation of Sir Roger's action that he is off his mental balance is likely true." Doyle's remarks were to upset Casement but his journalism was done as a kindness – offering as a defence that he was mad, not bad. Armour also reported "that Miss Casement of Ballycastle, his sister, is being watched by the police"[779] although suggesting it might be one of many unfounded rumours. True or not, Nina, never less than paranoid, had good reason to feel most of Co. Antrim society was against her. Outside of the Glens it did not warm to her views or her brother's presence in Germany.*

Setting-up the Irish Brigade, in contrast to the Declaration presented early and continued difficulties and was to be a total failure, that, with hindsight, would have been better not attempted. The first Irishmen that the Germans captured were by and large regular soldiers who were not going to be easily seduced from their comrades, unless at odds with them. This was not a problem faced by its forerunner and namesake in South Africa. A number of Irish-Americans assisted, as did Major John MacBride, and Colonel Arthur Lynch who, elected a Galway MP in 1901, was to be sentenced to death for treason when he came from France to take his seat. Unlike Casement, he was reprieved and released within months.

But the war in 1914 was still popular and, if anything, its *casus belli*, Belgium, was seen by many Irish soldiers as a small Catholic nation falling victim to the Protestant Germans (close to Carson and Ulster) while the very same Germans could be cruel in their treatment of British prisoners, especially when it came to food and medical assistance. NCOs of the Irish regiments at the biggest camp passed a message to the German commandant that they wanted no concessions unless shared by all prisoners. "In addition to being Irish Catholics, we have the honour to be British soldiers" they declared.[780]

Those less honourable in their comrades' eyes, who never numbered more than fifty-five, joined Casement. One of the first two, Timothy Quinlisk, was appointed quartermaster sergeant by the German Navy staffer, H.W. Boehm, who noted that this "while tickling his ambition eliminates him as much as possible."[781] Even Casement thought Quinlisk looked like a rogue while the Brigade's German interpreter, Joseph Zerhusen, wrote later: "Sergeant-Major Quinlisk, a very dubious character, apparently had had a good education, very conceited, suave, seldom gave trouble, a fellow who gave one always a peculiar

---

* The Dublin-born novelist, Iris Murdoch, in The Red and the Green has a character who argues of Casement, "It must be a lonely bitter business out there in Germany. He's a brave man and a patriot. He does it purely for love of Ireland. To love Ireland so much, to love anything so much, even if he's wrong-headed is somehow noble."

inexplicable feeling of distrust."[782] The son of an RIC constable from Co. Wexford, Quinlisk was later, in February 1920, to be shot in Ballyphehane, Co. Cork, apparently on the orders of Michael Collins as a spy or British agent.[783] It is suggested he had gone to the area to try to set Collins up. He had sent a letter from 21 Gardiner Place to the Under Secretary at Dublin Castle, dated 11 November 1919 which was intercepted by the IRA. In it, he wrote: "I was the man who assisted Casement in Germany, and in coming home I have been connected with Sinn Féin. I have decided to tell all I know of that organisation and my information would be of use to the authorities. The scoundrel Michael Collins has treated me scurvily." His betrayal was allegedly prompted by Collins's refusal to bankroll a gambling habit.[784]

The Irish Brigade soldiers were reckoned by the Germans to be the disaffected, for the most part undisciplined, and certainly susceptible to drink. Several were gaoled for a crime involving the theft of "Algerians money" although Casement felt obliged to admonish the German guards for striking his soldiers. Their uniforms, one of which is displayed in Dublin's National Museum, were, however, masterpieces of design, colour and cut. Few recruits were ideologically attracted by, or to, Casement's message of Irish freedom and independence, although several had genuine, and in one case reborn, Gaelic League or Fenian sympathies.

In time they became an albatross around his neck as he could neither abandon them nor risk bringing them with him to Ireland where, on capture, they would immediately have faced a firing squad. Some indeed were spotted in Danzig in 1919 on the side of the Communist revolutionaries and had to be detached for their own protection by the Brigade's former liaison officer, the Hibernophile Joseph Zerhusen.

In the end it was to be the evidence of repatriated wounded prisoners, who had refused to join the Brigade, which produced the worst moments at Casement's trial, and blackened his character with many ordinary people. The prosecution, under F.E. Smith, made out that soldiers who did not become turncoats were treated badly. Casement responded in his speech from the dock by saying "the horrible insinuation that I got my own people's rations reduced to starvation point because they did not join the Irish Brigade is an abominable falsehood…the other suggestion that men were sent to punishment camps at my instance for not joining the Irish Brigade is one that I hardly pause to refute. It is devoid of all foundation." And of course that was true. He was a stickler on such issues. But his reputation suffered from the suggestions as Smith realised it would.

Casement finally managed to get a meeting with the Imperial Chancellor, Bethmann Hollweg, on 18 December. They spoke in French: "I said I was aware, fully aware, that today, with the British fleet barring the way and keeping all Ireland in jail, to think of an independent Ireland was 'fantastic' and he agreed to that. But I begged him to have an Irish policy for Germany in the future, for the next war would be a war for the seas, and then the cause of Ireland would be the cause of Germany."[785] Despite this pessimistic perspective on the present war, Casement effected with the Chancellor a formal ten article German-Irish Treaty setting out the arrangements for the Irish Brigade "with a view to securing the national freedom of Ireland."

Unwisely, Articles 7 and 8 allowed for the Brigade "to be attached to the Turkish Army in the effort to expel the British from Egypt" if the German navy failed to open up a sea route to Ireland.[786] This was contrary to Devoy's advice "Don't send the Brigade if you get one to Egypt. 'Fighting for the Turks' would be a fatal cry in Ireland."[787] But Casement did not take kindly to instructions from his superiors, whether English or Irish. By such personal initiatives (and because of Adler) he turned Devoy into something close to an enemy who in the wake of the 1916 fiasco and defeat, as he first saw it, was not slow to rubbish Casement, saying of his homosexuality, "Well it's all true. I know it myself." These words were spoken to two Gifford sisters and quoted by Nina to Gertrude Parry in a letter of 1 November 1924.[788]

Article 10 firmed up the earlier Declaration: "In the event of the Irish Brigade landing in Ireland, and military operations in that country resulting in the overthrow of British authority and the erection of a native Irish Government, the Imperial German Government will give the Irish Government so established its fullest moral support, and by public recognition and by general goodwill, will contribute with all sincerity to the establishment of an independent government in Ireland."[789]

Casement was at a low ebb throughout much of 1915 having little more to do after these initial successes. Isolated, and at times malarial, he found solace in two new Irish-American friends, the U.S. consul in Munich, St. John Gaffney and Dr Charles Curry a family man and yet another who fell victim to Casement's charismatic charm, writing to Nina in December 1916 to "the sister of a man I worshipped and adored."[790] Gaffney, unfortunately for Casement, was soon to be dismissed by Washington for serving two masters.

With the Irish Brigade failing to prosper or grow, Casement's diplomatic work was largely complete except for securing the necessary military assistance for a rebellion. But the Germans adamantly maintained a policy, as Casement put it, of "No Revolution. No Rifles." Since no definitive plan was put to Berlin in 1915 there was only frustration in that department, the IRB having a revolutionary strategy but as yet no firm date for action.

At home, Redmond had suffered a political blow when Asquith set about forming a coalition government. Instead of the Irish Chief Secretary's job he was, it is said, offered and refused the pitiful post of Postmaster-General, while Carson, in contrast, became Attorney General. In coalition with the Conservatives, the Liberals no longer had to rely on the votes of Irish Party MPs. And with the Unionists in government, Redmond was widely seen to have been side-lined and diminished. Carson was, however, to throw over his post in October 1915 over Grey's failure to honour his promise to assist Serbia with "all the support in our power." Casement reckoned that Carson, being Irish, resigned "because he saw the truth and detested the deception."[791] He was to return to office as First Lord of the Admiralty when Lloyd George replaced Asquith.

As the war became increasingly unpopular, the suggestion of conscription in Ireland was a key development, drawing the various revolutionary forces into preparation for action. Not only was conscription an overall necessity but Irish recruitment had tailed off drastically after the initial surge, and was at a vastly lower level than it was in England. This provided evidence of a growing disenchantment with Redmond's politics and a growing resentment about Home Rule's postponement. With Unionists and Tories in the coalition the exclusion of six or more Ulster counties seemed guaranteed. Although Tories in government also meant the Unionists had lost an automatic ally when it came to Irish policy, the tendency worsened when Lloyd George became prime minister in 1916.

A memorable illustration of the population turning against parliamentarianism and toward separatism was the magnificent turnout for the funeral of Jeremiah O'Donovan Rossa, another old Fenian from 1867, who had died in America. This was on 1 August 1915, in Dublin, which now had the worst record for army recruitment in Ireland. Glasnevin cemetery was also to be the stage on which Pearse played his best speaking part: "They think that they have pacified Ireland. They think that they have purchased half of us and intimidated the other half. They think they have foreseen everything, think that they have provided against everything; but the fools, the fools, the fools! They have left us our Fenian dead, and while Ireland holds these graves, Ireland unfree shall never be at peace." That same cemetery was to be the scene of many more such memorable political funerals over the next ten years although Casement had to wait fifty before he was permitted to join his comrades of that era.

Back in Germany, in certain departments, Adler was not idle. He had met a German girl from a good family in Berlin by the name of Margarette Werschmidt and inveigled her into a relationship although they were not formally married. He called her Grete and she was encouraged to use his second name of Eivind. Later she explained her foolishness by saying she "never had any doubt in his sincerity or faith."[792]

What Adler did not tell her was that he was married to a woman living (at some point) in Somerton, Pennsylvania, variously described by Joe McGarrity as a half-breed and the "Indian wife of Christensen."[793] Sadie Weaver by name and a Nansemond native American, she was the recipient of Casement's generosity in April 1915 when he asked McGarrity to pay her the equivalent of 1,000 marks – about $220 – which he had obtained in Germany, adding that Adler did "not want any questions asked of Mrs C – simply that the money should be paid to her, as from her husband in Germany for her use and that of his son Albert Aksel."[794] A letter from Adler was enclosed.

Adler Christensen's first wife Sadie Weaver, a Nansemond Indian and mother of Albert Aksel

She was then staying at the house of a friend, Miss C.L. Meyers of 919 Locust Street, Philadelphia. By 1917, Sadie had no knowledge of Adler's whereabouts while as late as 1924 Margarette was still only beginning to discover the extent of his deceits, including the fact of their being a child of that primary marriage. She was therefore having to ask McGarrity "Did you see the son too? How old

Roger Casement in Germany on 17 April 1915, when he was being "kinematographed"

can he be? Adler must be married with her about 10-12 years. Is that right?"[795]

Initially, Casement appears to have managed to get Adler employment since Joe McGarrity wrote, with due caution, on 13 May 1915 (only received on 19 June in Berlin): "You have done the proper thing in keeping Christensen in Germany. You cannot tell what they might do if they got him away from there. I am glad you got him a position. That will be a load off your mind."[796] Casement's friend Charles Curry paints a picture of Adler whose "English was too deficient and his knowledge of Germany very limited [being] obliged to have recourse to 'friends' – internationalists of an inferior type whose acquaintance he had little difficulty in making during his sojourn in Berlin." These cosmopolitan fellows he believed were the source of scandalous reports on the veracity of Adler's Findlay saga. From names and context these may well have been Jewish socialists. According to Curry, they had become spiteful when Casement upset "their little business scheme"[797] of publishing the saga. Once Casement refused to assist or permit it, they apparently turned on Adler, suggesting it was false.

Such an interpretation is hardly credible, but Curry was determined to absolve Adler of blame. It is more likely that these individuals were perfectly aware of Adler's capacity for duplicity. One was probably Dr George Chatterton-Hill, an internee born in Ceylon of an Irish father and a Sinhalese mother, whose release Casement had obtained. Casement apparently traced the source of these reports to him. He pleaded that he had never stated that he "personally held Christensen to be a liar or swindler." Indeed in a later letter he told Casement that having now met Adler "every doubt in my mind has entirely vanished." Either Adler's charm had again worked or he was lying to keep in with Casement. He was keen to assist the Irish cause, despite being coldly warned "There is no living in being an Irish patriot. It is the lost cause of history."[798]

Nonetheless Chatterton-Hill continued with his involvement, turning up at socialist events to speak on Ireland, and in the 1920s being considered by Dublin as a diplomatic assistant in Germany. MI5 had it that he was a *soi disant* Irishman who disagreed with everybody and "joined nothing that would not pay" something Casement had supposedly "written and told him."[799]

Plainly things were not going Adler's way so when the opportunity of him acting as a courier arose, he was returned to the United States in mid-1915, leaving Berlin on 20 July. He left with Casement's farewell letter of 3 July from Munich, one that must have made him feel the well was never going to dry up: "I cannot get your face out of my head – I thought of you all the time – I know what you felt – and I love you for it, you faithful loving soul. I do not want to add to your grief by any show of mine. But one thing be sure of, in life and death I will never forget you, and your devotion, affection and fidelity to me...God bless you, dear faithful friend of my heart – you who are true to the death."[800] Joe McGarrity, on 25 September, his advice ignored, reported: "Your friend got here safely and delivered me some of Findlay's souvenirs. Brave boy but foolhardy. We have placed him in a good job and he likes it and is grateful. He would, as he says die for you. His personal troubles I will not mention as he made a confident of me and the matter rests there."[801] The unexplained personal troubles suggest that a request for extra financing had been made. This would have required Adler to explain that he needed sufficient extra funds to maintain two wives in America, the second of whom, if not then expecting a baby, would be soon. The evidence for this is a sad letter from Margarette's mother Leni, dated 7 November 1916, lamenting the fact that her grandson had died without ever being seen by her.[802] The boy died in Philadelphia although a daughter Margarethe was born in 1917.

Not long after his return to America, Adler was asked to make another round trip to Germany, this time in the interests of the Irish Brigade. Tom Clarke in Dublin requested Robert Monteith to go to Germany, in effect to take command of the Brigade and expand its numbers. This required Monteith, who was in internal exile in Limerick, to go first to New York and thence to Germany. Since no neutral ship would risk taking him as a crewman through the blockade back to Europe, it became necessary to call on Adler's ingenuity once more. He took passage on a ship going from Hoboken, New Jersey to Copenhagen, and by bribing a steward enabled Monteith to stow away. All went well until the Royal

Navy boarded the ship, taking her into Kirkwall in the Orkneys. For whatever reason, Adler chose not to betray Monteith and by moving him around the ship's empty cabins confused the British search parties. All Monteith suffered were burns from being jammed up against a heating pipe while under a bunk – with a drunken sailor oblivious to his presence, snoring only inches above him.

For once Adler was loyal and true but that did not mean he was not following his own interests. Instead of going on to Copenhagen as arranged, Adler insisted on disembarking at Christiania, at great risk to Monteith who had no papers for Norway. He told him he had discovered the ship would be stopped and searched again by the Royal Navy, between Norway and Denmark. "Later I discovered this to be pure subterfuge" recounted Monteith "he merely wanted to see his people who lived a short distance outside Kristiania."[803] Further adventures included a stay with Adler's parents in Moss, now at 43 Storgaden, probably engineered by another lie, this time about the police asking questions at the hotel regarding the foreigner Monteith who added "I began to think that if I ever did get to Berlin, it would not be because of Christensen, but in spite of him."[804]

When Monteith finally reached Berlin and reported to the Foreign Ministry he was to discover that Casement was in Munich. He was unwell. Von Wedel advised that he "was prone to take too little care of himself." Going to Munich he found Casement on the mend. "His deeply tanned face and lithe, wiry figure seemed strongly out of place with his surroundings. I noticed his movements were sinuous and panther-like, bringing to my mind the rolling veldt and trackless forests of Africa."[805] Monteith like so many others was instantly and permanently captivated. He took over the day-to-day running of the Brigade and started a further recruitment drive as Dublin had ordered, which despite considerable effort, was no more successful than that of Casement and the Irish priests whom he had summoned.

Adler did not linger in Germany this time. Carrying messages and money from Casement he was leaving Bergen on 8 November, heading back to America with Margarette, having only arrived in Berlin in late October. By 24 November he was writing to Casement from Jersey City confirming in a letter signed "Olsen" that he had "arrived safe and sound" and indicating cryptically "Joe has got 2 more irons in the fire".[806] But it was not long before he was up to his old tricks. Writing on 16 December 1915 Joe McGarrity, in a long letter, was now giving Casement advice and warning. It was not received in Berlin until 19 February 1916 over two months later: "My dear Rory, Our hero has done certain things that has made matters very unpleasant and has made Uncle John lose confidence in him. No break of course has occurred so far but there was ample cause for a break. While ample provision has been made for him and every courtesy and kindness shown he appears to be criminally neglectful of his duty or he has been trying to take advantage of his friends. I do hope matters will come right but things are in a very unsatisfactory condition on account of his actions. Were it not for his splendid service and loyalty to you a break would have been created recently. We, of course take into consideration the great services rendered and the shortcomings of the man and overlook his faults. Now of course this is confidential. You must not reprimand him but should you meet him shortly a little friendly advice might have a good effect."[807]

For the first time there is a hint of Adler's reputed sport of blackmail. He may have been suggesting he had valuable information which could find its way to hostile forces should more money not be forthcoming. There is confirmation from Devoy in a two-page diatribe of 19 December (received on the same date) that he was swindling the Clan by getting money for his wife who was discovered to be the German Margarette and not Sadie, and worse, of his effective treachery.[808] We also know that bank notes for Nina, entrusted to him by Casement, were never handed over. In gaol in 1916, Casement, by then a considerably wiser man, told his solicitor, "I sent her £50 from Germany in November 1915 but it was stolen by the bearer, I learned by letter from Devoy."[809] He was at this point seriously worried about the possibility of Adler turning up as a witness at the treason trial, and with good reason. As there was an alternate or second trial on a buggery charge being mooted, he was now having to contemplate and confront the possibility of Adler testifying in that regard too. In his brief to counsel Casement wrote a last misapprehension about Adler, "He would sell himself to them – although I don't think he would injure me."[810]

Joe McGarrity's letter had the required effect in that Casement seemed finally to accept reality where his relationship with Adler was concerned. Writing one of many "last words", before his submarine departure "for my true friend Charles Curry" he declared on 26 March 1916, "Christensen has turned out very badly since he went back to America in November 1915 [and] turned into a regular scoundrel…I trusted him absolutely. I was a fool."[811] The Germans had also apprised Casement of "Christensen's perfidy in U.S.A." by showing him a December 1915 letter from John Devoy "with the names cut out." "They stupidly thought it would intimidate me to see that Christensen, the man I trusted and sent to America had turned into a ruffian"[812] he added.

Luckily for all concerned in Irish conspiracy, on both sides of the Atlantic, Adler was now off duty. Not trusted by anyone, he was no longer party to new information. This was especially critical as plans and dates for the imminent coup d'état were firming up in early 1916. The key personnel, including Connolly and the IRB's inner circle were getting into, or being put into, position. Military backing from Germany was and would be vital. The diplomatic support brought about by Casement had been immensely valuable in actual and propaganda terms but now arms, ammunition and artillery and, it was also felt, German officers were required.

Had it not been for the Irish Brigade, Casement could have returned to America once a safe route was found. The Germans were more than keen for him to do so and had issued him with the necessary documents. As he was so obviously disturbed ("agitated and unpredictable") they could see little value in him staying. While Casement sought leave to travel to Constantinople, Gaffney also tried to arrange his passage to America on a Swedish warship,[813] Casement having been warmly offered "the protection and hospitality" of that country by the Swedish minister in Berlin.[814] The Foreign Ministry was now dealing directly with Devoy who was effectively the co-ordinator for the rising. Dublin had also sent Count Plunkett's son Joseph Mary to Germany in May 1915 to act for them separately and to get a handle on what was going on. Casement, on Devoy's advice, was being kept out of the loop, or at least maintained in the outer circle, like Bulmer Hobson. Knowing what he knew of Berlin's caution, Casement feared for the success of any rising and cast a damper, the first of many, on the project and thus on Plunkett's mission.

16

April-August 1916: Easter Rising and Casement's two trials

Word of a rising finally came through to Berlin, from the Imperial embassy in Washington, in a message dated 10 February 1916. It took the form of a request from John Devoy with the first mention of a start date and was duly intercepted by British Naval Intelligence. Headed by the embassy, "Extract from report of Confidential Agent John Devoy" it read, the words being largely Dublin's, "Unanimous opinion that action cannot be postponed much longer. Delay disadvantageous to us. We can now put up an effective fight. Our enemies cannot allow us much more time. The arrest of our leaders would hamper us greatly. Initiative on our part is necessary. The Irish regiments which are in sympathy with us are being gradually replaced by English regiments. We have therefore decided to begin action on Easter Saturday. Unless entirely new circumstances arise we must have your arms and ammunition in Limerick between Good Friday and Easter Saturday. We expect German help immediately after beginning action. We might be compelled to begin earlier."[815]

The confusion between days and dates started here. There are two versions of the next message – that dated 17 February 1916 from Ambassador Bernstorff. London deciphered it as "The Irish leader, John Devoy, informs me that rising is to begin in Ireland on Easter Saturday. Please send arms to arrive at Limerick, west coast of Ireland between Good Friday and Easter Saturday. To put it off longer is impossible. Let me know if help may be expected from Germany."[816] That received in Berlin as printed in Captain Spindler's book, *The Mystery of the Casement Ship*, however, correctly reads "Irish leader (name deleted) tells me that revolution begins Ireland Easter Sunday stop requests delivery arms between Goodfriday and Eastersunday Limerick West-coast Ireland stop protracted waiting impossible comma desire cabled answer whether may promise help from Germany."[817]

Both versions had been translated from German, the former after being first decoded by London. While the Germans have the action starting on the Sunday, the British have Saturday as Devoy earlier stated; the Germans have the arms landing between Friday and Sunday while London's decoders reckoned between Friday and Saturday. Whether starting on Saturday or Sunday it should have been sufficient to put London on high alert. The Military Council of the IRB, on reflection, realised it would be foolhardy to bring in the arms before the rising started, and thus ultimately insisted on Sunday night or Monday for the landing. But so late was the decision and subsequent message, it made it impossible to inform Captain Spindler on the arms ship *Aud* as he had no wireless.

The Germans, unable to guarantee or fix a precise day, had chosen to operate on a four day bracket of Thursday to Sunday which although relayed in time to Dublin, was itself so non-specific and elongated as to jeopardise the operation. In the event the *Aud* arrived on the Thursday in the late afternoon, and hung around Tralee Bay for nearly twenty-four hours waiting for the agreed signal from the Irish pilot's son, Mort O'Leary. He actually saw the ship but not expecting it until Sunday did not register its significance. Spindler also failed to make any contact with Casement's submarine.

The Royal Navy, knowing more than the military and the Castle, did take precautions although they were not effective. Here I particularly rely on Xander Clayton's monumental book, *Aud*.[818] Clayton, who lives near Tralee, has tracked down and published much original naval documentation, not least the secret orders[819] from Admiral Bayly to the blockading cruiser squadron off the west and northern coasts of Ireland. These warned accurately of "a rising which some say may be expected about Easter" and an arms landing.

The Navy's alertness however was not so keen as to unmask the *Aud*. It was stopped early on Friday morning (21st April) by *Setter 2* (or *Shatter*, as Spindler wrote), an armed outpost trawler commanded by a civilian Aberdeen fisherman named John Donaldson. He and his admittedly outnumbered boarding party were tricked by Spindler, despite being several hours on the ship. Drink was usefully provided and they failed to notice the fake Norwegian crew and the cargo of arms under open hatches. Instead the captain was provided with up-to-date newspapers. They even told the supposed Norwegians that it was intelligence had them on the lookout. Intent on staying for a while longer, Spindler realised his mission was doomed when the approach of a second British ship made him take to his marine heels.

The Navy version of the *Setter* incident was a "bare mention of some kind of encounter" which suggests embarrassment on the part of Sir Lewis Bayly, the Queenstown Admiral, who, almost alone in Ireland, knew exactly what he was looking for. Weisbach, the U-boat captain, did later describe Spindler's stories as "*wohl etwas romanhaft geschrieben*."[820]

This failure on the part of the Navy can be regarded as critical since it delayed knowledge of the ship's German origins for twelve more hours. Indeed that certainty only came via the Fenit Base Officer, Lt. A.S. Holmes, after he visited the RIC barracks in Tralee. He, together with Commander Francis Spring Rice RN (uncle of the gunrunner Mary Spring Rice), wired Queenstown to have the "Norwegian Steamer '*Aud*' [...] rearrested and taken to port for examination" as they were sure Casement's boat had landed from it.[821]

The Germans were as good as their word, in that with a date for the revolution a consignment of rifles and other arms was organised and the necessary shipping arrangements for men and *matériel* put in place. Devoy had intimated that enough men could be obtained for 100,000 rifles. He told the Germans there were 40,000 Volunteers "trained as efficient as the American National Guard" while 50,000 Redmond Volunteers should be anticipated. He "reckoned that practically all of them will join the revolution."[822] Such reckless optimism was ignored, without comment, by the German military as was a request for field artillery, officers and a submarine. Devoy was, however, advised in remarkably quick time, in a message dated 1 March, of the resulting decision: "Between 20th and 23rd April in the evening, two or three steam-trawlers could land 20,000 rifles and 10 machine guns with ammunition and explosives at Fenit Pier in Tralee Bay."[823]

Where Casement thought the German assistance hopelessly inadequate, Devoy believed otherwise, writing in July 1916 of the rifles and Casement: "They were good enough for the Russians to overrun East Prussia with and to drive the Austrians across the Carpathians and if our fellows had got them they'd be able to shoot a good many Englishmen with them. It is not true that the Germans treated us badly. They did everything we asked but they were weary of his impracticable dreams."[824]

In the event only one surface ship was used. Diversionary naval raids on east coast English towns were also decided upon. Lowestoft and Great Yarmouth were to be bombarded, with Zeppelin raids occurring in East Anglia, Essex and Kent. Ironically Casement's cousin Gertrude, on holiday in Frinton-on-Sea, was awakened by her bedroom windows shaking from the very Lowestoft bombardment designed to divert attention from Casement's landing and the imminent Irish rebellion.[825] The Germans also sent out six other submarines, two of which were lost or captured – for one British.

Although the Germans did not invest many men in the project, a properly professional effort was made. The arms (costed at £200,000) were sufficient, if landed and distributed, to change the balance of power in the west of Ireland and possibly Dublin. Although ultimate success remained a slender possibility, and thus the much-desired German submarine bases in Ireland, an unlikely reward, Berlin was well aware, as it had been when starting the war, that any trouble in Ireland made England vulnerable. Even if the Irish rebellion was not an immediate or total success it ought to be of sufficient length to weaken the British war effort and tie up troops for a very long time. This was especially true if the island was successfully split in two, leaving the southwest for a time out of British control, as was planned. In the fog of war who knows what the outcome might be; rarely what is expected or intended.

Several weeks passed before Casement was apprised of the precise nature of what was being planned, both in Ireland and Germany. It was Monteith who was summoned to hear the first news. Casement was deteriorating mentally and was in early 1916 in a sanatorium. As he put it to von Wedel: "Since the beginning of the year I have been for the most part, in a health 'cure' at Munich."[826] Monteith simply called it "a nervous breakdown."[827] The enormity of the whole venture was plainly beginning to crowd in on Casement. Although in many senses a loner, he craved company and would normally have been in a swirl of engagements and meetings.

In Germany, without Adler, he now had no official companion and with insufficient German he had few casual acquaintances. He was, as he said himself, isolated and he had no sexual outlet. The two Americans Curry and Gaffney tried to fill the social void, as did Monteith, but were unable to provide either sufficient time or intellectual stimulation. The life was ebbing out of Casement. When forwarding some letters to the sanatorium, Monteith, knowing the tendency to scribble incessantly, had to warn, "I am afraid you are going to start writing again & if I was sure of it, I would not send on these things, a spade and a garden rake would be better."[828]

Previously unnoticed correspondence[829] consisting of 16 postcards and letters to a Bavarian school boy called Max Zehndler living in Augsburg, or, more precisely, Landsberg a/Lech, tells of one new friend. Casement seems to have met him through his uncle and aunts (no names given) when staying in Riederau on the Ammersee in 1915. There are 8 personal letters and 8 cards dating from 28 July 1915 to 4 April 1916. Many of the postcards are written in tolerable German.

In an introduction to his series of articles in *The Nation* on 30 November 1921, Dr Curry (d. 1935) explained how Casement came to the area, "We soon became such intimate friends that, when I moved out with my family to the Ammersee for the summer vacation at the end of May, Sir Roger requested me to engage quarters for him there. I succeeded in securing two comfortable rooms for my friend in the country inn at Riederau; whereupon Sir Roger left Munich and joined us on the rural shores of the great lake. He was so happy and contented in his new environments – away from the noise and bustle of the city, that he remained in Riederau till late into the autumn."

The incoming correspondence from Max is not to be found. Was it destroyed by Dr. Curry or Gertrude Parry for fear of it revealing Casement's tendency to grooming? Who kept these outgoing items, and how did they end up in the NLI?

The number, MS 17033, indicates it is part of the Curry collection. MSS 17000-17033 were acquired by the NLI ca. 1970 via the US. The folder is marked "Dr Charles Curry Papers". MS 17000 is an "Account by Dr. Manfred

Curry of how his father acquired these papers and sketch of Casement's career (In German, with English translation) Nov. 1939."

Casement wrote this last letter to Max from Berlin on 4 April 1916. The envelope (stamp now removed) was addressed to –

"Max Zehndler,
Zögling des Stad. Realschul =
Pensionates,
Landsberg a/Lech."

This translates as 'Max Zehndler, Pupil Boarder of the Town Secondary Modern School, at Landsberg on the Lech.'

Casement pretty well tells his schoolboy friend in this letter, written a week before he leaves Germany, that something big is afoot i.e. his departure for Ireland and the Easter Rising:

"My dear Max,

I hope you are better now and enjoying this good weather at Landsberg. I am not going back to Ammersee for some time I fear and shall not see you for a long time I think as I have to go away now on a journey that will take up much time.

If I can I will come back to the dear old Ammersee – but if not you will know I am detained.

Meantime I hope for your welfare and success at school and that you may grow good, brave and strong and be very happy.

I hope your Easter holiday this year will be very pleasant and happy –

Please remember me very kindly to your Uncle and Aunt – and with all kind thoughts and wishes,

Your sincere friend,
Roger Casement.

– P.S. I send you some old stamps.

Also a small present. Don't answer this letter as I shall not get your reply.

Be a good boy and work hard and make your friends happy by obedience and cheerfulness. R.C."

He was so low, he noted of the German military officials, "They are swine and cads of the first water – not one of them with the soul of a rat or the mind of a cur – They certainly deserve to be thoroughly well taught in the first rudiments of humanity and kindliness – for as they are, they are lower than the Congo savages in most things that constitute gentleness of mind, heart or action."[830]

When Monteith reported that the rising was on for Easter, he also advised Casement, still in a sanatorium, that Devoy had wisely instructed him to remain in Germany as "Ireland's accredited representative until such time as the Provisional Government may decide otherwise."[831] This became the first matter to rearrange with the Germans. Initially he attempted to persuade them to send him immediately to Ireland to ensure that the arrangements for the shipment of arms were as clear as possible. The Admiralty only relented to the extent of helping a courier leave Germany to try and make his way to Ireland, and if possible return with accurate particulars as to place, date, method of landing and of dealing with the arms shipment.

The man chosen was a 30 year-old Irish-American, John McGoey (born in Scotland, although out of Chicago[832]) who had arrived in December 1915 with a letter from McGarrity stating he was a member of the "Irish Revolutionary Union."[833] He was then attached to the Irish Brigade although held free to serve Casement when required. On 19 March, the Admiralty provided a police agent "to get McGoey over the German frontier", Casement adding that he was smuggled into Denmark "without the knowledge of the General Staff".[834] He was then to try and get a ship to Scotland.

Casement, deceitfully, told McGoey to inform Dublin that he "strongly urged no 'rising'" because of the inadequate German help. McGoey apparently agreed, telling Casement, "It would be criminal, and he had long suspected the Germans of playing a double game." Casement further explained, "He would do anything I asked him. I told him it was necessary for me to keep silent as to my real opinions before the German General Staff and that when I took him to the Admiralty he must do the same."[835]

These then were Casement's "Instructions to John McGoey 19.3.16. Send word from Copenhagen when you start. This can be done through the German Legation. The German Minister can send word to the Foreign Office here to let Captain Monteith know when you sailed."[836] He was seen off on the stairs of the Hotel Saxonia, "with a last blessing and greeting in Irish". An unfinished, crumpled note to his comrades in which he tried to excuse his "apparently cold and feelingless departure" was retained by Casement.[837]

At the time, Casement recorded his own intentions for the McGoey mission thus: "He goes really to try and get the heads in Ireland to call off the rising and merely try to land the arms safely and distribute them…If he gets safely through to Dublin he is to seek out Tom Clarke and through him B. Hobson and try to 'call off' the rising."[838] With Clarke on the IRB's junta or Military Committee, and about to be the first signatory of the Proclamation of the Republic, one assumes that McGoey, had he ever made it to Ireland, would have been ignored, or arrested.

Ten days after his departure, Casement was dismayed to discover that the General Staff now knew of McGoey's journey. After two hours of heated argument where he repeatedly denied McGoey had any instructions to get the rising called off (only saying that certain advice was to be tendered) they threatened withdrawal of assistance if Casement turned "hand or finger" to communicate further with anyone outside Germany.

McGoey was not to be heard of again – for the best part of a century anyway. Maloney suggested he had been detained at sea and secretly executed at Kirkwall on Orkney. Another location for the execution was notioned as Peterhead Prison, north of Aberdeen, while a further writer suggested McGoey was instead a double agent working for British Intelligence.[839] The author, in this book's first edition notioned he had been murdered by the German military who did not want Casement's pessimism spread around Ireland, suggesting, alternatively, he had perhaps stowed away on a ship that had been sunk, or, maybe, returned discreetly to America.

McGoey's arrival in Dublin would probably have alerted Eoin MacNeill to the rising plans, and, perhaps, ensured better landing arrangements for the arms (and Casement). Either way, the course of history would have been dramatically altered. Casement later told his solicitor that McGooey (as he spelt his name – there are three variants), "formerly of Glasgow", had been "taken off ship at Kirkwall." He provided no source for that story.[840] McGoey's fate so unsettled him that he risked sending out a written message through Gertrude, written on the back of Cathal O'Byrne's letter of 22 June 1916: "I want Joe McGarrity told about him as it was Joe sent him over to me…I fear they have him in their clutches." He wondered if perhaps they (the English) had "sent him to the front in their army, a dreadful fate."[841]

The last word on Casement's messenger, in that era, came from MI5 in the person of Frank Hall who, in 1919, analysing the letters that Casement had left with the Blüchers, minuted: "With regard to John McGoey who is referred to further on in the same letter as 'the Volunteer who had come over from America in November (1915)' and whom Casement refers to further down on the same page as having been 'despatched on Sunday 19th March (1916), to Denmark with instructions to reach Dublin without delay'; I have failed entirely to trace this man or to connect him in any way with our records. The name is no doubt an assumed one but we have no record of any person who would appear to have come from America at the time stated or to have come to this country from Denmark."[842]

Recent intriguing research on the Irish Brigade by David Grant reveals McGoey survived the war.[843] He had the power to stymie the rising but didn't, which is not to say he couldn't be a quick worker. Last recorded in late March en route to Denmark, in Essex, by September, he was marrying a Miss Ethel Wells, having already joined the Royal Navy while serving on HMS Kildonan, an armed merchant cruiser.

So what precisely happened to him between April and September? Whether he was too late getting out of Denmark or just decided to disobey orders remains unclear. If he was stringing Casement along and had little antagonism to the Germans, he may simply have chosen not to go to Ireland. Why would an otherwise enthusiastic separatist (other than Casement) who had gone all the way to Berlin to assist in importing arms and making revolution, concur with such defeatism?

Did the Germans prevent him leaving mainland Europe before the rising? This was something reasonably assumed, especially as the GGS discovered that Casement had despatched McGoey to sabotage their efforts. Did he decide not to jeopardise the rising or did love of an Englishwoman get in the way of duty? Perhaps he decided to switch sides after experiencing the Germans close at hand, yet he did not tell London of his mission. We can deduce his loyalty to Irish separatism must have been – or have become – sufficiently shallow for him to join the Royal Navy, although he was plainly not averse to military involvement. It must be remembered that people are less ideological, more changeable, and more buffeted by events than often credited with.

Four years later in 1920, John McGoey, aged 37 and whose ethnicity was given as "British, Scotch", arrived in New York as a crew member on the cargo ship Huronian out of London, where he also resided. He was given as 5 foot 8 inches tall, weighs 144 lbs (10 stone 4 lbs) and a fireman on the ship, which he then deserted. By 1921, he was living in Detroit and applying for US naturalization, giving bricklayer as his occupation. His wife Ethel then emigrated with their daughter, born in 1918, and they had a second child, a son, John, born in 1924.

Sadly, McGoey died in Chicago in a building accident in 1925, taking his story to an early grave. However other questions remain. Knowing of his mission, and that the German Admiralty had granted Casement's repeated request for a submarine, once the GGS knew on 7 April, why did they allow him to proceed or, at least, ensure the orders about the timing of the arms landing were not tighter to minimise his ability to thwart matters? Indeed why did the Admiralty give in to Casement's request for a submarine at all? Was it a desperation to get rid of him, or did Casement pull sufficient of his many strings in Berlin?

As the date of departure for Ireland drew closer, Casement became frantic with worry both about his place in history and the men of the Irish Brigade. He expended great effort in ensuring the Brigade stayed put rather than act as defenders on the arms ship. Despite being trained with machine guns, he feared, with good cause, that his men would rapidly change sides. So fussed about their future, he even requested that a firing party of a dozen Germans instead of the recently trained Brigade should be furnished to cover the disembarkation in Kerry. He was accompanied by one ordinary member, Daniel Julien Bailey (who was crafty enough to join the Irish Brigade under the *nom de guerre* Beverley). Born in 1887, in Dublin, he had a French mother. A former regular soldier, he had been living in London and working as a porter at Paddington Station. He was then recalled to the colours on the outbreak of war. His loyalty to Casement and the Brigade lasted only until his capture, some forty hours after landing.

It was not cowardice on Casement's part that he did everything, short of informing the English enemy, to undo the rising. It was all of a part with his character. He was red hot in his hatred for England, both in his writings and conversation, yet being a humanitarian who could not bear anyone (especially those he knew) being killed or hurt because of him, he started to try and undo the damage he had caused. Without near-guaranteed success he opposed all their plans, presumably to the total exasperation of the Germans, who were in receipt of his inordinately long letters. That of 30 March to von Wedel was the longest and most vituperative. Nothing had been done right and he was more concerned about his fifty Irish Brigade members than those fifty plus Germans who were at risk in submarine and ship.

"My position is a hideous one. Let me restate it. First – entirely without consulting me and in opposition to my known views Mr Devoy and Irishmen at home decide to attempt some form of revolution in Ireland. I have always opposed such a course unless assured of ample external military aid – an assurance wholly impossible today...I do not think anyone was ever put in a more atrocious position. Whatever I do must of necessity be wrong...My instinct, as an Irish nationalist, is to be with my countrymen in any project of theirs however foolhardy; to stand or fall with them. My reason proclaims the project they have in view as a hopeless one. My judgment declares that I should oppose it...I know not what to do – whichever way I turn is equally dark. The one thing I see more and more clearly is that I <u>cannot</u> be the means of bringing the Irish ex-prisoners of war...into the terrible situation I find myself."[844]

Thinking more like an English Liberal than a revolutionary, he managed both to oppose and join, and to jeopardise the project. On 7 April he was informed that he had finally persuaded the Germans to send him, early and separately, in a submarine with just two companions. The Brigade was thus left to its own, and the Germans' devices although he asked Gaffney to take over responsibility for them. The three man team left Wilhelmshaven on 12 April in U-20, the boat that sank the *Lusitania* in May 1915. A day and a half out from Heligoland a breakdown in the crank operating the submarine's diving fins meant a return to port and a transfer to U-19, putting them three days

On German submarine U-19 in April 1916, west of the Hebrides, from left: Captain Robert Monteith, Roger Casement, Lt. Otto Walter, Daniel Julien Beverley (Bailey), and Captain Raimund Weisbach

behind the apparent schedule.

It was captained by Raimund Weisbach who had had the good fortune to be the torpedo officer that took out the *Lusitania* – a sinking celebrated by McGarrity, as he told Casement,[845] at a banquet for Kuno Meyer, with a toast to the submarine's captain. U-19 was to arrive in Tralee Bay just a few hours after the *Aud*. It also failed to find an assisting pilot. What he apparently never knew was that Captain Weisbach had been ordered that "under no circumstances however must a landing occur before April 20th [Thursday] in the event of a premature arrival."[846] Thus Casement would only ever have had hours to get to Dublin to persuade MacNeill (and the IRB) to abandon the appointed action. The Germans seem to have tricked him as there was no point in sending him separately if their timings were designed only to ensure he made a rendezvous with the *Aud* in Tralee Bay the same day.

Not the least of Casement's ill-considered behaviour was his loose tongue, as Monteith forcefully described: "I discovered that Casement had imparted the news of the projected rising to St. John Gaffney. Gaffney had, of course, been a good friend to Casement, but to tell him of the rising – it was inconceivable. When Gaffney spoke of it to me, I warned him to be very careful, and, to drive my point home, I slipped my hand into my pocket and told him that it would be a better and cleaner thing for me to shoot Sir Roger while he was still in Berlin than to let the English get hold of him. Gaffney immediately excused himself and Casement had the story in five minutes; he told me of it that night. He set me at ease by saying that he saw my point quite clearly."[847] But it was not a lesson learnt.

Shortly before his departure he landed up in Princess Blücher's Berlin hotel room in a seriously distressed state. She gave him a miniature prayer book as a keepsake (later found at Banna Strand and listed for the trial as "1 prayer book (Catholic Piety))," which suggests her sympathies were more with him than she was to write in her memoirs. There is probably a kernel of truth in her description of a nearly demented Casement talking in a husky whisper and sobbing like a child. His anxiety, she said, was to do with the Germans forcing him on an "errand which all my being revolts against."

The Princess probably failed to grasp that his concern about the mission was more to do with its potential for disaster than his rage at the Germans. But he felt she was one of the few people in Berlin to whom he could say such hateful things about them. And he was not a man to bottle up feelings about those in authority. Thus she probably described his state of near mania accurately. He was certainly on the edge: "They have a hangman's rope ready for me in England; and so the only thing to do is to go out and kill myself." Having, she reckoned, dissuaded him, the histrionics ended with Casement giving her "a bundle of farewell letters to be opened after his death", which they were, and then passed to MI5! Claiming he made a further plea to see her, now aware of some danger, she declined, saying she was "watched like everyone else here."[848]

Willing to wound but afraid to strike, Casement was now at his most dangerous not to the English but to the cause he loved and professed to uphold. He was desperate to get to Dublin in time to advise Eoin MacNeill and Bulmer Hobson of the low-level of German support, as he saw it, and of the Germans' mixed motives which were now beginning to take shape in, and dominate, his own mind. Like Hobson he believed only in a successful rising, or none at all. But success was always unlikely no matter the level of German assistance; what he could not contemplate or foresee was that an initial failure might be built upon – not just as a glorious failure or blood sacrifice to inspire future generations to worship, but the opening shots in a revolution that would rearrange southern Ireland, taking it entirely away from Britain. Casement was unaware that decisions were being made beyond MacNeill's control or authority by a secret military council, a conspiracy within a conspiracy. It was now about to unleash the potential of the Volunteers, whose arming Casement had initiated, yet he too was out of control.

Everything that could possibly go wrong with the Easter Rising went wrong. However, a creditable military operation was finally put in place which with seven years of further revolution and military conflict changed everything. Firstly the arms were never landed. The *Aud* effectively under arrest from Friday afternoon was scuttled by Captain Spindler the next morning, just outside Queenstown harbour, after leading the Royal Navy a long and merry dance. Secondly, Casement was captured.

MacNeill, now knowing all these facts and taking due account of Casement's despairing message (and Arthur Griffith's vehement opposition to any military action) changed his mind a second time and cancelled the Sunday mobilisation of the Volunteers. An advertisement to that effect was placed in the *Sunday Independent*: "Owing to the very critical position all orders given to Irish Volunteers for tomorrow, Easter Sunday, are hereby rescinded, and no parades, marches or other movements of Irish Volunteers will take place. Each individual Volunteer will obey this order strictly in every particular." Clarke's junta in the IRB had therefore to run a rising almost entirely in Dublin, and on the Monday instead of the Sunday, a day later than billed. Why having had the presence of mind to arrest Bulmer Hobson they did not complete the task by doing the same with MacNeill remains one of the many mysteries of that weekend.

An interesting sidelight on Casement's preparedness to actually go to war is his attitude to the gun he carried ashore. Monteith asked him if he knew how to load his pistol. He replied in the negative saying "I have never killed anything in my life." Once the method of loading the Mauser was explained Monteith then asked him to practice. Shaking his head, Casement declined, asking that it be done for him. Monteith handed it over along with his cartridge belt and a knife, noting that "as he took them from me an expression of intense pain and loathing crossed his face."[849]

Such fastidiousness was not shared by Countess Markievicz when at St. Stephen's Green three days later she apparently shot down a policeman taken unawares by her pointless seizure of the position. The war, however, had eaten away at any simplistic ideas of glorious sacrifice that Casement earlier entertained. A letter written in December 1915 to a friend, Miss Meyer, gives a rare insight into his thinking: "The war has killed Christianity in the life of nations." In an emotional and heartfelt outburst he further exclaimed that it was now "an orgie of Hatred, Lying and organised Murder! The Middle Ages were better – the <u>dark</u> ages even."[850] Casement would not have been pleased to know that his submarine after landing him at Banna Strand sped off and in the afternoon torpedoed a cargo ship, the S.S. *Feliciana*, that it had chanced upon.

Of the "three men in a boat – the smallest invading party known to history,"[851] who landed at 2 a.m. on Banna Strand, near Fenit, that Good Friday, the intrepid Monteith evaded capture entirely. Casement, unusually for him clean-shaven, masquerading as "Richard Morten an author of *The Savoy*, Denham, Bucks", was arrested in the early afternoon that 21st April by two armed policemen. The others had left him exhausted and wet, hiding out in McKenna's Fort, a Danish rath near the shore. Taken first to Ardfert RIC barracks, where locals had earlier reported suspicious activity on the beach and the discovery of handguns, he was transferred to Tralee. Amazingly the police allowed him to see (and see alone) a Dominican priest and a doctor in the barracks, both of whom passed his messages to the local Volunteers. He had told the police he "wanted to go to confession", explaining that his mother was a Catholic and saying "I am one at heart." They suspected he was Roger Casement but were not entirely sure, asking the doctor his opinion. He suggested not. Casement asked Father Ryan not to divulge his identity in the town, both to pacify his nervous captors and to avert premature action.

During the evening Casement began a series of self-justificatory conversations. Indeed before the night was out, first one and then another RIC man, Head Constable John Kearney and District Inspector Ambrose Britten respectively, became his confessors. They were responsive listeners, according to Casement's Notes to Counsel,[852] indeed to such a degree he was concerned not to have their nationalist views made known in court. There was apparently little left out: he spoke of the rising, the arms ship, who held his papers in Germany (posterity calling again), even of the messages he had sent to Dublin through the visitors arranged by Kearney. It is unlikely by morning there was anything except formal doubt as to his identity.

Whether the two officers were as sympathetic as he reckoned can perhaps be deduced by what they reported to Dublin. If even half this information had been relayed the mystery man would surely have been kept in Ireland. Had they had just been stringing Casement along with remarks such as those he attributed to Britten: "I pray to God it won't end the way of Wolfe Tone…We would be with you to a man if there was a chance of success", then they were masterful. Perhaps they toned down what they told their superiors because of the confessional nature of the whole night's talking or perhaps they believed in what they told Casement and left much information out; perhaps nobody at the centre bothered to ask for any detail once it was decided he was to be moved on, and out of Ireland.

Obviously the RIC was now on high alert and the suspiciously numerous cars in the area were being stopped. Monteith nonetheless managed to contact and see Austin Stack, the local Volunteer commander, who then had to hire a car to hunt for Casement. By late Friday, Stack had been arrested as had his second in command Con Collins. Beverley had been sent with them to look for Casement yet managed to remain at large for a further twenty-four hours. Neither of the Volunteer commanders, despite being armed, resisted. Stack believed, somewhat unimaginatively, that his orders for action on Easter Sunday remained paramount. For the same reason no rescue of Casement from the barracks was contemplated by the remaining Tralee officers. Indeed they were by now headless and permitted Monteith, without them so saying, to take command. He then prepared seriously for the Sunday rising.

On his train journey to Dublin, Casement became aware of the mysterious drowning of two men in a motorcar which had gone over a local pier the previous night. A policeman poked his head through the window at Killarney station asking "Did you hear what happened to the two lads in Puck...They ran into the sea and were drowned."[853] These two (of the three drowned) whose bodies were recovered early, were actually part of a five-man mission out of Dublin to dismantle the wireless station at Cahirciveen and set up their own transmitter to communicate with the German boat. They were under the orders of MacDermott and Plunkett. One of the two survivors (from a second car) was, on his return to Dublin on Saturday to be the man who unwittingly first told Eoin MacNeill of the gunrunning debacle.[854] It was the Kerry story which had MacNeill decide to countermand Sunday's mobilisation, after the day before's decision not to. Having only just heard of the rising he had reluctantly gone along with it. Apparently it was Bulmer Hobson's fiancée who bumped into The O'Rahilly and told him of the planned rising, a fact passed on to MacNeill.[855] Casement started to sob when he heard of the drownings.[856] He had jumped to the conclusion that they were his submarine companions, saying "I am sorry for those two men. They were two very good Irishmen. It was on my account they came over here."[857]

The assumption of deaths caused by him, made Casement even more depressed and it loosened further his never-firm tongue. He was contemplating suicide. Indeed it was anticipation of an early death that had earlier decided him to tell the RIC officers many things 'in confidence' in order to justify himself and mitigate any errors which others might reckon he had made. All this before the rising had even started! His message to Dublin was of a cautionary nature "Germany sending arms, but will not send men" and on much the same lines as those going separately from Monteith.[858] On his Saturday journey to Arbour Hill Barracks in Dublin, Casement was also shown a newspaper report of the *Aud's* interception. At the station in Mallow he changed trains, remarking evocatively to his police escort that he knew the place. This stemmed from his mother's supposed Jephson origins in the town's castle. An RIC sergeant escort finally told Casement he was sure the two drowned men were not his friends.[859]

By going to an army barracks, as opposed to staying in police custody it was plain that the critical decision had already been made as to who was going to have control of Casement and where. Instead of a night in a bed in Dublin which he was expecting and hoping for, he was swiftly moved on. But not before he experienced some rough treatment from soldiers. To his horror he was searched bodily by a brute of an English Sergeant-Major. He was not stripped as such but the search was done by the "pulling up of my shirt and pulling down of my trousers."[860] He was now in military custody and out of Irish police charge. But he was in Dublin, as F.X. Martin wrote "apparently without anybody knowing or caring."[861] Shortly he was taken from Dublin to Kingstown, to the mail boat and England.

By the Sunday morning he was entrained for London. At 5.45 a.m. Inspector Sandercock intercepted the train at Willesden Junction and relieved a taciturn army major who had escorted Casement thus far. After cautioning him – he had already been charged with illegal arms importation (three Mauser revolvers) in Kerry, Sandercock said he would be seen by certain parties at 10 a.m. after his breakfast. However, he was still in military custody as his interrogators would be that key amalgam of Naval Intelligence (Reginald Hall), War Office Intelligence – MI5 (Frank Hall) and Scotland Yard (Basil Thomson). They too were having a leisurely breakfast.

Who decided that Casement should go to England is unclear but it must surely have been someone in the War Office, once posted off by Naval Intelligence about his arrest. It was said to be the practice that suspected German spies were sent to London but this was no spy, rather an Irish revolutionary. Thomson diaried on Easter Saturday that Reginald Hall rang him at 10.30 p.m. (he was sleeping at the office) to tell him that the blighter Casement "was now in charge of the provost marshal" and on his way to London. His interrogation would "take place at Scotland Yard at ten o'clock next morning."[862]

The move to London was to be more critical for all concerned than is generally realised. It meant in the first instance Casement would not face trial in Ireland, perhaps because no jury in Dublin could be relied upon to bring in a guilty verdict. Rather his future, brief as it was, would be in England. Although he was seen as leader of the rebels – "a widespread delusion of the time" – he was also seen as a British traitor, someone deserving of distinct and different treatment. Those in London were therefore able to effect his extraction from Dublin.

Of more immediate significance, it revealed how Dublin Castle, the headquarters of the Irish administration, was failing to take the whole affair seriously. Any sensible intelligence officer would have maximised the interrogation of Casement (and any of his companions) there and then to elicit more information about planned events – not least because it was public knowledge that the

Volunteers were preparing for a general mobilisation the next day, Sunday 23 April. Mobilisations presage war – and they are normally taken to mean such. Yet Eoin MacNeill, like Matthew Nathan, his opposite number in Dublin Castle, had not been unduly suspicious of the mobilisation. To MacNeill it was still a mass parade, a route march with arms, and mock attack manoeuvres.

More intelligence gathering was being done in Kerry when Beverley (now also using the name Mulcahy) was taken prisoner on the Saturday, as by the next day he made it known from his cell that he was prepared to talk if he could get protection and be guaranteed indemnity from punishment. He had decided to throw himself on the mercy of the authorities and make a confession or at least a statement about his activities. If he had chosen not to, he was, undoubtedly, as a deserting, treasonable soldier, a dead man. No guarantee was given and in the event he was charged alongside Casement "as otherwise the army would be dissatisfied" diaried Basil Thomson, adding "if necessary he would be used as King's evidence." The Solicitor-General was, however, said to be strongly opposed to letting him off the hook.[863]

Beverley averred that he had only joined the Irish Brigade as a means of escaping back to Britain. Now revealing his real name to be Daniel Julien Bailey, he provided D.I. Britten, if in an exculpatory manner, with a certain amount of critical information. Most of his statement, dated Sunday 23 April, is an account of the events and people he saw after he landed, which probably interested the local RIC most. Even so he gave away little actionable detail about his contacts in Kerry. Six lines at the statement's end tell of overheard conversations involving an arms shipment going into Fenit with 20,000 rifles, 10 machine guns and one million rounds of ammunition in a "small Wilson Liner." In fact he was seriously understating his knowledge, considering he had just spent ten days in a German submarine with his two revolutionary colleagues. Casement recorded later that Bailey had been fully apprised of plans before their departure from Germany, so he was, in his statement, definitely holding back on information.

The arms shipment was no longer news as the *Aud* had been scuttled at 9.28 a.m. on Saturday although this mention of only one ship ought to have been of great interest. The last line of Bailey's statement read simply "I heard that Dublin Castle was to be raided." In a later statement for the trial he expanded a little, writing of a "ship to be piloted into Fenit on the following (Monday) morning and perhaps sooner" and that "there was to be a general rising in Ireland simultaneously and Dublin Castle was to be attacked or raided."[864] Inspector Britten, in receipt of such key information did not delay. "I left him and went to send some telegrams" he later affirmed. According to the RIC's April 1916 report the "intelligence was telegraphed in cipher to the Inspector General early on Easter Monday morning 24th April and was transmitted before 6 AM to the Under Secretary."[865] It is not clear where or when Bailey was then moved.

Britten's telegram, obviously with a degree of detail, reached Nathan in time for action but it was a slow enough process getting it to him. Nobody seems to have considered using the telephone at this point although it is unclear how extensive or secure the network then was. In his evidence, Nathan recounted to the Commission of Enquiry that the D.I. at Tralee reported "in the early hours of Monday morning the arrest of one of the men who had landed with Casement: A private in the RIR."[866] Although he confirmed the day as Monday it is possibly an error as Leon Ó Broin writes of Sunday in his book.[867] It is difficult to believe so many hours passed before Nathan was told of Bailey's statement, but if so, communication was plainly inadequate, or possibly the chain was so long as to be counter-productive. Mixing up these days and dates at Easter was happening even then, so it is often difficult to be sure of the exact sequence of events.

The Royal Commission on the Rebellion in Ireland, chaired by Lord Hardinge of Penshurst and two other minor luminaries (and briefed by Basil Thomson) reported on 26 June, barely six weeks after the last Dublin execution. It had insufficient time for precision or accuracy or for spotting contradictory evidence. Mistakes about the precise days of events were commonplace in the evidence. It did not help that the Commissioners treated official witnesses with the utmost deference while showing most interest in the confused chain of command in Ireland. With Casement's trial unconcluded, his story was largely bypassed.[868] J.B. Armour pointed out at the time what is obvious from the Commission's questioning, "There was nobody on it who knew anything of Ireland." Indeed Hardinge underwent minor surgery during its brief existence.[869]

It is necessary at this juncture to review the state of knowledge of the authorities about the plans for a rebellion, the reasons for their reactions and the consequences of Casement's being taken immediately to England. The confusions and mistakes of the Volunteers are well known but rebels have only one real advantage – surprise. That they still had although they were to be surprised themselves. Fortuitously, by virtue of changing and reversed orders and through the carelessness and ill-preparedness of their enemy, surprise was maintained. England's famed providence was not to be found working that well over Easter, although the capture of Casement was, for many, sufficient sweet success. It is said that the IRB's difficulty was that to avoid the informer problem so much key information was kept secret that many who needed to know were paralysed from lack of knowledge. The diverse strands of the government's authority and the intelligence secrecy led to an exactly similar problem in that quarter: Nathan and MacNeill were sharing a remarkably similar position.

Although the usual informers were not producing much for the RIC or the DMP, other techniques were bearing great fruit. Best of all, with the capture of Casement on Friday, Dublin had several days to respond to what ought to have appeared a fully-fledged conspiracy and an imminent rising. At the very least they now had confirmed the arrival of a massive arms shipment and the landing of the probable leader from Germany off a submarine. There was every reason to believe that the arrival of other arms ships and submarines was also likely. Given the known fact of the Volunteers' mobilisation there was little doubt as to what was afoot.

Such was the information now flooding in to Sir Matthew Nathan, the Irish Under-Secretary and the senior official in Dublin Castle. He bore a number of remarkable similarities to Casement, being Jewish and thus something of an outsider, and a bachelor with African experience, being once Governor of the Gold Coast in West Africa (as mentioned in Casement's 1903 printed diary notes). He had to a degree been relying, like Casement, on Alice Stopford Green for advice. She had told him a week earlier, probably without any intention to deceive, that her organiser contacts in the Volunteers were honest and straight young men who were not susceptible to evil counsels.[870] Nathan was not inclined to listen to southern Unionists who warned him of mounting trouble and advised of a need for drastic measures, as they would, he probably thought. In particular their leader, Lord Midleton, who wanted the Volunteers proscribed was disregarded, yet his sister the Hon. Albinia Broderick (Gobnait Ní Bhruadair*) lived in Kerry in a Gaelic League and Volunteer milieu. Midleton therefore had to have some better feel for what was developing than the Castle and its often nationalist advisers. He was aware that an administration that permitted an alternative and opposing locus of military power was asking to be subverted.

Nathan was so unconcerned he had brought his sister-in-law Estelle and her children over for an Easter holiday. They were staying at the Under-Secretary's Lodge in Phoenix Park (along with Dorothy Stopford, Alice's niece) where Mrs Nathan was to be trapped and terrified for five days. Augustine Birrell, the long-serving Chief Secretary was in London on conscription matters. Indeed

---

* Gobnait Ní Bhruadair (1863-1955) who trained as a nurse when a mature woman, was elected for Sinn Féin to Kerry County Council in 1920, only leaving the party in 1933 to form the right-wing Mna na Poblachta with Mary MacSwiney. Sheltering IRA men on the run, she was shot by the Black and Tans. Later, during the civil war, she was gaoled in Kilmainham by the Free State government. Learning Irish thoroughly in the Donegal Gaeltacht, she was a stalwart of the Gaelic League. She converted to Roman Catholicism, and never married. A typical Casement woman, although there is no record of a meeting.

for the last two of his nine years in that office, with Parliament in near continuous session, he was rarely able to be in Ireland although he too was invited to the Easter house party.

A somewhat more concerned Lord Wimborne, the Governor-General and Lord Lieutenant, was in Dublin. He was technically the head of the triumvirate but as he explained to the Royal Commission he was the youngest, least powerful, and least experienced of the three, being appointed only in February 1915. Indeed he was not even sure he had the authority to give the army direct orders. He had, he later discovered, except the General Officer Commanding (GOC) explained he would not have obeyed any until the War Office endorsed them.

Even on Easter Saturday, Nathan was sufficiently unfazed that he told Birrell in writing "I see no indications of a 'rising'."[871] This was stated when advising him of the next day's, as yet uncancelled, Volunteer mobilisation. As in the 1971 internment fiasco in Northern Ireland, he had eyes only on the previous rebels – old Fenians and dynamiters, who with the exception of Tom Clarke had retired. A very few new leaders like Ernest Blythe and William Mellowes had been exiled to England, Mellowes surreptitiously slipping back. This fate was being planned for Denis McCullough, Herbert Pim and possibly Tom Clarke, amongst only a small number of others.

Had the Castle simply relied on the front-page story in Saturday's *Dublin Evening Mail* they would have been sufficiently informed to batten down the hatches. Its headlines told in telegraphic messages of "Arms seized – A Kerry Sensation – Collapsible Boat – Captured by the Police – Some Arrests Reported – Further Sensational Developments are Expected – Stranger of Unknown Nationality Arrested." One police informer did tell the DMP that Easter Sunday was for real, and there was another separate report of an intended attack on Dublin Castle. Combined with Bailey's confirming statement it is amazing that at the very least the guard was not strengthened. Lord Wimborne, in his evidence, said that at 10 a.m. on the Monday, having heard of Bailey's story at 6 a.m., he "urged that the Castle guard be strengthened, but the Under-Secretary demurred."[872]

As it turned out the rebels, only twenty strong, when they came later that Monday were too cautious. Nervous of being trapped within the Castle's extensive yards, they pulled back after shooting a policeman sentry dead. Despite disarming and locking up the rest of the guard, they withdrew, seizing instead the adjacent City Hall as their orders required them. Major Ivon Price, the Director of Military Intelligence was talking to Nathan at the time, not 25 yards from the gate with (it is said by Basil Thomson) Casement's automatic Mauser in his hand. He was obliged to hare downstairs and fire a few shots, "at the half a dozen Volunteers in green coats dashing about"[873] hitting one.

With the gates now closed, Price held the Castle with a tiny Corporal's guard until relief slowly came.

Wimborne was later sarcastically asked, given his assumption that any attack would have started by 10 a.m., if his nonchalance suggested "a rebellion ought to begin immediately after breakfast."[874] He pleaded that that was Nathan's view too, although it was the reason he did not press (at 10 a.m.) for an increased guard on the Castle. Too many points of command, a spread of authority and a political nervousness made a pre-emptive strike against the Volunteers impossible but the complacency that led to minimal defensive measures being taken is hard to fathom. The Easter holidays and MacNeill's countermanding advertisement were probably the root cause on the day, although all were not entirely convinced since Wimborne said of MacNeill's advertisement "I was afraid it might be a trap."[875] Others felt the same.

But there was also a wealth of detail gleaned from intercepts by Naval Intelligence which ought to have ensured that the fact of it being a holiday period, at least, was ignored by both the army and administration in Ireland, and all leave cancelled. Since February, deciphered messages from the German embassy in Washington told of a plan for an uprising, and then an April date, in fact differing and multiple dates in April. In March, the messages to and from Berlin went into great detail about the transhipment of arms. Steamers and trawlers were mentioned. Confusion also reigned as to whether Limerick or Tralee was the destination for the arms, the precise number of ships, and whether submarines would go into Dublin Bay.[876] This explains the relief detectable in Scotland Yard when during Casement's interrogation he advised (for no useful gain) that only one arms ship was ever sent.

Given this plethora of information what actually ended up in Dublin Castle was negligible and came second or third hand. The greatest problem with the successful breaking of an enemy's codes is just how much of the precise deciphered information, and what, should be told to commanders in the field. Admiral Sir Henry Oliver, Chief of the Admiralty War Staff, to whom all intercepts from Room 40 went, was apparently a believer in protecting his secret source at all costs, to the point where he pared down and even distorted what little he passed on. Naval historians believe he was instrumental in allowing the *Lusitania* to go unprotected, and the Battle of Jutland to end as a draw, with terrible losses on both sides, rather than a British victory. Indeed his intelligence came to be doubted. As the source and strength of its origins went unrevealed, it was also not given the high level of credence it ought to have been. A differing Royal Navy view from Admiral Bayly at Queenstown was that other government departments "refused to take seriously naval intelligence hints of coming trouble in Ireland."[877]

The American secret service raid on 18 April on the Wall Street offices of a German diplomat and spy, Wolf von Igel, masquerading as an advertising agent, gave rise to the notion at the time that Devoy's messages which were seized there, were passed to London and gave warning of the rising and the arms ship. Certainly that was believed by both Devoy and the Germans. But such a theory was erroneous. The Department of Justice agents apparently did not get round to reading the Irish material or passing it to the State Department until after Casement had landed.[878] The German sabotage operations in America, revealed there, were of far more interest to them.

With Casement in London, Nathan lacked the immediacy and the potential intimate understanding of the plans for the rebellion, he (and also Bailey) would have provided. To save his skin Bailey was singing. To save lives and protect his reputation for posterity, there was very little Casement would not have told, especially if shown the newspaper advertisement where MacNeill cancelled the Sunday mobilisation. But that did not happen, and Nathan, who with Birrell was later to be sacked, was oblivious as to what was still to come. When this happened, the Liberals were cleared out of Dublin Castle in one fell swoop – which had its own effect, while the military under General Sir John Maxwell took command for a fortnight in Dublin in a way that may have changed the face of Irish life for a century.

Nathan despite being the political head in Dublin was not given direct knowledge of any of the key intercepts until the Monday of Holy Week, 17 April. General Lovick Friend, the top soldier in Ireland, showed him a letter that day which he had received from Brigadier-General W.F. Stafford in Queenstown (Cork) on foot of a conversation with his naval counterpart Admiral Bayly. As Nathan recounted to the Royal Commission on 18 May 1916, it told of a "contemplated landing from a German ship rigged up as a neutral and accompanied by two submarines, of arms and ammunition on the south west coast with a view to their reaching Limerick and of a rising timed for Easter.[879] The source of the information was not disclosed but it had reached the Queenstown command a whole month earlier. It was the reason for the extra patrolling that eventually closed in on the *Aud*. The Royal Navy's alertness, however, was not so keen as to stop Captain Spindler conning the first British boarding party. This can be regarded as critical since it delayed certainty about the *Aud's* German Navy origins for more than twelve more hours. Nathan and General Friend did agree to arrange for "armed pickets of 100 men to be nightly available at each of the four main barracks", a contingency that seems to have provided no cover of any value, if it ever happened.

Indeed the second and final *Aud* interception may only have been prompted by the emerging news of strange events on Banna Strand. Earlier, on 22

March, the intelligence had been described within the War Office as from "an absolutely reliable source."[880] Despite being communicated in writing to the "Irish staff" and to General Friend in some unspecified way it seems to have been kept largely within the operational sphere of the navy.[881] Nathan also advised the RIC chief but both remained sceptical, Sir Matthew describing it as "a rumour" to Birrell, several days later on 22 April, its supposed absolute reliability utterly unrecognised. Police guards were heightened but nothing else. Indeed there appear to have been no contingency plans made for such an event – no routine established for putting a visible or armed presence on the streets, no daytime pickets and none at or around crucial buildings.

As it turned out, Dublin Castle's decision-making process was still governed by the events following the Howth gunrunning and the consequent Bachelor's Walk deaths of July 1914. The Commission of Enquiry that followed had censured W.V. Harrel, the Assistant Commissioner of the (unarmed) DMP, for provocatively invoking military assistance at Howth. He duly resigned. Thereafter no response at all to the Volunteers or the Irish Citizen Army was to be operational policy. Even when a sham attack on the Castle "during manoeuvres" was observed on 6 October 1915, no special precautions were taken to provide any greater defence for this key position.[882]

Major Ivon H. Price DSO was Nathan's liaison officer and security adviser. He was an RIC County Inspector (with a law degree) seconded as Director of Military Intelligence to Irish Command HQ immediately war broke out. Price was the key intermediary between the military, the RIC, the DMP and Dublin Castle. Indeed Leon Ó Broin believes he was the person who first provided General Friend with the deciphered intelligence information from the War Office. But only the one substantive message made it through to Dublin Castle, long after its interception and even then it was indirect.

If Price did know in March he appears to have been more than negligent for he alone could inform Nathan – indeed that was his very job. Yet he too seems to have been kept in the dark about all other intercepts. His evidence to the enquiry contained implied criticisms of Nathan and Birrell insinuating they took more notice of outsiders than of their own advisers. Price was, however, on record as stating, on 10 April 1916, that "the general state of Ireland apart from recruiting and apart from the activities of the pro-German Sinn Féin minority is thoroughly satisfactory."[883] In mitigation, he pleaded that on that date he had not been advised of Casement's intended journey or by implication of any rising. This seems to negate the notion of Price knowing anything in March that he might have passed to General Friend.

Naval Intelligence and Captain Blinker Hall knew of many other more up-to-date intercepts which never got through to Nathan, let alone the army, navy or police; one fact, that of Casement's departure from Germany was apparently known, although no specific, published intercept tells of this. Blinker's confidential secretary, H.C. Hoy, wrote that the news of Casement's departure, when it came on 12 April, through the use of Devoy's code word "Oats", was such that "our excitement at the Admiralty may be imagined."[884] According to the 1921 publication *Documents Relative to the Sinn Fein Movement*, over a dozen despatches about the rising were intercepted and read in London; some ten wireless messages to and from Berlin were decoded, while three letters shipped from Washington to Germany via supposedly safe addresses in Holland and Denmark were also opened and read.

The final absurdity of the week's defensive inaction was the departure of the GOC, General Friend for London on leave, after hearing of the landing on Banna Strand. At the enquiry he was asked "You heard of Casement?" "I heard of Casement before I started. It was not known at the time it was Casement. I heard that on Friday evening." He then promptly quit Ireland leaving it in the administrative charge of Colonel H.V. Cowan, the assistant Adjutant-General. Otherwise Brigadier-General William Lowe was, he said in command. He told Wimborne nothing of Lowe's more senior status but only of Cowan and his deputy, Major Owen Lewis.

General Friend probably also knew Casement was going to be taken to London as his informant would surely have been aware of Military Intelligence's intentions on that score. The General, who further obfuscated his evidence by talking of meetings he perforce attended in London over the weekend, did not return to Ireland until Tuesday – in the middle of a revolution. Remarkably, he escaped censure. His absence was even defended by Lord French, his commander in London, who felt that it was reasonable to assume the danger had passed with the capture of Casement. This according to Alice Stopford Green was also Nathan's view, he having told her "they thought all was over on Roger Casement's arrest and they therefore deferred precautions which had been decided upon."[885] As is well known, other officers were also taking Easter Monday off to attend the races at Fairyhouse, west of Dublin, although Friend stressed to the enquiry that most of these men were on leave from England or the front.

The Dublin administration had one criterion for draconian action – evidence of German military involvement in Irish affairs. As Casement was not interrogated in Dublin, definitive evidence only came with Bailey's confession on Sunday although Casement that day in London would, and earlier in Kerry had, revealed a considerable amount both voluntarily and involuntarily of the German aspect. Wimborne felt that the "events of the 22nd of April [Saturday] revolutionised the situation" but Nathan did not accept that until told of Bailey's statement. Why the *Aud's* scuttling was insufficient evidence is another mystery. Nathan did tell Wimborne on Saturday evening that Casement, now identified, was on his way to England under a strong guard but it was to be Bailey's account that first changed his mood. He said in his evidence to the Royal Commission that it was the deciding factor in his decision to arrest and intern the separatist leadership, in view of a definite association with the enemy having been established.[886]

In summary, Nathan rotated from Friday to Monday in day and night-time meetings but no significant defensive step was ever taken. Wimborne got windy about the proposal to raid Liberty Hall without artillery to look for gelignite stolen from a Tallaght quarry on Sunday morning. He was told a gun would have to come eighty miles from Athlone, taking four or five hours. As an alternative, the Lord Lieutenant wanted arrests that Sunday night, sixty or a hundred, on his say-so alone if necessary, as he reckoned, accurately, the leaders "having countermanded their Easter Day Parade are probably sitting in conclave conspiring against us."[887] Major Price wanted Liberty Hall surrounded by a thousand men.

An impasse ensued, solved only by the postponement of the Liberty Hall raid and Nathan's insistence on wiring Birrell, seeking approval, "subject to concurrence of the Law Officers, Military Authorities and Home Office" for the arrest and internment of the leaders.[888] That would take time. Nathan felt Monday would be a bad day what with the holidays and a lot of disgruntled Volunteers wandering around Dublin. So it was agreed to put the start of the response back a day to Tuesday. And then the first shots rang out. The rising had started.

Lord Wimborne's parting shot on Casement's future came in a letter on Easter Sunday to Birrell, "I hope there will be no nonsense about clemency. He must be made an example of. He expects nothing else I understand. These fellows have enjoyed too much immunity already."[889] This suggests he already had some detail of Casement's admissions, presumably through Major Price and the Kerry police. To bring the enormity of it home ("the landing – the invasion") he wanted a public trial for Casement. Many like General Maxwell preferred courts-martial to avoid political pressure.

In London, Captain (later Rear-Admiral Sir) Reginald Hall's team of like-minded operators assembled at Scotland Yard. They were preparing to inspect their trophy and prize. The three were all politically motivated intelligence gatherers and in the case of Blinker Hall and Basil Thomson ultimately fell foul of political opponents, who knew they were crossing the line between politics and administration. Sir William James, Blinker's biographer, was to overstate the particular cause when he wrote "Several men holding prominent positions had sworn vengeance against Hall for his part in disclosing the contents of the diaries."[890] Thomson, Assistant Commissioner of the Metropolitan Police, was needed to enable suspects to be legally and properly held and if necessary processed. He and Blinker, responding to Adler's concoctions, had already teamed up in a complex (and silly) scheme that involved chartering a yacht, the *Sayanora*, which was sent out in 1915 along Ireland's Atlantic coast and whose crew masqueraded as German-Americans, sympathetic to Sinn Féin, in order to gather information and, if possible to trap Casement.

Thomson's diary and memoirs reveal a well-connected man with an immense number of contacts in London and abroad. One minute he was working on achieving American entry to the war, then squashing Spanish intrigues and later conversing with various double agents and questioning alleged spies. Thomson naively diaries his foreign sources, especially when they tell of trouble in Germany. He was a very political policeman who could not stop meddling. Neither a fantasist nor a particularly cruel man, his diary, however, reveals a person who seemed to do almost everything himself, and who in this confusion of dabbling could not see the wood for the trees. In April 1915, he confided to his diary that he had enough ample evidence for a charge of high treason against Casement. He had Casement now but he wanted more than a treason charge when the diaries were brought out.

The third member of the team was Hall's homonym – Major Frank Hall. Even Casement wrote of him as "Basil Hall"[891] an elision of Thomson and Blinker's names but one that has confused authors ever since.[892] Such confusion suggests he did not play a dominant role in the interrogations. Perhaps for a secret reason he stayed in the background, a reason Casement never seems to have discovered: Hall was Irish, although his accent may not have suggested that. Indeed there were actually <u>two</u> people in that room who had been involved in importing arms into Ireland from Germany. Casement, however, had done it twice, in peacetime in July 1914, and now in wartime; Frank Hall only once – in April 1914. There was another difference. Hall had been in the Ulster Volunteer Force, Casement in the Irish Volunteers. And Frank Hall was now in the British Army – as an MI5 officer.

Lt. Col. Frank Hall D.L. J.P. of Moygannon, Kilkeel and Green Park, Rostrevor was a classic Ulster Tory imperialist of the old school, impatient and ill tempered. Born in 1876, he was from a seventeenth century landowning family in Co. Down. Its seat is the gothic Narrow Water Castle on Carlingford Lough near Warrenpoint. Indeed the family still owns a thousand acres in the area including most of that town's land. This was the coast where Casement weekended with Millar Gordon in May 1910. Educated at Harrow and the Royal Military Academy in Woolwich, Frank joined the Royal Artillery in 1895, being commissioned as a Captain in 1901. His army career was initially fairly brief as by 1911 he was retiring on a pension of £120 p.a. with the brevet rank of Lieutenant Colonel.

Still only thirty-five, he was soon involved in the developing political crisis. His skills were noticed and he was appointed to reorganise the Ulster Clubs, that same year "to bring in the staunch Unionists who are not Orangemen" as Carson told him. It was to be the militia to the Orange Order's standing army, the way Hall put it.[893] He was then the key organiser behind the Ulster Day demonstrations of 28 September 1912, which climaxed in the mass signing of the Solemn League and Covenant. On the formation of the UVF he became its Military Secretary.

Although unaware of the obtaining of the arms in Hamburg, he was on a twelve-man committee tasked to arrange their landing and distribution. Indeed he was the figure who predominated in the argument as to whether the guns should be brought into Belfast. Craig wanted a political demonstration, Hall a smuggling operation. He also feared sectarian trouble so he went to London to see Carson and get the landing points moved away from Belfast. A continuing rift between the military and political wings of the UVF ensued. Hall explained in 1964 "I never fell in with Craig. Craig had no use for me because I wasn't an Orangeman." Thereafter he and Craig conversed in shouting mode.

Hall admitted he was wrong on one matter and that was the UVF turnout for the 'manoeuvres' on Friday 24 April 1914. As it was pay night in the mills and factories he warned of a rate of 15%. In the event he was taken aback by a 50% response.[894] During the arms landings in Larne and Bangor he played an intelligence role, diverting and confusing the RIC and the Army in and around Belfast as well as "short-circuiting", not cutting critical telegraph and telephone lines. Confirmation of Frank Hall's peppery nature comes in a letter of April 1914 in which T.C. Platt, secretary of the British League for the Support of Ulster and the Union, complained "according to Hall all the idiots in the universe are in the League…I am nearing the greatest contempt for Hall."[895]

Much of this information is gleaned from an interview Hall gave to a representative of PRONI on 14 April 1964 at his home in Hambledon near Portsmouth.[896] He was then aged eighty-eight and almost blind. Although said not to be doting, he was described as dozing off after periods of lucidity and then lapsing into jumbled statements of fact. Six days later he was dead. Awarded a DSO for his war work, Hall finally retired from the Army on 31 December 1921. He married twice, first in 1919, Violet Brooke from the leading Fermanagh family and secondly in 1937, the year after her death, when in Australia to one Joan Kynaston. He had no children from either marriage. In 1964 he was still enraged by the marriage in 1919 of his nephew to a "Roman Catholic Jew woman in Gibraltar." The nephew, he said, had turned his own mother "out of Narrow Water" drinking himself to an early death in 1939. The estate was then put in trust to minimise the perceived damage of a Catholic heir. The trusteeship repercussions rumble on to this day.

Earlier in 1913 with Fred Crawford and his brother Roger Hall he also imported Vickers maxim machine guns from London – in boxes labelled Wireless Apparatus. Roger and he test fired one at Narrow Water (scene in 1979 of the British Army's worst casualties in the modern Troubles when eighteen paratroopers were killed by the IRA). The bullets, in 1913, fired from the tennis court ricocheted off a bank a thousand yards away only to rain down on complaining estate workers. Frank Hall had another row with Craig when the UVF was being re-organised for eventual absorption into the British Army. He offered him the job of "Assistant Paymaster at Newtownards" in the Ulster Division. Duly enraged, he said "I cleared out" and went over to Great Britain intent on rejoining the Royal Artillery but through a Unionist contact Adjutant-General Sir Henry Sclater (a member of the Army Council) he was instead offered, in September 1914, a job in Military Intelligence. Thus did Frank Hall join MI5 becoming its fifth most senior official. His job was to form "an extra section to cover the Dominions, and Colonies and Ireland. It was very hush-hush."

Hall is remarkable also for his MI5 codename, one later utilised by Ian Fleming in his Bond novels. For Major Frank Hall was MI5's first 'Q' in Army Intelligence – probably Fleming's source if not his model.

Hall's memories of Casement were unfortunately sparse and governed by prejudice. His interviewer in 1964 records him saying that "M.I.5D issued a Q report (Colonel Hall was Q)" disclosing that "three men would land at midnight, between midnight and 2 a.m. on such and such a date." Hall remained peeved since "Dublin Castle refused to believe the Q report" his explanation being that "Dublin Castle was of course well known to be controlled by the Nationalists anyway." He did recall that on his appointment he checked what MI5 had on himself and the UVF, and discovered nothing. He is, however, to be found on the RIC files being mentioned in particular as present at a UVF meeting in Newry on 17 September 1913. "We were all blackguards" then, he chortled. "When Casement was taken to Scotland Yard" all he recounted, nearly half a century later, was that he was certainly present along with Blinker Hall and one Diel Herschall – a name the PRONI interviewer says he was unable to confirm. There was another officer, one Lt. Claud Serocold, from Blinker's staff present. David Ramsay's 2008 book, *'Blinker Hall' – Spymaster,* explains that Richard 2nd Lord Herschell and Claud Serocold were Hall's personal assistants in Room 40. Herschell had been Lord Aberdeen's private secretary from 1905 to 1907 when Lord Lieutenant of Ireland.

Frank Hall continued, in the interviewer's words, with "an outburst against homosexuals" saying that "Casement arrived 'with his two boyfriends' on the beach." The only further revelation was that the wireless message from Valentia cable station on Casement's arrest read "Tom operated on successfully today." No other intelligence detail was provided and certainly not the faintest whiff of a forgery operation. This is a dog failing to bark. Given Hall's age, the confused state of his mind, and the imminence of his death, it would be reasonable to have expected some fragment of any such memory to slip out. None did. For such a scheme of forgery to be put in train without the knowledge of Q at MI5 is quite improbable. Although the most junior of the interrogating trio, Frank was politically in tune and quite necessary in terms of Irish knowledge. The only potentially forgery-linkable item on record is his mild letter in July 1916 to Ernley Blackwell about the discovery of Millar Gordon's identity, which is not even suggestive of rigorous law enforcement let alone a campaign of deceit and forgery.

We do have one political appreciation of Casement by Hall. This came in the MI5 files released in 1999. On 4 November 1914, after Casement's appearance in Norway, Frank is to be found passing on his tuppence worth: "I have never met Sir R. Casement but was invited to do so by a mutual acquaintance last June who then described him as a 'sincere nationalist' I declined the honour and said I was a 'sincere imperialist' and heard no more."[897] Thus were his colleagues informed – more about Hall than Casement. The mutual acquaintance is likely to have been Rose Young of Galgorm Castle (or her Unionist brother), as in her diary she records a visit on 8 March 1911 from "Capt. Hall of Narrow Water."[898] Hall had acted as MI5's Belfast bureau chief, keeping tabs on Casement and other Irish revolutionaries from 1914 on, as is revealed by various memoranda in the organisation's files. Although not signed they are written in the Major's irrepressible and self-regarding style. One of his final naive comments came in a note complaining about a news cutting from an American Home Rule supporting newspaper which he said "throws a curious sidelight on the imperial sentiments of at any rate their supporters in America."[899]

Casement defenders then, and the forgery school in particular now, however, missed a golden opportunity in not spotting the fact that one of Casement's interrogators was the former Military Secretary of the UVF, an actual gunrunner himself. Enough was properly made of the trial prosecutor, the Tory Attorney-General F.E. Smith, being Carson's 'Galloper'. Another such involvement could have proved that the prosecution was little more than a persecution of one set of 'disloyalists' by another.

Basil Thomson stated that "after some time hunting up the Casement file" the prisoner was brought in. Memorably described, as always, Thomson wrote that he was "Tall and thin, and rather cadaverous, with thick black hair turning grey and a long pointed chin. He had thin nervous hands, mahogany coloured from long tropical service; his forehead was much wrinkled, his complexion deeply sunburnt. He was very vivacious and at times histrionic in his manner."[900] Official papers confirm this, saying during his interrogation by "Major Hall of MI5G" and others, including Inspector Sandercock, that Casement "showed some signs of becoming emotional and even hysteric."[901] Unbeknownst to the interrogators there was a Casement sympathiser in the ever more crowded room, the male shorthand writer, P.C. Charles Gill, by the sound of it an Irish nationalist or a member of the homintern, who at one point was able to whisper to the prisoner "Greater love hath no man than this, that he lay down his life for his country."[902]

Cautioned once again, Casement said that his great fear was to avoid betraying others or to appear treacherous to his German hosts, but he did communicate detail on the proposed Easter Sunday rising, "He was very insistent that the news of his capture should be published, as it would prevent bloodshed. Hall pointed out that most likely it would have the opposite effect."[903] Not a plausible argument since his capture was already public. However, Blinker Hall and his colleagues had a different view of how matters should proceed, one in tune with their high Tory politics and despite Asquith still being prime minister of an admittedly Liberal-Unionist coalition.

Margot Asquith, and of course her husband the Prime Minister, were apparently aware of the intelligence.[904] Indeed the whole Cabinet may have been informed by Arthur Balfour, the First Lord of the Admiralty, his source being Sir Henry Oliver, the Naval Secretary.[905] This however has not been confirmed and seems unlikely in that Birrell was plainly not *au fait* with the impending rebellion. Asquith unwisely discounted the intelligence, apparently as he had heard so much of a similar nature.

In two places, in slightly different words, Casement assessed the policy pervading that room in relation to the imminent Irish rebellion – and the possibility of it being abandoned before it started. Hall remarked when Casement proposed trying to stop the rising, "No better let this festering sore come to a head. Basil Thomson nodded approval."[906] Otherwise it was "It is better a festering sore like this should be cut out."[907] For precisely this reason Casement was brought to London and kept out of the hands of Dublin Castle – if not to enable the rebellion to proceed, then to ensure that he would not muddy the waters there, and instead serve the greater imperial interest both in terms of waging the World War and of assuaging the public's demand for vengeance. It has to be said that when this allegation about bringing the "festering sore" to a head was made known to a nervous Ernley Blackwell, through Eva Gore-Booth, there was a swift denial on 18 July from Basil Thomson of anyone making such a statement. He also explained that it had been decided not to announce Casement's arrest, as it would be "useful to the Germans"! Blackwell, a details man, dryly noted alongside this response "? published in Dublin evening papers on Sat."[908]

Nonetheless these three security chiefs plainly operated in a political manner at odds with their government. They chose in effect to encourage the rising and in the case of Blinker Hall may have limited the distribution of intelligence about its arrangements to nurture and help bring it about. By this point they were in effect projectors but without the skill of their Tudor predecessors. Hall was certainly no Francis Walsingham. Extracting Casement from Ireland did untold damage to Dublin Castle's knowledge and ability to respond. The consequence was undoubtedly an uprising that cost some five hundred British and Irish lives (almost all in Dublin) thus ensuring Ireland (or twenty-six counties thereof) left the United Kingdom, and thence the Empire. Ironically, even Casement, in 1906, had not argued such an extreme measure, presciently writing "The British Empire must become a great Commonwealth of Free States bound together by love and interest and fellow feeling, not kept chained to heel."[909] But Hall preferred, in a laissez-faire imperial fashion, to observe just what would happen if there was to be a big shooting match and the Irish separatist boil lanced, as he foolishly expected.

But which Hall? The assumption has been that the person who spoke of a festering sore was Captain Blinker Hall. Yet it is possible it was Major Frank Hall who used the phrase. According to Alice Stopford Green, Casement told her it was the higher in rank of the two who alluded several times to the festering sore.[910] A Major is a higher army rank than Captain but junior to a naval Captain, so confusion has lingered. However, the rank of 'Captain' is given by Casement in his 64-page typed brief to counsel,[911] so it was Blinker Hall not Frank Hall, although they were two of a kind.

Birrell's response to Casement, as described by an admittedly, hostile colleague, came in an Easter Monday meeting. Basil Thomson diaried: "I described my interview with Casement and detailed the Sinn Féin plans. Birrell remarked "You fellows get all the fun; in my long term of office I have never had a bit of fun like that...He laughed at the idea of a rising taking place on account of Casement's arrest saying that the Irish were secretly ashamed of Casement. He was just off to see Mr Redmond."[912] Shortly afterwards there was a total cessation of telegrams from Dublin. The G.P.O. had been seized. Later that day, in the House of Commons, Birrell would be hearing Noel Pemberton Billing MP asking (of Casement), to cheers, whether "this traitor will be shot forthwith?" Oddly Sir Matthew Nathan was not so puerile, rather he was significantly understanding, indeed overly so, being quoted in Horace Plunkett's diary on 27 April 1916 as deploring the way "this poor dupe had been duped by the Germans."

Close up of Casement, uniquely without beard, at sea, April 1916

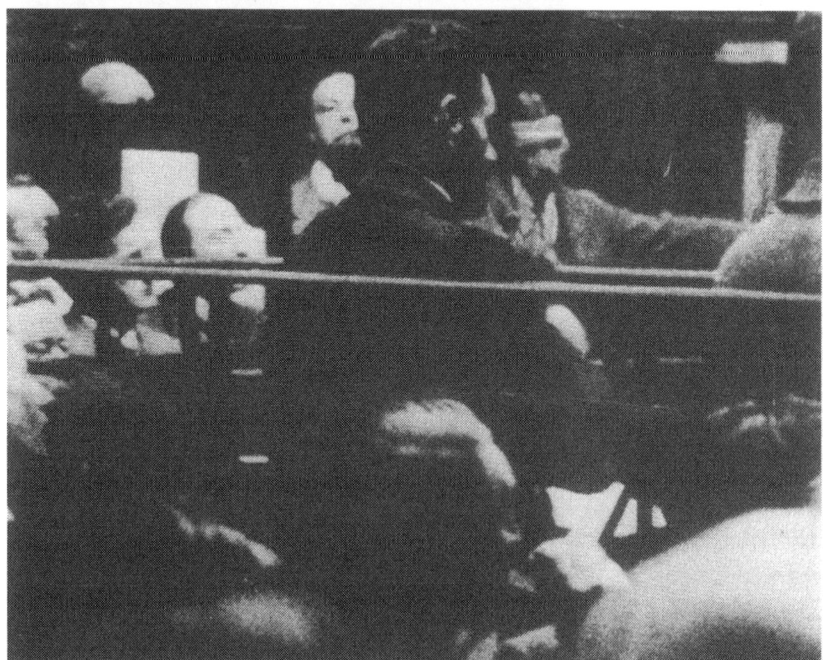

Casement in the dock at Bow Street magistrates court, May 1916

Casement was held incommunicado for over a fortnight. Until Easter Tuesday, he was lodged in Brixton Prison, and then in the Tower of London in deteriorating health and miserable conditions. He managed nonetheless to charm his army guards who told him certain pieces of unwelcome news and passed a number of communications to the outside. Gertrude and Elizabeth Bannister worked ceaselessly in London to track down their cousin and get to see him. After an initial period of shock when Alice Stopford Green was in something of a blue funk, calling his journey madness and the rising "a calamity brought on by an insane desire of Roger as well as the rest of the Irish rebels to follow Wolfe Tone", she rallied round. Her position was somewhat delicate as she was a confidante of Liberal Cabinet ministers in London and in Dublin but she had funded the importation of German arms for the Volunteers. In some ways, like Casement, she was willing to wound but afraid to strike. For her pains her house was, however, raided and searched.

As the possibility of a court martial and summary execution receded what Casement needed now was a defence team and a defence. Alice Stopford Green's major contribution was getting George Gavan Duffy (1882-1951) to act as Casement's solicitor. He first saw Casement on 9 May. From that start a defence team was built up. George was the son of Sir Charles Gavan Duffy, the Young Irelander, founder of the *Nation* and land reform agitator who ended his political career in Australia as Prime Minister of Victoria. His son's career would take many legal and political turns before it ended in Dublin as President of the High Court. Elected a Sinn Féin MP, he was the reluctant fifth signatory to the Treaty in 1921 and thence Minister of Foreign Affairs, soon resigning his Dáil seat over the refusal to treat captured Republicans as POWs. In his later legal work he was a champion of individual rights, and, at the same time, of a very Catholic state.

Leading counsel would be Gavan Duffy's brother-in-law, Serjeant Alexander Sullivan (1871-1959), an Irish prosecution lawyer without senior standing at the English Bar whose father had been a Home Rule MP. Sullivan was to feature subsequently as a thorn in the side of the diary forgery school. He was also a dedicated opponent of Sinn Féin throughout his life. Contemptuous of the men of 1916, he referred to them as gangsters which suggests he may not have been the best choice. Top English QCs, however, were not queuing up to take the case. Sir John Simon declined the brief as did Tim Healy MP, the future Irish Governor-General, who had tormented Dublin's homosexual community in the 1884 Dublin Castle scandal. Like most lawyers, Sullivan was to end up with a dissatisfied client.

Junior counsel was a Welsh barrister (and stonemason's son) Artemus Jones, later a judge. The team was advised by J.H. Morgan, a Professor of

Constitutional Law at London University and attached as staff officer to the War Office, latterly as a Brigadier-General, dealing with conscientious objectors and other military legal issues. He was also a friend of Dick Morten and had met and corresponded with Casement before the war. Morgan acted as an adviser to Liberal politicians and was working on amendments in 1914 to the ludicrous Amending Bill when he wrote to Casement on 12 July about the Volunteers, "It is wonderful what you have done. You have saved us from the consequences of Birrell's wretched laissez-faire attitude...Your work has changed the situation and saved Ireland." Despite the effusion, he was actually hoping to give Ulster administrative autonomy within Home Rule, seeing full Ulster exclusion as "vicious and impractical."[913]

Another adviser, Michael Francis Doyle, was also brought on board. A Democrat from Philadelphia, he was very much the American political lawyer. He too knew Casement, having acted for him when the *New York World* printed a story about Casement accepting 'German gold'. Doyle had obtained an apology and a retraction where John Quinn had refused to assist. He was an ardent supporter of the separatist movement. Part of his task was fund raising in the US, and later, trying to look after Nina, both financially and otherwise – not an easy task. Ironically, given Casement's scrupulous refusal to take German money, the equivalent of £1,000 was ultimately forwarded from Berlin to Bernstorff in America for his defence. It was to repay John Devoy who had provided $5,000 of his own money in emergency (from his brother's estate). Doyle brought the money over in the form of a cheque or draft made out to Casement.

Montgomery Hyde later interviewed Michael Francis Doyle about the money. He was suspicious as he mistakenly thought that the Doyle recorded as giving the largest amount to the defence fund was Sir Arthur Conan Doyle and that no American money had ever been handed over. Indeed in his trial book he said that exactly, transcribing "Doyle £700/0/0" from Gavan Duffy's hand written entry in his REX V. CASEMENT costs and expenses accounts to read "Sir A. Conan Doyle £700.0.0".[914] Curiously, with his Unionist politics and their contrary views on the diaries, Hyde dedicated his 1964 paperback book to the memory of Michael Francis Doyle, "Late of the American Bar: Defender of Sir Roger Casement no less after his execution than during his trial."

The American Doyle told Hyde he gave the Devoy cheque (or draft) to Gavan Duffy after he had seen Casement to get it endorsed and that he had then been given £250 of it by Gavan Duffy. Hyde asked to see the receipt but Doyle said he could not locate the "photographic copy of the check".[915] The 5,000 dollars was probably then worth about £1,000 and after Doyle took out a quarter the remainder went to Duffy. This is only confirmed in a set of accounts that Gavan Duffy provided to Mrs Sidney Parry, and others, after

Sketch of Casement at the Old Bailey by Alice Milligan, June 1916 (NLI 49154/20/1)

the execution which has been inappropriately filed by the NLI amongst South American papers. It went unnoticed until 2018.[916] Included, as received on 28 June, is "M.F. Doyle Esq. (American Contribution) £698.4.4."

The total income and expenditure for the trial was £1750.11.4, with fees to Counsel coming to £1086.6.0. Gavan Duffy for his months of dedicated work was only to be provided with the balance of £537.0.0. The confusion over names was to mislead writers, including this one, for a long period casting an unfairly poor light on Michael Francis Doyle.

Devoy later wrote, "After the trial the lawyers were constantly insisting that Doyle should get more money from us for them, although he had conveyed our message that we could pay no more than the $5,000 he had brought over. I believe it was Mr. Sullivan who made the demands. He wanted to appeal the case to the House of Lords, but that would be only prolonging Casement's agony. The Lords would certainly confirm the sentence. I was informed that Mr. Sullivan showed a considerable temper in his criticisms of us for not sending the money which he had been told we had not got. Everybody in Ireland expects money from America and seems to think there is no limit to the amount available."[917]

Indeed on 5 July, Doyle was telegraphing the US to seek an additional amount, immediately, by cable, saying, "COUNSEL ASK FIVE HUNDRED POUNDS".[918] However it was actually Gavan Duffy not Sullivan who was seeking greater US funding. In the event, Sullivan charged £530.0.0 for the case and said in July, "Fifty guineas is quite enough for the appeal"[919]

Gavan Duffy wrote bluntly to Doyle on 20 July to no avail, "The non-arrival of the American cheque, on which I counted in briefing Counsel for the Appeal is very disappointing. We want at least £300 more up to date and if the case goes to the House of Lords it will cost me out-of-pocket another sum of 250 guineas in Counsels' fees even at a moderate estimate so I trust that when you get over the other side you will be able to help in the matter."[920]

A final word on the shortfall went to Gavan Duffy who was to suffer financially, even though Sullivan ultimately waived the appeal fifty guineas.[921] Overall, counsel fees were £1,086.6.0. Total costs, excluding Duffy's fee, were £1,213.4.2 while donations came to £1,750.11.4, leaving him well short of the £800 fee he had agreed. Telling off Doyle, he wrote: "Your friends there have not treated me well in the matter. I suppose they believe in payments by results."[922] A rare flash of (gallows) humour in an otherwise cheerless story.

The American's involvement was not to the liking of the London establishment and Doyle clashed with them frequently. He was also economical with the truth, as Ernley Blackwell and others were shocked to discover, and anxious to point out – especially to Cecil Spring Rice, lest the issues were raised in America. Sir Ernley described Doyle's assertions as "pure invention", in particular the charge that application had been made, and refused, for him to go to Germany to bring back defence witnesses.[923]

By the time America entered the war, Doyle and many other Irish-Americans had faced up to the quandary it put them in and made a decision. As he told a doubtful Gertrude in April 1917, "Our country is your Ally in this awful war. Our people at large really do not want war. I have been active for peace [but] it is the duty of every American to sustain him [the President] and to fulfil the duties which the great crisis forces on us."[924] Doyle's later career was not as successful as he hoped, suffering as it did from proven allegations of unprofessional conduct. Despite bringing Irish-American support over to Roosevelt in 1931 as opposed to the 1927 candidate, the Catholic Al Smith, and ceaseless self-promotion he was only rewarded (late) with a judgeship at the Hague Court of International Arbitration – much of it served during the Second World War when the Court was inoperable. He died in 1960.

Casement knew he was technically guilty of treason, having said exactly that many times in Germany and before, and even at Scotland Yard. Indeed he admitted to his solicitor that when in custody "I said a great deal I should not have said. I mean for the purposes of this trial."[925] In May 1915, in Germany, he was writing "It used to be prophesied of me as a boy in Ireland that I 'would be hanged' – and I am beginning to think the prophecy may come true. Meantime I shall do my best to justify the hanging."[926] A month before, he rather unwisely wrote "I believe I am today in law as much a British subject as I ever was."[927] Earlier in 1906, it was "I ought really to be in jail instead of under Lion and Unicorn…I am sowing seeds of treason even here in Brazil."[928] Nonetheless he became increasingly determined to resist the prosecution case as his voluminous notes to counsel demonstrate.

If the country to which he was loyal was not the United Kingdom, but Ireland an unrecognised state, he had a case to argue, albeit hopeless, unless before a jury of Irishmen. There was a technical aspect to the statute of Edward III under which he was charged, one of some complexity. It hinged essentially on the existence or otherwise of a notional set of commas, or whether the absent punctuation marks might be present under a crease in the parchment. The interpretation on treasonable adherence to the King's enemies committed *outside the realm* as written in Norman-French in the 1351 Treason Act was ultimately judged, on precedent, against Casement, despite great efforts by Sullivan and the learned advice of Professor Jackie Morgan. As Casement later, eloquently, put it in a prison letter to Dick Morten, it was as if "to hang a man's life upon a comma, and throttle him with a semi-colon."[929] But in truth, law depends entirely on syntax and punctuation.

Initially he thought of representing himself, but London was determined on a full trial with a host of witnesses, particularly repatriated soldiers who would testify to his attempts at inducing them to join the Irish Brigade. All but one of the specific charges related to such attempts at disaffection, the other concerned the armed landing. The rules of evidence would not permit a politicisation of the case – it would be impossible to do more than allude to the fact that the Attorney General and Carson had been allied in the 1914 (arguably not illegal) importation and distribution of arms in Ulster. It was done, and attempted, on a number of occasions by the defence team, and duly resisted by the judges who induced a literal breakdown in Sullivan during his summing-up. He lost his thread and had to be replaced by Artemus Jones.

At Bow Street magistrates court on 15 May Casement saw Bailey for the first time since McKenna's Fort, while Frank Hall sat watching in the packed court alongside Casement's women. After the charge was read Casement intervened. Pointing to Bailey he said "That man is innocent. I think the indictment is wrongly drawn up against him."[930] He then asked that his own defence team be made available to him. Whether he knew precisely what Bailey had specified in his attempt at a life-saving deal with the police in Kerry is unclear, but it illustrates the consistent humanity and concern of the man, ever helping the unfortunate even at risk to himself. As Casement put it "My heart went out with a bound, always to the weaker man or thing, and right or wrong I had to champion it."[931] Such an outlook, however, made it impossible for Casement to be ruthless. Gertrude Bannister had no doubts about Bailey – describing him as a traitor and informer. The co-joined defence only lasted until the end of the three day magistrates court hearing when a proposal was wisely made, and accepted, for Bailey to instruct separate counsel. The evidence given had suggested a potential conflict of interest between him and Casement.

The trial proper has been well documented but what remains less known are the tensions and difficulties in and around the small group of Casement defenders and supporters. Little assistance of value came out of Ireland. The country was initially still in shock, if not hostile, while with hundreds of separatists rounded up and court-martialled there were few available to assist politically. On 30 April, Maurice Moore wrote to Alice Stopford Green asking "Do all you can to save the lives of these foolish people, infinite harm though they have done to our cause, worse will happen by their execution. Even Casement must be saved; nothing can be said to palliate what he has done but mercy will have more effect than revenge...de Wet was pardoned. Why not Casement. If not, his blood will breed another rebellion."[932] Harsh, if prescient swords from a friend, so the defence task therefore fell largely to women and so it happened that Casement's group of friends on which he used to rely when in England was largely reconstituted.

The problem of the second unofficial trial was one that had to be faced as newspapers started to publish reports of, and comments on, the existence of the diaries. In a sense Casement was well prepared for this eventuality having warned his friends in Germany of exactly that and the likelihood of his being hanged. Writing on 26 March 1916 in "a last word for my true friend Charles Curry", Casement explained "The English government will try now most to humiliate and degrade me. They will not honour me with a High Treason trial. I am convinced of that. They will rob Ireland of that and they will charge me with something else – something baser than 'high treason' – God knows what…I feel convinced they will seek through some dastardly means to assail me otherwise and break their vengeance on me and Ireland by a coward's blow…It is the most hopeless position a man was ever in…I go to a show trial to be wounded in my honour, to be defamed and degraded with no chance of defence probably and then to a term of imprisonment that will end my days in jail – a convict. For I should not long support the indignities and miseries I should be subject to."[933] Elsewhere in the letter he mentioned that Adler had been found to have misbehaved in America, which provides a certain context to his remarks. There is also a strong echo of Oscar Wilde's terrible treatment in prison and a fear of experiencing the same.

Not content with "a last word" Casement wrote Curry "a final word" on 6 April repeating these fears. In justification, he explained "I am wholly pro-German always for the sake and cause of the German people…It is not my own honour is at stake alone but the cause of Irish nationality in the extreme form I have stood for. The British Government will seek to injure both – and one through the other. By assailing me and my character they will hope to blacken my cause too – at any rate to gravely weaken it."[934] These letters, although in some senses just thinking aloud, were an attempt to soften the impact of disclosures which Casement reckoned could not fail to emerge. Even without the diaries there were, he knew, so many other letters and individuals around the world available to incriminate him.

Once the trial started Casement also prepared the ground for his lawyers on the looming homosexual charge. "If they should succeed in insinuating or implying anything discreditable to my character I must bear it – and carry the war into their camp by saying 'allright – you knew all that long ago; yet you suggested my return to your service on 26 October 1914 and three days after were offering a bribe of £5000 for my betrayal and when that failed too you spread this libel or lie about me all over the world. If you believed it how can you justify to the British people your suggestion of 26 October'…If the worst comes to the worst (as I always dread) and my strength can support the ordeal I will save the situation for others – for Ireland and Germany – even if I suffer worse than death."[935] He felt the trial's main purpose was an assault on Germany and by this defence against the sexual slur he could save the day, even if he would be sacrificed in the process. Quite how Ireland's case would be enhanced is not clear but if it was self-deception on Casement's part it was nonetheless wisely precautionary as it prevented him becoming dejected and broken.

Gavan Duffy was very much the captain of the good ship *Casement* over the three months of trial until the execution on 3 August – and beyond. Like a good ship's master he was calm, accessible, thorough and effective and did everything with a kindly grace. Luckily he was methodical in his treatment of documents and the bulk of his correspondence survived, with some obvious exceptions. He was plainly a very honest and principled man. He and the other lawyers developed a strategy for the second charge, one that did not involve untruths. At its simplest, as Artemus Jones put it, the diary should be dismissed with the statement "that there never was any kind of proof that it was in Casement's handwriting."[936] Similarly Duffy advised Mrs Nannie Dryhurst, "If I were you I would not pay the slightest attention to this kind of rubbish."[937] Nonetheless it was a leaky ship and some of the crew did not listen to, or grasp, orders.

In an early attempt to calm Casement, Gavan Duffy pressed that he be permitted cigarettes. On 20 May he wrote to the authorities pleading a medical case: "Sir Roger Casement is very unwell and his suffering is undoubtedly aggravated by the prohibition against smoking, since he is a heavy smoker and feels the abstention from smoking most acutely…I have little doubt that the MO of the prison would recommend this course." On 22 May, in response, he was advised that "on the recommendation of the MO at Brixton Prison this prisoner is being allowed to smoke."[938]

The greatest external danger seemed ironically to come from the prisoner's old friends, although the extended Casement family also presented various problems to Gavan Duffy. The one piece of good fortune was that Nina remained in America throughout, leaving Gertrude in charge. She was assisted in London by her own sister Elizabeth, Ada McNeill, Alice Stopford Green, Alice Milligan (who sketched him in the dock) and later by Eva Gore-Booth, whom Casement had never previously known. At the end Casement changed his will, leaving his entire estate to Gertrude, rather than Nina. This was presumably done because of her inaccessibility, but perhaps also on account of her volatility.

Dick Morten was the first of the crew that Gavan Duffy had to come down hard upon. He had seen Casement with their mutual friend Jackie Morgan. Writing to Duffy on 9 June, Morgan apologised: "I am sorry indeed that Dick Morten talked as he did…Had I known he was going to talk thus I should not have left him behind." His letter quoted Dick as having asked "What about the other things Roddie?" to which Casement made no reply, except to say "Dick you've upset me." Morgan was relieved that "Morten said not a word about it being common talk" reporting that Casement talked to Dick (his friend for twenty-six years) "as he would talk to no one else not even Miss Bannister." She reported separately that a sleepless and emotional Roger, in his distress had clasped Dick's hand for several minutes. What worried Professor Morgan most, he said, was that Dick's tactlessness revealed to Casement that he knew of the stories. He felt Dick was "probably the last man he would wish to hear of them."[939] Casement was later to write to his friend pleading opaquely, "Don't mind what anyone says about me, Dick – It is easy to pelt the man who can't reply or who is gone."[940]

The capacity of these stressed people at least to get used to the notion of Casement being homosexual is quite illustrative and significant. They did, and were in most instances the better for it. Duffy immediately wrote to Dick, to the Savoy Hotel rather than his house of the same name! Nervous of the harm arising from indiscreet talk, he warned "Dear Mr Morten, my client begs me to impress upon you the great importance of talking to nobody under any circumstances about any of the matters you discussed yesterday."[941] However, Gertrude, reporting later to Nina, wrote that once Morten had "blurted it out we could discuss it more or less – for there were always warders present."[942] Some weeks after the execution, Duffy felt able to complain "Morten has not paid anything! Though he originally promised a lot." In reply, defending his friend, Professor Morgan pointed out that he was the "very soul of honour" but hard hit by the war as he and his wife's money was largely in Belgian companies and they were getting no dividend.[943]

Sidney Parry turned out to be a worse problem than Dick Morten. Professor Morgan in his letter of 9 June explained that Parry "is going next week…and has been talking a great deal in my presence about the other charge. I have thought it wise to write today to him and request him if he does visit Roger Casement to avoid all references to those charges and such matters." Gertrude too was seriously worried about Sidney whom she said "has expressed a desire to go with me and thank Goodness I say, for then he cannot make any faux pas in that direction."[944] On 4 July 1916 he gaily advised "I am having a book sent to Roddie by Benson which seems fine and helpful: *The Friendship of Christ.* H.B. clearly was of the same nature as our friend and their spirits will understand each other." In hasty reply, Duffy realising he had to continue bailing out a very leaky ship wrote "Thanks for yours of yesterday. I shall be very glad of an early opportunity of meeting you as one cannot write about things but you will be very glad to hear that on the main issue everything is going splendidly."

H.B. was Monsignor Hugh Benson, a well-known religious writer whose father had been Archbishop of Canterbury. The son was obviously a convert to Rome. The Benson family held something of a record in that all three boys were homosexual while "all five grown-up Bensons never for one moment showed any interest in a person of the opposite sex."[945] According to a fellow priest Father Martindale, Hugh actively disliked women, adding "of marriage he loathed the thought, from congenital instinct." One writer has put it thus: "By the turn of the century there was a widely understood connection between Catholicism and male homosexuality."[946] This could be better phrased – the connection was actually to male converts. Sidney Parry's familiarity with Benson and his sexual nature strongly suggest that he too adhered to both Mgr. Benson's outlooks, but not, it transpired, to his view of marriage. Sidney was certainly a Catholic, and a convert in the 1880s, as the Parry family who ultimately and unexpectedly inherited Casement's literary estate in 1950, was otherwise sternly English and Protestant.

The earliest non-official reference to Casement probably being gay occurs in Edward Carpenter's diary when Sidney Parry weekended with him. Carpenter noted on Saturday 6 November 1915: "Sidney Parry at 6 p.m. Music in evg. Sunday. Morning walk with P. Talk about Casement (? homogenic), E.D. Morel, Northcliffe & the Govt. Robert Kay in to tea. Mon Parry off…"[947] He also diaried on 15 July 1916, "Talk of Casement" with Nevinson" and the next day, "Wrote to Asquith. Plea for Casement."[948] For Parry to have even stayed with the notorious homosexual and socialist writer, Edward Carpenter, indicates someone at least very tolerant, if not most likely gay himself.

Ironically, there was to be a bright and positive side to the tragedy; the unexpected union between Sidney Parry and Gertrude Bannister in the October of 1916 – literally in the shadow of the execution. Gertrude was then forty-three and cannot have expected to marry. Like her cousin Nina, there was really only one man she loved, "The outstanding glorious figure in my life", as she called him, while also lamenting to her young niece in Australia how "even his dear, dear beautiful body must be hidden away."[949] There had been mention ten years before of a young man named Baptist whose death Gertrude was mourning. He appears to have been the son of Casement's friend Dick Morten. Baptist Morten, if a son, can at most have been a teenager, Mrs May Morten being born in 1869 and married in 1889. The passing of "Poor Baptist", prompted the 42 year-old Casement to console Gertrude by writing rather tastelessly: "I am more and more coming to the opinion that an early death is best before the sadness of lost youth has robbed life of its worth…I wish I had died some years ago."[950] This low-level death wish, to die still with beauty in mind and face, was always an encouragement for Casement to risk a treason conviction.

Sidney and Gertrude's pre-nuptial contract implied that the marriage was not to have a sexual side, for on 3 September he was careful to confirm to his bride, "You will have the big front room and my room adjoins yours with my own little bed that I have slept in for over ten years but I am handy to see that you have all you need. So don't be anxious about anything and remember I have given you my promise to do all you ask of me."[951] Parry was also preoccupied with religious matters. On 30 September shortly before the wedding Father Murnane wrote to him to say "You are having many prayers answered. Miss Bannister's name and conversion are coupled with my prayers for you."[952] Plainly Gertrude was about to become a Catholic as her cousin had done the previous month. The American lawyer, Michael Francis Doyle, was revealingly candid about the wedding. In a letter to Gavan Duffy on 15 November he said "...the name of her husband. It certainly was a great surprise to me."[953]

Sidney Parry, an Oxford graduate, was in 1921 to write a short pamphlet with a long title: *Ireland's Claim to Independence – The Avenue to Peace: How England met this Claim in 1782*.[954] He was also fond of quoting Horace Plunkett's aphorism "Anglo-Irish history is for Englishmen to remember and Irishmen to forget."[955] Writing in the *Irish Statesman* on 29 January 1927, Parry, continuing Casement's noble tradition, was pressing for free school meals for the children in the Carraroe area and other "necessitous districts of the Gaeltacht." Casement had especially asked that "the wee souls out in the west by the western wave" be cared for.[956] In his final letter to William and Emmeline Cadbury, in what little was left after Ernley Blackwell had censored it, Casement pleaded "Please help the schoolchildren of Carraroe for my sake. I failed in that trust Alas!...Farewell dear gentle hearts." Cadbury gave £200 anonymously to the defence fund and privately pleaded for a reprieve by citing that "every organ in his body was soaked with malaria."[957]

The Parrys were to have twenty years of harmonious companionship. Sidney who died in 1937 was last remembered trying to start a branch of the Social Credit movement in Cushendall, the village where the couple took a summer house to be close to all Casement's friends. He was depicted to this author by someone who had heard him speaking from the platform as a very portly man of over twenty stone.[958]

Even a canny operator like Alice Stopford Green had not been properly buttoned up. In a letter dated 6 July 1916, given to Duffy by Robert Lynd's mother-in-law Nannie Dryhurst, one Mary Boyle O'Reilly opened up with both barrels. She announced "Ireland is not affected by Mr Casement's reputation or conduct" but she was raging about "Mrs Green's volunteered statement of his gross misconduct and his lawyer's curt refusal to speak with an American journalist who desired only a formal denial of Mrs Green's statement." The (anti-German journalist) complained about "Mr Casement's failure to take the witness stand" calling him "an English pensioner who became a German agent." She concluded "It needed only Mrs Green's assurance that the British Government had basis for the whispered moral charge to convince American editors how they should treat the Casement trial."[959] Alice wondered whether to respond, concerned that "rumours are swarming round me about what that woman says." Despite the earlier conversation with O'Reilly, a policy of no interviews was agreed for fear of journalists getting only more fixated on the issue, if any were allowed.

In an echo of the view expressed by the lady journalist, Alice Stopford Green writing to Gertrude Bannister from Dublin on 19 July 1916 explained "I hear Asquith has said Ireland does not care about this case. It is true enough at this moment. He was practically unknown here. The story that he was an English spy has been spread everywhere and is believed."[960]

To cope with the increasing mention of the diaries, Duffy was obliged to write to Gertrude on 15 July to make a general policy pronouncement: "The suggestion that I should take any notice of the allegations about a diary belonging to Roger Casement does not commend itself to me. No such diary has the remotest connection with the case on which I am engaged and these rumours are simply spread about from the lowest and most malicious motives, a proceeding which is beneath contempt and which it would be preposterous to expect me to notice."[961] The virtue of this lofty tack was that one did not deny the existence of the diary but simply declined to give the stories credence by offering any comment.

A further diversionary technique that Casement's solicitor adopted is exampled in a letter of 14 August sent to William Allan Hay, a man so upset by the newspaper allegations he had sent Gavan Duffy a copy: "Pay no attention to the kind of rubbish appearing in the enclosure. It is sufficiently obvious that if charges of the kind indicated could have been established at all they would have been the subject of the prosecution and aspersions of this kind defeat their own end."[962]

It is generally reckoned that the entire Casement family in Ireland was so aghast at the treason of their kinsman that they abandoned him to his just fate. And it was believed that all his inward letters and other documentation left behind in Magherintemple was destroyed. However, this was not the case, some did survive. It is true to say that for several generations their executed cousin was an occasion for family distress, derived from "a sense of shame that a member of the family let them down" as Hugh Casement put it on the 2002 RTE television programme. He was also someone whose Republicanism put them in an impossible bind in Ballycastle, as Unionists in a predominantly Catholic town. During the Second World War, the Mrs Casement of the day was collecting for the war effort and embarrassing local Republicans, one declining to contribute with the excuse "I've not enough money to give as would injure a mouse."

On top of this, for younger boys in the family, Casement's further notoriety as a homosexual added to their woes, especially at school. At its simplest and worst he was viewed by fellow Unionists as a traitor to the people of Ulster and Britain, and a pervert. The Casement family, however, felt deepest the hurt, in time of war, of his treason against their King and country. They were, and are not a significantly political family, being more British than Ulster. So many Casements were then serving during the First World War, and were to do likewise in the next, that this could be the family's only response. Military Casements pop up in the most unlikely places – even tending Rupert Brooke in his last hours.

However, contrary to the perception abroad, they were not inhumane or heartless about their doomed relative. Two members of the family, at least, were in communication with him while he was in prison. One, May (Charlotte Mary) Casement, who was living in Birchington, Kent, was to have several highly sentimental replies to her letters. On 3 June "Roddie" (he also signed himself "Davie") thanked May for her kind thoughts "and memory of me – and for what you say of Granny [John Casement's wife – his aunt Charlotte.] Hope you will be often over there again and up Glenshesk…I have often thought of those parts and of the kindly people there – and *Slogh-na-Morra* [the whirlpool of the sea, off Murlough Bay] and Fair Head."[963]

On 27 July, just days before the drop, he asked May "to write a nice kind letter to Mrs Dunlop – she is now Mrs Dunlop Williams with son 21 [Freddie] (on 7 May) and lives at San Diego California." He mentioned verse written "in Glenshesk at Alec Dunlop's in 1880…long long years ago when I was a boy and all the hills were gold and all the skies were blue." May Casement was to be given a book, *The Pilot*, in the final distribution of his belongings. Mary Dunlop Williams had written to him as early as 25 April 1916 saying "I who have known and loved you since a dear and enthusiastic boy of 19… with undying love and trust. Your dear old Irish friend."[964] A day later she was pleading with the London authorities, explaining how Casement's generous, self-sacrificing heart was "apt to go to extremes." Indeed he was not the only one of his immediate family who had "developed irrational traits at times. His own father was – to say the least – very 'eccentric'" as she had heard her mother say.

A more dramatic and generous gesture was made by his namesake, the head of the family. On 3 June 1916 he wrote to Gavan Duffy from Magherintemple, on a black edged letter, saying "I enclose a small contribution to go to the benefit of Sir Roger Casement, a cheque for £25.0.0, the money to be used in what ever way his friends think fit."[965] Somewhat needlessly, Duffy replied asking which friends were meant. On 6 June came the answer: "You may apply the money in whatever way the Misses Bannister may wish." Twenty-five pounds was a significant sum of money in those days, perhaps £1,250 in today's value. This generosity of spirit and charity has gone unnoticed to date. Although the list of those giving money for the defence included this £25 donated by "Roger Casement", most have assumed it was the prisoner's own money not his homonym's.

Casement acknowledged the gift on 6 June from Brixton Prison: "I heard yesterday of an act of kindness of yours that I much appreciate – and which I think shows a very good heart. I know quite well how you feel on the points where we differ so profoundly and so I can appreciate all the more your action – and the real good feeling that prompted it." Being Casement, he then launched into a political lecture on the 1848 Young Ireland movement and Charles Gavan Duffy, even suggesting his cousin read John Mitchel's *Jail Journal.* He told of meeting Mitchel's grandson, the Mayor of New York, and Teddy Roosevelt whom he "always regarded as a fraud." Casement warned Roosevelt (who apparently thought him charming) that England would come out of the war supreme. Teddy "grinned and said 'She won't – because she's finished'."[966]

Asking after various people including "Charlotte Young of Galgorm and Mya and Co", Mrs Robertson, the McCarrys of Murlough, Father Barnes and Father Cox, he ended "Don't forget the Old Cross at Broughanlea! Is it still on the fence or has it slipped into oblivion?" He did not expect or want a reply but in what was a difficult letter to write (and receive) remembered to "pray the boys may all come home to you safe and sound when peace comes." All five mercifully did.[967]

Gavan Duffy became involved with the problems of another Casement relative, Gertrude's brother Edward, also known as Squiggy. His choice of an acting career had perturbed Casement more than a decade earlier. There are tantalising references to an interesting story when he wrote on 1 January 1903 "Eddie has just been here to dinner…It is a pity I think he doesn't give up his theatrical aims and start on another tack." This meeting is not to be found in the 1903 diary as the pages for January were torn out. Later that year, on 20 April 1903, Casement was telling Gertrude "I am glad he has got a tour again but I wish for his own sake some more certain appointment. He is I fear wasting the young strong years of his life in what will never, or may never, I will say, bring him anything lasting for later life."[968] Such conventional concerns had of course no effect, so in July 1906, Casement was bemoaning "Poor Squiggy's trouble – that was hard lines."[969] Things did improve as he was reported a month later to be busy with a new part in *Raffles.*

When war came Eddie heeded his country's call and joined up. On 20 November 1915 Nina was to tell Casement in Germany "Poor Eddie is back in the trenches again." A month later the news about him was bad: Eddie "will be in hospital three months at the least. Pieces of shell are still in his head, a lot of teeth knocked out and poor soul a piece of his jaw blown away."[970] But he survived, with his enthusiasm for acting still intact. By the autumn of 1916 Lance Corporal Bannister was listed amongst those *hors de combat* now in H.Q. Coy 107th Provisional Battalion, based in Frinton on Sea. Casement, as ever, thinking of others' welfare and even after being sentenced to death the day before, pointed out "The clothes at Brixton might be very useful for Squiggy."[971] In that 30 June letter to Eddie's sisters, from the condemned cell in Pentonville, he joked about Sidney Parry's apparent scheme to rescue him in his motorcar and reminded them "all this came by sure and certain stages – an irresistible something – appointed since I was a little boy. I felt it then and have often felt sure of it in later days."

On 23 October 1916, Eddie was well enough to write to Gavan Duffy and ask, "Would you be good enough to use your influence with Morgan to get me out. I have a very good chance of good engagements if I only could get back to civil life and I'm certainly doing no good here either to the country or myself…I'm anxious about my future prospects which will be black if I have to remain in the service till after the war."[972] Duffy duly obliged with Professor Morgan. On 7 November he suggested to the then War Office Staff Captain, "As to Bannister it seems to me that in the special circumstances an exception might be made and that he might be discharged particularly as he has already been wounded, but of course you are the best judge."[973] Whether he got a discharge is unclear but he outlasted the war and continued his theatrical career. According to Gertrude he had in 1920 gone with a male friend to start a farm in the United States. That may not have prospered as the final news of Casement's Bannister cousin is his death in New York in October 1943, a detail confirmed by Actors Equity on whose books Eddie was held.

Three days after the execution another relative wrote to Gavan Duffy, from 42 Langham Street in London. She signed herself Emily Dundas Balharry and was last spotted in Casement's 1903 diary, and his address book of that time: "I must introduce myself to you as Roger's sister in law. I am writing to you today on behalf of Charles Casement, my sister Blanche who was married for a few weeks to Tom who is in South Africa and myself to thank you very sincerely for all the kindness and zeal you showed dear Roddie in his hour of need and sorrow.

"I received letters last mail from Melbourne asking if anything could be done through an American consul at Putumayo or some person of repute to clear his name of the foul slander that has so besmirched it. Charlie is feeling this terribly. I do not know if a report has yet reached you concerning Roger's residence at Campden Hill. I saw him as usual when he stayed at that address some years ago and understood it was lent him by a friend...the most horrible lies are being circulated concerning his tenancy of the place and I am naturally very indignant."[974] No reply is in Duffy's files but it can be imagined. Anyway stories of conduct unbecoming, a decade earlier in Count Blücher's apartment seem groundless and may be as much to do with the Count being a German as with Casement's guests.

A number of other people from Casement's past intervened, or failed to intervene, aside from complete cranks or one man who thought he had been to school with him in Armagh. He described him as of "an unstable temperament" only to discover it was the cousin of the same name he was writing about. Lady (Alice) Young of Formosa Fishery, Cookham wrote on 21 May to say "You are with one in thought so constantly in your present pain that I long for you to know it is so."[975] It was her son Winthrop, later a famous alpinist, who had bathed with Casement in the 1890s. Years later and less entranced than his mother (and other young people) he recalled how "Casement was a word spinner, a charmer. With his lovely soft beguiling voice he would spin you castles in the air – celestial rose-tinted shimmering castles. And while he was speaking, you felt that little else mattered. But he was humourless – had absolutely no sense of fun.""[976]

Lady Young was the daughter of a famous doctor, Evory Kennedy of Belgard, Co. Dublin. He was born in Carndonagh, Co. Donegal in 1806 and was an unsuccessful Home Rule candidate for Donegal in 1874. She was a member of the Anglo-Irish committee organising the acquisition of arms for the Irish Volunteers in 1914 along with her cousin Alice Stopford Green, Lord Ashbourne, Molly Childers, Mary Spring Rice and her cousins Hugh and Conor O'Brien. Her son, the mountaineer Geoffrey Winthrop Young (1876-1958), was gay. Another son was Hilton Young, the 1st Lord Kennet.

Lady Constance Emmott, daughter of the Duke of Argyll, and an intimate Casement correspondent, asked the Pentonville chaplain on 12 July (in vain), "Having known him in former years, it is a painful thought that anyone in such circumstances should think him or herself forgotten by former friends – so, if it is possible, or in your judgement advisable to convey to him merely the message that I have remembered him daily in intercession."

Joseph Conrad maintained a dismissive view of Casement's political efficacy and gave his old Congo acquaintance a wide berth. In a letter to his friend John Quinn in New York, he declared, "What he wanted to bring about would have been necessarily financial for the most part, with German money. As to German blood I imagine they would not have had any to spare in that quarter. It was a mere intrigue and they would have seen Ireland drained to the last drop of blood with perfect equanimity as long as it helped their military action on the continent forward, an inch or two." In an obscure rider, Conrad added that Casement in 1896 had been taken up by the then prime minister: "A Home Ruler accepting Lord Salisbury's patronage couldn't be taken very seriously."[977] This may refer to Casement's 1895 mission to Delagoa Bay. In his notes to Counsel in 1916 Casement described how Lord Salisbury had telegraphed him to go "as Special Commissioner to investigate the conditions there"; in other words to spy on whether the Portuguese were as neutral as they claimed to be.[978]

The intervention of Julio Arana in a pathetic letter from Manaos of 14 June addressed to Casement at the Tower of London, was intriguing especially to see what line of attack he would take. Arana had been in London in 1913 to give evidence at the select committee enquiry where he had received a mauling. Now he invoked divine justice and suggested Casement was controlled by Colombian agents: "You influenced the Judges in the Putumayo affair who by your ill-influence confirmed your own statements. You tried by all means to appear a humaniser in order to obtain titles fortune, not caring for the consequences of your calumnies and defamation against Peru and myself, doing me enormous damage. I pardon you, but it is necessary that you should be just and declare now fully and truly all the true facts that nobody knows better than yourself."[979] No mention was made of Casement's sexuality.

Adler was not to come to London for the trial. There was no need for his evidence. Indeed, knowing Adler as the Foreign Office did, they were well aware he could only be a loose cannon in the witness box. There was never any real intention to swap the treason charge for one of buggery as it would have entirely diminished the desired effect of destroying a traitor. The one attempt made by F.E. Smith to capitalise on the diaries, during the trial, was designed to tempt Casement's counsel into a plea of insanity, which would of course have destroyed the prisoner politically and in every other way except physically. (Casement had attempted suicide by poisoning himself on Easter Wednesday in the Tower of London. He rubbed curare, provided by the Germans, into a wound he made on his fingers.) Serjeant Sullivan declined even to be drawn into the projection and returned the typed diary copies unread.

The Scotland Yard officers in Philadelphia did see Adler a second time. But he returned without any of the promised documents, remarking "he had been led on to say a great deal more than he intended." He explained that he had wanted "to get even with Devoy." The two had come to blows over Devoy's attempt to stop him associating with a German lady, presumably Margarette. Devoy had also "remonstrated with him as to his gambling habits" which is an interesting new angle on his vices. Adler asked for fifteen dollars a week for his wife if he was absent in London giving evidence and a down payment of 700 dollars. The Yard report commented that he was "an unscrupulous person" who was in fear of the American police. He could not even be relied upon to fulfil his promise of a couple of days earlier. Indeed he was probably working-up to a double cross.

What is surprising is that his treachery became known to John Devoy. Perhaps Adler told him of it to extract money in a Christiania-style triple cross. Devoy, on 20 July 1916, in a letter copied to London by the American authorities, wrote of how Adler's betrayal had been prevented: "Christensen was going over from here to testify against him – and incidentally to give away all our secrets that he had got from Roger – *but we kept him here.*"[980] Oddly where any other Irish informer could expect to have been executed, both Devoy and McGarrity treated Adler like an errant child, the latter assisting both him and Margarette several times over the next few years.

In the meantime London invested considerable effort into the Norwegian end of the affair. In mid-July 1916 a number of statements were transcribed and sworn in front of the British vice-consul H. Charles Dick. A local private investigator called Jensen was put on the job and it is plain from some of the crude positioning what he thought was required of him. A number of the statements ring true while others are little more than accumulated gossip, possibly based on misinformation from Adler who was quite capable of laying a trail of confusion and contradictory stories.

The papers do not reveal the precise intention of this information gathering exercise except for two terse messages on the file from Basil Thomson to Ernley Blackwell, the co-ordinator of Casement information. At the end of a letter dated 26 July 1916, largely devoted to how he had provided diary copies to the American ambassador with the "filthy" parts pinpointed, Thomson added "I sent for some further statements, sworn and unsworn. Not much in them." They were forwarded the next day, Thomson minuting simply that these were "further police reports about R.C.'s doings in Norway."[981]

Casement was a week away from execution so a second trial on sex charges was now irrelevant. It is most likely that as with the despatch of the two policemen to see Adler in Philadelphia the team were hoping to dredge up some high quality evidence of Casement's homosexual activities, such that could be shown to ministers should the diary copies not work their charm. The Cabinet had already discussed the question of reprieve after Casement's appeal was lost on 18 July and would return to the matter on 21 July and 2 August. There were divisions of opinion of which Sir Ernley was keenly aware. Foreign interventions were growing apace. There was even a plea from the Colombian President recalling Casement's humanitarian efforts to save lives in the Amazon region (and Colombian territory). None came from his Peruvian counterpart.

Another unsuccessful plea came from Canon T.S. Lindsay, of Christchurch

Cathedral in Dublin, who wrote of Casement (and his effect on the Canon's wife), in fine Church of Ireland mode: "He lived in my parish for several months in 1914, and I had various opportunities of conversing with him & of observing his character.

"The impression left on me was that with much quick-witted intelligence, culture & experience of life, he was a crack-brained fanatic, & with such a distorted mind as to scarcely be responsible for his actions. He seemed to possess some strange psychic power which fascinated & almost paralysed the minds of those whom he sought to influence, & my wife thought him the most interesting & charming man she had ever met. But he had the habit of walking bareheaded and swinging his arms in the air, so that the people thought him mad. I have since been told that there is a strain of insanity in his family. This can be easily verified by enquiry in Co. Antrim.

"But looking at the case from the point of view of the welfare of Ireland, I am satisfied that to hang him, richly as his actions deserve it, would be to erect him into a popular hero, like Lord Edward Fitzgerald, or the 'Manchester Martyrs'. If possible, I would suggest that he should be confined to a criminal lunatic asylum. This would prevent invidious comparison with the fate of Capt. Bowen Colthurst."[982]

Blackwell's major effort against a reprieve in the form of his famous memorandum to Cabinet was already written, but he wanted back-up material and tried to ensure he had a reserve. The Norwegian research was in truth more damning of Adler than Casement. It was a poor crop and evidentially weak. Basil Thomson had the best (indeed only) witness brought over from Christiania who presumably travelled at some personal risk to himself. This was Gustav Adolph Olsen, the "Chief Reception-clerk" at the Grand Hotel, who was now installed in Piccadilly's Strand Palace Hotel. He alone could recount seeing some untoward activity of a sexual nature, actually in progress. Olsen's statement was taken on 21 July by Inspector Joseph Sandercock, Casement's escort in London, and someone he chose to write to, calling him an Englishman of "native good heart."[983]

In his signed and witnessed statement, Olsen recounted how just after midnight on 28 October 1914, the German Naval Attaché had asked to see Mr Landey (Casement). Going to room 442, Olsen said he "knocked and opened the door without waiting for an answer, and found Landey and Christensen half-naked and in a suggestive position over the bed." He reported also that the German stayed until six the next morning, while the chambermaid told him Adler's bed in room 443 had not been slept in. Olsen described him as "about twenty-two years of age and youthful appearance: he was clean shaved, fresh complexion and good looking." He recounted also how Adler had stayed there again in November and December 1914, carrying American gold coins, buying drinks all round and bragging that "his supply was far from drained." Once he was accompanied by two female relatives who had a separate room. Olsen had earlier reported on Adler's alcohol usage during these visits, saying he "was drunk in the Grand Café and complained of being refused drink" and that he later "went off to Moss with three bottles of Champagne."[984]

A somewhat different version of the same story occurs in a communication of 13 March 1915 from Findlay to Arthur Nicolson at the Foreign Office: "My informant (who is a respectable man) was asked to go himself to Landy's (Casement's pseudonym) room, he consented and found Casement and Christensen sitting on Casement's bed with their arms round each other. They were not undressed but the nature of their relations was evident."[985] The informant could only be Olsen yet his 1916 statement differs significantly in that the definite physical embrace is not mentioned and the two men's proximity is only described as "suggestive". Although one or both were said in the later statement to be half-naked, where previously it was "not undressed", Olsen is plainly pulling in his horns should his evidence be tested. Being half-naked in a hotel bedroom is hardly damning or unusual.

Olsen's statement was quite moderate compared to the others, which rose to a crescendo of orchestrated slagging-off of Adler, mediated only by an attempt to lay the blame on Casement for corrupting him. Two porters at the Grand Hotel, Messrs Suck and Russ, reportedly told of screams being heard from Adler's room when Casement was present, as well as "vociferous discourse." Adler later told friends how Casement had been brutal to him in the night and how he had then left his service. Suck and Russ also told of Adler using aliases such as Smith and Pederson and of the consequences of Casement's brutality: "Christensen was ill, he had pain in his rectum, and visited a surgeon several times." Neither Russ nor Suck would make written statements as "it was too filthy a job for them to have their names connected with in any way." These tales may have been told by Adler to lay a smokescreen in Christiania but their choice was nonetheless revealing. The point of forced anal sex can be discounted as it does not tally with the chambermaid's evidence of Adler's unused bed, apart from it being entirely unlikely.

Signor C. Gatti, the Head Waiter, "a well known personality among Hotel porters and waiters, Italien of nationality" wrote his statement in French. He did sign his, and it was sworn before Mr Dick. It contained identical stories and the same phrasings right down to Adler's aliases and the "*douleurs dans son rectum."* All three recounted very precisely how Adler had said the British minister did not request him to kill Casement rather he, Adler, wanted to kill him on his own account. This was plainly a piece of evidence sought out by the investigator to provide a defence for Findlay. His need for cover must have been made apparent to Jensen but the effect was so laboured as to be counter-productive. As it happened, Casement (for Adler reasons) had made it plain to his solicitor in 1916 he did not want the Findlay affair raised "at all."[986]

Porter Kurth at the Victoria Hotel had the most vituperative things to say about Adler "the biggest pig he ever had heard about." But all were second hand: "He was not only a sodomite but he was also a blackmailer, and he used it as a sport. When he had been with some people together, he tried to blackmail them later." The stories Kurth had heard ring true but for the fact that Adler had been away from Norway most of his adult life and had simply not had the time for much prolonged blackmail, neither then nor indeed later.

On 17 July a gentleman, H. Degerud, living at 12 Ovrevoldgate, concluded the evidence for the prosecution. He had seen Adler "in the company of a well-known 'sodomite' from Bergen, the German teacher of languages named Bauermeister." Degerud declared on oath that while staying at the Grand, Casement and Adler "provided sure proof that they were 'sodomites'" (*sodomitter* in the Norwegian original) and that that "opinion was general among the staff" who came into contact with them. He added a rider however: "It is beyond all doubt that it is Sir Roger Casement who has caused Christensen to become a homosexualist (*homosexuelle* in Norwegian) and so ruined him, and that is the general opinion among those people who knew Adler Christensen before he made Casement's acquaintance."

Degerud was probably accurate about the teacher as mention of such an individual turns up in Casement's papers. The question of his sexuality is not verifiable but it seems from the way Adler was behaving in Christiania that there was some sort of gay scene operating, indeed some of the hotel staff and witnesses may well have been part of it. In an undated letter Casement confirmed Bauermeister's existence when he drafted "Dearest Adler, Ask the schoolmaster to try and get these published in a Norwegian paper...the more the world knows about Ireland and what it is we are trying for and that our cause is really theirs too for until the sea is free no nation is really free and as long as England keeps Ireland she keeps the ocean chained."[987]

In the briefest, and penultimate, declaration, an Inspector of Taxes, E.W. Jacobsen, wrote on 19 July "I desire to state that I have ascertained that Adler Christensen is now known to be a 'sodomite'." Why or how a man in his profession had so ascertained, remains a mystery.

Only Kurth (and Jacobsen) failed to blacken Casement in one way or other but a certain defence of Adler was being mounted, and continued in the final statement. Jensen had remarkably obtained a signed, although unsworn declaration from Adler's mother Henriette, which must have been an embarrassing operation. She stated on 18 July 1916 that her son, Eivind Adler, had "previous to his journey to America in 1906 no homosexual tendencies." He was then sixteen. She conceded that "If Adler has since that time entered into relations of that nature with Sir Roger Casement I am convinced that Casement must have induced him to do it and thereby destroyed his previously pure character. When he was at home from Germany on a visit in November & December 1914 and until January 1915 he avoided all information about his relations with Casement."

In one area this reveals an Adler lie. He had told Casement it was twelve years since he had seen his parents. It was obviously no more than eight. While a mother's evidence can only be suspect, Adler, at home, was certainly not telling the same stories about Casement as those with which he was regaling the staff of the Grand Hotel. As Mrs Christensen in 1915 had assisted Captain Monteith by putting him up overnight, she was plainly keeping mum about what Adler had told her of Irish affairs. It is hard to believe Adler was silent about his earlier adventures since Monteith records considerable assistance from the Christensen family in enabling him to escape unnoticed from Moss.

McGarrity kept up a correspondence for a time with Adler, and with his second wife for over fifteen years. He helped her out financially and with the process of ending her later US marriage. Her new husband-to-be was a judge in Berlin and, as she advised McGarrity, someone who did not relish committing bigamy himself.[988] She had also been worried that on her father's death Adler might reappear "if he knew he had a chance to live a life of leisure at my expense."

Fragments of Adler's later life also appear in McGarrity's records, the most substantial being a letter from San Francisco of 25 May with a reference to influenza, which makes the year probably 1918. Adler, brazen as ever, suspects there may be something afoot to his advantage and cannot disguise his eagerness: "Dear Joe, Received your registered letter of May 20th after I had given up hope off ever hearing from you again after not receiving any answer to my letter of 6-7 months ago. I am doing fine. My wife is fine. Baby was borne Feb. 18th 1917. Her name is Margarethe Christensen. Please write your promised long letter at once, as we are both very anxious to know the real cause of your inquiries. Adres your letter to Ad. C. c/o United Railroads. I hope you and your family are allright did you have the flu. Please answer soon. With friendly regards from my wife and myself."[989] McGarrity even had a photograph of little Margarethe in his correspondence collection.

Margarette related on 16 September 1920 that McGarrity's promise of a loan for her and the baby to return to Europe was no longer necessary.[990] At another, later, point she tells of being five years with Adler in America and four in Germany, which makes it a nine year relationship – presumably with long gaps.[991] A cryptic 1922 note[992] from Adler now signing himself Olaf Olsen, a surname Casement had used as an alias for Christensen when writing to McGarrity[993] from Germany, read, "I will be out soon now" suggesting he was in prison. Margarette's repeated remarks about never wanting to see Adler again and of the torment of her time with him, indicate living with a charming sociopath had been deeply unpleasant. Adler then slid out of history.

However, it now appears he married again in 1928 in Winnipeg. His new wife was a 19-year-old German girl called Hedwig Kreppner whom he met on board a ship from Germany. The marriage did not last although they had a son, born in 1929. His family heard later Adler was 'in the opium dens in Vancouver'. Recent research by the author, Bjørn Godøy, who in 2016 published a biography, *Dobbeltspill*, of his fellow Norwegian, uncovered details of his pathetic death in Fresnes, a Paris prison, on 1 December 1935, aged 45, the proximate cause being suffocation due to the vomiting of blood (hematémèses). Since 1931, Adler (recorded as Edwind) had been convicted several times in France of robbery and of avoiding deportation, being sentenced on the last occasion (16 August) to eight months. His effects consisted of a white metal watch and forty francs. He was interred on 4 December at 10 a.m. as Ivan Christensen. Adler's life of crime was over.[994]

Casement believed in him until as late as 1916, himself by then in Brixton prison: "He never suspected Christiansen [sic] of treachery to himself until this year – he made no other comment", as he told Alice Stopford Green,[995]

On 26 June, Casement's trial opened in front of Sir Rufus Isaacs, the Lord Chief Justice, who had recently become Viscount Reading. It lasted four days. The charge of treason required evidence of adherence to the King's enemies. The Crown case was weak on specifics in this department while the prosecution certainly felt proof of actual linkage to Germany was a necessity. Relating Casement to the *Aud* and its arms importation was thought to be of critical importance once the defence failed in its motion that high treason was only appropriate to the Defence of the Realm Act and thus an invalid charge under the 1351 Treason Act.

The key to the arms aspect being proved as treason was reckoned to be the secret code found in Kerry which Casement had brought with him to communicate with the Germans – whether on the *Aud* or in Berlin was immaterial. It carried a host of possible messages such as "Keep agent back"; "Further rifles are needed"; and "Send more explosives" all with specific code numbers.[996] Not that these particularly damning details were ultimately considered of much significance by the Lord Chief Justice. He directed the jury that treason would have occurred if Casement knew that the Irish Brigade was designed to fight in Ireland. In other words if the German enemy could simply be assisted by such activity, even indirectly, there was no need to prove association with Germany itself. Suggestions about the Brigade preparing to fight in other theatres of war (such as against Russia, untruthfully evidenced in one instance) were largely irrelevant to the case, even if harmful to Casement.

The introduction into evidence of the 'Egyptian clauses' in the Brigade Treaty with Germany was Casement's other greatest concern. He feared that Bailey might mention them if he went into the witness box and asked that a message be got to his solicitor if it could be done "without fear of him blabbing." Casement was surprised that London had not got hold of details of the Treaty and its two treasonable articles which allowed the Brigade to fight with the Turks "for Egyptian national freedom." As he told Gavan Duffy: "It was 'all for Ireland' up to my reading them out" at one particular meeting in March 1915. Yet none of the soldier witnesses made mention of the offending clauses in their statements.

Another potential source for the Treaty details reaching the prosecution stemmed from the arrest on 1 May of Karl Liebknecht, the German socialist leader. He was charged with attempted war treason because of a speech he had made in the Reichstag on 8 April about Casement. While still in Germany, Casement had been advised of the speech. "How Liebknecht got a hold of this, goodness only knows"[997] he noted. The charging was reported on 16 May in the *Daily Chronicle* and Casement sent the clipping to Gavan Duffy, scribbling alongside it, "I am still anxious on this matter." It could be dangerous for several reasons, but the most obvious and immediate was that Liebknecht's alleged crime had been reading out the Brigade Treaty in the Reichstag. He had prefaced his remarks by saying that Germany had entered "a treaty with the arch-traitor Sir Roger Casement whereby English soldiers were to be used against England." Luckily, Liebknecht's quotation of the actual details had been suppressed in the German newspapers.[998] He was ultimately not so fortunate, being shot with Rosa Luxembourg by Free Corps officers in January 1919.

Casement, however, had a great many incriminating papers in his possession during the trial, including a copy of the Treaty which he lost between prisons.* Where he got it from remains a mystery. On 30 June, from Pentonville Prison, Casement asked Gavan Duffy to recover from the High Court of Justice or the Home Office, documents and papers contained in a canvas portfolio which he

* He told Gertrude and Elizabeth Bannister on 30 July 1916 (PRONI T3306/F/4), "I left a book for each of you at the High Court yesterday. I bought it in from Brixton to give you each – thinking I could have seen you at luncheon time – or later – but I was carried off after sentence – and the books and the papers with them were left on a side table in the waiting room where I had had my food – those excellent luncheons you sent me in each day."

had brought in from Brixton Prison to give to him, saying they were documents dealing with the trial and that it was "very important that they fall into no hands but yours".[999] Returned to him, Casement asked that the documents be sent out to Gavan Duffy! They were then, as usual, passed first for censoring to Ernley Blackwell who must have thought Christmas had come early. He made especial use of the Treaty and the boastful admissions of unfortunately inadequate treason he also found, to assist in averting a Cabinet reprieve.[1000]

Casement correctly surmised of "that fatal portfolio. That is really my death warrant I think. There are too many things in there to be passed over."[1001]

The result was probably a foregone conclusion although the trial was otherwise conducted in a thorough, and generally fair, manner. On 29 June, Sir Rufus Isaacs donned the black cap to pass sentence of death. Casement for the second time rose and was permitted to make his famous speech from the dock. His first intervention had been an unsworn statement – one consequently not subject to cross-examination, in which he dealt with certain false accusations made by witnesses about the Irish Brigade. A distressed Gertrude Bannister later wrote "to hear the Jew Isaacs pronouncing those dread words and ending up with 'May the Lord have mercy on your soul' – was so awful and revolting to me that I murmured 'And may he have mercy on yours'."[1002] Casement, when in Germany, had been obligingly provided by Richard Meyer with a copy of Robert Emmet's speech from the dock. In that 1803 case, the 1st Earl of Norbury, an ancestor of Casement's friend, had typically announced he did not sit on the bench to listen to treason, but Isaacs did not interrupt Casement. Emmet's epitaph would in five years be able to be written, thanks in no small measure to Roger Casement.

Sergeant Daniel Bailey of the Irish Brigade – a man captured in Tralee a day after the landing – then entered the dock. At the surprising request of the Attorney General, F.E. Smith, he was duly found not guilty by the jury and freed. He wisely slipped out of public history after the trial, although he does get a mention on the Casement monument at Banna Strand, but only as an unnamed "third man" who came ashore to further "the cause of Irish freedom."

After recall to the British Army and serving in former German East Africa and Egypt, Bailey emigrated to Canada in 1921. Firstly, however, in 1917, he married a widow he had known in London, Katerina O'Dea, née Friedrich, born in Germany in 1865. She died in 1924 and, in 1926, he remarried an 18-year-old girl called Clara Nash and they had a son. He died in Ontario in 1968.

It would be wrong to say Bailey betrayed Casement, not least because Casement was informing the authorities in Tralee, and most everyone else, of the imminent rising. Neither did he give 'King's Evidence' in court. Indeed

Bailey was far from frank with his local interrogators about the details and purpose of their mission, despite his, not unreasonable, efforts to escape the gallows. His motives seem mixed, much as McGoey's, although he was no sociopath like Adler Christensen.

The appeal, which was delayed to give Serjeant Sullivan time to recover from his breakdown, opened on 17 July, over a fortnight later. Sullivan concentrated entirely on the same area of argument he had made at the trial about the meaning and interpretation of the 1351 treason statute of Edward III. (Casement had usefully pointed out that that English King was never King of Ireland.) Ominously, the bench felt there was no need to call upon the Attorney General to reply. After a short retirement, the judges returned to dismiss the appeal, dealing at length nonetheless with the matters raised by Sullivan, and praising his efforts. As the other points "in the notice of appeal questioning the summing-up of the Lord Chief Justice had been entirely withdrawn by the appellant's counsel" the presiding judge said it was unnecessary "to say more about them."[1003]

Both Casement and Gavan Duffy were critical of Sullivan's decision to drop the attack on the Lord Chief Justice's direction to the jury regarding "aid and comfort to the King's enemies" and to his decision to admit certain evidence regarding recruitment to the Irish Brigade. Sullivan decided to sit on a one-legged stool and disregard both his client and his instructing solicitor, as barristers usually do, Casement observing wryly that he would have preferred his two Welshmen (Jones and Morgan) on their own. Gavan Duffy felt, in particular, that if those aspects had been argued by Sullivan it would have put the case for an appeal to the House of Lords on a stronger footing. He may well have been right but there was another hurdle to jump in that quarter, one that was insurmountable.

The only person who could grant leave to appeal to the Lords was none other than the Attorney, F.E. Smith. A point of law of exceptional public importance was required and Duffy argued cogently that there were several, not least the gravity of the crime; the bewildering nature of the 1351 statute; and the need to prove to Irishmen that justice was not being denied. Galloper Smith's decision to deny Casement that final avenue of appeal was a disgrace. Given his past involvement with Irish affairs and his present political position he should have erred on the side of transparency. Justice is not the same as fairness, but this was unjust.

Only a reprieve now stood in the way of the gallows. Despite petitions, none was ever likely to succeed. A changed mood on Ireland would in time have worked, or significant concern coming out of America, but there was insufficient momentum that July. The notable names on Irish petitions, although including Cardinal Logue who signed strictly "from motives of mercy and charity" (and several other bishops), Joe Devlin, Tim Healy and Stephen Gwynn, otherwise consisted of Casement's friends: Mary Spring Rice, Mrs Mary Hutton, Evelyn Gleeson, Douglas Hyde, Edward Martyn, AE, and Lord ffrench.*

And there were other voices in Ireland. One was quoted by Ernley Blackwell's superior, the Permanent Under-Secretary at the Home Office, Sir Edward Troup, in a memo of 17 July 1916 to the Cabinet, endorsing that of Blackwell. Troup remarked that if Casement's "execution is carried out, the knowledge of his immoral character, which is probably by this time fairly well spread [changed from "well known"] in Ireland, will tend to alienate sympathy from him and prevent him being treated as a martyr." He then quoted a letter from "a supporter of Home Rule" (possibly Sir Horace Plunkett) who argued that "if Casement, a Protestant, an ex-official, and a member of the 'ascendancy' class is let off the extreme penalty, while mere Catholic nationalists like Pearse and Macdonagh were executed out of hand, although their guilt was really less deep than his, a bad impression will certainly be made in Ireland."[1004] An opposite, and what should have been an alarming view, came from a JP in Co. Meath on 29 July: "If Roger Casement is hanged, England will get no more of my sons and I have nine."[1005]

Casement was finally guaranteed going to the gallows because of the co-incidental public outcry in England concerning the hanging by the Germans on 27 July of Captain Charles Fryatt. His cross-channel ferry, the *Brussels*, had rammed a German submarine leading to Fryatt being later seized, court martialled as a British *franktireur* and sentenced to death. A reprieve, never likely although Casement sometimes notioned it, would in these circumstances have been politically untenable. In truth, diaries or no diaries, nothing but time would have enabled him to escape the gallows.

As the execution drew closer Casement made his final dispositions. *The Confessions of St Augustine* given to him by Father Murnane went to Edward Bannister: "Roger Casement specially desired this should be given to you after his death" wrote Gavan Duffy in a final attempt to save Squiggy's soul.[1006] *Meditations for Lay Folk* went to Sidney Parry, while the only bit of Casement that Ada McNeill was ever to be granted were his spectacles, along with the hope that she "would never have any need to use them."[1007]

The conversion to Rome presented a series of well-documented difficulties and a surprise to most – Casement's early Catholic baptism in North Wales. It was duly confirmed from parish records in Rhyl. As a boy, probably more in an echo of his Irish political sentiments, he was wont to say (as reported by Lizzie Bannister) "If ever I left the Church of England I should become a

* The English petitions managed to get John Galsworthy, John Masefield and John Drinkwater's signatures, over and above the usual suspects like GBS and the Webbs.

Catholic…I am a Catholic at heart. I think I have always been one."[1008] In 1911, and for a number of years, Casement was happy to state privately "I am not Protestant"[1009] although politically he still traded on his ethnic Protestantism. He was to tell Gee on 20 July 1916, "I think I must become a Catholic before I die. I always wanted to – or felt inclined to I must say. And since beginning of the year I was taking definite steps & was in touch with a good Bavarian priest, Fr. Fischer. I shall be dead before the anniversary (5th Augt 1868) of our baptism in the Catholic church at Rhyl. Up to this I have not taken the necessary steps – because I want only to act on clearest acceptance and conviction – not from emotion. And this takes time. I am, and am not convinced. At times I think all is settled – but some fresh doubt arises within and pulls down the fabric – and now with my end so close I don't like galloping."[1010]

Yet Casement had certain intellectual problems hinged to whether he actually believed at all. In 1911 he was saying to Alice Stopford Green "There can be no heaven if we don't find it and make it here" and moreover, in an unusually frank remark about the Catholic Church, he wrote that "with its preposterous claims to be the beginning and end of all life [it] is a mental and moral stumbling block."[1011]

Casement expressed his doubts to Father Murnane on 16 July: "I have not been so happy of late in my mind, or in my spirit, as I was – doubts and perplexities assail me and leave me troubled – troubled always at myself and my own imperfect understanding. There are times when I feel that my doubts are settled and then they revive and I cannot say what motive actuates me. It is very hard to be sure of one's convictions – to be certain always one is convinced – I thought I was – and today and yesterday I am not sure – and questions come to me, from myself, that I find no answer to. The trouble is – am I convinced? Or do I only think I am? Am I moved by love or fear? I can only accept, in my soul, from love – never from fear – and part of the appeal seems, at times, to be my fear – the more I read the more confused I get – and it is not reading I want, but companionship. I am sure you understand.

And then I don't want to jump – or rush – or do anything hastily just because time is short.

It must be my deliberate act – unwavering and confirmed by all my intelligence. And, alas! to–day it is not so. It is still, I find, only my heart that prompts, from love, from affection for others, from association of ideas and ideals, and not yet from my full intellect. For if it were thus the doubts would not beset me so vigorously as they do. I am not on a rock, but on a bed of thorns."[1012] These somewhat Protestant uncertainties had a fortnight to be talked through and resolved with his spiritual advisers, who were by this time quite thick on the ground.

There was also the political problem faced by England's Cardinal Bourne who had a difficult balancing act in front of him. Casement would have known precisely what it involved, for his most sustained criticism of the Roman Catholic Church came from observing its preference for England's conversion over Ireland's freedom. This was true of even the Irish Church, "the fight with them is largely to Catholicise Great Britain and develop their hold on every department of Irish life" he once wrote.[1013] The Cardinal would be in enough trouble in England explaining the admission of a traitor into the Church but when the man was also a known "moral pervert" it put him in an impossible bind. Bourne had been duly advised of the diaries, noting "I was informed on the highest authority that his moral life had been deplorable" although he ultimately promised to offer his "mass for him on the day of his death."*

Bourne therefore sought a signed statement of sincere repentance for scandal caused, public or private. This referred not just to his sexual life but also to the trial evidence of the POWs in Germany. Casement declined "in all humility" to sign a paper "which would brand him as a man of ill-fame, a test which would not have been imposed in Ireland [and which] would strengthen the scandalous rumours as to his private life [that would circulate] with greater force afterwards if such an instrument were known to have been signed by him."[1014] Bourne's reluctance led to Gavan Duffy going over his head to Rome where he had good contacts. But he was ultimately advised by Father Murnane not to take the matter further. He pointed out that anti-clericals would only exploit it, adding "The Bishops and Priests of Ireland are doing their share for the new Ireland"[1015] which in due course would justify Duffy's public silence.

In the end the emergency posed by the execution overtook the normal rules and Casement was able, *in articulo mortis*, to become a confessed and communicant Catholic – for less than twenty-four hours. He died on the day he took his first communion. Father Thomas Carey told Sidney Parry, two days later on 5 August, "He sobbed like a child after his confession and his contrition for any sins he may have committed was intense. From the way he spoke repeatedly of you, I know you will be glad of all this. Don't think I exaggerate in the least – I was deeply touched by his death, and I had got to love him during the month he was under my care. I am going away for a month for a rest – I need it much."[1016]

---

* Quoted by Daniel Vangroenweghe at the April 2002 Goldsmiths College Casement colloquium and referenced to Westminster Cathedral's archives. He is a Belgian historian and anthropologist who has written extensively on the Congo. A Professor of African History at Ghent University, Vangroenweghe published an article, *Casement's Congo Diary, one of the so-called Black Diaries, was not a forgery,* in the Journal of Belgian History in 2002.

In reply to F.J. Bigger's message, "Has ship Hope arrived yet?", Gavan Duffy was obliged to telegram, "The ship has foundered." On 3 August he added the message: "Roger Casement's body is dead and he died like the man he is, but his spirit will live for many a long day in Ireland. He has not died in vain."[1017] When it came to finding an address for probate purposes Gertrude Parry was not so sympathetic, saying on 25 October, "I do not think that Bigger's address will do as he does not seem to have shown any sign of life during Roger's last months."[1018] She similarly, and sourly, excluded Magherintemple "as Roger's address. It is his cousin Mr Roger Casement's home and the same cousin was most anxious to disclaim any connection with him."[1019] She thus failed to give any credit for the generosity that came from that quarter. Perhaps she forgot, for as she said "I alternate between calm and the most awful storms of rage and despair and misery but…must live through it."

Casement appointed Gertrude and Gavan Duffy executors of his estate in his will, which was dated 1 August 1916, and witnessed by two warders. He left £135.0.10. In a final official insult, unintended but undoubtedly satisfying to the officials involved, there was attached to the probate document on 21 February 1917 a standard endorsement that no portion of the assets could go, or be paid to, any beneficiary in Germany, Austria-Hungary, Turkey or Bulgaria.[1020]

17

The authenticity controversies

Every writer brings to the Casement story their own prejudices. Each, like Casement himself has their own background and consequently a set of predetermined opinions. The facts may change a few of those opinions but the core ideology will usually remain. You are what you were born or at least what you were brought up. And after reaching a certain age, even more so. The reader must try therefore to be, or become aware of an author's background or make-up as a critical primary piece of information. Where the question of the authenticity of Casement's Black Diaries is concerned that admonition is yet more crucial – although appearances can at times be deceptive.

The literature on the diaries is now enormous, and growing. As no witnesses to Casement remain alive and all the Home Office's known documentation was finally released in 1998 it is unlikely any devastating or conclusive information is yet to be uncovered. The five previously unknown MI5 files to which the public first gained access in January 1999, contained nothing especially dramatic or revealing. Although rich in certain detail much of the material had been copied to, or originated from other government departments and had already been seen and read. A small number of MI5 documents from these files were retained which does indicate a continuing sensitivity on the issue. This fact alone can and will feed the forgery school. However, nothing like the record of Christopher Marlowe's inquest which was discovered in 1925, more than three hundred years after the event, was surely liable to turn up now. The unlikely exception is an, as yet unknown, personal memoir or photographs.

There is no smoking gun to come. But there is really no need for one. The Black Diaries are such a smoking gun; they were and are a nuclear bomb, the elephant in the room. It takes a peculiar kind of propagandist or dissembler to argue, indeed to start to argue with any sort of assurance against their authenticity. Yet it has been done a hundred times in books, newspapers, magazines or on TV, before and after the key year of 1959 when access to the diaries was first granted. And as soon as the rug is pulled out from under one set of contrary ideas a new set replaces it. The reverse for those who do not cry forgery is true to only a small degree.

After the diaries were published by Singleton-Gates that same year of 1959 the fact of Casement's homosexuality was proven beyond all reasonable doubt. The previous defence against the charge, if charge it be, was shattered. It is now incumbent upon anyone putting up an alternate view to make a positive case for another lifestyle for Casement, rather than just picking the odd hole in the provenance or content of the diaries. Unlike F.E. Smith who, as Attorney General and state prosecutor, was required at the trial to convince a jury of Casement's guilt, those who deny the diaries' authenticity must convince us of their entirely fictional nature and prove that Casement was fitted-up.

Proof positive of innocence of the charge (of homosexual activity) is also required – not assertions of shady or slanderous endeavours by the establishment. Even the author Angus Mitchell, who has worked tirelessly to reverse the penultimate conventional wisdom – that the diaries are genuine – accepts that Casement's sexuality "will always be an ambiguous issue." Or in the words of Dr David Hope, when Archbishop of York, about himself, "a grey area." The problem for Mitchell, a modern forgery theorist, is that Casement is convicted, in his words, of being "a psychopathic predator" and a "pederastic exploiter" particularly by virtue of the 1911 Diary, if it is genuine. It may indeed be homophobic, as Mitchell says, to ascribe such activities (and consequent epithets) to a man who did not so act or think, but if he did and you believe in such descriptions of his sexual character, his whole reputation and most of his life's work sink below the acceptable. If not, they do not need to.

It is next to impossible to deal with global forgery theories whereby every single fact is doubted, inverted and then used against the person introducing the fact. The resurrected suggestion of complete forgery, albeit with the diaries woven together over many years by use of both seized Casement material and of official files, is anti-historical since it involves the impossibility of any conclusions ever being reached on any past event or individual's character. The total forgery theory also fails by its reliance otherwise only on inconsistencies, and the introduction of innuendo about peripheral Intelligence characters, rather than evidence, let alone proof positive, of faking.

But indicating that some of the academics involved in Naval Intelligence, in Old Building (OB) Room 40, in the First World War, were probably homosexual is beside the point – just as relying on Alan Turing's homosexual status would be if such alleged activity had occurred at Bletchley Park, its Second World War successor. One of the latest characters said to be guilty, in this instance only of authoring the text of the diaries (an allegation made public by Owen Dudley Edwards at the Royal Irish Academy Casement Symposium on 6 May 2000) is one beloved by those who hunt out establishment homosexual candidates. The name was that of Sir Frank Ezra Adcock (1886-1968), Professor of Ancient History and Vice Provost of King's College Cambridge. From 1915, Adcock who had trained "in the rigours of German scholarship"[1021] in pre-war Munich and Berlin worked in Room 40 breaking German codes and cyphers.

His friendship with his boss, Captain Blinker Hall (1870-1943) is exemplified by the fact that a drawing of Hall by the Dutch artist Louis Raemakers hung in Adcock's Cambridge rooms ever after. Even before the outbreak of war in 1939, he was recruiting for Bletchley Park, particularly Kingsmen. Adcock, however, returned early to his academic life, perhaps overtaken by the increasingly technical nature of codebreaking.

Everything about Adcock suggests he was homosexual; from his classic bachelor don status; to his friends and heroes like the poet A.E. Housman (whose portrait hung alongside Hall's), 'Dadie' Rylands, and Maynard Keynes; his love of theatre; his speech quirk; his opposition to women in King's College; his fussiness; care for male students; the maintenance of contacts with former undergraduates; and his annual fishing holidays in Yugoslavia with an invited young friend. Yet there is no experience of life abroad equivalent to Casement's nor any suggestion of a vindictive obsession sufficient to devote many years of secret work to researching and writing Casement's diaries. His private life appears devoid of sexual partners. No lovers or rent boys have surfaced, although it is always possible that he had a full, if discreet, sexual career. Also, and like Casement, there is in his history absolutely no evidence of heterosexual activity.

What is clear is that although he was no liberal, being a man of *realpolitik*, Adcock was too much the individualist to be drawn into a long, sordid conspiracy to further destroy the reputation of a hanged man who was, like himself, homosexual. When Alan Turing, the computer codebreaking genius whom Adcock is thought to have recruited into Bletchley Park, was facing a charge of public indecency, Adcock did not desert him and rather encouraged Turing to sit tight and not resign his college fellowship. In the event Turing was to choose suicide. After the First World War, Adcock seems to have had more than enough on his plate with his classics teaching, publishing, and college administration to devote himself to forging. Neither did he display or leave the slightest sign of a guilty conscience.

Surprisingly little is made of the fact that Blinker Hall did not just retire gracefully after a good war. Having fallen foul of a number of establishment figures for crossing the line between matters political and matters military, he chose to go the whole hog and stand for Parliament. The seat for which he was effortlessly nominated, and then elected was that vacated by F.E Smith, who had become Lord Chancellor and 1st Earl of Birkenhead in 1919. Hall was to sit for Smith's Liverpool seat of West Derby until defeated in 1923, and then for Eastbourne from 1925 to 1929 when he retired. It would not have been a co-incidence that Galloper Smith handed over his seat to Hall. He obviously came recommended, having developed a taste for political activity when Director of Naval Intelligence.

The suggestion that a Swiss named Zwingleman, under orders from Blinker Hall, forged the diaries has only recently emerged.[1022] The source for the allegation, published in 1998, in *The Barnes Review*, an anti-Semitic American journal devoted to holocaust denial was deputy Gestapo chief, Heinrich Müller, a participant in the 1942 Wannsee conference which formally arranged (or confirmed) the extermination of European Jewry. He supposedly made his way to the United States after the war and chose to tantalise and divert his American interrogator with assertions of British perfidy. The story he told was of German agents going to Zwingleman's house in Chur, murdering him and seizing his forgery samples: "The papers he was working on at the time we visited him concerned the alleged German development of poison gasses that they were trying out in concentration camps. Not true of course but quite convincing." Not much else (and no actual evidence) was proffered by the top Nazi bar an allegation that many upper-class Englishmen were "fumbling aunties."[1023]

It seems only inevitable that such a series of claims would ultimately be made. On investigation, the Zwingleman story, not unexpectedly, turns out to be entirely false. The Californian journalist Gregory Douglas to whom the article (one of two on Casement in that issue) is attributed, is a German operating under an assumed name, while Müller was last seen alive in Hitler's bunker in Berlin in April 1945. His interrogation was posthumous. Further, Dr Roger Sawyer in his speech to the Royal Irish Academy Symposium on 6 May 2000, disclosed the results of his research on Herr Zwingleman: the Swiss Federal archives had no record of any such individual while the local Chur archives director stated that the name was "totally unknown in our region and does not compare in the registers of Swiss family names."

What also has yet to come is pure conspiracy theory – sword and sorcery or ufology. As time progresses it assuredly will, and the roots or seeds are already visible. They appear in the form of a proper scepticism laced with an ineradicable conspiratorial belief in the all-powerful British establishment, as exemplified by its Intelligence services. This heady brew can easily progress to paranoia. But it only takes one wrong fact, one ill-based supposition to create suspicion in the mind of a reader. A good antagonist can then turn that acorn error into an oak tree. Accuracy in matters Casement is therefore vital as is painstaking research into all new theories.

This author, who has literally typed out the four Black Diaries, knows the extent of them, the myriad pieces of information that lie within the hundreds of pages and the thousand plus daily entries. There is an enormous and varied cast of characters, and that is only for the three years of inscription, 1903, 1910 and 1911. If it took him the best part of two years to type them up, to put bones to some of that cast and flesh to a few more by consulting dozens of directories, genealogies, histories, official records, censuses, biographies and indexes, what measurement could then be put to the time, personnel and the artistic effort involved in inventing and writing them up from scratch?

It would have been a superhuman feat. But no matter. For those who believe in their forgery it is a fact of faith, and faith can accept the supernatural or the extra-terrestrial. Faith can also adapt to fresh climates. That faith was originally derived from the cause of Ireland which Casement died for. Indeed despite two early warnings about the potential for Casement's sanctification, by Alfred Noyes and Rev. J.B. Armour of Ballymoney, that was exactly what happened. Armour, a Protestant Home Ruler, wrote presciently, on 30 August 1916, "I fancy that it will take a great effort to establish Casement among the martyrs and saints of Ireland though there are curious specimens of Irish martyrs and saints in the calendar."[1024]

Casement's looming martyr status was only accentuated by the extra trial he experienced, after execution when his reputation was sullied by England. Having added to the whole overheated atmosphere by becoming a Catholic in the death cell, he was further guaranteed saintly status. His Jesus-like looks, as in much popular contemporary Catholic iconography, brought a dramatically visual aspect to the whole confection. Being thought seriously handsome, and having a large and adoring band of female followers, only added greatly to the potential for the creation of a hero – one whose public life had been dedicated to the poor and oppressed. Ironically the Black Diaries ended up convincing people more of his virtue, while enhancing his humanitarian role and Republican status.

That faith has its origin in the peculiar combination of myth and religiosity which was to revolutionise Ireland. The Catholic nation, numerically devastated by famine, but strengthened by a vastly extended land ownership and a modernisation that had required seeing off the Gaelic language, was in 1914, by virtue of Ulster's continuing recusancy, seriously out of step with its power potential. The English-speaking Catholic majority in the south had now been denied achievable Home Rule in their area for two generations.

An almost mystical alliance of Catholicism and separatism, laced with Gaelic revival, was to overthrow its own nationally minded Home Rule elite through the blood sacrifice of 1916. Because of the special circumstances of the First World War, that alliance had, within five years, also seen off London. It had taken power because of a substantive but failed coup, made hegemonic by the execution of its leaders – including Casement. Although the Easter Rising was only popular after the event, some from the originating conspiracy within the IRB were aware of ultimate success being generated by glorious failure, or at least that by challenging fortune anything could happen. Ironically Casement did not share that view.

In post-independence Ireland it was not the Gael that was to predominate but the Roman Catholic Church, in alliance with the separatists. An English Catholic state emerged, but one that was, and existed to be, anti-British. The revolutionaries had unintentionally replaced Gaelic Ireland with Catholic Ireland. There was no room for a return to the old language and lore. History was not going to be peeled back in this department, no matter what Irish and Gaelic Republicans wanted.

The new Irish state did not just start a new future, it first obliterated the past, especially the recent past. Out went the Home Rule party – overnight, both the personnel and the politics. The returning veterans of the Great War were immediately overwritten, departing Irish history for eighty years. The inevitable post-revolution civil war created a two party system in the Irish Free State – both parties being derived from the personnel of Sinn Féin. The emblematic event of the new Ireland was to be the Eucharistic Congress of 1932. Ironically this Catholic state lasted only fifty years, at least in its ultra-puritan and inward looking form, and has now, in the south, seemingly evaporated.

In those circumstances Casement presented both a problem and a challenge. As part of that sacrifice, and singled out to be judicially executed – hanged, not shot, months after the other leaders faced their firing squads or were reprieved, his death hurt Ireland and his friends in the new leadership greatly. As that elite took power his role was amplified and it could be seen how critical he had been for a number of reasons, not least in his involvement in the founding of the Irish Volunteers and their initial arming, but also in his laying out of a foreign policy for the new state that would hold it in good stead for nearly a century.

But he was not just a party to the founding of the state, he was himself a saintly martyred figure, a humanitarian who sacrificed (that word again) himself for others, both in Ireland and beyond. It was not and could not be conceivable to believers that he was a moral degenerate guilty of sex crimes that were once so awful that Christians could not name them, *Inter Christianos non nominandum*, as Sir Robert Peel stated. Consequently the unseen diaries were specious and could only have been concocted. No matter what the evidence, that will remain the view of a critical number of old believers. They must not contemplate anything else or their faith dies; nor can they ever be convinced to let up their campaign.

The huge change in attitude towards homosexuality which the Irish Republic has recently adopted, late but zealously, and which puts it now in advance of Northern Ireland, presents a new problem. But if the British did the forging then London's intention to libel Casement replaces that difficulty. Even if Casement was homosexual, several hurdles remain for many Irish people. He often did it with teenage boys, frequently out of doors and also wrote down the details. These difficult moral issues, however, need not be addressed, indeed can be avoided, if the forgery issue stays centre stage. Just as is the case with a fellow Irishman and Protestant nationalist, Oscar Wilde whose penchant for young rent boys would still land him in gaol, the prosecution itself became the issue.

Each biographer to date has dealt with the question of authenticity in an appendix or a preface, while earlier books were devoted entirely to the subject. It would take a long time to revisit all those discussions. And it would be especially tedious as there is, or was thought to be, a dividing line between those, like Dr William Maloney who was writing in 1936 with no knowledge of the content of the diaries beyond a few terse descriptions about immorality and perversion, and those who had read the 1959 publication, or seen the diaries themselves at the Public Record Office in London from August of that year, or who had earlier bought one of the copies Singleton-Gates was hawking around London. However, Maloney was aware of descriptions of the contents, such as that by Casement's second defence counsel Artemus Jones who wrote of (as if he may have read) being given typed diary entries describing "acts of sexual perversion he had committed with other men…at various places including Paris, also towns in Africa and South America.[1025] Maloney, however, ploughed on, regardless of such detail while Angus Mitchell attempts to discredit Jones, describing him as "the most junior member of Casement's defence counsel" and one "chosen by Casement's prosecutor the Attorney-General."[1026]

Casement's lawyers were to be involved in disputes and recriminations for forty years after the execution. Serjeant Sullivan, his senior counsel, took vigorous issue during the Casement controversy that raged throughout April 1956 especially in the columns of the *Irish Times* consequent on the publication of René MacColl's book for which Sullivan was a key source. The Serjeant had had many discussions with his client after his first consultation on 12 June 1916 and could thus illuminate the matters in dispute. However, his memory was poor (in 1956 he was 85) while he plainly relished, most of all, a proxy fight with his Irish separatist enemies. Indeed he wrote off his antagonists in letters to the editor as "Casement worshippers." Much of the dispute centred around what Casement had actually told him on the question of the diaries and his homosexuality.

Sullivan was so divorced from the diaries, which he had never seen that he even surmised Adler Christensen had provided them. In an interview with the distinguished historian and journalist Robert Kee, Sullivan retold the 1916 story. Kee initially noted on 15 February 1956: "I have absolutely no doubt as a result of this interview that Roger Casement asked Sullivan to explain to the jury if the matter arose that there was nothing wrong about being a homosexual – that it was even a mark of distinction to be one" and that "Casement discussed his diaries as being diaries in the possession of the Crown and containing detailed accounts of acts of sodomy."

By 21 February, Kee had had justifiable second thoughts about Sullivan's remarks and reinterpreted his notes, instead writing "If certain material concerning Casement's private life were introduced into the trial that there was nothing discreditable about the personal attitude revealed in it…I have little doubt that some diaries of Casement's were discussed between Casement and Sullivan and that these diaries contained evidence of some sort, either of Casement's homosexuality or at least of deep platonic affection for other men."[1027]

In the *New Statesman* of 18 May 1957 Robert Kee took his scepticism a stage further and made a series of points about the diaries themselves; he reckoned there was no corroboration in style and content with the innocuous material in the NLI; that many homosexual entries bore a vague relation to a perfectly harmless, trivial diary phrase just preceding; and that many sexual items appeared at the beginning of a day's entry. Two of these points are to a degree true but in essence amount to little. In the case of sexual material often appearing at the beginning – more often the end of a day – one must remark that much of Casement's sexual activity was nocturnal and would therefore be recorded late in the night and last thing in the diary, or first thing in the morning. The matter of the relationship between sexual and mundane items just does not stand up especially in the torrid 1911 diary which Kee had not seen. The style was in many ways of itself, a diary style, (or one of several such styles) while there are no other private diaries extant to compare.

In the *Irish Times* of 16 April 1956 Sullivan felt obliged to rephrase his previous statements, having checked his memory. He conceded "On reflection, I perceive that he neither affirmed nor denied authenticity. He took up the attitude that we pygmies could not understand the conduct of great men and had no right to pass judgment on it…He was neither glorifying nor repudiating what was alleged against him." Not to be outdone, Sullivan added "Everyone seems to have forgotten, as I have done myself that Casement was a megalomaniac."

Nine days later, in a further letter to the *Irish Times,* Sullivan was finally forced to come completely clean. He honourably admitted that Casement "told me nothing about the diaries or about himself." Sullivan had up until then been extrapolating an admission and a full discussion from Casement's generalised remarks, which were probably uttered in the manner in which Gavan Duffy had tried to drill all concerned. It was not like Casement to be precise about his sexual status as the Dick Morten conversation also reveals. But it was well within his argumentative style to mention famous homosexuals of history in some sort of elucidatory and diversionary response. Casement on 30 June

1916 did allude, cryptically as ever, to the diaries when he wrote to Gavan Duffy asking him "to protect my name" and saying "you know why I kept silent and why I did not refute many things as I might have done."[1028] But he was undoubtedly less precise with Sullivan, who retired from the *Irish Times* correspondence and the controversy, dying in 1959.

Sullivan's 1949 BMH statement adds a little more precision and contradiction: "The second matter that troubled him was the fear that the prosecution would introduce, in the trial, the deplorable entries in his Diary. In fact, the Attorney General sent me a number of messages asking me to inspect the Diary and wired me that the Home Office would be open to me, day and night, up to the moment of the trial.

Sir Travers Humphreys, by direction of the Attorney General, handed me a full copy of the Diary on the morning of the trial. I did not read it but passed it to one of my juniors. I formed a very definite opinion that it was the desire of the Government to assist in the establishment of a defence of insanity. It was impossible that they could put the Diary in evidence, but though never formed in plain language, it was clear to me that they were anxious to persuade me, by the Diary to make that defence.

I did not even discuss it with Casement, beyond assuring him that the Diary would not be alluded to during the trial. He was very nervous about it, and in spite of my efforts to avoid the subject, he intruded the observation that the matters recorded in the Diary were inseparable from the manifestation of distinguished genius. He meant, no doubt, that if the matter did appear at the trial, this theory should be put forward, coupled with the notorious historical proofs. Beyond this strange occurrence there is I think nothing that is not better known to the public and to myself in connection with the trial."[1029]

When W.J. Maloney was researching his book he turned to Michael Francis Doyle who was near at hand in Philadelphia. Doyle told him that Casement had emphatically repudiated the diary story and had "requested us to obtain quotations of it." When told no access to it was permitted, Casement explained that they were notes of official investigations. Gavan Duffy responded privately and firmly to this particular aspect of the story. He wrote in 1933, firstly to say he had never seen such a diary nor a copy. But secondly in relation to Doyle's version of events, including the statement that the two men had together with Casement conversed about the diary issue, emphasised "I am wholly unable to corroborate it."[1030] He did not call anyone a liar but he was adamant about the precise truth of the matter.

Ernley Blackwell had been very particular about Doyle, wanting to ensure the American did not receive the privileges of a lawyer. He ordered that no private interviews were permitted and that his visits had to be "within sight and hearing of prison officers" although his papers were permitted to enter the country unexamined. Doyle was therefore never able to see Casement either alone or without a warder present and listening. The Brixton governor indeed sat in on the visit of 15 June and sent a report of what he heard to Blackwell, including the fact that Doyle was giving the impression of being uninvolved in Irish political matters.[1031] There may have been an occasion at court when Doyle, Duffy and Casement were together alone but, as Duffy wrote, he could not corroborate any conversation about the diaries.

The question of forgery is not simple but one clouded by a number of differing theories, some developed on the hoof. The primary problem, which remained unclear until 2000 was the provenance of the five diaries or notebooks now kept in the Public Record Office at Kew. Where precisely did they come from and when? Allied to that is a second question; if they are authentic, were there other diaries (and letters) and, if so, what happened to them? If a man maintains a diary for each of three years entering it up reasonably faithfully, there could be, or have been, another thirty or more such volumes.

Casement left for Montreal from Glasgow on 4 July 1914 heading for New York. This was the last day he would be a free agent in the United Kingdom. He landed off the submarine in Ireland on Friday 21 April 1916. As a man who had no dwelling house, his property was spread over a number of locations in Ireland and England, as well as in Germany and the United States. The diaries turned up at his Ebury Street lodgings in London's Pimlico, not far from Eaton Square. There were, however, three different Ebury Street addresses used by Casement over the years – Nos. 45, 50 and 55. No. 50 was where he latterly stayed during May and June 1914. He also kept a considerable amount of other belongings in London at the premises of his regular shipping agents, W.J. Allison in Farringdon Road. "Several loads of valuable books"[1032] were also left with Stephen Clarke at *An Tuirne Beag* near Ballycastle. Francis Bigger at Ardrigh in Belfast – Casement's most used Irish address – had custody of at least one trunk containing clothes and papers.

Until 1959 the only official information available as to the discovery of the diaries was a series of five different, and at times, contradictory accounts given by the Head of CID, Sir Basil Thomson, in various books and articles. Thomson indicated in one account that the diaries taken from Ebury Street had been in Scotland Yard's hands before the prisoner's capture although the trunk or trunks in which they lay had not been opened until he was brought to London.

Despite the varied Thomson stories, all other witnesses are consistent in maintaining that nobody saw the diaries or, by implication, knew of their remarkable contents until after Good Friday 1916. Indeed in the interrogation record, Casement was at one point asked for a key to his trunks although that may simply have been a ploy to see how he responded. In the event Basil Thomson claimed that Casement replied by telling his captors to break them open as they contained only old clothes and other mundane belongings. Perhaps significantly, when Casement needed clothes for his trial, he sought them from Bigger's cache rather than provoke the police into gratuitously poking further through his trunks. However, in an unsigned Home Office minute of 1 January 1959, a different and less dramatic account has been given. It complained that Montgomery Hyde "has taken from Sir Basil Thomson's book *The Scene Changes* a purely fictitious account of how Casement having been asked for the keys of his trunks said that they could be broken open, and a few minutes later the obscene diaries were brought in and placed before him. In fact the keys were asked for right at the end of the final day's interrogation and the diaries did not figure in the proceedings at all."[1033]

An interesting variant of the story, as recounted by Gertrude Parry (and unsourced), was that Casement's landlady (note not landlord) in late 1914 handed over his property to the police "at the instigation of another lodger."[1034] The importance of the date on which the state came into possession of the diaries relates to the time that would have unquestionably been needed to counterfeit even a few such complex pages. But it matters little, in that no high official in his right mind could have either dreamt up such a scheme or been permitted to put it into effect. A single letter would have produced almost as much damage, and more, if it had been put into the public domain. In the late 1990s, Jerry Hayes, a Tory MP with a liberal reputation, had his political career effectively destroyed by virtue of a small number of emotionally-charged notes, written to his male 'researcher' on House of Commons notepaper, being sold to a tabloid newspaper. Any forging that starts to introduce other characters and events is inherently dangerous and open to error. To revisit the particular events being written about in order to assist the counterfeiting, itself leaves a trail. None has ever been discovered, revealed, or even hinted at.

The official line on the time and place of the seizure of the diaries was first given in the House of Commons on 23 July 1959. The Home Secretary, R.A. Butler, said "The Casement diaries consist of five volumes found in a trunk which the landlord of Casement's lodgings handed to the police at their request on 25 April 1916, two days after Casement had arrived in London under arrest. The diaries were retained in Scotland Yard until 1925, since when they have been in the Home Office." Butler also warned, lubriciously, that any publishers of extracts would be doing so "at their own risk" having regard to the law of obscenity. No documentary evidence, however, about the discovery was provided.

It ought to erode the forgery case beyond recall if the date of seizure of the diaries was proved to be 25 April. This would indicate that there was insufficient time to set about forging before diary copies are known to have started circulating. The suggestion is still bruited about that official papers have been withheld which might prove that Casement's belongings were seized from Ebury Street as early as 1914. Yet the Home Office assured this author that all their Casement-related records "have now been released to the Public Record Office following a re-review prompted by a request from Lord Kilbracken."[1035] However, that did not rule out records being held by other agencies. Consequently after writing to Scotland Yard the most likely custodian of further papers, this author was gratified to learn that "the Metropolitan Police Service has a number of files relating to the activities of Casement, his arrest, trial and execution. All of these records are, however, currently closed as they contain information which is still sensitive." In view of the request for access, a promise was then made "in accordance with the Open Government Initiative" that a review would be pushed ahead.[1036]

So some unsuspected material was yet to come, but as in most matters Casement, it was surely bound either to fail to fully clear up known mysteries or actually to lead to more unanswered questions, given that anything written in that era was put on paper for an entirely different reason than what motivates present-day researchers or readers. In 2000, these records were still being reviewed and assessed for public release "en masse", with no piecemeal release or "privileged access" permitted.[1037] A telephone call was able only to elicit the fact that a "filing cabinet drawer full" of Casement material existed.

The 1999 release of MI5 papers did provide an implied date and other circumstantial details suggesting late rather than early discovery of the diaries, but no facts about how the police came to possess them. Backing up a date in 1916, was firstly the lack of paperwork in the MI5 files revealing Casement's trunks in Ebury Street coming into the possession of the authorities earlier. This of course did not negate or deny a previous hand-over or seizure. But the absence of any minutes or correspondence about his private papers or of secondary hints of knowledge of a long sodomitical history does suggest the underdeveloped Intelligence services knew little, and indeed cared less, about the consul's private life despite knowing of his homosexuality (and imminent treason) from the British legation in Norway as early as October 1914.

Seven items were eventually discovered at Allisons and handed over to Inspector Sandercock of the Metropolitan Police on 27 April 1916. In a statement, Mr Allison described these as "one American studded trunk, one tin trunk, one wooden trunk, one tin trunk (marked Roger Casement), one large canvas bag and one deck chair." (A seventh item was omitted from the actual list.) He added that he was totally ignorant of their contents and could not say on what date they were delivered into his care, except that it was previous to the outbreak of war. He also stated, somewhat plaintively, that there was "an account of fifteen shillings owing" in respect of Casement's packages.[1038]

The seemingly languorous approach to inspecting Casement's belongings is of a part with the amateurish and half-hearted manner in which MI5 and Scotland Yard addressed the whole question. There was of course a problem of the necessary powers and the division of responsibility, not to mention an apparently low level of staffing in the Intelligence Services. Basil Thomson explained the scenario thus: "The War Office had none of the machinery for arresting and keeping men in custody: the Metropolitan Police had: and so we found ourselves playing the role of general servant to the Admiralty and the War Office. My room at Scotland Yard became the meeting ground of the two Services."[1039]

The police had to be aware of a particular crime before they would properly investigate an individual or enter premises, and only with a view to obtaining evidence, as opposed to just gathering information. The only crime suggested to them was treason and even then it was not until after Casement's chance arrest that they put into train such an evidence-gathering operation. The notion that there was material suggestive of treason to be obtained within the United Kingdom, given that Casement left Britain for America in July 1914 (before war broke out) was obviously, and not unreasonably, discounted. Thus Bigger was left with one lot of sexually explicit paperwork in Belfast and a Casement landlord in Ebury Street with another.

Although Bigger's house never appears to have been searched or raided, he was put under surveillance once Adler Christensen had named him as a co-conspirator. This was done when he first went to betray Casement at the British legation in Christiania in Norway on 29 October 1914. Adler explained that if Casement was arrested he had to communicate the fact to Francis Bigger, "Solicitor, Ardmore [sic] Belfast." London was advised, "the Informer believed Bigger to be in the plot as his friend has assured him that Bigger would be able to secure his release by bribery or otherwise."[1040] Bigger would have been petrified to hear of this intemperate and inaccurate statement, based presumably both on Adler's memory and his perfervid imagination.

Bigger must surely have known he was the subject of police observation, which he had been since at least 1905 when he was reckoned to be behind the printing of anti-recruiting literature. The Belfast Police Commissioner agreed with the Dublin Metropolitan Police on this, but pleaded that year that it was "difficult to probe the matter owing to Mr Bigger's position. He is a solicitor of long standing in Belfast. He, however, favours the Cumann na Gaedhal."[1041] When a German submarine was seen off Killard Point at the entrance to Strangford Lough in January 1915, this was reckoned to be especially suspicious as he had a "house [Castle Seán] at Ardglass close by and there is a strong party of Sinn Fein in the neighbourhood." Belfast's assessment was that he "probably has not the pluck to be an active agent for the disloyal party (although) he certainly would gladly be their passive agent."[1042]

In their naivety, the Belfast Intelligence operation even investigated a local photographer named W. Allison, of Donegall Square North, in case it was connected to Casement's London agents. Long after London knew of Casement's arrival in mainland Europe, Belfast was so under-informed it was reporting that "Sir Roger Casement has not been heard of in the North of Ireland lately, indeed not since the end of July." On 4 November 1914, Major Frank Hall, MI5's agent in charge of Ireland, wrote that he thought Casement was in America, stating "I am awaiting further information on this point and also as to his habits (natural and unnatural!)."[1043] This remark only adds to the confusion: how was Hall unaware of Casement's arrival in Norway yet managing to appear party to the confirmation of his sexual orientation made by Mansfeldt Findlay, the British minister in Christiania? Unless Hall was just under informed by the Foreign Office bosses about the Norwegian events, the probability is that Casement's homosexual status was known in Belfast and was already the source of casual jokes in communication with London.

In time, all else that was done in relation to W.J. Allison was to obtain an authorisation, on 12 February 1915, to open any postal packet addressed to any name at its Farringdon Road premises. In this way, one illegible letter was intercepted, written by Robert Cunninghame Graham from Montevideo in Uruguay.[1044] F.J. Bigger's mail to Ardrigh in Belfast was also being opened. One missive, and the only one mentioned in MI5's file, from Casement's brother Tom in South Africa, caused some excitement since he had written "Can't say much in letter for obvious reasons." Tom shared the anti-English sentiments of all four siblings – "a rebel too and would fight for Ireland if ever a chance came"[1045] as Casement informed Joe McGarrity in October 1914. Dated 22 November, the letter had been written before Tom knew his brother had gone over to Germany. Nonetheless it was not permitted to proceed, being marked "original detained." But Casement's extensive luggage at Allisons was to lie undisturbed for more than another year.

At this point MI5 had the most minimal information on Casement; no photographs, and a continuing propensity to mix him up with his cousin of the same name in Ballycastle and ironically with another eponymous cousin, Major Roger Casement of Cronroe in Co. Wicklow, a signatory of the Ulster Covenant as Nina sourly noted. The Major was to die of illness in 1917 after active service in Gallipoli. Indeed, until recently, the TNA at Kew had a file of the Wicklow Roger's 1880 entrance examination papers for the Royal Military Academy at

Woolwich, suggesting it refers to Roger David Casement.[1046] Requests were sent out to discover the names and whereabouts of his three siblings and to authenticate his non-existent land holdings in the Glens of Antrim.

The RIC at Dublin Castle collated the information they had gathered, and reported on 26 November 1914, less than accurately: "He had a sister Mrs Newman who lives in London and she is the only one of his relations who sympathises with his nationalist and pro-German views. He is regarded by the others as a visionary. He was adopted and brought up by people named Dickie of Ballymena where he is well known."[1047] Elsewhere, his brother Charlie in Melbourne was described as a "tramway driver." As late as 18 December 1914, a querulous request as to what to do if Casement was spotted was met with the definitive reply "He should be arrested."

Somewhat nervously, MI5 also set out to investigate his bank accounts. The results were uninspiring especially as no cheques had been recently processed in England or Ireland. A vignette of pre-war commercial life in Pimlico does, however, emerge as Casement's cheques progressed through a number of hands before they returned to Williams Deacon's, the issuing bank. In a report to Basil Thomson dated 16 January 1915 and based on information obtained from that bank, his last payments were outlined: one cheque had been endorsed "Edw. Peacock." He was pinpointed as "Tailor of 55 Ebury Street." Peacock had actually been a provider of Ebury Street rooms and storage to Casement on and off for at least a decade according to the diary entry of 18 February 1903. Another cheque was endorsed "W.P. Germain." His identity had been ascertained: "man of this name at 50 Ebury St. ?lodgings." A third was passed through A. Doubleday "no doubt the fishmonger. 63 Ebury St."[1048] (Thomson's failure to follow-up Germain meant the diaries went uncovered for another 15 months).

By means of checking with Casement's bank and with the Paymaster General's office who issued Casement's pension, Special Branch was able to obtain his addresses from 1906 to 1914, but this detail was only submitted by Superintendent Patrick Quinn on 22 June 1916. Miss Vigrass, for one, "proprietress of 110 Philbeach Gardens…with whom Casement resided from May 1906 to Easter 1912…said she knew very little of him beyond the fact that he was of a very reserved disposition and received very few friends. When he left Philbeach Gardens he left no property of any description behind."[1049]

Peacock confirmed his long acquaintance in a note to Casement's solicitor when he re-presented his account, two days after the execution. The £2.0.6 requested was made up of a "Storage" item from 9 May 1914 for a guinea, and an account already rendered for 19/6. Mr Peacock is described on his letterhead as a tailor dealing in "Jackets & Ulsters, Riding Habits and Breeches", also as making-up "Service Uniforms." He told Gavan Duffy, with genuine if buttoned-up feeling, that "When the man called from Scotland Yard some time ago to collect the late Sir Roger Casement's clothes etc. he took this account [originally dated 27 April 1916.] I understand you are managing his affairs so enclose another in case they did not pass it on to you. I made his clothes for the last twenty years and always found him a most charming man. I usually found him apartments in this street as I always stored his clothes. I certainly think when he turned so fanatical that he lost that keen judgment of his."[1050]

In a minute from Superintendent Quinn, dated 26 April 1916, there is the strongest inference in the MI5 papers, aside from the absence of contrary evidence, that Casement's papers were only recently uncovered. He wrote "A list of names and address found amongst property belonging to Sir Roger Casement, which was deposited by him at 50 Ebury St. S.W. is being prepared and will be submitted in due course." The submission is not present. If it were ever finished it would have been very long indeed. Nonetheless the remarks strongly imply that any Ebury Street hoard had only just been turned over, otherwise why the inordinate delay in excavating the material in search of suspicious characters?[1051] Casement did not appreciate Quinn, a type he knew and disparaged in different countries: "He is a sly old fox. Irish by birth but wholly English. One of the Irish sold body and soul to the enemy of his land."[1052]

It seems that Quinn, sly or not, had been unaware of Casement's precise Ebury Street addresses until his capture and thus had made no earlier effort to search them. It could be argued that people do not move house while leaving boxes full of their private papers and other belongings behind. There was thus no obvious reason to swoop on Ebury Street. But Casement was a nomad. Although the 1915 report on Casement's cheques in relation to "W.P. Germain" of 50 Ebury Street had a question mark beside the word "lodgings" this was a lead plainly not pursued. It now appears that had a visit to No. 50 been made, the diaries would have emerged long before Casement's arrest and the Easter Rising, in which event Irish history might well have taken a quite different course.

In May 2000, at the Royal Irish Academy's Casement Symposium in Dublin, a selection of the unseen Scotland Yard papers were to be unexpectedly revealed by the Foreign Office's Mrs Gill Bennett, who spoke on *Casement and Whitehall*. What she distributed was a veritable treasure trove answering those key questions which had baffled researchers for fifty years, and proof positive of when and where the Black Diaries came from.

In those Metropolitan Police papers there are two nearly identical references to the fact of the diaries arriving from 50 Ebury Street on the precise date mentioned in the House of Commons in 1959. In Quinn's Special Branch minute of 22 June there appears the paragraph: "During the month of May 1914 Casement deposited with Mr Germain of 50 Ebury Street, Pimlico, S.W. some boxes containing books, etc. These books which included three diaries for the years 1903, 1910 and 1911, a ledger, an address book and a memorandum book were brought to New Scotland Yard by Mr Germain on the 25th April 1916."[1053] So it was entirely the result of Germain's voluntary act that Casement's diaries resurfaced on Easter Tuesday. This is confirmed in a second reference, this time from a Metropolitan Police property list relating to Casement and dated 28 July 1916.[1054] There the contents of two trunks "brought to Scotland Yard by Mr Germain, 50, Ebury Street, on 25th April 1916" were enumerated and detailed as including "3 diaries, 1 ledger, 1 address book, 1 memorandum book." The last item was presumably the 1901 Army notebook while the sixth item was the apparently innocuous address book of Casement's returned to Gertrude Parry in 1917 (and now in the NLI).

Peacock, it turned out, had custody of similar property also left with him in May 1914, largely Casement's diplomatic clothing as well as a hat in a tin box and a sword, along with other formal dress apparel and ordinary clothes. These items were only "brought to Scotland Yard by police" the day after Germain's delivery. In other words the Yard did not search the other addresses at Ebury Street until after they knew for certain Casement had left items there.

Solved the mystery may now be, but there is already a suggestion on record that even if the diaries were first obtained in 1916 only a small amount of document cooking was necessary in the first instance; and that during the subsequent decades before the 1959 public access, the full task of forging five volumes of diaries was completed by a dedicated team. Eoin Ó Máille, the present doyen of the forgery camp, said as far back as 1976, that "the forgeries may have taken as long as forty years to get them the way the British Government wanted." He explained the techniques used over so many years: "All the forger-craftsman had to do was to select various words from genuine entries or reports by Casement, photograph them and then re-assemble them in whatever sinister context he wished. From then it would be a simple matter to re-photograph the new "entry" and, using negatives, to trace "genuine" examples of Casement's fluent handwriting into what are now paraded as his diaries." The lifetime's work of the forger-craftsman he explained as follows "Having started out with what was soon realised was an amateurish scheme to smear Casement's name, the British knew that to save their own face before the judgment of history they would have to do a much better job of providing proofs of Casement's depravity."[1055] And so the forgery school has *in situ* another leg to its stool.

Angus Mitchell has more recently repeated the somewhat crazed notion that, "The authorities actually had 43 years to perfect the look of the Black

Diaries", these years being from their delivery to Scotland Yard in April 1916 to the Kew release in 1959. However the typed versions filched by Sir Basil Thomson from Scotland Yard in the early 1920s (he was by then a renegade) are, typos aside, how the same items at Kew read.[1056]

Suffice to say, the forty years of official silence ensured the British would be blamed for either utilising the diaries, or manufacturing them, or most likely and more often, both. In truth the failure after Casement's execution to capitalise further on the find, which developed into the long forty year silence was based on a mixture of guilt (about having invaded a gentleman's privacy) and a certain common decency about further blackening a dead man's character. There was also an embarrassed fear of having to explain the details of the sexual activity involved – not to mention the more critical, and rapidly evolving, Irish political situation.

These conflicting sentiments were already apparent in 1916. London, and the Home Office in particular were sticklers for the legal niceties. One must remember Casement was on more than nodding terms with at least three members of the very Cabinet which was to dispute the question of a reprieve for him. Indeed the Marquess of Crewe, a former Lord Lieutenant of Ireland, for one, was circulating the Cabinet with the letter from Eva Gore-Booth which detailed Casement's intention to stop the rising as soon as he reached Ireland, as evidenced by Father Ryan of Tralee, in his 20 May interview in the *Dublin Evening Mail*. For a couple of months only there was to be no room for faint hearts. But from 1917, feeling it was in a no-win situation, London clammed up and unwittingly fed the conspiracy theories. Winning even a propaganda skirmish with Irish nationalism was never again a possibility. Guilt and indifference came instead to predominate.

Basil Thomson of Scotland Yard was the son of an Archbishop of York and suffered from a well-recognised syndrome, particular to a disproportionate number of the sons of clergy. Knighted in 1919, he fell spectacularly from grace in 1925 when he was convicted of indecent behaviour in a public place. That place was Hyde Park, a location also nocturnally frequented by Casement as he recorded in his diary. The only disappointment for the forgery school is that the other party was not male. She was the gloriously named Thelma de Lava – a moniker that confirmed she provided outdoor relief in a professional capacity. The name does, however, have something of a transsexual ring about it, which might be another splendid irony.

Thomson had had an earlier Colonial Office career in the Pacific, even becoming assistant premier in the independent Kingdom of Tonga, under King George I. Ultimately he was given the task of bringing Tonga into the Empire as a British protectorate in a 1900 side-deal with Germany, who in return obtained

Samoa. Thomson spoke Tongan and plainly appreciated the idiosyncratic culture of the islands although when push came to shove he forced the new King, George Tubou II, to sign a treaty under the guns of HMS Porpoise. The King's white suit was apparently covered with decorations which were all of the same Order – one he exclusively awarded himself. Described as obstinate, he took some time to agree the terms and accede to the treaty, but sign he would, so far as Basil Thomson was concerned.

He was later Governor of Dartmoor Prison. In what would have been a crushing disgrace to a more conventional man, or one less self-regarding, he was fined £5 for the indecency with Miss de Lava. By then Sir Basil, he had been sacked from his Assistant Commissioner's job by Lloyd George four years earlier in a purge of the old guard. Thomson gave the excuse as his lenient treatment of a number of Sinn Feiners who had broken into Lloyd George's official country home at Chequers and scrawled slogans there. Others have suggested he was caught red-handed with bogus copies of *Pravda*. Whatever the precise cause, and despite being something of a pragmatist on Ireland, he – like Blinker Hall – was too political and too close to the Conservative Party to survive at Scotland Yard. On his dismissal, never the dutiful public servant, it was stated "he left nothing for his successor to take over" having "filched" every scrap of paper in his office.[1057] Thereby he made implacable police enemies. Already a published author by the time of the Hyde Park incident, and apparently undeterred, he continued his career as a writer, ending up with over a dozen titles to his name. Contrary to Herbert Mackey's 'suicide in Paris' account,[1058] Thomson died of natural causes in Teddington, England.

Any evidence sourced to such a man was now forever suspect, although his inconsistent and disputed accounts of the first appearance of the diaries had already made any of the details he wrote unreliable. Indeed his own accounts of his Intelligence work do not reveal anyone logical, rigorous or ruthless, rather someone over-promoted and unable to see the wood for the trees. Herbert Mackey, in particular, made great play of both Thomson's unreliability and his obvious experience of the sexual underworld in London. He insinuated that the forger was not a million miles from the man in whose hands the diaries first came to light – a man familiar with "Hyde Park, that part haunted by degenerates of both sexes"; one who could "record his own debauchery and have the results counterfeited by his penman into a colourable imitation of Roger Casement's handwriting."[1059] Thomson, who unconvincingly claimed he was only in the park on some sort of evidence-gathering exercise, was not, however, without establishment support. Blinker Hall testified at the trial as to his "high moral character" but to no avail. Once down under the British system, you're out, although it used to take a lot for you to be downed.

Before Casement's belongings were handed over to Gertrude Parry, his solicitor George Gavan Duffy was told by the Home Office that three categories of papers would be withheld: "The prisoner's diaries and certain other papers which came into the hands of the Police in connection with the criminal charge must be retained by them: and certain documents which he wrote in prison for communication to persons were stopped under the Regulations and must also be retained." Duffy, whose partnership broke up when he took on the Casement brief, was also told of 128 books, 13 albums of photographs and newspaper cuttings, 21 photographs in frames, and a mass of other material, including two Blanco tins, two pots of "photograph mounter", a brass syringe, a "quantity of foreign grass", a button stick and a deck chair. Apart from "seven letters in envelope" the only other personal paperwork mentioned was "a quantity of envelopes, reports and manuscript dealing with the Putumayo Atrocities."[1060] Scotland Yard, for no explained reason, went carefully through Casement's Putumayo material, especially the witness statements, and reported that "nothing has been ascertained to show that that he obtained second hand information and made it appear to be first hand information."[1061]

Somewhat typically, there is a note on the file, by Basil Thomson, reading "I find that the landlord who housed the property claims £2.0.6 rent. I propose to ask Mr Duffy for this before handing over the property."[1062] He did, forwarding two bills, one from Allisons for 15 shillings and another dated 27 April 1916 from Edward Peacock. For his pains, he received a reply from Gavan Duffy pointing out with some pleasure that Casement had no money with which to settle the debts.[1063] Earlier Casement, concerned about the two debts, had requested Duffy to "ask Major Hall of the I.D. War Office" had they found any of the money he had secreted in Kerry: "I left about £47 in English gold and silver in a handkerchief hidden in some ferns."[1064] The answer unsurprisingly came back in the negative, leaving him with no ready cash but someone in Kerry with a smile on their face.

When a defence against the Black Diaries came to be mounted there were very few people available or willing to provide critical details about them. This was to be a lucky stroke of fate, enabling Casement's friends and supporters to develop an imaginative series of explanations for their existence. Only a couple of people came forward publicly to say they had ever seen something of them or knew of their contents. The details provided were limited and confusing; one journalist, Ben Allen of Associated Press, said he saw torn out original pages, not, he later stated, the first days of the 1903 diary which remain missing, although he was not precise as to what was written on what he had seen. He was to notion it was "a diary copied by Sir Roger Casement during the Putumayo investigations".*

---

* Brian Inglis, in a *Spectator* article of 13 April 1956, wrote of unimpeachable

But the intention was brutally clear, especially in the U.S. as a secret telegram to the Naval Attaché in Washington, Captain Guy Gaunt, indicates: "Photographic facsimile & transcript of Casement's diary, of which you have, no doubt, already heard is being sent to America by today's mail. Person receiving it will communicate with you when it arrives. In the meantime could you arrange to get Editors of Newspapers and influential Catholic and Irish circles informed indirectly that facts have transpired which throw an appalling light on Casement's past life, and which when known will make it quite impossible for any self-respecting person to champion his cause. Diary which is a daily record of amazing unnatural vice is quite unpublishable and is the worst thing which has ever come into the hands of persons with the widest experience of cases of this sort."[1065] Walter Page, the US ambassador in London, had early on been informed of the diaries and he was keen to advise Washington to have nothing to do with Casement "even indirectly", as he was of an "unspeakably filthy character."[1066] At his request, he was ultimately shown the diaries themselves by Basil Thomson and also provided with some photographs. Thomson "pointed out the innocuous passages that identified the writer as well as the filthy parts". Page was quite satisfied and reckoned he would have time to get the photographs to the President, it being a matter of international importance.[1067]

The Irish-American lawyer John Quinn, a friend and defender of Casement, although no supporter of his activities in Germany, was shown some photographic entries from the diaries at the British embassy in Washington. Writing to London on 22 August 1916, asking "for more Casement diary", Captain Gaunt spoke revealingly of the meeting: "Quinn who wrote the violent article in the *Times* I have played with for a week or two, and from being violently against us and swearing the whole thing was a forgery, got up by the British Government to vilify a dead man, he is bang round on the other side. I purposely played up to the Irish love of effect, got him in the centre of a room with two or three people and then pointed out that the question of authenticity rested entirely with one Quinn. After inspecting the copies sticking his left hand about the third button of his waistcoat and pointing the right at the floor above (or heaven, depending on the range) he said 'I declare this to be

witnesses to Casement telling them of copying "out a diary recording the perversions of one Armando Normand." He also quoted Ben Allen in similar support, while adding, as "guesswork", that the diaries "were probably not Normand's alone" but partially Casement recording "other erotica". It was his view that there are "misers of pornography, just as there are spendthrifts: men who collect and horde dirty stories, as others collect and distribute them." A visit from Singleton-Gates later that year, touting his typewritten copies of the diaries, disabused Inglis of any further notion of them being forged.

Ada McNeill (signed Íde nic Néill 1912) of Cushendun (Ellen McNally)

the handwriting of the late Roger Casement!'

All the foregoing you will think feeble but the point was that I got him then to write to that blackguard Kuno Meyer, his lifelong friend, 'advising him.' That tore it. He has written to Quinn telling him what he really thinks of him: 'Will denounce him on every platform in USA'. You never read such a letter. Quinn also stirred up Dan Cohalan and there is the loveliest three-cornered fight on, all cussing one another and all making it personal and entirely forgetting the original cause of the row. I have dropped out of it, not that I ever appeared really, but it is going to complicate the Irish question in the USA from the villains' side of it."[1068] Quinn went quiet on the subject but not before threatening his contact and the ambassador should the facsimiles be further distributed, adding "his private life had nothing to do with his public acts." He later advised Gavan Duffy "the handwriting looked like" Casement's.[1069] Others who were shown them in Washington included the singer Count John MacCormack. The embassy, given Quinn's influence in the State Department, was well pleased with his silence about Casement's execution and of course with the dissension the diaries had sown in Irish ranks.

The ambassador, Sir Cecil Spring Rice, disobeyed the Foreign Secretary Sir Edward Grey's express command not to show the diaries around any further, despite his initial efforts to adduce American concerns as good reason for a reprieve. Sir Cecil, with his Irish background, had a certain sympathy for, and connection to Home Rule. He also penned the patriotic anthem *I Vow to Thee my Country*, yet notably contributed to the Irish language college in Co. Clare, on whose management board his cousin Mary Spring Rice sat.

The ambassador's sympathies were known and noted in the Foreign Office, and quite probably his reports of potential American difficulties were more easily discounted as a result. On 14 May 1916, Sir Cecil was to be found soft-soaping a senior American friend of Ireland, Bourke Cockran (a former Congressman and relative of Winston Churchill and Shane Leslie), in a remarkably non-judgmental letter: "It seems that Casement has for years been abnormal sexually. But this might only make his case more difficult to deal with as it does not prove insanity. But if there is evidence that he is altogether abnormal mentally I think it should be supplied. I shall be ready to forward any evidence."[1070] This was written with a view to an insanity plea at the trial which was never a runner and only indicates that Spring Rice's sympathy for Casement's predicament was taking precedence over his professional judgment. Regardless of his good intentions, he was to be featured pejoratively alongside Alfred Noyes in Yeats's poem *Roger Casement* – "For Spring-Rice had to whisper it, Being their Ambassador."

Once sentence was executed the ambassador was not averse to capitalising further on the political value of the diaries. On 15 August 1916 he met the Apostolic Delegate in Washington. Advising caution, he told Archbishop Bonzano that Casement was "no model for the faith."[1071] But there were other tensions in the family as a cousin, the Hon. Thomas Spring Rice (1886-1934) later the 3rd Lord Monteagle of Brandon, was a third secretary in his Washington embassy. In a letter home to his father (the 2nd Baron) on 18 July 1916, Thomas wrote (at odds with cousin Cecil's approach) "I do wish the fate of that cur Casement were settled. I wonder if the wretched widow still holds to him. It really gave me quite a turn to hear Mary was staying with her! I happen to know for a fact a few things about Casement which make one positively sick. He is unfit for the company of anybody but Germans."[1072]

Presumably his gunrunner sister was living with the historian and widow Alice Stopford Green. In 1924, Mary Spring Rice, who died at the early age of forty-four, was to have her coffin carried by local Republicans into the family church at Foynes, Co. Limerick as a mark of appreciation for her part in the *Asgard* affair, the hugely significant 1914 arms importation into Ireland pioneered by Casement. Withdrawn from Washington, Sir Cecil Spring Rice died in early 1918 lacking the customary honours, only to be succeeded by Lord Reading.

The process of remaking Casement as a normal, red-blooded male continued for forty years. Indeed the final publication of *The Black Diaries* five years short of the centenary of his birth made it ever more necessary. When Dr Letitia Fairfield (1885-1978) returned to the fray with her analysis of the sexual content of the diaries, the moment had arrived for Bulmer Hobson to deliver what he hoped would be a decisive blow to the sceptics, and provide something to give succour to the beleaguered faithful. For Ada McNeill, Bulmer's old comrade and mentor, had finally passed away. She was a friend to three generations of Hobsons, taking refuge in 1922 with Bulmer's mother in Crawfordsburn when the killings and burnings intensified in the Glens, and providing 1930s holiday hospitality for Bulmer and his children.

Having died on 10 July 1959 at the age of 98, Ada Mary McNeill was buried under a small Celtic cross in the Church of Ireland graveyard in Cushendun. Around the corner, in a classic Antrim contradiction, and under an unusually substantial modern memorial, lies her Unionist propagandist cousin and friend, the Rt. Hon. Ronald McNeill, first and last Lord Cushendun (1861-1934), and briefly acting Foreign Secretary. Ada was born nearly four years before Casement on 27 September 1860 and was the linchpin of the Co. Antrim Gaelic revival, but she always claimed that in the early days it was the younger person, Casement, who influenced her. In a letter to the Dublin *Sunday Press*, published on 13 September 1959, Bulmer decided to try an ambush on Dr Fairfield:

"She does not know that the lady to whom Casement was engaged to be married when he was a young man died just six weeks ago. Circumstances (mainly financial) in the conventions of that time made it impossible for them to marry but they remained devoted to each other throughout their lives and neither ever thought of marrying anybody else. The few surviving friends who knew of these circumstances felt bound to respect her privacy while she lived."

The problem with this statement is that it was quite simply untrue. Casement was petrified of Ada's amorous intentions, for she would not take no for an answer. There never was such an engagement. Whether Bulmer had been told otherwise or was just using Ada's death to dissimulate, remains unclear but Gertrude Bannister for one had known differently. Casement had been obliged to write to her as late as January 1913 in no uncertain terms about the Ada question, presumably in the hope that Gertrude might caution her. "I wish poor old soul" he wrote, that "she would leave me alone. These repeated invitations to go to meet her are a bit out of place. I have very strong feelings of friendship for her, and good will, and brotherly Irish affection, but I wish she would leave other things out of the reckoning."[1073] Hobson's 1959 letter can only be construed as a smokescreen or an exercise in all round deception.

But Ada had been no shrinking violet and like so many of her female acquaintances immersed herself in the Gaelic League, and the national struggle in its various forms. She obviously had to be present at the famous 1913 meeting of anti-Carson Protestants in Ballymoney. Her house had been raided by the police in 1919, as was that of the Parrys in 1920. Not until the 1930s, after many visits to Italy did she succumb to the lure of fascism and the attraction of another strong-willed man. She became an "enthusiastic admirer of Mussolini whose portrait hung in the hall of Glendun Lodge" which apparently in the war years dismayed visiting refugees from fascism such as the Poppers."[1074] Only Bulmer Hobson and Dinny McCullough outlived her.

In her delightfully evocative 1929 memoir of Casement[1075] she wrote of her time with him, of when he was twenty-one and "we both discovered we could talk without ceasing about Ireland. This was a great joy to me, because there was no one to talk to on that subject except the country people who had sworn to make me a red-hot Republican and Fenian like themselves. I was in a Unionist milieu and Roger was too, on the other side of the mountain." Of the first Glens *Feis*, she wrote of how they "worked hard at it together, often sitting up writing till 1 or 2 o'clock, and then sitting by a dying fire to look into the future when the work we were starting would have grown beyond our control."

She recalled "how his earnestness influenced me on another subject beside Ireland. I had lost my faith and scoffed at religion, and I had a biting tongue and a certain power of influencing others. This gave my father great pain and vexation. I remember a long walk with Roger up the Glen. As we turned home he talked eloquently and earnestly against scoffing at religion. I listened – actually paid attention and listened. His enthusiasm was as great as my own, and he was far more earnest and simple. There was something always very young and boyish and yet so very true and earnest about his character that he made you pause and think." But she did not mention an engagement or any physical side of her feelings for him being able to be expressed.

"I saw him again in Brixton Prison in 1916. Today I took out of my dressing-case his goodbye letter to me from Pentonville. It had lain for twelve years successfully hidden there. I read it again, and oh, don't ask me to write any more."

When it came to protecting Casement's reputation no holds were barred as far as Ada was concerned either, and she enrolled the assistance of her cousin Ronald in 1925 to stop Singleton-Gates publishing the diaries. He intervened, from the Foreign Office, to have the journalist frightened off. Indeed he was forced by threat of prosecution to hand over his 1903 and 1910 Black Diary transcripts but obviously held on to copies which he finally published in 1959. Sidney Parry was also involved, writing to the Conservative Home Secretary "I know we have 'white' men at the head of affairs and they will not allow a dead man's memory to be blackened."[1076]

In these circumstances a first theory was developed in the circle closest to Casement, who Gertrude Parry said, never "had the smallest reason to doubt Roger's moral integrity." It revolved around half-remembered conversations Casement had supposedly had with Bulmer Hobson and P.S. O'Hegarty concerning recollections of sexual excesses in the diary of Armando Normand, the Peruvian gauleiter and Putumayo section chief. Whether Gertrude meant this to be a blanket denial of Casement's sexual identity is hard to believe, and it was perhaps carefully phrased to avoid so saying.

Hobson remembered Casement telling him, "He had got possession of this diary (Normand's) and had translated it and sent it to the Foreign Office along with his report...the diary was concerned with recording acts of sexual perversion."[1077] O'Hegarty, by then a senior Free State civil servant (and a noted bibliophile), in turn wrote "He told me that this man's private diary recorded in his own hand details of the most abominable and unnatural crimes. He said that he had sent the diary to the Foreign Office and had kept a copy of it. I cannot clearly recollect now whether the diary went in with his report or subsequent to it." The similarity of these two accounts is itself somewhat revealing and smacks of collusion or false recovered memory syndrome.

Another such version, from the loyal but utterly unreliable Captain Michael Kehoe, surfaced in a *Sunday Express* (Irish edition) review of Alfred Noyes

1957 book. The 'Captain' (a Sergeant-Major member of the Irish Brigade) dated Casement first connecting the Normand diary with allegations of sexual impropriety as December 1914. He elided the issue with Casement's known intention to sue an American newspaper for libel, after it had accused him in February 1915 of accepting German money. He was always careful to decline any such offer of cash gifts. Kehoe quoted him precisely as saying "the extracts must be from my translation of Normand's diary."[1078]

But no such document relating to Normand has ever surfaced. The only recorded item bearing any resemblance to it is a surveillance of Armando Normand that Casement ordered for the days from 22 to 28 October 1910. As he wrote in the 1910 White Diary on 28 October, he received from a Barbadian "a sort of written diary of his (Normand's) doings since he left." In the Black Diary entry for the same day he noted "Bishop brought a written statement of all that has transpired since he left me. Amusing in its way." But this is not the stuff of which so many daily diary entries, covering a decade and three continents, is made.

Serious doubt has to be cast on the veracity of the heard Normand diary stories let alone the theory. If Casement had had such a damning document he would have shouted it from the rooftops. In 1910 or later, the Foreign Office would have had no cause to conceal or hide such evidence, rather the opposite, and traces would unquestionably exist in the records, not least because reference would have been made to it by Casement. It is next to impossible to erase the existence of official records without leaving a further trail, and arousing proper suspicion and resentment amongst senior, and indeed junior, officials. Casement, in 1913, even provided the Putumayo select committee, through the Foreign Office, with his unexpurgated 1910 White Diary which is revealing not only of a fascination with young men, their looks and their bodies but also of his exotic political views.

Indeed Casement's first substantive biographer, Denis Gwynn, writing in 1930 of the "famous indecent diary" felt privately obliged to tell J.J. Horgan that "the evidence of the existence of its contents is so strong that I find that even the alternative story I had evolved which seemed to explain it away seems to break down. I find it hard to believe in face of what I have discovered, that the diary was something he had copied out and sent to the Foreign Office as evidence against some blackguard he was exposing on the Putumayo."[1079] Gwynn was politically sympathetic to Casement, and applying for a job at UCC, so this assessment did not appear in his book.

The term White Diary is something of a misnomer as entries are of considerable length. Casement himself described it as "less a diary than a reflection – a series of daily and weekly reflections."[1080] In truth, the document is an account of his official mission, although at times highly subjective and opinionated. One example of his overwrought political views, from 21 November 1910, are his words "No sight could be pleasanter than the flag of Teutonic civilisation advancing into this wilderness. The Americans have got their part of America, and it will take them all their time to civilise themselves. Germany with her 70,000,000 of virile men has much to do for mankind besides giving us music and military shows. Let loose her pent-up energies in this Continent."[1081]

Ingenuous, but illustrative of Casement's willingness to hand over any of his writings, if asked, regardless of what was revealed. It also indicates just how highly politicised he was and that he did not feel threatened by his bosses becoming aware of the extent. He did admit to Charles Roberts, the Select Committee chairman and MP for Lincoln, that there was much in it that "would expose me to ridicule were it read by unkind eyes." But away it went, with no Normand diary – neither extract nor mention.

Hobson and O'Hegarty purported to remain convinced of Casement's non-homosexual state – in the former case beyond the 1959 publication of *The Black Diaries*. Hobson had known him intimately over a number of years, had happily taken orders and advice from him and generally responded in a supine way to his demands and instructions, despite predating Casement in his revolutionary enthusiasm, although twenty years younger. But Casement did not mix Irish politics with pleasure, unless, one supposes, the hand was laid on him first. Anyway some like Francis Hackett had a low opinion of Hobson, describing him as "a dud and a bluff."[1082]

Assuming that they were not aware of any homosexual pattern to Casement and given their revolutionary anti-British politics, it is not impossible that the Normand story was largely the pair's invention. What is surprising is not just that it held together for over forty years, convincing anyone willing to be convinced, but that nobody has had the temerity to suggest it was itself a fake, that Irish Intelligence in its peripheral membership could be guilty of a tiny part of that which British Intelligence has been so long accused of.

Long interested in farming, Bulmer had been promised £150 by Casement in a letter of 8 August 1910 from Pará, to purchase land. "Look on it as a loan to Ireland" he told him before later withdrawing the offer.[1083] Countess Markievicz and Hobson had started a horticultural enterprise in a large north county Dublin house near Raheny. Named Belcamp Park, it was once the home of Henry Grattan. Rumour had it that Casimir Markievicz was none too pleased to discover his wife Constance and Bulmer together and there was talk of a duel. Their self-sufficiency 'good life' venture, however, did not last, despite the Count returning to his Ukrainian homeland around 1913. According to Intelligence papers, by 1916 he had become an officer in the Polish Army and was "a heavy drinker."[1084] That may, however, have come with the territory.

Bulmer was reckoned to be something of a sexual innocent. In a conversation with this author,[1085] Declan Hobson, Bulmer's only son related a story of an overnight trip into the Dublin mountains when Constance Markievicz insisted on accompanying Bulmer and a young *Fianna*. Without tents, they all slept in the heather, the Countess at a due distance, only for Bulmer, awakened by rustling, to discover Madame slipping in between the two males. She pleaded the freezing cold. Bulmer eventually met his future wife, Claire Gregan, in the office of the Volunteers where she was a secretary and he, Quartermaster General. Declan Hobson also remarked, on the authority of his aunt Florence Patterson, that Claire was the first woman in whom she was aware of Bulmer taking a serious romantic interest. The Hobson marriage did not last. There were two children.

Casement described the imagined diarist, Armando Normand as a thin, short, slimy individual with the most repulsive face he had ever seen "devilish in its cruelty and evil", also like a low type of "East-end Jew, with fat greasy lips and circular eyes".[1086] Normand was the archfiend of the Peruvian Amazon Company's staff of killers, with the blood of hundreds of Indians on his hands. He was a man who killed personally 'dashing children's brains out'. He beat a man on his testicles until he died. Indeed he cooked children alive, although much of the time he was ordering others to kill. O'Hegarty thought Normand a mixed breed whose "European training seemed to have made him more of a devil than any of his associates who had no contact with Europe." His diary he said in 1933 "recorded the most abominable and unnatural crimes."[1087] In the event Normand escaped from gaol in Iquitos in August 1915 and made his way to Brazil and freedom.[1088]

Normand operated out of Matanzas in the area between the Caquetá river and the Cahuinari and Igara-Parana, which was disputed territory. Colombia, Peru, Brazil and even Ecuador had conflicting claims in the area. Normand was no respecter of the Colombian frontier but his high crime was not homosexuality, rather barbaric and repeated murder. Not a whiff of that sort of sexual scandal attached itself to him. He was in 1910 living with a group of five women that Casement nicknamed "the harem." On 22 October in the White Diary he wrote "We could see...bringing up the rear, the blue and red costumes of the harem...The Mrs Normands appeared to be travelling fast, all were scurrying." The harem was entirely female.

Normand's diary perhaps fused to Casement's was the only ever suggested genuine source for the offending items. None at this time knew much beyond the word 'diaries' just what papers had been seized in London, although the Irish government's persistent attempt to damp down interest in having them inspected or returned, indicates there was more detailed knowledge of their form and content in Dublin circles. Both Michael Collins and Eamonn (Edmund) Duggan had been shown the diaries in London in 1922 during the Treaty negotiations by Lord Birkenhead – F.E. Smith as was. They had gone to a room in the House of Lords and were left alone with them. Collins knew and recognised Casement's handwriting. Duggan (1868-1927), Minister for Home Affairs in the first Dáil and a former director of IRA Intelligence, reported that the diary "in two parts – bound volumes" repeated "ad nauseam details of sex perversions – of the personal appearance and beauty of native boys – with special reference to a certain portion of their anatomy. It was disgusting."

When de Valera was told, third-hand, in 1966, of one Commander Clipperton who could attest to Naval Intelligence fabrication (by Blinker Hall), he wisely replied "the important thing is to get some positive proof. Nothing else will suffice." The informant added gratuitously that Hall's son had been about to be charged by Clipperton as he was "mixed up with a group of other young officers" but had been killed in an air raid.[1089] And de Valera's outlook was always, until 1999, the official Dublin line, if not of other Republicans. The then Sinn Féin President and West Belfast MP, Gerry Adams, writing as late as 1991, stated that the "British Government circulated forged copies of his diaries to undermine the campaign and try to make his execution acceptable." (*Who Fears to Speak*) The latter remark is certainly accurate. Even after the forensic results of 2002, Sinn Féin continued to favour the forgery theory.

Collins and Duggan presumably recorded and related to others some idea of the extent and range of the diaries, although there was a belief expressed by the Home Secretary in 1959 that Dublin had obtained a copy of at least some of them. The Home Office thought it "desirable to correct the impression that the copies…used by the authors of *The Black Diaries* had come from Dublin… to avoid giving offence to the Irish Government" and the earlier statement to the House was corrected.[1090] This supposition may have been derived from the fact that Dr Richard Hayes of the NLI had secretly bought copies from Singleton-Gates, promising not to release them for a decade. That Dr Hayes had worked as a code breaker in Irish Intelligence, during what was named in Dublin the Emergency, the Second World War, has not escaped the attention of those intent on finding evidence for conspiracy. Nor that he was working, discreetly and with official sanction, in liaison at times with British Intelligence.

Nonetheless the existence of five volumes – two more than Singleton-Gates had published or even mentioned in 1959, was something of a shock to everyone when finally revealed by R.A. Butler in the House of Commons. He was answering a question from H. (Harford) Montgomery Hyde, the Unionist MP for North Belfast who had made a name for himself by majoring on the

Casement diaries issue and the necessity for the Home Office both to admit they existed and to allow public access to them. The Home Secretary disclosed to Hyde the fact of a second, in the event, innocuous Congo item "a field service note book containing a few jottings apparently related to Casement's service in the Congo in 1901 and 1902" and a second, far from innocuous 1911 journal "a Letts' desk diary for 1911." This was over and above the known item of that year "a ledger containing accounts and notes relating to dates in 1911." Limited access to view them was also granted

Montgomery Hyde had courageously intervened in the House of Commons debate on the Wolfenden Report into Homosexual Offences and Prostitution on 26 November 1958. By January of the following year, he was facing a challenge for the parliamentary nomination from Air Marshall Sir George Beamish. Once an Irish rugby international, Beamish was born in Coleraine and had recently been the Air Ministry's director general of personnel. Before a Unionist Party selection committee meeting on 12 January 1959, Hyde, armed with a letter of endorsement from Carson's widow (which looks and reads suspiciously as if he had written it himself), scraped home by 77 votes to 72, knocking Sir George out of the running.[1091] His enemies, however, fought on. Unwisely, Hyde chose to miss the full North Belfast Imperial Association meeting, called for 13 February 1959 in the YMCA, to ratify the reselection. It was normally a formality. The alternative magnet was an arduous Commonwealth Parliamentary Association tour of the West Indies. Despite pleas from his wife and certain Belfast friends, to cut short his trip, he chose instead to appeal to the chairman, Mr D.A. McClelland, for a postponement.

That plea was in vain as McClelland was already hostile. He simply replied "Wire received. Regret you cannot attend meeting. Must go on. Management Committee decision." Writing letters from a hotel in Kingston Jamaica to his number one enemy, the association secretary Mrs Noble, was also bordering on the politically insane. In the event, Hyde was deselected by 171 votes to 152 and the Unionist Party lost its one respected voice at Westminster and its only MP who ever advised his people of changing times, while attempting to modernise and moderate Unionist opinion, both at home and abroad.[1092] Montgomery Hyde's dedicated Casement activities unfortunately only muddied already troubled waters so far as his constituency association was concerned. Nine years earlier, at his original selection meeting, he had been panicking over the possibility that he would be questioned about an article which he had written that William III, Prince of Orange, may have been homosexual. Luckily it was not mentioned so he was not called upon to use his somewhat unconvincing crib, that he was only quoting another author.[1093]

In the November 1958 debate, Hyde had contributed a lengthy half-hour speech on Sir John Wolfenden's report which had been published over a year earlier in September 1957. This was a debate Hyde had already called for in the House, fearing the matter was being shelved – as it was to be for a further decade. In a wide-ranging and thoughtful speech, he concluded by demanding equality for both the homosexual and the prostitute. Earlier he quoted a letter from a homosexual consenting adult who had been gaoled and released, only to be informed on again, losing his new job.

The North Belfast MP pointed out "three popular fallacies that have been exposed by the Report"; that "male homosexuality always involves sodomy"; that homosexuals are "necessarily effeminate" and that most relevant court cases "are of practising male homosexuals in private." Only one hundred men a year, he said, were convicted of sex in private with consenting adults.[1094] These ideas, novel to the wider public in 1958, can be directly traced back to the 1890s works of Havelock Ellis and J.A. Symonds.

But such seriously liberal views had already begun to pull Hyde down. He was also a convinced abolitionist on capital punishment. Indeed he was drifting toward Labour, as he had presciently begun to doubt the wisdom, or efficacy of the Unionist Party's rigid alliance with the Conservative Party. He vacated his seat at the general election of October 1959 despite having received many letters of support from within North Belfast including a number from his "Hebrew constituents", as he put it, and beyond, after he was deselected. There was (and is) a folk view that the North Belfast Unionist Association at that time was conducted out of the Synagogue, explaining to a degree its apparently liberal approach, although no such aspect to the dispute was to surface in the press.

The one (anonymous) antagonistic letter he did receive, addressed from Worthing, stated "Ulster has no time for an advocate for homosexuality" and also accused him of "gallivanting in the sunshine."[1095] He was replaced for fifteen years as North Belfast's MP by Mr Stratton Mills, a young Belfast solicitor who rose and sank without trace. Mills did, however, write to Hyde correcting and apologising for any impression that he had offered himself as a candidate before the surprise vote to deselect had occurred.

Montgomery Hyde nervously slipped a fortnight's worth of the erotic 1911 diary into the 1964 edition of his 1960 book on the trial of Roger Casement, which ensured it was banned in the Irish Republic. Regardless of the impression that the banning of the first ever extract from Casement's most sexual diary would leave, the Censorship Board ploughed on in its task of protecting the Irish people from sex and smut. In that month's blacklist, Hyde's book was joined by Alex Comfort's *Sex in Society* and Dr R. Swoop's *The Expert Way of Making Love*. Apart from such sex manuals and diaries, the Board also put a series of racy novels to the sword; *Cage of Passion* by I.C.A.

Mari, *The Love Go-Round,* Babes H. Deal's *Night Story,* and *The Wayward Wench* by Noel de Vic Beamish. Only Mike Baldwin's *A World of Men* had a whiff of homosexuality about it.[1096] That innocent, unblemished and decaying Ireland had only a few years left to run, as economic growth loomed. The tide of modernism was soon to sweep all before it.

Angus Mitchell, however, views Hyde in a different light. Not seeing him as a liberal or reformer, he instead draws attention to other facets of his life. He argues that although "best known as an author and barrister he also had a distinguished career as a British Intelligence officer and Unionist MP for North Belfast (1950-59) – whether such a combination of public posts made him a suitable voice to 'authenticate' the diaries is open to question."[1097] But with such a view, no one except the fully accredited true believer (or perhaps convert) can be trusted to judge the evidence.

Hyde had been an admitted member of the Intelligence services during the war. He was in fact Lt. Col. Hyde and was so addressed throughout most of his parliamentary career. His publications on intelligence and defence matters nearly outnumber those on homosexual characters or with gay themes. The Hyde oeuvre, of some fifty books and innumerable reviews and articles, was also peppered with works on pornography and aristocrats, some on peers like Lord Nathan commissioned by the family concerned, others like those on the Londonderrys (the Castlereaghs of Mount Stewart) contracted during and after his employment with that family.

When he took up the Casement controversy he was of course still MP for North Belfast and he was not as strapped for cash as he was later to become. His wife in 1959, had pointed out that, but for the fact he was a year short of the ten years necessary (at that time) to secure a parliamentary pension, losing his seat had compensations. As she put it, on 14 and 16 February 1959, writing to him in Jamaica: "SO THAT'S THAT. I'm sorry darling perhaps it's for the best. No more politics. No more Belfast politics. Oh bliss."[1098]

Apart from his money problems, Hyde had no obvious interest in hiding the truth. He was about as good an authenticator as one was likely to get in that era. A classic radical establishment figure, he working assiduously, right up until his death in 1989 just short of his eighty-second birthday. Hyde lived at Tenterden in Kent in the heart of the Home Counties, honoured more by a wide readership than by his country. He chose in death a non-religious cremation. "Harford was not a believer" explained Tim Brinton who provided the oration at his funeral in 1989, although, as he confusingly but accurately added, he was an Ulster Protestant.

Not having seen the diaries, W.J. Maloney was in an excellent position to erect a smokescreen of largely irrelevant 'facts' around the issue in his book. It was an article of faith for him that the diaries were forged, and even if they were not forged England was evil enough to have forged them. Ergo, if they could have been forged that was evidence itself of Albion's perfidy in the matter. He did make an especially memorable statement when he wrote "Of Casement's concurrent trials, one was a State trial at which he was legally condemned to death; the other a mob trial at which he was adjudged unfit to live."[1099] But Maloney made it impossible for a liberal argument to develop – that Casement may have dabbled a little (latterly a lot) in same-sex sex, but that that was a private matter. In the end he too, in the second trial, judged Casement unfit to live should the diaries have turned out to accurately depict his sexual life. There was as yet no middle way between seeing him as a treasonable pervert or as a Catholic nationalist saint.

The tale of the forging was developed by Maloney using the few facts as he knew them. "With the Normand diary at his disposal, the artist constructing the draft forgery had no lack of indecency to hinder him in the completion of his task…all that was needed was the changing of the dates so as to make them correspond to those of Casement's Putumayo investigations." The dossiers of "named people of appropriate criminal habit, in the archives both of Scotland Yard and of the police headquarters of England's ally at Paris" were woven in. Other people "had to be searched out, and considered, before the suitability of the tentatively chosen materials could be finally settled. And after that, there was the labour of pruning or expanding, the selected material and of inventing links to bind detached pieces together."[1100]

The Maloney book had a number of unexpected results in the literary world. When Yeats "after reading *The Forged Casement Diaries* by Dr Maloney" wrote his poem *Roger Casement*, he misused the name of the English poet Alfred Noyes who had worked during the war, most notably in America, as a British propagandist. It was there that Casement's sister Nina had bearded him in late 1916 at a public meeting in Philadelphia, calling him a blackguardly scoundrel. She also, as he wrote, poured out a torrent of invective against England. Noyes, having been briefly shown a transcript of the offending items in the Foreign Office News Department by Stephen Gaselee, had earlier written "And the chief leader of these rebels – I cannot print his own written confessions about himself, for they are filthy beyond all description. But I have seen and read them and they touch the lowest depths that human degradation has ever touched. Page after page of the diary would be an insult to a pig's trough to let the foul record touch it. The Irish will canonize these things at their own peril."[1101]

Yeats wrote two pieces on Casement, one *The Ghost of Roger Casement* a poem, and the other variously described as a poem, song or ballad to the tune of *The Glen of Aherlow*. The offending verse from the latter which provoked a plea from Noyes for forgiveness, read;

*Come Alfred Noyes, come all the troup**
That cried it far and wide,
Come from the forger and his desk,
Desert the perjurer's side.

Unfortunately, Noyes had had a conversion in the interim period both over Casement, and in 1927, religiously, to Rome. Described as an "implacable enemy of those who defied the moral code in the name of art" he later managed to stop the auction of a copy of *Ulysses* owned by F.E. Smith. Now he pleaded for a poetic rehabilitation. Yeats duly obliged by changing 'Alfred Noyes' to 'Tom and Dick'. Noyes, in expiation, was himself to author the year before his death in 1958 a book, *The Accusing Ghost – Justice for Casement*, described as a reader for the forgery school. Noyes's final effort was published before the next, watershed, year when the diaries were first made public. He had, however, been given a rough idea of what Singleton-Gates possessed, by Roger McHugh, who had had the diaries flashed before him at a meeting in London in January 1957. From McHugh's description of what the bemonocled Singleton-Gates described as his "investment", Noyes must have realised this was the same typescript he had seen in 1916.[1102] McHugh did in fact purchase typed copies, but it is unclear just when.

George Bernard Shaw, unlike Yeats, was not at all taken with Dr Maloney's book and told Gertrude Parry "It can do nothing but harm" although he was not sceptical about the Normand thesis (or the Soviet Union). In words a little less overwrought than those of Alfred Noyes in 1916, GBS had also advised her, in 1934, that if the alleged diary was Casement's it "proved him to be a disgustingly unpleasant person." He wanted, instead, something to vindicate the man and if nothing else, to provide an alibi. He declared of Maloney's book "It is a monument of zealous industry; but it does not clear the ground: it rather overcrowds it. It takes more trouble to put the British Government in the wrong than to put Roger in the right" adding, "The book that is needed to rehabilitate Roger must be written on a carefully cleaned slate. Dr Maloney has written his on one crowded with old sums."[1103]

Later, in 1937, GBS was to write in a letter in the press that "the documents existed and were authentic" which prompted the novelist, and soon-to-be

* Yeats's spelling of 'troup' may be a reference to Sir Edward Troup, the Home Office permanent secretary in 1916.

Nazi collaborator, Francis Stuart,* to respond angrily saying the diaries were a "concoction",[1104] however, that process had taken place.

When Dr Maloney published *The Forged Casement Diaries,* he got more than he bargained for. Operating out of America, he had relied for much of his background material on the good offices and efforts of Bulmer Hobson. Maloney's original intention was to write a full-scale biography of Casement. He then discovered he had so much material that a single volume, alone, was needed on Casement's family and upbringing, let alone one on his career, and a third on the diaries. Despite writing a manuscript on his hero's early days, only that on the diaries was ever to be published, or indeed to survive.

Bulmer corresponded with Ada McNeill about Casement's background in Co. Antrim while Travers King, the headmaster's son, located and transcribed the gravestone inscription of Captain Casement in Ballymena's New Cemetery. In the end, Gertrude Parry, apparently not the best correspondent, solved the mystery of exactly who Casement's grandfather was, and where he fitted in with the Casements of Magherintemple and Ballymena. In 1931, she provided "a pedigree."[1105] It offered some detail on his mother, Annie Casement, née Jephson, and her antecedents, but nothing sufficient to illuminate that mystery which may hold the key to fully understanding her youngest son.

Hobson was still out of favour with the new Dublin establishment. According to his son, Declan Hobson, he had never been forgiven by de Valera, and his 1917 attempt at a comeback ended when he was refused permission to speak at the big Mansion House meeting. He was critical of the Irish political parties, calling them economic Unionists, and argued for policies of self-sufficiency like reafforestation. In the 1930s he published plans of a social credit and Keynesian nature, and in the 1940s assisted *Clann na Poblachta* with its economic policy. That party was a strange mixture of radicals, pro-Axis elements and disaffected ultras, led by Maud Gonne's son, Seán MacBride, a former IRA Chief of Staff who spoke English with a French accent. He became Minister of External Affairs in the coalition of 1948-51 and was instrumental in declaring a Republic, taking Éire out of the Commonwealth.

In common with his associates, Bulmer Hobson remained loyal to his memory of Casement and determined that it would not be sullied by the homosexuality allegation. In a 1924 letter to Patrick McCartan he protested: "As

* Although he was born in Australia, Francis Stuart's parents were from Dervock in north Antrim and distantly connected to the Casements, by marriage. A Protestant Republican, married to Maud Gonne's daughter, Iseult (Seán MacBride's sister), he was interned during the civil war. In 1940, in Hamburg he published *Der Fall Casement,* a booklet on Casement's involvement with Germany over Ireland, based on Maloney's book.

regards what Gaffney or any other living man [?] says about Roger and vice, I hold it to be the dirtiest bit of English propaganda I ever heard of. I was Roger's intimate friend from 1902 or 3 until his death."[1106] However, Declan Hobson has said of his father that since he shared a tent and, at times, even a bed with Casement and had not been propositioned, let alone assaulted, he felt the stories could not be true. Declan added he never had the heart to tell his father it might just have been that Casement didn't fancy him.[1107]

In the United States, Maloney had collaborated with Joe McGarrity and McCartan in his researches. McCartan had been a doctor in Tyrone and founder in 1905 of an early Dungannon Club in Carrickmore. Indeed, he had, like Casement, welcomed the formation of the Ulster Volunteers and gone so far in his naïveté (or desire to drive a wedge between London and Ulster) to offer his car for use in the 1914 UVF gunrunning. On discovering that the Unionist driver had fallen ill and failed to turn up, he remarked that had he known the reason he would have driven the guns himself. In 1915 RIC intelligence for Tyrone marked him down as attempting to create a "pro-German party in the county."[1108] He became an early Sinn Féin MP, being returned unopposed for King's County North in April 1918 at a by-election, and was later sent as an envoy to the United States. His final claim to fame was as a candidate against Seán T. O'Kelly for the Irish Presidency in June 1945 when his significantly large vote of over 210,000 first preferences acted as a spur to the creation of *Clann na Poblachta*. He ended up in the Irish Senate, as did most of Casement's collaborators, from 1948 to 1961.

De Valera had declined to write a foreword to Maloney's book saying "the British allegations against Casement have never been believed by Irishmen and so far as they are concerned no refutation is needed." He added wisely "It is possible that his book might only result in a renewal of the campaign of defamation."[1109] No English publisher would take it on for fear of libel actions over the allegations of forgery against living individuals. Bulmer Hobson organised the edition brought out by Talbot Press in Dublin, right down to the photographs and the issue of review copies. While GBS dismissed the book and Yeats was moved to write his poem in response to its message, other unexpected tongues started to wag, bringing unwelcome news to those in America.

When the damage brought about by the publication became apparent, Patrick McCartan wrote, on 9 April 1937, to Bulmer Hobson from New York: "It seems the whispering campaign against Roger has started again but now in Ireland – from Trinity College. A few days ago Billy [Maloney] had a letter from Francis Hackett in which Hackett states that he and Shane Leslie had a statement from Dr Joseph Bigger of Trinity 'for private consumption' that Roger was a homosexual. The whole crusade here was mostly for private consumption and one wonders why a decent fellow like Bigger should lend himself to it. Why in the name of God send it to Leslie who is certain to send it to the Foreign Office."[1110]

Dr Bigger's statement, and his choice of Leslie and Hackett can only have been sparked off by Shane Leslie's review of Maloney's book in the *Irish Times* of 1 March 1937 which was followed by a letter on 8 March from Francis Hackett. He was critical of Leslie for failing sufficiently to indict the British government for its whispering campaign against Casement. Hackett also took the opportunity to repeat the Normand story, saying the account "of sexual depravity…is the translation Casement made of the diary kept by one of the pathological ruffians whose activities he sought to stamp out in the great work for which he was knighted by the King Of England." Bigger was unable to leave such nonsense unanswered.

Hackett (1883-1962) was a founder and former editor of the distinguished American magazine *New Republic*. He was married to a Danish novelist Signe Toksvig. Both had books banned in the 1930s – his, *The Green Lion*, in 1936, and hers, *Eve's Doctor*, a year later. They chose to leave Ireland for Denmark in July 1937 just after this publishing trouble began. By 1932, Hackett had already lost his illusions, complaining to his diary on 23 April, "They have transferred Catholic Ideology to Irish politics."

He seems to have had no time for Shane Leslie (Sir John Leslie), formerly a British diplomat in Washington, and a very Catholic convert, who (rather than Casement, one assumes) prompted Hackett's outburst to Maloney in a letter of 21 April 1937: "The tendency of weak-nerved people is to join a crew, and Foreign Offices must be full of queer fellows. The British F.O. is full of mincing Catholics." He then related a lurid story about Leslie, this time of a heterosexual variety. In fact Hackett had a fairly low opinion of most of his literary friends: "In Dublin you have to be a psycho-analyst to navigate through a tea party…Ireland is a country for a contortionist."[1111]

McCartan continued "Don't spread this but if you or P.S. [O'Hegarty] could find out what Bigger sent to Hackett and Leslie, Billy might be prepared, if the British spring something on him. P.S. or Mrs P.S. or Lil [O'Donnell?] is a friend of Bigger's but better not tell Lil. You or P.S. could find out yourselves. If you remember the Doctor's uncle Frank was charged with the same thing and his statement re Roger may be just as groundless as those about Frank. As the English knew of that rumour the Doctor may have been on purpose selected to start the whispering campaign. Find out all you can."

Only one side of this correspondence survives but enough remains to reveal the state of crisis the Bigger bombshell had put them all in. On 27 April 1937 McCartan wrote once more, somewhat repetitiously, to Hobson: "As I told you in a note about ten days ago the whispering campaign against Casement started again and from Trinity College this time and from the man who hopes to be the next Provost. Since I wrote to you Maloney got a copy of Dr Bigger's letter from Francis Hackett who said a copy had been sent to Shane Leslie... It seems there is one way to stop this – it is a rotten way but still – I shall pass the word to the IRA to give Bigger or any other Irishman found spreading the yarn one warning. The English enemy can do as they please...".

"If Leslie or any other Irishman help to substantiate the charges against Casement, Maloney will have a lot more to say. **Others who say nothing may act** [this author's emphasis]. Some of the men involved in shooting Wilson on his own doorstep are yet alive and they will get all the facts from me. I enclose a copy of Maloney's letter to Hackett...".

Field Marshall Sir Henry Wilson, born in Co. Longford in 1864, was by 1918 Chief of the Imperial General Staff and a member of the War Cabinet. He lived at 36 Eaton Place in London and was assassinated on his doorstep on 22 June 1922. Reginald Dunne and Joseph O'Sullivan were executed on 10 August for his murder although a wider 'organised conspiracy' was suspected. In the War Cabinet, Wilson had argued for conscription in Ireland and harsher military measures. By 1922 he had become Conservative MP for North Down and official security adviser to James Craig's new Belfast government, an appointment which sealed his fate.

Only an extract from Hackett's original letter to Maloney of 24 March 1937 survives. It was duly sent by McCartan to Hobson "for yourself and P.S. only." It read "Dr Joseph Bigger of Trinity has given Leslie and myself a statement for private consumption that Casement was a homo. You know this I assume. I'll copy the statement. Now Casement being a homosexual he was a perfect target for a criminal's diary to be pinned to him, granted. But de Valera knows that if Casement was in fact homosexual the rest of the game with Sir B Thomson will be played without a referee. You can't have a public vindication of a homo as an officer and a gentleman."

Hackett was still trying to marry the criminal Normand's story beloved by Maloney *et al* to the fact of Casement's homosexuality, which he now accepted, but in such a way as to warn the whole crew that London had the whip hand. These words were also written to explain why Dev was not exercising himself in Casement's defence and sticking instead to the government's sensible policy of avoiding the diaries at all costs and relying instead on Casement's reputation as a patriot and distinguished humanitarian.

On a separate undated sheet, McCartan advised Hobson "Burn what I write on this page and show the rest to Leslie. It will help to shut him up for he is 'yellow' as they say here. Show him also Maloney's reply to Hackett. Billy has enough on Leslie to make him run to cover. I hope to get Sean Russell or some of the boys to visit Bigger and give him some 'friendly advice'. He had no right to stick his nose in here."

Sean Russell (1893-1940) was Chief of Staff of the IRA, having succeeded Seán MacBride in 1937. His greatest achievement was the 1939 bombing campaign in England. Ironically he too made a submarine journey to Ireland from Germany, after seeing the Foreign Minister, Ribbentrop. He had also come there from America, although via Genoa. For the second time in the circumstances of a world war, the IRA/Irish separatists chose to ally themselves with Germany; this time with Hitler's regime. That journey too ended in disaster with Russell, accompanied by a left winger, Frank Ryan, dying on board the submarine from a ruptured duodenal ulcer. Russell has the distinction of being the only Irishman involved in the Second World War to have a statue raised in his honour in the Republic, in Dublin's Fairview Park.

McCartan ended with the instruction "Burn this. Yours &c. Pat." Oddly, Hobson did not do as he was commanded and the papers ended up, largely unnoticed in the NLI, although shorn of several key items and lacking his replies. Maloney and McCartan took their own advice on destroying correspondence concerning Dr Bigger's indiscretions. In the New York Public Library, the frequent, at times twice-monthly, letters from Hobson to America are absent from the archives after 20 March 1937 and do not recommence until October of that year.

A typed copy of a Maloney letter to Hackett, from New York and dated 25 April 1937, is the nearest we will come to the text of the Professor's traumatising original. Maloney comes on to Francis Hackett with leaden sarcasm in an attempt to belittle belief in the veracity of Bigger's disclosures. Having sent a "cable asking for the document", he wrote "It came safely, was very interesting but more so to me was your reaction to it…The proof [of sodomy] offered to you is the good faith of your informant, Joseph W. Bigger. You think Bigger is telling the truth…he seemed a straightforward chap. But he offered no evidence beyond his unsupported word.

"Bigger's uncle Francis Joseph, the one who lived at Ardrigh where Shane Leslie used to call, was interested in the boy scout movement about thirty years ago when I occasionally went to Belfast and never had any interest in what he was doing. Yet that did not spare my shocked ears from hearing that the Greeks had a name for Francis Joseph Bigger's habits and that he needed none to show him how to scout for boys. In this rumor he was I am sure misrepresented…As far as I can ascertain his sexual habits were not obtrusive and were presumably normal.

"But then no friend's nephew has come forward to tell with correct reluctance and with noble purpose of Bigger the sodomite's diary secretly burned at a midnight fire in the kitchen stove…I don't place the proper significance on the informer Bigger's statement that he learnt from the cook and his uncle that Casement went out much at night.

"Bigger tells you that his uncle, when Casement's activity in Germany became known (which was in October 1914) 'feared a search by the military authorities and got rid of his (Casement's) bags and old clothing'. As late possibly as September 1915 the nephew 'had found in the small room on the right of the hall at Ardrigh which Mr Leslie may remember' a diary telling of anti-British activities in organising the Irish Volunteers, in pitting German against British shipping interests in Ireland and in other spheres as well as exposing myself [sic] as a confirmed sodomist."

Joseph Bigger described his uncle Frank almost fainting on making the discovery, adding that the thing was destroyed "immediately in the kitchen fire – it was late at night – everyone but ourselves had gone to bed." Maloney's commentary intervenes again, "The only collateral statement that can be tested is the reference to Casement's brother being in debt in 1914." Finally, Bigger tried to explain: "My object in writing [to Hackett and Leslie] is to attempt to bring the controversy to an end because I am convinced that the British Government had and probably has diaries of Roger Casement which if published would establish beyond question that he was a pervert." His assessment of Casement nonetheless was that "his present position of national hero and martyr is one that is well deserved."[1112]

Bigger's nephew's story is undoubtedly true but there are problems with it. It may be that it is not all the truth. What he specified he burnt may have been only a small part of what went into the fire. He may have chosen, in his 1937 disclosures, to minimise the sheer quantity of the material discovered and destroyed. It is also possible Bigger had kept the hidden trunkful of Casement material elsewhere and it was still in 1915 to be excavated and weeded. He might, as his nephew stated, have "got rid of" Casement's clothes in the sense of secreting the trunk but, as we know, the clothes were not destroyed.

It is indicated by B.L. Reid that Bigger buried the Ardrigh trunk or box[1113] only later exhuming it, and then reading the papers he found inside. Disturbed by what he read – and had possessed – Bigger was then said to have burnt every scrap of paper therein. Herbert Mackey, in his 1962 book, accepts that Bigger set about destruction, stating, however, that it was "secret political papers" that were burnt.

Casement wrote on 26 March 1916,[1114] "These and many more letters & papers dealing with my past are in the custody of Francis Joseph Bigger, Ardrigh, Antrim Road, Belfast, a Solicitor. He was a close friend of mine & a nationalist

– but now doubtless has been swept off his feet.

However I am sure he would not give up my papers to the Govt. – & he buried them – or hid them I know, for I wrote to him from N. York before I sailed for Germany asking him to do this & got a reply that it had been done. So little had I "worked" against England or meditated treason that I have left all my other things at the mercy of the Govt.

I had boxes of valuable papers &c. &c. in store with Agents in London. Allison & Son, Farringdon Road E.C. Also others at Ballycastle, Co. Antrim, Ireland.

The former are surely long since in the possession of the Br. Govt. – the latter less important – chiefly books I had collected for years & are probably safe as they were in the hands of a staunch nationalist – Stephen Clarke."

What is hard to believe is that Casement's 1914 diary was just sitting out in a cloakroom open to Biddy, Tommie, or a stray visitor to find, unless in a locked trunk. The likeliest deduction is that Bigger wanted to consult his favourite nephew on his concerns and started by showing him the diary, perhaps saying he found it by chance. Maloney's suggested objective test on Tom Casement (or Charlie's) indebtedness was a reasonable one and would have gone in favour of the nephew's truthfulness except there was hardly a year when Tom wasn't in such difficulties. The cook's story (presumably Brigid Mathews), that Casement often went out at night, rings true but his recorded cruising successes in Belfast seem largely to have been in daylight or in the early evening. Belfast, at that time, was asleep by 11 p.m. so she may have been recalling that he went walking after he had dined.

On 4 May 1937, McCartan concluded the correspondence with Hobson, saying "I saw your letter with Billy which you sent to Hackett. You wrote in the right strain."[1115] And no more was heard of it until MacColl published his biography in 1956. Joseph Warwick Bigger (1891-1951), a distinguished Professor of Bacteriology, did not become Provost of TCD. He served in the Royal Army Medical Corps during the Second World War and like his father, was a Dublin University Senator, in his case from 1944 to 1951. Whether he ever received a visit from "the boys" or even Sean Russell himself, in his capacity as Chief of Staff, remains unknown. But the cover-up was to be enforced, as mention of Casement's homosexuality had now become a capital offence. Bigger certainly never went public with his insider knowledge on Casement. His silence suggests a warning message got through.

Shortly before his death, he did, however, detail the matter of his uncle Frank burning* the manuscripts and letters found in Casement's trunk, to

---

* See also the preface to the 1993 edition of Brian Inglis's Casement biography where the story of the burning is confirmed by Ernest Blythe, as told to him, innocently, by Bulmer Hobson.

John J. Horgan, the coroner who had presided over the *Lusitania* inquests in Cork. He in turn told the story in 1954 to René MacColl who kept Horgan's identity a closely-guarded secret until after he had died. At that point, MacColl disclosed the name in a letter to *The Times* of 18 August 1967. The desperate desire by Horgan to keep his name secret does suggest a carry-over of the IRA threat to Dr Bigger.

Horgan had been in close contact with Casement in 1913 and 1914, corresponding frequently about the controversy over the Hamburg Amerika Line getting to call at the port of Queenstown (Cobh). He was a Gaelic Leaguer and writer, as well as a council member of the Catholic Truth Society. Horgan's later, unflattering, assessment of Casement (provided to Denis Gwynn for his 1930 book) was in tune with a few other unsentimental acquaintances of Casement: "He was a Don Quixote. Any extreme or extraordinary project appealed to him and I should think he was a very difficult man to work with and easily upset if his impractical proposals were not carried out…I don't think he was altogether normal."[1116]

The trunk at Ardrigh was obviously the one Casement was sufficiently anxious about, to have the secret message sent in November 1914, from Berlin, through the German embassy in Washington to F.J. Bigger ordering concealment. Indeed Casement may have originally intended it to travel with him to America as there is a frantic telegram in Bigger's papers, addressed to his housekeeper Bridget, dated 4 July 1914 – the very day of Casement's departure across the Atlantic from Glasgow: "Box not come. Wire how sent at once. Casement."[1117] So he probably was mindful of leaving too many compromising papers behind. But in this instance he became parted from his property and it presumably returned to Belfast.

The Berlin message was duly intercepted and deciphered by Naval Intelligence in Room 40, yet London did nothing by way of seizing Casement's property. This strongly suggests they were not yet greatly exercised about him – not enough to probe his personal life in Belfast nor to consider the possibility of belongings in London. Inaction in the face of critical decryptions was something of a pattern in London and Dublin. Circumstantial evidence of the matter being so dealt with can be found, in Gavan Duffy's trial papers, from cryptic words written by F.J. Bigger on 1 June 1916, "You know I wish you and Ireland all credit and success…P is worrying about the papers. All Serene." A reasonable candidate for 'P' is Sidney Parry who was indeed worried. He was also talking, and talking too much about the "other charges." The gist of this message was a reminder that Bigger may be keeping his distance, as he was, but he remained sound and unaltered in his loyalties.[1118] It was Gavan Duffy who wrote to him asking for some of Casement's unearthed property. On receipt, he replied "Thanks for the clothes which Rory is wearing now. Everything is going splendidly."[1119] Keeping up morale was one of the gallant solicitor's duties.

There is no convincing reason for Casement to have given the concealing order in 1914 other than to have the evidence of his sexual activities hidden. Any notes or correspondence of a political nature in the cache predated his departure for America and also his defection to Germany. They would have provided little or no intelligence to his enemies. He did have at least one trunk's worth of valuable historical papers in America, leaving it with Joe McGarrity in Philadelphia. But Casement was too fond of his manuscripts to order the lot destroyed; too interested in how history would assess his actions. Hiding his letters and diaries, he felt, was sufficient for the moment. The war had, however, obliged him to dump overboard, through a porthole, those incriminating papers he could not pass to Adler, on the voyage to Europe in October 1914 when his Norwegian ship was stopped by the Royal Navy and taken into Stornoway.

René MacColl, whose book remained the only previous record of this event, can now be relied upon by virtue of this previously unknown attempt to suppress the truth and fake the historical record. One must, however, take into account the fact that the story is written in MacColl's own prose style and only came to him third or fourth hand. His presumption about the date of destruction ("after Casement's execution") is wrong as may be his view of Bigger's own state of knowledge about his friend's orientation. What he described sounds as if it refers to a different event or possibly a fusing of two incidents: "Bigger opened the trunk. What he discovered inside gave him a staggering shock...There lay a voluminous diary full of homosexual notations and reminiscences; and there was also a large quantity of letters from various young men, the contents of which left no doubt as to the nature of their relations with Casement."[1120]

F.J. Bigger presumably also knew what everyone else apparently did, that he was the subject of the same accusation of homosexuality as Casement was. If Roddie went down, Frank might well follow. He already felt himself at risk by virtue of his intimate connections to so many personnel in the 1916 Rising, to leading Sinn Féiners in Belfast, and of course to Casement himself – the man announced in newspapers, and reckoned by many in governing circles, to be the political leader of the rebellion.

The irony of course was that Bigger shared all the passion and prejudices that motivated Casement, but both he and Hobson had reckoned that he did not want to hear anything of conspiracy. In 1912 and 1913, when they stayed together at Ardrigh they protected him from unwelcome knowledge. As the TCD historian, R.B. McDowell, wrote, the pair felt it would be tactful to wait until Bigger had bustled off to his office before they discussed certain bold projects since he enjoyed the thrill of being against the government, but did not want to know too much.

Nina, in a typically harsh aside, added in November 1915, when justifying her dash to America to her brother, "Yes that beauty Bigger turned right over." She explained the alienation facing her in Co. Antrim after the war started, "I may as well tell you it was not one house in a thousand I could get into."[1121] In an ominous hint of what Casement's new Ireland might have been like, McGarrity wrote earlier, "Do not judge the Bigger boy too harshly. He may have thought she was one of those servants of the King that has made themselves such a plague to you for the last few months. In any case let us wait for an explanation. Bear up and think of the future when old scores will be settled and we will all be happy. He added in another letter, "Patrick did not drive all the snakes out of Ireland after all. Is it possible for you to get the names and addresses of your tormentors for future reference at least. When the day dawns as I think it will, these Vipers should get their chastisement."[1122]

The destruction of the Ardrigh cache may provide an answer to the mystery of the other missing diaries (if any ever existed) and the total absence in the surviving Casement papers of any boyfriend correspondence bar one innocuous letter from Millar Gordon and two postcards (now in New York). Given that various South American lads are recorded in the diaries as writing to Casement it is remarkable that their letters are otherwise absent from Casement's papers.

A likely explanation is that he had centralised his private notebooks and love letters keeping especially those papers and diaries associated with his official consular investigations in England. Scotland Yard would unquestionably have made much of any such revealing correspondence so one can assume that none was ever in their hands. There is some evidence from inscriptions on the back of a number of items, and the manner in which they have been folded, that Casement had been sifting, ordering and annotating his collected letters for the historical record, and ironically ultimate public access. It is therefore possible he might also have been availing of such an opportunity to excise his love life from the collection.

In a recently released Bureau of Military History (BMH) witness statement dated 5 May 1950,[1123] Gavan Duffy wrote of the Casement trial. He did this by providing the text of a "Lecture on Sir Roger Casement given by the Hon George Gavan Duffy to London-Irish Gaels, at 14 Parnell Square, Dublin, on 16th April, 1950." The BMH describes him as "Irish Envoy in Italy and France 1920-1921; Signatory of the Anglo-Irish Treaty 6/12/1921". Duffy explained how he had been staying with his family at Easter 1916 "in a remote part of Tírconaill" as news of the Rising filtered through. "I knew that Roger might have difficulty in finding a solicitor in London to defend him in the English atmosphere of the day, so, having known him earlier in County Antrim and in London, I went back to London [and] on 1st May, 1916, I applied in writing to see him as his solicitor".

In the middle of this explanation, he startlingly revealed, "I had in fact received the year before, from a friend of his, three cases of his papers which the friend thought it unwise to retain and he wanted to dispose of them. I remember spending an arduous week-end with Art O'Brien, whom I called in, going through these documents to see what might be utterly seditious in them."

The concerned friend is most likely to have been Dick Morten, given that the inspection probably occurred in London where both Duffy and O'Brien lived. Morten had earlier been a custodian of Casement papers at his house, The Savvy, as is revealed in a letter of 10 July 1906[1124] when Casement wrote, "Please ask one of your maids to do up all my things left at Savoy – books, papers, clothes, &c. &c. in one big bundle & then, very kindly, despatch them to me."

Art O'Brien, from an upper class Catholic family, was a cousin of Ignatius O'Brien (later Lord Shandon), the Lord Chancellor of Ireland from 1913 to 1918. 'Art Ó Briain', as he became, was born in England and was an early member of the Gaelic League, joining in London in 1899 where he would have met Duffy. He is described by Roy Foster in *Vivid Faces* as an "upwardly mobile sophisticate", and as having "an artistic temperament"[1125] which may suggest he was gay. It is plain that Gavan Duffy who was educated at Stonyhurst knew in 1916, if not earlier, that Casement was gay. Perhaps he asked O'Brien to help him sift the papers, knowing he would not be as shocked as some.

It is unlikely there was anything seditious in the three cases, given the material predated the outbreak of war so it must have been the mixed in sexual material that was so concerning. We know Casement was worried about his papers as he expressed concerns about those left with F.J. Bigger. Indeed he had written in 1914 asking that they be hidden (or buried) and been assured they were.

The absence of letters <u>to Casement</u> from a number of his key correspondents, with whom he was frequently in contact, confirms that a significant segment of his correspondence has disappeared. That group, for whom there is voluminous correspondence in archives written <u>by Casement</u>, comprises Gertrude Bannister, F.J. Bigger, Francis Cowper, Alice Stopford Green, Bulmer Hobson, E.D. Morel and Dick Morten. There is, in contrast, next to nothing, currently archived, <u>from them to Casement</u> written before 1913.

In the NLI, there are no Bigger to Casement letters nor any to Mrs Green. Only one item from Dick Morten to Casement survives there, an undated note about a repaid debt.[1126] Similarly the NLI has only one pre-war letter to Casement from Gertrude Bannister and one from Bulmer Hobson.[1127] In the case of E.D. Morel, only one such item is extant and just two in the NLI from Francis Cowper, the Lisbon Consul.[1128]

If the inspection took place in Belfast then the likeliest candidate is F.J. Bigger who certainly burnt other documents. Montgomery Hyde in an unpublished letter to *The Times*[1129] confirmed that F.J. Bigger's nephew, Joseph, then a medical student at TCD, when visiting his uncle "was shown the papers consisting of several diaries and also a number of compromising letters from homosexual correspondents." After talking it over, "the antiquarian [FJB] told him that that he thought the best thing to do was to burn the lot which he accordingly did."

Thus incoming boyfriend letters, especially those from South America mentioned in the diaries, disappeared. Gavan Duffy did not explain what happened to the three cases of papers after the pair's inspection but they must have been destroyed in their entirety. One way or another, in Belfast and London, any other diaries were also eliminated.

Dr Herbert Spencer Dickey was to be the next and alternate mainstay for the forgery school. His particular virtue was that he been in Casement's company for part of the period covered by the efflorescent 1911 diary. He was also thought especially credible, being a medical doctor employed as resident physician by the Peruvian Amazon Company in 1907-8. Casement did not particularly like or trust him. Indeed he called him "an unscrupulous rascal" in 1913 in a letter to Percy Browne for having later changed his testimony. In that respect anything Dickey says to bolster Casement's reputation (as he himself pointed out) has to be accorded extra validity, although balanced by his proven variable memory.

But he is no more important than dozens of others who were daily in Casement's company and were not aware of any homosexual mode or activity. Nonetheless Angus Mitchell describes him as "the most important and convincing witness to Casement's behaviour on his 1911 voyage."[1130] A less tendentious view is that he was not a mind reader and saw only behaviour that Casement allowed him to see, although he ultimately recorded more detail of their time spent together than did any other companion of the voyage.

To this day, gay men rarely advertise their intentions as regards outdoor cruising because of good taste, or shame over promiscuity, shame about homosexuality or simply shame about sex itself. If they are firmly closeted in their orientation then absolutely no hint of any of their true feelings or actual activities will emerge. The example of the Secretary of State for Wales who in 1998 lost his job and much of his reputation because of an event on Clapham Common, confirms this even now, some ninety years on. None of the MP's colleagues was able to explain, from pre-existing awareness of his nocturnal activities, why Ron Davies was there that night. All that was on offer in the media, initially, were assumptions based on Clapham Common's reputation as a cruising area and as a haunt of drug dealers. Davies later admitted to being "bisexual" when further outed in a Sunday newspaper, having been photographed in woods near his Welsh home. He then sought psychiatric assistance for what he called a compulsive sexual disorder.

Dr Dickey surfaced in 1936 after reading Denis Gwynn's book *The Life and Death of Roger Casement*, published six years earlier, and later provided an affidavit on what he had not seen in 1911. Dickey also came up with a Conan Doyle theory which was on a par with that concerning Armando Normand and about as unlikely. Not knowing the form or extent of the diaries, he was able, persuasively, to propose that his extended conversation on board ship with Casement about the sexual habits of the Amazon Indians, recorded at length in longhand in order to be sent to Arthur Conan Doyle (an author ever on the lookout for colour), was the source of the offending material in London. When Dickey asked for Conan Doyle's autograph, Casement "looked at the end of the letter and said it would be of no use to me as Sir Arthur had not signed in full." That story stands up only in part, which does not mean Dickey is not relating what he heard Casement say.

There is a letter of 8 June 1911 in the NLI from Conan Doyle, but the next is one dated 30 August 1911. It is marked as received in Iquitos, and answered from Manaos on 12 December. Unusually, it is signed "Arthur Conan Doyle" in full; others carry only initials.[1131] No new letter was therefore received and preserved during the time the two were together on board ship. But Casement could have been flourishing an older one, perhaps that of 3 July 1910 which is signed "ACD". In it, Conan Doyle wrote "Many thanks for all information which is duly filed and will in time be of great use."

A month later Doyle was sketching out the plot of an Amazon adventure story set on a high plateau cut off for millennia by cliffs, and inhabited by mastodons. In 1912 the book was finished and he was telling Casement "*The Lost World* has one character which is about the best I ever drew." This was Lord John Roxton "the spare, handsome, exquisitely dressed battler for the underprivileged" i.e. Casement. He then added quizzically "You are of the old faith are you not? I was but am no longer." Conan Doyle stood twice for parliament as a Unionist, but during the war he stuck by his 1910 promise "May our friendship survive all geographical separations."

It is interesting to read Dr Dickey's opinion of what Casement noted with some relish – that "sexual irregularities were openly and unashamedly practised among savage people and were not necessarily to be ascribed to the decadence they may connote under conditions of civilisation." He remarked that he had not had time in the Putumayo to delve into the matter.[1132]

Roger McHugh, a UCD professor, in his 1960 *Threshold* article, the first and longest post-diary publication, until Mitchell in 1997, to argue forgery, relies heavily on Dickey. Professor McHugh (1908-1987) could not believe the 1911 diarist to have been other than a gross pathic, "a compulsive or obsessive psychopath or neurotic of low intelligence with no sense of responsibility for his actions…A dull degenerate who has reached the last stages of abnormality"; one who described "impossible sights in an insane way" yet still managed to conceal his habits from the "trained eye of the American doctor." McHugh asserted, in rapid response to a substantive letter from Dr Letitia Fairfield in the following issue of *Threshold*, that Dickey "certainly knew him well enough to judge whether he was a psychopath of the kind revealed in the 1911 diary; his opinion was emphatically otherwise."

In further aid, Roger McHugh quoted the view of the noted Belfast psychiatrist Pearse O'Malley (husband of Mary O'Malley, the editor of *Threshold*) that "the disorganisation of personality manifested in them (the diary entries) should have been noticeable even to acquaintances." Dr O'Malley did, however, opine that the author was not of the schizophrenic or paranoid type. It is plain that O'Malley's homosexual patients did not include any who only a few years earlier, in 1943-44, had taken enormous advantage of the massive influx of American GIs into Northern Ireland and the fortuitous wartime blackout; but then psychiatrists' expertise was usually based on unhappy and unrequited homosexuals, not on those who enjoy themselves sexually and cheerfully report their adventures to the younger cohort.

From 5 September, in Casement's two 1911 journals, Dr Dickey gets a number of mentions but none that indicates he was in Casement's company, on land, for more than a few hours at a time. And it was not Casement's practice to be with anyone for long. He was always on the move, working as a solo operator, constantly seeing different people for relatively short periods. The two were together one evening in Pará (15 September) innocently working on a jigsaw puzzle with Ricudo, but only for an hour. They dined together another evening (18 September) although Casement, as he departed for an evening of unaccompanied cruising, noted that Dickey was ill. On a further occasion, in Manaos, he joined the doctor for breakfast.

During the fortnight's voyage from Manaos to Iquitos in early October, Dickey fell ill again, and took over Casement's cabin for a number of days. He compassionately recorded in his diary on 5 October, "bad with fever – poor beggar." But then Dickey appears to have begun to irritate him since he wrote on 7 October 1911, and then struck out, the harsh words "Damn Dr Dickey say I." Giving up his cabin was typical of Casement but then so was a later tirade against the beneficiary of his charity. Dickey does not appear to have been around Casement much during the first part of his stay in Iquitos and he apparently went on his way to Remate de Males after "four days" and a lunch together with an Englishman called Schultz (renamed "later Scott") who apparently annoyed Casement "by his presence."[1133] Dickey died in Ecuador in 1948.

The Normand theory and its Dickey variant were exploded in 1959 on publication by Singleton-Gates of three of the four incriminating volumes. Plainly Armando Normand was not involved in homosexual activity in Belfast, Dublin or the Canaries nor was he a habitué of London restaurants and salons nor English country houses (although he had lived in England). He was also not an intimate of the Casement family in Ballycastle and beyond.

Geoffrey Parmiter struck the final blow in an article in the *Quarterly Review* in April 1960. He recanted thus: "In my book *Roger Casement* published in 1936, I wrote that: 'It is possible that it [the Black Diary] formed part of the evidence which Casement collected during his enquiry in the Putumayo and was carefully copied by Casement, but never published owing to its indecent character'. This idea was developed in greater detail by Dr Maloney, also in 1936 and was adopted by Mr Noyes in 1957. An examination however, of the diaries now in the Public Record Office reveals that this conjecture is untenable."

But Normand and Dickey stood the forgery school in good stead for forty years and provided a bolthole, which was probably all that was needed, for those who knew and loved Casement. Dickey remained a weapon for the Casement defenders in a world lacking many others. By now it had become impossible to contemplate any other truth, for if Casement was (in their expressed view) that most degenerate of people, a rampant homosexual with a penchant for boys, it called into question the whole edifice of contemporary Irish nationalism which he had significantly helped to construct. For Protestant nationalists it was especially dangerous as it would confirm a then popular Catholic view of Protestants that they were heretical and thus capable of any and all vices.

Despite propagating the Normand theory, there are hints that Gertrude Parry may have had differing views of her beloved cousin, or at least different layers of knowledge. One sign comes in a letter of 24 June 1935, from Mrs Bernard Shaw, where mention is made of Lawrence of Arabia and his recent death which put a stop to Shaw's suggested project of writing about Casement. Charlotte Shaw twice quotes back to Gertrude her impression of T.E. Lawrence, "It is as you say he '*understood*'." Mrs Shaw continued "Perhaps, T.E. is better as he is – his life was not happy latterly." This last sentiment was surely uttered for Gertrude's sake to apply to Casement as well. Mrs Shaw added "This vulgar excitement over his death is horrible."[1134] Lawrence died alone in a motorcycle crash. Much of his life after the war was a sublimation of his own homosexuality and an escape from fame. Elsewhere, in a 1924 letter,[1135] Patrick McCartan privately remarks to Dr Maloney that Gertrude "does not know whether it is a forgery or genuine", suggesting at least that the matter was an open question with her.[1136]

Gertrude had one rare cross of infidelity to bear in the form of Herbert Ward's conviction as to the diaries authenticity. Ward, who had known Casement as well as any, and for longer than almost all others, had "alas, in his patriotic zeal", according to Gertrude "allowed his mind to be so poisoned against his old and true friend that he was ready to give his name as a guarantor that the diary was all in Roger's handwriting."[1137] He luckily died in 1919 before he was able to say more, although he had also stated, in her words, that "the whole idea came as an overwhelming blow to him and he had never suspected Roger." Ward's 'betrayal', although it predated the diary discovery, uniquely upset and concerned Casement in prison in 1916.

A balancing moment for Gertrude was the love token gift of Countess Markievicz's crucifix which, as she wrote, saved her "from going mad those awful hours at daybreak when I lay in my cell at Kilmainham listening to the English murdering our leaders and during Rory's last hours before he went out to die for us. I prayed for him with it in my hand."[1138]

We cannot tell what unrecorded conversations Gertrude may have had (or what comments she overheard) in those decades, with some who knew the secret, not least her own husband, but for the last fifteen years of her life she was to make no further public pronouncement. Her correspondence in the NLI peters out in the late 1930s. Although we will never know if she withheld some of Casement's papers or destroyed any, it is true to say that she did donate some that were incidentally revealing and many others that confirm the personnel and events in the Black Diaries.

Casement occasionally wrote comments at the top of correspondence, and at times used the back of letters as a notepad. Never having seen the diaries, Gertrude would not have known or recognised critical names like Millar, Ignacio Torres, Casaldo or Teddy that are to be found in the cache. She said herself, in 1930, when handing the papers to the NLI that she had "been quite unable to do more than look over them rapidly" although she promised to "go through them more carefully" on future visits to Dublin.[1139] The apparently innocuous, but unquestionably homoerotic, photographs of South American boys that reached the NLI say more than the poems and as much as many of the rampant diary entries. However, they represent a very small proportion of Casement's photograph collection, and few if any of those on Scotland Yard's list.[1140] None of the albums which were returned to Gertrude Parry seem to have been donated to the NLI.

Another conspicuous absence is that of the framed photographs of his friends, for which Casement had a particular penchant. Frequent references are made to the purchase of such frames, one in particular being bought at Harrods to memorialise the mysteriously deceased Belfast youth, Johnny Bell. Yet Scotland

Yard returned twenty-one of them while the Parry family who inherited the residue of Gertrude's estate in 1950 now recalls receiving only a few trinkets and no framed photographs.[1141]

The wills of Gertrude and Sidney Parry, dated 1944 and 1937 respectively, were both witnessed by the superb Ulster artist, James Humbert Craig, who had a cottage in Cushendun. Pictures by Craig with inscriptions that reveal they once belonged to Sidney Parry have appeared for sale in Belfast galleries. This suggests that Gertrude when in financial difficulties, during and after the war, may have disposed of valuable assets within Northern Ireland.

One other of Casement's famous literary friends and previous supporters was not so kindly disposed, as GBS in his idiosyncratic way, or W.B. Yeats in his apparent (but actually not*) simple faith, or as helpful as Doyle who petitioned for a reprieve while pleading tropically-induced insanity and getting no thanks for it. Joseph Conrad had first known Casement in the Congo a quarter of a century earlier. They had, as he recorded in his Congo diary, shared a bedroom for a fortnight in Matadi. However, writing to Lady Ottoline Morrell, on 10 August 1916, shortly after the execution, Conrad explained "Yes I knew Casement in the Congo in 1890...He was looked upon as a rather enigmatical personality. But all that is an old story of which the last chapter has been closed."

Conrad's opinions of his old friend had long been somewhat cold, if memorably composed, but when Casement took up a pro-German stance he had put himself way beyond the Polish-born writer's pale. Apart from having his elder son, Borys, in the trenches in France, Conrad was seriously anti-German. He had assumed, however, a reprieve would be forthcoming, just as de Valera and Markievicz had had their death sentences commuted by the military court in Dublin. In response to a letter from John Quinn, a Conrad manuscript collector, as well as an American oil company lawyer, he wrote on 15 July "No I don't suppose Casement will swing in any case. As to the (British) military action in Ireland one may regret it...In any other country it would have been a thousand times worse."

Quinn had written to Conrad on 29 June 1916, before his view was altered by inspection of Casement diary entries at the British embassy in Washington "I believe that he is a man of the utmost austerity and purity in his personal life, that the damn insinuations that came out of England that they had something on him in the way of degeneration of some kind were too filthy and nauseating to even think of." Conrad, in his response, declined to offer a comment on the filthy insinuations – a revealing silent statement. Nor did he sign the reprieve petition.

* Yeats wrote to his (lesbian) lover, Dorothy Wellesley, in 1937, "It would be a great relief to me if they [the diaries] were so submitted [to a tribunal] & proved genuine. If Casement were a homo-sexual what matter."

If anyone could have filled the bill as a forger it would have to have been someone with a magnificent imagination who was memorably eloquent on paper; in short a novelist or *litterateur* of great reputation, one either made or in the making. No mere scribe or bureaucrat could have mastered a day's diary entry let alone a year's worth. A man who had lived a mysterious life, an outsider who came from another culture fits the bill perfectly. Joseph Conrad was just such a person. And he also had a degree of motive. Not only did he have the skill to write the tale, he actually knew the man intimately, if briefly, while his handwriting bore an uncanny resemblance to Casement's. Better still, with his regular beard he looked like him.

Then throw in Rider Haggard, another Casement acquaintance, who significantly wrote that "sexual passion is the most powerful lever with which to stir the mind of man for it lies at the root of all things human."[1142] Haggard (whose diplomat brother, Sir William, was Casement's boss in Rio in 1908 and who attended the trial) was famous in his writing both for African colour and violent excess. If Arthur Conan Doyle, the creator of Sherlock Holmes, is added in for mystery and intrigue, plus T.E. Lawrence for a bit of rough homosexual experience, there is the making of just what a team it would have been necessary to put together to undertake the forging. However, an Irish contributor connected to Casement would also be essential; George Bernard Shaw had something of the same background and was notoriously contrary, if not perverse...But in truth only James Joyce, whose writing style was not dissimilar from some of the more impressionistic diary entries, could have concluded the task. He, however, was unavailable and would not have been willing, although he had in fact taken Casement under his notice, giving him a mention in *Ulysses* in relation to the 1904 Congo report, and on another, rarely noted, occasion when his September 1913 open letter is quoted anachronistically.

Conrad, like Herbert Ward, was not exercised to defend Casement. But another acquaintance, a minor character, one who would have been expected to give support, went into attack mode. Robert Cunninghame Graham, the radical travel writer, a former Lib-Lab MP, Catholic convert and "friend of Ireland", in a letter of 13 May 1916 to *The Nation* indulged, according to H.W. Nevinson, in venomous abuse of Casement, laced with "scornful innuendo." Casement's friend, the Belfast-born essayist Robert Lynd felt obliged to respond, writing that Casement had been blackened "with clichés of contempt."

If the diaries were not forged in their entirety or largely manufactured, then the alternative and vastly more plausible theory is one of interpolation of entries. This idea is encouraged by the fact that differing styles of handwriting and the use of different writing instruments on the same page occur throughout the volumes. Indeed the descriptions of sexual events and encounters are the most prone to such variations.

It is plain, however, that one of the diaries' functions was to enable Casement to avail of them as a sex substitute or erotic tool. When re-reading entries he would add remarks and exclamations, sometimes in amplification, sometimes, as one author has put it, in "ecstatic mode." But the idea of foreign insertion suffers from the fact that so many of the sexualised details form an integral and central part of the ensemble. It has to be accepted that amendments and additions will be placed in the spaces above, below and around entries, which they are. But then they would have to be. Nonetheless the enormous number of named characters, whether colleagues or partners or just young men whom Casement yearned over, would still have had to be either invented, or if drawn from life, researched. Such counterfeiting leaves traces. None have surfaced.

Handwriting experts, the first commissioned by R.A. Butler before the diaries were made accessible, and another in 1993, by the BBC, have concluded that they were written by one hand, and it was Roger Casement's. But such expertise is always open to question as to the nature of the science. However, the BBC's Dr David Baxendale asserted that even the apparent later insertions corresponded to Casement's handwriting. He has also stated there was no tremor of forgery, nor tell-tale break in the inkline in the entries he inspected. That individual letters of the alphabet were written in a variety of styles, depending on their placing in the word, as was the case, and as happens in genuine handwriting, was reckoned further proof of non-forgery. It has to be said, however, that some of the exclamation marks, numbers and **X**s are, by definition, too limited to be unarguably Casement's. The notion of further forensic examination turning up convincing evidence to prove forgery, or genuineness, was always implausible and has proved the case. Nonetheless a number of commentators maintain a naive belief in the ultimate proof of authenticity only being provided by amazingly complex, untried, scientific tests. But the diaries are like the Turin Shroud, an article of faith.

Peter Singleton-Gates and Letitia Fairfield did get an opportunity to view the diaries using an ultra-violet ray machine. This had been suggested in the House of Commons and agreed by Montgomery Hyde as the defining test. They reported that no erasures had been made and that there was a consistency of handwriting and of ink.[1143] But then they were already *parti pris*. Fairfield, a Catholic convert, was awarded a Papal Medal, *Pro Ecclesia et Pontifice*, in 1966 which suggests she was not driven by religious dislike of Casement. In truth, no forensic assessment could ever convince sceptics, as a counter-explanation or a smokescreen can always be summoned up in response to apparently convincing statements.

What is interesting is that London itself, in 1916, decided to assess the authenticity of the diaries once the cry came out of America that they must have been forged. Successful efforts were made to track down Millar Gordon in Belfast, while in Norway an extensive series of affidavits were sworn at the British consulate, by hotel staff and residents of Christiania, confirming a homosexual aspect to Casement's relationship with Adler Christensen. The references in the diaries to Casement's meetings and his correspondence with Foreign Office officials were also checked, although by no means exhaustively. A record of these investigations survived and was only released in 1995. It is difficult to believe that some of the very same people who would have to have been privy to any forging, if not instrumental in it, were also then risking further forging what would have to have been faked evidence of authenticity.

Ernley Blackwell (1868-1941), the Home Secretary's legal adviser for twenty years and Casement's chief tormentor, asked the Foreign Office to verify lists of dates on which Casement called or wrote. Although many could be linked to Foreign Office records, in some cases there were difficulties. Often the date mentioned in the diary did not correspond with that on Casement's letter, or the date of receipt or first reading at the Foreign Office was such that there was no certainty that they were one and the same item. If the diaries were forged or tampered with it could not have been done without the knowledge and assistance of Basil Thomson while Blackwell would have had to be complicit. Yet before the ink was dry, indeed before the execution, the establishment was testing the evidence with all the risks that could have entailed.

The problem of dating haunts contemporary researchers. When letters are started one day, perhaps finished the next and not posted until a third, there is no precise date to which they can be said to belong. Obviously Casement or any diarist will fix on only one particular day to mention (or initially date) a letter, but a recipient will rarely record its arrival using the same date. On occasion, one is helped by the recipient mentioning the sender's date in a reply. Sometimes, however, in Edwardian times both sides of a two-sided correspondence occurred on the one day – this being the era of multiple daily postal and telegram deliveries.

With regard to these official investigation, we are not talking here of the inner depths of the intelligence services, but of civil servants (and police), most of probity and integrity, and numbers of them. But then any good forger, we will be told, should have so covered his tracks as to withstand investigation. Common sense, however, requires one to believe that had the diaries been forged, their job being done with Casement executed, the nexus of Scotland Yard, the Home Office and Naval Intelligence would have slipped the material into the furnace. One thing is clear, the secret if it existed, has been kept a complete secret; no one boasted of it at the time, no one has spoken since. Yet the numbers of people involved in such a concoction would have run into hundreds while many of those required to provide the damning detail could not have been instructed to keep silent as they were not beholden to London nor privy to the scheme. And silence reigns.

The contemporary thrust of the forgery school, aside from building a collection of names of people associated with the intelligence community and letting the cluster influence the credulous, is to find, and detail, apparently revealing inconsistencies in the diaries. Where mistakes are made by authors in the field, so much the better, as error is the enemy of all. But differences in spelling, as between the 1910 White and Black Diaries, particularly with proper names, reveal only what we know – that Casement was quite variable in the way he spelt the names of people and places. Indeed in many cases he may never have seen the words written down and was just transcribing phonetically. Angus Mitchell notes as suspicious the differing spellings of 'yucca' and 'yuca' in the two diaries on 25 October 1910, and the same village being recorded as Murupa and then Muruka on 24 November. This may be the moment to call in aid F.J. Bigger who acclaimed the fact that there was "until recently no fossilisation of name spelling." Casement, respecting his friend, was unquestionably an exponent of the older, non-fossilised school of spelling.

The traffic in relation to authenticity has not been entirely one way. Although the forgery school had been devastated on Armando Normand, and defeated in relation to Dr Dickey, it remained chipper by virtue of it being impossible to disprove a global conspiracy theory, evidenced largely by minor diary inconsistencies, and by the modern computerised (although not always) textual analysis that Eoin Ó Máille was pioneering in Dublin.

Ó Máille's work has, however, been called into question by Hugh Casement, the family's genealogist, who shares a common descent from Casement's great-grandfather, the eponymous land agent and solicitor. Hugh, himself a computer systems analyst, states Ó Máille "does little credit to his cause by using a computer program which was designed to tell the 'reading age' of North American schoolchildren. Linguistic analysis is something more subtle than that."[1144] The programme apparently complains if words of more than three syllables, or sentences longer than a dozen words are used.

An example of the comparison of word frequency between Casement's two 1910 diaries – which are seriously dissimilar in form – is that the name of the American engineer and traveller, Walter "Hardenberg", as Casement spelt his surname, occurs eighteen times, and the recently deceased Indian rebel, Katanere, sixteen times in the White Diary yet neither even once in the Black (actually Hardenberg as spelt does appear twice). It was Hardenburg's account of the outrages of that state within a state, the Peruvian Amazon Company, which prompted Casement's investigatory appointment. But neither individual was available to be recorded as being met in a diary for 1910, Katanere being dead and Hardenburg absent. In the more discursive journal, the White Diary, their stories, and thus their names, do appear. The word 'actually' tops Ó Máille's linguistic fingerprint charts, appearing forty-six times in the former, and again not once in the Black Diary. Many of Ó Máille's high scores go to adverbs and prepositions which are, by definition, more likely to be used in what was the basis for an official report, as the White Diary, or more accurately draft report was, than in a diary proper.

Perhaps the most convincing and deepest evidence for Casement's homosexuality, outside of the diaries, yet in his own handwriting, is his poetry, in particular a seven verse poem entitled *The Nameless One.* It would be hard to argue, although it has been done, that this poem relates to anything other than the state of being a homosexual. It has been used to devastating effect by three Casement authors as a clinching piece of evidence. Nonetheless there are a number of immediate questions that arise for any historical researcher, not least when was the poem written, and when was the holographed document last in his possession?

However, not only has the poem's provenance become an issue but there are suggestions of an entirely different author which, even if true, would still reveal Casement's great interest in the subject matter in so far as he bothered to transcribe it:

No human hand to steal to mine
No loving eye to answering shine,
Earth's cruel heart of dust alone
To give me breath and strength to groan.

I look beyond the stricken sky
Where sunset paints its hopeless lie
That way the flaming angel went
That sought by pride love's battlement.

I sought by love alone to go
Where God had writ an awful no.
Pride gave a guilty God to hell
I have no pride - by love I fell.

Love took me by the heart at birth
And wrought out from its common earth -
With soul at his own skill aghast -
A furnace my own breath should blast.

Why this was done I cannot tell
The mystery is inscrutable.
I only know I pay the cost
With heart and soul and honour lost.

I only know 'tis death to give
My love; yet loveless can I live?
I only know I cannot die
And leave this love God made, not I.

God made this love; there let it rest.
Perchance it needs a riven breast
To heavenly eyes the scheme to show
My broken heart must never know.

It would be hard to read another interpretation, except perhaps one of incest, into these powerful verses, and even then the implication is that the forbidden love, so described, was innate. But this poem is not referenced separately, or detailed, in any Casement archive or catalogue in Britain or Ireland, and particularly not in the NLI. So where did it come from and where is it now? Did it ever exist and if so has it been sabotaged or stolen?

The poem was last reprinted in Brian Inglis's 1973 book *Roger Casement* and the mystery of its origin and whereabouts may usefully start there. Unfortunately, Inglis did not include quotation references in that book, instead pointing anyone sufficiently interested to a file he had deposited in Dublin[1145]. However, on inspection of his book's references there, all that the reader is told is that the poem was previously published in Peter Singleton-Gates and Maurice Girodias's 1959 book *The Black Diaries*. Inglis brought out two further editions of his book, both paperbacks, in 1974 and 1993, each with a new preface. He made only a couple of changes and did not amend the section dealing with the poem or choose to comment on its, by then, disputed authorship. He died in February 1993 before the *Blackstaff Press* edition of that year was published.

Most of *The Black Diaries* historical text was actually written in Paris by Maurice Girodias for whom it became something of an obsession. He presented the poem as exhibit one, writing on page fifteen that "It seems most unlikely that British Intelligence went so far as to forge incriminating poems in order to substantiate the charge of homosexuality made against him." In a footnote, the poem is not referenced to its original source, instead the following appears: "This poem by Roger Casement, entitled *The Nameless One*, is to be found at the National Library in Dublin. It was published for the first time by Mr H. Montgomery-Hyde, M.P. for Belfast North."

When Hyde died he left most of his papers to the Public Record Office in Belfast. That is except for the bulk of his Casement documentation, both books and manuscripts, which he had already sold, in 1970, to an Irish antiquarian dealer. In a letter to the Casement author, Roger Sawyer, he wrote "I no longer have the considerable collection of Casement material which I amassed over the years", not mentioning that this was his usual practice with such papers once he had mined a subject to exhaustion. It also provided further income for a man who, as he said "never had much money and always spent what I've made, pretty quickly."

All that remains in PRONI is the correspondence that came after the disposal, apart from the sale catalogue itself. A purchase was then made by Professor Roger Louis of the University of Texas at Austin for the Humanities Research Center there. He had earlier published extensively on E.D. Morel and the Congo – Casement inevitably figuring prominently in his work. Professor Louis told Harford Hyde, in a letter dated 3 October 1972, that he had largely completed about three hundred printed pages of a study or lengthy essay dealing with "the Congo episode…the Putumayo adventure…the Findlay affair" and a final part to be called 'A Re-Assessment of the Black Diaries Controversy' – based on your papers which are invaluable in this regard."[1146] This work, however, never appeared.

Professor Louis, a distinguished diplomatic historian, later described his work to this author as something that "now ranks as an abandoned project. In any event it would not have been a biography but a study of Casement in the Congo, the Putumayo, and the way in which his experience in Congo and Latin America helped to shape his views as a nationalist."[1147] There is apparently nothing available in the way of original material at Austin to illuminate the matter of the poem or whether Hyde recorded any details of his discovery of it.

Hyde himself was somewhat disingenuous in replying to a 1974 approach made on the poem by a Mrs Moira O'Scannlain, writing from an address in Sutter Street, San Francisco. She wrote first on 24 October, suggesting that the poem's author must have been Oscar Wilde, especially as she thought the title – "the exact title escapes me" might be "The love I dare not speak." Mrs O'Scanlainn did not attempt to disguise her sympathies, declaring "as a child of six, I sat on Casement's knee when he visited, with F.J. Bigger, my native city, Derry. I loved his gentle face and have never lost that memory. So pure a soul as I saw mirrored in his serene eyes (even a child has perception) could never have entertained the obscenities expressed in the (forged) diaries."

The author's response was to say "the manuscript of the poem is in the National Library in Ireland. I did not include it in any anthology of Casement's writings [as she had notioned.] The only book on Casement which I have written is an account of his trial." He then added "as for Casement being a practising homosexual there is no doubt about this either. Indeed he admitted it to his defence counsel, Serjeant Sullivan, at the trial and Serjeant Sullivan so informed me when I talked with him at his house in Dublin when I was writing my book." He concluded with a kindly paragraph saying this did not "detract from Casement's merits as an Irish patriot and his achievements in exposing terrible atrocities in the Belgian Congo and Putumayo."

Hyde's reward, dated 10 November, was a four page rambling missive indicating she had known him in the Department of Education in 1926 – when he was only nineteen and actually at university. It did, however, include some pertinent questions. O'Scannlain who had by this time procured a copy of *The Black Diaries* quizzed him again about the poem, raising both a doubt about its title and its authenticity. She pointed out that there was in print another poem by Casement with an identical title – one written in 1898 "on the massacre of the Armenians by the Sultan of Turkey, (which begins 'Embodied pest!')."

Then she asked "How and when did the poem beginning 'No human hand' come into your possession? How is it authenticated as Casement's? (I should also appreciate your conjecture as to the date of its origin)."[1148] By this time one has the feeling that she was not acting alone in the matter. Hyde apparently chose not to enter into any further correspondence as there is no reply in the file. Perhaps he felt he was on weak ground. But unfortunately by so omitting to reply there is no trace, in one place or another, of his answers to those critical questions.

It was no discovery that there was another Casement poem of the same title as that beginning "No human hand…". That other, written on 29-30 November 1898, "outside Lagos bar on the *Gretchen Bolen* on the way to London" dealt with that "Pharaoh in reverse (and)…anointed Kurd…Sultan 'Abdul the Damned'" and his role in the Armenian Massacres. It had been published as recently as 1958 in Herbert Mackey's collection of Casement poetry and writings, *The Crime Against Europe*. As one has come to expect with Casement matters, the confusion is further compounded by the fact that James Clarence Mangan used the same title for a poem in the 1840s.

And unnoticed until now there is yet another poem, so entitled, in Casement's papers in the NLI. It is to be found in a notebook along with certain items dated 1882 and 1883, when Casement was a teenager. The volume seems initially to have been a school exercise book but he also used it for writing poetry over at least a decade. This first of his three so-named poems opens with the line "And tell how chained to a spot he hates." It bears a resemblance to that in contention, indeed it could be described as an adolescent precursor, dealing with dark deeds and flagrant sins so drastic as to shake the author's faith in God.

Two memorable lines read "And tell how love in his bosom lighted/A hopeless passion that dried his blood." This nine verse poem also has a slight Ottoman aspect as it mentions Libya's deserts.[1149] One overly-simple explanation for the plethora of Casement poems so entitled may simply be that he was given to inscribing The Nameless One at the head of a poem, pending a fixed descriptor.

Perhaps Hyde could not respond to Moira's questions as the answers were in the papers he had sold a few years earlier. But we now have two distinguished authors and the journalist Peter Singleton-Gates quoting in full a poem without providing a scrap of other information about it – except for Hyde saying it was in the NLI. The only one of the three who actually said he had seen it there was in fact Montgomery Hyde. Its first appearance in print turns out to have been in the second of two *Sunday Times* articles written by him and published on 21 and 28 April 1957 respectively.[1150]

In these articles Hyde declared, "I have recently been able to examine the Casement papers in the NLI." He suggested that the hitherto unpublished poem by Casement would have "some bearing on the question of whether or not he was a homosexual." Describing what he saw there as a "manuscript of a poem by Casement entitled *The Nameless One*", he added "In my view it betrays strong homosexual feelings in its author." He then proposed that readers could now judge for themselves. But no NLI reference was provided for it – then or later – nor was one ever to be. To all intents and purposes the original, if original it was, no longer exists. This author had, over two years, inspected all the hundreds of likely Casement-related folders and not spotted it.

The reheated dispute brought about in 1957 by Alfred Noyes' book also produced a flurry of letters, claims, and counter-claims in both *The Sunday Times* and *The Observer*. On 12 May in the former, Frank MacDermot, a one-time TD and a regular contributor to this and other controversies, described Bulmer Hobson and P.S. O'Hegarty as "wishful thinkers and heated partisans" in relation to the Normand diary theory. O'Hegarty, who "values a book more than he does his wife or children" according to his old friend Dr McCartan, "is a first edition man so you know the type,"[1151] made no attempt to demolish the poem's provenance. Meanwhile stung by an attack from Noyes that totally ignored the poem and its implications, Hyde replied by reiterating that he at least had taken "the trouble to go to the NLI and look at the Casement papers there." Noyes was to be condemned since "he didn't even pay a flying visit", the phrase used to disparage Hyde's trip to Dublin.

On 5 May, in *The Observer*, Ernest Hambloch chipped in with the fact that Casement's sexuality "was not merely suspected; it was generally accepted as a fact in Brazil where I took over the Consulate General at Rio de Janeira from him in 1910." While Nigel Seymer on the same date valiantly defended his grandfather, Sir Basil Thomson, suggesting his slightly differing accounts of the diary discovery "do not to my mind constitute 'evasions' and contradictions." Desmond Berry, in a letter printed alongside Seymer's, naively added that his father, Colonel Berry of Richhill Castle, had been convinced that Casement was a changed man from 1903 due to the horrors he had witnessed "and to his belief that civil war in Ireland was inevitable", Casement's "devastating nightmares…often waking the whole house with his screams."

Oddly, the forgery school has not put forward the lack or absence of an original NLI holograph of the poem as critical evidence of further conspiracy by the massed ranks of British Intelligence. Their silence on the matter is revealing. Surely visits were made to the National Library to inspect this dramatic evidence? Yet none have been mentioned, and no one has triumphantly pointed out that the poem is not to be found there, which in itself suggests an explanation. Perhaps this was a dog that would not be barking. For if the document has been stolen or destroyed, the deed would probably have been done from love of Casement, and the culprit happy to know, that in time, its absence could undermine the case of those retailing such 'slanders'.

The first and only original defence relating to the poem was to emerge three months later in an article in the Dublin *Sunday Press* on 4 August 1957, where Clarence H. Norman, described as the author of *A Searchlight on the European War*, disposed of it. He first offered an identity for the master diary creator – an adventurer named Magnus whom he said had homosexual tendencies and was addicted to forgery. He had written in 1924 a book entitled *Memoirs of the Foreign Legion* which, for good measure, Norman added, had been provided with an introduction by D.H. Lawrence. This was "a diary of great similarity in style to the Casement diaries."

Turning to *The Nameless One*, he first said: "That the poem is capable of bearing only such an construction seems a wild assumption but the whole thing is a cock and bull story." Norman then offered his own fanciful provenance for it: "This particular poem was in circulation over fifty years ago and was generally believed to be the work of John Addington Symonds though there were other reputed authors. So much so that I put my copy of it over fifty years ago in a book entitled 'Ros Rosarum' or 'Dew of the Ever Living Rose' which contained a charming poem by John Addington Symonds on the subject with which the book was concerned."

There were no reasons given for his fondness for the poem or his in-depth knowledge of its supposed origins. But Norman was being misleading on a number of counts. The anthology *Ros Rosarum ex Horto Poetarum* was published in 1885 and edited by E.V. Boyle. She had collected poems on the motif of roses, not of homosexuality. That by Symonds, was a translation from Strato, a Greek poet who lived about the time of Hadrian. Strato's *Musa Paidike*, the twelfth book of the Greek or Palatine Anthology, was a collection of poems and epigrams mainly concerning boy love. Symonds' offering, *The Garland Weaver*, as published by Boyle, was supposedly about a female flower seller except that the weaver's sex in Strato's original was male:

> *...And whispering soft I to him offer made,*
> *'For how much will you sell to me your crown?'*
> *Redder than rose he blushed, and looking down,*
> *In sweet affront, he made me answer low,*
> *'Before my Father see, I pray you go'...*

On the face of it there is absolutely no cause to connect that volume with *The Nameless One* except co-incidentally through Shane Leslie and long after the event. Under the pseudonym Ion Ionicos, he wrote a prose translation of the *Musa Paidike*, entitled *Strato's Boyish Muse*, which was published in 1932 by Fortune Press. In this fragment of an epigram, the Monaghan baronet asked: "Venus is a woman and enflames us with a passion for women, but Cupid himself guides all desire for boys. Which way shall I turn?"[1152] The thread, through the Clarence Norman explanation, seems to point to his having had a peripheral connection to the tail-end of that Uranian literary movement of 1880 to 1930, one which Symonds actually deprecated for its fondness for boys. He would certainly have agreed with one critic, a Royal Navy surgeon, who after listening to an interminable discussion of their problems at a meeting of a homosexual front-group, the British Society for the Study of Sex Psychology, stormed out shouting "Go and do it instead of just sitting there jabbering about it."[1153]

The memoirs of a brief wartime stint in the French Foreign Legion written by Maurice Magnus (M. M.) were published (without the episodes of homosexual relief and abuse) in 1924. Magnus had committed suicide by taking prussic acid in late 1920 in Malta. His money had finally run out. He was an American, although also a Hohenzollern, as his mother was the illegitimate daughter of Kaiser Frederick. D.H. Lawrence had first met him in Florence in the company of Norman Douglas, a vagabond writer and "an ardent lover of both sexes." Later adventures occurred when Lawrence stayed at the Monte Cassino monastery with Magnus (who had become a Catholic in 1902 in England), and then in Taormina, in Sicily, where Lawrence and his wife were living.

Lawrence (and several Maltese) had loaned Magnus money, especially for hotel bills which he ran up freely. After his death, Lawrence tried to retrieve the outstanding debts by publishing the memoirs with his own lengthy introduction. They bear absolutely no resemblance to a diary such as Casement was reckoned to have written, being a harrowing account of pointless cruelty and mistreatment in the Foreign Legion. Given that Magnus joined to fight for the allies, it is ironic that he found himself amongst mostly German-born legionnaires. The book concludes with Magnus escaping from France and the Legion across the border at Menton, into Italy.

Clarence Norman featured prominently in the No Conscription Fellowship during the war, writing, in 1915, an ILP pamphlet entitled *British Militarism – a Reply to Robert Blatchford*. The only other occasion he surfaced in matters Casement was when he wrote to George Bernard Shaw in 1928 about *A Discarded Defence of Roger Casement*, written by GBS and printed in a limited edition of 25 copies in 1922 for Clement Shorter, who also provided an introduction. Shorter had signed one of the reprieve petitions in 1916.

In a reply, addressed to Clarence Norman at 74 Belsize Park Gardens, London, Shaw, warming to the subject, added by supplement "So Serjeant Sullivan after putting up the usual pickpocket's defence – 'Please, gentlemen, I didn't do it' got his compliments and Casement got his rope."[1154] GBS stated he had never met Casement but "knew his cousin" Gertrude. He described Clement Shorter as a collector "and an Irish patriot by sexual selection (having married Dora Sigerson)." The unfortunate poet, Dora Sigerson Shorter, daughter of Dr George Sigerson, committed suicide in 1918 due to a psychosis brought on by Casement's execution and the Easter Rising deaths. Her husband described to Gertrude Parry how "she suffered in anguish all the tortures of that execution and never recovered from it."[1155] She is best remembered for her poem *Sixteen Dead Men*. Shaw typically suggested that his own letter to Norman was probably worth as much as the defence pamphlet had recently fetched. He had earlier remarked "Clement died the other day…hence the fancy prices."

In a letter in the same NLI folder, Shaw declined to respond to a request in 1931 from Muriel MacSwiney (widow of Terence MacSwiney, the Lord Mayor of Cork and hunger striker who died in Brixton Prison in 1920) for support on the matter of the right of women to choose to have an abortion. The recent prosecution of two German doctors prompted her concerns. Shaw evaded answering. Writing to her at an address c/o James Larkin he said "It is not a man's subject." Muriel had earlier left Ireland and in Germany joined the Communist Party. After 1933 and Hitler's accession to power she fled to France, only to have her daughter removed from her charge, or as she said kidnapped, by her sister-in-law Mary MacSwiney. This was done with the diplomatic assistance of de Valera and his government on the grounds of her poor mental state.[1156]

So Clarence Norman, another Englishman, had uncovered an author or at least an assumed author. That was enough for the forgery school and Symonds was duly exposed and retailed as the poem's creator. Casement was exonerated. By some, Symonds was mistakenly spelt Symmons while Eoin Ó Máille in his revised 1995 pamphlet *The Vindication of Roger Casement* calls him Addington-Symonds, at the same time, unwisely remarking that for the Christian Irish "freedom by a pervert would be a perverted freedom and not acceptable." It was also suggested, adding authority to the farrago, that *The Nameless One* had been included in a 1902 Symonds anthology, but none has yet been put together or published.

John Addington Symonds (who just to confuse the issue shared identical names with his father and grandfather) was a homosexual and a poet of some repute, although his poetry on the theme was not published until after his death in 1893. Until then it had been circulated privately amongst friends in the so-called *Peccant Pamphlets*. Similarly his memoirs were locked up in the London Library until 1976, largely at his own behest, as he had "given pledges to the future in the shape of my four growing girls."[1157]

Like Casement, Symonds was particularly fond of Italy and Italians, and especially a Venetian gondolier named Angelo Fusato, as well as a Davos sleigh-driver called Christian Buol, although he had tried to repress his sexual instincts, partly in marriage. He memorably described how he was finally stung into acting out his homosexual nature by a particularly provocative etching: "My eyes were caught by sight of a slate pencil graffito so thoroughly the voice of vice and passion in the proletariat that it pierced the very marrow of my soul." The scrawl on the wall that so affected him read "prick to prick so sweet" and was accompanied by "an emphatic diagram of phallic meeting, glued together, gushing." It was "a moment of revelation", Symonds said, when "the wolf leapt out, converted into an appetite."[1158]

Symonds co-authored with Havelock Ellis, a man he never actually met, the first book, *Sexual Inversion*, which effectively made a case for homosexuality. It was to be published posthumously in England, with his name deleted, in 1897. That edition brought prosecution to the Legitimation League which was displaying it for sale. The book despite, or perhaps because of its legal difficulties, was to set the tone for advanced attitudes to homosexuality over several generations to come. Some of Casement's few recorded mentions of the subject, that regarding Sir Hector Macdonald's suicide in the 1903 diary, and the remarks he allegedly made to Serjeant Sullivan in 1916 praising the great homosexuals of history as being "inseparable from the manifestation of distinguished genius", suggest he may have read *Sexual Inversion*, or at least knew of the arguments.

The book, which eventually transmuted into Ellis's *Studies in the Psychology of Sex*, had devoted a number of pages to that theme of great men, and also offered many case studies written-up by Symonds (including his own). Ellis had argued for a congenital view of homosexuality's origin. However, love between men, the "Dear Love of Comrades", was what motivated Symonds, not theories of neuropathology. He would also have differed from Casement who by keeping his emotional life separate from his sexual, was enabled to devote his feelings and consequent efforts to causes other than his own socio-sexual freedom. Which is not to say that Casement failed to take the many opportunities available to him for sexual enjoyment. He did and seemed, certainly in later life, devoid of guilt or shame.

The foremost expert on the poetry of Symonds, Ian Venables, does not believe *The Nameless One* can be regarded as one of the perhaps 750 poems he is known to have written. He describes it as having "quite a Housmanesque lyric; not a form Symonds used, very often favouring as he did the 'In memoriam' style of Tennyson. The use of language and accent is not Symonds either."[1159] In fact it is not good enough to be written by Symonds which brings one back to Casement as the poet. It does indeed bear striking similarities in style and content to other verse that Casement did unquestionably write.

From 1957, as and when any press or media reference was made to the poem a brief rejoinder would be issued by Herbert Mackey, disclaiming authorship by Casement. This was particularly necessary in 1965 when his remains were brought back to Ireland, sparking off innumerable journalistic versions of the story, most often based on MacColl's book and *The Black Diaries.* Mackey took it upon himself to write to the offending publications, pointing out that the poem was "not written by Casement" but by J.A. Symonds. One case in particular was when *Time* magazine referred to the poem on 6 March 1965. Mackey took this opportunity to write to a number of Irish newspapers denying his hero's authorship of it. Such repetition, then and more recently, has worked to the extent that Symonds authorship is now widely, if not generally, accepted as fact.

The second stage, that of suggesting the poem was never in the NLI cache at all, and was therefore an invention, has either never needed to be stated or the document's apparent absence has not been realised. It was, to say the least, unlikely that Hyde either wrote the poem himself or completely invented its existence in the NLI. It presumably arrived within Gertrude Parry's largest donation of papers in 1930, which by 1957 still formed the bulk of its Casement archive. She understandably chose not to select it for her own 1918 publication of sixteen of his poems. Perhaps someone will yet find the third *The Nameless One* in the NLI and detail the form it takes, but it is has been attributed to Casement and disattribution requires more evidence than its absence in Dublin.

In May 1999, this author arranged to visit the United States, partly with a view to inspecting the Maloney Papers in New York's Public Library since preliminary research on his behalf had revealed non-specific mention of poetry in the catalogue. While at an American Conference on Irish Studies meeting in Virginia, the Casement enthusiast and lecturer, Lucy McDiarmid, confirmed what he hoped. A copy of *The Nameless One* in Casement's writing existed in New York. She too had been convinced it must be somewhere and, investigating locally at first, had found it in the NYPL. On going to Fifth Avenue the poem was finally seen. It covers one sheet of paper. On the reverse the title is repeated, suggesting that this is a copy and not the first version. In the final line the writer had hand-altered "my broken heart" to "a broken heart" although in Hyde's 1959 published version it read "my". This indicates again that what was seen by Hyde in Dublin was an earlier, and perhaps the original, manuscript.

Casement, however, chose also to specify on the back just where, when and why he had written the poem, providing incontrovertible proof of its authenticity. He explained that these were "Lines written in Very Great Dejection at Genoa. November 15 1900 before sailing on "Sirio" for Barcelona."[1160] These facts of Casement's travel can be confirmed elsewhere from letters (see below). A number of other poems like *Love the Overthrower* are also to be found in New York alongside the lost item. On one Casement inscribed a Dublin address for "Muiris Joy, 18 Longwood Avenue, S. Circular Rd., *Eblana*" – this was Maurice Joy who would in 1916 be his first biographer. Dejected in Italy, Casement had made the cardinal error of going back to follow up a holiday romance to find his welcome no longer warm.

Montgomery Hyde had risked his Unionist parliamentary career and ultimately lost it in 1959, not through homophobia or hyper anti-nationalism; rather the opposite. He was no charlatan nor anybody's pawn, least of all one of his own former comrades in the intelligence service. He was certainly not rewarded, indeed his widow Robbie was obliged to seek a benevolent grant from The Royal Society of Literature to survive. But he was no forger. If accused of any literary crime the only charge ever made was one of plagiarism. The missing poem was, however, not the only item in Dublin to have developed legs.

The absence of any evidence of diary forging in London's extensive Casement documentation is striking, and especially compelling. Given the complexity of any such operation, not least the checking of many thousands of facts, often trivial like the weather in Iquitos on a particular day, it is unimaginable it could be totally hidden with all evidence of forgery removed. Even arranging for people to destroy documents would have left a paper trail. Obviously there are some oddities in the diaries and lawyer-like deniers can, and do, pick holes in them making usually unevidenced assertions. One school argues for complete forgery, others, more sophisticated, suggest interpolation. But even interpolation – and it would have to have been extensive– would have been technically difficult, needed research and would leave traces. However it is hard to argue with faith and that is what much of this is based on.

There is however one rare, perhaps unique, occasion of possible forgery, in relation to Casement, to which historian Margaret O'Callaghan[1161] draws attention. It comes in a report to MI5 dated 8 August 1915 from "C", the Foreign Office representative in Copenhagen.

The file reads: "41408 Extract from a "C" report, dated 8-8-15: There is a curious though none the less persistent feeling amongst quite important persons in Germany that the above is in the pay of the British government. Amongst the many arguments for this are the following: (a) That as it is noticed that he is received into the best circles both officially and personally, it is obvious that he is not a person paid by these officials as they would never receive personally anyone they paid. (b) His manner is considered charming, but it is noticed that he appears to devote his chief attention to persons who influence, directly or indirectly, either the public opinion or relations with Foreign Powers. That he is kept informed to an extraordinary degree, as to movements, both prospective and in execution, of the troops on all fronts. (c) It is generally considered by persons of the above persuasion, that the whole story of his attempted assassination is an extremely well laid scheme, as is proved by the fact that the individual responsible still remains in his post etc. etc. (d) As a reward, if the above person escapes with his life, which some persons consider doubtful, he will be given a high position in the English Government, and, in order to still further enhance this position, he will be allowed to carry out with success a law sanctioning HOME RULE. I may say that there are many other statements but the above will show what is being said. Assuming that, after investigation as to the supporters of this movement, it was decided that there was something in it would you sanction a scheme being submitted whereby the matter could be so arranged that evidence could be manufactured by which the position of the man would be rendered untenable. If you wish for the names of the persons in Germany who are interested, I can furnish them at short notice. Please wire if this is required."

After ten days on 18 August 1915, M.O.5 (g) replied: "With reference to Contre Espionage report dated HELSINGFOR 3-8-15, last paragraph, we should be glad if you would ascertain the names of the persons in Germany who are interested in the matter of Sir Roger CASEMENT." The suggested 'manufacturing' scheme was not mentioned.

On receipt of the following, somewhat tardy, cable dated 20 September, an M.O.5 file was opened entitled, "Names of persons in Germany interested in matter of Casement, Sir Roger". "C" wrote: "Re Casement: I have had great difficulty in checking information owing to the renewed energy of German counter espionage agent.

The information checked up to date is as follows: VON VREDER one of Prince Rupprecht of Bavaria's Adjutants has stated upon several occasions that neither the Prince nor his friends can understand the folly of the Government in trusting Casement. The Prince has been in correspondence with Generals BESELER and YENISCH of the German diplomatic service, who state that until they can obtain definite proofs it will be futile to try to convince either the Chancellor or the Emperor.

The Prince doubts the sincerity of CASEMENT'S advice re South America and United States, he has also doubts as to the integrity of CASEMENT'S agents in Russia, Italy and India.[1162]

It is likely that London knew the circle of Prince Rupprecht of Bavaria. The name of von Vreder is not traceable although, if correctly spelt, it was probably someone from the von Wrede military family. The other two named were on the more liberal side of imperial Germany and, like Prince Rupprecht, non-Prussian.* General Hans Hartwig von Beseler (1850-1921) was a comparative liberal as military governor of the German-occupied Polish lands. 'Yenisch' again is misspelled but was probably the diplomat Martin Rücker Freiherr von Jenisch (1861-1924) who had served in Washington, Egypt, London, Vienna and Rome.

C's name is not on file but his English is slightly stilted while he cannot spell two of his German contacts' names. This suggests he was Danish. He rather desperately tries to explain why the Rupprecht circle did not trust Casement but, if anything, tells more of German naiveté and snobbishness. Making Casement's life in Germany "untenable" would of course have been welcome. However forging "definite proofs" that Casement was a British agent ("C" himself seems uncertain) was not going to be easy and could muddy MI5's waters. It is notable that no comment was inscribed on the paperwork nor is there a further response. Indeed Major Frank Hall ordered the file put away (P.A.) on 23 September. The idea was plainly not taken seriously nor advanced. And that is the closest one gets to forgery in the Casement documentation.

---

* Prince Rupprecht was to be exiled by the Nazis while his wife and five daughters were famously imprisoned in Sachsenhausen concentration camp.

18

Casement's homosexuality

Having proved to the reasonable reader's satisfaction that the Black Diaries were not forged, it is now necessary to display facts to see if it can be proved positively and beyond a reasonable doubt that they are genuine, using the same tests for authenticity. This requires corroborative evidence. Short of equivalent diaries by Casement's partners who understandably made themselves scarce after 1916, one starts with the diaries themselves which are an almost unique record of one homosexual's sexual life over three years in the early part of the twentieth century. After placing them in evidence and knowing there will be nothing more confirmatory ever found, it is incumbent on counsel not for the prosecution or the defence, but for posterity, to provide corroboration. Such evidence it must be said goes much more toward proving Casement's homosexual status than verifying actual sexual activities or adventures.

Alongside *The Nameless One*, there are several other exhibits which authors have laid out, designed to prove Casement's homosexual orientation which have either gone missing, or are inaccurate or are mistaken in their interpretations. Several relate to the early days of the teenager Casement, who presumably was sexually alert from about 1878, when he was fourteen. He was described in that year "as a dashing young fellow." Being tall for his age and with two older brothers it is unlikely he was totally uninformed about imminent puberty or sexual matters. It is also probable, by virtue of the myriad of addresses where the family lived before and during his adolescence, that he was not sheltered from the adult world.

Nonetheless his time at Ballymena Diocesan School was without his brothers Tom and Charlie who were nearly two and three years his senior respectively. Neither was it a hot house of love, sex and emotion like those English public schools attended by so many of the Uranian writers of Casement's era. It was, instead, in the tradition of most such Protestant schools in Ulster, puritan on sexual matters by means of a complete silence on such issues. With a standard, somewhat democratic, Ulster Protestant atmosphere, the school was probably neither cruel nor crude.

Up to the 1903 diary, apart from inferential material there is nothing of a specifically sexual nature to be found in Casement's remaining papers. But B.L. Reid was keen to flourish in his 1976 book several pieces of evidence that he felt substantiated "the testimony of the homosexual diaries." As he wrote,

"The earliest occurrence is early indeed: it appears in a Smith's *Scribbling Diary* for 1881. In the book the pages are torn out down to Monday, 16 May, and thereafter under various assigned dates in 1881-83, appear assorted notes and memoranda: titles of plays and operas, drafts of letters, drafts of poems or parts of poems, one of which is scrawled over in a very large hand "Rubbish." Under the date of 27 June 1881, when Casement would have been sixteen years old, and working as a clerk for Elder Dempster in Liverpool, the following lines are written in his already distinctive hand:

What hand hath reft Hope of her crown
Or ta'en her gems away
Oh! sweet boy of Dublin
Oft in my dreams do I see thee"[1163]

The emotional response seemed strong for a sixteen-year-old. Indeed Casement became sexually active quite young, given the earliest such reference in the 1903 diary where he makes a remark about cruising when aged twenty. The entry on 28 February, the day of his arrival in Madeira, reads in part, "Out at 8 to Old Town, same place as in Feb. 1885, eighteen years ago. Then to square. Two offers one doubtful." For such a young, middle class, and apparently conventional, English Irishman, Casement was quite advanced.

In the same decades, his recorded English contemporaries were largely riven with doubts, falling in love with schoolboys or converting to Rome to quell their desires. The fact of his being an independent young man, fending for himself, alongside the opportunities provided by foreign travel – with his life as a sailor, beginning at age nineteen, enabled him to do what many others never did. Certainly by the time of the 1903 diary his sexual needs, as described, were being met.

Having trumpeted his "Sweet boy of Dublin" discovery, Reid then provided a dud reference on page 482 of his book "MLI [sic] Ms. unclassified." This is not a term employed by the NLI but it was one Reid utilised a number of times in his book's references. A part explanation is provided by inspection of Reid's notes on his book's galley proofs: for the "Sweet boy of Dublin" reference he wrote "I beg pardon." These three words were to be transmuted, on publication into the unclassified mention. A reasonable explanation is that Reid was mortified that he could not find the NLI manuscript reference number, and was apologising for his failure, not to his readers, but to himself; the other that he could not find the item a second time he looked.

Even if the item could not be found again, that 1881 diary had a provenance beyond Reid's book. It cropped up in two different places in Casement records. Both were prompted by Dr Maloney as he sought to track the young Casement and his origins. Ada McNeill had written to Bulmer Hobson in

November 1931 reporting success in getting a Casement pedigree to assist Maloney in his biographical quest: "It's out of an old scribbling book of 1881 that this information is gotten. Roddie was then 17."[1164] Maloney also noted that, "These 30 sheets written in ink on one side are a written transcript by a cousin from the original in a large diary kept by Casement in his middle teens up to the age of 17½ showing the youthful attitude towards England, Ireland and his hunger for death."[1165]

The following lines from a poem, as then transcribed, entitled *A Dream,* certainly confirm that latter impression, revealing the young Casement's sense of hopelessness and doom, resulting from nameless snares:

I looked around the world, but saw
No path for me to tread
But spectres rose and seemed to draw
Me down unto the dead

The cousin was Gertrude Parry as the accompanying envelope containing these "scribblings… [and] scraps of poems"[1166] carries her name and address. The postmarked date is unreadable but the monarch on the stamp is George V, which means the package was sent before 1936. The address given was Rockport which was Gertrude's Co. Antrim residence after her marriage and up to 1942. By then a widow, Sidney Parry having died in 1937, Gertrude and her sister Elizabeth faced a financial crisis brought on by the Japanese invasion of Malaya. His investments had been in rubber plantations there. With most of her income stopped, Gertrude was forced, at the age of sixty-eight to return to teaching in Ilford while her sister went to stay with Ada McNeill in Cushendun. She moved on to Margaret Dobbs at Portnagolan in July (where Rose Young now also lived) before ending her days in December of that sad year, back near Gertrude, in a London nursing home.[1167]

The problem of lost or missing references was one Reid faced on several occasions when he was obliged to use the same 'unclassified' phrasing. Of particular importance in this context is his discovery of matching details for the boy, Francis Naughton, whom Casement mentions in his 1903 diary on 22 December: "Bad crossing to Dublin. At North Wall. Went Bray. Francis Naughton not there – back to Westland Row." The absent Francis, however, had a life beyond this one diary entry. Casement chose to outline it on what Reid describes as an undated "loose notebook page." It also had various notes on the reverse relating to 1901 and 1902 which help to fix its date.[1168] But it is not to be located in Dublin. There are literally thousands of pages of Casement material, much of it in folders classified under the broadest of headings but despite thorough checking, it seems to have disappeared.

Like all but one of Casement's sex partners in Ireland, Francis cannot be traced forward. His origins in Bundoran are detailed on the page found by Reid and may be verified by mentions in the 1903 and 1914 Ulster street directories of a wine and spirit merchant called T. Naughton in the Co. Donegal seaside village of Bundoran, at West End, operating furnished apartments in Cavan House. A decade later, in 1912, Casement was to visit Bundoran, staying on 7 August in the Northern Railway Hotel, but presumably Francis had not returned. The town disappointed him as he wrote in 1913, "It is hard to get the people of Ballyshannon to join the Gaelic League and Bundoran is even worse."[1169] There were to be many such boys of Dublin, and of Belfast, and beyond, like Francis, but few others were well documented or fully named.

B.L. Reid, who had won a Pulitzer Prize for his biography of the Irish-American company lawyer and art collector, John Quinn, was an inveterate researcher as well as a most elegant writer. By prolonged inspection of Casement's papers, both sides of the page and the envelopes, he turned up many items of great interest. His mission was memorably put when he wrote in an introduction to his *Necessary Lives* in 1990: "Biography is one of the things we need. For it tells us in signal instances, illustrious or infamous, in any case exemplary, what it has meant to be human, to live a life." But he failed in these instances to give good reference and he knew it.

If the *Scribbling Diary* had gone for ever it would have been a great loss, being such a rare and early Casement manuscript. This author looked long and hard for it but had effectively given up, assuming it had been illicitly removed, like the missing poem, 'The Nameless One' and the Francis Naughton document, seemed to have been.

Researching the provenance of the various Casement file donations and purchases, I asked the NLI about folders in the 17000 numeric series handed over by Éamon MacThomas, one, in particular, accession 2922, in December 1971.

The NLI replied: "Shortly after this accession, a second donation relating to Casement came to the NLI in January 1972 from an anonymous donor under the name of Department of Foreign Affairs. It contained 27 miscellaneous documents relating to Casement. Its accession number is 2924 and they are catalogued as MS 17401-17420."[1170]

Catalogued the donation may have been, but it never appeared on an index. It is likely B.L. Reid saw them before they were numbered, and they were then accidently omitted from the Hayes Irish Civilisation Supplement 1965-1975, or were too late for it. They then failed to get on to the later index cards which preceded computerisation. The manuscripts emanated from Gertrude Parry, but how they got to the Department of Foreign Affairs remains a mystery. They may actually have been bought in London like the rediscovery announced in 2012.

In that next year, the NLI advised of another file series which should have been in the Hayes Sources volumes by virtue of its numeric sequence, but intriguingly wasn't. This large batch of uncatalogued Casement papers, accession 1235, had been bought in London in 1952, possibly from the Parry family. It is now numbered MS 49154, and with its 22 folders, is a trove of interesting documents, the earliest dating from 1882. This rediscovery, however, was unconnected to accession 1235.

On periodic visits to Dublin, the twenty unindexed and unlisted folders, 17401-17420, were checked. Eventually, in November 2012, No. 17413 was reached and there in front of me was the missing Smith's *Scribbling Diary* with "R.D. Casement" neatly written at the top of the cover. Although for 1881, the diary was plainly used over a number of years and contained lines of verse, and much else, including notes written in Africa.

Desmond's Song, inscribed on the same Week 27 (June-July 1881) page of the diary and below the 'Sweet Boy of Dublin' lines is actually a transcription of Thomas Moore lyrics. The last two 'Sweet boy' lines were written in purple ink and further below, in the same colour of ink, are the words "…*Give none of your sass/My Colleen Dhas!*" The song *Colleen dhas cruthen na moe* ('The Pretty Girl milking the cow') is another linked to Thomas Moore. On this evidence, 'Sweet Boy' may well be from an untraceable song lyric and not related to a lad Casement knew.

On the matter of Cathal O'Byrne, Casement's American biographer got it badly wrong, in his otherwise superbly written book, at least with respect to a certain poem. This, B.L. Reid reckoned, was a homosexual poem, one that could count in evidence as such. It had been inscribed by Casement inside the front cover of a book of poetry by Rupert Brooke (*1914 and Other Poems*) given to him by Sidney Parry while in prison:

O Friend of my Heart!
'Tis a debt I pay in this telling
for hours of delight.
To lay my wreath of bays at
your feet I would climb afar
to your height,
I would walk the flints with
a terrible joy, if at the
journey's end
I would greet you, O Friend!

At the poem's end was written "Cathal O'Byrne 7.6.16."[1171] Reid noted that all he knew of O'Byrne, based on the surprisingly vague information of Bulmer Hobson's sister Florence Patterson, was that he "was a singer and one of the young men who made of F.J. Bigger's house in Belfast a Gaelic League enclave and a general hostel."[1172] Truly he was another talented young man, cultured or enabled by Bigger, but he had a long and varied career also as a poet, journalist, actor, dramatist and writer, largely in Belfast. In the early 1920s he was in America where his performances helped raise large sums of money for the White Cross Fund to assist Belfast Catholics made homeless by the troubles. Amcomri Street so named after the *American Committee for Relief in Ireland* was built on Cathal's efforts. Through his journalism, and especially his oft-reprinted volume of Belfast stories *As I Roved Out,* he is well-known to several generations of that city's readers.

Born Charles Burn in 1883, Cathal grew up in the early years of the Irish renaissance although like Casement he never mastered the revived language. He was largely self-educated and did not always derive an income from artistic efforts since at one early point of his life he ran a spirit grocers at 122 Beersbridge Road in east Belfast. He was a fine singer of ballads of which he was said to have a copious repertoire, one that others mined.

He would frequently wear his saffron kilt while performing, as at that time, explains one writer, "Irish-Irelanders believed in the authenticity of the kilt as an Irish costume, and he cut a striking figure in it, for he was a handsome man and had a good stage presence."[1173] The planter poet, John Hewitt in particular recalled, from Ulster Hall concerts attended as a boy, Cathal's black wavy hair and waxed moustache. Various other people recollected his part in early cultural efforts where he added a popular touch, being noted as an excellent musical artiste in a string band during the 1905 production of Bulmer Hobson's play *Brian of Banba* (Joseph Campbell played King Brian). In 1908 he was recorded as providing musical illustrations in St Mary's Hall in Belfast during a lecture by Bigger on "poets and writers of the nation." In an *Irish Times* appreciation of 23 July 1955 he is memorably dignified with the epithet "Shanachie of Belfast and its Red-Brick Gaeltacht."

That two verse poem *Friend of My Heart* was actually by Cathal O'Byrne himself, not Casement. He had first published it ten years earlier in 1905, with others by him and some by Cahir Healy (later a Stormont and Westminster MP for Fermanagh). The volume was entitled *The Lane of the Thrushes* and subtitled *Some Ulster Love-Songs*. Its cover is recognisably designed by John Campbell in that beautiful Gaelic revival, *art nouveau* style he and his brother both utilised.

The 'Friend' in question was F.J. Bigger, the breath of whose praise O'Byrne here likened to "the deep-throated music of thrushes in the windless quiet of day." He was also the man to whom Cathal dedicated *As I Roved Out* in 1946 with the words "To the memory of his life-long friend Francis Joseph Bigger of Ard Righ, Historian, Archaeologist and Antiquarian, whose erudition, generously shared, made the writing of it possible." The opening line and title (and obviously the poem) stuck in Casement's mind as he used it on several occasions, ironically once about Adler Christensen, and of course in 1916 he was able to quote its second verse precisely. But he did not author it nor was it dedicated to him. He inscribed it in his book of Rupert Brooke poems in no sense other than as a touching memory of times together at Ardrigh.

In the October 1937 edition of *The Irish Monthly* (subtitled *A Journal of Catholic Action*) Cathal O'Byrne wrote of some of those remarkably numerous last exchanges of letters, remembrances, medals and other religious items. In the tiny address book Gertrude brought into the various gaols to make notes, she recorded, "Message to Cahill O'Byrne – R would like to hear from him. He got his pc from L Derg."[1174] Cathal had recently been at Lough Derg, a famous Catholic place of pilgrimage and penance in south Donegal and was an habitué of its island, St Patrick's Purgatory.

In a letter responding to one from Bigger's housekeeper, written "from his prison cell", which Casement visioned as "a glimpse of the garden, with the wallflowers and the Japanese cherry", [*Roger Casement's Last Will*] the prisoner sent messages to a number of those from the Ardrigh days: "Do you remember the cradle song I liked so much? [by Padraic Colum] Get Cathal to sing it for me, and give him my love and thanks from my heart, also to Colm, if he is near you, and Dinny [Denis McCullough] and *Seaghan Dhu* [John Campbell] whenever they come back to you and the old room again. I dreamt last night I was lying before the fire in it, and the boys were there telling stories." It was that same ever-summer acre of garden that Joseph Campbell was to memorialise in the title poem of his first volume of poetry, *The Garden of the Bees*, published in 1905. The garden may still exist as there is a secret walled segment behind the modern Ardrigh Court flats.

These were the boys who had organised the sending of a statue of Our Lady to Casement once they heard he was becoming a Catholic. In an unsigned note for Gavan Duffy to pass on it is surely Cathal who writes to Casement, "The sender hopes he still has the Lourdes souvenir." He also enclosed a song to be given to him, assuring his imprisoned friend "of the unaltered devotion of the singer who used to sing it for him long ago."[1175] For these gifts, Gertrude, in 1917, thanked Cathal: "Your friend spoke of you many times to me. Your last letter to him was a great comfort, and he cherished to the end the little statue of Our Lady, and left it to his sister."[1176]

On 14 July 1916, Casement was advising Brigid about the newspaper stories now being published, "Don't pay any attention to the lies. They are a compliment really – and we need not mind compliments, you and I Biddy dear."[1177] He then added about Cathal "Give him my love and thanks from the heart." Later, Cathal O'Byrne was to describe Miss Mathews as "a merry-hearted kindly Irish woman" (only aged thirty at the 1911 census), who had mothered Casement "on the many occasions when he was ill, and who had understood him and loved him as perhaps no other human being did."

O'Byrne would have first met Casement at Ardrigh sometime around 1904. There is, however, no record or trace of an early or continuing correspondence, which can mean one of two things; they did not correspond, or *both* sides were entirely destroyed or lost. The latter seems unlikely and a small clue is that Gertrude had to ask Brigid Mathews "Have you Cahill's address?"[1178] when she wanted to give him the inscribed Rupert Brooke volume as a souvenir of "our dear dead friend." Cathal would have been one of the first Belfast Catholics that Casement could have been intimate with. Someone he was able to speak frankly to, indeed someone he may have been influenced by. They certainly shared a sentimental nature.

He was also twenty-one and markedly handsome, if in an actorial way, so it is likely that he impressed Casement visually even if his manners put him off. One journalist spoke of his luxuriant head of hair and magnificent moustache, assets confirmed by a particular studio photograph where Cathal's nostrils are flaring above a wide-open billowing white shirt.[1179] Florence Patterson, in her nineties, was still able to recall a sighting in period costume at Castle Seán in Ardglass of "the handsomest young man I ever saw." This was someone she thought was its custodian who may well have been Cathal.[1180] He was as quick as Frank Bigger, not to mention Joseph Campbell, to don an Irish kilt on any festive occasion, to which he would add a flowing blue bow.

While the politics of Ardrigh were largely the preserve of Bulmer Hobson and Dinny McCullough (and later Joseph Connolly) the culture was more the remit of Frank himself, Cathal, Herbert Hughes and his folksinger brother Frederick, and John Campbell and his brother Joseph (*Seosamh Mac Cathmhaoil*). Hobson did write plays, duly staged by the Ulster Literary Theatre, but he was the initiator and leader amongst the earliest of those who today would be recognisable as Republicans. The Belfast Catholics among them, although in their own eyes Wolfe Tone Republicans, were inevitably if unconsciously to see their coming political emancipation in different terms from the Protestants.

Joseph Connolly (1885-1961) was later to become a Fianna Fail Senator, Cabinet minister and Ireland's chief wartime censor. He was perhaps the most important Belfast man after Sean MacEntee in the politics of the Irish Free State. Connolly remembered afternoon garden parties followed by evening céilidhes at Ardrigh. It was there Casement and Alice Stopford Green stayed "for long periods as Frank's guests" under the shadow of the venerated MacArt's Fort where, in June 1913, Joseph Connolly addressed a Wolfe Tone commemoration pilgrimage in front of six *sluaighte* of *Fianna*, one of girls. In Ardrigh's library, in front of the big fireplace with the rugs rolled back, there was room for forty or fifty people to dance, he wrote, and still space "for the less active to sit around and talk and argue." The house was "the high spot of our meeting places" especially for the contacts made there.[1181]

Ardrigh could be said to have been the seedbed of Republican, Gaelic and literary Belfast as well as the literal supplier of seasonal fruit and vegetables to guests and friends as far away as Dublin. Joseph Connolly remains little known but he was something of a polymath, being also a writer of plays, an accomplished businessman, and a progressive on labour matters. These modes he combined, like Cathal, with a rigorous adherence to Catholic truths which he took to some extremes when censoring foreigners' love letters in Dublin during the Emergency.

Professor Seamus O'Neill in 1979 in an article in *Studies* refuted B.L. Reid's assertion about the poem being homosexual, and the implication of a passionate physical relationship between Casement and Cathal O'Byrne. This he did by exposing the evidence of Reid's error as to authorship. But he took the matter further and tried to exonerate O'Byrne of the charge, as he saw it, of being homosexual. Reid's wish, he wrote, had become father to the thought. This was probably true in Reid's case but it became obvious that O'Neill, who had been a guest speaker at Casement commemorations at Murlough Bay, was similarly guilty.

He protested Cathal's innocence far too much and betrayed his own antagonism, where he had earlier appeared unconcerned about the possibility of one or both parties being gay. The negative evidence was that if Cathal was homosexual he, the Professor "must have been exceedingly unattractive to him" for on visits to his parlour house in Cavendish Street off the Falls Road in Belfast, where Cathal lived with his sister "he made no advances" towards him. Indeed he declared, "If Cathal had been a homosexual I should not have been visiting him because in a close community like that of the Cavendish Street area his repute would have been known to everyone, and ill-repute it would have been and Cathal a man to avoid."[1182]

He did, in an attempt at absolution for his theatrical or effeminate manner, mention that O'Byrne "had some of the airs and graces that come naturally to a man who spent his life on a stage." Cathal had also been a friend of the famous Father Fullerton who tussled with both socialists and Unionists and was on Dublin Castle's list in early 1916 of those next to be sent into internal exile. O'Neill, however, felt this Gaelic League priest would not have been seen "cavorting around with homosexuals": nor he thought would Dinny McCullough whose daughter he quoted as saying, "Morally my father was a very strict man and he would not have allowed Cathal O'Byrne within a mile of our house if there had been the slightest suspicion attached to him."[1183] This remark has to be set against the fact that McCullough was associated with the Gate Theatre and thus with Micheál MacLiammoir and Hilton Edwards, Dublin's most regal gay couple.

It is difficult to believe that such Belfast Catholic revolutionaries, even if pious, could be quite so po-faced or narrow-minded as they are portrayed. In their circles there were undoubtedly sinners and if Cathal were such, so long as he was not constantly drawing it physically to their attention he would surely not have been ostracised. His reputation as an important and popular local cultural figure with an impeccable Catholic nationalist pedigree would have granted him at the very least a pardon, and a reprieve from social exclusion, as it did, if his large funeral is anything to go by. Indeed if recently unearthed stories about MacLiammoir and General Eoin O'Duffy are to be believed, the far-right Monaghan hero of the independence struggle and the famous actor were sexual intimates in the 1930s.

The notion that all males (no matter their looks) are in imminent danger of being molested by any and every homosexual as soon as they join them on a sofa was, until recently, a standard heterosexual view. The response is now also standard. But it is oddly true to say that Cathal himself was seriously pious and if anyone was going to be excluded he might have been in the vanguard of those doing it. He was a regular writer in the Catholic press and held, especially in the 1930s, what might now be thought ultra-right (or ultra-left) positions, casually including in religious stories comments on the Jews' responsibility for the murder of Jesus.

In England, especially around the turn of the century, as stated, it was almost *de rigueur* for men with a homosexual sensibility to convert to Roman Catholicism, one modern writer, Colin Cruise saying, "Nineties converts found a correspondence in the marginality of their religious beliefs and their sexual practices, a kind of acceptance, 'a returning home' when they 'came to Rome'. Two marginalities in British culture were brought together."[1184] But Cathal was already there and he was Irish. He simply agreed with the sentiments, ultimately expressed by Casement that there was really no choice "between the Catholic Church and religious anarchy, between the infallibility of the Pope and religious chaos." [*Roger Casement's Last Will*]

In later years Cathal O'Byrne's reputation waned. John Hewitt described him latterly in his 1982 introduction to *As I Roved Out*, as small "with a flushed face and scant blackish hair" wearing an enormous ring on the little finger of his left hand. He was "from the northern margin of the Celtic Twilight" Hewitt added, a view that chimed with another published in 1957: "Of his politics one can only say that they were rather narrow. Being formed in the early days of the Gaelic revival he did not take much account of the changing times since partition. There is at times a bitterness with planters and their work."[1185] That 1950s Ulster liberal view has in turn been overtaken by changing political styles and the rebirth of Belfast Republicanism. It could and would not be written today.

Cathal O'Byrne died from senile dementia in 1957 aged seventy-four. He had remained a bachelor all his life. And plainly a fairly camp one. There is no evidence to suggest he was gay but none to suggest he was not. It just seems unlikely, again, that a man who could be so emotional and passionate, was unable to arrange any sexual life for himself, as Casement did so vigorously, according to the considerable evidence of the diaries. Yet Cathal, who was given to quoting Casement's sentimental credo that "no one could love the Irish people without loving the religion that made them what they were" [*Roger Casement's Last Will*] was plainly someone who took religion seriously all his life. It could have been an insurmountable barrier to sexual expression. Had he nothing to confess? These line from *Love's Cares* certainly tell of Casement's view of sexual expression: "'Tis only those who have loved the best/Can say where the wounds of loving are."

In his extensive trawl of the Casement papers, B.L. Reid discovered another spontaneous expression of frustrated love, this time about a holiday romance in Italy. Given Casement's gargantuan output of correspondence and other writings, it is perhaps surprising that more such expressions of private feelings do not crop up. They do in his poetry but lack the names of those he loved. Reid wrote of "An incoherent note scribbled at the end of two pages of drafts of verses, also incoherent, treating of unhappy love":[1186]

"Casaldo's friend – R.C.
Naples, 3 September 1900
Written going to lunch at Naval & Military
on Saturday, Sept. 22 1900
- Oh Sad! Oh! grief stricken."[1187]

Reid took this to mean "that before going to lunch on 22 September 1900 at the Naval and Military Club in London (Cambridge House, Piccadilly) Casement tried to versify his feelings about an unsuccessful amorous event of three weeks earlier in Naples. It seems to me to express homosexual feelings about a homosexual relationship. That neither the poem nor the affair came off makes no difference as evidence."[1188] The poem on which Casement inscribed this *cri de coeur* is titled *The Unforgotten,* and although a rough draft, could well apply to Casaldo. Rather than being incoherent, it reads tolerably well, and seems another forerunner to *The Nameless One:*

Beat on sad heart O beat thyself away
I would not loveless hold my life a day
Yet never may thy willing hand seek mine
Yet never may the tumult of my heart
Beat to a rhythm caught from pressing thine
O thou art everywhere save in my arms.

On 7 September 1900 Casement was in London writing to Dick Morten from the Wellington Club, telling him he had taken a friend's studio or rooms at 12 Aubrey Walk, Campden Hill Road, in Kensington, for two months. That friend was Count Blücher. The address was to figure later in 1916. It is therefore likely that 3 September 1900 was the date he parted from Casaldo. Not that Casement was averse to taking his pleasure in Italy whenever he was able. This is best illustrated by his 1903 diary where, on 1 August, he recalls with pleasure a successful encounter three years earlier with a soldier called Fortunato in the Coliseum.

The manuscript of the poem *Love's Awakening*, published in Mackey's 1958 anthology, is also to be found in this batch of papers at the NLI.[1189] Its first verse could well be a poem prompted by Casaldo or any number of Italian boys met in Sicily or Naples, or in Dublin, boys who had brought Casement to life emotionally. The probable first draft, however, was written on "19th May 1895, Sunday on Rathlin Hills":

O! God of love, how can it be accurst -
This love that wakes, that thrills me thro' the night?
This love that fills my being with delight -
Of all the ills that stamp man's lot the worst?

He then crossed out:

Why were we given hearts to pant & thrill
And eyes to blaze & soften at a touch?

From diary evidence, by the early 1900s, Casement had long been sexually active, but rarely permitting a relationship to develop beyond a quick encounter: these Italian affairs or romances taught Casement that there could be joy in living out what is now (and may even then have been) called a gay life, but as ever the relationships would be uneven. The circumstances of the time, and the age and income disparities meant his partnerships would be largely commercially based, incapable of being integrated into his political or consular life. But they had one great advantage over the loves of so many of his English contemporaries who were stuck in a form of arrested development, panting over boys in their early teens, or even younger: these relationships could be consummated, and Casement undoubtedly did so. References to love in Italy, both in the diaries and in his other writings, abound. That country had a profound impact on him, as it did on so many other of his contemporaries.

The southern Italy of that time was becoming something of a Mecca for gay men and other literary and bohemian types. The key character was Baron Wilhelm von Gloeden of Mecklenburg who by the early 1890s was firmly established in the area as a purveyor of pictures of nude adolescents. His business was selling "to connoisseurs, photographs of the local male youth, unclothed or archaically draped in home-made togas and wreathed with laurel crowns."[1190] Another writer tells how von Gloeden "posed his models in intimate situations allegedly representing classical ideas of friendship or fraternity, but his depiction of brotherly love, two boys holding hands and looking into each other's eyes" could plainly be taken as one of lovers. If a harder presentation was required, a range of his studies of naked and sexually aroused youths was also available "under the counter."[1191] These pictures are still being reprinted.

The Baron's fame spread far and wide, and Taormina in Sicily became a point of pilgrimage for enthusiasts, including Oscar Wilde who visited after his release from Reading Gaol. Other visitors reputedly were both Kaiser Wilhelm's son Friedrich and his doomed favourite Prince Philip von Eulenburg. They were able to purchase pictures for their collections, and, at a cost, partake of the favours of some of the models. Rival photographers both in Taormina and in Rome entered the same lucrative market which was just beginning to emerge from under, and detach itself from, health and fitness publications. By publishing prominently a von Gloeden study of Sicilian boys bathing, a German *Korperkultur* title had opened the door for the Baron. The pictures were so great a hit with readers that it provided him with the incentive to concentrate on what would become his life's work. Before his arrival in Taormina there was apparently not one villa or hotel but, in time, he made the town's fortune, rather than his own, as he was wont to say. He wanted to be happy not rich. Through the pictures of his ephebes he managed both.

Casement was apparently in Taormina as early as November 1890, when he was twenty-six, according to a note inscribed on one poem. And he was to be back a decade later. Writing to Francis Cowper on 5 November 1900 from G. Floresta's "Hotel Timeo" in Taormina, Sicily he was excusing himself for failing to make a promised visit to Lisbon: "I find I can get from Genoa to Cape Verde by excellent Italian steamer...the Genoa alternative is so much nearer and gives me so much more time with my friends here", he dissembled.[1192]

As stated, he had inscribed "Lines written in Very Great Dejection at Genoa, November 15 1900, before sailing on 'Sirio' for Barcelona." He was in Barcelona by 26 November 1900, describing a bullfight he attended there in a letter to Dick Morten. This was a spectacle which he abhorred, writing off the Spanish as "ineffable swine" for their cruelty to animals. Given that he was in London in late September 1900 yet in Naples earlier that month when he was emotionally involved with Casaldo, it appears he had swiftly returned to Italy by November with a view to re-establishing this love affair – only to find it blocked for some reason. The most likely cause of his dejection has to be the fact that Casaldo was indifferent or unfaithful; probably both.

While he awaited his trial and execution Casement never stopped writing. His solicitor's papers are stuffed with pages of text from various gaols, so much that Serjeant Sullivan pleaded on 6 June, "There are parts of his notes that should be burned. Tell him he must stop scribbling. Papers get mislaid, overlooked and spied upon sooner or later. He has told us as much as can be of use – and everything else that is worse than useless."[1193] A wise warning since a mislaid file of incriminating papers did end up with the prison authorities and thence the Home Office. The description of the novelist Anthony Trollope who overheard his own publisher saying he had "the fecundity of a herring" might be also be thought applicable to Casement. The problem of his incriminating papers and especially the fear of his erstwhile friend Herbert Ward ending up with his picture collection of Italian boys, prompted one particular note from Casement to his solicitor. It of course revealed his appreciation of unclothed lads of Sicily, but on balance he seems to have reckoned it was better for Gavan Duffy to be aware of their existence and to take the heavy hint to get rid of them.

"There are a great many photographs scattered thro' all my belongings some of my travels of African types etc. Many of these are in the trunks at Allisons in London (and were originally, the Sicilian ones bought many years ago) in a package addressed "to be given to my friend Herbert Ward at my death." Don't give them to him now. He has turned against me and would only insult me now. They are mostly Sicilian types that I intended for his studio – or mine, when I lived at Campden Hill with Count Blücher. They might be destroyed now I think by my solicitor unless he cares to keep any of them. There are other Italian and Sicilian photos that used to be on the wall of my studio at C. Hill Gdns (with Count Blücher) I should like Mr Gavan Duffy to accept."[1194]

It seems Casement was carefully trying to shift some of the responsibility for possession of these Sicilian photographs to his old friend Count Blücher who was safely out of range in Germany. Earlier he was writing about Scotland

Yard having "no right to retain any papers or documents of mine – diaries, books or anything not used at the trial against me" so his concerns about these documents were growing. His problem was to get them back from the police but not to appear so keen as to draw attention to them, nor to seem too eager to have them destroyed in case it looked like his ownership of them was suspicious. The trick was to suggest that if they were not to be binned, or burned, as surplus to requirements, his solicitor, a man known to be of great piety and impeccable propriety, might be happy to take them.

If he did extract and retain Casement's Italian boys, Gavan Duffy, a man who combined compassion with common sense, certainly never displayed them. As someone who was generally punctilious about following legal etiquette and instructions it is likely he did go through the returned property and remove them. He may also have given advice on disposal of the framed pictures of young men and the many photograph albums which were never seen again after their return from Scotland Yard in early 1917[1195] although he may have left that task to Gertrude Parry.

Casement's infatuation with Italy and Italians, and the influence they had upon him, is revealed in another defining note: "I love Naples. It has all its sins and all its beauties upon its face; it hides nothing; it is the most human town in Europe. People there do what they think and as they are in the privacy of their own room (if they are among the fortunate Neapolitans who possess separate rooms) so they are in the streets…Whether it is better to hide our hearts to muffle up our lives and to live the truer part of our lives in secret as we do today, the future only knows. For my part I cannot help feeling that the world lost something when discretion became the first of the ten commandments."[1196]

His visiting the city of Naples is confirmed in a letter to Gertrude, dated 31 January 1902, when he enclosed "a present from Rod from Naples."[1197] It is further borne out by a gift to his fellow consul in Loanda, the German Dorbritz in whose company he chose frequently to be. On 2 November 1903, Casement recorded in his diary, after a farewell dinner, "Gave him my last neapolitan pin as a keepsake." The 1901/2 winter visit was to be described as "my long Italian spell" when Casement came to make his now traditional excuse to Cowper (from Ballycastle) on 17 February, "I had as I wrote you, intended going to Portugal but fate took me to Italy instead. I have just got back."[1198]

Casement had the habit of obtaining addresses of young men and sending on photographs he had taken of them, and there is mention of someone in Rapallo being such a recipient in one of his letters. The habit crops up in South America particularly in relation to the much sought-after Ignacio. Mr D. Brown of Booth & Co. writing from Iquitos in April 1911 dutifully reported to Casement: "I have delivered the photographs to Perez [Antonio Cruz Perez, a Booth's customs' clerk] on the Muelle; but up to the present I have not been able to find the boy Ignacio Torres. Some of our men are looking for him and as the Steward of the "Liberal" informs me that the boy is somewhere in Iquitos we should be able to find him."[1199] Back in Iquitos himself, Casement twice records in the 1911 Black Diary, in December, further attempts to get such photos to Ignacio.

Alongside the poem *The Nameless One* and outside of the diaries, the remarks about the freedom Casement felt in Naples are the most interpretable as a defiant exposition of a homosexual orientation. There is simply no other way they can be read except relating to sexual acts of a homosexual kind; no matter how easy-going Naples was, it certainly did not permit its girls the freedom that some of its boys took, and still do take, even if they are now too worldly-wise to let themselves be photographed in such poses.

However, on three occasions when Casement came tangentially to discuss homosexuality, twice in the Black Diaries; the suicide of General Hector Macdonald (on 17, 19 and 30 April 1903), and on native boys playing sexually with each other in public (on 4 October 1910), and once in a letter to Dick Morten, he took what appears at first sight to be an, at least distant, if not disapproving view of the matter.

In that letter, dated 2 January 1905, discussing the introduction of Chinese labour to South Africa he wrote: "No man who has travelled but knows that Chinamen hold views on sexual intercourse not in favour in Europe since the days of Greece and Rome. They come from their country without their womenfolk and they are enclosed in compounds for three years. It is not difficult to imagine that, with such men, with such natures, the results are not entirely healthy and charming to contemplate." He further described the system as "slave labour pure and simple."[1200] No evidence for this supposed Chinese predilection was provided.

Casement's brother Tom, when a commissioner of mines in the Transvaal, is said to have campaigned to abolish indentured Chinese labour in the Rand, which may have prompted discussion of the issue.[1201] The question was agitating London anti-slavery circles, with allegations that "the Chinese were teaching sodomy to the blacks."[1202] After two (unpublished) enquiries the first which reported in 1906 into "the prevalence of unnatural vice among Chinese indentured labour" and secondly in 1907 into such vice "among the natives in the mines of the Witwatersrand" the Chinese were unsurprisingly exonerated. Sodomy was apparently already common among east coast immigrant miners. It was, however, noted that some of the most enthusiastic participants in the 'boy wife' system were Portuguese soldiers and police.[1203]

What Casement actually wrote to Dick Morten was couched in an arch and knowing manner despite his recorded knowledge of matters Chinese being sparse to say the least. It was not condemnatory as such, merely observing that heterosexual men without women, will in time, and especially if with such "Chinese natures" descend into some form of primitive and unregulated homosexual behaviour. Of course being gay at this time and doing same-sex sex did not guarantee guiltlessness, still less admiration for such activity, as is illustrated by the lives of other contemporaries who practised what they did not preach; and preached against what they practised.

A notorious example of such contradictory, or mixed, attitudes comes from the most prominent Uranian writer after Baron Corvo, the teacher John Gambril Nicholson (1866-1931), author in 1911 of *A Garland of Ladslove.* He penned a pamphlet for his pupils, to instil into them "an awareness of the dangers of homosexual affection."[1204] Entitled *A Story of Cliffe School,* and probably written when employed at Rydal School in Colwyn Bay, it enjoined boys "swamped by the waves of sin" to leave "behind you those terrible habits which would work your eternal ruin." Nicholson, later a teacher at Stationers' School in London until his 1925 retirement, unlike many of his Uranian contemporaries was not chaste and was plainly a shameless hypocrite. Corvo, writing in 1908, was amazed that Nicholson despite the matter of his sonnet publishing, "held his mastership in a big school for quite a dozen years, and still holds it"; he being someone who wrote to Corvo of his own experiences "in a style precisely like that of the storiettes pencilled up in the jakes at the Marble Arch."[1205]

Casement's poem *The Streets of Catania* has previously figured in the controversy about his sexuality. According to the copy he wrote out for Father Murnane in Pentonville on the day before his execution, it was originally composed in Sicily in that finest of years, 1900. One stanza – that after the first – he said he had forgotten but his memory appears to have been faulty as it all appears present. Casaldo may well have prompted the poem, for a number of people see it as decidedly homosexual. It has been suggested that the gift to Father Murnane of such an otherwise inapposite poem was an attempt to validate a lifestyle that may just have been revealed to him, for it was this Bermondsey priest who had taken Casement through his intellectual doubts and brought him through his conversion:

All that was beautiful and just,
All that was pure and sad
Went in one little moving plot of dust
The world called bad.

Came like a highwayman, and went,
One who was bold and gay,
Left when his lightly loving mood was spent
Thy heart to pay.

By-word of little streets and men,
Narrower theirs the shame –
Tread thou the lava loving leaves, and then
Turn whence it came.

Aetna, all wonderful, whose heart
Glows as thine throbbing glows,
Almond and citron bloom quivering at start,
Ends in pure snows.

Casement's own less than enlightening commentary on the poem, reprinted in Mackey's *Crime Against Europe* was: "The streets of Catania are paved with blocks of the lava of Aetna." In a letter in the *Irish Times* of 21 April 1956, Monk Gibbon, who was a cousin of W.B. Yeats, joined the correspondence that was raging in the wake of René MacColl's recent biography. He wrote that he believed Casement was homosexual, in particular because of his failure to state to his barrister Serjeant Sullivan, simply: "This is false. The diary is a forgery." Furthermore, he stated "a poem by Casement…entitled if I remember rightly, 'Catania' is bound, to those who know the reputation of Capri and Sicily in this respect, to suggest that it was written by a homosexual. It is a remarkably fine sonnet, and I suppose I am starting another argument now which can be carried on till doomsday. I can only say that in my opinion that sonnet was written by a homosexual."*

The reputation of Catania, in particular, was described by the journalist Michael Davidson some thirty years later in *Some Boys*. He was a notorious pederast who also authored the infamous *The World, The Flesh and Myself*. In a chapter about Catania, a town that might not have changed much in this respect between the turn of the century when Casement visited and Davidson's time, he wrote: "Were a trophy to be offered for competition among all the

* Other literary figures expressed views on Casement and the diaries: Hilaire Belloc recorded in June 1916, "I had an instinctive repulsion for him when I met him years ago", adding that he had a "sudden unbalanced enthusiasm about anything." He also reported, wrongly, that he was a Freemason. Frank O'Connor wrote in 1957, it was "unquestionable that Casement was temperamentally a homosexual" while asserting Adler Christensen was both homosexual and a traitor. In 1961, Ethel Mannin recanted her previous view that the diaries were authentic (NLI 31741/3 & 4).

municipalities of the world for the most unashamed, ingenuous and confiding display, open to the public gaze, of juvenile eroticism, I believe it would be easily won by the city of Catania." Along a line of rocks below the harbour wall of this eastern Sicilian city, he reported that boys will unblushingly indulge in a "marathon of masturbation." Prizes, he felt, ought to be awarded for their tireless interest in sex. Davidson also suggested, not entirely tongue in cheek, that the proximity of Mount Etna, Casement's "Heaven attesting hill", might be the cause of such "lubricious exuberance." Catania he felt could not be recommended for friendship but was certainly "a wonderful place for sights to see."[1206]

Other occasional verse of Casement tells the tale of a man of strong passions, one emotionally labile and keen to justify himself to himself. In this 1899 jotting there is again little doubt as to why he feels it necessary to explain how love can transform what would otherwise be seen by his fellow men as degraded behaviour:

Were it not that the lowliest act can be
Stripped of unworthiness by love, and made
One tiny wave of a heaven reflecting sea...[1207]

The "Malay Love Song", so entitled by Casement, and written, as he noted, on 9 April 1900 at the "Capetown CS Club" is an anguished response to an apparently unrequited adoration of a Malay boy, from whom he was separating. Casement was leaving South Africa for a new appointment in the Congo State:

There's a star that set for ever,
when I said farewell to thee

There are joys that live for ever;
there are joys that last a day;

There are hopes that blossom never
on life's slowly dying spray -

Tho' I die - and Death's hereafter
hold no promise of the Dove

O! I'd sink with lips of laughter
for one moment of thy love.[1208]

It would be inconceivable in the South Africa of those days for the object of this affection to have been a woman; not least because he would not have been allowed into a position of proximity with a Muslim girl, let alone develop an acquaintance with her that could be publicly observed. His lover was probably a servant or waiter, possibly at the same Capetown Club where he may have been staying. The evidence of later passions suggest a pattern of infatuation with young working men met on board ship or in the course of the business of his consular activities. Lovers taken or wanted, and replaced, but not forgotten.

Amongst a number of apparently over-enthusiastic assumptions made by authors, including some dubious assessments of Adler Christensen, was one by Catherine Cline. In her book on Casement's friend, soul mate and Congo Reform Association ally, E.D. Morel, Cline devotes considerable space to their relationship. They and their careers bore remarkable similarities and Sir Alfred Jones who employed them both at different times must have wondered about his judgment, or the hand fate had dealt him, hiring so often hands which later bit him.

Oddly only one side of their extensive correspondence seems to have survived – that of Casement to Morel, which is in the London School of Economics Library. There are only a couple of letters from Morel to Casement in the NLI which suggests the destruction of a large cache.

Cline, in 1980, wrote, "Casement's biographers agree that he was successful in concealing his sexual proclivities almost until his arrest and that the charges circulated concerning his homosexuality, which probably sealed his fate by discouraging efforts for a reprieve, came as a total surprise to his friends." This seems to have been the case with most, although some may have suspected and chosen not to enquire. She continued, "The allegations may not, however, have been completely new to Morel. In an exchange of letters in late June 1911 Morel and Casement discussed in highly elliptical terms some shocking rumours which Casement reported were being spread around about himself. Morel assumed the stories to be false, an impression that Casement encouraged."[1209] His responding letter dated 27 June 1911 and lacking an address read, in full:

"My dear Bulldog, Just got your letter enclosing one addressed to Sir Roger Casement which I shall pass on to that man but I am sure he will not answer it except thro' me! What I said to you a few days ago was in confidence and I cannot discuss it further on the lines of your letter to Sir R.C. You must see that, if you will think on how I said it. No names of anyone were mentioned to me and I laughed at the story and ridiculed it. Why make up a fairytale and lose good energy fighting a myth that no real man ever believed? I don't think you are called on to deal with second hand liars and idiots and you make me feel an awful ass for having been such a fool as to mention it to you – but to tell you the truth I thought you knew already! – I had an idea that somehow or other the silly lie had reached you – but I see now (and saw in the taxi too) I was wrong and I was very sorry the thing slipped out from me as it did. I have not the slightest idea of who it referred to. I know my ideas are just as fallible as other men's – and in any case I should not give the thing another thought. The Testimonial wiped out that story from the minds of the few it could have influenced at all.

"I am overwhelmed with letters and worries too – among them that I find it hard to tackle and I beg of you my dear Bulldog, display some of the generosity of your animal prototype and release your hold! If I noticed all the rot said of myself I'd be a raving lunatic instead of only a mild one. But I beg you to desist from taking further notice of what should never have reached you ever had I not been such a fool! You make me ashamed of myself. In haste – yours ever Tiger."[1210]

The writing on this letter is difficult at times to decipher and it is true to say that there is ambiguity in most of the statements as to who is the object of the accusations. But the "silly lie" on close reading seems to have been one directed against Morel who is reacting badly, especially to Casement, who in this instance was the messenger. In his hurt, Morel had gone so far as to address Casement by his title. From other material it seems that there had been whispering about the sources of Morel's income, and the possibility that he was beholden to those traders like John Holt who provided the larger part of it. The suggestion of Casement that Morel's Testimonial would put an end to the stories surely clinches the matter as one definitely referring to Morel.

The letter therefore bore no relation to Casement's sexual activities and, if anything, indicates Casement was confident that his private life was unknown to Morel or perhaps just not an issue between them. Morel initially chose not to visit Casement in prison and was seriously disturbed by Gertrude Bannister's "indiscreet" letter in May 1916 asking him to request such a visit. By 21 July, as the end neared, he had changed his mind and decided he could risk public criticism. He wrote asking to see Casement but Duffy advised "he is being guarded from contact with the outer world with extraordinary jealousy."[1211]

It has been observed that as Casement was a person of strong feelings, "all emotion" in the words of Joseph Conrad, the fact of no known history of love affairs with women, requited or not, is evidence of great significance, another loud non-barking dog. The view remains that such a self-assured man with vast reserves of passion could not have failed to be a sexual being. Such indifference does not happen outside of monastic life. It is not as if Casement was afraid of women or that he stuck to male company. In the years of his life in England or when devoted to Ireland he was never long out of women's company.

Eligible females of all ages gathered round him with an unerring frequency that says much to the modern mind. Indeed a needlessly cruel term applied to such women, by gay men, springs to mind. Opportunity was ever present but he was certainly not partaking. Outside of taking a wife, Casement lived abroad in places where heterosexual services could be easily obtained at a price, and he was plainly aware of that, but he did not pay. While in England especially, he also moved amongst, or was within reach of, a new class of women in the arts movement or radical world who were now willing, and at times eager, to take male lovers without or beyond marriage, but again no action.

On a number of occasions Casement was pressed on the matter of marriage. He had several ready-made excuses which were sufficient to satisfy those who were happy to leave the matter alone. Ada McNeill, for one, (whom he thought of only as a "brick") was unwilling to let the matter rest and as we know Casement had to enrol his other favourite females to get her to call off the dogs of love. For those few of the marrying kind amongst the Protestant women of the Gaelic League, Casement must have been especially tantalising, as there were not enough Protestant gentlemen available, the sex ratios being very antagonistic. And he was also a fine catch by reason of intellect and beauty.

Mary Colum was first introduced to Casement in London soon after her marriage in 1912 to Padraic Colum. He had met Casement in Belfast at Ardrigh when collaborating with Herbert Hughes on collecting airs and writing lyrics. Mary Colum was to meet Casement again in Dublin and in New York in 1914. She described him later in terms that illustrate once more just how affecting his presence was. As a young newly-married women she wrote of her impressions of "a bearded, tanned, Castilian-looking man…magnificent looking", someone with an "aristocratic figure and face." She further noted, "There was about him that strong psychic life that was characteristic of so many of the elder generation of Irish people of the time", suggesting also an undertone of hysteria that others have mentioned. Alongside Wilfrid Scawen Blunt, she reckoned that "Yeats and Casement were the handsomest and most romantic looking men I have ever seen."[1212]

There were early signs of Casement's reluctance to marry or of excuses being tendered. His sister Nina writing in 1918 recalled him saying as a young man, "When I marry it will be an Irish woman but I have no time to think about such things and I certainly will never marry to leave a wife in Europe while I am at the other side of the globe."[1213] In itself it served, but allied to other remarks it wore thin. Gertrude, describing the episode involving Eve Symons and the young Roger, reported that he was serious so "I ventured 'Will you marry Eva?' He said 'How can I? I have no money – I'll have to earn some'."[1214] In 1924, Dr Patrick McCartan, an admittedly slow-to-marry bachelor himself, wrote to Maloney suggesting fibbing over Casement's sexuality was really not necessary, "If I were her (Gee) I'd let them do their worst though I knew the diary stuff were true. We know all about poor Oscar Wilde but who thinks now of his sins."[1215]

Judging someone else's sexual behaviour is a hazardous exercise since we are all uniquely limited to our own sexuality: one person's temptation is never precisely another's. The only secure stance is to refrain from judgment, except where clearer social morality pertains. Once the sexual behaviour of others is historical, the pitfalls on judgment increase dramatically. It is extremely hard to think oneself into the mores of another age and other cultures, to remember the different circumstances, laws and attitudes, the dissimilar perceptions, the alien rhythm of life itself. In addition, history is a very crude instrument; we speak of the sexual morality of the Victorian period, and with such a phrase history irons out the nuances and quirks of a generation into a conveniently simplified format that is describable and conceivable. In fact of course, life is never simple, least of all sexual life.

Modern discussion of the Wilde trial is a case in point. The attitude of newspaper prudery at the time of the scandal is usually taken to be the then societal norm. Public opinion it is said was outraged at Wilde's involvement with male prostitutes. Their age was then a minor issue. Yet such blanket condemnation cannot be an accurate view of opinion in 1895. It would be nearer the mark (but still a crude generalisation) to posit the theory that the norm was for late Victorian society to accommodate the fact of male prostitution, other societies in history have.

Several of those who most vehemently question the authenticity of the Black Diaries also maintain the view that the diarist was unusually gross in his sexual behaviour. In one case, the Dublin author Ulick O'Connor has gone so far as to describe the diarist as a "dangerous, degenerate monster."[1216] Others, more modish, now suggest that to believe in their authenticity is itself homophobic as the forger/author was trying to disparage such a lifestyle, making it appear ceaselessly depraved. Some who were until recently wont to talk of the writer as a degenerate pervert, are now, hesitatingly, learning to get their tongue around the word homophobe.

The evidence is, however, there. Casement was the author/diarist. He was a homosexual and he was no celibate. He did it often. He did it in public places. He did it with young men and with boys. He was promiscuous and he did not worry about laws and sexual morals.

The Black Diaries are authentic. They reveal the secret sexual thoughts of many homosexual men, then and now (and of heterosexual males if the gender of the individual being desired was switched). In respect of Casement's sexual manners, except for the mention of a number of younger boys, the diaries would today be unremarkable, if historic documents.

Several weeks ago (as I write in June 2002), Channel 4 showed a documentary on homosexual sex which featured in graphic verbal detail, and blurry visuals, cottaging in the very toilet frequented by Casement at Hyde Park Corner nearly a century earlier. And that was not the item later subject (in the gay press) to most hostile commentary. The world, where gays (and myself) are concerned, has turned upside down in little over a quarter of a century. Certain basic male manners seem, however, not to change.

Appendix: Nina, Tom and Charlie Casement

The explanation for Nina Casement's behaviour, over the years, lies within the family. It is quite simply the case that she, Tom and Roger were three remarkably unconventional, and in the first two cases, unstable characters. Only Charlie, the oldest boy, and the least mobile of the four led a relatively ordinary life in Australia, although he was never financially sound. The secretive nature of his second marriage indicates a complicated domestic life, while the two girls by his first Balharry wife appear to have been raised, in part, within that family. The same traits were also visited upon the three Bannister cousins, despite them having a more conventional upbringing, albeit with a father absent in Africa for much of their childhood. Of the seven cousins, only Charlie had children.

But where Roger and Tom were loved for their character, eccentricities and charm, Nina was almost feared for her extremity of opinion and harshness. Had she been a boy she might have been another Roger, but that option was never to be developed. No career ever seems to have been mooted for her. Born in 1856, and as the oldest child, and a girl, she had domestic responsibilities, being also obliged, in her teens, to become a substitute mother. Gertrude and Elizabeth Bannister both became schoolmistresses but Nina never had any employment. As a consequence, although reliant on her brother Roger's quarterly allowances, she was left to her own devices.

Gertrude perhaps hit on part of an explanation for Nina's continuing oddity, one with she was herself familiar, when she remarked "Nina always looked with jealous rage on anyone on whom she thought Roddie was likely to bestow his affections."[1217] In the family memory, Nina is still seen as quarrelsome and possessive. When it came to Roddie's last letter from the death cell on 25 July 1916, he finally reciprocated her love, writing "I have always cared for you more than anyone else."[1218] But his feelings had not always been so apparent, given that he was also obliged to apologise for "that day in Berkshire when I said such unkind things to you in your cottage." To Nina, he was forever the boy who "would come and confide all his troubles to me"[1219] and, as such, in the decade after 1916, she fired a host of angry letters at the London establishment about the "murder" of her dear brother.

In 1896, writing from Lourenco Marques, Casement expressed his regular exasperation about his siblings' marriage problems, and Nina's in particular, saying, "I wish she would take a kindly view and sensible of her affairs and return to her husband."[1220] That husband, George Henry Newman, goes entirely unrecorded in the wider Casement papers apart from his name. They married

Nina Casement (Mrs George Newman) with pony and cocker spaniel, NLI 49154/20/5

Charlie Casement, brother, Melbourne studio

in 1887 but where he was met, and where he went, is a mystery. He had however a number of convictions, one for trespassing in a field of turnips (fined 5s.) and several for embezzlement which resulted in a two year jail sentence. Marriage did not suit Nina and the rest of her life was hinged to her brother, his friends, and his enthusiasms.

Like her parents she was never long at one address, Casement noting, for example, in 1901, that Nina was again shifting her lodgings at Portrush in Co. Antrim. She was an early and steadfast adherent to Irish nationalism despite moving back and forward from Ireland to live at times in England. Once in America, she took up the cudgels on behalf of her brother. Her public attack on Alfred Noyes "who propagated the most unspeakable filth concerning my brother"[1221] was her most famous intervention. But there were others. One that she graphically described herself, concerned a woman in a restaurant who wanted her seat. In the ensuing squabble Roddie was called "an Oscar Wilde" by the woman, and Nina a "vile filthy painted old rip." In enraged response, as she reported, "I struck her several blows with my Irish blackthorn stick" adding, as if to excuse the violence, that there were English spies everywhere.[1222] In 1924, Bulmer Hobson, forgetting that one valiant episode which eventually came to haunt Alfred Noyes, indicated his low opinion of Nina, "Unfortunately

Mrs Newman was quite unfit to defend his character – her extravagance would ruin any cause she defended."[1223]

Although she managed to write a series of sentimental articles for the Irish-American press about her brother and their family upbringing, nobody, friend or foe, was spared the rough side of her tongue or pen. In September 1916, Michael Francis Doyle who had been asked by Gavan Duffy to effect the payment of a £150 annuity which he had organised, wrote of his discovery that Nina was "a very peculiar person. She has made the most bitter attacks on Mr McGarrity, John Devoy and others who were her brother's closest friends in this country. Many regard her mental condition as questionable. I am the only one whom she apparently has confidence in. This is because of her suspicious nature and her peculiar mental attitude."[1224]

A month later, he added that Nina "has the unfortunate faculty of quarrelling" with everyone and was now refusing to have anything to do with her brother's former friends "because she claims they are responsible for his death in obliging him to cross the ocean at the time he did."[1225] The annuity to which a number of people contributed was largely funded by the Cork-born writer and composer, Mrs Ethel Voynich (née Boole) whose Fenian-influenced novel *The Gadfly* sold over five million copies. Voynich also composed a cantata in memory of Casement.

As early as 15 August 1916, to pacify Nina, John Devoy was writing "in spite of the utterly undeserved abuse and epithets you fling at me I have the utmost sympathy with your misfortunes." But she could blow hot and cold as on 15 October when she was able to remind Joe McGarrity, "You were a good and dear friend of the blessed one who is gone."[1226] The state of Gertrude's irritation with Nina is exemplified by a long cautionary letter, dated 27 June 1920, sent to explain the current state of play as regards the diaries. At several points Nina is admonished by Gertrude, "For God's sake don't write and abuse me and worry me if there is anything you don't grasp."[1227]

Nina did return from America, and in December 1926 was permitted to visit her brother's unmarked grave in Pentonville. Then, shortly before her death, she sent an angry letter to the authorities over a prison officer's alleged use of the word "murderer" in relation to her brother. The Governor denied the word had been so used: "No doubt in her over-wrought and distressed condition at the grave side [she had] misconstrued the meaning" of what had been said about the occupants of adjoining graves.[1228]

Her raging letters reached a final low just before she died. The vexed issue of Casement's body being taken out of the prison and buried in Ireland was concerning her, especially as her cousin Gertrude was Casement's heir and executor. She wrote to the Home Office trying to ensure that they refuse any request from her. His remains, she felt, had to "be given to his only sister the one he loved best in this inhuman world. Mrs Parry is after all only a cousin on the maternal side – not Irish at all but a mongrel mixture who has been spoiled by a foolish and absurd husband of considerable means... [she] has become that most objectionable of all human beings, an English snob of the lower middle class." For good measure Nina added that her mother was 970 years in Ireland and a direct descendant of the Herveys of Tara Hall, forgetting that, if genealogically true, so also was Gertrude's mother Grace.[1229] However, there was to be no relenting on the issue of reburial of the remains for another forty years.

Nina died in 1927 aged seventy, in Atlantic City, another resort whose hotels were her usual home, probably alone. Only an Alice Stopford Green comment is on record after her death. Writing to Brigid Mathews (Bigger's housekeeper) on 22 April she reckoned "It is a mercy that Mrs Newman was taken away... The good people who got together an income for her were worn out by the difficulties she blew up around them."[1230]

A career at home for Charlie and Tom Casement was, for financial reasons, not considered and in 1878, aged fifteen and seventeen respectively, they were sent to sea apprenticed to a sailing ship in the Australian trade. In due course Charlie, and later Tom, who was by then an officer, "swallowed the anchor and took to the beach." This relocation in Australia required further financial assistance from their uncle John in Magherintemple and the hospitality of cousins there. Tom did not keep up with some of these relatives due to a falling out over his manners. According to the family historian, he was staying with Brabazon Casement and was "very rightly kicked out for discourtesy towards his wife." This was in 1888 shortly before the two brothers headed off to the Queensland gold fields for the first of Tom's mining adventures. Charlie, at least, returned to settle down in Melbourne where he worked for the Tramway and Omnibus Company and lastly the Melbourne Steamship Company. Their first marriages were to two sisters Minnie and Blanche Balharry, daughters of James Balharry and Emily Perry. She was the daughter of Charles J. Perry (1817-1893) who married as his second wife Isabella, the widow of Hugh Casement, their only full uncle. The Perry and Casement families were therefore linked through membership of the Catholic Apostolic Church. A third Balharry sister, Emily, migrated to London.

Money, presents and letters flowed over the years to Australia from that youngest and most successful of the brothers. Asking in December 1904 for a loan to finance his formal wedding to Beatrice, his second wife, Charlie politely suggested "I often have wondered is it because you have such a lot of poor relatives that you are helping, that you have never married yourself."[1231] Later he correctly predicted "I am very much afraid you and I will never meet on this earth again."[1232] In October 1916, Beatrice Casement wrote to Gertrude about Charlie's distress at the hanging of his brother. Having had a heart attack while at work after the execution, he was only able to scribble a note on the top of her letter saying "Dear Old Girl am very sick at heart and too miserable to write."[1233] It was their only child of whom Beatrice also wrote, "Joan is a little dear but has too tender a heart for this world. She never forgets to pray for her Uncle Roddie as she calls him." In an earlier letter Charlie had told his brother "Joan sends Uncle Rod a big kiss and thinks he is a very nice Father Xmas." Charlie died in 1932. It was to be his two older daughters who represented the family in Dublin in 1965, Joan having died before her uncle's reburial.

Tom did not stay in Australia, being drawn to South Africa by the Boer War where he reputedly "fought like a Trojan". More prospecting, this time for mercury, and employment as an Inspector in Johannesburg's diamond mines followed. The breakdown of his marriage to Blanche Balharry, as is evident in the 1903 Black Diary, when attempts at reconciliation or divorce were both reportedly failing, must have been another key factor in Tom leaving Australia. Indeed the marriage had only lasted a few weeks. As late as 1910 Tom was still writing about obtaining a divorce: "[Charlie] is seeing Blanche but has not succeeded in doing anything yet. He says she is very bitter against me and has her knife into me. Then why try to hold on to me and create a scandal when she can fix things up so easily over there."[1234] A year later the divorce had been effected and Tom was free to wed Katje Ackermann in 1912.

Another war intervened with service in German East Africa where Tom was made Captain. It was while in Tanganyika that news came through of his brother's trial and execution. He attempted to quit the army but after an intervention from Jan Smuts was persuaded to see "the damned business through". In June 1916 a despairing Casement had written to Katje reminding her of his visit three years earlier: "It was a pity I ever left you both that day", remarking ironically that his brother was now on Kilimanjaro's slopes, fighting Germans: "Poor old Tom I grieve for him and never forget the last look I got of him that day across the veld."[1235] Captain Tom Casement in 1919, just home from South Africa, did attempt to prise his brother's "detained letters" out of the Home Office. Perhaps aware that a last letter to him had existed (which was destroyed), he was fobbed off with a deceitful reply that nothing had been detained "after hostilities ceased."[1236]

That Tom should have fought for the British empire in the First World War was at odds with his anti-Redmond activities in South Africa and his violent views on England, as expressed in letters sent to Ireland after Casement's departure for America in July 1914. Then it was "all the d--- English & Co. are only waiting for a chance to throw mud at us...Personally I would far sooner die for Ireland and her cause than be a wealthy man and no use" and "the only thing that will bring prosperity to dear old Ireland is the gun and some blood spilling. The only way. And the sooner it is begun and finished the better"[1237] In late August, it was "I would sooner fight against the English than any nation under the sun except the Mexicans" but by September, not having heard from his brother, he was wondering, presciently "if they have laid you by the heels for 'Treason' or shot you. They (England) when in a d--- funk are up to any villainy."[1238]

Perhaps, in Tanganyika, Tom Casement saw himself as fighting for his great friend General Smuts and South Africa, not England. It was that friendship with Smuts that prompted de Valera to seek out Tom's services for an introduction to the South African prime minister at the Imperial conference of June 1921 in order to further Ireland's case. Dev was advised by his London representative that Tom could be found at Lord ffrench's brother's home near Ballinasloe, but that all his expenses should be met as "he is not blessed with much of this world's wealth."

The war interrupted Tom's marriage to Katje which seems to have already fallen apart if for no other reason than a series of failed touristic enterprises. Such economic disasters normally put relationships under intolerable stress. He eventually returned to Dublin in July 1920, starting up a coastal lifesaving service round Ireland, as after the departure of the British, most coastguard stations had fallen into disuse (indeed many were destroyed).

Although seen as an immensely amiable eccentric, Tom did have a way of getting things done. Serving in two wars, he must have been able to hold his own with men. Lady Glenavy describes him as tall, resembling his brother but without the beard, "dressed in Irish tweeds with a double breasted coat and a tweed hat" taking "a pride in his appearance, knowing that he always looked distinctive and original. Tom, she added, was quite incapable of keeping his money", collecting, as he did, in the haunts and hostelries of Dublin, "an extraordinary set of odd characters round him as drinking companions, who might all have come out of Joyce's *Ulysses*."[1239] In 1932 Gertrude summed up her Casement cousins: "Tom is an uncertain character – you can't be sure of his acting in a sensible business-like way. In some ways he is like Nina, apt to go off at a tangent."[1240] Indeed he had such a remarkably similar outlook (and character) as his younger sibling Roger, on so many issues, that they might as well have been twins. Their Irish nationalism and hatred of England was certainly sourced from within the immediate family and did not develop spontaneously.

When retirement threatened although approaching (if not over) seventy years of age, Tom resisted fiercely. Through having no birth certificate he denied his age. Writing to Dr Charles Curry in March 1934, Tom, enclosing some shamrock, advised "You will be sorry to hear the Irish government have dispensed with my services…it has been a real bad knock…I really can't believe why de Valera did it, but they are a queer crew. I really wish I had gone over to Germany when I was thrown out."[1241]

A last detail of his life is a letter to Gertrude Parry from Tom's landlady, Patricia Hudson, at 25 Mespil Road, Ballsbridge, regarding his enclosed account which covered "stout…full board, and fires." Miss Hudson added "he now gets out a bit every day but he is still very weak."[1242] On 6 March 1939, in old age and increasing ill health, Tom chose to end his life in the Grand Canal, his body being found at Baggot Street bridge near his Mespil Road lodgings. There was an extensive obituary in the *Irish Times* the next day, by Denis Johnston (under the penname *Nichevo*) who was bewildered that an old salt like Tom should meet such an incongruous end. He had depicted him as George, an ageless Peter Pan character, in his 1931 play *The Moon in the Yellow River*. "Tom above all other men I have known" Johnston wrote, "ought to have had a Viking's funeral, like the character in *Beau Geste;* for Tom was a heroic character in his queer, Quixotic, irritating but always lovable way. He ought to have lived centuries ago when knights were bold."

Mourners at the well-attended, Dean's Grange burial, included his cousins Gertrude Parry and Elizabeth Bannister, W.T. Cosgrave, Erskine Childers, Lord Glenavy, Dan Breen T.D., Lord and Lady ffrench, Cathal O'Shannon, Lennox Robinson, Sean Milroy, and Bulmer Hobson as well as many former life-saving colleagues. The Prime Minister, Eamon de Valera, who was in Rome, was represented by the Minister of Education. Later a whip round for a headstone was organised by Beatrice Glenavy, to which even Smuts subscribed, on which was carved a ship in full sail.

Twenty years on there was a final echo of Tom's complex personal life and the controversies surrounding his brother. In 1960 and 1961, Katje Casement, by then in her early eighties, wrote to Roger McHugh from Bournemouth, strongly objecting to a proposed TV drama. She declared that Casement whom she had first met in 1902 was never a "moral pervert", rather a saintly man. She also revealed that "being homeless, and my own breadwinner since 1916, now the Royal Artists Benevolent Institution give me board and assistance" while indicating that her "last trip to Ireland was in 1949 to see Gertrude Parry." She claimed the BBC had put her into a mental hospital.[1243] Katje, the last of Casement's generation, lingered on there until 1970.

Epilogue: 1965 Reburial

In the 1950s Casement could still upset and worry Unionists. In 1953, in particular, many Stormont MPs like Brian Faulkner, keen to ingratiate themselves with their constituency hard-liners, peppered the Minister of Home Affairs with their concerns. The visit that year to Murlough Bay by de Valera, Frank Aiken and Seán MacBride, and the related parade and speeches, provoked considerable correspondence. Some MPs had wanted the parade banned. The minister, Brian Maginness, tried to sooth his angry back-benchers by suggesting the police were well in control and taking a valuable opportunity to observe those locals involved. To Teddy Jones, the Derry City MP and later Attorney General, he wrote, somewhat patronisingly, "I don't think you need worry unduly about the matter." Maginness, a noted liberal, was choosing the tactic of emollience to pacify his parliamentary party.

Nonetheless, behind the scenes, Stormont civil servants had been told to draft legislation to deal with the eventuality of Casement's body being released from Pentonville for reburial at Murlough. They were tasked to prohibit its entry to Northern Ireland. This was duly done, but came perilously close to farce with one official pointing out a critical omission from the suggested law – that if Casement was first cremated in England "he could be sent through the post."[1244] David Rudkin's superb play on Casement would have benefited from knowledge of such a black comedy being played out, but the draft Bill was never published. The Home Office in London (the government at Stormont's minder) was furious about the talk of legislation, indeed with any talk at all of such intangibles. It was a waste of effort. Belfast was sternly instructed to damp down local interest and forget it.

The campaign for the return of the remains was kept alive by Frank Aiken, a South Armagh militarist during the so-called War of Independence, and later Fianna Fail's long-serving External Affairs minister. In 1961 he tried to disarm the British ambassador by saying there was no question "in present circumstances" of Casement being reburied in the north. "Clearly what he had in mind was, 'pending the reintegration of the national territory'" the ambassador told his London bosses who were duly unimpressed. The Conservatives maintained the prohibition on exhumation.[1245]

But the change of government to Labour in October 1964 and the development of better trading ties heralded a change of policy, and at a Cabinet meeting, on 14 January 1965, a secret deal with Dublin was agreed. The Home Secretary, Sir Frank Soskice, pointed out that it was "wholly unacceptable to the Government of Northern Ireland for him (Casement) to go there." Consequently the "condition of our agreeing to the proposal of the Government of the Irish Republic [was] an undertaking that the remains would be interred in Republican territory and would not be subsequently moved."[1246]

When the announcement of Casement's imminent return to Ireland was made, it came out of the blue. Indeed when the news was made public, his body had already been exhumed by prison warders "with a great deal of humanity and even reverence,"[1247] being placed overnight in the Catholic chapel at Pentonville prison. Some prisoners were observed by the Irish officials watching the operation by means of extending mirrors from their cells, and examining the reflection. Identification was based on the grave's location, number 27, between one for a man called Kuhn and one for a Robinson, and the size of the femurs. Black hair and an element of scalp were clearly visible on an otherwise very white skull while one tibia showed signs of having been broken and reset. Along with his disarticulated bones, calcified remnants of the shroud and several teeth with lead fillings were also taken from the grave and placed in a lead-lined casket for which the British officials insisted on paying. All the principal members of the skeleton were apparently uncovered although in 1916 there had been no coffin with quicklime being laid down. On 23 February 1965, the bones were flown from RAF Northolt into Baldonnel military air base near Dublin, soon to be renamed Casement Aerodrome. The British ambassador stood dutifully, if incongruously, in the welcoming party, alongside Frank Aiken.

The new prime minister, Harold Wilson, had chosen, in the year before the fiftieth anniversary of the Easter Rising, to mend that particular fence with Dublin. He called it "a satisfactory end to an unhappy chapter" although the reburial would not be at Murlough Bay. Casement was instead to have a memorable state funeral in Ireland's capital. The President of Ireland, Eamon de Valera, spoke on behalf of those few of Casement's contemporaries, still surviving, by saying "Now thanks be to God he is back here."

The colossal figure of 665,000 people, pretty well the then population of Dublin, came to pay their respects to Casement during the five days of his lying-in-state at Arbour Hill, the last place he had been in Ireland before being shipped out through Kingstown. No relatives travelled from Magherintemple or Co. Antrim but his two surviving nieces, Charlie's daughters, were brought from Australia for the funeral. They were in their seventies and looked somewhat bewildered and overwhelmed. In an old-fashioned fur coat Mrs Nina Ayers and her sister Mrs Kathleen Vaughan (with the unmistakeable classic Casement long jaw) came to bury their beloved uncle Roddie, who had written and sent presents to them but whom they had never met. Tom's widow Katje, the last Casement of his generation, was in no fit mental state to travel from her English hospital bed.

Mrs Ayers, interviewed by the *Irish News* on 3 March, said "My sister and I were absolutely amazed at the thousands and thousands of people who stood in the snow and rain to honour my uncle." She recalled that "When the news of his trial and execution came to Australia, people used to cross the street when they met us as if we had a disease or something. The reaction in Australia was very bad...My stepmother was a very nervous woman. She was afraid that the house might be raided and the letters (of Roger Casement) discovered so she disposed of them. She did it out of fear. All I have left is one letter which I discovered among my papers last week." Her younger sister Kathleen said "My parents kept the news of his execution from me."

The Glens *Feis* chairman, P.J. O'Clery, brought a sod from the Murlough gravesite to Glasnevin and laid a wreath. To the government's relief there were only the most minimal of semi-military demonstrations from the Republican movement, by one notorious IRA dissident Richard Behal. There was also a Sinn Féin manifestation involving the future Workers Party leader, Tomás MacGiolla. Meanwhile from the opposite side of the house, and with Montgomery Hyde out of the Commons, it was left to his erstwhile colleague, the South Antrim MP Knox Cunningham, to make a graceless intervention. Sir Knox, oddly (at first glance) Forrest Reid's friend and executor, asked Harold Wilson if Lord Haw Haw (the fascist William Joyce, executed for treason in 1946) was next for digging up. Cunningham's own reputation in relation to boys' boxing clubs in the East End was to be the subject of comment after his death.

On Monday 1 March, after a solemn Requiem Mass in the Pro-Cathedral, Casement set off on his final journey (to date). A national day of mourning had been declared and the event was televised by the fledgling RTE. The state funeral proceeded with his tricolour-draped coffin on a gun carriage. Accompanied by ranks of soldiers in Irish Army green, it wended its way through the centre of Dublin to Glasnevin cemetery. As the cortège moved into O'Connell Street, amidst enormous crowds and swirling snow, there was a flash of lightning and a roll of thunder. One God's salute to another? Many must have choked back tears as Ireland's last hero, so long dishonoured in an unmarked grave in an English gaol, passed by. Sadly Nina and Gertrude were never to know of this event but they were surely there in spirit.

Although old and blind, a hatless Eamon de Valera, 82, could not be dissuaded from delivering the graveside oration, in a blizzard, at the cemetery. "Casement deserves better" he reportedly said. Speaking first in Irish and then in English, he declared to his wide audience, "I do not think it presumptuous on our part to believe that a man who was so unselfish who worked so hard for the downtrodden and the oppressed and who so died, that that man is in heaven." Then, through sleet and a heavy wind, he recited the burial places of the men of 1798, many themselves hanged: Bodenstown (Wolfe Tone), Greyabbey (Rev. James Porter), Downpatrick (Thomas Russell), Templepatrick (Jemmy Hope) and the name of William Orr, executed in 1797 near Carrickfergus. Later that year, de Valera presented the original of Casement's last (20 July 1916) letter to Gertrude, to the National Library. It mentions Orr, and asks his cousin to "defend my honour and my name…in all this tangled web." Re-reading it probably prompted much of President de Valera's speech, which attempted that very task.

The return of Casement's remains, although a patriotic rather than irredentist affair, was the harbinger for the next year's 50th anniversary celebration of the Easter Rising. It was to spark off a renewal of nationalist fervour over partition and presage another round of conflict, starting in 1968, seven years before the death of de Valera, the last 1916 leader. But the feelings so aroused had never really been dampened for long; indeed there had been continuous low-level military activity, since partition, on both sides of the border. Romantic race-based nationalism was, however, about to predominate entirely over radical democratic Republicanism, in a very long war. Sadly, Casement might not have objected.

Primary bibliography to 2002 (annotated)

Books, articles, radio and TV exclusively about Casement, in date of first publication or transmission order

Books, pamphlets and articles

L.G. REDMOND-HOWARD *Sir Roger Casement – A Character Sketch Without Prejudice*, Hodges, Figgis & Co., Dublin 1916: pamphlet published between imposition of the sentence of death on Casement and his execution.

Roger CASEMENT *Some Poems of Roger Casement* (with an introduction by his cousin Gertrude Parry), Talbot Press, and T. Fisher Unwin, Dublin and London 1918: a selection of sixteen poems.

Dr Charles CURRY *Sir Roger Casement's Diaries – His Mission in Germany and the Findlay Affair*, Arche, Munich 1922. These diaries and other commentaries commence in 1914 and cover much of his time in Germany. They were not private diaries and were edited by a close American friend living near Munich who was the custodian of Casement's German papers. Curry omitted much that was critical of Germany or America including discussion of the German atrocities in Belgium in 1914. The full text is in NLI files 1689 and 1690 and now re-published in this author's *Roger Casement's German Diary*, 2016.

Denis GWYNN *Traitor or Patriot – The Life and Death of Roger Casement*, Jonathan Cape, London 1930, 444pp. Well-meaning though dull book, heavily derived from the officially published Congo and Putumayo reports, exhibiting some suspicion that the diaries may be authentic. Gwynn wrote a long article in *Studies* (Spring 1965) entitled *Roger Casement's Last Weeks* dealing with his religious conversion and his mother's origins.

Captain Karl SPINDLER *The Mystery of the Casement Ship – by its Commander*, with a foreword by Florence O'Donohue, Anvil Books, Tralee, Co. Kerry 1965 (first published by Kribe Verlag, Berlin 1931): a good naval yarn that also includes dramatic POW-escape accounts from camps in England although some of the author's facts have been disputed by other Germans involved.

Robert MONTEITH *Casement's Last Adventure*, Chicago, 1932; revised with a foreword by Franz von Papen, Moynihan, Dublin 1953 (this edition quoted):

a loyal and thoughtful account of the author's involvement with the Irish Volunteers and Casement's Irish Brigade in Germany. Having landed off the submarine in Kerry in 1916 and evaded capture, Monteith also tells something of his later involvements.

Geoffrey de Clifton PARMITER *Roger Casement*, Arthur Barker, London 1936: an empathetic book with much on the early days of Casement, based on the memories of his cousin Gertrude. Parmiter, a "very English" barrister, recanted some of his forgery theorising in a useful April 1960 article in *Quarterly Review* (Vol. 298). He died in 2000.

Dr William J.M.A. MALONEY M.C. *The Forged Casement Diaries*, Talbot Press, Dublin 1936, 275pp: partisan, if thorough, journalistic exposé of British perfidy in misuse of the diaries (and their contradictory statements thereon) which prompted Yeats to write his two poems on Casement. They in turn brought Alfred Noyes to disavow his 1916 denunciation that had so enraged Casement's sister Nina in America. The book is destroyed by the fact that the author had never seen the diaries in question and most of his conjectures and suppositions do not stand up against the actuality. His was, however, an accomplished precursor of the later and thinner Herbert Mackey efforts. Maloney, a Scots-born doctor, returned from America in August 1914 to enlist. He was wounded at Gallipoli in 1915, yet devoting his life (back in America) after 1916 to the cause of Ireland, although suspected by John Devoy of being a British spy. He married Margaret, the daughter of New York's most famous architect Charles McKim. Maloney died in 1952 having put Casement and Ireland aside since the Second World War.

Herbert O. MACKEY F.R.C.S.I. *The Life and Times of Roger Casement*, C.J. Fallon, Dublin 1954: interesting if sketchy account of Casement's life with some documentation and many errors that others have replicated. The dust cover reproduces a drawing of Casement "courtesy of Miss Ada McNeill."

René MacCOLL *Roger Casement: A New Judgment*, Hamish Hamilton, London 1956, 328pp and Four Square paperback, 1960 and 1965: matter-of-fact biography, first modern professional attempt at a comprehensive and definitive life, accepting truth of the Black Diaries, antagonistic to Casement, the person – windy and unstable – but praising of his humanitarian efforts and Irish patriotic activity. Brisk, journalistic and judgmental, it was written at a time when witnesses were still living, and was consequently informed by MacColl's interviews, especially with Serjeant Sullivan. He was a friend of Singleton-Gates and thus had access to the diaries although was obliged, he felt, by the Official Secrets Act not to mention that fact.

Jeffrey Dudgeon, David Rudkin and Fearghus Ó Conchúir, The Casement Project Symposium, Hospitable Bodies, British Library, London 3 June 2016

Alfred NOYES *The Accusing Ghost or Justice for Casement*, Victor Gollancz, London 1957, 191pp: a compendium of the forgery school's position to date, with a title prompted by the Yeats poem which attacked Noyes. He died before the diaries were published in 1959 although, working in collaboration with Roger McHugh, he actually had some idea of their contents.

Herbert O. MACKEY F.R.C.S.I. (ed.) *The Crime Against Europe – The Writings and Poetry of Roger Casement*, C.J. Fallon, Dublin 1958: well presented, collected works with several of Casement's articles, some letters to newspapers, and fifty-one poems, including his innocuous poem *The Nameless One* (that about the Armenian massacres by the Turks) as opposed to Mangan's or the disputed homosexual version. Some of Casement's youthful poetry is unintentionally revealing of his sexuality and illustrates also his very early Irish nationalism.

Peter SINGLETON-GATES and Maurice GIRODIAS *THE BLACK DIARIES – an account of Roger Casement's life and times with a collection of his diaries and public writings*, Olympia Press, Paris 1959, 626pp., limited edition of 1500 copies. The 1903 and 1910 Black Diaries are reprinted, in full, from the Scotland Yard typescripts – with a goodly number of misreadings and errors. The 1911 Black Cash Ledger, however, is only reprinted in the limited and numbered edition (1,500 copies) while the 1911 Black Diary is not included at all. That diary, as opposed to the ledger, is sexually the most detailed of all the five diary/notebook items at Kew. Quite substantial on the 1916 Rising, the book is bulked out with reprints of the official Congo and Putumayo reports, and has many excellent and evocative photographs. The somewhat haphazard, Irish historical material is of a nationalist disposition and was written by Maurice Girodias who apparently became quite obsessive about his task. Olympia's other authors included Henry Miller. Issues of 536 pp. without the Ledger also appeared in 1959 in London (Sidgwick and Jackson) and New York (Grove Press).

Roger McHUGH *Casement – The Public Record Office Manuscripts*: a thirty page study in *Threshold* (editor Mary O'Malley), Vol. 4, Spring/Summer 1960. Professor McHugh tried to deal with the actual content of the diaries now that they were available (from 10 August 1959) to historians, and concentrated on inconsistencies, interpolation theories, and the unlikeliness of Casement escaping detection during his heavy-duty sexual period, as recounted in 1911. McHugh wrote as a nationalist (a *Clann na Poblachta* Senator 1954-57) not capable of believing in their authenticity, therefore anything and everything goes into the pot including, then, contemporary psychiatric ideas about "promiscuous pathics."

H. (Harford) Montgomery HYDE *Trial of Roger Casement*, William Hodge, London 1960 in the *Notable British Trials* series: introduced with an account of the arrest and execution by the former Unionist MP for North Belfast. Hyde also reproduced, only in the revised 1964 Penguin edition entitled *Famous Trials 9: Roger Casement*, a fortnight's extract from the 1911 Black Diary which, up to this volume, remained otherwise unpublished. The MP's parliamentary efforts to get the diaries examined by experts form another appendix. An earlier, censored, transcript of the trial proper was published, in 1917, in the same series, edited by G.H. Knott.

Hyde's *The Other Love*, Heinemann, London 1970, remains the definitive book on British homosexual history. It is written in a racy no-holds-barred style with original accounts of lives lived as sexual outlaws. He was an indefatigable biographer and author on historical subjects, but sex, and homosexuality in particular, dominated his output. He was unusually liberal and freethinking, a product of the 1920s. He died, thrice married, on 10 August 1989 at the age of eighty-one, proving that Unionists are not always what they are presumed.

Herbert O. MACKEY *Roger Casement - The Secret History of the Forged Diaries* (within also entitled *Roger Casement - A Guide to the Forged Diaries*), Apollo Press, Dublin 1962: although published after *The Black Diaries*, this book (with its strong photographs) ignores the diaries content and concentrates almost entirely on discrepancies and the deceits of the British establishment. It is written from the viewpoint of a dedicated Catholic nationalist zealot. Mackey's views continue to live on in O Máille, Ui Callanan and Payne's 1994 pamphlet, *The Vindication of Roger Casement - Computer Analysis and Comparisons*, and into a new generation of forgery conspiracy buffs. Mackey also published a noisy, assertive 1959 pamphlet *I Accuse! - A Monstrous Fraud that Deceived Two Continents* (written after inspection of the diaries at Kew). His last work, *Roger Casement - The Truth About The Forged Diaries* (within also entitled *Roger Casement - The Forged Diaries*) C.J. Fallon, Dublin 1966 (95 pp.), was a pamphlet described as "a history of the Casement affair" and written just after the remains were returned to Dublin. It includes detail of Mackey's examination of the diaries in both 1959 and 1965.

John de COURCY IRELAND *The Sea and The Easter Rising 1916*, Maritime Institute of Ireland, Dublin 1966: a pamphlet largely concerned with Casement's voyage(s) to Ireland from Germany by submarine, and that of the arms ship. It is memorable for the first publication of a photograph depicting Casement without his torpedo beard and revealing his conspicuous elongated jaw. One can see why the beard never came off – except as an attempt at a disguise.

Brian INGLIS *Roger Casement,* Hodder and Stoughton, London 1973, 448pp. Well-written, extensive, historical and political biography by a former *Irish Times* journalist who accepted the Black Diaries were not forged, having held a different view earlier. Inglis is cheerful about Casement's sexuality, seeing him as an effective patriot and Irish nationalist, if a bit of an hysteric. Only a few pages deal with Casement's upbringing since Inglis concentrates on the African, Irish and First World War aspects. Three paperback editions have also been published since the hardback; by Coronet in 1974; Blackstaff in 1993; with a third, a *Penguin Classic,* in 2002.

David RUDKIN *Cries of Casement as his Bones are Brought to Dublin,*, BBC, London 1974, 84pp. Highly praised radio play, first broadcast in 1973 (with Norman Rodway as Casement) dramatising his sexuality and sexual activity from the text in the Black Diaries, juxtaposing Irish Catholic and Ulster Protestant hypocrisy with British humbug. It suffers from an idealistic ending, with Casement calling on an Ulster Protestant youth, guilty about his people's history to come together in a new Irishness with southern Catholics – and perforce abandon his own nationality. See also Rudkin's articles in *The Listener,* 8 February 1973, and *Encounter,* August 1973 (Vol XLI). David Rudkin was born in Ulster, his grandfather an Orangeman from Slieve Gullion.

B.L. (Benjamin Lawrence) REID *The Lives of Roger Casement,* Yale University Press, New Haven and London 1976. This is a little-known, thoroughly researched biography that majors on the German episode 1914-16. It is written in a literary and immensely readable style. Reid who died in 1990 was a Humanities Professor at Mount Holyoke College in Massachusetts and had already published a book on the Irish-American lawyer John Quinn. He attempts, evidentially, if not always accurately, to prove the diaries genuine and psychologically consistent. Reid deals with the homosexuality issue in an interesting and amusing mode, clearing away his own prejudices and treating Casement very much as a human sexual being with all the absurdity that can appear to involve for the outsider looking in. This novelised history was overshadowed by Brian Inglis's biography. The two authors' paths frequently crossed in those source rooms of *Casementia* – the National Library of Ireland in Dublin's Kildare Street and the Public Record Office in London.

Roger SAWYER *Casement: The Flawed Hero,* Routledge & Kegan Paul, London 1984: biography dealing for the first time, at some length, with Casement's family background and upbringing. Sawyer majors also on the Belgian Congo and South American investigations on rubber slavery for the Foreign Office. The consular service, and Casement's role in it, is a key part of this work which enters much new territory. The author writes as an Englishman from a radical, anti-slavery tradition, accepting, reluctantly, that the diaries have been proved genuine. Sawyer is now the doyen of the Casement authors, with a probably, unequalled, private, documentary archive.

Michael CARSON *The Knight of the Flaming Heart,* Doubleday, and Black Swan, GB and London 1995 and 1996, 272pp: a novel and comic fantasy, by a gay man, detailing Casement's return to Ireland and the Congo, in apparition form, becoming a gay saint because of his modern miracles performed on Africans, gays with AIDS, and (in an unlikely concept for Casement) decommissioning IRA active service units in England. Amazingly it succeeds in holding the reader's attention despite the absurdities and wish fulfilment.

Roger SAWYER (ed.) *Roger Casement's Diaries – 1910: The Black & The White,* Pimlico (imprint of Random House), London 1997, 274pp: consists of the 1910 Black Diary, unabridged and extensively annotated, alongside an abridged version of the 1910 White Diary. Sawyer's outlook is humanitarian. Believing the diaries to be authentic, he knocks down many of the forgery assumptions with hard evidence. A liberal where homosexuality is concerned, Sawyer is opposed to the "penetrative sex" aspect. Sympathetic to Ireland (and with an Irish wife), he writes from an understanding British viewpoint.

Angus MITCHELL (ed.) *The Amazon Journal of Roger Casement,* Lilliput Press Dublin, in association with Anaconda Editions London, 1997, 534pp: consists of the complete 1910 White Diary or 'Putumayo Journal' of 23 September - 6 December 1910, now in the NLI. It is well, if at times controversially, annotated and sits alongside comprehensive allied correspondence and a chapter on the Black Diaries controversy. Mitchell's outlook and specialism is Amerindian tribal extermination and the Amazon rubber trade. Born in 1962, he is from a British establishment family. His father Colin Mitchell, or 'Mad Mitch', was a colonial soldier-hero, notably in Aden, and later a Scottish Tory MP, who ultimately became disaffected from the London establishment which had taken him up.

Angus Mitchell believes the Black Diaries were forged by British Intelligence (involving a continuing cover-up), since Casement was too good a man and too serious an anti-imperialist to prey sexually and promiscuously (as he would put it) on native boys and colonial peoples. The author disputes at times whether Casement was gay but states the diaries are "clearly homophobic documents." He has lived in Brazil and knows the Amazon area. See also his *History Ireland* articles, *Casement's Black Diaries – Closed Books Reopened,* Autumn 1997 and *The Casement 'Black Diaries' Debate – the story so far,* Summer 2001, also *Forgery or Genuine Document* in History Today, March 2001, and his edited pamphlets of *Casementia* distributed by the Roger Casement Foundation in Dublin.

Reinhard R. DOERRIES *Prelude to the Easter Rising: Sir Roger Casement in Imperial Germany*, Frank Cass, London & Portland 2000: by translating and publishing original German Foreign Office material amongst 159 documents, Dr Doerries, a distinguished US/German diplomatic historian, provides for the first time the Berlin view of Casement.

ROYAL IRISH ACADEMY *Roger Casement in Irish and World History*, Dublin 2000: a collection of articles put together to be the programme for the Academy's prestigious Casement Symposium, 5-6 May 2000, with three articles by Casement including one on the Putumayo Indians, his 1913 Ballymoney speech, and the Irish government's 1965 report on the exhumation and return of his remains.

Adrian WEALE *Patriot Traitors: Roger Casement, John Amery and the Real Meaning of Treason*, Viking, London 2001: Weale, a former intelligence officer, compares the sociopathic, anti-Semite John Amery (son of Leo Amery, Churchill's Secretary of State for India) who was hanged in 1945, with Casement whom he boldly suggests was guilty of youthful exploitation of Africa while later being a compulsive, predatory, promiscuous homosexual. The Amery section is interesting and original, that on Casement is not, being almost entirely derivative and uncomprehending.

W. J. Mc CORMACK *The Forensic Examination of Documents and Handwriting*: The Report of Dr Audrey Giles on the Black Diaries, 47pp, The Giles Document Laboratory, Amersham, Bucks, 12 March 2002. The Giles Report was published in *Roger Casement in Irish and World History* in 2005.

Notable articles

Cathal O'BYRNE *Roger Casement's Last Will*, The Irish Monthly p. 668-672, Dublin, October 1937 and *Roger Casement's Ceilidhe* in the Capuchin Annual 1946-47.

Giovanni COSTIGAN *The Treason of Sir Roger Casement*, American Historical Review, 1955 Vol LX p. 283-302; elegant and sympathetic article utilising in particular the E.D. Morel correspondence in the LSE library.

John SPARROW (anon.) review of *The Black Diaries*, Times Literary Supplement, 26 February 1960, and correspondence *et seq* (later republished in *Independent Essays*, Faber & Faber, London 1963). Sparrow was a (gay) luminary of the English academic establishment.

Brooks THOMPSON *A Letter of Roger Casement (1888) in the Sanford Collection*, English Historical Review, January 1962, Vol LXXVII p. 98-102: reveals the dislikes and quarrels around Casement during his time with the Sanford Exploring Expedition in the Congo.

Galen BROEKER *Roger Casement: Background to Treason*, Journal of Modern History, September 1957 – a rare, unsympathetic assessment.

Professor Wm. Roger LOUIS *Casement and the Congo*, article in the Journal of African History, 1964, Vol V, No. 1 p. 99-120; at times critical of Leopold's critics.

Gearoid Ó CUINNEAGAIN *Casement Slanders Refuted*, Dublin 1967: disorganised pamphlet by the leader of the southern Irish fascist group, *Architects of the Resurrection*.

M.J.P. SCANNELL & O. SNODDY *Roger Casement's Contribution to the Ethnographical and Economic Botany Collections in the National Museum of Ireland*, Éire-Ireland 1968, Winter, Vol III, No. IV.

Jeffrey MEYERS *To Die for Ireland*, London Magazine April/May 1973: long article that tries, somewhat unconvincingly, to link Casement's 'guilty' sexuality and his emotional development, with his politics.

Alan WHARAM *Casement and William Joyce*, Modern Law Review, Vol. 41, November 1978: a comparison of two British treason trials ending in execution, the second being that of Irish-American fascist William Joyce (Lord Haw Haw).

Owen DUDLEY EDWARDS *Divided Treasons and Divided Loyalties: Roger Casement and Others*, Transactions of the Royal Historical Society, Vol. 32, 1982 (p. 153-174): an Irish historian (son of Robert and brother of Ruth) at Edinburgh University who puts the trial in the context of First World War events. He is not convinced the diaries are genuine, or that they are fake. In an *Irish Times* letter of 23 May 1956, when a teenager, he suggested the anti-homosexual hysteria of the war, encouraged by the maverick MP, Noel Pemberton Billing, and Lord Alfred Douglas, provided a mood for forgery.

Jeffrey DUDGEON *A Gay View of Roger Casement*, article in *Fortnight*, a Belfast magazine, October 1984: prompted by Roger Sawyer's 1984 book, this was the author's first Casement printed effort – analysis largely sound but grasp of the facts less than accurate; also articles in *Gay Community News*, Dublin, September 2000 and July 2001, and the *Belfast Telegraph* 9 October 2001.

Gerard J. LYNE *New Light on Material Concealed by Roger Casement near Banna Strand*, Kerry Archaeological and Historical Society 1987: excellent pamphlet by NLI staffer, documenting, detailing and explaining some of the 1916 Kerry mysteries.

Paul BEW *The Real Importance of Sir Roger Casement*, *History Ireland*, Summer 1994: Professor Bew (of Queens University, Belfast) reckons Casement ought on his many long walks in Co. Antrim "to have stopped to chat to the inhabitants."

Séamas Ó SÍOCHÁIN *Roger Casement, Ethnography, and the Putumayo,* Éire-Ireland, Summer 1994; and *Evolution and Degeneration in the Thought of Roger Casement*, Irish Journal of Anthropology, Summer 1997.

Lucy McDIARMID *The Posthumous Life of Roger Casement*, lively essay on the controversy and passion evoked since 1916 in *Gender and Sexuality in Modern Ireland*, University of Massachusetts Press, Amherst, published in co-operation with the American Conference for Irish Studies, 1997.

Colm TÓIBÍN *A Whale of a Time,* long article in London Review of Books, 2 October 1997 by a writer who admires "Casement more because of his Diaries...his passionate nature, his erotic complexity...his sexual energy." This article was expanded to form a Casement chapter in *Love in a Dark Time: Gay Lives from Wilde to Almodóvar*, Picador, 2002.

THE BARNES REVIEW Vol IV, Number 2, March/April 1998 edition, Washington, one of two articles is by John Garton and Moire O'Sullivan of the Roger Casement Foundation, *'We Accuse' – A Vindication of Roger Casement*, the second by Gregory Douglas is an imagined interview with Gestapo chief, Heinrich Müller on the supposed Swiss forger of the diaries. *The Barnes Review* is an unashamed pro-Nazi, anti-Jewish journal based on an American nationalist and mystical Celtic ideology. It is both pro-German and Anglophobic, because of England's supposed Jewish ruling class.

Richard KIRKLAND *Rhetoric and (Mis)recognitions: Reading Casement,* Irish Studies Review, Vol 7 No. 2, August 1999 (pp. 163-172): floats the notion that the diaries are both genuine and fantastic.

Public and private records

The National Library of Ireland in Dublin has several collection lists of Casement papers, in particular Special List A15, which details manuscript folders numbered 13073-13092. This set is largely Gertrude Parry's donation of 1930 and another made after her death. Collection list A15 earlier mentioned a superb 1994 acquisition of thirty-one folders, Accession 4902. Since publication in 2002, this accession has been fully catalogued as MSS 36199-36212. It is detailed in collection list 103 entitled: 'Roger Casement Additional Papers'.

Other Casement papers were to be found in the NLI card index, on computer file for the latest accessions, and the earliest in the volumes of *Hayes Manuscript Sources for the History of Irish Civilisation* (1965) plus the First Supplement thereto (1975). Hayes Sources and the card index have since been digitised by the NLI in its *Sources Database*. (N.B. Only some of the special collection list items appear in NLI's computerised Main Catalogue.) Increasingly, the NLI has digitised a portion of its enormous Casement collection and put some of the images freely online.

The provenance and origin of many NLI papers remain a mystery, while new items continue to appear in auction houses, most notably a big cache at Sotheby's in 2008 emanating from the Parry family. In 2012, the NLI, rediscovered a large batch of uncatalogued Casement papers, bought in London in 1952. Accession 1235, unseen before, was described as "some documents not included (presumably by error) by Mrs. Parry when she handed over to N.L. her Casement Mss. just before her death." Many emanated from Elizabeth Bannister and are numbered MSS 49154 (1-22). They date between 1882 and 1934 and include a unique photograph of Nina Casement.

PRONI with its Casement family document donations and the leftovers of Montgomery Hyde's papers (the bulk is the Harry Ransom Humanities Research Center in Austin, Texas), and the NYPL with its extensive Maloney Collection of Irish Historical Papers, are two other key depositories. Séamas Ó Síocháin's 2008 biography of Casement revealed three more significant locations for documentation – Farmleigh House, Dublin, Trinity College, Dublin, and the collection of Oliver McMullan in Cushendall. The TCD cache is notable for Casement's correspondence with Fritz Pincus, Farmleigh for his correspondence with Major Robert Berry of Richhill Castle, and also with Lady Constance Emmott (most also copied into PRONI), and the McMullan papers for material, some probably last owned by Gertrude Parry, including transcriptions from the *Scribbling Diary*. More and more Casement material is becoming available at the Military Archives of the Irish Defence Forces at Cathal Brugha Barracks – http://www.militaryarchives.ie/home.

In June 1998, TNA at Kew, London, released the final batch of documents on Casement held by the Home Office, including the key Millar letter and the post-mortem results. All were previously to be held back until 2006 for security reasons but were made available earlier, by the new Labour government. A previous, big batch in October 1995 provided many new leads including the full name of Casement's Belfast boyfriend, Joseph Millar Gordon. In January 1999, the first release of MI5 papers (KV series) included five files on Casement, and many on German spies in both world wars. These are now digitised. A small number of MI5's Casement documents in TNA remain "retained" or redacted.

While those in Scotland Yard were still being reviewed, a selection was released for the Royal Irish Academy Symposium on Casement in May 2000, distributed there by the Chief Foreign Office historian, Gill Bennett. They were something of a treasure trove especially on the details of how and when the diaries came into the possession of Scotland Yard in April 1916, with more material on Adler Christensen's treachery in Christiania. They were put fully into the public domain at TNA in June 2001.

TV, radio and films

All known attempts to make cinema films or dramas of Casement's life, or about his activities, have been called off for various reasons usually involving pressure from one or other political establishment. Parties to these efforts to prevent even Hollywood from making such a film included Eamon de Valera, Sidney Parry and Lord Tyrrell, President of the British Board of Film Censors and formerly of the Foreign Office. The possibility of a film of the "life of this great Irish patriot" was mooted by Julius Klein of Universal Pictures in the early 1930s. He was, as he pointed out a noted German-American, so in that sense would be a safe choice. But the idea was not relished in Ireland.

Ada McNeill reported to Bulmer Hobson on 25 July 1934 that Gertrude Parry was distressed at the proposal. She concurred, saying: "I think the idea of a film with some vulgar utter lie of a love interest and strong anti-English propaganda dragging in Roger and exciting more dirt-throwing is horrible. Forgive my thrusting my snout into it."[1248] "*Entre nous*", Gavan Duffy told Maloney in 1933, Sidney Parry got the project squashed.[1249] The Parrys' success at stopping any film was matched only by the blocking of Singleton-Gates' publication of the diaries. Candidates recently suggested for casting as Casement, should a film or drama series be made, include Liam Neeson who was also educated in Ballymena, and Daniel Day Lewis.

Granada TV did, however, dramatise the 1916 treason trial in July 1960 in the first of a series of *On Trial* programmes. It was produced by Peter Wildeblood who wrote the book *Against the Law* which described his own trial and imprisonment for gross indecency in a case that also involved the gaoling of Lord Montagu of Beaulieu. Casement was played to great effect by Peter Wyngarde ('Jason King') an actor who later fell foul of the public indecency laws himself. He died in 2018 at the age of 90 having two years earlier introduced a showing of the programme at the British Film Institute alongside this author. On 2 March 1961, BBC radio broadcast in the Home Service *The Trial of Sir Roger Casement* written by Montgomery Hyde. BBC TV also dramatised the trial on 12 May 1970 with Richard Wordsworth playing Casement and Ulster actor Denys Hawthorne, Serjeant Sullivan. Conor Cruise O'Brien "filled in the inexpedient facts." *On Trial – A Question of Allegiance* was directed by Christopher Burstall. On 23 September 1993, BBC Radio 4 transmitted *Document: The Casement Diaries*, produced and narrated by Roisin McAuley, in which a handwriting expert Dr David Baxendale gave a convincing verdict that Casement was their author.

Kenneth Griffith produced a 1992 television programme in the BBC *Timewatch* series on Casement, majoring on the Congo episode in a relentlessly hagiographic and anti-English mode. He played the title role himself (and all others, some in consular headdress), partly in the hall at Magherintemple in front of photographs of British-uniformed Casements (not including Sir Roger), much to the annoyance of the current chatelaine, Mrs Lesley Casement.

RTE and BBC broadcast historical films on Casement in March 2002 entitled *The Ghost of Roger Casement* and *The Secret Diaries of Roger Casement* respectively, both hinged to a new forensic examination of the diaries by Dr Audrey Giles. She had been commissioned by a steering group put together by Professor Bill Mc Cormack of Goldsmiths College, London, constituted after the Royal Irish Academy symposium of May 2000.

Dr Giles reported that the writing in the Black Diaries was a single population and that the vast majority of what she had inspected could be identified conclusively as in Casement's hand. Perhaps most importantly, she said she noted no significant differences from his handwriting, neither was there any evidence of the "contentious" entries having been added.

The second, hour-long, RTE programme, broadcast after the Giles Report was published, was remarkable for its attempt to counter the result of the forensic examination – despite RTE and the Irish government having part-funded it. A significant accusation repeatedly levelled at Dr Giles was that her previous employment by the London Metropolitan Police made her report fatally flawed. That programme closed with a hesitant series of afterwords by Angus Mitchell who in the words of the *Sunday Times* reviewer "sought refuge in his quotations bank. 'All truths are oppressive statements by the authorities,' he declared, parroting Michael Foucault. Realising that this may have sounded pretentious, not to mention dumb, he called W.B. Yeats to the stand. 'There is no truth save that in thine own heart,' he proclaimed. So now you know, ignore history books and television documentaries. Buy a stethoscope instead." The RTE commentator after all his efforts could only conclude "Casement remains elusive and enigmatical."

No openly gay voice was heard on either of the TV programmes nor was any historian from Northern Ireland featured. Both productions were marred by a tendency to depict Casement simply as a hero or patriot, or as a victim, losing many of the subtleties and contradictory facts in their desire to avoid the controversial issues of Ulster and the nature of his sexual lifestyle.

At a further Goldsmiths College Symposium in April 2002, a New York police forensics expert, James Horan, asked to peer review the Audrey Giles report, stated that it would not pass muster in an American court (although that was not in her brief). This gave the forgery theorists new legs, confirming that the authenticity of the diaries cannot be proved to everyone's satisfaction, nor can it be proved by science, only by historically-based evidence, and the application of common sense.

Peter Wyngarde and Jeffrey Dudgeon at the British Film Institute screening of the Trial of Roger Casement, London 17 March 2016

Secondary bibliography to 2002 (annotated)

Excludes books or articles *entirely* on Casement himself, and includes others not specifically about him, in alphabetic order by author

Betty ASKWITH *Two Victorian Families – The Bensons and the Stracheys,* Chatto & Windus, London 1971 (Father Hugh Benson and his gay and lesbian siblings).

Jonathan BARDON *A History of Ulster*, Blackstaff Press, Belfast 1992, 914pp. (invaluable guide and source book).

Sam Hanna BELL *The Theatre in Ulster,* Gill & Macmillan, Dublin 1972.

John BOYD *The Middle of My Journey*, Blackstaff Press, Belfast 1990 (literary and progressive life in Ulster from the 1930s to the 1950s including a lengthy impression of Forrest Reid).

(Sir Charles) C.E.B. BRETT with photographs by **Michael O'CONNELL** *Buildings of County Antrim*, Ulster Architectural Heritage Society and the Ulster Historical Foundation, Belfast 1996 (Magherintemple, Kintullagh, Castle Dobbs etc).

(Sir Charles) C.E.B. BRETT *Five Big Houses of Cushendun and Some Literary Associations,* Lagan Press, Belfast 1997 (especially useful on Ada McNeill).

Joseph BRISTOW *Effeminate England – Homoerotic Writing After 1885*, Open University Press, Buckingham 1995.

BRITISH GOVERNMENT REPORTS (Command Papers):
Royal Commission on the Rebellion in Ireland (Cmd. 8279, 26 June 1916) with *Minutes of Evidence and Appendix of Documents* (Cmd. 8311);

Documents Relative to the Sinn Fein Movement, XXIX (Cmd. 1108, 1921); intercepted and decrypted transatlantic messages and letters to and from the German embassy in Washington, on Ireland and Casement, during and after the First World War.

Patrick BUCKLAND (ed.) *Irish Unionism, 1885-1923: A Documentary History*, HMSO, Belfast 1973 (especially for details on Frank Hall).

Flann CAMPBELL *The Dissenting Voice: Protestant Democracy in Ulster from Plantation to Partition,* Blackstaff, Belfast 1991 (a son of Joseph Campbell; *progressiste* and thus angled detailing of the Protestant influence on Irish Republicanism).

Catherine CLINE *E. D. Morel 1873-1924: The Strategies of Protest*, Blackstaff Press, Belfast 1980 (hard hitting political biography).

Mary COLUM *Life and the Dream*, The Dolmen Press, Dublin 1966 (wife of Padraic Colum; previously published in London 1947 and New York 1958).

Joseph CONNOLLY *Memoirs of Senator Joseph Connolly (1885-1961) – A Founder of Modern Ireland*, edited by J. Anthony Gaughan, Irish Academic Press, Dublin 1996 (very informative on the early 1900s in Belfast and the personnel of Sinn Féin in the 1920s and later in Fianna Fail).

Joseph CONRAD (Jozef Korzeniowski), *Heart of Darkness* (1899) with Conrad's 1890 *Congo Diary*, Robert Hampson (ed.), Penguin, London 1995.

S.J.S. COOKEY *Britain and the Congo Question 1885-1913*, Longmans, London 1968 (especially for Casement's uncle, Edward Bannister).

Michael DAVIDSON *Some Boys*, The Gay Men's Press, London 1988 (World Copyright 1970); author born 1897 (sections on the boys of Catania and Naples).

Herbert Spencer DICKEY *The Misadventures of a Tropical Medico,* The Bodley Head, London, first published in 1929 (the Peruvian Amazon Company doctor who met and travelled with Casement in 1911).

James GARDINER *A Class Apart: The Private Pictures of Montague Glover,* Serpent's Tail, London 1992 (gay architect and amateur photographer who served in the First World War and photographed his companions).

Beatrice, Lady GLENAVY *Today We Will Only Gossip*, Constable, London 1964 (Beatrice Campbell's impressions of Ireland before and after independence with details of Tom Casement's life and his last years in Dublin).

Ernest HAMBLOCH *British Consul – Memories of Thirty Years' Service in Europe and Brazil,* Harrap, London 1938 (colleague of Casement's in Brazil).

M.W. HESLINGA *The Irish Border as a Cultural Divide*, Van Gorcum Assen, The Netherlands 1979.

Adam HOCHSCHILD *King Leopold's Ghost – A Story of Greed, Terror and Heroism in Colonial Africa*, Macmillan, London 1999 (readable account, much from new Belgian sources on the Congo's history, the Leopoldian regime being excoriated, with extensive evidence, for most of the ills of that country as the narrative model used only allows for good and bad.)

Ronald HYAM *Empire and Sexuality – The British Experience,* Manchester University Press, Manchester 1990 (extensive and readable account of the sexual opportunities taken by the personnel of empire – at times quite torrid; Casement is given tolerance for his sexual, but not his political activities).

H. (Harford) Montgomery HYDE *The Other Love: An Historical and Contemporary Account of Homosexuality in Britain*, Heinemann, London 1970 (unequalled history of homosexual trials and scandals), and *A Tangled Web: Sex Scandals in British Politics and Society*, Futura Publications, London 1987.

Sir William JAMES *The Eyes of the Navy; a Biographical Study of Admiral Sir Reginald Hall,* Methuen, London 1955.

Maurice Denham JEPHSON *An Anglo-Irish Miscellany,* Allen Figgis, Dublin 1964 (family history and genealogy that includes Casement's 1895 correspondence regarding his mother's antecedents).

James H. JONES *Alfred C. Kinsey: A Public/Private Life*, Norton, New York 1997 & London (biography of the American sexologist, a driven man with secrets, remarkably like Casement).

Maurice JOY (ed.) *The Irish Rebellion of 1916 and its Martyrs – Erin's Tragic Easter,* Devin-Adair, New York 1916 (Joy, one time secretary to Sir Horace Plunkett, wrote the section on Casement; several items are by Padraic Colum, amongst others).

Maurice LEITCH *The Liberty Lad,* MacGibbon & Kee, 1965 (excellent novel set in Co. Antrim with a prominent homosexual character and the earliest description of an Ulster gay venue – *The Royal Avenue* bar in Belfast's Rosemary Street).

Wm. Roger LOUIS & Jean STENGERS *E.D. Morel's History of the Congo Reform Movement*, Clarendon, Oxford and OUP, London 1968 (with a critical commentary especially good on depopulation, and Leopold's supposed profits).

R.B. McDOWELL *Alice Stopford Green: A Passionate Historian*, Allen Figgis, Dublin 1967.

J.R.B. McMINN *Against The Tide: J.B. Armour, Irish Presbyterian Minister and Home Ruler,* PRONI, Belfast 1985 (the correspondence of Armour of Ballymoney who put together the famous 1913 meeting of Protestant Home Rulers).

M.M. (Maurice MAGNUS) *Memoirs of the Foreign Legion (with an Introduction by D.H. Lawrence)*, Martin Secker, London 1924 (Lawrence, writing in Taormina, explains his connection with Magnus and how he came to possess the manuscript concerning his brief and inglorious military career).

A.P.W. MALCOMSON *The Extraordinary Career of the 2nd Earl of Massereene 1743-1805,* PRONI, Belfast 1972 (features Roger Casement, the land agent great-grandfather).

F.X. MARTIN *Leaders and Men of the Easter Rising,* Methuen, London 1967 (especially good on Denis McCullough, Bulmer Hobson and Sir Matthew Nathan).

Patrick MAUME *The Long Gestation – Irish Nationalist Life 1891-1918*, Gill & Macmillan, Dublin 1999 (excellent on the minor characters and lesser known events of the era).

Austen MORGAN *Labour and Partition: The Belfast Working Class 1905-23,* Pluto Press, London 1991 (valuable fact-based history).

Eoin NEESON *Birth of a Republic,* Prestige Books, Dublin 1998 (one section extensively reworks the forgery theory with first mention, from Nazi sources, of the supposed Swiss forger Zwingleman). Mr Neeson, a former director of the Government Information Bureau, in an *Irish Times* article of 4 April 2002 after the forensic examination results, conceded that it looked now as if Casement was the diarist. He maintained all his previous arguments on the culpability of the British, adding it would be a pity if Casement was portrayed "merely as some kind of homosexual icon rather than as the great man that he was."

Charles NICHOLL The *Reckoning – The Murder of Christopher Marlowe, Jonathan* Cape, London 1992 (gripping, literary detective history on the Tudor intelligence service and Marlowe's death – not in a tavern).

Leon Ó BROIN *Protestant Nationalists in Revolutionary Ireland – The Stopford Connection,* Gill & Macmillan, Dublin 1985, and the excellent *Dublin Castle in the Easter Rising – The Story of Sir Matthew Nathan,* Helicon, Dublin 1966 (1970 edition Sidgwick & Jackson, London – page numbers quoted are from this edition unless otherwise stated).

Kit & Cyril Ó CEIRIN *Women of Ireland: A Biographic Dictionary*, Tir Eolas, Co. Galway 1996 (especially good on the females of the Irish revolution).

Ulick O'CONNOR *Celtic Dawn – A Portrait of the Irish Literary Renaissance,* Hamish Hamilton, London 1984.

Diarmaid Ó DOIBHLIN *Womenfolk of the Glens and the Irish Language,* Monaghan 1996 (long article on Rose Young and Margaret Dobbs).

Professor Seamus O'NEILL *Note: Roger Casement, Cathal O'Byrne and Professor Reid,* Studies, Vol. LXVIII, Spring/Summer 1979 (article).

Padraig Ó SNODAIGH *Hidden Ulster: Protestants and the Irish Language,* Lagan Press, Belfast 1995 (pamphlet, largely listing names).

Thomas PAKENHAM *Scramble for Africa 1876-1912,* Weidenfeld & Nicholson, London 1991 (good context for understanding the Congo).

Forrest REID *Private Road*, Faber, London 1940 (early-life autobiography of the Belfast novelist and helpmeet of boys).

Trevor ROYLE *Death Before Dishonour – The True Story of Fighting Mac,* Mainstream Publishing, Edinburgh 1982 (life of Major-General Sir Hector Macdonald who committed suicide in 1903).

Norah SAUNDERS & A.A. KELLY *Joseph Campbell, Poet & Nationalist 1879-1944*, Wolfhound Press, Dublin 1988 (detailing the key intellectual in the Gaelic literary revival in Edwardian Belfast).

Timothy d'Arch SMITH *Love in Earnest,* Routledge & Kegan Paul, London 1970 (a literary and detective history, 1880-1930, of the men of Urania and their (largely) unrequited boy love).

A.T.Q. STEWART *The Summer Soldiers – the 1798 Rebellion in Antrim and Down,* Blackstaff Press, Belfast 1995 (features Dr George Casement under attack by the United Irish in 1798 in Larne).

A. (Alan) J.P. TAYLOR *The Trouble Makers – Dissent over Foreign Policy 1792-1939*, Hamish Hamilton, London 1957 (especially E.D. Morel).

Sir Basil THOMSON *The Scene Changes,* Collins, London 1939 (autobiography on his colonial, prison and police service up to 1921, and his ultimate enforced departure from Scotland Yard).

John URE *Trespassers on the Amazon*, Constable, London 1986 (succinct chapter on the whole Putumayo controversy from Hardenburg, through Casement, to the House of Commons select committee enquiry).

Eibhear WALSHE (ed.) *Sex, Nation and Dissent in Irish Writing,* Cork University Press, Cork 1997 (especially Colin Cruise on Forrest Reid).

Jeffrey WEEKS *Coming Out: Homosexual Politics in Britain, from the Nineteenth Century to the Present,* Quartet, London 1977 (an excellent history, especially useful on J.A. Symonds and Havelock Ellis).

Captain J.R. WHITE D.S.O. *Misfit – An Autobiography,* Jonathan Cape, London 1930 (son of General Sir George White VC of Broughshane, Co. Antrim, hero of Ladysmith. Jack White was an anarcho-socialist who helped train Connolly's Citizen Army. He died in 1946).

Patrick WILKINSON *Frank Ezra Adcock 1886-1968 – A Memoir,* Kings College, Cambridge 1969 (the classics don, who worked alongside Blinker Hall in Naval Intelligence's Room 40, recently accused by Owen Dudley Edwards of being the diary forger).

Additional bibliography (annotated) for 2nd and 3rd editions

Covering new items from November 2002

Books, pamphlets, talks and other media on Casement in date of publication order. Titles of books exclusively on Casement are in **bold**

The first three publications predate the 1st edition's publication and were omitted from its bibliography:

Roger McHUGH *Dublin 1916*, Arlington Books, London 1966: chapters entitled *Dilemma in Berlin* (from Casement's last diary), *Casement's Last Expedition* (Robert Monteith's Story), *Arms off the Kerry Coast* (the story of Captain Spindler of the Aud), and *the Last Days of Roger Casement* by Gertrude Parry.

Richard COLLIER *The River that God Forgot,* Collins, London 1968. The story of the Amazon rubber boom told through Julio Arana and Walter Hardenburg, and the Putumayo Commission. Good photographs including one of the *Liberal.*

Deirdre McMAHON *Roger Casement: An account from the archives of his re-interment in Ireland,* Irish Archives, Spring 1996, http://www.nationalarchives.ie/topics/AAE/Article_2.pdf

W. J. Mc CORMACK *Roger Casement in Death or Haunting the Free State*, UCD Press, Dublin 2002, on Dr Maloney's book by the Professor of Literary History at Goldsmiths College, London. The publisher wrote "Forensic tests commissioned in 2001 by Professor Mc Cormack on the so-called 'black diaries' of Roger Casement have confirmed beyond all reasonable doubt that they were indeed written by Casement, and not forged by British intelligence, either in part or wholly. How then did the idea take hold that the diaries had been forged? *Roger Casement in Death* provides a fascinating answer. The story is centred on W. J. Maloney, whose 1936 book, *The Forged Casement Diaries,* brought the topic to the attention of the Irish public. Mc Cormack raises questions about intelligence work, archival engineering, IRA unofficial action, and Nazi propaganda. He reveals an Irish-American campaign to influence the domestic politics of the Irish Free State, and sheds new light on such figures as Eamon de Valera and W.B. Yeats, as well as on a cast of colourful bit players."

Jeffrey DUDGEON *Roger Casement: The Black Diaries - With a Study of his Background, Sexuality, and Irish Political Life*, Belfast Press, November 2002 (1st edition), 679pp.

This book was launched by Professor Paul Bew (now Lord Bew of Donegore) of Queen's University Belfast on 21 November 2002 at the Linen Hall Library in Belfast. Full-page previews and photo-led extracts appeared in the Belfast Telegraph (18 November 2002) and Ireland on Sunday (17 November), with a news story in the Observer (Irish edition) the previous week. The author gave interviews on BBC Radio Ulster's *Talkback*, and *Sunday Sequence*, and RTE Radio 1's *Tonight with Vincent Browne* in an hour-long discussion of the Casement controversy. RTE TV's *The View* chose it as book of the week and broadcast a three-person panel review (including a authenticity sceptic, Margaret O'Callaghan of QUB) after a filmed reading by the author in the National Museum pictured beside Casement's Irish Brigade uniforms.

It was reviewed in the *Daily Telegraph*, on 28 December 2002, by the former Taoiseach, John Bruton; on 5 January 2003 in the *Sunday Telegraph* by Christopher Andrew, the MI5 historian (both reviews are on the *Telegraph* website or accessible through www.nuzhound.com) and in the *Irish Independent* on 11 January 2003; favourably in the *Belfast Telegraph* on 4 January 2003 by John Hunter, a barrister journalist with Ballycastle connections; and also by Brendan O'Connell in the January 2003 issue of Dublin's *Gay Community News*.

The *Irish Times* review on 19 January 2003 was by Senator David Norris. Brendan Clifford discussed the book (and the author's life and times) at some length in the *Irish Political Review/Northern Star's* January and February 2003 editions, and again in October 2011 alongside another article by Manus O'Riordan. The diary controversy continues as the Roger Casement Foundation and the Aubane Historical Society/*Irish Political Review*/B&ICO/Athol Books maintain a forgery position.

Fortnight carried a page-long review in its March 2003 edition by the BBC's William Crawley entitled 'God's Own Bugger?'. *GI*, a glossy Dublin gay magazine, had an article with several pages of extracts and commentary about the book in its March 2003 issue. The April 2003 edition of *Gay Times* had a review by the late Scottish novelist, Graeme Woolaston which, almost uniquely, concentrated on the Irish political aspects. The *Belfast News Letter* finally printed an (edited) review by Roger Sawyer in October 2003.

History Ireland carried an extensive review by Margaret O'Callaghan of QUB in its Winter 2003 edition. She was not convinced of the diaries' authenticity. *The Irish Economic and Social History Journal* (2003 edition) published a rancorous review by Angus Mitchell which accused this author of homophobia.

The Spring 2004 edition of the *Irish Literary Supplement* published by Boston College for the American Conference on Irish Studies (ACIS) carried a hostile three-page review of the book by Coilin Owens of George Mason University. He did however accept the authenticity of the diaries. A correspondence ensued in the Fall 2004 issue with a response from this author.

In its edition of 27 May 2004, the *New York Review of Books* published an extensive 6,000-word article/review by the novelist Colm Tóibín of *Roger Casement: The Black Diaries* and three other Casement books (those by Angus Mitchell, Bill Mc Cormack and Séamas Ó Síocháin). Tóibín described Dudgeon's book as "perhaps the most complete and interesting so far." Mc Cormack criticised Tóibín in a response in September 2004 who replied in the same issue.

BBC 2 broadcast its hour-long television documentary on the Casement diaries on Tuesday 20 May 2003 (first shown on BBC 4 in 2002 as its opening programme) which sent the author W.G. Sebald to sleep. It was repeated in March 2004, after a programme on King Leopold, which aroused, in England, new interest in Casement's life.

The diaries controversy re-ignited somewhat over articles in the *Guardian* and *Daily Telegraph*, and consequent correspondence, over the display at the National Portrait Gallery in London of Sir John Lavery's picture of Casement's appeal hearing and a BBC Radio 4 *Today* interview with the author on 1 July 2003.

In September 2008, Professor Roy Foster wrote a long review in *The Times Literary Supplement* of Séamas Ó Síocháin's definitive *Roger Casement: Imperialist, Rebel, Revolutionary*. The review was variously entitled 'Casement Cults – The best account yet of the campaigner whose radicalism, execution and homosexually explicit diaries made him a hero of Dublin, the Congo and Peru' and 'Roger Casement versus the British Empire – The story of an Irishman with two diaries, one for his sex life, and one for his humanitarian campaigns'. Take your pick, but the review was something of a tour de force, and referenced this book extensively and glowingly.

No nationalist or Republican paper in the north published a review, despite promises and even provision of duplicate review copies. Similarly, despite giving interviews to both BBC and RTE for their TV programmes, no reference to the author's work was carried and neither interview used. Both ignored the gay and the Ulster aspects of Casement although the authenticity of the diaries featured.

The Peruvian novelist and 2010 Nobel Prize Winner for Literature, Mario Vargas Llosa, visited Belfast in the autumn of 2009 when he was researching his novel on Casement. The author took him to Galgorm Castle in Ballymena where he was shown round by Christopher Brooke, and to the Glens of Antrim. *Dream of the Celt* was published in November 2010 and acknowledges this author's assistance.

Mario Vargas Llosa with the author, Jeff Dudgeon, at his Belfast home, 22 September 2009

Angus Mitchell, finally, in 2012, and frankly, expressed his view:[1250] "This somewhat eccentric publication which included extensive passages from all the disputed diaries, along with fresh interpolations, and thoughtful omissions amounted to little more than an updated and camped-up version of the 1959 edition, with a few original insights into Casement's early years in Antrim. Dudgeon upheld the diaries as the heart and soul of Casement's biography and used them provocatively as a means of destabilising (or queering) the martial spirit of Northern Irish Protestant nationalism and representing it as some deviant youth movement. The book baffled academics, and was as unashamedly political as it was scholastically unsound."

Angus MITCHELL *Casement*, Haus Publishing (Life & Times series), London 2003, brief, unreconstructed, pedagogic political biography, taking little or no account of recent new facts.

Angus MITCHELL (ed.) *Sir Roger Casement's Heart of Darkness: 1911 Documents*, Irish Manuscripts Commission, Dublin 2003. An extensive volume (816 pp.) dealing largely with Casement's second, return, visit to Peru replicating his associated correspondence and reports. Well produced and annotated although with a tendentious introduction. The 1911 Black Diary and 1911 Cash Ledger are excluded. It has two appendices, the first being the dubious memories of Dr Dickey and the second *The Paredes Report: Debunking the myth of the Normand diary*. "In an alternative version to the Millar story", Mitchell writes, without evidence, that he "was involved in advanced nationalist activities from 1911 onwards", and from a humble family. (He was a bank manager's son and signed the Ulster Covenant!) Contains one of two Rothenstein sketches in the National Portrait Gallery and a Harry Kernoff woodcut of Casement in the dock (NLI Prints Collection) along with numerous anthropological photographs and some of Peruvian politicians etc.

Colm TÓIBÍN *Love in a Dark Time, Gay Lives from Wilde to Almodóvar,* Picador, London 2003 (Casement chapter: *Sex, lies and the black diaries.)*

William BRYANT *Iquitos 1910: Roger Casement and Alfred Russel Wallace on the Amazon,* Xlibris, USA 2003, a fiction which links Casement knowledgeably with earlier botanists and explorers; written in a post-modern idiom and replete with unrelenting sexual fantasies. Second such book by Bryant.

Séamas Ó SÍOCHÁIN and the late Michael O'SULLIVAN (eds.) *The Eyes of Another Race: Roger Casement's Congo Report and 1903 Diary*, University College Dublin Press, Dublin 2003. Comprehensive and definitive account of both report and diary – anthropological, historical and political: "In 1903, Roger Casement, then a British consul, left his consular base on the Lower Congo River and made a journey through the regions of the Upper Congo to investigate at first hand reports of alleged atrocities. His subsequent report was a crucial instrument in the British government's efforts to bring about change in King Leopold's Congo Free State. This edition brings together Casement's report, together with his diary of that year, which have been carefully edited for publication. Names which were omitted from the original published report have been reinstated, and explanatory notes have been provided to both report and diary. The editors' introduction addresses the scramble for Africa, the role of Leopold and the Congo Free State, Britain and the Congo question, Casement's career, publication of the report and the humanitarian campaign, 1904-13" Exceptionally well referenced with hard-to-find biographical information on many of the Congo characters. Séamas Ó Síocháin was then Senior Lecturer in the Department of Anthropology at the National University of Ireland in Maynooth. Their 1903 diary is unabridged and contains many favourable references to this author's book.

Kathryn A. CONRAD *Locked in the Family Cell: Gender, Sexuality and Political Agency in Irish National Discourse,* University of Wisconsin Press 2004, pp. 26-33 *Perverted Justice: Roger Casement and the Treason of Ambiguity.*

James MORAN *Being Sir Rogered: George Bernard Shaw and the Irish Rebel,* Cló Ollscoil na Banríona, Belfast 2004, in *To the other shore: cross-currents in Irish and Scottish Studies,* Alexander N., Murphy S. and Oakman, eds. pp. 128-136: Tells of Julius Klein and the film about Casement that has never been made.

Brendan CLIFFORD *The Casement Diary Dogmatists,* Belfast Magazine, 2004, 68 page pamphlet from the Athol Street B&ICO stable defending Casement's separatist and pro-German policies while vigorously attacking Dudgeon and Mc Cormack's views.

Lucy McDIARMID *The Irish Art of Controversy*, Lilliput Press, Dublin 2005; one of whose five chapters *The Afterlife of Roger Casement: Memory, Folklore, Ghosts, 1916* is devoted to Casementistas and the Black Diaries. Many favourable references to this author's book.

Ovidio LAGOS *Arana, rey del caucho: Terror y atrocidades en el Alto Amazonas*, emecé, Buenos Aires 2005. Biography of Julio Arana with excellent photographs.

CLARE COUNTY ARCHIVES LIBRARY 2005, pamphlet collection of the papers of Roger Casement, transferred to the archives from Clare County Library's Local Studies Centre in October 2003. The papers were originally donated in 1969 by the late Ignatius M. Houlihan, solicitor and friend of Count Blücher. The collection contains mainly correspondence as well as receipts, essays, leaflets and newspaper cuttings. Of particular interest are the letters, which provide a glimpse of the Irish-German background to the Easter Rising. They date from Casement's arrival in Germany in 1914 to the month he leaves Germany in 1916 on the U-19 submarine bound for Ireland and provide an insight into Casement's state of mind (c. 50 documents).

Eamon PHOENIX (ed.) *Feis na nGleann – A Century of Gaelic Culture in the Antrim Glens*, Stair Uladh (Ulster Historical Foundation) 2005; chapter 7: *Roger Casement and North Antrim* by Stephanie Millar includes many references to Dudgeon's work on the early Casement.

ROYAL IRISH ACADEMY (ed. Mary E. DALY) ***Roger Casement in Irish and World History***, Dublin 2005. Not the proceedings of the Academy's May 2000 Symposium as this author's presentation (and others) is excluded, leaving no gay or non-nationalist Irish voice. The chapters by Angus Mitchell, Owen Dudley Edwards and Margaret O'Callaghan (all pro-forgery theorists or sceptics) are entirely original and were not delivered at the Symposium, only the last adding any value although it was published elsewhere the year before. Reinhard Doerries, for one, declined to have a truncated version of his talk published in it. Amazingly badly proofed and copy edited. Includes the Giles Report on the forensic examination of the diaries.

Brian LEWIS *The Queer Life and Afterlife of Roger Casement*, Journal of the History of Sexuality (Texas), October 2005, 19pp. Rare excursion into Casement's sexual nature.

Richard KIRKLAND *Cathal O'Byrne and the Northern Revival in Ireland, 1890-1960*, Liverpool University Press, 2006. Interesting and important book with a key Casement chapter. It uniquely addresses the cultural and political position of the northern Catholic minority post-partition. Kirkland pays homage to "Jeffrey Dudgeon's *Roger Casement: The Black Diaries*...a work which transformed understanding of the Northern revival as much as it sent reverberations through the world of Casement's studies."

Xander CLAYTON ***Aud***, George Alexander Clayton, Plymouth 2007, 896 pp., paperback, extensive account with full documentation of the Casement arms ship and the landing in Kerry. The cover says, "The true and in depth history of the German arms ship, which battled its way into Tralee Bay for the 1916 Easter Rising".

Séamas Ó SÍOCHÁIN ***Roger Casement: Imperialist, Rebel, Revolutionary***, Lilliput Press, Dublin, 2008, 656pp., the essential, definitive biography.

Jeffrey DUDGEON review of *Roger Casement: Imperialist, Rebel, Revolutionary*, by Séamas Ó Síocháin, Dublin Review of Books, issue 7, Autumn 2008: http://www.drb.ie/more_details/08-09-28/He_Could_Tell_You_Things.aspx

Roy FOSTER review of Séamas Ó Síocháin's *Roger Casement: Imperialist, Rebel, Revolutionary*, Times Literary Supplement 24 September 2008. Contains many favourable references to this book.

Brian LACEY *Terrible Queer Creatures: Homosexuality in Irish History*, Word*well* Books, Dublin, 2008. Reviewed by Jeffrey Dudgeon in *History Ireland*, 'Sodom and Begorrah' March/April 2009.

David RAMSAY *'Blinker' Hall - Spymaster*, Spellmount, Stroud, 2008 pp. 130-138, hagiography with less than accurate segment on Casement.

Christopher ANDREW *The Defence of the Realm: The Authorized History of MI5*, Allen Lane, London 2009.

Jordan GOODMAN ***The Devil and Mr Casement***, Verso, London 2009, the Putumayo investigations and aftermath are detailed with occasional use of the Black Diaries for colour despite the author's scepticism as to authenticity.

Angus MITCHELL *Beneath the Hieroglyph: Recontextualising the Black Diaries of Roger Casement*, Irish Migration Studies in Latin America, July 2009, wherein Mitchell colourfully states, "Jeff Dudgeon uses the Black Diaries to update the queer geographies of Ulster and to re-imagine Northern Protestant nationalism as some high camp drama driven by a cabal of queer crusaders."

Michael LAUBSCHER ***Who is Roger Casement? A New Perspective,*** The

History Press, Dublin 2010. "Who is Roger Casement? is history with a difference; it is an excursion into the early twentieth century, when the final dramatic events of Roger Casement's life were unfolding. The controversial tale of Casement's life is brought to us through the dispatches of a fictional journalist."

Lesley WYLIE *Rare models: Roger Casement, the Amazon, and the ethnographic picturesque*, Irish Studies Review (18: 3, 315-330) 2010 with previously unseen, shirtless photographs of Ricudo and Omarino taken in England and found in Cambridge University's Museum of Archaeology and Anthropology. Wylie writes, "In 1910 Roger Casement was sent by the British government to investigate the alleged humanitarian abuses of the Peruvian Amazon Company in the Putumayo, a disputed border zone in North West Amazonia. Casement brought more than verbal and written testimony back to London. On 26 June, some six months after he returned from the Amazon, Casement collected two Amerindian boys – Ricudo and Omarino – from Southampton docks. This paper will reconstruct the brief period that these young men spent in Britain in the summer of 1911 and assess, in particular, to what extent they were treated as 'exhibits' by Casement, who not only introduced them to leading members of the British establishment but also arranged for them to be painted and photographed following contemporary ethnographic conventions." See also her 2013 book *Colombia's Forgotten Frontier: A Literary Geography of the Putumayo* (Liverpool University Press).

Mario VARGAS LLOSA *El sueño del celta*, Alfaguara, Madrid 2010; in English ***The Dream of the Celt***, Faber June 2012, historical novel that views Casement as a humanitarian hero if something of a sexual fantasist. There is little trace of any of this author's influence. The novelist's views seem already to have been formed by others before he visited Northern Ireland.

Elizabeth JAEGER *Roger Casement: How Effective Was the British Government's Smear Campaign Exposing the Homosexual "Black Diaries"?*, Éire-Ireland, Volume 46:3 & 4, Fall/Winter 2011, pp. 132-169. She concludes the diaries had no effect on American public opinion and little coverage.

Jeffrey DUDGEON reply to Manus O'Riordan's *The 1934 Larkin Affidavit* articles on Casement, Larkin and US sabotage, *Irish Political Review*, November & December 2011; reply March 2012 (with further response by Brendan Clifford).

Patrick MASON *The Dreaming of Roger Casement*, RTE radio play, broadcast on 13 May 2012, with Ciarán Hinds as Casement. "Patrick Mason's drama follows the last days of Roger Casement's life." Script in *Breac*: http://www.rte.ie/drama/radio/genres-history-thedreamingofrogercasement.html

Angus MITCHELL *Field Day Review* 8. 2012, University of Notre Dame, Indiana:

- 'A Strange Chapter of Irish History': Sir Roger Casement, Germany and the 1916 Rising.
- Diary of Roger Casement, 1914-16, Part I: 'My Journey to the German Headquarters at Charleville', annotated by Angus Mitchell.
- Roger Casement 'A last Page of My Diary' 17 March to 8 April 1916, with an introduction by Angus Mitchell.
- 'Phases of a Dishonourable Phantasy', full and frank discussion of the Black Diaries controversy to date (pp. 85-125).

Casement's End, Dublin Review of Books, January 2013 on the NLI's release "of a file of Casement papers that had sat for over sixty years on the 'Not for Consultation' shelf."

Jeffrey DUDGEON Dublin Review of Books (drb), March and June 2013, reply to Angus Mitchell's *Field Day Review* articles on Casement in Germany and the Black Diaries, in two parts:

- Part I, *Casement's War*, Issue 31, 25 March 2013: http://www.drb.ie/essays/casement-s-war;
- Part II *Casement Wars*, Issue 36, 4 June 2013: http://www.drb.ie/essays/casement-wars

Jeffrey DUDGEON *Roger Casement: Controversies in Script and Image*, talk given at School of Creative Arts, Queen's University Belfast, 22 April 2013.

Mark McCARTHY '*1916 as Spectacle*' review of *Ireland's 1916 Rising: Explorations of History-Making, Commemoration & Heritage in Modern Times*, Dublin Review of Books, 6 May 2013: http://www.drb.ie/essays/1916-as-spectacle

Jeffrey DUDGEON 'Ethics of Archives' paper, Institute for the Study of Conflict Transformation and Social Justice, Queen's University Belfast (ISCTSJ), 7 June 2013.

Angus MITCHELL ***16 Lives: Roger Casement***, The O'Brien Press, Dublin 2013, 414 pp. Mitchell's first substantive work on Casement, placing him in a modern globalist, human rights-oriented setting, in opposition to 'western hegemony'; anti-imperialist yet pro-German, and nationalist. A couple of previously unseen photographs are used including an early one of Casement, probably in the Congo, on the back cover. Martin Mansergh in his *History Ireland* review of May 2014 concurs with Mitchell's "scepticism" over the diaries: "Few who accept the 'Black' content as genuine believe it to be literally credible. As the Hitler diaries show, people can go to great lengths to construct something so plausible as to take in the greatest expert." This author responded, especially on Michael Francis's Doyle's dubious report of a discussion with Casement in Brixton Prison where he "emphatically" repudiated the Black Diaries: http://www.historyireland.com/uncategorized/roger-casement/

Jeffrey DUDGEON *Cult of the Sexless Casement with Special Reference to the Novel The Dream of the Celt by Mario Vargas Llosa (Nobel Prize Winner for Literature 2010)*, Studi irlandesi. A Journal of Irish Studies, n. 3 (2013), pp. 35-58 ISSN 2239-3978 (online) Firenze: http://www.fupress.net/index.php/bsfm-sijis/article/view/13792

Jorge Luis Chavez MARROQUIN (ed.) *Álbum de Fotografías Viaje de la Comisión Consular al Río Putumayo y Afluentes*, Lima 2014. Striking photographs of an up-river investigatory voyage from August to October 1912 by consuls Michell, Fuller and Rey de Castro, with Julio Arana and Juan Tizon. https://issuu.com/jorgeluischavez/docs/album_de_fotografias_viaje_comision/101

Roy FOSTER *Vivid Faces: The Revolutionary Generation in Ireland 1890-1923,* Allen Lane, London 2014, 496 pp. Emblematic book on the, largely disappointed, progenitors of the intellectual side to Irish independence and consequent partition. Deals extensively with Casement and F.J. Bigger in the *Loving* and *Arming* chapters. (I met the author several times, co-incidentally, when we were both researching in the NLI Manuscripts room in Kildare Street, and pointed him to a number of documents and photographs I had spotted.)

Jeffrey DUDGEON *Casement and Ulster: seeding separatism and misunderstanding,* 'The North Began? Ulster and the Irish revolution 1900-25' lecture, TCD Centre for Contemporary Irish History/St Patrick's College Drumcondra History Department, 20 June 2015, 'Influences and Inspirations' section.

Keith JEFFERY *1916: A Global History*, Bloomsbury, London 2015, by the QUB historian of MI6, includes the Easter Rising, the Somme and German East Africa.

Lucy McDIARMID *At Home in the Revolution: What Women Said and Did in 1916*, Royal Irish Academy, Dublin 2015, evocative and comprehensive account of varied female opinions and actions during the Easter Rising, with particular coverage of Gertrude Bannister's efforts to assist Casement in London. Lucy kindly acknowledges my provision of information, saying Gertrude "had no direct descendants but fortunately for me Jeff Dudgeon knows as much about her life as any grandson and has given me information I could not have got otherwise."

Jeffrey DUDGEON (ed.) ***Roger Casement's German Diary 1914-1916 including 'A Last Page' and associated correspondence,*** Belfast Press, 2016, paperback (and Kindle), 367 pp., 45 illustrations, ISBN 9780953928750: https://amzn.to/2MpNaaD This definitive, unabridged version of Roger Casement's German Diary covers the years 1914 to 1916 when, after the war started, he went to Berlin seeking support for Irish independence. It is another and the last surviving Casement diary, and deals with that most interesting, dramatic and penultimate period of his life in Germany and Berlin prior to his departure to Ireland for the Easter Rising. It was not a private diary in any sense as he left instructions for its future publication. Much of what he wrote was designed to provide a record justifying his time in Germany. He was of an age to have his eye on history while knowing the accusations of treason he had, and would, face, Casement was desperate to have his actions understood. A secondary prompt in the last months was to indicate just how disgraceful and intransigent he felt the behaviour of the Germans had become and how the decision to start the rebellion in Ireland was something he did not agree with for tactical reasons, being an event he thus hoped to prevent or at least postpone. The final section describes his frantic attempts both to get sufficient arms shipped to the separatist Irish Volunteers and to travel by submarine to Kerry with a view to getting the Easter Rising called off. This latter effort failed and had no useful effect on the campaign for a reprieve.

The diary and many linked letters give a vivid impression of a man under stress in an alien environment who still manages to observe, describe and appreciate what he sees around him. He writes as an outsider of a nation at war with England and France. His growing frustrations however come to the point where his own mental health is destabilised.

There is a cast of the usual characters that Casement mixed with, political, often aristocratic, although also frequently military men. There were to be none of the street people or lovers that his earlier, more sexual, diaries detailed. In Germany, probably for security reasons and lacking the language, he chose not to go out at night or to cruise for sex. He was also getting on. His Norwegian companion and betrayer, Adler Christensen, looms large, tricking and twisting his way round Germany and America, while draining much of Casement's time and common sense.

The text is laid out in as close a way as possible as the actual manuscripts to provide an impression of the original. The appendices include correspondence and newspaper articles from the time, while bringing the reader up to date with recent articles in relation to Casement in Germany, the Easter Rising and the role of British and German Intelligence, as well as the ongoing Black Diaries authenticity debate which is, if anything, accelerating. That controversy tells of a still contested issue in modern-day Ireland, despite the immense strides made towards gay equality and emancipation, most recently in the Republic.

The diary manuscript is in two notebooks in the National Library of Ireland and essentially covers the eight months from July 1914 to February 1915. It begins to be written on 7 November 1914 and takes Casement retrospectively from England, to the US and to Germany and then includes a tour of war-torn Belgium. It effectively concludes on 11 February 1915 with him in a sanatorium. At the end, however, there is a brief account dated 28 March 1916 of events later in 1915. Separately, 'A Last Page' picks up the narrative on 17 March 1916 running it to Casement's final days in Berlin.

Casement, a man who wrote too much, drafted many hundreds of other letters and memos when in Germany of which a number of the more significant, particularly those related to the arrangements for his departure to Ireland, are reprinted here along with the full, unabridged diary where another writer, Angus Mitchell, has edited out nearly a quarter of the original text in his book sub-titled *The Berlin Diary*. Those cuts are at times from the most sensitive of areas, including the behaviour of the German Army in Belgium and Casement's increasing disillusionment with the Kaiser's Imperial Government and Prussian militarism. Being complete in its narrative, makes this book vastly more readable and comprehensible.

Angus MITCHELL (ed.) ***One Bold Deed of Open Treason: The Berlin Diary of Roger Casement 1914-1916***, Merrion Press, Sallins, Co. Kildare 2016, 280 pp.; abridged version of the German diary with some 20,000 words, cut out, dedicated to Dr Charles Curry. *Irish Catholic* review by W.J. Mc Cormack: http://www.irishcatholic.ie/article/odd-thoughts-republic%E2%80%99s-man-berlin

Colin MURPHY *Roger Casement's 'Apocalypse Now' - Africa & 1916,* RTE broadcast 25 March 2016: "Murphy who narrated and produced, visited the Casement childhood home in Antrim in search of the seeds of Casement's anti-imperialism. There, amidst the paraphernalia of an ascendancy family with a tradition of military service, Casement had soaked up Irish history and lore in the library of the Big House, while looking out on Rathlin Island, scene of a massacre by English forces centuries before. The empathy fostered there for the native Irish would be the seed of his empathy for the Congolese; and that, in turn, would reinforce his hostility to Empire.

Casement's "treason" and "black diaries" brought shame on his family but, in Antrim, Colin Murphy discovered that contact and affection between them endured right up to his execution in London in August 1916. And a new generation of Casements is now embracing his complex legacy – foremost within it, his groundbreaking work in Congo": http://www.rte.ie/radio1/doconone/2016/0318/775719-roger-casements-apocalypse-now-africa-1916/

Arnold Thomas FANNING *McKenna's Fort*, 2016 play premiered at the New Theatre Dublin. Saoirse Anton wrote: "Directed by Paul Kennedy, this one-man show telling the story of Roger Casement is an engaging and unusual exploration of the experiences of a 1916 rebel. As Casement hides in the McKenna's Fort rath, having returned from an unsuccessful journey to Germany to acquire arms, ammunition and support for the Easter Rising, he brings the audience on a stream-of-consciousness trip through his memories of the failed mission, his older tales, and his plan for his new personal mission; to have the rebellion called off."

Tim O'Sullivan however says, "The Casement that emerges is a disjointed personality, compassionate yet with a violent streak, idealistic yet madly vain, capable yet delusional, desirous of doing great deeds yet lacking depth of character. His views on Ireland or on Germany and the war are not explained save for the suggestion of mild psychosis which in the script hovers over and about the main character."

Jeffrey DUDGEON *Roger Casement and the Easter Rising: Berlin, Dublin and British Intelligence*, article in Vol. 23, Dúiche Néill, Journal of The O Neill Country Historical Society (ed. Brian Gilmore), Armagh 2016.

***BREAC:* A Digital Journal of Irish Studies**, Keough-Naughton Institute for Irish Studies, University of Notre Dame, Indiana April 2016: https://breac.nd.edu/articles/category/roger-casement/. "The nineteen contributions in this special issue of the online journal *Breac* delve deep into Casement's life and exploits, and examine various aspects of his legacy and motivations; in so doing, they shed new critical light on previously unknown and unexamined aspects of his career". An extensive range of articles, some from the October 2013 Tralee conference *Roger Casement: The Glocal Imperative*. In particular, scripts of the RTE play by Patrick Mason and of an unmade film by John Banville are published. Several of the papers relate to the German period while one of interest tells of the Belgian response to Casement. They include 'Introduction: The ghost of Roger Casement is beating on the door', by John Gibney, Michael Griffin, and Brian Ó Conchubhair; *The Three Lives of the Casement Report: Its Impact on Official Reactions and Popular Opinion in Belgium*, Pierre-Luc Plasman and Catherine Thewissen (Université Catholique de Louvain, Belgium); *Ireland, Empire, and British Foreign Policy: Roger Casement and the First World War*, Margaret O'Callaghan; *Lost to History: An Assessment and Review of the Casement Black Diaries*, Paul Hyde; *Casement (An Original Screenplay)* by John Banville, with an introduction by Bridget English; *The Dreaming of Roger Casement: A Play* by Patrick Mason; *From Fragments to a Whole: Homosexuality and Partition in 'Cries from Casement as his Bones are Brought to Dublin', by David Rudkin*, Mariana Bolfarine (University of São Paulo); *History and Imagination in 'The Dream of the Celt' by Mario Vargas Llosa*, Leopoldo M. Bernucci; *A Note on the Casement Papers in the Benjamin Iveagh Library, Farmleigh House*, John Gibney; *Ruairí Mac Easmainn agus an Ghaeilge*, Nollaig Mac Congáil; *The Afterlife of Roger Casement's Irish Brigade, 1916-1922*, Justin Dolan Stover; *Guns in the Water: Quilty's Car, Spindler's Aud, and the First Casualties of the Easter Rising of 1916*, Eoin Shanahan; *Roger Casement and America*, Robert Schmuhl; *Roger Casement's Long Journey to Ballyheigue*, Michael Cronin (Boston College); Angus Mitchell, In Conversation with John Gibney; and a review of Angus Mitchell's *Roger Casement: 16 Lives* by Gearóid Ó Tuathaigh.

Jessica O'DONNELL (ed) *High Treason: Roger Casement*, Hugh Lane Gallery Dublin 2016, 96 pp., exhibition catalogue with illustrations and essays by Sinead McCoole, Mr Justice Donal O'Donnell, Angus Mitchell, Chris Clarke, Charles Esche, Tacita Dean and Elizabeth Magill.

Bjørn GODØY *Dobbeltspill, Kjærlighet og forræderi i skyggen av første verdenskrig/ Double Game, Love and betrayal in the shadows of World War I,* Spartacus Forlag AS, Oslo 2016 https://spartacus.no/boker/dobbeltspill with family photographs from Adler's nephew Per Rolf Christensen. "Roger Casement was possibly the most hated man in England during World War I. In 1916, he was hanged for high treason for having sought German support for a rebellion in Ireland. Two years earlier, he had travelled to Berlin just as British men were being massacred on the battle fields in Europe. Flaming Irish nationalism emboldened him to make the fateful trip – along with blind confidence in a young Norwegian sailor.

Eivind Adler Christensen escorted Casement into Germany, and remained to serve as his closest aide and companion. Shortly after his arrival, Casement launched a fantastic offensive designed to bring the British Empire to its knees, using Christensen as his field agent. The plan was to tarnish Britain's reputation to such an extent that the global community would turn on the self professed world leader.

Bjørn Godøy, author of Dobbeltspill (2016), the story of the life and death of Adler Christensen

Per Rolf Christensen (2015), son of Adler Christensen's brother Rolf

Still, many in the Irish rebel community wondered why Casement was so dedicated to a man nobody could vouch for. The truth would have shocked them beyond words. Christensen was not only Casement's assistant, he was also his lover.

Double Game is the incredible story of the unlikely relationship between two men in a ruthless and manly world. It is a story of a lover who mainly loved himself, and of a traitor who ended up being betrayed."

Jeffrey DUDGEON *Getting Casement right: the early influences,* Irish Times website, 12 June 2016: Roger Casement: a campaigner, not a conspirator or even an Ulster Protestant: http://www.irishtimes.com/culture/books/roger-casement-a-campaigner-not-a-conspirator-or-even-an-ulster-protestant-1.2680244?utm_source=dlvr.it&utm_medium=twitter

Roger CASEMENT *The Crime against Europe: A possible outcome of the war of 1914,* reprint with an introduction by Angus Mitchell, Dun Laoghaire Rathdown (dlr) County Council Roger Casement Summer School 2017: https://www.academia.edu/35390173/_2017_The_Crime_against_Europe_A_possible_outcome_of_the_war_of_1914_Dublin_Dun_Laoghaire-Rathdown

Sabina MURRAY *Valiant Gentlemen*, Grove Atlantic, New York 2017. "A historical novel about Roger Casement, defender of indigenous rights in the Congo and the Amazon, covert homosexual and eventual martyr to the cause of Irish independence" – on Herbert Ward and Casement and their relationship…This essential book introduced me to some of the people in Casement's circle, Millar Gordon and Frank Bigger, among others. Jeffrey Dudgeon solidly places Casement within a gay cultural reality and provided a lot of necessary orientation and detail." One critic stated, "On this side of the Atlantic, Sabina Murray is our Hilary Mantel."

John GRAY *Roger Casement: 'Realities and Illusions of Colonialism'*, Vol. 24, Dúiche Néill, Journal of The O Neill Country Historical Society (ed. Brian Gilmore), Armagh 2017.

Jeffrey DUDGEON *H. Montgomery Hyde: Ulster Unionist MP, Gay Law Reform Campaigner and Prodigious Author*, Belfast Press 2018, ISBN 9780953928798. http://amzn.to/2BCOp0J (Amazon). http://amzn.to/2GtS705 (Kindle): Montgomery Hyde died in 1989 by which time he had become history. Only a very few remembered him or his gay campaigning role let alone the fact he had been an Ulster Unionist MP throughout the 1950s. Thirty years later, he can hardly be conceptualised. Too many, at best, see him as an aberration for Belfast, but he was a recognisable type of progressive, yet traditional, British politician. No one else played as long or as effective a part in changing views towards gays when only a handful of people, let alone MPs, put their head above the parapet.

"Harford" as he was known to his friends, "H. Montgomery Hyde" to his readers, and "Montgomery Hyde" to the electors of North Belfast, led the battle in the House of Commons for decriminalisation of homosexuality. And he paid as great a price as any parliamentarian could for his courage – he lost his seat.

Very much a child of the 1920s, he was dedicated to researching and writing about those two most prominent gay men of the 20th century – Oscar Wilde and Roger Casement, both Irish outlaws. None the less, he managed to publish another forty books on a wide range of subjects including perhaps his finest works 'The Rise of Castlereagh' and 'The Other Love'. A cheerful and good natured figure, Harford lived and loved well and is deserving, at the least, of this short book outlining his struggles and achievements.

Mariana BOLFARINE *"Between Angels and Demons": Trauma in Fictional Representations of Roger Casement*, Humanitas-FFLCH/USP, São Paulo 2018, literary comparisons within trauma theory on works involving Casement, including *At Swim Two Boys*, and those by David Rudkin and Mario Vargas Llosa.

Martin DUBERMAN *Luminous Traitor: The Just and Daring Life of Roger Casement: a Biographical Novel*, University of California Press 2018. David Norris, a member of the Irish Senate and human rights activist wrote: "This remarkable and very readable book deserves a wide audience. The late Sir Roger Casement's wonderful and tragic life, from his first experiences in the Congo to his effective challenge to the brutal exploitation of indigenous people in the Putumayo region of the Amazon, is dramatized beautifully. Episodes including Casement's voice are persuasively achieved. During my lifetime Casement's homosexuality was aggressively denied by a Republican who refused to allow that an Irish patriot could be both such and also gay, but Casement's diaries are both convincing and representative of the sexual encounters of many gay men right up into my own lifetime. Here his sexuality is finally woven into the narrative naturally and compellingly."

Endnotes

1 Reviewed unfavourably by Frank MacGabhann in the Dublin Review of Books 2017, *Proof or Imagination?*: http://www.drb.ie/essays/proof-or-imagination-

2 Quoted in Stephen Coote's 1997 biography of Yeats and referenced to Nancy Cardozo's *Life of Maud Gonne*

3 *Field Day Review* (Mitchell 2012), 'Phases of a Dishonourable Phantasy' pp. 100, 117, and 102 respectively.

4 See NLI 49164: letter of 15 January 1903 from Casement to his uncle who has taken in Charlie's older two daughters. "I am very sorry for Charlie & his hardships." £20 is promised.

5 Mackey 1959 p. 14 & NLI 13088

6 TNA HO 144/1637/176

7 TNA HO 144/1637/182

8 Hyde 1964 p. 82

9 Mackey 1959 p. 14

10 Quoted in an article by Montgomery Hyde, *Books & Bookmen* September 1976

11 NLI 7946

12 NLI 13088

13 Joy p. 307

14 Mackey 1959 p. 15

15 NLI 22986

16 TNA PCPM 9/2331

17 TNA HO 144/1637/141

18 TNA HO 144/1637/182

19 NLI 13075/1

20 TNA HO 144/1636/40

21 TNA HO 144/1636/49, 14 July 1916

22 See Scotland Yard MEPO 2/10672 on Blackwell accessing "Casement's diary and ledger" and typed entries to show Harris.

23 Mitchell (1997) p. 32-33 and TNA HO/144/1636/49 (Blackwell)

24 Quoted in R. Barry O'Brien article 'Fresh Light on Casement Diaries', *Daily Telegraph*, 12 March 1959

25 Sawyer 1984 p. 140-1

26 TNA HO 144/1636/311643/3A, and British Library Add. 46912, Miscellaneous Letters and Papers, 11 June 1916

27 Quoted in R. Barry O'Brien article 'Fresh Light on Casement Diaries', *Daily Telegraph*, 12 March 1959

28 NLI 17046

29 UCD McCullough Papers P120/17

30 Sparrow p. 162-3

31 Quoted in Glenavy p. 90

32 NLI 12114

33 TNA HO 45/10772/276022

34 NLI 17428

35 Malcomson p. 121

36 Malcomson p. 123

37 PRONI T810/166

38 Brett 1996 p.210

39 PRONI HA/32/1/954

40 NLI 31722

41 Bob Pollock, known to author when a child as a neighbour and Communist Party family

42 Boyd p. 18-19

43 TNA HO 161/2

44 NYPL Maloney Collection of Irish Historical Papers, Box 3 Fol 3
45 Brett 1996 p. 210
46 PRONI D3027/5
47 PRONI T810/4
48 PRONI T810/4
49 PRONI D1905/2/45/10
50 From Hugh Casement's will, probated in London 30 May 1863
51 PRONI D1905/2/45/10
52 NLI Acc 4902 Folder 16 (now in 36199-36212)
53 TNA WO 31, Abstract 823
54 Sawyer 1984 p. 12
55 NLI 13080/6/ii
56 NLI 10464/2
57 Sawyer 1984, pp. 12 & 13
58 Letter of 8 December 1872 in possession of Casement family
59 Letter in possession of Casement family
60 NLI 13159
61 NLI 17594
62 NLI 9932
63 NLI 13079
64 NLI 17604
65 PRONI T3787/1/1
66 NLI 13080/6/ii
67 Letter in possession of Casement family
68 Letter in possession of Casement family
69 Letter in possession of Casement family
70 PRONI T3787/2/1
71 Sawyer 1984 p. 15
72 NLI 12115
73 NLI 12114. A further Casement notebook was purchased in 2003 by the NLI. Now MS 39120 and dating from 1895 to 1900, it was probably sold by the Parry family. It includes many African and Irish poems and some military details relating to Lourenco Marques.
74 NLI 14100
75 NLI 17594
76 NLI 9932
77 NLI 13077/3
78 NLI 13077/3
79 Sawyer 1984 p. 15
80 NLI 9932
81 Transcribed by John O'Loughlin
82 NLI 13074/3/ii
83 NLI 10764
84 NLI 9932
85 NLI 13074/2
86 *Morning Post* report 26 January 1876 in Southwark court.
87 NLI 17604
88 NLI Acc 4902 Folder 19 (now in 36199-36212)
89 NLI 18459
90 Sawyer 1997 p. 35
91 NLI 13074/2/ii
92 Jephson p. 259
93 NLI 17594
94 NLI 9932
95 NLI 13082/1/iii
96 NLI Acc 4902 Folder 30 (now in 36199-36212)
97 Jephson, Pedigree No. 5
98 Jephson p. 260
99 NLI 17595
100 NLI 13077/2
101 NLI Acc 4902 Folder 30 (now in 36199-36212)
102 PRONI T3787/15/1
103 Jephson p. 261
104 NLI Acc 4902 Folder 19 (now in 36199-36212)
105 PRONI D3027/7/14
106 This 26 April letter (Hugh Casement) indicates the boy stayed with John and his wife, Elizabeth Dickey.

107 NLI 17604/1
108 NLI Acc 4902 (now in 36199-36212) and PRONI T Folder 19
109 NLI 17594
110 Information supplied by George Glass of Ballymena, from local newspapers.
111 NLI 9932
112 NLI 10464/2
113 NLI 13082/1/iii
114 Letter in possession of Casement family
115 PRONI T3382
116 NLI 13088/13
117 Ó Doibhlin p. 123
118 PRONI T3787/3/1
119 NLI 41654
120 NLI 9932
121 NLI 17594
122 NLI Acc 4902 Folder 12 (now in 36199-36212)
123 NLI Acc 4902 Folder 12 (now in 36199-36212)
124 NLI Acc 4902 Folder 17 (now in 36199-36212)
125 NLI Acc 4902 Folder 17 (now in 36199-36212)
126 Hyam p. 70
127 NLI 17594
128 NLI 13082/2/ii
129 Introduction to *Some Poems of Roger Casement*, 1918
130 Mackey 1958 p. 172
131 NYPL Maloney Collection of Irish Historical Papers, Box 2 Fol 19
132 NLI Acc 4902 Folder 17 (now in 36199-36212)
133 NLI 13073/4/ii
134 NLI 13086, 8 September 1903
135 NLI 13073/46
136 Sawyer 1984 p. 20
137 PRONI T3787/4/1
138 PRONI T3787/5/1
139 BLPES F8/18/1430/147
140 TNA FO 403/304
141 TNA FO 10/730
142 TNA FO 10/731
143 TNA FO 10/730
144 TNA FO 10/730
145 TNA FO 10/730
146 TNA FO 10/731
147 TNA FO 10/731
148 TNA FO 10/731
149 TNA FO 10/464
150 Letter to author 30 June 2000
151 Cookey p. 27
152 NLI 9932
153 TNA FO 10/464
154 NLI 17594
155 NLI Acc 4902 Folder 16 (now in 36199-36212)
156 TNA FO 13/748
157 TNA FO 13/761
158 TNA FO 13/761
159 NLI 13081/2
160 Correspondence of Sanford Exploring Expedition, Africa Boxes 21-32
161 See Ó Síocháin (2008) ch. 2 pp. 21-43 for an illuminating account of Casement's earliest times in the Congo Free State (1884-91).
162 Another old comrade who wrote to those gathering signatures for the reprieve, said, "Can you get a message through to the one of whom we are all thinking? It is only this. I saw a dead man in a fight/And I think that man was I – Masala at Vivi in 1886. Perhaps you have not forgotten." There is no name or date on this 4-sided note (NLI 13088/9) but it has to be the enclosure mentioned in A.

Werner's letter of 31 July 1916 to H.W. Nevinson (NLI 13078/3) where Deane, Glave, Swinburne, and Skagerstrom are described as Old Congo comrades who "are all gone" who would otherwise "have come forward", even Coquilhat would, adding "You? did not know 'Masala'. He went before the others, except Deane." Years earlier, Casement wrote to Herbert Ward (NLI 13078/1) saying he had been told by Tanqueray that "poor old Ingham is dead too! Killed by an elephant [in November 1893] – his rifle having jammed…Alas, another of our dear friends gone". He added that Tanqueray himself was also killed by an elephant! The other recently deceased were Reginald Heyn on 2 June 1892 in St Paul de Loanda, and Major William Parminter on 24 January 1894, of liver disease in Nice, not long after his 8 June 1892 marriage to Miss Heyn.

163 Correspondence of Sanford Exploring Expedition, Africa Box 28, folder 1

164 Correspondence of Sanford Exploring Expedition, Africa Box 26, folder 14

165 Correspondence of Sanford Exploring Expedition, Africa Box 27, folder 14

166 NLI 13082/2/ii

167 From *The life of Edmund Musgrave Barttelot, captain and brevet-major Royal fusiliers, commander of the rear column of the Emin Pasha relief expedition; being an account of his services for the relief of Kandahar, of Gordon, and of Emin, from his letters and diary*, Richard Bentley, London, 1890, edited by W.G. Barttelot.

168 Thompson p. 98-102

169 PRONI D3027/6

170 Conrad p. 150

171 Conrad p. 150

172 Cookey p. 315-317

173 Inglis p. 30

174 PRONI T3787/14/1

175 PRONI T3787/13/1

176 TNA FO 2/336

177 NLI 10464/2

178 NLI Acc 4902 Folder 7 (now in 36199-36212)

179 NLI 17590/4

180 Sawyer 1984 p. 29

181 TNA FO 2/64

182 NLI 13082/1

183 PRONI D3301/CA/7

184 TNA FO 2/64

185 NLI Acc 4902 Folder 18 with sketch of hair-do (now in 36199-36212)

186 PRONI T3787/12/1

187 NLI Acc 4902 Folder 1 (now in 36199-36212)

188 PRONI T3787/14/1

189 NLI 13088/1/iii

190 NLI Acc 4902 Folder 16 (now in 36199-36212)

191 NLI 13081/2

192 NLI 10464/3

193 TNA FO 10/731

194 MacColl p. 26

195 TNA FO 403/304

196 TNA FO 10/739

197 PRONI T3787/14/10

198 NLI Acc 4902 Folder 5 (now in 36199-36212)

199 NLI 13047/1

200 TNA FO 403/305

201 NLI 18923
202 MacColl pp. 34 & 35
203 Inglis pp. 75 & 76
204 TNA HO 161/1
205 TNA FO 2/491/166-175
206 TNA HO 161/2
207 NLI Acc 4902 Folder 14 (now in 36199-36212)
208 NLI 21814
209 Extract from Countess Blücher's *An English Wife in Berlin: A Private Memoir of Events, Politics, and Daily Life in Germany Throughout the War* (1920)
210 NLI 13073/46/v
211 Inglis p. 65
212 B.L. Reid p. 484
213 NLI Acc 4902 Folder 7 (now in 36199-36212)
214 NLI 13083
215 NLI 13074
216 TNA FO 811/55/65161
217 NLI Acc 4902 Folder 6 (now in 36199-36212)
218 TNA FO 811/55/65161
219 NLI Acc 4902 Folder 7 (now in 36199-36212)
220 NLI Acc 4902 Folder 7 (now in 36199-36212)
221 TNA FO 811/55
222 NLI 12117
223 PRONI T3787/15/1
224 Royle p. 129
225 Sparrow pp. 163 & 164
226 NLI 13074/3
227 NLI 13074/1
228 NLI 13074
229 PRONI T3787/16/1
230 TNA WO 100/299
231 NLI 13081/2
232 NLI 10764/1
233 NLI Acc 4902 Folder 6 (now in 36199-36212)
234 TNA FO 10/805, S.C. Bentill in Africa 24
235 NLI 13074
236 NLI 13073/46/vii
237 NLI 12117. See also T Butler Blunt (McIntosh county) in Georgia State Gazetteer, Business and Planter's Directory, Vol. II, 1881-82.
238 Jones p. 756
239 NLI Acc 4902 Folder 6 (now in 36199-36212)
240 BLPES Morel F8/16/5 and TNA FO 403/338 (Africa 38, 30 September 1903)
241 In 2014, the Faroe Islands issued a stamp to mark Danielsen's crusading contribution to the Congo with a picture of him, Casement and the Henry Reed.
242 BLPES Morel F8/16/5
243 TNA FO 10/805
244 NLI 13086
245 BLPES Morel/F8/16/5
246 NLI 13073/27/ii
247 Hochschild p. 204
248 NLI 13083
249 BLPES Morel F8/16/13.13v
250 Louis p. 107
251 NLI Acc 4902 Folder 17 (now in 36199-36212)
252 Mrs French Sheldon, an American writer, became a well-paid Leopold defender, regarded by Casement as a threat, being like Mary Kingsley "a woman who had been there" which would "count for much with the popular point of view". See Inglis p. 135 and Hochschild p. 237-8.
253 NLI 13073/7
254 NLI Acc 4902 Folder 16 (now in 36199-36212)

255 NLI Acc 4902 Folder 7 (now in 36199-36212)
256 NLI Acc 4902 Folder 8 (now in 36199-36212)
257 NLI 13074/1
258 NLI 13073/21
259 PRONI T3787/17/1
260 PRONI T3787/15/1, and information from Hugh Casement
261 Louis and Stengers p. 162
262 MacColl p. 33
263 NLI Acc 4902 Folder 16 (now in 36199-36212)
264 Louis and Stengers p. 160
265 BLPES Morel/F10/13/675-6
266 NLI 13073/30
267 Inglis pp. 78 & 79
268 BLPES Morel/F8/23/453
269 NLI 10763/2, 14 and 22
270 NLI 13074/1/ii
271 NLI 13074/1/i
272 NLI 12117
273 B.L. Reid p. 483-4 (and pp. 53-4 and p. 515)
274 NLI 9932
275 *The Times* 7 February 1917, and information from Hugh Casement
276 Scannell & Snoddy p. 46-47
277 Scannell & Snoddy p. 50
278 PRONI D3027/7/14
279 ?? John Young quote
280 NLI 13082/2/ii
281 PRONI D3027/7/14
282 NLI 12115
283 NLI 13073/2
284 BLPES Morel/F8/16/13
285 Cline p. 7
286 Information from Hugh Casement
287 NLI 12117
288 Louis and Stengers p. 140
289 BLPES Morel F8/18/149-150
290 NLI Acc 4902 Folder 5 (now in 36199-36212)
291 NLI Acc 4902 Folders 5, 6 & 7 (now in 36199-36212)
292 NLI Acc 4902 Folder 6 (now in 36199-36212)
293 NLI Acc 4902 Folder 8 (now in 36199-36212)
294 NLI 21531
295 NLI Acc 4902 Folder 16 (now in 36199-36212)
296 NLI 14100
297 NLI 13073 & 13081
298 Joy p. 296
299 NLI 15138/2
300 BLPES Morel/F8/16/20.20v
301 NLI Acc 4902 Folder 10 (now in 36199-36212)
302 NYPL Maloney Collection of Irish Historical Papers, Box 1 Fol 15-20
303 Singleton-Gates p. 339
304 NLI 13073/21
305 NLI 5461
306 Louis and Stengers p. 176
307 NLI 17675
308 NLI 31726
309 McDowell p. 50
310 NLI 10464/4
311 NLI Acc 4902 Folder 2 (now in 36199-36212)
312 NLI 10464
313 Joy p. 296
314 Joy p. 298
315 Facsimile reproduced by the Roger Casement Foundation, Dublin
316 NYPL Maloney Collection of Irish Historical Papers, Box 3 Fol 3
317 NLI Acc 4902 Folders 10 & 13 (now in 36199-36212)
318 Author's telephone conversation

with Declan Hobson 2 March 1999
319 NLI 13158/3
320 NLI 14100
321 Martin p. 99
322 Morgan p. 201
323 TNA CO 904/117
324 TNA CO 904/117
325 PRONI Belf/1/1/2/18/6
326 NLI 10764
327 TNA CO 904/117
328 Morgan p. 202
329 NLI 17675
330 NLI Acc 4902 Folder 16 (now in 36199-36212)
331 NLI 8358
332 Campbell p. 364
333 NLI Acc 4902 Folder 16 (now in 36199-36212)
334 NLI 13073
335 NLI 18574
336 NLI 13073/4
337 NLI Acc 4902 Folder 16 (now in 36199-36212)
338 NLI 13158
339 NLI 13158
340 NLI 10464/3
341 *The Month* Vol. 15, June 1956
342 NLI 13158
343 NLI 5459
344 NLI 13158/2/1
345 NLI 13158/6/34
346 NLI Acc 4902 Folder 17 (now in 36199-36212)
347 NLI 13074
348 NLI 17580
349 NLI 13074
350 NLI 10464/6
351 NLI 13074
352 NLI 12117
353 NLI 18273
354 NLI 13080/1/ii
355 Quoted in Mackey 1958 p. 93
356 NLI 1689
357 NLI 13079
358 NLI 10464
359 NLI 13081
360 NLI 10764
361 NLI 17580
362 NLI 10464
363 NLI Acc 4902 Folder 17 (now in 36199-36212)
364 NLI 13074/5/i
365 NLI 1690
366 NLI 13085/9/ii
367 Quoted in Campbell p. 237
368 NLI 15072/2
369 NLI 5459
370 Bigger photograph collections in the Ulster Museum and BCL; NLI 21536 & 21543
371 NLI 8824/1
372 NLI 16994
373 Saunders & Kelly p. 23-4
374 NLI 21531
375 NLI 13078/4
376 *vide* Dr J. S. Crone's 1927 memoir
377 NLI 15072
378 NLI 16995
379 *vide* J.K. Owen's pamphlet, BCL
380 BCL Bigger catalogue
381 NLI 10464/2
382 NLI Acc 4902 Folder 16 (now in MS 36202/3)
383 NLI 10464/2
384 Morgan p. 200
385 BCL Bigger collection
386 NLI 15072/1
387 Bigger scrapbook No. 3, Ulster Folk and Transport Museum
388 Armagh Guardian 27 September 1912
389 TNA CO 904/194/46
390 TNA KV2/6-5
391 Connolly p. 96
392 TNA CO 904/99

393 Bigger archive, Ulster Folk and Transport Museum
394 NLI 21537/1
395 NLI 21537/1
396 TNA FO 369/63
397 NLI 13074/3
398 Sawyer 1984 p. 64
399 NLI 13087/1
400 NLI 13073/4
401 NLI 13080/4, 4 March 1908
402 TNA FO 128/324
403 NLI Acc 4902 Folder 2 (now in 36199-36212)
404 TNA FO 2/491/147
405 NLI 13074/6/ii, 1 September 1909
406 TNA FO 128/324
407 All quotations from TNA FO 369/198
408 NLI 13073/2/i
409 NLI 13087/2
410 TNA HO 161/3
411 B.L. Reid p. 486
412 NLI 10464/3
413 NLI 13073/16
414 NLI Acc 4902 Folder 16 (now in 36199-36212) and NLI 13074/6/ii
415 NLI 13073/16
416 NLI 15138/4
417 NLI 13075/1
418 F. Reid p. 33-37
419 Phoenix Park is still a cruising area. An Irish Government Minister, Emmet Stagg, was, in the 1990s, outed after being questioned by police there, a detail then passed to a tabloid newspaper. Remarkably, he held on to his job whereas, in 1998, a London opposite number, Welsh Secretary Ron Davies, robbed when out cruising on Clapham Common, had to resign after what he said was "a moment of madness". He, however, compounded his problem by lying to the police about his stolen car. It is the cover-up that corrodes.
420 NLI 13074/1/i
421 NLI 13073/16/ii
422 NLI 35456
423 Bell p. 19
424 Royal Irish Academy Vol. XXX, May 1912
425 NLI 31722
426 Sawyer 1997 p. 52
427 NLI 31722
428 Belfast Natural History and Philosophical Society Proceedings, 2nd series, Vol. 3, 1948
429 Sawyer 1997 p. 52
430 NLI 10880
431 Hambloch pp. 75 & 76
432 NYPL Maloney Collection of Irish Historical Papers, Box 3 Fol 3
433 Information from Cathy Gage now Doig
434 NLI 13158
435 July 1999 conversation in Cushendall
436 Ó Doibhlin p. 103
437 NLI Acc 4902 Folder 23 (now in 36199-36212)
438 McDowell p. 94
439 NLI 10880
440 NYPL Maloney Collection of Irish Historical Papers, Box 7 Fol 16-17
441 All quotations from NLI 13073/46/xvi; other details from author's conversation in 1999 with Mrs Macha Mackay, Shelagh's niece, of Centreville, Nova Scotia

442 NLI 13073/8/ii
443 NYPL Maloney Collection of Irish Historical Papers, Box 3 Fol 1 to Mrs Gavan Duffy
444 NLI 13080/1/ii
445 NLI 13073/9
446 NLI 13073/13
447 NLI 13087/5
448 NLI 13081/2
449 Sawyer 1997 p. 150
450 Mitchell (1997) p. 169
451 Mitchell (1997) p. 308
452 NLI 13087/25, 31 October 1910
453 NLI 13087/26
454 Dickey p. 165 *et seq*
455 NLI 31735
456 NLI 15138/3 & 4 (cheque stub)
457 NLI 13087/25
458 NLI 13087/25
459 PRONI T3787/13/1
460 Mitchell (1997) p. 483
461 NLI 13087/26
462 NLI Acc 4902 Folder 23 (now in 36199-36212)
463 BCL Bigger Collection
464 TNA HO 161/5
465 Meyers p. 44
466 Sawyer 1997 pp. 21 & 59
467 NLI 13073/29/iii; 9 June 1911
468 Mitchell (1997) p. 137n, with a note on the cover in Casement's handwriting.
469 NLI 13073/12/ii
470 TCD 10676/17/66
471 NLI 17582
472 NLI 13088/13
473 NLI 13073/46/ii
474 NLI 1690
475 NLI 13073/46
476 NLI 13081
477 Copy of page supplied to author by Roger Sawyer where Ward wrote of Morten that he was "an old friend of my father, and his family had lived for centuries at the Savoy Farm (always known as 'The Savvy') an ancient house containing some delightful Elizabethan frescoes...Dick had recently sold 'The Savvy' to the Mosleys."
478 NLI 13073/26/i
479 NLI 15138/4
480 NLI 15138/4
481 Costigan p. 297
482 NLI 10464/4
483 NLI 13073/20 and 24i
484 NLI 31724
485 NLI 13081/2
486 PRONI T2646/10
487 NLI 35456
488 NLI 15138/4
489 TNA HO 144/1637/194A
490 NLI 13158/7
491 NLI 10464/4
492 BCL Bigger Collection
493 TNA HO 144/1637/100 & 1636/44
494 NLI 31741/3
495 NLI 15138
496 NLI 15138/1/28
497 Tim O'Sullivan and Paul Hyde argue very different versions of events concerning Millar Gordon and the motor bike purchase in *Irish Political Review* articles in 2018 involving, they suggest, considerable MI5 deception, documentary tampering and diary forgery to ensure Casement was not reprieved.
498 NLI 15138/1/12
499 NLI 22317
500 NLI 13081
501 NLI 15138/4
502 NLI 15138/1/16

503 NLI 15138
504 NLI 15138/1/18
505 NLI 13082/2
506 TNA HO 144/1636/58
507 NLI 15138/1/31
508 NLI 13073/19
509 NLI 15138/1/30
510 NLI 13088/1
511 BLPES Morel F8/25/592
512 NLI 15138/1/5 & 6
513 TNA FO 371/1201 Casement's 22 June 1911 letter also outlines his considered view that nothing valuable will come out of Lima's remedial actions given their understanding of the Indians ("the internal South American slave trade"). Peruvians are "a gang of bandits of certain blood and social standing who oppress and enslave the vast bulk of the people they pretend are their fellow countrymen."
514 NLI 13073/46/x
515 NLI 13073/17
516 NLI 13073/24/ii
517 NLI 13073/45/ii
518 NLI 8358
519 NLI 15138/1/29
520 NLI 15138/1/32
521 NLI 8358
522 NLI 13081/2
523 NLI 13080/1/ii
524 NLI 13073/41
525 NLI 13081/6
526 NLI 15138/1/17
527 NLI 15138/2
528 NLI 13073
529 NLI 13074/1
530 TNA HO 144/1637/182
531 NLI 15138/1/34
532 NLI 13073/6/ii
533 NLI 13078/1
534 NLI 13073/2/i
535 Ó Broin, p. 47
536 NLI 14100
537 NLI 10464
538 NLI Acc 4902 Folder 16 (now in 36199-36212)
539 NLI 10763/18
540 NLI 8358
541 B.L. Reid p. 142
542 NLI 13089/6
543 NLI 13073/38
544 TNA HO 144/1637/139
545 NLI 17601/3
546 NLI 15138/1/27
547 Mitchell (1997) p. 35
548 NLI 17443
549 NLI 12117
550 NLI 15138/1/38
551 TNA FO 317/1201
552 NLI 13073/2
553 TNA HO 161/4
554 NLI 13074/1/i & 9932
555 NLI 21536
556 NLI 13073/46/xvii & 10464/5
557 NLI 9932
558 NLI 13082/2
559 All quotations from NLI 13073/46/xi
560 Costigan p. 292
561 NLI 13158/4
562 NLI 15138/3/9, bill dated 4 September 1911
563 NLI 15138/1/38
564 NLI 13073/13
565 Hambloch p. 74
566 NLI 13081/2
567 NLI 13073/8/i
568 NLI 13081/2
569 PRONI T3787/9/1
570 TNA FO 63/1375
571 NLI Acc 4902 Folder 6 (now in 36199-36212)
572 NLI 5588

573 NLI 31722
574 NLI 13081/2
575 NLI 13087/25
576 NLI 13073/9
577 NLI 1689-90
578 NLI 31725
579 Jones p. 497
580 Ure p. 88
581 NLI 13081/2
582 NLI 13080/2/i
583 NLI 13073/46/xi
584 Letter of 20 December 1872 to John Casement
585 NLI 15138/4
586 NLI 12117
587 NLI 13073/46/xvi
588 White Diary 18 November & 1 December 1910
589 NLI 13080/1
590 NLI Acc 4902 Folder 16 (now in 36199-36212)
591 NLI 12117
592 TNA FO 128/324
593 NLI 13089/6
594 NLI 13073/46
595 NLI 8358
596 NLI 15138/1/42, bill dated 31 December 1911
597 NLI 15138/4 (cheque stub)
598 Inglis p. 197
599 NLI 13073/13/iii
600 NLI 13073/26
601 BLPES Gardiner/1/6
602 NLI 13087/34
603 NLI 13073/20/ii
604 NLI 13087/18
605 NLI 13080/2/i
606 Numerous photographs from this 1912 voyage can be found in *Álbum de Fotografías Viaje de la Comisión Consular al Río Putumayo y Afluentes*, edited by Jorge Luis Chavez Marroquin, including one of the two boys in European clothes.
607 NLI 13073/10/ii
608 NLI 31745
609 NLI 17582/4
610 TNA HO/144/1637/139
611 TNA HO/144/1637/139
612 All quotations from TNA HO/144/1636/53, 15 July 1916
613 BLPES F8/19/189
614 NLI 10464
615 NLI 13073/1
616 NLI 13073/16
617 B.L. Reid p. 486
618 Eoin Ó Máille, Roger Casement Foundation conference 1999, Dublin
619 NLI 13073/46/xii
620 B.L. Reid p. 486
621 NLI 13080/2/i
622 "Statement prepared for the John Hewitt Summer School, Glens of Antrim 29 July 1999".
623 BCL Bigger collection, Gordon scrapbook
624 *Ballymena Observer* 3 May 1907
625 NLI 31735
626 NLI 31735
627 "Statement prepared for the John Hewitt Summer School, Glens of Antrim 29 July 1999"
628 NLI 31725 and NLI Acc 4902 Folder 16 (now in 36199-36212)
629 NLI Acc 4902 Folder 23 (now in 36199-36212)
630 NLI Acc 4902 Folder 23 (now in MS 36202/3)
631 NYPL Maloney Collection of Irish Historical Papers, Box 1 Fol 14
632 NYPL Maloney Collection of Irish Historical Papers, Box 1 Fol 14

633 NLI 10763/23
634 NLI 10763/14
635 Letter to author 9 September 1998 from J.N. Simpson, Northern Bank archivist.
636 Hambloch p. 145
637 NLI 13074/7/ii
638 NLI 49154/5 postcards; 31,725/5 letters
639 NLI 17411
640 NLI 13073/46/xix
641 NLI 36200/2 '2 sheets.' (typescript only); missing original letter now found in NLI 17402.
642 NYPL Maloney Collection of Irish Historical Papers 18
643 NLI 36199/4 & 36200/2
644 NLI 10464
645 NLI 13088
646 NLI 8358
647 NLI 10464/7
648 White p. 183-4
649 White p. 185
650 NYPL Maloney Collection of Irish Historical Papers, Box 1 Fol 6-10
651 NLI 10464/7
652 McMinn p. 132
653 McMinn p. 131
654 NLI 17675
655 PRONI D1792/A3/4/33
656 McMinn p. 136
657 *The Times*, 31 October 1913
658 NLI 13082/5
659 PRONI D1792/A1/3/58
660 White p. 184-5
661 White p. 194
662 Letter to author February 2000
663 *Oration II*, Roger Casement Foundation pamphlet 1999
664 Quoted in Brett 1997
665 McMinn p. *lvi*
666 NLI 13074
667 James Craig's family owned a distillery of this name in Belfast.
668 McMinn p. 138
669 NLI 13073/15
670 NLI 13080/2/i
671 Neeson p. 93
672 Neeson p. 93
673 Maume p. 140
674 *An Claidheamh Soluis* 1 November 1913
675 Maume p. 146
676 Monteith p. 15
677 Monteith p. 15
678 NLI 10464
679 MacColl p. 121
680 NLI 31725
681 NLI 15072/3
682 NLI 13074/8
683 NLI Acc 4902 Folder 14 (now in 36199-36212)
684 NLI 18273
685 NLI 18273
686 NLI 13080/6/ii
687 NLI 10464
688 NLI 13080/6/ii
689 NLI 10464
690 NLI 10464
691 NLI 17582/3
692 NLI 10561
693 Inglis p. 252
694 NLI 17675/5
695 NLI Acc 4902 Folder 16 (now in 36199-36212)
696 Martin p. 104
697 Morgan p. 144
698 NLI 17582, 2 August 1914
699 NLI 13173
700 Inglis p. 265
701 NLI 10464/10
702 NLI 13173
703 von Papen quotations from NYPL Maloney Collection of Irish Historical Papers, Box 2 Fol 4

704 NLI 13074/9 to Gertrude Bannister
705 BLPES Morel/F8/23/431
706 BLPES Morel/F8/23/436
707 NLI 13082
708 NYPL Maloney Collection of Irish Historical Papers, Box 3 Fol 1
709 NLI 17582
710 NLI 17602
711 *Irish Independent* 5 October 1914
712 Costigan p. 295
713 NYPL Maloney Collection of Irish Historical Papers, Box 2 Fol 3
714 Costigan p. 298
715 Costigan p. 289
716 *Documents Relative to the Sinn Fein Movement* p. 3
717 Doerries p. 75
718 *Documents Relative to the Sinn Fein Movement* p. 8
719 *Documents Relative to the Sinn Fein Movement* p. 8
720 Inglis p. 357
721 NLI Acc 4902 Folder 17 (now in 36199-36212)
722 NLI 10464/10
723 NLI 13173/3
724 *Documents Relative to the Sinn Fein Movement* p. 5
725 NLI 1689-1690
726 Dudgeon (*German Diary* 2016) p. 14-15
727 PRONI T3787/21/7
728 NLI 5459
729 Moss Parish Church Record no. II-2a
730 MacColl p. 151
731 Curry p. 55
732 NLI 17023
733 All quotations from TNA KV2/9-3
734 PRONI T3787/20/1
735 NLI 13084/1
736 Scotland Yard MEPO 2/10660
737 Curry p. 39
738 NLI 13084/1
739 Scotland Yard MEPO 2/10660
740 TNA FO 95/776
741 Scotland Yard MEPO 2/10660
742 Scotland Yard MEPO 2/10660
743 Noyes p. 83-86
744 NLI 13073
745 *Documents Relative to the Sinn Fein Movement* p. 4, and Doerries p. 57
746 NYPL Maloney Collection of Irish Historical Papers, Box 1 Fol 15-20
747 TNA FO 337/107, and KV 2/6-3, 3 January 1915
748 TNA FO 95/776
749 Scotland Yard MEPO 2/10660
750 NLI 13085/17
751 NLI 13081
752 Dudgeon (*German Diary* 2016) p. 112-3 and Curry p. 134
753 NLI 13084/3
754 NLI 1689/1690 and Dudgeon (*German Diary* 2016) p. 113
755 Dudgeon (*German Diary* 2016) p. 72
756 Dudgeon (*German Diary* 2016) p. 113
757 MacColl p. 163
758 NLI 13084/1
759 Dudgeon (*German Diary* 2016) p. 114
760 TNA HO 144/1637/194A
761 MacColl p. 154
762 Curry p. 95
763 MacColl p. 152 and Curry p. 206-7
764 NLI 17008
765 Noyes p. 87

766 NLI 31735
767 NYPL Maloney Collection of Irish Historical Papers, Box 1 Fol 15-20
768 NLI 17007
769 NLI 17008
770 TNA FO 95/776
771 NLI 31783
772 Doerries p. 108-110
773 *Documents Relative to the Sinn Fein Movement* p. 4
774 *Documents Relative to the Sinn Fein Movement* p. 4
775 NLI 13084
776 Inglis p. 295
777 *Documents Relative to the Sinn Fein Movement* p. 6
778 Inglis p. 282
779 McMinn p. 155
780 *The Times* 27 October 1915
781 NLI 13085/17
782 NLI 31728/3 statement dated 10 November 1966
783 TNA KV2/6
784 *Cork Constitution* 24 and 25 February 1920
785 Singleton-Gates p. 383
786 Monteith p. 265
787 NLI 13073/44/i
788 NLI 13075/4
789 Monteith p. 266
790 NLI 17029
791 NLI 13081/6
792 NLI 17433
793 NLI 17433
794 NYPL Maloney Collection of Irish Historical Papers, Box 1 Fol 15-20
795 NLI 17433
796 NLI 13073/31
797 Curry p. 42
798 NLI 17018
799 TNA KV2/10
800 NLI 13085
801 NLI 13073/31
802 NLI 17433
803 Monteith p. 69
804 Monteith p. 72
805 Monteith p. 80
806 NLI 13073/46/xiv
807 NLI 13073/31/ii
808 NLI 13073/44viii "The proof is conclusive and overwhelming that he has been swindling us and recklessly and foolishly lying."
809 NLI 10764/1
810 NLI 13088
811 NLI 17026
812 NYPL Maloney Collection of Irish Historical Papers, Box 2 Fol 14-15
813 Doerries p. 138
814 NYPL Maloney Collection of Irish Historical Papers, Box 1 Fol 4
815 *Documents Relative to the Sinn Fein Movement* p. 9
816 *Documents Relative to the Sinn Fein Movement* p. 10
817 Spindler p. 188
818 Xander Clayton, *Aud*
819 Clayton pp. 68 and 69. Admiral Bayly's orders of 14 and 16 April 1916.
820 De Courcy Ireland p. 18. Hugh Casement advises "Spindler wrote 'romanhaft' not 'romanschaft' which de Courcy Ireland translated as romantically. That would be romantisch, which I maintain was not the intention. A better translation would perhaps be 'in the manner of a romance' – a tale of derring-do."
821 Clayton p. 656

822 Spindler p. 192
823 *Documents Relative to the Sinn Fein Movement* p. 10
824 *Documents Relative to the Sinn Fein Movement* p. 20
825 NLI 7946
826 TNA HO 144/1637/194A
827 Doerries p. 179
828 NLI 13085/24, 1 February 1916
829 NLI 17033
830 NYPL Maloney Collection of Irish Historical Papers, Box 2 Fol 1, pencilled note on letter of 22 February 1916 from Monteith
831 Spindler p. 195
832 Doerries p. 150
833 NLI 13085
834 NLI 13088
835 NYPL Maloney Collection of Irish Historical Papers, Box 2 Fol 14-15 and Singleton-Gates p. 408
836 NLI 17580 and NYPL Maloney Collection of Irish Historical Papers, Box 2 Fol 17
837 NLI 13085/25
838 NYPL Maloney Collection of Irish Historical Papers, Box 2 Fol 14-15, entitled 'Last Page' – actually runs over thirty sheets; see also NLI 5244 (original).
839 Doerries pp. 29-30
840 NLI 10764
841 NLI 14100
842 TNA HO 144/1637/194A
843 http://www.irishbrigade.eu/other-men/goey/goey.html
844 TNA HO 144/1637/194A
845 NLI 13073
846 Spindler p. 203
847 Monteith p. 219
848 Singleton-Gates pp. 408-9
849 Monteith p. 148-9
850 NLI 5459
851 Monteith p.151
852 NLI 13088
853 Singleton-Gates p. 422
854 Neeson p. 131
855 NLI Acc 4902 Folder 29 (now in 36199-36212)
856 TNA KV2/7
857 Hyde 1964 p. 19
858 MacColl p. 212
859 NLI 13088/4
860 NLI 10764
861 Martin p. 7
862 Thomson p. 273
863 Thomson p. 282
864 NLI 10764
865 TNA CO 904/99
866 *Royal Commission on the Rebellion in Ireland* Cmd. 8311 p. 8
867 Ó Broin p. 83
868 Report, Cmd. 8279; Minutes of Evidence and Appendix of Documents, Cmd. 8311
869 McMinn p. 170
870 Martin p. 5
871 Neeson p. 378
872 *Royal Commission on the Rebellion in Ireland* Cmd. 8311 p. 37
873 *Royal Commission on the Rebellion in Ireland* Cmd. 8311 p. 59
874 *Royal Commission on the Rebellion in Ireland* Cmd. 8311 p. 37
875 *Royal Commission on the Rebellion in Ireland* Cmd. 8311 p. 40
876 *Documents Relative to the Sinn Fein Movement* Cmd. 1108
877 De Courcy Ireland p. 18
878 NLI 13173/3
879 *Royal Commission on the Rebellion in Ireland* Cmd. 8311 p. 7
880 Ó Broin p. 135-6
881 Ó Broin p. 135-6
882 *Royal Commission on the Rebellion in Ireland* Cmd. 8311 p. 13

883 Neeson p. 138
884 Ó Broin p. 155
885 NLI Acc 4902 Folder 22 (now in 36199-36212)
886 *Royal Commission on the Rebellion in Ireland* Cmd. 8311 p. 8
887 Ó Broin p. 84
888 Ó Broin p. 84
889 *Royal Commission on the Rebellion in Ireland* Cmd. 8311 p. 37
890 NLI 21814
891 NLI 10764
892 *vide* B.L. Reid p. 359
893 PRONI D1496/9 *et seq*
894 PRONI D1496/8
895 Buckland p. 286
896 PRONI D1496/9
897 TNA KV2/7
898 PRONI D3027/16
899 TNA HO 144/1636/311643/44
900 Thomson p. 274
901 TNA KV2/7
902 NLI 13088 & TNA HO 144/1636/311643/3A
903 Thomson p. 275
904 BBC Radio 4 *Document* programme, *The 'Easter Rising' – the Dublin Rebellion of 1916*, broadcast 11 March 2013: http://www.bbc.co.uk/programmes/b01r55x9
905 Ramsay, p. 134
906 NLI 10764
907 NLI 13088
908 TNA HO 144/1637/311643/176
909 NLI Acc 4902 Folder 17 (now in 36199-36212)
910 NLI Acc 4902 Folder 19 (now in MS 36207/2)
911 NLI 17420
912 Thomson p. 278
913 NLI 17582
914 Hyde 1964 pp. 183-5 and NLI 10763/11, 21 June 1916
915 Michael Francis Doyle to Montgomery Hyde, 4 November 1958, Series 1.23 Harry Ransom Humanities Research Center Austin, Texas
916 I spotted it in NLI 15138/3/11: "Cheque-stubs, vouchers, statements of account, etc., relating to Expenditures by Roger Casement, mainly in South America, 1910-1911".
917 NYPL Maloney IHP 56, *Gaelic American,* 11 October 1924, p. 1
918 NLI 18081/13 Devoy's record of Michael Francis Doyle's debriefing
919 NLI 10763/15, Sullivan to Gavan Duffy, 7 July 1916
920 NLI 10763/17
921 NLI 10763/28, Gavan Duffy to Doyle 27 January 1917
922 NLI 10763/27, 8 December 1916
923 TNA HO 144/1636/65
924 NLI 13075/1
925 NLI 10764
926 NLI 5459
927 NLI 13081
928 NLI Acc 4902 Folder 16 (now in 36199-36212)
929 Hyde 1960 p. 147
930 Hyde 1960 p. 57
931 NLI 10764
932 NLI Acc 4902 Folder 21 (now in 36199-36212) – 36207/3
933 NLI 17026
934 NLI 17027
935 NLI 31730
936 NLI 17601/9
937 NLI 10763/15
938 TNA PCOM 9/2318
939 NLI 10763/8

940 NLI Acc 4902 Folder 3, 8 July 1916 (now in 36199-36212)
941 NLI 10763/8
942 NLI 14100
943 NLI 10763/24
944 NLI 10763/9
945 Askwith p. 207
946 Bristow p. 118
947 Sheffield Archives Carp Mss 259 (film 27)
948 Sheffield Archives Carp Mss 260 (film 27)
949 NLI 22317
950 NLI Acc 4902 Folder 16 (now in 36199-36212)
951 NLI 13078/3
952 NLI 13075/1
953 NLI 10763/27
954 NLI Acc 4902 Folder 26 (now in 36199-36212)
955 NLI 13082/1/iii
956 PRONI D3905/A/4
957 NLI 8358
958 Author's 1999 conversation in Cushendall
959 NLI 10763/15
960 NLI 13075/1
961 NLI 10763/16
962 NLI 10763/22
963 Reproduced in *Irish News* 26 March 1965
964 NLI 13073
965 NLI 10763/6
966 NLI 10464
967 PRONI T3787/19/1
968 NLI 13074
969 NLI 13074
970 NLI 13076/2/ii
971 PRONI T3306/F4
972 NLI 10763/26
973 NLI 10763/27
974 NLI 10763/20
975 NLI 10763/3
976 MacColl p. 301-2 & PRONI T3072
977 NLI 17601/2
978 NLI 13088/1/iii
979 TNA FO 371/2798
980 *Documents Relative to the Sinn Fein Movement* p. 20
981 All Norwegian investigation quotations from TNA HO 144/1637/140
982 TNA HO 144/1637/311643/67: 22 July 1916 to the Home Secretary
983 NLI 17045
984 TNA FO 337/107
985 TNA FO 95/776
986 NLI 10764
987 NLI 17007
988 NLI 17433
989 NLI 17600 spelling as in original
990 NLI 17600
991 NLI 17433
992 NLI 17433
993 NYPL Maloney Collection of Irish Historical Papers, Box 7 Fol 5
994 I have recently had extensive email correspondence with the descendants of Adler's wives, Sadie and Hedwig who are now aware of each other. In Sadie's case, the family had met some of the Norwegian relatives but none knew of his death in Paris until I linked them with biographer Bjørn Godøy who so advised them.
995 NLI 36207/2
996 NLI 13088/1/ii
997 NYPL Maloney Collection of Irish Historical Papers, Box 2 Fol 14-15
998 NLI 13088/4/i

999 George Gavan Duffy Papers UCD P152
1000 TNAHO144/1636/311643/32A "Note enclosure: Casement's personal prison papers July 1916", presumably the contents of the portfolio.
1001 NLI 14100
1002 NLI 7946
1003 Hyde 1964 p. 132
1004 TNA HO 144/1636/311643/53
1005 NLI 13088
1006 NLI 10763/26
1007 NLI 10763/21 & 26
1008 NLI 17594
1009 NLI 13080/6
1010 NLI 14100
1011 NLI 10464/4
1012 NLI 14100 and Gwynn 1965 p. 64
1013 NLI 5459
1014 Mackey 1962 p. 131
1015 NLI 17603
1016 Gwynn 1965 p. 69
1017 NLI 10763/20
1018 NLI 10763/26
1019 NLI 10763/23
1020 NLI 10765
1021 Wilkinson p. 6
1022 Neeson p. 312
1023 *Barnes Review* pp. 11 & 12
1024 McMinn p. 169-70
1025 Hyde 1964 p. 76
1026 Mitchell (1997) p. 34
1027 NLI 31744 McHugh papers
1028 NYPL Maloney Collection of Irish Historical Papers, Box 1 Fol 3, and George Gavan Duffy Papers UCD P152
1029 BMH WS253, 25 May 1949: http://www.bureauofmilitary-history.ie/reels/bmh/BMH.WS0253.pdf#page=1
1030 NLI 17601/4 & 5
1031 TNA HO 144/1636/311643/17
1032 NLI 10764
1033 TNA HO 144/23486
1034 NLI 11488
1035 Home Office Record Management Services, 5 February 1999
1036 Metropolitan Police Records Management Branch, 11 March 1999
1037 Metropolitan Police Record Officer, 16 March 2000
1038 TNA KV2/7
1039 Thomson p. 227
1040 TNA FO/95/776
1041 TNA CO 904/117
1042 TNA KV2/6
1043 TNA KV2/6
1044 TNA KV2/6
1045 NYPL Maloney Collection of Irish Historical Papers, Box 1 Fol 15-20
1046 TNA CSC 11/47. TCD has made a similar mistake regarding Casement schoolbooks.
1047 TNA CO 904/194/46
1048 TNA KV2/6-3
1049 Scotland Yard MEPO 2/10672
1050 NLI 10763/20
1051 TNA KV2/8
1052 NLI 10764
1053 Scotland Yard MEPO 2/10672
1054 NLI 10763/24 and Scotland Yard MEPO 3/2415
1055 *Irish Independent* 3 August 1976
1056 *Field Day Review* (Mitchell, 2012) pp. 97-8 and 120; TNA HO 144/23425
1057 TNA HO 144/23425/207
1058 Mackey 1954 p. 114
1059 Mackey 1954 p. 114
1060 See TNA HO 144/1637/178 and Ernley Blackwell's note of 23

August 1916 when he wrote, “As regards the diaries it is open to the Executors if they think fit to apply to Bow Street for an order under sec. 1 of the Police Property Act 1897. They are not likely to do that”, and the list in Scotland Yard MEPO 3/2415, dated 17 August 1916, where it is also stated the luggage was eventually collected on 14 February 1917 by Gertrude when a lorry took it to her new Surrey residence of Oxmead.

1061 Scotland Yard MEPO 2/10660
1062 TNA HO 144/1637/178
1063 NLI 10763/17
1064 NLI 10763/2
1065 TNA FO 395/43 of 29 June 1916
1066 Inglis p. 358
1067 TNA HO 144/1637/311643/140. The diaries were shown to the US Ambassador on 26 July 1916.
1068 Scotland Yard MEPO 2/10664
1069 NLI 17603
1070 NLI 17601/13
1071 TNA CO 904/194/46
1072 PRONI Monteagle Papers B/7
1073 NLI 13074/8
1074 Brett 1997
1075 NYPL Maloney Collection of Irish Historical Papers, Box 3 Fol 3
1076 TNA HO 144/23425/207
1077 Maloney p. 198
1078 NLI 23419
1079 NLI 18273
1080 Mitchell (1997) p. 37
1081 NLI 13087/25
1082 NYPL Maloney Collection of Irish Historical Papers, Box 5 Fol 12
1083 NLI 13158/7 (both letters)
1084 TNA KV 2/10
1085 2 March 1999
1086 Quoted by Bill Mc Cormack on p. 187 of *Roger Casement in Death* where many pages are devoted to his researches into Armando Normand, who was apparently educated in England.
1087 NLI 17601/6 (Duggan) and NLI 18776 (Clipperton)
1088 Maloney p. 268
1089 NLI 18776
1090 TNA HO 144/23508
1091 PRONI D3084/I/A/2
1092 PRONI D3084/I/A/3
1093 PRONI D3084
1094 *Hansard* cols. 390-399 26 November 1958
1095 PRONI D3084/I/A/2
1096 PRONI D3084/W/A/4/2
1097 Mitchell (1997) p. 26-7
1098 PRONI D3084/I/A/3
1099 Maloney p. 18
1100 Maloney p. 199-200
1101 *Philadelphia Ledger* 30 August 1916
1102 NLI 31745
1103 NLI 17601/1
1104 NLI 5460
1105 NLI 17604
1106 NYPL Maloney Collection of Irish Historical Papers, Box 6 Fol 9
1107 Conversation with author, March 1999
1108 TNA CO 903/19
1109 NLI 17604/5/14
1110 NLI 17604/3/15
1111 NYPL Maloney Collection of Irish Historical Papers, Box 5 Fol 11
1112 NLI 17602
1113 B.L. Reid p. 472 & NLI 17021. Reid gave an incorrect reference of 17026 for the burying story.

1114 NLI 17021, from notes left in Germany
1115 NLI 17604/3
1116 NLI 18273
1117 NLI 21531
1118 NLI 10763/6
1119 NLI 21535
1120 MacColl p. 284
1121 NLI 13076/2/ii
1122 NLI 17599/2 McGarrity wrote to Nina under the pseudonym Catherine Bigley on 17 April 1915 and a second time without a date, possibly also in 1915.
1123 BMH WS 381. Before the Gavan Duffy lecture text, there are several pages listing, "Material Collected by Bureau Regarding Roger Casement."
1124 NLI 36199/3
1125 See his NLI profile http://www.nli.ie/pdfs/mss%20lists/150_OBriain.pdf
1126 NLI 13073/46xiii 'n.d.'
1127 NLI 13076/2/i "1 letter 7 Oct. [1909/10]". There are also three to Gertrude written in 1914 in the NYPL. The one (undated) Hobson letter is in NLI 13073/46x.
1128 NLI 36201/5, 30 September 1904, and NLI 13073/13ii, 11 March 1905 from Cowper (not The O'Neill), also a 1913 letter.
1129 Letter dated 1 October 1967, Harry Ransom Humanities Research Center Austin, Texas
1130 Mitchell (1997) p. 35
1131 NLI 13073/3
1132 NLI 17601/3
1133 NLI 17601/3
1134 NLI 13075
1135 NLI 13075/1
1136 NYPL Maloney Collection of Irish Historical Papers, Box 6 Fol 10-16
1137 NLI 11488
1138 NLI 13075/1
1139 NLI 13075/3
1140 NLI 10763/24
1141 Author's conversation with a friend of Mrs Elspeth Parry, 1999
1142 1887, *Contemporary Review*
1143 Sawyer 1997 p. 22
1144 Letter to author 22 December 1998
1145 NLI 17804
1146 PRONI D3084/T/1/11
1147 Letter to author 14 September 1998
1148 PRONI D3084/T/1/16
1149 NLI 12114
1150 NLI 22986 & 23419
1151 NLI 17675
1152 d'Arch Smith p. 185
1153 d'Arch Smith p. 138
1154 NLI 3229
1155 NLI 13075/2/ii
1156 NLI 3229
1157 Weeks p. 55
1158 Bristow p. 138
1159 Letter to author 12 December 1998
1160 NYPL Maloney Collection of Irish Historical Papers, Box 2 Fol 19
1161 *Breac* (2016) O'Callaghan article, footnote 32
1162 TNA KV 2/6-2
1163 B.L. Reid p. 482
1164 NLI 17604/4/1
1165 NYPL Maloney Collection of Irish Historical Papers, Box 2 Fol 19
1166 NLI 17602
1167 Rose Young's diary, PRONI D3027/7/14 & 16.
1168 B.L. Reid pp. 54, & 483-4

1169 NLI 13073/4
1170 Eimear Walsh, NLI Department of Manuscripts, email to author 5 July 2011
1171 NLI 14220
1172 B.L. Reid p. 487-8
1173 O'Neill p. 118
1174 NLI 13088/13
1175 NLI 10763/4
1176 O'Byrne p. 668
1177 NLI 13092 (quoted by Eva Gore-Booth)
1178 NLI 21535
1179 PRONI T3306/D1
1180 B.L. Reid p. 175
1181 Connolly pp. 76 & 77
1182 O'Neill p. 120
1183 O'Neill p. 120
1184 Walshe p. 63
1185 PRONI T3306/D3A
1186 B.L. Reid p. 482
1187 NLI 13082/2
1188 B.L. Reid p. 482-3
1189 NLI 12115
1190 d'Arch Smith p. 62
1191 Gardiner pp. 69 & 72
1192 NLI Acc 4902 Folder 5 (now in 36199-36212)
1193 NLI 10763/7
1194 NLI 10764/1
1195 NLI 13075
1196 NLI Acc 4902 Folder 20 (now in 36199-36212)
1197 NLI 13074/1
1198 NLI Acc 4902 Folder 6 (now in 36199-36212)
1199 NLI 13073/2/ii
1200 NLI Acc 4902 Folder 17 (now in 36199-36212)
1201 Redmond Howard p. 9
1202 Hyam p. 99
1203 TNA CO 537/540 & 542
1204 d'Arch Smith p. 131
1205 d'Arch Smith p. 131-2
1206 Davidson p. 157-162
1207 NLI 12116
1208 NLI 12116
1209 Cline p. 151
1210 BLPES Morel F8/23/517-9
1211 NLI 10763/15
1212 Colum pp. 153-5, 188-90
1213 NLI 9932
1214 NLI 17594
1215 NYPL Maloney Collection of Irish Historical Papers, Box 6 Fol 10-16
1216 In public discussion with this author at the John Hewitt Summer School 29 July 1999
1217 NLI 17594
1218 NLI 14220
1219 NLI 9932
1220 NLI 13074
1221 NLI 23422
1222 TNA HO 144/23429
1223 NLI 17675/3
1224 NLI 10763/25
1225 NLI 10763/26
1226 NLI 17599
1227 NLI 14100
1228 TNA HO 144/23428
1229 TNA HO 144/23429
1230 NLI 21537/1
1231 NLI 13076
1232 NLI 13078/2
1233 NLI 13075/4
1234 NLI 13076/1/ii
1235 NLI 13776
1236 TNA HO 144/1637/194
1237 NLI 17582
1238 NLI 13076
1239 Glenavy p.123
1240 NLI 17602
1241 PRONI T3787/23/1
1242 NLI 13075/2
1243 NLI 31735a
1244 PRONI HA/32/1/954

1245 TNA DO 161/168
1246 TNA CAB 128/39
1247 National Archives of Ireland, Department of Taoiseach files, S 7805D
1248 NLI 17604/4/5
1249 NLI 17601/4
1250 *Field Day Review* (Mitchell, 2012) p. 110

Index

If a name is qualified, it is usually in relation to Casement.

Printed in Great Britain
by Amazon

85970142R00454